Merry Christmas to Robin

1995 JAC

With Love from Mother

DEAR MOTHER – GUESS YOU WANTED THIS ONE A LOT – YOU GAVE ME TWO! SORRY I TOOK SO LONG TO GET YOUR COPY BACK TO YOU!

MERRY X-MAS 1997

Love, ROBIN
JENNY
JESSE
JAMIE

HEADLINES

HEADLINES

FRONT PAGE NEWS FROM THE San Francisco Chronicle 1865-1988

■

EDITED BY PHELPS DEWEY

CHRONICLE BOOKS / SAN FRANCISCO

Printed in the United States of America.

Library of Congress Cataloging in Publication Data

Headlines: front page news from the San Francisco chronicle / Phelps Dewey, editor.
p. cm.
ISBN 0-87701-542-2
1. San Francisco (Calif.) — History — Sources. 2. United States — History — 1965-1898 — Sources. 3. United States — History — 1898- — Sources. 4. History, Modern — 20th century — Sources. I. Dewey, Phelps. II. San Francisco chronicle.
F869.S3H39 1988
979.4'6105—dc19 88-12673
CIP

Book and cover design by Eric Jungerman

10 9 8 7 6 5 4 3 2 1

Chronicle Books
275 Fifth Street
San Francisco, California
94103

Contents

1865-1899	11
1900-1909	19
1910-1919	29
1920-1929	43
1930-1939	57
1940-1949	87
1950-1959	121
1960-1969	153
1970-1979	181
1980-1988	213

Preface

When we read our newspaper, we really are reading history viewed from the perspective of the present. Since 1865, Northern Californians have been witnessing history in the making through the front pages of The San Francisco Chronicle.

A lot has happened in that time. There was the assassination of Lincoln and the completion of the transcontinental railroad, which transformed San Francisco from an outpost to a thriving American city. There was the great earthquake and fire that decimated that city. There were great world wars and wars not so great. There were battles closer to home, like Custer's last stand at the Little Bighorn, and the U.S. Army's vengeful invasion of Mexico in pursuit of Pancho Villa. The splendor of King Tutankhamen's tomb was revealed, millions of people perished in numerous cataclysms, and presidents came and went, some dispatched by an angry electorate, others at the hands of assassins.

Looking back over these newspaper pages, we can relive hundreds of great events that shaped the history of the last century and a quarter. Reading history from the front pages of The Chronicle is different from reading about it in a history book, where the writer has the perspective of hindsight: Newspaper stories give us a feeling for what it was like to be there at the time.

After seeing the hundreds of front pages contained in this book, the reader may get the impression that The Chronicle's editors were overly aware of calamities, wars and deaths (whether by natural or unnatural causes). These events hit the front page because they are easily recognized as the stuff of history. From all the thousands of things that happen every day, newspaper editors must, as a daily ritual, sit down and sort out the important. They have to decide quickly which events are historically significant and which are not. Many of these decisions are made while stories are still evolving and leading to an unknown end.

Over the 123 years covered by this book, The Chronicle editors have done a pretty good job of picking the big stories that have withstood the test of time. Many relate to events that still have a profound effect, however indirectly, on the way we live today. The editors missed a few, of course: the events at the Little Bighorn were given only a couple of paragraphs on an inside page, for example, and the Wright brothers' flight at Kitty Hawk also failed to make page one. The 1945 San Francisco conference that gave birth to the United Nations was a daily story for months, but because of the continuing coverage, it never became front page material. To prepare this book, a chronology of historic events since 1865 was compiled and then checked against The Chronicle of the following day. The front pages reproduced here, selected from the nearly 45,000 published by The Chronicle, provide a fascinating view not only of the news but also of the editors' perspective at the time.

A good newspaper reflects the interests of the community it serves, and the San Francisco of earlier times was quite different than it is today. Before the turn of the century, San Francisco was isolated from the rest of the country and the world by vast distance and primitive communication. It is no wonder that the city was much more interested in itself than in the rest of the world. This provincial attitude is reflected in The Chronicle, perhaps explaining why so many stories of towering international importance were eclipsed on the front pages by local matters that in hindsight appear to be relatively trivial. Nonetheless, these headlines give us a glimpse of what San Franciscans were talking about and feeling on that day.

During the ferment and transformation of the years recorded here, it is interesting to note that one thing has not changed: The Chronicle has remained in the ownership of the same family. The present publisher is the great-grandson of Michael de Young, who with his brother, Charles, founded the paper in 1865. During the four generations of publishers, the newspaper, like its city, has undergone profound changes. Richard Thieriot, publisher since 1977, is as much a product of modern San Francisco as his great-grandfather was the product of a city enjoying the spoils of the Gold Rush. They, and the two publishers in between, are directly responsible for giving us this fascinating look into our past.

PHELPS DEWEY
San Francisco, 1988

Acknowledgments

The idea of compiling a book of front pages commemorating momentous events in history was a product of The San Francisco Chronicle's Centennial Celebration in 1965. At the time, it seemed like a simple task, but I was soon to learn how difficult it can be to sort out 100 years' worth of events. That first deadline has been missed by nearly a quarter of a century.

During that time, I have depended on many dedicated Chronicle staff members without whose help this book could have taken another quarter century to compile. Among those to whom I am especially indebted are the late Hubert Buel, Richard Geiger, Bob Cochnar, Johnny Miller, William Van Niekerken, Dennis Gallagher, Eric Jungerman, Aida Gamez, John Boring, Bruce Krefting and Bill Smith.

1865-1899

JANUARY 16, 1865
First Chronicle Brings Hope

APRIL 15, 1865
Lincoln Assassinated

OCTOBER 21,1868
Earthquake

MAY 9, 1869
Trans-Continental Railroad Completed

FEBRUARY 28, 1888
Steamer Julia Sinks

FEBRUARY 16, 1898
Battleship Maine Blown Up

OCTOBER 13, 1899
Boer War Starts

THE DAILY DRAMATIC CHRONICLE

A DAILY RECORD OF AFFAIRS—LOCAL, CRITICAL AND THEATRICAL.

Volume I. SAN FRANCISCO, MONDAY, JANUARY 16th, 1865. Number 1.

PRIVATE

Medical & Surgical Institute

ESTABLISHED IN 1850 BY

DR. J. C. YOUNG,

Formerly Professor of the University, Penn.

No. 540 WASHINGTON STREET,

BELOW MONTGOMERY,

FOR THE CURE OF ALL DISEASES OF A PRIVATE, SPECIAL OR CHRONIC NATURE, WHETHER ARISING FROM IMPURE CONNECTIONS OR THE DEGRADING AND DESTRUCTIVE HABIT OF SELF-ABUSE; ALL FEMALE IRREGULARITIES; ALL DISEASES OF THE SKIN, GLANDS AND BLOOD, AND ALL AFFECTIONS OF THE URINARY ORGANS IN EITHER SEX, IN THE MOST SPEEDY, PERFECT AND PERMANENT MANNER,

☞ **Without the Use of Mercury.** ☜

Consultation, by Letter or otherwise,

FREE.

The Doctor can be consulted privately and with the utmost confidence by the afflicted, at all hours daily, from 9 A. M. until 8 P. M.

☞ CURE ALWAYS GUARANTEED, OR NO PAY REQUIRED. ☜

During the Fourteen Years since this NOW CELEBRATED INSTITUTE was opened, it has met with an unparalleled success. Upwards of Five Thousand are discharged annually cured, making a record unsurpassed by any similar Institute in the World, and unapproached by any in America.

ITS MOTTO; *Quick Cures Guaranteed at Moderate Compensation, or No Pay Required.*

THE BEST SKILL, CARE AND ATTENTION GIVEN TO EVERY CASE.

Recent Cases Cured in a few days, and Chronic Cases in a very short time, without change of diet, hindrance from business or danger of exposure.

The Remedies used are free from Mercury or any deleterious substance whatever, Balsams or other nauseous drugs. They are private compounds unknown to any other Physicians.

Address: **Dr. Benj. F. Josselyn,**

Box 735.

WORRELL'S OLYMPIC

(Formerly Gilbert's,) N. E. Corner Kearny and Clay Streets.

WM. WORRELL...LESSEE AND PROPRIETOR | H. WILLIAMS...LEADER OF THE ORCHESTRA
HARRY COAD..............STAGE MANAGER | W. G. RYDER ....TREASURER

FIRST NIGHT OF THE GROTTO NYMPH

☞ CONTINUED SUCCESS OF THE FAIRY SISTERS,

SOPHIE, IRENE & LITTLE JENNIE WORRELL.

Monday Evening, January 16, 1865

PART FIRST.

Bones..................Geo. Wallace | Tamborine................Walter Bray
OVERTURE....................................ORCHESTRA
OPENING CHORUS....................................COMPANY
SILVERY MOONLIT HILL....................................F. B. TAYLOR
I'D CHOOSE TO BE A BABY....................................GEO. WALLACE
JUST BEFORE THE BATTLE, MOTHER....................................W. STEPHENSON
DRAFTED....................................WALTER BRAY
BREAK IT GENTLY TO MY MOTHER....................................MISS IRENE WORRELL
FINALE....................................COMPANY

CHARACTER DANCE....................................LITTLE JENNIE
CHARACTER ACT....................................WALTER BRAY

After which the Screaming Farce entitled

CROSSING THE LINE

Wouverman....................FRED FRANKS | Bluebag....................G. MITCHELL
Wouter....................F. WOODHULL | Estelle....................Miss LOUISA FRANKS
Pomona....................................LITTLE JENNIE

DOUBLE DANCE, Misses SOPHIE and IRENE WORRELL
UNCLE SNOW....................................G. WALLACE
SONG....................................F. WOODHULL

To conclude with a Nondescript Fantastico Morceau of Absurdity, arranged expressly for this House, entitled The

GROTTO NYMPH

Sarsaparilla, (Princess of Goat Island)..........**Miss IRENE WORRELL**
Cygarita, (her femme de chambre)..........**LITTLE JENNIE**
Prince Klevaphella, (Sovereign of Gnomore, and a good singing voice)...W. STEPHENSON
Marquis of Walkynge Stycke, (Lord High Constable of Goat Island)........FRED FRANKS
Sir Apropos des Bottes, (known in the Police Courts)........GEO. MITCHELL
Sylva, the Fairy Queen, (with a conventional brevity of skirts)........KATE ARCHER
Floreta, (her left-bower)........Mrs. FRANKS
Pggspheet, (her right-bower)........Mrs. EVERARD

The Scene lies near a Fairy Lake; the precise locale of which, like that of Kyd's Treasure, has never been discovered.

GRAND WALK AROUND

In which will appear

THE THREE GRACES—SOPHIE, IRENE AND LITTLE JENNIE,

SATURDAY AFTERNOON—GRAND MATINEE

For the Accommodation of Ladies and Children. SUNDAY EVENING, A SACRED CONCERT. On which occasion the First Musical Talent of the City will appear.

Admission, Twenty-Five Cents | **Arm Chairs..........Fifty Cents**
Private Boxes,..Three Dollars | **Proscenium Boxes, Five Dollars**

DOORS OPEN AT SEVEN O'CLOCK; PERFORMANCE TO COMMENCE AT EIGHT.

PRIVATE MEDICAL INSTITUTE,

Established in 1850 by

DR. J. C. YOUNG,

540 WASHINGTON STREET,

BELOW MONTGOMERY.

HOPE TO THE AFFLICTED

[**From the Tuolumne Courier.**]

If you are sick and would have health; if you are in trouble and would have happiness, read the advertisements of the PRIVATE MEDICAL INSTITUTE, established by DR. J. C YOUNG in 1850, and follow its advice. The reputation of that renowned INSTITUTE needs no applauding word of ours. The thousands annually cured under its treatment, speaks its fame. Do not hesitate, if you require medical aid for any ills to which flesh is heir.

Seminal Weakness.

There is no disease more common, nor more dangerous, than that arising from the weakness of the generative organs. It is the source from which spring so many of those troubles which are treated under the various titles of Liver Complaint, Indigestion, Dyspepsia, Heart Diseases, Lung Complaints, etc. *It arises most frequently, though not altogether, from self-abuse*, and I set it down as an incontrovertable fact *that no one who has practiced that vice, even in the slightest degree, is free from the seeds of the disease.* He may feel well now, or only notice transitory symptoms; but so insidious is it, it will appear in some distressing form sooner or later. Let all who have reason to fear its baleful pressure, submit his case at once to the INSTITUTE, 540 WASHINGTON STREET, *where a perfect and permanent cure is warranted in all cases.* Do not be deterred by a false sense of shame, for delay may prove most disastrous. All communication held perfectly sacred.

Venereal.

If the reader of this has contracted the VENEREAL DISEASE, in any of its various forms, he should look to it at once, and consult only such physician as he knows is qualified to treat successfully that most destructive of all poisons. MERCURY only drives it on the surface to drive it into the blood, whence it is liable to appear in some more terrible form. *In all cases I guarantee perfect and permanent cures in the most speedy manner, without hindrance from business, change of diet, or danger of exposure, by purely vegetable remedies.*

Important to Females.

The various troubles and irregularities to which, as a sex, females are liable, requires the nicest judgment and best knowledge in discerning, as the greatest skill in treating. Having been, for years, a PROFESSOR OF OBSTETRICS AND FEMALE COMPLAINTS, and having been favored with an extensive practice in families, I fell warranted in guaranteeing a cure in all troubles of the Urinary and Generative organs, whether requiring Medical or Surgical treatment. Families can rely upon me with every assurance of confidence. *All Consultations and Communications held perfectfly sacred.* ☞ Apartments privately arranged for the benefit of ladies desirous of consultation. The Preventative Powders for Married Ladies; the French Lunar, or Female Monthly Pill, and other celebrated Female remedies, compounded from the private prescriptions of DR. J. C. YOUNG, can be procured only at the Institute.

To Correspondents.

If you are prevented by any cause from visiting the Institute a candid and full description of the complaint, in a letter, will obviate the necessity of a personal interview. *All Communications returned or destroyed, and the contents held perfectly sacred.* Address,

Benj. F. Josselyn, M. D.

Box 735, P. O. **No. 540 Washington Street.**

Daily Dramatic Chronicle

PUBLISHED AT

No. 417 CLAY STREET,

Between Sansome and Battery.

☞ THE DAILY DRAMATIC CHRONICLE is published every morning (Sundays excepted), and distributed GRATUITOUSLY in all the restaurants, saloons, hotels, reading-rooms, stores, boats, cars, and among the audience at WORRELL'S OLYMPIC, and broadcast through the marts of trade around about the city, making it one of the BEST advertising mediums in the State.

Star Notices Twenty Cents per Line Each Issue.

DAILY CIRCULATION, ... 4,000

"All the world's a stage,
And all the men and women merely players."

SATURDAY, APRIL 15th, 1865.

AMUSEMENTS.

GILBERTS MUSEUM.—This ever attractive place for young and old, Gilbert's Museum, will have its doors thrown open as usual to the public to-day. The Chinese Jugglers and Learned Pig are still among the attractions.

THE ANATOMICAL MUSEUM is one of the great attractions of the day, where a lesson of vital interest will be obtained by all who visit and see for themselves the many forms of "*The House we live in.*"

THE WILLOWS.—There will be sport of all kinds at the Willows Sunday, such as Shuffle Boards, Ten Pin Alleys, Shooting Galleries, together with Flying Horses, Revolving Carriages, Swings, etc., for the amusement of the little folks.

HAYES PARK will be open Sunday, for dancing and other amusements.

High Art.

We don't go a cent on Ruskins theory of pre-Raphelite art. If an artist undertakes to delineate Nature let him represent her as she is,—not as he conceives she ought to be. Such, too, is the theory of FRED MORSCH, who, prefering the useful and practical branch of his profession to that which is purely ornamental, prefers painting houses and signs, to painting landscapes. Nevertheless, Morsch is powerful on the "fresco," which has always been recognized as a department of "high art." He holds forth at No. 540 California street below Kearny, where the public can at any time inspect specimens of what he can do when he feels like trying.

Woman's Friendship.

The satirists insists that there is no such word as "friendship" in the female vocabulary; that with the gentler sex "love is the only reality, while friendship is a shadow, a pretence and a myth." Rochefaucauld, declares that women *might* be sincere friends if there were no men in the world, but that the moment a man appears, women's friendship are destroyed by vanity and jealousy. Rochefoucauld ought to be lynched.

Four and Five.

Four papers of the finest and purest and most fragrant chewing tobacco (fine cut) for two bits,—or five plugs of "Virginia Leaf" for fifty cents, seems a ruinous rate;—but VAN SCHAACK, of 706 Kearny street, stands it. And he says he means to keep on doing so.

Inhuman.

A brutal saloon keeper refused our canine friend, Bummer, a night's lodging's during the recent cold weather. Before shutting up his whisky mill, he *turned him out* in the street. After which he turned his gas—in the pipe.

Extensively Read.

Everybody reads the CHRONICLE. Go where you will, it is to be seen; and wherever it is seen it is seized with eagerness, and read with avidity. At Maguire's and Worrell's the audience read it between the acts, advertisements and all.

LATEST DISPATCHES.

ASSASSINATION

OF

ABRAHAM LINCOLN

[FIRST DESPATCH.]

Washington April 15.

Gen. B. W. Carpentier: His Excellency President Lincoln was assinated at the theatre last night.

[SECOND DESPATCH.]

President Lincoln died at 8:30 this morning, and Secretary Seward a few minutes past 9.

[THIRD DESPATCH.]

Reports of are contadictory. It is reported that President Lincoln died at 7:22.

Narrow Escape.

Yesterday, Mr. Henry Jones, of the firm of Tompkins Jones & Co., on Battery street, was passing an unfinished building, an eight inch redwood plank fell upon his head from the second story. Fortunately, he wore at the time, one of MCGANN'S best "stove-pipes," which was made of such excellent material, and with such remarkable skill, that it broke the force of the blow, and prevented him from receiving any serious injury. MCGANN (of 654 Washington street) knows how to combine the useful with the ornamental. His new style of hat is acknowledge to be the perfection of elegance and symmetry,—but this is the first instance where it has been the means of saving life.

Played Out.

Gwin and his friends appear to be "played out" in the United States and in Mexico. They are good for nothing in this world. The *Spectator* suggests that they may serve *for fuel* in the next.

☞ Carte de Visite, $2 per dozen; Ambrotypes, with Cases, 25 cents, at No. 20 Third street, a few doors above Howard.

CARD PHOTOGRAPHS—Only $2 per dozen, and Vignettes $2.50, at the NEW YORK GALLERY, Nos. 25 and 27 Third Street, east side, near Market. Call and see our specimens.
B. F. HOWLAND & CO.

DENTAL.—No branch of Medical or Surgical science has made such rapid strides as Mechanical Dentistry. No man or woman, or child, need suffer the curse of decayed, or crooked, or repulsive looking teeth in our day. All such annoyances and deformities vanish before the practical skill of DR. C. E. DAVIS, No. 145 Third street, between Mission and Howard.

Interesting to Ladies and Gentlemen—Messrs. Rohenschild & Melsted would respectfully call the attention of Ladies and Gentlemen to their comfortably furnished Saloon, known as TAYLOR'S RESTAURANT, Nos. 718 and 720 Market street, above Kearny, where every delicacy of the season, well prepared, can be obtained at any hour of the day and night. Give them a call. They are very accommodating.

Mrs. Chapman's Hair Dye.—The attention of the Ladies and Gentlemen of San Francisco is respectfully called to the superior merits of Mrs. Chapman's preparation of Hair Dye. It is warranted to restore hair, to any shade or color, and make it soft and glossy; it cleanses the hair, and removes scurf and dandruff. This excellent Hair Dye and Restorative was awarded First Premium by the late Mechanics' Fair, on account of its superior qualities. Those afflicted with baldness will, by using it, procure a beautiful head of hair. For sale by Mrs. Chapman, 687 Market street, room 29

EVENING EDITION.

DISTRIBUTED FREE.

CHRONICLE OFFICE - - 3½ P. M.

DEATH OF THE PRESIDENT.

MURDEROUS ATTACK ON MR. SEWARD.

Wilkes Booth Supposed to be the Murderer of the President.

WASHINGTON, April 14th.—President Lincoln and wife, with other friends, this evening visited Ford's Theatre for the purpose of witnessing the performance of the "American Cousin." It was announced in the papers that General Grant would also be present, but that gentleman took a late train of cars for New Jersey. The theatre was densely crowded, and everybody seemed delighted with the scene before them.

During the third act, and while there was a temporary pause for one of the actors to enter, a sharp report of a pistol was heard, which merely attracted attention, but suggested nothing serious until a man rushed in front of the President's box, waving a long dagger in his right hand, exclaiming, "*sic semper tyrannis!*" and immediately leaped from a box which was in the second tier to the stage beneath, ran across to the opposite side of the stage, making his escape, amid the bewilderment of the audience, from the rear of theatre, and, mounting a horse, fled.

The screams of Mrs. Lincoln first disclosed the fact to the audience that the President had been shot, when all present rose to their feet, rushing towards the stage, many exclaiming "Hang him!" The excitement was of the wildest possible description. Of course there was an abrupt intermission of the theatrical performance. There was a rush towards the President's box when cries were heard of "Stand back," "Give him air," "Has any one stimulants?"

On a hasty examination it was found that the President had been shot through the head above and back of the temporal bone, and that some of the brain was oozing out. He was removed to a private house near by. The Surgeon-General of the army and other surgeons were sent for to attend him. On the examination of the private box, blood was discovered on the back of the cushioned rocking chair on which the President had been sitting, also on the partition, and on the floor; a common single-barreled pistol was found on the carpet.

About 10 o'clock a man rang the bell, and the call having been answered by a colored servant, he said he had come from Dr. Viede, with a prescription, and at the same time holding in his hand a small piece of paper and saying, in answer to a refusal, that he must see the Secretary, as he was entrusted with particular directions concerning the medeine, he insisted on going up. Although repeatedly informed that no one could enter the chamber, he pushed the servant one side, walked heavily toward the Secretary's room, was met there by Mr. Fred. Seward, of whom he demanded to see the Secretary, making the same representations which he did to the servant. What further passed in the way of colloquy is not known, but the man struck him on the head with a billy, badly injuring the skull, and felling him senseless. The assassin then rushed into the chamber and attacked Mr. Seward, a paymaster in the United States Army, and Mr. Hunsell, a messenger of the State Department and two male nurses disabling them. He then rushed upon the Secretary, who was lying in bed in the same room, and inflicted three stabs in the neck, but severing, it is thought and hoped, no artery, though he bled profusely. The assassin rushed down stairs, mounted his horse and rode off before an alarm could be sounded and in the same manner as the assassination of the President. It is believed the injuries of the Secretary are not fatal, nor those of the others, although both the Secretary and Assistant Secretary are very seriously injured.

DEATH OF SECRETARY SEWARD.

Secretary Seward has since died.

The "Democratic Press" Office has just been thrown into the street by an infuriated Mob of outraged Citizens.

An Attempt is now being made to destroy the "News Letter" Office.

The Monitor office has just been MOBBED!

REMOVAL.

MESSRS. GODCHAUX, WEIL & CO. would respectfully inform their friends and customers they have removed their store to corner of Natoma and Second streets. Thankful for past patronage of their friends, they hope they will all call at their present corner.
Godchaux, Weil & Co.

N. P. HOPKINS' Livery and Sales STABLES, 679 and 681 Market St

CHOP HOUSE.

THE UNDERSIGNED HAS PURCHASED the well known Chop House, formerly known as BALL'S CHOP HOUSE, corner **Merchant and Montgomery Sts.,** In the rear of Robinson's Saloon, adjoining the "Bulletin" Publication Office, where he intends to serve the best the market affords.
Henry B. Fisher.

No. 598 WASHINGTON ST.

J. STOCK & CO., Proprietors.

Ladies' Dining Saloon,

No. 611 Sansome Street.

All the delicacies of the Season THAT THE MARKET AFFORDS.

THE ARIEL,

320 MONTGOMERY ST.,

EUREKA THEATER BUILDING.

The "ARIEL" has recently been fitted up in magnificent style, at great expense.
The Bar is constantly supplied with the choicest **WINES, LIQUORS and CIGARS.**
☞ PRIVATE CARD ROOMS.

HARRY BRISTOL, Proprietor.

Bradley & Rulofson

PROPRIETORS OF THE

CELEBRATED

Photograph Gallery

CORNER

SACRAMENTO AND MONTGOMERY,

Entrance 429 Mongomery Street.

(Vance's Old Stand.)

This magnificent establishment has more room, larger lights, greater facilities, and produces FINER PHOTOGRAPHS than any other gallery in the city.

TELEGRAPHIC.

MR. C. EWING HAS OPENED his School for the instruction of the art of Telegraphing, at 729 Bush street, above Montgomery, Room No. 12. Those desirous to become Operators will do well to call. Terms moderate.

The Hotel of this Fashionable and Popular Place of Resort

WILL BE

RE-OPENED

—ON—

SUNDAY, APRIL 2, '65

Under the management of that well known caterer,

JACOB WIMMER.

THE GROUNDS ARE NOW highly Improved and Ornamented, and contain Rare Facilities in the way of Amusement and Recreation. A Restaurant, with a Ladies Department and a Ladies' Refreshment Saloon, will be in readiness for occupancy. Among the varied resources of the Willows, are Shuffle Boards, Ten Pin Alleys Shooting Galleries, together with Flying Horses, Revolving Carriages, Swings, etc., for the amusement of the little folks. Ample stabling accommodations, under the charge of watchful grooms, are attached to the premises. The Theatre has been newly decorated and refitted; and attractive Afternoon Performances, embracing popular Minstrelsy, etc. will be given every Saturday.

A GRAND BALL

Will be given on each Sunday.

THE GROUNDS are thrown open to Military Companies, Schools and Pic-Nic Parties which will meet with every attention.

The North Beach and Mission Railroad Cars leave the corner of Montgomery and California streets every eight minutes for the Willows.

N. B.—Bills and Posters will be distributed throughout the city for the Saturday and Sunday performances.

JACOB WIMMER.
Manager.

"OURSELVES,"

HOW WE LIVE,

MOVE, AND HAVE OUR BEING!

Now open at the

New Hall on Pine Street,

Between Montgomery and Sansome.

FOR GENTLEMEN, ONLY

THE

PACIFIC MUSEUM

—OF—

ANATOMY AND SCIENCE.

This magnificent collection has been culled from the best SCHOOLS OF ANATOMY IN THE WORLD, and contains innumerable preparations of every portion of the Human Frame also, full length Figures, which dissect into the most minute proportions. Prominent among them is the

Life-Like "Florentine Venus."

Which takes into SEVEN HUNDRED PIEC

Here may be seen every

Nerve, Artery, Muscle, and Bone

Of the wonderful fabric "THE HOUSE W LIVE IN." This truly beautiful figure is wonder and admiration of every beholder, a universally pronounced to be the acme of A tomical Science and Skill.

The evils resulting from

TIGHT LACING

Are shown and illustrated by a FULL LENGTH TRUTHFUL AND LIFE-LIKE FIGURE proving the prejudicial effects frequently foll ing this absurd practice.

The Egyptian Mummies!

Five in number, curiously show the custom by-gone ages.

☞ Important LECTURES every eve at 8 o'clock.

☞ Every attention has been paid for comfort of visitors.

Catalogues describing the thousand inter objects in the Hall, may be had at the door.

Open Daily from 10 A. M. till 10 P.

ADMISSION, - ONE DOLL

GRANT HAS TAKEN RICHMON

—AND—

E. KIEL & CO.

Have Taken the

EAST INDIA TEA STO

(Formerly owned by Chas. Strassman,)

OPPOSITE Maguire's Opera House, where they are now selling choice Green and Black Teas, of Chinese and Japanese production. Also, Coffees, Sugars, and Chocolates, and all kinds of Family Groceries, which they sell at the lowest prices. ☞ Goods delivered Free of charge any part of the city.

R. F. ROCCHICCIOLI,

Engraver, Electrotyper and Silver-Plat Brass Founder and Finisher,

No. 523 CALIFORNIA street, between Kearny and Montgomery, San Francisco. Engraving of every description done at the shortest notice; all kinds Seals and Pressers; Iron, Steel, Brass and Wo Stamps made to order, besides Door Plates, Numbers, all kinds of Brass and Plate Letters Work in the Military line; also, Bell-Hanging by practical workmen; Repairing of Silverware Silver-Plating, Bronzing, etc. Particular attention paid to the repairing of articles in this line and satisfaction guaranteed. All kinds of Hanging material, of our own manufacturing, on hand, and for sale at very reasonable prices. Orders from the country promptly attended to.

WATCH REPAIRING

AT NEW YORK PRICES, BY

H. TRAUBE, Practical Watchmaker,

717 Clay Street,

Six doors from Kearny, San Francisco.

Watches, Clocks and Jewelry

NEATLY REPAIRED.

Jewelry, Diamond Setting and Engraving to order. Watch glasses fitted for TEN CENT

Daily Morning Chronicle

PUBLISHED BY

CHAS. DE YOUNG & CO.,

No. 604 Montgomery street, between Sacramento and Commercial.

SERVED BY CARRIERS AT

12½ CENTS PER WEEK.

SINGLE COPIES, FIVE CENTS.

THE OFFICIAL LIST OF LETTERS, published by the Postmaster, is published in the CHRONICLE every Wednesday, in consequence of a large city circulation.

OFFICIAL LIST OF LETTERS

Remaining in the Post Office, October 21, 1868.

LADIES' LIST.

Window—A to M.

Window—M to Z.

THE DAILY

Morning Chronicle

VOL. VIII. SAN FRANCISCO, WEDNESDAY, OCTOBER 21, 1868. NO. 84.

Daily Morning Chronicle

EXTRA

WEDNESDAY, OCTOBER 21...1½ P. M.

Earthquake

THE SEVEREST EVER FELT IN SAN FRANCISCO.

SEVERAL PEOPLE KILLED AND A LARGE NUMBER SEVERELY INJURED.

Buildings Tossed About, and Immense Damage Done.

THE GROUND OPENS IN NUMEROUS PLACES THROUGHOUT THE CITY.

A MORNING OF HORRORS LONG TO BE REMEMBERED.

The Greatest Calamity that Ever Befel San Francisco.

GREAT EXCITEMENT—THE PEOPLE FILLED WITH TERROR.

Business Suspended and the Whole Populace in the Streets.

Never in the history of San Francisco has so great a calamity befallen it as we have met with to-day. In the natural excitement of the moment when the streets are crowded with the affrighted populace and the people are crazed with terror, it is difficult to calmly write up the

At the corner of Fifth and Folsom streets the street has perceptibly sunk.

The building of the Pacific Woolen Mills, corner of Folsom and Eighteenth streets, is badly crushed and is unsafe for occupation. The Chinamen and other employees have refused to work.

At the Pacific Tannery and Boot and Shoe Company's works a panic ensued. Several men were injured in the rush to get out, and the men kept the women from escaping first.

The telegraph wires are down on Market street above Fifth.

The Brevoort House, corner of Fourth and Mission, is badly cracked.

Two horses became frightened, and dashed through the windows of a dry goods store on Fifth street near Folsom.

On Ellis street, the front wall of Mrs. Samuel Marks' house fell out in the street.

At the corner of Brannan and Seventh streets the ground is reported as having sunk four feet.

A painter on Kearny street is reported as having been thrown from his ladder and killed, but the news is not confirmed, nor any name given.

A lady at the Mission jumped out of a window and had her head severely cut.

At the corner of Folsom and Fourteenth streets a house has sunk four feet. All the gas and water pipes are reported as bursted, and the ground open two inches for a distance of forty feet, in this vicinity.

The Denman School building is badly cracked.

On Fremont street the gas works are badly damaged.

There is a large seam through the Pacific Brewery on Tehama street.

The front wall of a brick building on Main street, between Howard and Folsom streets, is in danger of falling.

All of the foundries are badly strained and cracked.

The drug store on the corner of Folsom and Fifth streets is filled with broken glass, the contents being entirely destroyed.

The walls of the Cosmopolitan School are badly cracked.

At the corner of Clay and Sansome streets two men were covered in the debris of a falling wall, and the fire alarm was rung to dig them out.

While the firemen were engaged in this duty a fire was discovered in the building on the northeast corner of Clay and Battery streets, but extinguished without much damage.

A lady on Main street jumped out of a third-story window into a sand lot.

A. De Tavel's stable, on Howard street above Fourth, is badly cracked.

The building No. 739 Howard street, is badly cracked, and considered in a dangerous condition.

At McDonald's mill, on Market street below Front, the ground sunk in the rear letting down the wall some eight feet and opened.

At the northwest corner of Mission and Third streets the top line of the wall came down.

At the corner of Fourth and Harrison, the ground sank and raised about one and a half feet, stopping the cars.

A woman is reported killed by the falling of a cornice on Sansome street.

On Bush, below Sansome, the ground opened.

The plate-glass window of the Women's Co-operative Union was smashed, and also of the Hibernia Bank.

The building on the southwest corner of Kearny street and St. Marks place is badly cracked.

The chimney at the Lick House fell, and a man jumped from a window and broke his leg. Several men are reported hurt at the Miners' Foundry.

A. M. Boyle's drug store on Washington street, near Sansome, was injured to the extent of $2,500.

In the County Jail the scene was horrible, the prisoners shrieking and yelling with terror.

A man named Blumenbery was cut by a falling brick when at the Empire Restaurant on Sansome street.

The chimney of the Mint is in great danger of falling, as also is the granite front of Blake's hat store on Montgomery street.

The rear of the *Alta* office on Sacramento street is badly cracked.

In the hurry of getting out of the *Bulletin* composition rooms, Crabb, one of the printers, was knocked senseless on the sidewalk.

A printer named Phair jumped through a sky light in Bacon & Company's to the Pacific Fruit market and was badly cut.

Patrick Warren, one of the pressman at Deffebach's, was hurt by falling bricks and bruised about the head. Four of the men were injured.

A German in Goodwin's furniture store had his leg broken.

A lady, whose name we could not learn, had her leg broken on Clay street east of Montgomery, in front of the City Restaurant.

The rear of the clothing store of G. Broderick, on Sacramento near Montgomery, was entirely crushed in by the adjoining walls falling. Nobody hurt. It was a one-story frame building.

The fire wall of the Pacific Mail Steamship Company's office was thrown down.

The front walls of the stores of A. J. Plate, No. 510, and Wigmore, No. 512, Sacramento street, sunk about six inches. The floor of the cellar raised up two feet. A crack extended along the street about one hundred feet.

The walls between the Coso House and adjoining building were separated at the top five or six inches.

The fire-wall of Howard's building, Sansome and Clay—the entire Sansome street front—fell into the street. Blumenthal, the proprietor of the restaurant in the building, was badly hurt and another man reported killed.

A fire-wall on the west side of Leidesdorff street fell on the adjoining frame building.

The fire-wall at the top of Sam Brannan's building fell and broke through the sidewalk. Nobody hurt.

At Trainer's block, on the corner of Kearny and Sutter streets, the top of the building fell off and broke down the awning.

At No. 20 Kearny street, the building cracked at both ends.

At No. 8 Kearny street the windows were all broken.

At B. P. Wilkins', No. 648 Market street, the ceiling fell down and threw the goods all over the floor and broke the front windows.

At I. C. Talbot & Co.'s, No. 620 Market street, the ceiling fell down and the glass in the front windows were broken.

A Chinaman, name unknown, was killed on Sacramento street.

The chimneys from the Nucleus building fell upon the roof of the dining-room, smashed through and fell between two tables while people were breakfasting at them. The front wall of the dining-room is badly cracked to the top.

Mrs. Chamberlain's house on Third street sustained much injury, large plates of glass being broken from the stores beneath.

The Pacific Insurance building, on the northeast corner of California and Leidesdorff streets, shows numerous small cracks in the walls.

Squarza's building, on Liedesdorff street, is badly cracked from top to bottom; also the continuation of building forming the southeast corner of Sacramento and Leidesdorff streets.

J. G. Hodge & Co.'s building, on the southwest corner of Sacramento and Sansome streets, was considerably cracked and the shelving in the store was twisted out of place.

The American Exchange building was badly cracked, especially on the Halleck-street side.

The Bank of California building, northwest corner of Sansome and California streets, had the stone ornaments on top and balustrades thrown down; also in the arches of the doors and windows the joints between the stones opened with the shock of the earthquake. On the California-street side the stone cornice was broken in places, and the main west wall showing a decided crack.

Northeast corner Sansome and Halleck street, front and side wall of old building, American theater parapet wall thrown down and rest of building in a very dangerous condition. Brick building south side Sacramento street, No. 425, occupied by A. Wasserman & Co., badly cracked.

No. 415 Sansome street, front wall badly cracked, occupied by Williams, Bornstein & Co.

Nos. 221 and 223 Battery street, east side, are very badly injured, the front wall having fallen in; probably will have to come down.

The southwest corner of the building at the southwest corner of Battery and Halleck streets is badly cracked, as also parapet wall of the building adjoining.

Building southeast corner Battery and Halleck streets, corner parapet wall down and main wall very badly cracked; may have to come down.

Brick store, northwest corner California and Front streets, occupied by DeWitt, Kittle & Co., east parapet wall almost all down.

At the northwest corner of Halleck and Front streets, a brick store occupied by Castle Bros. with parapet walls on south side are all down with part of the main wall. Some of the roof bracing timbers also came down. The north parapet wall fell down.

At the southwest corner of Sacramento and Front streets a brick building occupied by Weil & Co., north wall was so started that it will probably come down.

A building, No. 317 south side of Sacramento, was cracked and the goods of L. Fieldman & Co. badly injured.

Buildings Nos. 319 and 321 Sacramento street were also much cracked and damaged.

On Sacramento street, just below Montgomery, the roof of a building fell in on a clothing store underneath.

The back part of Smith & Beasson's carpet store, on Washington street, is all down.

The building corner of Polk lane and Stockton street is badly damaged. The front wall is very much cracked, and is likely to fall at any moment.

The Jewish church between Broadway and Vallejo streets is somewhat damaged. Brick and mortar cover the sidewalks.

The new building on Bush street, near Battery, fronting on Market, in process of erection, fell and covered up, it is supposed, three persons. Jasper Shawl has been taken out, badly cut about the head and with an arm broken.

The store on the corner of Front and California streets is badly damaged.

The building occupied by the California Shirt Factory will have to be torn down. Ropes are stretched across the street to keep pedestrians from going near.

The building occupied by Weil & Co., No. 225 Front street, corner of Sacramento, is twisted two feet out of place.

J. C. Noonan, the porter of the Lick House, was asleep, and hearing the noise jumped out of the window, about ten feet from the ground, and broke his leg.

It is rumored that the porter of the Bank of California is killed.

From Alvarado and Hayward's it is reported that all is in ruins. Not a chimney is standing. The large storehouse in Alvarado is destroyed.

A man on the Presidio road was thrown out of his buggy. The chimneys in that neighborhood are nearly all down.

The fire wall of the new building corner of California and Battery is down.

John Vannie, head cook at the Empire Restaurant, got his right leg badly crushed.

Andrew Folley had his right arm broken at the Pacific Lodging-house, in jumping from a second story back window.

No. 318 California street, brick building occupied by California Powder Works, etc., front wall considerably cracked.

Wooden building, south, occupied by O. F. Willey, badly settled on south side by Reese's building adjoining.

Reese buildings, seven two-story brick, extending to Battery street, very badly injured; the west end, adjoining Willey's, ready to fall down at a moment's notice; store underneath occupied by S. Reinstein, considerable injury to goods; end of store settled about a foot and must come down; all the other buildings of the row more or less cracked, and cornice on southeast end thrown down.

Building southwest corner of Halleck and Battery, south wall badly cracked and leaning off from balance of the building on Halleck street; front wall may have to come down; occupied by Enestein, Brothers. Front wall of Newhall & Co's warehouse badly cracked at southeast corner, on Halleck street.

The building on the corner of Battery and Merchant streets, used as a carriage warehouse, is badly shattered, the awning falling and crushing one or more carriages.

The earth at the corner of Battery and Commercial streets has settled about three feet below the regular grade.

The building at the corner of Clay and Battery streets, occupied by Breed & Chase and Sherwood, Buckley & Co., is considerably shattered.

At Meigs & Gawley's lumber yard on Stewart street W. T. Halsey, the bookkeeper, on attempting to gain the outside when the shock was felt this morning, had his ankle and arm broken by the falling of lumber. He was removed to the house of Mr. Gawley.

All the lumber piles on Stewart street have been more or less shaken by the earthquake. No damage done save in the expense of repiling.

The Empire Mills, Fremont street, were also damaged. The floor settled in some places nearly two feet, while in others the planks were thrown up by the shock. The earth cracked about eight or nine inches, and the water gushed through the fissures. The dam

By Telegraph

[SPECIAL DISPATCHES TO THE CHRONICLE.]

UPHEAVAL IN SAN LEANDRO.

FALLING OF THE JAIL—PRISONERS CRUSHED.

GREAT DAMAGE TO BUILDINGS AT HAYWOOD.

OPENING OF THE EARTH.

SAN LEANDRO, October 21st.

The earthquake which visited us this morning was not less destructive than across the bay.

At San Leandro the jail has tumbled and entombed its inmates. It is not yet known how many lives have been lost.

Mr. Tocklin, the County Treasurer, was killed. All the frame buildings at Haywards are reported damaged, and the brick ones have been levelled to the earth. The earth has opened several feet. The stage from Pleasanton to Alameda Books tumbled down the hill.

SECOND EDITION

WEDNESDAY, OCTOBER 21 ... 3:30 P. M.

BY TELEGRAPH.

[SPECIAL DISPATCHES TO THE CHRONICLE.]

FROM THE INTERIOR.

Marysville.

MARYSVILLE, October 21st.—The shock here was very slight, being noticed only by a few.

Grass Valley.

GRASS VALLEY, October 21st.—Quite a severe shock of an earthquake was felt here this morning about eight o'clock, causing lamps to vibrate and the occupants of second stories to vacate briskly. About five minutes after there was another very slight shock.

Sonora.

SONORA, October 21st.—A slight earthquake shock was felt here at four minutes past eight o'clock this morning.

Mare Island.

MARE ISLAND, October 21st.—No injury done. Shock very light. The Convent of Notre Dame is all safe. No damage.

Los Angeles.

No report has been received from Los Angeles, and the rumor of great destruction there is unfounded.

Petaluma.

A passenger from Petaluma by this morning's boat, states that a severe shock of an earthquake was experienced at five minutes to eight o'clock. Its violence was so great that all persons ran into the street and the front wall of a stone building (name unknown) was thrown down. The walls of the grain warehouses were also badly cracked. The cars being about to leave he could obtain no further particulars of damage.

The Earthquake in San Mateo County.

REDWOOD, October 21st.

The American Hotel at this place is very much shaken. The Court-house is standing, but is unsafe. The public school building was damaged so much that the school was dismissed. Many chimneys were shaken down. The wall on Merrill's block was shaken down. No one has been killed or injured.

SAN MATEO, October 21st—1 P. M.

The first earthquake was felt here at two and one-fourth minutes of eight o'clock A. M., the severe one lasting fifteen seconds. Barometer 29.92 inches; thermometer 48. The vibration was from north to south, according to memoranda made by F. A. Bishop. The damage done to property here is not less than $5,000.

CITY INCIDENTS.

J. B. Mansfield was killed in front of Graves' store on Clay street, and taken to Gray's, on Sacramento street. He was a tanner by trade, and worked at Bullard's place, No. 18 Geary street.

Daily Morning Chronicle

SERVED BY CARRIERS AT

12½ CENTS PER WEEK.

DAILY MORNING CHRONICLE—Is published every morning, excepting Monday, and served by Carriers at 12½ cents per week; single copies, Five Cents.

DAILY EVENING CHRONICLE—Is published every evening, excepting Sunday, ...

WEEKLY CHRONICLE—Due notice will be given of the issuance of this edition.

Terms by Mail:

ONE YEAR (in advance) ... $8 00 | Six Months ... $5 00 | Three Months ... $3 00

To the getter up of a Club of Ten Subscribers a free copy will be sent.

Daily Morning Chronicle
PUBLISHED BY
CHAS. DE YOUNG & CO.,
— AT —
No. 504 Montgomery street, between Sacramento and Commercial.
SERVED BY CARRIERS AT
25 CENTS PER WEEK.
SINGLE COPIES, FIVE CENTS.
The Official List of Letters (furnished by the Postmaster) is published in the CHRONICLE every Wednesday, in consequence of its large city circulation.

THE DAILY Morning Chronicle

VOL. IX. SAN FRANCISCO, SUNDAY, MAY 9, 1869. NO. 104.

CELEBRATION.

Completion of the Trans-Continental Railroad.

SAN FRANCISCO APPROPRIATELY CELEBRATES THE EVENT.

One Hundred Thousand People Participate.

Immense Procession of Military and Civic Societies.

The City Magnificently Decorated.

LITERARY EXERCISES—POEM—ORATION—BANQUET—SPEECHES, ETC.

BRILLIANT ILLUMINATION OF THE CITY.

VARIOUS INCIDENTS AND ACCIDENTS.

THE CELEBRATION ELSEWHERE.

Grand Celebration in Sacramento—Full and Complete Report.

Stockton, Petaluma, Yreka, Vallejo, Mare Island and Placerville Join in the General Celebration.

The Preparations for the Event.

At sunrise the signal guns fired at the forts in the harbor informed the community that the day was ushered in, on which was to be celebrated the great event of the nineteenth century. As the bright sun rose and shed his radiance over the scene, workmen began the work of decorating the various streets through which the procession would pass; and as if by magic, in a few hours forests of evergreens and myriads of flowers of the gaudiest hues were entwined around balconies and trellis-work until some streets were literally covered with flowers, the perfume of which filled the early morning air with fragrance. Many of the houses of wealthy citizens were festooned with banners and red, white and blue cloth from top to bottom. Others had the front handsomely decorated with pictures in gilt frames, and a few had transparencies and mottoes. The notice given of the intention to celebrate was too short to admit of this kind of ornamentation. From nearly every house floated "Old Glory;" on some there were scores of miniature copies of that grand old flag, while on others they were of mammoth proportions, almost sweeping the streets when suspended between the palatial residences of our merchant princes. The flags of almost every nation, from the ancient Chinese to the new North German Republic; the Irish green with its golden harp and the English red with its tri-color crosses, hung side by side, wrapping their folds in a fond embrace over the gay scene. The decorations on Montgomery street by 9 A. M., made that busy thoroughfare appear as if floating in a cloud of red, white and blue, so numerous were the stars and stripes. As an illustration of the rapidity with which the preparations were made, it may be stated that the Committee of Arrangements at ten o'clock decided to erect seats for the accommodation of the ladies on Montgomery street, and before 11.30 a stand with seven rows of seats, extending from the corner of Bush street to near Pine, capable of seating 1,000 persons, was erected and a white canopy put up the whole length to shelter the ladies from the sun. The city authorities had the streets thoroughly cleaned the day before and they were well sprinkled in the morning, so there was but little dust. Long before the hour for the procession to arrive the sidewalks along the route were fringed with women and children waiting for the sight. So great was the crowd behind this margin of women and children that the streets were impassable during the progress of the procession. It has been estimated that there were nearly 100,000 people on the sidewalks and in the procession, numbers coming from all the surrounding country. At 11 o'clock, pursuant to notice, all the steam-engines throughout the city blew their whistles, which created an almost deafening noise, but a fitting chorus to the music of the many bands in the procession. Everything in the shape of bunting was flung to the breeze. The whole city front, from the Oakland ferry-boat, appeared like a flower garden full of brilliantly-colored flowers. The occasion being one that all mankind have an interest in, the ships of all nationalities displayed their country's banners in recognition of the universal joy at the completion of the work that shortens the distance between all nations.

The Last Spike Driven.

At ten o'clock the Grand Marshal received a telegram from Governor Stanford, informing him that the last spike had been driven at that hour. This news soon spread among the excited multitude, and everybody was anxious to proceed with the celebration of the event.

The Procession.

At precisely 11 o'clock A. M. the pageant started from Washington Square along Stockton street, in the following order:

Platoon of mounted police, under command of Chief Crowley.
Mounted trumpeters.
The American flag, with escort.
Grand Marshal—A. P. Stanford, yellow sash.
Chief Aid—A. W. Von Schmidt, red sash.
Marshal—Charles L. Wiggin, purple sash.
One hundred Aids, blue sash, mounted.

FIRST DIVISION.

Major General E. O. C. Ord and Staff; escort from United States Dragoons.

Second Artillery Band, 20 pieces; United States troops, under command of Colonel Miller; 12th Infantry; 12th Infantry Band, 17 pieces; Company K, 28 men, Captain Trippler; Company G, 40 men, Brevet Major Ford; Gibbon's Light Battery, four Parrott guns, 40 men, under command of Colonel Pennington, U. S. A., and Lieutenant Curtis.

Second Brigade, N. G. C., Brigadier General John Hewston Jr. and staff.

First Regiment Infantry, Major G. W. Granniss—Walcott's Band, 20 pieces; Ellsworth Rifles, 43 men, Captain Carson; Oakland Guard, 35 men, Captain Little; Tigers, 29 men, Captain Traynor; National Guard, 55 men, Lieutenant Vaughn; Sumner Light Guard, 40 men, Lieutenant Younger; Light Guard, 35 men, Captain Badlam; City Guard, 35 men, Captain Dunn.

Second Regiment, Colonel M'Kenzie—Ninth Infantry Band, 18 pieces; Excelsior Guard, 28 men, Captain Wilkinson; German Rifles, 45 men, Captain Sneider; Franklin Light Infantry, 30 men, Lieutenant Pierce; Veteran Guard, 40 men, Captain Hughes; San Francisco Cadets (Zouaves), 45 men, Captain McDonald.

Irish Battalion, Colonel M. C. Smith—Alper's Band, 17 pieces; Montgomery Guard, 61 men, Captain Quinn; Emmet Guard, 46 men, Captain Cleary; Wolf Tone Guard, 60 men, Captain Wasson; the Irish national flag and stars and stripes; Sarsfield Guard, 60 men, Captain O'Donnell; Meagher Guard, 60 men, Captain Egan; Shields Guard, 60 men, Captain Flannagan. California Light Battery, 60 men, 6 Parrott guns, Captain Bluxome.

Cavalry—San Francisco Hussars, 33 men, Captain Macdonald; Haight Light Guard, 65 men, Captain Knox; Jackson Dragoons, 50 men, Captain Rafferty. The two latter companies made a splendid appearance with their new brass helmets.

SECOND DIVISION.

Jacob Deeth, Marshal, and Aids; band of 30 pieces; MacMahon Guards, 80 men, Captain Canavan; band of 15 pieces; California Pioneers, 80 men; Veterans of the War of 1812; Veterans of the late War, with Societies' banners and stars and stripes.

In carriages—Major General Halleck, commanding Division of the Pacific; civic officials, 5 carriages.

THIRD DIVISION.

H. Droste, Marshal, and Aids; band of 17 pieces; San Francisco Schuetzen Verein, 70 men, Captain [illegible]; San Francisco Turn Verein, 78 men; Turner Boys, 40 in number; Turner truck, with implements of the Club, and going through gymnastic exercises; German Yagers, 50 men; Eureka Turn Verein, 80 men; German Benevolent Society; Eureka Sewing Company. Each Society carried its banners and the stars and stripes.

FOURTH DIVISION.

A. D. Splivalo, Marshal, and Aids; band of 15 pieces; Garibaldi Guard, 50 men; 30 Italian fishermen, with full-rigged boat mounted on truck, four horses, with flags flying; Italian Benevolent Society, 75 men; Italian National Association; Universal Republic; Mexican Benevolent Association—with national flags and Society's banners; barouche, drawn by four grays, containing Italian Consul.

FIFTH DIVISION.

James V. McElwee, Marshal; John Hanna, Captain John Short, Aids; Walcott's Band, twenty pieces; fifteen men of Fire Department; open carriage containing Fire Commissioners Freeman, Torrey and Merrill and Secretary Martin; Chief Whitney and his two assistants, foreman and ten men of No. 1; No. 1 Engine, with steam up and whistle blowing; Hose Cart No. 1; Hose Company No. 1, eight men; hose cart; hose company, eight men; Engine No. 2, foreman and seven men; Hose Cart No. 2, foreman and eight men; Engine No. 3 and hose cart, foreman and eight men; hose cart, foreman and seven men; Engine No. 4 and hose cart, foreman and seven men; Hook and Ladder Truck No. 1, neatly decorated with evergreens and flowers—foreman and seven men; Engine No. 5 and hose cart, foreman and ten men; hose cart, decorated with evergreens—foreman and seven men; Engine No. 6 and hose cart; assistant engineer, with elegant silver trumpet; [illegible] Engine No. 7 and hose cart, foreman and eleven men; Hook and Ladder Truck No. 2, elegantly decorated with festoons and garlands of flowers; twelve boys in white shirts and red caps, drawing miniature fire engine; truck drawn by four horses containing sample of main pipes and new hydrants used by the Spring Valley Water Company.

SIXTH DIVISION.

H. S. Homans, Marshal; George W. Barter, Henry N. Chauncey, Aids; band, fifteen pieces; open barouche drawn by four elegant grays, containing Mayor McCoppin and the orator, poet and chaplain of the day; six carriages containing foreign consuls, naval officers and other invited guests; twenty carriages containing Board of Supervisors, Board of Education, Chamber of Commerce, officers of the United States Coast Survey, officers of the United States Revenue service.

SEVENTH DIVISION.

John O. Earl, Marshal, and Aids; band, seventeen pieces; Independent Order of Red Men, 200 men in red regalia, banners and emblems of the order; band, fifteen pieces; Scandinavian Society, thirty men; Philharmonic Society, twenty-five men; Boot and Shoe Manufacturing Company with a large wagon drawn by four horses, with the artisans working at their trade, each Society carrying its banner and the Stars and Stripes. [illegible] "United we stand, divided we fall," and below, "Patronize Co-operative Associations." The wagon was followed by seventy-four Knights of St. Crispin, the French Benevolent Society, forty-eight members, and thirty-six butchers and market men, mounted.

EIGHTH DIVISION.

H. J. Booth, Marshal, and Aids; band; Improved Order Red Men, two hundred and fifty men.

Union Iron Works, marshaled by I. M. Scott, the men and boys, one hundred and thirty in number, each bearing a white cape with "Union Iron Works" painted in black letters. This party had a locomotive boiler made for the Virginia and Truckee Railroad, on a truck drawn by four large bay horses, with workmen hammering at the rivets and making as much noise as possible.

[illegible]

Two wagons belonging to Wheeler & Wilson's Sewing Machine Company.

TENTH DIVISION.

The colored citizens led by Mr. Bell, editor of the *Elevator*, Thomas Dyer, Marshal, and Aids.

Pacific Brass Band, 14 pieces; Brannan Guards, 29 men, Capt. Jones; Lincoln Zouaves, 25 men, Captain Phillips; delegation of colored citizens; Young Men's Beneficial Association.

The colored citizens made a very handsome turnout. The little vivandiere, who very properly marched beneath the folds of the stars and stripes, was an interesting feature of the division. The colored Band has greatly improved since its last appearance in a procession.

The procession occupied an hour and a half passing a given point, and was estimated to have contained nearly 3,000 men.

At the Pavilion.

The procession arrived at the Mechanics' Pavilion at ten minutes to two o'clock P. M. Mayor McCoppin then ascended the platform at the end of the building, on which we observed Major General Ord, Colonel Sherburne, Eighth Cavalry; Captain Preston and Major Brown, Thirty-sixth Infantry, and Aids to General Ord; Commodore Alfred Taylor, United States Navy; General Shanahan, Governor Blasdel, of Nevada; Lieutenant Governor Holden, Dr. Scudder; Colonel Holt and a large number of other prominent citizens. To the left of the stand was a large motto, "Public School Teachers of California—Pioneer Developers of California Mind;" and on the right, "The Ladies of California—Delighted Guests at the Iron Wedding of the East and West." The large building was well filled with an enthusiastic crowd. Mayor McCoppin called the meeting to order, and, after a few appropriate remarks, introduced Mr. Kennedy, the Scotch songster, who sang "The Star Spangled Banner" in a style that called forth much applause—the audience rising and joining most enthusiastically in the chorus. Mr. Kennedy was loudly encored, when he said that as he knew nothing better or more appropriate, he should sing the same song over again, which he did with, if possible, increased applause. This gentleman may very appropriately be called a patriotic songster, as, added to the advantage of a clear, fine voice, he is an eloquent elocutionist.

Rev. Dr. Cox made an impressive prayer, offering up thanks for our preservation as a nation and the completion of the great national work that we had assembled to commemorate.

John Mayer then sang "America," the audience, as before, joining in the chorus.

THE POEM.

Mr. Rhodes (Caxton) was then introduced as the Poet of the day, and was heartily applauded. He stated that he could not better introduce his poem than by quoting a stanza from one of the first of American poets (Whittier), who says:

"I hear the tramp of pioneers
Of nations yet to be—
The first low wash of waves, where soon
Shall roll a human sea."

After this preface, he read a most excellent poem, which was received with much applause, but which he did so much injustice to himself as to decline permitting its publication, [illegible]

Sierra Nevada's [illegible] of snow and Utah's desert of sand
Shall never again turn backward the flow
Of that human tide which may come and go
To the walls of the golden land.
We bid you welcome, brothers, to California's shores,
To her hills of golden granite and her flower-enameled floors,
To her streams whose waves run amber as they sparkle to the sea,
Where the heart is ever open and the hand ever free.

At the conclusion of the poem, Judge Nathaniel Bennett was introduced, and, in a clear voice that could be heard in all parts of the building, delivered the following

ORATION.

Ladies and Gentlemen: The great work is accomplished. On this day the vast undertaking, deemed at first chimerical and visionary, [illegible]

[illegible] Nay, starting at a later period, and reverting only to the time when the unfortunate John Fitch, whose soul was filled with the unextinguishable fire of the highest order of genius, first entertained an unbelieving Congress with a pleasure trip on the Schuylkill at the rate of progress of four miles an hour, on the first boat ever driven by steam; or, still later, to the time when Fulton, grasping, without thanks or acknowledgment, the great thought which had worn out the life of Fitch in poverty to develop, first treated the deriding Knickerbockers to a ride on the Hudson in his infant steamer *Hudson*. And what wonders, what magical achievements, have not been performed by the intelligent application and use of a little boiling water. What to-day would have been the Father of Waters himself, and the immense valley he enriches, were it not for the steamboat? What would have been the internal commerce on the waters of the United States? What, indeed, would have been the commerce of the whole world, had the same never-flagging, never-weary motive power remained yet undiscovered? Solitude would have brooded over the now busy streams, and the cries of wild fowl and beasts of prey only would have been heard in the places where the shrill scream of the steam-whistle now awakens civilized life on a thousand cultivated fields and hilltops.

But the triumph of steam is most complete in its conquests upon land, and it is in its application to the propulsion of the railroad car that it attains the highest degree of usefulness. It is considerably less than half a century since the first railroad for the use of commerce went into operation. The railroad system was then in its infancy. [illegible]

It is computed that the yearly revenue of the forty thousand miles of railroad in the United States is about $350,000,000. This amount is a simple tax on travel and production. It is perfectly true it is a necessary tax, and one gladly paid; [illegible]

[illegible] that additional sum, however fairly earned by the services rendered, is nothing more nor less than a tax of 200 per cent. on the consumption of tea in New York, which again reacts and affects the profit on production in China. The process of removal from one point to another—from the point of production to the point of consumption—has, in the case supposed, added nothing to the wealth or possessions of the world. It has indeed distributed, but it has in no way increased or intrinsically qualified human possessions; for after it, as before, whether in Canton or in New York, the world possessed the same number of pounds of tea of a given quality. So of flour, of cotton, of gold, or of every other product of the earth. Transportation cannot add to wealth, though it does to the cost; it is simply a distribution of wealth already in existence; and the cost of distribution constitutes a tax on consumption, levied indifferently on the producer, the manufacturer and the consumer. Could that tax be wholly abolished—could, for instance, breadstuffs be transported without cost to London, the exchangeable value of flour would rise in San Francisco and fall in Liverpool. Could that tax be wholly abolished, society would at once be relieved of a tax in comparison with which all the imposts of Government are trivial. In like manner everything which adds to the necessary cost of transportation aggravates the tax, and anything which diminishes it removes one more burden from human toil.

These facts and principles must be clearly borne in mind, else the great interest which communities have in all questions of transportation cannot be appreciated.

[illegible]

conclusion he sat down amid a tempest of plaudits. Rev. Dr. Cox being called upon, delivered a few brief, pointed remarks, and in conclusion toasted "The Day we Celebrate," to be drank, the reverend gentleman stipulated, "in cold water." Toasts were drank to "The President of the United States;" "The Central and Union Pacific Railroads and their officers and men;" "Leland Stanford, President of the Central Pacific Railroad;" "Major General Ord and his Staff;" "A. P. Stanford, the Grand Marshal of the Day," and numerous others, whom we have not space to mention. Colonel Von Schmidt proposed three cheers for the Union and moved that the party adjourn, which motion was carried.

Meeting of the Pioneers.

The Pioneer Society held a meeting previous to the procession, Mr. Brannan in the chair. The accompanying address of congratulation, by Mr. H. Kimball, was sent to the Directors of the road and ordered published in the daily papers:

"The present is a most eventful period in the history of California, for we are about to celebrate the completion of the great Pacific Railroad, one of the most grand enterprises ever achieved by man. This great work, in its conception, in carrying it forward and in its completion, is peculiarly the work of Pioneers. The early advocates of it—those who wrote for it, spoke for it, worked for it—were Pioneers, and the present Board of Managers, the entire Executive Board, are Pioneers. This great work is a Pioneer enterprise and one worthy the Pioneer's devotion, and if there is any class of our citizens who should take the deepest and most earnest interest, and act a most conspicuous part in this grand celebration it is the Pioneers of California, for they have always pioneered every great and good enterprise, from the earliest day of our State's history to the present time. We, therefore, as the Society of Pioneers of San Francisco, should take immediate steps to send the warmest congratulations of this Society to the President and the Board of Managers of the Central Pacific Railroad for the triumphant completion of that great and grand highway.

"Never in the history of the world has there ever been conceived such a grand enterprise, nor has there ever been accomplished such a work against such almost, and, we might say, such apparently unsurpassable obstacles; and this triumph, now about to be consummated, has only been brought about by that indomitable fortitude and heroism and that deathless energy which belongs peculiarly to the Pioneers of California.

"At the present most auspicious event it is the imperative duty of Pioneers to take an active part, and their first duty is to congratulate the President and Board of Directors, who have, amid such fearful obstacles, sustained themselves and brought about results that will soon be felt in our city and over this State with electric power.

"This is no ordinary event; its effect will be to revolutionise almost all the enterprises among us, by bringing us into close connection with and almost in speaking distance of the Atlantic States, and also with the nations of Europe.

"California holds the keys to the Golden Gate of the commerce of the world. 'Her hills and mountains are full of gold and silver;' 'her cattle are upon a thousand hills,' and her land 'is flowing with milk and honey.' It is a 'land of perpetual fruits.' The present grand and successful achievement is but the fulfillment of a prophecy in the completion of 'a great highway across the desert.'

"How many of our Pioneers there are now living in our midst who can recall their perils in 'Crossing the Plains;' their long, fearful and perilous journeyings of weary months, that now will be accomplished in less than one week, and that, too, across the very pathway of our early Pioneers? Some there may be here with us, while some near and dear ones have laid down to rest to await our coming.

"But the day of great things has come: the triumph is near at hand, even at our doors; and it is this great opportunity of performing a duty which should prompt the Pioneers of San Francisco to send a message of warm congratulation to those who have achieved this mighty triumph.

[illegible]

The Illuminations.

[illegible]

Gathering at the Lick House.

[illegible]

Incidents and Accidents.

[illegible]

every family in the city who could boast of an American flag, no matter how small, flung its starry folds to the breeze yesterday.

As Company M, Second Artillery, was passing Platt's Hall on Montgomery street, one of the gun-carriages came in contact with the underpinnings of a stage platform that had been erected to accommodate the young ladies of the State Teachers' Institute, and part of the platform suddenly collapsed. Fortunately no one was seriously injured. A boy named David Levi had his ankle sprained by the falling timbers, and some of the young ladies were somewhat bruised.

Colonel George T. Knox was kicked by a vicious horse in front of the City Hall, and narrowly escaped being run over by a railroad car, as he fell directly in front of the forward wheels, and but for the prompt action of the car-driver would have met with a shocking death. Sorely bruised he was extricated from his perilous position and managed to keep in his saddle and command his men all through the line of march.

At sundown the California Guard, under command of Captain I. Bluxome, fired a salute of thirty-seven guns, in front of the City Hall, on Kearny street.

On Montgomery street a fight took place between a driver of one of the Pacific Union Express wagons and the driver of a milk wagon—the latter of whom was seriously injured by being struck over the face and head with a whip. Both men were arrested.

A soldier named Haley, a gunner belonging to Company M, United States Artillery, was thrown from his seat on one of the gun carriages while the procession was passing the corner of Sutter and Montgomery streets. The wheel of the carriage passed over his breast. He was picked up by the bystanders and carried into a neighboring drug store. He was not seriously injured.

Several runaways occurred, and in some cases serious damage was done. Two powerful horses, drawing a heavy wagon loaded with grain, ran down Jackson street from Powell, and smashed up several buggies and lighter wagons on their way down to Stockton, when one of them fell and the other was caught. In one of the buggies was Mrs. Gatley and two children, one of whom was badly hurt.

THE CELEBRATION ELSEWHERE.

SACRAMENTO.

Immense Enthusiasm—Large Delegations From Abroad—The Streets Crowded with People.

[SPECIAL DISPATCH FROM OUR OWN REPORTER.]

SACRAMENTO, May 8th.

The streets are crowded with an immense throng of people. It is estimated that there are not less than seven or eight thousand strangers in town. Trains arrived at an early hour bringing delegations of firemen and military from Virginia City, Marysville, Placerville and other points on the lines of the different railways. Along the line of the railroad on the city front were twenty-three locomotives and the "Union Boy" gun, with the wire attached, waiting for the signal. The gun bore the following inscription: "I announced its opening, November 9, 1863; I proclaim its completion, May 8, 1869." The locomotive No. 1, the "Governor Stanford," the center of the group, bore the following: "We have met the light from the East in the tie and the rail." Precisely at ten o'clock the gun was fired, and from the throats of the locomotives issued sounds the like of which was never before heard. Bells and guns over the city accompanied them. The San Francisco boat and the cars from Vallejo arrived on Friday night heavily loaded with visitors. A train of eighty platform cars arrived from Nevada and Grass Valley, packed with passengers and fancifully decked out with flags and evergreens.

Delegations from Across the Mountains.

Early on Saturday morning a train from Nevada brought the Liberty Company, of Gold Hill, the Washoe Company, of Virginia, and the Truckee Eagles. These delegations were received by the Sacramento fire companies, and after being escorted through the streets were hospitably breakfasted. All the delegations were received with the like formality and hospitality.

Street Decorations and Displays.

The city presented a novel and most beautiful appearance. The principal streets were lined on both sides with cottonwood and evergreen branches and spanned by arches festooned with flags, and adorned with appropriate mottoes. Many of the houses and balconies were richly and tastefully decorated; J and K streets, in particular, presented a most picturesque appearance. The locomotives ranged at the city front were magnificently ornamented with banners, streamers and flowers. Pains had been taken to water all the main streets, so that they were free from dust.

The Procession.

FIRST DIVISION.

Escort—Sacramento Hussars, Captain Ebner, 49 men.

Grand Marshal—General Josiah Howell. Aids—Major L. H. Foote, W. J. Robertson, Major W. A. Anderson, E. M. Fry, Major G. L. Simmons, Captain J. D. Yost, Major E. M. Howison, Major T. J. Blakeney, Edw. Cadwalader, A. J. Nichols, John H. Carroll, C. T. Wheeler, D. A. Bender, L. A. Upson.

Willis' Band; Marshal—Major W. L. Campbell, with Aids; Nevada Light Guard, Captain Lancaster, 50 men; Union Guard, Grass Valley, Lieutenant Ruhl commanding, 25 men; Howell Zouaves, Grass Valley, Lieutenant Chas. Wells commanding, 30 men; Sacramento City Guard, Captain Turton, 35 men; Placerville City Guard, Lieutenant Wiley, 45 men; Emmet Guard, Captain Sheehan, 57 men; Sacramento Light Artillery, Captain Davis, 66 men.

SECOND DIVISION.

Marshal—E. J. Robinson, with Aids; Alper's Band; escort, Sacramento Pioneer Association, 125 men; carriages, containing Superintendent, Directors and officers of the Central Pacific Railroad, engineer corps and clerks, carpenters and car-builders, etc.; also the shovel used in turning the first sod and a piece of the "last tie;" Truck, with mechanics' lathes, etc.; men from the Sacramento Iron Works, 200 in number; trucks, containing implements from the boiler and coppersmiths' shops, with men at work; carriage, containing 11 men, with the inscription, "These are the men who laid ten miles of track in one day;" boiler makers, with locomotive boiler on truck; truck, carrying a printing press, printing the *Daily Record*.

THIRD DIVISION.

Marshal—John Donnellan, with Aids; Kidd's band; Chief Engineers of the Virginia, Gold Hill, Nevada City and Marysville Fire Departments; Chief and Assistant Engineers of Sacramento Fire Department; Confidence Engine Company No. 1, 54 men; Confidence Hose Company No. 1, 22 men; Nevada band; Nevada Engine Company No. 1, Nevada City, 27 men; Pennsylvania Engine Company No. 2, Nevada City, 50 men; Protection Engine Company No. 2, Sacramento, 42 men; Protection Hose Company No. 2, Sacramento, 17 men; Cornet band; Sacramento Engine Company No. 3, 45 men; Sacramento Hose Company No. 3, 14 men; Liberty Engine Co. No. 1, Gold Hill, 51 men; Eureka Engine Company No. 4, Sacramento, 61 men; Eureka Hose Company No. 4, 21 men; Washoe band; Washoe Engine Company No. 4, Virginia City (including a delegation from Truckee), 78 men; Kidd's second band; Knickerbocker Engine Company No. 5, Sacramento, 63 men; Knickerbocker Hose Company No. 5, Sacramento, 17 men; Young America Engine Company No. 6 (with engine drawn by four horses), 50 men; Young America Hose Company No. 6, 21 men; delegations from Protection and Eagle Engine Companies of Grass Valley, 45 men; Neptune Hose Company No. 1, Sacramento, 29 men; Alert Hook and Ladder Company No. 2, 17 men.

FOURTH DIVISION.

Marshal—W. F. Knox, with Aids; Band; Sacramento Commandery, 41 men; Carriages containing Hon. C. H. Swift, President of the Day; His Excellency H. H. Haight, Orator; Albert Hart, Reader; Rev. J. A. Benton, Chaplain; Ex-Governors of California; Judges of Supreme Court; District and County Judges; Present and past State and Municipal Officers of Sacramento and adjoining counties and cities, and others.

FIFTH DIVISION.

Marshal—F. A. Hornblower, with Aids; Band; Improved Order Red Men; Grand Lodge, I. O. O. F.; Grand Encampment and all the Sacramento Lodges; Stockton Band; San Joaquin Delegation, with banners; Mexican and Chilean Clubs.

SEVENTH DIVISION.

Marshal—Captain J. D. Yost, with Aids; Cars containing Templars' Band of Hope; School Children in carriages; Omnibuses and wagons.

EIGHTH DIVISION.

Marshal—John T. Carvy with Aids; Placerville Band; Wells, Fargo & Co.'s "pony;" express wagons with transparency, a man carrying the mail to New York from San Francisco with letter for U. S. Grant; Capital Woolen Mills—two cars with machinery and men at work; Union Iron Works with implements of trade; mounted men and citizens in carriages.

The procession was fifty-five minutes passing a given point. It reached the depot at about two o'clock, where the following services were held: Mayor Swift called the meeting to order; Music, Railroad Galop, Willis' Band; Invocation, Rev. J. A. Benton; An Original Ode, by L. E. Crane, sung to "America;" Poem, by L. E. Crane, read by A. Hart; Music, vocal, by The Twelve; Oration, Governor H. H. Haight; Music, vocal, by The Twelve; Benediction, Rev. J. A. Benton; Music, by Band.

Illuminations—Appearance of the City at Night.

At night the the principal streets of the city presented a most splendid and imposing appearance. The illumination was general and magnificent. The whole city was ablaze with light, and 20,000 people were abroad to enjoy [illegible]

[Continued on Third Page.]

San Francisco Chronicle.

VOL. XLVII. SAN FRANCISCO, CAL., TUESDAY, FEBRUARY 28, 1888. NO. 44.

A FATAL EXPLOSION.

A Terrible Disaster at Vallejo.

The Steamer Julia Blows Up and Sinks.

Fifteen Dead Recovered and Fourteen Missing.

All the Others on Board More or Less Severely Injured.

The Old Boilers the Cause of the Calamity.

Narrow Escape of the Survivors—Losses by Fire—Stories of Eye-Witnesses.

One of the worst steamship explosions that ever occurred on this coast wrecked the Southern Pacific Company's steamer Julia at South Vallejo yesterday morning and resulted in the killing or injuring of every one of the forty-nine persons on board. Fifteen bodies of the dead have been recovered and identified, and fourteen persons are missing, all of whom are believed to be lying dead among the wreckage of the ill-fated steamer. Most of the killed and injured were workingmen going from Vallejo to the Contra Costa shore to their daily labor in the mills and factories at the Junction. The explosion occurred just as the steamer was about to start from the wharf. The Julia was broken in two, the crude petroleum used for fuel took fire, the vessel soon burned to the water's edge and the flames spread to the adjoining wharf, burning the offices and four cars. Starr's flourmill was saved with difficulty. The entire loss is estimated at $250,000.

The saddest feature of the disaster was the grief of those who lost husbands and fathers. The identification of the recovered bodies was attended by terrible scenes. None of the survivors could give any clew to the cause of the explosion, but late last night a diver settled the mystery by discovering one boiler with the end blown clean out, while the petroleum tanks were found to be intact. The Julia was an old boat, built in 1864, and the boilers, though frequently overhauled, were never renewed. They were inspected last June and declared to be sound. Full details of the disaster, with the condition of the wounded up to midnight, will be found below.

Special Dispatches to the CHRONICLE.

STORY OF THE DISASTER.

Terrible Scenes at the Recovery of the Bodies.

VALLEJO, February 27.—Vallejo was shaken to its foundation this morning, and throughout the day the wildest excitement has prevailed in this usually quiet little place. The cause was the terrible boiler explosion which occurred at 6:10 o'clock this morning on board the ferry-steamer Julia, as she lay at her berth at South Vallejo. As far as can at present be learned twenty-four lives were lost and twenty-four were seriously injured, while the steamer is a total loss, having sunk almost immediately after the accident.

THE CROWD OF WORKINGMEN.

The Julia belonged to the Southern Pacific Company and made several trips daily between North and South Vallejo and across the bay to Vallejo Junction. Every morning she left South Vallejo to call at North Vallejo, return to the starting point and then cross to the Junction, having on board the many workingmen who found employment at the smelting works, iron works, lumber yards and grain warehouses of the latter place. To-day the little side-wheeler had been up to North Vallejo, which she left at 6 o'clock in the morning and had returned to South

The Julia's lower deck.

Vallejo, with her usual complement of passengers. As the men came on board, the morning was chilly and many crowded into the room around the smokestack in order to benefit by its warmth. Below them were the two boilers, fed with petroleum, and the ruddy glow shone on their faces as they looked out into the gray dawn and chatted pleasantly together, little dreaming that the next moment would be for many their last.

THE EXPLOSION.

The order to throw off the ropes had been given and the engineer's gong from below had sounded an answer to Captain Gedge's order to "go ahead." Before the sounds of the gong had died on the air and before the order could be obeyed, a terrible explosion took place, filling the air with human beings and shaking the country for miles around. As nearly as can be learned the explosion took place immediately under the feet of the men who had congregated round the smokestack. Scarcely had the sound of the explosion died away when the red flames and dense smoke of burning petroleum rose from the wrecked vessel. Many of those who were not near the smoke-stack were thrown violently toward the bow of the boat while others were hurled into the water, thankful to escape with a wetting and a few bruises. Almost immediately

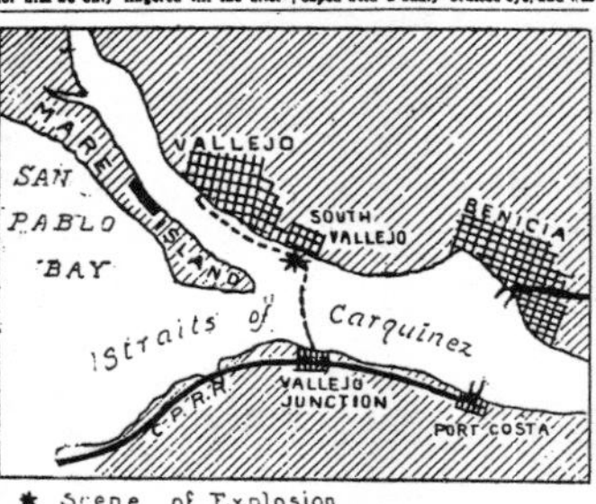

Map showing location of disaster.

... ner of the shed lay a mass of human remains, charred, bruised and mangled beyond recognition. Close by lay a second, the skull frightfully disfigured and one hand blown off. A third was the body of a young man, the face raw with burns, the legs broken, and presenting at the same time a pitiable and horrible spectacle. Many of the men were married and leave families.

IDENTIFYING THE VICTIMS.

In the shed only the jurors and press representatives were allowed, but outside stood crowds of anxious ones, and many a cry was heard as peering over the gates or between the bars a glimpse was caught of some familiar body, the identification of which the jury sought to determine. When their labors had suspended they had identified thirteen.

At 5 o'clock, when the work of the jury was suspended, there still remained one unidentified body, and the searchers were still at work on the wreck, trying to find more of the missing men.

A QUARTER OF A MILLION LOST.

The fire destroyed the wharf sheds, the telegraph station and ticket office, as well as four passenger and freight cars. The loss in all amounts to about $250,000. The wharf was almost entirely destroyed, and Starr's Flouring Mills, which are only separated by a few yards from the end of the wharf, were at one time in great danger.

CREW OF THE JULIA.

The crew of the Julia consisted of eleven hands: George Gedge, captain; Charles Heath, pilot; Joe Waite, Manuel Frictas, Frank Williams, Gus Anderson; engineers, John Long and George Wallace; fireman, M. Degner. It is believed the last-named was not on duty this morning, but that his place was filled by Henry Peterson.

NOTES AND INCIDENTS.

A full telegraphic outfit arrived from Sacramento to-night. Although the telegraph station was burned at 8 o'clock this morning a temporary table had been put up and messages were flying over the wires, to the great credit of George Hanscom, the telegraphic superintendent at South Vallejo.

The inquest will be continued at 10 o'clock to-morrow morning.

The steamer Modoc replaced the Julia to-day, and the El Capitan arrived this evening to run regularly over the Julia's course.

The force of the explosion broke the Julia in half, though Captain Gedge said that she remained afloat long enough to enable several of those aboard to get ashore.

THE KILLED.

A List of the Victims of the Explosion.

VALLEJO, February 27.—At the Coroner's inquest this afternoon thirteen bodies were identified. From the result of the inquest and from other sources the following is a complete list of the killed:

Brandon, John—Laborer, 38 years old, native of Ireland; leaves a wife and two children.

Branneley, Michael—Laborer in a lum- ...

South Vallejo depot and ferry-boat Julia immediately after the explosion.

FROM THE EAST.

A California Swindler Arrested.

Burgess Designs Four New Yachts.

A Singer's Miserable End—An Audacious Cadet—A Terrible Crime.

George von Reinalds of San Francisco, has been arrested at Fall River, Mass., for passing worthless drafts.

Burgess has designed four yachts of different models, but all measuring forty feet on the water line.

Charles Richard, a once famous singer, died in New York yesterday.

Cadet W. C. Davis is in the guardhouse at ...

... murdered by Zeph Davis, a mulatto, at Chicago, yesterday.

Ex-Senator Tabor and W. T. Carleton were arrested at Denver yesterday for giving a sacred concert on Sunday.

Special Dispatches to the CHRONICLE.

WORTHLESS DRAFTS.

They Cause the Arrest of a San Franciscan at the East.

BOSTON, February 27.—George von Reinolds, who was arrested in Fall River yesterday, was brought here this morning to answer a charge of passing worthless checks. Reinolds belongs in San Francisco. He claims to have spent $1400 in gambling and drinking. He boarded at the Hotel Temple and on Tuesday morning ...

... ment is with the Mayor in his endeavors to close all variety theaters on Sunday nights; but considerable indignation is expressed and the general opinion is against him in his course toward Tabor in not permitting the grand concert performance given last night.

A BRUTAL CRIME.

A Young Girl Assaulted and Murdered by a Mulatto.

CHICAGO, February 27.—Maggie Gagen, 15 years of age, was assaulted and murdered and her body concealed in a closet in Gregg Brothers' boot-heel factory in this city, early this morning. Zeph Davis, a mulatto, 29 years old, is supposed to be the murderer. He left the store before the discovery of the body and has not yet been found. The girl worked in the factory, and is supposed that she reached there about 6:30 o'clock. Davis at that time was there alone, and it is supposed that he criminally assaulted her and then murdered her with a hatchet, her skull being beaten to pieces. The clothing and body gave evidence of the girl having made a desperate struggle.

LOCKE'S LUCK.

How the Manager Was Relieved of a Serious Charge.

WASHINGTON, February 27.—The case of Ella Sylva and Mrs. Pierson of the defunct National Opera Company against Manager Locke, for swindling them by means of worthless checks, was dismissed in the Police Court this morning, the evidence showing that Locke really had opened an account with the bank in question and had a balance there of 55 cents. ...

PUBLIC BUILDINGS.

THE DEMOCRATS OPPOSING THEIR CONSTRUCTION.

The Administration Is Fighting Against Appropriations Which Would Reduce the Surplus.

WASHINGTON, February 27.—The House has endeavored to take up and pass a number of bills providing for the erection of public buildings in various parts of the country. Among the bills on the calendar are one for a public building at Portland, Or.; another for the purchase of a postoffice site at San Francisco and one for increasing the ...

AFFAIRS ABROAD.

Gladstone's Home Rule Article.

Critical Condition of the Crown Prince.

A Sensational Story Spoiled—Deaths Caused by an Avalanche.

Gladstone's article on Ireland receives much praise in England.

The latest reports regarding the Crown Prince are unfavorable.

The British Government denies that it is negotiating with Turkey for Salonica.

An avalanche killed many people in Valtorta, Italy.

The Russian garrisons on the Austrian frontier have been re-enforced.

Prince Ferdinand's birthday was celebrated ...

GLADSTONE'S APPEAL.

His Article on the Irish Question Received With Favor.

[THE NEW YORK WORLD CABLE SERVICE; COPYRIGHTED, 1888 — SPECIAL TO THE CHRONICLE.]

LONDON, February 27.—The newspapers here to-day are twenty-four hours behind the New York *World* and San Francisco CHRONICLE in representing copious extracts of Gladstone's article on Ireland from advance copies of the *Contemporary Review*. From the Liberal papers Gladstone gets laudatory praise, and the Tory papers, while dissenting from his conclusions, give him stinted credit for a fair and impartial review of the Irish question ...

San Francisco Chronicle.

VOL. LXVII. SAN FRANCISCO, CAL., WEDNESDAY, FEBRUARY 16, 1898. NO. 32.

BATTLE SHIP MAINE BLOWN UP IN THE HARBOR OF HAVANA.

Terrific Explosion Rends the Magnificent Machine of War and Brings Death to Hundreds of the Brave Fellows Upon Her.

CAPTAIN SIGSBEE, COMMANDER OF THE MAINE.

Captain Sigsbee, who commanded the battle-ship Maine in Havana harbor, one of the most trusted officers of the Navy. He has a splendid record, ever from his graduation from Annapolis in 1863, but the incident that gave him the most prominence was his presence of mind in New York City last year, when, by the quick handling of his ship, he saved the lives of a thousand river excursionists.

NEW YORK, February 16.—A cable to the World from Havana says: Captain Sigsbee says that one-quarter of his crew of 600 men are dead which is precisely the same estimate as that of Paglierei, Chief of Police of Havana.

Captain Sigsbee says he is not able to state officially the cause of the explosion until he has made an investigation with his officers. He said the magazine was well guarded, [illegible]

"[illegible] the American people," he said, "that nearly all the [illegible] are saved."

[illegible] ship is lying near the head of the bay. Proof that [illegible] not the magazine only that exploded is shown by the [illegible] the bow was entirely blown to pieces. The crew are [illegible] ignorance of the cause of the disaster.

[illegible] force of the explosion was something frightful. Part of the marines were taken on board of the Alphonso XII, the crew of which rendered very effective service in saving the lives of the American sailors. Others of the crew were picked up by a Ward Line steamer in the bay. There is much excitement here, but there is no riot and no danger to Americans.

DETAILS OF DISASTER.

A Terrific Explosion That Cost Hundreds of Brave Men Their Lives.

HAVANA, February 15.—At 9:45 o'clock this evening a terrible explosion took place on board the United States cruiser Maine in Havana harbor.

Many sailors were killed or wounded.

The explosion shook the whole city. The windows were broken in many houses.

The wounded sailors of the Maine are unable to explain it. It is believed that the cruiser is totally destroyed.

A correspondent says he has conversed with several of the wounded sailors and understands from them that the explosion took place while they were asleep, so that they can give no particulars as to the cause.

All the boats of the Spanish cruiser Alfonso XIII are assisting.

HAVANA, February 16. — The wildest consternation prevails in Havana. The wharves are crowded with thousands of people.

It is believed the explosion occurred in a small powder magazine.

The first theory was that there had been a preliminary explosion in the Santa Barbara (magazine) of powder or dynamite below the water.

Admiral Manterola believes that the first explosion was of a grenade that was hurled over the navy yard.

Captain Sigsbee and the other officers have been saved. It is estimated that over 100 of the crew were killed, but it is impossible as yet to give exact details.

Admiral Manterola has ordered that boats of all kinds should go to the assistance of the Maine and her wounded. The Havana firemen are giving aid, tending carefully to the wounded as they are brought on shore. It is a terrible sight.

General Zolano and the other Generals have orders by Captain-General Blanco to take steps to help the Maine's crew in every way possible.

A correspondent has been near the Maine in one of the boats of the cruiser Alfonso and seen others of the wounded, who corroborate the statement of those first interviewed that they were asleep when the explosion occurred.

Captain Sigsbee says the explosion occurred in the bow of the vessel. He received a wound in the head. Orders were given to the other officers to save themselves as best they could. The latter, who were literally thrown from their bunks in their night clothing, gave the necessary orders with great self-control.

At 1:15 the Maine continues burning.

THE NEWS IN WASHINGTON.

WASHINGTON, February 15.—The Secretary of the Navy received the following telegram from Captain Sigsbee:

Maine blown up in Havana

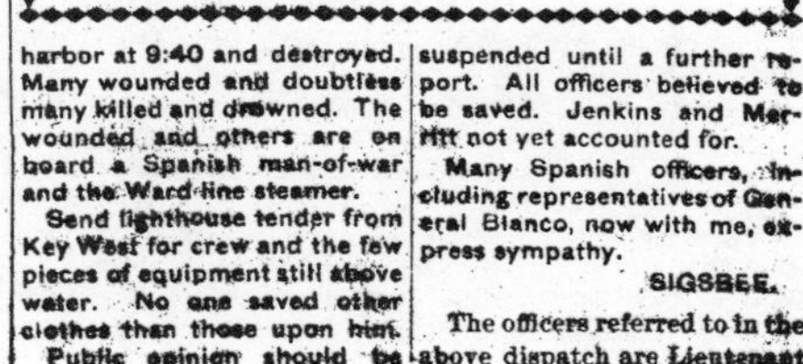

harbor at 9:40 and destroyed. Many wounded and doubtless many killed and drowned. The wounded and others are on board a Spanish man-of-war and the Ward line steamer.

Send lighthouse tender from Key West for crew and the few pieces of equipment still above water. No one saved other clothes than those upon him.

Public opinion should be suspended until a further report. All officers believed to be saved. Jenkins and Merritt not yet accounted for.

Many Spanish officers, including representatives of General Blanco, now with me, express sympathy.

SIGSBEE.

The officers referred to in the above dispatch are Lieutenant

BATTLE SHIP MAINE BLOWN UP IN HAVANA.

OFFICERS OF THE MAINE

The Men Who Had Charge of the Splendid Warship Destroyed in Havana Harbor.

The officers of the Maine are:

CHARLES D. SIGSBEE, Commander.
RICHARD WAINWRIGHT, Lieutenant-Commander.
G. F. HOLMAN, Lieutenant.
JOHN HOOD, Lieutenant.
C. W. YUNGEN, Lieutenant.
C. W. BLOW, Lieutenant (junior grade.)
J. T. BLANDIN, Lieutenant (junior grade.)
F. A. JENKINS, Lieutenant (junior grade.)
J. H. HOLDEN, Cadet.
W. T. CLUVERIUS, Cadet.
AMOS BRONSON, Cadet.
D. F. BOYD Jr., Cadet.
L. G. HENEBERGER, Surgeon.
RYAN, Paymaster.
L. G. HOWELL, Chief Engineer.
E. C. BOWERS, Passed Assistant Engineer.
J. R. MORRIS, Assistant Engineer.
D. R. MERRITT, Assistant Engineer.
POPE, Cadet Engineer.
WASHINGTON, Cadet Engineer.
ARTHUR GRENSHAW, Cadet Engineer.
J. P. CHADWICK, Chaplain.
A. W. CATLIN, Lieutenant of Marines.
FRANCIS E. LARKINS, Boatswain.
JOSEPH HILL, Gunner.
GEORGE HELMS, Carpenter.

[illegible] of Havana, in Which the Maine Was Destroyed.

MORRO CASTLE, HAVANA HARBOR

San Francisco Chronicle.

VOL. LXX. SAN FRANCISCO, CAL., FRIDAY, OCTOBER 13, 1899. NO. 90.

BOER FORCES MARCHING ON FIVE BRITISH POINTS.

ENGLISH ARMORED TRAIN DESTROYED.

Fears at Cape Town That Many Lives Were Lost in the Disaster.

The British Troops at Mafeking and in Northern Natal in Grave Danger.

Special Dispatches to the "Chronicle."

CAPE TOWN, October 13—9:45 A.M.—A dispatch from Vryburg says that an armored train has been destroyed. It is feared that much loss of life will result. The news has been unofficially confirmed.

JOHANNESBURG, October 12.—War was declared yesterday. The formal declaration goes into effect at 10 o'clock this morning.

PARIS, October 12.—Secretary Vanderhoeven of the Transvaal European agency officially notified the French Government this morning that a state of war between the South African Republic and Great Britain exists, and has existed since last evening.

LONDON, October 13.—When the Cabinet meets at noon to-day it is evident the Boer advance will be in full swing. Judging from present appearances the Boers are preparing for a simultaneous invasion at five separate points, Laing's Nek, Kimberley, Vryburg, Mafeking and Lobatsi. Therefore, it is almost impossible to guess the plan of campaign. A dispatch from Durban, dated Thursday morning at 8 o'clock, announces that the Boers seized Albertina station and demanded the keys, which were delivered to them by the station master, who reached Ladysmith on a trolley car. The excitement at Ladysmith is increasing and the troops are ready to act at a moment's notice.

It is now definitely known that the British Government sent no final proposals to Pretoria. The Transvaal's ultimatum forestalled that intention.

So far as news received thus far shows not a shot has yet been fired. The evacuated district between Charlestown and Newcastle, Natal, has an area of 250 square miles, and consists chiefly of hilly moorland sparsely populated.

The Jacobsdal commando of the Free State Boers is marching on the Modder river.

In reply to the formal inquiry of Sir Alfred Milner, Governor of Cape Colony and British High Commissioner in South Africa, President Steyn of the Orange Free State announces that that state will make common cause with the Transvaal.

The home preparations for war are growing apace. The reservists are responding more actively to the proclamation ordering their mobilization and the Government has engaged more transports.

In military circles no apprehension is felt at any of the movements yet reported on the part of the Boers, and it is not believed they will make any serious attack, preferring to wait for the British to advance.

There is no abatement in the anti-English feeling on the Continent. The Times' Berlin correspondent declares that the German nation as a whole is unfriendly to England and that there would be rejoicing on all sides if England should suffer disaster or damage, just as the people were ready to rejoice had America suffered defeat at the hands of Spain.

Advices from Vienna report that at an anti-Semitic meeting there Burgomaster Lueger included both the United States and England in a charge of ruthlessness and thirst for gold, especially criticising America in her economic dealings with Europe. Herr Lueger, in the course of his speech, paid homage to the patriotism and love of liberty displayed by the Boers

BOERS PLAN TO CUT OFF BRITISH FORCES.

Burghers Now Marching Against the Troops at Ladysmith—May Attack From Two Sides.

NEW YORK, October 12.—A cable to the Sun says: A dispatch to the Telegraph from Ladysmith, Natal, says that a column of Boers, numbering 8000 men, is now at Tugel river. Others are at Middledale Farm, below Tintwa mountain.

Judging from the Telegraph's dispatch, the Boers' move apparently aims at cutting off the British northern garrisons. They will probably be joined south of Ladysmith by a column which is believed to be advancing from the river.

DURBAN, October 12.—The imperial reserves in Natal have been called out. Everybody has left Charlestown, the last train bringing away the railway staff to Newcastle, while the exodus from Newcastle also continues. The Fifth Dragoons arrived this morning from India, landed immediately and at once proceeded to the front.

CAPE TOWN, October 12.—All available troops of the garrison of the district were dispatched to a point nearer the western border last night.

NORVALS PONT, ORANGE RIVER, ON THE BOUNDARY OF THE CAPE COLONY AND THE ORANGE FREE STATE.

BRITISH TROOPS AWAIT ATTACK.

Believe They Will be Able to Hold Mafeking Against Transvaal Army.

CAPE TOWN, October 12—Morning.—Advices from Mafeking say that precaution has been taken against attack, and all the streets are barricaded. According to these advices the Boers intend to shell the town before delivering their attack. They are said to possess twelve guns. Every man in Mafeking is carrying a rifle, and the military authorities are confident that they will be able to repel the attack, but they lack the force necessary to follow a Boer retreat.

The town is fairly quiet. The convent sisters and many ladies have elected to stay and nurse the wounded and many houses have been converted into hospitals. The searchlight on the fort is kept working across the veldt. Three Boer spies have been arrested in the town. Railway communication to the southward is practically at the mercy of the Boers, over 200 miles of the line being within easy striking distance of the enterprising commandos.

Sad scenes occurred at the railway station on the departure of the women and children by train. It is thought that even should the main line be blown up at any point, the damage can be repaired within a few hours.

Wednesday evening three carriages containing women and children, but not a single white man, except sick ministers, were dispatched from Mafeking.

MAFEKING, October 12.—Half a battery of artillery from Kimberly has just arrived. The police at the outlying stations have been ordered to concentrate within the town limits. No one is allowed to leave either by road or train without special permission, which is not granted to any able-bodied man. Nearly all the women and children have left. Confidence in their ability to repulse the Boers is increasing among the British.

The news of the ultimatum created no excitement at Mafeking. A transport rider, suspected of carrying details daily across the border, has been arrested there.

KIMBERLEY, October 12.—The authorities at Mafeking are hourly expecting an attack, in which event the wires between Mafeking and Kimberley will be cut and information entirely shut off. The latest information regarding the number of burghers assembled along the Kimberley border is that it does not exceed 3500. The Boers have only four field guns. A successful attack upon Kimberley is therefore considered impossible.

LONDON, October 12.—A dispatch from Kimberley states that the artillery stationed there has been out practicing at a dummy force at a range of from 2500 to 2900 yards. The practice showed excellent results. According to the same dispatch defenses have been erected in all directions and the garrison declare that they are "quite ready to meet the tortoise and give him a warm reception when he puts his head above the kopje."

A dispatch from Mafeking under today's date says that Colonel Baden-Powell has just sent a strong British force from Mafeking toward the border with field guns and ambulances, presumably with a view of occupying advantageous defensive high ground.

ENGLAND'S REPLY TO THE BOER ULTIMATUM.

LONDON, October 12.—Following is the text of the British reply to the Boer ultimatum: "Chamberlain to Milner, High Commissioner, sent 10:45 P. M., October 10, 1899: Her Majesty's Government has received with great regret the peremptory demands of the South African Republic, conveyed in your telegram of October 9th. You will inform the Government of the South African Republic in reply that the conditions demanded by the Government of the South African Republic are such as Her Majesty's Government deems it impossible to discuss."

MAP OF THE SEAT OF WAR IN SOUTH AFRICA.

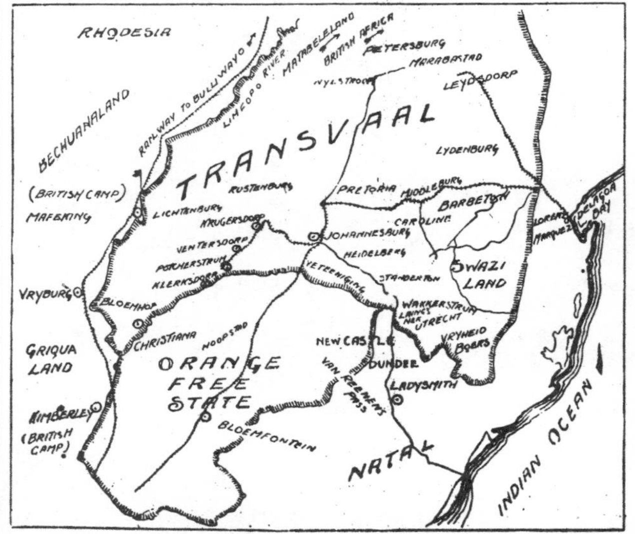

THE BOER campaign appears to have been planned for simultaneous attack on all the important British positions near the border. A Boer force entered yesterday through Van Reener's pass and took Albertina, which is between the pass and Ladysmith, in Natal. At the latter place, thirty-six miles from the Orange Free State border, about 8000 British troops are encamped. The other points threatened are Laing's Nek, Kimberley, Vryburg, Mafeking and Lobatsi. Colonel Baden-Powell, at Mafeking, is in the worst straits, as he has only a small force, variously estimated at from 600 to 1800 troops, and he is threatened by a big Boer force of 8000 men.

BRITISH DEFENSE AGAINST EUROPE.

Flying Squadron to Be Formed to Overawe the Jealous Powers.

Former Home Secretary Asquith Intimates That England Looks to America for Aid Should the Nations Interfere.

Special Dispatches to the "Chronicle."

NEW YORK, October 12.—The World's London cable says: The proposed formation of a British flying squadron is a purely defensive measure and inspired by the bitter hostility to England displayed by the Continental press. The Russian official organs are foremost in threats and incitements to joint action against Great Britain, and though official Germany proclaims itself neutral the German press is second only to Russia in its denunciation of England's South African policy. Though not believing at present that these outbursts of rancor will materialize the British Government is taking precautions against eventualities.

The difficulty and delay in mobilizing an army corps for South Africa is regarded as most unfortunate and calculated to induce Great Britain's enemies abroad to take advantage of the present crisis to satisfy old animosities. The formation of an Irish corps with Krueger excites violent resentment. The Globe advises commanders of British forces that their duty, should they capture any Irishmen among Krueger's forces, would be to "shoot them like dogs."

The meeting of the Cabinet to-morrow furnishes occasion for a big demonstration by the supporters of the Government and elaborate police arrangements are being made to cope with the anticipated crowd. This is an innovation. Heretofore the assembling of the Cabinet, even at the most critical times, has been witnessed by only small gatherings of idlers or casual passers-by.

ENGLAND LOOKING TO AMERICA FOR SYMPATHY.

Former Home Secretary Recalls Incidents of Spanish War—Indications That Intervention Is Feared.

LONDON, October 12.—Henry Herbert Asquith, former Home Secretary, speaking at Newburgh this evening on the Transvaal situation and referring to the attitude abroad, said:

"The Americans have not forgotten, and I believe they will not forget, the attitude which this country, almost alone among the nations, assumed toward them recently when they were enduring times of crisis and emergency similar to those which seem now before us. The sympathy shown in those hours of danger and need engendered a warmth of gratitude and, I might say also, a tenderness of sentiment which is no less genuine and strong between the nations than between individuals.

"Looking backward two years, there is nothing which we have more reason to congratulate ourselves upon, nothing that has added more to our international assets, than the fact that we established this tie of affectionate, reciprocal sympathy with our great kindred nation beyond the Atlantic."

Lee Henry Courtney, Liberal member of Parliament for the Bodwin division of Cornwall, addressing his constituents at Liskenard, was frequently interrupted. Mr. Courtney lamented the failure of the principles enunciated at The Hague, and in a lengthy criticism of the Government's policy declared that "our policy has been of a shifting character, causing the Boers to distrust us."

He said he did not believe the prevalent idea that there was a conspiracy to expel the British from South Africa and he regretted the Boer ultimatum, but he said he was unable honestly to condemn it. After his speech Mr. Courtney was followed by hostile demonstrations. The customary vote of confidence was moved, but was met by an amendment, which was adopted by a large majority, expressing regret that Mr. Courtney should be at variance with the Government's policy and expressing complete confidence in Lord Salisbury. Mr. Courtney, after the passage of the amendment, said it was the first time he had encountered a hostile vote, and he admitted its gravity and seriousness. The audience then sang "Rule Britannia."

Although a considerable minority of the English public regard the war with grave misgivings, it is practically impossible for this feeling to get voice at the present juncture. An attempt of the Peace and Arbitration Association to hold a meeting at Bristol last evening occasioned an extraordinary scene. Directly the doors were opened the jingoes crowded into the hall, sang patriotic songs, waved union jacks and refused any hearing to the peace orators, finally taking possession of the platform and passing a vote of confidence in the Government.

At Cardiff the Conservative Association adopted a vote of want of confidence in James Mackensie Maclean, their representative in the House of Commons, because he recently attacked the policy of Mr. Chamberlain and the Government. The Duke of Marlborough addressed a mass meeting at Oldham. In his speech the Duke justified the policy of the Government, which, he declared, had not been driven into war by overexcited enthusiasm or unwise agitation.

Winston Churchill, who spoke at the same meeting, said he felt no animosity toward the Boers in connection with Majuba Hill. "We were worsted," said Mr. Churchill, "in a fair fight, and I hope now there will be no cant about avenging Majuba Hill. The Government throughout have displayed admirable patience, but there is ample evidence of the existence of a deliberate conspiracy against British supremacy and they have been practicing patience on top of a powder magazine."

UNITED STATES CAN TAKE NO ACTION.

Official Statement Issued at Washington in Reply to the Petitions Urging Mediation.

WASHINGTON, October 12.—The following statement was issued by the State Department to-day:

"The President has received a large number of petitions signed by many citizens of distinction, requesting him to tender the mediation of the United States to settle the difficulties existing between the Government of Great Britain and that of the Transvaal. He has received other petitions on the same subject, some of them desiring him to make common cause with Great Britain to redress the wrongs alleged to have been suffered by the Uitlanders and especially by American citizens in the Transvaal, and others wishing him to assist the Boers against alleged aggression.

"It is understood that the President does not think it expedient to take action in any of these directions. As to taking sides with either party to the dispute, it is not to be thought of. As to mediation, the President has received no intimation from either of the countries that the mediation of the United States would be accepted, and in the absence of such intimation from both parties there is nothing in the rules of international usage to justify an offer of mediation in the present circumstances. It is known that the President sincerely hopes and desires that hostilities may be avoided, but if, unfortunately, they should come to pass, the efforts of this Government will be directed—as they are at present—to seeing that neither our national interests nor those of our citizens shall suffer unnecessary injury."

1900-1909

SEPTEMBER 12, 1900
Galveston Flood

JANUARY 23, 1901
Queen Victoria Dies

SEPTEMBER 7, 1901
President McKinley Shot

DECEMBER 1, 1901
San Rafael and Sausalito Ferries Smash

APRIL 19, 1906
Earthquake and Fire — San Francisco in Ruins

APRIL 23, 1906
Five Hundred Die in Great Disaster

JULY 9, 1907
Mayor Schmitz Sentenced to San Quentin; Chief Geronimo Tries to Escape

DECEMBER 11, 1908
Power Broker Abe Ruef Convicted

SEPTEMBER 7, 1909
Peary Reaches North Pole

San Francisco Chronicle.

VOL. LXXII. SAN FRANCISCO, CAL., WEDNESDAY, SEPTEMBER 12, 1900—FOURTEEN PAGES. NO. 59.

HORRORS OF THE GALVESTON FLOOD STEADILY GROW.

Twenty-Three Hundred Bodies Have Already Been Taken From the Ruins.

Belief That Five Thousand Died—Ghouls Who Robbed the Dead Are Killed by Soldiers—Terrible Scenes of Horror in the Stricken City.

GALVESTON, (Tex.), September 11.—Mayor Walter C. Jones estimates the number of dead at 5000, and he is conservative. Over 2300 bodies have already been taken out to sea or buried in trenches. Other hundreds are yet to be taken from the ruins. These bodies are now all badly decomposed and they are being buried in trenches where they are found. Others are being burned in the debris where it can be done safely.

There is little attempt at identification and it is safe to say that there will never be a complete list of the dead.

Chief of Police Ketchum is in charge of the work of burying the dead. There are large bodies of men engaged in this work, tearing up the ruins and getting out the corpses. Some of those whose bodies are being taken out were probably only injured when they were first struck down, but there was no getting relief to them, and they perished miserably.

The remnant of the force of regular soldiers who were stationed here, and it is a very small remnant, have joined the police in patroling the city.

Several persons have already been shot, it is reported. A soldier of Captain Rafferty's battery, while patroling the beach this morning, ordered a man to desist from looting. The fellow drew a weapon and the soldier shot him dead. The soldier was attacked by four other men and he killed all of them. He had five cartridges in his rifle, and each of them found a victim.

Other men have also been shot, but the details are not known, nor can the exact number be ascertained. It is probable that twenty-five were killed. Some of these were shot for failing to halt when ordered to do so. Others were shot for vandalism.

The ruins of the brick buildings have not yet been searched for the dead, and there is a large number in them. In the mass of rubbish which marks the site of the Lucas Terrace Bridge House forty or fifty people were killed outright, and their bodies are still in the ruins.

The Orphans' Home is totally demolished. Ninety-two children and eleven nuns were killed. It is rumored that one sister escaped, but if she did no trace can be found of her.

Of the regular soldiers few remain. Twenty-three were drowned at the barracks at Camp Hawley and seven at Bolivar. One man drifted about in the bay until Monday morning and was taken out alive.

"The correspondent stood at the foot of Tremont street and counted nine floating bodies without moving, and this is only one instance. It is not known whether these were water-front victims or dead beings cast up by the sea. A lot of rubbish was being loaded on barges and this stuff had many bodies in it."

Order is being slowly brought out of chaos, and something like a systematic attempt is being made to clear the debris and remove the dead. Idlers are being pressed into the service at the point of the bayonet and made to work, and a military cordon is being drawn tighter and tighter about the place. Every horse and mule that was left in the city is in service. Supplies are coming in from Houston, and the first line of communication with the outside world was obtained to-day via Texas City. The forces are working on railroads, and in a few days the people of Galveston believe the situation will be greatly improved.

HOUSTON (Tex.), September 11.—More bodies have been picked up on the beach at Virginia Point and Texas City, and searching parties are now going into the country between the two points. One member of the life-saving crew said he believes that not one-third of the [illegible] are being recovered. Many sank before reaching the beach and he believes that a week will pass before the bay gives up all the dead. Scores of people are here trying to get into Galveston. Many of them claim to have relatives there, but it is not possible to reach that city at present. All the small boats and tugs in the bayou have been taken down to the bay to be used in ferriage.

The great storm covered a large area of the cotton-growing section of Texas and did tremendous damage to the crops. A traveling man who covers a big area of the State reports that for a hundred miles west of Houston the wind and storms have wrought great havoc, and all chances for a crop have been destroyed. Southwest of Houston the fields are ruined. In large cotton-growing counties around Houston it is said crops have been beaten into the ground and are worthless.

THE LONG IRON BRIDGE AND BATHHOUSES SWEPT AWAY BY THE STORM.

IRON BRIDGE TO GALVESTON.

BIG BATH HOUSES ON THE BEACH.

General Chambers McKibben, Sent to Galveston by the War Department.

STORY OF THE STORM WHICH RUINED GALVESTON.

People Warned of Its Coming, but Unable to Escape—Wind a Hundred Miles an Hour.

GALVESTON (Tex.), by Western Union dispatch boat to Houston (Tex.), September 10.—The terrific cyclone that produced such a distressing disaster in Galveston and all through Texas was predicted by the United States Weather Bureau to strike Galveston Friday night, and created much apprehension, but the night passed without the prediction being verified. The conditions, however, were ominous, the danger signal was displayed on the flagstaff of the weather bureau, shipping was warned, etc. The southeastern sky was sombre, the gulf beat high on the beach with that dismal roar that presaged trouble, while the air had that stillness that betokens a storm.

From out of the north, in the middle watches of the night, the wind began to come in spiteful puffs, increasing in volume as the day dawned. By 10 o'clock Saturday morning it was almost a gale; at noon it had increased in velocity and was driving the rain, whipping the pools and tearing things up in a lively manner, yet no serious apprehension was felt by residents remote from the encroachments of the gulf. Residents near the beach were aroused to the danger that threatened their homes. Great waves began to send their waters far inland, and the people began a hasty exit to safer places in the city. Two gigantic forces were at work. The gulf force drove the waves with irresistible force high upon the beach, and the gale from the northeast pitched the waters against and over the wharves, choking the sewers and flooding the city from that quarter. The streets rapidly began to fill with water, communication became difficult, and the helpless people were caught between two powerful elements, while the winds howled and rapidly increased in velocity.

Railroad communication was cut off shortly after noon, the track being washed out; wire facilities completely failed at 3 o'clock and Galveston was isolated from the world. The wind momentarily increased in velocity, while the waters rapidly rose, and as the night drew on apprehension was depicted in the face of every one. Already thousands were bravely struggling with their families against the mad waves and fierce wind for places of refuge. The public school buildings, Courthouse, hotels, in fact any place that offered apparently a safe refuge from the elements, became crowded to their utmost.

At 6:28 P. M., just before the anemometer blew away, it had reached the frightful velocity of 100 miles an hour. Buildings that were considered safe tumbled and crashed, carrying death and destruction to hundreds of people. Roofs sailed through the air, windows were driven in or shattered by flying slate. Telegraph, telephone and electric light poles, with their mass of wires, were snapped off like pipestems and water pipes were broken. What velocity the wind attained after the anemometer blew off is purely a matter of speculation. The lowest point touched by the barometer in the press correspondents' office, which was filled by frightened men and women, was 28.04½; this was about 7:30 P. M. It then began to rise slowly and by 10 P. M. had reached 28.09, the wind gradually subsiding, and by midnight the storm had passed. The water, which had reached a depth of eight feet on The Strand at 10 P. M., began to ebb and ran out very rapidly and by 5 A. M. the crown of the street was free of water. Thus passed out one of the most frightful and destructive storms which ever devastated the coast of Texas.

The city is filled with destitute, bereft and homeless, while in the improvised morgues are the rigid forms of hundreds of victims. Whole families are side by side. The city beach in the southwestern part of the city was under ten feet of water and the barracks, located there, are destroyed, the soldiers having a miraculous escape from drowning. Many substantial residences in the southeastern and southwestern part of the city were destroyed and the death list from there will be large.

A heavy mortality list is expected among the residents down the island, where there are several small towns, and adjacent to the coast on the mainland, as both were deeply flooded and the houses were to a great extent insecure. The heaviest losers by the storm will be the Galveston Wharf Company, the Southern Pacific and Gulf, Colorado and Santa Fe Railroad Companies and the Texas Lone Star Flooring Company.

GALVESTON PLACED UNDER MARTIAL LAW.

State Troops Ordered to the Island City to Preserve Order and Assist in Burying the Dead.

DALLAS, September 11.—A bulletin received here states that Governor Sayers has placed Galveston city and island under martial law. Adjutant-General Scurry is ordered to have State troops to take charge at once. The order includes instructions that the troops compel the people to bury the dead.

BEARING NEWS OF DISASTER TO THE WORLD.

Story of a Terrible Trip Over the Raging Water and Flooded Country to a Telegraph Point.

HOUSTON (Tex.), September 11.—A newspaper writer, who got through from Galveston to-day, made the following statement: "The condition at Galveston is heartrending in the extreme. The list of dead will not be fully known for weeks. The list of missing will swell rapidly as soon as the people have begun to report their losses to the authorities, and gradually this list of missing will change into the list of dead as the bodies are recovered from the ruins in the city or are picked up on the beach of the mainland, where many of them lie, it is believed. A meeting was held at the Tremont House and at this meeting measures were considered for the relief of the stricken. The conclusion was quickly reached that the citizens are not equal to the task, do what they may.

"Five miles of Laporte track, just north of Texas City junction, were submerged during the storm. All the drawbridges between Virginian Point and Galveston are gone. The county bridge, which cost $265,000 and which was the longest wagon structure in the world, collapsed before the storm got under good headway. An ocean steamship plowed its way through the piling in two other bridges. As far as known the bridge tenders are dead.

"The first vessel to leave Galveston after the storm contained the party delegated to inform the outside world of the catastrophe and to ask for help. It consisted of Lieutenant J. J. Delaney of the Southern Pacific, E. G. Cox of the firm of Thomas Taylor & Co., E. L. Porch of Welch & Porch, South Galveston, correspondent of the Houston Post and Richard Spillane of the Galveston Tribune. Their boat was the steam yacht Pherabe, owned by Colonel W. L. Moody and the crew was made up of volunteers, Lawrence V. Elder, superintendent of the Galveston Cotton Mills, acting as engineer and all hands being stokers.

"The trip across the bay was one of the most tempestuous imaginable. Many squalls struck the bay just as the Pherabe got into the channel from the Galveston wharves to Texas City. The boat was one time pointed toward the sky and the next movement downward. The engineer declined to take the boat any farther than Texas City, declaring that she could not live in such a sea. Lieutenant Delaney, who was an officer in the Japanese navy and commanded one of the war ships in the battle of the Yalu river and was later a Lieutenant in the United States Navy, said the trip across the bay was a far more desperate struggle for life than that during the hurricane of the night before, and he also said that in all his experience at sea he never knew of a craft surviving such a strain. To get into Texas City we had to break a way through a lot of wreckage, and then had to make our way for fifty or seventy-five feet over wreckage before we could get to shore.

"From Texas City to La Marque the party went over the flooded prairie in a buggy. A work train on the Galveston, Houston and Henderson Railroad was below La Marque toward Virginia point, and we tried to stop this train to get to Houston. The conductor would pay no attention to our signals for him to stop, and with brutal indifference signaled the engineer to go ahead faster. At La Marque we [illegible] car and pumped our way to about five miles north of Dickinson, where, just at dusk, we met a train from Houston. This train we managed to stop."

BODIES TOWED TO SEA AND THROWN OVERBOARD.

Railroad Man Tells a Shocking Story of the Situation in the Hurricane-Swept City of Galveston.

HOUSTON (Tex.), September 11.—G. L. Russ, passenger conductor on the International and Great Northern Railroad, was among a party of refugees who reached this city at midnight. Mr. Russ said: "I will not attempt to describe the horror of it all; that is impossible. When I left Galveston men armed with rifles were standing over burying squads and at the point of the guns compelling them to load the corpses on drays to be hauled to barges on which they are towed into the gulf by tugs and tossed into the sea. As I left I saw a barge freighted with dead on its journey to the gulf. This manner of burial is imperative; the living must be protected now."

Mr. Russ' story was confirmed.

SAW WIFE AND CHILDREN PERISH.

Only the Husband and Father of a Family Survives—One of the Incidents of the Flood.

HOUSTON (Tex.), September 11.—At a local undertaking establishment in Houston are resting the remains of five Houston people who perished at Seabrooke in Saturday's hurricane. They are Mrs. C. H. Lucy, her two small children, Haven McIlhenny, and the five-year-old son of David Tyce. The latter was visiting the family of Mrs. McIlhenny at the time of the disaster. All the bodies are so badly mangled as to make it difficult to identify them. They were washed ashore near Seabrooke.

The same train brought the bodies of Mrs. Vincent and her two children, who were drowned at Morgan's Point. Mr. McIlhenny was rescued alive, and is completely prostrated. He said the water came up so rapidly that he and his family and Mrs. Lucy and her children sought safety on the roof. He had his little son Haven in his arms, and the other children were strapped together. It was not long before a heavy piece of timber struck Haven, killing him. Young Tyce was washed off and drowned. Mrs. Lucy's eldest child was next killed by a piece of timber, and the younger one was drowned.

Then Mrs. Lucy was washed off and drowned, thus leaving Mr. and Mrs. McIlhenny the only occupants on the roof. Finally the roof blew off the house, and as it fell into the water it was broken in twain, Mrs. McIlhenny remaining on one-half and Mr. McIlhenny on the other. The portion of the roof to which Mrs. McIlhenny clung turned over, and this was the last seen of her.

Thus in a very brief space of time Mr. McIlhenny witnessed the loss of his family one by one. He held to his side of the roof so distracted in mind as to care little where or how it drifted. He finally landed on terra firma about 3 P. M. Sunday.

GHOULS AT WORK IN RUINED CITY.

Vandals Mutilate Corpses to Get Jewelry—Dead Even Stripped of Clothing.

DALLAS (Tex.), September 11.—A horrible story is told by Dallas citizens who returned to-night from Galveston. They declare that negroes and many white persons are hourly committing the most atrocious acts of vandalism. J. N. Griswold, division freight agent of the Gulf, Colorado and Santa Fe Railroad, who was in that city during the storm and had a narrow escape from death, said:

"Ears and fingers bearing diamonds were hacked off with pocketknives and the members placed in the pockets of the vandals. The bodies of women who wore fine clothes were stripped of their last thread and left to fester in the sun.

"The residences left standing have been broken into and jewelry and silver plate stolen. I saw a negro woman carrying a large basket of silverware that was not hers.

"At Texas City I saw an old man considerably under the influence of liquor. From his pocket protruded a roll of bills as big as my arm, which he claimed to have found. Upon all hands this horrible work is going on. The offenders are generally negroes, although there are some white men who had demonstrated that they are sufficiently devoid of honesty and manhood to participate in these ghoulish deeds.

"As soon as the storm subsided the negroes stole all the liquor they could get and, beastly drunk, proceeded with their campaign of vandalism. Troops are needed at once. If they are not sent without delay, God help the survivors in Galveston."

This is confirmed by a dozen men of the highest standing here.

Cutters Wanted to Carry Food.

HOUSTON (Tex.), September 11.—Messages were sent from here to-day asking that revenue cutters be ordered to Galveston bay to assist in transporting provisions to the city. Telegrams were also sent to New Orleans and Mobile asking for tugs. It is quite probable that in the next day or two free communication will be established.

SMALL TOWNS SWEPT AWAY BY THE FLOOD.

All the Houses in Entire Counties Destroyed—Desolation Marks the Track of the Water.

HOUSTON, September 11.—The Santa Fe ran its first relief train to Hitchcock to-day, finding conditions along its line similar to those prevailing along the Galveston, Houston and Henderson. In many places homeless inhabitants of the section traversed were housed in empty cars, while others were sitting on the wreck of their household effects. Many sufferers are destitute and will have to be given free transportation to places where they are sure of obtaining shelter and sustenance. Every building in Pearland was either damaged or destroyed, but no lives were lost there.

At Alvin the story is also gloomy. Besides the great damage to property, that town has the following deaths to report in addition to seven previously reported: Mrs. J. C. Collins, killed by falling timbers; W. P. Hawley, crushed by debris. W. C. Mebham and wife were seriously injured by flying timber.

The town of Angelton suffered severely from the storm and assistance is greatly needed.

Algoa, Arcadia and Alto Lomax show signs of a severe visitation and many are in need of help. The twelve-year-old son of James Rodacher was killed at Arcadia. Two children lost their lives at Alto Lomax.

At Hitchcock sixteen lives were lost. Two Italian families of thirteen people lost twelve of their number by drowning. The following were killed by falling timbers: Mr. and Mrs. Hiram Johnson, William Robinson and a child named Dominico.

A number of bodies floated in from across the bay, but could not be identified.

The prairie is covered with drift of all kinds, dead cattle, water craft of all sizes, buggies and wagons. Searching parties had up to noon found a dozen bodies in Hall's bayou and buried them. The railroad track from Hitchcock to Virginia Point has been washed out.

News from the coast along the Gulf and Interstate Railroad between Sabine and Bolivar indicate that no one has been killed. There are no houses left standing at Patton or Bolivar. The rescue party has not reached Bolivar opposite Galveston. It is reported that the village was swept off the earth and has few inhabitants left. The railroad tracks are under water and the relief party is on foot.

At Wharton an immense amount of damage was done. In the country about town all crops were laid waste. Three negroes are reported killed on various plantations in Wharton and Matagorda counties. In the latter county only two houses were left standing.

Richmond is reported to have been very nearly wrecked. Eighteen persons are reported killed, most of them negroes, in the country immediately about the town, and for twenty-five miles from town there is not a house standing on the prairie. Most of the dead so far located are in the two small villages of Heedville and Beasly. One man was killed on the Booth plantation, and the plantation was wrecked.

At Prairie View the Normal School has been badly damaged, but no one was killed.

San Francisco Chronicle.

VOL. LXXIII. SAN FRANCISCO, CAL., WEDNESDAY, JANUARY 23, 1901—FOURTEEN PAGES. NO. 8.

DEATH COMES TO QUEEN VICTORIA AFTER SHE HAS RECOGNIZED HER CHILDREN AND SAID GOOD-BY.

Conscious for Some Hours and Then Sank to Sleep and Passed Away---Remarkable Manifestations of Grief Throughout the Empire.

NEW YORK, January 23.—A cable to the Sun dated East Cowes, January 22d, says: Victoria, R. I., by the grace of God Queen of the United Kingdom of Great Britain and Ireland, defender of faith and Empress of India, is no more. She passed away without pain or suffering at Osborne House at 6:30 o'clock this evening. King Edward VII rules in her stead. England is silent with grief. The sense of personal bereavement is so overwhelming that Englishmen will be unable for a season to join in the loyal cry of "Long live the King."

The fateful news came in the following simple bulletin: "Her majesty the Queen breathed her last at 6:30, surrounded by her children and grandchildren."

A glimpse of the last moments of the beloved sovereign which the nation and world also so earnestly craved has been vouchsafed by a representative of the stricken family. We are permitted to know not only the brief, but eloquent facts stated in the frequent bulletins, but some few details which make very human this deathbed of the most illustrious sovereign of her times.

It was when the cold, gray day dawned that a renewed decline of the vital powers warned the watchers that the struggle against nature could not much longer succeed. The Queen was then completely unconscious, and from moment to moment the exhaustion of the small remaining store of vitality became perceptibly greater. Shortly after 9 o'clock the doctors sent a summons to all members of the family and also to the rector of the Royal Chapel. Before they all arrived there took place that prudential phenomenon which nature sometimes grants to the dying. The Queen became conscious and free of all suffering.

It was under these circumstances of precious memory that the last interviews with her children and grandchildren took place. The world will never know, and has no right to know, what took place. The Queen received them all singly and by twos and threes within the next four hours. She recognized most of them. Then the curtain of unconsciousness fell for the last time and the physicians made known that the Queen was dying. All assembled and remained until the very end. It was so quiet and peaceful and gentle that it was difficult to realize that the shadow of death was present. Nothing more can be said of those last moments. Even the fierce light which beats upon the throne did not penetrate that chamber, and the tender memories of the last hours belong to those who mourn Victoria, not as Queen, but in the dearer relationship of the family.

The circulation of all manner of imaginative reports during the past three days led the authorities at Osborne House to authorize the publication of these simple facts in addition to the foregoing:

The Queen was attended throughout her illness by two nurses and four dressers in charge of Miss Soal, who is matron of the sanitarium in Osborne Park. They had long been her personal ministrators when her majesty was at Osborne. The Queen was nourished throughout her illness with warm milk, invalids' prepared food, champagne and brandy. She was never fed artificially. The doors of the wing of the palace where the Queen lay were kept locked during her illness, so she was entirely isolated from the rest of the establishment.

The strictest precautions were taken Saturday, Sunday and Monday nights that in case of sudden death no unauthorized person should communicate the fact to the Prince of Wales in violation of the strict traditions. The Earl of Clarendon, Lord Chamberlain, and Arthur Balfour, First Lord of the Treasury, arrived just in time to perform this duty. Balfour did not see the Queen. The most significant point of the present situation is the statement of the authorities of the court that absolutely no preparations have been made for any feature of the elaborate proceedings now forced upon the nation. One would imagine that the great age of the sovereign would have led to some consideration of the inevitable problem now presented. It is only another evidence of the marvelous hold that the Queen had upon the affections of all classes, including, of course, most of all those personally attached to her. These simply refused to consider the possibility of her death.

Within an hour of the Queen's death the vicinity of Osborne House was deserted, and it was difficult to believe that one was almost in the presence of the first great event of the new century. Then came one of those little signs which even Englishmen are sufficiently superstitious to notice. The day had been damp and chill and heavily overcast. Presently, when the tragedy had been enacted, the evening became mild, the clouds rolled away and the stars shone brightly. It is now traditional "Queen's weather," but the phrase has become a mournful memory.

While the court is not prepared for the great public functions attendant upon the change of sovereigns it, of course, is settled that the body will be taken to Windsor and buried beside that of the Prince Consort at Frogmore. The funeral will certainly be delayed more than a week. It has not yet been decided whether the body will lie in state in Osborne House or be removed immediately to St. George's chapel, Windsor. The King will go to London early in the morning, where a meeting of the Privy Council will be held in the course of the day. The German Emperor will accompany him. The latter's future movements have not been decided upon. The remainder of the palace party will stay at Osborne House until further arrangements are decided. The new sovereign remains to-night under the same roof as his dead mother, the chief mourner among a larger gathering of children than often meet round a parent's deathbed anywhere in the world. They are in their own secluded world inside the gates of Osborne lodge.

COWES (Isle of Wight), January 23.—Queen Victoria is dead and Edward VII reigns. The greatest event in the memory of this generation, the most stupendous change in existing conditions that could possibly be imagined has taken place quietly, almost gently upon the anniversary of the death of the Queen's father, the Duke of Kent. The end of this career, never equaled by any woman in the world's history, came in a simply furnished room in Osborne House. This most respected of women, living or dead, lay in a great four-posted bed and made a shrunken atom, whose aged face and figure were a cruel mockery of the fair girl who in 1837 began to rule over England.

Around her were gathered almost every descendant of her line. Well within view of her dying eyes there hung a portrait of the Prince Consort. It was he who designed the room and every part of the castle. In scarcely audible words the white-haired Bishop of Winchester prayed beside her, as he had often prayed with his sovereign, for he was her chaplain at Windsor. With bowed heads the ruler of the German empire, and the man who is now King of England, the woman who has succeeded to the title of Queen, the Princes and Princesses and those of less than royal designation listened to the Bishop's ceaseless prayer.

Six o'clock passed. The Bishop continued his intercession. One of the younger children asked a question in shrill, childish treble and was immediately silenced. The women of this royal family sobbed faintly and the men shuffled uneasily.

At exactly 6:30 Sir James Reid held up his head and the people then knew that England had lost her Queen. The Bishop pronounced the benediction.

The Queen passed away quite peacefully. She suffered no pain. Those who were now mourning went to their rooms. A few minutes later the inevitable element of materialism stepped into this pathetic chapter of international history, for the court ladies went busily to work ordering their mourning from London.

The world was jarred when the announcement came, but in the palace at Osborne everything pursued the usual course. Down in the kitchen they were cooking a huge dinner for an assemblage, the like of which has seldom been known in England, and the dinner preparations proceeded just as if nothing had happened. The body of Queen Victoria was embalmed and will probably be taken to Windsor Saturday. The coffin arrived last evening from London.

It was thought that the Queen was dying about 9 o'clock in the morning, and carriages were sent to Osborne cottage and the rectory to bring all the Princes and Princesses and the Bishop of Winchester to her bedside. It seemed then very near the end, but when things looked the worst the Queen had one of the rallies due to her wonderful constitution, opened her eyes and recognized the Prince of Wales, the Princesses and Emperor William. She asked to see one of her faithful servants, a member of the household. He hastened to the room, but before he got there the Queen had passed into a fitful sleep.

Four o'clock marked the beginning of the end. Again the family were summoned, and this time the relapse was not followed by recovery. The Prince of Wales was very much affected when the doctors at last informed him that his mother had breathed her last. Emperor William, himself deeply affected, did his best to minister comfort to his sorrow-stricken uncle, whose new dignity he was the first to acknowledge.

When the 4 P. M. bulletin announced that the Queen was sinking all the watchers at the gates of Osborne House made up their minds to remain to the end. The cold was intense and a few favored ones sought shelter in the royal lodge, just inside, where they waited in absolute silence. The telephone bell rang at 7:04 P. M., but before a royal servant had time to take the message the chief of the Queen's police emerged from the darkness, and, with bared head, said: "Gentlemen, the Queen passed away at 6:30."

All present reverently uncovered, and then shrill whistles and ringing of the bells of bicycles in waiting were the signals for messengers to race to Cowes with the news. In a few moments the place was deserted. Simultaneously mounted messengers on white horses dashed from Osborne. On their arrival at Cowes the correspondents found the news known both at East and West Cowes fully fifteen minutes before it had been announced to those in waiting at the gates of Osborne House. The streets were already filled with sorrowful crowds discussing her majesty's death.

From all parts of the world there are still pouring into Cowes messages of condolence. They come from crowned heads, millionaires, tradesmen and paupers, and are variously addressed to the Prince of Wales and the King of England.

Emperor William's arrangements are not settled. His yacht will arrive here to-day (Wednesday), but it is believed that he will not depart until after the funeral. Several other royal personages are likely to be present at the function.

The record of the last days of the reign of Victoria is not easy to tell. The correspondent of the Associated Press was the only correspondent admitted to Osborne House, and his interview with Sir Arthur John Bigge, private secretary of the late Queen, was the only official statement that had been sent out. For several weeks the Queen had been failing. On Monday week she summoned Lord Roberts and asked him some searching questions regarding the war in South Africa. On Tuesday she went for a drive, but was visibly affected. On Wednesday she suffered a paralytic stroke, accompanied by intense physical weakness. Then her condition grew so serious that, against her wishes, the family were summoned. When they arrived her reason had practically succumbed to paralysis and weakness.

The events of the last days described in the bulletins are too fresh to need repetition. At the lodge gates the watchers waited nervously. Suddenly along the drive from the house came a horseman who cried "The Queen is dead!" as he dashed through the crowds.

Then down the hillside rushed a myriad of messengers passing the fateful bulletin from one to another. Soon the surrounding country knew that a King ruled over Great Britain. The local inhabitants walked as if in a dream through the streets of Cowes, but they did not hesitate to stop to drink the health of the new monarch.

NEWS SPREADS PALL OVER ALL ENGLAND

London Theaters Close and Everywhere There Is Mourning.

LONDON, January 23.—The Queen's death has cast a pall over the British people. The shops closed as soon as the bells began to toll, and the blinds of the Mansion House were drawn down as soon as the message from the Prince of Wales was received by the Lord Mayor. The bell rung in St. Paul's Cathedral was the gift of William III, and is used only on the occasions of the death of royal personages, Archbishops of Canterbury, Lord Mayors of London and Bishops of London. The tolling continued for two hours to-day at intervals of a minute and could be heard for miles in the direction of the wind.

Some hundreds of people stood in front of the cathedral around the spot where Queen Victoria prayed on the sixtieth anniversary of her accession to the throne.

At the usual dinner of the Hilary term of Gray's Inn the master teacher said: "Amid great sorrow we must follow the practice of the constitution and recite 'God Save the King.'" The chapel bell tolled eighty-two times and the benchers drank the health of the King.

All theaters, music halls and places of amusement voluntarily closed and not until Queen Victoria has been laid to rest beside the Prince Consort at Frogmore will they reopen. Moreover, business will come to a practical standstill. The music in all the halls and public places has ceased. Fashionable resorts were empty and very few of the nightly habitues were in evidence. The St. James, Princes' and other prominent restaurants have already discarded alluring colors for somber black.

Americans who have passed through great national calamities may remember the crape covered buildings, but they can ill conceive since the death of Lincoln, any such expression of gloom as has already fallen upon the United Kingdom. Marlborough House, so long the home of the new monarch, Buckingham Palace, where Queen Victoria made her last stay in London and St. James' Palace, the residence of so many former monarchs, were all black and deserted. Sentries in black overcoats kept silent vigil before the closed gates and bolted doors. The population therefore slowly dispersed as the night wore on. Shortly before midnight an official announcement was issued calling Parliament to meet at 4 o'clock this (Wednesday) afternoon to enable members of the House of Lords and Commons to take the oath of allegiance to King Edward VII.

Telegrams pouring in from all parts of the Continent re-echo the deep feeling of sorrow pervading all classes. These show that everywhere bells have been tolled and public performances and private functions suspended.

In Dublin the expressions of regret were universal. The bells of St. Patrick's Cathedral were tolled. Earl Cadogan, the Lord-Lieutenant, was absent from Dublin yesterday, but it is expected he will return immediately to preside at a meeting of the Irish Privy Council to proclaim the new King. The Privy Council will meet in London to-day and the proclamation of the King will occur thereafter at all places required by custom. The King will come to London to preside over the Council.

SOME CHANGES THAT DEATH WILL BRING.

London Likely to Become a Gay Capital When Mourning is Ended.

LONDON, January 22.—Absolute silence reigned to-night in the vicinity of Buckingham Palace and Marlborough House. A small bill, signed "Balfour" was posted outside announcing the demise of the monarch.

Everywhere to-night the topic of conversation was what would happen under the new reign. Much interest is evinced in what way the fortune of the Queen will be distributed, the general notion being that Osborne House would go to Princess Beatrice, and that she and Princess Christian would come into a considerable portion of Victoria's wealth.

The probability that King Edward will take up a practically permanent residence in Buckingham Palace was much canvassed. This is a question that comes very much home to Londoners. Queen Victoria's preference for Balmoral Castle and Osborne House has been a complaint of long standing in the metropolis and it is hoped that the new reign will see a change in this respect. The presence of the court in London would give a brightness and gayety which have long been absent.

EX-EMPRESS FREDERICK IN A SERIOUS CONDITION.

LONDON, January 22.—"The news of her mother's death was tenderly broken to Dowager Empress Frederick late this evening," says a dispatch to the Daily Mail from Frankfort. "It was a terrible shock, but the Empress is bearing up bravely. The trials of the last few days have exercised a most prejudicial effect upon her health, which causes serious anxiety."

THE DEAD QUEEN

THE NEW KING

San Francisco Chronicle.

VOL. LXXIV. SAN FRANCISCO, CAL., SATURDAY, SEPTEMBER 7, 1901—SIXTEEN PAGES. NO. 54.

PRESIDENT M'KINLEY SHOT BY AN ANARCHIST AT BUFFALO FAIR.

Two Bullets Fired by the Assassin, but Only One Penetrates the Body—Surgeons Hopeful of Recovery—An Attempt Made to Lynch the Cowardly Murderer.

WOUNDED AT A PUBLIC RECEPTION.

Stricken by a Man Who Grasped His Hand---Crowd Sought to Mete Out Swift Punishment.

BUFFALO (N. Y.), September 6.—President McKinley was shot by an anarchist assassin in the Temple of Music at the Pan-American Exposition grounds this afternoon. One bullet entered his stomach, and the doctors who are in attendance upon him are extremely apprehensive as to the result of this injury. Frederick Nieman, an avowed disciple of the principles of anarchy, fired the bullets that threaten to deprive the Nation of its ruler. He is a prisoner now in a dungeon at the police headquarters in Buffalo, but it was only by the most desperate efforts that the police succeeded in saving him from the vengeance of the maddened thousands on the Exposition grounds, who were clamoring for his life. He is calm and cool, and not inclined to discuss his mad act beyond the single statement: "I am an anarchist, and have only done my duty."

The daring attempt at assassination was made, according to the closest possible calculations, at 4:12 o'clock. It was the second day of the President's appearance at the fair grounds, and arrangements had been made for a public reception. The Temple of Music, being one of the most spacious and centrally located buildings in the grounds, was selected for the reception. Promptly at 3:30 o'clock Mr. McKinley, accompanied by President John G. Milburn of the Exposition, Secretary Cortelyou and a guard of detectives, arrived at the railroad station on the grounds. About two minutes before the time for the reception, 4 o'clock, his carriage drove up to the entrance of the Temple. Twenty thousand people were gathered in and about the building, and as the President bowed to right and left a mighty shout of welcome went up on every side. Then the great organ in the temple pealed forth the national air, and the throngs fell back from the entrance, through which Mr. McKinley was to pass.

Inside the Temple a place had been made in the center of the floor for the President to stand and greet the thousands who were waiting to grasp his hand. Two aisles led diagonally from the entrance at either corner of the reception room, and the people passed in one doorway, halting at the central point to meet the Chief Executive, then passed on and out through the opposite door. Perhaps 100 men and women and children had gone slowly up the long aisle and looked into the kindly face that met each comer with a smile of welcome. Then there was a break in the line and a rush of the Exposition guards toward the door through which the crowds were entering. At that moment a woman was standing before Mr. McKinley. The trouble at the door apparently subsided and the woman gave way to a well-dressed man. He grasped the President's hand warmly and spoke a few words, but the crowd pushed him along and he gave way to Fred Nieman.

Secret Service Agents Foster and Ireland were standing directly across from the President, closely scanning each man and woman passing along the line. When Nieman paused before McKinley, the Government officers saw before them a quietly dressed, intelligent appearing young man with reddish hair and smooth shaven cheeks. His right hand was thrust beneath the lapel of his coat and a handkerchief was wrapped about it in such a way as to give the impression that it had been injured.

Nieman turned his eyes squarely upon the President's face and extended his left hand. Mr. McKinley observed that the man before him was offering his left hand instead of the right, and his eyes wandered to the hand thrust beneath the coat. Then his own right hand closed about the fingers of the man who was ready to slay him.

The touch of McKinley's hand seemed to rouse the assassin to action. He leaned suddenly forward, at the same time gripping the President's hand in a vise-like hold. He drew Mr. McKinley's breast a trifle toward him and the hidden right hand flashed from beneath his coat lapel. The hand and fingers were hidden by the folds of the handkerchief. Nieman thrust his hand fairly against the President's breast and pulled the trigger of the weapon that the white bit of cloth was concealing. Then he fired again, the second shot following the first so quickly that the report was scarcely noticeable. President McKinley dropped the hand of the assassin and staggered back a pace toward his secretary, Mr. Cortelyou, and President Milburn, who had been standing at his side. They caught him as he was falling, and drew him tenderly toward a chair. Nieman's every act had been watched by the secret service officers, but they were not quick enough to stop him.

As the second shot was fired the meaning of what was happening dawned upon half a hundred of those who were nearest the place occupied by the President, and there was a mad rush to seize the murderer. Homer James, an exposition guard, was probably the first man to reach Nieman. He sprang upon the backs of those who blocked his way and dashed his club down upon the anarchist's skull. Then there was a rush from every side, and Nieman was borne from his feet and swept to the floor. He was trampled on and kicked and pushed from side to side, everybody seeking to lay hold of him.

The strains of the great organ died away as the President staggered back from the line where he had encountered his assailant. Thousands who were too far off to even see the place where the reception had been in progress guessed that something was wrong, as a wonderful silence fell upon the great room and its hundreds of occupants. Then the word went through the assembled throngs like wildfire, "The President has been assassinated."

One bullet had struck the President in the left side of the abdomen and ranged downward through the groin. It lodged in the region of the back. The other, probably the first shot fired, had struck the topmost button of Mr. McKinley's vest and torn its way through his clothing, carrying the button with it. The button bruised the flesh over the breast bone, but the bullet did not go through the skin. An ambulance was brought from the Emergency Hospital upon the fair grounds, and the President was placed upon a stretcher and borne out of the building. He was conscious and smiling faintly. He was carried to the Emergency Hospital at a mad rate of speed, a mounted infantryman galloping ahead of the vehicle and warning the crowds out of the way.

The prisoner was hurried into the little room just off the west stage of the Temple of Music, being dragged by patrolmen through the crowd. His lip was bleeding and his face was swelling from the blows he received. Around him there was a group of officers. Once inside, the door was closed with a bang and the mob surging against that part of the building with the blind impulse to get near him, fairly made the walls creak. The entire scene in the room was

(Continued on Page Two.)

A RECENT PORTRAIT OF PRESIDENT M'KINLEY.

FAVORABLE REPORT ON PRESIDENT'S CONDITION.

BUFFALO, N. Y., September 7.—At 3 A. M. the following bulletin was issued: "The President continues to rest well. Temperature 101:6, pulse 110, respiration 24. "P. M. RIXEY."

BUFFALO, September 6.—Secretary Cortelyou to-night gave out the following statement:

"The following bulletin was issued by the physicians at 7 P. M.:

'The President was shot about 4 o'clock. One shot struck him upon the upper portion of the breastbone, glancing and not penetrating; the second bullet penetrated the abdomen five inches below the left nipple and one and one-half inches to the left of the median line. The abdomen was opened through the line of the bullet wound. It was found that the bullet had penetrated the stomach. The opening in the front wall of the stomach was carefully closed with silk stitches, after which a search was made for a hole in the back wall of the stomach. This was found and also closed in the same way.

'The further course of the bullet could not be discovered, although careful search was made. The abdominal wound was closed without drainage. No injury to the intestines or other abdominal organs was discovered. The patient stood the operations well; pulse of good quality, rate of 130. His condition at the conclusion of the operation was gratifying. The result cannot be foretold. His condition at present justifies hope of recovery.'

"GEORGE B. CORTELYOU, Secretary to the President."

"The following bulletin was issued by the President's physician at 10:40 P. M.:

'The President is rallying satisfactorily and is resting comfortably, 10:15. Temperature, 100.4; pulse, 124; respiration, 24.—P. M. Rixey, M. B. Mann, R. E. Parke, H. E. Minter.

The President continues to complain of painful character of the chest wound. Surgeons, however, assert emphatically that the wound is a slight affair.

DOCTORS DECLARE INJURIES SEVERE.

The Chances of Recovery Said to Be Against President---Cheering Reports Untrue.

CHICAGO, September 7.—Late advices from Buffalo show that the President is desperately wounded. There is absolutely no authority for the bulletin that he will surely recover. Seventy-five per cent of abdominal gunshot wounds are fatal. Physicians say that with the President's strong constitution and fine physical condition that he may pull through, but the chances are three to one that he will die. It is evident that Wall street is using every effort to put an optimistic twist into the news to-night to avoid a big stock panic. At 2 o'clock, Buffalo time, the physicians on watch said that the President was suffering great pain, but holding his own.

NEW YORK, September 6.—New York surgeons were to-night asked to give their opinions as to the nature of the President's wounds, based on the report of physicians in attendance.

"The only way to save the President," said Dr. Allen H. Oliver, who served as a surgeon in the Franco-Prussian war and who is assistant superintendent of the Presbyterian Hospital, "is to perform the operation of laparotomy; that is, make an incision in the stomach and go right in after the bullet. That should be done right away.

"It is to be hoped that the feeling that held back the able surgeons who attended President Garfield will not deter President McKinley's surgeons from performing the operation—that is, the fear that if the patient died after the operation the operator would be held to be responsible. I believe President Garfield would be alive if an operation had been performed.

"Dr. Agnew, one of his surgeons, told me that if President Garfield had been a poor man and had been treated as a poor man would have been, laid on the table and an operation performed, he believed he would have got well."

"There is danger of death from hemorrhage and from blood poisoning in the President's case. I think in a case such as the President's is described to be the chances are about 90 in 100 against his recovery."

"The chief danger to recovery of the President," said Dr. George Woolsey, the eminent surgeon, "is blood poisoning. If the ball went through the stomach it may not be as bad as if it had passed through the intestines. The walls of the stomach are thicker than those of the intestines, and sometimes close up of their own motion, preventing leakage.

"There is, of course, danger from hemorrhage and danger from shock. A sound constitution will go a great way in enabling the President to stand his injury."

"The treatment of the President's wound is, from a surgeon's point of view, very simple," said Dr. Schulese. "One danger is that he may have already suffered from internal bleeding. Another great danger, which will remain for several days, is that some foreign particle might be left in the intestines after the incision is sewed up, causing peritonitis later on. It will take several days before the President may safely be pronounced out of danger."

Dr. George E. Doty, instructor of surgery in the Post-Graduate Medical School, expressed the opinion that the recovery of President McKinley was doubtful. "If the second bullet entered the abdomen or intestines," said Doty, "the prospects of the President's recovery would be extremely doubtful. In the latter case complications of a serious nature would undoubtedly arise, probably followed by acute peritonitis, which would be very apt to prove fatal. Should the President live three or four days his ultimate recovery could be hoped for."

Cleveland Says He Must Have Been Crazy

WINSTEAD (Conn.), September 6.—Ex-President Cleveland was fishing at Darling lake when he received the news regarding the shooting of President McKinley. He at once started for the shore in order to hear the details, and anxiously asked for the latest news from the President's bedside. Cleveland was horrified at the news, and said: "With all American citizens, I am greatly shocked at this news. I cannot conceive of a motive. It must have been the act of a crazy man."

CARING FOR THE WOUNDED CHIEF.

The Buffalo Surgeons Probe for the Bullet but Fail to Find It.

BUFFALO, September 6.—As soon as the crowd in the Temple of Music had been dispersed sufficiently the President was removed in the automobile ambulance and taken to the exposition hospital, where an examination was made. The best medical skill was summoned, and within a brief period several of Buffalo's best-known practitioners were at the patient's side.

The President retained the full exercise of his faculties until placed on the operating table and subjected to an anaesthetic. Upon the first examination it was ascertained that one bullet had taken effect in the right breast just below the nipple, causing a comparatively harmless wound.

The other took effect in the abdomen, about four inches below the left nipple, four inches to the left of the navel, and about on a level with it. Upon arrival at the exposition hospital the second bullet was probed. The walls of the abdomen were opened, but the ball was not located. The incision was hastily closed, and after a hasty consultation it was decided to remove the patient to the home of President Milburn. This was done, the automobile ambulance being used for the purpose.

Arriving at the Milburn residence, all persons, save the medical attendants, nurses and the officials immediately concerned, were excluded and the task of probing for the bullet which had lodged in the abdomen was begun by Dr. Roswell Parke, but the bullet was not found.

Secretary Cortelyou to-night said that a telegraph office would be established at once in the Milburn residence, and bulletins, giving the public the fullest information possible, would be issued at short intervals.

At the Milburn house were Secretary of Agriculture Wilson, President Milburn, Director-General Buchanan of the Pan-American Exposition, Dr. Rixey and Secretary Cortelyou. Telegrams poured in by hundreds, and Secretary Cortelyou was kept busy replying to them. Two stenographers, with their typewriters, were placed in the parlor, which was quickly transformed into a bustling room.

PITTSBURG, September 6.—Attorney-General P. G. Knox left at 1 P. M. for Buffalo. Just before leaving he said: "I can only express common sentiment of horror of the dastardly blow inflicted upon a lovable and beloved man, who has stood for all that is best for the people, who have so implicitly trusted him. His bodily wounds, grievous as they are, will cause him less pain than the thought that any human heart could have harbored against him the malice that inspired the deed."

San Francisco Chronicle.

VOL. LXXIV. SAN FRANCISCO, CAL., SUNDAY, DECEMBER 1, 1901—FORTY PAGES. NO. 139.

FERRY SAN RAFAEL RUN DOWN AND SUNK IN FOG--LOSS OF LIFE AS YET UNCERTAIN.

IN THE DENSE FOG which shrouded San Francisco bay last evening a collision occurred between the steamers Sausalito and San Rafael, the latter going to the bottom within twenty minutes. The number of lives lost is still unknown, but many passengers were severely injured. One child is known to have been drowned, and passengers declare that when the San Rafael went down she carried a score or more of people with her. This statement, however, is denied by Captain McKenzie, who says he was the last to leave the vessel. The collision occurred at 7:15 o'clock in the evening, about half way between Lombard-street wharf and Alcatraz. The two vessels were approaching one another, each hidden from view by the dense fog, when suddenly, through some error in the signals for passing, the bow of the Sausalito crashed into the starboard side of the San Rafael, entering the restaurant, where many people were eating, many of them being severely injured.

The San Rafael at once began to sink and panic prevailed. Some of the crew and passengers kept their presence of mind, and worked bravely to convey the women and children to the Sausalito, which had been lashed to the side of the sinking boat. As the vessel settled nearer to the surface of the water, her lights went out and the terror of the passengers once more became unrestrained. Ropes were thrown from the Sausalito and many persons were dragged up by ropes. Many jumped overboard and were picked up by the boats of the two steamers. When the San Rafael had sunk the Sausalito brought the rescued passengers to this city.

THE SURVIVORS COMING ASHORE.

SCENES OF HORROR AS THE FERRY SANK.

Heroic Work Done by Crews and Passengers Dragging Helpless People to Places of Safety.

IN A black and blinding fog, the heaviest that has visited this city for many years, the ferry-boat San Rafael of the North Pacific Coast Railroad line collided last night with the ferry-boat Sausalito of the same line, and sank within twenty minutes to the bottom of the bay. Of the 200 or more passengers whom the San Rafael carried on her run most, if not all, were saved through the coolness and bravery of the men aboard. For fifteen minutes she lay lashed to the other vessel, which was not injured, while the San Rafael's passengers were passed aboard. Owing to the darkness and the terrible fog, which hid everything and rendered navigation on the bay a thing of deadly peril, it is impossible to state the loss of life. Some of the passengers place the loss of life as high as thirty or forty, while the officers of the San Rafael say that all were saved. It is almost certain, however, that the three-year-old son of Mrs. Waller of Ross station is lost. The preparation of accurate lists will be possible only after the fog lifts to-day.

About twenty people were injured, only five seriously, although many more were carried from the wharves half unconscious from the water which they had taken into their lungs before they were drawn from the water.

The collision came on the regular 6:15 o'clock run of the San Rafael from San Francisco out. Owing to the thickness of the night the start had been postponed, and it was twelve minutes later than schedule time when the ferry-boat cast off her lines and left the slip. She carried a load of about 200 passengers, mostly residents of San Rafael and Sausalito, going home for Sunday. The restaurant was crowded with people, snatching their dinners en route.

So dense by that time was the fog which had settled down that the lights of piers a few hundred yards from the boat's course were not discernible from the bridge. The ferry-boat felt her way past Lombard-street wharf, steering by compass and tide calculation, until about half way to Alcatraz island. She was sounding her fog whistle at intervals.

Suddenly, out of the blackness, the lights of another boat glimmered through the fog. Just what happened next is a matter of doubt. The captain of the Sausalito says that the San Rafael sounded the signal to turn to port, across his bows. The captain of the San Rafael says that he gave no such signal and kept his course.

However it happened, both vessels, backing with all the might of their engines, crashed together. The San Rafael was turned broadside on to the rush of the Sausalito. They collided with a crash that threw passengers and crew off their feet. The strong bow of the Sausalito crashed sheer through the starboard side of the other steamer and burst into the crowded restaurant, killing at least one person.

In a moment there was the wildest panic on board. The passengers, huddled into the cabins for shelter against the chilly night, rushed for the doors. They blocked the entrances, they smashed the windows, they piled up against the partitions. Captain McKenzie, from the bridge, sent his first officer to report on the damage. The man returned in a moment.

"The boat is sinking, sir," he said.

The officers ran to the decks and cabins and warned the frightened passengers of their danger. For a moment there was a rush, almost a panic. Women ran from one side of the cabin to the other calling for help. Children shrieked. Many of the frightened passengers seized life preservers and threw themselves into the water. Some of the crew made their escape to the decks of the Sausalito; others remembered their duty and manned the boats. The crew of the Sausalito, cooler when they saw that they themselves were not in danger, threw lines from the rail, which were caught by the men of the San Rafael, and the vessels were lashed tight together. To this act of foresight hundreds of the passengers owe their lives.

At the height of the panic the nerve of the officers and the coolness of some passengers came to the rescue. The frightened women were calmed, and the men from both boats began to pass them over the rails to the opposite deck. The rush at the doors blocked all entrances, and men threw themselves against windows and frames, breaking them and letting out the imprisoned women and children. A score of men, working like heroes, dragged them over the rails into safety.

Then, when order was coming out of chaos, it was seen that the San Rafael was settling rapidly. The water rose to the rail, submerged the lower deck, and slopped over the cabin floors. Working ankle deep in water, the rescuers dragged the last of their charges out to the cabin roof. The panic was almost over now, and the heroes, though working like madmen, were perfectly cool. Some of the passengers, men and women, half crazed with fright, sobbed and prayed and struggled until they were passed over the rail.

Lower sank the doomed boat, and it became impossible to reach the lowest rails of the Sausalito from the very highest cabin of the San Rafael. The men and women remaining on deck were lashed to ropes passed over the rails and dragged up in such feverish haste that many of them were injured in scraping over the rail. Others, lashing themselves to life-preservers, jumped into the strong current. Two boats had been launched by the cool heads among the crew, and these loaded themselves to the bulwarks with the struggling people in the water. Two more boats from the Sausalito aided in the work of rescue.

Then, suddenly, with a rush and a sob, the ferry settled bow first and sank to the bottom, leaving the few that were on her decks struggling and shouting in the water. The boats scoured the waves in the darkness, picking up the half-drowned. One, an after boat from the San Rafael, was overturned by the clutches of the drowning, leaving a dozen of her passengers clinging to the bottom. The boatmen, rowing with all their strength, drew load after load to the rails of the Sausalito and passed them up by ropes. And finally, when no more cries were heard from the water, they themselves were dragged aboard.

Captain McKensie, standing by his duty to the last, stayed with his boat until the moment she sank. He saw most, if not all, of her human freight carried to safety, and then jumped for his life. The steamer had been about twenty minutes in sinking; in the last ten minutes her lights had been out, and she finished her career in total darkness, which may have hidden some who would otherwise been discovered and taken off. As it is, no one could say last night for a certainty whether the dead are three or thirty.

The decks of the Sausalito were like a hospital with maimed and mangled and half-drowned survivors. The men who had forgotten their own peril and remembered only the ethics of "women and children first" became nurses, binding up wounds and chafing limbs. Passengers, collapsing under the release of the strain, became hysterical, and for a few minutes the scene on board the lucky vessel in the collision matched the panic that followed the crash.

All this time the engines of the Sausalito had been stopped, and she was broadside on to the treacherous current. When the last boat was unloaded on her decks, the fog lifted a little and a light showed to the south close abeam. At that moment the tug Sea King loomed up through the dense fog.

"Where are we?" yelled the captain of the ferry from the bridge.

"Off the Presidio light and heading out to sea," came the answer.

The Sausalito put about and under her own steam felt her way through the fog to her own slip. On the way she had

(Continued on Page Two.)

SAN RAFAEL'S CAPTAIN SAYS ALL WERE SAVED

M'Kenzie Declares He Was Last Person to Leave the Vessel--Knows of Few Casualties.

JOHN T. M'KENZIE, captain of the lost ferry-boat San Rafael, told what sounded like a clear and straightforward account of the events and circumstances attending the disaster, when seen after the landing of the Sausalito last night, although in many important particulars it differs from the stories told by surviving passengers. First of all, he declares with seeming earnestness that he did not believe one life was lost in the accident, in the face of the accumulative testimony of many passengers that many of their number perished in the waters of the bay.

"The San Rafael left her slip on the 6:15 o'clock trip for Sausalito about ten or twelve minutes late," he said, in starting to give a connected story of the accident. "The fog enveloped the bay in impenetrable blackness, and we had to be guided almost entirely in our efforts to pass the Sausalito safely by the fog signals. Under usual conditions the ferry-boats on the Sausalito run sail on widely divergent courses in going to and from Sausalito, the boat from this side passing to the north of Alcatraz island and the boat bound toward the city taking a course around the southerly side of the island. During the progress of the dredging work about Arch rock, however, boats going in both directions have followed the northerly course. In foggy weather these conditions necessitate extreme precautions against collisions, but I do not see how greater precautions than those taken by me could possibly be employed.

"The San Rafael was right on her course and should have passed the Sausalito safely. To guard against accident we were feeling our way slowly until we should pass the other boat. As a signal to the Sausalito and other bay craft we kept our fog signal going from the moment we left the slip. This signal consists of repeated sharp blasts of the whistle. The Sausalito did the same. Before we reached Alcatraz island we heard the approaching signals of the Sausalito, and we stopped our machinery. Then we reversed our wheel and were making back when the Sausalito struck us.

"I was in the pilot-house at the time with First Officer Charles Johnson. My first act was to send him below to find out how badly we were damaged. He hurriedly returned and informed me that the bow of the Sausalito had crashed into the restaurant; that we were making water rapidly, and would probably sink. All my efforts from that instant were directed toward the saving of the passengers.

"It is impossible to tell a connected story of the events that followed. No one person could grasp it all, and every person had a different experience. Briefly, however, I can say that as quickly as the thing could be done we had the two boats lashed together to facilitate the transferring of the passengers from the sinking steamer to the Sausalito, and the transferring of the passengers was done as quickly and with as little difficulty as the prevailing disorder would permit. You must consider that intense excitement prevailed among the passengers, while the panic that prevailed in the main cabin, where the women and children were running around in a circle, screaming and frantic, made it difficult for the steamer's officers to carry out any orderly plans. We broke out the windows of the cabin to permit an exit from the cabin of the other boat, and I simply had to force women to climb out and get aboard the Sausalito. The officers and crew of the San Rafael acted well, and did their duty to the last moment. We lowered our two forward boats at the beginning of the trouble, and the Sausalito also lowered two boats. These did valuable work in rescuing our passengers. People on the lower deck of the San Rafael were passed into the small boats, and by them transferred to the Sausalito.

"The Sausalito remained with us until everybody was safe aboard her decks. Then, as the sinking steamer

The Call=Chronicle=Examiner

SAN FRANCISCO, THURSDAY, APRIL 19, 1906.

EARTHQUAKE AND FIRE: SAN FRANCISCO IN RUINS

DEATH AND DESTRUCTION HAVE BEEN THE FATE OF SAN FRANCISCO. SHAKEN BY A TEMBLOR AT 5:13 O'CLOCK YESTERDAY MORNING, THE SHOCK LASTING 48 SECONDS, AND SCOURGED BY FLAMES THAT RAGED DIAMETRICALLY IN ALL DIRECTIONS, THE CITY IS A MASS OF SMOULDERING RUINS. AT SIX O'CLOCK LAST EVENING THE FLAMES SEEMINGLY PLAYING WITH INCREASED VIGOR, THREATENED TO DESTROY SUCH SECTIONS AS THEIR FURY HAD SPARED DURING THE EARLIER PORTION OF THE DAY. BUILDING THEIR PATH IN A TRIANGUAR CIRCUIT FROM THE START IN THE EARLY MORNING, THEY JOCKEYED AS THE DAY WANED, LEFT THE BUSINESS SECTION, WHICH THEY HAD ENTIRELY DEVASTATED, AND SKIPPED IN A DOZEN DIRECTIONS TO THE RESIDENCE PORTIONS. AS NIGHT FELL THEY HAD MADE THEIR WAY OVER INTO THE NORTH BEACH SECTION AND SPRINGING ANEW TO THE SOUTH THEY REACHED OUT ALONG THE SHIPPING SECTION DOWN THE BAY SHORE, OVER THE HILLS AND ACROSS TOWARD THIRD AND TOWNSEND STREETS. WAREHOUSES, WHOLESALE HOUSES AND MANUFACTURING CONCERNS FELL IN THEIR PATH. THIS COMPLETED THE DESTRUCTION OF THE ENTIRE DISTRICT KNOWN AS THE "SOUTH OF MARKET STREET." HOW FAR THEY ARE REACHING TO THE SOUTH ACROSS THE CHANNEL CANNOT BE TOLD AS THIS PART OF THE CITY IS SHUT OFF FROM SAN FRANCISCO PAPERS.

AFTER DARKNESS, THOUSANDS OF THE HOMELESS WERE MAKING THEIR WAY WITH THEIR BLANKETS AND SCANT PROVISIONS TO GOLDEN GATE PARK AND THE BEACH TO FIND SHELTER. THOSE IN THE HOMES ON THE HILLS JUST NORTH OF THE HAYES VALLEY WRECKED SECTION PILED THEIR BELONGINGS IN THE STREETS AND EXPRESS WAGONS AND AUTOMOBILES WERE HAULING THE THINGS AWAY TO THE SPARSELY SETTLED REGIONS. EVERYBODY IN SAN FRANCISCO IS PREPARED TO LEAVE THE CITY, FOR THE BELIEF IS FIRM THAT SAN FRANCISCO WILL BE TOTALLY DESTROYED.

DOWNTOWN EVERYTHING IS RUIN. NOT A BUSINESS HOUSE STANDS. THEATRES ARE CRUMBLED INTO HEAPS. FACTORIES AND COMMISSION HOUSES LIE SMOULDERING ON THEIR FORMER SITES. ALL OF THE NEWSPAPER PLANTS HAVE BEEN RENDERED USELESS THE "CALL" AND THE "EXAMINER" BUILDINGS, EXCLUDING THE "CALL'S" EDITORIAL ROOMS ON STEVENSON STREET BEING ENTIRELY DESTROYED.

IT IS ESTIMATED THAT THE LOSS IN SAN FRANCISCO WILL REACH FROM $150,000,000 TO $200,000,000. THESE FIGURES ARE IN THE ROUGH AND NOTHING CAN BE TOLD UNTIL PARTIAL ACCOUNTING IS TAKEN.

ON EVERY SIDE THERE WAS DEATH AND SUFFERING YESTERDAY. HUNDREDS WERE INJURED, EITHR BURNED, CRUSHED OR STRUCK BY FALLING PIECES FROM THE BUILDINGS, AND ONE OF TEN DIED WHILE ON THE OPOPERATING TABLE AT MECHANICS' PAVILION, IMPROVISED AS A HOSPITAL FOR THE COMFORT AND CARE OF 300 OF THE INJURED THE NUMBER OF DEAD IS NOT KNOWN BUT IT IS ESTIMATED THAT AT LEAST 500 MET THEIR DEATH IN THE HORROR.

AT NINE O'CLOCK, UNDER A SPECIAL MESSAGE FROM PRESIDENT ROOSEVELT, THE CITY WAS PLACED UNDER MARTIAL LAW. HUNDREDS OF TROOPS PATROLLED THE STREETS AND DROVE THE CROWDS BACK, WHILE HUNDREDS MORE WERE SET AT WORK ASSISTING THE FIRE AND POLICE DEPARTMENTS. THE STRICTEST ORDERS WERE ISSUED, AND IN TRUE MILITARY SPIRIT THE SOLDIERS OBEYED DURING THE AFTERNOON THREE THIEVES MET THEIR DEATH BYRIFLE BULLETS WHILE AT WORK IN THE RUINS. THE CURIOUS WERE DRIVEN BACK AT THE BREASTS OF THE HORSES THAT THE CAVALRYMEN RODE AND ALL THE CROWDS WERE FORCED FROM THE LEVEL DISTRICT TO THE HILLY SECTION BEYOND TO THE NORTH

THE WATER SUPPLY WAS ENTIRELY CUT OFF, AND MAY BE IT WAS JUST AS WELL, FOR THE LINES OF FIRE DEPARTMENT WOULD HAVE BEEN ABSOLUTELY USELESS AT ANY STAGE. ASSISTANT CHIEF DOUGHERTY SUPERVISED THE WORK OF HIS MEN AND EARLY IN THE MORNING IT WAS SEEN THAT THE ONLY POSSIBLE CHANCE TO SAVE THE CITY LAY IN EFFORT TO CHECK THE FLAMES BY THE USE OF DYNAMITE. DURING THE DAY A BLAST COULD BE HEARD IN ANY SECTION AT INTERVALS OF ONLY A FEW MINUTES, AND BUILDINGS NOT DESTROYED BY FIRE WERE BLOWN TO ATOMS. BUT THROUGH THE GAPS MADE THE FLAMES JUMPED AND ALTHOUGH THE FAILURES OF THE HEROIC EFFORTS OF THE POLICE FIREMEN AND SOLDIERS WERE AT TIMES SICKENING, THE WORK WAS CONTINUED WITH A DESPERATION THAT WILL LIVE AS ONE OF THE FEATURES OF THE TERRIBLE DISASTER. MEN WORKED LIKE FIENDS TO COMBAT THE LAUGHING, ROARING, ONRUSHING FIRE DEMON.

NO HOPE LEFT FOR SAFETY OF ANY BUILDINGS

San Francisco seems doomed to entire destruction. With a lapse in the raging of the flames just before dark, the hope was raised that with the use of the tons of dynamite the course of the fire might be checked and confined to the triangular sections it had cut out for its path. But on the Barbary Coast the fire broke out anew and as night closed in the flames were eating their way into parts untouched in their ravages during the day. To the south and the north they spread; down to the docks and out into the resident section, in and to the north of Hayes Valley. By six o'clock practically all of St. Ignatius' great buildings were no more. They had been leveled to the fiery heap that marked what was oncethe metropolis of the West.

The first of the big structures to go to ruin was the Call Building, the famous skyscraper. At eleven o'clock the big 18-story building was a furnace. Flames leaped from every window and shot skyward from thecircular windows in the dome. In less than two hours nothing remained but the tall skeleton.

By five o'clock the Palace Hotel was in ruins. The old hostelry, famous the world over, withstood the seige until the last and although dynamite was used in frequent blasts to drive

Continued on Page Two

BLOW BUILDINGS UP TO CHECK FLAMES

The dynamiting of buildings in the track of the fire, to stay the progress of the flames, was in charge of John Bermingham, Jr., superintendent of the California Powder Works. Several experienced men from the powder works, assisted by policemen and members of the fire department, did the hazardous work of blowing up the buildings. They were razed in sets of threes, but the open spaces where the shattered buildings fell were quickly turned into holocausts of flame. The work was most effective in the business blocks east of Kearny street.

WHOLE CITY IS ABLAZE

At 10 o'clock last night the Occidental Hotel was destroyed by the flames which swept unchecked across Montgomery street and attacked the block bounded by Montgomery, Sutter, Bush and Kearny. The new Merchants' Exchange building was a mass of flames from basement to tower.

The Union Trust building and Crocker-Wolworth Bank were both ablaze and the Chronicle building and other buildings in that block were threatened by the flames.

Shortly after 10 o'clock the fire had eaten its way southward from Portsmouth Square to Kearny and California streets. The entire section fronting on the west side of Kearny street seemed doomed.

All the building adjoining the Hall of Justice were ablaze and the firemen were striving to save the structure by using dynamite. It is almost a certainty that every building contained in the section bounded by Clay, Kearny, Market and East streets will be consumed.

The flames had eaten their way westward in the residence section as far as Gough street. There, by dynamiting blocks after blocks, the firemen succeeded in checking the devouring element.

CHURCH OF SAINT IGNATIUS IS DESTROYED

The magnificent church and College of St. Ignatius, on the northwest corner of Van Ness avenue and Hayes street represents in its destruction a material loss of over $1,000,000. The actual cost of the great building was over $900,000, but during the years which have elapsed since its erection the church has been enriched by paintings and frescoes, which were priceless. Some of them were works of art which can never be replaced, however willing those interested in the church might be to meet any expense in the effort.

MAYOR CONFERS WITH MILITARY AND CITIZENS

At 1 o'clock yesterday afternoon 50 representative citizens of San Francisco met the Mayor, the Chief of Police and the United States Military authorities in the police office in the basement of the Hall of Justice. They had been summoned thither by Mayor Schmitz early in the forenoon, the fearful possibilities of the situation having forced themselves upon him immediately after the shock of earthquake in the morning, and the news which at once reached him of the completeness of the diaster. He lost no time in making out a list of citizens from whom to seek advice and assistance, and in summoning them to the conference. It was called at the Hall of Justice, as virtually the first news which reached the Mayor regarding the extent of the disaster was that of the ruin of the City Hall. He did not realize that even while the conference was to be going on cornices would be crashing down and windows falling in fragments in the Hall of Justice also, and that before sunset desperate efforts would be made to blow the structure up in the vain endeavor by this means to check the advance of the flames in the northern section of the down town district.

All, or nearly all of the citizens summoned to the conference

Continued on Page Two

San Francisco Chronicle.

VOL. LXXXVIII. SAN FRANCISCO CAL., MONDAY, APRIL 23, 1906. NO. 93

FIVE HUNDRED DIE IN GREAT DISASTER

PROPERTY LOSS IS PLACED AT $300,000,000

SEARCH OF THE RUINS BEGUN

Facts Will Never Be Known as Many Lie in Unnamed Graves.

As nearly as can be estimated by the authorities of the Health Office approximately 500 bodies of victims of the earthquake and conflagration have been recovered thus far and disposed of either by burial or cremation. The difficulty of obtaining a correct list of the killed lies in the fact that many bodies that have been recovered in the last five days have been hastily interred or cremated without reference to the regulation regarding the issuance of burial permits. The Health Board hopes from this time on, however, to preserve more regularity in the matter of burials.

The first systematic search for bodies started yesterday. The ruins throughout the burned district are now cooled enough to permit searchers to work to advantage, and as bodies are found wagons from the Coroner's office are dispatched to the scene. The city has been divided into districts and it is believed that all bodies, except probably those that have been reduced to mere ashes, will be recovered and disposed of during the next few days. The Coroner's office has fifteen wagons engaged in the work of removing the remains of the dead to the various cemeteries.

Not all of the recovered bodies have found a resting place in the cemeteries. Owing to the lack of adequate transportation facilities and the necessity for prompt interment of bodies, there have been a number of burials at the foot of Van Ness avenue, at Bernal Heights and in other vacant spaces. There have also been a number of cremations. Most of the burials have taken place at the cemeteries, however, and the health authorities announce that hereafter, so far as it is within their power to do so, they will require all interments to be made within cemetery grounds. The crematory at Odd Fellows' Cemetery has been placed at the disposal of the health authorities. About forty bodies a day, or something like two an hour, can be disposed of at the crematory.

The remains of Annie Webster, 38 years of age, were removed yesterday from 14 William street and interred at Mount Olivet.

The remains of an unknown male were found at Pine and Jones streets and buried by the city undertaker.

The remains of a man supposed to be H. Delaranelle of San Jose were found at California and Jones streets. They were interred at Laurel Hill.

Frank Nunan died at the City and County Hospital.

The remains of an unknown man and an unknown baby were found at Dupont and Union streets. They were buried at Laurel Hill.

William Stanisis died at the Children's Hospital yesterday and his remains were sent to Laurel Hill.

The body of a man supposed to be Houston was found on Silver street, between Third and Fourth. The charred remains were interred at Bay View and Van Ness avenue.

The bodies of three unknown men were found at Harrison and Brannan streets and were buried at Laurel Hill.

N. A. Hiestel died on the street at Fifth and Montgomery streets yesterday and his body was cremated at Odd Fellows' Cemetery.

The body of an unknown man was found in the burned district and taken to Laurel Hill.

The remains of two Italians, names unknown, were also delivered at Laurel Hill for burial yesterday.

Cornelius McCarthy and his son Robert lost their lives at First and Minna streets. Their bodies were recovered yesterday and taken to Laurel Hill.

An effort is being made to locate the body of Miss Blaney, who died Thursday morning and whose body was at Monahan's undertaking establishment, Twenty-second and Mission streets, when that establishment was destroyed by fire. The Coroner has been asked to notify relatives at 2..9 Fifteenth street should the body be found.

The Coroner's office was notified yesterday that Mrs. Elisabeth Reece Richards perished when the building at Seventeenth and Valencia streets was destroyed. Her body has not yet been recovered.

The finding of the bodies of two children in the Potrero district was reported to the Coroner yesterday. It is believed that they died from exposure.

The following died at the Presidio General Hospital during the twenty-four hours ended at noon yesterday: Nansen, Patrick Dockery, F. D. Sullivan, Bernard Shay, Jules Zaliski, Amalia [illegible], 210 Cypress avenue, Alameda; A. Hustel, John Fauth, Hughes Home, San Francisco.

The public is requested to report the [illegible] bodies to the main office of [illegible] located at Mowry's Hall, [illegible] Grove streets, or to the [illegible], Portsmouth square, opposite [illegible] of Justice.

It is believed that the charred bones of seventeen human beings repose in the ashes of the frame lodging-house at 119 Fifth street. Yesterday the fragments of one body were recovered, and according to the story of one occupant of the house who escaped with his life, at least seventeen bodies must have burned up when the building was reduced to ashes.

The building at 119 Fifth street was a four-story frame structure, the ground floor being occupied by a saloon and restaurant, and the upper floors as a lodging-house. The lodging-house was conducted by a Mrs. Murray.

The building was completely wrecked by the earthquake. It fell against the building on the opposite side of Minna street, crushing it like an egg shell and crushing itself at the same time. The wreckage was piled high in Minna street. Instantly a fire broke out in the mass of twisted timbers, presumably from the stove in the kitchen on the ground floor. J. Armstrong of Armstrong & Co., steam fitters, who were located at 905 Market street, was one of the first men on the scene. Armstrong, who is at present encamped in the neighborhood, rescued one man from the ruins. This latter occupant of the house said that seventeen other people were in the house at the time of the catastrophe, and Armstrong declared that none of them escaped. He saw a man and woman in the wreckage, pinioned in bed by a heavy timber that lay across their chests and that had apparently crushed out their lives. He also heard an infant crying a short distance away. He attempted to rescue the infant, but was driven away by heat and smoke.

Adam Gill, member of the Vallejo relief committee and wearing a red cross insignia, visited the ruins of the building and talked of having the debris searched for the [illegible] of Mrs. Murray, the landlady of the house, who, he declared, was his [illegible]-in-law. The latter is supposed to have had considerable money in her possession. She leaves a husband, who is now at Fort Bragg.

RAPHAEL WEIL WILL REBUILD

"The White House will be rebuilt, and it will be better than ever," said Raphael Weill yesterday. "I have enough left to buy an annuity and live like a fighting cock for the rest of my days; but none of that for me. I am going into the work of rebuilding with all my soul. I am 70 years old, but I love San Francisco with a love that is filial, and I am going to work at the restoration of the city as if I were only 30."

The Risdon Iron Works at the Potrero are absolutely uninjured and start in tomorrow with a full force.

DOCKS IN FAIR SHAPE.

The Ferry building is sound, except the clock tower, which is injured and leans toward the south. From Market street north the wharf line is unimpaired to pier 7, collapsed. Pier 6 of the Northern Pacific Steamship Company is in ruins, as is Broadway wharf No. 2. The N. P. R. R. sheds are in good condition and the Custom-house is unharmed; but from it along sections 1 and 2 of the seawall for a quarter of a mile the warehouses are smoking ruins. Onfarther to Fisherman's wharf the destruction is heavy, but the quarantine office and Merchants' Exchange station are safe.

Bread Line n Jefferson square.

Ruins of the Valencia-Street Hotel, showing the depression in the street. This is the best photograph of the effect of the earthquake itself yet published.

WASTE OF WATER DELAYS SUPPLY

The city will be well equipped with water by noon to-day, according to the announcement of the Spring Valley Water Company. The task of restoring the supply has been great owing to the depletion of the reservoirs during the fire, the breaking of the mains by the shock and the subsequent waste through broken mains in the burned district. The work of repairing these breaks has been carried on by large squads of men divided into districts.

The Mayor has issued a warning to consumers of the great danger from fire from the wasteful use of water and leaks. Urgent appeal is made to all users of water to use the same for drinking and cooking purposes only, and to prevent all leaks and waste. All citizens are required to stop leaks where possible and to notify the committee on water supply, 1849 Fillmore street, of all leaks and extravagant use. Engineer Schussler of the water company says:

The Spring Valley authorities complain about the action taken by some of the National Guardsmen and a great many special policemen in hindering their employes from working. Only yesterday morning a large squad of men was held up and sent away from their work. They were not allowed to return until the Spring Valley officials held a conference with the Mayor and secured 500 passes for workmen, who were put to work immediately.

LOOTERS SHOT BY THE POLICE

Patrolman Charles Fennell reported to Captain Duke yesterday that he had shot a looter in the shoulder and that the man had been taken in charge by the soldiers and put in the Presidio Hospital. The man, a big burly fellow, had been turned over to Fennell by two citizens who found him in a cigar store. He had a bottle of whisky, some watches and jewelry, and a revolver. When Fennell took him from his captors he made a break and was shot. A soldier coming along made a lunge with his bayonet, but stumbled and the thief was not much hurt.

Policeman Flood reported that he killed a man near his home for looting. The man was not identified.

TRIPLETS BORN IN CAMP.

On Saturday night triplets were born to one of the homeless at the Presidio, and the same night eight little tots made their first appearance on the reservation at Fort Mason. Six were born in the Emergency Hospital and two out on the vacant space adjoining the fort, where the mothers had taken refuge. The babies all are reported to be healthy youngsters.

UNION LEAGUE MEMBERS.

The members of the Union League Club of San Francisco are requested to register at Union League rooms, third floor, Bacon block.

FIFTEEN CHOSEN TO HANDLE FUNDS

The finance committee of the Citizens' Committee was enlarged and reorganized yesterday. As now constituted the body which will manage the money end of the relief work is as follows: James D. Phelan, chairman; J. Downey Harvey, secretary; I. W. Hellman Jr., Herbert E. Law, Rudolph Spreckels, M. H. de Young, James L. Flood, Thomas Magee, William F. Herrin, William Babcock, Hubert J. Tobin, Charles Sutro Jr., Allen Pollok, Rufus P. Jennings, Lester Herrick, assistant secretary.

The committee has engaged permanent headquarters at the northwest corner of Fillmore and Pine streets, and will be in session each day at 3 P. M.

Lester Herrick, the assistant secretary, was selected for that post because of his being an expert accountant. He will regulate the system of accounts of the committee so as to avoid any embarrassing errors, and conduct its bookkeeping department with as much system as is adopted by the banks.

The following are the money subscriptions received by the committee yesterday:

Thomas J. Lipton	$ 5,000
Victoria Licensed Vintners' Association	200
Colusa Sun	2000
City of Little Falls, N. Y.	1000
Robert G. Cottrell, Newport, R.I	1000
Pelham State Bank, Pelham, Ga	45
Citizens of Marysville, Cal.	2000
City of Charleston, S. C.	5000
People of Charleston, S. C.	927
City of Meridian, Miss	500
City of Terre Haute, Ind	2000
Davenport Clearing-house	500
Columbus Insurance and Banking Co., Columbus, Miss	190
Cincinnati Chamber of Commerce	10,000
Citizens of District of Columbia	10,000
City of Joplin, Mo	2000
Denemouro Powder Co., Wilmington, Del	5000
St. Louis Live Stock Exchange	1000
Sacramento Comfort	500
Citizens of Thomasville, Ga.	58
Chicago Commercial Association	100,000

BOHEMIAN PICTURES SAVED.

President Fred Hall of the Bohemian Club states that all the historical and other important pictures in the club's gallery were saved and are now at the Park Museum. The office books and records were also saved.

ELECTRICIANS' HEADQUARTERS.

Electrical Union, No. 6, has established headquarters at 2315 California street. All executive officers will report there at once.

LOSS AS GIVEN BY THE AGENTS

Insurance Commissioner Places the Amount of Policies at $175,000,000.

The Insurance Commissioners and Underwriters yesterday made a thorough inspection of the burned district and they now state that their belief is that the insurance loss will be approximately $175,000,000 and that the total loss will be about $300,000,000.

State Insurance Commissioner E. Myron Wolfe made a very reassuring statement covering the condition of the insurance companies that will be called upon to make good the losses incurred through the fire.

"I estimate," Commissioner Wolfe said, "that the total insurance loss will aggregate close to $200,000,000. This will, of course, be divided among a great number of companies, nearly four score in all. It is probable that two or three of the very smallest companies will be unable to meet their losses in full, but with these exceptions I have every reason to believe that the companies will pay dollar for dollar on the policies held by property owners.

"An organization was perfected yesterday at a meeting held during the afternoon in San Francisco. On Monday the underwriters will meet in Reed Hall in Oakland and at that time a plan will be perfected covering the adjustment of losses. The result of that conference will be promptly announced and within a short time those who have suffered loss will know where they stand. The companies that go under will, of course, pay in part, but just what extent we are unable to say as yet."

Mayor Schmitz has been notified by the insurance companies that if any attempt is made to build fires in any of the houses of San Francisco except the bakeries already authorized to have fires for preparing bread, all insurance will be invalidated.

CITY LIGHTS WILL SOON BE RESUMED

The resumption of street lighting is now believed to be not far distant, possibly within five or ten days. As yet there has been no official test of the mains and conduits for the reason that the manholes are too hot to permit of their being entered. However, enough is known to warrant the statement that the installation of the service need not be long delayed.

As a matter of course the resumption of street railway traffic is of paramount importance owing to the congested condition of the various concentration camps. The opening of traffic will permit many thousands of refugees to seek friends in the district that escaped the fire. With this purpose in view, employes of the electric company have been working day and night inspecting the trolley lines and removing all dead wires that may come in contact with those on the trolley poles. When that is completed, probably by this morning, the current will be turned on and the lines tested. After that the installation of the current for lighting the streets, dwellings and business houses will be a matter of a few hours.

The city's Department of Electricity has established headquarters at 2034 Steiner street, where Chief Hewitt has collected the nucleus of a strong working force, has had it employed night and day and has now restored a semblance of order out of the chaos of the past four days. He is inspecting buildings in the district that escaped the fire and as rapidly as one is found with its wires intact and in condition to receive the current the San Francisco Gas and Electric Company is notified. One of the buildings reported safe yesterday afternoon was the Home of the Little Sisters of the Poor at 318 Lake street.

The work of testing the gas mains and the conduits will be begun this morning. Some of the mains are known to be broken, but it is thought that the break may be repaired in a day or two. The plant of the San Francisco Gas and Electric Company is said to be comparatively uninjured and Mr. Naphtaly says that the company can start with a production of 500,000 feet of gas per day, and inside of a week increase it to 10,000,000 feet, ample for all purposes of the city as it now exists.

SURGEON SHOT BY HIS OWN PISTOL

Dr. C. F. Taggart, one of the foremost physicians of Los Angeles, who volunteered his services with the Red Cross brigade, was shot and killed yesterday by the accidental discharge of his pistol.

While running up the steps of the Crocker school building the weapon dropped from his hip pocket and the hammer struck the stonework.

Dr. Taggart came here a week ago to attend the meeting of a medical society. He was a native of Sparta, Ill., and 44 years of age. He was a graduate of St. Louis Medical College and took a course at Berlin. He leaves a wife and daughter. His twin brother, Dr. Thomas Taggart, is practicing here.

STEALS MANY TRUNKS.

Representing himself to be an expressman, A. R. Hoskins took six loads of trunks from Union square. He charged $5 for each trunk. When the trunks could not be located complaint was made to the police and Hoskins was found and locked in the Stanyan-street Police Station. He refuses to divulge the whereabouts of the trunks.

FURNISHING FREE BREAD.

Schwabacher Brothers, agents for the Stockton Milling Company, sent 300 barrels of flour to Oakland for baking last Wednesday, the day of the earthquake, and had the bread brought to this city for free distribution. Since then the firm has contributed one carload of flour each day, and will continue to do so as long as there is need.

DEATH COMES TO FIRE CHIEF

Dennis T. Sullivan, chief of San Francisco's Fire Department, died at 10 minutes past 1 o'clock yesterday morning from the effects of injuries received on the morning of the earthquake. When the tremendous convulsion came, Chief Sullivan and his wife were sleeping in the firehouse adjoining the California Hotel. The chimney of the hotel was shaken down by the shock and came crashing through the firehouse. The chief and Mrs. Sullivan were carried two stories to the ground floor and were extricated from the debris with great difficulty.

Teh injured chief and his wife were conveyed at once to the Southern Pacific Hospital at Fourteenth and Mission streets, but when the flames reached the Mission district, they were again moved, this time to the General Hospital at the Presidio, where the Chief died yesterday morning. Mrs. Sullivan, whose injuries also looked serious, has progressed and, it is confidently expected, will recover.

WILL UTILIZE SCHOOLHOUSES

President Roncovieri of the Board of Education yesterday issued general orders which, in effect, are as follows:

The school year is now terminated.

All employes and especially male teachers of the department or directed to report this morning at 9 o'clock on Vallejo street, between Steiner and Pierce, where an open air meeting will be held to plan for the future conduct of the schools and the payment of salaries.

All schools standing shall be thrown open to the public, but those occupying them shall maintain good sanitary conditions under the direction of the janitors. Janitors whose schools have been destroyed shall report to schools still standing. They shall police the schools and see that neither lights nor fires are permitted in them.

President Roncovieri recommends that as many women teachers as can do so report to the relief committee for duty.

CONVENIENCE STATIONS.

The Street Sweeping Department was kept busy cleaning up around the public parks and squares, and all public places where the homeless are camping. Convenience stations are being constructed as rapidly as possible.

The Board has made a special appeal to all persons whose houses are in the vicinity of public parks and squares to keep their houses open for the convenience of women and children camping in public places.

San Francisco Chronicle.

VOL. XC. SAN FRANCISCO, CAL., TUESDAY, JULY 9, 1907. NO. 175

SCHMITZ SENTENCED TO SAN QUENTIN FOR FIVE YEARS

Trial of Louis Glass Begins  *Six Jurors Accepted and Sworn*

CONVICTED MAYOR CREATES A SCENE

He Brazenly Affronts Judge Dunne When the Court Pronounces Judgment.

EUGENE E. SCHMITZ, for five years Mayor of San Francisco, was yesterday sentenced by Judge Dunne to serve a term of five years—the extreme penalty for his crime—in the penitentiary at San Quentin.

Turbid with the outbursts of unrestrained passion, the scene in the courtroom when sentence was pronounced on the convict Mayor was marred by ugly retort and clamor, and justice strove with riot for a voice. Five times the defendant broke in upon the Judge and interrupted him with vehement demands that he be sentenced and not lectured, and when the Court's last words were spoken that pronounced the sentence of five years of penal servitude upon the arrogant Schmitz a cheer broke from the crowd.

Jerry Dinan rose from his seat, but one in the back of the crowd cried out: "Send Dinan with him!" and the Chief of Police, who was himself in court as a defendant, slunk back into his chair beside his attorney.

"This is rather an abnormal proceeding," Attorney Fairall said to the Court, but the noise was such that only the stenographer and the Judge heard him. The bailiffs stood by as though they had been petrified.

Judge Dunne Rebukes the Sheriff.

"If we had a Sheriff worthy of the name, this exhibition would not happen!" exclaimed the Judge, and Tom O'Neil came to life with the retort:

"We could not stop that," your honor."

"I think you might clear the courtroom," suggested the Judge, and the Sheriff made a rush into the crowd and, singling out a detective in the employ of Burns, whose affidavit had been used to disqualify him in the course of the Ruef trial, seized him by the coat collar and started him doorward, pushing the crowd in front.

When order had been restored, Fairall was addressing the Court and asking that the clerk be instructed to enter "the cheering and the hissing" on the record.

"We ask the stenographer to enter what happened just now—the cheering, the sneering and the hissing of this mob," he said.

With the picturesque braggadocio of a pirate of romance, Schmitz had attempted to preside at his own judgment and tell the Court what he should and should not say about him. In this course he was aided by his attorney, William H. Metson, who also broke in upon the stringent words of denunciation which preceded the actual passing of sentence with the declaration:

"We take an exception to any cruel or unusual punishment by the Judge of this court."

Metson Arouses Wrath of Court.

Judge Dunne, who had remained calm while struggling with the defendant for a chance to speak the words he had prepared, lost control of his temper and shouted:

"If I am interrupted again I will send you to jail, Mr. Metson. You would be better engaged if you were asking this Court to set a day to inquire into an accusation made against you here, that you willfully and deliberately attempted to tamper with and influence a witness in this case."

Violence seemed imminent, and all the while Schmitz was standing with both hands in his trousers pockets, demanding that the Court do its duty and sentence him.

"I am ready to meet any charges that your honor may make in court or without," came like a truculent challenge from Metson, and the hearing suggested by the Judge was not set.

When it was all over Schmitz turned to the newspaper men and dictated another statement that he would be a candidate for Mayor in November, and, with the yells of the crowd still in his ears, said that "the people were always right," and that he would leave it to them to decide whether he was innocent or guilty. Bathos rounded out the anticlimax of turbulence.

SPECTATORS IN COURT THROW RESTRAINT ASIDE

THE defendant, Schmitz, was one of the first to arrive at the Temple. He came in his red automobile, and was accompanied by his three attorneys, Frank Drew, William H. Metson and Charles H. Fairall.

It was soon evident that the proceedings were to attract a large crowd to the courtroom. Before the Judge entered every seat in the room was taken, and crowds were standing in the aisles. Among those who struggled for standing room in the mob were a dozen women.

As several of the other graft cases were on the calendar, the seats immediately outside the railing were occupied by an array of defendants and their counsel. Behind the Mayor and his lawyers, who sat in the first row, were the indicted members of the Parkside Company, with Attorney Hoefler. Dinan and Attorney Byington occupied adjoining chairs, and behind them was Theodore V. Halsey, whose trial will commence before the week is over.

[Heney?] came late, attended by his bodyguard, Hess, and followed by Cobb. The party had to elbow their way through the press of the crowd in the aisle. Soon after them Rudolph Spreckels entered, and a bailiff found a chair for him. Langdon was the last of the prosecutors to arrive, somewhat flushed from his struggle to force his way to the front of the room.

CALLS THE SCHMITZ CASE.

The door of the Judge's chambers opened, the bailiff rapped for silence, and Judge Dunne, quickly taking his seat, called his calendar, disposing of the other graft cases in advance of the Schmitz case. In the same monotone in which the cases of a host of other criminals have been called he pronounced the words:

"Case of the people vs. Schmitz."

There was a hush of expectancy in the courtroom as District Attorney Langdon arose to say:

"We are ready to proceed to judgment."

The Court asked to be advised by

(Continued on Page Two.)

The convict Mayor and two of his attorneys in Judge Dunne's court yesterday morning. In the group from left to right are Eugene E. Schmitz, John J. Barrett and W. H. Metson.

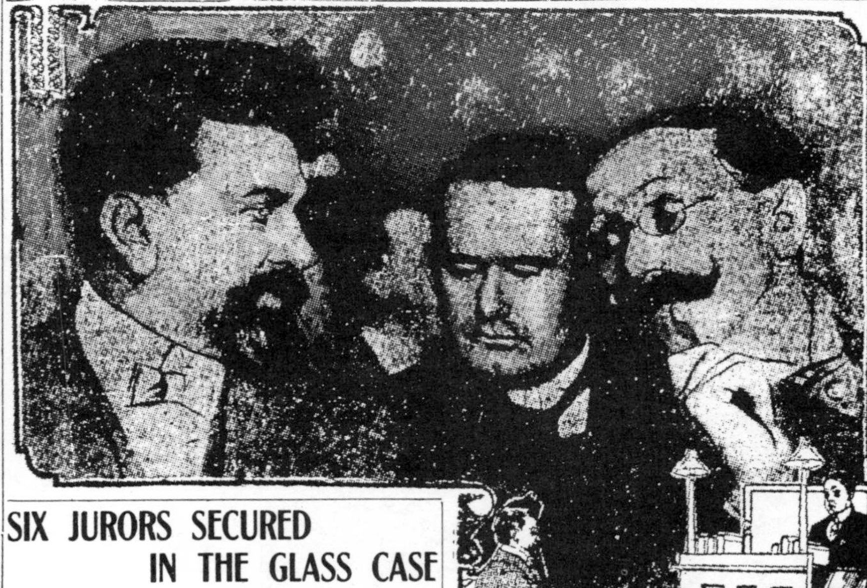

SIX JURORS SECURED IN THE GLASS CASE

Trial of the Indicted Magnate Is Proceeding Rapidly in Lawlor's Court.

SIX JURORS were secured and sworn yesterday in Superior Judge Lawlor's court to try Louis Glass, vice-president and general manager of the Pacific States Telephone Company on the specific charge contained in one of the eleven indictments found against him, namely, of having paid a bribe in the sum of $5000 to Supervisor Charles Boxton. The jurors are: Patrick Lyons, 1927 Bush street; Joseph H. Robinson, 3978 Nineteenth street; Michael A. Samuels, 1139 Stanyan street; George A. Kohn, 2110 Scott street; John G. North, 133 Third avenue, and John W. Shields, 2584 California street.

After a delay of several months, devoted largely to preliminary skirmishes in the courts, the actual trial of Louis Glass, was begun yesterday, and in two brief sessions of the Court one-half of the jury was secured. At this rate, it is believed that to-day's session will produce a full jury box and probably the opening statement of the prosecution. The six jurors were taken from a drawing of eighteen, all of whom were rigidly examined as to bias, opinion and affiliations with public service corporations on the one side, and trades unions on the other. After twelve jurors had been passed for cause, the prosecution exercised two peremptory challenges and the defense four. This leaves three peremptory challenges for the prosecution and six for the defense.

ARRAY OF LEGAL TALENT.

A trio of prominent attorneys has charge of the defense of the telephone magnate. Henry C. McPike, who shared with D. M. Delmas the honors that attached to the defense of Harry Thaw, was yesterday added to Glass' array of legal talent. With these two prominent lawyers is associated T. C. Coogan, who had charge of the case at its inception. The trial, which was set for 11 o'clock, did not commence until 11:30, when Assistant District Attorney Francis J. Heney and associates arrived from Judge Dunne's courtroom below, where Eugene E. Schmitz had just been sentenced to five years in San Quentin. The graft prosecutors were followed by a large crowd, which struggled into the big auditorium.

Before taking up the Glass case Judge Lawlor continued the case of Abraham K. Detweiler, the indicted fugitive, until July 23d. Heney then asked that the names of witnesses be read. The names of the witnesses attached to indictment 476 were read. They included the confessed Supervisors, several directors and officers of the telephone company and Miss Nellie Smith, stenographer. A number of the city fathers were present and answered to the roll call. The witnesses were then dismissed until this morning.

District Attorney Langdon conducted the examination of the jurors. McPike held the fort for the defense. Delmas merely stroked his Napoleonic curl and offered suggestions in whispered tones, while Coogan concerned himself with perusing law books.

VENIREMEN ARE CALLED.

Judge Lawlor ordered that the names of the panel of seventy-three be called. A number of the jurors were absent. The names of the following twelve were then drawn from the box by Clerk Welch: Fred A. Kaufmann, James H. Robertson, William Jones, Thomas Kirby, Sol Schloss, Patrick Lyons, Joseph A. Robinson, Joseph S. Silverberg, Michael A. Samuels, John Tiedemann, Frank Wentworth and Henry Sieroty. After being sworn by the clerk Heney informed the veniremen that Glass was to be tried on the charge of paying the sum of $5000 to Supervisor Boxton.

Fred A. Kaufmann, residing at 525 Lyon street, was the first juror examined. He said that he was in the grocery business. The prosecution challenged him for bias. James H. Robertson, 316 Bartlett street, was next examined. He said that he was in the insurance and brokerage business and had lived in San Francisco fourteen years, that he knew no reason why he could not render a fair and impartial verdict in the case. He satisfied both sides and was passed.

William Jones, retired, of 1059 Haight street, admitted that he was acquainted with the father of Supervisor Sanderson and that he knew Assistant District Attorney John O'Gara. McPike, for the defense, made it a particular point to question each juror as to any connection with trades unions, and went so far as to ask if the jurors' relatives or friends belonged to unions.

Solomon Schloss said that he could not sit on the case unless it could be concluded by Sunday, as he had made arrangements to leave town. He was excused by consent.

HAD FORMED OPINION.

At the afternoon session Thomas Kirby, formerly a non-union carpenter, and now an insurance broker at 40 Hayes street, was the first venireman examined. He said that from reading the papers he had formed an opinion that the defendant was guilty, but he had never expressed that opinion. He had discussed the cases with his son, who is a member of the Typographical Union, and with others, "but if sworn as a juror," continued the venireman, "I would honestly try to do right." Kirby was temporarily passed.

Patrick Lyons, a retired dry goods merchant living at 1927 Bush street, said that he knew no reason why he could not give the defendant a fair and impartial trial. He was temporarily passed.

Joseph A. Robinson, a retired retail grocer, formerly of the firm of Robinson & Knox, testified that he had never expressed an opinion relative to the case at bar, and had none. He would give an honest verdict regardless of consequences. He was passed temporarily.

Joseph S. Silverberg, a wholesale clothier, was excused on his statement that he had a fixed opinion.

Michael A. Samuels, a photographer on Golden Gate avenue was challenged by the defense on his testimony that he had an opinion that the defendant was guilty and it would take fairly strong evidence to remove that opinion.

To Judge Lawlor the venireman stated that from what he had read and

(Continued on Page Two.)

CHIEF GERONIMO TRIES TO ESCAPE

Aged Apache Wants to Go to El Paso to Fight With His People.

Special Dispatch to the "Chronicle."

LAWTON (Okla.), July 8.—Geronimo, the old Apache warrior, while attending a celebration Saturday at Cache, as a guest of the Comanche, Chief Quanah, made an attempt to escape across the Texas panhandle into Mexico. A detail of soldiers from Fort Sill rounded him up and brought him back. He had been missing overnight, but was overtaken several miles out, and made no resistance.

He said he had heard of recent trouble with the Apaches near El Paso and wanted to help his people fight. He also said his domestic affairs were irksome and his eighth wife has left him. He has been drinking heavily and recently stole out and remained away all night.

When the invitation came for him to attend the celebration near the mountain home of Chief Parker, Geronimo was highly pleased. Several hundred Indians participated in a sham battle and stage-coach robbery, and the old man became highly enthusiastic. During the excitement he slipped quietly away and was not missed for several hours.

EX-SENATOR JOHN P. JONES SUED ON OLD NOTE.

NEW YORK, July 8.—Sheriff Hayes has received an attachment against Ex-Senator John P. Jones, formerly of Nevada, for $7000 in favor of the National Bank of North America. The writ was granted by Justice Platzek of the Supreme Court. Jones, it is stated, is now a resident of Santa Monica, Cal. The claim is on a note made by Jones and F. W. Pratt, at Washington, D. C., March 30, 1905, in favor of Eugene Davis, who assigned it to the bank. The note was not paid. The Sheriff served the attachment on Laidlaw & Co., bankers, to attach any account Jones might have with them.

RUNS AMUCK WITH HATCHET.

NEW YORK, July 8.—Becoming suddenly insane, probably from the heat, while at work upon the new building of the Trust Company of America today, a plasterer ran amuck with a hatchet among his fellow workmen. He attacked three of them, two of whom were probably fatally injured.

FAIRBANKS SAVES LIFE OF A WOMAN

Rescues a Hotel Waitress From Drowning in Yellowstone Lake.

Special Dispatch to the "Chronicle."

YELLOWSTONE PARK (Wyo.), July 8.—Vice-President Fairbanks is a hero. His long legs and presence of mind stood him in good stead yesterday evening, when he plunged into the lake and rescued Miss Lena Wallace, a waitress at the hotel where he is stopping.

Mr. Fairbanks and J. I. Gibbs, proprietor of the hotel, were sitting on the piazza overlooking the lake, exchanging stories, when they saw a boat coming across the lake containing several persons. A piercing shriek alarmed both of them and they noticed that the boat had capsized. Two women and two men were making for the pier, but another woman was floundering in the water. Fairbanks leaped over the railing of the piazza and ran to the pier. The woman had sunk twice, and was going down for the third time when he reached her, half swimming and half wading, and seized her clothing. Water was over his head, but he managed to bring the woman in. It required half an hour's work to restore her to consciousness.

LOADED DICE, BEYOND REACH OF POSTOFFICE.

No Law Enables the Authorities to Strike at the Mischievous Industry.

WASHINGTON, July 8.—The "loaded" dice industry has passed the scrutiny of the Postoffice Department, which finds it cannot interfere. Not long ago the postal inspectors in Chicago got after the firm that advertised for sale "loaded" dice. When the legal advisers of the department went over the papers in the case it was found the firm's business was legitimate as far as the use of the mails is concerned. The firm openly advertised their dice for sale, the purchasers got what they bought and were satisfied. There was no fraud against the purchaser, and the department consequently found it could not legally issue a fraud order against the concern.

MONEY FOR RUSSIAN NAVY.

ST. PETERSBURG, July 8.—The Council of Ministers to-day authorized an annual expenditure of $15,500,000 from 1908 to 1911 for the construction of new war ships and their armaments.

RIDICULE ALL TALK OF CONFLICT AS SENSELESS

Officials of Japan and United States Say There Will Not Be War.

RELATIONS ARE PEACEFUL.

Tokio Declares That the Fleet Would Be Welcomed in Those Waters.

Special Dispatches to the "Chronicle."

WASHINGTON, July 8.—Representatives of Japan, as well as of the United States, regard with impatience the talk of war between the two countries. While realizing the danger of unbridled jingoism, they declare that there is absolutely nothing but the best of feeling existing between the two governments, and it seems almost impossible that the equilibrium could be disturbed.

At the Japanese Embassy it was remarked that "semi-official" statements about the negotiation of a new treaty with the exclusion feature could not be discussed seriously, but it can be said here that no such negotiations are under way. No draft of a treaty has been submitted by Secretary Root to Foreign Minister Hayashi, and, therefore, the latter could not have rejected any such proposal.

The Embassador declares that there is nothing but the kindliest feeling in Japan toward this country, and that this state of affairs would have continued had not American papers printed things about Japan and Japanese which were read there and caused comment.

The Japanese papers replied to editorials advocating exclusion and the feeling was fanned by the discussion. Naval officers, of course, are gladly speculating on the chances of war, with its accompanying glory and prospective promotions, but the facts seems to be against them.

TOKIO, July 8.—The Asahi to-day published an interview with an influential Japanese naval expert, who says: "It would be improper to infer a demonstration in the transfer of the American fleet to the Pacific. This movement is part of a prearranged plan, and is a result of the constant growth of the American Navy and the increasing importance of Pacific interests from the strategical point of view."

The Asahi also publishes an editorial setting forth the same views. It regrets that the American fleet cannot visit Japan in order to enable Japan to reassert her sincerity and reciprocate the naval hospitality extended to the visiting Japanese war-ships at Jamestown. The paper also urges the abrogation of article II of the existing commercial treaty in order to put an end to the cause of the anti-Japanese feeling at San Francisco.

Almost all the newspapers treat the matter with calmness, finding it is natural for the United States to distribute its naval forces as a result of its imperial policy. They, too, generally express regret that it will be impossible for Japan to extend hospitality to the American officers in return for that shown the Japanese officers at Jamestown.

The Asahi is an independent newspaper, prominent among all classes and has probably the widest circulation in Japan. It is not considered, however, to carry great weight editorially.

PACIFIC WILL BE THE BATTLE-FIELD.

LONDON, July 9.—The Daily Mail, in an editorial article on the Japanese-American situation, says: "Around the immense area of the Pacific ocean the

(Continued on Page Three.)

San Francisco Chronicle.

VOL. XCIII. SAN FRANCISCO, CAL., FRIDAY, DECEMBER 11, 1908. NO. 119

JURY PRONOUNCES RUEF A FELON BY CONVICTING HIM OF BRIBERY

ABE RUEF FOUND GUILTY BY A JURY

Twenty-Four Hours' Deliberation Ends in Grafter's Conviction.

JUDGE THANKS THE JURORS.

He Tells Them They Have Well Performed Their Duty.

ABE RUEF, who once held the government of San Francisco in the hollow of his greedy palm, is now a condemned felon. A jury has pronounced legally the verdict which the people long ago arrived at, and the man who at his first trial said that he was guilty has now heard the word echoed by twelve men sworn to mete out to him nothing but even-handed justice.

The verdict was returned at 3:55 o'clock yesterday afternoon, after a period of suspense lasting almost exactly twenty-four hours, just as the friends of justice were beginning to despair. Five ballots were had before an agreement was reached. On the first, taken before the dinner hour on Wednesday evening, Jurors Harrison, Murphy, Sullivan and O'Brien voted for acquittal. Later in the evening Sullivan shifted to the side of the prosecution, only to change his mind the next morning, and later still to shift back to his original position. Murphy several times voted "undecided." On the next to the last ballot, taken at 2:30 yesterday afternoon, the vote was ten to two for conviction, Sullivan and O'Brien having come over permanently to the majority. Half an hour later Harrison and Murphy also swung into line and the welcome word was sent to Judge Lawlor that an agreement had been reached.

A great crowd, which the walls of Carpenters' Hall could by no means contain, had been waiting [illegible] morning, notwithstanding the fact that the most discouraging reports were current and a general impression that a disagreement was more than probable. The air was heavy and vitiated; the prospect of any good news extremely thin; but the patient multitude waited on, like the leaders of a forlorn hope. Many were standing in the aisles, and the vestibule and the sidewalk were packed with humanity. Yet these were but a handful compared to the thousands who waited and watched throughout the city for the last act of the great drama of justice which had been playing since August 26th.

When Judge Lawlor finally ascended the bench it was exactly 3:55 o'clock by the watch of the official clerk. Utter silence prevailed as the mandate of the Court was delivered.

"I desire that the strictest order be maintained in the courtroom," said Judge Lawlor in quiet, but impressive tones. "Any person who is guilty of any form of demonstration will be severely dealt with."

The group about the defendant's table, including Ruef's aged father, Meyer Ruef, his attorneys, Dozier and Kirk, and Charley Hagerty, his office boy, huddled closer together as this dictum protecting them from any expression of the feelings of the assemblage was uttered. The jury, whose faces were so familiar to the regular attendants of the trial as to seem like the faces of old friends, filed in from the rear door in charge of Deputy Sheriff Coyle, and answered to their names as they were called by Clerk Welch.

THREATENED OUTBREAK QUELLED

"Gentlemen of the jury," continued the clerk, "have you agreed upon a verdict?"

"We have," said James McNamara, the foreman, rising.

A sigh of relief breathed from the crowd, for there were many who had not caught the significance of the preliminary proceedings.

"Let the verdict be recorded," ordered the Court, as the momentous bit of paper was handed him.

While the clerk entered the decision which branded Ruef as a felon the excitement in the courtroom grew, it being all the more intense because it was forbidden utterance. Although there had never been any suggestion of a possibility of acquittal, there were people who remembered the common saying, "You can never tell what a jury will do."

When the entry had been completed the clerk read the verdict aloud:

"We, the jury, find Abraham Ruef, the defendant in this action, guilty as charged in the indictment herein."

"Silence! Silence! Sit down! Keep your seats!" cried a dozen officers as the crowd half rose to its feet and seemed about to break into spontaneous cheers.

It was all quiet again as Dozier, who, since Ach's attack of illness after his long effort of Monday, has been in charge of the defense, made the conventional demand:

"We demand to have the jury polled."

The roll was accordingly called for the second time since the coming of

(Continued on Page 2, Column 1.)

Abe Ruef and the Twelve Jurors by Whose Verdict of Guilty He Becomes a Convict.

BEAR RAID BREAKS A RAWHIDE STOCK

Sensational Collapse of Coalition on the New York Market.

Special Dispatch to the "Chronicle."

NEW YORK, December 10.—Nat Goodwin's Rawhide Coalition Company mining stock was the subject of an irresistible bear attack early this afternoon, and after the opening price had been cut in two, feeling ran high on 'Change and the curb. Between 80,000 and 90,000 shares changed hands, and those behind the deal must have reaped a rich harvest.

The anger that the coup aroused was [illegible] generally known that only a few insiders knew that the man behind the stock-floating operation was a man who some years ago in this city had been at the head of an extensive racing tip concern which had been forced by the authorities to go out of business.

The opening price to-day was $1 40, which was maintained until shortly after noon, when somebody began unloading, and the stock fell, while scenes of excitement were enacted both on 'Change and on the curb. The climax came when sales were made at 75 cents. The stock closed at 85 cents. E. A. Manice & Co., members of the Stock Exchange, had been giving out orders on the stock, but that firm says it was acting merely as a broker for customers in the regular course of business.

JACK DALTON IS BADLY CRIPPLED

Famous Alaska Pathfinder a Victim of Severe Attack of Rheumatism.

Special Dispatch to the "Chronicle."

SEATTLE (Wash.), December 10.—Crippled with sciatica and unable to make use of the once sturdy legs which for years carried him through Alaska, Jack Dalton, known in every part of the United States as the man who made the Dalton trail from Haines' Mission to the Yukon in 1896, was tenderly removed from the steamship Yucatan on her arrivel fram Valdez this afternoon, and will proceed from Seattle to Hot Springs, Ark., in charge of his sister.

Dalton is one of the early characters of the north and earned fame as a musher in the pioneer days. He has made and lost several fortunes in different lines of business in Alaska. He is suffering from a bad case of sciatic rheumatism, due, no doubt, to the exposure and hardships he suffered in Northland. He is really unable to walk, and it is doubtful if he will ever be able to return to Alaska. He came out from Cordova, where he now has large mining interests.

RUSTIN TRIAL ENDS IN VERDICT OF ACQUITTAL.

OMAHA, December 10.—After thirteen hours' deliberation the jury in the case of Charles E. Davis, charged with the murder, on the morning of September 2d, of Dr. Frederick Rustin, this morning agreed upon a verdict of not guilty and ordered the discharge of the prisoner.

CHILE MAY ORDER LIGHTSHIPS.

VALPARAISO (Chile), December 10.—The naval authorities of Chile are greatly interested in the presence here of the six American vessels comprising the fleet of tenders and lightships which arrived at this port last week from New York. It is probable that the Government will place an order in the United States for a number of vessels of this description.

CASTRO LANDS ON THE SOIL OF FRANCE

Belief That Visit Will Result in the Settlement of Conflicts.

BORDEAUX, December 10.—Cipriano Castro, President of Venezuela, was allowed to land on French soil to-day when he arrived at Pauiluo, thirty miles from Bordeaux, on the steamship Guadelupe. It was announced that the President would go to Paris to-morrow.

It was believed to be the intention of the Government to exact an apology from Castro before permitting him to land, but apparently a communication received by the Government from M. Merlo, the French Minister to Peru, who was also a passenger on the Guadelope, to the effect that Castro was anxious to arrange a settlement of the difficulties between the two countries brought about a change in the plans.

This evening an agent of Foreign Minister Pichon informed President Castro that he would be welcomed as a private citizen and that as a chief of state he would be given every protection during his sojourn in France. Upon Castro's arrival in Paris he will send a representative to Pichon to convey his thanks. This may furnish the desired opening for negotiations with France.

President Castro did not deem it advisable to make a public declaration about the international position of Venezuela because this might be misunderstod and provoke discussion which would embarass any prospective negotiations.

President Castro refused to receive newspaper representatives, but it was announced that he expected to undergo an operation and would visit Spain afterward.

Several Dutch journalists who had come here in the hope of securing a statement regarding the dispute between Venesuela and Holland, pleaded in vain for an interview. Castro and his party remained closely in their rooms as a tempest was raging outside.

SEVERE SHOCKS IN ITALY.

MESSINA, December 10. — Severe earthquake shocks at Mount Albano today caused a panic. The church and a number of buildings were badly damaged.

AUSTRIA MUST PAY HIGH FOR PEACE

Turk, at First Willing to Take a Million, Now Wants Forty Million.

Special Dispatch to the "Chronicle."

VIENNA (Austria), December 10.—The obstacle that prevents Austria from coming to an understanding with Turkey in the matter of the boycott and other pending differences is believed to be purely a question of compensation.

From well-informed sources it is learned that Turkey at the beginning of the trouble would gladly have accepted $1,000,000 as compensation for the annexation of Bosnia and Herzegovina. Foreign Minister Aehrenthal contemptuously refused to entertain this proposition, and his blustering attitude toward the Porte is likely to cost Austria dear, for Turkey now demands $40,000,000, but probably would accept half that amount.

Some agreement must speedily be reached, because without Turkey it would be impossible to arrange a conference. Unless diplomats hasten their movements it is feared that the spring will find the Balkans still in a state of ferment, and then it may be impossible to restrain the patriotic impetuosity of the Servians and Montenegrins from starting a European upheaval.

CHAUFFEUR GIVEN TWO YEARS FOR KILLING MAN.

MILWAUKEE (Wis.), December 10.—"We must teach the lesson that chauffeurs, rich or poor, must have due regard for the value of human life," said Judge Brazee in the Municipal Court to-day in sentencing William Goston, colored, to the reformatory at Green Bay for two years for running down and causing the death of Mathias Kurath, an art student, on September 27th last.

KING EDWARD ONLY HAS A COLD.

LONDON, December 10.—In view of the disquieting rumors abroad, the Lancet is authorized to state that the health of King Edward gives no cause for anxiety. The King contracted a slight cold, but he improved under treatment.

WILL BUILD DOCKS WITHOUT BOND ISSUE

Commissioners Adopt Plan to Improve Water Front on Advance Rent.

LESSEES FURNISH MEANS.

Passengers Complain Against the Methods of Agent for Transfer Company.

The State Harbor Commissioners have adopted a plan by which, if successful, they expect to improve the water front, have docks and slips constructed, without crippling the revenue of the harbor and without a bond issue. The first step in that direction was taken yesterday, and the Commissioners are confident that the plan will succeed.

The Board at its meeting yesterday opened bids for the construction of the proposed wharf along Illinois street south from Santa Clara street in what is known as Central basin. The eight bids received ranged from $57,741 to $93,700. The lowest bid appeared acceptable to the Commissioners, as the wharf is to be built upon concrete piles, but the contract was not awarded. Instead the Commissioners adopted a resolution inviting bids for the lease of that wharf when completed, on the following conditions: The lease shall be executed upon the lessee paying the amount in advance which it will require to construct the wharf and take a lease upon it for the shortest period of time, not to exceed fifteen years. The rent is to be exclusive of dockage and tolls. The lessee is to maintain the wharf in good condition, pay for all repairs, and at the expiration of the lease the dock is to revert to the State in good condition.

[illegible] slightest doubt that the proposed wharf will be readily leased on the terms named, and that subsequent docks which are now in contemplation will find lessees readily.

WILL BRING GOOD REVENUE.

President Stafford of the Harbor Board said in reference to the proposed building of the dock on money obtained in advance for a lease:

"We are not going to stop the construction of permanent improvements. The wharf to be constructed in Central basin, for which the contract is to be given out, will bring a good revenue in tolls and dockage. The cost of construction will be borne by the lessee, whoever that may be, who will be amply repaid by having the exclusive use of the wharf for a term of years. The State, at the termination of the lease, gains the improvement without outlay. The wharf will be just as permanent in the character of its construction as though it were built from the harbor revenue or with money obtained from a bond issue.

"We expect to be able to construct a high class dock by the same method on the seawall just contracted for, and in this way eke out the $2,000,000 bond issue, so that we can cover considerable space on the unimproved water front and yet maintain a high standard in the type of construction."

COMPLAINS OF SOLICITORS.

W. H. Fogarty, a resident of Fruitvale, in a lengthy communication to the Board, complained of the reprehensible methods practiced by solicitors for transfer and express companies, plying their vocation in the Ferry building. Relating his personal experience with one of the solicitors, he tells of deception and cheating, which caused the writer loss of time and money and much vexation. The Harbor Board, unable to control the conduct of solicitors licensed by the city authorities, ordered the complaint referred to the local Police Department.

The Board accepted the offer made by M. M. Finlayson, the contractor engaged in making alterations in the Ferry building, to lay new floors in the north wing of the building, and to replace the asphalt on the driveways and to the curb line with concrete and cement finish, at a cost of $1067, also to cover steam pipes with iron plates.

The Downtown Merchants' Association and the Ferry District Improvement Association sent a joint communication conveying thanks to the Harbor Board for promising to illuminate the Ferry tower on New Year's eve, and requested that the Board have the grand nave in the Ferry building illuminated on that evening. The request was granted.

The Healy-Tibbitts Construction Company was awarded a contract to remove certain portions of Beale street wharf and of Brannan street wharf at a cost of $1000.

TAFT SOON TO REACH AUGUSTA.

AUGUSTA (Ga.), December 10.—President-elect Taft and the family, with the exception of Miss Helen, will arrive here Friday next to become the guests of Mr. and Mrs. Landon Thomas until the following Monday. Miss Helen will come from Bryn Mawr for the Christmas holidays. A letter from Taft asks that he be allowed to spend the first few days in complete rest, as he is greatly fatigued.

NO CANAL FUNDS FOR AMERICAN SPECULATORS

Cromwell Gives the Lie to Those Who Seek to Cause Scandal.

TELLS STORY IN DETAIL.

Shows That Money Paid by the United States Went to the French Investors.

NEW YORK, December 10.—**In concluding a sweeping and detailed statement contradicting the charges that an American syndicate secured a large part of the $40,000,000 paid by the United States Government for the Panama canal, William Nelson Cromwell says:**

"The whole story of Americans, or some American syndicate, buying up the Panama canal securities at a low price, or at any price, and then turning them in upon liquidation at a profit is a fiction and a concoction. The money of the United States went to France and was distributed to the hundreds of thousands of foreign owners, none of whom, so far as I know, were Americans."

The statement says in part: "I wish to call attention to the fact that on the first day of the hearings before the Committee on Interoceanic Canals of the Senate of the United States in February, 1906, I voluntarily made an explicit and detailed statement showing how the $40,000,000 was paid by the United States through Messrs. J. P. Morgan & Co., as their agents, to the Bank of France at Paris for account of the new Panama Canal Company and also explaining the subsequent payment of the full amount to the liquidators of the new Panama Canal Company and to the liquidator of the old Panama Canal Company, who in turn distributed the same to their respective stock and bond holders, numbering [illegible]

STATEMENT MADE TO SENATORS.

"I further submitted to the Senate committee, with the permission of the Panama Government, a detailed statement of the disposition by the republic of Panama of the $10,000,000 paid by the United States to Panama in 1904, accounting for the payment of the whole amount, and showing the investments and disposition by the Panama Government of every dollar.

"On the same public inquiry I further stated, with reference to the proposed Americanization of the Panama Canal Company in the year 1899, and the proposed formation of a syndicate for the purpose in that year, that the proposed plan 'never matured into anything. It was never consummated either by subscription or by assent, and it is obsolete and an impracticable thing—proved to be so. It has no life or force of being, did not exist and never has existed, and is as dead as a door nail. That was a fruitless suggestion of the company, which came to naught, and under which I acted as their counsel only.'

"The testimony taken by the Senate committee is a public record, and was available to the editors of the News and the World, and had either of them been as interested in publishing the truth as they were to create a possible sensation, they doubtless would have taken the pains to publish the above facts which I quote.

AMERICANIZATION PLAN FAILED.

"I again denounce the statement, wherever published or by whomsoever made, that there was a syndicate formed by American citizens to purchase the Panama canal and to sell it to the United States as absolutely and unqualifiedly false and untrue. The Americanization plan was an entirely different matter. It was a project proposed by the company to the Rivers and Harbors Committee of the House and to President McKinley on February 27, 1899, and was formally authorized by the board of directors October 10, 1899, subject to the necessary approval of the stockholders.

"The initial steps were taken by me in October, November and December, 1899, and a company formed for the purpose, under the laws of New Jersey, carrying out the instructions of my clients. While the certificate of incorporation of the Panama Canal Company of America was filed in New Jersey, no capital stock, except the nominal capital of $5000, set forth in the certificate of incorporation, was ever issued, and nothing further was ever done by that company, as the records in the office of the Secretary of State of New Jersey will show. The project adopted by the board of directors failed of approval by the stockholders in December, 1899; the board of directors, in consequence, resigned in a body, and the plan then and forever ended. The period covered by this project was less than three months; not a dollar was paid in under it, nor a transaction conducted by the New Jersey company for the reason stated."

HOW MONEY WAS PAID.

He further says: "Now, with regard to the distribution of the $40,000,000, it has been made to appear in newspaper comments that there was some

(Continued on Page 2, Column 6.)

EXTRA SESSION TO REVISE THE TARIFF

Taft and Members of Ways and Means Committee in Harmony.

PLEDGES TO BE FULFILLED

Plans for Legislation on This Subject Outlined in Statement.

WASHINGTON, December 10.—William H. Taft said to-night that it was his belief that the House would make an "honest and thorough revision of the tariff" at the extra session which he will call for that purpose.

This belief he bases on a conference he had yesterday with Speaker Cannon and in a session to-day with the Republican members of the Ways and Means Committee. Taft said he had not as yet consulted with Senators on the subject, indicating the tremendous pressure upon his time as the reason. When the suggestion was made that the Senate would undoubtedly have something to do with the tariff bill, he replied, with no uncertainty in his demeanor, that there was some one else who also would have something to do with the bill, which, interpreted through the medium of previous utterances, indicates clearly that Taft is determined, even to the exercise of veto power, to execute the party's pledges.

CONFERENCE WITH CANNON.

Taft dictated a statement which covered his interview late to-day with the Republican members of the committee, with the exception of Representatives McCall of Massachusetts and Crumpacker of Indiana. With the latter Taft had a satisfactory interview at Hot Springs.

He was asked the substance of the interview he had yesterday with the Speaker. His reply was that Cannon had said that he was in favor of [illegible] tariff in accordance with the party promises. The question of the Speakership of the next Congress, Taft said, was not discussed, but many other matters of legislation were.

He added that he had been somewhat misled regarding his interpretation of the attitude of the Speaker by the reports of Cannon's speech before the Cleveland Chamber of Commerce. The official report of that speech, he said, had given him an entirely different impression.

REVISION TO BE THOROUGH.

"I had an interview with Mr. Cannon yesterday," said Taft, "and with his concurrence and at the suggestion of a member of the Ways and Means Committee, with the Republican members of that committee this afternoon. From my conversation with them and with the discussion that followed as to the examination which they are now conducting and expect to conduct, I have every reason to be confident that they are keenly alive to the obligation which is on them as Representatives

(Continued on Page 2, Column 7.)

San Francisco Chronicle.

XCV. SAN FRANCISCO, CAL., TUESDAY, SEPTEMBER 7, 1909. NO. [illegible]

PEARY REACHES POLE ONE YEAR AFTER COOK

BRIEF MESSAGES FROM LABRADOR TELL OF AMERICAN'S SUCCESS

Details Will Not Be Received for at Least Another Day.

Confirmed by One of His Party

Everywhere the Explorer Is Hailed as Victor and No Doubts Are Raised.

[illegible]INS (N. F.), September 6.—Commander Robert E. Peary, who [illegible]nced to-day that he had discovered the North Pole on April 6th [illegible] present year, found no trace of Dr. Frederick A. Cook, who [illegible]t he had made the same discovery in April of the preceding [illegible] news reached here to-night through Captain Robert Bartlett of [illegible] Peary's ship.

[illegible]eary does not expressly repudiate Dr. Cook's contention in so [illegible] his statement may have an important bearing upon determining [illegible] Dr. Cook's explorations. Coming south the Roosevelt passed [illegible]pernivik, where Dr. Cook had preceded Peary.

[illegible]sevelt to-night is bound for Chateau Bay, Labrador, with Peary [illegible]board, where she is due to-morrow. Chateau Bay lies north-[illegible]ide and Henley Islands on the northern shore of Belle Isle straits [illegible] of Belle Isle.

[illegible]ORK, September 6.—Peary has reached the North Pole. It has [illegible] doubly discovered. From the bleak coast of Labrador Commander [illegible] to-day flashed the news that he had attained his goal in the [illegible], while at the same moment in Denmark Dr. Frederick Cook was being dined and lionized by royalty for the same achievement.

Yankee grit has conquered the frozen north and there has been created a coincidence such as the world will never see again. Two Americans have planted the flag of their country in the land of ice which man has sought to penetrate for four centuries; and each ignorant of the other's conquest, has sent within a period of five days a laconic message of success.

STORY TOLD IN BRIEF MESSAGE FROM NORTH.

[illegible] are the various messages received to-day announcing Peary's [illegible]

"Indian Harbor, via Cape Ray, September 6. The Associated Press, New [illegible] Stars and stripes nailed to North Pole. PEARY."

"Indian Harbor, via Cape Ray, (N. F.), September 6, 1909. Herbert L. [illegible], Brooklyn, N. Y.: Pole reached, Roosevelt safe. PEARY."

"Indian Harbor, via Cape Ray, (N.F.), September 6, 1909. To the New [illegible], New York: I have the Pole. April 6. Expect arrive Chateau [illegible] 7th. Secure control wire for me there and arrange expedite trans[illegible] story. PEARY."

[illegible] his first message to his countrymen was brief but non-committal; Peary's even briefer, but specific.

"[illegible] and stripes nailed to the Pole," he said.

[illegible] days ago, September 1st, Dr. Cook sent out from the Shetland [illegible] first message of his success, a message which has aroused a [illegible] controversy around the world. To-day Robert E. Peary, lost from [illegible] land of ice and unheard from since August, 1908, startled the [illegible] similar message sent from Indian Harbor, Labrador. There was no [illegible]tion; it left no doubt.

AWAIT DETAILS FROM THE EXPLORER.

[illegible] a word from Peary, the world waits for details, but none will be [illegible] until he arrives at Chateau Bay, Labrador, to-morrow.

[illegible] the old and the new world were apprised of Peary's great achieve[illegible]ically at the same moment and the excitement which followed [illegible] the high pitch of interest aroused over this climax of man's perse[illegible]

[illegible]paper extras were rushed from the press and those who read marveled.

It was comparatively a simple matter to ascertain that the April 6th referred to by Peary was April of this year, as his expedition did not start from New York until July 7, 1908.

IT IS A STRANGE SITUATION.

Two explorers, Dr. Frederick A. Cook and Commander Robert E. Peary, both Americans, are in the Arctic seeking the goal of centuries, the North Pole, whose attainment has at times seemed beyond the reach of man. Both are determined and courageous, and both leave expressing the belief that their efforts will be crowned with success. Peary is well known to both scientists and the general public as a striver for the honors of "farthest north." Dr. Cook, on the other hand, has held the public attention to a lesser degree. He made his departure quietly and his purpose was hardly known other than to those who are keenly interested in polar research.

FIVE DAYS BEHIND COOK'S NEWS.

Then, suddenly, and with no word of warning, a steamer touches at Lerwick and Dr. Cook's claim to having succeeded where expedition after expedition of the hardiest explorers of the world had failed, is made known. Three days after Dr. Cook arrived at Copenhagen and was given a welcome to an explorer unprecedented in history.

Five days after the receipt of the Lerwick's message, almost to the hour, comes the sensational statement from Indian Harbor that Commander Peary has been successful on his third expedition to the coveted goal.

Commander Robert E. Peary was detached from regular duty with the Navy Department July 2, 1908, and assigned to special duty with the Coast and Geodetic Survey.

His explorations in the Arctic regions before that date had been conducted under technical leaves of absence from the Navy Department. This status was satisfactory neither to Commander Peary nor to his associates in the naval corps of civil engineers and it was believed that he could prosecute his scientific investigations with a freer hand if he were attached to one of the Government scientific bureaus and relieved from the tedious form of naval reports at set intervals which had embarrassed him.

STATEMENTS OF PEARY WILL BE ACCEPTED.

One point of supreme importance in this report of his success which has attended his last efforts to reach the North Pole is that the statement must remain absolutely unchallenged in all probability; there can be no question of the fact, because Peary undoubtedly is able to confirm his statements by creditable white witnesses who made up the personnel of his party.

Rear-Admiral W. S. Cowles, chief of the Bureau of Equipment of the Navy, expressed his delight over the Peary announcement.

"It was my understanding," said Admiral Cowles, "that when he left here it was his hope to reach the Pole [illegible] is a deserving officer. He has pursued his purpose under all sorts of adverse conditions and only a man of his energy and persistence could hope to win so great an undertaking.

"Peary had an exceptionally fine equipment. It would be no great wonder at all if he has at last achieved what he set out to do."

Admiral Cowles also said that he believed that Dr. Cook discovered the Pole last year.

"At any rate," he said, "I believe in the interest of fair play, adverse judgment should be suspended until it has been demonstrated that he has not made the discovery he claims."

LAST WORDS FROM EXPLORER.

From the time Peary wrote his last letters home from his depot of supplies at Etah in August 1908, until he flashed the magic words from Indian Harbor, nothing was known of the fight he had been making across the frozen crust of the north.

Access was obtained to-day, however, to a number of personal letters which Commander Peary had written to friends and business associates in New York between the time he sailed on July 6 and the time he left his supply depot at Etah in the following August. The last words from him came in the mails of September 1, 1908. The letters were written in August aboard the Roosevelt, but were not dated. Some were to Mrs. Peary and others to personal and business friends. These letters told little of conditions at Etah nor did they speak of what his hopes or misgivings might be.

Mrs. Peary in writing to a friend in June, 1909, said:

"Nothing has been heard from Mr. Peary since last fall when the letters dated Etah in August were delivered. I hope to have news in September and will be very much disappointed if I do not see the commander himself."

HIS STATION AT ETAH.

At Etah Peary had established a station for training Esquimaux and dogs and accumulating supplies. On former expeditions it had been his plan to take his ship as far north as he could penetrate and there put into winter quarters, using Etah as a base of supplies.

This time he divided his party into three groups—one to make geological observations, another to make meteorological notations and a third of five or six picked men, with dogs, for the last dash to the Pole, while the first two followed more slowly as supporting parties and established bases of supplies [illegible]

Commander Peary and His Ship, The Roosevelt

Peary's Many Voyages to the Far North

ROBERT EDWIN PEARY has probably made more Arctic voyages than any other explorer of the north. In 1898 he wrote a two-volume account of his voyages previous to that time, which included the narratives of four separate expeditions. More recently he published his "Nearest the Pole," in which he gave the account of his voyage of 1905 and '06 in the Roosevelt, at which time he won the record, reaching latitude 87 degrees and 6 minutes north, and coming within 200 miles of the pole. Only an open lead in the ice prevented the consummation of his hopes then, and his success was freely predicted when he again sailed in the Roosevelt on July 17th of last year.

Peary's first trip was a summer voyage in Greenland waters in 1886. Five years later he spent two years in Northern Greenland, determining the insularity of that country, and again in 1893 he was off in the Falcon, returning in 1895. On this expedition he made a 1200-mile sledge trip and surveyed in detail the Cape York meteorites; 1896 and 1897 found him again in the Arctic, and he said that he had come to look upon the journey as most men regard a trip to Europe.

It was the 1905-06 expedition that aroused the greatest hopes in the scientific world and among the financial backers of the enterprise. When Peary failed to reach the Pole on this occasion his friends said that the next time would surely bring success, and their prediction has been justified.

Peary is an officer in the Navy, of the rank of Commander, and it was with some difficulty that he obtained leave of absence for this last voyage.

FALLS THOUSAND FEET BEFORE GREAT CROWD

Illinois Balloonist Still Alive, Although Terribly Crushed.

Special Dispatch to the "Chronicle."

CHICAGO (Ill.), September 6.—More than 6000 persons, more than half of whom were women, saw Fred Banter, a balloonist, fall nearly 1000 feet this afternoon at a Labor day picnic at Dekalb. Nearly every bone in Banter's body was broken and he is internally injured, but at a late hour to-night he was still alive.

Banter was to have made a parachute leap and his ascension was made directly in front of the grandstand at the fair grounds. When it came time for him to make his leap, however, his parachute wire failed to work, and he fell the entire distance directly in front of the grandstand. His body was crushed into a shapeless mass, but there was still a spark of life left and numerous physicians who were in attendance are making a desperate effort to save the man's life.

Banter, while falling, missed a haystack about twenty feet. Had the wind been blowing in the right direction he would have alighted on the stack and his life probably would have been saved. Banter was an Aurora man and has made more than one hundred ascensions.

HUNDREDS DROWNED IN MEXICAN FLOOD

Death List in Nuevo Leon Officially Placed at 1500.

MEXICO CITY, September 6.—The town of Tula, in the State of Tamaulipas, was swept by another flood yesterday, houses being carried away and rich plantations destroyed. General Trevino places the deaths for the State of Nuevo Leon officially at 1500. A number of towns on the Rio Grande have not yet been heard from. The towns of Aldama de Cos and Aramberri are reported destroyed, making ten towns in all affected by the floods.

POPE SHOWS HIS INTEREST.

ROME, September 6.—The Pope is keenly interested in the story of Dr. Cook's achievement. He expressed the opinion to-day that one must believe in the truthfulness of a man whose character had been tried by such perils and who had faced death [illegible]

MESSAGES TELL THE STORY OF PEARY'S SUCCESS

Member of Party Sends Dispatch Confirming the Leader's Story.

SOUTH HARPSWELL (Me.), September 6.—Commander Robert E. Peary announced his success in discovering the North Pole to his wife, who is summering at Eagle island here, as follows:

"Indian Harbor, via Cape Ray, September 6, 1909.—Mrs. R. E. Peary, South Harpswell, Me.: Have made good at last. I have the old Pole. Am well. Love. Will wire again from Chateau. "BERT."

In replying Mrs. Peary sent the following dispatch:

"South Harpswell (Me.), September 6, 1909.—Commander R. E. Peary, Steamer Roosevelt, Chateau Bay. All well. Best Love. God bless you. Hurry home. JO."

FREEPORT (Me.), September 6.—Confirmation of Peary's success was received here to-day in a telegram from D. B. McMillan, who accompanied Peary. The message sent to McMillan's sister, Mrs. W. C. Fogg, follows:

"In[illegible] Harbor, September 6, 1909. Mrs. W. C. Fogg, Freeport, Me.—Arrived safe. Pole on board. Best year of my life. BEN."

ST. JOHN'S (N. F.), September 6.—Commander Peary has just telegraphed the Governor of Newfoundland by wireless from Indian Harbor, Labrador, announcing he has discovered the North Pole and congratulating Newfoundland on its part in the discovery, seeing that the captain and crew of Peary's steamer are Newfoundlanders.

HARRIMAN SAID TO SUFFER RELAPSE

Condition of the Railway King Reported to Be Serious.

TRAINED NURSES ATTEND

All the Family and Judge Lovett Now at Arden House.

DOCTOR ADMITS A CHANCE

Asserts, However, That Patient's Condition Gives No Alarm.

Special Dispatch to the "Chronicle."

ARDEN (N. Y.), September 6.—Edward H. Harriman has suffered a relapse and is thought to be in a serious condition to-night. Dr. William G. Lyle, the family physician, admits that there has been a change in the financier's condition, but insists that there is no cause for alarm.

"Mr. Harriman suffered a sharp attack of indigestion yesterday, but he is resting comfortably to-night," Dr. Lyle said.

Dr. Lyle to-day sent a message to Miss Taylor, superintendent of St. Luke's Hospital central registry in New York, requesting that a professional nurse be sent on the first fast train. The nurse reached Arden at 1:15 o'clock this morning and was taken to the Harriman house in an automobile. She said that she understood that Harriman was critically ill and required the attention of a nurse both day and night.

CONDITION CONSIDERED SERIOUS.

While no authentic information other than Dr. Lyle's brief statement has come from Arden House, the impression prevails, both here and in Turner, that Harriman is dangerously ill. The entire family is at Arden House, and Judge Robert S. Lovett, general counsel for the Union and Southern Pacific Railroads, was summoned here last night.

Inquirers at Arden were referred to the Union Pacific offices in this city. These offices were closed. Judge Lovett, who is in close touch with Harriman's affairs, was not in the city, and at his home information was refused as to whether he had gone to Arden to see Harriman.

On Monday last the newspaper men at Arden were withdrawn after the issuance of Harriman's statement to the newspapers, in which he said: "If there was or should be anything serious I will let the press know, and as I have never deceived them, I ask that the press now withdraw its representatives and rely upon me."

SPAIN SENDS ANOTHER DIVISION AGAINST THE MOORS.

MADRID, September 6.—The twelfth division of the Spanish army, consisting of 11,000 men under the command of General Solomayo, has been ordered to Melilla, Morocco, to take part in the campaign against the Moors. Premier Maura said that another division might be mobilized immediately.

Advices received from Melilla say the Spanish position at El Arba and Resinga have been re-enforced and that the Moors have partly abandoned Mount Guruga and are massing at Nador and Zestuan.

FRENCH SAILORS SLAIN IN THE NEW HEBRIDES.

SYDNEY (N. S. W.), September 6.—The captain and crew of the French schooner Qualite, engaged in recruiting laborers, have been murdered by natives of Mallicollo islands in the New Hebrides. The vessel was driven ashore by a storm and while stranded she was attacked. In spite of stubborn defense, all of the crew were massacred. A British war ship is investigating the occurrence.

1910-1919

DECEMBER 25, 1910
250,000 Hear Diva Sing At Chronicle

APRIL 16, 1912
Titanic Sinks

JUNE 29, 1914
Archduke Ferdinand Shot

AUGUST 15, 1914
Panama Canal Opened;
Kaiser Increases Attack on Belgium

FEBRUARY 20, 1915
San Francisco World Exposition;
Submarine Warfare Begun by Germans

MAY 8, 1915
Lusitania Torpedoed

MARCH 10, 1916
U.S. Troops Chase Pancho Villa Into Mexico

MARCH 11, 1916
President Orders Pershing to Invade Mexico;
Intense Fighting at Verdun

JULY 23, 1916
Bomb Explosion Kills Preparedness
Parade Spectators

APRIL 6, 1917
War With Germany Voted by Representatives;
French Hurled Back by Germans;
American Vessel Sunk

JUNE 5, 1918
Americans Turn Tide on Marne

NOVEMBER 11, 1918
Great War Over

JULY 1, 1919
S.F. Saloon Licenses Voided

San Francisco Chronicle.

VOL. XCVII. SAN FRANCISCO, CAL., SUNDAY, DECEMBER 25, 1910. NO. 163

TWO HUNDRED AND FIFTY THOUSAND HEAR TETRAZZINI SING IN THE OPEN AIR BEFORE THE CHRONICLE BUILDING

Madam Tetrazzini Singing to 250,000 People in Front of the Chronicle Building Last Evening.

QUEEN OF SONG SINGS FROM HER HEART TO WORSHIPFUL THRONG IN SAN FRANCISCO'S STREETS

Buildings the Sounding Boards for Magic Voice of Luisa Tetrazzini

By FREDERICK WOOD

TETRAZZINI kept her promise last night. From the great platform in front of the main entrance to the Chronicle building she lifted her wonderful voice and animated face to 250,000 people. No detail was lacking, no preparation disarranged. She came to the editorial rooms of the "Chronicle" at 7 o'clock and spent the time from then until 8:30 in conversation with friends. Most of the time she talked delightful English, but once in a while she would have recourse to French, and, when talking to her husband, Bazelli, spoke in Italian. In all San Francisco, Christmas eve saw no one more joyous than was this great diva. She laughed and joked away the hours, singing snatches from "Yip I Addy I Aye" and "There Was an Old Soldier Who Had a Wooden Leg." She was gayety personified, and after a while infected every one in the room with her with an abandon of joy so that before long all were singing and she was having what she called "mos' fun my life." Impresario Leahy was everywhere in evidence, and while he was at the platform perfecting arrangements for her appearance, she amused herself by waving her handkerchief at the thousands and thousands that thronged the streets.

NOTES AS TRUE AS THE LARK'S.

Under the hazy blue of an English June sky, with the hurly burly noises of raucous London all about her, Tetrazzini is to sing at the coronation of England's King. No eager lark, swinging in the whitened spaces of the heavens, will sing a truer note.

Last night, under the torchlike stars of a California sky, with the monolithic buildings of Market street for acoustic boards, she sang to the kings of the West—and to their queens.

In London she will be acclaimed by the people of the earth, and there will be a double coronation, for she will be queen of song; but there will be lacking the Latinized greetings and the warmth of welcome that was given her by those who live in this city of her discovery and who love her because she was once a part of them.

It was a night and an hour of regality. The spiritualized faces of such a throng as never before stormed the approaches to the "Chronicle" building framed the thousands of eyes that watched with patient longing the draped platform immediately in front of the main entrance to the "Chronicle," where stood this Italian daughter of the West, courtiered by her friends and heralded by her admirers.

She was happy—happy, as she is always happy, because God placed in her golden throat the gushing wells of such glorious music that those who heard her last night now know something of the songs the angels sing. I was happy—happy as Tetrazzini, because I had been permitted to walk the wavering paths of life until the time when such a spectacle was given to my eyes to see and my ears had heard the mingled music of the woman glorious and the throng worshipful.

Ah, but it was wonderful! The hush of admiration was so vast and deep, the cadences of her voice were so beautiful, the stage setting was so unusual, the occasion was so unique that the lexicographers have failed me in my hour of greatest need, and I am made to realize that words were never fashioned to tell the story of Tetrazzini's concert in the triangle surrounding Lotta's Fountain. It is a pity that Lotta Crabtree, grown serenely old in her Boston home, could not have heard the benisons of song, as that marveling crowd heard them, poured upon her splendid gift to the city, which has for so long withstood sunshine and storm in front of the "Chronicle" business office.

EACH PAYS DEBT OF GRATITUDE.

It was like Tetrazzini and it was like San Francisco that this thing should have been done. Each met the other in graceful salutation; one graciously acknowledging a debt of gratitude to those who had made possible her eminence, the other paying liege tribute to such a voice as must have startled into eye-rubbing wakefulness the guard that kept somnolent vigil on the Hill of Golgotha that spring morning when the Master fulfilled the phophecy and walked, alone, the sun-touched road to Jerusalem.

It has been given to me as a heritage of memory to have heard Patti and Nevada in my impressionistic boyhood, and to have sat at the knees of one who told me of Jenny Lind and the tempest of adulation that received her in old Castle Garden, but I am constrained to believe that not since the loving stars sang their anthems to the roses of the first dawn has such music, without money and without price to pay, been heard by finite ears.

Every intaken breath was a caress; every exhaled sigh was a prayer; each upraised hand was a benediction; every tintinnabulating scale of molten notes was a hallelujah. Tetrazzini has come and gone to win plaudits otherwheres, but every enthusiast of last night has fast locked in his or her heart a

(Continued on Page 28, Col. 1.)

GREAT ARTIST REVEALS HER VERY SOUL TO THE PEOPLE SHE LOVES

Deeply Moved by the Tribute Accorded Her, Tetrazzini Thrills Vast Audience With Bounty of Song

By RALPH E. RENAUD.

JUST before she went down to sing her heart out for the people she loves, Tetrazzini leaned from a window in the "Chronicle" building and gazed upon the crowd that stretched away below for block on block, a monumental microcosm of humanity itself. Every gem of the hundreds on the diva's gleaming gown quivered and flashed with her quickening heart throbs.

As she turned inward there was an expression on her face I had never seen there before. She was quite serious. No smile turned the corners of her lips. No flush incarnadined her cheeks. There was a film over her eyes.

A timid soul would have shriveled from fright. In the recorded history of mankind no artist had ever sung before so vast a throng; no singer, with a voice of gold to risk, had ever dared so much; no woman had ever faced a similar occasion.

From the street a faint buzzing only arose. In a multitude so huge this might almost be taken for silence. An imagination that excitement had terrified would have considered it ominous—they would expect too much, they would rush forward and engulf her, so many thousand ears would absorb her voice until it shrilled and faded to an unheard whisper.

Was Tetrazzini frightened?

Ah no! Her eyes were filmed with tears. Clasping her hands upon her breast, she cried:

"Look! Look! My grrreat familee! See! Evarybody my brudder! Evarybody my sister!"

And, spreading her arms and stretching her gloved fingers, she spoke once more, with almost a sob in her tones:

"My 'eart eet is so beeg lak dees! Way out to 'ere an' 'ere! Oh, I am so 'appy!"

THE DIVA IS HAPPY.

In a moment she was smiling again with the familiar, dimpled, roguish smile. Her robe—an old rose, like the flower in her first sweet song—was placed about her shoulders, and she passed down stairs and out upon the platform, as ready to bestow her richest love as the opulent magic of her voice.

Fortunately, there are others to describe the half hour's miracle that followed then. My feelings are much like those of George Bazelli, who, when it w[illegible] over, shrugged his shoulders, sighed, and, addressing space, observed: "Ah, I can say nothing—nothing!"

I have only a confused and emotional recollection of an event that is too big to grasp at once. It is all like a brilliant dream that leaves one a little dazed upon awakening and only comes back bit by flashing bit. I know that I heard a roar that broke into a long-drawn thunder, like the pounding of storm waves upon a pebbled beach, as the spot-lit figure moved to the raised dais from which she sang. I remember listening to the words of a speaker and then feeling a hush clear to the distant edges of the crowd. Then came those spirit-piercing, sweet, sweet tones that fluttered, rose and floated into the enamored night air, carrying peace and good will to the Christmas throng, speeding a message to the whole world, and pumping the love of a great-souled woman through the valves of every heart.

Surely it was "one of God's choristers" I heard.

When the last note died on the darkness the multitude, as I looked across it from the platform, seemed to convulse itself into sudden motion. Heads were flung back, wild arms sprang upward, shaking hats and caps, while a hoarse and deafening shout issued from I'd hate to say how many thousands of throats, repeating itself again and again. It was a crowd "where the best was like the worst," bootblacks rubbed elbows with bankers, and painted creatures with the fat and wholesome mothers of families; but I'll guarantee that but one emotion, indeed but one sensation, moved them all. Curiosity, excitement, criticism, selfish impulses to push forward, irritation at being pushed backward were sunk in a single, binding wave of gratitude. Before the amazing demonstration ended this found definite direction in the hymnal sentiment of "Auld Lang Syne," carried by the orchestra and welling from the concourse, and the intensely Anglo-Saxon function of three rousing cheers.

When the emotional side of our natures is greatly strained by grief, joy or sudden delight little, inconsequential things stand out with great distinctness in our memories. It was so with me. Looking over the edge of the railing, I saw an obscure Italian listening to his famous countrywoman. His head was bent down and he was making no attempt to see, only listening. As Tetrazzini sang the tears dripped steadily from his eyes and rolled ludicrously into his mustache. Near by stood a young woman with a boy, both keyed to rapt, ecstatic attention. Yet she was not so forgetful as the diva began "The Last Rose of Summer" that she did not remember to raise her hand and gently remove the lad's cap. I recollect, too, the silhouetted figure of one of the musicians, rubbing his bald head with one hand and wiping his eyes with the other.

And, naturally enough, every move, every gesture of Tetrazzini herself is engraved upon my memory. Closing my eyes for a moment, I can even bring her back as she bowed and smiled to the crowd, waving her handkerchief and wiggling her extended fingers. As she stretched her throat for a high, aspiring note I see her robe slip from her shoulders, revealing the dazzling white of her gown and the rounded lines of her form against the glowing gloom that surrounded her. I see her shaking hands with Paul Steindorff, receiving her basket of scarlet poinsettias. Then I see her leaving the platform, thrilled with pleasure in every nerve that she had been able to give so much pleasure.

Perhaps the miracle could have happened in no city of the world but San Francisco, but no woman alive, except Tetrazzini, would have performed it. To be sure Providence was kind and gracious, and the night was as soft and clear as one of the last evenings of an Eastern spring. She had declared her wish to sing in the streets for San Francisco, and sing she would. It is the tenderest tribute ever made to the people of a big city.

Must it not be a happy thought to her that of all the Christmas gifts that are passed in all the Christian lands of the world today, she had the loveliest to give, and gave it where she loved the mos

ONE LITTLE WOMAN, PRODIGAL WITH TALENT, CHARMS GREATEST CROWD THAT EVER HEARD SINGER

Vast Throng Moved by Voice of One of God's Own Choristers

By HELEN DARE.

"O-H-H! My hear-r-rt, eet feel so-o-oh beeg!!!! Comme ca!" and she made a circle with her plump, pretty arms to the utmost limit, a comprehensive, stretched-to-the-bursting-point circle, when the moment came for her to face the greatest audience of her joyous life, and the Mayor offered her his arm.

"Oh, my! Now I am sorree eet ees feen-eesh! I am sorree eet ees oll o'faire, an' donn weet!"

There you have Tetrazzini, happy, laughing, prodigal Tetrazzini, of the child-heart, with the joy of life turning up the corners of her mouth in curving smiles and rippling laughs, and sparkling in her roguish eyes.

Tetrazzini—artist, child and woman. Tetrazzini—who went to sing to San Francisco with eagerness and enthusiasm, who finished with regret!

She came sparkling, radiant, charming—and laughing, always laughing, breaking out delightfully in the unexpected places when every one else was down and self-conscious—like one of our own California mountain brooks that murmurs along smooth places for a little space and then breaks into song and chatter over fall and bowlder.

She came in her rose-pink cloak and her iridiscent, trailing white gown, and big, transparent hat, sparkling with brilliants, and her white ostrich boa fluffing under her round chin, her white gloved hands waving friendly little salutes and acknowledgments, and her round, healthy, sweet, smooth, radiant, smiling child's face beaming with friendliness and happiness.

Nothing was too good for San Francisco. She had made a most careful toilette, wearing her most sumptuous, dazzling gown—and she looked charming.

ATTENDED LIKE A QUEEN.

She was attended like a queen with a retinue of friends and protectors, gay and carefree in their midst; she bowed right and left and waved fluttering hands in response to the plaudits rolling up and down the street.

She looked down out of the window, from the beautiful room in the Chronicle building, where she was the center of interest, and the crowd, looking up, caught sight of her and cheered, a cheer that rolled toward Twin Peaks and the Ferry building and out into the by-streets. From every window of the buildings across the street and round about on the gore and on Kearny came cheers and a fluttering of handkerchiefs and waving of hats.

"Oh—h! Eet is lufly! Eet is gran'; it make my hear-r-rt to feel like so-o-o beeg till it hur-r-rt me," she said, raising her hands in eloquent ecstasy.

"They ar-re my brothaire an' my sistaire; everybody out there waiting for me. Eet ees all one beeg fam'ly—MY fam'ly!"

And in this spirit, with this enthusiasm and prodigality of self, she went out to sing to you—San Francisco!

With all her heart!

Without reserve!

Without restraint; or selfish fear; or condescension.

WAS PRODIGAL WITH HER GIFT.

Generously, warmly, prodigally of her gift she gave you, San Francisco!

Surely it is something to have been there around Lotta's fountain—we folks around our town pump—and had a part in such an event.

Sweet, clear and pure, in all its artless beauty rose that rare voice in the simple, appealing strains of "The Last Rose of Summer."

Sparkling, liquid, bird-like—like a nightingale on a summer bough, when the moon is at the full, or like the high-shot slender spray from a fountain playing full strength in the sun-

(Continued on Page 29, Col. 4.)

San Francisco Chronicle.

VOL. C. SAN FRANCISCO, CAL., TUESDAY, APRIL 16, 1912. NO. 92

GIGANTIC LINER TITANIC SINKS; 1500 LOST

OF 2200 SOULS ABOARD ONLY 866 ARE RESCUED

Women and Children Placed in Life Boats Are Picked Up

LOSS OF FLOATING PALACE ON HER MAIDEN VOYAGE WORST DISASTER IN MARINE HISTORY

Titanic Goes Down Soon After Colliding With Wall of Ice in the Ocean Graveyard---Women and Children Are Rescued by Steamship Carpathia

Special Dispatches to the "Chronicle."

BOSTON, April 15.—A wireless message picked up late tonight relayed from the Olympic says that the Carpathia is on her way to New York with 866 passengers from the steamer Titanic aboard. They are mostly women and children, the message said, and it concluded:

"Grave fears are felt for the safety of the balance of the passengers and crew."

NEW YORK, April 15.—Latest reports indicate that 1800 persons probably perished when the Titanic went down.

The text of the message from the steamer Olympic reporting the sinking of the Titanic and the rescue of 675 survivors, which reached here late tonight, expressed the opinion that 1800 lives were lost.

"Loss likely total 1800 souls," the dispatch said in its concluding sentence.

It is hoped and believed here that this is an error, unless the Titanic had more passengers on board than was reported. The list as given out showed 1310 passengers and crew of 860, or 2170 in all. Deducting 675, the known saved, would indicate a loss of 1495 persons.

The Olympic's dispatch follows:

"Carpathia reached Titanic position at daybreak. Found boats and wreckage only. Titanic sank about 2:20 A. M. in 41:16 N., 50:14 W. All her boats accounted for containing about 675 souls saved, crew and passengers included. Nearly all saved women and children. Leyland liner Californian remained and searching exact position of disaster. Loss likely total 1800 souls."

LONDON, April 15.—At the White Star office here it was said the total number of persons aboard the Titanic was 2358, divided as follows:

Cabin, 350.
Second cabin, 305.
Steerage, 800.
Crew, 903.

This differs considerably from the number given out in New York, adding 170 to the total.

NEW YORK, April 15.—More than 1500 souls, men, women and children, were lost, it is feared, in the wreck of the White Star liner Titanic, latest and greatest ship of the seas, which collided with an iceberg at 10:25 o'clock Sunday night and sank off the banks of Newfoundland at 2:20 A. M. Monday, less than four hours after she had struck.

The White Star line early this morning gave out the list of those who were saved.

Captain Haddock of the Olympic sent this dispatch by wireless to the White Star Line last evening:

"Carpathia reached Titanic's position at daybreak. Found boats and wreckage only. Titanic sank about 2:20 A. M. in latitude 41 deg. 46 min. north, longitude 50 deg. 14 min. west. All her boats accounted for, containing about 675 souls saved, crew and passengers included. Nearly all saved are women and children. Leyland liner California remained and searched exact position of disaster. Loss likely to total 1800 souls."

1800 REPORTED LOST.

The exact text of this dispatch was closely guarded until after midnight by Vice-President Franklin of the White Star line, who received it at 7 o'clock. It gave the first definite news of the sinking of the Titanic and of the great loss of life. But it is believed that the words "loss likely total 1800 souls" is an error due to the ignorance of Captain Haddock and the rescued passengers of the total number of persons aboard.

There were, according to the White Star Company, 325 first cabin, 285 second cabin and 710 steerage; a total of 1320 passengers, and a crew of 860. This would make 2180 persons on board, and some late comers not on the passenger lists are believed to have brought the total up to 2200. Deducting 675 from this, the loss would only be 1505, which Franklin believes to be correct.

A wireless dispatch from the Olympic was picked up by a Boston operator late last night in which it was stated that the Carpathia was on her way to New York with 866 passengers rescued from the Titanic. The rescued, the dispatch read, were mostly women and children and the dispatch concluded, "Grave fears are felt for the safety of the balance of the passengers and crew."

Captain E. J. Smith of the Titanic is believed to have gone to the bottom with his vessel.

Among the 1320 passengers of the giant liner were Colonel John Jacob Astor and his wife, Isador Straus, Major Archibald W. Butt, aid to President Taft; George B. Widener and Mrs. Widener of Philadelphia, Mr. and Mrs. Henry S. Harper, William T. Stead, the London journalist; Charles M. Hays, president of the Grand Trunk Railway, and many more whose names are known on both sides of the Atlantic. The news that few besides women and children were saved has caused the greatest apprehension as to the fate of these.

PLUNGES AGAINST ICE WALL.

When the Titanic plunged headlong against a wall of ice at 10:40 P. M. Sunday night her fate established that no modern steamship is unsinkable and that all of a large passenger list cannot be saved in a liner's small boats.

The White Star line believed that the Titanic was practically invulnerable, and insisted until there was no doubting the full extent of the catastrophe that she could not sink. The great ship was the last word in modern scientific construction, but she found the ocean floor.

LOST ON MAIDEN TRIP.

On her maiden trip the Titanic, built and equipped at a cost of $10,000,000, a floating palace, found her graveyard.

Swinging from the westerly steamship lane at the south of the grand banks of Newfoundland to take the direct run to this port, she hurled her giant bulk against an iceberg that rose from an immense field drifted unseasonably from the Arctic. Running at high speed into that grim and silent enemy of seafarers, the shock crushed her bow. From a happy, comfortable vessel, she was converted in a few minutes into a ship of misery and dreadful suffering. Through rent plates and timbers the water rushed so swiftly that her captain, E. J. Smith, the admiral of the White Star fleet, knew there was no hope of saving her. That much the faltering wireless has told.

BRINGING WOMEN AND CHILDREN.

At midnight tonight the officials of the White Star line were struggling to get into communication with the Cunarder Carpathia, which has on board the 675 women and children saved from the Titanic, but not one word of news could they obtain.

All they could get by wireless was the fact that the Carpathia, which left New York on April 13th for the Mediterranean, was retracing her course to this port, bringing here the women and children who were widowed and orphaned by the disaster.

The Marconi stations were striving, also, to get in touch with either the Carpathia or the Allan liner Virginian, to find out if all of the rescued were on board the Carpathia or whether the Virginian carries others that were saved, but the Marconi people were unsuccessful, and it is not known whether the Virginian transferred all of those she picked up to the Carpathia.

The latest news was that the Carpathia had started for New York. She should reach here some time on Wednesday.

WORST IN MARINE HISTORY.

Accepting early estimates of the fatality list as accurate, the disaster is the greatest in marine history. Nearest approaching it in magnitude were the disasters of the steamer Atlantic in 1873, when 547 lives were lost, and of La Bourgoyne in 1898, with a fatality list of 571.

Should it prove that other liners, notably the Allan liners Parisian and Virginia, known to have been in the vicinity of the Titanic early yesterday, had picked up other of her passengers, the extent of the calamity would be greatly reduced. This hope remains.

News of the sinking of the liner and of the terrible loss of life came early this evening with all the greater shock because hope had been buoyed up all day by reports that the steamship, although badly damaged, was not sinking, and that all her passengers had been taken off safely.

The messages were mostly unofficial, however, and none came directly from the liner, so that a fear remained of possible bad news to come.

TITANIC SOON SINKS.

Shortly after 7 o'clock last night there came flashing over the wires from Cape Race, within 400 miles of which the liner had struck the iceberg, word that at 2:20 o'clock this morning, three hours and fifty-five minutes after receiving her death blow, the Titanic had sunk. The news came from the steamer Carpathia, relayed by the White Star liner Olympic, and revealed

(Continued on Page 2, Column 4.)

Giant liner Titanic, which sank off Newfoundland. The lower pictures show some of the steamer's luxurious apartments.

MEN ON THE TITANIC HAVE VAST FORTUNES

NEW YORK, April 15.—John Jacob Astor was among the passengers who went down with the ship, according to a wireless dispatch received by Bradstreet's last night from the liner Olympic. Mrs. Astor was saved and is being brought to shore by the Carpathia.

NEW YORK, April 15.—Wealth aggregating something like half a billion dollars is represented by seven of the passengers on the Titanic. If calamity befell only a few of these even, it would materially affect the vast business enterprises in the United States and England. The seven are:

Colonel John Jacob Astor—$150,000,000.

J. Bruce Ismay—$40,000,000.

Colonel Washington Roebling—$25,000,000.

Isidor Straus $50,000,000.

George D. Widener—$50,000,000.

Benjamin Guggenheim—$95,000,000.

J. B. Thayer—$10,000,000.

Total—$420,000,000.

If the fortunes of the first-class passengers alone were placed together they would easily make $1,000,000,000.

MEN OF GREAT WEALTH.

Foremost among the passengers in point of wealth is Colonel John Jacob Astor, who was returning to New York with his bride, formerly Miss Madeline Force. Colonel Astor's holdings may amount to $150,000,000, and he is connected with nearly a score of corporations, besides attending to his realty interests.

Next in financial importance comes Benjamin Guggenheim. Guggenheim is in the American Smelting Securities Company, a great mining corporation which was founded by his father, Meyer Guggenheim. He is connected with the following corporations: Blake and Knowles Steam Pump Works, president and director; Henry R. Worthington Company, president and director; International Steam Pump Company, president and director; Laidlaw Dunn Gordon Company, president and director; Power and Mining Machinery Company, president and director.

George D. Widener is connected with the Widener Elkins Traction Syndicate of Philadelphia. He is one of two sons of P. A. B. Widener. George D. Widener's fortune is estimated at $50,000,000.

Colonel Washington Roebling, builder of the Brooklyn bridge, is president and director of John A. Roeblings Sons Company. His fortune amounts to about $25,000,000.

STRAUS WORLD FAMOUS.

Isidor Straus is one of the best-known merchants in the world, and is worth about $50,000,000. Straus is connected with the following organizations: R. H. Macy & Co., L. Straus & Sons, Abraham & Straus, the Birbeck Investment Savings and Loan Company, vice-president and trustee; Educational Allians, president and director; Hanover National Bank, director; Second National Bank, director.

John B. Thayer is vice-president of the Pennsylvania Railroad. His son, J. B. Thayer Jr., who was on the Titanic with his parents, formerly was a noted fullback on the University of Pennsylvania football team. Young Thayer was known as one of the best fullbacks that ever played on the college team.

J. Bruce Ismay is president of the International Mercantile Marine Company and is one of the founders of that organization. It was Ismay and J. P. Morgan who consolidated the American and British Steamship lines. It also was Ismay who conceived the idea of building the Titanic. He is worth probably $50,000,000.

LINER'S DEATHBED TWO MILES BELOW SURFACE.

HALIFAX, April 15.—The deathbed of the $10,000,000 steamer Titanic and of probably many who must have been dragged down with her is two miles below the surface of the sea.

The calculation was made by an official of the Government marine department, who finds that the depth on the marine chart at a point about 500 miles from Halifax and about seventy miles south of the Grand Banks, where he believes the Titanic went down.

This location is midway between Sable island and Cape Race, and in line with those dangerous sands, which, however, might have proved a place of safety had there been time to run the Titanic there and beach her.

San Francisco Chronicle
LEADING NEWSPAPER OF THE PACIFIC COAST

Weather Report
San Francisco, Oakland and Vicinity: Fair Monday, except foggy in the morning and at night; light northwest wind.
G. H. WILLSON, Local Forecaster

VOL. CV. SAN FRANCISCO, CAL., MONDAY, JUNE 29, 1914. X CITY NO. 14

HEIR TO AUSTRIAN THRONE AND WIFE SLAIN

Archduke Francis Ferdinand and Consort Shot Down by Assassins

BRYAN'S COLOMBIAN TREATY IS ATTEMPT TO LOOT UNITED STATES BY LOBBYISTS—LOOMIS

Photographs of the four principals who knew the secret of the dealings with Colombia in regard to acquiring the Panama route for the canal, and a map showing the location of the big ditch. About 13,000 square miles of land was lost to Colombia when the United States obtained this canal route, and it is in payment for this that President Wilson and Secretary Bryan urge the $25,000,000 warrant.

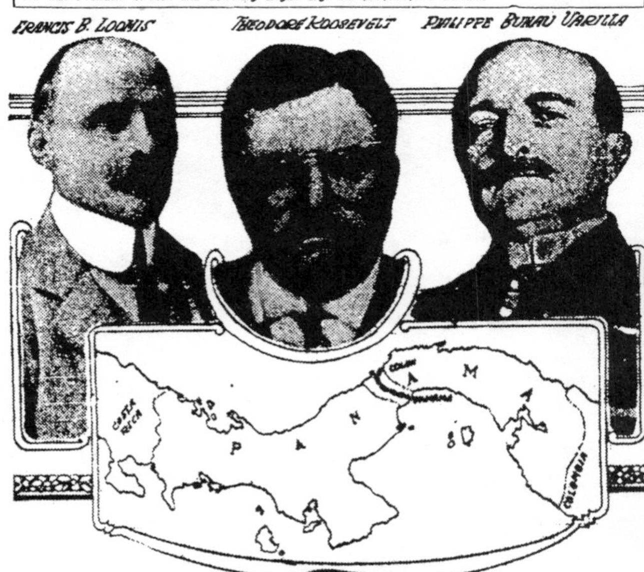

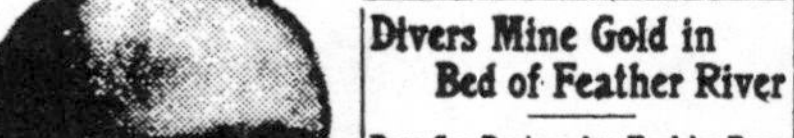

ANCHOR LINER HITS ROCKS DURING DENSE FOG

The Steamship California Goes Aground Off Irish Coast and Bows Are Damaged.

Special Dispatch to the "Chronicle."

LONDON, June 28.—The Anchor line steamship California, on its way from New York for Glasgow, went aground today on the rocks near Tory island off the northwest coast of Ireland in a dense fog.

Wireless messages calling urgently for assistance were picked up by the wireless stations along the coast. The messages said that the steamer's bows were badly damaged and water was pouring in through two gaping holes opened when she drove into the rocks.

NAVAL SHIPS TO RESCUE.

Naval vessels were dispatched from Londonderry to the steamer's assistance. These ships are now standing by her. Late messages received from Londonderry denied the earlier ones to the effect that the passengers had been transferred from the California. They stated that they were all still on board and that the steamer was stuck fast between two enormous rocks and in no immediate danger of sinking.

The pumps have been manned and the crew are sticking to their work steadily. No panic prevailed on board after she struck and the passengers are taking their dangerous situation calmly.

LIES IN FIVE FATHOMS.

The California, according to the wireless, lies in five fathoms of water forward and seven fathoms aft. The Government ships which have reached her are those which are patrolling the northwest Irish coast to prevent gun runners slipping in and landing cargoes of arms and munitions of war for the Ulsterites. They were the first to pick up her wireless calls for assistance, and lost no time in dashing to her aid.

They steamed through the fog at reckless speed, disregarding all danger to themselves. The California has on board 115 first cabin passengers, 300 second cabin and 500 steerage, a total of 915.

NECK BROKEN WHILE DOZING.

WICHITA (Kan.), June 28.—When Alfred Brinkloew, a farmer, 46 years old, finished his day's work in the wheat field near Derby, Kan., Saturday, he climbed into a buggy, lighted his pipe and fell asleep. As he dozed he [illegible]

OLYMPIA TO SHARE HONORS WITH OREGON.

Dewey, Like Clark, to Have Chance to Come With Exposition Fleet.

Special Dispatch to the "Chronicle."

WASHINGTON, June 28.—In arranging for the largest and most interesting naval display ever known at the Panama-Pacific Exposition at San Francisco, beginning early next year, Secretary Daniels has decided that the old cruiser Olympia shall share honors with the battle-ship Oregon, and that Admiral George Dewey, like Rear-Admiral Charles E. Clark, shall have opportunity again to stand on the bridge from where he directed the successful fighting in 1898.

Neither Dewey nor Clark has visited his ship since they surrendered their commands shortly after the end of the Spanish-American War. Rear-Admiral Clark already has the invitation to command the Oregon on her voyage leading the American Navy and visiting squadrons of the world from Hampton roads through the Panama canal and up to San Francisco. On the Oregon will be the President, Secretary Daniels and other Cabinet members.

Secretary Daniels will extend a formal invitation to Admiral Dewey to make this cruise, or at any rate to visit the Olympia at San Francisco.

The two historic ships will be moored at San Francisco, where they will be easily accessible to visitors. Behind them will be anchored seven of the newest vessels of the Navy, each representing a different type.

REPUBLICANS MEET.

SANTA FE (N. M.), June 28.—The Republican State Central Committee [illegible]

Divers Mine Gold in Bed of Feather River

Deep-Sea Devices Are Used by Prospectors in Hunt for Precious Metal Near Oroville.

Special Dispatch to the "Chronicle."

OROVILLE, June 28.—Delving for the golden gravels of the Feather river by means of deep-sea diving apparatus, J. W. Wright and A. B. Knapp, both of Reno, are now at a point near Belden and are making good wages at their work.

At the present time they are working in about ten to fifteen feet of water, and the diver stays down about half an hour at a time, enabling him to scratch in the crevices of the bedrock for the precious metal.

The banks and bars of the Feather have yielded millions of dollars to the prospector and the miner since the early fifties, but not until recently did anyone hit upon the scheme of getting at what is supposed to be the richest part of the river—its bed.

Postoffice Safe at Broderick Blown Open

Small Sum Is Secured by Cracksmen in Town Across the River From Sacramento.

Special Dispatch to the "Chronicle."

SACRAMENTO, June 28.—The safe of the Broderick postoffice, across the river from Sacramento, was blown open by three men at 4 o'clock this morning, and about $10 in money, $400 in stamps and a pad of money order blanks stolen. Constable William Russell of Broderick saw three men, well dressed, hurrying across the bridge into Sacramento shortly after the safe had been rifled.

The Sheriff of Yolo county informed the local authorities tonight he had found some papers and the stolen money order blanks in the brush outside of Woodland.

Hottest Day of the Year in the Valley

Thermometer Registers 105 Degrees in Fresno, Driving Residents to the River for Relief.

Special Dispatch to the "Chronicle."

FRESNO, June 28.—Today was the hottest day of the year, and the thermometer registered 105. Last year the hottest day in June was only 97. The heat drove hundreds to Riverview, where the Commercial Club held its annual picnic. Other resorts of the river were crowded. [illegible]

SECRETARY PREY OF POLITICAL BRIGANDS

Former Official Declares the President and Bryan Would Discredit Republicans.

BLUNDER IS STUPENDOUS

Proposed "Gift" of Twenty-Five Million Dollars Said to Be Vicious in Purpose.

Proposed Treaty Is Criticised
F. B. Loomis Issues Statement

BRYAN'S Colombian treaty is a covert attempt to loot the United States Treasury by lobbyists and political brigands, into whose hands the Secretary of State is playing.

"Bryan and the President are trying to besmirch and discredit the achievement of the previous administration, which made the canal a reality.

"The treaty is one of the most stupendous blunders made by Bryan, who is running wild with his "world peace" theories.

"The United States owes Colombia nothing, either by treaty or otherwise.

"Bryan has made false public statements concerning the attitude of other South American republics on the Colombian question. He is in danger of placing himself in the position of seeming willingness to sacrifice our national prestige for a petty and temporary partisan advantage.

"The provision of the treaty permitting free passage through the canal of Colombian war material and to the citizens and merchandise of Colombia is one of the most amazing features of the most amazing treaty ever submitted to the Senate, and in a violation of the 'most favored nation' clause in our other treaties."
—Statements by Former Assistant Secretary of State Francis B. Loomis.

BRYAN'S proposed treaty between the United States and the republic of Colombia, now before the Senate for ratification, was declared to be vicious both as to motives and purpose last night at the Bellevue Hotel by Francis B. Loomis, former assistant Secretary of State and acting Secretary of State, one of the four men who alone know the inside of the dealings with Colombia and the republic of Panama which made it possible for the United States to build the Panama canal.

The Bryan treaty provides, it is said, that this Government pay Colombia $25,000,000 indemnity, offer a humble and abject apology to her, and permit Colombian munitions of war, citizens and cattle to pass through the Panama canal free of tolls.

Loomis declares that we have at no time violated our treaty obligations with Colombia, but on the contrary have borne Colombia's disregard of our treaty rights, with patience and at much risk and expense. He said:

"That the whole business of obtaining the canal zone and constructing a canal across the isthmus of Panama was accomplished without infringement on the sovereignty of Colombia.

"That Bryan and the President seek without cause to attack, stultify and besmirch the achievements of previous national administrations in a great international undertaking—the first attempt of its kind in the history of the country.

"That Bryan has made false public statements concerning the attitude of other South American republics with regard to the Colombian question.

"That the Secretary of State has played into the hands of the lobbyists and political 'brigands' active both in Washington and Bogota.

"That the treaty represents an attempt to involve in a cloud of mean suspicion and downright scandal a vast historic work that has been brought to completion without corruption, and that Bryan has put himself in a position of seeming willingness to sacrifice our national prestige for a petty and temporary partisan advantage."

STUPENDOUS BLUNDER.

Loomis also expressed the opinion that the part of the Bryan treaty permitting free passage of Colombian war material through the canal, as well as citizens and merchandise of Colombia, is one of the most amazing features of the most amazing treaty ever submitted to the Senate, and is in violation of our treaties with other powers. The treaty will pass into history as [illegible]

THE late Archduke Francis Ferdinand of Austria, his wife, the Duchess of Hohenberg, and his three children—the Princes Maximilian Charles and Ernest Alphonse and Princess Sophie Marie. The Archduke had been given practically full power by the old Emperor, Francis Joseph.

Flag on White House in Electrical Storm

Old Glory Left Flying by Mistake Is Revealed by Flashes of Lightning.

Special Dispatch to the "Chronicle."

WASHINGTON, June 28. — Vivid flashes of lightning that featured the heavy rainstorm in Washington tonight revealed the Stars and Stripes flying from the top of the flagstaff on the White House. The flag is supposed to fly there when the President is in the White House, but only between sunrise and sunset. Rumors spread over the city that President Wilson had nailed his flag to the mast and that such was his answer to his advisers who insist that he must surrender in his campaign for trust legislation and permit Congress to adjourn.

However, newspaper men who called up the White House and inquired the why and wherefor of the unusual display of Old Glory were promptly assured that the flag had been left up through the mistake or oversight of a servant. Five minutes later when the lightning flashed, the flag no longer waved, and only the black line of the flagstaff stood out against the sky.

Bride of Six Hours Granted a Divorce

Marion Ellsion of This City, Who Was Married in Chicago, Wins Freedom in Court.

Special Dispatch to the "Chronicle."

BUFFALO (N. Y.), June 28.—Justice Creuch late Saturday, in Syracuse, N. Y., granted a final decree of divorce annulling the marriage of Marion Ellsion of Syracuse to Elias Ellsion of San Francisco, who lived together only six hours in Chicago, where they were married August 25, 1912, the bride being under 17.

The reason for the separation was never revealed. When the San Francisco girl was unable to come to Syracuse the bride's mother arranged for a wedding at Chicago and accompanied her to that city.

DEATH DUE TO THE HEAT.

FORT SMITH (Ark.), June 28.—One death and temperatures ranging from 100 to 106 degrees marked the thirty-eighth day of the earliest and longest drought in thirty-three years in this section. G. A. Blanton, a prominent planter of Steigler, Okla., was found unconscious on a horse. He died soon [illegible]

BOMB IS THROWN BEFORE THE SHOTS

Archduke and Morganatic Wife Are Victims of Bullets Fired by a Young Student

SERAJEVO, June 28.—Archduke Francis Ferdinand, heir to the Austro-Hungarian throne, and his morganatic wife, the Duchess of Hohenberg, were assassinated today while driving through the streets of Serajevo, the Bosnian capital. A youthful Servian student fired the shots which added another to the long list of tragedies that has darkened the reign of Emperor Francis Joseph.

VICTIMS OF SECOND ATTEMPT.

The Archduke and his wife were victims of the second attempt in the same day against their lives. First a bomb was thrown at the automobile in which they were driving to the Town Hall. Forewarned, however, of a possible attempt against his life, the Archduke was watchful and struck the missile aside with his arm. It fell under an automobile which carried members of his suite, wounding Count von Boos Waldeck and Colonel Merizzo.

COUPLE MORTALLY WOUNDED.

On their return from the Town Hall the Archduke and Duchess were driving to the hospital when the Servian, Gevrio Prinzip, darted at the car and fired a volley at the occupants. His aim was true, for the Archduke and his wife were mortally wounded. With them at the time was the Governor of the city, who escaped injury. The [illegible]

collapsed [illegible] him from [illegible]
The Governor [illegible] chauffeur [illegible] top [illegible] prompt [illegible]

Fourth Tragedy in Ruler's Life
Relatives Meet Violent Deaths

THE assassination of Archduke Francis Ferdinand and his wife is the fourth great tragedy in the life of the aged Emperor Francis Joseph, now in his eighty-fourth year.

The Emperor has seen the object of his three younger brothers, the Archduke Ferdinand and the Emperor Maximilian of Mexico, executed; his only son, the Archduke Rudolph, die under mysterious and scandalous circumstances, either murdered or a suicide; his wife, the beloved Empress Elizabeth, assassinated, and now his second heir and the latter's wife assassinated.

The attempt of the Archduke Ferdinand Maximilian of [illegible] to establish himself [illegible] of that turbulent [illegible] made against the [illegible] of his elder [illegible] Joseph.

San Francisco Chronicle

LEADING NEWSPAPER OF THE PACIFIC COAST

SIXTH EDITION

VOL. CV. SAN FRANCISCO, CAL., SATURDAY, AUGUST 15, 1914. XX NO. 61

JAPAN'S FLEET SAID TO HAVE JOINED BRITISH

Forces of the Kaiser Increase Attack on the Liege Forts

PANAMA CANAL OPENED TO COMMERCE OF WORLD

First Ocean-Going Steamer, Government-Owned Ancon, Will Make Its Initial Trip From Atlantic to the Pacific.

JOURNEY WILL TAKE ABOUT TWELVE HOURS

Governor Goethals, President Porras of Isthmian Republic and Other High Officials to Be on Board the Vessel.

PANAMA, August 14.—The canal was the scene of activity tonight, in preparation for its opening tomorrow.

On board the steamship Ancon, officers and men were busy setting everything shipshape for her start early in the morning on the first voyage of a big ocean-going steamship through the new highway. The Ancon, 10,000 tons register, owned by the United States War Department and leased to the Panama Railroad for New York-to-Colon trade, has not discharged her cargo, as it is planned to have her make the journey fully loaded.

On her trip down from New York she received a new coat of paint, and, with the finishing touches given her tonight, will look as though fresh from the builder's yard. The first thing in the morning signal flags will be strung from foretruck to keelson, and the flags of all nations hoisted on the ship to mark the national aspect of the occasion. Inside and out, the ship will be gay with bunting. Even the deck hands will be rigged out in spotless new white uniforms.

START AT 7 A. M.

Orders have been issued for the Ancon to leave her dock at Chrystobal promptly at 7 o'clock, in order that she may arrive at the Gatun locks at about 8. She was boarded tonight by John Constantine, canal pilot, who will have charge of the ship during her passage tomorrow. He hopes to get her through to the Pacific within eleven hours, although twelve is the set time for the average trip.

Entering the Gatun locks at 9, the eleven-hour run would bring the Ancon to the end of the deep water channel in the Pacific at 6 in the evening. The passage of the Cucaracha slide in Culebra cut will be made shortly before noon. The usual regulations provide a speed limit of fifteen knots in the wider and deeper channels of Gatun lake, but in the Culebra cut not more than six knots an hour will be allowed. Every move which the ship makes will be recorded on plotting charts in the port captain's offices at either end of the waterway.

SUSPEND OTHER TRAFFIC.

In order that the Ancon's journey may be wholly unimpeded, all other traffic on the canal will be suspended.

Those aboard will include Governor Goethals, the builder of the canal, and numerous other high officials and President Belisario Porras of the Republic of Panama and members of his Cabinet. Most of them will be accompanied by their wives. During the voyage a buffet luncheon will be served, but without wine, as the canal zone is "dry" territory.

Panama Republic and canal officials who have been asked by Secretary of War Garrison to make the trip will arrive at Colon early tomorrow morning on a special train. There will be about 200 invited guests on board the Ancon.

Much disappointment has been expressed because the Secretary of War was unable to come for the trip. It is understood that there will be no ceremonies of any kind in view of the absence of official Washington.

Weather Report

San Francisco, Oakland and Vicinity:

Fair Saturday, except foggy in the morning; light west wind.

G. H. WILLSON, Local Forecaster

Sun Rises.......5:24 | Sun Sets........7:04

Full Meteorological and Hydrographic Reports on page 14.

WAR NEWS SUMMARY

Reports of the continued advance of the Germans toward Brussels, the march extending through the heart of Belgium on a line extending relatively from Namur to Haelen, and of continued fighting at the Liege fortresses, were the chief items of news of the warfare in Europe that winnowed through the sieve of the censor last night.

Of the movement of the armies of the Germans and the allies, it was stated that it had progressed to a point where it seemed apparent that the first great battle of the war could not long be deferred.

A dispatch from Brussels said the concentration of French troops in Belgium was complete, and that all the troops that had been expected were in battle order.

A German report from in front of Liege said the Fortress Pontisse had fallen into the hands of the Germans. Belgians denied this, and asserted the Germans had suffered heavy losses in the attack.

A special dispatch received in London said the Japanese purposed to carry out their treaty obligations with Great Britain and that the Japanese fleet had put to sea to co-operate with the British ships.

Greece, it was stated, probably would engage Turkey again should the report that the Ottoman Government had purchased the German cruisers Goeben and Breslau prove true.

The German cruiser Karlsruhe, after coaling at San Juan, Porto Rico, following her fight with British cruisers, put into the Dutch island of Curacao last Wednesday.

MARCONI ISSUES GERMANY'S VERSION

Imperial Chancellor Appeals to Sense of Justice of the American People.

Special Cable to The Chronicle.

LONDON, August 14.—Marconi's wireless press has issued to all the London papers the following German war news, officially circulated through the German wireless stations and received by the Marconi Company:

"BERLIN, August 14.—In an interview the German Imperial Chancellor stated today:

"The war is a life and death struggle between Germany and the Muscovite races of Russia, and was due to the recent royal murders at Serajevo.

"We warned Russia against kindling this world war. She demanded the humiliation of Austria, and while the German Emperor continued his work in the cause of peace and the Czar was telegraphing words of friendship to him, Russia was preparing for war against Germany.

"Highly civilized France, bound by her unnatural alliance with Russia, was compelled to prepare by strength of arms for an attack on its flank on the Franco-Belgian frontier in case we proceeded against the French frontier works. England, bound to France by obligations disowned long ago, stood in the way of a German attack on the northern coast of France.

"Necessity, therefore, forced us to violate the neutrality of Belgium, but we had promised emphatically to compensate that country for all damage inflicted.

"Now England avails herself of the long-awaited opportunity to commence war for the destruction of commercially prosperous Germany. We enter into that war with our trust in God. Our eternal race has risen in the fight for liberty as it did in 1813.

"We expect that the sense of justice of the American people will enable them to comprehend our situation. We invite their opinion as to the one-sided English representations, and ask them to examine our point of view in an unprejudiced way.

"The sympathy of the American Nation will then lie with German culture and civilization, fighting against a half-Asiatic and slightly cultured barbarism."

Declares Roumania Would Fight Austria

Special Cable to The Chronicle.

LONDON, August 14.—The Daily Express' Paris correspondent says news has been received here that public opinion in Roumania is strongly in favor of joining in the fight against Austria, with the object of reconquering Transylvania. The Bratalno Ministro is in favor of siding with the triple entente.

FIELD MARSHAL SIR JOHN FRENCH, in command of the British troops with the allied armies, who has joined General Joseph Joffre, the commander in chief of the French forces.

WAR BULLETINS

PARIS, August 14.—The Havas Agency announces that Field Marshal Sir John French, the commander in chief of the English field army, joined General Joseph Joffre, the French commander in chief, at headquarters today. The locality is not mentioned.

LONDON, August 14, 11:07 P. M.—It is officially announced from Nyassa-Land, British Central Africa, that the Government steamer Guendolin yesterday surprised and captured the German armed steamer Von Wissonar on the eastern shore of Lake Nyassa.

WASHINGTON, August 14.—President Wilson issued a proclamation today of the war between Great Britain and Austria-Hungary.

BRUSSELS (via London, 5:45 P. M.), August 14—In a sortie near Namur yesterday 200 military cyclists, after surrounding 400 Germans, killed a large number, captured fifty and routed the rest.

LONDON, August 14, 11:28 P. M.—A Reuter dispatch from St. Petersburg says a message has been received there from Vilna stating that a German aeroplane, which was making observations of Russian military movements in the Polish government of Suwalki, was fired upon and brought down with a crash. Its occupants, four German officers, were killed, according to the dispatch.

LONDON, August 14, 10:20 P. M.—The Brussels correspondent of the Exchange Telegraph says the transportation of French troops into Belgian territory is now complete, and that all the troops that had been expected are in battle order at a place fixed according to the plans of the chief of staff.

LONDON, August 14.—A German who was suspected of espionage was arrested at Aldershot last Saturday. In his rooms were found a number of tubes containing millions of cholera bacilli.

ROME, August 14, 2:05 P. M. (via Paris, 7:06 P. M.)—Serious troubles in Albania are causing anxiety. Insurgents are threatening Durazzo and Valona.

COLON, August 14.—The French steamship Guadalupe sailed for Bordeaux today with 300 reservists aboard. The soldiers came from Peru, Chile, Costa Rica and Panama.

DESPERATE FIGHTING IS PROCEEDING AGAINST WEST DEFENSES OF BELGIANS

Germans No Longer Rely Upon Siege Artillery in the Prolonged Siege of Liege and Try to Rush Fort Pontisse by Overwhelming Force

Object of the Besiegers Is to Seize Forts on the Left Bank of the Meuse River and Turn Captured Guns on the Courageous Defenders

LONDON, August 14.—The Daily Telegraph says the Japanese navy has put to sea and will co-operate with the British fleet in taking effective action against enemy ships in the Pacific.

PARIS, August 15, 3:20 A. M.—The Petit Journal, the editor of which is Stephen Pichon, who was formerly Minister of Foreign Affairs, says today that it learns on absolutely unimpeachable authority that Japan is resolved to declare war on Germany and that official action probably will be taken today, following the return of the Emperor to Tokio.

ST. PETERSBURG, August 15 (via London, 8 A. M.)—The Russian Government has offered Poland freedom in religion, language and autonomy if the Poles are loyal in the present struggle with Germany and Austria-Hungary.

LONDON, August 14.—About one hundred and fifty of the passengers and crew of the Austrian Lloyd steamer Baron Gautsch were killed or drowned when the vessel was blown up by a mine off the Island of Lussin, on the Dalmatian coast, according to a Reuter dispatch from Triest. She carried about three hundred passengers and crew, of whom one hundred and fifty were rescued.

LONDON, August 14, 9:05 P. M.—A dispatch to the Exchange Telegraph Company from its Brussels correspondent says that Fort Pontisse and its neighboring forts to the west of the city of Liege are resisting extremely well the fierce German attack. The Germans have been trying to rush Pontisse by main force, no longer relying upon siege artillery. They have been unable, however, to get beyond the glacis of the fort, where they have been mowed down by the fire of the defenders. The besiegers are provided with bundles of wood and mattresses with which to fill up the ditches about the fort, but they have been unable to make use of them. Fort Liers, which is just west of Pontisse, has lent efficacious aid to the latter fortification.

SEEKS FORTS ON LEFT BANK.

The object of the Germans obviously is to seize the forts on the left bank of the Meuse, which in the hands of the Belgians would be terrible weapons against the invading forces, should the Belgian main army march toward Liege. On the other hand, these forts in the hands of the Germans would serve as a base for action directed against the Belgian center for defense against the Belgian attacks.

NEW MOVEMENT PLANNED.

A dispatch from Brussels to Reuter's Agency says the following official announcement was issued at noon today:

"The Germans are planning a new movement against us, but all dispositions have been made to repel it, like the preceding ones.

"Reports show that the situation continues favorable to us and our allies, while the news from Lorraine is highly favorable to the French.

"The general staff has heard noth-

(Continued on Page 2, Column 4.)

GERMAN ADVANCE IS BECOMING GENERAL

Attack by Several Army Corps Is Expected in the Direction of Diest and Aerschot

TIRLEMONT (Belgium), August 14 (via London).—The German advance became more pronounced and general today. Their infantry is advancing in the direction of Tongres and St. Trond, and another attack is expected in the direction of Diest and Aerschot, to the northwest of Brussels, by several army corps.

The German troops are marching on a front stretching from St. Trond to Hasselt. Their cavalry occupies a position to the right of Hasselt.

Formidable defensive works have been erected by the Belgians around Namur. To obviate any pretext for reprisals on the part of the Germans all the inhabitants of Namur are being disarmed.

LONDON, August 14.—A dispatch from Brussels to Reuter's Agency says that a battle near Eghezee, north of Namur, which occurred yesterday at Noville Taviere, on the Namur-Tirlemont railroad line, was keenly contested.

The Germans, according to the dispatch, were mostly cavalrymen. They were surprised by the Belgians and sustained severe casualties. Eventually they fell back hurriedly on Huy, between Namur and Liege.

SHOTS BRING DOWN AIRSHIPS.

The dispatch adds that three German aeroplanes flying over Diest were brought down by the Belgian artillery. Two of the aviators were killed by being dashed to earth and the third was terribly injured.

A dispatch to the Central News from Amsterdam says the Mayor of Aix la-Chapelle, Germany, has issued a proclamation announcing that great masses of German troops are to pass through the town on Saturday.

WOULD FORCE A RETREAT.

BRUSSELS (via Paris), August 14.—Technical observers of the military operations of the last two days declare their opinion is confirmed that the German army is seeking to reach the French border through the southern part of the Belgian province of Brabant crossing that section where the plain of Waterloo is situated and forcing the Belgian army to retreat on Antwerp.

Prince William of Lippe, who fell at Liege, is reported to have had in his helmet 10,000 marks in German bank notes.

FRENCH TROOPS MARCH.

PARIS, August 14.—An official announcement says that a large number of French troops has entered Belgium and are proceeding from Charleroi to Gembloux, ten miles to the northwest of Namur.

A telegram from Brussels to the Havas Agency says a fresh engagement between Germans and Belgians occurred yesterday between 5 and 6 o'clock in the evening at Geet-Betz, five miles south of Haelen. The Belgian troops fired heavily on a detachment of 400 Germans, who retired hastily.

PATROLS IN SKIRMISHES.

An official report issued here today says:

"No fact of striking importance took place in the theater of operations yesterday. There were, however, several skirmishes between German and French patrols and encounters between outposts, notably at Chambrey in German Lorraine, where two companies of the Eighteenth Bavarian Infantry regiment were surprised by the French troops and driven off, leaving numerous dead and wounded on the field."

FALSE NEWS ALLEGED.

An official communication issued today says that since the beginning of the war the German people have been systematically deceived by false news circulated by a large German agency.

(Continued on Page 2, Column 2.)

San Francisco Chronicle
LEADING NEWSPAPER of the PACIFIC COAST

Weather Report
San Francisco, Oakland and Vicinity: Unsettled weather, with showers. Saturday; light southwest wind.
G. H. WILLSON, Forecaster.
For Meteorological and Hydrographic Reports see Page 6.

VOL. CVI. SAN FRANCISCO, CAL., SATURDAY, FEBRUARY 20, 1915. NO. 36

NOW'S THE DAY AND NOW'S THE HOUR

San Francisco Opens the Doors of the Greatest of World Expositions Today

MARCHING HOST TO ENTER GATES IN CELEBRATION

President Wilson Will Start Wireless Spark From White House to Set the Wheels in Machinery Palace Going, and the Fountain of Energy Playing

SECRETARY FRANKLIN K. LANE WILL DELIVER CHIEF ADDRESS

City Will Awake at the Sunrise Salute and Big Noise Will Herald the Fact That the Panama-Pacific Exposition Is Ready for the Initial Festival

THIS is the morning of realization. The day of anticipation and preparation passes; and the words of prediction are lost in the Big Noise that heralds the opening hour of the greatest of world expositions.

San Francisco becomes the host city of the world this morning, and offers its guests amusement, enlightenment and beauty.

Everyone is an optimist today. The last of the pessimists, entering the open gates of the exposition, becomes an optimist. With 299,999 others, seeing for the first time the completed poetry of the exposition architecture, he gets a shock; exclaims, "OH!" In a breath the last doubt expires. The exposition is a reality.

Of course, the weather is fair. We have made it so. It took five years. So if the weather man hints of showers, just tell him: "None but the brave deserve the Fair." That ought to be enough to reform even the barometer. And if it isn't, then remember that it is a "rain or shine" programme today, and that it takes more than a shower to make San Franciscans turn back.

Everything is ready to ring up the curtain. Don't imagine for a moment that because you have watched the progress of the exposition building up to the time when the gates were closed to the public a month ago that you have any adequate conception of what the Panama-Pacific International Exposition looks like this morning. In that last month there has been a marvelous transformation. Scaffolding has been torn down, the finishing touches have been put on the grounds, fountains completed, and the last note of color added in the banners, so that when the great crowd marches in through the gates at 10 o'clock this morning the revelation will come.

Representatives From All Sections.

And the great crowd that will assemble in the south gardens between the Horticultural Palace and the Festival Hall in front of the south facade of the main buildings will itself be something to remember.

Secretary of the Interior Franklin K. Lane, the personal representative of the President for the occasion, and on all occasions the personal representative of San Francisco and California, will be there with the board of directors of the exposition, the city and

(Continued on Page 4, Column 1.)

WILL EXCHEQUER BROWN PLEASE COME TO FRONT?

Man Recently Appointed Postmaster at French Gulch, Shasta County, Is Not Known in That Community.

Special Dispatch to The Chronicle.

FRENCH GULCH, February 19.—A recent press dispatch from Washington, enumerating several postmasters who have been appointed for offices in Shasta county, stated that Exchequer Brown had been appointed for French Gulch.

Diligent inquiry has failed to reveal any one in this neighborhood by the name of Exchequer Brown.

Mrs. Clara E. Jones is still acting as postmaster, she having been appointed to the position temporarily after Miss Bessie Maxwell went to Kennett to teach school.

Tulare Produces the Finest Oranges

Prizes Are Awarded at National Show for Best Golden Fruit Produced in World.

SAN BERNARDINO, February 19.—For the first time in the history of the annual National Orange Show, first prizes designating their products the best oranges and lemons in the world were awarded today to citrus districts outside the Southern California orange belt. The world's sweepstake prize for oranges was awarded by the judges to Lindsay, Tulare county. Carpinteria, near Santa Barbara, won the sweepstake for lemons. Etiwanda, the district near here which won both prizes last year, took second in both today.

The judges who awarded the prizes were A. J. Cook, State Commissioner of Horticulture; B. A. Woodford of Claremont and W. L. Moulton of San Francisco.

The fortieth anniversary of the Washington navel orange industry in California will be celebrated Monday, and the orange show will close Wednesday. Millions of oranges and lemons are on display.

Steals Dahlia Bulbs From a Rival Grower

William M. Hollenbeck, Prominent Pacific Grove Resident, Convicted of Raiding Garden.

SALINAS, February 19.—William M. Hollenbeck of Pacific Grove was found guilty last night by a jury in the Superior Court, of stealing rare dahlia bulbs from the gardens of Lester E. Doolittle, a rival grower. Sentence will be given next Tuesday.

The arrest and conviction of Hollenbeck has been a mild sensation in Monterey county on account of the prominence of the defendant, he being one of Pacific Grove's most highly respected citizens for over twenty-five years. Hollenbeck's undoing was brought about by a thin trail of dirt dropping from the stolen bulbs, which led up hill and down dale from Doolittle's gardens to those of the defendant.

There was great rivalry between these two men in the culture and propagation of dahlias, and Doolittle had several rare varieties coveted by the defendant.

Royal Indian Maid in Today's Parade Will Lead Native Daughters' Column Honor for Princess Ah-Tra-Ah-Saun

THE PASSING AWAY OF A RUGGED PEOPLE.

PRINCESS AH-TRA-AH-SAUN, at top to the right, as she appears in the century-old dress of her royal Indian ancestors, the Klamaths. To the left are two poses, typical of the artistic Indian heads from life, photographed by Mrs. Emma B. Freeman, whose picture appears at the bottom. The Princess and the pictures will be a part of Humboldt county's Indian exhibit at the exposition.

SHERIFF KILLS MARSHAL.

LOCKHART (Tex.), February 19.—City Marshal John L. Smith of Lockhart was shot and killed today by Sheriff J. M. Franks. Two years ago Smith, who had been deputy Sheriff, made the race for Sheriff against Franks. Franks surrendered and was released under $3000 bond.

POLICEMEN IN NEW UNIFORMS.

ALAMEDA, February 19.—Members of the Alameda Police Department were inspected this afternoon by Police Commissioners Al Latham, W. H. L. Hynes and E. J. Bevan, the occasion being the christening of the new uniforms, which comprise blue suits with short coats and natty caps.

LAST OF ROYALTY OF THE KLAMATH TRIBE

She Is Now Graduate Nurse and Has Accepted Modern Ideas.

MARCHING at the head of the Native Daughters' column in this morning's exposition opening parade, keeping step to music that a few short years ago would have sounded in her ears as the weirdest of the weird, will be Princess Ah-tra-ah-saun, last of the royal lineage of the Klamath tribe of Indians.

Princess Ah-tra-ah-saun, known in civilized life as Miss Burtha M. Thompson, has an ancestry running back so far into the mists of time as to be—she expresses it naively—"as ancient as the world." She is to be a feature of Humboldt county's Indian exhibit at the exposition, forgetting for a time that the stamp of progress is upon her.

For, be it known, the Princess, as Miss Thompson, is a graduate nurse, having received her diploma from the City and County Hospital in 1911. Those traditions that came down from her noble ancestors she had somewhat relegated to the background of her life with her acceptance of twentieth century enlightenment. But for a few months at least she will renew her acquaintance with those things that surrounded her bringing up, to grace the exhibit of which Mrs. Emma B. Freeman is in charge.

IS LAST OF HER LINE.

Princess Ah-tra-ah-saun left the forests and mountains of Northern California but a few years ago, coming out into a world of wonders that she knew only by hearsay. Until she was past 12 years of age she never saw a white woman. Practically the only white man she had known was her father, whose name she assumed when she left her native haunts.

Being the last of her line, her mother being the only other surviving royal Klamath, the Princess is one of the sole two Klamaths to whom has come down all that mysterious lore of a mysterious tribe. Even she

(Continued on Page 2, Column 3)

VINCENT ASTOR'S AMBITION IS TO RAISE APPLES

Young Millionaire, Launching Plan to Have Largest Orchard in New York State, Orders 2100 Trees.

Special Dispatch to The Chronicle.

POUGHKEEPSIE (N. Y.), February 19.—Vincent Astor, in ordering 2100 trees today as a starter, has launched a plan to have the largest apple orchard in the State. The order was placed by a representative with a Maryland nursery concern. The trees are to be delivered at once. Among the varieties to be planted are 120 Northern Spies, 120 Rhode Island Greenings, 360 Baldwins, 930 Hubbardston Nonesuch, 320 Gravensteins and 200 Duchess of Oldenburgs. Astor's experimental farm at Ferncliff will hereafter be devoted to the cultivation of apples.

CHINA WORRIED BY DEMANDS OF THE JAPANESE

Lu-Cheng-Hsiang, Foreign Secretary, Would Discuss Note With Nipponese.

PEKING, February 19.—Lu-Cheng-Hsiang, the Chinese Foreign Minister, yesterday paid a visit to Eki Hioki, the Japanese Minister to China, and inquired whether the Minister was willing to discuss with him twelve of the demands Japan has made on China, which China has agreed to consider. It is stated in Chinese circles that Lu-Cheng-Hsiang took the initiative in the matter in order to refute accusations of the Japanese newspapers that the Chinese Government was delaying the negotiations.

According to information from Chinese sources, the Japanese Minister told Lu-Cheng-Hsiang that he was awaiting further instructions from Tokio. It is stated that the Chinese Government cannot accept even the twelve debatable demands unless they are materially modified.

The following is said to be a special article in the Japanese demands, the wording of which has disturbed officials:

"The Japanese Government and Chinese Government, with the object of effectively protecting the territorial integrity of China, agree to the following special article:

"The Chinese Government agrees that no island, port or harbor along the coast shall be ceded or leased to any third power."

The word "third," it is declared, was omitted from the Japanese communication to the powers. That the number of "forcible Japanese advisers in political, financial and military affairs" which Japan desires to place in China is not mentioned is said to be causing concern to the Chinese. This is the foremost question which the Chinese are said to have declined to discuss.

Kennedy Is Coming as General Freight Agent

Popular Hill Railroad Official to Represent Great Northern Steamship Line Here.

SEATTLE, February 19.—H. N. Kennedy, former general agent of the Northern Pacific Railroad in Seattle, has been appointed general freight agent of the Great Northern Steamship Company, with headquarters at San Francisco. Kennedy had been promoted to be general agent of the railroad company's freight department at Milwaukee, and notice of his new promotion was wired to him en route. He immediately started for San Francisco. The new post is the highest one Kennedy has held in twenty-five years of service for the Hill railroads.

Say "Bill," Was It You or Twin "Jim"?

NEVADA CITY, February 19.—William Allen, charged with battery in the District Court here, went free today because the witnesses were unable to say positively whether it was William or his twin brother, James Allen, who committed the offense. Although the prosecuting witness knows the brothers well, he was unable to swear which assaulted him.

DUKE OF MANCHESTER BETTER.

LONDON, February 19, 10:07 P. M.—The Duke of Manchester, who is suffering from pleurisy, was reported as slightly better tonight.

SUBMARINE WARFARE BEGUN BY GERMANS

Torpedo French Steamer Off Dieppe; Norwegian Craft Strikes Mine and Goes Down With All of Her Crew.

ANOTHER DAMAGED, BUT MAKES PORT

England Suspends Travel Between Its Coast and Continent; Enemy's Blockade Campaign Opens Seriously.

LONDON, February 20, 2:15 A. M.—The Norwegian steamer Nordkyn has been sunk through striking a mine near Bornholm island, in the Baltic sea, according to a dispatch from Copenhagen to the Central News. All of the crew were drowned.

LONDON, February 19, 11:30 P. M.—An official statement issued by the Admiralty tonight says the Norwegian tank steamship Belridge was struck by a torpedo fired by a German submarine today near Folkestone. Pieces of the torpedo, it is asserted, have been found on the ship.

DIEPPE (France), February 19, via Paris, 4 A. M.—A German submarine torpedoed this morning without warning the French steamer Dinorah, from Havre for Dunkirk, at a point sixteen miles off Dieppe.

The Dinorah did not sink, but was towed into Dieppe. No mention is made of the loss of any of the crew.

A plate on the portside of the steamer below the water line was stove in by the torpedo. Nevertheless, the Dinorah managed to keep afloat by hard pumping. Word of the occurrence was taken into Dieppe by fishing boats and assistance for the Dinorah was promptly sent out. She was towed into port and her cargo will be discharged here.

The presence of a German submarine off Cape Ailly was reported four days ago.

The daily steam traffic service between Dieppe and England has been suspended.

NORWEGIAN SHIP DAMAGED.

Vessel Bound for Amsterdam Hits Mine Off Dover.

DOVER (via London), February 19, 3:08 P. M.—The Norwegian tank steamer Belridge, which sailed from New Orleans January

(Continued on Page 2, Column 1.)

San Francisco Chronicle
LEADING NEWSPAPER of the PACIFIC COAST

FAIR
Weather Report
San Francisco, Oakland and Vicinity:
Fair weather Saturday; light west wind.
G. H. WILLSON, Forecaster.

VOL. CVI. SAN FRANCISCO, CAL., SATURDAY, MAY 8, 1915. XXXX NO. 113

HUNDREDS PERISH WHEN LUSITANIA IS TORPEDOED

Submarine Sinks Liner, With 2160 Persons, Off Irish Coast

CHINA YIELDS TO THE MODIFIED DEMANDS OF JAPAN; CLASH AVERTED

Pending Receipt of Reply to the Ultimatum the Tokio Government Rushes Military and Naval Preparations; Warships Sail on Secret Missions and Five Transports Depart From Hiroshima Troop Laden

DR. SUN YAT SEN PREPARES TO STRIKE AT YUAN SHI KAI BY REVOLT

Warfare in the Orient Probably Checked by the Decision of the Peking Officials to Submit Without Qualification to More Lenient Proposals Made by Threatening Nipponese at the Eleventh Hour

TOKIO, May 7, 9:45 P. M.—The Japanese await China's reply to the Japanese ultimatum. The Government, it is stated, has been deeply desirous of avoiding a rupture with China, which, it was admitted, would prove embarrassing.

Pending the receipt of China's reply, however, military and naval preparations are being pushed vigorously. Five transports laden with troops have sailed from Hiroshima in the direction of China, and numerous warships have left for secret destinations.

Waseda University has deprived Professor Ariga, Japanese adviser to President Yuan Shi Kai, of his professorship, and he has disappeared. Previously he had been denounced as a spy and the police were protecting him.

Dr. Sun Yat Sen, the first Provisional President of China, has been seen frequently in Tokio recently. The Yokohama Hochi declares that if war between Japan and China develops, the revolutionists in China who side with Dr. Sun are likely to seize the opportunity to strike against Yuan Shi Kai.

CHINESE LEAVING JAPAN.

Some Chinese are leaving Japan, while preparations are being made by many of those in Korea to depart from that country.

In presenting its ultimatum to China, Japan omitted from the present negotiations all items in group V of the amended list of demands, with the exception of the portion dealing with concessions in Fu-Kien, on which an agreement already has been reached. The demands in group V are reserved for future discussion.

Group V included the stipulations against which China raised the most vigorous objections. The decision of Japan to defer these matters is made known in an official communication of 2400 words, which was issued here today in regard to the Japanese ultimatum.

The principal provisions of Group V have to do with the appointment of Japanese military and political advisers for China and for Japanese supervision over the manufacture or purchase by China of munitions of war.

REPORT SATISFACTORY REPLY.

The Japanese Government has instructed Eki Hioki, Japanese Minister at Peking, to advise China to give due regard to Japan's wishes and to the conciliatory spirit of the Tokio Government, in view of which Japan believes China should give a satisfactory response.

The press generally deprecates the necessity of further concessions to China. Some newspapers express the fear that the impression will go abroad that the Elder Statesmen are still the power behind the throne.

WARSHIPS ARE PREPARED.

More than forty warships, including the battleship Hizen and the battle cruiser Kongo, are preparing at Sasebo for possible operations against China. A second squadron under Admiral Nawa has arrived and is hastily embarking supplies.

Rear-Admiral Kamimura's fleet, including the battle-ships Sagami and Suwo, has been ordered to the Gulf of Pechili, to be in readiness to take aboard Minister Hioki in case of necessity.

CHINA ACCEPTS DEMANDS.

PEKING, May 8, 3:05 A. M.—The attaches of the Foreign Office were at work all night translating Japan's ultimatum and drafting the terms of China's compliance with the demands, which were to be submitted to Yuan Shi Kai and the State Council this morning at 10 o'clock.

The reply will be delivered to M. Hioki, the Japanese Minister, this evening or Sunday morning. The Chinese will review China's case,

answer the charges contained in the ultimatum and accept the demands without qualification.

The Government expects no serious revolutionary outbreak from the people. The military leaders have assured Yuan Shi Kai that their support would continue.

ULTIMATUM PRESENTED.

PEKING, May 7, 6 P. M.—Eki Hioki, the Japanese Minister to China, went to the Chinese Foreign Office between 3 and 4 o'clock this afternoon and presented the Japanese ultimatum which insists that China accede to the demands presented by the Tokio Government.

Previous to this action on the part of the Minister, the secretary of the legation visited the Foreign Office and informed Vice-Minister Tsao Yulin that the ultimatum of the Japanese Government contained certain modifications of the twenty-four demands presented by Tokio.

GROUP FIVE SUSPENDED.

The handing in of the Japanese ultimatum to China has brought out knowledge of one point which has caused surprise here.

It seems that Japan, after insisting upon the acceptance of her demands, suspended in her ultimatum discussion of all of group 5, with the exception of the demand bearing upon Fukien province, to which the Chinese had agreed in their reply of last Saturday. The records now show that China, last evening, offered to concede to the Tokio Government more than the ultimatum now exacts from her.

It was learned today that in the course of Vice-Minister Tsao Yulin's visit to the Japanese legation yesterday evening he proposed verbally to meet the Japanese railroad demands, to grant school and hospital privileges, offered to bestow land without compensation upon Japanese, and proposed to withdraw China's three requirements regarding Shantung province, namely, the return to the status quo before the war, China's participation in the peace conference and compensation for damages in the Kiao-Chow campaign.

CHINA'S FINAL PROPOSALS.

In its final Chinese proposals, therefore, refused only to authorize Japan to supply half the arms used by China; to participate in the conduct of Chinese arsenals; to appoint Japanese advisers to China, and to preach Buddhism in the republic.

The Chinese dislike the requirement insisted upon by Japan that China recognize Tokio's right to reopen these questions at a future date, but they will accept these features unless the few irreconcilables in the councils of President Yuan Shi Kai

(Continued on Page 2, Column 3.)

THE swift Cunard liner Lusitania, which was torpedoed by a German submarine off Old Head of Kinsale on the Coast of Ireland, and which sank soon after. Most of the 1251 passengers on board escaped in small boats. Among the passengers were Alfred G. Vanderbilt, Elbert Hubbard and many other prominent Americans. The sinking of this favorite British passenger steamer, following the German warning printed in the leading American cities just a week ago, created a profound impression throughout this country.

LOSS OF LIFE IS ESTIMATED TO BE MORE THAN 1500

Rescue Steamers Landing Dead and Survivors, Many of the Latter Wounded, at Various Points in Ireland; List of Saved Not Known Until Today, Says Admiralty

TWO TORPEDOES STRIKE SHIP, CAUSING EXPLOSION

Deadly Missiles Reported to Have Been Launched Without Warning While Passengers Were at Lunch; Craft Goes Down in 30 Minutes; Members of Crew Tell of Attack

LONDON, May 8, 5:58 A. M.—Signals have been received at Queenstown that an armed trawler and two fishing trawlers are bringing in 100 more bodies. The Cunard Line agent stated that the total number of persons aboard the Lusitania was 2160. The number of known survivors is 658. This would make the list of dead and missing 1502.

WASHINGTON, May 8.—A dispatch to the State Department from American Consul Lauriat at Queenstown stated that the total number of survivors is 634.

The consul's latest message added the names of four Americans saved to those mentioned in his previous dispatch, making a total of 51 Americans saved.

QUEENSTOWN, May 8.—Survivors of the Lusitania, who have arrived here, estimate that only about 650 of those aboard the steamer were saved, and only a small proportion of those rescued were saloon passengers.

Officials of the Cunard line are attempting to prepare a list of the saved, but their task has been rendered extremely difficult by the indiscribable confusion which prevails. The names of those landed at Kinsale and Clonakilty are not yet available here.

Four torpedoes were fired at the Lusitania, her officers say, but two of them missed. The steamer was flying the British flag when she was struck.

LONDON, May 8, 5:55 A. M.—A statement issued by the British Admiralty says the total number of survivors of the Lusitania is 658. It is believed that only a few first-class passengers were saved, as they thought the ship would remain afloat and made little effort to escape.

LONDON, May 8.—The Cunard liner Lusitania, which sailed out of New York last Saturday with more than 2000 persons aboard, lies at the bottom of the ocean off the Irish coast. She was sunk by a German submarine, which sent two torpedoes crashing into her side, while the passengers, seemingly con-

(Continued on Page 4, Column 1.)

Ammunition Aboard Lusitania
War Munitions Worth $200,000

Special Dispatch to The Chronicle.

NEW YORK, May 7.—One of the items of the Lusitania's cargo was ammunition, valued at $200,024. The ship carried 5471 cases of cartridges and ammunition, according to the ship's manifest. Such a passenger ship, it was explained, would not carry high explosives, for those articles are shipped on the British cargo ships.

The Lusitania had a cargo of 1200 tons, which is practically all she could carry. Its value was put at $850,000. Included in her manifest are the following items:

Sheet brass—260,000 pounds, value $49,565.
Copper—11,762 pounds, value $20,053.
Copper wire—58,465 pounds, value $11,800.
Three hundred and forty-nine packages of furs; value $119,220.
Military goods, 189 packages, value $66,221 00.
Cases of leather, value $31,317.
Three hundred and forty-two thousand one hundred and sixty-five pounds of beef.

GRANDSON BORN TO MILLIONAIRE COPPER KING

New Arrival Is at Home of Mr. and Mrs. Charles W. Clark in San Mateo.

A son was born yesterday to Mr. and Mrs. Charles W. Clark at their country home, El Palomar, in San Mateo county.

When William Andrew Clark III was born twelve years ago, his grandfather, Senator William A. Clark of Montana, announced that a check for $1,000,000 had been placed to the credit of his grandson. That sum is said to have increased until today it exceeds $2,000,000. The boy is now on his way across the continent unaccompanied, and is expected to arrive in San Francisco the latter part of next week. He will be taken at once to the home of his new cousin in San Mateo.

The name of the new grandson of the millionaire has not been decided upon, as it is the wish of the parents to consult the grandfather on that subject. This is the fourth child born to Mr. and Mrs. Clark, the other three being daughters. Mrs. Clark before her marriage was Miss Celia Tobin.

BURGLARS STEAL FURS.

Complaint was made to the police yesterday by Mrs. John Briscoe, 759 Page street, that burglars had entered her home and stolen silverware and furs valued at $125.

Mrs. Vanderbilt Says Husband Is Not Lost

Wife of Noted Lusitania Passenger Still Hopes That He Has Been Saved.

Special Dispatch to The Chronicle.

NEW YORK, May 7.—Mrs. Alfred Gwynn Vanderbilt refused to believe that her husband had been lost with the Lusitania, and after the first shock of the news made every effort to secure tidings of him by telephone from the Hotel Vanderbilt. Late tonight she had heard nothing.

"I will not believe Alfred is drowned," she said to friends. "None of the reports thus far is conclusive, and until absolutely reliable information comes to the contrary I shall believe he is safe."

Mrs. Vanderbilt heard of the sinking of the Lusitania as she was arising from a luncheon given by Mrs. Alexander D. B. Pratt at the Ritz-Carlton. She telephoned Frank Crocker, her husband's private secretary, and arranged to have the press bulletins sent her every few minutes.

LONDON, May 7.—Messages from Queenstown and Cork received by way of Dublin say that Alfred G. Vanderbilt was lost. One dispatch says both Vanderbilts were lost, but Alfred G. Vanderbilt is the only one of that name on the passenger list.

Kills Girl in Taxi and Then Himself

BALTIMORE (Md.), May 7.—A man believed to be Dr. C. V. Drien of the medical corps of the United States Navy late tonight shot and killed Miss Grace Eichorn of this city, in a taxicab. He then killed himself. Jealousy is given as the motive.

CHAUFFEUR ROBBED BY TRIO AFTER A LONG RIDE

Pay for San Jose Trip in Advance, but Get Fare and More.

Engaged to transport two men and a woman, strangers to him, to San Jose and return yesterday afternoon, then to be robbed by the trio of all his money after the journey had fairly begun, was the experience of Edwin A. Seely, 609 Ashbury street, a jitney bus driver, as related by him to the San Francisco police last night.

Seely says that he was accosted by the trio at Sixth and Market streets, when one of the men asked the price of transportation to and from San Jose. Seely quoted them $15 for the round trip.

"All right," said the man, "take us. Here's $20, and keep the change."

The man who did the bargaining, and whom the others called "Fred," sat with Seely. The other man and the woman, addressed as "Grace," occupied the rear seat. At a point a mile this side of Millbrae "Fred" kicked the battery switch, which turned it off and "killed" Seely's engine.

While Seely was on the ground cranking his car, the man in the front seat said: "I guess we've gone far enough. Give us back our money."

Seely said something about having spent part of it before leaving the city, whereupon "Fred" engaged him in a fight, the other man aiding, and the two took all the chauffeur had, $37 10.

"Now get in and beat it," threatened one of the men, "and don't stop until you're out of sight or I'll shoot you dead."

Seely drove hurriedly back to the city and the trio started to walk in the opposite direction.

Flying Boat Owned by Astor Wrecked

Special Dispatch to The Chronicle.

MARBLEHEAD (Mass.), May 7.—Vincent Astor's flying boat, which was being given its final tests before shipment to New York, was wrecked today and Aviator Clifford Webster received a broken left wrist and cuts when the machine fell on the rocks on the harbor side of the causeway.

Daughter of Wealthy Chicago Man Killed

Miss Marion Farwell Falls to Her Death From Bridge on Father's Estate.

CHICAGO, May 7.—The body of Miss Marion Farwell was found yesterday at the bottom of a deep ravine which marked the boundary of the Lake Forest estate of her father, Francis Farwell, of the John V. Farwell Dry Goods Company.

The young woman had been in ill health and only Wednesday returned home from Tryon, S. C., where she had spent the winter. A trained nurse who had been in attendance on the young woman missed her and the search which was instituted resulted in the finding of the body.

Miss Farwell was engaged to be married to Reginald Foster of Boston, and their wedding, which was to have taken place May 19th, had been postponed because of ill health.

A coroner's jury, which held an inquest last night returned a verdict that Miss Farwell left her home while depressed, following a serious illness, and fell from a bridge near her home.

Alameda Man Was One of the Drowned

Special Dispatch to The Chronicle.

REDDING, May 7.—The body found in Trinity river in Hoopa Indian reservation has been identified as that of Arthur C. Hussey of Alameda, who, with Curtis Louk of Weaverville, was drowned at Taylor's flat, sixty miles up stream in Trinity county April 2d. At first the body was reported to be Louk's. The inquest settled it that the body was Hussey's. It was in a good state of preservation, and has been shipped to relatives in Toledo, Ohio. Hussey, a dredger worker, left a wife and one child in Alameda.

Excursionists Arrive Via the Celilo Canal

ASTORIA, May 7.—The trip from Lewiston, Idaho, of the fleet celebrating the completion of the Celilo canal ended here today with the arrival on steamers of more than 200 excursionists, including Governors, Senators, and Representatives from three Northwestern States. Tomorrow the six-day festivities will conclude with exercises ashore, and a brief cruise upon the Pacific ocean. As a feature of the celebration, the annual convention of the Columbia Waterways Association opened tonight. Governor Withycombe of Oregon and Governor Lister of Washington spoke.

"Wild Bill's" Wife Is Granted Divorce

Manager Donovan of New York Americans Loses Spouse Because of Failure to Provide.

RENO (Nev.), May 7.—Helen M. Donovan, wife of W. E. (Wild Bill) Donovan, manager of the New York Americans, was today granted a decree of divorce in the District Court. Failure to provide since September, 1913, was alleged in the complaint. Donovan did not contest the suit. The couple were married at Windsor, Ontario, March 4, 1903. Before her marriage Mrs. Donovan was Miss Nellie Stephen of Windsor. She was recently left a considerable estate through the death of her mother.

San Francisco Chronicle
LEADING NEWSPAPER of the PACIFIC COAST

Weather Report.
San Francisco, Oakland and Vicinity: Fair Friday, continued warm; light northerly wind.
T. R. REED, Forecaster.

FOUNDED 1865 SAN FRANCISCO, CAL., FRIDAY, MARCH 10, 1916 VOL. CVIII, NO. 55

U. S. TROOPERS RETURN TO BORDER AFTER CHASING VILLA INTO MEXICO

Turks to Fight on the West Front

VAUX IS SCENE OF BLOODY BATTLE

Germans Repulsed in Series of Desperate Attacks, Being Mowed Down by French Curtain of Fire

TEUTON TRENCHES IN ALSACE ARE CAPTURED

Paris Claims the Enemy Has Been Pushed Back at Several Points on the Line Around the Verdun Fortress

ODESSA (via London), March 9.—It is reported here that Germany has given formal assurance to Turkey that she will not make a peace without compensation to Turkey, and that Turkey has consented to send Turkish troops to assist the Germans on the western front. Several contingents have already been withdrawn from Asia Minor to Constantinople.

LONDON, March 9.—Fighting between the French and the Germans northwest and north of Verdun has in nowise slackened. Particularly violent have been the attacks of the Germans to the north of Verdun, around Douaumont, the village of Vaux and Fort Vaux, but according to Paris they went for naught.

The Germans were thrown in solid formation against trenches of the French bordering the foot of the ridge dominating Fort Vaux, which the latest German official report said the Germans had captured, but the French drove back the attacking forces with "enormous losses."

Northeast of the fort the Germans essayed an assault against the village of Vaux, from which they previously had been driven by the French, but here also they were repulsed with heavy casualties, says the Paris statement.

DRIVE GERMANS FROM WOOD

To the west of the Meuse, midway between Bethincourt and the river, the French have continued on the offensive in the Corbeaux Wood, and are officially reported to have driven the Germans from almost all of that point salient.

The French also claim the capture of a section of German trenches in Alsace.

In the eastern theater the Russians at various points have taken the offensive against German advanced positions, but Berlin declares they have nowhere met with success.

The Russians on the Black sea coast continue to press on toward Turkey's principal port, Trebizond, and also are making progress against the Ottoman positions in the Persia sector.

The Russian Foreign Office denies that Turkey has made any peace proposals.

Germany has declared war on Por-

(Continued on Page 6, Column 4.)

War With Portugal Declared

Germany Breaks With Lisbon Government; Hands Minister His Passports

Germans Prepare Ships for Battle In the North Sea

By ARTHUR S. DRAPER
London Correspondent of The Chronicle
By Special Cable

LONDON, March 10.—Indications that the German fleet is about to put to sea and the long-expected gigantic battle with the British fleet will shortly take place, are contained in a Rotterdam dispatch to the Daily Mail.

Unwonted activity has been shown by the German navy, the dispatch states, and already large forces of marines have been sent from Hamburg and Bremen, where they have been stationed, to the Kiel canal.

The Germans have recently constructed a large number of submarines, which each requires a crew of from forty-five to fifty men to operate. Great difficulty is being experienced by the German Admiralty in getting trained men to man them. The loss of a large number of U boats has left the Germans with comparatively few trained men capable of putting to sea in a submarine.

BERLIN, March 9 (by wireless to Sayville)—Germany declared war on Portugal at 3:30 o'clock yesterday afternoon, and handed his passports to the Portuguese Minister.

"The German Government therefore considers itself from this time in war with the Portuguese Government," is the conclusion of a declaration handed today by the German Minister at Lisbon to the Portuguese Government and in Berlin to the Portuguese Minister, a semi-official Overseas News Agency announcement states.

"The German declaration," says the News Agency, "emphasized the fact that this step was made necessary by the recent illegal seizures of German ships in Portuguese ports, which is the gravest sort of breach of neutrality and of special treaties. Germany, therefore, is obliged to give up her former attitude of forbearance, which she has maintained because of Portugal's awkward situation.

CITES MANY BREACHES

"The declaration enumerates a long series of breaches of neutrality by the Portuguese Government, such as the permission of free passage to English troops through the colony of Mozambique; the permission given to English men-of-war to use Portuguese ports for a time exceeding that given by neutrals; the permission given the English navy to use Madeira as a naval base; actual engagements between Portuguese and German troops on the frontier of German Southwest Africa and Angola; frequent insults to the German nation by members of the Portuguese Parliament, who never were reprimanded.

"The declaration further points out that the seizure of German ships in neutral Portuguese ports on February 23d was an act against the law and

(Continued on Page 6, Column 1.)

COMPROMISE IS OFFERED TO EASTERN WINE MEN

California Producers Will Forego Fight on Claims of Ohio and Other Producers

IS EFFORT TO REDUCE EXCESSIVE WAR TAX

Willing to Admit That U. S. Government Can Declare Pure Wine Can Be Made With Grain and Grapes

In an effort to reduce the excessive war tax on the wine industry which has so seriously crippled both the production and consumption of California wines, the State Viticultural Commission yesterday in special session here offered to compromise with the Eastern wine men—all the issues over which the two groups have struggled during the past year or so.

The meeting was held at the Palace Hotel, and in addition to the members of the Commission, some of the biggest wine grape growers in the State were in attendance. The action of the Commission had the united support of all those present.

CONGRESSMEN INSTRUCTED

In a telegram to the California delegation in Congress the members were instructed to accept the recommendation of the Treasury Department if no better tax rate and alcohol percentage rate can be secured.

The message further set forth that the California wine men would agree not to oppose the new definition of the proposed by the Ohio wine men, if the Government's sanction can be obtained. In part, the instructions read:

"We agree not to fight the use of grain spirits in fortification, if Administration is willing to pass a law agreeing that the United States Government can go to the extreme in declaring by statute that pure wine can be made by a combination of grain and grapes in manufacture.

FOREGO THE FIGHT

"In other words, in order to get a reduction of the tax so we may make our normal production, we forego fighting Eastern contentions. If it could be brought about, we would like to simplify the tax schedule so as to make it 2 cents on dry and 12 and 7 cents on sweets to 20 with higher alcohol than that taxed at commercial brandy rate."

The present emergency revenue tax on brandy used in fortification of sweet wines is 55 cents. In addition all wines are subjected to a stamp tax of 8 cents a gallon. A month ago Congressman Kent introduced a relief measure proposing the abatement entirely of the fortifying tax and the stamp tax. In lieu of these the bill provided for a revenue on a measure basis, amounting to 2 cents a gallon wines, up to 20 per cent.

The Treasury Department, however, recommended to the Ways and Means Committee a schedule running from 2 cents a gallon on wines of 10 per cent alcohol up to 20 cents a gallon on dry wines and 6 cents on sweet wines, up to 20 per cent.

The Ohio and Missouri wine makers have proposed an amendment to this, allowing them to use extensively water and sugar and the use of grain spirits in the fortification of their wines.

Famous Inventor Has Passed Away

Julien P. Fries Made First Telegraph Key and Sounder

Special Dispatch to The Chronicle.

BALTIMORE, March 9.—Julien P. Fries, leading manufacturer of meteorological instruments, has died at the Church Home Infirmary. He was with the General Electric Company for a number of years, and made the first key and sounder for telegraph service for the company. He invented a musical telephone, a device now out of existence. He was a pioneer in the manufacture of heliograph signal apparatus used by the Government before electricity came into use. He worked with Professor Henry A. Rowland on the Rowland multiplex telegraph and aided in perfecting the Mergenthaler linotype machine.

NATION BACK OF COLONEL SLOCUM ON VILLA'S TRAIL

Lansing Informs Carranza He Hopes There Will Be No Objection to Pursuit and Punishment of Marauding Bandits

WASHINGTON, March 9.—Washington stands squarely behind Colonel Slocum in sending his cavalrymen into Mexico in pursuit of Francisco Villa and his band of outlaws who raided Columbus, N. M., today, murdering American soldiers and citizens and firing the town.

Tonight Secretary Lansing informed the de facto government of Mexico through Eliseo Arredondo, its Ambassador designate here, that he trusted no objection would be made to the action of the American troops, they having followed what is known in military circles as a "hot trail." No orders have been issued for the return of the soldiers, and it is not probable any will be issued for the present.

SHOCK FOLLOWED BY OFFICIAL SATISFACTION

Shocked indignation occasioned by news of Villa's outrage was quickly succeeded by undisguised satisfaction in official and Congressional circles over the knowledge that after three years of patient forbearance United States troops actually were on Mexican soil to avenge the death of their comrades and bring to justice the outlaws whose depredations have terrorized Americans on both sides of the border.

Reports that the American troopers were in action tonight [illegible] miles south of the border against a much larger force of bandits were heard with anxious interest in official circles.

Five troops of cavalry crossed the border early in the day. At a late hour tonight it was not known officially just where they were or just what account they had given of themselves.

While no formal word of the policy of the administration was given out, it was reliably stated that the Army would be given free rein to catch the bandits if possible. It was not considered in Administration circles that Colonel Slocum's act in any sense constituted an invasions of Mexico, a policy which the Administration has opposed in the past and will continue to oppose.

(Continued on Page 2, Column 1)

TERRIFIC BATTLE FOR CAURES WOOD

Chasseurs of France, Led by Heroic Colonel, Show Unyielding Gallantry as Ring of German Infantry Closes In

PARIS, March 9, 1 P. M.—An officer who has returned from the Verdun front gave the following description today of the battle for possession of Caures wood:

"The affair of the Caures wood was one of the most dramatic and most glorious episodes of the battle of Verdun. The chasseurs who were charged with defending this part of the sector were under the orders of Lieutenant-Colonel Driant. They have added a magnificent page to contemporary history by their unyielding gallantry.

"It was 7:15 in the morning of February 20th when the Germans commenced preparations for their attack. We had then been holding the trenches for four days, and our chief, Lieutenant-Colonel Driant, was making a tour of inspection. We had one battalion on the firing line and another held in reserve at the Moronat farm.

STORM OF IRON BEGINS

"Everybody was immediately on the alert. The bombardment began with an unusual violence and our listening posts, according to orders, fell back on the first line, where we awaited the attack.

"A storm of iron began to pass over. It was in fact, more than a storm—it was a deluge. Our shelters, even the best constructed, were demolished. About 11 o'clock the post at which I was was wiped out under the hail of shells, and fourteen chasseurs and one officer were buried in the debris. However, our men did not hesitate, but pressed forward to the aid of their wounded comrades as if it was simply a question of some common accident. Sergeant Caplain, with some assistance, rescued nine victims, and each one courageously prepared again to face the enemy. Under the fire of the enemy the soldiers labored to reinforce our fortifications in the wood.

SHELTERS ALL DEMOLISHED

"About 3 o'clock the effects of the bombardment were tremendous. There did not remain a single shelter worthy of the name. The officer next in command to Lieutenant-Colonel Driant was seriously wounded, and many of our chasseurs also were stricken.

"About 5 o'clock the enemy's artillery slackened its fire and we no longer suffered so much. The reason of this was that the Germans were about to hurl themselves on Haumont.

"The front ranks of the enemy were dressed in capes somewhat resembling ours and they wore armlets similar to those on our men. This ruse was quickly seen through and they received a warm welcome. However, at the end of a certain time they were able to penetrate our first-line trenches and establish themselves there. Counter attacks were made by us during the whole night, and after a hot grenade fighting our positions were practically maintained.

COURIERS NEVER RETURN

"On the 22d the bombardment was resumed with the greatest violence. Our trenches, hammered by shells, were rapidly leveled, the communicating trenches were destroyed and even the wood itself was mowed down in large spaces. However, our chasseurs maintained the same impassability.

"Toward midday we perceived large parties of the enemy, who, after having advanced toward the wood of Haumont, turned toward the Caures wood with the intention of taking us in the rear. All our telephonic communications had been destroyed the evening before, and we were no longer able to communicate with the main body of our troops except by couriers. Many volunteered for this service, but none of them ever returned. The devotion of the chasseurs was inexhaustible in these critical circumstances.

TERRIFIC INFANTRY ATTACK

"The German attack increased in violence. A lieutenant sprang to the head of his company to repel the enemy. He was wounded in the hand immediately. He wrapped it in his handkerchief and sprang forward again, crying, 'Forward.' A second bullet cut the word short in his mouth. As he fell to the ground, another officer leaped automatically forward to take his place. He had only gone a few yards when a bullet pierced his throat. The enemy, with very superior forces to ours, including an entire new brigade, swept down upon us. From the evening before until the morning our two battalions had suffered under a most murderous fire.

The enemy was endeavoring to turn both our flanks, and we fought

(Continued on Page 2, Column 6)

Wires for Cavalry to Hunt Villa

Colonel Slocum in His Report to Funston Describes Fight

SAN ANTONIO (Tex.), March 9.—Major Frank Tompkins, commanding the detachment of American troops which pursued General Villa and his bandits into Mexico after the attack early today on Columbus, N. M., has returned to the border, after engaging in three running fights with the Mexicans, who finally made a stand which stopped the advance of the American soldiers. This information was conveyed tonight to Major-General Frederick Funston, commanding the Southern Department, United States Army, in an official report on the situation from Colonel H. J. Slocum, in command at Columbus.

"All peaceful as a summer morning at this writing," was the way Colonel Slocum described the situation in Columbus tonight.

Following is the text of the report as given out by General Funston at Fort Sam Houston:

"When Villa troops fell back before daylight we followed them with a dismounted line. At the same time I sent Major Tompkins with three troops mounted to attack. Tompkins followed them for about five miles into Mexico, having three running fights with them, and they finally made a stand with their entire force and stopped Tompkins' advance, and he returned here.

CORPORAL KILLED IN PURSUIT

"We had one corporal killed in the pursuit. The Mexicans dropped considerable material and loot that they had gotten in town. I am reliably informed that it was Villa who made the attack with 1500 men, leaving about 1000 on the river east of Boca Grande. From his spies in Columbus he was informed that there was but four troops here with three machine guns. [illegible] he took this opportunity to attack.

"He intended capturing the town, looting the bank and killing all Americans. Our casualties were five wounded, seven killed. Lieutenant Benson was shot in the arm. Captain Williams, adjutant, received a slight wound in the hand. Eight civilians were killed in the town, including one woman. We have already buried twenty-seven Mexican soldiers, most of them killed in the camp, some near the bank, and there are many other dead Mexicans on Villa's line of retreat, about one mile west, not yet collected.

ATTACK A FAILURE

"Mexican troops under Villa's personal command and by his orders made the charge through the camp. Our troops turned out quickly and drove the Mexicans out, killing seventeen in or about the camp. About ten or twelve Mexicans were killed in the

(Continued on Page 2, Column 3)

WOMEN KILLED BY OUTLAW BAND IN NEW MEXICO RAID

Sixteen American Citizens Slaughtered in Ear[illegible] Dawn as They Seek Safety From Band[illegible] Torch Applied to Homes and Business Hous[illegible] by Incendiary Bands Told Off by Mexica[illegible] Ravisher; Two Perish in Hotel Firetr[illegible]

Wives of Army Officers Have Narrow Escap[illegible] From Raiders' Bullets; Seven Troop[illegible] of Thirteenth Cavalry Killed in Rep[illegible] ing the Attack; Scores of Bandits Slain [illegible] Steady Return Fire; Burn Raided Vi[illegible]

COLUMBUS (N. M.), March 9.—Francisco Villa, out[illegible] Mexican bandit, raided United States territory today. With [illegible] men he attacked Columbus, killed at least sixteen Americans [illegible] fired many buildings before he was driven back across the [illegible] national border.

Approximately 250 troopers under Majors Frank Tomp[illegible] and H. L. Lindsley, who pursued the Villa bandits to a p[illegible] fifteen miles south of the border were halted when Villa's f[illegible] outnumbering them ten to one, made a stand at the po[illegible] guarded by a force of 1000 bandits left in reserve.

CIVILANS AND SOLDIERS, ON ALERT, GUARD BORD[illegible]

American cavalry border patrols, New Mexico militia[illegible] cowboys and civilians were alert tonight against another [illegible] attack by Francisco Villa's Mexican bandits. Heavy guard[illegible] trolled Columbus and vicinity.

The raid to American territory proved costly to the b[illegible] chieftain. The bodies of twenty-seven Mexican bandits, inclu[illegible] Pablo Lopez, second in command, had been gathered and bu[illegible] before night, and troopers reported an undetermined number [illegible] dead still lying in the brush and along the line of flight.

Led to the attack under the slogan, "Death to the Am[illegible] cans," Villa's followers fought with desperation. Just be[illegible] dawn they crept along ditches skirting the United States cav[illegible] camp and rushed the sleeping town, firing heavily.

The first volley brought American troopers into al[illegible] instant action. While a portion of the raiders engaged the [illegible] alrymen, others detailed by the bandit chieftain began apply[illegible] the torch and shooting American civilians who ventured from [illegible] buildings. Lights in homes and public buildings immed[illegible] became targets for snipers posted at Villa's direction. O[illegible] bandits creeping close to American homes enticed a number [illegible] civilians into the open with English-spoken invitations. A [illegible] ber of fatalities are attributed to [illegible] ruse.

Stores were looted, oil was p[illegible] upon frame structures and the [illegible] applied by still other bandits. [illegible] postoffice was raided, furniture [illegible] smashed, but the looters secured [illegible] one small registered package.

Many civilians barricaded [illegible] selves in their homes and fired at [illegible]

(Continued on Page 2, Column [illegible])

Two Plucky Boys Overtake and Stop Runaway Car Laden With Dynamite

Run Race With Engine in Automobile and Reach It in Time to Stop Its Wild Flight as It Bumped Along Following Passenger Train

Special Dispatch to The Chronicle

DRYAD (Wash.), March 9. — Two boys in an automobile after a race through the railroad yards here Tuesday night captured and stopped a runaway switch engine that was bumping a carload of dynamite on to the main track following a passenger train just leaving Doty. The train was sidetracked at Littell and derailing crews were sent out to catch the runaway.

Leaping from the automobile, one of the boys jumped into the cab of the engine and stopped its flight through the yards just before it reached the derailing point. Clyde Smothers and Roy Eubanks were in the machine.

The engine belonged to the Doty Lumber and Shingle Company. As it progressed through the yards it picked up an empty stock car and proceeded on to the main line of the Northern Pacific. The agent at Dryad was instructed to derail it, but decided to let it pass through the town, fearing a disastrous explosion. Both cars were badly damaged when the engine was stopped, and the explosive was scattered about the loaded car.

Hillsborough to Hold an Election To Annex the A. M. Easton Estate

Millionaire Will Be Provided With a Polling Place in Which to Cast Lone Vote

HILLSBOROUGH, March 9.—The mountain didn't come to Mahomet, but Hillsborough is going to come to Ansel M. Easton, millionaire landowner, after whom the little town of Easton, just north of Burlingame, is named.

In order that Easton and his extensive chattels may be part and parcel of the exclusive suburban haven de luxe, Hillsborough has planned to annex the seventy-acre estate of its wealthy neighbor.

To accomplish this feat the Town Trustees today called a special election for April 10th.

Easton will not only go Mahomet one better, but he will also possess the distinction of having a special polling place provided for him, in which he will be the one lone voter. As it is necessary, according to the law of the county, for both annexors and annexed to pass on the proposition, and as Easton is the only one involved on his side of the line, he will cast a lone ballot.

His polling place will be his residence and it will, as the law makes necessary, be kept open from daylight to sunset, with election officers present.

San Francisco Chronicle
LEADING NEWSPAPER of the PACIFIC COAST

Weather Report
San Francisco, Oakland and Vicinity: Fair Saturday, continued warm; light southerly wind.
T. R. REED, Forecaster.

FOUNDED 1865 SAN FRANCISCO, CAL., SATURDAY, MARCH 11, 1916 xxx VOL. CVIII, NO. 56

PRESIDENT ORDERS PERSHING TO INVADE MEXICO

TOLL IS HEAVY AS FOREST IS TAKEN

Corbeaux Wood Is Scene of Severe Fighting When the Teutons Advance With Huge Force Against Defenders

ATTACKS AT VAUX REPULSED BY FRENCH

Great Activity of Artillery Marks Big Battle Which Takes Place on West Bank of the River Meuse

PARIS, March 10.—The Germans in infantry attacks, launched with a huge force but with losses described as beyond all proportions to the objective they sought, have occupied a part of the Corbeaux wood, to the west of the Meuse and northwest of Verdun, according to the French official communication issued tonight.

German attacks to the west of the village of Douaumont and against the village of Vaux were put down by the French.

Intense Fighting Goes on at Verdun

LONDON, March 10.—Throwing large masses of infantry against the French in the Corbeaux to the northwest of Verdun, the Germans after several attacks in which they are declared by Paris to have suffered large casualties, have retaken part of the wood from which the French had previously ejected them.

The entire region about Verdun continues the scene of intense operations. West of Douaumont and the sector embracing the village of Vaux have been points against which the Germans have launched vicious infantry attacks, but at both places their efforts to advance broke down under the heavy fire of the French, according to Paris.

Berlin, however, counters this assertion by announcing the taking of a ridge west of Douaumont by the Germans and says also that the Germans have succeeded in pushing forward their line through the wooded sector southeast of Damloup, which lies a short distance from Fort Vaux.

The announcement is made in the German official statement that the French have succeeded in gaining a firm foothold in Fort Vaux. Paris had previously categorically denied that the Germans had captured either the fort or the village of Vaux.

East and southeast of Verdun, over a front of about seven and a half miles the Germans have been directing a heavy bombardment on the towns of Eix, Moulainville, Villers-Sous-Bonchamp and Bonzee with the

(Continued on Page 6, Column 3.)

Siege at Verdun Is At Climax

Assault by Germans Is Called Failure After Three Weeks of Slaughter

By ARTHUR S. DRAPER
London Correspondent of The Chronicle

By Special Cable

LONDON, March 11.—The climax of the German assault upon Verdun is now thought to have been reached, and the position, for possession of which a bloody three weeks' battle has been waged, remains in the hands of the French.

What was undoubtedly the last bitter effort of the Germans was made yesterday afternoon, according to a message to the Times, when for two hours on a front of more than two miles around the fort at Vaux, German guns poured 80,000 shells on the French positions.

When the frightful bombardment ceased the German troops charged in columns of four. The resistance from the French was as unexpected as it was effective, and as the Germans came on under the direct fire of the defenders' guns they were mowed down with perfect accuracy.

The German losses are reported as enormous.

That there is no longer doubt that Roumania is about to join with the allies is indicated in a dispatch which the Geneva correspondent of the Daily Express sends from the Cologne Gazette. The Roumanian army, it is declared, is mobilized and in condition to enter the war at a moment's notice. Ready to take the field are from 400,000 to 450,000 men, with 600 modern guns, 18,000 cavalry, and 300 machine guns. The attitude of Roumania is declared unmistakable.

For the time being the German people have ceased to implore divine vengeance upon England, and the cry last night in Berlin was "Gott strafe Portugal." A message in the Daily Express from The Hague states that the German Minister at Lisbon has received instructions to demand his passport at once, while a request to the allied governments asking his safe conduct back to Germany has been made through the American Embassy at the Portuguese capital.

Fairbanks Far Ahead In Indiana Primaries

Republican Has 17,282 Votes More Than President Wilson

INDIANAPOLIS, March 10.—Practically complete returns from Tuesday's primary, tabulated here unofficially today, shows that former Vice-President Charles W. Fairbanks, candidate for the Republican nomination for President, received 17,282 votes more than were cast for President Woodrow Wilson, candidate for renomination on the Democratic ticket. Fairbanks received a total of 176,129 votes to Wilson's 158,847.

Willis Booth Will Be Candidate for Senate

Los Angeles Republican Will Seek Job of U. S. Senator Works

WASHINGTON, March 10.—Willis Booth, of Los Angeles, who is here conferring with Republican leaders, will be a candidate for the United States Senate, to succeed Senator Works in 1917. Booth has authorized friends here to state that when he returns to California in a few days he will make formal announcement of his candidacy.

CRISIS IN WESTERN PACIFIC WRANGLE

U. S. District Judge Van Fleet Ordered Before Court of Appeals to Explain the Blocking of Foreclosure Sale

WRIT OF MANDATE TO BE ARGUED THURSDAY

Reorganization Committee Is Hopeful of Saving Plan and $20,000,000 Underwriting Pact, Which Expires July 15th

United States District Judge Van Fleet was ordered yesterday by the Circuit Court of Appeals to appear before that tribunal Thursday and explain why he does not allow the foreclosure sale of the Western Pacific to proceed in accordance with the wishes of the bondholders' reorganization committee and the Equitable Trust Company, the trustee under the first mortgage issue.

This order of the appellate court was issued on the request of Jared How, attorney for the Equitable Trust, who wants the Circuit Court of Appeals to mandamus Judge Van Fleet to issue the order for the sale of the Western Pacific at once, so that the reorganization plan, with its $20,000,000 underwriting contract, expiring on July 15th, may not fall flat.

LOOK FOR MOTIVES

General interest, which was aroused by the peculiar circumstances surrounding the unforeseen delay in the consummation of the reorganization plan, continues to express itself in the form of surmises at the motives behind the opposition to the reorganization under the plan already approved by a large proportion of the bondholders.

John Drum's announcement that he is about to bring forth an entirely new scheme of reorganization for the Western Pacific has also provoked surprise, and the majority bondholders say they are unable to understand how it would be possible for John Drum to do the reorganizing while his brother, Frank Drum, is one of the receivers appointed by Judge Van Fleet.

However, the bondholders' committee still expresses itself as believing the obstacles in the path of a more speedy reorganization, and the consummation of the underwriting agreement already secured, may yet be overcome, and in this particular the interest centers in the hearing before the United States Circuit Court of Appeals on Thursday.

RESENT BOWIE'S APPEARANCE

Judge Van Fleet's friends yesterday criticised the appearance of John F. Bowie before the appellate court in making the motions for a speedy hearing of the appeal from Judge Van Fleet's order that the interest guarantee from the Denver and Rio Grande should be tried before the bondholders should be permitted to foreclose on the property. They claimed that Bowie, as the attorney for the reorganization committee, did not represent a party to the suit, and consequently had no authorization to appear in the case.

Bowie explains that he was appearing for Jared How, counsel for the Equitable, and so stated to the Court. The bondholders resent the criticism, and ask if they are to be denied an opportunity to ask for a speedy decision, when the opposing interests are aiming, as the bondholders believe, to defeat reorganization and make the receivership last through a period of years.

Ablain Wood Is Taken by Germans

BERLIN, March 10 (via London).—Capture of the Ablain wood was announced today by German army headquarters. It was stated that the French had regained a foothold in the fort of Vaux.

Six Villa Spies Arrested in El Paso; Infantry Pursues Gun Runners

EL PASO, March 10.—Six Mexicans, suspected of being Villa spies, were arrested late tonight by the El Paso police. Among the number was General Manuel Banda, formerly Villa commander of the Juarez garrison, and Colonel Pablo Luna, formerly a member of Villa's personal bodyguard. A party of fifty soldiers from Fort Bliss tonight began the pursuit of a number of Mexicans, who, with a wagon train of small arms and ammunition, were said to have taken a westerly course along the Rio Grande on the American side. Reports received by military authorities stated that the ammunition had been loaded into wagons in the Mexican quarter of El Paso early tonight

S. F. Post May Send Its Quota

General Orders Hold All Available Troops Ready for Trip to the Border

"Hold every available man in the Western Department of the Army in readiness for field service on the border."

This was the word flashed from Washington yesterday to the commanding General of the Western Department, General J. Franklin Bell. And from the headquarters of the department to every commanding officer of the Third Division was relayed the order to prepare for active service.

The order was considered more than significant, inasmuch as the Western Department has contributed more than its share of troops for border patrol work, having sent the entire Eighth Infantry Brigade from the Presidio, the Twentieth Infantry and many cavalry troops to guard the Texas-New Mexico-Arizona border.

MUSTER ROLL LIGHT.

The Western Department today musters but thirty-five companies of Coast Artillery, the Fourteenth and Twenty-first Infantry, a small amount of cavalry and hospital and ambulance troops—scarcely enough men to adequately man the different posts in the department. It would take a big crisis to call out the Coast Artillery troops, and so leave the fortifications of Puget sound, the Columbia river, San Francisco and San Diego defenseless, yet General Bell has orders to hold all the defense troops in readiness to proceed at once to the Mexican border.

The only explanation here of the order to the department is that intervention in Northern Mexico is considered, in the opinion of Army officers.

INTERVENTION NECESSARY

General Carranza is able to care for the situtaion in Central and Southern Mexico, according to officers who are conversant with the situation, but only American intervention can calm the troubled waters of Northern Mexico.

American soldiers have been on the border line—12,000 strong—from two to five years. In the opinion of Army men, these soldiers are the best trained in the world and can be trusted to give a good account of themselves under any conditions.

Fleet in Flurry to Prepare for Sailing

The possibility of orders coming from Washington sending the Pacific fleet to Mexican waters to co-operate with United States troops in their expedition against General Villa, yesterday caused a flurry of excitement at Mare Island Navy Yard. No orders were received, according to Commandant Bennett.

Practically all of the Pacific fleet warships are at present stationed at San Diego, having recently been holding war maneuvers off the Southern California coast. The vessels there include the cruisers Milwaukee, San Diego and Maryland, the transport Buffalo, the torpedo-boat destroyers Perry, Paul Jones, Preble, Whipple and Stewart and the tender Iris. The cruiser Chattanooga is stationed at Mazatlan, Mexico, and the gunboat Yorktown is at Topolobampo. The cruiser Raleigh is at Mare Island, undergoing repairs, and the supply ship Glacier is also at the naval station.

Cavalry May Leave San Diego Exposition

SAN DIEGO, March 10.—Orders for the First United States Cavalry, 300 strong, in camp at the Panama-California International Exposition, to entrain for duty with the Mexican expeditionary force were expected momentarily tonight by Captain Frank B. Arnold, squadron commander.

Four troops of the First Cavalry are stationed here. Troop A is commanded by First Lieutenant C. Enos, Troop D, by First Lieutenant W. W.

(Continued on Page 2, Column 5.)

LEADER OF U. S. FORCES AT BORDER

Brigadier-General John J. Pershing, who has been ordered to invade Mexico and capture Francisco Villa, the Mexican bandit, who raided the New Mexican town of Columbus.

Villa Off on a Mormon Raid
U. S. Troops Ready for Trail

Five Hundred Mexican Regulars Unable to Save Settlers From Slaughter

EL PASO (Tex.), March 10.—Villa is headed directly for Casas Grandes, Chihuahua, in order to attack the 500 Mormons settled in that section, according to a report received tonight at Juarez by General Gavira from General Bertani.

Small hope is felt that General Bertani will be able to bring help to the Mormons, as the cavalry force of 500 he commands is stationed at Palomas, 100 miles distant, over a broken, roadless country. Ten trains, containing 2000 men, left Chihuahua City this afternoon to act as railway patrols and train guards, Gavira said.

ATTEMPT TO RESCUE

It was to rescue these people that the Mormon colony of El Paso dispatched a messenger immediately with news of the Columbus massacre, and special trains were expected to start immediately with the refugees. Bishop Hurst, head of the local church, received urgent messages today from the Salt Lake headquarters of the Mormon sect, asking that he take all possible precautions against his co-religionists being caught in a trap in Casas Grandes. The Bishop conferred with the Mexican railway officials over train arrangements and with General Gavira regarding military protection.

Since troops had already started from Chihuahua City, it was decided that they would be first on hand, and the protection of the refugees was intrusted to their care. The question now is whether the refugees can be gathered in in time.

MAS RELAY OF HORSES

From the reports received from General Bertani, Villa and his men early in the day were dashing through

(Continued on Page 5, Column 4)

Columbus Tense With Excitement as Big Pursuit Nears Its Launching

COLUMBUS (N. M.), March 10.—Francisco Villa, with the Mexican bandit army, whose raid on Columbus was beaten off by the Thirteenth United States Cavalry with severe losses Thursday morning, was at Boca Grande, twenty-five miles southeast, at last reports brought here today by scouts. American military authorities here were impatient for orders to cross the border and assail the bandit leader before he had time to retreat farther into the interior of Chihuahua.

With plenty of cavalrymen available tonight, Colonel Slocum and his officers were convinced that an order to cross the line now would mean a quick disposition of Villa. When Major Frank Tompkins of the Thirteenth, with hardly 200 men, took up the pursuit of the entire Villa force, estimated at 2500 men, yesterday, the Mexicans fled fifteen miles. Six troops of cavalry were ready and eager tonight to start the chase.

Meanwhile residents of the town of Columbus were in a state of high tension tonight. A report today that Villa had recrossed the border and surrounded the town stampeded nearly all the inhabitants.

The funeral of Mrs. Milton James, one of the American civilians killed by Villa's raiders when they burst into the town Thursday morning before daylight, was held today. A throng attended. Every man and even boys in knickerbockers in attendance were alert and armed with rifles and revolvers. Rifles captured from the Mexicans when the American troops drove them from the town supplied arms for many of the civilians. Tonight the report that Villa was again advancing gained currency. Armed civilians supplementing

(Continued on Page 5, Column 2)

CARRANZA TO BE IGNORED IF HE PROTESTS

Capture Villa and Stop His Forays, Command Sent Out From White House; Secrecy to Mark Expedition Through Spy-Infested Cactus Plains on Bandit Chase; Navy to Protect Citizens in Seaboard Towns From Uprising

Carranza Sorry Villa Perpetrated Columbus Massacre, but Withholds Consent to American Pursuit of Villa and His Cutthroat Band; Marauders, 3000 Strong, Intrenched in Mountains; Constitutionalist Troops Scattered

WASHINGTON, March 10.—American troops were ordered across the Mexican border today by President Wilson to take Francisco Villa and his bandits, dead or alive.

Indications late tonight were that the carrying out of President Wilson's order that American troops re-enter Mexico to capture or kill Villa and his bandits would be left to the man on the ground, Major-General Funston, who ended the Philippine insurrection by taking Aguinaldo single-handed. American columns are expected to be moving into Mexico before tomorrow night. They go to meet about 3000 guerrilla troops in a mountainous region from which Carranza troops have fled. Whether this long-deferred armed action, which begins purely as a punitive measure to clear Northern Mexico of menacing bandit bands over which General Carranza has no control, shall grow into a general armed intervention or occupation of Mexico, depends, in a large measure, upon General Carranza and the Mexican people.

TO PUT A STOP TO VILLA FORAYS AT ANY COST

It begins with President Wilson's declaration that it is entirely in aid of the Carranza government, and without thought of aggression. This statement, prepared by the President himself, was given out at the White House:

"An adequate force will be sent at once in pursuit of Villa with the single object of capturing him and putting a stop to his forays.

"This can be done and will be done in entirely friendly aid of the constituted authorities in Mexico, and with scrupulous respect for the sovereignty of that republic."

President Wilson's intention to depart from the policy of watchful waiting, ended by the Columbus massacre yesterday, was announced today after it had been unanimously approved by the Cabinet and Administration leaders in Congress. The President's position was explained fully to the latter, who agreed that he should not be embarrassed at this time by discussion of a minority, which might arouse trouble in Mexico.

BAKER ORDERS TROOPS TO PURSUE BANDITS

After a brief Cabinet meeting, at which the President was described as being as determined to eliminate Villa as he was to eliminate Huerta, Secretary Baker hurried to the War Department and sent orders to the border troops.

Soon afterward the Army General Staff assembled and con-

German Flotilla Seen By a Norwegian Crew

Dreadnaught Fleet Headed by the New Hindenburg

COPENHAGEN, via London, March 11, 2:19 A. M.—A local newspaper says the Norwegian steamer Bergen met on Thursday in the southern part of the North sea a German flotilla of fifty dreadnaughts, cruisers and large destroyers of the latest type. The largest ship in the fleet was the new dreadnaught Hindenburg. One squadron was steaming in an easterly direction, followed by two airships.

A London dispatch on March 8th said that a German fleet of at least fifty large warships had been sighted Monday afternoon in the North sea.

San Francisco Chronicle

LEADING NEWSPAPER *of the* PACIFIC COAST

Weather Report
San Francisco, Oakland and Vicinity:
Fair weather Sunday; light to moderate west wind.
T. R. REED, Forecaster.
(Complete Weather Report on Page [illegible])

FOUNDED 1865 | SAN FRANCISCO, CAL., SUNDAY, JULY 23, 1916 | xxxx | VOL. CIX, NO. 8

BOMB EXPLOSION KILLS 6 AND MAIMS 40 PREPAREDNESS PARADE SPECTATORS

TIMED INFERNAL MACHINE WORKS HAVOC IN CROWD

Pipe, Filled With Dynamite, Surrounded by Slugs of Jagged Metal and Bullets, More Deadly Than Shrapnel Used in Grim Work of War, Strikes Down Innocent and Peaceful Citizens, Among Them Mothers With Babes in Arms

Rolph Orders Sweeping Investigation; Police Drop All Else to Hunt Down Human Monster; Finnish Sailor Arrested as Suspect; Grand Army Veterans, Schooled Amid Shot and Shell, Prevent Panic of Paraders by Coolness

WHILE veteran soldiers of the Grand Army of the Republic, symbolizing liberty and the preservation of the Union and government, swung into the line of the preparedness parade at Steuart and Market streets, shortly after 2 o'clock yesterday, a bomb exploded six lives were snuffed out and two scores of persons, all spectators, were injured. Two of these are dying.

The police theory of the explosion is that it was the act of an anarchist or fanatic. Threatening letters had been received by proponents of the parade, the police and the newspapers for a week preceding yesterday.

No one had taken these warnings seriously. The bomb which exploded, it is thought by the police, was placed on the sidewalk, next to the brick wall of the Ferry Exchange saloon, with a time fuse or clock attachment.

As near as can be ascertained, the explosive in the deadly machine of destruction was dynamite incased in a lead pipe, surrounded by missles. The fanatic who prepared the bomb filled it with steel rivets, cartridges, sections of steel auto tire and bullets of .32 and .22 caliber. When it exploded the effect was like that of a shrapnel shell.

BOMB TIMED TO REAP HARVEST IN THRONGS WATCHING PARADE, WORK OF ANARCHIST OR FANATIC

The massed crowd around the corner was mowed down as if the bomb had been a machine gun. The concussion of the explosion was terrific. It shattered the plate-glass windows near by, knocked people off their feet, and left almost a shambles of Steuart street for 150 feet off Market.

The police are divided as to whether the bomb was contained in a suit case. Across the street they found the handle of a suit case of yellow leather.

The bomb outrage failed to disrupt the parade. Two minutes after it happened the columns of marching men and women were making their way along Steuart and up Market street to martial airs played by bands, while the clanging bells of ambulances and police patrols made hubbub around them.

PARADE OF MARCHING MEN AND WOMEN REFORMS AND PROCEEDS ON WAY UP MARKET

To it all the marchers seemed oblivious.

It fell to the lot of the Grand Army men, who, years ago, faced exploding shells in the trenches of Vicksburg, Gettysburg and Grant's campaign for Richmond, to avert a panic.

Some grayed Grand Army veteran, the commander of a fast diminishing post, through the bomb's smoke, called "Attention!" and the command to march was given.

With limping and yet measured tread, the column in blue marched on past the dead and dying and injured victims lying in huddled heaps on the street and sidewalk.

GRAND ARMY MEN, SCHOOLED ON FIELDS OF CARNAGE, AVERT PANIC BY THEIR CALMNESS

"It is war," one elderly veteran said as he hobbled under the hot sun from Steuart into Market street.

Mayor Rolph, who led the parade, waving an American flag, has ordered a sweeping investigation.

Chief White has demanded the arrest of the fanatic. Frank Josefson, a Finnish sailor, was taken into custody fifteen minutes after the explosion by Police Sergeant Brasfield.

He was standing near the explosion and, according to the police, he said: "That's what they get for talking preparedness too much."

Josefson was grilled by Captain of Detectives Patrick Shea and District Attorney Charles Fickert after his arrest. He declared he was on Front street, more than a block away, when the explosion occurred. He lives at the Scandinavian Sailors' Home on Drumm street.

He admitted he thought the parade was an exhibition of rankest foolishness but denied affiliation with any anarchistic society.

District Attorney Fickert intimated that his office had a suspicion as to the identity of the ringleaders in the bomb plot, but, further than that, would make no statement.

HOSPITALS FILLED WITH VICTIMS OF TRAGEDY, MANY FRIGHTFULLY MANGLED BY SPLINTERS OF BOMB

The Harbor Emergency Hospital was filled with victims of the bomb tragedy and there were not sufficient ambulances to convey the dead and wounded to the hospitals or Morgue. Several inclosed motor-truck delivery wagons were pressed into service to remove the wounded.

The dead and injured were frightfully mangled by the explosion. Pieces of human bodies were found within a radius of 100 feet. Many narrow escapes were recorded.

The bullets and metal which the bomb contained spread for yards. It was more than half an hour before the marchers at the head of the parade, which was just passing Eighth street when the explosion occurred, learned of the dastardly deed.

MARCHERS PASS SCENE OF BOMB HORROR FOR HALF AN HOUR AFTER EXPLOSION FAILED TO HALT PARADE

Many of the injured victims went home without medical attention or were removed to private hospitals. It is doubtful if an accurate estimate of the number of wounded can be had.

The Grand Army men were in the Eleventh division of the parade. It had been in progress from the Ferry building about a half hour when the explosion occurred.

For almost a half hour other divisions passed the scene of the tragedy, not without fear of a repetition of the outrage, but they passed it.

LIST OF DEAD, DYING AND INJURED

THE DEAD

FOX, ADAM, 3227 Sacramento street; G. A. R. veteran, 72 years of age; died from shock of explosion.
KNAPP, MRS. H. E., 1438 Sixth street, Alameda; badly mangled.
LAMBORN, L. H., 1516 St. Charles street, Alameda.
LAWLOR, GEORGE G., lumber salesman, Mill Valley.
NELSON, ARTHUR, commissary clerk, Fairmont Hotel; residence, Larkspur, Marin county.
PAINTER, DR. GEORGE L., physician, 3016 Telegraph avenue, Berkeley; lungs punctured through both sides; ribs fractured; died at Central Emergency at 6 P. M.

THE DYING

At Central Emergency Hospital.
SEEMANN, MISS PEARL, 619 Forty-fifth street, Oakland; left leg blown off.
TURNBULL, THOMAS H., 1680 California street; fractured skull.

THE INJURED

ANDERSON, A. B., printer, San Anselmo, lacerations of both legs and of the body.
ANDERSON, THOMAS, 50 Clay street, powder burns in the face and cuts.
BRYDON, C. A., 1612 Minton avenue, Alameda, contusions and abrasion of face.
BRYDON, MRS. C. A., 1612 Minton avenue, Alameda; contusions and abrasion of right leg.
BRADY, JOHN, San Bruno, severe lacerations of both legs.
CLAUSSEN, HENRY J., 725 Santa Clara avenue, Alameda, right leg fractured and severe contusions of both legs.
DETRICK HENRY L., stationer, 1815 Third avenue, Los Angeles, brother of Charles R. Detrick, secretary State Railroad Commission, severe lacerations of scalp.
GADDY, FRANCIS D., traffic officer, 327 Twenty-fifth avenue, slightly injured.
GAMMEL, RAY, traveling salesman, 556 Jones street, lacerations of legs.
KENNEDY, CAPTAIN THOMAS, 619 Forty-fifth street, Oakland; contusions of body.
KENNEDY, GEORGE, 6, son of Captain Thomas A. Kennedy, 619 Forty-fifth street, Oakland; legs cut to bone.
KENNEDY, MRS. ELEANOR, his mother; cut.
KNAPP, HOWARD E., 1436 Sixth street, Alameda, side and shoulder torn. (Mrs. Knapp was killed.)
KNAPP, WILLIAM, two and one-half years old son of Howard E. Knapp, forehead bruised and legs cut.
LOZOVSKY, GIRSH, clerk, 1389 Golden Gate avenue; right leg broken, both legs lacerated.
MEYERS, HYMAN, 1281 Vallejo street, advertising man, contusions of legs.
McARTHUR, JAMES, 32, driller, 3361 Sixteenth street; lacerations and abrasion of left leg.
McCARTHY, JERRY, Oakland, right leg cut.
McDERMOTT, JAMES, 2532 Army street; on opposite side of street; cut by glass.
MRS. McDERMOTT, his wife; shock.
MOFFET, SAMUEL, Harbor Hotel, San Francisco; laceration of hip, fractured finger.
MONROE, GEORGE D., 4096 Seventeenth street; lacerated wound of right fore arm.
NELSON, H. K., 1004 Fifty-Ninth street, Oakland; puncture wound, back.
NORN, EMIL, mechanic, American Hotel, 718 Howard street, laceration of legs.
PELSINGER, FRANCIS, 192 Sixth street, employe of Emporium.
POWELL, A. B., stevedore, 132 East street, left leg broken.
TOY SING, 15, Chinese, 658 Jackson street; laceration of back.
TCHI ONG, 14-year-old Chinese boy, 873 Washington street; cuts.
TERRY, T. J., Nevada State Superintendent of Schools, East Ely, Nev.; shock and superficial neck wounds.
TERRY, MRS. T. J., shock and neck wounds.
TOWNSEND, MISS MYRA; cuts, right leg.
VAN LOO, MRS. KINGSLEY, 384 Clark street, Oakland, gashes on leg, cuts on breast.
VAN LOO, MARIE, aged 7, cuts on left leg.
VAN LOO, RICHARD, aged 9, right foot mangled.
VAUGHAN, REUBEN J., captain of river steamer Sacramento, 2917 Lorina street, Berkeley, right leg badly mangled.
WYMORE, MRS. CECIL, 1238 Fifty-third avenue, Oakland, one leg almost blown off, and the knee on the other punctured.
WYWOOD, ROBERT, 370 First street, lacerations and bruises.
WOO YUNG, 924 Dupont street; contusions left thigh.

BRITISH PREPARING FOR FINAL DRIVE AT GERMAN THIRD LINE

Massing of Cavalry in Picardy Leads to Belief That Allies Are Preparing for Hard Drive at Remaining Trench Defenses

By ARTHUR S. DRAPER
Special Correspondent of The Chronicle in London

LONDON, July 22.—While the censorship has again drawn a blanket over the allies' activities on the western front, and the official bulletins record nothing beyond scattered and minor engagements and a heavy artillery fire from both sides, the paucity of the news deceives no one here. All recognize that the British are now concentrating their forces for the assault on the third and strongest German line before Bapaume.

The presence, reported from Berlin, of British cavalry on the lines indicates what may shortly happen. The present comparative quiet may represent the hush before the most important events of the allied offensive. Cavalry can only be of use when trench fighting is over and the enemy has been driven into the open.

THIRD TRENCH IS LAST

The line of trenches which the British now face is understood to be the last of the German "permanent defenses"—those tremendous works of cement and iron which represent months of labor, millions in money and the most highly developed skill of military engineering science. Beyond lies open country and use for cavalry.

The report of the intense bombardment which is bathing the trenches on both sides along the British front in a flood of steel and gas may mean either or both of two things—a preparation by the British to renew their offensive, and a preparation by the Germans to launch another desperate counter attack in a final effort to save their front from being pierced.

It is taken for granted here that the British are planning fresh efforts. General Haig's report that the Germans are using tons of explosive and tear-producing shells, and both British and French reports of German attacks, which, while not important, may have been in the nature of feelers, causes the belief that the Germans, too, contemplate an attack.

Which will be launched first, and how great a force the Germans have been able to gather, can only be guessed. The British are confident of holding their gains, confident, too, that the German charge will break down, as the last one did, and that the British will again sweep forward, and soon, for the first time since the Marne, will have their enemy in the open, except for such defenses as can be thrown up during the battle.

FIGHT TO BE DESPERATE

There is no tendency to underestimate the strength which such a German thrust will show. It is realized that the general staff is desperate; that unless it can check the offensive on either the east or west fronts, so that it can again swing its reserves back and forth across to the threatened points, it knows that it faces a series of defeats, each greater than the last.

It is expected, therefore, that it will throw into its counter-attacks every
(Continued on Page 30, Column 4.)

51,000 MARCHERS CARRY FLAGS IN IMPOSING PARADE

Well-Known San Franciscans Take Places Among Thousands of Their Fellow Citizens, Who March Quietly in One of the Most Notable Street Pageants in History of City—Seriousness of All Who Take Part Is Striking

American Emblem Displayed by Tens of Thousands and Heads of All Are Bared as National Anthem Is Played by More Than Fifty Bands—Cumulative Force of Great Display by Men and Women Proves Tremendous In Effect

Facts About the Parade

Number in line	51,329
Time occupied in passing	3 hours
Length of march	1 1-2 miles
Organizations in line	213
Bands	52

IN UNBROKEN ranks San Francisco told its determination yesterday that the United States be prepared.

It was not a holiday sentiment that the 51,000 marchers expressed, when for three hours they filed through the length of Market street, in ranks that reached from curb to curb. For in the long list of street pageants that San Francisco has known, the Preparedness of July 22 stands alone in the seriousness of its purpose and the magnitude of its declaration.

Of color there was little, and the decorations were the American flag—tens of thousands of flags. Cheers did not seem to tell the spirit of the hour, and for the most part they were omitted. Gold lace and military title also were absent, and the armed forces were represented alone by the citizen soldiers—a thousand of them from the training camp. But without color, titles, or cheers, the Preparedness Parade told a story, and told it more forcefully than studied pageantry can.

CUMULATIVE POWER OF PARADERS PROVES TO HAVE GREAT EFFECT ON SPECTATORS

It was the cumulative power of repetition; the ceaseless recurrence of ranks on ranks of citizens, familiar friends, distinguished men, common people, judges, clerks, bankers, workers, and leaders; that made for greatness. And it was no less than great.

Promptly at 1:30 o'clock the signal sounded for the start, and on the instant the head of the column swung into Market street from the Embarcadero. Forty minutes later Grand Marshal Thornwell Mullally halted the front ranks in front of the reviewing stand in Marshall square, and at that moment every band in the long line played the national anthem, and a hundred thousand heads were bared.

Traffic had been cleared for the entire length of Market street. As far as the eye could see the ununiformed paraders filled the street.

Marching at the head of the line came Mayor Rolph. Governor Johnson, who had signified his intention of joining in the

Fourteen-Year-Old Girl Weds Her Uncle

Idaho Miss Becomes a Bride With Consent of Her Mother

Special Dispatch to The Chronicle.

CALDWELL (Ida.), July 22.—Mary Dotson, 14 years old, daughter of Wesley Dotson, a rancher, living near Caldwell, Idaho, married her mother's brother, T. B. Smith, 32 years old.

Today the girl's mother accompanied the couple across the line to Oregon and helped them obtain the license, after which they were married and returned to the home of the parents of the girl.

Mrs. Dotson said she saw no reason why her daughter should not marry the man of her choice, and all parties declined further to discuss the matter.

EXTRA **San Francisco Chronicle**
LEADING NEWSPAPER of the PACIFIC COAST

Weather Report
San Francisco, Oakland and vicinity: Fair weather Friday; light to moderate westerly wind.
T. R. REED, Forecaster.

FOUNDED 1865 SAN FRANCISCO, CAL., FRIDAY, APRIL 6, 1917 XXXXXX VOL. CX. NO. 81

WAR WITH GERMANY VOTED BY REPRESENTATIVES 373 TO 50

RESOLUTION PASSED IN EARLY MORNING AFTER LONG DEBATE

President to Sign Document After Vice-President Marshall Signs in Senate, and Hostilities Will Then Officially Be Commenced; Army and Navy Appropriations Are Rushed

House Refuses All Amendments Without the Formality of a Roll Call; Democratic Leader Kitchin Unexpectedly Takes Stand Against War and Draws Number to His Side

WASHINGTON, April 6.—The resolution declaring that a state of war exists between the United States and Germany, already passed by the Senate, passed the House shortly after 3 o'clock this morning, by a vote of 373 to 50.

President Wilson will sign the resolution as soon as Vice-President Marshall has attached his signature in the Senate. It formally accepts the state of belligerency forced by German aggression, and authorizes and directs the President to employ the military and naval forces and all the resources of the Nation to bring war against Germany to a successful termination.

HOUSE REJECTS ALL AMENDMENTS AND PASSES RESOLUTION IN ITS ENTIRETY

Without roll calls, the House rejected all amendments, including proposals to prohibit the sending of any troops overseas without Congressional authority.

Passage of the resolution followed seventeen hours' of debate. There was no attempt to filibuster, but the pacifist group, under the leadership of Democratic Leader Kitchin, who declared conscience would not permit him to support the President's recommendation that a state of war be declared, prolonged the discussion with impassioned speeches.

MISS RANKIN BOWS HEAD AND THEN, RISING, SINKS BACK WITHOUT VOTING

Miss Rankin of Montana, the only woman member of Congress, sat through the first roll call with bowed head, failing to answer to her name, twice called by the clerk.

On the second roll call she rose and said in a sobbing voice, "I want to stand by my country, but I cannot vote for war."

For a moment then she remained standing, supporting herself against a desk, and as cries of "Vote, vote," came from several parts of the House, she sank back into her seat without voting, audibly. She was recorded in the negative.

CHEERS GREET ANNOUNCEMENT OF VOTE; FIFTY VOTE NO

Cheers greeted the announcement of the result. A few minutes later Speaker Clark signed the resolution and the House then adjourned, to meet again Monday and take up the Administration's recommendations for war legislation.

The fifty who voted against the resolution were:

Almond	Fuller of Illinois	McLemore
Bacon	Haugen	Mason
Britten	Hayes	Nelson
Browne	Hensley	Randall
Burnett	Hilliard	Rankin
Carey	Hull of Iowa	Reavis
Church	Igoe	Roberts
Connolly of Kansas	Johnson of S. D.	Rodenburg
Cooper of Wisconsin	Keating	Shackleford
Davidson	King	Sherwood
Davis	Kinkaid	Sloan
Decker	Kitchin	Stafford
Dill	Knutson	Van Dyke
Dillon	La Follette	Voigt
Dominick	Little	Wheeler
Esch	London	Woods of Iowa
Frear	Lundeen	

California Representatives voted as follows: Curry, Elliston, Kahn, Kettner, Lea, Nolan, Raker and Osborne voted for the

(Continued on Page 3, Column 3)

Late War Bulletins

WASHINGTON, April 6.—It is understood that orders for the seizure of all German ships in American ports went out this morning immediately upon the passage of the war resolution by the House. The vessels will be held for the present as a measure of safety. So far there has been no decision as to whether the Government shall take them over and pay for them after the war.

NEW LONDON (Conn.), April 6.—The North German-Lloyd steamer Willehad, which came here from Boston last August in order that accommodations might be provided for the members of the crew of the German merchant submarine Deutschland, was ordered seized this morning by Collector of the Port James A. McGovern.

BOSTON, April 6.—Five German steamships which have been in refuge at this port were ordered seized and their crews dispossessed by Collector of the Port Edmund Billings early today. The vessels taken over are the Amerika and Cincinnati, passenger ships, and the Wittekind, Koln and Ockenfels, freight steamers.

BALTIMORE, April 6.—Three German steamships, the Rhein, Neckar and Bulgaria, were ordered seized at this port this morning. United States marshals, assisted by a company of National Guardsmen, have boarded the vessels.

PORT COLLECTOR READY TO SEIZE GERMAN VESSELS

Arrives at Offices in Early Morning Prepared to Carry Out Orders

To put into operation the machinery of the local Customs Bureau in connection with the seizure of German vessels here, Collector of the Port John O. Davis hastened to the Custom-house early this morning from his home in Berkeley.

Collector Davis refused to comment on his orders from Washington, but they are believed to be similar to those sent out to all collectors and Federal officials following the passage of the war resolution in the House.

The German vessels which will be seized here are the steamer Serapis, the bark Ottawa and the power schooners Atlas and Neptun, aggregating 5891 tons, which are lying off Sausalito. Armed guards are already aboard the vessels and it is expected their crews will be interned at the Angel island immigration station early today.

Edward White, commissioner of immigration, while admitting the receipt of instructions, which he will put in force today, refused to reveal the procedure that will be carried out by his department here.

It is believed the plan will include the internment of Franz Bopp, former German Consul-General at this port; E. H. von Schack, former vice-consul and Wilhelm von Brincken, who was attache of the consulate, the Germans recently convicted of violating the neutrality of the United States.

BILLIONS NEEDED FOR YEAR OF WAR

Congress Asked to Provide Immediately $3,502,517,000 to Finance Army and Navy Departments Twelve Months

INCREASED TAXES AND BOND ISSUE PROBABLE

Secretary McAdoo Says Government Will Have No Difficulty in Raising Money; Big Incomes May Pay Large Share

WASHINGTON, April 5.—Congress was asked today to provide immediately $3,502,517,000 to finance the war for one year, approximately as follows:

For the War Department, $2,952,-537,923.

For increasing the authorized strength of the Navy to 150,000 men and the marine corps to 30,000 men, $178,855,762.

MEANS BOND ISSUE AND BIGGER TAXES

For other necessary expenditures for the naval establishment, at the direction and discretion of the President, $292,538,790.

For the coast guard, so that it may perfect and bring to a high state of efficiency its telephone system of coastal communication, $600,000.

A bond issue, increased taxation, including higher taxes on estates with large incomes, whisky, beer, tobacco and new methods of taxation probably will be resorted to to raise the huge amount.

FEDERAL RESERVE BANKS TO TAKE $2,000,000,000

Unofficial estimates to the Federal Reserve Board are that the banks of the Federal Reserve system are in a position to absorb up to $2,000,000,000 of war bonds at once at a rate of interest not exceeding 3½ per cent. Secretary McAdoo authorized the statement that he thought the Government would have no difficulty in raising the necessary finances, but declined to indicate the probable methods that will be adopted.

Treasury Department experts are assembling a mass of data for consideration of the President and Congressional committees in drafting the war revenue measure. Leaders in the House and Senate conferred with Secretary McAdoo during the day with reference to proposed increases and new taxation and a call was issued for a meeting tomorrow of the House Appropriations Committee to consider the situation.

POSSIBLE LOANS TO ALLIES NOT INCLUDED

The estimates calling for the appropriation of money for carrying on the war were couched in general terms and lacking in detail. The great total does not include possible loans to the allies, part of the Administration's programme as outlined in the President's address to Congress, and demands upon the country's finances will be increased by whatever amount it is decided to place at the disposal of the entente governments.

Secretary McAdoo, into whose hands will be placed the task of suggesting methods for raising large sums by increased taxation so that the war may be paid for as far as possible during

(Continued on Page 3, Column 6)

Mayor Responds to Timely Suggestion Made by Chronicle

SAN FRANCISCO'S public demonstration of loyalty to the President and Congress will take place at 3 o'clock Sunday afternoon, in connection with the dedication of the big pipe organ in the Exposition Auditorium.

Following the suggestion made editorially in The Chronicle Thursday morning, Mayor Rolph yesterday said he would take advantage of a large crowd Sunday to speak of the international crisis and to urge that San Francisco go on record as back of the President to a man.

Resolutions to this effect probably will be drawn up and adopted, said the Mayor, to be wired to President Wilson and his Cabinet.

AMERICAN VESSEL, UNARMED, IS SUNK WITHOUT WARNING

Steamer Missourian, With 32 Americans on Board, Is Diver's Victim

WASHINGTON, April 5.—Sinking without warning of the unarmed American steamer Missourian, which left Genoa April 4 with thirty-two Americans among her crew of fifty-three, was reported to the State Department today by Consul-General Wilbur at Genoa. The crew was saved.

Destruction of two more vessels, one British and one Norwegian, with Americans on board, also was reported to the State Department today by Consul Lathrop at Cardiff. The Norwegian steamer Handvikgoole was sunk by a submarine, believed to have been German, while the British steamer Lincolnshire was sunk without any submarine being seen. Crews of both vessels were in small boats for two hours in dangerous positions before being rescued. There were no casualties in either case.

NEW YORK, April 5.—The Missourian, owned by the American-Hawaiian Steamship line, left here March 6 for Italian ports. The Missourian was first named the Missouri. For many years she was engaged in the New York-Panama trade, and was transferred to the Atlantic trade shortly after the beginning of the Europan war. She was for a time in the service of the United States Government, having been taken over as a transport shortly after General Funston was sent to Vera Cruz in 1914.

TWO RELIEF SHIPS SUNK

NEW YORK, April 5.—The Belgian relief steamship Feisten, has been sunk in the North sea while approaching Rotterdam, according to a cablegram received here today by the Belgian Relief Commission. It is believed she struck a mine. It is believed no Americans were on board.

The cablegram did not state how or when the Feistein was sunk or whether any lives were lost.

It was stated definitely by A. W. Duckett & Co., agents for the Belgian commission, that there were no Americans on the Belgian relief ship Trevier, reported in London dispatches as sunk by a submarine. If twenty-four men were landed at Ymuiden, as reported, then the entire crew was saved.

When the Trevier left here she carried a safe conduct pass, signed by the Swiss Consul, in compliance

(Continued on Page 3, Column 6)

STRIKE OF BOATMEN TIES UP FERRIES

Deckhands on Santa Fe Craft Unexpectedly Quit Work and Ultimatum Is Sent to Shipowners by the Officers' Union

MEN DEMAND 56-HOUR LIMIT ON WEEK'S WORK

Strikers Declare Traveling Public Is Endangered by Hours Now Required of Employes on Transbay Vessels

CREWS of the Santa Fe ferry-boats San Pablo and Yerba Buena, under charter to the railroad, unexpectedly quit work early last night after an ultimatum threatening a walkout of the deck and engine-room officers of the ferry lines had been ratified by the Marine Engineers' Beneficial Association and the Masters, Mates and Pilots' Association. The other lines were not affected and the Santa Fe expects to have its steamers operating this morning.

The deckhands quit when the company, as the result of the new thirteen-hour day limit, announced a nine-hour work day on the San Pablo and a nine and one-half-hour day on the Yerba Buena. The men insisted upon the old working basis of twenty-four hours on and twenty-four hours off.

WALK-OUT OF OFFICERS MAY COME TOMORROW

Action of the Santa Fe crews was not joined in by the officers. The general walkout of ferry-boat officers is scheduled for tomorrow night unless their demands are granted.

The officers are demanding that fifty-six hours be recognized as a week's work. The decision for the action followed a meeting of more than 150 ferry-boat officers with Steamboat Inspectors James Guthrie and Joseph Dolan yesterday.

The ferry-boat officers who appeared before the inspectors were from the Southern Pacific, Santa Fe, Northwestern Pacific, Key Route and Western Pacific ferry systems and are all members of the Engineers and Masters, Mates and Pilot associations.

Henry Taylor, a maritime lawyer, acted as spokesman for the officers. He said the growth of travel on the bay has greatly increased the risk of collision, and that the officers could not remain on duty thirteen hours and remain in an alert and active state of mind.

SAFETY OF TRAVELING PUBLIC SAID IN DANGER

"The officers feel that the safety of the traveling public requires that their hours of labor be reduced," continued Taylor. "The thirteen-hour day is more of a hardship than the twenty-four-hour day previously in effect, and the short time allowed the men off does not give them the required rest."

Inspectors Guthrie and Dolan told the men their authority did not allow the reduction of the hours less than thirteen and directed them to take the matter up before their employers.

After the meeting in Maritime Hall Captain Taylor said:

"The men have decided to walk out after the last trips tomorrow evening if their demands are not acceded to. The officers would go out tomorrow morning but for the inconvenience the public would suffer."

Americans Adjured By Cardinal Gibbons To Preserve Loyalty

BALTIMORE, April 5.—"In the present emergency it behooves every American citizen to do his duty and to uphold the hands of the President and the legislative department in the solemn obligations that confront us," said Cardinal Gibbons tonight in response to requests for an expression from him on the National crisis. "The primary duty of a citizen is loyalty to his country. This loyalty is manifested more by acts than words; by solemn service rather than by empty declamation. It is exhibited by an absolute and unreserved obedience to his country's call.

"The members of both Houses of Congress are the instruments of God in guiding us in our civic duties. It behooves all of us, therefore, to pray that the Lord of Hosts may inspire our National Legislature and Executive to frame such laws in the present crisis as will redound to the glory of our country, righteousness of conduct and to the future permanent peace of the nations of the world."

CARDINAL GIBBONS

Colonel Ziegler Forced to Quit Island Militia

Charge of Disloyalty Is Revived and Pressed by Army General

HONOLULU (H. T.), April 5.—The resignation of Lieutenant-Colonel Charles W. Ziegler of the Hawaiian National Guard was tendered today after it had been demanded by Governor L. E. Pinkham, who made the demand at the instance of Brigadier-General Frederick S. Strong, United States Army, commanding the Department of Hawaii.

General Strong based his demand for Colonel Ziegler's resignation on the fact that the Colonel presided February 7 at a meeting here of the German-American Alliance, at which a resolution was adopted demanding that the question of war with Germany be submitted to popular vote, and at which speeches, which General Strong regarded as disloyal, passed unrebuked by Colonel Ziegler.

The Governor ordered an investigation at the time, at the request of the Army authorities, but later ordered the investigation dropped. The Governor revived the orders and requested Colonel Ziegler's resignation from the Guard today, at General Strong's request.

Thirty-Six Colliers Perish at Fernie, B.C.

FERNIE (B. C.), April 5.—Explosions in No. 2 and No. 3 mines at Coal Creek at 10 o'clock tonight are believed to have killed thirty-six men. All but two of the men in No. 2 mine escaped, but no hope is entertained that any of the thirty-four men in No. 3 will come out alive. According to latest reports here, two bodies have been recovered.

Foreigners in U. S. Are Not to Suffer

WASHINGTON, April 5.—Official announcement was made today that foreigners in the United States who conduct themselves properly will suffer no loss of property or liberty as a result of a declaration of a state of war.

FRENCH HURLED BACK BY GERMANS

Secret Concentration of Force on Hindenburg Line Near Rheims Strikes Staggering Blow to Men of Nivelle's Army

EIGHT HUNDRED TAKEN CAPTIVES BY SURPRISE

Russians Cross Mesopotamia Border, Link With British, and Thus Envelop Turk Empire Completely on East and South

By ARTHUR S. DRAPER
Special Correspondent of The Chronicle in London

LONDON, April 5.—Hindenburg struck back hard at the French today. Picked German troops tore into the French lines northwest of Rheims on the Aisne canal and, according to Berlin, inflicted on the enemy a shattering reverse, taking 800 of them prisoners.

The night report from Paris, however, minimizes the defeat. The attack was thrown forward over a mile and a half front, but it is declared it was completely checked over the bulk of the line, Nivelle's soldiers forcing their way back into their first line trenches almost at once.

FRENCH DRIVING HOME COUNTER-ATTACKS

For those portions of trenches which the Germans still cling to the battle still continues, and tonight the French are driving home repeated counter-attacks.

The operation was an example of what has been known as "the Hin-

THE FRENCH INVINCIBLE
Tests by blood and fire have strengthened France's Army to fight until Allied victory is assured, says Grant Singleton in
Next Sunday's Chronicle

San Francisco Chronicle
LEADING NEWSPAPER of the PACIFIC COAST

FAIR
WEATHER REPORT
SAN FRANCISCO, OAKLAND AND VICINITY
Wednesday fair, cloudy or foggy in morning; moderate westerly winds. E. A. BEALS, Forecaster.
Complete Weather Report on Page 15

FOUNDED 1865 — SAN FRANCISCO, CAL., WEDNESDAY, JUNE 5, 1918 — VOL. CXII, NO. 141

AMERICANS TURN TIDE ON MARNE.
DIVER RAID MISSING ROLL, 58

Outfight Enemy At Every Turn; Take Prisoners

All France Rings With Praise of American Brothers in Arms, Who Thrash Germans Both on Offensive and Defensive and Come Through Victors in Every Action

WASHINGTON, June 4.—A terse announcement is made in General Pershing's evening communique of the actions announced today by the French War Office, in which Americans, by a brilliant counter-attack, repulsed the Germans near Chateau Thierry, and French and American troops drove back an enemy force which had crossed the Marne farther south.

WITH THE AMERICAN ARMY IN PICARDY, June 4 (by the Associated Press).—American troops co-operating with the French west of Chateau Thierry, north of the Marne, the nearest and most critical point to Paris reached by the enemy, have brilliantly checked the onrushing Germans, beaten off repeated attacks and inflicted severe losses, adding to the glory of American history.

The troops began to arrive on the battle front on Saturday and participated in the fighting almost immediately. They not only repulsed the Germans at every point at which they were engaged, but took prisoners, without having any prisoners taken in turn by the Germans.

The Americans entered the battle enthusiastically, eager to fight, after a long march. On their way to the battle line they were cheered by the crowds in the villages through which they passed. Their victorious stand with their gallant French allies so soon after entering the line has electrified all France.

AMERICAN MACHINE GUNNERS WIPE OUT WHOLE ATTACKING FORCE AND WIN AT HAND-TO-HAND

The work of the American machine gunners was particularly noteworthy. There was at least one instance where an entire attacking party was wiped out.

Owing to the fierceness of the battle, it has been difficult to verify details, but there were instances of the stiffest of hand-to-hand fighting. In this the Americans acquitted themselves in a manner which won the greatest praise from their French comrades.

The most determined attack against the Americans occurred last night. Preceded by a heavy bombardment, the Germans came in waves. They penetrated the American trenches, but were quickly ejected, leaving many dead.

Two earlier attacks Monday and three Sunday had the same result.

WITH THE FRENCH ARMY ON THE MARNE, Monday, June 3 (by the Associated Press).—American machine gunners, only an hour or so after their arrival on the banks of the River Marne, on the 31st of May, took a most active part in the defense of Chateau Thierry, which then was menaced with imminent capture by the Germans.

Scarcely had the Americans alighted from their motor lorries when they were ordered into Chateau Thierry with a battalion of French colonial troops. The Americans immediately organized their defenses and by rapid action and excellent shooting caused the approaching enemy to hesitate.

PERSHING'S MEN COVER FRENCH TROOPS WHILE THEY BLOW THE ENEMY TO KINGDOM COME

In order to mask their movements the Germans used smoke grenades, rendering shooting difficult for the defenders, and at the same time opened a severe bombardment on the town. The enemy started across the bridge, but when many had reached the center of the structure a terrific explosion behind them heralded the destruction of the central arch. Dozens of the Germans were hurled into the water, while the few that reached the south side were captured.

The Americans, who held the south end of the bridge and banks of the river, covered the whole operations and protected the French troops while crossing before the explosion. The French officers fighting with them declare that the Americans displayed wonderful qualities of coolness and courage in the most difficult situation, and in the course of the trying struggle in the streets,

(Continued on Page 2, Column 2)

ALLIED WAR COUNCIL IS UNSHAKEN IN CONFIDENCE

"After Review of Situation" Is Convinced Enemy Will in Due Course Be Defeated

COMPLIMENTS ARE PAID TO PRESIDENT WILSON

No Fear of Final Outcome Is Felt, Although Critical Days Are Still to Be Expected

LONDON, June 4 (by the Associated Press).—The Supreme War Council, which has had under advisement the entire war situation, has expressed in an official statement made public tonight full confidence in the outcome of the war, with the aid of the American forces.

Complete confidence in General Foch also is expressed and tribute is paid to President Wilson for his co-operation in the work of transporting and brigading American troops.

"The Supreme War Council held its sixth session under circumstances of great gravity for the alliance of free peoples," says the statement. "The German Government, relieved of all pressure on the eastern front by the collapse of the Russian armies and people, has concentrated all its efforts in the west.

TRYING TO FORESTALL AMERICA'S ARRIVAL

"It now is seeking to gain a decision in Europe by a series of desperate and costly assaults upon the allied armies before the United States can bring its full strength effectively to bear.

"The advantage it possesses in its strategic position and superior railway facilities has enabled the enemy command to gain some initial successes. It will undoubtedly renew its attack, and the allied nations may be still exposed to critical days.

CONVINCED ENEMY WILL BE DEFEATED

"After a review of the whole situation the council is convinced that the allies, bearing the trials of the forthcoming campaign with the same fortitude they have ever exhibited in defense of the right, will baffle the enemy's purpose and in due course bring him to defeat. Everything possible is being done to sustain and support the armies in the field.

"The arrangements for unity of command have greatly improved the position of the allied armies and are working smoothly and with success. The supreme war council has complete confidence in General Foch. It regards with pride and admiration the valor of the allied troops.

TRIBUTE IS PAID TO WILSON'S CO-OPERATION

"Thanks to the prompt and cordial co-operation of the President of the United States, the arrangements which were set on foot more than two months ago for the transportation and brigading of American troops will make it impossible for the enemy to gain victory by wearing out the allied reserve before he has exhausted his own.

"The supreme war council is confident of the ultimate result and the allied peoples are resolute not to sacrifice a single one of the free nations of the world to the despotism of Berlin. Their armies are displaying the same steadfast courage which has enabled them on many previous occasions to defeat a German onset. They have only to endure with faith and patience to the end to make victory for freedom secure. The free peoples and their magnificent soldiers will save civilization."

Wilson Opposes All Further 'Dry' Laws Till Hoover Decides on Need

President Takes Stand in Letter to Senator; Food Chief's Report To Shape Action

WASHINGTON, June 4.—President Wilson today declared his opposition to further prohibition legislation until the Food Administration decides it is necessary to conserve foodstuffs. His position was made known in a letter to Senator Sheppard of Texas. A House amendment to the agricultural appropriation bill would prevent the expenditure of $6,000,000 unless the President prevents the use of grain in the production of alcoholic liquors.

Senator Sheppard said he would not make public the letter at this time. He said he conferred with Food Administrator Hoover today regarding the situation and was awaiting his report. Upon this answer, he said, will depend future action.

Auto Kills Child Running Errand

Driver Held for Death of John Wisloh, Aged 5

While returning from an errand to a neighborhood store, John Wisloh, five-year-old son of Harry C. Wisloh, was killed by an automobile in front of his home at 1028 Golden Gate avenue yesterday afternoon. The boy, according to witnesses, stepped off the curb in back of another automobile and ran directly into the path of the machine driven by Alexander V. Stevens, 170 Margaret avenue.

Stevens rushed the boy to the Central Emergency Hospital but he died on the way. The driver of the machine then surrendered himself to the police and was arrested on a charge of manslaughter.

Kaiser 'Sorry' France Didn't Make Peace

AMSTERDAM, June 4.—"When I see such horrors of war rendering thousands of people homeless and converting flourishing stretches of the French country into hideous deserts, the thought is forced upon me: 'What suffering and misery France might have spared herself and her people if the peace offer of December 12, 1916, had not been so criminally rejected,'" said Emperor William, while journeying through the devastated Marne region, according to Karl Rosner, the war correspondent of the Berlin Lokal Anzeiger.

146 Die, 150 Hurt as Allies Raid Cologne

WASHINGTON, June 4.—A recent allied air raid on Cologne caused the death of 146 persons, the State Department was informed today. About 150 were injured. The people of Cologne, the department's advices said, were thrown into a state of "the most absolute panic."

Dr. Roberts Held for Illicit Relations

MILWAUKEE, June 4.—Dr. David Roberts, for the murder of whose wife Grace Lusk was found guilty on May 29 at Waukesha, was arrested tonight on charges of illicit relations committed here with his wife's slayer. He was brought to Milwaukee.

Bavarian General Killed On Marne

WASHINGTON, June 4.—A diplomatic dispatch from Switzerland today says that Prince von Buchau, the commanding General of a Bavarian division, has been killed in the fighting on the Marne.

British to Employ Women as Aviators

LONDON, June 4.—Employment of women as aviators is intended by the British Government, George H. Roberts, Labor Minister, declared in a speech at Sheffield. The Minister said he believed women would make good aviators.

VERDUN MAY NEXT FEEL MIGHTY BLOW OF GERMANY

Revealed Enemy Strategy, Says Frank H. Simonds, Indicates Smashes to Date Only Preliminary

KNOCKOUT IS HELD UNTIL ALLIES ARE DISLOCATED

Kaiser Plays Dangerous Game as Long as Foch Spares His Reserves for the Supreme Moment

By FRANK H. SIMONDS

(Copyright, 1918)

Special Dispatch to The Chronicle.

NEW YORK, June 4.—The next blow!

The multiplying signs that the German drive in Champagn is approaching its term must be accepted with the full understanding that a new German blow is imminent. Thus we may assume that if the allies have weakened their forces before Amiens, or between Lille and Arras, the Germans will follow up their earlier successes on one of these fronts.

If the first purpose of the Germans be to produce a dislocation of the entire allied line between the Meuse and the sea, preliminary to the delivery of a supreme blow, nothing is more likely than that they will now attack somewhere between Rheims and Verdun for the express purpose of disorganizing this very strong and important section of the allied defense.

WHERE DID FOCH DRAW UPON HIS RESERVES?

Moreover, since the situation between the channel and the British front is critical, it is more likely that Foch has drawn reserves from the east than from the west and that he has exposed an important, but a less vital region, to attack rather than invite a new assault on a front dangerously weakened in the March and April attacks.

The thing that is of utmost importance to remember now is that the German has not sought a "knock-out" by any one of the thrusts that he has undertaken, although his first drive toward Amiens had a weight which suggested that it was intended to achieve a final decision if possible.

STRATEGY SEEMS TO BE TO DISLOCATE ALLIES

His strategy has seemed, and seems, rather, first by a series of blows delivered from the interior positions to dislocate and disorganize the entire system of allied defenses, and then—and only then—to risk all in a final thrust.

So far he has contented himself with brief efforts only after he has felt himself to be checked by the arrival of reserves. The danger for the German in this strategy is obvious. He is steadily consuming a limited reserve. If he consumes it too rapidly in advance of the moment when he is to make his decisive thrust, he will lack the numbers to enforce his local victory.

NAPOLEON FOLLOWED SAME POLICY IN 1814

Bernhardi has a very interesting reference to precisely this same difficulty which confronted Napoleon in his brilliant 1814 campaign, where he won many local successes, but found himself without the reserves to enforce any of them. All things considered, the logical place to look for the blow that is to be expected would be eastward of Rheims, between that city and Verdun.

An attack between Rheims and the Argonne in the "dusty" Champagne would immensely strengthen the German position by relieving the front

(Continued on Page 2, Column 6)

Twelve Ships Sunk Is Submarine Toll Off American Coast

Empty Boat From Carolina Picked Up With Riddled Hull And Splintered Oar, Giving Evidence That It Was Shelled by Diver; Sixteen Drowned When Little Craft Is Swamped During Terrific Thunder Storm

LEWES (Del.), June 4.—Firing was heard off the Delaware capes tonight, but the cause of it could not be learned.

CAPE MAY (N. J.), June 4.—Firing was heard off Cape May this afternoon and again about 8 o'clock tonight. Small boats containing women and children were reported to have been seen this afternoon several miles off shore by an aviator. The report could not be confirmed.

Airplanes tonight were flying low over the mouth of Delaware bay.

AN ATLANTIC PORT, June 4.—Latest reports indicate that at least twelve vessels have been sunk by German submarines off the Atlantic coast during the past ten days. This list includes the steamers Winneconne, Herbert L. Pratt, Texel and Carolina and the schooners Edward H. Cole, Jacob M. Haskell, Isabel B. Wiley, Hattie W. Dunn, Edna, Hauppauge, Edward R. Baird Jr. and Samuel Hathaway.

NEW YORK, June 4.—Reports came to shipping authorities today that another American tank steamship had been sunk by a German submarine. No details were disclosed.

WASHINGTON, June 4.—The tank steamer Herbert L. Pratt, sunk yesterday by a German submarine off the Delaware Capes, has been floated and is now being towed to harbor for repairs, the Navy Department announced tonight.

NEW YORK, June 4.—News reached here today that an American tanker damaged as a result of a fight with a German submarine off the American coast had arrived at an Atlantic port. Naval tugs picked up the crippled vessel at sea and towed her in. Details were withheld for the time. The tanker's hull was punctured and she had shipped a considerable quantity of water.

AN ATLANTIC PORT, June 4.—The City of Columbus of the Savannah line, which it was feared had been sunk by a German submarine, is safe in another port. While the City of Columbus was anchored some distance from shore, there was no evidence that she had been damaged by submarines.

NEW YORK, June 4.—The toll of dead and missing from the raid of German submarines against shipping off the American coast apparently stood tonight at fifty-eight, all from the steamship Carolina of the New York and Porto Rico Line.

Sixteen of this number are known to have perished when one of the ship's boats capsized in a storm Sunday night after the vessel had been sunk. The fate of the others is not known, but it is hoped they have been picked up by a passing ship and will yet reach shore safely.

Officials of the company have placed the number of passengers aboard the Carolina when she was attacked, 125 miles off Sandy Hook, at 220, and the crew at 130, making 350 in all.

Captain Barbour of the Carolina reported to the company today that he was on board the schooner Eva B. Douglass, with 150 passengers and ninety-four of the crew. The schooner is being towed to this port by a tug and is expected to arrive tomorrow morning.

A boat containing twenty-eight survivors, twenty-one passengers and seven of the crew arrived at Atlantic City this afternoon.

Another lifeboat, with ten passengers and nine members of the crew, arrived at Lewes, Del., with the report that sixteen of the thirty-five who had started from the ship had lost their lives in the storm Sunday night.

If the company's figures as to the number aboard the ill-starred liner are correct, this leaves forty-two unaccounted for. That number might have been crowded into one lifeboat. The only possible clew to their fate was found in the fact that an empty boat, marked with the name of Carolina, was picked up at sea by a British steamship which arrived here today. It had every evidence of having been riddled by gunfire. It may have carried the passengers and sailors who still are missing.

Another ship was added to the list of victims of the U-boats when the American schooner Edward B. Baird Jr., was found in

(Continued on Page 2, Column 3)

DESTROYER'S ACTION SAVES FRENCH SHIP FROM U-BOAT

American Warship Also Rescues Two Survivors of Schooner Bombed by Foe Invaders

COAST PATROLS AND SEAPLANES ON GUARD

Theory That Only One Submarine Operated Dispelled by Reports From Vessels Attacked

WASHINGTON, June 4.—Enemy submarines still were operating off the American coast today. A French tank steamer, the Radioleine, first transatlantic craft to be attacked by the raiders, was rescued from destruction at 9:30 o'clock this morning by an American destroyer, sixty-five miles off the Maryland coast.

The same destroyer found the coasting schooner Edward H. Baird Jr. sinking after having been bombed in the same vicinity, making seven schooners and four steamers known officially to have been sunk by the raiders.

Announcement by the Navy Department of these facts late tonight disclosed that the raid in American waters had not ended with yesterday's tale of destruction, upsetting the theory that the raiders probably were speeding homeward.

Coast patrol vessels had not acted on theory. They now are closing in from all directions on the scene of the raider's last exploit, scouring the sea for further trace of enemy U-boats as they come. Seaplanes also are on lookout.

Secretary Daniels directed tonight that a brief report from the destroyer be made public. The destroyer herself, with two survivors from the Baird, a 279-ton craft hailing from Wilmington, Del., was still hunting for the enemy.

The announcement, which, naval of-

THIS NEWSPAPER IS ONE HUNDRED PER CENT AMERICAN

FAIR — WEATHER
San Francisco, Oakland and Vicinity
Monday fair, light northwesterly winds.
T. Francis Drake, Forecaster.
Complete Weather Report on Page 16

FOUNDED 1865 — SAN FRANCISCO, CAL., MONDAY, NOVEMBER 11; 1918 — VOL. CXIII, NO. 119

GREAT WAR OVER

Foe Signs Truce; Fighting Ceases On French Front

WASHINGTON, November 11.---The world war will end this morning at 6 o'clock, Washington time, 11 o'clock Paris time. The armistice was signed by the German representatives at midnight. This announcement was made by the State Department at 2:50 o'clock this morning.

The announcement was made verbally by an official of the State Department in this form:

"The armistice has been signed. It was signed at 5 o'clock A. M., Paris time, and hostilities will cease at 11 o'clock this morning, Paris time."

The terms of the armistice, it was announced, will not be made public until later. Military men here, however, regard it as certain that they include:

Immediate retirement of the German military forces from France, Belgium and Alsace-Lorraine.

THE ARMISTICE TERMS

Disarming and demobilization of the German armies.

Occupation by the allied and American forces of such strategic points in Germany as will make impossible a renewal of hostilities.

Delivery of part of the German high seas fleet and a certain number of submarines to the allied and American naval forces.

Disarmament of all other German war ships under supervision of the allied and American navies, which will guard them.

Occupation of the principal German naval bases by sea forces of the victorious nations.

Release of allied and American soldiers, sailors and civilians held prisoner in Germany without such reciprocal action by the associated Governments.

There was no information as to the circumstances under which the armistice was signed, but since the German courier did not reach German military headquarters until 10 o'clock yesterday morning, French time, it was generally assumed here that the German envoys within the French lines had been instructed by wireless to sign the terms.

Forty-seven hours had been required for the courier to reach German headquarters, and unquestionably several hours were necessary for the examination of the terms and a decision. It was regarded as possible, however, that the decision may have been made at Berlin and instructions transmitted from there by the new German Government.

Germany had been given until 11 o'clock this morning, French time, 6 o'clock Washington time, to accept. So hostilities will end at the hour set by Marshal Foch for a decision by Germany for peace or for continuation of the war.

The momentous news that the armistice had been signed was telephoned to the White House for transmission to the President a few minutes before it was given to the newspaper correspondents. Later it was said that there would be no statement from the White House at this time.

EX-EMPEROR FLEES WITH HINDENBURG TO HOLLAND

Wilhelm Hohenzollern Seeks Asylum After Abdication at Middachten Castle, Across the Dutch Border

GENERAL STAFF ATTENDS FORMER RULER ON TRIP

Deposed Monarch, in Uniform, Alights at Station and Smokes Cigarette as He Paces Platform

WASHINGTON, November 10.—The American general staff today received from The Hague this message: "Press reports state that the Kaiser arrived this morning in Maastright, Holland, and is proceeding to Middachten castle in the town of De Steeg, near Utrecht."

LONDON, November 10 (midnight).—Both the former German Emperor and his eldest son, Frederick Wilhelm, crossed the Dutch frontier Sunday morning, according to advices from The Hague.

LONDON, November 11, 12:31 A. M.—The former German Emperor's party, which is believed to include Field Marshal von Hindenburg, arrived at Eysden, on the Dutch frontier, at 7:30 o'clock Sunday morning, according to Daily Mail advices.

Practically the whole German general staff accompanied the former Emperor, and ten automobiles carried the party. The automobiles were bristling with rifles and all the fugitives were armed.

KAISER SEEMS NOT DISTRESSED

The ex-Kaiser was in uniform. He alighted at the Eysden station and paced the platform, smoking a cigarette.

Eysden lies about midway between Liege and Maastricht, on the Dutch border.

GENEVA (Switzerland), November 10.—It is reported here that William Hohenzollern may come to the chateau of his friend, Baron von Kleist, at Zug, thirteen miles northeast of Lucerne.

The first member of the Austrian royalty has arrived in Switzerland with an Italian permit. He is the Duke of Braganza. Additional members of the royal family are expected.

Chatting with the members of the staff, the former Emperor, the correspondent says, did not look in the least distressed. A few minutes later an imperial train, including restaurant and sleeping cars, ran into the station. Only servants were aboard.

EMPRESS WITH FORMER MONARCH

A dispatch to the Exchange Telegraph Company from Copenhagen quotes the Politiken as saying that when the former German Emperor arrived at Maastricht he was accompanied by the former Empress.

The flight of Emperor William to Holland is confirmed from several sources, but there is a divergence in reports relative to the identity and number of his companions. A Copenhagen dispatch to Reuter's says it is semi-officially reported in Berlin that the Emperor, accompanied by ten men, has arrived at Arnheim, and occupied Count von Bentinck's chateau.

(NOTE—De Steeg is on the Guelders Yssel, an arm of the Rhine river about forty miles east of Utreqht and

(Continued on Page 2, Column 3)

Berlin Seized by Red Forces in Big Popular Uprising

People's Government Instituted, General Strike Declared and Garrison Taken Over as Workmen and Soldiers Fraternize; Dreadnaught Crews at Kiel Join Revolt and Marines Fight Down Resistance From Artillery

COPENHAGEN, November 10.—The crews of the German dreadnaughts Posen, Ostfriesland, Nassau and Oldenburg in Kiel harbor have joined the revolution. The marines occupied the lock at Ostmoor and fought down a coast artillery division who offered resistance.

BASEL (Switzerland), November 10 (Havas).—Wilhelm II, the reigning King of the monarchy at Warttemberg, abdicated on Friday night.

BASEL, November 10 (by the Associated Press).—Hesse-Darmstadt has declared itself a republic,

BASEL, November 10.—An official dispatch received by the Havas Agency from Berlin today says:

"Official. The revolution has resulted in a striking victory almost without the effusion of blood. A general strike was declared this morning. It brought a cessation of work in all workshops at about 10 o'clock."

COPENHAGEN, November 10.—At Stuttgart the new government has issued a proclamation to the people announcing the formation of a provisional republic.

BERLIN, Saturday, November 9 (German wireless to London, November 10, 12:56 P. M., by the Associated Press).—The German People's Government has been instituted in the greater part of Berlin. The garrison has gone over to the Government.

The Workmens and Soldiers' Council has declared a general strike. Troops and machine guns have been placed at the disposal of the Council. Guards which had been stationed at the public offices and other buildings have been withdrawn.

Friedrich Ebert (vice-president of the Social Democratic party) is carrying on the Chancellorship.

The text of the statement issued by the People's Government reads:

"In the course of the forenoon of Saturday the formation of a new German People's Government was initiated. The greater part of the Berlin garrison, and other troops stationed there temporarily, went over to the new Government.

LEADERS OF DEPUTATIONS DECLARE AGAINST USING ARMS ON PEOPLE

"The leaders of the soldiers' deputations to the Social Democratic party declared that they would not shoot against the people. They said they would, in accord with the People's Government, intercede in favor of the maintenance of order. Thereupon in the offices and public buildings the guards which had been stationed there were withdrawn.

"The business of the Imperial Chancellor is being carried on by the Social Democratic Deputy, Herr Ebert."

With regard to the incidents of November 9 in Berlin, the semi-official Telegraph Bureau, working under the control of the Workmens and Soldiers' Council, issued the following report:

GENERAL STRIKE INAUGURATED BY WORKERS OF BIG INDUSTRIAL CONCERNS

"This morning at 9 o'clock the workers of the greatest industrial undertakings commenced a general strike.

"Processions hastened from all the suburbs to the center of the city. Red flags were carried at the head of the processions in which marched armed soldiers and all classes.

"The first procession arrived from the Ackerstrasse and Brunnestrasse. As a preliminary the soldiers and officers were urged to

(Continued on Page 2, Column 4 and 5)

DEATH METED OFFICERS WHO RESIST REBELS

Red Forces Occupy Greater Portion of the German Capital

"MARSEILLAISE" IS SUNG

Violent Bombardment Shakes City as People Throw Off Hohenzollern Yoke

LONDON, November 10.—Severe fighting took place in Berlin between 6 and 8 o'clock last night, and a violent cannonade was heard from the heart of the city.

The revolution is in full swing in Berlin and the red forces occupy the greater part of the German capital, according to a Copenhagen dispatch to the Exchange Telegraph Company, quoting Berlin advices sent from there at 2 o'clock this morning.

REVOLUTION RAPIDLY EXTENDING IN NATION

According to dispatches from Amsterdam and Copenhagen the revolution in Germany is extending rapidly, but in most places the desired effect is being achieved without violence or serious disorder.

In some places, notably in Anhalt, Hesse-Darmstadt and Mecklenburg-Schwerin, the princely houses are cooperating with the reforming parties in establishing a new order of things.

Up to the present the most serious conflict has taken place in Kiel. The soldiers and workmen's councils in most of the larger cities appear to be devoting their first efforts to organizing the food supplies.

REVOLUTIONISTS SEIZE CROWN PRINCE'S PALACE

The Crown Prince's palace was seized by the revolutionists. The people shouted "Long live the republic!" and sang the "Marseillaise."

When revolutionary soldiers attempted to enter a building in which they supposed a number of officers were concealed, shots were fired from the windows. The reds then began shelling the building.

Many persons were killed and wounded before the officers surrendered. The red forces are in control and have restored order. Strong guard is marched through the streets.

When the cannonade began the people thought the Reichsbank was being bombarded, and thousands rushed to the square in front of the Crown Prince's palace. It was later determined that other buildings were under fire.

LEIPSIC, STUTTGART AND COLOGNE JOIN REVOLT

Leipsic, the largest city in Saxony; Stuttgart, the capital of Wurttemberg, and Cologne and Frankfort have joined the revolution, according to reports from the Danish frontier. The soldiers' councils at Stuttgart, Cologne and Frankfort have decided to proclaim a republic.

Delegates of the revolutionary German navy arrived in Berlin Friday. They conferred for several hours with the Minister of Marine and with members of the Reichstag majority parties.

It is stated that Hugo Hasse, a Socialist leader in the Reichstag, has the situation at Hamburg in hand.

Essen, where the great Krupp steel works are situated, is reported to be in the hands of the revolutionaries, says a dispatch from Amsterdam to the Exchange Telegraph Company.

Lieutenant Krupp von Bohlen und Halbach, the head of the Krupp works, and his wife, have been arrested.

This news was brought from Essen by Dutch workmen arriving by special train at Zevengar on Saturday.

Hungarians Insult Austrian Escutcheon

BASEL (Switzerland) November 10.—The palace of the Austrian delegation at Budapest has been stormed by a mob which threw down the Austrian escutcheon, according to a Vienna dispatch received here.

CITY SHOUTS ITS JOY IN WELCOME TO PEACE NEWS

Bells, Bonfires, Horns and Whistles Acclaim Victory of Heroic Troops of Free Nations

ASSOCIATED PRESS GIVES WORD OF WAR'S ENDING

Civic Center Is Thronged by Cheering Hosts Who March by Thousands in Great Peace Parade

SAN FRANCISCO went wild with joy when it received news that the world war was ended and a victorious peace once more has rested upon American arms.

The Associated Press flashed the news that the greatest war of history had ended in the greatest victory for democracy and humanity of all time. Ten minutes later bonfires were burning on the highest point of the Twin Peaks, Scott's Hill at Twenty-second and Wisconsin streets and Telegraph Hill. Fire Chief Murphy, who had caused the bonfires to be in readiness two days before, had only to telephone to men waiting at each point to strike a match that was to light the fires for which the people of San Francisco and vicinity have been waiting anxiously, hopefully, for several days.

WHISTLES AND SIRENS JOIN IN ACCLAIM

But it did not take ten minutes for Chief Murphy to get all the whistles and sirens in San Francisco blowing. Just a few minutes after the Associated Press news had been flashed to The Chronicle, and the news in turn relayed to Chief Murphy, San Francisco took on the aspect of New Year's eve. Men, women and children hurried to the Civic Center, where the programme of celebration of the greatest victory American

THIS NEWSPAPER IS ONE HUNDRED PER CENT AMERICAN

Page of Labor News
Another full page will be devoted to news about the trades unions in San Francisco and other California cities, prepared by competent writers for
NEXT SUNDAY'S CHRONICLE

San Francisco Chronicle
LEADING NEWSPAPER of the PACIFIC COAST
REG. U. S. PAT. OFF.

FAIR
WEATHER
SAN FRANCISCO, OAKLAND AND VICINITY
Tuesday fair, except cloudy or foggy in the morning; moderate westerly winds. E. A. BEALS, Forecaster.
Complete Weather Report on Page 2

FOUNDED 1865—VOL. CXIV. NO. 167 | S | SAN FRANCISCO, TUESDAY, JULY 1, 1919—TWENTY-TWO PAGES | DAILY 5 CENTS, SUNDAY 10 CENTS

S. F. SALOON LICENSES VOIDED; STRONG LIQUOR DOOMED TODAY

PALMER WAITS COURT'S RULING ON LIQUOR ACT

Law Ordered Enforced on All Drinks Containing 2 3-4 Per Cent Alcohol

BEER SALE TO CONTINUE

Later Prosecutions Hinted by Attorney-General if Test Cases Are Lost

WASHINGTON, June 30.—As war-time prohibition took effect tonight, the Department of Justice announced that its agents throughout the country would not attempt tomorrow to stop the sale of 2¾ per cent beer.

This eleventh-hour development, a flat reversal of an earlier ruling today by the department, was due to the uncertainty as to how the Federal District Court of New York might rule on a pending claim by brewers that beer containing that much alcohol was not intoxicating.

But while this uncertainty existed as to beer of lighter alcoholic percentage than that sold generally heretofore, full warning was given that with respect to whisky and all beverages as to whose intoxicating powers there was no doubt, every Government legal agency would be set to work in a determined effort to prevent their manufacture and sale.

Congress Expected to Act To Make Ban Effective

How long the sale of 2¾ per cent beer might continue would depend dinarily upon the speed of the courts, but Congress meanwhile will step to the front in an effort to complete the effectiveness of the war-time law.

Exactly what they have refused heretofore to do prohibition members of the House will now attempt—passage of a straight, clear-cut bill for enforcement of war-time prohibition.

When word spread tonight that the Attorney-General by his ruling had permitted beer saloons and breweries to remain in operation, members of the Judiciary Committee counted noses to find a sufficient number ready to go to the front to demand separation of the enforcement measurers so as to get through at once a bill that would stop the sale of all beer containing more than one-half of 1 per cent alcohol.

Prohibition Measures Will Be Held Up for Week

Congressional leaders, it was said, refused to abandon plans for a recess beginning probably tomorrow in order to put the bill through as an emergency measure, and the whole question of prohibition will be held up until next Monday, at the earliest. There were indications tonight that a hard fight would be made in behalf of an amendment to be offered by Representative Igoe, Democrat, of Missouri, which would permit the President to set aside the war-time act in so far as it relates to light wines and beers.

While the Attorney-General's staff was wrestling with the question of intoxicating and non-intoxicating beer, the Judiciary Committee sent to the House its report, in which the bold assertion was made that anything over one-half of one per cent alcohol was intoxicating within the purview of the general law and construction that Congress, and not the Court, should fix the alcoholic percentage of all beverages sale of which is restricted by prohibition statutes.

County and State Officers Asked to Enforce Law

Attorney-General Palmer, in his statement as to the policy of the department, called attention to the fact that the authorities in county and State had been requested to give the utmost co-operation in the matter of enforcing all undisputed provisions of the war-time law. The temporary refusal not to proceed against those selling 2¾ per cent beer—although

(Continued on Page 2, Column 2)

Beer and Wine Sales Waived by City Authorities

While Legal Knot Is Discussed Crowds Give Booze Joyous Farewell

SAN FRANCISCO saloons may sell beer and wines of an alcoholic content of 2¾ per cent or less without observance of any city, State or Federal license requirement.

That is the policy of the Police Commission as announced last night by Theodore Roche, its president.

"The Government has ruled that wines and beer of 2¾ alcoholic content are not intoxicating," Roche said. "Therefore it is the opinion of the Police Commission that prohibition and other laws regulating the sale of liquor do not apply to such beverages."

Roche said the police were prepared to assist the Federal authorities to enforce the law.

By ordder of the mommission, all liquor licenses of every sort in San Francisco were suspended at 12 o'clock last night. Under the Commission's policy, however, any person was privileged to sell wine or beer of the limited alcoholic content without restriction.

Police captains that reported to the Commission at 8 o'clock last night were ordered to return to their stations to enforce the 12 o'clock closing law.

S. F. Crowds in Wild, Joyous Carnival

That official chaos in the administration in San Francisco of prohibition enforcement by the local Federal agencies—due to the admitted failure of the Washington, D. C., authorities to furnish specific instructions—was not attended by flagrant abuses up to an early hour this morning, when jollification began to abate, was described as due to "gratuitous" services performed by the San Francisco Police Department. Uncle Sam laid down on the job, as it were, and the city did as best she could under the circumstances.

Wine-inspired happiness, to be followed by an epidemic of headaches, reigned from sundown to today's daybreak, but the dying hours of booze presided over by the spirits of carnival and merry conviviality were no more unholy than could be expected under conditions imposed by the absence of a well-defined enforcement policy for an epoch-making statute.

Press Advices Give No Comfort to Wine Men

Semi-official advices from the East telling of court decisions that permitted the sale of beverages of not more than 2.75 per cent alcoholic volume served only to add to the confusion in law-administration circles. These advices, carried by press wires, gave no comfort to California wine growers with a $12,000,000 crop on the vines, or to consumers or sellers. Horatio F. Stoll, secretary of the California Grape Protective Association, said:

"No wines are produced in California with as little as 2.75 per cent alcoholic volume, so no relief is afforded to one of the State's biggest industries, even though the decision of the New York courts is sustained."

Cafe Crowds Take No Account of New Lease to Beer

The tens of thousands of celebrants in the local hotels, cafes and restaurants concerned themselves not at all with the legal aspects of the occasion as applicable up to midnight. Until then, the "lid" was off indeed. Drinking undoubtedly was somewhat more intensive and a lot more pep developed in the jazz dancing, but an undercurrent of restraint seemed to check objectionable boisterousness. As a matter of fact, San Francisco, outside observers said, may well be proud of the manner in which she

(Continued on Page 2, Column 4)

City Ponders What to Do About the Lid

CALLING upon Chief of Police White to disregard the enforcement of war-time prohibition until the Federal Congress enacts an enforcement law, Supervisor James E. Power yesterday presented a resolution to the Board of Supervisors which was finally referred to the Mayor.

The resolution sets forth that the Department of Justice is issuing instructions relative to the enforcement of the prohibition act, but that the interpretation of the law is somewhat clouded and it appears that necessary laws for the enforcement of prohibition have not yet been enacted. The Chief of Police having announced that he will enforce the law after midnight last night, the resolution calls upon him to refrain from carrying out his intentions until such time as he has received further instructions and information from the proper Federal authorities.

An attempt was made to refer the resolution to the Police Committee, but it was finally sent to the Mayor, who will confer with the Chief of Police and other city officials.

BRITONS PLAN PACIFIC FLIGHT

Former Canadian Flyer Makes Statement That Surprises Aero Officials

MILES CITY (Mont.), June 30.—Several British airplanes will start across the Pacific on August 15, from San Diego, Cal., bound for Australia, according to a statement made here yesterday by Captain William McDonald of Melbourne, formerly in the Canadian flying service, who is here on his way to Southern California, via Seattle. He stated that while full details of the trip have not been decided upon, the date of the start has been set and that the trip would be made with stops at Honolulu, Gutta Percha, a small British island near Guam, and Nagasaki. He said he will pilot one of the planes himself.

SAN DIEGO, June 30.—Aviation officers here received with surprise the statement of Captain William McDonald that several British airplanes would be brought to San Diego for the start of a flight across the Pacific. The statement by Captain McDonald, it was said, is the first intimation they have received of any such plan and until more details are received they stated that they could not talk for publication.

French to Announce Triple Defense Pact

PARIS, June 30 (Havas).—The first public announcement of the text of the defensive pact between France, Great Britain and the United States will be made in the Chamber of Deputies, the Echo de Paris says. The document, according to the newspaper, contains clauses intended to justify it before British and American public opinion.

FALL ATTACKS NATIONS' LEAGUE AND PEACE PACT

Senator Declares Ratification Would Brand Signers as Falsifiers

MORGAN AGENT ACCUSED

Representative Says Adoption of Covenant Will Kill Original U. S. Ideals

WASHINGTON, June 30.—The League of Nations covenant and the influences at work to secure its acceptance by the United States furnished the vehicle today for another long debate in the Senate.

Renewing his charge that international bankers are sponsoring the league for selfish purposes, Senator Borah, Republican, of Idaho, charged that Thomas W. Lamont, a partner in the Morgan banking house, had purchased the New York Evening Post as part of a propaganda to force Senate acceptance of the covenant. He charged the League to Enforce Peace, headed by former President Taft, also was controlled by the bankers.

Senator Hitchcock, Democrat, of Nebraska, defending Taft and his organization, replied that not only business men, but organized labor, the churches, the farmers and the people generally were demanding ratification of the covenant.

Popular Opinion Favors League, Asserts Hitchcock

Every test of popular opinion that had been taken anywhere, he said, had shown an overwhelming sentiment for the league.

The league covenant was defended also by Senator Gerry, Democrat, of Rhode Island, in a speech declaring it the only hope of Europe during reconstruction, and was attacked by Senator Fall, Republican, of New Mexico, who said he could not vote for its ratification without violating his oath as a Senator.

Many others were drawn into the debate, which occupied virtually the entire day's session.

Covenant Makes Treaty Scrap of Paper, Says Fall

"By ratifying the treaty and League of Nations covenant," said Senator Fall, "we make a scrap of paper of the Declaration of Independence and brand its signers as falsifiers. The adoption of the treaty with or without the covenant marks an entire reversal of the policy of this country in foreign affairs, to say nothing of its limitations upon our municipal law.

"We went to war with Germany because of specific acts of war of Germany against us; we indulged with President Wilson in the hope that peace might bring conditions which would make for the betterment of mankind and render wars less likely to occur.

Wilson Not Commissioned To Form League, Fall Says

"I will, to attain these objects, go as far as my sense of obligation to the people of the United States and to their and my Government justify. I would have voted, and will vote, to bind this country to abide the decisions upon international questions, not affecting our national honor or the Monroe Doctrine or municipal regulations, such as naturalization. I would agree to an additional limitation of sovereignty in enforcing such decrees by blockade or other means, to be decided by us; but I could not vote to allow even that court to declare war for us, nor to exercise the powers which its decisions by our agreement might limit or restrain.

"The President holds no commission from the people entitling him to form or join in creating or forming any other government. Attempt to ratify such act by the Senate would, in my judgment, be a violation of the Senatorial sworn duty.

"The mask of hypocrisy will be torn off," said Borah, "and even the sacred name of an ex-President cannot be

(Continued on Page 2, Column 6)

RUSSIANS KILL 18 AMERICANS, WOUND OTHERS

Yankee Soldiers Slain in Attack by Anti-Kolchaks on Railway Guards

OFFICER AMONG WOUNDED

Forty-Three Names on Casualty List After Engagement With Bolsheviks

WASHINGTON, June 30.—Eighteen American soldiers were killed, one officer and seven men severely wounded and seventeen slightly wounded in an engagement with anti-Kolchak forces near Romanovka on June 25.

Major General Graves, commanding the American expedition in Siberia, informed the War Department today that the engagement followed an attack by the Bolsheviki on railroad guards.

Apparently Company A of the 31st Infantry was the only unit engaged. Second Lieutenant Lawrence Donald Butler was reported severely wounded.

The official cablegram consisted of only the single line, "Anti-Kolchak forces attacked railroad guards at Romanovka, Suchan Branch, 5 A. M. June 25th," and then gave the following casualty report:

KILLED—Company A, 31st Infantry: Sergeant Henry P. Casey, Corporals Thomas B. Mason and Herbert Tell; Privates Brook Lee, George Love, James R. Love, Cecil T. Parson, William Roberts, Albert Simpson, Dart H. Balek, Walter H. Cole, Wesley Davis, Dave William Ivie, John Montoya Lopez, Walter Edward Roberts and Frank Schwab.

DIED OF WOUNDS—Corporal Louis Carter, Private Louis A. Schlichter.

SEVERELY WOUNDED—Corporal Valeryan J. Brodnicki, Cook Louis K. Boneau, Privates Edgar Curston, Aleyszuk Lukaslisch, Ray Ray Reader, Walter J. Renaes and Steward Reeves.

OFFICERS DENY STORY OF AMERICAN MUTINY

NEW YORK, June 30.—Reports of a mutiny on the Archangel front last March among members of the 339th Infantry were vehemently denied today by Major J. Brooks Nichols of Detroit and Captain H. G. Winslow of Madison, Wis., commanding Company I, the unit said to have been involved. Both officers returned on the transport Von Steuben, which brought back the first complete units to return from service in the Archangel sector.

"I have heard more 'bunk' about this mutiny than could be written in a dozen books," declared Major Nichols. "The incident which gave rise to the rumors was a misunderstanding between a sergeant and one private. The men of the 339th are the best disciplined and most courageous of any outfit I know, and all any officer could desire. They are second to none as soldiers."

Reports of the alleged mutiny and the refusal of troops to go to the front were confirmed last April by General March, who stated that the incident was due to bolshevik propaganda.

KUBAN COSSACKS TAKE 4000 BOLSHEVIKI

EKATERINODAR, Friday, June 20.—The army of Kuban Cossacks, operating in the bend of the Don river, has captured 4000 Bolsheviki and ten guns. The Don Cossacks, who also are advancing northward, have captured 1500 prisoners and three armored trains.

The Don Cossacks have occupied Millerovo and broken the Bolshevik front north of Millerovo.

In their successful advance the Kuban Cossacks put to rout four infantry and two cavalry regiments of the Bolshevik forces.

West of Ekaterinodar the Bolsheviki have been defeated on the Kertch

(Continued on Page 2, Column 1)

Californians Who Want Good Roads Have Duty to Perform by Voting Today

VOTE for the good roads bonds before you go to your business this morning! Don't leave it to the other fellow! It will take but a few minutes.

Every good Californian is for good roads and for the bond issue.

Naturally there are always some voters who oppose progressive measures. They always go to the polls

Because you hear your neighbor boost good roads and the bond issue do not take it for granted that the measure will carry without your vote.

The ballot of every Californian may be needed to carry the day when the votes are counted.

If you should neglect this duty that you owe yourself and the reputation of your State and the bonds should be defeated because you took too much for granted, and if there were a whole lot of others who followed your course, wouldn't it make you mad if you had to take upon yourself a big share of the blame for defeating a great public enterprise?

DEAD IN ITALY'S QUAKE HUNDRED

Several Thousand Injured, Hospitals Filled, Airplanes Search Devastated Area

FLORENCE, June 30 (by the Associated Press).—The victims of the earthquake so far reported number more than 100 killed and several thousand injured. A million and a half of the people of the provinces of Florence, Arezzo and Siena, where the shocks were especially severe, spent the night in the open air.

All the hospitals here are filled with wounded and the work of rescue is going on under difficult conditions.

This earthquake is the most sever that Tuscany has suffered in the last fifteen years. Vicchio, a village of 1200 inhabitants, suffered heavier, most of the local doctors being among the victims. In Dorgo San Lorenzo, with a population of more than 5000, factories, schoolhouses, churches and railway stations were destroyed.

It is feared that some region might be entirely isolated through the destruction of communications and airplanes have been dispatched in all directions on scouting missions.

Twelve Men Killed In Mine Explosion

McALESTER (Okla.), June 30.—Twelve miners are known to be dead and three more are expected to die as a result of an explosion in a mine of the Rock Island Coal Company at Alderson, Okla., five miles east of here. Rescue crews are at work.

Canada to Furnish Wheat for Greece

TORONTO, June 30.—Wheat in all Canadian elevators has been commandeered by the board of grain supervisors in order to provide Greece with 15,000,000 bushels within the next twelve months, it was announced tonight.

IRISH SLAIN BY BRITISH FLYERS

Towns Bombed, Women and Children Murdered, American Delegates Charge

PARIS, June 30 (by the Associated Press).—Irish-American delegates here in the interest of the Irish independent movement sent a new note to Premier Clemenceau today in which they charge the British with bombarding Irish towns from airplanes, "wantonly murdering women and children." They also said the British are issuing frequent orders of banishment. They asked the appointment of a special investigation commission.

BOSTON, June 30.—Eamonn de Valera, the Irish leader, today placed a wreath beneath the historic elm in Cambridge under which General Washington took command of the American revolutionary army, and another on the "minute man" monument on the green in Lexington. He was a guest during the forenoon of the city of Cambridge, with a reception at the City Hall, a luncheon at Riverbank Court and an automobile tour that showed him the landmarks of Cambridge and Boston.

Dutch Asked to Hold Ex-Kaiser in Holland

LONDON, June 30.—The allied governments have represented to the Government of Holland the necessity of taking steps to prevent the departure of the former German Emperor from Holland, C. B. Harmsworth, Undersecretary of State for Foreign Affairs, announced in the House of Commons this afternoon.

Germans Quit Riga As Letts Draw Near

COPENHAGEN, June 30.—(By the Associated Press)—Lettish troops are within nine miles of Riga and the Germans are evacuating the city, according to a dispatch received by the Lettish press bureau from Libau.

FRENCHMEN AND U. S. POLICE FIRE ON EACH OTHER

More Than 100 Wounded in Fighting and Two Civilians Are Killed

NAVY OFFICER BLAMED

Declared to Have Torn Down French Flag and Trampled It; Crowd Attacks Him

BREST, June 30.—Two [illegible] civilians were killed and [illegible] American soldiers and [illegible] were injured severely and more [illegible] 100 wounded in riots here last [illegible] Two of the American soldiers are [illegible] pected to die.

The casualties occurred as a [illegible] of the exchange of shots betw[illegible] American military and naval [illegible] and French sailors.

The trouble began, according [illegible] available accounts, when an Ame[illegible] naval officer, who is said to have [illegible] [illegible] a French flag [illegible] trampled on it. A [illegible] men attacked the officer [illegible] said, kicked and beat him [illegible] was unconscious.

Americans who passed by and [illegible] were not aware of the cause of [illegible] fight went to the aid of the naval [illegible] ficer. The fight then became [illegible]

A mob of French civilians and [illegible] diers and sailors attempted to [illegible] the Hotel Moderne, where Ameri[illegible] officers were quartered. They bu[illegible] a sentry box and threw stones [illegible] Americans in uniform wherever [illegible] found them. The Americans, it is [illegible] retaliated.

A company of marines with [illegible] bayonets was hurried to the scene [illegible] the Americans soon restored [illegible] Admiral Henri Salaun, the [illegible] naval commander at Brest, ord[illegible] the marines to return to their [illegible] racks. As the marines marched [illegible] to their quarters, it is declared, [illegible] were pursued by a mob throw[illegible] stones and bricks.

The city is quiet today.

Serbian and Italian Clash Near Di[illegible]

PARIS, June 30.—Serbian and [illegible] ian troops have clashed near [illegible] according to unofficial reports rec[illegible] here today.

1920-1929

JULY 3, 1921
Dempsey Wins in Fourth Round

JULY 9, 1921
Britain and Ireland End War; Asylum Fire Frees Maniacs

DECEMBER 7, 1921
Ireland Wins Fight for Freedom

FEBRUARY 17, 1923
King Tut's Tomb Opened

AUGUST 3, 1923
President Harding Dead

SEPTEMBER 3, 1923
100,000 Perish in Japanese Fires, Quakes

SEPTEMBER 18, 1923
Fire Sweeps Berkeley

JULY 21, 1925
Bryan Under Merciless Goad of Darrow

MAY 10, 1926
Byrd Circles North Pole

SEPTEMBER 24, 1926
Tunney Defeats Dempsey

MAY 22, 1927
Lindbergh Safely in Paris

MARCH 14, 1928
Dam Disaster Toll 1,125

OCTOBER 30, 1929
Record Stock Slump

The Sunday Chronicle
CONSISTS OF EIGHT SECTIONS TODAY
(COUNT THEM)
1—Rotogravure Pictorial (Eight Pages)
2—Magazine
3—Comics
4—Editorial and Features
5—Automobiles
6—Society
7—Main News
8—Classified

San Francisco Chronicle

LEADING NEWSPAPER of the PACIFIC COAST

REG. U. S. PAT. OFF.

FAIR
WEATHER
SAN FRANCISCO, OAKLAND AND VICINITY
Sunday fair, moderate westerly winds
E. A. BEALS, Forecaster.
Complete Weather Report on Page 97

FOUNDED 1865—VOL. CXVIII. NO. 169 CC SAN FRANCISCO, CAL., SUNDAY, JULY 3, 1921—SEVENTY PAGES DAILY 5 CENTS, SUNDAY 10 CENTS

DEMPSEY WINS IN 4TH ROUND; CARPENTIER INJURED IN SECOND

HARDING SIGNS MEASURE ENDING STATE OF WAR

Signature Affixed by Chief Executive at Home of Senator Freylinghuysen

U. S. IS NOW AT PEACE

"That's All," Says President as He Completes Historic Document

Special by Leased Wire to The Chronicle.

RARITAN (N. J.), July 2.—War with Germany ended as it began by Congressional decision and Executive signature on American soil.

At 4:10 P. M., local daylight saving time, in the living-room of The Hill, Senator Joseph S. Frelinghuysen's home here, President Harding today placed his signature to the Porter joint Congressional resolution declaring peace with Germany and Austria, just two years and four days after the ill-fated treaty of Versailles was signed

Acceptance Speech Begun Year Ago

By a coincidence, a year ago to the day, Warren G. Harding, United States Senator from Ohio, the Republican nominee for President, left Washington for his Marion front porch to prepare his speech of acceptance containing the promise of "formal and effective peace so quickly as the Republican Congress can pass its declaration for a Republican Executive to sign."

Scarcely thirty people in a country home in the hills of Somerset county witnessed the last act that concluded the World's war, while a few minutes before, fifty miles away in another part of the State, 90,000 persons saw a war-time riveter in a shipyard knock to the floor of the ring a former French enlisted man and aviation pilot.

Ink Drips From Pen Upon Paper

"That's all," said President Harding, as he held his pen above his signature on a broad vellum typewritten page. The ink dripped from the pen and made a blot the size of a 5-cent piece on the page, almost effacing the "g" of the President's signature.

War against Germany was declared on April 6, 1917, and against Austria-Hungary on December 7, 1917.

RESOLUTION TAKEN BACK TO CAPITAL

RARITAN (N. J.), July 2 (by the Associated Press).—So that there might be no unnecessary delay in consummation of the long deferred state of peace the resolution was brought here by special messenger from Washington, where it had been given final Congressional approval yesterday. The messenger left for the capital again tonight to complete the formalities of the declaration by depositing the document in the archives of the State Department.

Widow, 77, Drowns Herself in Bathtub

Mrs. Ester A. Campbell Ill, Despondent

Mrs. Ester A. Campbell, a widow, 77 years of age, was found dead, fully dressed, in a bathtub filled with water in her home at 204 Hugo street yesterday afternoon. The case is believed to be one of suicide through despondency over ill health.

The body was discovered by Anna Olson, a domestic in the household, who was attracted to the bathroom after hearing the water running for two hours. She found Mrs. Campbell's body, partly submerged, face downward in the overflowing tub. There was every indication, according to deputy coroners, that the woman had drowned herself.

Mrs. Campbell lived with her daughter, Miss Nettie Campbell, a school teacher, from whom it was learned that she had been ill for a long time and a year ago had been stricken with paralysis, which affected her speech.

Kidnaped Woman Socialist Orator Eludes Captors

Mrs. O'Hare Reaches Pocatello With Story of Escape From Abductors

POCATELLO (Ida.), July 2.—Mrs. Kate Richards O'Hare, widely known Socialist writer and lecturer, kidnaped at Twin Falls by eleven men and taken across the desert into Nevada, in an automobile, arrived in Pocatello at 6:30 o'clock this evening from Ogden, Utah, where she changed cars from Montello, Nev. Mrs. O'Hare, attired in a light green summer dress, with no hat and no personal possessions, upon alighting from the train at this city, stated that she escaped her captors when about one-quarter mile from Montello. The kidnaping party was composed of three cars. The escape was effected when the first car had a puncture and the gasoline supply in the second was exhausted.

SLIPS AWAY FROM CAPTORS

During the excitement over the accidents Mrs. O'Hare slipped out of the rear car and made her way across the desert to Montello, where she secured the assistance of the marshal, who arrested nine of the captors while they were repairing the puncture and searching for gasoline, according to her story.

Upon arriving in Pocatello Mrs. O'Hare found that her daughter had arrived from Twin Falls intent upon filling her mother's lecture engagement, but found that the doors of the hall in which they were to appear had been locked. The owners of the hall stated that the Twin Falls incident was sufficient to warrant the closing.

TIRED OF LECTURING

Mrs. O'Hare said she was tired of lecturing and that she would try to cancel her remaining engagements, devoting her time to preferring charges against her nine captors.

"Certain members of the party," declares Mrs. O'Hare, "stated that if I dared return to Twin Falls I would be killed. They again reiterated the threat to the Marshal of Montello."

Mrs. O'Hare plans to remain in Pocatello tomorrow, later returning to Twin Falls.

TWIN FALLS (Ida.), July 2.—Ten men, alleged kidnapers of Mrs. Kate Richards O'Hare, arrived here today in three automobiles with Deputy Sheriff Bert Robinson, of Montello, Nev. The Nevada officer declared he had no warrant for any member of the party. There were no charges here against them, according to Sheriff E. R. Shearman, and no arrests had been made at a late hour tonight.

Mrs. O'Hare told the Nevada officer, he said, that she had been well treated and that her abductors had conducted themselves in a gentlemanly manner.

H. H. Friedheim, sponser here for Mrs. O'Hare, from whose residence she was yesterday taken by the kid-

(Continued on Page 2, Column 7)

Soldiers Discharged To Get 3 Years' Pay

Special by Leased Wire to The Chronicle.

WASHINGTON, July 2.—It is going to be expensive for the Government to discharge enlisted men in the army to meet the Congressional order that the army may be cut to a maximum of 150,000 men. Enlisted men must be paid their three-year enlistment allowance, and that is one of the obligations which President Harding referred to in his request to Congress stating that it may be necessary for him to ask for emergency legislation so that the Government may meet the obligations to the soldiers.

Salvers Work Upon Wrecked Naval Plane

MONTEREY, July 2.—Efforts to salvage the naval seaplane N-9, which fell into the ocean off the mouth of Little Sur river, thirty miles south of here, while making a trip to this place, are being continued today. The combers have washed the seaplane high up on the beach. Lieutenant Guy McLaughlin, who was in command, was washed overboard when the machine landed, but was uninjured. The other members of the crew escaped injury also.

FIRE DESTROYS TWELVE BLOCKS IN MARYSVILLE

Hundreds Left Homeless and $500,000 Damage Done by Big Blaze

CAUSED BY FIRECRACKERS

Aid Sent From Chico, But Wind Carries Flames to Yuba River Levee

Special Dispatch to The Chronicle.

MARYSVILLE, July 2.—Three twelve-year-old boys playing with firecrackers, precipitated a $500,000 fire here this afternoon, which swept twelve city blocks and leveled more than 100 buildings. The flames, fanned by a strong north wind, consumed two hotels, three apartment houses, two small lumber yards, two warehouses, four blocks of Southern Pacific trestle and several scores of dwelling houses.

Several hundred men, women and children, whose small homes were in the direct path of the flames, are homeless, and the citizens made arrangements to house them and care for them.

Boys' Firecrackers Said to Be Cause

The police say the conflagration was started by three small boys playing with firecrackers in the rear of the Pavilion livery stable, at Sixth and B streets at 2 o'clock this afternoon It is believed that several lighted firecrackers were carried by a gust of wind to the roof of the livery stable, which soon was in flames. Three small dwellings to the north of the blazing building were destroyed and the flames then leaped across the street to a small lumber yard. Within an hour two blocks were a raging inferno, the conflagration spreading rapidly in all directions and soon was out of control of the Marysville Fire Department.

Chico responded to a call for help by sending a fire engine, and a Southern Pacific fire engine also aided the forces combating the fire.

Flames Stopped By River Levee

The flames swept on until checked by the Yuba river levee at 4:30 this afternoon.

Among the buildings leveled was a large warehouse of the California Packing Corporation. The Southern Pacific station was damaged by fire, but employes saved the structure. Had the wind been from the east, firemen say, the entire city of Marysville would doubtless have been wiped out.

The burned area extends between Sixth and First streets, between A and B streets. Last night the fire fighters confined their operations to holding the flames within the area already destroyed, and tonight it was stated that unless the wind changes the fire will not spread further.

So swift was the sweep of the flames that in many cases those living in their path were unable to save anything but the lightest personal property, and the streets were crowded with hundreds of persons carrying large bundles on their backs, presenting the appearance of refugees fleeing before an invading army. All those whose homes were destroyed will be cared for by other citizens. Two men suffered burns while fight'ng the fire.

County Assessor Thomas Bevan, after going over the tax rolls here tonight, estimated that the fire loss would exceed $500,000.

SACRAMENTO UNABLE TO HELP MARYSVILLE

SACRAMENTO, July 2.—Constantly present danger of spread of grass fires about the city of Sacramento caused the city authorities to inform Marysville officials, who had asked that the fire department send apparatus to help check the flames in that city, late today that the hazard was too great to send the fire department or any of its equipment out of the city. The department responded to several calls during the day and momentarily was expecting others, as a strong north wind was blowing.

Referee Ertle Explains How Dempsey Won

By HARRY ERTLE
Referee, Carpentier-Dempsey Fight

Special Dispatch to The Chronicle.

NEW YORK, July 2.—The better man won—there is no question in my mind about that. I was never more surprised in my life than when the bell clanged to end the second round, Carpentier showed his wonderful comeback in this session.

* * * *

Carpentier showed remarkable cleverness in infighting and in being able to punch Dempsey around the ring.

* * * *

The blow that finished Carpentier was the right hook to the jaw, delivered with force and precision. The same wallop put Fulton out at the Harrison Ball Park, and the same wallop won the championship at Toledo two years ago tomorrow.

* * * *

Carpentier went down the first time and I began to count—the Frenchman scrambled to his feet, so I dropped my arm. It was a big surprise, for I hadn't expected him to come up again.

* * * *

But he was badly hurt. Again Dempsey sprang at him. I finished my count.

Mercury Volplanes From 92 Degrees to Snowstorm in Idaho

IDAHO FALLS (Idaho), July 2.—A drop from ninety-two degrees two days ago to a snowstorm today was reported from Heise and Amoon, two towns near here. An inch of snow fell at Heise.

Judge Unable to Send Man Back to Mexico, But Selects San Quentin Instead

San Quentin Next After Mexico, Judges Opinion

Special Dispatch to The Chronicle.

STOCKTON, July 2.—"Do me the grand favor, Judge, of sending me back to Mexico," answered Jose Malava, when asked by Judge Buck in the Superior Court if he had any legal cause to show why judgment should not be pronounced on his conviction for burglary.

"I can't do that," replied Judge Buck, "but I will send you to San Quentin, the next best place."

Mystery Man Comes Out Of Three Years' Sleep

FORT SMITH (Ark.), July 2.—Jim Eschlinger, the mystery man, whose strange sleeping sickness case has baffled leading medical experts of America, has awakened from his three-year sleep in a hospital here. His first words were:

"The Lord help me."

He is still awake. During the three years he never ceased taking food.

Lightning Strikes Man Listening to Fight News

ATLANTIC CITY (N. J.), July 2.—Casper Risley, sitting at a wireless telephone instrument in his Margate City home listening to the bulletins from the fight at Jersey City, today was struck by a bolt of lightning and slightly injured. The instrument was shattered.

Jury Prays All Night and Sends Slayer to Gallows

DALLAS (Texas), July 2.—After praying virtually all night for divine guidance in arriving at a verdict in the case of Charles E. Gaines, a jury early today condemned Gaines to the gallows. He was tried for murder in connection with the death of G. W. Street, register clerk in the postoffice here, last January.

Several of the jurors offered prayers for the salvation of the doomed man's soul, it was said.

Carpentier Breaks His Thumb And Sprains Wrist by Blows

MANHASSET (N. Y.), July 2.—Georges Carpentier broke his right thumb in two places and suffered a slight wrist sprain in the second round of his fight with Jack Dempsey in Jersey City this afternoon. This was reported by Dr. Joseph Connolly of Glen Cove, N. Y., who examined him at his training camp tonight.

Dr. Connolly's report follows:

This is to certify that I examined Georges Carpentier after his fight with Jack Dempsey and found him to be suffering from a compound fracture of the metacarpal bone of his right thumb and a slight wrist sprain. These injuries have rendered his right hand useless.

Dr. Connolly said Carpentier's hand was swollen to three times its normal size.

Challenger Is Toy in Hands of Jack Dempsey, the Champion

Bell in Third Round Welcomed by Tired French Pugilist

By JAMES W. COFFROTH
Famous San Francisco Boxing Expert and Promoter

Special Dispatch to The Chronicle.

JERSEY CITY (N. J.), July 2.—The "wonder man" from France was a mere toy in the hands of Jack Dempsey, the world's champion.

JAMES W. COFFROTH

The American ended it midway in the fourth round with a succession of heavy uppercuts.

Two punches decided the greatest sporting spectacle of the decade. The first, a heavy uppercut to the jaw, laid Carpentier flat. He took the count of nine, then he sprang to his feet with a surprising suddenness. Dempsey lost no time. Another terrific jolt to the heart and down went the French idol. He could not rise. Referee Ertle gave him a full ten count, but Descamps had already leaped into the ring, before the uplifted hand had descended for the tenth time, knowing his pet was an utter wreck.

LIFTED TO HIS CORNER

Carpentier was tenderly lifted to his corner. It was several minutes before he revived. Pandemonium broke loose among the spectators with the conclusion of the bout of the century. Dempsey was cheered to the skies. The great mob of humanity went wild. A score of blue coats prevented an invasion of the ring by the seething crowd.

CHALLENGER IS PUNISHED

In victory Dempsey was great. Carpentier fought capably and surprised me by staying as long as he did. However, the challenger was woefully lacking on defense. In the fourth, shortly before the end, Dempsey rained wicked short chops to Carpentier's jaw, without an arm being raised by the foreigner in his own protection. He was a wide open target for all Dempsey had to offer.

Jack was not bashful in his serving. The finish might just as well have come about in the opening round, for the champion punished the challenger severely. Dempsey was slow in following his advantage. He preferred to wait.

Realizing his magnificent superiority, gained in the opening session, Dempsey became careless in the second and Carpentier displayed his talked-of right hand. Shooting thrusts, particularly after clinches. Carpentier sent a series of these lightning rights to the champion's head. Jack assumed a worried look for the moment. The rally brought Carpentier's followers to their feet in a wild

(Continued on Page 4, Column 5)

Follow Fight By Rounds on Second Page

THE full details of the big fight, every blow, every move, just as flashed from the ringside, will be found on Page 2, Columns 3 and 4. This is the chronological history of the battle. The experts watched every angle and this was flashed over the wire just as it occurred, one move after the other.

As fast as the optic nerve carried the message to the expert's brain, just so fast did it leap across the continent on the direct wire to The Chronicle office. The crowds before the bulletin boards received the news immediately.

The fight by rounds on Page 2 is the fight as the ringside experts saw it.

Ninety Thousand Witness Contest

RINGSIDE, JERSEY CITY July 2.—Announcement was made after the contest that 90,000 persons witnessed the battle. The receipts totaled $1,600,000.

Dempsey's share $300,000
Carpentier's purse $200,000
Cost of arena $250,000
Estimated tax to be collected by Government from all sources, $1,000,000.

Heavy Punches to Body and Broken Thumb Beat French Championship Contender

Challenger Shows Brief Flash in Second Round, but Hard Blows Slow Him Up Until Ertle Counts the Fatal Ten

By HARRY B. SMITH
Sporting Editor of The Chronicle
Special Dispatch to The Chronicle

RINGSIDE, JERSEY CITY (N. J.), July 2.—Jack Dempsey is still champion of the world. The big Westerner, rated two years ago as one of the best heavies the game has produced, ran true to form.

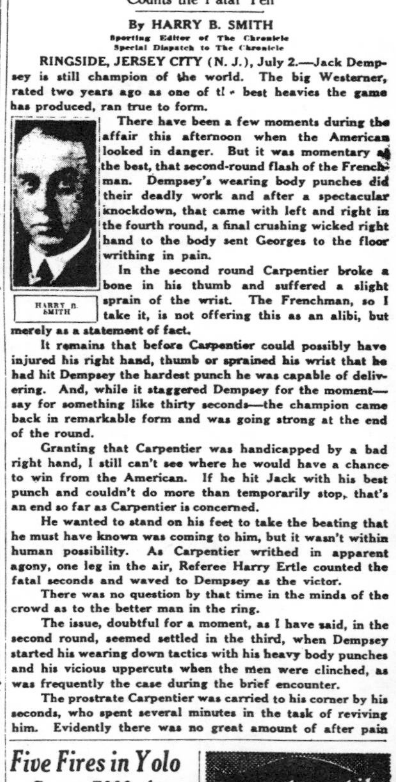

HARRY B. SMITH

There have been a few moments during the affair this afternoon when the American looked in danger. But it was momentary at the best, that second-round flash of the Frenchman. Dempsey's wearing body punches did their deadly work and after a spectacular knockdown, that came with left and right in the fourth round, a final crushing wicked right hand to the body sent Georges to the floor writhing in pain.

In the second round Carpentier broke a bone in his thumb and suffered a slight sprain of the wrist. The Frenchman, so I take it, is not offering this as an alibi, but merely as a statement of fact.

It remains that before Carpentier could possibly have injured his right hand, thumb or sprained his wrist that he had hit Dempsey the hardest punch he was capable of delivering. And, while it staggered Dempsey for the moment—say for something like thirty seconds—the champion came back in remarkable form and was going strong at the end of the round.

Granting that Carpentier was handicapped by a bad right hand, I still can't see where he would have a chance to win from the American. If he hit Jack with his best punch and couldn't do more than temporarily stop, that's an end so far as Carpentier is concerned.

He wanted to stand on his feet to take the beating that he must have known was coming to him, but it wasn't within human possibility. As Carpentier writhed in apparent agony, one leg in the air, Referee Harry Ertle counted the fatal seconds and waved to Dempsey as the victor.

There was no question by that time in the minds of the crowd as to the better man in the ring.

The issue, doubtful for a moment, as I have said, in the second round, seemed settled in the third, when Dempsey started his wearing down tactics with his heavy body punches and his vicious uppercuts when the men were clinched, as was frequently the case during the brief encounter.

The prostrate Carpentier was carried to his corner by his seconds, who spent several minutes in the task of reviving him. Evidently there was no great amount of after pain

Five Fires in Yolo Cover 7000 Acres

Damage to Buildings and Grain Set at $200,000

WOODLAND, July 2.—Five fires, in different sections of Yolo county today, burned over 7000 acres of grain and pasture land and caused damage estimated at $200,000. The drying sheds and other buildings of the Yolo Orchard Company, north of here, were destroyed. All of the fires were reported under control at 10 o'clock tonight.

Damage estimated at $35,000 was caused when the grain fields of the A. W. Morris and the F. Meyers ranches east of here were burned over and approximately 400 acres of grain and grazing lands burned on the R. L. Ogden ranch to the west.

Anglo-Japanese Pact In Force for Year

LONDON, July 2.—Great Britain has notified Japan that owing to the decision of Lord Birkenhead, the Lord High Chancellor, the Anglo-Japanese treaty, even if denounced July 15, will automatically run for another year.

Ship Brings 5824 Bodies of Soldiers

HOBOKEN (N. J.), July 2.—The United States Army transport Wheaton arrived today with the 5824 bodies of American soldier dead.

San Francisco Chronicle

LEADING NEWSPAPER *of the* PACIFIC COAST

REG. U. S. PAT. OFF.

FOUNDED 1865 — VOL. CXVIII. NO. 175 CC SAN FRANCISCO, CAL., SATURDAY, JULY 9, 1921 — TWENTY-TWO PAGES DAILY 5 CENTS. SUNDAY 10 CENTS: DAILY AND SUNDAY PER MONTH, $1.00

BRITAIN AND IRELAND END WAR

San Francisco to Observe Diamond Jubilee Today.

Fight on Anti-Beer Measure Develops in Senate

PEACE AGREED ON AT MEETING HELD IN DUBLIN

Terms of Truce to Be Given Out Today When Details Are Arranged

ALL FACTIONS ASSEMBLE

Crowds Cheer Both Sides, Even English General, in Enthusiastic Scene

By JOHN STEELE

Special Cable to The Chronicle

DUBLIN, July 8.—The Irish war is over. Peace was agreed upon at a conference at the Mansion House today between General Sir Nevill Macready, commander in chief of the British forces in Ireland, and representatives from all sections of opinion in the south of Ireland.

The terms of the truce will be announced tomorrow morning, the details yet remaining to be worked out, and until then no statement will be made; but it is understood the Irish will not be required to surrender their arms. The truce is to take effect Monday noon.

All-Day Conference Brings Result

The agreement for the cessation of hostilities was the result of an all-day conference beginning at 11 o'clock this morning and breaking up at 9 o'clock tonight. The members of the conference were the same as those attending the previous session, neither Sir James Craig nor General Smuts attending. Eamonn de Valera and Arthur Griffith represented the Sinn Fein and the Earl of Midleton, Sir A. Woods, Sir Maurice Dockrell and Andrew Jameson appeared for the southern Unionists.

The first session broke up at 1 o'clock this afternoon, when it was announced the meeting would be resumed at 4 o'clock. Shortly after 4 o'clock an aide-de-camp arrived from the British headquarters, bearing a dispatch. He was taken to the conference room and soon dashed out again.

"It's All Over," And General Smiles

A little before 5 o'clock General Macready, in full General's uniform and unescorted for the first time in Dublin streets, drove up and entered the conference room, where he remained for an hour. When he left he said he was going to consult with Prime Minister Lloyd George by direct wire, and in less than an hour he returned. When he came out again he was smiling and whispered to the Lord Mayor that it was all over.

A little later the Southern Unionists emerged and the Earl of Midleton smilingly thanked the Lord Mayor for his peace efforts, which he said had been fully justified.

Lloyd George Concurs In Opinion of De Valera

Shortly after the conference disbanded the Lord Mayor, speaking from the Mansion House steps, said it was the proudest and happiest day of his life and he introduced Eamonn Duggan, a leading member of Dail Eireann, who read a short statement saying at the first conference that De Valera informed the assembly of the terms with which he proposed to reply to Prime Minister Lloyd George's invitation to go to London, but he expressed the view that fruitful results were impossible while bloodshed continued.

This morning a letter from Prime Minister Lloyd George to the Earl of Midleton, concurring in these views, was read to the conference, Duggan said. The Prime Minister indicated the willingness of the British Government to consent to the suspension of active operations by both sides. The statement concluded by saying a truce would be announced tomorrow.

Immediately at the close of the conference Mr. de Valera telegraphed the following acceptnce to Prime Minister Lloyd George's letter:

"The desire you express on the part of the British Government to end the centuries of conflict between the peoples of these two islands and to establish relations of neighborly

(Continued on Page 2, Column 3)

Explains Heat Wave

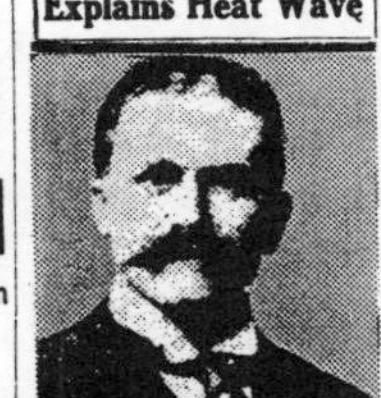

Professor T. J. J. See, Government astronomer at Mare Island Navy Yard, who says the hot summer is due to a heavy downpour of meteors upon the sun.

PEGGY AWARDED $1350 MONTHLY

Special by Leased Wire to The Chronicle

CHICAGO, July 8.—Peggy Hopkins Joyce must struggle along with $27,500 for solicitors' fees, $12,500 for other legal expenses and $1350 a month temporary alimony from her husband, James Stanley Joyce, millionaire lumberman.

This was the award made today by Judge Sabath. Peggy had asked for $100,000 attorneys fees and $10,000 a month temporary alimony. Her request was based upon the statements of her husband during their honeymoon that he was worth $40,000,000 and wanted her to live accordingly. In his testimony Joyce said his total assets would not exceed $3,000,000.

PROPERTY NOT MENTIONED

Joyce had asked for the return of jewelry worth many thousands of dollars which he had given Peggy, and also the home he built for her in Miami, Fla. He has since given title to the Miami property to his brother. The Judge made no mention of jewelry or the home in his award. He said that if it should subsequently develop that actual and necessary expenditures were more than $12,500 allowed for taking depositions and hiring detectives and investigators, he would entertain further motions.

Joyce's attorneys had sought to prevent the allowance of any attorneys' fees, claiming that Peggy had sufficient money of her own with which to prepare her case. After the award had been announced they asked permission to file an appeal from the decision. This was granted and a bill of exceptions will be filed within forty days. Joyce will give bond of $15,000 to insure the payments and then the case will be taken to the Appellate Court.

"FIFI" WON MORE IN COURT

The alimony award, while considered high for local courts, is small compared with the temporary alimony allowed "Fifi" Stillman, who was granted $7500 a month, $35,000 lawyers' fees and $12,000 suit money. Mrs. Stillman had asked for $10,000 a month alimony, the same figure set by Peggy.

Neither party to the suit was present in court. Peggy is still in New York. Judge Sabath ruled two weeks ago that she need not come to Chicago to undergo cross-examination. Joyce is believed to be in Chicago, but he was not in evidence today. Peggy's attorneys seemed well pleased with the decision.

Four Charged With Plot to Start Riots

CHICAGO, July 8.—Four men were arrested in Gary, Ind., today in connection with recent alleged attempts to incite riots among the negroes there by the distribution of Communist literature. Three were turned over to Department of Justice agents to face deportation proceedings.

Weather Forecast

Full reports of the weather will be found on page 19.

METEORIC RAIN ON SUN BLAMED FOR HEAT WAVE

Mare Island Astronomer Says Orb's Radiation Has Been Increased

HAPPENS AT INTERVALS

Downpour Accelerates Speed of Earth Upon Its Solar Orbit

VALLEJO, July 8.—The extraordinary hot summer being felt all over the world is due to an unusual downpour of meteors upon the sun, by which the radiation and effective surface temperature of the sun is temporarily increased, Professor T. J. J. See, Government astronomer at the Mare Island Navy Yard today said his researches had led him to conclude. He said:

Since a mass of meteoric matter greater than our moon is falling into the sun every century, it is very improbable that the downpour proceeds at a uniform rate. If it comes down in gusts under the action of the chief planets Jupiter and Saturn, which are now near conjunction and are seen together in our evening sky, then we should have sudden increases of the sun's radiation just such as we now witness all over the world.

Sun's Radiation Found to Be Variable

Within the last twenty years Dr. Abbott of the Astrophysical Observatory, Smithsonian Institution, Washington, has gathered observational data to show that the sun's radiation is variable to an appreciable degree. In practice it is not easy to overcome all local effects within our own atmosphere, yet such unprecedentedly hot summers over the whole world will appeal to our common sense as showing that the radiation of our sun is sensibly variable.

In the year 1909-10 I was led to investigate the average amount of meteroric matter falling into the sun. It proved to be larger than had been generally supposed, making a solid layer about two meters deep all over the sun's surface in a century, when the matter is of the average density of the earth, which is 5.5 or twice the density of the earth's crust. In a century this downpour accumulates and exceeds the total mass of our moon.

Light Thrown Upon Mystery After Research

This is a sufficient explanation of the unprecedentedly hot summer and so simply and directly connected with the established secular acceleration and increase of the sun's mass by meteoric downpour that public attention should be called to the nature of the cause at work. It has been at work also in all past ages, but now, for the first time, by profound researches, as-

(Continued on Page 2, Column 1)

Missing Woman's Body Found Starved

COMPTON (Cal.), July 8.—The body of Mrs. P. Maxwell, formerly of Fresno, was found under a sanatorium here today. Mrs. Maxwell had been missing for some time. A Coroner's deputy, who investigated, said the woman had evidently crawled under the floor of the building when it was being repaired about two weeks ago, and had starved to death. She was at the sanatorium because of a mental condition. When she disappeared search was made for her and it was believed she had wandered away and would be found in time. She was about 30 years of age.

American Music at British State Ball

Special Cable to The Chronicle

LONDON, July 8.—Strains of American music filled Buckingham Palace last night, where the first state ball since 1913 was given by the King and Queen of England. More than 2000 guests were present, including Ambassador and Mrs. Harvey, other members of the diplomatic corps and a host of British notables. Dukes and Duchesses, glittering in satin, diamonds and gorgeous uniforms, danced to the strains of American popular music.

Parade and Historical Pageant to Be Features of Anniversary Celebration

Flag-Raising of 1846 To Be Re-Enacted By Citizens

Some San Franciscans who can still remember the cheer of Commander Montgomery as the Stars and Stripes were flung to the breezes in Portsmouth Square July 9, 1846, and hundreds of their descendents who were present on the memorable occasion, will gather on the same historic spot today and observe the seventy-fifth anniversary of Montgomery's action.

The mighty armada in the bay will fire a salute, just as the tiny U. S. S. Portsmouth did seventy-five years ago today. Two thousand soldiers, sailors and marines, will take the place of the two score sailors who accompanied the gallant commander and a throng representative of 600,000 people will cheer, just as that small body of pioneers cheered.

Uniforms of Old Guard to Be Worn

When Commander Montgomery ran up the flag a band of Americans hastily organized the first California Guard, which was enrolled on the spot. In today's parade will be twenty men and an officer dressed in the uniform of the old California Guard. They will lend a hand to the flag raising just as the original unit did seventy-five years ago. The detachment will be led by George H. Howard Jr., whose father, George H. Howard was the nephew of W. D. Howard, who commanded the hurriedly formed guard on July 9, 1846.

In the parade will be Stephen Richardson who was a boy of fifteen when Commander Montgomery landed and who threw his hat into the air and cheered when the Stars and Stripes were run up. And in line also will be Mrs. George Bucknall, 2845 Green street, the first white child born in San Francisco.

Flags to Fly Throughout the City

Observance of the Diamond Jubilee will begin this morning at 10 o'clock, when flags will be raised on public and private buildings throughout the city. Mayor Rolph, in a proclamation issued yesterday, requests that no flags be put up before that hour, as it is the wish of those in charge of the celebration to have the flags raised simultaneously all over San Francisco. The siren at the Ferry building will give the signal for the flag raising promptly at 10 o'clock.

The exercises in Portsmouth square will follow a review of the parade this afternoon. The men and women in the line of march will follow the route Commander Montgomery took when he went to the plaza to raise the Stars and Stripes. Montgomery landed just east of Montgomery street, at Clay, and the paraders,

(Continued on Page 2, Column 5)

Hardings Celebrate 30th Anniversary

WASHINGTON, July 8.—Today was the thirtieth anniversary of the marriage of the President and Mrs. Harding, but they planned no formal observance. They were married at the same house in Marion from which the front-porch campaign was conducted last year, and George B. Christian Jr., now secretary to the President, was the chief doorkeeper of the occasion.

San Franciscan in Yellowstone Burned

OGDEN (Utah), July 8.—Mrs. Henry Cendagorta, wife of an Ogden business man, was severely scalded Sunday at Yellowstone Park when she stumbled and fell into a hot pot near Old Faithful geyser, and Dr. Mario Isnada of San Francisco was painfully burned in dragging her from the water, it was learned today when Mrs. Cendagorta was brought to an Ogden hospital for treatment.

Navy Yard Employes May Lose Positions

VALLEJO, July 8.—Employes at the Mare Island Navy Yard were paid today to include June 30, Captain E. L. Beach, commandant of the yard, announcing that this would be the last pay day until Congress passes the naval appropriation bill. It is expected employes will continue at work until the new appropriation becomes available to make up back pay.

Every San Francisco Building Asked to Display Old Glory

MAKE San Francisco's Diamond Jubilee an event to be remembered. Run your flag up promptly at 10 o'clock this morning when the siren on the Ferry Building will give the signal. Hoist Old Glory to the top of your building or house top. If you have no building or house top, display it in your window. Remember the hour, 10 o'clock and not before. The official programme for the day follows:

10 A. M.—Siren at the Ferry Building will be sounded as signal for raising of flags throughout the city.

2 P. M.—Parade starts from the Civic Center, arriving at Portsmouth Square at 2:30.

2:30 P. M.—Literary exercises start at Portsmouth Square.

FIRE FIGHT LED BY PADEREWSKI

Special Dispatch to The Chronicle.

SAN LUIS OBISPO, June 8.—Personally directing a force of more than 200 men, Ignace Paderewski, world renowned pianist and former Premier of Poland succeeded today in saving the beautiful home on his estate near Paso Robles from destruction by fire. A blaze that started last night swept over the Paderewski ranch, burning twenty-six acres of grain and pasturage.

While the blaze on the Paderewski place was being combated, several hundred citizens were fighting a stubborn fire that has been sweeping for two days over the Eagle ranch, owned by Frederick Peabody. Another large force was battling a fire at Creson, where 1000 acres of grain were burned and the Creson Hotel destroyed. Other firefighters were trying to check flames at Atascadero and in Stone canyon, just west of Paso Robles.

Both this city and Paso Robles were without electric lights tonight, the fire at Atascadero having burned power line poles of the San Joaquin Light and Power Company.

Every available man in the countryside near Paso Robles and in the vicinity of the Eagle ranch was being used to save the Peabody estate, and tonight a call was sent out for reinforcements. The millionaire owner of the ranch offered firefighters $1 an hour.

The damage following the various fires is expected to total thousands of dollars. The Peabody residence is one of the show places of the county and herculean efforts are being made to save it.

Fifty-Three Chinese Stowaways Captured

GALVESTON (Texas), July 8.—Fifty-three Chinese stowaways aboard the American steamer Ausable were taken into custody by immigration officials when the vessel docked here late today from Havana, Cuba.

ASYLUM FIRE FREES MANIACS

UKIAH, July 8.—M. Machada of Sonoma, said by the hospital authorities to be a dangerous maniac; John O'Neill of Eureka, George Rustico and Arthur Fime, patients of the Mendocino State Hospital at Talmage, near here, were still at large late today after having escaped with eight other patients during a fire in the hospital early today. The remaining fugitives were returned to the hospital by Ukiah police and deputy sheriffs.

Hospital authorities expected that the four who are still out would be driven back to the hospital tonight by hunger, or rounded up by hospital and police guards.

Chief concern is being felt on account of Machada, who is described by hospital executives as a "bad man." It is believed that all of the remaining escapes are in the brush back of the institution. He was not confined in the violent ward.

The fire raged worst on the roof above the ward in which 118 violent patients were confined. They were aroused and led from the room, while guards counted them at the door. They were then taken down a back stairway into an inclosed structure on the ground, where they were counted again. Today they were subjected to a third count, and it was determined that none of them is missing.

Superintendent D. R. Smith and John Murphey, an attendant, personally prevented the fire from catching the main building by taking turns at a big fire hose in a tiny, smoke-filled room in the path of the flames. Each man held the hose for a few minutes at a time, while the other sought relief in the fresh air. All of the patients endangered by the fire were

(Continued on Page 2, Column 3)

Four Meet Death In Swimming Pool

Mother, Uncle, Die Trying to Save Two Children

Special by Leased Wire to The Chronicle

LEWISTOWN (Ill.), July 8.—Grim tragedy was enacted in a little swimming pool on the Shaw farm near Canton, Ill., shortly after noon today. The victims are:

Lefley, Charles, aged 54.
Shaw, Mrs. David, aged 35.
Shaw, Ruth, aged 14.
Shaw, Dorothy, aged 12.

The two girls, accompanied by their brother, Robert, aged 10, had gone to the pool to bathe. Soon after they left the boy came running back and said the girls had gone under the water and had not come up.

Mrs. Shaw, their mother, and Lefley, her uncle, ran to the pool half a mile from the house. What befell them can only be conjectured. When they did not return neighbors called by Robert found the four bodies in ten feet of water.

Muskegon Forbids Bathing Suit for Women on Street

Shore Costume Worn by Shoppers in Michigan; Unique Sign Warns Auto Tourists

MUSKEGON (Mich.), July 8.—Mrs. Sarah McVeigh, police matron, has asked Muskegon women to discontinue wearing bathing suits while shopping. Women recently have appeared on the streets and also in some of the downtown stores here clad in bathing costumes. The police matron announced bath robes must be worn over the bathing suits when women appear on the streets.

Autoists Go Slow to See Town, Fast and See Jail

AMESBURY (Mass.), July 8.—"Go slow and see our town; go fast and see our jail."

This combined invitation and admonition posted conspicuously along the State highway has proved an effective means of stopping automobile speeding.

Tourists pass through Amesbury in large numbers and the good roads have tempted fast traveling. Chief of Police [illegible] decided to post the signs, [illegible] effectiveness was shown [illegible] Sunday the signs [illegible] no overnight [illegible]

Berkeley [illegible] Crowing [illegible]

BERKELEY, July 8.—[illegible] to stop a rooster from cro[illegible] Berkeley is to have it prosecuted [illegible] a charge of disturbing the peace, according to Patrolman W. A. Wiltberger of the Berkeley Police Department. He told this to Mrs. O. A. Phillips, 1511 Walnut street, early this morning when she complained to the police after being awakened at daylight by a crowing rooster. Wiltberger told her the police were powerless to muzzle the bird and referred her to Police Judge Robert Edgar for a warrant, providing the Judge would issue one.

160-Pound Arbuckle Gets "Fatty's" Calls

Special by Leased Wire to The Chronicle

CHICAGO, July 8.—For several days it has been rumored that Roscoe ("Fatty") Arbuckle would descend upon our city to take pictures in the stockyards and along the lake front.

Today a Mr. Arbuckle registered at the La Salle Hotel. A reporter called him by telephone.

"Yeh, this is Arbuckle," a worn and weary voice said dejectedly. "No, it isn't "Fatty" Arbuckle—F. for fat man. It's P. for Peter, H. for Henry, Arbuckle for short. I'm not a movie actor and I don't think I ever will be. I'm not from California. I'm from Houston, Texas, and I don't weigh a pound over 160. You're the 216th person to call me!"

The receiver banged.

Germ-Proof Wedding Performed in Hospital

VANCOUVER (B. C.), July 8.—Love refused to be swerved by illness when Miss Kate O'Brien of Philadelphia and Charles Barker of Vancouver were married at Moose Jaw, Sask., according to word received here today. On the date set for the wedding Miss O'Brien was in a hospital at Moose Jaw with scarlet fever. Nothing daunted, the couple had the ceremony performed on either side of a germ-proof sheet of glass. The priest read the servic into a disinfected speaking tube. Medical attendants said the bridegroom would have to wait six weeks before taking the bride away for the honeymoon.

Death Judgment of $11,875 Is Upheld

SACRAMENTO, July 8.—An award of $11,875 damages made by the Stanislaus County Superior Court to Robert L. Dallas of Modesto against N. E. de Toe for the death of his wife, Mrs. Martha Dallas, who was killed by De Toe's automobile, was affirmed by the Third District Court of Appeal. De Toe attempted to set aside the judgment of the trial court on the ground the accident was unavoidable. He claims that while backing his car on a business street in Modesto his foot caught between the brake and the accelerator, causing the machine to leap backward over the sidewalk. Mrs. Dallas was pinned between the machine and a wall and died from the injuries.

LENGTHY DEBATE OVER BILL NOW SEEMS PROBABLE

Senator Shortridge, Others Insist on Debate Before Vote Is Taken

'WETS' PLANNING BATTLE

New Yorker Denounces Act, Saying it Will Increase Law Violations

Special by Leased Wire to The Chronicle

WASHINGTON, July 8.—Determined opposition to the Campbell-Willis bill, designed to prohibit the prescription and sale of beer as medicine, developed in the Senate today.

Although the bill was taken up by a vote of 43 to 16, clearly indicating its ultimate passage, so much debate resulted that virtually no progress was made toward its final disposition.

Senator Wadsworth of New York made it plain that the bill would not be permitted to go to an immediate vote and Senators Broussard of Louisiana, G[illegible]y of Rhode Island, Short[illegible]e of California and others insisted [illegible] fullest discussion. There [illegible] no opposition to filibus[illegible] measure, but it was [illegible] considerable con-

D[illegible] Meas[illegible]

After seve[illegible] bill was autom[illegible] the soldiers' bonus, [illegible] right of way as unfinishe[illegible] Senator Sterling of South Dakota, who has charge of the bill, will endeavor to bring it up again next week.

Senator Wadsworth made a sharp attack upon the bill, predicting that it would increase violations of the law.

Senator Wadsworth especially denounced those provisions of the bill with respect to the exemption of distilled spirits stolen from warehouses from the assessment or collection of taxes thereon. The Senate provisions would have the effect of exempting the owner or person legally accountable for such distilled spirits if he was not in collusion with the thief, regardless of whether there had been a conviction of the thief. The House bill would not grant exemption from taxes on the stolen liquor unless the person guilty of the theft had been convicted.

Senator Wadsworth contended that

(Continued on Page 2, Column 3)

San Francisco Chronicle
LEADING NEWSPAPER of the PACIFIC COAST
REG. U. S. PAT. OFF.

FAIR WEATHER
SAN FRANCISCO, OAKLAND AND VICINITY
Wednesday fair, frost in morning; northwesterly winds.
G. H. WILLSON, Forecaster.
Complete Weather Report on Page

FOUNDED 1865—VOL. CXIX, NO. 145 CC SAN FRANCISCO, WEDNESDAY, DECEMBER 7, 1921—TWENTY-TWO PAGES DAILY 5 CENTS, SUNDAY 10 CENTS

PALATIAL YACHT SEIZED BY DRY AGENTS

Supervisors Open Way to Buy Street Car System

Ireland Wins Fight of Centuries for Freedom

BOAT PUTS INTO MONTEREY WITH LIQUOR ABOARD

Wealthy Shipbuilder on Pacific Cruise Stores 100 Cases Whisky in Craft

$100,000 BOND PREPARED

Part of Wet Cargo Stolen After It Was Taken to Bonded Warehouse

Arrest of James Shewan, New York shipbuilder, and seizure of his palatial private yacht, the Patricia, were ordered yesterday by United States Commissioner Silas W. Mack of Monterey, following the finding last Monday night of 100 cases of whisky in the boat's hold. The yacht is anchored in Monterey bay. Shewan and a party of New York friends are stopping in Del Monte.

After the liquor was seized and placed in a bonded warehouse at New Monterey, thieves broke in and stole at least three cases, and possibly more. The disappearance of the liquor was discovered by Government agents when they went to the warehouse to inspect the stock of liquor. They said they believed they would be able to trace the stolen liquor.

Warrant to Be Issued For Shewan's Arrest

The warrant for Shewan's arrest will be issued this morning at 9 o'clock, according to Mack, and will be served by United States Marshal James Holohan, who arrived in Monterey last night. Mack said last night that the warrant will charge Shewan with illegal possession and transportation of liquor in violation of prohibition laws.

Mack said that the reason the warrant was not issued yesterday when sought by the San Francisco authorities, was because he "had not yet got around to it." He said that yesterday his men were carrying out instructions under a search warrant he had issued. The warrant called for the search of the yacht Patricia, property of Shewan, and the confiscation of its stock of wine.

Shewan's Counsel Arranges For $100,000 Bail

The liquor which has forced Shewan into a clash with the Federal authorities was found aboard the yacht Monday night by Assistant Prohibition Director Thomas A. Brown and, Prohibition Agent James Doyle, working with Federal officials from Monterey.

Shortly after the appearance of the prohibition agents, Shewan engaged Gavin McNab of San Francisco as his attorney. McNab and Herbert Rothschild of the California Theater prepared a bond of $100,000 for the release of the yacht.

Liquor Sealed at U. S. Ports, Says Owner

The Patricia, recently purchased by Shewan, left New York October 26 with a crew of forty men. Shewan was accompanied by a party of guests and had 100 cases of liquor on the boat. He stopped at Bermuda and in American ports, at each place having the liquor sealed by customs officials under the prohibition regulations.

When Shewan put into San Diego and had his liquor sealed by customs officers, A. B. Stroup, special agent for the treasury department, witnessed the operation. He followed the Patricia up to Monterey and sent to Prohibition Director Brown for help in seizing the yacht. Brown took Doyle and hastened to Monterey Monday, where they took possession of the Patricia.

The seizure of Shewan's yacht and supply of liquor is similar to the raid conducted on the private Pullman car belonging to Harry St. Francis Black, New York multimillionaire, while he was traveling through Florida last March. Black and his porter were arrested and his stock of liquor, consisting of fifty-five cases of whisky, seized. Black's car was not seized. Black was fined $500.

She's Not Jealous

Mrs. Dudley Field Malone, who divorced the politician and suffrage advocate, does not object to his marriage to Doris Stevens.

MALONES ARE STILL FRIENDS

Special Dispatch to The Chronicle.

NEW YORK, Dec. 6.—Although Mrs. Dudley Field Malone has obtained a divorce in Paris, she and her husband still are good friends, according to Malone, who is planning to go to Paris to practice law.

Malone is at the Vanderbilt hotel here, and his friends say he and his wife had been living apart for years when she got her decree last summer.

SOON TO REWED

Malone and Miss Doris Stevens, a leader in the suffrage movement, soon are to be married, according to their friends. Whether the ceremony is to be here or in Paris has not been disclosed.

Malone, who was assistant secretary of state during Wilson's first term and later was appointed collector of the port of New York, resigned because he objected to Wilson's attitude toward suffrage, of which Malone long had been an ardent supporter. At the last New York state election Malone ran for Governor on the new Farmer-Labor ticket.

FORMER SENATOR'S DAUGHTER

Mrs. Malone was the daughter of former Senator James A. O'Gorman of New York.

"Mrs. Malone did me the honor to become my wife; we still are very good friends," was Malone's comment on the divorce and his reported engagement to Miss Stevens.

Japanese Liner Sends Out S. O. S.

Three Steamers Now Rushing to Vessel's Aid

Distress calls from the Japanese steamer Karachi Maru, en route to Kobe from Seattle, were picked up early yesterday morning by the Government radio station at St. Paul island, Alaska. The St. Paul station said that it received a number of S. O. S. calls from the Karachi Maru at 2:10 Tuesday morning, but the calls failed to give the location of the vessel. The United States ship West Jester, British steamer North Eagle and the Japanese steamer Mikaah, which are now in Alaskan waters, also picked up the calls, and advised the St. Paul station that they would search for the Karachi.

The Karachi Maru left Seattle for Kobe November 10.

PEOPLE TO GET VOTE ON ISSUE IF DEAL IS MADE

Official Body to Investigate Purchase Plan and Have Price Set

SPEAKERS FAVOR MOVE

Addition of Market-Street Company Held Necessary to Needs of City

The Board of Supervisors approved a resolution yesterday to open negotiations with officials of the Market Street Railway Company regarding the proposed purchase of the system by the city.

It was made plain by every member of the board that this action would in no wise obligate the Supervisors to present the issue to the voters at an election.

It was also made plain that the proposal to purchase the rights and properties of the street car company would go before the people for ratification, should the Market Street Railway be willing to sell and the price and terms of purchase be agreeable to the city officials.

Proceeding First Step to Purchase

The proceedings of yesterday mark the first actual step toward the purchase by the city of a public utility under amendment 30, approved at the election November 2, 1920, and designed with the purchase of the Market-street system in view, to establish a uniform street-car system in San Francisco, a 5-cent fare and transfer system to all parts of the city.

Amendment 30 provides a pay-as-you-go basis of purchase, whereby a utility may be paid for out of its own earnings, and paid for on the installment plan, covering a number of years. It is the amount of installment, as well as the price, that the Supervisors voted must be ascertained before a decision to submit the proposal to the people can be made.

Board Sits As Committee

The Board sat as a committee of the whole yesterday, and will continue to do so throughout the entire negotiations, on a resolution by Supervisor John D. Hynes, the Board approving the "open door" investigation on the matter, that all the facts may be placed before the entire Board at once. Citizens will be invited to attend the meetings, and to enter into the discussion.

While City Engineer M. M. O'Shaughnessy placed a valuation of $40,000,000 on the rights and properties of the railway company, it is the opinion of many of the Supervisors that the system may be acquired at a lower price.

The matter will be up before the Supervisors next Monday as a committee report. It is expected that officials of the street car company will be present at the next meeting with the Supervisors acting as a committee of the whole, when the price and terms will be discussed.

A large crowd of citizens, most of them representatives of civic organizations, attended yesterday's meeting, and the proceedings were listened to practically in silence. Only one speaker actually opposed the proposed purchase. He was W. H.

(Continued on Page 6, Column 4)

Complete text of President Harding's address to Congress will be found on page 4

National Guard Called Out in Packers' Strike

Will Patrol Packing Plants in South St. Paul, Scene of Much Disorder

CHICAGO, Dec. 6 (by the Associated Press).—Violence marked the second day of the strike of packing-house workers in several cities, and resulted in the calling out of National Guard troops tonight in South St. Paul.

At Fort Worth, Texas, two strike sympathizers were shot and wounded and a negro, who it is said did the shooting, was severely beaten.

At Omaha missiles were thrown by various persons, including women, in clashes between strike sympathizers and workmen.

300 PERSONS HELD AT BAY

Policemen with drawn revolvers held a crowd of 300 persons at bay here today until reserves arrived, after arresting strike sympathizers said to have beaten a workman. A man and his daughter, packing plant employes, were twice attacked by strike sympathizers as they started to leave a packing plant, and several arrests were made for minor disturbances.

400 MEN TO GUARD PLANTS AT ST. PAUL

ST. PAUL, Dec. 6.—Announcement that National Guard troops had been called out to patrol the packing plant district in South St. Paul, where close picketing by strike sympathizers has prevented the use of strikebreakers, was made tonight.

The announcement was made at the adjutant general's office after Adjutant General W. F. Rhinow had conferred over the telephone with Governor J. A. O. Preus, who is in Washington.

Four hundred members of St. Paul companies of the guard will be sent to South St. Paul as soon as they are mobilized. About 200 men will be sent to the Swift plant and 200 others to the Armour plant.

Adjutant General Rhinow, who will take personal charge, said he informed Governor Preus that the strikers and pickets had failed to keep a promise made to him earlier in the day that pickets would allow workers access to and from their places of employment without molestation.

TWO SERIOUSLY WOUNDED

Calling out of the troops follows unsuccessful attempts of both the Swift and Armour companies to bring in men to take the place of strikers and after conferences with labor leaders had failed to effect an agreement for a discontinuance of the picketing.

TWO STRIKERS INJURED IN TEXAS DISORDERS

FORT WORTH (Texas), Dec. 6.—Two brothers—Tom and Tracy Macklin—said by friends to be striking packing house employes, were shot and seriously wounded late today in disorders growing out of the local packing house strike. Fred Rouse, a negro who is said to have been responsible for the shooting, was taken to a hospital following a severe beating he received at the hands of a large crowd. The shooting occurred in front of the Armour & Co. plant.

6000 JOIN STRIKERS

CHICAGO, Dec. 6 (by the Associated Press).—Union officials after the second day of the strike of packing house employes asserted six thousand more had joined the strikers in Chicago, while the packers reported that between 90 and 95 per cent of their men were working, and that the places of strikers had been filled from the hundreds of unemployed.

While spokesmen for the packers admitted that more employes here had joined the walkout, they also asserted that part of those that went out Monday had returned and that there was no difficulty in hiring men.

HARDING STIRS LABOR'S IRE IN CONGRESS TALK

Friends of Organized Workers Hostile to "Nationalization" Inference

LOWER TAXES ARE URGED

President's Recommendations on Agriculture Meet General Approval

By ARTHUR S. HENNING
Special by Leased Wire to The Chronicle

WASHINGTON, Dec. 6.—President Harding, in the message he read to Congress today, submitted a program of legislation comprising a number of innovations of government, some of them of radical character, designed to remedy existing evils and curb abuses of power.

He aroused the opposition of organized labor to his proposal of a labor court to prevent strikes, ruffled the feelings of agrarian legislators with his remarks condemnatory of the agricultural bloc, and shattered party lines in the reception accorded some of the policies and reforms he suggested.

Among his recommendations were the following:

Here Are Some of His Recommendations

FIRST—Establishment of judicial or quasi-judicial tribunals for the adjudication of disputes between capital and labor which subject the public welfare to the menace of the strike, the lockout and the boycott.

SECOND—Encouragement to the development of co-operative marketing by organizations of farmers as an "economic solution for the excessive variation in return for agricultural production."

THIRD—Decentralization of industry, which tends to concentrate in large cities, with retarding effect on agriculture and wasteful economic results, such decentralization to be brought about by readjustment of freight rates in favor of smaller communities and extension of good roads.

FOURTH—Amendment of the constitution to prohibit the issuance by states and municipalities of non-taxable bonds investment in which results in avoidance of income taxes and the withdrawal of capital from industry and commerce.

Early Passage of Tariff Bill Urged

FIFTH—Early passage of the tariff revision bill, with provisions authorizing the President functioning through the tariff commission to increase or decrease duties and to substitute American for foreign valuation of specific imports.

SIXTH—Reclamation of 20,000,000 acres of potentially arable lands and Government advances to ex-service men and others desiring to settle thereon; Government advances, in co-operation with states and individuals, for the reclamation of 79,000,000 acres of swamp and cut-over lands largely situated in the southern states.

SEVENTH—An appropriation to supply 10,000,000 bushels of corn and 1,000,000 bushels of seed grains to the 15,000,000 starving people of Russia.

EIGHTH—Passage of the bill authorizing the funding into definite long-term obligations of the $11,000,000,000 war loans by the United States to the allies.

The President intimated his dissatisfaction with the new tax law in some respects and promised to lay before Congress later some pro-

(Continued on Page 4, Column 7)

Tumulty's Story: 'Woodrow Wilson As I Knew Him' Will Be Found Today on Page 2

Harding Not To Override Congress In Conference

By H. WICKHAM STEED
Editor of The London Times
Special Dispatch to The San Francisco Chronicle

WASHINGTON, Dec. 6.—The House of Representatives, where the members of Congress gathered to hear President Harding inaugurate their first ordinary session, was, on Tuesday, the scene of a notable gathering. The large hall and the galleries were crowded, while some of the principal foreign delegates attending the Washington conference were accommodated on the floor of the House. By the special courtesy of some of the Congressmen violence was done to the rules of the House in order to permit the chief correspondents of foreign journals likewise to sit in the body of the chamber—a characteristically American act of courtesy, which its recipients keenly appreciated.

The President, whom Congress received very cordially, took his stand at a desk below the speaker's chair, and read a remarkable address in a clear, deliberate voice. The impression of spaciousness which his person makes upon all who approach him was revived as he passed from topic to topic, seeking to convey the largeness of his meaning rather by cautious under-statement than by over-emphasis.

President Lauds Work of Envoys

Indirect reference to the Washington conference ran through several points of his address. The audience applauded loudly his initial statement that not only was the country free "from every impending menace of war, but there are growing assurances of the permanency of the peace which we so deeply cherish." But the cheering was loudest at the close, when, leaning over the desk, the President mentioned the conference explicitly and said in impressive tones: "It is easy to believe that a world hope is centered on this capital city. A most gratifying world accomplishment is not improbable." More than this the President could not well say. To have said less would have been to belie his own expectations and those of the American delegation. But, as he said them his words sounded as the announcement of a certain hope that the conference will be a great and enduring success.

U. S. Interest In Nations Emphasized

Apart from his declaration the speech was notable for its repeated recognition of the essential community of interest between the United States and other nations of the world. In these days of disorder, said the President, "no permanent readjustment can be effected without consideration of our inseparable relationship to world affairs in finance and trade," and the note thus struck was sounded again and again. While insisting that the nations most cruelly stricken by war and its consequences must themselves apply heroic remedies, he held out the prospect of help. "Then we can help, and we mean to help," he declared, giving the assurance gravely and emphatically amid warm cheers. He was

(Continued on Page 7, Column 5)

MEIGHEN LOSES IN CANADA VOTE

OTTAWA, Dec. 6.—Premier Meighen was defeated in his home constituency, Portage La Prairie, Man., in the Canadian general election today. His opponent was Harry Leader, progressive.

Returns received tonight indicated defeat of the Meighen government and a landslide for the liberals, led by W. L. Mackenzie King. Eleven members of the cabinet were defeated.

DEFEAT CONCEDED

Premier Meighen, in a statement admitting the fall of his government, said: "I accept the verdict of the people. I have no further comment."

King, liberal leader, was elected in North York, Ontario, a division normally conservative, by 1000 majority. T. A. Crerar, leader of the progressive party, was elected in Marquette, Manitoba.

In the eastern part of the dominion the liberals made a clean sweep. Quebec, with sixty-five members in Parliament, will be represented entirely by liberals.

Border Airplane Liquor Smugglers Held in San Diego

Pilot, Auto Driver, 48 Gallons of Whisky Netted by U. S. Officials

SAN DIEGO, Dec. 6.—W. H. Helvey, an aviator, J. S. Stewart, airplane pilot, and Louis Balincourt, automobile driver, were arrested here late this afternoon after a cargo of forty-eight gallons of whisky had been successfully transported from Lower California by airplane. The three men were lodged in the county jail here and Federal officials stated that a Federal charge of smuggling would be placed against them tomorrow morning.

Although many cases of liquor smuggling by automobile have been uncovered, this is the first time, so far as known that an airplane has been employed in the traffic in this vicinity.

Mayor, Trustees, Police on Fire Wagon Scare Robber

Special Dispatch to The Chronicle.

REDDING, Dec. 6.—The monthly meeting of the City Trustees last evening was thrown into a commotion when a telephone call came from the wife of the Mayor stating that a burglar was trying to break into the home. The Trustees, reinforced by the police force, jumped aboard the chemical fire engine and were at the Mayor's home, four blocks away in quick time. The burglar was probably scared away by the approach of the fire engine, but he already had pried open the front door screen and was at work on the lock of the front door. Mayor Norton was grateful to the City Council for service rendered in time of peril.

SINN FEIN AND BRITAIN SIGN NEW CHARTER

Takes Form of Treaty With an Oath to "Be Faithful to the King"

ULSTER IN FREE STATE

Has Right to Get Out of Contract by Petition Within a Month

By JOHN STEELE
Special Cable to The Chronicle

LONDON, Dec. 6.—Ireland's ... years' struggle for freedom is ... A formal peace treaty between Ireland and England was signed at 2:15 this morning.

The main points of the ... are, first of all, that ... a treaty, thus recognizing Irish nationhood. Ireland shall have constitutional place in the empire with Canada, Australia, New Zealand and South Africa, and her constitution shall be specifically based on that of Canada. The representative of the crown in Ireland ... be chosen in the same way as Canadian viceroy.

Question of Allegiance Settled Satisfactorily

The difficult question of allegiance has been got over by an ingenious formula for an oath, which must be taken by all members of the parliament of the Irish Free State—which is to be the name of the new dominion—as follows:

"I do solemnly swear in true faith allegiance to the constitution of the Irish Free State as by law established and that I will be faithful to his majesty, King George V, his heirs and successors by law, in virtue of the common citizenship of Ireland and Great Britain and her adherence to membership in the group of nations forming the British commonwealth of nations."

Ireland to Have Army And Coast Defense

Other clauses in the document set out Ireland's right to have an army and coastal defense, her financial independence, her admission of liability for a share in the British debt, British right to control certain ports, etc.

Ulster is to be included in the Irish Free State, but has the right by petition to the king within a month to get out of the contract and regain her present status, while if she remains in she retains her autonomy under the Irish State.

The treaty must be ratified by parliament and Dail Eireann, which

'SLOW MOVIES' of Stanford Sparkle," the new dance that is creating sensation. The inventor poses in "Slow Movies" in Tomorrow's Chronicle

San Francisco Chronicle

LEADING NEWSPAPER OF THE PACIFIC COAST REG. U.S. PAT. OFF.

FOUNDED 1865—VOL. CXXII, NO. 33 CC SAN FRANCISCO, SATURDAY, FEBRUAYR 17, 1923—TWENTY-SIX PAGES DAILY 5 CENTS, SUNDAY 10 CENTS

S. F. AMATEUR BANDIT SHOT IN HOLDUP AT PALACE HOTEL

YOUNG ROBBER NEAR DEATH OF BULLET WOUND

Joe Levy Dying of Punctured Lung After Attack on Women With Toy Gun

CLEARS PISTOL WIELDER

Victim in Hospital Shakes Hand of J. E. Burman and Apologizes for Act

Rushing to the defense of his wife, who had been followed into her room, on the sixth floor of the Palace Hotel, by Joseph Levy, 2713 Sacramento street, brandishing a "revolver" and demanding her jewels, Joseph E. Burman, a stock broker and former naval officer, shot Levy through the chest with a 45-caliber revolver yesterday afternoon.

Taken to the Central Emergency Hospital, where it was found that a lung had been punctured and that he would probably die, Levy made a signed confession in which he absolved Burman of all blame, and said that he was discouraged at being out of work and was trying to rob Mrs. Burman of her jewelry.

Victim Asks Pardon Of Man Who Shot Him

Burman, Mrs. Burman and Mrs. W. E. Jones, who was a witness to the shooting, visited Levy's bedside at the hospital last evening. Gasping for breath, Levy asked the pardon of Mr. and Mrs. Burman for his act, declared that Burman did the manly thing in defending his wife, and only urged in his own behalf the fact that his "revolver," with which he threatened Mrs. Burman, was a toy. Burman, in turn, expressed his regrets at having to shoot Levy.

Guests at the Palace Hotel were alarmed at 5:20 o'clock to hear revolver shots resound through the corridors. It was the first warning of a tragedy in the busy hostelry. Assistant managers rushed upstairs to find Joseph Levy lying near the elevators on the second floor in a state of collapse. In his chest there was an ugly wound.

Women Followed to Rooms by Robber

In two rooms on the sixth floor, Burman, his wife and Mrs. W. E. Jones were awaiting the arrival of the police to tell of one of the strangest holdups and shootings in recent years.

As the facts were pieced together, it developed that Mrs. Burman met Mrs. Jones, a friend, by appointment in the lobby on the main floor of the hotel. After a short chat, the two women decided to join Burman in his suit on the sixth floor. They took the elevator. Another passenger was a stout man of medium height, dressed sufficiently well as not to attract undue notice. He, too, alighted from the elevator on the sixth floor.

Women Ordered to Throw Up Hands

This man, who proved to be Levy, followed the women to the Burman suite. Then he produced what appeared to be a formidable weapon, but which later proved to be a toy pistol. Pointing this at Mrs. Burman, who wore an expensive bar pin at her throat, Levy told her gruffly to hold up her hands.

Instead of complying, Mrs. Burman grew Mrs. Jones into their room. In the inner of the two rooms Burman was seated near a table. Mrs. Burman thought the intruder would leave, but as she tried to shut the door in his face, he forced his way into the suite.

Within the Burman rooms and within call of her husband, Levy again demanded that Mrs. Burman hold up her hands.

"Joe! Joe!" she called to Burman. "There's a strange man out here!"

Burman hurried to the connecting door. When he observed Levy in the presence of his wife and guest brandishing a weapon, he returned to the bureau in his room, pulled a heavy service revolver from a drawer and rushed back.

At the sight of the business end

(Continued on Page 6, Column 3)

Principals in Shooting Tragedy at the Palace Hotel

Mrs. J. E. Burman

Captain J. E. Burman

Mrs. W. E. Jones

An amateur holdup man, Joseph Levy, known in local sporting and political circles, was shot and may die as the result of an effort to rob a woman guest at Palace Hotel yesterday. Above is a diagram showing how Levy "trailed" his intended victim and how the shooting took place. In the picture, from left to right, are Mrs. Burman, Burman and Mrs. Jones.

FRENCH SEIZE ESSEN POLICE HEADQUARTERS

Chief Burgomaster of Oberhausen Sent to Prison for Disregarding Orders

ESSEN, Feb. 16 (by the Associated Press).—Essen was the storm center today in the Ruhr, where the friction between the French and the Germans has increased because of Thursday night's shooting of two French soldiers by security police in a cafe brawl.

In retaliation for this shooting General Fournier ordered a battalion of French infantry to occupy the German police barracks. The chief of police was arrested, all the files and documents at police headquarters were taken by the French and the disarming of the police was begun.

The shooting of the French soldiers occurred when eight of them, off duty, entered the cafe. The waiters refused to serve them because of the boycott against the French, started last Monday night, and fighting immediately broke out.

French Say German Policeman Began the Shooting

A member of the security police appeared at the door of the cafe when the brawl began, and the French say he was the first person to begin shooting.

The director of the Essen electric light plant, Bussmann, was sentenced by the French court-martial at Bredeney today to pay a fine of 5,000,000 marks for alleged interference with the French on Monday after the taking over by the French of the Kaiserhof Hotel, which is the headquarters of General Coste, head of the industrial mission in the

(Continued on Page 2, Column 3)

Idaho House Acts to Ban Japanese Leases

BOISE, Idaho, Feb. 16.—The Assembly of the seventeenth Idaho Legislature today passed a measure to prohibit the leasing of land in the State to Japanese. The vote was 54 to 6.

The land lease measure, according to its author, Representative Gillis, Republican, of Twin Falls, while aimed primarily at the Japanese, is likewise applicable to all aliens.

RICH ENGINEER FOUND SLAIN IN LOS ANGELES

His Wife, Mrs. Earle Remington, Had Consulted Lawyer About Divorce

Special by Leased Wire to The Chronicle.

LOS ANGELES, Feb. 16.—Shadows of the underworld late this afternoon fell on the mystery surrounding the slaying of Earle Remington, widely known electrical engineer and aviator, and mingled with reports of a bitter domestic clash of recent date between the slain man and his beautiful and socially-prominent wife, Mrs. Virgiria Lola Stone Remington.

Less than two weeks ago Mrs. Remington discussed divorce proceedings with Deputy District Attorney Burton Fitts and later retained Attorney H. L. Geisler. Then she went to San Francisco to visit friends and only returned to this city two or three days ago. No divorce action had been filed before she left the city and no papers had been drawn up, according to the attorneys.

Shortly after Remington is believed to have been shot by a hidden assassin as he stepped from his automobile in the driveway of his home at 1409 South St. Andrew's

(Continued on Page 4, Column 3)

Resignation of Forbes Accepted

WASHINGTON, Feb. 16.—The resignation of Colonel Charles R. Forbes as director of Veterans' Bureau, has been accepted by President Harding, effective February 28, it was announced today at the White House.

Without comment, White House officials made public an undated letter from the retiring director, who now is in Europe, assigning ill health as the reason for his resignation.

House Votes Quiz On Legation Rum

WASHINGTON, Feb. 16.—An inquiry into the importation of intoxicating liquors by foreign diplomats was ordered today by the House by a vote of 189 to 113.

The inquiry is directed to Secretary Mellon, who already has informed the House Judiciary Committee that he could not "properly" give out the information which the House now asks for.

The resolution calling upon Mellon for a statement of the amounts of liquor imports for all embassies and legations was introduced recently by Representative Cramton, Republican, Michigan, after publication of statements by police authorities that foreign diplomatic establishments here formed the source of much of the illicit liquor supply in Washington. The resolution had been referred to the Judiciary Committee, but the House on Cramton's motion today discharged that committee from further consideration of the resolution and then voted to adopt it.

Nevada Assembly Overrides 'Dry' Veto

CARSON CITY, Nev., Feb. 16.—The State Assembly voted, 29 to 7, today to override Governor Scrugham's veto of a Senate bill repealing the Nevada initiative prohibition law.

Hero Left Legacy For Defining Word

Philip C. Katz, California's representative in the "Living Hall of Fame," is to receive a bequest of 1000 francs because he took the time to define the word "perspicacity" to an elderly Frenchman, who was struggling to learn English. Katz was notified yesterday by the French Consul-General in San Francisco that he had been named a beneficiary in the will of Gustave Chauffant of Saulxures, France.

It was in July, 1918, that Katz, then a sergeant in the Three Hundred and Sixty-third Infantry first met Chauffant, while billeted in Saulxures. Chauffant was struggling with an English dictionary and stumbled at the word, "perspicacity." Katz helped the Frenchman over "perspicacity" and thus began a friendship that lasted until Chauffant's death.

"I didn't know the old fellow was dead until I received a Christmas card I sent him with the notation that the addressee was dead," Katz said yesterday. "When I left Saulxures the old fellow made me promise to write to him. I did so after I returned to America, but it was the word 'perspicacity' that began our friendship."

The will bequeathing Katz 1000 francs is now in the French courts, according to the local French Consul-General.

PRINCE'S SHIP LOCATED OFF POINT REYES

Grave Fears Had Been Entertained for Safety of Waldemar of Denmark

TUSCAN PRINCE FOUND

British Steamship Discovered at Village Point, Vancouver Island

Fears as to the safety of Prince Waldemar of Denmark, passenger on board the Danish motor ship Peru, due in port yesterday morning which had failed to reply to more than thirty wireless calls, was dispelled last night, when the ship reported shortly after 8 o'clock giving its position as seventy-five miles north of Point Reyes. It will dock, according to advices at 8:30 o'clock this morning.

Since late Thursday night, the Radio Corporation of America at the request of the ship's agents, the East Asiatic Company, Inc., has been steadily trying to get into "air" communication with the Peru, but without success. The Peru was due to arrive here Thursday.

[illegible] Also Located

At the same time the Peru reported, messages from Seattle announced the finding of the wrecked British steamer Tuscan Prince at Village point, Vancouver Island, late yesterday afternoon.

Word of the discovery of the Tuscan Prince for whom dozens of craft have been searching since she flashed "We are going to drown" was received here in dispatches from the Coast Guard cutter Snohomish.

The Snohomish at that time reported having removed fourteen members of the ship's crew of forty-two and is to remove the others this morning.

Every Member of Crew Reported Safe

While the Tuscan Prince was reported as a total loss it was stated that every member of the ship's crew of forty-two persons was safe and, although suffering from the extreme cold, well.

In reporting to the Radio Corporation of America last night, the Danish motorboat Peru failed to explain its failure to reply to any of the countless messages flashed seaward.

(Continued on Page 2, Column 3)

Young Prince May Wed Half-U.S. Girl

British King's Third Son Favors Lady Curzon

Special Cable to The Chronicle.

PARIS, Feb. 16.—A half-American girl may enter a British royal family through marriage, according to Riviera gossip.

Assiduous attention is being paid by Prince George, third son of the British Sovereign, to Lady Alexandra Curzon, youngest daughter of the British Foreign Minister by his first wife, who was Miss Leiter of Chicago. Lady Alexandra is at Cannes, where she is being chaperoned by her sister, Lady Cynthia Moseley. Prince George is continually in the company of Lady Alexandra.

(Copyright, 1923, by the Chicago Tribune Co.)

Follies Girl Marries, But Not a Millionaire

Special by Leased Wire to The Chronicle.

NEW YORK, Feb. 16.—A Ziegfeld Follies girl was married yesterday. It was learned today. To the general amazement of all, she announced that her husband was not a millionaire. This is a record, as thus far a Ziegfeld Follies girl has never failed to pick a millionaire. The bride is Fern Oakley. The bridegroom is John Wilton Crosby, formerly a moving picture leading man and now personal representative of several screen stars.

Senate Approves Bill Giving British Sixty-Two Years To Pay War Loan

Debt Commission Enlarged So as to Make Room for Democratic Members

By ARTHUR S. HENNING

Special by Leased Wire to The Chronicle.

WASHINGTON, D. C., Feb. 16.—Approval of the British debt funding agreement was given by the Senate tonight when it passed the administration bill amending the Debt Commission act by a vote of 70 to 13. Four Republicans voted against the bill, while twenty-four Democrats were recorded in the affirmative.

Amendments were made which will necessitate an adjustment of differences in the Senate and House bills. An agreement will be reached by conferees of the Senate and House without delay and the bill will go to the President when the conference report is approved by the two Houses.

PERIOD OF 62 YEARS

The British agreement as approved [illegible] provides for the payment of the $4,600,000,000 principal over a period of sixty-two years with interest at 3 per cent for the first ten years and 3½ per cent thereafter.

Another amendment added by the Senate without a roll call was one by Senator Harris, Democrat, Georgia, providing for the enlargement of the Debt Commission from five to eight members, the three new members to be Democrats. President Harding is selecting the present five members named only Republicans.

The four Republicans who voted against the bill on the final roll call were Senators Borah, Idaho; France, Maryland; La Follette, Wisconsin, and Norris, Nebraska. The nine Democrats voting against it were Ashurst, Arizona; Gerry, Rhode Island; Heflin, Alabama; Hitchcock, Nebraska; McKellar, Tennessee; Reed, Missouri; Trammell, Florida; Walsh, Massachusetts, and Walsh, Montana.

LIVELY DEBATE

Before passing the bill the Senate had a lively debate, with many Senators participating. Senator Glass, Democrat, Virginia, who served as Secretary of the Treasury during a part of the war period, made one of the most effective speeches of the day in support of the bill. The Virginia Senator described war conditions in an impassioned manner, and pictured what the possibilities might have been if the United States had not made its loans to the allies. He declared that assertions by opponents of the British debt agreement that it would mean a gift of $1,666,000,000 to the British Government, this amount representing the difference between the proposed interest rates and a rate of 4¼ per cent, were nothing but "a figment of the imagination."

Senator La Follette, Republican, Wisconsin, made a lengthy speech condemning the British settlement. He declared that the American commission has been too lenient with the British and that interest equal to that paid by the United States on its bonds should be insisted upon.

Zula Prince From Flapperless Clime Sees Laxity Here

CHICAGO, Feb. 16.—There are no flappers in Zululand, Prince Bullawa Cetawayo, chief of a Zulu tribe, said today. He said he found moral laxness here. One thing he said always caused surprise was the knowledge that in Zululand the people are civilized and eat canned food.

"People are always surprised when I tell them that my country is almost as thoroughly civilized as, say Nebraska," he said. "Most Zulus go to church on Sunday, eat canned foods and use the telephone."

ANCIENT KING'S TOMB REVEALS RICH SPLENDOR

Exploring Scientists Open Mortuary Chamber of Pharaohs

TREASURES ARE FOUND

Immense Gilded Canopy Richly Inscribed Cause for Amazement

LUXOR, Egypt, Feb. 16 (by the Associated Press).—Opening of the mortuary chamber in the tomb of King Tutenkhamun today showed the sarcophagus of the Pharaoh to be still in the same position in which it was placed by his mourners more than 3000 years ago.

When the exploring scientists, after removing the delicate seals, broke their way through the masonry of the inner chamber door, they were confronted with splendors which, upon the first cursory examination, appear to surpass even those of the ante-chamber which have held the interest of the entire world.

Immense Gilded Canopy Is Found

The exploring party, headed by Howard Carter, exclaimed with amazement at finding the central chamber, which is about fourteen feet square, occupied by an immense gilded canopy, richly inscribed.

The canopy was closed, but there was a door, and the opening of this revealed inside what undoubtedly is Tutenkhamun's coffin. For the present, however, this was left undisturbed.

Two Chambers Full of Treasures

The sarcophagus was inclosed in a huge canopy which alone has been opened so far.

The exploration revealed two chambers, each filled with splendid treasures. Many articles of furniture also were in the mortuary chamber.

A canopy jar, which probably contains the heart and other internal organs of the king, was found inside the canopy.

One feature of the discovery in the inner chamber was a magnificent statue of a cat, richly painted, which has stood sentry over the dead Pharaoh through the centuries. The chamber is filled with splendid furniture, in orderly array. It also holds several superb gold chariots.

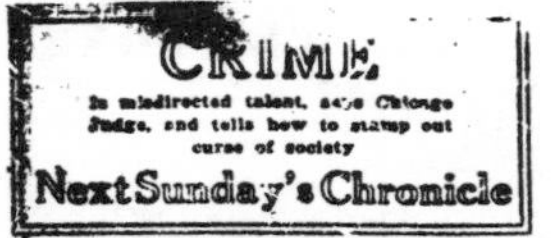

CRIME
Is misdirected talent, says Chicago Judge, and tells how to stamp out curse of society
Next Sunday's Chronicle

San Francisco Chronicle

LEADING NEWSPAPER OF THE PACIFIC COAST — REG. U.S. PAT. OFF.

FAIR
WEATHER
Friday fair, cloudy morning; moderate westerly winds.
Mount Tamalpais—Fair; fresh northwesterly winds.
E. A. BEALS, Forecaster.
Complete Weather Report on Page 13

FOUNDED 1865—VOL. CXXIII, NO. 19 — CCCC — SAN FRANCISCO, CAL., FRIDAY, AUGUST 3, 1923—TWENTY-EIGHT PAGES — DAILY 5 CENTS, SUNDAY 10 CENTS

HARDING DEAD

Beloved President Succumbs Suddenly In Early Evening

Death Caused by Apoplexy Stroke; Mrs. Harding Reading to Executive When Famous Leader Expires

President Harding died at 7:30 o'clock last night in his suite at the Place Hotel.

A stroke of apoplexy that came while Mrs. Harding was reading to him from a magazine, at the bedside, ended his life suddenly.

It is notable that the President's death came about in precisely the same manner as one of his sisters died. This was revealed after midnight this morning, when the five attendant physicians issued their last formal joint statement, detailing completely the entire history of the President's last illness, and concluding with the succinct sentence:

"One of his sisters died suddenly in the same manner."

The news of the Executive's death, after two days of steadily more optimistic bulletins from the five attendant physicians, came with a suddenness that left stunned unrealization in its wake.

Authoritative reports of the last moments told how Mrs. Harding was reading to the President. Miss Ruth Powderly and Miss Sue Dausser, the two nurses in attendance, and Dr. Charles E. Sawyer, the President's personal physician, were also in the room.

Suddenly and without warning, a shudder passed over the President's body. He raised one arm, but not a word came from his lips. The arm dropped back and the President lay still.

For an instant the three women in the room stared, unrealizing. Then with one accord they knew that death had come.

In a few moments Dr. Boone joined Dr. Sawyer at the bedside. They could do nothing.

And in a few more minutes the Nation was hearing that its chief had gone.

First inklings of the catastrophe came to the few persons who were about the President's suite when a sudden stir and commotion behind the "deadline" which barred the way to the President's sick chamber gave portent of some extraordinary happening.

It being dinner time, there were few persons present. A small group of newspaper men were there, but not the crowd that had been thronging the corridors earlier during the President's illness. Of his official family, the majority were elsewhere in the city, and some were on their way out of town.

The favorable reports of the last two days had so relieved apprehension that no one—not even his physicians—feared trouble.

Newspaper men, noting the sudden activity behind the deadline screen, scented a momentous happening.

A moment later Dr. Boone, his face a mask of unbelief, strode madly down the corridor to the President's suite.

Over the newspaper wires flashed the message: "Something's happened!"

Others of the President's doctors came. Waiting newspaper men gathered anxiously about the deadline.

A secret service man came out and returned within a few moments with Judson Welliver, the official press representative with the Presidential party.

The newspaper men flung whispered questions at the grim-faced detectives at the barrier.

"No news, boys. We can't tell a thing," was the reply.

Then Judson Welliver, his face gray, hurried to the bulletin room and, a moment later, handed out the message that left newspaper men of years' experience staring wide-eyed for moments before they dashed to telephones to broadcast the news that the

(Continued on Page 2, Column 1)

Nation Mourns Beloved President

©EDMONDSON

TRAIN BEARING HARDING'S BODY LEAVES TONIGHT

Special of 12 Cars Pulls Out of S. F. at 7 O'Clock for East

NO STOPS TO BE MADE

Presidential Party Will Accompany Remains; Burial in Marion

Funeral services of the simplest nature will mark the rites over President Harding at the Palace Hotel. They will be held late this afternoon, just prior to the removal of the late President's body to the special train which is to convey them to his home at Marion, O. The simplicity of the arrangements is in accordance with the wishes of Mrs. Harding.

At 7 o'clock tonight, a Presidential special of twelve cars, bearing the last remains of America's chief executive, Warren G. Harding, will leave on its sad journey across the country toward the national capital.

There will be no delays in its procedure. With a right of precedence over all other traffic in the country, it will travel on a seventy-two hour schedule to Chicago, from which point arrangements have been made to hurry it onward to its destination.

Body Will Leave Hotel At 6 o'Clock Tonight

The body of the President will leave the Palace Hotel at 6 o'clock tonight and will be placed aboard the Presidential special at Third and Townsend streets an hour later. The details of the transportation will be worked out at a conference with the immediate members of the President's party at 9 o'clock this morning.

In the rear coach, the lights of which will burn until its duty is discharged, and under official military escort, the body of the late President of the United States will be conveyed toward its last resting place, while the eyes of a sorrowing Nation will follow its solemn pilgrimage from Coast to Coast.

Presidential Party Will Accompany Train

Accompanying the train will be the Presidential party, as it has traveled happily together until the grim shadow of death brought a tragic and unexpected end to the official tour. The party will be augmented by General Pershing, Attorney-General Daugherty, Mrs. E. E. Remsberg, sister of President Harding, and her husband and family.

Sixteen enlisted men of the army and navy will accompany the cortege as the official escort, accorded a President in his final journey. They will be under command of two officers and will represent both army and navy. All through the long hours of the days and nights, encompassed by the journey across the continent, two soldiers and two sailors will stand at motionless attention beside the basket—a military honor that will not be withdrawn until the President has passed to his last resting place at Marion, O.

Train Will Make Only Necessary Stops

Despite the desire of mourning thousands to view the remains of their beloved President, the train will make no stops other than those necessary for the operation of the special. The train will have the right of way over everything before it, and train after train will remain waiting on sidetracks until the special with its sad burden has passed on its way East.

The train will proceed from San Francisco via Reno, Ogden, Cheyenne, Omaha, Chicago and thence to Washington, D. C. From that point it is expected that President Harding's body will be taken to his former home at Marion, O., for interment. All along the line dipped flags, draped mourning, and other

(Continued on Page 2, Column 3)

COOLIDGE TAKES PRESIDENTIAL OATH OF OFFICE

Policies of Late Executive Will be Continued by His Successor

MOURNS NATION'S LOSS

New Executive Sworn in by Father at Plymouth, Vt., Home

WASHINGTON, Aug. 3 (by the Associated Press).—Calvin Coolidge took the oath as the President of the United States at Plymouth, Vt., at 2:47 a. m. today.

The new President was sworn in by his father, who is a notary public, and at whose home he was visiting. The text of the pledge, as prescribed by the Constitution, was telephoned to him from the White House.

PLYMOUTH, Vt., Aug. 3. (by the Associated Press).—President Coolidge plans to leave here about 7:30 a. m. by automobile for Rutland to catch the 9:35 train for New York, due in that city at 5 p. m., Eastern standard time. He will be accompanied by Mrs. Coolidge and Congressman Porter H. Dale.

Special by Leased Wire to The Chronicle.

PLYMOUTH, Vt., Aug. 3.—Vice-President Calvin Coolidge received news of the death of President Harding and of his own elevation to the Presidentcy at ten minutes before midnight, standard time.

The new President will be sworn in this morning as soon as the proper form of oath can be obtained by his father, John C. Coolidge, who is a notary public. Coolidge will leave for Washington soon afterward.

Receives News of Harding's Passing

Coolidge received the first news of the death of President Harding through telegrams from George C.

(Continued on Page 2, Column 6)

San Francisco Chronicle

LEADING NEWSPAPER OF THE PACIFIC COAST

REG. U.S. PAT. OFF.

FAIR WEATHER

Monday fair, cloudy in morning; moderate west winds.

Mt. Tamalpais—Fair; moderate northwest winds.

E. A. BEALS, Forecaster.

Complete Weather Report on Page 2

FOUNDED 1865—VOL. CXXIII. NO. 50 CCCC SAN FRANCISCO, MONDAY, SEPTEMBER 3, 1923—TWENTY-FOUR PAGES DAILY 5 CENTS, SUNDAY 10 CENTS. DAILY AND SUNDAY PER MONTH, $1.00

100,000 PERISH

OSAKA, Sept. 3 (by the Associated Press).—Lieut. Ishida, who flew over Tokyo and the stricken district in an airplane yesterday, has reported to commander of the Nagoya division that the imperial palace was only partially damaged. Tokyo itself is devastated, with the exception of Ushirome Ward, part of Koishigawa Ward, virtually the whole of Yetsuia Ward and the north side of Asyamaderi. Nearly all the concrete and brick buildings collapsed. Fukagara Ward was flooded by the tidal wave.

Allied Forces of Death Reap Fearful Harvest

Mountainous Tidal Waves Wipe Peninsula Community Out of Existence; Toll Grows; Historic Capital of Nippon in Ruins; Famine Stalks

NAGASAKI, Sept. 2 (by the Associated Press). --- A number of volcanoes are reported active in the earthquake-stricken zone. Several more earth shocks were felt at Yokohama at 1 o'clock Sunday afternoon. Tokyo is still burning and explosions there are frequent. Only those with food may enter the city.

SHANGHAI, Sept. 3 (by the Associated Press).---Bulletins received here from Japan report that 100,000 persons perished in Tokyo and Yokohama alone in Saturday's earthquake and fire.

The bulletins said fires in the Tokyo arsenal caused explosions, destroying the arsenal and the adjoining printing bureau, killing several thousand persons. The Nichi Nichi was the only newspaper in Tokyo to escape destruction. The Japanese community here is grief-stricken.

The most serious damage was done to the tract covering the Yamanote district, including the Tokyo wards of Honjo, Fukagawa, Akusaka, Shitaya, Nihonbashi and Kanda, where hardly a single structure was left standing.

At Ito, on the Idzu peninsula, more than 500 houses were washed away by tidal waves. Six hundred persons are said to have perished when the railway tunnel at Sasako, the largest in Japan, collapsed.

The British light cruiser Dispatch, the only foreign war vessel at Shanghai, sailed at 4 o'clock this morning for Yokohama, expecting to arrive in eighteen hours.

Thousands are without water and food. The famed twelve-story tower of Asakusa was demolished. Among the larger buildings destroyed were the Mitsugoshi department store, the Imperial Theater, the Marunouchi building and the Imperial Hotel.

When the Kaijo and Marunouchi buildings collapsed there were thousands of casualties. Many lofty buildings that lined the street opposite the Tokyo Central Railway station were burned, although the main building of the station remained intact.

In Yokohama the fire following the earthquake started in the Bund (the foreign section), and spread first through Benten and Isezaki streets, wiping out the business district. Tens of thousands of guests in the mountain resorts of the Hakone district, many of whom were foreigners, were panic-stricken. There were repeated quakes at Mount Hakone, and the town of Atana, in this district, was demolished. Six or seven thousand persons perished.

Holocaust Epitomized

1—One hundred thousand reported dead in Tokyo and Yokohama alone from earthquake, fire and tidal wave.

2—Two hundred thousand houses are in ruins in the Japanese capital.

3—Fears for the safety of the Japanese fleet and merchant ships and vessels of other nations in and near Japan felt in government circles, as no radio messages have been received from them, the Japanese warships in particular being equipped with powerful wireless.

4—No word received regarding the 1000 or more Americans in Japan.

5—Between 6000 and 7000 perished at Atama in destruction of city.

6—Refugees need food and water.

7—Three liners from the United States landed passengers at Yokohama shortly before the earthquake.

8—Odawara on the bay of Odawara swept away by tidal wave.

9—The city of Nagaya, which numbered about 620,000 inhabitants, destroyed.

S. F. Girl on Ship Due in Yokohama

SHANGHAI, Sept. 3 (by the Associated Press).—The Canadian Pacific liner Empress of Australia, which sailed from this port for Yokohama August 27, carried three Americans on her passenger list. They were Miss Mary Ellerce of San Francisco and R. C. Allen and O. E. Taylor of Shanghai.

Anxiety Felt for Judge Lobingier, Associates, and Wives in Japan

SHANGHAI, Sept. 3 (by the Associated Press).—Fears are entertained here for the safety of Judge Charles Lobingier of the United States Court for China, his wife, United States District Attorney Leonard Husar, his wife, and United States Marshal Thurston Porter, all of whom are believed to be in Yokohama.

Porter went to Yokohama to greet his fiancee, Miss Louise McCoubrey. They were planning to marry in Japan.

Judge Charles Sumner Lobingier of the United States Court for China at Shanghai, is one of the best known jurists in the Orient. He has served on the Shanghai bench since 1914, and before that was judge of the court of First Instance in the Philippines for ten years.

Going to the Philippines from Nebraska in 1904, he was active in reforming the island primary courts, held the first justice of the peace assembly in the archipelago and subsequently conducted schools of instruction for native magistrates. He was chairman of the preliminary committee to codify the Philippine laws in 1907.

Later he declined the appointment as a member of the Permanent Code Commission. Since 1908, however, he has been a member of the National Conference of Commissioners on Uniform Laws. He is chancellor emeritus of the Philippine Academy.

(Continued on page 2, column 2)

Bride Who Recently Left S. F. Missing in Yokohama

Mrs. Leonard G. Husar as she appeared on the transport leaving San Francisco recently for Shanghai, where she became the bride of the U. S. District Attorney there. Grave fear is felt for her safety.

Many San Franciscans In Midst of Orient Quake

Among the 1500 citizens of the United States living in the foreign colonies of Tokyo and Yokohama, in the districts where casualties and damage were reported heaviest, are eighty San Franciscans. In addition to these, registered and engaged in business there, are many tourists from California. It is believed scores of other United States citizens, either registered permanently or visiting in the stricken cities are among the dead and suffering. The San Franciscans whose names appear in the official registry of the Empire are:

Mr. and Mrs. Marcus Harlow, Yokohama. Harlow is a member of the United States Shipping Board.

W. R. Lynch, Yokohama. Lynch is also a member of the Shipping Board.

Mrs. Earl Ransom and family, Yokohama. Ransom is attending the University of California at Berkeley.

Mr. and Mrs. W. R. Devin, Yokohama.

Three members of the Klinger family, Tokyo. Harry Klinger is registered at the Whitcomb Hotel here. Klinger's mother is court costumer at Tokyo.

Mrs. William Scott and family, Yokohama. Scott is in San Francisco on a business mission.

Miss Josephine Cook, Yokohama.

Miss Mullins, Yokohama. A sister of Miss Mullins resides in Berkeley.

Miss J. Manley, Yokohama.

A. Kaufner, Yokohama.

M. Frank, Yokohama. Mrs. Frank is in San Francisco.

Miss Josephine Laffin, Yokohama.

Mr. and Mrs. E. Lord, Yokohama.

Mr. and Mrs. E. J. King and two children, Yokohama.

Mr. and Mrs. Herbert Hall, Yokohama.

W. W. Baer, Tokyo.

A. E. Bennett, Tokyo. Manager of the Grand Hotel, Tokyo. Bennett's daughter is living in San Francisco.

Roger (Dinty) Moore, Tokyo. Assistant manager of the Grand Hotel, Tokyo. Moore's family is in San Francisco.

Mrs. D. H. Wainright, Tokyo. Wainright is at present in Oakland.

J. E. Moss, Yokohama. Mrs. Moss and family are at Catalina Island.

(Continued on Page 2, Column 5)

Japan Stricken by Fire, Quake; Cities in Ruins

Tokyo Populace Flees Before Flames Spreading Desolation and Death; City Under Martial Law; Yokohama Foreign Section Escapes Disaster

LONDON, Sept. 2.---The foreign section of Yokohama, which is situated high on a hill, escaped destruction, according to an Osaka dispatch to the Daily Express.

Martial law in Tokyo, which is without an adequate supply of food.

Not a single house standing in the cities of Yokosura and Kamajura, as the result of a tidal wave.

Flames sweeping through eight of the leading wards of Tokyo and inhabitants fleeing to other sections of the city.

All six bridges spanning the Sumita river in Tokyo destroyed, crippling communication.

These startling developments are contained in an epitome of the destruction wrought by earthquake, fire and tidal wave in Japan since Saturday, as flashed across the Pacific last night by the lone operator of Station JAA at Tomioka and received here by the Radio Corporation of America.

In brief sentences, the Japanese operator at the lonely station—the same man who voluntarily stepped into the breech on Saturday when the cables were "out" and flashed the news of the disaster—reported additional information.

Tokyo now is under martial law and, with the military in control, nobody is admitted to the city unless they have their own provisions. A railroad man from Tokyo estimated the casualties in that city at 100,000.

The fire following the earthquake broke out in more than twenty places and spread over the wards of Honjo, Fukagawa, Asakusa, Nihombashi, Akasaki, Kojimachi and Shiba. The Nihombashi ward apparently suffered the most, being reported as "practically annihilated" by the wireless operator.

The flames also devastated the wards of Kokugikwan, where the wrestling tournaments of Tokyo were held.

Inhabitants of Tokyo were fleeing to the wards of Ushigome, Yotsuya, Koishikawa, Azabu and northern Hongo, where apparently the fire has not spread.

Tokyo buildings completely destroyed were the two largest department stores, Mitsukoshi and Shirokiya; the army arsenal, military academy, metropolitan police headquarters, Imperial Theater, the home office of the finance department of the printing bureau and the Imperial University buildings.

The message contained the

(Continued on Page 2, Column 5)

Japanese Cities Are in Ruins and Streets Strewn With the Dead

PEKING, Sept. 2.—Wireless dispatches reaching here today tell of possibly the greatest disaster in the history of the world, following tremendous earthquakes and subsequent tidal waves which have caused widespread death and desolation throughout aJpan.

The fragmentary messages tell of thousands of dead lying in the streets of Tokyo and Yokohama. All the important buildings of Toky chave been demolished or consumed by fire. Yokohama is in ashes. Many other cities have been hit equally as hard.

The death list is mounting hourly. Those who escaped the disaster are without food or water. The number who lost their lives in other cities is still unknown.

No word has been received from the more than 1000 American residents of Japan.

Martial law has been declared in Tokyo.

The United States warship Huron is proceeding to the stricken area bearing a corps of physicians, nurses and medical supplies.

The first earth shocks that hit Tokyo toppled practically every big building. These in turn crushed smaller ones, piling mountains of wreckage. Fire broke out immediately, resulting in a vast conflagration. Bridges across the Tokyo canal were destroyed by fire, preventing the escape of thousands of panic-stricken people who perished. The business sections of

(Continued on Page 2, Column 4)

EXTRA

San Francisco Chronicle

LEADING NEWSPAPER OF THE PACIFIC COAST REG.U.S.PAT.OFF.

FOUNDED 1865 — VOL. CXXIII, NO. 65 — O — SAN FRANCISCO, TUESDAY, SEPTEMBER 18, 1923 — THIRTY-TWO PAGES — DAILY 5 CENTS, SUNDAY 10 CENTS; DAILY AND SUNDAY PER MONTH $1.10

FIRE SWEEPS BERKELEY

Fifty Blocks Razed; 6000 Left Homeless

Many Periled As Flames Cut Through City

Cragmont Residential District Is in Ruins; Dynamite Used to Block Path of Destruction; 600 Homes Destroyed

Six hundred of Berkeley's finest homes, fifty blocks in the restricted Cragmont residential section, went up in a whirlwind of flame and smoke yesterday afternoon, when a brush fire swept down the hills and struck treacherously at her back, as she helped her sister community Oakland fight the same enemy.

Within a few hours, 6000 persons were rendered homeless, millions of dollars worth of property was destroyed, and two persons are supposed to have lost their lives as the flames bit deep into the heart of the city before 7500 fire fighters rallied to victory.

For hours during the afternoon, it was nip and tuck in fight to save the business section. Time after time, the flames drove into the down town district, only to be beaten back.

And not until well after dark, not until fashionable Cragmont remained only a black scar rimmed with ruins of dynamited buildings, did Berkeley know her business section was safe.

Thousands Join Forces to Battle Flames; Homes Dynamited to Block Fire; Large District Swept

The city was not saved until firemen from San Francisco, Oakland, Albany and Richmond had worked for hours side by side with every Berkeley fire fighter; not until 5000 University of California students and thousands of other Berkeley citizens had thrown their force into the battle; not until a row of homes at the edge of the fire zone were dynamited to stay the spread of the flames.

The territory swept by the worst fire the east bay has ever known, extends from Hearst avenue and Hillcrest road west, to Walnut and north to Eunice, thence northeast into the hills. Block after block of homes was destroyed on Virginia and Hilgard streets and Le Conte and Euclid avenues.

Piles of furniture from the destroyed homes, carried by scores of vehicles of every description during the progress of the fire, today dot streets, parks and open spaces in the sections surrounding the blackened district. Six thousand persons, from university students and professors to business men and just plain folk, who lost their homes, are anxiously seeking shelter in Berkeley, Oakland and San Francisco until they can start the task of rebuilding their houses.

Red Cross Assists in Caring for Injured; Damage To Property Will Total Millions of Dollars

The Berkeley General Hospital cared for scores of burned and injured, while the Berkeley Red Cross Chapter is caring for the more seriously hurt and homeless in an emergency hospital and dormitories at the Y. W. C. A.

The total damage will not be known for several days. But the figures will run well into the millions, since among the ruins are some of the finest homes in Berkeley, sevreal churches, fraternity and sorority houses, and apartment buildings.

The flames struck the city with suddenness. While some of her fire fighters were still aiding in the battle Oakland was waging against a fire which for hours had threatened Mills College and other buildings there, flames which had been consuming brush and grass and timber in Waldcat canyon crept over the ridge of the Berkeley hills and swept down Codornices canyon.

Before the city was aware of the magnitude of her danger, the fire had attacked in full fury. At first a few houses went. Then, beyond all control, the fire leaped from building to building until block after block of Cragmont flamed.

(Continued on Page 2, Column 7)

Above photo shows the flames that spread rapidly over the college city yesterday, burning 600 homes to the ground, reducing to ashes whole blocks of residences and other buildings and leaving thousands of persons homeless. The fire swept down the Cordonices canyon into the Cragmont district first, where everything was leveled before it.

Private Houses, Fraternity Houses Destroyed Listed

Buildings That Were Razed by Disastrous Blaze, With Names of Residents, Compiled

Here is a list of private residences and fraternity houses destroyed:

CHESTER ROWELL, University Regent, 1204 Tamalpais avenue.
EMIL GREPS, 1212 Tamalpais avenue.
MRS. ANNA B. TABER, 1412 Hawthorne street.
A. H. WEBER, 1515 Euclid avenue.
MISS ANN WOODAL, 2113 Delaware street.
MRS. R. W. CORTELYOU, 1830 Walnut street.
DR. STEWARD DAGGERT, 1427 Hawthorne street.
IRVING WHITNEY, 1431 Hawthorne street.
COLONEL UPTON LANDON, 1439 Hawthorne street
E. R. ZARAEILE, 1414 Le Roy avenue.
CHARLES F. SHAW, 1415 Euclid avenue.
MRS. NELLIE STAFFORD, 1409-1411 Euclid avenue.
PROFESSOR E. B. BABCOCK, 1601 Spruce street.
A. S. PILLSBURY, 1537 Spruce street.
JACOB BAUMIEL, Berkeley Hillside Club.
MRS. EMMA E. TAYLOR, 1544 Spruce street.
MRS. RUBY MITCHELL, 1540 Spruce street.
MRS. JOHN BOWERS, 1631 Oxford.
BRUCE McCRAD, 2617 Virginia street.
HOMER WHITING, 1783 Walnut street.
WILLIAM EDGAR, 1783 Walnut street.
J. E. HAVENS, 1735 Walnut street.
THE BRAEMER HOTEL, Home for University Girls, 2417 Le Conte avenue.
LOIS and MARGARET AUSTIN, 1741 Euclid avenue.
PROF. L. W. ALLEN, 1556 Le Roy avenue.
PROF. L. O. BORRINGER, 1689 Le Roy avenue.
PROF. J. H. HILDEBRAND, chemistry professor, 1836 Le Roy avenue.
PROF. L. R. BOYD, military science, 2524 Virginia street.
PROF. J. F. BOLIN, associate professor in education, 1600 Scenic avenue.
PROF. H. F. BOLTON, history, 1526 Scenic avenue.
L. E. BOMAR, 2706 Virginia street.
W. Gerard, 1589 Le Roy avenue.
H. N. Gjelnes, 1730 La Loma avenue.
Miss H. M. Gladding, 2555 Buena Vista way.
G. Glockler, 1601 Marin avenue.
Professor L. W. Godden, 1262 Euclid avenue.
H. F. Grady, 1574 Le Roy avenue.
Miss A. R. Green, 2322 Virginia street.
Mrs. B. N. Grimes, 2563A Buena Vista way.
Professor E. E. Hall, 1501 Le Roy avenue.
R. L. Holl Jr., 1707 Euclid avenue.
C. M. Herring, 1325 Arch street.
Professor H. R. Hatfield, Dean of Faculty, 2632 Le Compe avenue.
Miss L. Helber, 1700 Euclid avenue.
PROF. W. B. HERMS, 1424 LeRoy avenue.
MISS F. A. HICKS, 1700 LaLoma avenue.
E. F. HILL JR., 1726 Euclid.
E. C. HILLS, 2539 Buena Vista way.
F. E. HINCHLEY, 1627 Scenic boulevard.
MISS F. HOLLIS, 1415 LaLoma avenue.
H. M. HOLMAN, 2706 Virginia street.
J. J. HOPFIELD, 1135 Walnut street.
W. T. HORNE, 2527 Virginia street.
J. C. HOWARD, 2596 Buena Vista way.
PROF. A. E. HOWARD, 1401 LeRoy avenue.
A. F. HURD, 962 Euclid avenue.
F. IRWIN, 1625 Arch street.
J. C. JOHNSTONE, 1504 LeRoy avenue.
B. M. JONES, 1737 Virginia street.
R. M. JONES, 1012 Euclid avenue.
F. L. JORY, 1420 Scenic boulevard.
M. S. BRADINER, 1535 Euclid avenue.
W. C. BRAY, 2708 Virginia street.
MISS H. BREWSTER, 2550 Buena Vista avenue.
MISS E. G. CADWALADER, 1709 LaLoma drive.
G. M. CALHOUN, 1056 Euclid avenue.
C. L. CAMP, 1584 Le Roy avenue.
W. R. CAMP, 2731 Virginia street.
MISS E. L. CAMPER, 1516 Le Roy avenue.
L. G. GLEDD, 2312 Virginia street.
PROFESSOR IRA B. CROFF, head of department of economics, 1418 Le Roy avenue.
W. V. CRUESS, 1434 Scenic avenue.
MRS. M. B. DAVIDSON, assistant dean of women, 1523 Le Roy avenue.
R. E. DAVIS, 1801 Thousand Oaks boulevard.
MISS S. R. DAVIS, 2611 Virginia street.

(Continued on Page 2, Column 2.)

List of Known Injured In Big Fire in Berkeley

Following is a list of the injured in yesterday's fire at Berkeley. Many other persons are believed to have suffered minor hurts, for which they received home treatment:

AARINE, John, aged 60, 2510 Buena Vista street, burns and shock.
BECKETT, P. E., 2139 Berkeley Way, minor burns; treated at Berkeley General Hospital.
BLUNT, H. F., 2537 First avenue, severe burns; Berkeley General Hospital.
BOOTH, Mrs. Emma S., 80 years of age, 2414 Cedar street, collapse and minor bruises; Berkeley General Hospital.
DONOVAN, Mrs. E. E., 70 years of age, address unknown, collapse; Berkeley General Hospital.
GEORGE, Mrs., treated at University Infirmary for shock and minor cuts.
IRELAND, William R., minor cuts and burns; Berkeley General Hospital.
JOHNSON, Arlington, university student, collapse; Berkeley General Hospital.
JORGENSON, Ray, 2911 Beacon street, contusions on arms; Berkeley General Hospital.
PRESTON, E. J., cuts and burns; Berkeley General Hospital.
RAZUM, Joseph, 2924 Shattuck avenue; sprained groin; Berkeley General Hospital.
ST. CLAIR, Orla, university student, collapse; Berkeley General Hospital.
SULLIVAN children, suffering from effects of smoke; treated at University Hospital.
WARD, Kenneth, university student, broken arm; Berkeley General Hospital.
WOLD, H. W., address unknown, burns; Berkeley General Hospital.

Revolution Breaks Out in Trans-Jordania

JERUSALEM, Sept. 17.—Authoritative reports say that a revolution has broken out on Trans-Jordania against the Emir Aboullah.

Advices from Jersalem on September 5 report a revolt by 3000 Arabs under the leadership of the Sheik of Es Salt. The rebels submitted an ultimatum in which they demanded an equitable system of taxation, the expulsion of all forcigners and the formation of a parliamentary government.

4 Men Buried Alive In River Under Mortar

SCHENECTADY, N. Y., Sept. 17.—Four men are believed to be buried in the Mohawk river near this city under tons of wet concrete, which forced them under water when wooden scaffolding on the Great Western Gateway bridge gave way late this afternoon. One of the men is Kenneth Davidson, superintendent of construction for the entire bridge. S

20 Families Entrapped in Flame-Surrounded Canyon

Sonoma Valley Fire-Swept; Band of Volunteers Desperateley Battle to Save Menaced Victims

Dynamiting a perilous path through the ravaging flames that have been sweeping Sonoma Valley for more than twenty-four hours, a band of volunteers from Petaluma were fighting desperately last night to reach more than twenty families entrapped in Cavedale Canyon, four miles north of Boyes Springs, which, with Fetter's Springs, has been completely destroyed.

Early last night two boys managed to break through the inferno and report the peril of the fifty or more persons hemmed in between the narrow walls of the canyon over which the flames were slowly creeping.

It is feared the entire settlement in the canyon will be burned to death unless the rescuers break through by noon today.

AID LEAVES SAN FRANCISCO

At 10 o'clock last night, answering an appeal from the district, Fire Chief Thomas Murphy ordered three chemical and hose wagons sent to the scene on a special train, under command of Captain Hanrohan.

According to the two boys who, suffering from burns and exhausted, carried the call for help from the entrapped families to Petaluma, barriers against the insatiable flames are being destroyed almost as fast as the frenzied little group can erect them.

Escape cut off on the higher levels, the families retreated again to the canyon, throwing up trenches between the oncoming flames and the walls of Cavedale canyon. Restrained but shortly, the fire crossed these trenches, the boys reported, and crept on to the very walls of the retreat.

LAST FUTILE BATTLE

At the time they were dispatched to seek help, the boys said, the little band were stripping the sides of the canyon of all brush and vegitation in an effort to prevent the flames from swooping from the higher level down into the canyon. Sparks carried on the high winds, however, made these attemps futile, the boys said, and unless a path can be forced into the canyon before noon today, everyone there will perish.

New perils were felt late last night when the flames that had already laid waste Fetters spring and Boyes springs veered westward again on the outskirts of Sonoma, creeping up on the Sonoma mountains, threatening to race through the dry brush lowlands and pastures into Petaluma.

Every available man and woman in the vicinity was pressed into service last night and huried to the crest of the mountains an dynamite a broad stretch of timber in an effort to check the flames.

PETALUMA MENACED

Should the fire eat over the Sonoma mountains and into the lowlands, ePtaluma will be lost, fire officials there stated last night. However, they said, there is little doubt that the conscriped forces of fighers shall be able to halt the flames at the crest of the mountains, adding tha reports from Sonoma stated that forces from there were succesfully fighting fire on the other side.

The fire started Sunday morning on the Napa county side of the mountains, skirting Sonoma valley, in the heart of the Valley of the Moon, where practically every summer home and building was consumed by the flames.

The Boyes Springs Hotel was one of th eprincipal buildings in the district completely destroyed. The gusets fled as the hotel burned. Every structure at Fetter's resort was lost.

New Pictures of Japanese Disaster—Page 11

Temperature Comparisons

	High	Low		High	Low
San Francisco	71	56	New York	90	66
Los Angeles	80	65	Chicago	82	70
Seattle	78	54	Kansas City	82	70
Denver	78	62	New Orleans	92	74

San Francisco Chronicle

LEADING NEWSPAPER OF THE PACIFIC COAST — REG. U.S. PAT. OFF.

WEATHER Tuesday: Fair and mild, but cloudy mornings; gentle westerly winds. Complete Weather Report on Page 15.

FOUNDED 1865—VOL. CXXVII, NO. 6 — CCC — SAN FRANCISCO, CAL., TUESDAY, JULY 21, 1925 — DAILY 5 CENTS, SUNDAY 10 CENTS

BRYAN, UNDER MERCILESS GOAD OF DARROW, HOLDS FAST TO HOLY WRIT

DEFENSE LEADER, IN CONTEMPT, RECANTS

COMMONER, IN ANGER, FLAYS ALL SCIENCE

Reaffirms His Literal Belief In Every Biblical Miracle And Parable

COURTYARD PLATFORM, DAYTON, Tenn., July 20 (I. N. S.)—The Scopes anti-evolution trial took a sensational turn this afternoon when William Jennings Bryan, outstanding fundamentalist, was called as a witness for the defense of John Thomas Scopes.

This maneuver was taken by Clarence Darrow to prove that the Bible was not believed literally even by the best fundamentalist American.

Before he took the witness chair Bryan obtained permission from the court to put Darrow and Dudley Field Malone on the stand, too.

Introduces Testimony of Modernist Churches

Out in the courtyard Arthur Garfield Haynes arose to conclude his discussion of the defense's scientists. Haynes introduced testimony from clergymen, who reconciled evolution to the Divine creation. He called attention to the statement by Dr. Herman Rosenwater, a Cincinnati rabbi, who said the "King James version was not an accurate translation of the old Jewish Bible." To support his contention, Rabbi Rosenwater pointed out that the Jewish word "Bara" was translated as "Create" when its true meaning is "set in motion."

This error, the rabbi said, changed the whole sense of the original version of the Divine creation.

"Read Our Bible" Sign Is Cause of Clash

The defense projected a new clash in the open air courtroom by demanding the removal of a nearby sign which said "Read Our Bible," when Darrow objected to it. General Ben J. McKenzie made a slighting reference to Darrow's agnosticism.

This provoked Dudley Field Malone to "read the riot act" to McKenzie and to demand that Darrow's religion be left out of the trial.

"The counsel for the defense are not on trial," Malone shouted and the crowd applauded him.

Darrow again protested against the sign. He urged the court to place a sign reading "Read Evolution," alongside the religious sign.

The Commoner took the stand with a declaration that he was ready to defend the Bible against every attack of science. He said, too, he denied the truth of all the findings of science. He said, too, he be-

(Continued on Page 4, Col. 1)

William J. Bryan (above), Biblicist, and Clarence Darrow, suspender-snapping cross-examiner, who raged at each other during the Scopes case hearing yesterday.

COURT QUOTES BIBLE, GRANTS FORGIVENESS

Leader of Nation's Criminal Lawyers, Capituates to Judge of the Hills

COURTHOUSE, DAYTON, Tenn., July 20 (I. N. S.).—The fires of human passion which have blazed in the Scopes trial were partly quenched this afternoon when Clarence Darrow, one of the leading members of the American car, apologized to Presiding Judge John T. Raulston for th remarks which caused him to be cited for contempt of court.

The Judge then withdrew the contempt citation which he had ordered.

Darrow told the court that he regretted his words from the moment that he read them in the stenographic record.

The Judge replied to Darrow by saying he would forgive even as Christ forgave his critics.

Lawyer and Judge Shake Hands in Amity

The incident was ended when Darrow and Raulston shook hands in open court.

Because of the great crowd, Judge Raulston then adjourned his court to the courthouse yard, where a speaking stand and benches were erected at the opening of the trial for a series of open-air prayer meetings. Before taking this extraordinary action the court announced that the tremendous crowds in the courtroom had cracked the first floor ceiling, causing the building to become unsafe.

Darrow made his apology as soon as the afternoon session started.

Darrow Embarrassed, But Stands to His Guns

The Judge nodded consent and the great criminal lawyer arose, obviously embarrassed, but determined to wipe out the stain upon his legal record.

"Whatever took place there was hurried," said Darrow, his arms folded. "The truth was that I did not know at the time how it sounded and when I read it over I was sorry. I determined on Friday that I would speak to the court about it. Some of the newspapers seemed to think that you should do something about it, so this morning I waited for you to speak first.

"I speak now not to influence your decision, but because I think I ought to say it for myself.

Disclaims Premeditation In Any Degree

"I do believe, however, your honor, that I went further than I should have done. So far as it was premeditated, there was nothing of the sort. So far as the people of Tennessee are concerned, I don't know that I have been in a community in my life where my religious beliefs have been accepted as quietly as here in Tennessee. I have been treated kindly here.

"I certainly did this and I don't see how your honor could fail to take notice of it.

"I deeply regret my action and I apologize for it," said Darrow. In replying, Judge Raulston's voice shook with emotion.

"If this little incident had been personal between Darrow and myself," said the court, "it would have passed unnoticed.

"When a judge speaks from the bench, he is a part of the great State, and I could not afford to pass these words by. To do so would not do justice to the great State for which I plead from the bench."

"I believe in the mercy of Jesus Christ. I accept Mr. Darrow's apology. I do not believe his words were premeditated. We forgive him and we forget the incident. The citation is dismissed."

Bryan's Belief Told on Stand

Called by Clarence Darrow as a witness for the defense in the Scopes trial, William Jennings Bryan testified to his belief in the literalness of the Bible. The following are the highlights of the Commoner's testimony:

I believe:

That Jonah was swallowed by a whale. It might have been a big fish. God could make a man or a fish do anything he wanted to.

Jonah was in the fish's belly for three days.

That the flood took place in the year 5929 B. C. and it wiped all life from the face of the earth.

That scientists who say that life existed on the earth 25,000 years ago are wrong.

That God sends the pains of childbirth to women because of the transgression of Eve.

That God made the earth in six days, but that "days" might have been periods of millions of years.

That Eve was the first woman and that she was created from Adam's rib.

OH! MARGY

BY JOHN HELD, JR.

Margy wonders if "scratching the favorite" isn't just another cruel form of horse branding.

(Copyright, 1925.)

Mary Pickford Avoids Service of Subpoena

LOS ANGELES, July 20 (A. P.).—Serving a subpoena on Mary Pickford is almost as difficult as trying to kidnap her, Deputy Sheriffs decided today after trying in vain since last Friday to catch a glimpse of the motion picture actress off the screen, in person. They were armed with a summons for her to appear at the trial in Superior Court Wednesday of two truck drivers and an automobile salesman accused of plotting to kidnap her and hold her for $200,000 ransom. They had to give up trying to serve the subpoena and tonight were counting on the assurance of Miss Pickford's attorney that she would be produced in Court at the proper time.

$5,000,000 Paid for Property In Uptown Business District

S. P. TERMINAL RUMORED AS NEW VENTURE

Move by Railway Would Be Followed by Electrification of Peninsula Lines

The biggest cash realty deal involving one piece of property in the history of San Francisco, which was announced yesterday, has coupled with it one of the deepest and most tantalizing realty mysteries that have ever agitated local real estate circles. The property is the holding of the Marian Realty Company at Eighth and Market streets, occupied by the Crystal Palace Market and other buildings, which has been sold to the Mercantile Trust Company, as agent, for the sum of $3,500,000.

At the same time agents are active in acquiring other holdings in the same block, bringing the total sales up to $5,000,000.

Block Gives Lengthy Frontage on Market

The block bounded by Seventh and Eighth, Market and Mission streets is 825 by 550 feet in size. Acquisition of the entire block, with its enormous frontage on upper Market street, will give the owners an ideal site for whatever purpose it is used.

Who are the buyers? is the question that everyone cognizant of the deal was asking yesterday. None of the principals or the agents could or would answer the question. Some of them professed to be as much mystified as "the street."

Three plausible answers were advanced by realty men. They were:

1—Site of the long rumored peninsula system terminal for the Southern Pacific Railway.

2—Huge new department store, with the name of B. F. Schlesinger and the May Department Stores Company most prominently mentioned.

3—New hotel project with which the name of a large Eastern chain hotel corporation is linked.

All of these conjectures were juicy morsels of gossips and discussions yesterday. Attractive arguments in favor of each one were made. As one realty man said:

"The deal covers such an enormous piece of land, it has been carried through with such secrecy, and the buyers are evidently possessed of such great resources that one has to have an active imagination to picture what it is all about."

Rumors of New S. P. Terminal Prevalent

Talk of the Southern Pacific acquiring the block was especially prevalent. It has long been anticipated that the railroad company would at no distant date acquire a site on upper Market street for a passenger terminal which would put their trains into the heart of the city. High officials of the company several years ago admitted that such was the plan. More recently officials have stated that electrification of the peninsula system would go hand in hand with the construction of a new terminal.

The steady growth of upper Market street as a retail district, the evident trend to make the Civic Center the heart of the business district would make it likely that the Southern Pacific is behind the new deal. It would be an ideal location, according to engineers.

The present peninsula line makes a turn to reach the Third and Townsend station near Seventh street. From there to Market is a straight line, between Seventh and Eighth, and the level at which the line could be constructed would make it possible to excavate the right of way, passing under Harrison, Fol-

(Continued on Page 3, Column 6.)

Fails in Attempt To Slay Husband

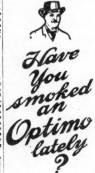

Mrs. Della Keating, Denver wife, who tried to kill her husband yesterday a few minutes before his divorce suit against her was to be heard in Kansas City.

Angry Wife Sorry She Did Not Kill

Special Dispatch to The Chronicle

KANSAS CITY, July 20.—Thrusting a revolver at her husband's chest and announcing that she intended to kill him, Mrs. Della Keating, Denver beauty, caused a panic in the corridors of the Circuit Court here today. The husband, Stephen E. Keating, who is suing the woman for divorce, seized her arm and took the pistol from her. Keating had just stepped from an elevator when Mrs. Keating leaped from a bench. Crossing the corridor, she brandished the revolver and shouted:

"Stephen, I'm going to kill you!"

"I wish I had waited until he turned his back," she told officers later, "then he could not have caught my arm before I fired."

Keating was granted a divorce by default on July 2. The decree was set aside July 16 when Mrs. Keating alleged she had not been notified of the filing of the suit. Keating said his marriage was annulled on July 2 after he had learned that she had another husband from whom she had not yet obtained a divorce.

She admitted today that she had been married three times and that she had another husband from whom she is not divorced.

"He is an English nobleman whom I married in Denver," Mrs. Keating said. "Three weeks after the marriage I learned that he had a wife and three children. I just left him."

Harry Thaw's Mother Sues Her Grandson

NEW YORK, July 20.—Mrs. Mary Copley Thaw of Pittsburg today sued her grandson, Lawrence Copley Thaw, in the Federal Court here for the recovery of $600,000 which she alleges had been taken from her when she was weak in mind and body and easily influenced. Mrs. Thaw is 83 years old. She is the mother of Harry K. Thaw, whose half-brother, the late Edward Thaw, was the father of the defendant. The complaint in the action, which was drawn by Mrs. Thaw's attorneys, Reed, Smith, Shaw and Beal of Pittsburg, is brief.

Chicago Broker Leaps 15 Stories to Death

Special by Leased Wire to The Chronicle

CHICAGO, July 20.—Emil Wagner, once head of one of the largest stock and commission houses in the country, and reported to have had a private fortune of $8,000,000, today committed suicide by leaping from the fifteenth floor of the Westminster buildi g.

COOLIDGE TOLD OF NEED FOR ALAMEDA BASE

Senator Hale Advocates Early Remedying of Pacific Weakness

By ARTHUR S. HENNING

Special by Leased Wire to The Chronicle

SWAMPSCOTT, Mass., July 20.—Imperative necessity of remedying the weaknesses of the American system of naval defenses in the Pacific was urged upon President Coolidge today by Senator Fred Hale, Republican, Maine, chairman of the Senate Committee on Naval Affairs.

The major recommendations submitted by Senator Hale, as the result of observations on a tour of Hawaiian and Pacific Coast naval establishments, from which he has just returned were:

1—That a naval base of the first rank be established at Alameda on San Francisco bay, there being now no base on the Pacific Coast capable of supplying and repairing the fleet in time of war or accommodating the entire fleet even in time of peace.

2—That Pearl Harbor in the Hawaiian islands be developed into an adequate naval base by the deepening of the entrance channel sufficiently to allow ingress of our largest battle ships, the dredging of the inner anchorages and the construction of a new drydock capable of accommodating warships of the greatest draft.

President Promises Serious Consideration

The President assured the Senator that he would give the recommendations the most serious consideration, remarking that he had been studying the question of our Pacific defenses for some time.

"The fact is," said Senator Hale, after his call at White Court, "we have only the beginning of a naval base in the Hawaiian Islands and in my talk with the President I emphasized the steps that should be taken at the earliest possible moment to remedy the situation.

"What is the value of a naval base harbor which our battle ships cannot get into? The present entrance channel of Pearl harbor is too shallow for our battle ships, which it was necessary to anchor outside in the open sea after the recent maneuvers in the Hawaiian islands.

Need of Big Naval Base on Pacific Coast

"We ought to have a naval base on the Pacific Coast comparable to Norfolk on the Atlantic," the Senator continued. "We have no adequate base there now, as our fleet has outgrown Mare Island. I am in favor of the establishment of a real base at Alameda without abandoning Mare Island, which can still be used for subsidiary purposes. If the Pacific Coast Senators and Congressmen will get together the Alameda plan can be put through. There ought to be no jealousy in a matter like this, which means providing adequate protection for the whole West Coast."

Alameda Had Been Urged as Base

The Navy Department and a special Congress committee have urged the adoption of the Alameda project repeatedly as a vital feature of naval defense, but it has been defeated by influences aiming to compel the further development of Mare Island, which has been pronounced officially incapable of expansion commensurate with the needs of our present day navy.

Senator Hale told the President he believed the navy is pursuing the proper policy in the development of aviation.

NEWS ODDITIES OF THE DAY

$1500 Cobwebs On Rockefellers' 1920 Taxes Paid

IT MAY be a hard winter for the Rockefeller family. A penalty of about $1500 was collected from the oil magnates yesterday by State Controller Riley because an inheritance tax of $2490 was overlooked for five years. Mrs. Almira C. Rockefeller, wife of William Rockefeller, had $96,000 worth of stock in the Standard Oil Company of California when she died at her New York home in January, 1920. She was a sister-in-law of John D. Rockefeller. When Riley recently reminded the Rockefellers' New York attorneys of the debt a check for the tax, plus the penalty, promptly followed. Judge Shortall confirmed the settlement yesterday.

Wife Sues Widow for $50,000 as Spouse Angler

NEW YORK, July 20 (I. N. S.).—An action to obtain $50,000 from Mrs. Ruth Marlow Bush, for "wilfully, wickedly and maliciously" gaining the affections of her husband, was filed today in Brooklyn by Mrs. Hattie Nathan. Mrs. Nathan alleged that "by offers of money," Mrs. Bush, described in the papers as "a pretty widow, 32 years of age," sought to induce her husband to leave her and go with Mrs. Bush to various cities in the United States. Mrs. Nathan alleged her husband and Mrs. Bush were now living together in San Francisco.

Landscapes on Girls' Knees Latest Novelty

CHICAGO, July 20 (A. P.).—Landscaping such feminine knees as may from time to time be exposed by rolled stocking and perverse winds is advocated by beauty specialists, who began a week's convention here today.

"Painted knees are the latest thing," said Mrs. Ruth Maurer, presiding at the opening session. "Hand-painted pictures on the knees are intriguing. Some designs are simple, some elaborate, some girls prefer a flower or a group of blossoms. Others like a portrait or a little landscape."

Young Cyclone Takes 1500 Union Chicks on Air Dash

Special Dispatch to The Chronicle

PASO ROBLES, July 20.—Picking up a chicken house containing 1500 chickens, scattering it over a large-sized lot, after having selected that building from a group of others, and killing but two fowls in the operation is the freak record of a wind which swooped down upon the property of Hans Iverson, a rancher of Union, near here. So far as can be learned, his place was the only one to suffer damage, other sections in the vicinity reporting no unusual wind manifestations.

Burglars Take Star of Lassen County Sheriff

SUSANVILLE, July 20 (I. N. S.).—Thieves invaded the room of G. W. Carter, Sheriff of Lassen county, at Reno last night and robbed the officer of his star, a suit of clothes and other valuables, it was learned here today when Carter returned from the Nevada city. Carter's companion, whose identity could not be learned, also lost his clothing and personal effects.

Solon From Colorado Operated On in S. F.

Representative E. T. Taylor of Colorado was operated on at Letterman Hospital yesterday for tumor. This is the second operation performed on Congressman Taylor at the Presidio hospital. The first one was several weeks ago, after his return from a voyage with the fleet in Pacific waters.

S. F. LIQUOR TRADE CHIEFS NEAR ARREST

General Roundup Planned to Clean Out Narcotic, Whisky Rings

Warrants for the arrest of eight men, powerful leaders in the rum-running and bootlegging industry, the discovery of an alleged hijacker beaten, bound and gagged and left to die in an isolated spot near Eureka, and the arrest of another marked the Government's onslaught yesterday in the Pacific Coast rum war.

A general roundup of a combination rum and narcotic ring was momentarily expected with the issuing of eight secret warrants by United States Commissioner Krull. The names contained in the warrants were closely guarded, but it is believed they are connected with the gang that participated in the fatal machine gun battle at Moss Landing.

Rum Runners Busy in Eureka

While Government agents prepared to serve the warrants issued here, the activities of rum runners—possibly a San Francisco gang frightened away by the Government investigation—were disclosed at Eureka when Thomas Gist was badly beaten and bound to a post in a deserted barn. He released himself and was being taken to Eureka by a Deputy Sheriff when he recognized two of his assailants. The deputy arrested Frank Nelson, an alleged hijacker, but Nelson's

TEMPERATURE COMPARISONS

	High	Low		High	Low
San Francisco	58	54	New York	64	54
Los Angeles	63	51	Chicago	80	50
Seattle	62	44	Kansas City	72	60
Denver	60	40	New Orleans	86	68

San Francisco Chronicle

LEADING NEWSPAPER OF THE PACIFIC COAST

REG. U.S. PAT. OFF.

WEATHER

MONDAY

Fair and warmer; gentle northerly winds

Complete weather report on Page 19

FOUNDED 1865—VOL. CXXVIII. NO. 115 CCC* SAN FRANCISCO, CAL., MONDAY, MAY 10, 1926 DAILY 5 CENTS, SUNDAY 10 CENTS

BYRD CIRCLES NORTH POLE IN PLANE

Flies 1620 Miles in 16 Hours on Nonstop Dash

Leak in Oil Line Menaces Airship At Top of World

Commander and Pilot Alternate in Handling Machine on Trip; Perfect Weather Aids in Verifying Peary's Observations

By WILLIAM E. BYRD

Exclusive Dispatch by Leased Wire to The Chronicle
Special to The New York Times

KINGS BAY, May 9.—America's claim to the North Pole was clinched tonight when, after a flight of fifteen hours and fifty-one minutes, Commander Richard E. Byrd and Floyd Bennett, his pilot, returned to announce that they had flown to the Pole, circling it several times and verifying Admiral Peary's observations completely.

When they were within sixty miles of the Pole the oil system of the right-hand motor began leaking badly and it seemed necessary to choose between proceeding with two motors or attempting a landing to make repairs.

Byrd Gives Up Idea of Landing

In the neighborhood of the Pole numerous stretches of smooth ice were seen and a landing was favored by Bennett, but Commander Byrd, remembering his difficulties in starting at Kings Bay, vetoed his proposal.

Both agreed, however, to continue the flight to the Pole, even if they went on with only two motors. To their surprise the right-hand motor continued to work effectively, despite the ruptured tank, and when the Fokker returned to Kings Bay all three motors were hitting perfectly.

Circles Kings Bay, Lands Safely

The Josephine Ford, after making three circles over Kings Bay, landed at the takeoff runway and taxied to her original starting position.

Commander Byrd and Bennett hurried a mile and a half to the shore, where a motor boat rushed them to the Chantier. The crew aboard her went wild with joy, waving flags and their caps. Many of the crew completely broke down with emotion and with tears streaming from their eyes embraced the flyers.

They were favored by continued sunlight and there was never the slightest fog, enabling Commander Byrd to use his sun compass and bubble sextant and obtain the most accurate observations possible.

Three Magnetic Compasses Chart Course

There were three magnetic compasses in the plane, but all of them deviated eccentrically after reaching high latitudes. Bennett declared that when he was piloting the magnetic compasses were wholly useless and would swing almost a quarter turn, returning very slowly.

Without the sunlight navigation would have been almost impossible. Bennett and Commander Byrd alternated in the piloting, Bennett refilling the gasoline containers while the Commander piloted and navigated.

Commander Byrd found that the Bumstrad sun compass worked perfectly, even when held in the hand, so when he was in the pilot's seat he held the throttle in one hand while he got his direction from the sun compass held in the other.

Sirens Screech When Plane Appears

Special Cable to The Chronicle

KINGS BAY, Spitzbergen, May 9.—Commander Byrd and his companion had not been expected to return from the airplane dash to the Pole before 8 o'clock tonight. At 5:25 p. m. a tiny speck was seen in the distance by the eager watchers here. As the speck grew larger and larger, the American ship Chantier and the Norwegian ship Heimdal ran their flags up to the topmasts and started their sirens to screeching, for it was realized that the flyers were returning. It was hard for the crowds to believe, but it was true.

The giant Fokker landed lightly on the spot where it had started this morning.

Throng Rushes to Greet Birdmen

The throng rushed toward the flyers before their propellers had stopped and lifted Commander Byrd from his machine amid wild cheering. Captain Roald Amundsen and his partner in the projected dirigible flight over the Pole, Lincoln Ellsworth, were among the first to welcome Commander Byrd and his companion.

Captain Amundsen embraced the pair and called for three cheers.

Questions were hurled at the flyers.

"Did you reach the Pole?" "Did you find land?" were the queries.

But the flyers only smiled, too tired to reply. They were borne on the shoulders of the crowd to the ship Chantier, which brought them and their planes to Spitzbergen.

Band Strikes Up National Anthem

On the Chantier the crew went wild with joy and the band on the Heimdal struck up "The Star-Spangled Banner."

Commander Byrd told this correspondent: "We flew three times in a circle over the Pole, then dropped the American flag, with an account of our flight, in a box."

Commander Byrd also told Lieutenant Riiser Larsen of the Norge's crew that he was sure he had reached the Pole, and it is generally agreed here that he did.

Asked if he had found new land, Commander Byrd said he had found none, affirming Captain Amundsen's account after his flight last year. Only one opening was found in the ice.

The average speed was 98.75 miles an hour, the time for the flight being 15 hours 51 minutes.

The three-motored Fokker plane carried a load of two tons.

NEW YORK, May 9 (A. P.).—By flying over the North Pole today, Lieutenant Commander Byrd completed his first flight six

(Continued on Page 2, Col. 3)

Wins Honor For America

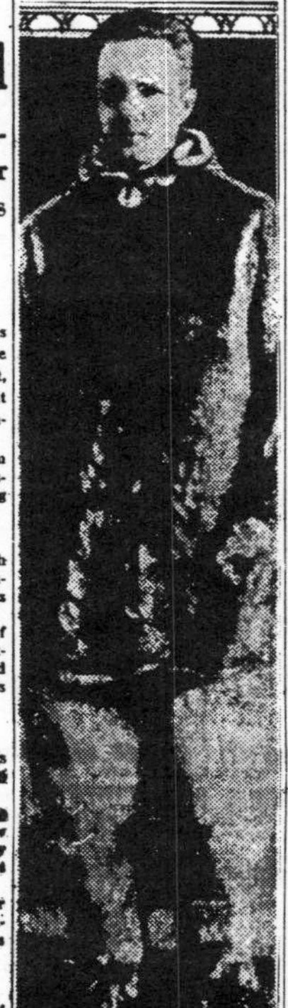

—Wide World Foto

Commander R. E. Byrd, whose airship is first to reach the North Pole.

160 Hurt When Paris Royalists Battle Police

Students Smash Cordon to Place Wreaths on Joan of Arc Statues

PARIS, May 9 (A. P.).—Joan of Arc day national fete was marred in Paris by a conflict between the police and royalist forces, in which 118 policemen were injured. Two policemen were taken to a hospital and four others were unable to return to duty. About forty of the Camelots du Roi, a royalist organization, for the most part young students, were injured.

The clash grew out of the refusal of Minister of the Interior Durand to permit formal processions for the purpose of placing wreaths on the two monuments to the Maid of Orleans, one in the Place Saint Augustin and the other in the Place des Pyramides, abutting the Rue Rivoli. Two hundred and twenty-one arrests were made, but thirty-one persons were released after examination of their credentials.

Despite the mobilization of a vast force of police and Republican guard, the royalists planted floral tributes at the bases of both statues, forcing their way through the police cordon and battling with canes against night sticks.

Iron Ore Discoverer Of Minnesota Dies

DULUTH, Minn., May 9 (A. P.).—Leonidas Merritt, 82, discoverer of the first iron ore on the Mesaba range, died today at his home here of heart disease.

CHURCH FRONT WRECKED IN SECOND BOMB BLAST PLOT

Parish Priests of SS. Peter and Paul Alarmed, but Escape Injury

Work of Vandals Who Planted Dynamite There Jan. 31, Police Believe

With a roar that aroused the neighborhood for blocks around and sent scores of startled residents to the street in their night attire, a dynamite bomb early yesterday morning exploded at SS. Peter and Paul's Church, 666 Filbert street, in what was the second attempt within less than three months to wreck the edifice.

Sleeping in the parish house not more than fifty feet away, were Father Oreste Trinchieri, pastor of the church; Father Rafael Piperni and several others. They were uninjured.

The bomb was planted at the front entrance to the building and exploded shortly after 3 o'clock. It tore a hole in the concrete more than a foot deep, shattered marble walls and windows in the vestibule, splintered wooden wainscoating and loosened a heavy door.

Bombs Identified In Two Plots

The instrument, comprising from three to five sticks of dynamite bound together with wire, was identical in construction to the bomb planted back of the church on the morning of January 31.

Detectives are sure that both explosions were set by the same person. But whether it is the vandalism of a religious fanatic or of some enemy of the church who is using too light a charge of explosive in a serious aim to wreck the building, is undetermined.

Paper and Fuse Offer Clues

A burned fuse ten feet long and some fragments of oiled paper in which the dynamite was wrapped are being held by the police as clues.

It is believed the bomber hid in Columbus square, across the street from the church, awaiting the early morning hour when the street was deserted. The bomb was placed in a corner where the stairs meet the main floor. A heavy steel and rubber mat was thrown over the bomb to confine the explosion and give it more power.

Long Fuse Used To Insure Escape

The length of fuse probably gave the bomber fully five minutes to escape before the detonation occurred.

The deafening report sounded as

(Continued on Page 3, Col. 1)

Margy says: "When a fellow takes a girl out for just a little ride, he shouldn't go too far."

C. S. HOWARD'S SON KILLED UNDER TRUCK NEAR WILLITS

Week-End Fishing Party of Three Boys Brings Death to Its Leader

Parents Charter Train and Hurry North From San Francisco

Frank Robert Howard, 15-year-old son of Charles S. Howard, automobile distributor, was instantly killed yesterday morning at Ridgewood ranch, the Howard estate in the mountains near Willits.

He was driving a truck and with two companions was on his way to the ranch house returning from an early morning fishing trip, when the truck overturned.

In attempting to dodge a rock in the canyon road about two miles from the ranch house, the front wheel went over the side of the grade, causing the truck to topple over and pinning the boy underneath.

Week-End Vacation Brings Tragedy

Young Howard, accompanied by Richard Penniman, son of L. E. Penniman, 816 Crescent avenue, San Mateo, and schoolmate at the Peninsula Avenue School, had gone to Ridgewood to spend the week-end vacation, while the adult members of the family went to Del Monte to attend the opening of the new hotel.

On Saturday, the two boys were joined by a third, Lawrence DeBree of Willits. They planned to spend Sunday fishing for trout in streams on the Howard 15,000-acre ranch. They got an early start and were on the return trip, rejoicing over a big "catch," about 9 o'clock when the accident occurred.

His Companions Thrown Clear of Truck

Young Penniman and DeBree were thrown clear when the truck went off the grade. Penniman was unhurt, but young DeBree was cut and bruised on the legs. The two notified the ranch superintendent of the accident and attempts were made to revive young Howard. A physician, summoned from Willits, announced after his examination that the boy had died instantly. His back was crushed and the skull fractured.

Charles S. Howard was notified of the accident at Del Monte, and accompanied by Mrs. Howard, departed immediately for Ridgewood. Dr. Harry Warren, the family physician from San Mateo, accompanied them.

The body will be brought to San Francisco this morning by special train.

Pulitzer Air Trophy Race Off for 1926

NEW YORK, May 9 (A. P.).—The annual Pulitzer trophy race, usually the closing event of the national air races, will not be held this year, the New York World announced tonight, after learning that the army and navy, for several years the only contenders, would have no entries for the 1926 air contest.

Fishing Jaunt Proves Fatal

Frank Robert Howard, who was instantly killed when a truck he was driving overturned at Willits.

Woman Plunges Into Bay; Fails To Rescue Youth

Dives Into Estuary in Heroic Effort to Save Boy Caught in Tide Waters

The heroism of a woman bather, who plunged into the Oakland estuary in an effort to save a drowning boy, was in vain yesterday and George Boerner, 18 years old, of 2885 Carmel street, Oakland, drowned when caught in the swirling tide of the channel.

The woman was walking along the bank at the foot of Garfield street, Alameda, when Boerner, who was climbing down the bank toward the water, slipped and fell into the stream.

Wearing her bathing suit under a long coat, the woman stepped to the edge of the estuary, threw off her coat, and dove for Boerner. Several times she dove but could not find him.

Boerner's body was found just before dark by Patrolmen George Resso and James Threne of the Alameda police force, who had been dragging the estuary channel for several hours.

Boerner lived with his stepfather, William Davis and his mother at the Carmel street address.

World's First Rotor Ship Crosses Atlantic to N. Y.

NEW YORK, May 9 (A. P.).—The world's first rotor ship, the Baden-Baden from Hamburg, Germany, arrived in New York harbor today. Flying the flag of the new German Republic, she came up the harbor on wind power alone at a nine-knot clip, while tugs and shipping tooted and ferry boat passengers stared.

The 600-ton ship with its two huge rotor towers revolving an average of ninety-five revolutions a minute, was carrying a cargo of building stone. It completed an experimental trip of 6200 miles in thirty-eight days.

Anton Flettner, inventor of the rotor, met the ship at quarantine. After receiving the reports of Captain Peter Callsen he announced that he considered the voyage had demonstrated the success of the rotor principle. A considerable saving in Diesel oil is practical evidence, he said.

The rotors, which act in place of sails and have no connection with the propellers were in operation about 70 per cent of the voyage, frequently unassisted by the six-cylinder, 250 horsepower main Diesel engine.

"The daily rotor mileage was greater on this trip than ever reached before, and greater than was thought possible," Flettner said.

On one of the best days the ship made 212 miles, although the average daily run was about one hundred and sixty-eight miles for the trip. Once in rough weather, when the main engine was shut down for repairs, the Baden-Baden made five knots on the rotors alone for several hours.

British Workers' Third Army Waits Orders to Strike

Walkout of General Laborers to Swell Unionist Ranks to Five Million; Negotiations Remain at Standstill

HULL, England, May 9 (A. P.).—Trams and busses reappeared on the streets of Hull today, with their windows protected by wire netting. These measures were taken because of the hectic happenings of yesterday, when crowds pelted vehicles of all sorts with missiles and the police were compelled to make baton charges. More than forty persons were injured, including two constables.

LONDON, May 9 (A. P.).—The British government utilized the greater part of Sunday in developing its preparations to combat the general strike, which now has been in progress for nearly a week, and which seems no nearer settlement than the day it began.

Troop movements went along with a vim. Soldiers, all steel helmeted, passed through the main thoroughfares at intervals on their way to outlying districts and various vital points where the government deemed their services might be needed. The early morning Sabbath calm was broken as 158 motor trucks, heavily loaded with food and conveyed by sixteen armored cars and flanked by cavalry, rumbled from Victoria docks to Hyde Park.

Authorities Spend Anxious Sunday

Sunday was full of anxiety for the authorities because the rest day gave labor's second and third lines of defense an opportunity to discuss the situation with their striking comrades; hope springing from the pulpit and other peaceful sources that some way would be found before another Sabbath came to end the struggle which already has brought deprivation and suffering to millions.

For so great an upheaval there has been little disturbance or disorder. Even at the mass meetings held today there was little evidence that so mighty a battle was being fought. J. H. Thomas, once Minister of the Crown in the Macdonald Cabinet and recognized leader of the labor men in the present strike, addressing strikers at Hammersmith

(Continued on Page 7, Column 2)

ODDITIES IN THE NEWS OF THE DAY

Surgeons Operate On Mining Man As Train Speeds

KANSAS CITY, May 9 (A. P.).—As his special car, attached to the Golden State express, sped across Western Kansas toward Kansas City this morning, Besley W. Mudd, mining engineer of Los Angeles, was operated on for abdominal trouble.

The operation was decided upon when examination by physicians indicated he otherwise might not live until the train reached St. Louis, where he was to be taken to a hospital. His brother, Dr. Harvey G. Mudd, is chief surgeon of the hospital. Dr. Rae Smith, Los Angeles, performed the operation with the aid of Dr. Donald Frich, also of Los Angeles, two other assistants and four nurses.

Money Buyers in France Must Show Passports

Special Cable to The Chronicle

PARIS, May 9.—Foreigners in France henceforth must show their passports to purchase more than 1000 francs ($31.50) worth of any foreign money, according to instructions from the Minister of Finance sent to all the banks. Tourists wishing to obtain foreign moneys in order to travel may obtain 5000 francs ($157.50) worth on showing their passports vised to the country of destination.

Ex-Governor Odell Of New York Dies

NEWBURGH, N. Y., May 9 (A. P.).—Benjamin Barker Odell, former Governor of New York, died at his home today, aged 72. Odell was Governor from 1901 to 1905.

As chairman of the Republican State Committee and as a lieutenant of Thomas C. Platt, he so welded the Republicans in the upstate counties that to him was attributed the nomination and election to the governorship of the late Theodore Roosevelt.

Ex-Grecian King to Visit San Francisco

THE HAGUE, May 9 (A. P.).—George, formerly King of Greece, is going to the United States toward the end of the summer for a tour extending as far as San Francisco. He will travel as a private person, but will carry letters of introduction to Americans of distinction in Washington and various other cities, from American diplomatists and other Americans whom George knows. George has expressed a desire to meet President Coolidge.

Senator Capper's Wife Passes Away

BALTIMORE, May 10 (A. P.).—Mrs. Arthur Capper, wife of Senator Capper of Kansas, died at 3:20 this morning at the Hospital for the Women of Maryland. Senator Capper and members of the family were at her bedside when she died. Mrs. Capper had been a patient at the hospital about five weeks, having been admitted for a major operation.

Actual Action Photos of Dempsey-Tunney Ring Battle in Sporting Green

TEMPERATURE COMPARISONS

	High	Low		High	Low
San Francisco	79	57	New York	76	62
Los Angeles	76	57	Chicago	78	60
Seattle	54	42	Kansas City	90	70
Denver	74	46	New Orleans	88	76

San Francisco Chronicle

LEADING NEWSPAPER OF THE PACIFIC COAST REG. U.S. PAT. OFF.

WEATHER FRIDAY
Fair and moderately warm; light variable winds
Complete Weather Report on Page 28.

FOUNDED 1865—VOL. CXXIX. NO. 71 CCC SAN FRANCISCO, CAL., FRIDAY, SEPTEMBER 24, 1926 DAILY 5 CENTS, SUNDAY 10 CENTS

Tunney Defeats Dempsey; Battle Thrills Thousands; New Champion Acclaimed

TITLE HOLDER IS OUTFOUGHT AND OUTBOXED EVERY ROUND

Challenger Finds "Tiger Man" Mere Shell of Old Self

Masterly Battle Waged by Marine in Annexing Golden Crown

Special by Leased Wire to The Chronicle

PHILADELPHIA, Sept. 23.—The receipts of the Dempsey-Tunney fight tonight were in excess of $2,000,000. On the basis of $2,000,000, the receipts were divided as follows:

Dempsey	$850,000
Tunney	200,000
Federal tax	200,000
State	100,000
Sesquicentennial	200,000
Preliminary fighters	40,000
Tex Rickard, promoter	410,000

By HARRY B. SMITH
(Sporting Editor of The Chronicle)
Special Dispatch to The Chronicle

SESQUI-CENTENNIAL STADIUM, PHILADELPHIA, Sept. 23. —"The judges are unanimous"—

The announcer withheld further information for the spectacular affect this half-way information carried.

On the one side was the grinning, cheerful, confident Gene Tunney, the ex-Marine, scarcely marked. story On the other side was Jack Dempsey, champion of the world up to that fateful moment. His left eye was almost closed and the cheek was badly swollen. Under the right eye was a bad gash, that had been left him as a memento from one of Gene Tunney's gloves.

Crowd Impatient, Roots for Verdict

The crowd roared in impatience. To ring followers, anxious to be in at the death, there was question as to what that decision was to be and all the more since the judges were unanimous.

"The judges," repeated the announcer impressively, "have agreed that Gene Tunney has won the decision and the championship of the world."

Some 125,000 rain-soaked spectators, with ardor nothing dampened because of the rain that started falling as the title bearer and his challenger entered the ring and thickened as the contest proceeded, rose en masse to cheer the new champion.

New King Rises In Boxing Realm

"The king is dead, long live the king!" rings as true today as in the old days when monarchs ruled the earth. The king had died. It was Jack Dempsey in this case.

A new king had come in his place, Gene Tunney, beloved of the marines, favorite with perhaps 90 per cent of the crowd had come into his own.

What cared the crowd that rain had fallen; that clothes were ringing wet?

Masterly Lacing Handed Dempsey

They had seen the champion humbled. They had watched Gene Tunney beat Jack Dempsey in no uncertain terms. Aye, more than that, they had seen the king of the heavies, who had held the championship for more than seven years, handed a beating that will go down into history.

Jack Dempsey was a sorry sight as the tenth round was closed. Strong hearted that he has always been in the ring, Dempsey was still trying. But it was a futile effort, and the challenger gaining confidence at every stage as the fight progressed, more and more proved he was master of the situation.

Dempsey can have no alibis. He was beaten from gong to gong tonight. Fairly beaten and squarely beaten, and beyond all question of doubt. I gave Gene Tunney every round of the ten. Others who have watched fights for many years, fig-

(Continued on Page 2H, Col. 3) Sporting Green)

Ex-Marine Crowned New King of Heavy Weights

Gene Tunney, the New Champion

Dempsey's Wife Wants Only Mate Scoffs at Fame

Estelle Taylor Speeding East to Comfort Her Fallen Fight Champion

CHICAGO, (Friday) Sept. 24 (AP)—Estelle Taylor of the movies, who married the world's heavy weight champion, hastened eastward today to comfort the Jack Dempsey she knows as a big, black-haired boy in the hour of his great disappointment.

"I don't care two whoops about fame, fights or fortune," she proclaimed, "so long as his name is Jack Dempsey and he's as crazy about me as I am about him. All I want to know is that he's all right."

Wanting only to hear the news of the championship battle from her husband, she sought retreat behind closed pullman doors as the Pennsylvania limited sped toward the seaboard last night, but she could not escape the hoarse cry of a station newsboy at Fort Wayne.

"Extra!" the boy cried. "Tunney beats Dempsey by a decision."

Etelle Taylor had promised the champion before he went into the Philadelphia ring she would be stoical, whatever the news, and she was.

"I have nothing to say," she said. "I'm just going to Philadelphia to see Jack, that's all. I want so much to be with him again."

She is due in Philadelphia this afternoon.

Aged Woman Hurt By Hit-Run Driver

A delivery truck carrying three young men last night seriously injured Mrs. Margaret Ford, 72, 161 La Martine street, and sped away without stopping to render aid. The accident occurred at Circular avenue and Monterey boulevard. Mrs. Ford suffered possible internal injuries and a broken right hip.

Admiral Fullam, Former Pacific Commander, Dies

Complications Following Pneumonia Is Fatal to Retired Officer in East

WASHINGTON, Sept. 23 (AP)—Rear-Admiral William F. Fullam, retired, died here today from complications of pneumonia. He was in his seventy-first year.

REAR-ADMIRAL FULLAM

Rear-Admiral Fullam was well known in San Francisco and throughout the Pacific Coast, having come here in 1915 to take command of the Pacific Reserve Fleet.

He was commander of the Patrol Force of the Pacific fleet in 1916 and 1917. During America's participation in the World war Fullam commanded the Second Division of the Pacific fleet and was senior officer in command of the Pacific.

He and his family were favorites in social circles along the coast until his retirement for age in 1919, when the family went to Washington, D. C., to live.

Born at Pittsford, N. Y., October 20, 1855, Fullam was appointed to the Naval Academy from that State and was graduated at the head of his class in 1877. He was married in 1885 to Miss Mariana Winder Robinson, a beauty of the eastern shore of Maryland and daughter of Chief Justice Robinson of the Maryland Court of Appeals.

During the Spanish-American war Fullam served on the New Orleans. From 1883 to 1904 he was instructor in various departments

(Continued on Page 2, Column 2)

FLORIDA BOOM HOUSES FALL IN THOUSANDS DURING STORM

Faulty Construction Noted in Wreckage Strewn Over Coast Area

State Reported Likely to Prosecute Promoters, Realty Men

Special by Leased Wire to The Chronicle

MIAMI, Fla., Sept. 23.—Florida's disaster is being pointed out as a direct reflection of the great forced land boom of just one year ago. The homes that were unable to stand under the strain of the whipping tropical hurricane of a few days ago are the boom houses, the pretty places full of beauty to the eye, risen like mushrooms overnight, thrown together for the money that was in them.

And now they lie in heaps under the stately palms that surrounded them or on the more open drained and reconstructed marsh land, leopard spots on the integrity of the boomers and the promoters that tossed them together.

There are mutterings here about all this.

Wreckage Evidence Of Hasty Promotion

All along the way for miles north and south of Miami and Miami Beach along the Atlantic coast, back west from Miami toward Hialeah, there is storm evidence enough that the buyers of the little homes paid for plenty that they did not get.

There is talk that Florida will take action against many more than the score or two of high powered real estate operators against whom action already has been started. The hurricane has revealed some real evidence of the lack of honesty on the part of many men.

Poor Construction Noted in House Ruins

House after house that lies in ruins all irredeemable is just the same kind of a house, thin walls of some composition, supposedly stucco. An inch or two possibly of some crumbly cement seemingly tossed up against some lath, or some wire mesh unbelievably frail and apparently of sinew to withstand not even a good man's-sized push.

In all directions such sights greet the eyes. The good houses, even the fair houses many even very shaky looking wood houses of thin board and plaster still stand, but the poorly built houses lie amangst them in ruins.

Splintered Structures In All Directions

Miami's citizens' committee in a statement say there are 5000 houses down in what is known as Greater Miami. And Miami looking on all

(Continued on Page 3, Col. 5)

Fame Too Much for Matzanauer's 'Ex'

Special Dispatch to The Chronicle

SALINAS, Sept. 23.—Because, he alleges, he is constantly pointed out as the ex-chauffeur husband of Margarete Matzenauer, famous Metropolitan opera singer, which causes him "great embarrassment and humiliation," Floyd F. Glotzbach has petitioned the Superior Court of Monterey county to have his name changed to Lloyd F. Howard. Glotzbach sets forth that when his famous wife secured a divorce from him in 1922 he was given "much publicity" because he was a chauffeur who had married his employer. He resides in Monterey.

Margy says, "Clothes make the man—foolish."

(Copyright, 1926)

Film Actress In Love Suit

Lady Peel

Lady Peel Sued For $100,000 in Alienation Case

Musical Comedy Star Involved in Hollywood Love Theft Scandal

Special by Leased Wire to The Chronicle

LOS ANGELES, Sept. 23.—Beatrice Lillie, also known as Lady Peel, famous English musical comedy star, now engaged in motion pictures in Hollywood, today was named defendant in a suit for $100,000, and as co-respondent in an action for separate maintenance filed in Superior Court by Mrs. Priscilla Whelan.

The husband involved in the two lawsuits is Timothy F. Whelan, motion picture gag man and scenario writer.

Mrs. Whelan charged the musical comedy star, said to be the wife of an English nobleman, with alienating the affections of Whelan and causing an estrangement between Whelan and his wife.

Miss Lillie came to America as the star of Charlot's Revue, famous London musical show. Following an engagement of Charlot's Revue at a Hollywood theater, she gave up the stage for the movies.

Whelan, it was said, is employed at the Metro-Goldwyn-Mayer studio.

Mrs. Whelan charged that her husband and Miss Lillie occupied the Whelan home together last September while Mrs. Whelan was at Avalon, Catalina. The Whelans were married August 20, 1920, and separated September 22, last, according to Mrs. Whelan, who valued the community property at approximately $30,000.

Mrs. Whelan, who asserted her husband has an income of $500 a week, asked a reasonable share of this for maintenance.

5 Americans Killed In Canal Ship Blast

Special Dispatch to The Chronicle

PANAMA CITY, Sept. 23.—Four American petty officers were killed outright and another died on the way to a hospital aboard the Finland at 4 o'clock this morning as the ship was entering the Panama Canal at Cristobal following the bursting of a steam pipe in the forecastle. The Finland is carrying members of the American Bankers Association to their convention at Los Angeles from New York. Canal Zone officials are investigating the accident. Those killed were: George Bourgette of Seattle, Harold Banks of Southampton, George Mendiar, James Young and James Harwood of New York.

(Copyright, 1926, by Chicago Tribune Press Service)

S. F. Woman Killed When Hit by Truck

Mrs. Mae Larabee, 45, of 147 Fillmore street, was killed yesterday afternoon when she was run down at Fillmore and Waller streets by an automobile truck driven by W. M. Karstaet, 559 Valencia street. Karstaet picked up Mrs. Larabee and took her to the Central Emergency Hospital, where she was pronounced dead. The truck driver told the police that he was driving out Fillmore street when Mrs. Larabee stepped in the path of his machine. He was arrested on a technical charge of manslaughter pending an investigation of the accident.

ALLEGED GRAFT MONEY LEAK IN DAUGHERTY CASE TRAILED

U. S. Completes Attempt to Show $50,000 Fee Went to Miller

Attorneys Charge Papers Mutilated in Effort to Cover Up Guilt

NEW YORK, Sept. 23 (AP)—Over a partly obliterated paper trail the Government today pursued its tracing of $200,000 reputed graft money from German ownership to its alleged final resting place in the pockets of Harry M. Daugherty and Thomas W. Miller, Attorney-general, and Alien Property Custodian of the Harding administration.

During the morning session prosecution completed its attempt to show that of $441,000 paid John T. King, Republican leader, to "help and speed" claims for $7,000,000 of impounded enemy interests in the American Metal Company through Government offices, $50,000 went to Miller.

Attorneys Claim Records Mutilated

The rest of the day was given over to testimony tending to show that $150,000 of the money King received from Richard Merton, German metal magnate, sent to this country to effect the claims, went to Daugherty. At the close of the day's session evidence had been given through witnesses and documents concerning some $22,000 of this account.

It was in tracing this latter amount that the Government attorneys had to follow a trail which they claimed had been mutilated by the defendant or his associates in an effort to destroy evidence of guilt.

Introduce Government Transportation Papers

Government transportation papers were introduced to show that on October 12 Daugherty and Jesse W. Smith, his confidential adviser, went to Ohio, and records of the Fourth National Bank of Cincinnati were shown revealing that on October 14 the King check was received there for payment indorsed by the Midland National Bank of Washington Courthouse, Ohio, of which Daugherty's brother, Mal S. Daugherty, is president.

Miss Vera V. Veail, assistant cashier of the Midland bank, was called in an attempt to show how the King check had come to the bank where she was employed.

Her testimony revealed that both the Daughertys and Smith had had regular accounts in the bank and that King had never had one there. She testified, however, that all documents which might show who had cashed the King check there or to whose acount it had been deposited, had disappeared. The Government contends that these records were wilfully destroyed as being incontrovertible evidence that the King money went to the former Attorney-General.

The case against Daugherty will be continued tomorrow and it is the hope of Buckner that the Government may be able to rest before adjournment is taken until Monday.

Operation Performed On King Ferdinand

SINAIA, Rumania, Sept. 23 (AP)—King Ferdinand has undergone an operation for varicose veins at his country residence here. Physicians announce his general condition is satisfactory. His illness is not believed to be serious enough to warrant a change in the plans of Queen Marie, who will leave for the United States next month.

Glenn Curtiss Safe In Hialeah, Fla.

NEW YORK, Sept. 23 (AP)—Glenn Curtiss, pioneer airplane builder, whose friends yesterday were reported as fearing he had been a victim of the Florida hurricane, is safe in Hialeah, Fla.

Schwab Ready to Retire, Now Intellectual Farmer

CHICAGO, Sept. 23 (AP)—Charles M. Schwab, head of the Bethlehem Steel Corporation, works only two hours a day in steel now, and is increasing his golf, he told the Chicago Association of Commerce today.

In a retrospective mood, he said he was getting "pretty near the end of my rope," and that he is interested in farming near Loretto, Pa. He reiterated, however, his faith in the continued growth of American industry.

He already is "on a higher intellectual plane than the rest of the steel men," he said, for he had "turned to the less profitable but more intellectual occupation of farming."

"I'll pass along to you," he said, "the advice a caddy gave me yesterday in Minneapolis. I asked him to advise me about improving my game. He said: 'You big slob, why don't you keep your eye on the ball?' I say the same to you, keep your eye on the business ball."

Keyes Bares Wires Linking Aimee and Ormiston in Hoax

Telegrams Found in Home of Doctor-Suicide Reveal New Carmel Evidence; K. G. O.'s Forwarding Order Discovered

SAN BERNARDINO, Sept. 23 (AP)—Efforts to trace K. G. Ormiston, former radio engineer of Angelus Temple, to San Bernardino last August when Mrs. Aimee McPherson was at Arrowhead Hot Springs and at Lake Arrowhead, near this city, developed tonight that a postal forwarding order in the name of K. G. Ormiston had been deposited in a mail box here on August 9. The order, written on the regulation change of address card of the Postoffice, directed that mail addressed to Ormiston be forwarded to Hollywood, Cal., until August 15. The card listed former addresses as Chicago, Ill., and Santa Barbara, Cal. Sheriff W. A. Shay inspected the card and Ormiston's signature. Mrs. McPherson was at the Arrowhead Hot Springs Hotel on August 8, visited at Lake Arrowhead, and was at the Hot Springs Hotel again on August 11.

Aimee Communication With Doctor Shown

LOS ANGELES, Sept. 23 (AP)—New evidence tending to show that Aimee Semple McPherson had been in direct communication with Dr. A. M. Waters shortly before his death has been added to the State's case against the Angelus Temple evangelist and her six co-defendants, the District Attorney's office announced.

At the same time, officials disclosed that evidence had been obtained which indicated that Mrs. McPherson and her mother, Mrs. Minnie Kennedy, secretly kept in touch with Ormiston while a widespread public search was being made for him and while the evangelist herself was appealing publicly over the radio for him to come forward.

Additional Evidence in Suicide's Apartment

Dr. Waters, who committed suicide here September 15, was definitely linked with the McPherson case when county detectives, earlier in the day, made a search of the doctor's apartment and found telegrams signed by Mrs. McPherson and her mother, Mrs. Minnie Kennedy, and other notes and documentary evidence bearing on the Carmel angle of the disappearance mystery.

The new disclosures were made when investigators for the District Attorney's office located a "mystery" witness who is said to have listened in on telephone conversations between Mrs. McPherson and Dr. Waters. The new informant is said to have verified that Dr.

(Continued on Page 2, Column 8)

ODDITIES IN THE NEWS OF THE DAY

There She Blows! Catalina Swim Off; 'Whales' Were Subs

Special Dispatch to The Chronicle

NEWPORT BEACH, Sept. 23.—Five United States submarines unwittingly broke up an attempt to swim the Catalina channel from Newport Beach this afternoon.

Accompanied by the power boat Dixie, and rowboats manned by life guards, the two swimmers, Nicholas Samoff, Newport Beach lifeguard, and Robert Foster, Ocean Park lifeguard, took to the water at 11:30 a. m. to swim the twenty-seven miles to Avalon.

According to the story brought back by the convoys the swimmers were six or seven miles out when five large black objects rose out of the water just ahead of them. The swimmers apparently thought the intruders were whales and clambered into the rowboats. The interlopers then were revealed as five submarines, bound for San Pedro from San Diego.

Hunting Judge Fines Hunters and Repents

Special Dispatch to The Chronicle

REDDING, Sept. 23.—To accommodate a game warden who had arrested three hunters in the Modoc county lava beds for killing a mule tail deer a day before the season opened, Justice of the Peace F. M. Callison of Fall River Mills, who chanced to come along on a hunting expedition, held court, imposed fines totaling $210 and collected the money.

Callison now learns that a Shasta county Judge has no jurisdiction in Modoc county, even in game law offenses. He has the $210 and he does not know what to do with it unless he gives it back to the three offending hunters with apologies, and he does not know now where they are.

Train Performs "Soosarean" Operation on Bossy Cow

MANITOWOC, Wis., Sept. 23.—A Soo Line train today performed what is termed locally as a "Soosarean" operation on a cow. A herd of prize Guernsey cows, owned by Edward Knutson, broke through a pasture fence and wandered onto the tracks at Madison station, the train killing four of the animals. One cow was almost cut in two in such a manner that her unborn calf was uninjured. Knutson took the calf home and will raise it on a bottle.

Traffic Cop's Siren No Good on 'Dummy' Autoist

Special Dispatch to The Chronicle

VISALIA, Sept. 23.—D. B. Phillips, State traffic officer, got his man, anyway. Phillips encountered a speeder, gave chase, opened his siren to no avail. The drived sped twenty miles before he stopped. Phillips lectured the driver on paying attention to the siren before he found out that the speeder was deaf and dumb.

FIRST INTERVIEW WITH CAPTAIN LINDBERGH IN PARIS

COMPARATIVE TEMPERATURES	High	Low		High	Low
San Francisco	64	51	New York	66	52
Los Angeles	70	52	Chicago	66	50
Seattle	56	46	Kansas City	82	68
Denver	74	54	New Orleans	74	72

San Francisco Chronicle

LEADING NEWSPAPER OF THE PACIFIC COAST

REG. U.S. PAT. OFF.

WEATHER SUNDAY

Fair and mild; moderate westerly winds

Complete Weather Report on page 15.

FOUNDED 1865—VOL. CXXX, NO. 127 CCC* SAN FRANCISCO, CAL., SUNDAY, MAY 22, 1927 DAILY 5 CENTS, SUNDAY 10 CENTS: DAILY AND SUNDAY PER MONTH, $1.10

LINDBERGH SAFELY IN PARIS 2½ HOURS AHEAD OF SCHEDULE

40,000 Crowd Acclaims 'Slim' in Greatest Paris Outburst Since Armistice

Gendarmes Trampled as Milling Hordes Battle for Sight of Flyer; Guided by Eiffel Lights, He Says, in Account of Trip

Special Cable to The Chronicle

PARIS, May 22 (AP)—At 1 o'clock this morning Captain Lindbergh went to salute the Tomb of the Unknown Soldier.

LE BOUGET FLYING FIELD, Paris, France, May 21 (AP)—Captain Charles Lindbergh, American aviator, landed here safely tonight, completing his nonstop flight from New York to Paris.

His plane, the Spirit of St. Louis, came down on the field at 10:21 p. m., Paris time, arriving about two and a half hours ahead of his schedule.

Lindbergh came over Le Bourget flying high slightly to the east of the field. He circled twice slowly, then settled down 800 yards east of the main building.

By HENRY WALES

Special Cable to The Chronicle

(Copyright, 1927, Chicago Tribune Press Service)

PARIS, May 21.—Slim Lindbergh arrived tonight, after flying from New York to Paris in a little over thirty-three hours.

[Lindbergh had covered the distance from San Diego to Paris, 5725 miles, in actual flying time of 56 hours and 46 minutes. He left San Diego on the afternoon of May 10 and arrived in St. Louis —1600 miles—the next day. After a rest there he hopped to New York—900 miles—crossing the American continent in an actual flying time of 23 hours and 15 minutes. After a few days' rest he started from New York to Paris—3660 miles. His time on this part of the trip was 33 hours and 29 minutes.]

"Am I in Paris?" were the pilot's first words as the French aviators and mechanics dragged him from the cockpit of the Spirit of St. Louis.

"You're here," I told him, as the mob jabbered in French, which was not in the least understood by the bewildered American. Enthusiasts hoisted the exhausted pilot on their shoulders and tried to fight their way across the field.

Excited Mob Acclaims Wrong American

The French pilots, however, spirited Captain Lindbergh to the hangar, rescuing him from the mob, and then dashed away to Paris with him aboard an automobile across the aviation field.

Meantime the crowd picked up an American who had fallen and been trampled on by the mob and carried him on their shoulders to the administration building, where American Ambassador Myron T. Herrick, French officials, and the welcome committee were awaiting him.

"Let me go, I'm not Lindbergh," shrieked the American, but the sturdy Frenchmen carried him upstairs. Ambassador Herrick, glancing at the man's disheveled business suit, wilted collar and torn necktie, realized it was a mistake, and spent an hour for Captain Lindbergh, fruitlessly.

The [illegible] yell that went out from the 40,000 Gallic throats when the plane finally picked its way through the obscurity to [illegible] only a prelude to the wild dash out to the field and [illegible] the [illegible] of the projectors, toward the shining Spirit of St. Louis. [illegible] historical gendarmes were trampled under foot as the [illegible] a full third of a mile toward the still moving plane. Lindbergh must have seen them start, for on landing [illegible] nose of his ship away from the stampeding thou[illegible] toward the group of military hangars, missing them [illegible] yards, when he turned his craft about and started to [illegible] into the crowd.

[illegible] Hauled From Plane, Carried Away

[illegible] dieu! Mon dieu! He cannot see, the projectors have [illegible]," many yelled in terror, while those in the lead scat[illegible] to be faced forward again by the thousands pushing [illegible]. But finally the monoplane came to a full stop on the terrified mob, which then threw fear to the winds [illegible] around it, under it and over it. The door of the [illegible] yanked open and the grinning pilot was hauled forth [illegible] off.

[illegible] riot had only begun. Fathers held youngsters, [illegible] they risked, dragging them up there to kiss, feel or [illegible] part of the great bird that came down among them so [illegible]. Others hopped into the pilot's seat and stared in [illegible] at its neatness and tidiness, especially the three neat [illegible] hanging in back of the pilot's seat, reliably rumored [illegible] change of linen.

[illegible] speedily eyed the maps and instruments that helped [illegible] his objective, but all refrained, if reluctantly, from [illegible] souvenirs. Then, howling still, they began to dash in [illegible]. As many as could took hold of the plane and shoved [illegible] the airport, where its pilot apparently was being carried

(Continued on Page 2, Col. 1)

He Flew to Paris—and World Fame

Captain Charles Lindbergh

'Lindy' Trained 2 Months to Keep Awake for Trip

Practiced Sleeplessness in Long Walks While Plane Was Prepared

SAN DIEGO, May 21 (AP)—Lindbergh is the most unusual flyer that local reporters have seen in some time. For more than a week they pleaded with him to permit the publication of his plans for his epochal hop.

"Wait until I have done some things," he said, forgetting that his four-time membership in the famous Caterpiller Club, during which he escaped death four times by thrilling parachute jumps, was worth more than casual mention.

During the two months that the monoplane was under construction at the Ryan plant, Lindbergh took long walks, remaining awake from thirty to forty hours at a stretch. One week before he hopped off from Rockwell Field on his now memorable flight he remained awake forty-nine hours. He was in superb physical condition and those who were close to him during his stay here felt confident he had a good chance to get to Paris.

Here's Chronological History of Epoch Flight

The flying log of Lindbergh's plane follows:

Eastern daylight saving time.

7:52 a. m.—(Friday) left New York for Paris.

9:05 a. m.—(Friday) sighted over East Greenwich, R. I.

9:40 a. m.—(Friday) sighted over Halifax, Mass.

12:25 p. m.—(Friday) reported over Meteghan, N. S.

1:05 p. m.—(Friday) reported over Springfield, N. S.

1:50 p. m.—(Friday) reported over Milford, N. S.

3:05 p. m.—(Friday) passing over Mulgrave, Nova Scotia, and Straits of Canso for Cape Breton.

5 p. m.—(Friday) cleared Nova Scotia at Main-Dieu, the Easternmost tip.

7:15 p. m.—(Friday) passed St. John's, Newfoundland, and headed over broad Atlantic.

6:30 a. m.—(Saturday) Independent Wireless says a vessel reports Lindbergh 200 miles off Irish coast. (Report seems doubtful).

8:10 a. m.—(Saturday) Cape Race has wireless from Dutch ship that Lindbergh was 500 miles off Irish coast.

2.30 a. m., Greenwich time—(Saturday) London Press Association dispatch says Lindbergh sighted 100 miles off Ireland.

10 a. m., Eastern daylight—(Saturday) Radio Corporation says its Paris office reports plane over Valencia.

10 a. m.—(Saturday) Halifax received a wireless dispatch that Lindbergh has passed over Valencia.

12:30 p. m.—(Saturday) Belfast, Ireland, reports Lindbergh over Dingle bay, Ireland.

2:06 p. m.—(Saturday) Valencia, Ireland, government wireless says Collier Nogi sights airplane near Dingle.

2:18 p. m.—(Saturday) Cork, Ireland, says civic guard reports Lindbergh plane passing over Smerwick harbor, Ireland.

3:02 p. m.—(Saturday) New York-French Cable Company says official advices report Lindbergh over Bayeux, France, at 8 p. m., French time.

3:20 p. m.—(Saturday) reported over Cherbourg, France.

5:11 p. m.—(Saturday) lands safely at Le Bourget field, Paris.

Pinedo to Hop for Azores This Morning

TREPASSEY, N. F., May 22 (Sunday) (AP)—As the first hint of dawn creeps on the eastern horison Commander Francesco de Pinedo, Italian four-continent flyer, will hop off on his long jump to Candelo Branco, Azores. Later weather reports from the Azores said that a storm which had swept over the islands had abated, and the Italian airman immediately announced he would fly with the coming day.

AIR HERO, IN AMBASSADOR'S SILK PAJAMAS, TELLS OF TRIP

Lindbergh Sleepy but Talkative as He Basks in Restful Luxury

Fuel Left in Tank for 1000 More, He Says; Feared He Would Crash Crowd

BY STAFF CORRESPONDENT

Special Cable to The Chronicle

(Copyright, 1927, Chicago Tribune Press Service)

PARIS, May 22.—At 1 o'clock this morning Captain Lindbergh, with M. Weiss, veteran French pilot, escaped from the hangar at Le Bourget and stealthily crossed the air field aboard an automobile and was whirled to Paris by roundabout roads to escape the glut of cars on the main highway.

Weiss stopped at the Arch of Triumph enroute to Ambassador Herrick's house, near the Trocadero, and "Slim" got his first glimpse of the tomb of the Unknown Soldier flickering in the flame.

Air Jockey Lounges in Flowered "P. J.'s"

Parmely Herrick, the ambassador's son, welcomed Captain Lindbergh at the embassy, escorted him to a room where a hot bath was awaiting him. "Lindy" swallowed a glassful of port and then a glass of milk and took a bath, combed his hair and donned a pair of Herrick's white flowered silk pajamas, blue embroidered silk bath robe and Moroccan leather slippers.

Captain Lindbergh received the correspondent in the bedroom, sitting on the bed, when I arrived to deliver his mother's telegram of congratulations.

"I have fuel enough for another 500 miles, maybe 1000 miles, left in the tanks," he said.. "I encountered no trouble on the trip. I did expect bad weather on the Newfoundland banks, but it was all right.

Struck Sleet, Squals, Rain and Fog

"After I passed that I ran into 1000 miles of bad weather over the ocean. That was last night. I struck, sleet, squalls, rain and fog. I flew at anywhere from ten feet to ten thousand feet altitude.

"When I ran into bad weather I had to try to ride over it or duck under it and I managed to avoid most of the sleet which would have weighted the plane. My compass worked fine. You know I studied navigation, although I don't pretend to be a navigator.

"I hit right over the Irish coast and recognized Cork and then veered over the Irish sea over England and saw Plymouth, I guess it was. Then I crossed the channel and hit the French coast near Cherbourg. I just took a chance, driving straight inland toward Paris, according to what the map and compass showed me to be the direction.

"Picked Up Eiffel Tower and Saw Seine"

"I was nearly to Paris and could see the lights before it got real dark. I saw a big flare at Mont Valerian and picked up the Eiffel tower and saw the Seine reflected and the lights of the city. I made lots of altitude going over Paris.

"I saw one ship at night. I saw the lights but I don't know if they signaled me.

"I was not sleepy at all—don't know why. I'm used to it, I guess. You know I trained for this flight. I didn't drink anything but water coming across.

"It wasn't hard. You know, driving an airplane is easier than driving an automobile. You have a couple of controls that are easy to handle and the well balanced ship handles herself.

"I started with five sandwiches and I ate one and a half and drank one bottle of water. I just had

(Continued on Page 4, Column 3)

President Sends Hero Felicitations

WASHINGTON, May 21 (AP) — President Coolidge, in a congratulatory cablegram to be delivered to Charles A. Lindbergh in Paris, told the transatlantic flyer that the "American people rejoice with me at the brilliant termination of your heroic flight."

The message of the President, sent to the American Embassy in Paris, for transmission to Lindbergh immediately on his arrival, follows:

"The American people rejoice with me at the brilliant termination of your heroic flight. The first nonstop flight of a lone aviator across the Atlantic crowns the record of American aviation and in bringing the greetings of the American people to France you likewise carry the assurance of our admiration of those intrepid Frenchmen—Nungesser and Coli —whose bold spirits first ventured on your exploit and likewise a message of our continued anxiety concerning their fate."

ODDITIES IN THE NEWS OF THE DAY

Victorian Pants Oxford Antidote For 'Bags' Plague

OXFORD, England, May 21 (AP)—Mid-Victorian trousers are now being worn by some Oxford students who are "fed up" with the famous bags. The newly-contrived trousers, cut without cuffs, have a slight flare at the bottom and a strap under the instep which holds the trousers down tight over the shoes. The effect is much the same as that given by the fashion prints of sixty years ago.

Docile Film Lion's Attack Kills Actor

LOS ANGELES, May 21 (AP)—Gordon Standing, 39, film and stage actor, died today in the General Hospital here from injuries received several days ago when he was attacked by a supposedly docile lion during filming of a picture at Selig Studios.

The Sunday Chronicle

CONSISTS OF TEN SECTIONS TODAY

1—Rotagravure Pictorial. (Twelve Pages)
2—Magazine.
3—Comics.
4—Society.
5—Screen, Drama, Music, Books and Art (Tabloid).
6—Automobiles.
7—Main News.
8—Classified
9—Main News II World Topics (Tabloid)
10—Sports.

BRADY GUILTY OF FALSIFYING PAYROLL, SAYS BAR REPORT

Dereliction in Office, Aiding Disorderly, Gaming Houses Also Charged

Official, Appraised of Accusations, Declares, "Christ, Too, Was 'Framed'"

District Attorney Matthew Brady is accused of dereliction of duty, falsifying his payrolls, intervening in behalf of disorderly houses and gambling places and habitually frequenting bootleg establishments, in the secret report rendered the board of governors of the Bar Association by its investigating committee, it became known yesterday.

"Father forgive them for they know not what they do," quoted Brady when the report was brought to him. A copy of "The Trial of Jesus," by George W. Thompson, was open before him on his desk. He was on page 102 and had reached the conclusion, audibly, that Christ, too, was "framed."

Undecided Whether He Will Appear Tuesday

Brady said he was undecided whether or not he will appear next Tuesday night before the board of governor of the Bar Association to defend himself against their charges. He declined to make known the contents of the report, brought to him by messenger yesterday forenoon.

"I want time to look it over and study the accusations," he said.

President Henry Monroe of the Bar Association and the investigating committee composed of Attor-

(Continued on Page 6, Column 1)

COMPARATIVE TEMPERATURES

	High	Low		High	Low
San Francisco	68	54	New York	50	44
Los Angeles	64	55	Chicago	48	48
Seattle	48	42	Kansas City	54	36
Denver	48	28	New Orleans	86	68

San Francisco Chronicle

LEADING NEWSPAPER OF THE PACIFIC COAST

REG. U.S. PAT. OFF.

WEATHER WEDNESDAY
Partly cloudy and mild with fogs in early morning; moderate westerly winds.
Complete weather report on Page 15.

FOUNDED 1865—VOL. CXXXII. NO. 59 CCC SAN FRANCISCO, CAL., WEDNESDAY, MARCH 14, 1928 DAILY 5 CENTS, SUNDAY 10 CENTS: DAILY AND SUNDAY PER MONTH, $1.15

DAM DISASTER TOLL 1125 IN DEAD, MISSING; TOWNS FLOODED; TROOPS MOBILIZE

Area for Miles Around Swept by Raging Torrent

Water Crushes Homes, Traps Sleeping Victims; $30,000,000 Damage Caused; Highway Bridges, Gas Mains Broken

CHRONICLE BUREAU, Newhall, March 13.—Two additional morgues, hastily improvised in the small towns of Moorpark and Bardsdale, situated in the path of the 12,000,000,000-gallon death rush of water from St. Francis dam in San Francisquito canyon, tonight added twenty-five bodies to the steadily growing death list.

While exact figures as to identified dead, unidentified dead and missing are totally lacking, it is estimated that the dead will total 275. **The missing runs up to 850.**

Some forty-two identified dead lie on slabs, covered with white linen, in the morgue at Fillmore; about the same number at Newhall; another twenty-six at Moorpark; ten at Santa Paula; one at Piru. **Beside them lie scores of unidentified dead, features and bodies so distorted by the mad race of water and boulders as to be unrecognizable.**

Mountaineers Bring Bodies From Remote Districts

Weary rescue workers, suspending operations over a thirty-mile zone for the night, expressed the belief their work was far from completed, that another day will reveal further bodies in small coves of the canyon and in the deposits of the raging river from Saugus to the sea.

There are nineteen bodies of men, women and children at Moorpark, eight miles below Santa Susanna pass, and six others at Bardsdale in the same region, which has for a day been rendered inaccessible.

Hardy mountaineers, who were among the first to volunteer in the relief work, still were bringing in bodies late tonight. They had packed into the more remote districts with horses, and the beasts were carrying out the bodies. Unlike the workers from the city, these men disdained to halt their labors at sundown.

Thousands of Acres of Orchards Are Destroyed

Details of the devastation in the lower reaches of the Santa Clara river valley came in tonight for the first time. The beautiful scenic country is devastated. Acres and acres of orange and walnut groves were laid waste by the flood. Farm after farm was ruined. Property damage will be high. City Engineer Harry Reddick of Santa Paula said damage to public works in that city alone would reach $2,000,000.

Approximately 400 houses located between the St. Francis dam and the town of Piru were demolished and the orchards and ranches rendered useless for agriculture.

Property damage is estimated at between $15,000,000 and $30,000,000.

What caused the collapse of the $1,400,000 dam has yet to be determined, and will be the subject of the usual official investigations. Sensational reports were current in Saugus soon after the break. One had it that the dam and its supporting earthen walls had been weakened by an earthquake last Saturday night.

A tremor was reported about 7:10 p. m. Saturday throughout Ventura county, lasting ten seconds. Water and Power Bureau officials scoffed at this suggestion.

Seepage From Dam Reported Break Cause

Another theory raised by a motorist, who said he observed signs of seepage from the base of the dam, was that the collapse was hastened by explosions of dynamite by workmen carrying on operations nearby. Still another version had it that San Francisquito canyon was visited by a cloudburst Saturday night.

Undoubtedly tremendous pressure from behind the dam forced it to crumple. Its appearance today is ample testimony of the force that caused it to topple. Of the 1200-foot-long arch-shaped symmetrical structure only the main arch, built on a bed-rock foundation now stands. This central arch is seventy-five feet in width. The east and west wings were carried away as if they were cardboard rather than concrete.

Lieutenant Earl H. Robinson of the National Guard, who

(Continued on Page 3, Col. 3.)

Wrecked Dam That Loosed Death on Valley in Night

All that remains of the St. Francis dam in San Francisquito canyon is a gigantic segment 200 feet high and 75 feet wide that stands as a grim monument to the death and destruction that followed its bursting without warning early Tuesday morning resulting in scores of deaths, unestimable damage.—Wide World Telephoto.

List of Persons Missing In Los Angeles Disaster

CHRONICLE BUREAU, LOS ANGELES, March 13.—Following is a list of persons reported missing from their homes in San Francisquito canyon following the bursting of the St. Francis dam early this morning:

MR. AND MRS. G. Q. HUGHES. Hughes was foreman at power house No. 2. Two children.

. J. ELY, wife and two children.

MRS. WILL NEILSON and two children.

A. HARNISCHFEGER AND FAMILY.

ROY PIKER AND FAMILY.

HOMER COE AND WIFE. Kenneth, 12, a son, is dead.

C. J. MATHEWS AND THREE CHILDREN. Bodies of Mrs. Mathews and one child recovered.

LEWIS BURNS AND CHILD, power hourse No. 2.

HARRY BURNS, WIFE AND TWO CHILDREN, power house No. 2.

FARRELL F. HOPPE and DONALD HOPPE, 10, dead.

H. F. MATHIS, WIFE AND ONE CHILD. Fay, 6, dead.

HARLEY S. BERRY, WIFE, power house No. 2.

D. C. LE BRUN AND FAMILY.

MISS CECELIA SMALL, school teacher.

CASPER MARLAND AND FAMILY.

C. F. HARDER, manager Harry Carey's ranch.

D. J. BIRD, manager Carey's ranch restaurant.

O. H. WILMOT, WIFE AND TWO CHILDREN.

LYMAN CURTIS AND ONE CHILD. Wife and mother and child found alive.

—— BROWSKY.

—— BROSS.

ETHEL COCHENS.

F. R. HOWE.

R. J. KERN.

C. A. MANN.

A. J. NEFF.

J. B. PARKER.

MRS. W. Y. NEINLAND AND CHILD. Husband dead.

TONY ——, WIFE AND CHILD.

21 Killed in Train Collision in Ceylon

COLOMBO, Ceylon, March 13 (AP)—Twenty-one persons were killed today when a passenger train collided with the Galle-Colombo express near Kalutarai. The engines and several coaches of both trains were wrecked.

U. S. Army Chiefs at Galveston on Flight

GALVESTON, March 13 (AP)—Assistant Secretary of War Trubee Davison and Major-General James E. Fechet, chief of the Army Air Corps, landed here at 1:35 p. m. today en route by air from Washington to Panama.

Victims of Dam Tragedy Listed As Bodies Found

139 Unidentified Dead Taken to Various Towns; 865 Are Reported Lost

LOS ANGELES, March 13 (AP)—Following is the partial, incomplete list of identified dead in the St. Francis dam disaster as reported from improvised morgues in the stricken area shortly before midnight.

Including these identified dead, a total of 274 bodies had been recovered. In addition the number of persons missing was variously estimated between 300 and 600.

IDENTIFIED DEAD AT NEWHALL:

SOLOMON J. BYRD.
MRS. RAY RISING.
MRS. NELL HANSON.
FAY MATHIS, 6.
JOHN PARKER, 60.
CARL J. MATHEWS JR., 2.
EARL PIKE.
ROLAND ERRETCHUO, 14 Mos.
MRS. ROSARI RUIZ, 46.
EDDIE GARCIA.

(Continued on Page 2, Col. 7.)

Muscle Shoals Bill Adopted by Senate

WASHINGTON, March 13 (AP)—The Norris resolution providing for Government operation of Muscle Shoals was adopted by the Senate today. The vote was 48 to 25.

FOUR SAVED BY MATTRESS

Father Swims Mile to Safety as Baby Clings to His Neck

Chronicle Bureau, Los Angeles, March 13.—An old feather mattress was the salvation of Mrs. Sisto Luna and her three children when their home near the outskirts of Santa Paula collapsed with the first rush of the water from the St. Francis dam.

With her three children, the youngest less than a month old, Mrs. Luna clung to the mattress when her home was swept away, and floated more than two miles, to be rescued when the mattress lodged in the top of a huge tree.

William Spring, a neighbor, proved one of the flood heroes. He swam almost a mile with his 6-month-old child clinging to his neck. Mrs. Spring, who was caught in the torrent, owes her life to the strong branches of an orange tree, to which she clung until rescued by workers from Santa Paula.

Fog Drives Lindbergh And Counsel to Land

COATESVILLE, Pa., March 13 (AP)—Colonel Charles A. Lindbergh and Henry Breckenridge, his counsel, who took off in an airplane from Curtiss Field, N. Y., this afternoon, were forced to land on a farm near here late today because of a dense fog

Briton Hops Off On East-to-West Atlantic Flight

Girl Financial Backer Accompanies Flyer; Plane Sighted by Steamers

NEW YORK, March 13 (AP)—What may be the first "at sea" report on the transatlantic flight of Walter Hinchliffe, British aviator, was picked up tonight by George W. Dawson, operating station 2YW here. He announced interception of a message, apparently relayed by the French steamer Roussillion from another steamer, reporting the passage of "a large plane, low overhead and heading west."

The message stated that on the wing of the plane a roman numeral was distinguished, while on the cabin were the letters "A-D-V-E-N," the first five letters of the name of Captain Hinchliffe's plane, the "Adventure."

Special Cable to The Chronicle

LONDON, March 14 (3:45 a. m.)—Captain Walter Hinchliffe, famous one-eyed British flyer, is believed to be far out over the Atlantic this morning on his way to America. With him, acting as relief pilot, is Elsie Mackay, third daughter of Lord Inchcape, the noted British ship magnate. The pair hopped off from Cranwell airdrome early this morning in his American-made Stinson monoplane, Endeavor, the flight at first being

(Continued on Page 7, Col. 3.)

HAYS ADMITS HE WITHHELD TRUTH ABOUT SLUSH FUND

Special by Leased Wire to The Chronicle

WASHINGTON, March 13.—Two pillars of the Republican party—Secretary of the Treasury Mellon and William M. Butler, chairman of the national committee—repudiated by their testimony today Will Hays' use of Harry F. Sinclair's Continental Trading Company Liberty bonds to lift the party's 1920 presidential campaign deficit.

Both refused, so they told the Senate's Teapot Dome investigators, to accept any of the bonds from Hays in return for subscriptions to the deficit raising fund.

And Hays, when they concluded, spent a wearing two hours trying to explain to the Senators how he finally disposed of the bonds, and why he did not tell the whole story

(Continued on Page 10, Col. 1)

COMPARATIVE TEMPERATURES

	High	Low		High	Low
San Francisco	68	57	New York	50	38
Los Angeles	72	51	Chicago	46	42
Seattle	52	38	Kansas City	66	45
Denver	28	26	New Orleans	84	66

San Francisco Chronicle

LEADING NEWSPAPER OF THE PACIFIC COAST

REG. U.S. PAT. OFF.

WEATHER WEDNESDAY
Fair and Mild
Complete Weather Report on Page 11.

FOUNDED 1865—VOL. CXXXV, NO. 107 CCC SAN FRANCISCO, CAL., WEDNESDAY, OCTOBER 30, 1929 DAILY 5 CENTS, SUNDAY 10 CENTS: DAILY AND SUNDAY PER MONTH, $1.15

RALLY CHECKS RECORD STOCK SLUMP

Crew of 50, Trapped by Forest Fire, Cheat Death. Steamer Sinks in Great Lakes Gale, Nine Drown

23,506,300 SHARES SOLD IN SINGLE DAY ON EXCHANGES

Heavy Buying Orders Avert Wall Street Stampede After Hectic Session

NEW YORK, Oct. 29 (AP)—Huge barriers of buying orders, hastily erected by powerful financial interests, finally checked the most frantic stampede of selling yet experienced by the securities market, which threatened at times today to bring about an utter collapse in prices.

All trading records were broken, with a turnover of 16,410,000 shares on the New York Stock Exchange and 7,096,300 shares on the New York Curb market. This contrasts with the previous records of 12,894,600 and 6,148,300 shares, respectively, established last Thursday and a Stock Exchange turnover of 9,212,800 shares yesterday.

Declines in Stocks Range From $10 to $70 a Share

Extreme declines in the active issues ranged from $10 to $70 a share, but many of these were cut in half in the rally which started in midafternoon and continued through to the close.

Thomas W. Lamont, senior partner of J. P. Morgan & Co. announced, after a second conference of bankers had been held tonight, that leading New York bankers were supporting the market in a co-operative way and would continue to support it.

Morgan Partner Pledges Support of N. Y. Bankers

"It was not an attempt of the group," he said, "to maintain prices, but to maintain a free market for securities in good order."

Unofficially, it was ascertained that large corporations, including United States Steel, had stepped into the market today to purchase stock for their employes stock purchase plans, as well as for their investment accounts, and that these purchases had been supplemented by the buying of wealthy capitalists for their individual accounts. Rumors that the banking group was a seller of stock were denied.

Blocks of 80,000 Shares Dumped Into Market

Bankers, who had been hurriedly called into conference last night and again at noon today, apparently stood aside at the opening as blocks of 10,000 to 80,000 shares were thrown into the market for whatever price they would bring. When this initial flood of selling had spent itself supporting orders began to make their appearance, not with the intention of completely checking the stream of selling, but with the avowed object of regulating their flow.

Several times during the day, particularly in the early afternoon and again towards the close, it looked as though a fresh collapse in prices bringing ruin in its wake was inevitable, but each time the holes were plugged and the threatened disaster was averted.

Prices of Thousands of Securities Cut in Half

Despite the fact that prices of probably half of the thousands of stocks listed on the exchange have been cut in half, or more, during the recent decline, and that the aggregate decline in quoted values of all securities from the high levels of the current year exceeds $25,000,000,000, only one casualty has developed among brokerage houses thus far.

Suspension of the New York Curb Exchange firm of John J. Bell & Co. for failure to meet its obligations was announced shortly after the market opened. Inasmuch as this firm was not engaged in a general commission business, the failure had no serious consequences.

Directors of the United States Steel Corporation and the American Can Company, supplementing the efforts of bankers to restore confidence which has been badly shak-

(Continued on Page 2, Col. 3)

S.F. Financiers Say Business In Good Shape

FROM the mouths of six of the city's leading financiers came yesterday the assurance that business is in a sound condition. Those signing this statement are executive heads of the city's leading financial institutions.

Business and industry are sound and generally prosperous here on the Pacific Coast as elsewhere throughout the country. The movement going on on the stock exchanges is evidently a correction of the technical condition brought about by over-speculation.

It is desirable, and it is recommended that the community and the banks themselves should regard values of securities rather than immediate quotation of a stock market that indicates hysteria rather than cool judgment.

C. K. McIntosh
F. L. Lipman
Fred T. Elsey
Herbert Fleishhacker
E. Avenali
A. J. Mount

Youth, Speechless From Operation, Dying After Fall

Child Is Found in Yard With Skull Crushed; May Result in Death

Unable to cry for help because of a silver tube in his throat, Clifford Rowe, 10, 776 Turk street, plunged ten feet off a concrete wall last evening to what may prove his death.

At the Central Emergency Hospital physicians held out little hope for his recovery.

Apparently the boy had been "cat walking" on the wall, when he lost his balance and fell.

For several hours police proceeded on the theory the boy had been a victim of a fiend, because beside him on the ground was a crowbar covered with hair and blood. But eventually found witnesses whose information led to the conclusion the boy's fall was an accident.

CLIFFORD ROWE

The youngster, who lived with his father, Earl Rowe, on the top floor of the Turk street boarding house, recently underwent an operation which required the placing of a tube in his throat. Since that time he has not been able to speak above a whisper.

Fireboats Battle Flames Sweeping S. P. Ferry Pier

Everyone who has ever been apprehensive of a fire at the Ferry building, with piers blazing furiously, thick clouds of smoke blackening the sky, and ferry boats darting swiftly out of danger, had his fears realized yesterday morning.

A pier did burn furiously, huge clouds of creosoted smoke shot upward, fireboats excitedly puffed streams of water onto the blaze, alert mariners backed their ferry boats off in a hurry—there were all the trappings of a spectacular blaze.

Five minutes after the Southern Pacific ferry boat Alameda had come in and out of Slip 5 at the Ferry building yesterday morning at 11 o'clock, Ray Dever, a State electrician, discovered the pier between Slips 5 and 6 on fire. Its origin was believed to have been in a cigarette thrown from the Alameda's decks.

Dever immediately rang in the auxiliary fire alarm box on the pier and looked for an ax and hose. William Morrison, a State fire marshal, passing at the time, joined in the fight. City firemen on arrival immediately turned in a second alarm.

Soon there arrived Acting Fire

(Continued on Page 3, Col. 6)

WIND SHIFT SAVES GANG; FLAMES DOOM SONOMA TOWN

Inhabitants of Kellogg Flee Homes as Blaze Sweeps Toward Village

Trapped for nearly three hours by flames which roared over a five-mile front, approximately fifty men, members of a forest fire fighting gang in Knights valley, thirty-five miles northeast of Santa Rosa, were saved at 11:30 o'clock last night when the wind shifted.

But the shift, fortunate for the men whose lives were despaired, apparently spelled doom for the town of Kellogg, which lay directly in the path of the advancing flames. More than 200 persons living in the settlement were rushing out their belongings at midnight, with the smoke so thick about them that visibility was impossible at ten feet.

Ring of Fire Hems in Crew as Wind Veers

The fire fighting crew was trapped shortly after 8:30 o'clock last night when the wind, which had been blowing briskly from the north, shifted to the northwest. Flames hemmed them in from all sides and backfires laid by the crew failed to break the fire wall.

State Forest Ranger Taylor Day of Lake county and Deputy State Fire Warden Will Kettlewell were leaders of the crew inside the trap. At 11:30 o'clock they dispatched E. A. Erickson, one of the crew, to Middletown with the news that they were safe, but unable to check the flames from reaching Kellogg.

Flames Repel Rescuers Seeking to Reach Crew

During the time that the fifty men were surrounded by the flames numerous attempts were made to effect their rescue.

Each attempt, according to State Forest Ranger Ernest Rupe, failed because of the intense heat which repulsed every man who tried to get inside the burning cordon.

Rangers conducting the fight against the flames characterized the fire as one of the most stubborn brush blazes they have ever had to combat.

Score of Ranches Burned; Blaze Sweeps 600 Acres

It was believed at midnight that more than a score of ranches had been swept by the flames, but only four were known to have been destroyed. These were the Sutherland ranch and the ranches of John O'Connor, John Carsons and William Harris.

All the buildings in each case were burned it was reported. In all approximately 600 acres had been burned over in Sonoma county. The

(Continued on Page 2, Col. 7)

Fire Chief Murphy Sinking Gradually

His vitality rapidly ebbing, Fire Chief Thomas R. Murphy was much weaker last night, his physician, Dr. J. H. O'Connor, said after two visits to the sickbed. Dr. O'Connor found the veteran firefighter clinging to life by sheer will power. No hope could be held out for Murphy, according to the doctor, who said that death was likely to come at any moment.

Navy Digs Up $47,000 Loot In Back Yard

WASHINGTON, Oct. 29 (AP)—Navy Department officials announced today they had found $47,000 buried in a chicken yard in Southeast Washington by Lieutenant Charles Musil, who disappeared from Charleston, S. C., several weeks ago with a $54,600 payroll.

Lieutenant Musil walked aboard the receiving ship Seattle in New York last week and surrendered. He turned over $1500 in cash at that time.

Musil told naval officials he had buried the money in the chicken yard behind a vacant house once occupied by him and his family.

Lost Sky Liner, 5 Aboard, Safe At Albuquerque

Pilot Lands at Remote Field When Storm Endangers Ship's Flight

ALBUQUERQUE, N. M., Oct. 29 (AP)—Fighting a snowstorm most of the way to Albuquerque from Trechando, N.M., Pilot Jimmy Doles and his co-pilot brought the lost Western Air Express Plane 113 safely to the Albuquerque Airport this afternoon under its own power.

Doles, Allan C. Barrie, co-pilot; R. L. Britton, steward, and passengers, Dr. A. W. Ward of San Francisco and W. E. Merz of Mt. Vernon, N. Y., were none the worse for their adventure and said the greatest inconvenience had been the loss of time.

The plane encountered a terrific snowstorm over Arizona yesterday morning, and Doles circled until he found a safe place to land.

He put the plane down at Trecrado, and he and his cargo spent the night there to await clear weather. Trechando is about seventy-five miles southeast of Gallup, and only about five miles south of the country of treacherous lava beds and extinct volcanoes.

Doles landed the huge trimotored passenger plane at the airport here at a time when the search had been temporarily held in abeyance until a snowstorm raging over the State had cleared.

The plane had been missing since 10:30 o'clock yesterday morning.

(Continued on Page 4, Col. 7)

WILL ROGERS

BEVERLY HILLS, Oct. 29—Editor The Chronicle: What's the matter with this for a laugh? When the stock market goes down Mr. Morgan, Lamont, Charley Mitchell and Mr. George Baker hold a meeting and let everybody see 'em in this huddle. Then the market perks up.

I was just thinking what a great idea it would be if we could just get these boys to room together for six months. There is no telling to what heights the market might go.

Just think what a calamity there would be if they forgot where they were to meet some day to inspire confidence. Yours,

WILL ROGERS.

SIXTY DRAGGED FROM WATERS AFTER 'HOODOO' SHIP FOUNDERS

Rescuers Battle 50-Mile Michigan Gale to Pick Up Survivors

Special by Leased Wire to The Chronicle

CHICAGO, Oct. 29.—A valiant captain gone down with his ship in a fifty-mile Lake Michigan gale, eight others of the crew drowned and three more missing and given up for dead, sixty saved in a wild night rescue — thus begins the obituary of the hoodoo ship Wisconsin, Goodrich passenger liner, which foundered today six and a half miles southeast by east of the city of Kenosha, Wis.

Hours of pumping against an ever rising flood in the racking, plunging hold of the leaking ship, until the fires were quenched and the engines stilled and the pumps choked with ashes and the water came higher and higher until the old ship sank—this is the story of the battle of the crew and its four passengers.

Rescuers Battle Furious Sea to Pick Up Survivors

Hours of struggling against a furious sea and rescues of men in lifeboats, on rafts, clinging to wreckage, rescues of men feebly swimming in the violent lake itself and a final battle to bring the dead, the rescued and themselves to morgues, hospitals and refuge in Kenosha—this is the epic spun by the heroes of the United States Coast Guard at Kenosha and Racine.

Tomorrow a triple inquiry by the United States Government, by the Coroner of Kenosha county and by the Goodrich Line officials, will be launched in the Courthouse of Kenosha.

Survivors Tell Thrilling Story of Lake Disaster

The blame will be fixed, if there be any to blame beside the gale which whipped the waters into such turmoil.

Not a woman nor a child was aboard, although one woman, the captain's maid, might have been. She went ashore to telephone a friend before the ship left Chicago, and while she was talking the ship left without her.

As they huddled around a huge stove in the Kenosha Coast Guard station the survivors told how Lake Michigan had proved too strong for the passenger-freight boat, which had weathered many fiercer blows

Hardly a minute after the Wisconsin poked her nose out of Chicago' arbor she was caught up in

(Continued on Page 6, Col. 1)

Woman, Asleep at Wheel, Crashes Tree

Falling asleep at the wheel, Mrs. Kate Simpson, 30, of 46 Entrada court, crashed her heavy car into a tree on El Camino real, near Sherman avenue in Burlingame, early yesterday morning. At the Mills Memorial Hospital, San Mateo, she was found to have a fractured nose, and after treatment she returned to her home.

Ishbel MacDonald Writes For The Chronicle Her Impressions of U. S. Life

Glimpsing of National Kaleidescope In Hurried Visit Leaves Premier's Daughter Yearning to See Inside of Homes

By ISHBEL MacDONALD

Daughter of Premier MacDonald of Great Britain, who recently visited the United States

Copyright, 1929, by New York Evening Post, Inc.

MY SECOND dash into the arms of American hospitality has ended, and still I have not had one glimpse of the inside of an American home.

The joy of being part of the peace mission, and the keen pleasure of filling a round of entertaining engagements made up for this lack, of course. But it is my nature to place such an importance on family life that my eyes turn at once in each country I visit to the homes out of which that country is made.

All I have been able to see in New York, Washington, Philadelphia, Buffalo and Niagara Falls is the outside of homes, the cheerful, beckoning brick and frame outside, with lights shining from windows behind which people live.

What is the atmosphere of an American home? How do parents and children get on? What attitude has a boy on the fifth floor of an apartment building toward his small sister lying in her crib by the window? How much is the care of these children left to nursemaids?

MISS ISHBEL MacDONALD

These are the intimate questions running through my mind as I contemplate the days, now come to a close. Because of the official nature of my visit I had no time to investigate these homely, friendly aspects of American life.

Indeed, I had no time even to inspect the outside of homes in the Middle West, the West and the South of the United States. I leave with a curiosity still within me.

Some day I must come back. I must return as a woman interested in meeting men, women and children. I shall not stay in hotels then, going out only to visit clinics, Government bureaus, settlement houses, juvenile courts, brilliant receptions. I shall try to live as Americans live. I shall absorb something of the real American atmosphere.

This has been a wonderfully interesting trip. From the moment I set foot on American soil—or shall I say on American boards, for the first step was to the deck of a welcoming tug in New York harbor?—until, regretfully I left the United States behind me with the roar of Niagara

(Continued on Page 8, Col. 2)

Sidney Ballou Dead of Heart Attack in N. Y.

Sugar Institute Official, Former Hawaii Judge, Ill but Short While

NEW YORK, Oct. 29 (AP)—Sidney Ballou, executive of the Sugar Institute in New York and formerly a Justice of the Supreme Court at Hawaii died at the Harvard Club in this city today after an illness of ten days. He suffered a heart attack, from which until yesterday it was believed he was recovering. He was 59 years old.

SIDNEY BALLOU

His widow, who was Lucia Burnett of Los Angeles, and two daughters survive.

ODDITIES IN THE NEWS

Hunger Striker Defies Jailors Atop Flagpole

Special Cable to The Chronicle

BUDAPEST, Oct. 29.—Flagpole sitting is the latest device employed by the communist hunger strikers to gain better treatment. Frantz Litzmann climbed up the 80-foot tower of the prison at Sopron and remained there for thirty hours. All attempts of the prison officials to bring him down, even high power streams of water, failed, until this afternoon, when Litzmann grew tired and came down.

Man Attempts Suicide, Bullet Wounds Neighbor

Special Dispatch to The Chronicle

PERHAU, Esthonia, Oct. 29.—Doctors hold little hope for the recovery of a woman who was shot by a man who attempted suicide here. Jan Toomp, an insurance agent, decided to rid himself of his life of poverty. He placed the muzzle of an army rifle under his chin and pulled the trigger. The bullet penetrated the ceiling, piercing the lung of the woman in the apartment above.

Carload of Wild Ducks Jails Hunter

When Berkeley police stopped Sam Plovsen, 1114 McAllister street, last night as he drove along San Pablo avenue they merely intended to check the headlights of his automobile. The headlights were all right, but Plovsen went to jail for the night just the same. As Patrolman C. E. O'Brien gave him a clear ticket on the lights he glanced into the back of Plovsen's car. Imagine the latter's embarrassment when the policeman found 238 wild ducks. Plovsen was held without bail for the State Game Commission, as he was only 223 ducks above the limit for one day's shooting.

Union Tobacco Head Plunges To Death From Hotel Suite

Special by Leased Wire to The Chronicle

NEW YORK, Oct. 29.—Albert Schneider, 60, president of the Union Tobacco Company, was killed today in a six-story plunge from his eleventh-floor apartment in the Hotel Beverly. His friends and hotel officials insisted his death was accidental. If such, police pointed out, it was strangely coincident with an amazing depreciation in the quoted value of the stocks in the big tobacco companies he heads.

Webster, Eisenlohr, Inc., stock on the New York Stock Exchange, selling at a high for the year of more than $133 some months ago, and at $68 a week ago, hit a bottom of $4 yesterday and again today. The company is a $12,500,000 corporation of the Schulte chain. Union Tobacco stock, which sold up to $20 a share earlier in the year, was down to around $1 a share on the Curb today.

Yet, according to Louis Morrell, a Beverly Hotel waiter, Schneider was leaning out a window of the apartment into which he moved last February, trying to repair a radio aerial when the waiter entered with his breakfast this morning.

Morrell told investigators he saw Schneider lose his balance and fall outward. Dropping the tray, the waiter asserts he reached the window in time to seize Schneider's left foot. Struggling briefly to drag the tobacco magnate back through the window Morrell says the string in the shoe broke and the shoe came off. Schneider plunged to the roof of a five-story extension of the Lexington Theater building.

GRUNDY URGES SENATE POWER BERATED BY STATE REVENUE

Lobbyist Charges Poorer Western Districts Have Too Much to Say

WASHINGTON, Oct. 29 (AP)—Joseph R. Grundy, president of the Pennsylvania Manufacturers' Association, took the breath of the Lobby Committee today when he frankly stated he thought the smaller Western States had too much voice in the Senate on tariff legislation.

Sharply questioned by the Senate investigators Grundy said it was a "tragedy" that the States contributing negligible amounts in Federal taxes and "with no chips in the game" could help breakdown a fundamental economic policy.

Senator Walsh, Democrat, Montana, wanted to know how Grundy proposed to silence "Senator Borah and myself for instance," on the tariff bill and the witness said "propriety" should dictate that.

Examined by Senator Borah, Republican, Idaho, Grundy persisted he stood by the Republican platform to give agriculture an equality with industry but he disagreed with the Idahoan that it would be necessary

(Continued on Page 7, Col. 6)

1930-1939

OCTOBER 24, 1931
Trunk Killer Captured

MARCH 2, 1932
Lindbergh Baby Kidnaped; Chinese Forces Flee Japan Trap

MAY 13, 1932
Lindy Baby Found Slain

JULY 29, 1932
Troops Use Gas, Bayonets to Break Up Capital Camps

NOVEMBER 9, 1932
Roosevelt Elected

MARCH 6, 1933
U.S. Banks on Holiday; Hitler Wins Reich Election

OCTOBER 15, 1933
Germans Quit League of Nations

NOVEMBER 27, 1933
Kidnapers Lynched

DECEMBER 6, 1933
Prohibition Wiped Out

MAY 25, 1934
Troops Kill Two Strikers

JULY 6, 1934
Bloodshed, Riots, As Police and Strikers War

AUGUST 2, 1934
Von Hindenburg Expires; U.S. Cuts Fleet

FEBRUARY 13, 1935
Dirigible Falls in Sea, Sinks

FEBRUARY 14, 1935
Bruno Hauptmann Must Die

AUGUST 17, 1935
Will Rogers Plunges to His Death in Plane

NOVEMBER 23, 1935
Giant China Clipper Takes Off for Manila

MARCH 8, 1936
15,000 Nazis Line Rhine As France Mans Border

JULY 20, 1936
Civil War Tears Spain

NOVEMBER 12, 1936
San Francisco-Oakland Bay Bridge Opens

DECEMBER 10, 1936
Edward VIII Abdicating Today

MAY 7, 1937
Hindenburg Destroyed

MAY 28, 1937
Golden Gate Bridge Opens

MARCH 12, 1938
Hitler Rules in Austria

SEPTEMBER 29, 1938
Hitler Defers War Plans

AUGUST 24, 1939
Nazis, Soviets Sign Pact

SEPTEMBER 1, 1939
Warsaw, Five Cities Bombed

SEPTEMBER 3, 1939
Great Britain Declares War

NOVEMBER 30, 1939
Russia Goes to War

DECEMBER 30, 1939
Bridges Wins Deportation Case

RAINFALL COMPARISONS

	Last 24 Hours	Seasl. to Date	Nrml. to Date		Last 24 Hours	Seasl. to Date	Nrml. to Date
San Fran	:19	:57	1:31	San Jose.	:02	:02	:89
Sacrmto.	:04	:10	1:03	Stockton	:24	:24	:69
Red Bluff	:11	:21	1:89	Fresno..	:00	:05	:61
Eureka..	:18	1:74	2:95	Los Ang..	:00	:31	:66
Sta Rosa.	:92	1:12	1:66	San Diego	:00	:24	:53

San Francisco Chronicle

LEADING NEWSPAPER OF THE PACIFIC COAST

WEATHER SATURDAY

Fair and mild.

Complete Weather Report on Marine Page.

FOUNDED 1865—VOL. CXXXIX, NO. 101 CCC•• SAN FRANCISCO, CAL., SATURDAY, OCTOBER 24, 1931 DAILY 5 CENTS, SUNDAY 10 CENTS: DAILY AND SUNDAY PER MONTH, $1.25

TRUNK KILLER CAPTURED, CONFESSES

Laval Talks World Crisis With Hoover

Heads of Two Nations Seek Basis of Cooperation to Restore Economic Health

Financial and Political Considerations Play Big Part

WASHINGTON, Oct. 23 (AP)—Two business men, President Hoover and Premier Laval of France, drew chairs together at the White House tonight and discussed ways of bringing the world out of its economic troubles.

Uppermost in the minds of each was the thought of closer cooperation between France and America to ease the increasing strain on world finance, with its entwinements of related political questions.

AIDS AT CONFERENCE

The chief executive, who put aside all else to devote his time to the opporunity, asked Secretary Stimson of the State Department and Undersecretary Mills of the Treasury to join in the conference.

Neither spoke the language of the other, but each spoke as a man with a long business background. Interpreters broke down the language barrier. Secretary Stimson and Undersecretary Mills, both of whom speak French, acted for the President. Jacques Bizot, a financial expert with the Premier's party, acted for M. Laval.

NO PACT PLANNED

They found immediately that each shared the view of the other that no definite agreement to be set down in words or figures on paper could result from their meeting. Each has hopes, however, that definite

(Continued on Page 4, Col. 1)

Mlle. Josette Would Meet Yankee Boys

Cocktail Party, Dinner at White House for Premier's Daughter

Special to The Chronicle

WASHINGTON, Oct. 23—In between a trip to Mount Vernon, where she saw George Washington's dental instruments, and a dinner at the White House, where she learned about Abigail Adams' wash line, once strung across the east room, Mademoiselle Josette (her father's pet name), Premier Laval's dashing daughter, went to a cocktail party.

MMLE. JOSETTE LAVAL

At least, that's what they called it over at the French Embassy. They sounded right rejoiceful over the phrase, too.

Mrs. Campbell Pritchett gave the party at the home of her aunt, Mrs. Sydney Cloman. Mrs. Cloman is the widow of a diplomat, so there were a lot of foreign young men drinking whatever it was they served.

WOULD MEET BOYS

Now, Gallic gentlemen are "very, very nice," Mlle Josette said. But what she'd "just love to meet," she said earnestly, "are some really truly, young American boys."

And so they routed her over to dinner at the White House to meet President Hoover, Secretary of State Stimson, Under Secretary of the Treasury Ogden Mills and a few other men.

But Mrs. Hoover had Mrs. Stimson and several other women in, so the ladies, all speaking English, got together in one room and talked of things feminine, while M. Laval and Mr. Hoover, each with an interpreter, went to the Lincoln study to discuss debts and pacts.

STAY AT WHITE HOUSE

Josette may have wanted to drop in at the reception which Ambassador and Mme. Claudel were giving for Marshal Petain at the Mayflower Hotel. But, of course, it isn't etiquette to walk out on a White House evening when you are a house guest. There was some talk of Mrs. Hoover taking the French visitor over for a few moments, but instead Mrs. Hoover took Mlle. Josette to see the magnificent Lincoln memorial by moonlight.

The huge marble pillared structure, upon which searchlights play every night, is one of Mrs. Hoover's favorite visiting places. The President's wife was readily admitted to the lighted interior, although visitors are not allowed at night.

SLEEPS IN WHITE HOUSE

Mlle. Laval spent the night at the White House in a room near her father's, and tomorrow, if she can, she's going to see a lot of American boys at a football game.

When she mentioned her profession of law the interviewers were quick to ask her that same old question, "Can a woman have a career and a happy marriage life?"

"Ah, that depends," a shrug of her blue chiffon shoulders, a wave of a pretty pink fingernail, "that depends on the husband."

TALKS OF PAPA

But it wasn't of husbands that she talked mostly; it was of "papa," pronounced, if you please, with the accent on the last syllable.

She wears so much blue because "papa likes it."

She has learned a lot about international affairs by an everlasting questioning of "Papa." "But so many times, Papa doesn't answer my questions."

She isn't the Diana of the chase that newspaper stories have made her out, but she does "go hunting a lot with Papa."

Three Slain, One Shot in Cell Break

New Jersey Convicts Wound Guard, Flee in Auto; Kill Policemen

Fugitive Turns Gun on Self as Pal Fatally Hurt by Posse

TRENTON, N. J., Oct. 23 (AP)—Shooting a guard and a policeman, four convicts fled from the New Jersey State Prison today in a spectacular getaway which brought death to two of them and the policeman.

Jack Wierman, 24-year-old prisoner, committed suicide in a Pennsylvania woods rather than face his airplane-directed pursuers, who fatally shot his companion, James A. McGrath, 30. McGrath had fatally wounded a Philadelphia policeman, Joseph V. Campbell Jr.

FLEE IN AUTOMOBILES

The other two fugitives, James Stoddard, 35, and Frank Seibert, 25, separated from Wierman and McGrath after shooting John D. White, a guard, near the prison wall. Each of the two pairs commandeered automobiles as they dashed away in opposite directions, one into Pennsylvania and the other toward Northern New Jersey.

The prison break came in midafternoon, shortly after the recreation period. White was on duty in a tower house on the Second street wall. Near him the prison electrician, a civilian, and a trusty were working.

ARMED WITH REVOLVER

A ladder they had used to get to the tower stood against the 30-foot high prison wall.

Armed with a single revolver, the four convicts dashed across the prison yard and swarmed up the ladder. Thrusting the electrician and the trusty aside, they fired two shots at White, one bullet piercing his shoulder and the other grazing his chest. They paused on the wall long enough to seize a riot gun, revolver and a rifle from the tower house, then dropped to the street.

Two cars parked in the vicinity of the prison walls were seized.

Stoddard and Sibert took possession of the automobile of Norman Fretz of Trenton at pistol point and

(Continued on Page 4, Col. 1)

Pauline Lord, Actress, Sued for Reno Divorce

RENO, Oct. 23 (AP)—Pauline Lord, actress and star of many stage productions, including "Strange Interlude," was sued for divorce here today by Owen B. Winters, nationally known advertising man. Winters' complaint charged cruelty on the part of his wife had seriously injured his health.

Woman Wed to Butler Wills Him $8000 Yearly

NEW YORK, Oct. 23 (AP)—Mrs. Antoinette L. Burden, socially prominent, who married her butler two years before her death, left most of her $1,191,000 estate to him and other relatives, a transfer tax appraisal showed today. The husband gets an $8000 annuity.

Mrs. Judd, With Bullet in Hand and Weak From Hunger, Surrenders in L. A.; Says She Slew Women in Battle for Own Life

Mrs. Judd's Own Story

Compelled to Shoot in Self-Defense, She Tells Lawyer

LOS ANGELES, Oct. 23—Former Judge Louis P. Russill, quoting Mrs. Ruth Judd, gave the first story tonight of what had happened in the Phoenix apartment when Mrs. Agnes Le Roi and Miss Hedvig Samuelson were shot to death and the body of the younger one dismembered.

"I had gone to the girls' home to remonstrate with Miss Samuelson for some nasty things she had said about Mrs. Le Roi," Mrs. Judd was quoted by Attorney Russill as saying.

"Miss Samuelson got hold of a gun and shot me in the left hand. (This is the hand bearing a serious wound.)

"I had struggled with her and the gun fell. Mrs. Le Roi grabbed an ironing board and started to strike me over the head with it.

"In the struggle I picked up the gun and 'Sammie' got shot.

"Mrs. Le Roi was still coming at me with the ironing board and I had to shoot her.

"Then I ran from the place."

Russill said this was as far as Mrs. Judd was able to get in her story of the Phoenix killings because of her critical condition. Further questioning of the woman, he said, will have to wait an improvement in her condition.

At the time of her surrender Mrs. Judd was attired in a green dress, a dark rough coat with a well-worn fur at the collar, black shoes and no stockings. Both her hands were bandaged.

Police Surgeon Kirkpatrick said after an examination that Mrs. Judd has numerous bruises all over her body and an injured right hand, in addition to the bullet wound in the left hand.

Paraguan Students Killed in New Riots

BUENOS AIRES, Oct. 23 (AP)—A dispatch to the newspaper Nacion from Asuncion, Paraguay, said today that several persons were killed and wounded in a renewal of student disorders in protest against the government's policy in the Grand Chaco boundary dispute. The students were fired on, the dispatch said, when they attempted to enter the government building. Minister of Justice Justo Prieto has resigned and has been replaced by Dr. Alejandro Arce.

DRAMATIC HUNT ENDS

Mrs. Winnie Ruth Judd, arrested for killing Mrs. Agnes Le Roi and Hedvig Samuelson, in Phoenix, Ariz. Photo shows Mrs. Judd with injured hand as she left the undertaking parlors where her surrender occurred; Attorney Richard Cantillon, at right, and Dr. William C. Judd, her husband, at left.

(AP) Photo by Telephone.

Slayer Feared Lockjaw, She Babbles Under Ether

Hit Them Once for Me, Woman Pleads With Her Husband

LOS ANGELES, Oct. 23 (AP)—"Oh, doctor, I gave myself up because it began to hurt so much," Mrs. Ruth Judd babbled under an anaesthetic at the Police Receiving Hospital, as surgeons worked over her wounded hand. "I was afraid of lockjaw."

She continued muttering, incoherently, with lapses of silence:

"Oh, doctor—I fought—I fought so hard. You'd have fought, too."

Dr. Judd stood beside her, great beads of perspiration breaking out on his forehead.

"Doctor, kiss me—I've been so mean.

"I wish I had a Catholic priest here.

"I always wanted to be a nurse, but I couldn't. I wasn't strong enough. I loved the clinic (the Phoenix clinic, where she had been employed).

"Oh, don't hurt my hand! I've been asked all those questions and I answered them. They're pinching my hand. It hurts! Oh, doctor, just hit them once for me."

Mrs. Judd moaned and screamed as the influence of the anaesthetic lessened.

A bullet was removed from the base of her middle finger, close to the joining with the index finger. The index finger is fractured. She was given an injection of anti-tetanus serum.

Quick Dye Aids Woman Escape Widespread Hunt

Special to The Chronicle

LOS ANGELES, Oct. 23—One of the reasons why Mrs. Winnie Ruth Judd, Arizona trunk killer, was not recognized during the week's intensive hunt here was revealed tonight as she lay on the operating table at Georgia Receiving Hospital while a bullet was removed from her hand.

Dark dye stains were discovered on the upper part of Mrs. Judd's body, and she was questioned by police officers. She said she went into a drug store two days ago, bought a brand of quick acting dye, and changed the color of her dress from brown to dark green in a women's rest room downtown.

Spain's First Women Jurors Convict Slayer

OVIEDO, Spain, Oct. 23 (AP)—Serving on a jury for the first time in Spain, four women concurred with four men today in finding Francisco Suarez guilty of slaying his niece and sentencing him to serve ten years in prison. Under new laws a jury trying crimes of passion is composed of four men and four women.

Spanish Cruiser Hunts Sharks to Aid Fishers

SANTANDER, Spain, Oct. 23 (AP)—Sharks which have been destroying fishermen's nets and eating their fish are being tracked down by the cruiser Miguel de Cervantes. Sharpshooters from the crew are hunting the sharks from launches and killing many along the North Coast.

Darkness Shrouds S. F. While P. G. E. Executives Hear Talks

While practically all of the higher executives of the Pacific Gas and Electric Company banqueted in Berkeley and listened to the silvery tongues of young orators, the San Francisco lighting system failed for twenty minutes last night and many portions of the city were plunged into darkness.

Apparently everyone who knew something of the huge cables and switches of the system was at the banquet, as the light cables were repaired after the first failure, only to plunge into darkness again ten minutes later for another five-minute period of blackness.

President A. F. Hockenbeamer, General Manager Paul M. Downing and nearly 200 other officers of the company nodded at the after-dinner speakers as the "hired hands" in San Francisco struggled to repair the system. The executives had left strict injunction with the hotel management that they were not to be disturbed at the banquet. So all were in ignorance of the accident until after the meeting.

The failure of the system was caused by the burning out of an 11,000-volt main cable in Station A, Third and Twenty-third streets, the main steam plant of the P. G. and E. in the city. The burned out cable threw out all the other substations in the city, with the exception of one station controlling part of the Mission district.

Working against time, the plant employes repaired the cable in fifteen minutes and the current went on. Ten minutes later the second cable burned out, and another five-minute period of darkness followed.

(Continued on Page 4, Col. 6)

Today's Features

	Page
Amusements	5
Chester Rowell	10
Church News	6-7
Comics	(Green) 4
Crossword Puzzle	(Green) 3
Culbertson's Bridge	14
Deaths	14
Dorothy Dix	14
Dr. Evans on Health	14
Editorials	10
Financial	15-16-17-18
Home Magazine	14
Jane Friendly	14
Marine	19
Ninon Fashions	14
Oddities in the News	12
Radio	12
Real Estate	22
School News	8-9
Society	7
Sports	Green
Want Ads	18-19-20
Will Rogers	1
Women's Club Calendar	7

Attorney Leads Officers to Mortuary in Few Blocks of Jail, Where Slayer Gives Up Before Curious Crowd

Special to The Chronicle

LOS ANGELES, Oct. 23—Dramatic surrender of Mrs. Winnie Ruth Judd, 26, at a mortuary establishment almost within the shadow of the Hall of Justice here this evening was climaxed by her assertion that she killed Miss Hedvig Samuelson and Mrs. Agnes Le Roi, Phoenix trunk murder victims, in a desperate battle to save her own life.

The meeting of police and the woman they had hunted for a week was arranged through her husband, Dr. William C. Judd, and attorneys he had retained. Mrs. Judd was found suffering from a bullet wound in her left hand and had eaten scarcely nothing since she vanished Monday after attempting to claim the two death trunks at the railway station here.

Says She Killed in Self Defense

With officers holding back the crowd, the woman's husband, Dr. Judd, and her attorney, Richard Cantillon, talked with her.

After a lengthy questioning by Chief of Detectives Taylor, which was reported to have revealed little additional light on the murders, Mrs. Judd was taken to the County Jail hospital, high up in the Hall of Justice. There she was permitted to rest for the balance of the night.

Mrs. Judd wearily admitted the slayings, and told them she had quarreled with Mrs. Le Roi and Miss Samuelson Friday night. Miss Samuelson shot her in the hand, she said, and Mrs. Le Roi struck her with an ironing board. Then, she said, she wrested the gun from Miss Samuelson and shot them both.

Attorney Cantillon led Sheriff Traeger and police to the undertaking place, to which Mrs. Judd had gone this morning, and from which she had sent a message to her husband at her attorneys' offices in the Subway Terminal building.

Mrs. Judd, it was disclosed, had remained in the undertaking parlors throughout the day and police indicated that she might have gone there late last night.

That she was not feigning illness was apparent to those who met her and took her in custody, they said. She was so nervous as to be close to a complete breakdown after her attempt to elude the army of peace officers who have sought her since last Monday.

Unattended Wound Proves Serious

The wound in her hand was serious largely because it had not been given proper attention. A bullet was removed from her palm at Georgia Receiving Hospital. She was then taken to the women's section of the County Jail atop the Hall of Justice.

The mortician parlors of Alverez & Moore at Court and Olive became the center of crowds of curious as soon as the news flew through the downtown district of the city that Mrs. Judd had been found.

Physicians were called by the Sheriff to determine how serious was the physical condition of Mrs. Judd before her removal from the scene of her arrest.

It was said by physicians that Mrs. Judd had apparently had no sleep and nothing to eat since last Monday night until today when she was fed at the undertaking place. The morticians said she had been in a sodden, deep sleep most of the day, but upon awakening asked for eggs, and ate all that were given her.

Attorney Hints Self-Defense Plea

A defense hint of self-defense was given by Attorney Richard Cantillon at the scene of the arrest. He pointed to the gunshot wound in Mrs. Judd's hand. The lawyer said no plans for her defense would be undertaken until the woman was able to stand the ordeal of a lengthy conference with him and his partner, former Judge Russill.

Piece by piece came information of how Mrs. Judd had eluded the police since last Monday.

She is said to have sought refuge in a sanatorium near Los Angeles during the four days that she was vigilantly sought. One of her many friends, a nurse, is reported to have hidden her.

Eludes Police in Sanatorium

Mrs. Judd's wounded hand was given an emergency dressing at the sanatorium, whose location the Sheriff held secret pending a check on the institution.

Even while the bandages were being placed around her injured hand, she told her questioners, two Los Angeles policemen entered the sanatorium and questioned her. She said she was able to give them the slip and escaped from the place.

Her final surrender tonight was the direct result of the published appeal of her husband, Dr. Judd, in which it was disclosed that adequate preparations had been made to defend her when she was ready to give herself up.

Later Attorney Louis P. Russill, one of the attorneys retained yesterday by Judd, admitted that he and the surgeon had been in communication with Mrs. Judd since 2 o'clock this morning. Russill said that at the first interchange of messages Mrs. Judd said she was willing to give herself up, but she de-

(Continued on Page 2, Col. 3)

Will Rogers Says:

BEVERLY HILLS, Oct. 23—Editor The Chronicle: Exclusive — Bernard Shaw come out this morning in favor of prohibition. He is also a vegetarian. Shows you what the influence of a good woman will do even on a writer. Lady Astor, a staunch believer in prohibition, accompanied Shaw to Russia. Your,
WILL ROGERS.

COMPARATIVE TEMPERATURES

	High	Low		High	Low
San Francisco	64	47	New York	44	38
Los Angeles	66	54	Chicago	34	34
Seattle	42	38	Kansas City	68	59
Denver	50	38	New Orleans	82	62

San Francisco Chronicle

THE CITY'S ONLY HOME-OWNED NEWSPAPER

WEATHER WEDNESDAY

Fair and Mild.

Complete Weather Report on Page 18.

FOUNDED 1865—VOL. CXL. NO. 47 CCC** SAN FRANCISCO, CAL., WEDNESDAY, MARCH 2, 1932 DAILY 5 CENTS, SUNDAY 10 CENTS: DAILY AND SUNDAY PER MONTH, $1.15

LINDBERGH BABY KIDNAPED FROM CRIB

Two Men Seize Child In Home; Ransom Note Found on Window Sill

Two States Combed for Auto Seen Near Estate of Flyer

Troopers Mobilized, Police Search Underworld

(Copyright, 1932)

PHILADELPHIA, March 2 (AP)—A man who said he is Albert Cramer, 35-year-old bakery truck driver for the American Stores, today told police he saw a bundle he thought was a "doll baby" in a ditch about a mile and a half from the Lindbergh home on the road to Somerville.

The driver, who told his story when stopped by Philadelphia police and informed of the Lindbergh baby's kidnaping, said that he did not stop because he thought the bundle contained a doll.

HOPEWELL, N. J., March 2 (Wednesday) — Charles Augustus Lindbergh Jr., 20 months old son of the Flying Colonel, was kidnaped last night from his nursery in the second floor of the Lindbergh country home near here.

He was spirited away in a dark green Chrysler sedan.

The window near his crib, which was open when his nurse discovered the kidnaping, is thirty feet from the ground.

Note Left in Window

On the window sill, police said, a note was found and, though they would not divulge its contents, it was indicated that it contained a demand for ransom.

A three-piece ladder was found a hundred feet from the house, as if it had been dropped in a hurry, and police believe this was used to reach the window.

Woman's Footprints Found

Possibility that a woman figured in the kidnaping developed, police said, when a minute examination of the grounds around the Lindbergh home revealed feminine footprints, along with those of a man.

A car containing two men, stopped at least two persons prior to the kidnaping and asked directions to the isolated Lindbergh home.

Chloroform Clue Found

Police at Hillside later reported the finding of a blue sedan early today at Route 29 and Field place. The rear seat yielded an odor resembling chloroform.

Police expressed the belief the car might have been the one used by kidnapers of the Lindbergh baby.

Within an hour after Colonel

(Continued on Page 5, Col. 2)

KIDNAP VICTIM

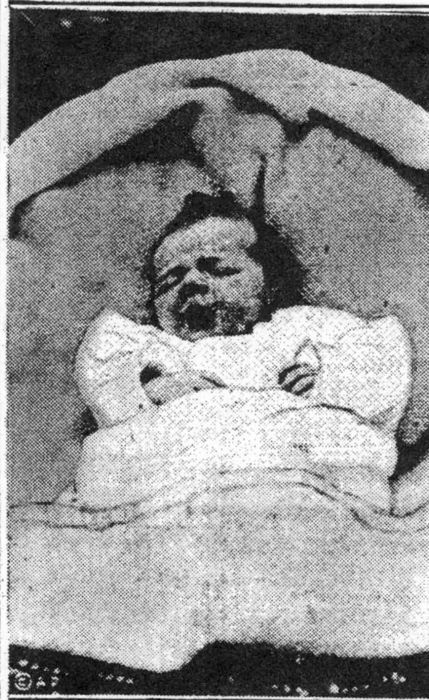

Charles Augustus Lindbergh Jr.

Anne, Sobbing, Gives Story To Troopers

Colonel Tells Details of Wife Finding Cradle Empty

Special to The Chronicle

HOPEWELL, March 1 — Mrs. Charles A. Lindbergh was the first to be told by the nurse that her baby was missing and rushed to the nursery to find the crib empty.

Mrs. Lindbergh and the Colonel started to search the room. An

EXPECT ANOTHER CHILD

NEW YORK, March 1 (AP)—It was said by close friends of the family tonight that Mrs. Charles A. Lindbergh is expecting another child within about three months.

open window was the first thing that caught his attention, but he put aside all thought of kidnaping and sought to reassure himself and his wife.

As the search of the entire house failed to locate the child, he called police.

While Lindbergh took command

(Continued on Page 4, Col. 6)

$17,000 Violin Crushed Under Wheels of Car

SYRACUSE, N. Y., March 1 (AP)—A $17,000 violin was crushed under the wheels of an automobile here today. The instrument, a Guarnerius, was valued at that amount by the owner, Andre Polah, head of the violin department, school of fine arts, Syracuse University. Polah slipped and fell as his wife was backing their car out of a garage.

Film Actress Arrested In Refrigerator Row

BEVERLY HILLS, March 1 (AP)—Esther Muir, film actress, was arrested here today on a charge of refusing to return an electric refrigerator after becoming delinquent in payments. She claimed she couldn't return the refrigerator because it had been stolen from her home.

Former Felon Given Life in New Isle Attack

Man Confesses Assault, Sentenced Few Hours After Crime

HONOLULU, March 1 (AP)—John Fernandes, 21-year-old former convict, was sentenced to life imprisonment late today when he pleaded guilty to an assault earlier in the day on a Japanese servant woman.

The speedy retribution which followed the second similar crime within four days bespoke the high feeling which an apparent recurrence of a recent series of such assaults has aroused among Honolulu citizens.

CONFESSES ATTACK

The report of the assault, perpetrated near the home of Harold Castle, sent police, army men and citizens hurrying to the scene.

Police soon arrested Fernandez at the dairy where he was employed.

He confessed, police said, and he was immediately indicted by the Federal Grand Jury. He was held without bond until brought into court for arraignment, where he pleaded guilty and was immediately sentenced.

SPEEDY JUSTICE METED OUT

Sentence, pronounced nine hours after the attack upon Mrs. Miwa Watanabe, mother of four children, was the first under the new law passed by a special session of the Legislature increasing penalties in such cases.

Answering criticism that he should have imposed the death penalty, Circuit Judge Albert M. Cristy told the Associated Press

(Continued on Page 9, Col. 2)

Driver Fined $50 For 90-Mile Speed

A. L. Goldsmith's automobile will go ninety miles an hour. In case anyone doubts this, Goldsmith can today produce a receipt from Judge Edward Farrell of South Francisco which shows that Goldsmith yesterday paid a $50 fine for making that speed on the Bayshore highway. Sir Malcolm Campbell's competitor lives at the Armour Hotel, San Francisco.

Wets Force House Vote On Rum Bill

145 Sign Petition Withdrawing Measure From Committee; Ballot March 14

Texan in Wheel Chair Last to Affix Signature to Document

WASHINGTON, March 1 (AP)—A House vote on considering a bill to give control of liquor to the States was assured today.

The wet block obtained 145 signatures upon a petition to withdraw from the Judiciary Committee a resolution to bring this about. A vote will be taken March 14 on the question whether the measure will be placed upon the calendar of the House for its consideration.

In previous Congresses 218 petitioners, one more than a majority have been necessary to discharge a committee from consideration of a bill. At the outset of this session the number was reduced.

WILL RECORD VOTES

Representatives Linthicum of Maryland and Beck of Pennsylvania, leaders of the Democratic and Republican wet organizations, respectively, said the vote will show "The American people exactly how every Representative stands on the vital question."

The 145th signer of the petition was Representative Mansfield, Democrat, Texas, a paralytic, who rolled himself to the desk in his wheel chair from his quarters in the House office building.

LAST SIGNER CHEERED

When Mansfield signed antiprohibitionists on both sides of the aisle stood up and applauded.

Representative La Guardia, Republican, New York, who had the floor, said amidst the confusion:

"I am very happy the last man who signed was a distinguished citizen of the State of Texas."

This brought renewed applause. Speaker Garner was not in the chamber at the time.

La Guardia said the antiprohibitionists will continue their fight to get action.

BEER MEETING CALLED

Elated, Representative Linthicum and Beck in midafternoon in a statement said "we believe that a new chapter was opened today in the history of this controversy and that the success of our efforts is assured."

They called the anti-prohibitionists to meet tomorrow to consider a beer bill, and said they would force a vote on this bill also through a petition if necessary.

Vote Roster on Page 9

Morgans Greet Scotch Marquis at Liner Pier

NEW YORK, March 1 (AP)—J. P. Morgan and his son Junius met the liner Berengaria tonight to welcome an old grouse-hunting companion, the Marquis of Lithingow of Scotland. Another passenger was Kathleen Norris, novelist, who will go to her home in Palo Alto, Cal., in a few weeks.

Gandhi's Youngest Son Gets Six Months' Term

MEERUT, India, March 1 (AP)—Davi Das Gandhi, youngest son of Mahatma Gandhi, who was arrested February 2 on a charge of abetting the civil disobedience campaign of the Mahatma, was sentenced today to six months imprisonment.

Yancey, Flyer, Injured By Autogiro Propeller

MONROE, La., March 1 (AP)—Lewis Yancey, transatlantic flyer, was knocked unconscious today when the propeller of an autogiro struck him. Physicians said his injuries were not serious.

Today's Features

Amusements	7
Army Orders	18
Chester Rowell	8
Comics	Green 14
Crossword Puzzle	Green 12
Culbertson's Bridge	Green 13
Deaths	9
Dorothy Dix	6
Dr. Evans on Health	6
Editorials	8
Financial	16, 17, 18
Home Magazine	6
Jane Friendly	6
Marine	19
Ninon Fashions	6
Oddities in the News	4
Radio	Green 14
Society	6
Sports	Sporting Green
Want Ads	19, 20, 21
Women's Club Calendar	6

One Just Has To Have Host's Suit in Velvet

Plum Colored, Mauve Coats, Vests Without Buttons Appear

Special to The Chronicle

NEW YORK, March 1—If you haven't a "host" suit for semi-formal evenings at home you might just as well go out and get run over by a beer truck. If your vest has buttons on it you will be as old fashioned as prewar Scotch this spring. And another thing, don't go near the beach this summer unless you own a pastel tinted jacket and canary colored flannel pants.

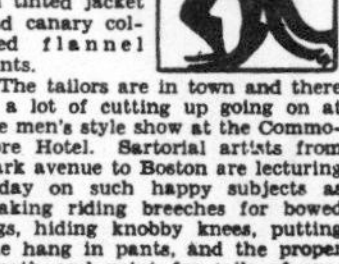

The tailors are in town and there is a lot of cutting up going on at the men's style show at the Commodore Hotel. Sartorial artists from Park avenue to Boston are lecturing today on such happy subjects as making riding breeches for bowed legs, hiding knobby knees, putting the hang in pants, and the proper length and point for tails of evening dress coats.

These snip and shear fellows are custom cutters. They are not designers. They are composers. James Sicatone of East Boston composed an overcoat with lapels cut like Ma in honor of Bellini, who composed his opera, "Norma," 100 years ago, when lapels such as these were popular.

Frank C. Nagle of the New York Custom Cutters' "club" composed the buttonless vest. The secret of this piece of apparel is a buckle in the back.

The "host" suits won the hearty approval of every chorus man in town.

The most saucy "host" suit comes in plum colored velvet. It is a gorgeous affair reminiscent of the eighteenth century and is quite likely to revive cambric jabots and brocaded waistcoats. The suit is cut like a tuxedo and comes in cashmeres as well as velvets. Blues, purples, greens, browns, lavender and mulberry suits are displayed.

The tails of the evening coat called for an extra lecture period due to argument over inches and points. It was decided to add three inches to the skirt of the coat and lift or reef the waistline. The tails are considerably more pointed (this may be taken as the last word).

Nicaragua Rebels Slain In Battle With Guardia

WASHINGTON, March 1 (AP)—The death of two Nicaraguan insurgents and the wounding of several others in a clash between twenty-one members of the Nicaraguan guardia and numerous insurgents at Nacascolo was reported to the navy today by Lieutenant Colonel C. B. Matthews, marine corps, commanding the Nicaraguan National Guard detachment. One member of the guardia was wounded.

Prehistoric Statues Of Bronze Age Found

(Copyright, 1932)

ROME, March 1—Sculptures believed to have been made by men of the bronze age have been discovered in the valley of Torrent Pell in Upper Adige. They consist of two large stone blocks cut in rudimentary fashion to present weird human figures, presumably idols. They are the first of their kind ever discovered in Italy.

Dudley Field Malone To Aid Massie Defense

NEW YORK, March 1 (AP)—Dudley Field Malone, international lawyer, announced tonight he would go to Honolulu to join Clarence Darrow in defending Mrs. Granville Fortesque and three others charged with second degree murder.

Mr. Darrow at Chicago today announced his decision to help defend the four persons. Mr. Malone said he and Darrow probably would sail March 19 from San Francisco.

Welsh Students Tear Down British Flag

CARNARVON, Wales, March 1 Welsh Nationalist students today hauled down the Union Jack from historic Carnarvon Castle and tore it to shreds in the market place.

Tokyo Votes Truce, Wants Victory First

Japan, Accepting League Proposal, Determined on Forcing Back China Troops

Conference to Seek Solution of Entire Shanghai Problem

By GLENN BABB
Associated Press Staff Correspondent
(Copyright, 1932, by Associated Press)

TOKYO, March 2 (Wednesday)—Acceptance of the League of Nations proposal for an international conference at Shanghai to end the conflict with China was announced by the Japanese government, but truce negotiations at Shanghai made no further progress, the Foreign Office said today.

Vice Admiral Sir Howard Kelly, commander of the British Asiatic fleet, presented Japanese negotiators with armistice terms yesterday. Dispatches said the Chinese previously had assured Admiral Kelly the terms were acceptable.

COUNTER-PROPOSAL OFFERED

The Japanese found them unacceptable, however, and presented counter-proposals. The Chinese had not yet replied to the Japanese terms, the Foreign Office indicated, and there the matter rested.

At the same time various government spokesmen made it clear that Japan believes a decisive victory in the field will be necessary to pave the way for the conference.

NATIONS IN NEGOTIATIONS

The League proposal, made by Joseph Paul-Boncour, French delegate to the League Council at Geneva, called for negotiations in which the United States, Great Britain, France and Italy would participate, as well as Japan and China.

It was understood the Japanese government interpreted the suggestion as meaning that the conference probably would cover a long period and would seek a permanent solution of the Shanghai problem.

In official quarters it was said that a decisive Japanese victory was expected to result in bringing the fighting to an early close, thereby producing the conditions

(Continued on Page 2, Col. 4)

State Aids Berkeley Annapolis Unit Move

SACRAMENTO, March 1 (AP)—As a step toward bolstering California's fight to get the Annapolis Graduate School for Berkeley, State Director of Finance Rolland Vandergrift set aside $37,000 today for reconditioning and maintenance of certain buildings on the University of California campus. Robert G. Sproul, president of the university, has approved the plan, Vandegrift said.

Hundred Dead or Hurt In Harbin Explosion

TOKYO, March 1 (AP)—The Rengo (Japanese) News Agency reported from Harbin today that 100 persons had been killed or injured in an explosion last night at a Chinese powder magazine on the southern outskirts of the city. The Rengo correspondent said police declared the plant had been blown up intentionally.

Will Rogers Says:

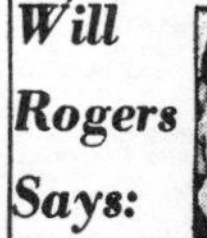

BEVERLY HILLS, Mar. 1—Editor The Chronicle: In one column of our morning papers the war had been called off. But they hadn't notified the other column. The Japanese say they don't want China, and it's a cinch the Chinese don't want Japan.

The Japanese say if the Chinese would get back twenty miles from Shanghai that they would quit fighting. The Chinese say if the Japanese would go on back home where they belong they would quit fighting. So nobody really knows what they are fighting over. It's almost like a civilized European war in that respect. Yours,

WILL ROGERS.

Chinese Forces In General Rout, Flee Japan Trap

Defense Army, Completely Demoralized, Pursued by Nippon Bluejackets; Chapei-Kiangwan Line Abandoned

By MORRIS J. HARRIS
Associated Press Staff Correspondent
(Copyright, 1932, by Associated Press)

SHANGHAI, March 2 (Wednesday)—The Chinese retreat became general at 1:30 p. m. today, when soldiers holding the front lines of Chapei began withdrawing from the vicinity of Liuying road, the official Japanese army report said.

Foreign military observers at the boundaries of the International Settlement verified the report. They said apparently the Chinese feared being trapped against the settlement by a fast enveloping Japanese right wing.

Japanese bluejackets crossed Hongkew creek to chase the fleeing Chinese.

CHINESE COMPLETELY DEMORALIZED

A Japanese spearhead occupied Tachang, four miles west of Kiangwan. The Japanese also said they occupied Miaochungchen, northward on the advancing battle line.

The Chinese, fleeing northward and westward, were completely demoralized, the enemy said.

JAPAN PLANES BOMB RAILWAY

The doughty Chinese 19th Route Army was flung back toward Kunshan, west of Shanghai, at a cost of 1800 lives, the Japanese said, while they lost only 60 dead. A retreat of other Chinese troops in Nantao, south of Shanghai, also was reported.

Another battle was under way near Liuho, 20 miles north of Shanghai, where Japanese flyers bombed Chinese troops attempting to block thousands of landing Nipponese reinforcements fighting their way through Chinese fire to join the left flank of their comrades.

Six Japanese airplanes bombed the Shanghai-Nanking Railway near Kunshan, thirty-five miles west of Shanghai, and cut the line apart, the flyers said, with their rain of 150-pound missiles. They had threatened to destroy the railway if the Chinese continued to transport reinforcements over it. The threat was carried out on schedule.

Important Objective Taken

The Japanese, the superiority of their war machines and men felt more strongly with every blow, said they had crushed the Chinese defense on the Kiangwan line.

Japanese army authorities said Tachang, an important objective, was occupied by Japanese troops at 12:30 p. m. today.

Right Wing Closes In

The Japanese pushed relentlessly on as the Chinese forces fled toward Kunshan and Tasang. The Japanese right wing was closing in from the north in a similar advance.

Toward Chapei the Japanese line bent eastward as the Chinese continued to hold the devastated battle ground of the conflicts beginning more than a month ago.

12,000 Troops at Liuho

Japanese officers said their forces in the vicinity of Liuho totaled 12,000. Their landing was virtually completed, they said, and the soldiers had begun a southward movement. Although Liuho itself was not yet occupied, the Japanese expected to take it over during the day or tomorrow.

Enveloping Move Seen

The Japanese seemed headed for Kating, as well as Tachang. Kating is a short distance north of Tachang.

In event the Japanese continued westward while the

(Continued on Page 3, Col. 1)

COMPARATIVE TEMPERATURES

	High	Low		High	Low
San Francisco	64	50	New York	60	48
Los Angeles	74	56	Chicago	52	46
Seattle	66	48	Kansas City	78	56
Denver	76	50	New Orleans	82	68

San Francisco Chronicle
THE CITY'S ONLY HOME-OWNED NEWSPAPER

WEATHER FRIDAY
Fair weather with high fog in the morning. Moderate temperature.
Complete Weather Report on Page 18.

FOUNDED 1865—VOL. CXL, NO. 119 CCC** SAN FRANCISCO, CAL., FRIDAY, MAY 13, 1932 DAILY 5 CENTS, SUNDAY 10 CENTS: DAILY AND SUNDAY PER MONTH, $1.15

LINDY BABY FOUND SLAIN IN WOODS NEAR HOME; KIDNAP ENVOYS GRILLED

Abductors Beat Child To Death, Body Hidden In Grave at Roadside

Special to The Chronicle

NEW YORK, May 12—The baby son of Colonel Charles A. Lindbergh was found dead this afternoon. The child had been murdered. Two tremendous blows on the head ended the life of the child, the official autopsy by Dr. Charles A. Mitchell, county physician, disclosed tonight.

The autopsy showed that the skull had been fractured on the left side, the fracture extending from the top to just behind the left ear. The second blow was dealt on the right side of the head just back of the right ear, and left a hole one-half inch in diameter.

It was as if some adult person had held the baby tightly in his arms and deliberately hammered the head with the purpose of causing instant death.

The diagnosis was: "The cause of death is a fractured skull due to external violence."

The body, lying face down in a depression, and partly covered with dead leaves and wind blown debris, was discovered by a negro truck driver in a patch of woods in the Sourland mountains less than five miles from the Lindbergh home near Hopewell, New Jersey.

KILLED SHORTLY AFTER KIDNAPING

The child evidently had been killed soon after he was stolen from his crib in the Lindbergh nursery on the night of March 1. The condition of the body indicated that the child had been dead at least two months. The kidnaping occurred 72 days ago.

John F. Condon of New York and John Hughes Curtis of Norfolk, Va., intermediaries in attempts to obtain the return of the kidnaped baby, were questioned late tonight by State police. They are believed to have important information regarding the kidnapers.

Mrs. Lindbergh was home at Hopewell when the body was discovered, but Colonel Lindbergh was absent.

MOTHER RETURNS TO HOPEWELL

Mrs. Lindbergh had been at the home of her mother, Mrs. Dwight W. Morrow, in Englewood, N. J., for the last few days and returned with Mrs. Morrow to the estate near Hopewell only a few hours before the body was found.

Finding of the body brought the search, which had covered much of the world, into a new phase. The indignation and sorrow, which the kidnaping had inspired, were intensified when the fate of the child finally was learned. Colonel Schwarzkopf and other officials, who have been in charge of the long hunt, declared their determination to press the hunt for the kidnapers with renewed vigor, freed now of the necessity of proceeding

(Continued on Page 4, Col. 1)

LINDBERGH REACHES HOPEWELL HOME

HOPEWELL, N. J., May 13 (Friday) (AP)—An automobile believed to have been occupied by Colonel Charles A. Lindbergh, John Hughes Curtis and Edwin B. Bruce of Elmira, N. Y., a friend of Mr. Curtis', entered the flyer's estate early today.

No official confirmation of Colonel Lindbergh's arrival could be obtained and it was understood the police would make public no further information for six or seven hours more.

Negro Relates How He Came On Baby's Body

Passing Through Woods and Saw Skull; Worries About Dinner

HOPEWELL, N. J., May 12 (AP)—William Allen, 46, negro, tonight gave the following account of how he discovered the body of the Lindbergh child:

"After I got into the woods, I went under a branch and looked down. I saw a skull sticking up out of the dirt, which seemed to have been kicked up around it. I thought I saw a baby, with his foot sticking out of the ground.

"I called Williams (Orville Williams, his companion) and he came into the woods. I said: 'I think it's a baby.'

LOOKED FOR POLICEMAN

"He said: 'Well, what are you going to do about it?'

"I said: 'I guess I'll report it to Charley Williamson' (one of the two members of Hopewell's police force).

"We stopped at Hopewell, and, after looking around for Charley, found him in the barber shop.

"I said 'Could you talk to me for a couple of minutes?' He said, 'Sure,' he'd talk to me for five if I wanted to.

WENT BACK TO DINNER

"Williamson went and got the State police. He took me back to the truck and after I delivered the load of blocks I had on the truck I took him to the road where we found the baby.

"The baby was about forty-five feet back from the road. After I showed it to Charley he went and got some State policemen and I

(Continued on Page 3, Col. 2)

Oil Man Robbed of Auto and Valuables

BAKERSFIELD, May 12 (AP)—Harry L. Gilespie, Long Beach oil operator, reported to the Sheriff's office today he was robbed of his car and valuables by three armed men who bound him and left him in a shack near Magunden. He escaped from the shack. The men came up while Gillespie was in his parked car.

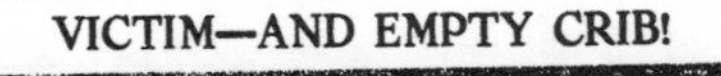

VICTIM—AND EMPTY CRIB!

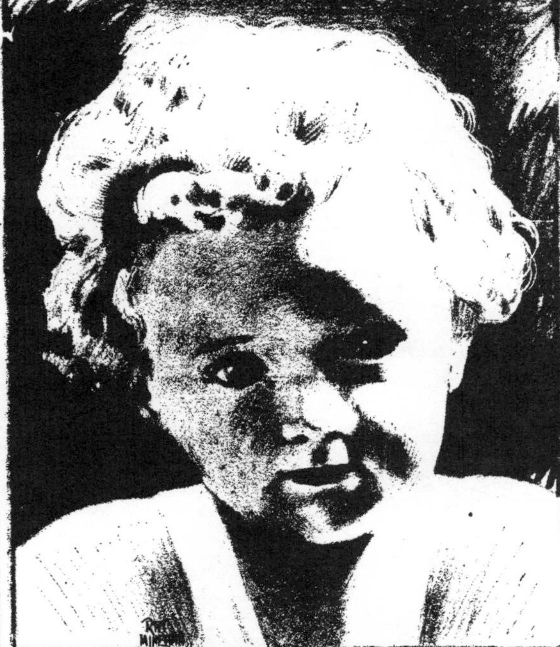

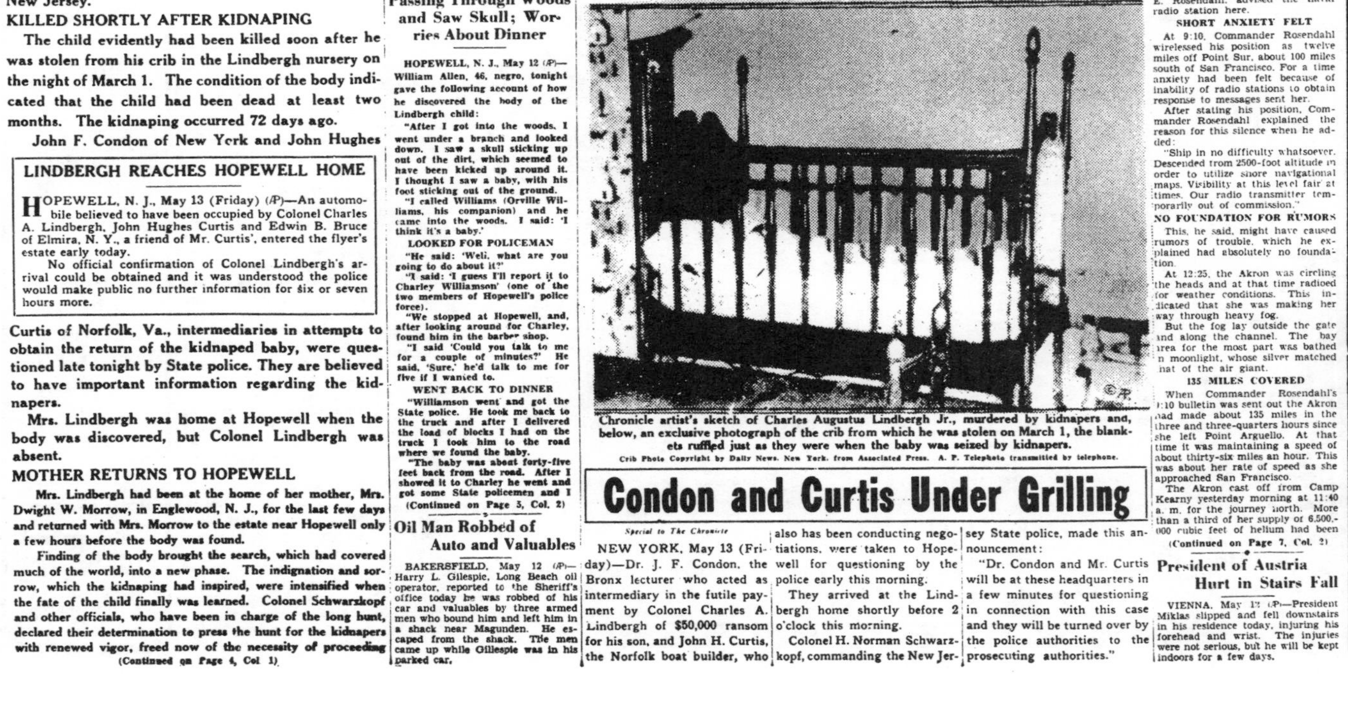

Chronicle artist's sketch of Charles Augustus Lindbergh Jr., murdered by kidnapers and, below, an exclusive photograph of the crib from which he was stolen on March 1, the blankets ruffled just as they were when the baby was seized by kidnapers.

Crib Photo Copyright by Daily News, New York, from Associated Press. A. P. Telephoto transmitted by telephone.

Condon and Curtis Under Grilling

Special to The Chronicle

NEW YORK, May 13 (Friday)—Dr. J. F. Condon, the Bronx lecturer who acted as intermediary in the futile payment by Colonel Charles A. Lindbergh of $50,000 ransom for his son, and John H. Curtis, the Norfolk boat builder, who also has been conducting negotiations, were taken to Hopewell for questioning by the police early this morning.

They arrived at the Lindbergh home shortly before 2 o'clock this morning.

Colonel H. Norman Schwarzkopf, commanding the New Jersey State police, made this announcement:

"Dr. Condon and Mr. Curtis will be at these headquarters in a few minutes for questioning in connection with this case and they will be turned over by the police authorities to the prosecuting authorities."

Akron Soars Over S.F., Welcomed by Midnight Crowds

The navy dirigible Akron soared over San Francisco at 12:40 o'clock this morning and headed toward Sunnyvale, there to be given a tumultuous welcome by assembled thousands.

Like a great silver fish in a giant, inverted, star-studded bowl, the world's greatest ship of the air made her bow to San Francisco, the hum of her motors roaring overhead like giant drums afar.

And San Francisco, despite the hour, greeted the great ship as its own.

Thousands crowded the heights of the city to acclaim her coming. Land's End, Twin Peaks, Telegraph Hill, the Cliff House and other points of vantage were crowded with enthusiastic thousands.

The roofs of the city's tall buildings held watchers awed into silence by the spectacle.

The sky over the city was clear. Wisps of fog scudded across the face of the moon. The city's lights gleamed and twinkled as though in sudden harmony with the stars overhead.

The Queen of the Skies, feeling her way over the Golden Gate, soared over the city and the bay, and circled her supply ship, the Patoka, which carries the Akron's mooring mast.

LIGHTS PICKUP SHIP

The Patoka's searchlights sought out the Akron with her penetrating beams.

And then, after circling over the buildings, back and forth, the Akron turned and moved majestically toward her base, Sunnyvale, for which The Chronicle waged a successful campaign.

The arrival of the Akron had been awaited with dramatic interest. At 11:26 the dirigible was over the Farallone islands, twenty-one miles west of San Francisco, her commander, Lieutenant Commander C. E. Rosendahl, advised the naval radio station here.

SHORT ANXIETY FELT

At 9:10, Commander Rosendahl wirelessed his position as twelve miles off Point Sur, about 100 miles south of San Francisco. For a time anxiety had been felt because of inability of radio stations to obtain response to messages sent her.

After stating his position, Commander Rosendahl explained the reason for this silence when he added:

"Ship in no difficulty whatsoever. Descended from 2500-foot altitude in order to utilize shore navigational maps. Visibility at this level fair at times. Our radio transmitter temporarily out of commission."

NO FOUNDATION FOR RUMORS

This, he said, might have caused rumors of trouble, which he explained had absolutely no foundation.

At 12:25, the Akron was circling the heads and at that time radioed for weather conditions. This indicated that she was making her way through heavy fog.

But the fog lay outside the gate and along the channel. The bay area for the most part was bathed in moonlight, whose silver matched that of the air giant.

135 MILES COVERED

When Commander Rosendahl's 9:10 bulletin was sent out the Akron had made about 135 miles in the three and three-quarters hours since she left Point Arguello. At that time it was maintaining a speed of about thirty-six miles an hour. This was about her rate of speed as she approached San Francisco.

The Akron cast off from Camp Kearny yesterday morning at 11:40 a. m. for the journey north. More than a third of her supply of 6,500,000 cubic feet of helium had been

(Continued on Page 7, Col. 2)

President of Austria Hurt in Stairs Fall

VIENNA, May 12 (AP)—President Miklas slipped and fell downstairs in his residence today, injuring his forehead and wrist. The injuries were not serious, but he will be kept indoors for a few days.

COMPARATIVE TEMPERATURES	High	Low		High	Low
San Francisco	68	52	New York	86	68
Los Angeles	80	51	Chicago	86	66
Seattle	66	56	Kansas City	94	74
Denver	88	66	New Orleans	92	80

San Francisco Chronicle

THE CITY'S ONLY HOME-OWNED NEWSPAPER

WEATHER IN S. F. BAY REGION
Fair and Mild
Complete Weather Report On Page 21

FOUNDED 1865—VOL. CXLI, NO. 14 CCC* SAN FRANCISCO, CAL., FRIDAY, JULY 29, 1932 DAILY 5 CENTS, SUNDAY 10 CENTS: DAILY AND SUNDAY PER MONTH, $1.15

FIRE AND SWORD ROUT VETS

Troops Use Gas, Bayonets; Bonus Seeker Slain

Capital Camps Burned; Police Beaten in Battle

Ex-Service Men Hurl Brickbats, Officers Wields Clubs; 50 Hurt; Cavalrymen, Doughboys Clear Out City

WASHINGTON, July 29 (Friday) (AP)—The four wretched encampments which for two months past have housed the bonus army lay burned to earth early this morning, and the veterans that have lived there sought haven in dark streets, on country roads and the path homeward.

One of their number had been shot dead by police.

That affray, near the Capitol yesterday afternoon, led to President Hoover's calling upon Federal troops to clear the camps—which they did with use of tear gas.

In late afternoon and early evening, they successfully attacked the three shanty sites in the city proper, applying the torch once the veterans had fallen back.

Blazes Light City

Late at night, after it had been decided to hold off drastic action in the main Anacostia camp until today at least, one after another blaze broke out in huts where the veterans were, and that portion of the city was cast in a lurid glare that could be seen by the President as he retired at the White House. Finally it was determined to let the troops complete the destruction. They did, and set up a guard there such as was watching over the other three scenes of attack.

Fires Start Dispute

The numerous blazes which swept across the Anacostia camp followed a few earlier, which started coincidentally with the arrival of the infantry and cavalry. It became a matter of dispute whether the soldiers set off these, or whether the veterans themselves had, or whether it had been the grim police.

But there was unanimity that the angered veterans themselves started the final conflagration, since no soldiers were at the huts where the fires originated.

General Praises Hoover

In a statement, General Douglas MacArthur, Chief of Staff of the Army, expressed his conviction that if the President had not taken his decisive action when he did "the Government would have been threatened."

The President, he said, "had gone the limit in the exercise of patience before he used force.

Tear Gas Used

"I believe he would have been derelict in his duty if he had not acted."

The main evacuation yesterday was of the shanty settlement and that in abandoned buildings in the shadow of the Capitol. That done, at the expense of much tear gas and cavalrymen riding into crowds of veterans and spectators, dispersing them, the soldiers broke up the encampment of the left wing or communist group and another which had been peopled by California veterans in southern Washington.

The number of troops employed was placed by the War Department at "not more than 700."

More in Reserve

Three troops of cavalry, comprising about 300 men, and a battalion of infantry, consisting of about 350, comprised the force.

In reserve at nearby Fort Myer, Va., were 1400 additional troops consisting of the 34th Infantry and the 13th Engineers. They had been called in from Fort Meade, Maryland, and Fort Humphreys, Va., a few miles away.

General, Hoover Confer

Before leaving Anacostia last night, General MacArthur made a final inspection of the troops.

The army chief returned to Washington and, joined by Secretary Hurley of the War Department, called on President Hoover at the White House to report on the situation. MacArthur and Hurley then went across the street to the War Department for a final conference about plans for tomorrow.

Out at Anacostia, meanwhile, the blazes spread in several sections of the camp.

Some of the property destroyed, besides the crudely constructed huts, included National Guard tents loaned to the veterans when they first came to Washington.

Men Moved in Dark

Military police of the bonus army went through the camp and told all the men to move out and offer no resistance.

Some men started almost immediately, although some declared they wished to stay and fight.

The men were moved forward unseen by having them advance behind the truck mounted floodlight. When the lights were extinguished the entire field appeared dark and figures could not be discerned moving about on it unless an observer approached within 100 feet.

Carries Bedraggled Flag

On foot, riding in overloaded trucks and passenger cars of every description, they poured up the narrow street leading from the camp.

Some of the men on foot carried blanket rolls, odds and ends of cooking utensils, and even articles of furniture. One man was carrying a bedraggled

(Continued on Page 5, Col. 1)

BONUS BRICK BARRAGE ☆ ☆ FIRST PHOTO OF RIOTS

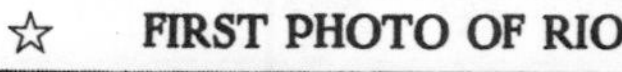

Bonus marchers throwing stones at Treasury agents and police who sought to evict them from Government property in Washington. This attack started the riot which cost one life and caused serious injuries to two men and resulted in Hoover's order for troops to restore order.
—Associated Press Telephoto, Transmitted by Telephone.

Cavalrymen Called to Beat Back Rioters

Infantry With Drawn Bayonets Drives Out Vet Marchers

WASHINGTON, July 28 (AP)—Mounted troops were called upon today to beat back the mob of bonus veterans after their riot with police in Washington, seeking to evict them from Government property.

Relentlessly, cavalry men rode on the sidewalks forcing spectators into doorways or up side streets. One man standing in the door of a telegraph office refused to move. Two cavalrymen converged on him, their horses beating him back into the doorway.

As the streets were being cleared, infantrymen—their guns in their hands and with their bayonets drawn—rushed at double quick time toward the area occupied by the marchers.

The first advance was made in a less crowded area.

GREETED WITH SONGS

One company of infantry turned from Pennsylvania avenue into Fourth street, dividing the bonus forces. They started to drive the bonus marchers across the foundations of torn-down buildings.

There was a constant array of comment from the veterans, they sang songs and shouted while the steel-helmeted infantry moved closer into the area with their guns slung over their shoulders.

Cavalrymen, after a start and then remaining still several minutes, began to clear the north side of Pennsylvania avenue, two or three riding into the crowd.

Spectators and veterans massed there dropped back to a vacant lot.

CAVALRY CLEARS STREETS

Meantime the almost solid group of veterans on the south side of the avenue did not move back an inch. Finally, the cavalry cleared the streets and surrounding lots of the throng preliminary to the evacuation move.

Police were put inside the lines of the veterans' camp as the cavalry undertook its task of getting the crowd away from possible danger.

At this point, numbers of the troops donned gas masks and began flinging tear gas bombs into the ranks of recalcitrant veterans.

A company of infantry deployed

(Continued on Page 5, Col. 3)

Hoover Pins Flying Crosses on Aviators

WASHINGTON, July 28 (AP)—Two transatlantic flyers walked from the White House today carrying distinguished flying crosses, authorized to them by Congress and pinned upon their breasts by President Hoover. They were Russell Boardman and John Polando, both of Massachusetts, who just one year ago today took off on a flight that carried them over 5000 miles of ocean and land to Istanbul, Turkey.

Hoover Statement Tells Reason for Army Call

Troops Needed to End Civil Disobedience, Says President

WASHINGTON, July 28 (AP)—President Hoover late today issued an announcement that in order to put an end to "rioting and defiance of civil authority" arising in clashes between bonus seeking veterans and the police, he had asked the United States Army to assist in restoring order.

The full text of the President's statement follows:

"For some days police authorities and Treasury officials have been endeavoring to persuade the so-called bonus marchers to evacuate certain buildings which they were occupying without permission.

"These buildings are on sites where Government construction is in progress and their demolition was necessary in order to extend employment in the district and to carry forward the Government's construction program.

ORDERED TO EVACUATE

"This morning the occupants of these buildings were notified to evacuate and, at the request of the police, did evacuate the buildings concerned.

"Thereafter, however, several thousand men from different camps marched in and attacked the police with brickbats and otherwise, injuring several policemen, one probably fatally.

"I have received the attached letter from the commissioners of the District of Columbia, stating that they can no longer preserve law and order in the district.

"In order to put an end to this rioting and defiance of civil authority, I have asked the army to assist the district authorities to restore order.

PROVISION FOR RETURN

"Congress made provision for the return home of the so-called bonus marchers, who have for many weeks been given every opportunity of free assembly, free speech and free petition to the Congress.

"Some 5000 took advantage of this arrangement and have re-

(Continued on Page 5, Col. 6)

Today's Features

	Page
Amusements	9
Book Reviews	11
Chester Rowell	11
Comics	Green 16
Crossword Puzzle	Green 15
Culbertson's Bridge	Green 15
Deaths	11
Dorothy Dix	18
Dr. Evans on Health	18
Editorials	10
Every Man's University	11
Financial	19, 20, 21
Jane Friendly	8
Marine	22
Ninon Fashions	18
Radio	Green 16
Society	18
Sidney Skolsky	11
Scotty's Column	11
Sports	Sporting Green
Want Ads	22, 23, 24, 25, 26, 27
Women's Club Calendar	18

Casualties In Capital Bonus Riot

WASHINGTON, July 28 (AP) —The casualty list in Washington today:

SHOT TO DEATH

WILLIAM HASKA, 37, 2316 West Twenty-third place, Chicago.

SERIOUSLY HURT

George Scott, policeman, skull fractured by brick.

Eric Carlson, 40, Oakland, Cal., veteran, shot in the abdomen.

John Hall, negro, Mocksville, N. C., veteran, gunshot wounds.

LESS SERIOUSLY INJURED

Allen Bradley, policeman, tear gas.
Richard Belfield, policeman, tear gas.
William Manning, Los Angeles veteran, tear gas.
Francis Conley, Pennsylvania veteran, gassed.
John C. Morton, San Angelo, Texas, hand burned.
Otto Green, Nashville, Tenn., saber cut on head and ear.
Earl Smith, Las Vegas, Nev., gassed.
Sergeant John T. Hellman, Fort Washington, hand burned.
Robert N. Floyd, policeman, head wounds from bricks.
Samuel H. Hartung, policeman, head wounds.
John E. Winters, policeman, head injury.
John O. Hite, policeman, cut with hatchet.
Henry Price, policeman, body wounds from bricks.
William Bankert, policeman, struck by bricks and bottles.
Philip K. Clark, policeman, head wounds from bottle.
Chief Mountain Heart, veteran, head wounds.
John Wyndom, Cleveland, veteran, head wounds.
Emmett Morris, veteran, gassed.
Harry Walters, 14, Washington, saber

(Continued on Page 5, Col. 2)

Accused San Bruno Officials Lose Jobs

Emil Bohm, city clerk of San Bruno, and Councilman William Maurer, under fire for irregularities in the conduct of the city's business, were stripped of their appointive offices yesterday at a meeting of the San Bruno Council. Bohm was ordered to vacate the offices of water clerk, deputy Tax Collector and city purchasing agent, reducing his income from $200 a month to $90. Maurer was removed from the Finance and Insurance committees of the Council, but was permitted to remain on the Streets Committee. The alleged irregularities concerned the collection of water bills.

Police Hunting Mystery Man In Knife Killing

Youth Tries to Hurl Note to Templeton's Fiancee in San Jose Jail

Into the eerie murder of Mrs. Lillian Babcock, wealthy Manila society matron, by her nephew, George Douglas Templeton Jr., there came last night a new and mysterious figure.

A tall, blond youth with curly hair made a daring but futile attempt to communicate with Dixie-ana Chapman Burnett, sweetheart of young Templeton and a material witness against him, as she sat with two matrons in the Detention Home at San Jose.

After twice trying to hurl a message wrapped about a stone through the girl's cell window, the youth fled with police and sheriff's deputies in pursuit. He escaped.

Other developments of the day in the weird case were:

1—Major Geo. Douglas Templeton Sr., father of the young slayer, announced his determination to delve to the bottom of Miss Burnett's relationship with his son, and determine what influence she held over him, if any. The first Major and Mrs. Templeton heard of the girl, they said, was after their son's arrest.

2—Young Templeton gave several "demonstrations" in his cell at San Jose, which jailers considered ground work for an insanity defense. The youthful knife murderer announced the ghost of his maternal grandmother had urged him to kill his aunt, and seriously stab his uncle, William Rider Babcock, as

(Continued on Page 3, Col. 2)

Lina Basquette to Wed Dempsey's Old Trainer

HOLLYWOOD, July 28 (AP) — Setting at rest rumors that she might become the bride of Jack Dempsey, Lina Basquette, motion picture actress, today announced her engagement to Teddy Hayes, boxing trainer. She said no date had been set for the wedding. Hayes formerly was Dempsey's trainer, but they became estranged. They traded heated words recently after Hayes was quoted as intimating that Dempsey had "stolen" Miss Basquette's affections.

Woman Lost in Wilds Found After 3 Days

LAKESHORE, Huntington Lake, July 28 (AP)—Mrs. Nina Newell, Fresno teacher, lost in this mountainous region for the last three days, was found today by Forest Ranger Oscar Fuller in Aspen meadows, six miles from the Kaiser Diggings Ranger Station. Mrs. Newell was dazed but in good condition despite the three days of hardships. She will remain at the ranger statioin pending the arrival of her husband.

Movies Pageant Ends Shrine Fete In Blaze of Color

Stars of Pictures, Beautiful Girls of Hollywood Appear in Striking Climax to Brilliant Session

By EARLE ENNIS

Amid the flame-tipped monoliths and gleaming electric jewels of the Civic Center's great O-shaped stadium, the Shrine convention climaxed last night in a pageant of beauty!

Only Hollywood with its glamor, romance, color and gift for spectacular pageantry could have evolved such a fitting peak event. Beautiful women from the National Hub of Beauty, stars of the celluloid firmament dipped down to rub elbows with common mortals, girls framed in light, floats of superlative charm—it ran the gamut of all adjective expression and left the grandstand breathless.

The Shrine provided the frame, but the picture was Hollywood's. Not only were beautiful women used as only Hollywood can use them, but every device of trick lighting, modernistic color effect, electrical genius and illumination was called into play. It was the reflected genius of one man and one woman—J. A. Biggam of Los Angeles, master designer of floats, and his wife Mrs. Biggam, who costumed and girled the displays.

Without contradition the closing parade was the most beautiful that

(Continued on Page 4, Col. 1)

Many Demand Film Pageant Be Repeated

Thousands Miss Final Spectacle; May Be Staged Saturday

THE Shrine's Motion Picture Pageant of last night should be repeated!

This is the consensus of a public demand as a result of the terrific last-minute seat jam which shut thousands of people out of the most beautiful spectacle that San Francisco has seen in many a day.

It is suggested that the Motion Picture Pageant be given again on Saturday night at popular prices, so that thousands who did not see it last night, through inability to obtain a ticket, or because of the price of the tickets, may see the great spectacle. Out of this demand has grown a hope that the thing may be done.

The bringing of floats of the magnitude and beauty of those which were shown last night is an expensive process and one that does not occur except at rare intervals. The stadium still stands ready for a vast crowd. The lighting effects are all up and the floats carry their own power equipments for the illuminative effects. It would be a simple thing to stage again this magnificent spectacle on a scale that would bring it within the reach of every man, woman and child.

The phrase of last night, heard oftenest in the grandstand was: "Oh, how I wish so-and-so was here!" It referred to people who couldn't get away to see the movie pageant, who hadn't been able to obtain a ticket, who through personal reasons or the jam of a huge crowd found it impossible to sit with the others more fortunate.

Out of this was born the idea that perhaps the pageant could be produced on Saturday night at popular prices for the general public—that the spectacle that thrilled the few could likewise thrill the many. The idea, first suggested yesterday, has gained momentum as those who saw the display broadcast its beauty and magnificent effects.

If the plan can be worked out there appears to be no reason why San Franciscans cannot see the closing event of the great Shrine convention staged again for their benefit with full light, color and pageant effects for the price of a downtown show, on Saturday evening.

Plot for Revolution Uncovered in Cuba

HAVANA, July 28 (AP)—Police disclosed today they had uncovered a plot for a revolution scheduled to take place between August 13 and August 15. The conspiracy was directed, they said, by members of the army detachment which rebelled last year under General Francisco Peraza.

FINAL ELECTION EXTRA

COMPARATIVE TEMPERATURES

	High	Low		High	Low
San Francisco	74	53	Kansas City	36	32
Los Angeles	90	65	New Orleans	72	60
Seattle	52	46	New York	56	50
Denver	50	22	Chicago	62	44

San Francisco Chronicle

THE CITY'S ONLY HOME-OWNED NEWSPAPER

WEATHER IN S. F. BAY REGION

Fair and Mild

Complete Weather Report on Page 22.

FOUNDED 1865—VOL. CXLI, NO. 117 CCC***** SAN FRANCISCO, CAL., WEDNESDAY, NOVEMBER 9, 1932 DAILY 5 CENTS, SUNDAY 10 CENTS: DAILY AND SUNDAY PER MONTH, $1.15

ROOSEVELT ELECTED!

McAdoo Defeats Tubbs in Senatorial Contest

STATE REPEALS WRIGHT ACT BY WIDE MARGIN

Governor Sweeps 42 States, With Congress Democratic and Wet

Winner Given 472 Electoral Votes to 59 for President Hoover

Veterans of Senate Go to Defeat in Ballot Wave

By Associated Press

A gigantic tide of votes rolling Westward with undiminished force has swept Democratic forces aligned behind Franklin D. Roosevelt into control of the national and many State governments.

In the Republican column of President Hoover only six States definitely were aligned, as returns from what promised to be a new record popular vote poured in early today from last Eastern districts and the West. The Hoover States were Delaware, Maine, New Hampshire, Connecticut, Pennsylvania and Vermont.

With over 14,000,000 votes counted in one-third the Nation's election districts, the Democratic standard held a plurality near the 3,000,000 mark, for an electoral vote already over 400 out of a possible 531. If popular balloting maintains this pace in the remaining district the aggregate vote promises to exceed 1928's record of 37,000,000 by 5,000,000.

EARLY FORECAST

INCOMPLETE returns compiled by the Associated Press still inconclusive as to many States, show totals which, if borne out by later figures, would give the following electoral vote:

Hoover 59
Roosevelt 472
Necessary to elect.......... 266

MARGINS MOUNT

Indicative of the Democratic strength were pluralities in such normally Republican States as Michigan, Indiana, Ohio, Iowa, Kansas and Utah, and mounting margins of victory on the West Coast, which apparently were engulfing President Hoover's own State of California.

With the national ticket, a Democratic Senate and House seemed assured, together with victories for this party in a majority of the thirty-five gubernatorial contests. Accompanying these shifts were evidences of an anti-prohibition sweep in many sections.

CONGRATULATES ROOSEVELT

President Hoover, watching the mounting returns turning with increasing favor to his opponent, sent to Governor Roosevelt, shortly after

(Continued on Page 7, Col. 1)

ELECTION BY STATES

STATE	Electoral	Hoover	Roosevelt
Alabama	11		11
Arizona	3		3
Arkansas	9		9
California	22		22
Colorado	6		6
Connecticut	8	8	
Delaware	3	3	
Florida	7		7
Georgia	12		12
Idaho	4		4
Illinois	29		29
Indiana	14		14
Iowa	11		11
Kansas	9		9
Kentucky	11		
Louisiana	10		10
Maine	5	5	
Maryland	8		8
Massachusetts	17		17
Michigan	19		19
Minnesota	11		11
Mississippi	9		9
Missouri	15		15
Montana	4		4
Nebraska	7		7
Nevada	3		3
New Hampshire	4	4	
New Jersey	16		16
New Mexico	3		3
New York	47		47
North Carolina	13		13
North Dakota	4		4
Ohio	26		26
Oklahoma	11		11
Oregon	5		5
Pennsylvania	36	36	
Rhode Island	4		4
South Carolina	8		8
South Dakota	4		4
Tennessee	11		11
Texas	23		23
Utah	4		4
Vermont	3	3	
Virginia	11		11
Washington	8		8
West Virginia	8		8
Wisconsin	12		12
Wyoming	3		3
Totals	531	59	472

Necessary for a choice, 266.

Roosevelt Will Have Democratic Congress

By ARTHUR EVANS

CHICAGO, Nov. 8 — Governor Franklin D. Roosevelt will have a Democratic Congress, both houses and Senate, when he takes office as President March 4. Incomplete returns indicate the Democrats made a net gain of five seats, possibly six, in the Senate today when Senators were elected in thirty-three States.

It indicates the Democrats will have fifty-three members of the next Senate, which gives the Democrats a larger control of the upper house than in 1913 when Woodrow Wilson became President.

Both houses will be wet, so the partial figures protend.

Four Republican leaders in the Senate appear to have been engulfed in the anti-Hoover wave. Some fell by the way in the primaries. Among the faces that will be missing in the United States Senate after March 4, it appears, will be the following:

Hiram Bingham of Connecticut.

Reed Smoot of Utah.

Otis F. Glenn of Illinois.

George H. Moses of New Hampshire.

James E. Watson of Indiana.

Smith Wildman Brookhart, Iowa.

John J. Blaine of Wisconsin.

Samuel M. Shortridge, California.

Senator Wesley L. Jones, author of the Jones five and ten law, also may be among the missing. Early returns from Washington indicated he is in a close race with Homer T. Bone, Democrat.

The Democrats up to midnight had not lost a Senate seat with the possible exception of Colorado. In New York the Democrats reelected Senator F. R. Wagner; in Ohio they reelected Senator Robert J. Bulkley; in Kentucky they put over Senator Alben W. Barkley—all wets, so the incomplete figures indicate.

The size of the Democratic ma-

(Continued on Page 7, Col. 5)

Californians Smash All Vote Records

Roosevelt Wins 745,045 Ballots to Hoover's 509,633; Racing Bill Close

L. A. Goes Wet, Turns Down School Fund, Drilling Plan

By EARL C. BEHRENS

In an avalanche of ballots which smashed all California vote records yesterday, President-elect Franklin D. Roosevelt won the State's twenty-two electoral votes from President Herbert Hoover; William G. McAdoo was swept into the United States Senatorship by the Democratic victory and at the same time the people knocked off the statute books the Wright dry law enforcement act.

Passage of the racing law, legalizing betting on horse races under the certificate form of wagers, hung in balance early this morning.

HUGE ROOSEVELT VICTORY

Complete and incomplete returns from 6805 of the State's 10,547 precincts gave Roosevelt, 745,045; Hoover, 509,633.

For U. S. Senator, 7070 complete and incomplete precincts gave: McAdoo, 441,411; Tubbs, 347,805; Shuler, 262,14-.

With the tremendous San Francisco majority of more than 138,000 recorded against the continuance of the State's dry law, the Wright act repealer was swept along toward victory as the returns from yesterday's election were tabulated from the fifty-eight counties.

MANY WET VOTES

Returns from 5845 complete and incomplete but widely scattered precincts out of the 10,547 on the Wright act repealer gave "Yes," 277,008, "No," 78,861.

San Francisco gave an overwhelming vote to President-elect Roosevelt to Tallant Tubbs, wet Republican, over McAdoo, and Bob Shuler, Prohibitionist, and to the racing measure.

From Los Angeles county 3160 of the 3537 precincts gave Roosevelt 445,554, Hoover 304,033. The same precincts gave McAdoo 265,868; Shuler, 148,384; Tubbs 136,067.

L. A. RACE VOTE CLOSE

On the Wright act repealer, the Los Angeles vote was "Yes," 37,334; "No," 16,306. The companion wet measure, the State liquor regulation act, had "Yes," 34,909, "No," 17,202. The first tabulation on the racing bill from Los Angeles was close, 23,977 for and 21,019 against it. Both the school fund and the tidelands leasing measures were being turned down by the Los Angeles voters. The votes were taken from 700-odd precincts.

It was once remarked that California is famous for beautiful

(Continued on Page 4, Col. 2)

City Ballots Wet; Favors Legal Betting

Roosevelt Leads S. F. by 68,690; Tubbs Far Ahead Here; Garbage Plan Carries

Veterans' Tax Exemption and Beach Drilling Defeated

By overwhelming margins yesterday, San Francisco voted for President-elect Franklin D. Roosevelt, for Tallant Tubbs, wet Republican candidate for U. S. Senator, for the repeal of the Wright dry enforcement act and to legalize the certificate system of betting on horse races.

In the Democratic landslide, Roosevelt piled up a lead over President Hoover, Republican nominee, of 68,690. Norman Thomas, Socialist candidate, received 5369 votes.

134,801 ROOSEVELT VOTES

For presidential electors, the complete San Francisco vote was Roosevelt, 134,801; Hoover, 66,111.

In the race for U. S. Senator, the final vote was Tubbs, 112,263; McAdoo, 61,043; Shuler, 14,253.

By the huge majority of more than 138,000, San Francisco voted to repeal the State dry law. The complete semi-official figures were: Wright Act repealer, "Yes," 173,457; "No," 35,380.

The second of the two wet measures on the ballot, the State liquor regulation act, also received a huge vote of approval. The margin for the measure was more than 60,000.

BET MEASURE APPROVED

The proposed legalization of the certificate system of betting on horse races also came in for a tremendous favorable vote. The first tabulation on the racing bill gave "Yes," 109,624; "No," 70,129.

All of the charter amendments, with the exception of No. 4, the revenue bond proposal to finance construction of municipal water department extensions and mains, were passed yesterday. The new garbage disposal ordinance also was approved.

Disapproval of the voters was expressed on the following State propo-

(Continued on Page 4, Col. 2)

Waiter Jumps or Falls To Death From Bridge

Boris Nazaroff, 25, 1483 O'Farrell street, a waiter, jumped or fell to his death from a 100-foot bridge at Nineteenth and Indiana streets, early yesterday. He was found lying beneath the bridge by a police patrol car. The body was later identified by a sister, Mrs. S. Bojko, 1775 O'Farrell street. Mrs. Bojko was unable to furnish any motive for suicide.

State Vote Tabulated

Returns from 6805 widely scattered precincts out of 10,5?? in California gave the following returns:

PRESIDENT

Hoover 509,633
Roosevelt 745,045

U. S. SENATOR

Tubbs 347,665
McAdoo 443,543
Shuler 265,432

STATE PROPOSITIONS

Incomplete Returns From 2664 Precincts

No. 1 (Wright Act)
Yes...277,008 No......78,861

No. 2 (Liquor Regulation)
Yes...192,192 No.....?8,916

No. 3 (Trust Deeds)
Yes....56,241 No.....17?,475

No. 4 (Highway Taxes)
Yes....65,242 No.....176,048

No. 5 (Racing)
Yes...149,421 No.....116,825

No. 9 (School Funds)
Yes....55,316 No.....153,411

No. 11 (Tideland Leases)
Yes....73,196 No.....114,485

S. F. Returns

Complete returns in San Francisco gave the following results:

PRESIDENT

Hoover (R.) 66,111
Roosevelt (D.) 134,801
Thomas (Soc.) 5,369

U. S. SENATOR

McAdoo (D.) 61,043
Shuler (Prob.) 14,253
Tubbs (R.) 112,263

CONGRESS

FOURTH DISTRICT

Kahn (R.) .... Elected

MEMBER OF BOARD OF EDUCATION

C. Harold Caulfield
Elected

STATE PROPOSITIONS

No. 1 (Wright Act Repealer)
Yes.......173,457 No........ 35,380

No. 2 (Liquor Regulation)
Yes.......126,000 No........ 63,384

No. 3 (Trust Deeds)
Yes....... 36,535 No........130,788

No. 4 (Highway Taxes)
Yes....... 44,621 No........121,917

No. 5 (Racing)
Yes.......109,624 No........ 70,129

No. 6 (Vets Exemption)
Yes....... 71,319 No........ 74,228

No. 7 (Legislation Expense)
Yes....... 21,564 No........132,293

No. 8 (Init. and Refnd.)
Yes....... 94,409 No........ 46,161

No. 9 (School Funds)
Yes....... 30,946 No........124,600

No. 11 (Tidelands)
Yes....... 45,619 No........119,414

No. 13 (Boxing Act)
Yes....... 81,192 No........ 6,332

No. 14 (Ship Exemption)
Yes.......113,408 No........ 38,013

No. 16 (Tax Liens)
Yes....... 92,249 No........ 45,927

No. 17 (City Charters)
Yes.......103,191 No........ 34,103

No. 18 (County Charters)
Yes....... 39,211 No........ 95,811

No. 19 (Charter Provisions)
Yes....... 74,819 No........ 58,380

CITY PROPOSITIONS

No. 1 (Emergency Appointments)
Yes....... 82,846 No........ 75,944

No. 2 (Residence Qualification)
Yes.......113,591 No........ 43,448

No. 3 (Temporary Loans)
Yes....... 92,792 No........ 54,423

No. 4 (Revenue Bonds)
Yes....... 65,495 No........ 88,117

No. 5 (Civil Service)
Yes.......102,985 No........ 96,607

Garbage Ordinance
Yes.......102,436 No........ 36,197

U. S. Envoy Denied Vote After Trip From Berlin

LOUISVILLE, Ky., Nov. 8 (AP)—Ambassador and Mrs. Frederick M. Sackett of Louisville came all the way from Germany to vote and then discovered they were not entitled to cast their ballots because neither had registered under a new law. Democratic attorneys agreed to waive objections but there was no legal way for the Circuit Judge to sign an authorization.

Gov. Hunt Ill With Pneumonia Attack

PHOENIX, Nov. 8 (AP)—As the electorate of Arizona was naming his successor, Governor George W. P. Hunt, seven times chief executive, was taken to a hospital tonight in a serious condition, suffering from pneumonia.

Wife of Trust Company Chief Commits Suicide

CHICAGO, Nov. 8 (AP)—A woman identified by police as Mrs. M. M. Dunbar, 40 years old, wife of the vice president of the Union Trust Company of Indianapolis, ended her life with poison this morning

Hoover Concedes Roosevelt Wins, Pledges Support

President Sends Wire Congratulating Governor; Hears Returns at Palo Home With Friends

By WILLIS O'BRIEN

With that candor and good sportsmanship which has been the mark of his life, President Hoover early last night conceded the national election to Franklin D. Roosevelt, in a telegram of congratulation to the President-elect in New York.

In simple and direct words from his Palo Alto fireside, Herbert Hoover pledged himself "in the common purpose of all of us" to serve the new administration in its great task of maintaining America's preeminence among nations.

The dispatch was the dramatic climax to the President's homecoming, when he had been only a few hours from his transcontinental train and while the overwhelming tide of votes was running to his opponent.

The historic telegram, sent at 9:18 o'clock, read:

"Honorable Franklin D. Roosevelt, Biltmore Hotel, New York City:

"I congratulate you on the opportunity that has come to you to be of service to the country,

WINS OWN PRECINCT

STANFORD UNIVERSITY, Nov. 8 (AP)—President Hoover's home precinct, where he and Mrs. Hoover cast their votes this afternoon, stayed in the Republican column. Hoover was given 175 votes.

and I wish for you a most successful administration. In the common purpose of all of us I shall dedicate myself to every possible helpful effort.

"HERBERT HOOVER."

Less than a day from the time the President "smelled the soil of California," the telegram went forth to his successor-elect. About him, as he sent it, were the lifelong friends of his youth. They were in the home, and their shadows marched in the flood-lighted yard on San Juan hill behind the Stanford University campus.

HOOVER "TIREDEST MAN"

But in defeat "the tiredest man in the United States," as his secretary characterized him, kept to the native dignity which has marked his public life. With Mrs. Hoover, he smiled and chatted with friends, and spoke of the heartening loyalty of

(Continued on Page 6, Col. 2)

Father of Girl Eloper Charged With Murder

SAN LUIS OBISPO, Nov. 8 (AP)—Murder charges were filed today by officials against G. A. White, accusing him of shooting to death Thomas Moses, who eloped two weeks ago with White's 14-year-old daughter, Audrey. The girl testified against her father last night at the Coroner's inquest, accusing him of which she termed the "cold-blooded killing" of her husband.

Motorist Loses Life Under Wagon Wheels

LOS ANGELES, Nov. 8 (AP)—A motorist, James Berry, is dead here from traffic injuries, but no automobile or power driven vehicle is responsible. Berry stepped out of his car and started across the street. He was run down by a wagon and a team of mules. The wagon wheel passed over his head.

COMPARATIVE TEMPERATURES

	High	Low		High	Low
San Francisco	71	46	New York	40	35
Los Angeles	76	57	Chicago	30	20
Seattle	56	45	Kansas City	40	33
Denver	36	24	New Orleans	66	48

Snow at Soda Springs, 50 inches.

San Francisco Chronicle

THE CITY'S ONLY HOME-OWNED NEWSPAPER

WEATHER IN S. F. BAY REGION
Fair and Mild, with Some Cloudiness
Complete Weather Report on Page 4.

FOUNDED 1865—VOL. CXLII, NO. 50 CCC SAN FRANCISCO, CAL., MONDAY, MARCH 6, 1933 DAILY 5 CENTS, SUNDAY 10 CENTS: DAILY AND SUNDAY PER MONTH, $1.15

GOLD EMBARGOED, U. S. BANKS ON HOLIDAY

Roosevelt Summons Congress to Meet Thursday

War Powers Invoked By President, Moving to Meet U. S. Emergency

All Finance Institutions Must Close Until Friday, Executive Proclamation Reveals

Secretary of Treasury Given Control of Currency Movements; Scrip Issuance Provided

By ARTHUR SEARS HENNING
Special to The Chronicle

WASHINGTON, March 5—President Franklin D. Roosevelt today called the seventy-third Congress to meet in extraordinary session next Thursday and tonight proclaimed a national holiday in banking operations ending next Thursday midnight.

In a proclamation designed to steady the financial situation until Congress can act, the President invoked the powers conferred on the executive by the war-time trading with the enemy act of 1917 to put an end to domestic hoarding and foreign withdrawals of gold.

Secretary of Treasury in Control

By the proclamation all banking business is placed under the regulation of the Secretary of the Treasury.

Restrictions are placed on withdrawal of deposits already in the banks, but provision is made for unrestricted withdrawal of deposits made from tomorrow morning.

The effect of the proclamation is to take the country off the gold standard for the period of the holiday, at least, for the reason that gold will not be procurable upon demand by the holders of obligations of the Government requiring redemption in gold.

Establishes National Holiday

Specifically the proclamation does the following things:

1—Established a bank holiday, national in scope, beginning tomorrow morning and ending Thursday midnight.

2—Suspends during the holiday all banking transactions except such as are permitted by the Secretary of the Treasury.

3—Prohibits hoarding.

4—Suspends specie payments.

5—Declares an embargo on the export of gold.

6—Authorizes the Secretary of the Treasury to permit performance of all banking functions under such regulations as he may impose.

7—Authorizes issuance of Clearing House certificates or other forms of scrip to be used in place of currency.

8—Authorizes segregation of new deposits which may be drawn upon by depositors without restrictions.

Proclamation Climaxes Exciting Day

The proclamation was issued at the White House late tonight at the close of an exciting day of conferences by the new President and his advisers on ways and means of ending the banking situation which has seriously affected the business of the country.

All day leading bankers of the country, Secretary of the Treasury William H. Woodin and members of the Federal Reserve Board were in session at the Treasury working out the plan for dealing with the crisis which was eventually embodied in the President's proclamation.

In the meantime, Mr. Roosevelt had held a meeting of his Cabinet and had called in Democratic and Republican leaders in Congress for council which finally resulted in the convocation of the new Congress.

The plan of action emerged from three hectic sessions of the financial powers that he assembled at the Treasury. There were Melvin A. Traylor, president of the First National Bank of Chicago, and a dozen other bankers of national reputation. There was the new Secretary of the Treasury, William H. Woodin. There were his predecessor, Ogden L. Mills, and the holdover Undersecretary of the Treasury, Arthur Ballantine. And there were Governor Eugene Meyer and other members of the Federal Reserve Board.

All sorts of plans for reopening the banks of the country under conditions that would preclude a revival of the disastrous drain of deposits by hoarders were discussed and thrown aside. Eventually the conferees united on the plan for creating the Secretary of the Treasury a virtual banking dictator under authority derived from the almost forgotten trading with the enemy act which was passed by Congress in 1917 to enable the executive to protect the country's gold reserve.

A decade ago most of the war-time legislation clothing the

(Continued on Page 3, Col. 3)

Here Is Text Of Roosevelt Proclamation

WASHINGTON, March 5 (AP)—The full text of President Roosevelt's proclamation on the banking situation follows:

WHEREAS, there have been heavy and unwarranted withdrawals of gold and currency from our banking institutions for the purpose of hoarding; and

WHEREAS, continuous and increasingly extensive speculative activity abroad in foreign exchange has resulted in severe drains on the Nation's stocks of gold; and

WHEREAS, these conditions have created a national emergency; and

WHEREAS, it is in the best interests of all bank depositors that a period of respite be provided, with a view to preventing further hoarding of coin, bullion or currency or speculating in foreign exchange and permitting the application of appropriate measures to protect the interests of our people; and

WHEREAS, it is provided in section 5 (B) of the act of October 6, 1917 (40 Stat. L. 411) as amended, "that the President may investigate, regulate, or prohibit, under such rules and regulations as he may prescribe, by means of licenses or otherwise, any transactions in foreign exchange and the export, hoarding, melting, or earmarking of gold or silver coin or bullion or currency; ..."

WHEREAS, it is provided in section 16 of the said act "that whoever shall willfully violate any of the provisions of this act or of any license, rule, or regulation issued thereunder, and whoever shall willfully violate, neglect, or refuse to comply with any order of the President issued in compliance with the provisions of this

(Continued on Page 4, Col. 2)

Move Acclaimed By Fleishhacker

"Splendid! Just what the banking world has been waiting for."

Mortimer Fleishhacker, chairman of the board of the Anglo California National Bank, expressed this enthusiastic approval when The Chronicle informed him last night of President Roosevelt's proclamation calling a national bank holiday and declaring a gold embargo. He evidenced optimism over the financial outlook in view of the President's action and the certainty of a congressional session Thursday.

President Roosevelt could have taken no more favorable and effective step at this time," he said.

Venizelos Leads In Greek Election

ATHENS, March 5 (AP)—A few returns tonight in the Greek Parliamentary elections indicated a trend toward Premier Elutherios Venizelos' Coalition party, but it was too early to forecast the final result.

Opposing the followers of Premier Venizelos, who is 69 years old and has been Premier seven times, was the coalition of Panagiotes Tsaldares, which includes three parties, having 105 members in the previous chamber.

Government finance and economies were the major issues.

Seattle Street Wrecked by Blast

SEATTLE, March 5 (AP)—A mystery explosion tore a hole in the middle of Ashworth avenue in the Wallingford district shortly before 1 p. m. here today. Police said there was nothing to indicate what caused the blast, which shattered plaster from the walls of nearby houses. No one was on the street near the spot when the explosion occurred.

Plan Drafted For Issuing Scrip in S. F.

Knowledge of Chicago, N. Y. Bank Closings Delays California Law Action

Schools, Courts, Public Offices to Reopen Tomorrow

President Roosevelt's proclamation declaring a modified national bank holiday until Friday morning finds California banks in as solvent a condition as banks of any other State in the Union, if not actually more so.

The State Legislature was ready on Saturday to enact new relief legislation that would have permitted reopening of the banks this morning, but the closing of New York and Chicago banks, which would have precluded normal functioning of California institutions, barred the way to legislative action.

In view of the President's proclamation and the imminent convening of a special session of Congress, the Legislature will probably delay its own action until it learns what program is contemplated by Roosevelt.

CLARIFIED BY BANK CHIEF

President J. F. Sullivan Jr. of the California Bankers' Association made the above clear last night at State and National Governments prepared to authorize and regulate immediate issuance of emergency clearing house certificates that will keep the wheels of business whirring as usual, while new safeguards for bank depositors and the National banking structure are drafted.

AGREE ON METHOD

With members of the San Francisco Clearing House Association informally agreed upon the mechanism of scrip issuance, pending formal ratification in executive session today, high lights in the local banking situation last night were:

1—Banks prepared to open Friday morning.

2—Courts, public offices and the like, except schools, will be closed today, a general State holiday, so proclaimed by Governor Rolph.

3—Public offices and courts will reopen tomorrow under a special holiday designation, both State and national; schools will continue as usual.

4—The San Francisco Stock and Curb exchanges will observe the holidays in the same manner as the banks.

5—The Oakland Clearing House Association will meet this morning at 8:30 o'clock to consider scrip issuance.

6—Superintendent of Banks Edward Rainey expressed confidence that all interests have been safeguarded in the emergency amendment proposed by the Legislature and forwarded to the Comp-

(Continued on Page 2, Col. 4)

Will Rogers Says:

SANTA MONICA, Mar. 5—Editor The Chronicle: America hasn't been as happy in three years as they are today. No money, no banks, no work, no nothing, but they knew they got a man in there who is wise to Congress; wise to our big bankers, and wise to our so-called big men.

The whole country is with him, even if what he does is wrong. They are with him, just so he does something. If he burned down the Capitol we would cheer and say, "Well, we at least got a fire started anyhow."

We have had years of "Don't rock the boat." Go on and sink it if you want to. We just as well be swimming as like we are. Yours, WILL ROGERS.

Vote on Beer This Month, Says Rainey

Speaker Designate Sees Quick Approval of Measure by Congress

New Wet Members Will Insure Action, Says Party Leader

WASHINGTON, March 5 (AP)—From the next Speaker of the House there came today most positive assurances that "the Democratic party will make good its promises and legalize beer at the earliest possible moment."

That moment, said Henry T. Rainey of Illinois, Democratic speakership nominee, who will be elected because of his party's large majority in the House, may come before April 1. In any event, he asserted, "It won't be many weeks."

SETS EARLIER DATE

Since the session is to begin Thursday, Rainey said, the House might even act March 20, on a bill to modify the Volstead act. House rules permit any measure to be brought up under a suspension of the rules the first and third Mondays in any month—and March 20 is the third Monday.

"Anyhow, the question of letting the House vote on that date is being considered," he said.

NEW MEMBERS AID

Rainey and other Democratic leaders are hopeful that because of the influx of 160 new members of their party to the House—many of whom supported the platform promise of "immediate modification of the Volstead act" — the necessary two-thirds majority for passage under a suspension of the rules on March 20, can be mustered without difficulty.

If need be, they are prepared once more to emphasize the tax feature of the proposal. The measure adopted by the last Senate included, as the new bill is likely to, a tax of $5 a barrel on the new beverage. Estimates of the anticipated revenue ranged from $75,000,000 to $300,000,000.

Farley Places $5 Tax on Victory Fete

Special to The Chronicle

WASHINGTON, March 5—Postmaster General Jim Farley's big dinner for the electors who cast the votes which put Franklin D. Roosevelt in the White House has resulted in some of those electors having something to say about Farley as a host. It develops that everyone had to dig up a $5 bill to pay for the Farley feed.

Anita Stewart Will Undergo Operation

LOS ANGELES, March 5 (AP)—Anita Stewart, star actress of the silent film days, is scheduled to undergo a major abdominal operation tomorrow morning in a Los Angeles hospital. In attendance with her has been her husband, George Peabody Converse, son of E. C. Converse, former United States Steel Corporation executive.

Mary Wister, Kin Of Novelist, Wed

PHILADELPHIA, March 5 (AP)—Miss Mary Channing Wister, daughter of Owen Wister, the novelist, and Andrew Dasburg, an artist of Santa Fe, N. M., were married today at Wister's home, "Longhouse," in suburban Bryn Mawr.

Woodin Denies U.S. Off Gold Standard

WASHINGTON, March 5 (AP)—Secretary Woodin, in amplifying the President's proclamation, said emphatically that the United States was not off the gold standard.

"Any such interpretation upon the President's pronouncement is a grave mistake," he said.

Hitler Wins Reich Election, Powers to Force Dictatorship

Nazis Attain Legal Tools to Wipe Out Last Vestiges of Democracy by Vote of 17,000,000

BERLIN, March 6 (Monday) (AP)—Seventeen million voters cut of 39,000,000 manifested their confidence in Chancellor Adolf Hitler in yesterday's Reichstag election and demonstrated to President von Hindenburg that he sensed the desires of the German people rightly when he asked the chief of the Nazi Brown Shirts to take the helm of the ship of state.

Germany now is well on the way to Fascist dictatorship. Chancellor Hitler, by the vote of the people, has been given the legal tools to annihilate the last vestige of the democracy which he considers a failure.

BALLOT TOTALS COMPARED

The following table shows the party standings compared with the last previous Reichstag election:

	March 5	Nov. 6
National Soc.	17,264,000	11,705,000
Nationalists	3,131,000	3,021,000
People's Party	432,000	660,000
Christian Soc.	382,000	412,000
Centrists	4,289,000	4,228,000
Bavarian P'ple's	1,206,000	1,081,000
State Party	335,000	338,000
Socialists	7,176,000	7,231,000
Communists	4,746,000	5,970,000
Scattered	220,000	

The Nazis alone will command nearly 44 per cent of the votes in the new Reichstag and can dictate to their Nationalist coworkers in the government what must be done to shape a new Germany in accordance with Nazi ideals.

REDS WILL BE BARRED

As the Nazis in their preelection campaign left no doubt that the Communist Deputies would never be allowed to take their seats, the followers of Chancellor Hitler will in fact command a majority in the new Reichstag.

In Prussia, which elected a State Diet yesterday, the Nazi victory was equally sweeping. Thus, in both the Reich and in its largest State, no popular election may be expected for a long time to come.

In accordance with the promise he gave President von Hindenburg when he was appointed Chancellor, Hitler does not intend to make any effort to rid himself of non-Nazi members of his Cabinet.

HITLER TO DICTATE

"It really does not matter who is at the head of the various ministries so long as we, on the basis of our overwhelming victory, have the right to dictate policies," a Nazi spokesman said.

"In Prussia we intend to claim influence in accordance with our strength. The commissionary government there will disappear and Nazi influence will be predominant."

It is understood that Chancellor Hitler, elected to the Reichstag as the head of the Nazi ticket, will not himself take a seat.

Hermann Goering, Minister Without Portfolio, said one of the first acts of the new Reichstag will be to declare the old imperial black, white and red flag the national colors instead of the republican black, red and gold.

Cermak End Near, Family At Bedside

All Hope Abandoned in Battle to Save Life of Mayor Victim of Assassin

Special to The Chronicle

MIAMI, Fla., March 5—The death of Mayor Cermak of Chicago was imminent tonight. All hope was abandoned for him today when a third blood transfusion failed to produce the beneficial effects hoped for, and shortly before midnight it was stated that he has only a few hours to live.

Around his death bed members of the family congregated late tonight. It was a dramatic scene, with a weird setting.

DAUGHTERS AT BEDSIDE

The Mayor lay gasping on his bed in the small, dimly lit oxygen room, while his three daughters bent over and kissed him. He stared before him with glassy eyes. For a moment he seemed to recognize them and made an effort to speak, but failed.

Mrs. Richey V. Graham, one of the daughters, fainted and was carried from the room. She was revived only to burst into hysterical sobs. The other two spoke to their father. Again he made an effort to talk. They bent low to catch his words.

WHISPERS CHILD'S NAME

"Vivian," he whispered. It was the name of his favorite grandchild, 15 years old, the daughter of Mr. and Mrs. Graham. She was immediately sent for.

Then the sons-in-law entered the oxygen room and stood looking for a moment at the man who meant so much to them and for whom they had conceived a great affection.

Mrs. Roosevelt Makes Jig-Saw Puzzle of Official Etiquette

WASHINGTON, March 5 (AP)—The century-old White House wore a startled air today, as though listening to the sound of shattered precedents.

One day with dynamic Mrs. Franklin D. Roosevelt as mistress, and the pattern of red-tape embroidered official etiquette was snipped into as many pieces as a jig-saw puzzle.

A first lady who greeted her dinner guests at the door, instead of waiting for them to assemble and then make ceremonious descent!

A White House hostess who served tea in the east room!

A President's wife who had invited in the women of the press, with the promise that she'd talk for publication and, who, indeed already had been "interviewed" in her new home!

Washington had never seen the like, and Anna Eleanor Roosevelt's tall figure became symbolic of an exclamation point as the capital dwellers talked of the social transformation that apparently had taken place with the "new deal."

The first function was that afternoon "tea," originally planned for a thousand, but assuming the proportions of a formal reception. Three thousand came—or at least food for that number was consumed.

But Mrs. Roosevelt's tea guests popped in at the front door, to find her standing by the blue room door ready to greet them graciously, to chat with them if it happened that way, to kiss an arriving relative. Tables offering coffee, tea, punch, sandwiches and cakes were spread in three rooms, including the east room, where the gold piano is.

Today's Features

Amusements 5
Book Reviews 7
Bright Sayings of Children 8
Chester Rowell 7
Comics ..... Green 12
Crossword Puzzle 14
Culbertson's Bridge 6
Deaths 7
Dorothy Dix 16
Dr. Evans on Health 6
Editorials 6
Financial 4
Ferry Tales 8
Jane Friendly 16
Looking About 7
Ninon Fashions 16
Radio ..... Green 12
Shipping 4
Society 16
Scotty's Column 7
Sports ..... Sporting Green
Want Ads 14, 15
Women's Club Calendar 14

China Makes Final Stand In Jehol War

Chang Hsiao-Liang Falls Back to Great Wall for Battle

PEIPING, March 5 (AP)—Japanese airplanes today bombed Chinese concentrations at several points in Jehol province as the forces of Marshal Chang Hsiao-liang, North China military leader, fell back to positions a few miles to the north of Koupeikow, a pass through the great wall leading to Southern China.

Jehol City, or Chengtefu, the capital of the northern Chinese province, Jehol, was occupied Saturday by a detachment of 128 Japanese soldiers. Jehol City is less than fifty miles from the Koupeikow pass.

General Sun Tien-ying, Chinese commander who was the defender of Chihfeng, strategic point to the north through which the Japanese swept in their conquest of the province

(Continued on Page 7, Col. 6)

COMPARATIVE TEMPERATURES

	High	Low
San Francisco	62	50
Los Angeles	72	57
Seattle	56	50
Denver	72	46
New York	60	38
Chicago	60	44
Kansas City	76	54
New Orleans	84	68

NRA MEMBER U.S. WE DO OUR PART

San Francisco Chronicle

THE CITY'S ONLY HOME-OWNED NEWSPAPER

NRA MEMBER U.S. WE DO OUR PART

WEATHER IN S. F. BAY REGION Fair and Mild; Overcast in Morning. Complete Weather Report on Page 6c

FOUNDED 1865—VOL. CXLIII, NO. 92 CCC** SAN FRANCISCO, CAL., SUNDAY, OCTOBER 15, 1933 DAILY 5 CENTS, SUNDAY 10 CENTS: DAILY AND SUNDAY PER MONTH, $1.15

TROJANS DEFEAT GAELS 14-7

Germans Quit League, Hitler Defies World, Cries for Arms Slash

Reich Hits Geneva Parley, Plans to Regain Its Equality

Election Called to Prove Backing of People

BERLIN, Oct. 14 (AP)—Germany, declaring inability as a "second-class nation" to participate longer in disarmament negotiations "which thereby could only lead to new dictates," today bluntly gave notice of withdrawal from both the League of Nations and the arms parley.

The German stand was made plain in an appeal to the German people by Chancellor Adolf Hitler and by another issued by the government.

Both minced no words in expressing dissatisfaction with the unwillingness of the other powers to give Germany the arms equality promised at Geneva last December.

REACHES END OF ENDURANCE

"As the Reich's government sees in this manner of procedure a discrimination against the German people, as unjust as it is humiliating," said the Chancellor's declaration, "it deems itself unable under the circumstances as a second-class nation deprived of the rights to continue to participate in the negotiations which thereby could only lead to new dictates."

The Chancellor's appeal spoke of the other nations' demands as "humiliating and dishonoring," but again expressed the German nation's "unshakable will to peace."

CLAIMS TREATIES SECURE

A government spokesman meanwhile hastened to add that "leaving the arms conference in nowise means Germany intends to disregard the treaties."

To provide the German population with a means of expressing their attitude toward the Nazi government of Chancellor Hitler, the Reichstag was dissolved by President Von Hindenburg and new elections set for November 12.

Under the election plan votes for the Nazi member of the Reichstag in effect would mean support for the government's policy.

In explaining this "plebiscite" plan, the Chancellor's declaration also made it clear that the Reich will not "turn a deaf ear to proposals for real peace."

WELCOMES PEACE MOVES

"On the contrary," the Chancellor declared, "she will welcome every suggestion."

The Statthalters, or state Governors, also were ordered to dissolve the state Diets, but no dates for elections to fill those seats immediately were set.

Notice of the German intention to withdraw from the arms parley was telegraphed to Arthur Henderson, the president of the assembly, at Geneva, by Foreign Minister Konstantin von Neurath.

"The last discussions of the participating powers anent disarmament," the Foreign Minister's message said, "have proved conclusively that the Arms Conference will not fulfill the sole task of bringing about a general disarmament.

BLAMES ARMED STATES

"At the same time it is certain that the failure of the Arms Conference is due solely to the lack of the will on the part of the highly armed states now to make good their obligation to disarm, as laid down in treaty.

"Thereby, the realization of Germany's acknowledged claim to equality has been rendered impossible, and the condition under which Germany, the beginning of this year, declared its willingness again to participate in the con-

(Continued on Page 7, Col. 6)

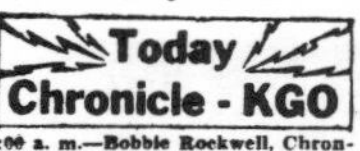

8:00 a. m.—Bobbie Rockwell, Chronicle comics.
9:15 p. m.—Joseph Henry Jackson, Readers' Guide.

Shakes Nations

Adolf Hitler

U.S. Backing Proposal That Led to Break

Washington Stands on Plan for Adjusting Arms Quotas Gradually

WASHINGTON, Oct. 14 (AP)—The United States tonight was disclosed as standing firmly with its onetime allies in opposition to German rearmament and in support of the arms reduction plan which led the Reich to bolt both the Geneva conference and the League of Nations.

This was made clear in a statement that followed official expressions of concern and great disappointment at the Hitler government's sudden action and an assertion by Secretary Hull that the German withdrawal would halt the entire movement toward disarmament.

SEQUEL UNPREDICTABLE

As to the dangers inherent in the determination of Germany to go it alone, neither the Secretary nor his foremost advisers would undertake to predict in the absence of complete official advices from Ambassador Dodd at Berlin concerning the import of the move.

Privately they agreed, however, that the logic of events pointed in a dangerous direction.

BOLT SEEN ARMS DEMAND

Germany apparently had left the arms conference and the league because it was denied the right to planes, light tanks and artillery asserted to be of a defensive character but withheld from Germany under the treaty that ended the World War.

Therefore, there was seen at least a possibility that Germany, having now abandoned diplomatic methods, might go ahead and acquire the weapons anyway.

CANNOT USE IT TO ARM

In direct language, the Roosevelt administration asserted its position that "a disarmament convention could not properly be made an instrument for rearmament and that qualitative equality in armaments should primarily be sought through the reduction in the armaments of the heavily armed powers and not through acts on the part of others to attempt to build up."

The statement of policy read to a private session of the Geneva conference by Ambassador at Large Norman H. Davis and made public by the State Department, added that German equality in armaments "cannot be achieved at one stroke" and "under present conditions, steps are necessary" for its attainment.

On behalf of the United States,

(Continued on Page 7, Col. 3)

Let All Nations Discard Weapons, Chancellor Demands

France Is Not Foe, Reds Nazis' Only Enemy

BERLIN, Oct. 14 (AP)—Chancellor Adolf Hitler in a worldwide speech tonight rapped the treaty of Versailles, reiterated that Germany was not responsible for the World war, thanked the French Premier for "the noble sense of justice" contained in a recent speech and declared there is little or no possibility of conflict between the two nations.

"After the return of the Saar territory to the Reich," said the Chancellor, "only a crazy man" could believe a war between the two countries possible.

MARCH TO CURB REDS

Hitler, replying directly to questions of the French Premier Edouard Daladier, as to why "the German youth marches," said:

"I reply, not to demonstrate against France, but to show its determination to keep communism down."

The army, said the Chancellor, is the only organization which bears arms in Germany, adding the explanation that the only enemy of the Nazis is communism.

At the same time the speaker declared Germany is ready to go to the limit in disarmament, but warned that the Reich demand for equality, if other nations are to be armed, must not be sidetracked.

READY TO DISARM

"If the world decides to remove all weapons to the last machine gun," the speaker said emphatically, Germany will fall in line, and the same applies to certain other categories of weapons.

"He warned, however, that if certain weapons are allotted to other powers, the German nation is not ready "to permit ourselves to be excluded therefrom as a nation of inferior rights."

The Chancellor furthermore said there was no possibility of territorial conflict with Germany's neighbor, France, as far as the Reich is concerned, for "after the return of the Saar territory to the Reich only a "crazy man could think" such a conflict possible.

CASTS ASIDE WAR BLAME

The Chancellor also bitterly assailed the treaty of Versailles and reiterated the conviction of the German people that they were not to blame for the World war.

Discussing the close of the Great war when the German people "in trustful faith and in the assurance of President Wilson's 14 points" lowered their arms, the Chancellor said:

"The people could fully have

(Continued on Page 7, Col. 2)

Two-Story Fall Kills Girl, 22

Victim Found on Sidewalk; Expires

Miss Erminie Bassetti, 22, was fatally injured last night when she jumped from the roof of a house at 1631 Cabrillo street.

The girl's body was found in the driveway of the Cabrillo street address by Edward Lawson, the owner, when he returned and started to enter the garage.

She was rushed to the Park Emergency Hospital, but died from a fractured skull shortly after arrival.

According to police, she was employed as a maid at the home of Arthur Blumenthal, 1623 Cabrillo street. She crawled from the bathroom window of the Blumenthal home to the Lawson roof adjoining. The girl came here four weeks ago from Williams, where her parents own a ranch.

Rossi Flays Uhl 'Attempt At Boss Rule'

Lafayette Club Hears Bristling Answers to Attack on Administration

Colleagues on Supervisor Ticket Held Rubber Stamps

By EARL C. BEHRENS

In a bristling answer to an attack upon the administration by Adolph Uhl, Mayor Rossi last night assailed Uhl as attempting to create a "rule by boss" in San Francisco policies and branded Uhl's colleagues on the latter's ticket for Supervisor "as rubber stamps."

The Rossi-Uhl spat occurred at what up to that time had been a very calm and sedate banquet, high jinks and reunion of the Lafayette Club at Scottish Rite Hall.

LAUNCHES COUNTER ATTACK

Aroused by Uhl's statement that "a $2,000,000 saving can be made at the City Hall by adopting ordinary business methods," and by charges that violations of the charter were being permitted by nonresident employes, the Mayor took the platform and vigorously launched a counter attack.

The Mayor characterized some of Uhl's charges and statements "as an insult to your intelligence."

Uhl had criticized the handling of unemployment relief, the use of water department funds for reducing the tax rate and had declared that the claims of incumbent Supervisors that they were responsible for the tax reduction were fallacious. Uhl claimed that the sales tax refunds from the State for support of the schools and other revenues were responsible for the cut in the taxes.

SPEAKERS YIELD TIME

When Uhl appeared on the platform he was accompanied by his colleagues, John M. Ratto, Dr. Adolph Schmidt, Charles T. Phillips and Frank B. Lorigan. The others yielded their time to Uhl. This brought forth the Rossi charge that Uhl was attempting to make himself a boss and dictate to his group.

"I do not control nor attempt to dictate to any member of the Board of Supervisors," Rossi declared with much heat.

The Mayor defended his administration, declaring that "you have a business administration and that's why you have a balanced bulget."

500 ATTEND AFFAIR

More than 500 members of the Lafayette Club and their guests gathered for the annual affair last night. Edmond P. Bergerot, Deputy City Attorney, was toastmaster.

Members of the judiciary, holdover officials and the various candidates were given a hearing. Among those who spoke were City Attorney O'Toole, Treasurer Matheson, Charles J. Gavin Jr., Neil Hickey, Municipal Judges Prendergast, Steiger and Lazarus; Allen Spivock, Harold J. Boyd, and the candidates for Supervisor. Among the letter were Supervisors Canepa, Hayden, Spaulding, Stanton, Miles, Peyser and McSheehy; Louise Todd, John P. Courter, John G. Lawlor, L. Raymond Holmes, Sam McKee, Charles S. Delany, Walter G. Remley and others.

Martial Law Faces Cotton Strike Area

Pickers Vote Solidly to Stay Out; Will Call State Troops Says Commissioner

Workers Stage Martyr Funeral, Then Denounce 'Ruse'

By CLIFFORD FOX
Chronicle Staff Writer

TULARE, Oct. 14.—The threat of military law hung over the strike-torn cotton fields of the San Joaquin valley tonight.

With striking cotton pickers voting solidly to stay "out" until their demands are met, Edward H. Fitzgerald, U. S. commissioner of conciliation, virtually admitted that State troops will be called in unless strikers return to work pending arbitration of their difficulties.

Although publicly voicing confidence that the strike would be settled speedily, Commissioner Fitzgerald and State labor officials said they are greatly worried over the gravity of the situation.

MARTYR'S FUNERAL HELD

Following a spectacular "martyr's funeral" for Delores Hernandez, slain striker, 3000 cotton pickers branded efforts to get them to return to work pending mediation as a subterfuge on the part of cotton planters, and voted to remain on strike until their demands are met.

They are asking $1 a hundred pounds wages, as against 60 cents per hundred offered by the cotton growers.

Strikers expressed bitter resentment against what they termed propaganda of Federal and State officials, who announced earlier in the day that the strike had been settled.

[illegible]

At the same time representatives of the growers expressed dissatisfaction with the mediation board appointed by Governor Rolph and NRA Commissioner George Creel of the Western district. The committee, comprised of Archbishop Edward J. Hanna, Professor O. K. McMurray of the University of California and Dr. Tully Knoles, president of the College of the Pacific, is not sufficiently conversant with conditions in the cotton belt to mediate the difficulties, many growers maintain.

This was the information forwarded Governor Rolph in a confidential telegram from State Farm Bureau representatives in the field here.

Commissioner Fitzgerald, however, announced tonight that the authorized committee of cotton growers had accepted arbitration, and are satisfied with the committee as named.

CITES DUTY OF ALL

"It therefore," Fitzgerald declared, "becomes the duty of the striking pickers to proceed with the picking of California's cotton crop, subject to the decision of the Federal-State Arbitration Commission's findings and decisions.

"It is also the duty of the cotton growers to reemploy the cotton pickers who have been on strike.

"The Federal Government and the State of California will undertake to furnish food, clothing, and, if necessary, medical attention to cotton pickers and their families

Continued on Page 3, Col. 3

Sunnyvale Set to Greet Air Queen in Afternoon

Residents of all Bay Cities will probably have an excellent view of the giant navy dirigible Macon today, it was reported at the Sunnyvale base last night.

LOG OF THE MACON

Thursday, 6:05 p. m.—Weighs off at Lakehurst, N. J.
Friday, 8:30 a. m.—Passed over Macon, Ga., city for which she is named.
Saturday, 9 a. m.—Entered New Mexico, slightly west of El Paso, Texas.
Saturday, 12:30 p. m. (Mountain time)—Passed Safford, Ariz., following Gila river west.
Saturday, 3:30 p. m.—Again passed over Safford, turned back 90 miles by formidable Mescal mountains.
Saturday, 5:05 p. m.—Passed over Phoenix.
Saturday, 8:35 p. m.—Passed over Gila Bend.
Saturday, 10:55 p. m.—Passed over Yuma.
Saturday, 11:07 p. m. (Pacific time)—Passed near El Centro.
Sunday noon—Due over San Francisco.

The Macon will arrive here about noon, according to schedule, but will remain in the air until 4 p. m. before mooring.

DIRIGIBLE FORCED BACK

The navy's newest queen of the skies strayed from its course into the Arizona mountains and was forced to turn back 90 miles, according to Associated Press dispatches from Safford, Ariz.

After following the Southern Pacific railroad mainline into Arizona from New Mexico, the dirigible turned north at Bowie, junction of the mainline and the Globe branch. It followed the branch line to Safford and went on to Coolidge dam, where it circled over San Carlos lake for half an hour.

CLIMB AVOIDED

The dirigible than turned back, its commander apparently deciding against an attempt to climb over the Mescal mountains.

Safford again saw the big ship at 3:30 p. m. heading south for Bowie and the main line of the railroad, which it could follow west, approximately along the southern air mail

(Continued on Page 9, Col. 2)

U.S.C. Converts Two St. Mary's Penalties Into Winning Scores

Many East Grid Games See Big Victor's Scores

U. S. C. 14, St. Mary's 7.
Stanford 0, Northwestern 0.
California 23, Olympic Club 0.
Oregon State 12, U. S. F. 7.
Yale 14, Wash. and Lee 0.
Army 52, Delaware 0.
Princeton 45, Williams 0.
Pittsburgh 34, Navy 6.
Pennsylvania 9, Franklin-Marshall 0.
Fordham 20, W. Virginia 0.
Columbia 15, Virginia 6.
Colgate 25, Rutgers 2.
Ohio State 20, Vanderbilt 0.
Michigan 40, Cornell 0.
Georgia 30, N. Carolina 0.

Fred Canrinus Scores on 32-Yard Pass, Ties Count 7-7, While 88,000 Watch

Troy Registers 26th Win, but Moragans Force Gruelling Play

By HARRY B. SMITH
Chronicle Sports Editor

LOS ANGELES COLISEUM, Oct. 14—A crowd of more than 80,000, the largest ever attending a noncoference game in these parts, watched the St. Mary's Gaels go fighting down to defeat this afternoon at the hands of a Southern California team by a score of 14 to 7.

Defeat though it was for the Northern Californians, it was by no means disgrace, and their thousands of supporters who followed them from the San Francisco area were almost as pleased as if the Moragans had tucked that game away for themselves, as they did a couple of years ago.

STANFORD HELD SCORELESS

Stanford University's football team was held to a scoreless tie by Northwestern University at Chicago yesterday. Stanford's most promising scoring threat was halted by the half time gun, just after Bill Sim carried the ball to Northwestern's 1-yard line.

The victory was the twenty-sixth consecutive one registered by the sons of Troy.

PENALTIES AID U. S. SCORES

Penalties aided the Trojans materially in their first period touchdown, when they started a drive from the middle of the field that, aided by twenty yards handed them for offside and unnecessary roughness, netted them the first score of the afternoon.

And later, just after the Gaels, thanks to a passing attack, had tied the score, another penalty—because Big Ed Gilbert, thrown in the fray, was charged with doing some talking—saw the Gael team losing 15 yards at a critical stage in the game and then remain helpless as the Trojans drove their last nine yards for the touchdown that gave them the coveted honors.

TALK IS MYSTERY

Just what Gilbert, reinforced by a huge shoulder pad that Dr. Gyinan brought all the way from San Francisco, said, nobody knows. Just why he should have talked, with his team on the defensive and backed up on their own 26-yard line, is another of those posers we can only wonder about.

But talk he did, evidently, for the officials marched the Trojans 15 yards closer to the goal line and the U. S. C. boys were nine yards to go for the winning touchdown.

GOING HAD BEEN TOUGH

It was just the touch they needed. The going had been none too easy for the Howard Jones team and even Homer Griffith, who had been shining all afternoon at quarter, found it more and more difficult to gain his yardage.

Then Gilbert talked the ball down the field and after that, with spirit renewed, the U. S. C. men carried it

(Continued on Page 12, Col. 4)

Fresno Wife Hunted for Gold Hoard

Fugitive Warrant Issued for Woman Accused of Holding $85,000 Coin, Notes

Charged in a Federal warrant with hoarding $85,000 in gold coin and certificates, Mrs. Effie L. Martin, wife of a wealthy Fresno county vineyardist, was being sought by Department of Justice agents here last night on a fugitive warrant.

The case marks the Pacific Coast's first charge under President Roosevelt's ban against gold hoarding issued last August and the second on record in the United States, it was declared.

WOMAN LEAVES HOTEL

Mrs. Martin was reported to have left the Hotel Oakland for the week-end with her son, John D. Martin Jr., Oakland attorney.

The complaint against Mrs. Martin, wife of J. D. Martin, 120 North Fulton street, Fresno, was filed yesterday by United States Commissioner Samuel F. Hollins at Fresno at the request of a special agent for the United States Department of Justice. Later a fugitive warrant for her arrest was issued by U. S. Commissioner Ernest E. Williams in San Francisco.

DEMANDS REFUSED

Assistant U. S. Attorney Jack Powell at Fresno said that the issuance of the warrant culminated an investigation of several months by Department of Justice agents and declared numerous demands had been made upon Mrs. Martin to tur over the gold.

The hoarded gold, Federal agents said, is being kept in a San Francisco safety deposit box.

Her hearing at Fresno has been set for 10:30 Saturday morning. Her bond was fixed at $5000.

Did You Hear Those Explosions? Shake!

Police stations and newspaper offices were swamped with telephone calls in frightened voices at 1 a. m. today—voices wanting to know whether the Macon had arrived in the night and exploded over the city, or an earthquake was in progress, or we'd gone to war.

The calls came from all Bay Cities.

The people learned that night blasting was in progress on the Golden Gate bridge construction—and went back to sleep.

Oregon Chief Faces Recall

Petition Filed Charging Governor Unfit

SALEM, Or., Oct. 14 (AP)—A preliminary copy of a recall petition charging general neglect of duty was filed against Governor Julius L. Meier here today.

F. W. Stevens of Goldson, Lane county, filed the petition with Secretary of State Hal E. Hoss.

The Stevens petition declared that Meier "is utterly devoid of that leadership necessary to the office of Governor," that the "real duties of the office of Governor * * have been left to persons whom the people have not selected * * the incompetency of (the Governor) and his inattention to duties * * have placed the State * * in an impossible condition," and that "for the reasons above set forth, the welfare of the State of Oregon demands the recall."

Police Chief Tired, Demoted at Request

BAKERSFIELD, Oct. 14 (AP)—Saying he was tired of the turmoil of his job, Police Chief Font Webster resigned today and asked City Manager Fred Nighbert to demote him to the rank of patrolman—which Nighbert did.

Today's Features

Amusements ....Special Section
Art ....Drama 3
Aunt Dolly ....Society 8
Automobiles ....Special Section
Books ....Drama 4
Comics ....Comic Section
Contract Contacts.....Main News 8
Crosswords ....Main News 11
Culbertson's Bridge ....Autos 4
Deaths ....Main News 12
Fashions ....Society 9
Ferry Tales ....Main News 11
Financial 13, 14, 15
Wm. P. Golden ....Autos 4
Magazine ....Special Section
Music ....Drama 3
Ninon ....Society 6
Radio ....Main News 12
Rotogravure ....Special Section
Shipping ....Classified 8
Society ....Society Section
Sports ....Sporting Green
Veterans' News ....Autos 4
Wants Ads ....Special Section
Washington-Merry-Go-Round ....Main News 8
Will Rogers ....Drama 4
Women's Clubs......Society 7, 8, 10
World Topics..Tabloid Special Sec.

Siam Rebels Driven Back With Losses

Two Airplanes Shot Down; Battle Now Rages on City Outskirts

Government Artillery Roars Without Let Up

BANGKOK, Siam, Oct. 14 (AP)—The Siamese government, besieged by rebellious forces which reached the outskirts of the city smashed back today in a counter attack which was officially described as victorious.

Official communiques said the government forces had recaptured the Donmuang Airdrome, the headquarters of the royal aeronautical service, which were taken two days ago by rebels unde the command of Prince Bovaredej, a member of the royal family and former Defense Minister of the nation.

ARTILLERY ACTIVE

Government artillery roared all night in the counter attack, which ended in a rebel retreat. Official communiques did not state that the rebellion had been suppressed, but merely that the government was confident it would be able to subdue the rebellion.

The rebel casualties were heavy, said announcements, which also reported that many persons were injured in minor clashes.

Air fighting occupied a spectacular part in the day's battle.

Two airplanes circling the city were shot down in the river, one of them crashing directly in front of the royal palace.

Three flyers of the royal aeronautical service won immediate pro-

(Continued on Page 2, Col. 3)

EXTRA

COMPARATIVE TEMPERATURES

	High	Low
San Francisco	68	52
Los Angeles	72	61
Seattle	56	46
Denver	70	36
New York	56	44
Chicago	32	32
Kansas City	54	38
New Orleans	65	54

San Francisco Chronicle

THE CITY'S ONLY HOME-OWNED NEWSPAPER

WEATHER
IN S. F. BAY REGION
Cloudy, Cooler
Complete Weather Report on Page 21

FOUNDED 1865—VOL. CXLIII. NO. 135 CCC •• SAN FRANCISCO, CAL., MONDAY, NOVEMBER 27, 1933 DAILY 5 CENTS, SUNDAY 10 CENTS: DAILY AND SUNDAY PER MONTH, $1.10

KIDNAPERS LYNCHED!

Mob Storms Jail, Hangs Slayers in San Jose Square

Avengers of Hart Defy Tear Gas Bombs to Drag Thurmond and Holmes From Cells to Death

By ROYCE BRIER
Chronicle Staff Writer

SAN JOSE, Nov. 26—Lynch law wrote the last grim chapter in the Brooke Hart kidnaping here tonight.

Twelve hours after the mutilated body of the son of Alex J. Hart, wealthy San Jose merchant, was recovered from San Francisco bay a mob of 10,000 infuriated men and women stormed the Stanta Clara County Jail, dragged John M. Holmes and Thomas H. Thurmond from their cells and hanged them in historic St. James Park.

Swift, and terrible to behold, was the retribution meted out to the confessed kidnapers and slayers. As the pair were drawn up, threshing in the throes of death, a mob of thousands of men and women and children screamed anathemas at them.

HOWLING MOB BESIEGES JAIL

The siege of the County Jail, a three-hour whirling, howling drama of lynch law, was accomplished without serious injury either to the seizers or the 35 officers who vainly sought to defend the citadel.

The defense of the jail failed because Sheriff Emig and his forces ran out of tear gas bombs. Bombs kept the determined mob off for several hours.

Help from San Francisco and Oakland officers arrived too late to save the Hart slayers.

HOLMES PLEADS AGAINST HANGING

"Don't string me up, boys. God, don't string me up," was the last cry of Holmes as the noose was put about his neck in the light of flash lamps.

Thurmond was virtually unconscious with terror as the mob hustled him from the jail, down the alley and across the street to his doom.

Great cheers from the crowd of onlookers accompanied the hoisting of the two slayers. Some women fainted, some were shielded from the sight by their escorts, but the gamut of human nature was here in the park. Old women with graying hair and benign faces expressing satisfaction at the quick end of the murderers, and young women with hardened faces broke down and wept.

KING MOB TAKES LAW TO ITSELF

King Mob was in the saddle and he was an inexorable ruler.

And here was a sovereign whose rise in invincible power stunned San Jose and will stun the Nation and the world.

Brooke Hart's torn body was found in the water this morning. Barricades went up before the County Jail and the crowd gathered and stayed all the day. It was a good natured crowd. It knew the deputies and the police and the State highway patrolmen who stood guard. It bandied words with them.

There had been talk of an organized mob, and as the crowd grew in the evening there was no organization. There was shouting, and good nature still ruled.

"This crowd won't do anything," was the constant reiteration of Sheriff Emig's deputies.

Yet as their words of confidence were being spoken there flashed, like a prairie fire, the word through San Jose—11 o'clock! 11 o'clock!

The constant bombardment of that hour on the ear was monotonous and ominous.

(Continued on Page B, Col. 3)

PORTALS OF DOOM CRACKED!

The fall of the Santa Clara County Jail after a determined siege of three stormy hours by a howling mob of 10,000 persons. Heavy iron pipes were used for battering rams to smash in the jail door as officers inside the building hurled tear gas bombs from upper windows at the besiegers. The mob fought on blindly with eyes burning from the gas.
Associated Press photo.

Deputy Tells Own Tale of Fight in Jail

Following is an eyewitness story by one of the officers participating in the struggle, of what happened inside the Santa Clara County Jail after the mob broke in to seize and lynch Jack Holmes and Thomas Thurmond, slayers of Brooke L. Hart, last night.

By DEPUTY SHERIFF JOHN MOORE

The inside of the County Jail was fogged with tear gas when the mob rushed in behind a battering ram. Most of the windows were broken and all but a few dim lights were out.

I was standing on the stairs, inside the second steel mesh door, with Deputy Sheriffs Earle Hamilton and Howard Buffington. We had only a few gas bombs left and we knew they had us.

They began battering down that second door—our last hope—and we waited. When they came through we gave them two more bombs but they charged through the cloud of smoke as though it were fog.

TRUSTIES PERILED

Just then some of the trusties on the third floor started to come down above us, trying to escape and not knowing they were headed right for that mob. I shouted for them to go back and promised them that no innocent man would be hanged.

The mob brushed past us to Holmes' cell on the second floor, and four men stood me against a wall, searched me and took my keys. Then they went in for Holmes, who was hiding in the lavatory of his cell.

He came out crying, "I'm not Holmes! I'm not Holmes!" — but one of the lynchers rushed up and grabbed him by the neck and told him to shut up.

Another man stepped up to Holmes and said, "The hell you're

(Continued on Page D, Col. 8)

Hell Rips Loose--Women Laugh--Women Sob and Cheer On Frenzied Mob

By CAROLYN ANSPACHER
Chronicle Staff Writer

SAN JOSE, Nov. 26—Hell turned loose here tonight and women laughed.

Their laughter and cries rose shrilly above the shouts of the men of an avenging mob as two men were hanged by their necks until they were dead.

From the heavy boughs of darkened trees in St. James Park, across the street from the Courthouse and County Jail, John M. Holmes and Thomas H. Thurmond, the confessed slayers of Brooke Hart, paid for their crime at the hands of a howling mob.

HUNDREDS ARE WOMEN

Hundreds of that mob were women. Old women, young women and girls in their teens.

Not all the women laughed. Some fainted. Some of the laughter was hysterical. They knew not what they did.

Women milled with the men and surged around the gas-infested courtyard of the little jail. And when Thurmond and Holmes were seized from their jailers and dragged to their doom women followed and were in at the finish.

Earlier many of them had whispered words of encouragement to the men—egged them on.

"I hope they hang them. This is one case where I believe in lynch law."

All evening long, as the mob of thousands massed in front of the jail, which later was stormed and captured when the guards' supply of tear gas bombs ran out, this admonition was heard from many feminine lips.

RECALL HART'S FATE

During the day they had recalled Brooke Hart's fate, stirring their men folk on to taking the law into their own hands.

A few of the hundreds of women who witnessed the lynching tonight as if it had been a garden fete, yielded to feminine impulses. Some wept softly. Others shrieked.

Still others dropped soundlessly to the gray sidewalks and on the lawns and there were forgotten by all save their male attendants. There were women there without men. And if they fainted, that was just too bad.

But others among the women all but danced around the death trees. They hurled maledictions against the dying men. They clawed at their dangling bodies like avenging furies.

The scene was like the hell of Dante—the awful avenging hell of the New Testament—a hell peopled by women.

FORGOT COUNSELING

Many of these women were gently bred and for days had been counseling that the law be permitted to take its course.

Then, as the rising tide of frenzy grew higher, and steel smashed with resounding and implacable force against the brick walls of the little red brick jail, there came a metamorphosis.

It was amazing—as if a magician had waved his wand over the gathering.

These gentle, timid housewives and stenographers and ranchers' wives, these debutantes and subdebs and school girls, seemed to hear the voice of Mephisto himself.

DROP ALL REFINEMENT

From them dropped all vestige of refinement. They became beings who were guided by instinct rather than by thought.

Impelled by the Biblical edict of "an eye for an eye, a tooth for a tooth," they cast their robes of femininity from them and roared their approval of the fate meted

(Continued on Page A, Col. 7)

Rolph Calls Mob Action Best Lesson

SACRAMENTO, Nov. 26 (AP) — When Governor Rolph was advised tonight the slayer-kidnapers of Brooke L. Hart had been lynched in San Jose he said: "This is the best lesson that California has ever given the country. We show the country that the State is not going to tolerate kidnaping."

The Governor was in the executive mansion when he was told Thomas L. Thurmond and John Holmes had been taken from the Santa Clara Jail by a mob and lynched. He said E. Raymond Cato, chief of the California Highway Patrol, and Theodore Roche of San Francisco, director of the State Department of Motor Vehicles, had telephoned to him the men had been lynched.

Before he received word of the lynching, while the mob was being repulsed with tear gas bombs, the Governor had canceled his airplane flight to Boise, Idaho, where he was going to attend a conference of Western Governors. The airplane was due to leave Sacramento about 10 minutes after the lynching occurred.

"I want to be on the job," the Governor said in giving a reason for postponing his air flight. He also said when he announced he was not going to leave the State tonight that Sheriff William Emig of Santa Clara had been trying to reach him by telephone.

If conditions are normal in San Jose by tomorrow night the Governor said he will depart for Boise by airplane.

Rabied Mouse Bite Fatal to Boy, 14

ADA, Okla., Nov. 26 (AP)—Bitten by a mouse, William Ryan Coopedge, 14, died here today of rabies.

Kidnap Victim's Body Found in Bay by Hunters

Intensive Search for Murdered Youth's Remains Terminated by Chance; Knife, Tape Aid Identification

The body of Brooke Hart, 22, slain November 9, by kidnapers seeking to mulct his father, wealthy San Jose merchant, of $40,000 in a fantastic plot, was recovered yesterday from San Francisco bay. It was found floating in five feet of water about a mile west of the Alameda shore and half a mile south of the San Mateo-Hayward bridge by two duck hunters.

Removed to a branch morgue at Hayward, it was identified by friends of the dead youth and by department heads of the Hart Department Store, of which he had recently been made a vice president by his father, Alex J. Hart.

Because of the condition of the body after 17 days in the water identification was established by the clothing, by a pearl handle knife found in the clothing and by the fact that the right foot was wrapped in tape. The torso and head of the victim were practically a skeleton.

The chance find terminated a search that had called into play all the agencies of four counties and the assistance of the Government—a search employing divers, Coast Guard boats, airplanes and even a navy blimp.

Climaxes Long Search

The discovery of the body, for which a reward of $500 was recently offered by Brooke Hart's father, was made shortly after 9 o'clock by Leonard L. Dalve, a civil engineer, 628 Maple street, Redwood City, and Harold E. Stephens, Redwood City store proprietor, living at 174 Jeter street.

The two were in a skiff and were hunting ducks. They had started out from an Alvarado duck club on the Alameda shore at daylight, having slept at the club the night before.

Tow Body Ashore

They sighted the body floating about 400 feet from their small boat and at first thought it was a seal. Moving closer, they realized they had undoubtedly come upon the body for whom hundreds had been making a systematic search since November 16, when Holmes and Thurmond, captured in an elaborate trap, made their astounding confession.

Wrapping the body in a piece of canvas the two duck hunters towed it to a peninsula of mud on the Alameda shore.

Officials Notified

Making their way on foot through deep mud the discoverers notified a traffic officer, who immediately telephoned Sheriff M. B. Driver of Alameda county and Coroner Grant D. Miller.

Within a few minutes these officials and others, including Sheriff Emig of Santa Clara county and Sheriff James J. McGrath of San Mateo county,

(Continued on Page A, Col. 1)

COMPARATIVE TEMPERATURES	High	Low
San Francisco	56	46
Los Angeles	68	48
Honolulu	80	71
Seattle	50	44
Denver	32	24
New York	44	34
Chicago	44	40
New Orleans	82	64

NRA U.S. WE DO OUR PART

San Francisco Chronicle

THE CITY'S ONLY HOME-OWNED NEWSPAPER

WEATHER IN S. F. BAY REGION: Cloudy and Unsettled. Complete Weather Report on Page 8

FOUNDED 1865—VOL. CXLIII. NO. 144 CCC* SAN FRANCISCO, CAL., WEDNESDAY, DECEMBER 6, 1933 DAILY 5 CENTS, SUNDAY 10 CENTS

Prohibition Wiped Out; Canada Rum Approved To Meet Big Demands

Medicinal Liquor Also Will Be Released for Beverage

Utah's Vote Ends 14 Years of Dry Rule

WASHINGTON, Dec. 5 (AP)—Prohibition today was wiped from the constitution.

With a dash of ceremony, Utah late today wrote an end to the dry law in a decree that opened the doors of liquor shops in 18 States.

Almost half a dozen other States were completing plans for legalizing sale under their own laws. The remainder of the Nation remained dry.

FLASHED TO CAPITAL

Word that Utah—the 36th State—had ratified repeal was flashed to the capital a few hours after Pennsylvania and Ohio. A little later the final formalities were completed with the issuance of proclamations by the State Department and President Roosevelt declaring prohibition at an end.

There was little ceremony at the signing of the presidential or the State Department proclamation, but in wet States and some dry ones there were celebrations.

CONTROL RULE READY

Nearly 14 years of alcoholic draught, enforced by the 18th amendment of World war day inception, was ended by the Utah vote.

It found the Federal Government prepared to control the flow of liquor in wet States, through a virtual dictatorship over the industry, and to protect the arid ones.

Several of the 18 States where liquor could be sold immediately, however, were without regulations.

SUPPLY RESTRICTED

Repeal celebrations, however, found liquor supplies for immediate consumption restricted in some sections.

In a hurried effort to meet the demand and thereby thwart the bootlegger, the Government today decided to allow large importations of American type bourbon and rye whiskies from Canada. It also planned to release for beverage purposes medicinal liquors held in bonded warehouses and customs houses.

A move of the International Reform Federation to block the issuance of the repeal proclamation was turned down in District of Columbia Supreme Court, when Justice F. Dickinson Letts rejected a petition filed by Canon William Sheafe Chase of Brooklyn, N. Y., on the ground there was no basis for the action.

He ruled repeal was effective upon ratification by the 36th State and not through the proclamation.

Repeal was brought about through the convention system, authorized under the constitution, but used for the first time in this case.

FIRST TO LOSE

The eighteenth amendment is the first to be rejected from the constitution.

Thirty-three States, beginning with Michigan, had ratified the twenty-first amendment previously. Pennsylvania's delegates were the first to ratify today. Ohio soon followed. Utah had determined to have the 36th position.

To assure itself of it being the final State, the delegates had

(Continued on Page 9, Col. 2)

Here Is Proclamation Ending Rule of Dry Law

WASHINGTON, Dec. 5 (AP)—The text of President Roosevelt's repeal proclamation follows:

Whereas the Congress of the United States in 2d session of the 72d Congress, begun at Washington on the fifth day of December in the year one thousand nine hundred and thirty-two, adopted a resolution in the words and figures following, to wit:

JOINT RESOLUTION

Proposing an amendment to the constitution of the United States.

Resolved by the Senate and House of Representatives of the United States of America in congress assembled (two-thirds of each House concurring therein), that the following article is hereby proposed as an amendment to the constitution of the United States, which shall be valid to all intents and purposes as part of the constitution when ratified by conventions in three-fourths of the States:

"Article—

"Section 1. The eighteenth article of amendment to the constitution of the United States is hereby repealed.

"Section 2. The transportation or importation into any State, Territory or possession of the United States for delivery or use therein of intoxicating liquors, in violation of the laws thereof, is hereby prohibited.

"Section 3. This article shall be inoperative unless it shall have been ratified as an amendment to the constitution by conventions in the several States, as provided in the constitution, within seven years from the date of the submission hereof to the States by the Congress."

Whereas section 217 (A) of the act of Congress entitled "an act to encourage national industrial recovery to foster competition, and to provide for the construction of certain useful public works, and for other purposes," approved June 16, 1933, provides as follows:

Sec. 217 (a). The President shall proclaim the date of:

(1) The close of the first fiscal year ending June 30 of any year after the year 1933, during which the total receipts of the United States (excluding public debt receipts) exceed its total expenditures (excluding public debt expenditures other than those chargeable against such receipts), or

(2) The repeal of the eighteenth amendment to the constitution, whichever is the earlier."

Whereas it appears from a certificate issued December 5, 1933, by the Acting Secretary of State that official notices have been received in the Department of State that on the fifth day of December, 1933, conventions in thirty-six States of the United States, constituting three-fourths of the whole number of the States had ratified the said repeal amendment;

Now, therefore, I, Franklin D. Roosevelt, President of the United States of America, pursuant to the provisions of section 217 (A) of the said act of June 16, 1933, do hereby proclaim that the eighteenth amendment to the constitution of the United States was repealed on the fifth day of December, 1933.

Furthermore, I enjoin upon all citizens of the United States and upon others resident within the jurisdiction thereof, to cooperate with the Government in its endeavors to restore greater respect for law and order, by confining such purchases of alcoholic beverages as they may make solely to those dealers or agencies which have been duly licensed by State or Federal license.

Observance of this request, which I make personally to every individual and every family in our Nation, will result in the consumption of alcoholic beverages which have passed Federal inspection, in the break up and eventual destruction of the notoriously evil illicit liquor traffic and in the payment of reasonable taxes for the support of government and thereby in the superseding of other forms of taxation.

I call specific attention to the authority given by the 21st amendment to the Government to prohibit transportation or importation of intoxicating liquors into any State in violation of the laws of such State.

I ask the wholehearted cooperation of all our citizens to the end that this return of individual freedom shall not be accompanied by the repugnant conditions that obtained prior to the adoption of the eighteenth amendment and those that have existed since its adoption. Failure to do this honestly and courageously will be a living reproach to us all.

I ask especially that no State shall by law or otherwise authorize the return of the saloon either in its old form or in some modern guise.

The policy of the Government will be to see to it that the social and political evils that have existed in the pre-prohibition era shall not be revived nor permitted again to exist. We must remove forever from our midst the menace of the bootlegger and such others as would profit at the expense of good government, law and order.

I trust in the good sense of the American people that they will not bring upon themselves the curse of excessive use of intoxicating liquors, to the detriment of health, morals and social integrity.

The objective we seek through a national policy is the education of every citizen towards a greater temperance throughout the Nation.

In witness whereof, I have hereunto set my hand and caused the seal of the United States to be affixed.

Done at the city of Washington this fifth day of December, in the year of our Lord, nineteen hundred and thirty-three, and of the independence of the United States of America the one hundred and fifty-eighth.

By the President,

By the Secretary of State.

Will Rogers Says:

BEVERLY HILLS, Dec. 5—Editor The Chronicle: Talk about the "noble experiment." "The noble experiment" is just starting. Every State is in doubt as to how their liquor will be handled. Say it's not how the State will handle its liquor, it's how the folks will handle theirs. States are going to have a scandal over the sale of it, and politicians will fight over the taxes on it. But anyhow, the first week will be the hardest. Yours,

WILL ROGERS.

High-Power Tag Fixing Jails Man for 3 Months in Cotati

The alleged combined efforts of the State Treasurer's office, a secretary to the Governor, the Mayor of Petaluma and the attorneys of a railroad to "fix" a traffic tag yesterday put Walter Emes, 53, in the Sonoma County Jail for three months and cost him just $250!

It was Justice of the Peace Harry Richardson's way of showing the "high pressure boys" that Cotati, where men are still men, is one place where a traffic tag is a traffic

(Continued on Page 2, Column 3)

Repeal Flash Starts Bulk Sale in State

Bars Prohibited, Serving Minors Banned, With New Legal Tangles in Prospect

Rolph Ponders Special Session to Smooth Out Snarls

By EARL C. BEHRENS

SACRAMENTO, Dec. 5—California's official machinery for the control of licensing and regulation of liquor sales started without a single creak a few minutes after Utah ended national prohibition this afternoon.

With thousands of applications for liquor sale licenses pouring into offices of the State Board of Equalization, the body which administers California's liquor control law, legalized sale of liquor was begun in all parts of the State.

ISSUE TO BE SPEEDED

Formal licenses will be issued during the next few days.

As Governor Rolph sat in his office in the capital and awaited word from Utah that the end of the national dry law had been voted, members of the Equalization Board, headed by Chairman Richard E. Collins and Fred E. Stewart, prepared instructions to the enforcement officers representing the board.

TWO BASIC INSTRUCTIONS

Two principal instructions were given out:

No hard liquor sales are to be permitted over bars.

Sales to minors not to be tolerated.

While the State set machinery in operation to enforce provisions of the liquor act passed by the last Legislature, in conformity with the amendment to the constitution approved by the voters last November, moves were made in various directions to begin initiative campaigns to change the law, now only a few hours in operation.

Opposing groups, however, may force a worse tangle in the California liquor law than now exists.

Wine men reiterated their disinclination to support the initiative which the hotel men, cafe, restaurant and kindred interests expect to have out for voters' signatures Friday.

Edmund Rossi, speaking for the wine men, declared that his group had not been consulted in the framing of the measure and had no intention of moving to aid its passage unless a change of sentiment is expressed by the vintners.

LOCAL CONTROL DEMANDED

Threats of county and local officials to frame a counter proposal so that there will be more home control and that the local political subdivisions, rather than the State, shall control the liquor traffic, added more confusion.

The presence of a proposed initiative measure on the streets for signature, changing only a word or two of the present constitutional provision, has added more trouble. This measure is frowned upon by larger hotel and restaurant groups, which desire a change in the law so as to permit the sale of hard liquor by the drink in their establishments.

EXTRA SESSION DOUBTFUL

Governor Rolph had no special comment to make today as the prohibition law died. He has decided to withhold a decision on the proposals for a special session of the Legislature to deal with the liquor situation.

The Governor has been advised that a 2-cent-a-gallon tax will be imposed by the State Board of Equalization on wine, as well as on beer. Hard liquor, however, will escape the levy.

Whether the Governor will call a special election early next year for the submission of the proposed initiative amendments to the liquor provision of the constitution is yet undecided.

The Governor had before him today the hotel mens' proposed amendment, which would permit

(Continued on Page 7, Col. 6)

'What?' Asks U. S.; 'Liquor!'—'O.K. Pal'

NEW YORK, Dec. 5 (AP)—When the liner Majestic put in from Europe today Marc Connelly, the playwright, Laura La Plante, actress, and Ethel Levy, comedienne, trooped down the gangplank with certain mysterious packages.

"What's in them packages?" asked the customs men.

"Liquor," they yelled.

"O. K.," said the customs men.

It was an historic moment.

Woodin Recuperating In Arizona Camp

TUCSON, Ariz., Dec. 5 (AP)—Contemplating a long rest, William Woodin Sr., Secretary of the Treasury, was settled comfortably here today after a trip from the national capital.

Suffering from throat trouble, Mr. Woodin said he came here "to recover my health."

Roosevelt Plea Brings $3900 to Ousted Farmer

WILLOWS, Cal., Dec. 5 (AP)—Wm. L. Vaughn, a farmer, who appealed to President Roosevelt after the Farm Credit Administration had delayed the making of a loan to him and foreclosure proceedings were started against his home, announced today he had received a $3900 Federal commissioner loan as the result of presidential intervention.

Rossi Called East by Ickes On Bond Bid

Secretary Hits Syndicate in 6 Per cent Interest Demand for New S. F. Issue

By PAUL C. SMITH
Financial Editor The Chronicle

Fireworks flared from Washington to San Francisco and back again yesterday as an aftermath of the city of San Francisco's rejection of a lone bid by a Nation-wide banking syndicate for a part of the $20,480,000 bond issue approved by the voters November 7.

The bankers offered to buy the bonds at a price to yield 6 per cent, but the bid was rejected by the Board of Supervisors "because San Francisco never has paid in excess of 5 per cent on its bond issues and the electorate was advised during the campaign for the issues involved that the bonds could be sold on a 4 per cent basis."

ICKES RESENTS BID

Yesterday Secretary Ickes, Public Works Administrator, charged that "the attitude of the syndicate which made the bid is, to say the least, one of noncooperation in the recovery program. It is difficult to arrive at any other conclusion when even the banks say they are bursting with money."

On the heels of the Ickes blast, Mayor Rossi was summoned to Washington to confer with the Public Works Administration at once in order to expedite action on San Francisco's application for the $20,480,000 loan which the Mayor was authorized to negotiate at the close of Monday's meeting of the Board of Supervisors.

THREE GOING EAST

This request was interpreted by Mayor Rossi as "a favorable indication" that the loan will be granted at an early date. He will leave for Washington tonight or early Thursday and will be accompanied by City Attorney O'Toole and Controller Leavy, whose presence also was requested by Secretary Ickes.

Rossi and Ickes conferred by long distance telephone before noon yesterday. Ickes stated that he believed action on the loan would be taken promptly. He added that he would confer with President Roosevelt at once in order to expedite matters, Mayor Rossi said at the close of the conversation.

MAYOR OPTIMISTIC

"We will have the five bond projects under way sooner than expected," Rossi said in announcing his trip to Washington. "The Secretary told me that the Government's sole concern is getting men to work without delay. It therefore can only mean that our presence in Washington will speed things up

(Continued on Page 12, Col. 2)

Gandhi's Assistant Goes to Hospital

CALCUTTA, India, Dec. 5 (AP)—Miss Nila Cram Cook of Iowa, who recently quit the seminary of Mahatma Jandhi, was placed in a hospital here today following her disappearance from a new Delhi hotel yesterday.

Today's Features

Amusements	10, 11
Book Reviews	12
Captain Riordan	10
Chester Rowell	12
Comics	22
Crossword Puzzle	21
Contract Contacts	20
Culbertson's Bridge	20
Deaths	13
Dorothy Dix	20
Dr. Evans on Health	21
Editorials	12
Ferry Tales	13
Financial	22, 23, 24, 25
I Saw You by Wolo	10
Jane Friendly	20
Looking About	12
Mallon	14
Ninon Fashions	20
Oddities in the News	4
Radio	10
Safety Valve	12
Shipping	8
Society	21
Sports	Sporting Green
Veterans' News	6
Want Ads	26, 27
Washington Merry-Go-Round	12
Women's Club Calendar	21

Edwin A. Lee Takes Gwinn Job in 1934

Resigned Superintendent to Get Post of Technical Adviser to School Board

New Chief Professor of Education at California U.

Dr. Edwin Augustus Lee, professor of education and director of vocational education at the University of California, was yesterday appointed superintendent of schools of San Francisco.

By unanimous vote of the Board of Education, he succeeds Dr. Joseph Marr Gwinn, who resigned last summer after a stormy school controversy, but who is expected to remain as an educational adviser—at least until next June.

NOTIFIED IN DETROIT

Apprised in Detroit of his appointment yesterday, Dr. Lee pledged his best effort toward San Francisco education, according to the Associated Press. He said:

"I shall approach the task with humility of spirit, and an absolutely open mind."

Dr. Lee's appointment came as a surprise, although it was known that the Board of Education was sifting a list of seven educators recommended jointly by Dr. Ray Lyman Wilbur, president of Stanford University, and Dr. Robert Gordon Sproul, president of the University of California.

NEW POST FOR GWINN

Dr. Gwinn's retention in an advisory capacity depends upon the creation of a new position at a salary of $8200 a year by the Board of Supervisors. The school board recommended this new post yesterday. It will be known as technical educational adviser, and is to cover a period, December 15, 1933, to June 30, 1934, when Dr. Gwinn will be eligible for retirement.

APPOINTEE'S RECORD

Apparently Dr. Lee's appointment also depends upon the creation of the new job for Dr. Gwinn. The committee resolution of the board recommends Dr. Lee's appointment "effective at such date as Dr. J. M. Gwinn may be assigned to the newly created position." Dr. Lee's salary will also be $8200 a year.

The appointee's record is that of a California country boy, who fought his way rapidly to educational heights. He was born in Redding on August 9, 1888, and 21 years later graduated from the State Teachers' College at Chico.

He took a bachelor's degree in Columbia University in 1914, a master's degree in 1915 and a doctor's degree in 1926. Meanwhile he had been associate professor of vocational education at Carnegie Institute, Pittsburgh, and head of vocational work at Indiana University. Before his college work he was supervisor of music and industrial arts at San Rafael. He came to the University of California post in 1921.

TEXTBOOK AUTHOR

Dr. Lee has written several books in the educational field, and has held numerous posts of honor in national educational organizations. He was married in Chico in 1912 to Miss Edna Canfield, and they have three sons. They live at 1546 Le Roy avenue, Berkeley.

Dr. Lee planned to leave Detroit Saturday for San Francisco.

"The Francisco superintendency is one of the major educational posts in the Nation," he said.

(Continued on Page 5, Col. 6)

Aged Widow, Son Burned

Pair Near Death Dragged From Blazing Home

Trapped in a gas explosion that wrecked their flat at 1144 Oak street, a 71-year-old woman and her son were taken to Park Emergency Hospital in dying conditions last night.

The explosion occurred when the son lit a match in exploring a dark corner for a leak in the old-fashioned gas fixtures. The blast set fire to the house.

Found unconscious on the floor, Mrs. Louise Dashwood and Walter Dashwood, 51, were carried from the blazing building by firemen.

They had suffered major burns of the face, hands, arms and body, and physicians at the hospital held little hope for their lives.

A daughter, Miss Ethel Dashwood, escaped unharmed. A disorder from which she has been suffering was apparently aggravated by the shock, however, and she was transferred to the Detention Hospital for observation.

The house was apparently filled with gas when the explosion occurred, shaking the neighborhood.

Lindys Start Hop of Atlantic; Hit Squall at Dawn

Anne Radios Plane Progress on Africa to Brazil Journey

Wind Favors Pair At Takeoff in Africa Port

BATHURST, Gambia, Dec. 6 (Wednesday) (AP)—Colonel Charles A. Lindbergh lifted his heavily laden red monoplane into the air at 2 a.m. today (9 p.m., Tuesday, E. S. T.), and with Mrs. Lindbergh at the radio headed across 1900 miles of open sea toward South America.

After a score or more unsuccessful attempts to lift the plane in an almost dead calm, he was helped on his way by a light breeze from the interior, which rippled the surface of the lower Gambia river.

SQUALLS ENCOUNTERED

A message direct from the Lindbergh plane to Bahia, Brazil, relayed to Pan-American Airways in New York at 2:15 a.m., E. S. T. (11:15 p.m. Tuesday, Pacific time), reported the plane was 630 miles over the Atlantic (about one-third of the distance). It was daybreak, the sea was calm, wind zero, and the sky was overcast. The message said they were encountering frequent squalls.

ANNE SAYS O. K.

NEW YORK, Dec. 5 (AP)—A message from Anne Lindberg two hours after she and her famous husband took off tonight in a flight across the South Atlantic, reported "everything O. K."

The wireless was relayed to New York after being picked up in Bahia, Brazil.

Anne was reported sending like a professional.

DOZEN SEE TAKEOFF

For four days the Lindberghs had been balked by inability to lift the heavy load of fuel required for the longest hop yet attempted in their aerial survey tour of Atlantic ocean airways.

It was a still, clear night and the moon was shining brightly when the Colonel and Mrs. Lindbergh took off.

There were about a dozen spectators who had foregone sleep for the purpose of wishing the American flying couple luck and of witnessing a sight most unusual here.

The German steamer Westfalen, which had been in Brazil securing supplies, was due to return to its midatlantic post yesterday, affording further security for the Lindberghs on their long flight. The Westfalen is used by the German Lufthansa Line as a base for transatlantic flights, and officials of the line previously had offered the

(Continued on Page 6, Col. 2)

Dr. Work Will Wed Widow in Denver

DENVER, Dec. 5 (AP)—Dr. Hubert Work said today he and Mrs. George W. Gano, widow and prominent member of Denver society, will be married Friday.

Dr. Work, formerly Secretary of the Interior and a former Republican national committee chairman, is a widower and has three children, Dr. Philip Work and Mrs. A. W. Bissell of Denver and Mrs. Guy H. Work of Evanston, Ill. Mrs. Gano has no children.

SAID A PROF TO HIS PUPIL MISS DEE,
YOU WERE NOT AT MY LAST SECTION B"
SAID MISS DEE, "I CUT CLASS TO BUY GIFTS, FOR ALAS!
THERE'S JUST 16 SHOPPING DAYS. SEE?"

I. Jones, 1157 Stanyan street, San Francisco, takes the Christmas Limerick dollar today. Every shopping day between now and Christmas The Chronicle will pay $1 for the best Shopping Limerick submitted. Address, the Limerick Editor, The Chronicle, Fifth and Mission.

Tax Plan Hits Big Incomes, Aids Wages

Higher Surtaxes, Fewer Exemptions Seen as Blow to Wealthy

WASHINGTON, Dec. 5 (AP)—Striking at large incomes and personal holding companies organized to save taxes, a House Ways and Means subcommittee today recommended changes in the revenue law to bring in an estimated additional $237,000,000 to the Government.

The full committee headed by Representative Doughton (D., N. C.), met and received the report of the subcommittee, but took no action pending hearings to be held later. The proposals were designed to simplify the present law and plug up holes through which wealthy persons have avoided taxes.

FLAT 4 PER CENT

The subcommittee, which said it later would make more recommendations, especially with respect to new sources of revenue, did not disturb the lower income brackets, but proposed a single normal rate of 4 per cent on all net income, instead of the present 4 per cent on the first $4000 and 8 per cent on the balance.

Other recommendations included higher surtaxes, with only 27 brackets against the existing 57; increased rates on dividends and partly tax exempt interest; a 35 per cent tax on the "undistributed adjusted net income" of personal holding companies, abolition of consolidated returns and withdrawal of the right of partners to

(Continued on Page 12, Col. 4)

COMPARATIVE TEMPERATURES

NRA — WE DO OUR PART

San Francisco Chronicle

THE CITY'S ONLY HOME-OWNED NEWSPAPER

WEATHER in S. F. Bay Region Cloudy, With Occasional Showers. Complete Weather Report on Page 10

FOUNDED 1865—VOL. CXLIV, NO. 130 CCC SAN FRANCISCO, CAL., FRIDAY, MAY 25, 1934 DAILY 5 CENTS, SUNDAY 10 CENTS

TROOPS KILL TWO STRIKERS

Bricks, Bottles, Gas Attack Reply

S. F. Merchants to Open Port

Reserves Called to Foil Dynamite Plots on Factories

TOLEDO, Ohio, May 25 (Friday) (AP)—A jeering crowd of 6000, refusing to be cowed by rifle fire and gas barrages, battled 740 National Guardsmen for hours with bottles and bricks at the Electric Auto-Lite plant last night.

At midnight (Eastern standard time) the casualties had mounted to two dead, killed by the militia's fire, 11 known injured and perhaps scores of others hurt but unaccounted for in hospital lists.

As the battles continued military authorities began to investigate the circumstances of the rifle fire yesterday afternoon. The guardsmen opened fire during a major skirmish again last night. Commanding officers said the afternoon firing had not been ordered. They were silent about tonight's outburst.

GENERAL STRIKE LOOMS

Although three moves for peace were under way, the threat of a general strike, discussed for two weeks in labor unions, again appeared to be gaining ground. Last night 275 union electrical workers voted to authorize their business agent to call them out on strike at any time he desires.

FEAR DYNAMITING

Another company of troops was dispatched to guard the Bingham Tool and Die Company plant, another company affected by the automotive strike, last night, so gravely did guard officers take the rumor that an attempt would be made to dynamite factories.

At Central Labor Union headquarters, unverified reports were heard that machine guns to arm the rioters were being sent in from Detroit.

One man was oveheard to say he "hadn't seen so many guns and so much ammunition since I left the army as when I passed through the mob."

The guerilla warfare which slackened early today until only 300 of yesterday's crowd of 5000 were on hand, came as a climax to three days of rioting at the Auto-Lite plant. Some of the workers have been on strike for five weeks, demanding a 10 per cent wage increase, recognition of their A. F. of L. union and other concessions. The company has refused to concede the closed shop. Before yesterday 100 persons had been slightly hurt in occasional rioting.

TROOPS CAUSE OF RIOT

Continuous warfare did not break out until National Guardsmen had been ordered here to bolster local authorities yesterday.

By midafternoon 5000 strike sympathizers were pressing close to guard details that were thrown about the plant. The militiamen resorted to tear gas to stop the barrage of stones and bottles and the bloody encounter was on.

The throng surged close. Guardsmen fired a volley overhead. Fifty more soldiers came up. Still the crowd came on. The soldiers low-

(Continued on Page 5, Col. 2)

Excerpts From Statements In S. F. Strike Controversy

DECISION of San Francisco business leaders actively to participate in the longshoremen's strike was revealed last night in the following terse announcement of J. W. Mailliard Jr., president of the Chamber of Commerce:

"We do not wish to make a statement pending the outcome of negotiations with Mr. Ryan and his group, *following which the merchants will open the port of San Francisco to commerce.*"

Simultaneously with this, the Waterfront Employers' Union last night issued a statement replying to allegations made by the International Longshoremen's Association strike committee yesterday morning, and denying them in their entirety.

They declared they are willing to submit wage demands to impartial arbitration; that there is no issue of the right of collective bargaining nor union recognition; that longshoremen were forced to join the I. L. A. under threat that if they remained in the "blue-book" union they could not work on the waterfront.

The complete text of the employers' statement will be found on Page 4.

Ryan Tells of Peace Hope, Addressing Meet

Expressing hope of an "early and equitable settlement" of the Pacific Coast longshoremen's strike, Joseph P. Ryan, national president of the International Longshoremen's Association, addressed a mass meeting of nearly 3000 striking stevedores in Eagles Hall last night.

Ryan, recognized as one of the most powerful figures in New York city labor circles, had a busy time following his arrival by plane late in the afternoon.

He had dinner with Mayor Rossi and a group of business and civic leaders, conferred with Pacific Coast executives of the longshoremen, addressed the strikers' mass meeting, and then conferred some more.

"I have just arrived and am glad to be here, and sincerely hope for early settlement of the situation which confronts you," Ryan told the mass meeting. "I hope to be able to effect an early and equitable settlement as quickly as possible, and I hope you men will bear with me in my efforts."

The national chief, who technically has no executive status with the Pacific Coast district of the longshoremen, was given a rousing cheer by the hundreds of men, after a group of radicals who had parked in the forefront of the hall attempted to "boo" him.

The meeting, representing San Francisco Local 38-79 of the I. L. A., adopted an ultimatum to the effect that should the ship operators refuse to concede the closed shop and hiring hall control of the union by Saturday, that all negotiations would be ended, and a "fight to the finish" would follow.

District officers were said to be opposed to such an ultimatum, and urged more time for negotiations.

Police Jail Three Here in Drive to Clean Out Radicals

Aroused by the deadlock in the Pacific Coast longshoremen's strike, San Francisco business leaders yesterday took an active hand in the controversy with the announced intention of reopening the port to commerce immediately.

In a virtual ultimatum to striking longshoremen a group headed by J. W. Mailliard Jr., president of the Chamber of Commerce, announced that "merchants of the city will open the commerce of the port."

With the strike in its 16th day, business in a large number of industries is virtually at a standstill, thousands of tons of cargo are tied up on the docks, factories are being closed, and thousands not involved in the strike have been thrown out of work.

As a result importers and exporters and retail merchants are suffering heavily as well as other business dependent upon shipping and its affiliates.

PARLEY ACTION AWAITED

Announcement of the exact plan of action is being held in abeyance pending the outcome of negotiations between ship operators, strikers, and Joseph P. Ryan, national president of the International Longshoremen's Association, who arrived from New York yesterday.

Coincident with the merchants' decision that cargoes must be moved, San Francisco and Oakland police joined with conservative labor leaders in a determined drive to rid striking longshoremen groups of alleged communistic agitators, held by both employers and labor leaders to be responsible for violence on the bay water fronts.

SOME BELIEVED ALIENS

A number of the more radical leaders are not even citizens of the United States, it was declared. As the first move in the drive San Francisco police arrested a woman and three men on the complaint of conservative strike leaders, who objected to radical speeches of the trio at water front meetings.

At the same time Oakland police aroused by the two shootings Wednesday night, ordered the East Bay water front cleared of pickets and announced that no San Francisco communists would be permitted in Oakland.

RYAN ARRIVES

The drive to rid the ranks of the striking longshoremen of radical agitators came a few hours before Ryan arrived in San Francisco to take a leading part in peace negotiations.

Twelve men, described as strikers by James O'Dowd, special Southern Pacific officer, boarded an electric train at the Oakland mole and got into a fight with strikebreakers. The fight lasted for several minutes as the train proceeded. The strikers got off at Seventh and Willow streets, and escaped in two waiting automobiles. Several car windows were broken, and there were bloodstains on the seats, but no one reported for hospital treatment, O'Dowd said.

Ryan arrived via United Air Lines late in the day, fresh from a successful settlement of a one-line New York dock strike and a general strike of Gulf Coast stevedores.

Ryan was met at the San Francisco Municipal Airport by district officers of the International Long-

(Continued on Page 4, Col. 5)

Woman Dies So Love for Mate May Live

Mrs. Louise B. Crocker Takes Poison Eighteen Months After Husband's Demise

By CAROLYN ANSPACHER

SUICIDE: Mrs. Louise B. Crocker, 52, 550 Geary street; died by poison; body discovered at 9:20 a. m. by hotel attendants.

These words, written yesterday into a great book at the City Morgue spelled the end and the beginning of a love greater than life, greater than death.

The story of Louise Crocker's suicide is a strange one, built on the death a year and a half ago of her husband, Dr. Harry B. Crocker.

DIED SO LOVE MIGHT LIVE

Into its simple tapestry is woven the thread of a love transcending the limits of time and space.

For Mrs. Crocker died that the love she bore her husband "might endure forever." To her friends she confessed that in seeking death she was achieving the ultimate in life.

For one year and a half she prepared for the hour of her departure. For one year and a half she

SEEKS LOVE IN DEATH

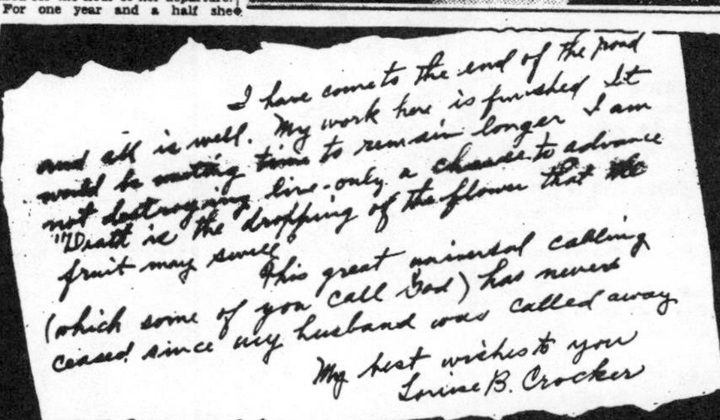

I have come to the end of the road and all is well. My work here is finished. It would be wasting time to remain longer. I am not destroying life — only a chance to advance. "Death is the dropping of the flower that the fruit may swell." This great universal calling (which some of you call God) has never ceased since my husband was called away.

My best wishes to you
Louise B. Crocker

Mrs. Louise B. Crocker and excerpt from suicide letter, in which she explained her act as due to an overwhelming desire to join her dead husband.

planned the moment of her triumph, using as her guide the last letter of her husband, written just before his death, in which he told her that already he was lonely without her . . . that death would be a dreamless sleep without her.

BEGGED HER TO LIVE LONG

In this letter, Dr. Crocker begged his wife to live long and beautifully, and added he hoped she would join him soon.

Seven times Mrs. Crocker crossed the continent in airplanes, praying they would crash.

She courted danger, laughed at fear. Then, in desperation, when she felt life's grip too strong upon

(Continued on Page 2, Col. 4)

Japan to End Naval Pacts, Admiral Says

Ship Ratios Menace Safety of Empire, Claims Chief of Propaganda

TOKYO, May 24 (AP)—Maintaining that the 5-5-3 naval ratios "menace the Japanese empire's safety," Rear Admiral Tsuneyoshi Sakano, chief of the navy's propaganda bureau, today gave notice of Japan's objections to an extension of the present limitations beyond 1936.

"New agreements fairer and more reasonable and affording Japan genuine assurance of security" must replace the London and Washington treaties, Sakano said in a written statement to the press, which, however, did not mention the matter of parity with the United States and Great Britain.

INSIST ON NEW PACTS

"The Washington treaty was framed to meet special conditions immediately after the war," the statement said, "and now long outdated.

"Armaments compacts must be offered in accordance with changed political, scientific and technical conditions. The London treaty was a temporary compact and was not intended to extend past 1936.

"Both treaties are undesirable in many respects. We insist upon new agreements."

Vernacular newspapers in report-

Robinson Picks Up Following Isle Operation

Picture on Page 9

LOS ANGELES, May 24 (AP)—William Albert Robinson, wealthy explorer critically ill with appendicitis aboard his tiny world-circling craft, Svaap, at Tagus Cove, Galapagos islands, was operated upon tonight and later reported "doing as well as could be expected."

Naval medical officers aboard the destroyer Hale reached Tagus bay late today and the operation was started immediately.

"Destroyer reached Tagus bay," said a wireless message flashed from the trawler Santa Cruz, which has been standing by the Cambridge, Mass., textile engineer's ketch. "Operation being performed on Robinson."

Two naval medical officers flew nearly 1000 miles from the naval air base at Coco Solo, Canal Zone, to the volcanic islands yesterday. They found Robinson's appendix apparently was ruptured and hesitated to operate until better equipment arrived.

6000 Killed, 12,000 Injured In Chaco War

LA PAZ, Bolivia, May 24 (AP)—More than 6000 Paraguayan soldiers were killed and at least 12,000 wounded in a Bolivian counter attack before Fort Ballivian, according to an official dispatch today.

The action was regarded as a master stroke by Colonel Bernardino Bilbao Rioja, in command of the Bolivian forces in the Canada and "strongest" sectors.

WASHINGTON, May 24 (AP)—The Senate today adopted and sent to the White House the House resolution to prohibit the sale of arms in the United States intended for use in the Gran Chaco conflict between Paraguay and Bolivia. The House approved it yesterday.

GENEVA, May 24 (AP) — The League of Nations announced officially tonight eight nations have accepted in principle the proposal of an embargo against further shipment of arms to Paraguay and Bolivia so long as they continue their war in the Chaco.

The eight nations are Argentina, Peru, Chile, Belgium, Canada, Guatemala, Panama and Mexico.

Protocol Settling Leticia Row Signed

RIO JANEIRO, May 24 (AP)—The protocol providing for a peaceful settlement of the Leticia dispute between Peru and Colombia was signed tonight. Roberto Urdaneta Arbelaez signed on behalf of Colombia and Dr. Victor Maurtua for Peru.

Notre Dame Chief Still Near Death

SOUTH BEND, Ind., May 24 (AP)—The condition of Rev. Charles L. O'Donnell, president of Notre Dame University, was reported as critical tonight

Statue of Bryan Is No Beer Bust!

ONTARIO, May 24 (AP)—Decrying the erection of a statue of William Jennings Bryan adjacent to a Washington, D. C. brewery, a hundred members of the Women's Christian Temperance Union of Western San Bernardino petitioned President Roosevelt to have the brewery or the statue moved.

Barrow Death Car Will Be Exhibited

TOPEKA, Kas., May 24 (AP)—The automobile in which Clyde Barrow, Southwest desperado, and Bonnie Parker, his girl, met a violent death, is to be placed on exhibit.

Jesse Warner, owner of the car, which was stolen here April 29, contracted today with a promoter to use it for exhibition purposes. It is to be taken to the World's Fair at Chicago.

Quezon Confined In Manila Hospital

MANILA, P. I., May 24 (AP)—Manuel Quezon, president of the Philippine Senate, entered a Manila hospital today for observation of a kidney ailment, from which he has been suffering since his recent trip to Washington, D. C.

French Ace Claims New Speed Record

ETAMPES, May 24 (AP)—Raymond Delmotte, French pilot, claimed a new world's airplane speed record for a 100 kilometer course today after racing over the distance at 431.664 kilometers (268.06 miles) an hour.

Dillinger Hand Seen in Slaying Of Two Officers

EAST CHICAGO, Ind., May 25 (AP)—Two detectives were shot to death here tonight and the killers suspected of being members of John Dillinger's mob, escaped without leaving a single clue.

The two dead officers were found huddled in the front seat of their speedy little squad car on Gary road in one of the most deserted spots of the city by a workman on his way home from toil.

Each had 10 or 15 bullet holes in his head and neck and the car was riddled with bullets. Police, reconstructing the crime, said that the bullets had been fired from a machine gun.

The slain officers, Martin O'Brien, 44, and Loyd Mulvihill, 28, were both veterans of the force. Both were married.

There were no witnesses to the killings and the bodies had been dead about half an hour when discovered, the Coroner said.

Suspicion was pointed to John Dillinger and his mob as the slayers, but officers said if this was true the men were shot before they even knew their assailants were at hand, as both had their pistols in the holsters.

Five States Post Reward Of $5000 for Dillinger

SPRINGFIELD, Ill., May 24 (AP)—Governors of five States today officially posted a reward of $5000 for the capture of John Dillinger.

A proclamation signed by the Governors of and bearing the official seals of Illinois, Indiana, Ohio, Minnesota and Michigan, offered the reward to anyone who "delivers said John Dillinger to any Sheriff or Sheriff's representative in the five States.

Hepburn Altar Trip Halted by Mrs. Hayward

Special to The Chronicle

NEW YORK, May 24—That trip to the altar by Katharine Hepburn, talkie idol, and her manager, Leland Hayward, which all the Broadway and Hollywood gossips expected in a week or so, is off indefinitely.

The wedding isn't going to be held for the good reason that Hayward's wife, the former Lola Gibbs, has decided not to go through with the divorce action she filed against him in Mexico early in April, it was learned today.

News of her suit followed by a few days the announcement that Miss Hepburn had divorced her first husband, Ogden Ludlow Smith, Philadelphia blueblood, on May 8, in Yucatan.

Mrs. Hayward, admitting today that her divorce was postponed indefinitely, said: "Oh, I think it's too hot in Mexico now," when asked her reasons.

"As far as the friendship between Leland and Miss Hepburn is concerned, I've always thought it just proved that Hollywood press agents are hard up for methods of getting their stars into the papers," she added.

Covert Moderator Of Presbyterians

CLEVELAND, May 24 (AP)—Dr. William Chalmers Covert of Philadelphia, general secretary of the Presbyterian Board of Christian Education, today was elected moderator of the Presbyterian Church at the general assembly here.

Two ballots were required to reach the decision. Rev. Herbert Booth Smith of Los Angeles and Rev. James C. McConnell of Upper Darby, Pa., were the other candidates for the office.

Today's Features

Amusements 12, 13
Book Reviews 15
Chester Rowell 14
Comics 24
Crossword Puzzle 10
Contract Contacts 15
Culbertson and Sims 12
Deaths 15
Dorothy Dix 22
Editorials 14
Ferry Tales 8
Financial 24, 25, 26, 27
Foods and Markets 6, 7
Junior Baseball 28
Mallon 8
Ninon Fashions 22
Oddities in the News 11
Radio 12
Rogers 9
Safety Valve 14
Shipping 10
Society 23
Sports ....Green
Veterans' News 9
Want Ads 28, 29
Washington Merry-Go-Round 21
Welo 12
Women's Club Calendar 23

The Modoc Massacre • In 1873 Indian peace commissioners were slain as they met with the Indians in council tent. The later battle with the treacherous Indians will be retold, along with a reproduction of The Chronicle page of April 13, 1873 **In SUNDAY'S CHRONICLE** • **A Feature by Tom Bellew**

EXTRA

COMPARATIVE TEMPERATURES

	High	Low
San Francisco	63	52
Los Angeles	74	62
Honolulu	82	74
Seattle	76	53
Denver	90	56
New York	84	66
Chicago	94	74
New Orleans	84	78

San Francisco Chronicle

THE CITY'S ONLY HOME-OWNED NEWSPAPER

WEATHER in S. F. Bay Region: Fair, with Fog. Complete Weather Report on Page 30

FOUNDED 1865—VOL. CXLIV, NO. 172 CCC* SAN FRANCISCO, CAL., FRIDAY, JULY 6, 1934 DAILY 5 CENTS, SUNDAY 10 CENTS: DAILY AND SUNDAY PER MONTH, $1.15

TROOPS GUARD FRONT!

2 DEAD, 109 HURT IN RIOTING

S.F. Embarcadero Rocked By Death, Bloodshed, Riots

Governor Merriam Ends Day of Terror by Ordering National Guard to Take Charge of Piers

PICTURES—The story of yesterday's rioting in pictorial form is told by The Chronicle on this page, page A, page B (a page of illustrations), page C and page D, another complete page of pictures.

By ROYAL W. JIMERSON

Troops of the California National Guard—1750 picked men with full war equipment—moved with swift military precision last night into a San Francisco water front rocked by death, wholesale bloodshed and wild rioting.

With two dead, 31 wounded by gunfire, and 78 seriously injured by bricks, clubs and tear gas, Governor Merriam yesterday ended a day of terror by ordering the National Guard to take control of the Embarcadero with the greatest possible speed.

In a statement issued at Sacramento last night, the Governor pleaded with "sane, clear-thinking workers" to avoid becoming involved in the maritime strike along San Francisco's water front.

STRIKE IN HANDS OF REDS

He warned that strike activities were in the hands of communists.

The Governor further warned that "the National Guard shan't be overridden or overpowered." The maritime strike, he said, has "gone beyond the point of common sense and good citizenship."

EMBARCADERO OCCUPIED

Long before midnight, guardsmen from San Francisco, the East Bay and Santa Clara county had completed their occupation of the Embarcadero, battle ground of the maritime workers' strike for the last 58 days.

Guardsmen on duty last night included complete units from the 250th Coast Artillery, the San Francisco regiment, and the 159th Infantry, comprising the East Bay, San Jose and Gilroy groups. Major General David P. Barrows of Berkeley is in general command of the militia on the Embarcadero, with Colonel R. E. Mittelstaedt commanding the San Francisco unit.

SENTRIES LINE WATER FRONT

Sentries armed with rifles and fixed bayonets made a wall of steel on the south side of the water front from Fisherman's Wharf to China Basin, and their orders, as bluntly revealed by commanding officers, were to preserve law and order at all costs.

"Avoid shooting if possible," the men were told, "but if it becomes necessary to discharge your rifles, shoot for effect."

In army parlance, this means that the guardsmen are not to fire their weapons in the air, but at a human target.

As the arrival of the troops intensified the quiet that descended on the water front after a day of fighting, there

(Continued on Page 2, Col. 6)

Here Is List of Men Who Fell In Bloody S. F. Strike Warfare

Following is a list of dead and injured, casualties from one day's rioting on the San Francisco water front:

THE DEAD

HOWARD SPERRY, 50, 445 Gough street; shot in the back with buckshot near I. L. A. headquarters.

GEORGE COUNEOURAKIS, member of the Cooks and Waiters' Union, said to be an "intelligence officer" of the International Labor Defense. Shot in abdomen. Was among those injured in riots of May 30, when he suffered scalp wounds.

THE INJURED

Joseph Camarato, 27, seaman; contusion of leg, tear gas; pier 32.

James Engle, 36, 1409 Geary street; shot in head, fractured skull, in a serious condition.

Edwin L. Hodges, 60, 3530 Sacramento street; bullet wounds hands and stomach; First and Harrison streets.

Jerry Hart, 38, 909 Guerrero street, longshoreman; bullet wound back of knee; First and Harrison streets.

Nick Nicholas, 54, 277 First street; hit by tear gas bomb, contusions of scalp; pier 32.

Vassili Zakharoff, 41, 1377 Ellis street, striking cook; hit by policeman, lacerated scalp; pier 32.

Policeman Emmet Grimm, 41, 531 Rolph street; tear gas; pier 38.

Albert Simmons, 920 Montgomery

(Continued on Page 2, Col. 2)

FIRST OFFICIAL ACT OF MILITIA!

SOLDIERS ON THE JOB!—Here is the first official move on the part of the National Guard after it had taken charge of the water front last night. An enlisted man, followed by an officer, is escorting Capt. Michael Riordan and his prisoner.

Military Rule Put Into Effect on Water Front

By NEIL HITT

Troops now occupy the water front. The rule there is the rule of the bayonet. None comes or goes without military permission.

The State of California is maintaining her sovereignty—the right of access to her port of San Francisco, and what a spectacular gesture it is.

Not since the fervored days of 1917 and the later homecoming of troops has the city seen anything like it.

MILITARY ATMOSPHERE

Again the cadenced tread of marching feet, the command to halt, the grounding of rifles, the slinging off of heavy packs. Hundreds of boys from the city itself and from the inland valleys are in uniform—olive drab, with olive drab trench helmets. Their officers are spick and span in polished boots and Sam Brown belts. Most of them are war-scarred veterans of the World war about to engage in something that may not be child's play either.

The water front strikers have withdrawn into the darkness. Their watchfires are allowed to go out after a bloody day. Here and there fire apparatus has been called to put out small fires along the front.

ALONG EMBARCADERO

The State troops are being deployed along the magic crescent of the Embarcadero, where ships have come and gone unmolested for nearly a century.

Troops pour in from Gilroy, from San Jose, from Oakland—State troops—National Guardsmen. Hundreds more come in trucks from the San Francisco Armory.

Bayonets are being affixed to Springfields. Youthful hands finger riot guns. Machine guns are being unpacked and there are even howitzers.

READY TO BATTER

"We may have to batter down brick walls or other barricades," says a Lieutenant.

Every thing is orderly. A squad of men is stationed in front of each pierhouse to keep an all night vigil. Sentries are gravely walking their posts, coming down to the port with their rifles at the approach of officers.

The men will sleep in the big sheds. They expect cots to arrive but if they don't come they will spread their blankets out on the hard floors and make pillows of their shelter tent halves. A chill wind is blowing along the front and the lads from the warm inland valleys do not appear to have brought overcoats. They will miss them before morning.

LOCALS STATIONED

The "overbay" troops are stationed along the odd numbered side of the Embarcadero; the locals on the even side.

Temporary headquarters have been established on the second floor of the Ferry Building.

Police, who have had long tours of duty during the day, their eyes still red from tear gas, watch the incoming of the National Guardsmen. They do not feel any particular relief about it.

POLICE PESSIMISTIC

Says one:

"It won't make any difference. They will only have charge of the State's property along the water front. They will see that the State's Belt Line railroad moves its cars in and out of piers. But when the trucks get loaded and get out-

(Continued on Page C, Col. 6)

Governor Calls State Troopers For Protection

By EARL C. BEHRENS

SACRAMENTO, July 5—For the protection of life and property in the San Francisco longshoremen's strike, Governor Merriam, as commander in chief of the militia of the State of California, at 3:03 o'clock this afternoon issued the proclamation which sent National Guardsmen for duty along the San Francisco water front.

Two hours earlier in the day the Governor had directed Adjutant General Seth E. Howard to order certain of the National Guard units to stand by for immediate service. Most of these troops were in readiness at the San Francisco Armory while Deputy Attorney General Jess Hession was preparing the proclamation for the Governor.

"STATE OF TUMULT"

Declaring that "a state of tumult, riot and other emergencies or immediate danger thereof, existed and that riotous and unlawful assemblies with intent to do violence," are present in San Francisco, Governor Merriam called upon his Adjutant General to order into active service all troops necessary to handle the situation.

The Governor's proclamation does not restrict the National Guard troops to any particular part of San Francisco for duty, but they are available for service in any part of the city their commander, Major General David P. Barrows, a former president of the University of California, should direct.

The Governor was ready to make his official call upon the troops at 2 o'clock. He had given Adjutant General Howard a two-hour period to warn the troopers that they must

(Continued on Page 2, Col. 4)

Blood Floods Gutters As Police, Strikers War

By ROYCE BRIER

Blood ran red in the streets of San Francisco yesterday.

In the darkest day this city has known since April 18, 1906, 1000 embattled police held at bay 5000 longshoremen and their sympathizers in a sweeping front south of Market street and east of Second street.

The furies of street warfare raged for hour piled on hour.

Two were dead, one was dying, 32 others shot and more than three score sent to hospitals.

Hundreds were injured or badly gassed. Still the strikers surged up and down the sunlit streets among thousands of foolhardy spectators. Still the clouds of tear gas, the very air darkened with hurtling bricks. Still the revolver battles.

As the middle of the day wore on in indescribable turmoil the savagery of the conflict was in rising crescendo. The milling mobs fought with greater desperation, knowing the troops were coming, the police held to hard-won territory with grim resolution.

It was a Gettysburg in the miniature, with towering warehouses thrown in for good measure. It was one of those days you think of as coming to Budapest.

The purpose of it all was this: The State of California had said it would operate its water front railroad. The strikers had defied the State of California to do it. The police had to keep them off. They did.

Take out a San Francisco map and draw a line along Second street south from Market to the bay. It passes over Rincon Hill. That is the west boundary, Market is the north, of the battlefield.

Not a street in that big sector but saw its flying lead yesterday, not a street that wasn't trampled by thousands of flying feet as the tide of battle swung high and low, as police drove them back, as they drove police back in a momentary victory.

Don't think of this as a riot. It was a hundred riots, big and little, first here, now there. Don't think of it as one battle, but as a dozen battles.

And with a nonchalance which was dumfounding at times, San Franciscans, just plain citizens bent on business, in automobiles and afoot, moved to and fro in the battle area.

It started with a nice easy swing, just as great battles in war often start. The Industrial Association resumed moving goods from pier 38 at 8 a. m. A few hundred strikers were out, but were held back at Brannan street, as they had been in Tuesday's riots, by the police.

Technically the strikers had lost that battle Tuesday, but now there was something else. The State Belt engines were puffing up and down.

POLICE HURL TEAR GAS

At Bryant and Main streets were a couple of hundred strikers in an ugly mood. Police Captain Arthur de Guire decided to clear them out, and his men went at them with tear gas. The strikers ran, scrambling up Rincon Hill and hurling back rocks.

Proceed now one block away, to Harrison and Main streets. Four policemen are there, about 500 of the mob are on the hill. Those four cops look like good game.

"Come on, boys," shouted the leaders.

They tell how the lads of the

(Continued on Page A, Column 4)

Paris Denies Part in Hitler Revolt Plot

French Envoy Puts In Strong Protest; Cardinal Held Prisoner

Copyright, 1934, by the Associated Press

BERLIN, July 5 (AP)—France, through her Ambassador here, tonight formally and vigorously denied she was involved in the plot against Chancellor Hitler's government which was broken up by the week-end executions.

The denial was given out and it was stated a formal protest will be made to the German government after the Nazi press had accused

(Continued on Page 11, Col. 3)

COMPARATIVE TEMPERATURES

	High	Low
San Francisco	65	53
Los Angeles	82	67
Honolulu	83	76
Seattle	78	56
Denver	90	66
New York	80	66
Chicago	84	70
New Orleans	88	76

NRA MEMBER U.S. WE DO OUR PART

San Francisco Chronicle

THE CITY'S ONLY HOME-OWNED NEWSPAPER

WEATHER in S. F. Bay Region
Fair; Clouds Night, Morning
Complete Weather Report on Page 6

FOUNDED 1865—VOL. CXLV, NO. 18 CCC* SAN FRANCISCO, CAL., THURSDAY, AUGUST 2, 1934 DAILY 5 CENTS, SUNDAY 10 CENTS: DAILY AND SUNDAY PER MONTH, $1.15

VON HINDENBURG EXPIRES!

Germany's Grand Old Man Dies as Hitler Plots To Take Over Control

Chancellor Visits Bedside of Dying Man; Calls Cabinet

BULLETIN

BERLIN, Aug. 2 (Thursday) (AP)—Immediately following the death of President Paul von Hindenburg, Chancellor Hitler assumed the presidency.

NEUDECK, Aug. 2 (AP)—President von Hindenburg died at 9 a. m. today.

The President's death was indicated to correspondents by the disappearance of the house flag from the flagstaff.

Death came to the 86-year-old leader of the German people and former war marshal after a valiant fight against a complication of ailments.

Chancellor Adolf Hitler, who returned to Berlin for a Cabinet meeting last night after visiting Hindenburg's death bed, many believed, will assume the presidency.

By Associated Press

BERLIN, Aug. 1—Paul von Hindenburg, President and hero of Germany, grew weaker tonight and his stout heart beat more slowly.

He lapsed into unconsciousness at Neudeck, his country estate, and at Neddeck, his country estate, and at one time it was announced he was in death throes.

HITLER COUP BARED

About an hour and a half later, at 9:50 p. m., his physician, Dr. Ferdinand Sauerbruch, telephoned to Berlin that he was amazed at the President's power of resistance and that he might linger for some time.

The news followed the revelation by a close friend of Adolf Hitler that the Chancellor planned, in the event of Von Hindenburg's death, to become both President and Chancellor.

This step, say political observers, would give Hitler a dictatorship as absolute as any in the world.

At 10 o'clock tonight Chancellor Hitler called the Cabinet into session.

The session lasted into the early morning hours, it was said, but the Chancellery and official news agencies declined to divulge details of what happened.

Earlier today he visited Von Hindenburg, whose son, Colonel Oskar von Hindenburg, is in constant attendance on his father.

FLIES TO BEDSIDE

With his immediate entourage, the Chancellor flew to Marienburg and then motored to Neudeck. He was with the President for an hour and a quarter.

Hitler said that when he arrived in the sick room at Neudeck, Von Hindenburg's condition already was serious, but his mind still

(Continued on Page 4, Col. 6)

Today's Features

Amusements	8, 9
Book Reviews	11
By the Way	10
Chester Rowell	10
Comics	20
Contract Contacts	24
Crossword Puzzle	Green
Culbertson and Sims	24
Deaths	11
Dorothy Dix	18
Editorials	10
Financial	20, 21, 22, 23
June Friendly	18
Mallon	17
Merry-Go-Round	17
Navy Orders	6
Ninon Fashions	18
Radio	6
Safety Valve	10
Shipping	6
Society	19
Sports	Sporting Green
Veterans' News	6
Want Ads	24, 25
Will Rogers	11
Wolo	5
Women's Club Calendar	18

FATHERLAND MOURNS

President Paul von Hindenburg
Died Today at Country Home

U. S. Bans Navy Ratio Shift, Urges Fleet Cuts; To Build Fewer Planes

WASHINGTON, Aug. 1 (AP)—Secretary Swanson frankly told Japan—and the world—today that while the United States might favor a slash of 20 per cent in naval armaments, it would oppose vigorously any re-alignment of existing naval ratios for the principal powers.

The Secretary of the Navy said he gave only his personal opinion but his naval officers surrounded him as he spoke and apparently he laid down the position of his department—if not that of the Administration.

"I take the same position I always have," he said. "The naval powers met in London and distributed naval strength as they thought just and right. Naval strength is relative. If we abandon the ratios there is no telling where we shall go."

Swanson's statement was prompted by questions regarding his reaction to a statement by Keisuke Okada, the new Japanese Premier. It was interpreted by observers as a reply to Okada's recorded desire for a further reduction in sea power and his expression of dissatisfaction with the existing 5-5-3 naval ratio between this country, Great Britain and Japan.

WOULD HAVE TO SCRAP SHIPS

Since Japan is virtually at treaty strength and England much nearer than the United States, the Secretary said, these powers would have to make a reduction in actual fighting craft and not merely tear up blue prints. He added that for the United States a 20 per cent cut would mean abandonment of some naval construction.

URGES 20 PER CENT CUT

"I am willing to abandon over-age ships and refrain from replacing them to an extent of 20 per cent," Swanson declared. "I have already advised a 20 per cent reduction in public statements and reports."

Swanson said he did not believe the United States could agree to

(Continued on Page 4, Col. 1)

(Copyright, 1934, by Associated Press)

WASHINGTON, Aug. 1 (AP)—The naval high command was disclosed authoritatively tonight to have determined on a sharp reduction in naval aviation construction.

Present plans, which may be altered, call for 274 fewer planes than the 2184 which the navy had decided would be necessary under the Vinson bill authorizing a treaty strength navy by 1942. A thousand planes now comprise the naval air force, and plans had evolved to build the other 1184 in annual installments.

High officials now have chopped down the total to a tentative figure of 1910 planes as adequate for peacetime navy requirements. The total may be cut slightly again before a final one is reached.

The reduction includes 34 craft which would have been assigned to a proposed flying deck cruiser which the navy has decided not to lay down.

'How You Doing?' U. S. Asks Factories

WASHINGTON, Aug. 1 (AP)—The Government today began asking small manufacturers how they've been doing lately and if they've got anything they can use for money.

Questionnaires were sent out to 16,000 firms employing between 30 and 190 workers, said William L. Austin, director of the Census Bureau, to determine their comparative financial standing in 1926, 1929 and 1933, and ask suggestions for sources from which credit should be made available.

Pope Departs for Summer Residence

VATICAN CITY, Aug. 1 (AP)—Pope Pius XI left the walls of the Vatican at 5:37 p. m. today for his summer residence at Castel Gandolfo.

He and his suite made the trip in four American automobiles.

ThirdAustria Slayer Hangs, Fourth Jailed

Pay of Suspect Federal Workers Stopped as Schuschnigg Plans Mussolini Visit

Vienna Officially States Revolt Was Mapped in Germany

VIENNA, Aug. 1 (AP)—With the hangman's rope, a sentence of imprisonment and empty pay envelopes, the government of Chancellor Kurt Schuschnigg today pressed its fight against the defeated Nazi rebels of Austria.

Friedrich Wurnig, a Nazi, was hanged at 8 o'clock tonight at Innsbruck, three hours after he was sentenced to death for killing Police Commandant Franz Hickel in that city last Wednesday.

Wurnig, the third Nazi to die on the gallows in two days, collapsed when he was told that clemency was refused. He had to be carried to the gallows.

NOT LINKED TO REVOLT

Although his crime occurred about the same time that Chancellor Dollfuss was killed by Nazi putschists, it had no direct connection with that outbreak.

An alleged accomplice, Christian Meyer, was sentenced to 20 years' imprisonment, receiving clemency, it was reported, because he had revealed Nazi secrets to the government.

Trial of another Nazi is scheduled to begin here tomorrow.

REDS' WAGES STOPPED

Economic pressure against Nazis in government employ was ordered. The salaries of all persons in the public employ who are suspected of aiding or encouraging the Nazi revolt will be withheld.

The suspects will be denounced, the order says, to the nearest police station, and will remain without pay until their cases are investigated.

The order recalled that 20 Federal employes were reported to have cried, "Heil Hitler!" when the Nazi putschists seized the Chancellery last Wednesday.

VON PAPEN HELD UP

The decision as to acceptance by the new government of Franz von Papen as special German Minister was held up today.

This friendly gesture of Chancellor Hitler remains unrecognized, and it was said in government circles that it is expected nothing will be done during the uncertainty attending President von Hindenburg's illness.

A possibility was reported that Chancellor Schuschnigg and Vice Chancellor Von Starhemberg will go to Rome some time this month for a conference with Premier Mussolini.

The semiofficial newspaper, Weltblatt, summing up today the Nazi rebellion in the provinces, reported that the majority of the rebels were peasants. Others, said the paper, were public officials, policemen, postmasters, teachers, customs officers and physicians.

RINTELEN CONFESSION DENIED

Police executives denied today a report that Dr. Anton Rintelen, pro-Nazi former Minister to Rome, had "confessed" to taking part in the putsch.

On the other hand, Austria officially pointed an accusing finger at Germany for the blood which flowed. An announcement approved by the Cabinet said directions to Austrian Nazis were sent into the country several weeks ago from Germany.

The plans, which included the possibility of civil war, said Walter Adam, propaganda chief, in a radio address, were seized in the shoes of a man arrested in Upper Austria.

Altar-Bound?

Ishbel MacDonald
Dutiful Daughter

Hint Romance For Daughter Of MacDonald

Ishbel Believed Meeting Swain During Canadian Visit

By GENEVIEVE HERRICK

(Copyright, 1934, by the North American Newspaper Alliance, Inc.)

WASHINGTON, Aug. 1—Ishbel MacDonald, on holiday in Canada with her father, Great Britain's Prime Minister, may be merely acting her usual role of dutiful daughter to a doting, if somewhat demanding, parent. Or she may have plans of her own.

Once upon a time—more than a year ago—there was a Canadian suitor when Ishbel accompanied her father to Washington. In March, 1933, the suitor hurried down from Canada. He came frequently, if not too publicly, to call on Ishbel at the White House, where the MacDonalds stayed.

The day she was interviewed by the newspaper women, she was 20 minutes late because she had tarried to talk with the gentleman. She talked to us on everything—then hurried back to the tete-a-tete.

Now, 'tis said, she's renewing that acquaintance in Canada.

Film Firms Sued Over Love Song

LOS ANGELES, Aug. 1 (AP)—D. Acosta, a citizen of Mexico, but who resides here, today filed a damage suit against Warner Brothers Pictures Inc., the Vitaphone Corporation, Vitagraph Inc., Mervyn Leroy and others for asserted copyright infringement on his Mexican love song, "Las Cuatro Milpas."

Acosta asks for an accounting of the profits from the picture, "Heat Lightning," wherein the song allegedly was used, for $250 for each public use of the song, attorney fees of $10,000 and a restraining order against further use of the piece.

Senator Wagner Hurt in Auto Crash

WESTPORT, N. Y., Aug. 1 (AP)—Swerving his automobile to avoid hitting a truck, United States Senator Robert F. Wagner was injured when the machine plunged off an Adirondack mountain highway into a brook near here today.

Representative S. Prall of Staten Island, en route with Senator Wagner to a fishing camp in Quebec, was more severely hurt.

One or two of Senator Wagner's ribs were fractured and Prall has a compound fracture of the right leg.

U. S. Selects Location for New Mint

Site Will Be Bounded by Duboce, Herman Webster, Buchanan and Streets

Impregnable Vaults Will Be Built in Solid Rock

San Francisco's new mint, replacing the famous old structure at Fifth and Mission streets, will be built on the fortress-like, rocky citadel comprising the block bounded by Duboce, Herman, Webster and Buchanan streets, The Chronicle learned upon good authority yesterday.

While the Treasury Department was reported not to have finally closed the deal, approval of the site and the price were expected to come from Washington within a short time, possibly 24 hours.

Federal authorities declined to comment on reports preliminaries had been disposed of and plans for construction soon would be under way.

JAGGED HEAP OF ROCKS

The block at present is a jagged heap of rocks, rising like a miniature Yosemite. It is a familiar sight on upper Market street, which is touched by one corner of the block. Treasury officials are said to regard it is a natural site for the building, which eventually will house a large share of the Nation's gold supply.

The entire area rests upon solid rock, which will provide an ideal foundation for the heavy structure. The subsurface vaults will be sunk into the rock, instead of being built on "made" land or in a sandy bottom, which would be the condition in the downtown area.

VAULTS TO BE IMPREGNABLE

The same circumstances will make it impossible for thieves to tunnel into the vaults—assuming this were possible—from some nearby locality. Nothing less than a major contracting operation with generous use of explosives will penetrate the rock.

The foundation will be blasted into the rock to a depth of several stories, to provide for impregnable storage vaults. The rock above street level will be blasted away to make room for the building, which will involve unusual architectural features to blend it with the surroundings.

Location of the mint away from the downtown business area will cause no inconvenience, it was point out. The mint business involves a comparatively small amount of trucking, and but few employes. Meanwhile plans were being pushed to transfer the huge gold reserve here to Denver during the period of construction.

(Picture on Page 7)

Nannys' Appetites Get Jeanne's Goat

CHICAGO, Aug. 1 (AP)—No kidding, these goats at the World's Fair will eat your shirt and all, complains Miss Jeanne Goodner of New York.

She added their appetite up to $200 today and put in a bill in Municipal Court, asking that the fair's Swiss village be told to settle, along with some unpleasant legal remarks about the three "hollow-horned, ruminant goats, possessed of omnivorous propensities." She appended their menu for one day: Her hat, $10; her gloves, $9; her purse, containing $150.

San Diegan Named As Aid by Kelly

Special to The Chronicle

SACRAMENTO, Aug. 1—Appointment of Edward J. Neron of San Diego as deputy State Director of Public Works was announced today by Earl Lee Kelly, Public Works Director. He succeeds Morgan Keaton of Los Angeles.

Neron is a former commander of the California-Nevada Department of the Veterans of Foreign Wars.

E. W. Scripps Wed To Seattle Woman

SEATTLE, Aug. 1 (AP)—E. W. Scripps, chairman of the board of the Scripps League of Newspapers, and Mary Oldham, daughter of Mr. and Mrs. Robert P. Oldham, were married here today. The bride is a graduate of Annie Wright Seminary in Tacoma and of Whitman College.

Retreat Sounded In New Orleans War by Kingfish

Mayor's Big Police Force Ready to Do Battle With Senator's Guardsmen

Machine Guns Aimed at City Hall; Governor Orders Vice Probe

NEW ORLEANS, Aug. 1 (AP)—As Mayor T. Semmes Walmsley mustered more men and guns than Senator Huey P. Long in their police-militia "war," Adjutant General Raymond H. Fleming announced tonight that half of the Senator's National Guardsmen were being demobilized.

Nearly 1500 city police under Mayor Walmsley, armed with pistols, rifles and riot guns, were ready to engage the guardsmen if an attempt was made to usurp the New Orleans government.

ADJUTANT EXPLAINS

Adjutant General Fleming from his headquarters at Jackson Barracks, where 500 militiamen were under arms, said he had dismissed "half of the 300 men called out" because "they were not needed."

HUEY LONG

"We are just going to keep as many men on duty as are necessary," he said. "We can get the others out at a moment's notice, anyhow. We might even let some more men go tomorrow."

Governor O. K. Allen at Baton Rouge broadened his proclamation of partial martial law and ordered the soldiers to scurry throughout the city and uncover, "without the use of any force," asserted evidence of vice, gambling and graft.

Adjutant General Fleming said he had not yet received Governor Allen's order which would turn the guardsmen into a huge detective force to investigate the "red light district" and "miscellaneous gambling."

The new proclamation directed the adjutant general, "without the use of any force, unless otherwise ordered by me hereafter, to make a survey and investigation to determine when and where red light districts are operating" with the "sanction of city authorities"; who, if anyone, is "collecting from the inhabitants," and "for what offices, if any, the said collections are being levied."

T. S. WALMSLEY

A like order was issued for the investigation of "lotteries, roulette games, blackjack, faro games, dice games, handbooks, keno games and other gambling activities."

Mayor Walmsley quickly answered the new thrust of the Long-controlled Governor.

"The proclamation of the Governor apparently is designed to usurp powers, duties and functions of the District Attorney," he said. "I particularly note that the Governor in his proclamation excludes any investigation of graft and paid for operation of gambling dives in the parishes surrounding New Orleans."

The Mayor has charged that Senator Long is connected with the operation of luxurious casinos in nearby parishes, which have ceased operation along with city establishments since the present political war started.

Leaders of both sides said any overt act would bring bloodshed.

Mayor Walmsley had been in-

Long Branded • • • • *'Drunken Rat'*

NEW ORLEANS, Aug. 1—Sheriff George E. Williams of the Parish of Orleans, recently reelected by an overwhelming majority, tonight sent the following open letter to Senator Huey P. Long:

"Sir: During your drunken radio speech last night which lasted for several hours, your statement to the effect that I had a brother running a gambling game—no brother of mine has ever run a gambling game in this city or anywhere else. Simply a drunken slam from a drunken United States Senator.

"You are just as I have branded you, a lying, drunken, cowardly rat.

(Signed) George E. Williams, Criminal Sheriff of the Parish of Orleans."

Bryan's Son Quits Nomination Race

LOS ANGELES, Aug. 1 (AP)—William Jennings Bryan Jr., son of the great commoner, today announced his withdrawal from the race for the Democratic nomination for Lieutenant Governor.

Paris Dressmakers Hem, Haw And Then Go to Great Lengths

PARIS, Aug. 1 (AP)—Longer skirts appeared in today's display of winter fashions as the occasion began to get down to serious business.

Although the largest dressmakers have not yet exhibited, the others have almost unanimously decreed that sports tailleur skirts must reach to 11 or 12 inches from the ground, day clothes to eight or 10 inches, and afternoon frocks to six.

This is in keeping with the slender silhouette, with tubelike skirts, slit at the back, front or sides, generally favored.

The greatest display of two toned or multicolored tweeds, woven in a harmonious blend of colors, which Paris ever has exhibited, is notable this season, indicating they will be all the rage this fall.

The hats were dark felts turned up in back and down in front and trimmed with brilliant features.

The afternoon frocks were designed with stemlike lines fashioned of new changeable velvets, taffeta velvets and such cushiony fabrics as quilted crepes and heavy corduroy wools.

EXTRA

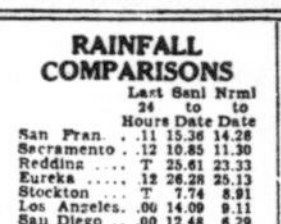

RAINFALL COMPARISONS

	Last 24 Hours	Seasl to Date	Nrml to Date
San Fran.	.11	15.36	14.28
Sacramento	.12	10.85	11.30
Redding	T	25.61	23.33
Eureka	.12	26.28	25.13
Stockton	T	7.74	8.91
Los Angeles	.00	14.09	9.11
San Diego	.00	12.48	6.29

San Francisco Chronicle

THE CITY'S ONLY HOME-OWNED NEWSPAPER

WEATHER in S. F. Bay Region
Occasional Rain
Complete Weather Reports on Page 20

FOUNDED 1865—VOL. CXLVI. NO. 29 CCC SAN FRANCISCO, CAL., WEDNESDAY, FEBRUARY 13, 1935 DAILY 5 CENTS, SUNDAY 10 CENTS: DAILY AND SUNDAY PER MONTH, $1.15

MACON FALLS IN SEA, SINKS; 81 RESCUED BY NAVY SHIPS OFF POINT SUR; 2 MISSING

Explosion on Dirigible Told by Eyewitness on Shore; SOS Brings Aid

Airship Sighted on Water Following Desperate Two-Hour Search by Vessels; Three Men Slightly Hurt

By ROYCE BRIER

The great dirigible Macon went to her grave in the sea last night off Point Sur, 100 miles south of San Francisco.

Two are missing from a crew of 83, and 81 were rescued by vessels of the naval fleet, which was sweeping northward with the Macon above.

The disaster followed an accident aboard, believed to have been an explosion. The commander referred to it as a "casualty" in the stern. The ship crumbled aft, and her life was a matter of minutes.

She went down in an offshore drizzle, just as night was closing down. Her gray length was last seen dipping toward the ocean. Then she soared in her death throes, and was lost to view in the mist.

The doomed ship flashed an SOS to the world, saying she was "falling" and saying "wait!" and she rested on the water.

Gas cells under the fins had disintegrated, and fuel tanks had been thrown overboard, but the sky mammoth had come down stern-first, broken beyond all help.

Then began a desperate two-hour search of the dark seas. Naval vessels, with their giant searchlights, made a murky daylight of the scene. Lifeboats were put off, and ultimately the stricken airship was sighted. Seven lifeboats filled with survivors, including Lieutenant Commander Herbert V. Wiley, were taken aboard the cruisers.

As the rescue was completed, nothing but calcium flares and wreckage marked the descent of the dirigible. Late last night the survivors were being brought to San Francisco, and patrols were ordered out to search for the two men unaccounted for.

The first SOS came at 5:19 sharp.

Then began a drama of the air and sea such as the Pacific Coast has never witnessed. Fragments came

(Continued on Page A, Column 4)

SHIP LOST, ITS CHIEF SAVED

LIEUTENANT COMMANDER HERBERT V. WILEY of the dirigible Macon, who was rescued in the disaster off Point Sur when his craft dived into the sea, and above, the giant ship when she was moored at her Sunnyvale base.

Wiley Tells Own Story of Macon Crash

'Discipline Excellent' Commander Radios Admiral

Here is the story of tragedy of the Macon as described by Lieutenant Commander Herbert V. Wiley in a radio message to Admiral Thomas J. Senn received at 9:10:

"While off Point Sur course north all engines standard speed 63 knots, altitude 1250 feet, ai-squally at times about 5:18 p. m. Casualty occurred in stern. I thought elevator control carried away. Ship took bow up inclination and rose rapidly. Ordered all ballast and fuel slip tanks dropped aft of midships. Received prompt word No. 1 gas cell under fins was gone and stern was crumbling and finally that No. 2 cell was gone.

"Tried to land ship near cruisers

(Continued on Page A, Col. 8)

Tense Messages From Sea Tell Story of Great Disaster

By CAROLYN ANSPACHER

At twilight last night a message flashed through the storm clouds that terrified the world.

It was a single word that in its seven letters spelled the doom of the Macon, last of the Nation's giant silver dirigibles.

"Falling," radioed the airship at 5:19 o'clock.

Just that, followed by the single cryptic word, "wait." And the heart of America turned cold in memory of a similar message flashed from the dirigible Akron less than two years ago.

From then on the tragedy of the Macon was told in dispassionate messages that reached into millions of homes and offices through millions of radios.

They came with maddening irregularity, with fearful deliberation.

The second message from the ship came at 5:34.

"Will abandon ship as soon as we land on water somewhere within 20 miles of Point Sur about 10 miles at sea," it said.

Nearly an hour passed before the next message. It finally came at 6:30 from the U. S. S. Maryland.

"The Macon reported sighted about 0 point 20 from Maryland" the vessel radioed.

"Proceeding in that direction. Maintain the same position." the last words were directed to the Macon.

Two minutes later the next mes-

(Continued on Page A, Col. 7)

Bruno Death Demanded; Case to Jury by Noon

FLEMINGTON, N. J., Feb. 12 (AP)—An angry demand for Bruno Richard Hauptmann's death sealed New Jersey's case against him today for the murder of Baby Lindbergh.

His voice raised in scorn and fury, Attorney General David T. Wilentz cried out in his all-day summation for a jury mandate which will put Hauptmann in the electric chair, but as he finished he was interrupted and the courtroom thrown into confusion by a spectator-clergyman's shout.

From his perch on a window sill of the jammed courtroom, Rev. Vincent G. Burns, a North Jersey pastor, interrupted the summation to cry: "A man confessed that crime to me in my church."

Struggling, he was hauled down and taken away. Later Justice Thomas W. Trenchard ordered him released after instructing the jury to disregard the incident. The preacher had told his story before to both prosecution and defense, but neither called him as a witness.

TO JURY BY NOON

By tomorrow's noon hour the jury of eight men and four women will be locked up to decide Hauptmann's fate. Then Justice Trenchard will charge the jury at 10 a. m.

Hauptmann had sat tight-lipped through Wilentz's fiery, all-day summation, as the prosecutor swung his fist and called him "the lowest form of animal," a pariah who "contaminates the air."

Anna Hauptmann was statue-like in her chair, but the jurors, by slight gestures and fleeting expressions, frequently betrayed their feelings.

Savagely, Wilentz demanded that Hauptmann be put to death like a dangerous beast, and told the jury that a verdict of conviction with a recommendation of mercy would be "wishy-washy."

Only the electric chair, he cried, would "thaw out" Hauptmann's coldness—he is cold, yes, but he will

(Continued on Page 5, Col. 1)

Navy to Call Investigation

Action Awaits Preliminary Reports

WASHINGTON Feb. 12 (AP) — With President Roosevelt keeping a vigil on reports from the Macon crash, the calling of a naval board of inquiry into the disaster tonight awaited only preliminary reports from the fleet commander.

The board, it was indicated at the Navy Department, would be appointed promptly upon initial direct information from Admiral J. M. Reeves, commander of the fleet, and the skipper of the Macon, Lieutenant Commander H. V. Wiley.

Onto President Roosevelt's desk during the night were dropped from hour to hour a file of all messages relating to the story of the crash. Mr. Roosevelt himself called the Navy Department shortly after word of the wreck reached Washington.

RELIEVED

Both the chief executive and the navy high command were known to be relieved that here would be no mounting casualty list. The memory of the Akron with its towering

(Continued on Page A, Col. 6)

Abyssinia Defies Italy; Army Ready

We Have Million Men, Won't Pay Indemnity, Says Envoy

ROME, Feb. 12 (AP) — Ethiopia's diplomatic envoy to Rome announced tonight Ethiopia would not pay a cent to Italy as indemnity, that the African empire had one million men available to fight Italy, that no foreign power was expected as an ally, and that "Ethiopia does not need one."

This statement was made directly to the Associated

(Continued on Page 2, Col. 5)

LIST OF THOSE MISSING AND RESCUED OF MEN ABOARD WRECKED DIRIGIBLE

Following is the list of missing and rescued in the Macon disaster, showing vessels survivors were taken aboard, compiled from official navy reports:

MISSING

E. E. Dailey, Chief Radioman.
E. Edquiba, mess attendant. tendant.

SURVIVORS

Reported Aboard U. S. S. Concord

LT. COMDR. HERBERT V. WILEY, commanding.
LT. COMDR. JESSE L. KENWORTHY, executive officer.
J. B. CONNOLLY, coxswain.
H. H. ASHCRAFT, seaman.
A. FRANCES, chief aerographer.
K. H. McARDLE, aviation machinist's mate.
W. F. GERMAINE, av. machinist.
A. F. GLOWASKI, seaman 1c.
C. E. ADAMS, boatswain's mate, 2c.
L. E. GENTILE, coxswain.
W. M. CONOVER, aviation machinist's mate.

Reported Aboard U. S. S. Cincinnati

EMMETT C. THURMAN, chief machinist's mate.
V. T. MOSS, pharmacist's mate.
P. M. JACKSON, boatswain's mate, internally injured.
J. N. GARNER, aviation machinist's mate, internally injured.
J. B. HALL, fireman.
J. C. JENNINGS, aviation chief machinist's mate.

Reported Aboard U. S. S. Richmond

COMDR. ALFRED T. CLAY, guest officer and slated as new commander of Sunnyvale base.
LT. COMDR. EDWIN COCHRANE, engineering officer.
LT. COMDR. GEORGE H. MILLS, tactical officer.
LT. COMDR. SCOTT E. PECK, navigator.
LT. DONALD M. MACKEY, gunnery officer.
LT. CALVIN BOLSTER.
LT. HOWARD N. COULTER.
LT. ANTHONY L. DAVIS.
LT. HAROLD B. MILLER, airplane pilot.
LT. JOHN D. REPPY, airplane pilot.
LT. FREDERICK N. KIVETTE, airplane pilot.
LT. GEORGE W. CAMPBELL.
LT. GERALD L. HUFF.
LT. LEROY C. SIMPLER.
LT. C. S. ROUNDS.
LT. EARL J. VAN SWEARINGEN.
T. C. BRANDES, quartermaster 1c.
E. KLASSEN, av. machinists mate 1c.
D. W. BOUNDS, fireman 2c.
W. F. BUCHER, hcief commissary steward.
W. J. BAKER, av. machinists mate 3c.
W. G. BIGHOUSE, radioman, 2c.
F. M. CULBERT, or Culvert, av. machinists mate 3c.
M. CARIASA, mess attendant.
T. CLASS, ship's cook 2c.
W. H. CLARK, coxswain.
A. E. CARROLL, av. machinists mate 3c.
C. L. DE FOREST, av. machinists mate 3c.
G. L. DUNN, fireman 1c.
F. S. DOMIAN, boatswains mate 2c. swain 2c.
M. FEIT, carpenter's mate.
M. G. FRASS, av. machinists mate 2c.
J. C. GILMORE, electricians mate.
D. R. SAFFORD, av. machinists mate.
A. B. GALATIAN, av. chief machinists mate.
E. H. HERRINGTON, boatswains mate 1c.
W. H. HERNDON, coxswain.
W. M. HAMMOND, coxswain.
C. S. SOLAR, chief machinists mate.
E. W. KIRKPATRICK, boatswains mate 1c.
W. S. KOSAR, radioman, 1c.
W. F. LEONARD, av. machinists mate, 2c.
L. E. LETONEN, av. machinists mate 3c.
M. O. MILLER, chief petty officer.
J. E. MALAK, av. machinists mate, 1c.
W. A. MacDONALD, coxswain.
C. W. MILLER, [illegible]
E. R. MORRIS, av. machinists mate, 1c.
B. G. PERKS, quartermaster.
C. C. PADGETT, or Padette, fireman, 2c.
H. G. ROWE, seaman.
H. B. SULLIVAN, radioman, 1c.
L. T. SHELLBERG, boatswain's mate, 1c.
W. A. THOMPSON, signalman, 2c.
J. F. TODD, av. machinists mate, 3c.
M. T. WALTERS, radioman, 2c.
W. A. BUCKLEY, chief boatswain's mate.
W. BROOK, chief boatswain's mate.
R. J. DAVIS, chief boatswain's mate.
J. E. STEEL, aviation ordnance mechanic.
R. F. RANDOLPH, chief radioman.
T. M. SLEEK, fireman, 2c.
E. M. OLIVER, coxswain.
SYDNEY [illegible]

EXTRA

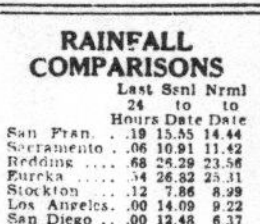

RAINFALL COMPARISONS

	Last 24 Hours	Ssnl to Date	Nrml to Date
San Fran.	.19	15.55	14.44
Sacramento	.06	10.91	11.42
Redding	.68	26.29	23.56
Eureka	.54	26.82	25.31
Stockton	.12	7.86	8.99
Los Angeles	.00	14.09	9.22
San Diego	.00	12.48	6.37

San Francisco Chronicle

THE CITY'S ONLY HOME-OWNED NEWSPAPER

WEATHER in S. F. Bay Region
Clearing with Showers
Complete Weather Report on Page 24

FOUNDED 1865—VOL. CXLVI, NO. 30 . CCC* SAN FRANCISCO, CAL., THURSDAY, FEBRUARY 14, 1935 DAILY 5 CENTS, SUNDAY 10 CENTS: DAILY AND SUNDAY PER MONTH, $1.15

BRUNO HAUPTMANN MUST DIE; ELECTROCUTION SET IN MONTH; CARPENTER FAINTS IN CELL

Jury Finds Defendant Guilty of Murdering Charles Lindbergh Jr.

Courtroom Tense as Justice Pronounces Doom of Convicted Kidnaper of Infant

Special to The Chronicle

FLEMINGTON, N. J., Feb. 13—While a howling mob of 5000 men, women and children cheered and screamed their approval around this old courthouse, Bruno Richard Hauptmann, as white as death and cold as ice, stood erect before the court at 10:47 p. m. (E. S. T.) tonight and was sentenced to the electric chair for murdering Charles A. Lindbergh Jr.

Neither Hauptmann nor Mrs. Anna Hauptmann, the deepened lines of her face drawn into a defiant stare, shed a tear or showed a trace of emotion during the long, tense ordeal. But 281-pound Mrs. Verna Snyder, who held out for life imprisonment for Bruno until the seventh and deciding ballot of the jurors, was crying.

HAUPTMANN ERECT

Hauptmann stood erect, as stiff as a ramrod and apparently just as nerveless, for a full three minutes of dreadful tension during the ordeal. First he stood while Charles Walton, sober foreman, read from a paper:

"We find the defendant, Bruno Richard Hauptmann, guilty of murder in the first degree."

Bruno's deep-set eyes—they seem an inch deeper in their sockets than a week ago—blinked, but not a muscle in his body moved.

"Please poll the jury," Edward J. Reilly, defense counsel, said.

Walton, whose voice wavered and sunk when he was originally asked for the verdict, didn't understand and said:

"Here."

READS GUILTY VERDICT

He was told the jury was being polled, and he read the entire guilty verdict again. One by one, each of the jurors followed suit. Mrs. Rosie Pill had difficulty in saying the words, and next to her, Mrs. Snyder simply mumbled, on the point of bursting into tears.

Until late tonight, after they had argued with nine other jurors from 11:13 a. m. today until they arrived at their verdict at 10:20 p. m., Mrs. Snyder and the stout, kindly Mrs. Pill held out for guilty with recommendation of mercy—which meant life imprisonment for Hauptmann. Until the third ballot, shortly

(Continued on Page 8, Col. 4)

FLEMINGTON, N. J., Feb. 13 (AP)—When word that a verdict had been reached in Bruno Hauptmann's trial for murder of the Lindbergh baby flashed through the courtroom confusion reigned briefly.

In transmitting the verdict from one part of the courthouse to another the Associated Press' report of the decision was garbled and first word to reach waiting newspapers was that the jury had found Hauptmann guilty, but with a recommendation for life sentence instead of the death penalty.

Bruno Faints After Doom Is Sounded

Slayer Falls Insensible on Reentering Cell; Powerful Drugs Restore Him

FLEMINGTON, N. J., Feb. 13—Bruno Richard Hauptmann, an iron man when he faced the jury that decreed his death, collapsed into unconsciousness a few moments afterward, when he reached his cell, a short walk from the courtroom.

Dr. Barclay H. Fuhrman, who was quickly summoned, administered powerful restoratives, but it was nearly half an hour before the doomed man came to his senses.

FALLS UNCONSCIOUS

Hauptmann walked steadily when he started out of the courtroom, manacled to two guards. He hung back a little as they neared the door of the Courthouse library, which lay en route to the jail.

His guards pulled him on roughly. When he walked into the bullpen, the barred inclosure on which his cubicle opens, he still appeared steady enough. At the door of the cell he uttered an exclamation—"O-o-o-o-o!" and fainted. He would have fallen, except that the manacles of his guards held him up.

WIFE IS DISTRAUGHT

The unconscious man was quickly unlocked from the handcuffs, while half a dozen State troopers supported his relaxed body, and then was laid on the narrow cot which has been his bed for four months, ever since he came to Flemington's jail from the Bronx.

In the meantime, Mrs. Haupt-

(Continued on Page 8, Col. 3)

S. F. Boy Named Stanford Editor

The editorial staff of the Stanford Daily, university student publication, yesterday named Julius Jacobs, San Francisco, editor for the remaining half of the college year.

Frank Orr of San Diego and Robert Jones, Oakland, were named associate editors; Bob Calkins of Ceres, managing editor, and Charlotte Burridge, San Diego, woman's editor. Jacobs succeeds Stanlet Beaubaire as editor.

BRUNO HAUPTMANN The camera's history of kidnaping, search and trial—Pages 6 and 7.

Wiley's Own Story of Macon Disaster Places Blame on Collapsed Cells

ERECT, gray-haired Herbert V. Wiley, Lieutenant Commander of the United States Navy and survivor of the Akron and Macon disasters, yesterday gave a detailed explanation of the Macon's plunge into the Pacific off Point Sur.

Holding a prepared statement in a steady hand, Lieutenant Commander Wiley leaned forward in a chair of the U. S. S. Concord's ward room and told his story calmly, alternately reading from the script and interjecting explanations. Here is his story:

By LIEUT. CMDR. HERBERT V. WILEY
Commander of the U. S. S. Macon

It was at 7:10 a. m. on Monday, February 11, 1935, that the Macon left Sunnyvale for exercises in conjunction with the fleet in accordance with approved schedule. Scouting for the fleet was conducted on Monday and continued on Tuesday. The exercises were completed in so far as the Macon was concerned at 3 p. m. Tuesday and the Macon proceeded toward its base at Sunnyvale.

About 20 miles off Point Buchan the course was set to pass near Monterey, as it was desired to enter the Santa Clara valley at Watsonville if visibility permitted. You know, there's a low point there which would permit access to Sunnyvale without having to rise to any great altitude.

In order to reach the base before the visibility became any worse, all engines were run at standard speed, the air speed being about 63 knots.

We ran into some rain squalls then. Altitude was decreased from 2700 feet to 1600 feet to pass under one squall, and then decreased to 1250 feet to pass under another.

Visibility, which had been bad, was somewhat better near Point Sur, and two divisions of heavy cruisers were observed in that locality.

Two or three minutes after passing Point Sur, about three miles distant, I felt a short jar and the helmsman said the wheel had slipped out of his hand.

I seized the wheel, myself, and it swung loose in my hands. At the same time the ship tilted upward, a bow up inclination, and she started to rise.

Out of Control

You see, with the ship tilted up the motors were still driving her forward and she drove up into the mist. Apparently the man at the elevators had no control.

At the same moment, and things were happening quickly, I received a phone call from aft that No. 1 cell was gone. That's one of the gas bags containing the helium.

There was no explosion, I know that. What the "casualty" to the gas bag was I do not know.

At any rate, I immediately ordered all ballast and emergency fuel dump tanks in the afterpart of the ship to be jettisoned. At the same time I ordered gas to be valved from the forward gas cells to regain the trim, put the ship on an even keel.

Relieved the Strain

The inclination of the ship had reached 23 degrees and she ascended rapidly. The engines were ordered

(Continued on Page 3, Col. 5)

Win Ball Prize: Good-by Appendix

TORRANCE, Feb. 13 (AP)—The Torrance Memorial Hospital today announced something new in the way of prizes for a benefit ball it is holding in a Hermosa Beach club on February 22.

First prize is an appendix operation, valued at $200.

Shanghai Greets Aimee McPherson

SHANGHAI, Feb. 13 (AP)—The docks rang with hymns today upon the arrival of Aimee Semple McPherson, who is paying a brief visit before proceeding to Hongkong to visit the grave of her former missionary husband, Robert Semple.

Survivors Relate Macon Tragedy, Mute on Cause

Chief Radio Operator, Man Who Flashed SOS, Stuck to Post Until Last, Then Plunged to His Death

By ROYCE BRIER

Sullen death which snatched at four score men with the destruction of the dirigible Macon, and lost, was beaten into the background yesterday as 81 came home.

The officers and men, saved by heroism and a miracle, told what had happened to their great silver airship.

They stood huddled on three rescue cruisers in San Francisco bay, laughing, begging cigarettes, between puffs relating an epic of sea and air such as has seldom been told.

But though they could describe the first alarm and the fall, the flying minutes, after she struck, and dragging hours as the navy swept the misty seas in search of them, they were mute on the initial cause of the catastrophe.

FIGHT FOR LIFE

Some fabric tore away on her fins, along her backbone, gas cells burst, the great length shuddered and soared and descended and hit,

INQUIRY TODAY

Admiral J. M. Reeves, commander in chief of the United States fleet, last night called a court of inquiry to convene at 9:30 a. m. today on board the U. S. S. Tennessee to investigate the Macon disaster. The board will consist of Rear Admiral Orin G. Murfin, Captain W. R. Van Auken, Captain H. E. Shoemaker, as members, and Commander T. L. Gatch as judge advocate.

and suddenly they tumbled pell-mell out, they were in the water, fighting for their lives.

Flaming gasoline was about them, ignited by calcium flares of mercy.

This was the story in brief, different for every man, yet somehow merging into one great story of men against the sea—and the air.

BLOCK FROM TROUBLE

The Richmond, the Cincinnati and the Concord had these men yesterday, with Lieutenant Commander Herbert V. Wiley aboard the Concord. He described what happened, talking in terms of telephone calls, buoyancy and lack of it, jettisoned gasoline and crumbling gas cells and frames. He was in the control car a city block from the source of trouble.

The story of men is another story.

The Macon was humming along not far at sea south of Monterey bay. The weather was dark gray and filled with drizzle, but the world's greatest dirigible had seen many such days. She had met the fleet plowing northward toward San Francisco, she was accompanying it, and soon she would go to her home in Sunnyvale.

The time was a little after 5 o'clock in the afternoon, and daylight was already failing.

There was a little jar. It jerked at the wheel in the helmsman's hands. Some said they didn't feel it—the jar—but immediately no-

(Continued on Page 2, Col. 1)

17-Day-Old Baby Can't Eat, Dies

GRANITE CITY, Ill., Feb. 13 (AP)—Ending his stubborn fight for life, 17-day-old Robert Jenkins died of starvation at St. Elizabeth's Hospital today.

Medical science had stood by helplessly, unable to aid the infant, born with a strictured esophagus which prevented it from taking food.

Two Dogs Added To Poison List

Special to The Chronicle

SAN JOSE, Feb. 13—Death of two more valuable dogs caused officers to renew their efforts to apprehend the "phantom" poisoner, who has operated extensively here during the last three weeks.

EXCLUSIVE -::- IN THE CHRONICLE -::- EXCLUSIVE

WILL ROGERS' LAST STORY!

COMPARATIVE TEMPERATURES

	High	Low		High	Low
San Francisco	66	52	New York	86	72
Los Angeles	76	65	Chicago	80	70
Seattle	72	52	Kansas City	102	76
Denver	76	62	New Orleans	88	78

San Francisco Chronicle
THE CITY'S ONLY HOME-OWNED NEWSPAPER

WEATHER in S. F. Bay Region
Fair and Mild
Complete Weather Report on Page 24

FOUNDED 1865—VOL. CXLVII, NO. 33 CCC SAN FRANCISCO, CAL., SATURDAY, AUGUST 17, 1935 DAILY 5 CENTS, SUNDAY 10 CENTS: DAILY AND SUNDAY PER MONTH, $1.35

Rogers and Post Plunge to Their Death in Plane

Flyer Arrives to Bring Back Bodies of Famed Pair Killed in Alaska

For Editorial Comment see Page 8

(Copyright, 1935, by the Associated Press)

POINT BARROW, Alaska, Aug. 16 (AP)—Death, reaching through an Arctic fog, overtook Will Rogers, peerless comedian, and Wiley Post, master aviator, when their rebuilt airplane faltered and fell into an icy little river near this forlorn outpost of civilization last night.

They had just taken off for a trifling ten-minute flight from their river position to Point Barrow. Sixty feet in the air their motor misfired. The plane heeled over on its right wing and plummeted to the river bank.

The lives of both the gentle master of the wise-crack and the champion aerial globe trotter were crushed out as the impact drove the heavy motor back through the fuselage.

ESKIMO RUNS 15 MILES

A terrified Eskimo ran 15 miles to Point Barrow with the news. Sergeant Stanley R. Morgan of the United States Army Signal Corps dashed to the scene, recovered the bodies and brought word of the tragedy that shocked millions throughout the world today.

President and pauper alike expressed sorrow, for both men were known over virtually the length and breadth of civilization.

TO RETURN BODIES BY AIR

In Washington it was learned tonight that Pilot Joe Crosson of the Alaska Airways would return to Fairbanks tomorrow with the bodies of Rogers and Post from Point Barrow.

The Coast Guard was informed that Crosson arrived at Point Barrow at 4 p. m., Eastern Standard Time.

He planned to proceed from Fairbanks to Juneau, the Coast Guard was informed.

At the same time, in Burbank, Cal., it became known that the multi-millionaire humorist and the famous globe trotter were using a plane made up of second-hand parts and operating under a restricted Government license.

Dr. Henry Greist, Presbyterian medical missionary, who received the bodies here pending their removal home, said both men apparently had died instantly.

"Both men's limbs were broken and both suffered severe head wounds when they were crushed in the wreckage," said Greist.

Rogers and Post had landed on the river when the Arctic fog had made them uncertain of their bearings on a 500-mile flight from Fairbanks to Point Barrow.

The Eskimo pointed out the way a few seconds after the takeoff the plane's engine spluttered. The ship dropped into the river, striking first on its right wing and then nosing into the bank head-on.

POST'S WATCH STOPS

"The Eskimo said he ran to the water's edge and called, but that there was no answer," said Dr. Greist.

"Alarmed, he turned and ran the 15 miles to Barrow and informed Sergeant Morgan.

"Several motor boats, under the sergeant's command, sped to the scene.

"The rescuers had to tear the plane fragments apart to extricate the bodies.

"The Eskimo was three hours running the 15 miles to Barrow, over the rough tundra, with many small lakes to encircle and many streams to cross.

"Post's watch stopped at 8:20, probably when his arm dropped into the water after death.

USE WHALE BOAT

"The native runner," Dr. Greist went on, "in his excitement on first arriving here,

(Continued on Page C, Col. 3)

Today's News Summary on Page 2

In Memoriam

Will Rogers' last winged dart of wit or wisdom is spent. The last rope is flung, the last bright quip has sparkled, the last searching epigram has found its mark. America mourns its gayest comedian and most popular philosopher. There is an end of wisecracks and of wise saws, but most of all, there is the end of a fine life, which gave and received much love. The man who never threw down a friend nor earned an enemy, whose words and thoughts and deeds were all of kindness, whose playful motley covered a gentle heart and a keen mind, died as he had lived, in high adventure.

Will Rogers feared nothing and had done almost everything. He would have been the last to shrink from an experience because it was dangerous, and the first to undertake it if he could thereby bring a little more helpfulness or cheerfulness into the world. His last message from the North was one of appreciation of the problems and charity for the blunders of the Alaskan "spinach pioneers," and his last weekly article, now published after his death, is one of homely affection for the folks at home.

There was only one Will Rogers, and this day will be sadder in millions of homes by the knowledge that he is gone.

DEATH STRIKES---WORLD LOSES

Will Rogers and Wiley Post. Smilingly they posed beside their doomed plane.

WILL ROGERS' LAST STORY

(Here is Will Rogers' column originally written for release in tomorrow's Chronicle.)

By WILL ROGERS

ODD McINTYRE is always writing "Thoughts While Strolling." Well, suppose you are not a "Stroller." I am what you might call a mighty poor "Stroller." The feet are bad and the legs are worse, so I take mine out in riding. So with all due apologies to Odd this is "Thoughts While Flying."

Away here a week or so back I went out to the flying field at midnight in Los Angeles to catch the plane for Seattle. You see, day or night means nothing to 'em now. With the courses all lighted they run schedules in the night time the same as in the day. Bill, that's the first born, and his Mother were with me, and I was off on a little sightseeing trip with Wiley Post. When my wife knew it was with Wiley, it dident matter where it was we was going and she was mighty fine about it.

Well she is about everything. You can't live with a comedian long without being mighty forgiving. The same field a couple of years or more ago she had seen me off to Vancouver to catch a boat to go to the Japanese Manchurian war, and then fly on around the world and meet her in Geneva, Switzerland, at one of those Dissarament Conferences where I used to always go for my amusement. Then around South America on 21 thousand miles jaunt one time, and by the way, she is no mean aviation enthusiast herself. She will make all the short trips with you. In fact she was flying the next night after I left on this trip clear back to New York and to Maine to see our Mary.

* * * *

BUT THIS has nothing to do with "Air Strolling" as I haven't started strolling yet. Pretty night, nice stars, I dropped off in Frisco to tend to some business early the next morning and caught a plane out of there at eleven the next morning, and then to Seattle at five in the afternoon. That's a pretty trip. The pilots in the big Boehing just scraped Mount Shasta. Snow all over the old ant hill. We flew right up and over what I think they call the Redwood highway. Lots of pretty little towns nestled back in little valleys and canyons. First stop out of Sacramento was Medford, Oregon, where a few days before some ambitious reporter had sent out a Dispatch that he had seen Wiley Post and I flying over there, when we were at that time crossing Arizona. So this time he is liable to report that I arrived there by horse and buggy.

* * * *

SAY, THERE is some Mountains over that route. South of Medford, north of Medford, that's the town where they raise the fine pears. I was forced down there on my previous flight to Vancouver and they kept telling me about the fine pears and I afterward wrote about them, but said they never did offer me any, they just kept telling how great they was. Well, sir, when I returned from around the World, they sent me practically all they raised in the Valley that year I think. Every time a box would come it would be more pears, and better pears (if possible).

* * * *

WE LOOKED down and saw a big forest fire in the Mountains. Pilots said it had been burning for days. Lots of great timber going to waste. Beautiful country Northern Cal., and Oregon and Washington, everything green, rivers galore. Into Portland, Ore., a beautiful air field on an Island, and a beautiful located city. Asked for Tex Rankin, a flyer that had hauled me over that Country in the early days. He was a fine flyer, and is yet, which means that he is good. If "You are a fine flyer" means a lot more than saying "You was a fine flyer." Girl stewardess come along somewhere in the story here with a fine lunch. It had more dainty little sandwiches, and knicknacks than I had ever seen in any lunch in my life, it was arranged lovely. They say it was made up at the St. Francis Hotel in San Francisco.

* * * *

THEN INTO the Puget Sound Country, beautiful Bays, and Islands. Tacoma, who had the first slogan that I can ever remember, it was when I played there in vaudeville about 1908, "Watch Tacoma Grow." I have never watched it much since, but it did. Seattle? That's a whole story in itself. The Gateway to Alaska, to the Orient, to Canada. Have to tell you about that and seeing the big bombing plane they was just finishing for the Army. Biggest in the World.

Yes, sir, a plane is a great place to see anything, only the wings are right under where you want to look and you can't see anything. Did really see Mount Shasta. They couldent hide it under the wings.

His Epitaph

BOSTON, Aug. 16 (AP)—The death of Will Rogers recalled remarks he made in a speech here in 1930 concerning the epitaph to be placed on his grave.

"When I die, my epitaph, or whatever you call those signs on gravestones, is going to read:

"'I joke about every prominent man of my time, but I never met a man I didn't like.'

"I am proud of that," Rogers added. "I can hardly wait to die so it can be carved. And when you come around to my grave, you'll probably find me sitting there proudly reading it."

Ethiopia Offers Concessions to Italy at Parley

Duce Unwilling to Tell France, Britain What He Wants

Tripower Parley Balked in Peace Efforts

PARIS, Aug. 16 (AP)—Ethiopia offered Italy economic concessions tonight, but Premier Mussolini's unwillingness to tell France and England exactly what he wants balked efforts to avert war.

In a message from Ethiopia to the tri-power conference, Emperor Haile Selassie emphasized he would not accept a military occupation.

His offer climaxed long deliberations by Premier Pierre Laval of France, Anthony Eden of Great Britain and Baron Pompeo Aloisi of Italy as the talks formally were opened.

A British spokesman said Aloisi

(Continued on Page 2, Col. 1)

G-Man Slain In Gun Fight With Robber

Accused Man Wounded by Justice Agent, Who Fires Shot as He Falls

WASHINGTON, Aug. 16 (AP)—Nelson B. Klein, a Justice Department agent, was killed tonight in a gun battle at College Corner, Ohio, about 35 miles from Cincinnati, with George Barrett, who was being sought as an automobile thief.

J. Edgar Hoover, chief of the Federal Bureau of Investigation, announced the death of the "G-man."

ACCUSED MAN WOUNDED

Barrett was wounded by Klein and a fellow agent, he said, and will be charged with the murder of a Federal officer. Barrett was taken to a Cincinnati hospital.

Klein and his companion approached Barrett in the small Ohio town, Hoover said, but before they could identify themselves the man sought for automobile theft opened fire and Klein fell.

SHOOTS AS HE FALLS

Klein shot as he fell, Hoover said, and bullets from his gun and that of his companion cut Barrett down with wounds in the legs.

Klein was the fourth Justice Department agent to lose his life in the line of duty during the last two years, Hoover said. A Federal Agent since 1926, Klein is survived by a wife and three children.

Rogers Says:

(Reprint from Friday's Chronicle)

FAIRBANKS, Aug. 15—Visited our new emigrants. Now, this is no time to discuss whether it will succeed or whether it won't; whether it's farming country or whether it is not, and to enumerate the hundreds of mistakes and confusions and rows and arguments and management in the whole thing at home and here.

As I see it, there is now but one problem that they are here, and that's to get 'em housed' within six or eight weeks. Things have been a terrible mess. They are getting 'em straightened out, but even now not fast enough. There is about 700 or 800 of 'em. About 200 went back; also about that many workmen sent from the transient camps down home (not CCC), and just lately they are using about 150 Alaskan workmen at regular wages. But it's just a few weeks to snow now, and they have to be out of tents, both workmen and settlers.

There is plenty food and always has been and will be. They can always get that in, but it's houses they need right now, and Colonel Hunt, in charge, realizes it.

You know, after all, there is a lot of difference in pioneering for gold and pioneering for spinach.

Yours, WILL ROGERS.

MANILA — 1500 MI. — GUAM — 1450 MI. — WAKE — 1242 MI. — MIDWAY — 1380 MI. — HAWAII — 2410 MILES — SAN FRANCISCO

COMPARATIVE TEMPERATURES

	High	Low		High	Low
San Francisco	60	52	Denver	56	30
Los Angeles	64	58	New York	56	46
Seattle	48	40	Chicago	24	18
Honolulu	....	66	New Orleans	64	52

San Francisco Chronicle

THE CITY'S ONLY HOME-OWNED NEWSPAPER

WEATHER in S. F. Bay Region
Fair, With Clouds
Complete Weather Report on Page 6.

FOUNDED 1865—VOL. CXLVII, NO. 131 CCC SAN FRANCISCO, CAL., SATURDAY, NOVEMBER 23, 1935 DAILY 5 CENTS, SUNDAY 10 CENTS: DAILY AND SUNDAY PER MONTH, $1.15

Clues Show Manno Firm Sold Barrel Of Fluoride

Deadly Powder Believed Shipped Through Error

Mystery Expected to Be Cleared Up Soon

Clues indicating that the poison which killed three persons and imperiled several hundred when sold as soda in a Mission street store, came directly from the basement of the Manno Sales Company, assertedly were in the hands of police last night.

Inspector George Engler of the homicide squad made this statement after day-long investigation:

"I am convinced that one barrel, containing deadly fluoride, was mistakenly included in the shipment of six barrels of supposed baking soda, sold by the Manno firm to Rosenthal's.

"From various bits of evidence gathered, I am further convinced this fluoride barrel was the one used to refill the barrels of uncontaminated soda as they were depleted through sales to customers of the Rosenthal store.

"I intend to act at once on my conviction, and expect to have a definite announcement to make that will clear up this mystery."

Engler's theory was fortified by interrogation of an employe of Nich Manno, proprietor of the salvage firm, and of Rosenthal's.

EMPLOYE QUIZZED

From August J. Weiler, employed at Manno's, the inspector obtained this statement:

"I loaded three barrels of soda on our truck, and they were delivered to Rosenthal's. Then the driver made a second trip. This time, three more barrels were brought up from the basement I don't know what was in them. Manno stuck his finger in one, tasted the suff, and said 'that's soda—take it along.'"

Proceeding to Rosenthal's, Engler questioned Jack Dineen, and reported the latter made this declaration:

"I am certain that the barrel we got back from the cooper to whom we sold it, was one of the barrels that came from Manno's."

FLUORIDE IN BARREL

(The barrel referred to had two pounds of a white substance still inside when it was retrieved, and this substance, tested under direction of Dr. J. C. Geiger, city health officer, proved to be death-dealing fluoride).

Engler said Dineen further explained:

"I used the contents of that barrel

(Continued on Page 7, Col. 3)

Doris Cromwell Marks Birthday

HONOLULU, Hawaii, Nov. 22 (UP)—Doris Duke Cromwell, generally considered the world's richest girl, quietly observed her 23d birthday today, happily married and eager to keep out of the limelight.

---AND HISTORY IS MADE!

China Clipper shown as she soared out of S. F. Bay and over the Golden Gate bridge on her maiden flight to Hawaii and the Philippines.

CLIPPING OFF THE MILES

Log of the China Clipper flight to Manila.

By United Press, (all times Pacific Standard).

3:46 p. m.—Took off from Alameda, Calif., to start first regular trans-Pacific air mail flight.

4 p. m.—Captain Edwin C. Musick radioed the following message: "Over lightship 20 miles off the Golden Gate, altitude 6000 feet. Climbing. Weather clear, visibility unlimited, and ceiling unlimited."

5 p. m.—Flying between two layers of dense clouds at 7000 feet altitude; sea invisible; 125 m. p. h.; bucking 18 miles-an-hour wind; 140 miles from Alameda.

7 p. m.—A message from Captain Musick: "390 miles out; 0300 GCT; latitude 3502, long. 1380; temperature 47 degrees; altitude 8000; wind 15; direction west; speed 124 m. p. h.; weather cloudy; visibility unlimited, ceiling 10,000; sea invisible; all well."

8 p. m.—495 miles out of San Francisco; altitude, 8600 feet; sky, sea, invisible; flying between two strata of clouds; weather colder, 47 degrees. All well.

9 p. m.—595 miles out, flying at 9000 feet between two cloud strata, visibility unlimited. Speed reduced to 100 miles an hour by a strong head wind.

9:30 p. m.—660 miles out, flying at 130 miles an hour after bucking through a stiff head wind.

10 p. m.—710 miles out; flying at 9000 feet altitude; bucking a 20-miles an hour headwind; unlimited visibility; weather clear; sea visible.

11 p. m.—820 miles out of San Francisco, flying 9000 feet, bucking a 17-mile-an-hour wind. Clear overhead, with scattered clouds beneath.

Officer Aboard Clipper Describes Pacific Hop

Engines Drone Steadily, Men Go About Duties Like Clockwork

By GEORGE KING
Second Flight Officer of the China Clipper, Writing for United Press

ABOARD THE CHINA CLIPPER, EN ROUTE TO HONOLULU, Nov. 22—As the sun goes down, casting a flaming mantle over bulbous clouds beneath, scattered strips of cumulus high above the circular world sink into impenetrable blackness.

A cloudy ceiling shuts off the stars, and the clouds below shut off the Pacific swells, 7000 feet below.

Tiny pilot lights, seen through the flight deck, grow brighter. The radium painted dials on the 197 flight and engine instruments on the board, glow eerily.

A faint yellow pilot light on Radio Officer Jarvoe's receiver blinks with his rapid fire transmission of the punctual, brief, dramatic position reports back to the base at San Francisco, ahead to Honolulu, to Midway, to Wake, to Guam, and to Manila, their goal.

SULLIVAN AT CONTROLS

At the controls is First Officer R. O. D. Sullivan, veteran of eight Pacific crossings connected with the Pan-American Airway's survey flights for the coming China Clipper.

Directly behind him is Radio Of-

(Continued on Page 3, Col. 8)

Child Poisoned By Burglar Loot

Special to The Chronicle

PATERSON, N. J., Nov. 22—A quirk of fate today killed a child or two as the aftermath of a burglary.

Robert Mayer died after eating poison tablets. They were thrown in his backyard when the robbers discarded them during a midnight division of spoils.

Wed Day, Sailor Leaps to His Death

SANTA BARBARA, Nov. 22 (UP)—Henry Mellus Tilestone, 28, yeoman attached to the battle ship West Virginia and bridegroom of one day, leaped to his death from the fashionable Santa Barbara hotel today.

California's new unemployment insurance law, affecting hundreds of thousands of employers and employes, becomes operative January 1, 1936. The State law is complementary to the new Federal social security act. The provisions of the new law will be outlined in a series of articles by Earl Behrens in The Chronicle, beginning Sunday.

Giant China Clipper Hops For Manila

25,000 Watch Huge Airship Take Off From Bay on Epochal Flight

Inaugurates Plane Service From S. F. to Orient

By ROYCE BRIER

America's history and the world's reached some giant new age yesterday when the China Clipper took flight with the trans-Pacific mail, and a prophet of old would be needed to fortell it.

The Clipper soared from Alameda Airport at 3:47 p. m., lifting slowly and spreading proudly her silver wings against the setting sun, flashing 150 years of Yankee tradition in her propeller blades.

Five minutes later she passed through the Golden Gate, and at 11 o'clock she was 820 miles down the Western sea.

25,000 WATCH

Twenty-five thousand people—such an outpouring as the Bay District has never given an airplane—waved her good-bye. There were 7000 at the airport, where a brief ceremony preceded the departure, and other thousands were at the Marina and on San Francisco's housetops.

Their acclaim was given to an idea rather than to aviation audacity, for Captain Musick and his crew of six are piloting the most advanced airliner of the day, over a course charted and proof, as nearly as man's technical ingenuity can make it, against the unforeseen.

It is the unfathomable future latent in this sleek and roaring machine, not the 25-ton Pan American Airway's plane itself out there over the sea, which holds the drama and the meaning.

BON VOYAGE FETE

Something of this was manifest in the bon voyage ceremony, and it was stamped with clarity on the faces of the thousands who watched.

Outside the air harbor, when she was a mile away, the China was just another seaplane. She taxied almost lazily in the subdued silver sunlight, warming up her four motors, until some grim fury seemed to seize her and her roar cut the air for 60 seconds.

Then, "She's up!"

The cheers died, the thousands stared at the Clipper, silent at the majesty of her rise. Thirty planes had been circling overhead, and they dropped toward the monarch,

(Continued on Page 3. Col. 5)

San Francisco Chronicle
The City's Only Home-Owned Newspaper

TODAY'S NEWS HIGHLIGHTS

Saturday, November 23

LOCAL

China Clipper hops on first flight to Manila with U. S. mail. Pages 1 and 3
Clues indicate Manno Company sold barrel of fluoride. Page 1
90,000 grid fans revel in city on eve of Big Game. Page 1
Proposal to set up unicameral legislative system in California hit. Page 7
State to call bids for three-lane bridge approach to Golden Gate span. Page 12
Anita Whitney, Communist party aid, tried for perjury. Page 12
Public Administrator Katz must turn in law fees to city. Page 28

DOMESTIC

U. S. exerts pressure to halt shipments of supplies to war zone. Page 1
Secretary of Labor Perkins leads move to halt I. L. A. Gulf strike. Page 7
U. S. seeks case to test constitutionality of utilities act. Page 11

FOREIGN

River of lava flowing from Hawaii volcano to the sea. Page 1
Complete coverage of Italian-Ethiopia war news. Pages 1-2
Japanese troops massing in North China as Tokyo studies next move. Page 2

Today's Features

Amusements	8, 9
Army, Navy News	25
Book Reviews	11
By the Way	10
Chester Rowell	10
Church News	4, 5
Comics	20
Coming Events	11
Crossword Puzzle	26
Deaths	11
Dorothy Dix	18
Editorials	10
Financial	21, 22, 23
Irvin Cobb	8
Labor News	17
Lichty	11
Merry-Go-Round	17
Ninon Fashions	18
Off the Record	27
Radio	8
Real Estate News	5
Safety Valve	10
Small Town Girl	8
Smoke Rings	20
Shipping	6
Society	19
Sports	Green
Veterans' News	7
Want Ads	26, 27
Will Rogers	8
Women's Club	18

Betting Odds Favor Bears In Big Game

Greatest Grid Throng in Coast History Revels on Eve of Palo Alto Battle

90,000 to See Struggle at 'Farm'; Tickets Gobbled Up

History's biggest sports crowd on the Pacific Coast surged into San Francisco and neighboring cities last night jubilantly celebrating the eve of the 43d annual coronation ceremony of King Football.

The king's 1935 reign ends at Palo Alto this afternoon.

While 90,000 cheering, loyal subjects acclaim his greatest post-depression season from the seats of Stanford stadium, the football teams of University of California and Stanford will enact their annual pageant in the king's honor.

Last minute odds quoted by

18 SPECIAL TRAINS

BECAUSE of the super-stupendously-colossal crowds expected at the Big Game, special transportation has been arranged.

The Southern Pacific announces 18 special trains of 12 coaches each, starting at 10 o'clock this morning from Third and Townsend streets. They will load and get away when full. The last rain will arrive about 1:30 o'clock. This service will be additional to the six regular trains.

Similarly six extra trains will leave Oakland starting at the same hour, the last one leaving at 11:50 and arriving at 1:30 p. m.

Similar return service will be given after the game, the company announces.

bookmakers indicated that California continues to rule as favorite.

5 TO 4 ON BEARS

Five to four odds the undefeated, untied Golden Bears will be the unanimous choice for Rose Bowl honors.

By airplane, by steamer, by train, by automobile and afoot will come more than 100,000 partisan rooters. Most of them had arrived last night, but additional thousands were clogging highways, straining transportation facilities, and adding to a gay, mad disorder that will border on frenzy at 2 o'clock this afternoon.

Scalpers' prices skyrocketed as it became known all but 3000 end zone seats had been sold. These will be snapped up at stadium booths. University authorities were quietly checking reports good seats were being retailed for as high as $100 a pair.

GAYETY RULES

Hotels and homes were jammed. Night club reservations were exhausted. Florists worked late into the night filling rush orders. Cocktail bars were packed to the doors.

Added "pep" was given celebrations of down town crowds when the California band, resplendent in full uniform, cavorted through the business district streets and hotel lobbies while the crowds roared the choruses of favorite college airs.

Queen Gayety was being acclaimed consort of King Football.

PLAYING FIELD FAST

Stanford's playing field was reported to be fast and dry and was expected to remain in ideal condition with the announcement by weather forecasters that the day would be fair and mild.

Can California check Stanford's plunging All-American Bobby Grayson or Stanford's All-American Monk Moscrip, whose magic toe has won three games for the Cards this year by goals from field?

Can the great California passer, Floyd Blower, be checked in his attempted goal line aerial shots?

Mad, gay, delirious night!

Expectant, nervous, voluble morning!

Hysterical afternoon!

The Big Game of 1935!

(For more Big Game news see Page 7 and Sporting Green)

New Girl Makes Tenth in Family

BURLINGTON, Iowa, Nov. 22 (AP)—A tenth daughter was born today to Mr. and Mrs. Melvin Lietsch of West Burlington. The eldest of the girls, all living, is 11.

U.S. Puts Pressure On Ship Lines to Halt War Trading

Threat of Financial Reprisal Made by Shipping Board

Exports to Italians Gain Despite Embargo

WASHINGTON, Nov. 22 (AP)—The financial pressure of a principal mortgage holder was applied, in effect, to the shipping industry today by the Administration to prevent shipments of potential war materials to Italy and Ethiopia.

An implied threat by the Shipping Board to become a tough creditor was reported to have held in port several vessels already loaded with supplies for the East African war zone.

EXPORTS SHOW RISE

Even as this move was disclosed, **a sharp jump in exports** to Italy during October was shown in newly compiled Commerce Department figures. Despite the frequent application of moral pressure by both President Roosevelt and Secretary Hull, intended to prevent shipments of any character to the belligerents, the export figures to Italy were:

October, $6,821,366; September, $4,795,887.

It was on October 5 that the President proclaimed America's neutrality policy; placed an embargo on arms and ammunition, and first enunciated the frequently reiterated policy of discouraging all trade with the warring countries. Some observers saw the apparent failure of this moral pressure as leading to the move disclosed today.

THREAT IN LETTERS

With some banks and railroads deeply indebted to the Government, the step aroused prompt speculation over how far the Administration might go in using its creditor position to discourage commerce with Italy and Ethopia.

The hinted threat to steamship owners and operators was inclosed in letters from the Shipping Board Bureau to lines owing money to the Government. In itself, the letter was given over principally to a reiteration that the Administration's neutrality policy deeply opposes all commerce with the beligerents.

Revealing this action today, J. C Peacock, director of the bureau and president of the Federally controlled Merchant Fleet Corporation, said: "As a Government organization, the Shipping Board naturally would be in sympathy with a Government policy so clearly stated as the one which seeks to restrict our trade with belligerent nations."

The bureau has over $97,000,000 outstanding in ship construction loans and ship owners are in its debt for millions more, due on vessels purchased from the Government.

On another front, Jesse W. Donaldson, Postoffice deputy in charge of ocean mail, said no action has been proposed to stop possible violation of the embargo by ocean mail contract carriers.

Three American lines carry mail to Italian ports, Donaldson said, adding:

"If any other mail carriers are touching Italy, they're making sailings outside their mail contracts."

Even in advance of the Shipping Board Bureau's letters and Peacock's statement, spokesmen in Rome hit out against any embargo on oil shipments to Italy. Officials close to the Italian government said such a course would be "tantamount to following the lead of British imperialism."

Czech President Plans to Resign

PRAGUE, Czechoslovakia, Nov. 22 (UP)—President Thomas G. Masaryk, 85-year-old head of the post-war Czechoslovakian republic, decided today to resign immediately.

300 Latins Slain

Africs Cite Victory In 11-Hour Battle

ADDIS ABABA, Nov. 22 (AP)—A ten-day-old Ethiopian victory in which 300 Italian soldiers and three of their officers were reported slain behind the Fascist northern lines was claimed tonight by Emperor Haile Selassie's high command.

An official communique said the 11-hour battle, reputedly fought in the Womberta region north of Makale, was "the first real fighting on any scale since the war began."

The Italians fled in utter disorder before Ethiopian rifles, spears and cutlasses, the Negus was informed by Dedjazmatch Kassa Sehabet.

Sehabet said the Italian commander was shot down and wounded seriously and that 200 rifles and four machine guns were captured. Nothing was said about the Ethiopian losses.

The government also announced a battle in the Tembien mountain region in which an Italian commander and many of his men were said to have been killed when they were surprised by Ethiopian forces while advancing on Kolel.

Surviving members of the Italian detachment fled to Makale, the communique said.

(Additional War News on Page 2)

COMPARATIVE TEMPERATURES

	High	Low		High	Low
San Francisco	67	50	New York	40	16
Los Angeles	64	51	Chicago	40	30
Seattle	52	46	Denver	60	36
Honolulu	78	66	New Orleans	70	54

San Francisco Chronicle

THE CITY'S ONLY HOME-OWNED NEWSPAPER

Weather in S. F. Bay Region: Fair and Mild. Complete Weather Report on Page 13

FOUNDED 1865—VOL. CXLVIII, NO. 53 CCC* SAN FRANCISCO, CAL., SUNDAY, MARCH 8, 1936 DAILY 5 CENTS, SUNDAY 10 CENTS

15,000 Nazis Line Rhine As France Mans Border

Taxes Mount, Jobs Decline, Hoover Tells G.O.P. Youth

Opportunities for New Generation In Peril, He Declares

American System of Liberty Held Menaced

COLORADO SPRINGS, Colo., March 7 (AP)—Former President Herbert Hoover charged tonight the New Deal had failed in "the outstanding governmental job of reemploying the jobless" despite an increased tax burden of which "the new taxes of today are but a part."

"Certainly your freedom and your opportunities in life are being mortgaged," Mr. Hoover told the Colorado Young Republican League. He criticized Administration policies as endangering the American system of Liberty.

The Colorado Springs Auditorium, seating 3100, was filled virtually to capacity. As he read his address,

Speech in Full on Page 6

Mr. Hoover clasped and unclasped his hands in front of him, then drummed his fingers upon the table. His sallies against the Roosevelt Administration brought frequent applause.

Gordon Allott of Lamar, Col., permanent State chairman for the Young Republicans, introduced Mr. Hoover as "a real liberalist, not the anarchistic, communistic, socialistic type that we have now."

The "money changers" that President Roosevelt "promised to drive out of the temple" are the only ones

(Continued on Page 7, Col. 1)

Felons in Quentin Submit Program To Smash Crime

Convicts Willing to Divulge to Government Secrets of 100 Rackets; Demand Nonpolitical Consideration

By DON CASTLE

(Copyright, 1936, Chronicle Publishing Company)

A 14-point program to smash crime in America has been submitted by San Quentin Prison convicts to United States Attorney General Homer S. Cummings and the California State Board of Prison Directors.

At the same time, the convicts have offered to divulge to the Federal Government and prison authorities the secret workings of more than 100 rackets that each year mulct the American public of billions of dollars.

GUARANTEE SOUGHT

Developed through the cooperation of more than 3000 of the so-called better-type convicts of San Quentin, the proposal is predicated on the guarantee that the revelations receive the attention of a strictly nonpolitical body completely free of the suspicion of hampering entanglements.

The convicts' offer embraces a willingness to reveal to officials everything they know concerning graft, crookedness and racketeering in the communities from which they come.

Their solution to the Nation's crime problem, as epitomized in the 14-point program, follows:

1—Control of all law-enforcement machinery by the Federal Government.

2—Fingerprint everybody.

3—Abolish the jury system. A jury is too easily fixed.

4—Let all criminal cases be heard by three Judges, appointees for life at high salaries, and consequently immune to intimidation and bribery. Let the decision of two of the three Judges decide the question of guilt or innocence.

5—Substitute certainty of punishment for severity of punishment.

6—Make restitution of stolen property compulsory. Let prisoners work at decent wages, maintaining their dependents, paying their own prison expenses, and paying off the stolen property in cash earned by themselves. Thus sentences will fit the amounts involved in the crimes. If this is done there will be no $10,000,000 crooks doing the same sentences as the men who stole $20.

7—Make it compulsory for the defendant to appear as a witness at his own trial.

8—Permit but one postponement of a criminal trial.

9—Make executions of the death sentence public in the county in which the crime was committed.

10—Abolish all useless and out-of-date laws.

11—Let Judges administer an elastic form of penalty for first offenders.

12—Positive segregation in all prisons and county jails.

13—Show movies in the schools of prison life. Show movies in the schools of criminals who have made

(Continued on Page 13, Col. 2)

Split Widens In Townsend Ruling Board

Surprise Meeting Called by Founder Points to Revamping of Control

By EARL C. BEHRENS

In a surprise move which may cause a national schism in the Townsend old age pension ranks, Dr. Francis E. Townsend has called a special meeting of the governing board of his organization for Kansas City tomorrow.

An open break between Dr. Townsend and Robert E. Clements, the cofounders of the $200 a month plan, is imminent over the financial and political management, nationally, of the Townsend movement.

At present Dr. Townsend, Clements, secretary and in charge of the Washington activities of the Townsend organization, and Gomer Smith of Oklahoma constitute the national governing board of the movement.

CHOSEN AS ARBITRATOR

For a time Townsend and Clements constituted the board, but, due to differences between the two men, a third member was named by them to act practically in the capacity of arbiter when the two could not agree on policies.

Now Dr. Townsend proposes to increase the membership on the national board to five. He will suggest the name of Gilmour Young, San Francisco, and A. J. Wright, Cleveland, as the new directors, according to reports here.

CLASH ON SALARY BOOSTS

Dissatisfaction is understood to have been expressed by Dr. Townsend over the increases in salaries and expense accounts as approved by Clements at Washington. These increases were revealed in the congressional inquiry recently of the Townsend and other old age pension movements. Salary increases are said to have been disapproved by Dr. Townsend.

Dr. Townsend, Young and Sheridan Downey, Democratic nominee in 1934 for Lieutenant Governor, are en route to Washington and will stop off in Kansas City for the meeting tomorrow.

DOWNEY TO BE COUNSEL

Downey is accompanying Dr. Townsend to Washington to appear both as a witness and as counsel for Townsend at the congressional hearings on the old age pension movement.

It is understood the sudden calling of the meeting for tomorrow at Kansas City rather than at Washington is occasioned by a desire on the part of Dr. Townsend to steer clear of the Washington influences that might be brought to bear upon the governing board by Clements.

COURT SMITH NEW WARDEN AT QUENTIN

Warden Court Smith of Folsom Prison, ruler of the State's penitentiary for "repeaters," will take over the job of ruling the congested ominous San Quentin Prison April 15.

His appointment was officially announced yesterday by the State Board of Prison Directors, after the resignation of Warden James B. Holohan was accepted. The board action confirmed announcements first made by The Chronicle several days ago.

For more than 30 years, Smith has been identified with police and prison work in the State. Nine years ago this month he took over the duties at Folsom.

He was previously city marshal o Tulare city and then Sheriff of Tulare county and later chief of police at Visalia.

ction of the board was announced by Judge T. N. Harvey, who said a resolution had been adopted unanimously commending Holohan on his devotion to duty, bravery, hon-sty and general ability.

(Story of Smith's plans on page 14)

Students Win School War In Alameda

City Attorney, Warren Rule Paden's Ouster in Political 'Coup' Was Illegal

Special Guards Quit Hall; Classes to Be Resumed Monday

Alameda's school and municipal war appeared yesterday to have been won by student strikers. In tabulation, the situation appeared to be as follows:

1—School Superintendent William G. Paden, whose removal in a political maneuver precipitated a strike of 3000 students, was back in the saddle, fortified by opinions from the City Attorney and District Attorney his removal was illegal.

2—Einer Sorenson, seventh grade teacher, elevated to Paden's position in the ouster, was back where he started. On advice from the City Attorney he turned over keys and papers he had seized when he thought Paden was out and he was the superintendent.

3—Mayor Roebke withdrew his armed guards from the City Hall, ending possibility of armed strife with police.

4—City officials of the majority group, faced with a May election, were explaining the whole embroglio was a school matter and not one that concerned them.

5—Student leaders called a meeting for 8 o'clock Monday morning, and told all striking students to be prepared to return to classes.

WARREN TAKES HAND

Action of District Attorney Earl Warren in warning officials he would hold them responsible to the full extent of the law for anyone injured in their private fight, was said to have been a material factor in ending the trouble.

Warren later notified the Board of Education their action in deposing Paden was illegal. He pointed out there was a conflict between the city charter and the State law, and said that in a test the State law would prevail. Warren's ruling marked the end of clique resistance.

The student strike, which had the backing of 10,000 voting parents, precipitated a crisis in municipal affairs in which a recall election already is awaiting a court ruling. With the whole town boiling at fever heat, and the Mayor and city manager burned in effigy on the streets, somebody decided it was time to quit. And everybody quit.

ATTORNEY RULING GIVEN

City Attorney Locke handed down the unusual opinion yesterday when he told the Board of Education it was entirely in error in trying to fire Paden. State law provides the superintendent shall be elected for four years, Locke said, adding, in his opinion, the appointment of Paden by the board had complied with that requirement. Then there was the matter of a contract the board had signed with Paden and which

(Continued on Page 16, Col. 1)

New Greek Chief To Form Cabinet

ATHENS, March 7 (AP)—Themistokles Sophoulis, Venizelist leader, who yesterday was elected president of the Greek Assembly, accepted an assignment today from King George to form a new Greek government.

Countess Salm Granted Divorce

RENO, March 7 (AP)—Countess Maud Coster Salm-Hoogstraeten, socially prominent in New York, won an uncontested divorce decree today from Count Otto Salm-Hoogstraeten.

State's Pension Setup Approved

SACRAMENTO, March 7 (AP)—California's setup for the administration of old age pensions has been approved by the Federal Government, Governor Merriam said today.

Mrs. Mellie C. Ford, statistician of the State Department of Social Welfare, brought the word back from Washington, he stated.

Mrs. Hewitt Still On 'Danger List'

NEW YORK, March 7 (UP)—Mrs. Maryon Cooper Hewitt still was on the "danger list" in Jersey City Medical Center, physicians said today.

Paris Prepared to Use Army; Russ, Czechs Back Her

Belgium, Britain, Italy Aid Is Sought

PARIS, March 7 (AP)—French officials declared that tonight France was ready to use her army, supported by her allies, to compel Germany to evacuate the Rhineland, but that France first would exhaust the peaceful methods possible under the League of Nations.

This declaration followed an order by military authorities that all fortifications along the northeast frontier be garrisoned immediately with their full quotas of troops.

The order was issued shortly after the French government decided to do its "utmost" under the League of Nations' covenant to compel Germany to take its troops out of the Rhineland.

VIOLATES TREATY

Officials declared France would ask the league to vote economic and financial sanctions against Germany. Remilitarization of the Rhineland violates the treaty of Versailles, the pact by which the League of Nations also was created.

In authoritative quarters it was stated France would ask Great Britain, Italy and Belgium, cosignatories of the Locarno pact, which

(Continued on Page 2, Col. 7)

Berlin Jubilant

Defiance Celebrated

Parades, Songs

(Copyright, 1936, by United Press)

BERLIN, March 8 (Sunday)—Jubilant Germans paraded and sang in the streets until the early hours of the morning, celebrating Fuehrer Adolf Hitler's defiance of the powers in sending an estimated 25,000 troops into the demilitarized Rhineland.

They celebrated also the end of the last of the repressive clauses of the Versailles treaty, which he sank without a trace by his single-handed action.

The celebration started last night and lasted for many hours. Its high point started at 10 p. m., when a stream of flame poured through the Brandenburg gate down the Wilhelmstrasse as 20,000 excited Nazis honored the Fuehrer in a torchlight parade.

Led by Hitler's elite guards with fixed bayonets, representatives of all Nazi men's organizations surged through cheering, waving crowds to salute Hitler, Paul Joseph Goebbels and other Nazi dignitaries standing on the Chancellory balcony in the blaze of a searchlight.

In a two-minute radio broadcast to the Rhineland at 10:15 p. m., Goebbels insisted the reoccupation is really a "gesture of peace," foreshadowing a new and better future, not only for Germany, but for all Europe.

What May Happen

Crisis Analyzed by Expert

War Nearer Than in 1914

By CHESTER H. ROWELL

Editor of The Chronicle

The news dispatches relate what is happening in this new threat of war in Europe. This is to explain, briefly, the background out of which these events have come, which also gives them their significance.

Ever since the treaty of Versailles, which imposed certain restrictions on Germany which did not apply to the victor countries, there has been an impasse between Britain and France as to what should be done in case Germany should violate these provisions.

The position of Britain was that if Germany should commit aggressions abroad or invade territory of other nations, it should be met by force, in which Britain would join, but that if it merely violated the treaty at home, in its internal policy, other remedies than war should be used, and Britain would not join in any war of invasion to enforce this part of the treaty, within Germany.

When, in 1922, France declared that Germany was in default and invaded the Ruhr, Britain protested that the invasion was illegal and impolitic, and finally joined perfunctorily in it only to be able, when it should later lead the way out, to assure that the French troops would come out also. America, it will be remembered, joined the Siberian invasion for the same purpose, and was enabled, thereby, to bring out the large Japanese force when the small American force withdrew. The same thing happened with the British and French, on the Ruhr.

Invasion Disapproved

Ever since, the British have insisted that they would not again join or approve such an invasion, while the French have been seeking to maneuver them into a position where they would have to do so.

The Treaty of Versailles made provision for changing its own conditions, by consent, but France and its "status quo" allies have adhered to the theory that they would not give that consent. However, by tacit acquiescence, they had already acceded to the practical abrogation of most of the restrictions, including the reparations payments, even before Hitler came in.

What were left were the territorial arrangements, the colonies, limitations of German armaments, and the frontier zone which France was permitted to fortify and garrison on the one side, while Germany was required to dismantle its fortifications and withdraw its troops on the other side.

Merely by Violation

Hitler adopted the tactics of abrogating these restrictions, one at a time, simply by violating them. He rearmed, on land and sea, and secured British acquiescence in so doing. The French, while not recognizing his right, did nothing about it. He at first threatened to take the Polish corridor by force, and then made a 10-year agreement with

(Continued on Page 4, Col. 6)

Roosevelt Guest At Press Dinner

WASHINGTON, March 7 (AP)—President Roosevelt, Cabinet members and diploma :: were honor guests tonight at the fifteenth annual dinner of the White House Correspondents' Association.

Frederick A. Storm of the United Press was installed as the new president of the association, succeeding Albert L. Warner of the New York Herald Tribune.

Duce Willing To Consider Afric Peace

Acceptance of League Parley Plan Hinges on Large Grant of Ethiop Land

ROME, March 7 (AP)—Flanked by an imposing array of conditions, Italy's reply to the League of Nations' appeal for peace in Ethiopia was dispatched to Geneva today in a tenor bespeaking Premier Mussolini's determination to get what he started after.

The reply resolved down to this, after a meeting of the Cabinet:

1—Italy's peace conversations will be conditioned on realization, by both the league and Emperor Haile Selassie, that Italy is in Ethiopia to stay, both in territories conquered and in others where a semi-mandatory influence will be wielded.

2—Italy does not intend to let her African armies stagnate. If Ethiopia wants peace, it must seek it with an eye on the Italian mailed fist.

TWO NOT EQUAL

Il Duce made it plain "equality" as between Italy and Ethiopia does not exist. Hostilities cannot cease, he said, until Italy's needs and demands are satisfied.

Thus did Mussolini accept "in principle" the appeal of the league for peace in East Africa.

The dictator's demands on which he based any move for ending his campaign of occupation, recently marked by outstanding victories on the northern front, included influence on sections of Ethiopia such as the Lake Tana district and areas west, south and southeast of Addis Ababa.

OLD PEACE PLANS BASE

Significant was the point the Italian conditions include the zone of influence which would have fallen to Italy under the peace proposal formulated by Sir Samuel Hoare, the then British Foreign Minister, and Pierre Laval, then the French Premier.

An excellent authority divulged the inclusion of the Lake Tana area. The lake is the headwater of the River Nile.

Ethiopia had accepted the peace proposals of the League of Nations Committee of 13 without reservation.

SANCTIONS IN ABEYANCE

(The league asked for consideration of a peace formula, holding in abeyance the question of imposing additional sanctions, including one on oil, against Italy.)

Fuehrer Stirs World, Offers New Peace Treaties

Calls for Vote of People March 29

(Copyright, 1936, by Associated Press)

BERLIN, March 7—Adolf Hitler, thundering to his brown shirt Nazi Reichstag that the Locarno pact was dead, sent triumphant German troops goose-stepping into the demilitarized Rhineland today and pronounced the fight for Germany's freedom finished.

In swift, world-stunning thrusts, the fuehrer offered Europe a new western demilitarized frontier on a cooperative basis, declared he was ready to sign a new 25-year nonaggression treaty, and an air pact with his western neighbors and expressed willingness—if these things transpire—to return to the League of Nations.

Then he dissolved his standing, shouting Reichstag and called a plebiscite for March 29 to prove to the world the German people are behind him. In these general elections Hitler and his followers expect to get a majority even greater than their previous 90 per cent.

Traditional Prussian precision, orderliness and speed marked the

Full Text of German Repudiation on Page 2

large-scale army movements into the Rhineland zone today. The movements, it was announced officially will be completed Sunday.

15,000 MOVE IN

The exact number of men going into the zone could not be established, although one Reichswehr official estimated it at about 15,000.

A carnival spirit seized the populace of the first towns to greet the troops. They moved in even as the citizens stood listening to Hitler's speech.

In all, 18 infantry battalions of 500 men each and 13 artillery units of nearly 200 men each were being transferred from the interior of the country into the zone today and tonight.

In addition to ground forces, two groups of pursuit flyers were being moved in and two antiaircraft units were designated for Cologne and Mannheim.

FRANCO-RUSS PACT HIT

Exhorting the Reichstag in classic Hitler style, Der Fuehrer pleaded his friendship for France, detailed what he said were his constant efforts for a rapprochement with that country and castigated the new Franco-Russian mutual assistance pact as one which might lead to "unpredictable consequences" for Europe.

This pact, he shouted, with its danger to Europe of bolshevik "chaos," freed Germany from Locarno.

To begin his day of extraordinary action, Hitler told foreign

(Continued on Page 3, Col. 6)

Today's Features

Airplane Models	Green 6
America Speaks	Main News 9
Amusements	Special Section
Art	Amusement Section
Army, Navy News	Main News 19
Automobile	Special Section
Books	Amusement Section
Comic	Comics Section
Coming Events	Main News 16
Contract Contacts	Main News 12
Crossword	Classified 2
Deaths	Main News 16
Fashions	Society Section
Financial	Main News 17, 18, 19
Merry-Go-Round	Main News 9
Music	Amusement Section
Ninon	Society Section
Radio	Main News 15
Robin Hood	Green 5
Rotogravure	Special Section
Schools, Colleges	Main News 7
Shipping	Main News 12
Skylines of N. Y.	Green 6
Society	Special Section
Sports	Green
Veteran's News	Main News 20
Want Ads	Special Section
Weekly News Review	Classified 8
Will Rogers	Green 6
World Topics	Main News 10, 11
Women's Clubs	Society Section

THIS IS FOR AMATEURS ONLY

THIS is for amateurs of all ages who are ineligible to appear on amateur radio programs by virtue of the fact they cannot play musical saws, imitate homing pigeons, warble the "Bell Song" from "Lakme" or the like.

This is for amateur writers, poets, cartoonists who yearn for an opportunity to see their brain children on paper.

It is for these aspirants to literary or artistic fame that The Chronicle will open its pages each Sunday beginning one week from today.

IF YOU have talent The Chronicle will give you the chance to prove yourself, and, each week, will give prizes for the outstanding contributions.

The Chronicle's great reading public will be the judge. Each Sunday a coupon will be printed so that readers of the amateur page may designate their choices for first, second and third prizes.

All manner of contributions will be welcomed. Short stories, either fiction or based on experience, not exceeding 500 words in length, comic strips, cartoons of various kinds, caricatures, neighborhood feature stories that may be illustrated photographically if you are camera-minded.

Serious poems, jingles limericks, timely and snappy wisecracks, all these things may be entered in this weekly contest.

THERE are only two admonitions editors of The Chronicle offer: Firstly, contributors MUST BE AMATEURS, and secondly, contributors must dare to be original.

Material copied from any sources will not be acceptable.

Depending upon your response to this great opportunity, The Chronicle's first amateur page will appear next Sunday. Material for the first page must be received at The Chronicle office, Fifth and Mission streets, by Thursday.

ADDRESS contributions to The Chronicle Amateur Editor.

No contributions will be returned.

Remember, this is for amateurs only, amateurs of all ages, and that the deadline for the first issue will be Thursday.

First Prize $20—2d $10—3d $5

COMPARATIVE TEMPERATURES

	High	Low		High	Low
San Francisco	64	53	New York	82	64
Los Angeles	94	72	Chicago	74	72
Seattle	84	60	Denver	96	66
Honolulu	82	74	New Orleans	94	78

San Francisco Chronicle

THE CITY'S ONLY HOME-OWNED NEWSPAPER

Weather
Fair and Mild
Complete Weather Report on Page 15

FOUNDED 1865—VOL. CXLIX, NO 5 — CCC — SAN FRANCISCO, CAL., MONDAY, JULY 20, 1936 — DAILY 5 CENTS, SUNDAY 10 CENTS: DAILY AND SUNDAY PER MONTH, $1.15

Civil War Tears Spain

Rebels March on Madrid

Government Soldiers Surrendering, Ships Sent to Quell Uprising Desert to Franco Forces

(Copyright, 1936, by Havas News Agency and New York News)

Rebellious Spanish army officers, apparently in control of all Spanish Morocco and of Southern Spain, were marching on Madrid last night (Sunday) in a grim drive to capture the capital, still in control of the Leftist government.

At midnight the situation was as follows:

In Madrid, the government now headed by Jose Giral Pereira, began arming all civilians. Fifty thousand Asturian miners arrived in the capital to help fight the Fascist-Monarchist rebels. Strict censorship was clamped down.

Gibraltar sources reported rebel Moroccan troops had landed at Cadiz, had joined Seville insurgents, and were marching on Madrid. Thousands of refugees fled to Gibraltar.

Reports from Rabat said three government warships sent to bomb the rebels at Ceuta, Spanish Morocco, had joined the revolt.

In Tangier broadcasts received from Seville and Ceuta indicated all Spanish Morocco was in the hands of the rebels, and General Gonzalo Queipo de Llano y Sierra had taken over Seville in the name of the insurgents. The rebels also claimed to be in control of all Andalusia.

At Algeciras, a torpedo boat commanded by rebels fired six shots over the city and took it over after the white flag had been hoisted by government forces.

By Associated Press

The long struggle between Fascists and a united leftist front for supremacy in Spain apparently had become last night (Sunday) the most widespread and bloodiest civil war in the country since the unsuccessful leftist revolt of October, 1934.

REBELLION SPREADS

An organized and, apparently, well-timed rightist revolt, which began simultaneously at several points in Spanish Morocco Friday morning, has spread to practically every important city of Spain except the capital.

An air bombardment of Barcelona, largest city of the five-year-old republic, was reported by travelers. Government planes also were attacking Morocco cities, while the rebels, claiming control of all Spanish Morocco as well as the Canary and Balearic islands, were reported landing troops in South Spain to aid allies already rising up in many cities.

MALAGA BURNING

Despite a rigid censorship the government in Madrid admitted rebellion "had started" in various important cities on the peninsula, but predicted all uprisings would be quickly stamped out. It announced reinforcements were being rushed to Seville and admitted fierce fighting in Malaga, center of a large foreign colony, which was reported half in flames.

An estimate of total casualties was impossible, but various reports indicated nearly 100 killed in various battles in Morocco and 25 killed in one clash at Seville. Rebels claimed that three of four naval vessels sent to Morocco had gone over to their side.

General Francisco Franco, recently named military governor of the Canary Islands, is the active leader of the Fascist revolt. He has established himself in Morocco, describing himself as "Commander-in-Chief in Africa."

LEADER IN EXILE

Jose Maria Gil Robles, the Spanish rightist leader, was in exile in Biarritz, France, but some reports credited him with issuing secret orders to Franco and other Fascist commanders. The idol of the

New Chief Of Cabinet

Jose Giral Pereira
Premier takes helm

BULLETINS

LISBON, (Monday) July 20 (U.P.)—A radio announcement from a Seville station heard here today claimed that rebelling soldiers dominated all provinces of Spain except those of Galiza, Asturias and Catalonia.

LONDON, July 19 (Havas)—Telephone service between London and Gibraltar, vital source of news regarding the revolt reportedly sweeping Spain, was suddenly interrupted tonight. Communication with Portugal also was severed.

HENDAYE, Franco-Spanish Frontier, July 19 (U.P.)—French officials tonight posted strong detachments of gendarmes along the Franco-Spanish frontier after Spanish frontier guards were summoned to reenforce police fighting rebels, leaving the border unprotected.

French forces took up positions along the River Bidassoa with instructions to prevent armed incursions into French territory.

Eye-Witness Story of Battle

Jay Allen, Chicago Tribune correspondent, who was reported wounded by a mob at La Linea, but was unhurt, has written the following eyewitness account of the Spanish rebellion.

He describes his narrow escape from death thusly:

By JAY ALLEN

(Copyright, 1936, Chicago Tribune Foreign Cable Service)

I have never been a war correspondent and the noisy battle that has been going on the last 24 hours for La Linea, within spitting distance of where I am writing this, has got me stumped. I helped start it, too.

Here are my notes:

Sunday, at 1 o'clock in the morning, at a Red Cross clinic at La Linea. Nobody told me there was any trouble here. I drove from Malaga in hopes of getting to Gibraltar before the gates closed and on to Africa. The carburetor coughed all the way, thus affording me the privilege of arriving at La Linea 11 to 20 yards behind a small car with the lights of the republic's khaki. Now was I to know this contained officers from the garrison at Algeciras that rebelled half an hour before, going over to call out the battalion at La Linea?

How was I to know the loyal troops of the republican militia were waiting for them behind the barricade and they would stop in front of me, pile out and blaze away at said barricade?

Anyway, there are 21 bullet holes in my friend, Mark Hawker's Chrysler, one in my chauffeur, Eduardo's left shoulder, and none at all in me, which seems odd.

HIS STORY FOLLOWS:

GIBRALTAR, July 13—Civil war, for a long time now smouldering and intermittent, has at last broken into flame over Spain.

A clique of political generals, survivals of King Alfonso XIII's praetorian guard, are leading a savage assault on the republic voted by an immense majority of the Spanish people in 1931, lost for a time, redeemed in February of this year and in recent months weakened by strikes and violence.

Under the leadership of General Francisco Franco, 43, youngest general of the Spanish army, they led off from Spanish Morocco where they have undisputed control, and now (midnight Sunday) they seem to be the masters of a large part of Andalusia.

CLAIM VICTORIES

They claim victories in the north, but it is obvious their plan is to advance from the southern coast on the republic's stronghold, Madrid, with the dread foreign legionaires and Moors in the vanguard.

General Franco crossed from Ceuta, Spanish Morocco this morning by plane to Algeciras, to lead the parade which the generals expect will bring the garrisons of the north, which are now hesitating, to the standard of revolt and military dictatorship.

His advance guard appeared on the peninsula today. Hard bitten Legionaires landed from the war ship Churrucca at Cadiz and turbanned Moroccans, Moors and Blackamoors landed from a transport at Algeciras, whence they advanced upon, and took, La Linea, frontier town

(continued on Page A, Col. 6)

Morocco Soldiers Shed Blood Near Gibraltar

GIBRALTAR, Monday, July 20 (U.P.)—At least 50 persons were believed killed and more than 100 wounded at La Linea, Spain, early today when Fascist rebels and Moorish troops from Spanish Morocco clashed with leftists loyal to the popular front government.

The rebellious forces sprayed the left wing adherents with machinegun and rifle bullets. Streets of La Linea, nearest Spanish point to Gibraltar, were littered with dead and wounded.

Truck loads of invading troops fired ruthlessly after the populace gave a hostile reception to the Moorish forces sent into Southern Spain by rebel leaders in Spanish Morocco. Sounds of the fighting were clearly audible in Gibraltar.

GRENADES FIRE HOUSES

Moors, who crossed the Mediterranean straits of Gibraltar and swept into Southern Spain under command of leaders of the Fascist revolution, opened fire with rifles and hand grenades.

Several houses were set afire and a new stream of refugees poured into Gibraltar.

Many arrived in fishing boats. They disembarked at the eastern beach where heavily armed British troops halted them half a mile from the frontier. Only those traveling with their families and obviously civilian refugees were permitted to enter the city.

MOORS OPEN FIRE

Eye witnesses said that La Linea fighting began when civilians gathered to watch the rebel Moorish forces of occupation. They were ordered to disperse. When they refused the Moors opened fire and Leftist elements began resistance.

La Linea and Algeciras, across the bay from the British fortress, were the first points on the main land to fall before the advancing Moors.

A Spanish warship joined the revolutionary forces and escorted a steamer loaded with rebellious Moors across the bay of Gibraltar to Algeciras. Communications were cut. It was not known whether the Algeciras garrison surrendered or resisted.

REBELS IN CONTROL

However, all indications were that the rebels were in complete control of the city before nightfall.

Other anti-government disturbances were reported at various points between La Linea, Algeciras and Seville, 100 miles north of Gibraltar, causing fears the Moors

(Continued on Page A, Col. 3)

Los Angeles Heat Claims Two Lives

LOS ANGELES, July 19 (AP)—Continuing hot weather resulted in two deaths in Southern California today and drove an estimated 700,000 persons to the nearby beaches where they attempted to escape heat that reached 95 degrees in Los Angeles and was much higher inland.

Balloon Altitude Record Claimed

MOSCOW, July 19 (AP)—Soviet scientists announced today a radio balloon had been sent to a height of 47,500 meters (approximately 154,000 feet), claimed a new record.

The balloon, sent up at Tixie Bay at the mouth of the Lena river, made the ascent in 59 minutes, carrying only instruments.

Lemke Describes Self as '100 Per Cent for Pension'

Union Party Leader Lauds Townsend Organization; Doctor to Stump for Roosevelt Defeat; Meet Ends

By EARL C. BEHRENS

CLEVELAND, Ohio, July 19—Before an outdoor audience 10,000 the big Townsend national convention came to a close here early tonight with Representative William Lemke, presidential candidate of the National Union for Social Justice, and Dr. Francis E. Townsend, joining in pleas for more adequate security for the aged of the Nation.

Lemke, second of the presidential candidates to appear before the Townsendites, described himself as "100 per cent for an old age revolving pension" but he did not unqualifiedly indorse the Townsend $200 a month pension plan.

Dr. Townsend presented to his followers the report on his old age pension program which he had intended reading before the congressional committee at Washington which investigated his movement.

Lemke declared, "The Townsend organization has challenged the attention of the whole world."

Dr. Townsend followed him with the statement that 20,000,000 Americans were committed to it. "Mobilize our neighbors into our movement," urged Dr. Townsend. "Elect those candidates who are loyal to our program."

AFTER BIG GAME

Dr. Townsend told his members to elect their Congressmen for "I am going after bigger game." Townsend is going on the stump with Lemke, Father Coughlin and Rev. Gerald Smith, Huey Long's successor to the Share-the-Wealth organization.

Dr. Townsend's statement was a warning to his members that he intended to participate actively in the campaign to defeat President Roosevelt.

"I will go with anybody and speak with anybody whose purpose is to put the stamp of condemnation on this present administration in Washington," Dr. Townsend said.

(Continued on Page B, Col. 3)

Tax Policy Of U. S. Hit By League

Powers Misused, Says Liberty Group

WASHINGTON, July 19 (AP)—Contending that the New Deal had been "thwarted in its attempt to extend the authority of the Federal Government through laws held unconstitutional by the Supreme Court," the American Liberty League asserted today the Administration had turned to the use of taxing power to attain those ends.

The league, in a statement, said that "the New Deal has prostituted the taxing power under the constitution to accomplish social and economic ends remote from the raising of revenue."

The league contended that "through the power of taxation the New Deal has sought to experiment with economic theories, regiment industry, penalize big business, redistribute wealth and otherwise interrupt and obstruct the free flow of individual initiative and business activity."

"Diversion of a greater part of the national income into spending channels by punitive taxes upon undistributed profits of corporations.

"Graduation of taxes on corporate income as a means of penalizing bigness.

"Redistribution of wealth by higher surtaxes on individual incomes, by higher estate and gift taxes and by making subject to high individual surtaxes a larger part of corporate earnings."

Coed Murder Probe Turns To Violinist

Musician's Alibi Denied by Two Witnesses; His Fiancee Held for Quizzing

Medical Report Shows Latest Suspect Has Bruised Foot

ASHEVILLE, N. C., July 19 (U.P.)—A medical report revealing that Mark Wollner, concert violinist detained for questioning in the assault-murder of pretty Helen Clevenger, has a badly bruised right foot was called the "most significant development of the day" by Sheriff Lawrence Brown tonight.

When the injured foot was reported by Dr. H. L. Sumner, county physician, after examination of the 35-year-old musician, Brown pointed out that the unidentified man seen running through the lobby of the Battery Park Hotel at about the time the girl was killed, had leaped a high wall to the hotel grounds.

MUSICIAN'S ALIBI

The physician's report climaxed 24 hours of efforts by authorities investigating Wollner's story that he was in his room from 9 p. m. Wednesday until 8 a. m. the next morning, and knows nothing about the case.

Miss Clevenger was slain, a Coroner's Jury found, shortly after 1 a. m. Thursday by a man who attacked her, then slashed her face with scissors or a knife and finally shot her with a small bore revolver.

The report was revealed shortly after Miss Mildred Ward, 19-year-old semiinvalid and fiancee of Wollner, was arrested and taken to the matron's quarters of the County Jail for questioning.

FIANCEE QUIZZED

Miss Ward had told officers the German born violist, whose American debut was made in Town Hall in New York city, was at her mother's home the night of the slaying. Two witnesses, however, gave Sheriff Brown statements to the contrary.

The Sheriff said the girl and Wollner, as well as two other persons held for questioning—Joey Urey, Negro bellboy at the Battery Park where Miss Clevenger was a guest, and the hotel's nightwatchman, Daniel Gaddy—were held without charges being filed against them.

Wollner, arrested last night while he visited friends, was locked in solitary confinement tonight.

(Wirephoto of Wollner on Page 3)

North Spain Overrun by Red Hordes

Civil War Spreads to All of Peninsula; Radicals Seek Vengeance on Fascists

San Sebastian Called a Nightmare; Railroads Blocked

(Tribune copyright)

HENDAYE, France, July 19—Civil war, perhaps the bloodiest in Spanish history, has broken out and fighting is occuring throughout virtually the whole peninsula.

Although the border has been closed to both rail and automobile traffic in either direction since 4 p. m. today, and no phone communication between France and Spain exists, the Chicago Tribune Press Service correspondent, on arrival at Hendaye tonight, learned from refugees who succeeded in getting across the frontier before it closed that fighting had spread to Northern Spain.

As in Madrid, where a proletarian army reinforced by police and loyal troops was marching south to meet the insurgents who landed at Cadiz from Morocco this morning, and in Asturias, where an army of 50,000 miners armed with dynamite and rifles were moving toward the front by forced marches, a civilian red army has sprung up in the Basque provinces.

RED FORCES CONCENTRATED

Tonight this force, which is half mob and half army, was roaring through the streets of San Sebastian and other large towns of the region seeking to exterminate civilian fascists before swinging into action against insurgent army units.

Red forces were concentrated, ready for a march on Pampeluna (Pamplona), which was reported to be in the hands of monarchists, whose principal stronghold it is and where tomorrow it is feared important garrisons under the command of General Mola, chief of police under the regime of Dameso Berenguer, president of the Council of Ministers before the revolution, will join the insurrection.

A general strike was called in the region and train movements between the border and Madrid were cut off. All highways were blocked by armed workers who only allow their own forces to pass.

Their aim is to cut off the monarchist and fascist insurrection centering at Pampeluna and keep it from spreading toard Burgos, or getting reinforcements from the royalist refugees waiting across the border in France.

CITY IS NIGHTMARE

A vivid description of the fighting at San Sebastian was given by a young British tourist, Richard Smith of London, who was the last person to cross the border line into France—in fact, the border police let him through exceptionally after the frontier was closed officially. Smith had motored from Hendaye to San Sebastian early today. This is what he saw:

San Sebastian is a nightmare. Red hordes armed with shotguns, rifles, revolvers and bombs and carrying red flags, were marching by the thousands through the

(Continued on Page A, Col. 1)

U.S. Revolt Plotters To Have New Trial

SAN JUAN, P. R., July 19 (AP)—Federal Judge Robert A. Cooper informed the jury could not agree, ordered a mistrial today in the case of eight Puerto Rican Nationalists charged with conspiring to overthrow the government of the United States by force. A second trial was set for July 27.

Pedro Albizu Campos, leader of the eight defendants, objected to the early retrial, asking that it be set for the next term of court. The eight were accused of fomenting rebellion against the government and attempting to conscript a rebel army.

Baseball Bat Beating Kills Man, Kin Accused

A family quarrel between husband and wife ended in tragedy yesterday when Joel Eugene Mathis, 23, of Watsonville, died at University of California Hospital here from head injuries received when he was struck a week ago with a baseball bat wielded by his brother-in-law, Henry W. Richards, 35, also of Watsonville.

Richards, who claimed Mathis tried to pull a knife during their dispute and that he struck in self-defense, was held without bail in Watsonville City Prison and will be arraigned today in Police Court.

QUARREL AFTERMATH

The fight between the two men was the tragic aftermath of a trifling quarrel between Mathis and his wife, Dorcas, at their home, 236 Locust street, Watsonville, police were told.

Mathis "became angry over something," the wife said, during a party a week ago Sunday night at which friends, Alfred Morrow and Christine Gordon, were present.

Mrs. Mathis walked out of the house and, accompanied by Miss Gordon, went to the home of Richards, her brother, at the ball park camp grounds, where the brother lived with his wife and four children.

SECOND QUARREL

The husband followed her, there was another quarrel and Mathis pulled his wife out into the street, Richards following them. From that point on witnesses' stories vary. Richards declared Mathis reached for a knife; another witness said it was an ice pick, according to special dispatches to The Chronicle.

A blow from a baseball bat wielded by Richards, according to his own admission, dazed Mathis and he wandered off. He was found later in another part of town, taken to Watsonville Emergency Hospital, then transferred to Santa Cruz County Hospital.

When his condition did not improve, he was brought here for a head operation in an attempt to save his life. Mathis was the son of Mrs. Maynard Tate, well known ranch woman of the Watsonville area.

SAFE DRIVER STOPS AUTO, FALLS DEAD

A dying man's presence of mind probably averted a serious traffic accident yesterday.

Pedestrians saw an automobile suddenly turn out of the line of traffic and stop near the Mission street curb at Twenty-ninth street. The driver turned off the ignition. Then he crumpled over the steering wheel.

When the ambulance arrived William H. Pond, 57, 357 Head street, was dead. He had been suffering from heart trouble. Attendants said he probably felt the attack coming on and, with his last strength, stopped his automobile. Had his car gone wild an accident in the heavy Sunday traffic would have been almost certain, police officers said.

Farm Nude Feud Reaches Peek

Special to The Chronicle

LONG VALLEY, N. J., July 19—Farmer William A. Searles, who (as he puts it) was raised up to be respectable, today enlivened the summer season here for the second successive year by inaugurating his annual peeking campaign to drive nudists from the vicinity of his land near Long Valley.

Flanked by reporters and crouching in the shrubbery on the edge of the nudist encampment, the North Jersey Health Institute, Searles, using binoculars, spotted a plump, middle aged woman, wearing only a floppy straw hat. The corpulent woman waddled within 100 yards of the ambush and then splashed into a creek. Then two fat, bald headed men hove into view, entirely unclothed. When they came within throwing range, Searles whooped, leaped up and hurled sticks at them.

"You ought to be ashamed of yourselves," he cried. The bald headed men fled into a woods in their best imitations of startled gazelles.

Satisfied with his initial foray of the season, Searles, snapped his galluses and harangued his guests as follows: "Gentlemen, this is a helluva situation. There's a Y. M. C. A. camp on one side of these nuders where there's about 100 boys around 15, 16 years old spending the summer. Suppose some kids out on a nature study trip should come across these nuders?

"I'm going to confer with these Y. M. C. A. people and see if they won't set up a grandstand where the public can come and eat baked clams and drink beer and peek these nuders out of the neighborhood. They can't stand having an outsider look at them. I'm against nuders because I was raised up to be respectable and wear clothes. It's disgusting to see a lot of bare folks running around. 'Taint decent."

Searles disclosed that two accidents caused him to renew his crusade. One occurred when his son, William Jr., was out driving in the family car on a back-country road. Young Searles' girl friend was in the car. Suddenly they espied a nude woman swimming in a creek. The girl driver couldn't keep her eyes off the nudist and, as a result, the Searles machine collided with a tree, smashing a headlight and a fender.

The other mishap occurred on the property of a neighbor, G. M. Dilley. Dilley was having a carpenter repair his farm house roof. The carpenter got a glimpse of the nudists and tried to get closer. He took a thoughtless step and nearly broke his neck when he hit the ground.

(Wirephoto on Page 2)

SHIPS HUNT CRAFT WITH 21 ABOARD

TAMPA, Fla., July 19 (AP)—The third day of a search by American and Cuban craft passed today without a trace of the British motorship Nunoca, unreported since leaving the West Indies for Tampa July 4 with 21 persons aboard.

Nine Americans, four Britons and a crew of eight, under Captain Moses I. Kirkconnell, were aboard when the Nunoca sailed from Georgetown, Grand Cayman island. The cutters Nemesis of St. Petersburg, the Tampa of Mobile, Ala., and the Kimball of Key West combed waters of the lower gulf and Florida straits.

Today's Features

Alice Longworth	7
Among the Argonauts	7
Amusements	8, 9
Army, Navy News	26
Book Reviews	7
Chester Rowell	7
Comics	22
Coming Events	14
Crossword Puzzle	24
Contract Contacts	14
David Lawrence	6
Deaths	8
Dorothy Dix	13
Editorials	6
Financial	17
Irvin Cobb	7
Labor News	26
Lichty	7
Merry-Go-Round	12
Ninon Fashions	13
Oddities in the News	16
Off the Record	6
Passing Show	14
Radio	14
Safety Valve	6
Shipping	12
Skill-Words	8
Society	12
Sports	17, 18, 19, 20, 21
Ticking Terror Murders	25
Veterans' News	10
Want Ads	23, 24, 25
Women's Clubs	13

FOUNDED 1865—VOL. CXLIX, NO. 120 CCCC* SAN FRANCISCO, CAL., THURSDAY, NOVEMBER 12, 1936 DAILY 5 CENTS, SUNDAY 10 CENTS: DAILY AND SUNDAY PER MONTH, $1.15

TODAY--Mighty Bridge Opens!

At Last the Dream Comes True

Governor Merriam Will Sever Chains at Both Approaches; Roosevelt Will Turn on Green 'Go' Signal

By FLOYD HEALEY

San Francisco today reaches deeply into the glory and tradition of its past to salute a milestone it has taken 100 years to reach—and ten times that many will have been folded away in history's pages before another event of such vital import to its future will have come to pass.

The San Francisco-Oakland bay bridge will be opened.

Inspiration of dreams for nearly a century, it boldly holds its sinews of steel and columns of concrete against the heavens, a visible challenge to the forces of nature that decreed it should not be.

DEEPEST BAY SPANNED

It stands stanchly above the deepest body of water ever spanned, the fulfillment of human will, courage and resourcefulness, one more prideful step in an indomitable progression that dates backward to the Garden of Eden and beckons the future illimitably.

Nature rimmed San Francisco bay with hills towering high, and gouged deeply down their flanks to create a reservoir of water. From prehistoric times, the rolling waves within the Golden Gate have defied the brains and brawn of man.

Some were awed, and beaten, at the gage thus flung.

Others took it up.

Today they accept the conquerors' acolade and dedicate the fruits of their victory to the common weal.

The bay bridge is a reality, mocking those who said it would never be.

TRAFFIC STARTS TODAY

Wheels of motor cars will start rolling on the highway of the mightiest bridge that ever was built at 12:30 o'clock this afternoon.

Preceding them will be the wheels of a select caravan housing the notables who will praise it, thrill to it, and give it to the public.

Following it will come a celebration lasting until Sunday, in which the 2,000,000 persons of the Bay Area may join and echo the wonder of it all.

THREE-DAY CELEBRATION

There will be three more days of fiesta, with spirits high and hearts aglow.

The anticipatory thrill was evident all over the Bay Region last night, with nearly 300,000 visitors milling among the inhabitants of the sister cities of the bay, eager to be part of the unforgettable picture, avid with the desire to be one of the first to drive over this bridge which has no equal.

Governor Merriam will cut its bonds, President Roosevelt will open it.

Arriving in Oakland early this

Continued on Page A, Col. 3

Rebel Guns Roar In Savage Attack

Loyal Legion of Poles, French, Italians and Germans Defends Madrid

MADRID, Nov. 12 (Thursday) (AP)—Fascist insurgents launched a desperate attack on Madrid from Los Franceses bridge toward the university city in the northwest section of the capital at 11:20 p. m. last night.

The incessant tat-tat-tat of machine guns and rifles, punctuated by heavy gunfire, especially from the university city area, sounded ominously close to the population in the center of the city.

Madrid citizens feared a general attack on the capital was being signalled as sudden, crackling fire was heard all along the lines from Casa de Campo to the Toledo bridge.

The sector near Los Franceses bridge was stoutly defended by an international regiment of Poles, Germans, French and Italians, many of whom served in the World war and who had built there the strongest lines of trenches Spain has ever seen.

The insurgents were believed to have started their sortie in two sections, one fording the Manzanares river at Puerta de Mirro, and the other following the Escorial railroad to Los Franceses bridge.

SHELL OVER RIVER

Earlier the Fascists' batteries, a quarter of a mile west of Carabanchel Bajo and north of Cuatro Vientos, had rained shells across the river into sections of Madrid.

One insurgent battery was brought a mile nearer to the capital, between Carabanchel and the Talavera highway, to a point only 200 to 300 yards from the government front-line trenches.

Observers on the telephone building in Madrid witnessed shells exploding near the opera house, the old cathedral, the unfinished new cathedral, the royal palace and the north station.

Two large fires broke out near the opera house and an evacuated ammunition factory alongside the Segovia bridge in the wake of the blazing insurgent gunfire.

POWDER PILE FIRED

The Socialist gunners returned the insurgents' withering barrages with desultory fire. They scored one hit on Carabanchel Bajo, sending up a Fascist ammunition dump in clouds of black smoke and lurid flames.

Members of the Scottish ambulance brigade described the ghastly scene in a shelled house at Paseo de San Vicente above the north station.

There the family of seven was having dinner when a shell burst under the table, killing five and wounding two children.

Two new battalions arrived to reinforce the international legion in the university city sector as the newly arrived 4000 Catalans opened fire on insurgent trenches with machine guns and rifles.

(Columns of militia arrived daily in Valencia, a dispatch said, en route to join the government forces defending Madrid. Several thousand have been dispatched to the capital from Barcelona, it was reported.

(At the same time it was expected President Manuel Azana would arrive Thursday in Valencia to summon Parliament into session.)

Weather
Partly Cloudy and Mild
Complete Weather Report on Page 22

Wally Dined With Queen, Says Rumor

Heart to Heart Talk Over King Held at Mother's Invitation, Declare Throne Sources

(Copyright, 1936, Chicago Tribune-New York News Syndicate Co., Inc.)

LONDON, Nov. 11—Sources close to the throne said tonight Queen Mary, mother of King Edward, had dined this week with his American friend, Mrs. Ernest (Wally) Simpson, at Marlborough House, upon the queen mother's invitation.

The Queen's invitation, tantamount to a command, wasn't prompted so much by a desire for friendship with the Baltimore-born beauty, the sources said, but by a desire to have a heart to heart talk, as woman to woman, over her son's friendship with Wally and the uproar it has created.

FRIENDSHIP SAME

No one knows how the conversation ended, but as far as can be seen, it has not caused any difference in the friendship of the King for Wally.

At the opening of Parliament, Wally was definitely in the distinguished visitors' gallery, it has been established. She escaped detection despite the fact society and the press were looking for her avidly. Somehow she was able to enter and leave unnoticed.

She also occupied a special place in the balcony of the home office today to watch the King at the Armistice day ceremonies. Queen Mary and the Princess-royal, as well as the Duchesses of York and Kent, sisters-in-law of the King, were also in the balcony.

MARRIAGE RUMORS

Insurance brokers on the stock exchange are doing a brisk business in policies against the King's postponing the coronation. This is the direct result of the rumors of his intent to marry Wally.

Brokers are now quoting a special 8 per cent insurance for the first time against postponement of the coronation "for reasons other than the death of a member of the royal family, the King's illness or war."

The idea behind the new rate is the belief in the King's determination to marry Wally in spite of all opposition as well as in his possible abdication.

Three Perish, 31 Injured in Bus Accident

Truck Crashes Headon Into San Francisco-Bound Stage; Driver One of Victims

A terrific head-on crash between a Pacific Greyhound bus and a 12-ton truck on a steep grade a mile north of San Luis Obispo, killed the driver and two women passengers at early dawn yesterday. At least 31 other persons were injured.

THE DEAD

LAWRENCE P. BAKER, 33, the driver of the bus, who resided at 1256 Nineteenth avenue with his wife and 9-year-old son.

MRS. NORA EMRICK, 56, of 1005 First avenue, Inglewood.

MRS. ANNA B. SINGLETON, 1663 Murchison street, Los Angeles.

The bodies of the two women were disfigured almost beyond recognition, and were not identified until late last night.

A third woman, Mrs. Christina Boss of San Francisco, lay in a coma, her chest crushed in San Luis Sanitorium.

The crash occurred on Cuesta grade when a truck driven by Erwin Honeyball of Pasadena, with Forest Stroh of Los Angeles as a passenger, came south bound down the grade at an estimated speed of 60 miles per hour, striking the north bound stage and overturning it into a ditch.

THROWN THROUGH ROOF

The bus was crumpled for more than half its length. Baker was pinned between the wheel and driver's seat. Firemen worked for three hours under floodlights with acetylene torches to remove the injured. The truck was demolished, and Honeyball was seriously injured.

Nels Peterson of El Monte was thrown through the roof of the bus, and remained there for three hours with his feet caught in the steel framework as firemen sought to extricate him.

PASSENGERS TELL HORROR

Late yesterday, passengers arriving here, told of horrors experienced after the streamlined, $20,000 stage plunged off of the highway.

J. F. Ogeltree, a pharmacist's mate aboard the U. S. S. Oklahoma, who aided in the rescue work, said he was sitting near the women who were killed, and saved himself by dropping behind a seat just before the crash.

Ogeltree said that he was recovering from a wound received in the

(Continued on Page 4, Col. 5)

Pilgrims Hear Song, Ave Maria, Rising From Lay Nun's Grave

CLEVELAND, Nov. 11 (AP)—Thousands of persons in recent months have visited the "singing grave" of Helen Pelczar, listening for "miraculous music" said to filter from beneath the trampled sod.

A woman said she could hear plainly a voice singing "Ave Maria." Another said she could hear the sound.

Men came, too. One spread a newspaper and knelt. Wide-eyed children watched expectantly. Some pilgrims bring little bunches of chrysanthemums, holy medals, rosaries, to place by the stone, which reads:

HELEN PELCZAR
1888-1926
"AVE MARIA"

Some scooped up earth, wrapped it in their handkerchiefs and put it away in pocket or purse. Their faith was unshaken.

Catholic church officials said today that a "thorough investigation" was being made of the reported miracle.

"It is the policy of our church to proceed very carefully and make a most thorough investigation when a miracle is reported," said Monsignor Floyd L. Begin, secretary to Bishop Joseph Schrembs of the Cleveland Catholic diocese.

Monsignor Eugene P. Duffy, director of cemeteries, said he knew nothing of Helen Pelczar except she belonged to the Third Order of St. Francis, Catholic lay organization, and that she was buried in the robes of the order.

Quarter of a Million Here for the Show

Hotels Are Jam-Packed for First Time In Ten Years . . . Huge Stream of Gold Pouring Into the City

All previous crowd records in San Francisco yesterday appeared on the verge of being shattered as 250,000 visitors poured into the city for the biggest of all big celebrations—opening of the San Francisco-Oakland bay bridge.

By bus, train, airplane and private autos, they surged in to see the latest engineering wonder of the world and to join in festivities Thursday, Friday and Saturday.

Hotels were dusting off their "sold out" signs as they prepared for the first capacity crowd in 10 years.

Already one place on Market street has turned down 900 requests for accommodations affording a view of the two parades, it was reported.

For once it appeared possible that the 75,000 hotel rooms that places San Francisco third in the Nation in regard to accommodations, might be inadequate.

More than $2,000,000 of outside money will be dumped into the stream of local commerce during the three-day period of gayety, according to Walter Swanson of the Convention and Tourist Bureau.

Police were preparing for a street crowd record of around 750,000 during the Saturday night parade. The largest crowd so far was 600,000 during the Shrine convention in 1932.

All days off have been canceled for the entire police department for the three-day holiday. Extra officers have been assigned to the traffic and hotel details.

Down town San Francisco was flooded with autos yesterday as the heavy inflow of machines began making itself felt. The California Automobile Association reported requests for tourist maps were ten times the usual number. Out-of-State licenses were in evidence everywhere.

The Southern Pacific Railway has added an extra sleeper to its Salt Lake City train for passengers, San Francisco bound, and are preparing extra sections for Valley and Coast lines.

The bulk of the passengers will come from within a 200-mile radius, officials forecast. The company also plans to have additional ferry boats beginning today to augment normal service.

Wallace Plans Unrestrained Crops in 1937

WASHINGTON, Nov. 11 (AP)—Unrestrained crop production next year was indorsed today by Secretary Wallace as a means to convince the public that production control is a national necessity.

At a press conference he said the Administration would press for crop insurance legislation and some changes in the present soil conservation act, under which, he added, $500,000,000 would be paid farmers next season.

But, despite the recent urgings of a conference of farm leaders here, Wallace asserted the Administration would not ask the new Congress for production control legislation.

"That is a matter for Congress and the farmers," he said.

Adding that drought and high prices had caused many farmers to want unrestrained production next year, he expressed belief "it would be a good thing from a public and political point of view."

"They could fill up their bins," he said, and big surpluses probably would push down prices.

"With normal weather and large production of wheat and corn next year, I think just about everybody in the United States would then favor some kind of production control."

Bridges Calls On Public, U. S. To End Strike

Charging the shipowners are prepared for a three to four months' lockout to smash the Maritime Federation and all organized labor on the Pacific Coast, Harry Bridges, longshore leader, addressed 6500 people at a mass meeting in Dreamland Audtiorium last night.

He demanded the public and a pro-labor government exert pressure on the shipowners to bring the water front strike to an immediate cessation.

"If you, the public, and the Government, now in office chiefly through the labor vote, fail to do this," he charged, "then we are prepared to carry this fight to a finish. It goes beyond the water front. This attack is an assault on all organized labor. If we lose there is no doubt as to what will happen to the labor movement on the Pacific Coast, if not throughout the country."

His address, the high light of the meeting, came on the heels of a scorching dissertation on the maritime situation by Harry Lundeberg, leading figure in the Sailors' Union of the Pacific. Lundeberg, insisting that "conditions in the American merchant marine are rotten," attacked the shipowners for "yelling we're reds because we ask for living wages and decent conditions."

He termed the Copeland discharge book bill a "fink bill which seeks to

(Continued on Page 8, Col. 4)

Inter-City Link Feted By Oakland

Parade Launches Celebration of Victory

By FRANCIS B. O'GARA

Almost in the shadow of the great bridge which links them, two cities joyously celebrated their union yesterday.

In the sunny warmth of a perfect day, 25,000 bright-clad marchers paraded through the streets of down town Oakland in the first major event of a four-day program long awaited by all Northern California.

Dual motives inspired the great celebration—the bridge and the Armistice day anniversary.

Veterans and their organizations played prominent part in the day's program.

The rebirth of peace in the world in 1918 and the birth of the great bridge mingled in minds and hearts of the thousands who participated.

Mindful of the honor that was theirs in formally launching the fete, San Francisco's neighbors across the bay presented a spectacle seldom surpassed for color and feeling during recent Bay District history.

Tens of thousands of spectators, many of them from San Francisco and the Peninsula, lined Oakland's gayly bedecked streets. Other thousands peered out from office buildings and hotels as the procession passed below.

As reviewing officer, Governor Merriam, surrounded by civic digni-

(Continued on Page 10, Col. 1)

Today's Features

Feature	Page	Feature	Page
Amusements	14	Labor News	27
Army, Navy News	27	Lichty	13
Book Reviews	13	Mallon	17
Chester Rowell	12	Merry-Go-Round	18
Comics	21	Ninon Fashions	18
Coming Events	20	Passing Show	13
Crossword Puzzle	28	Radio	20
Contract Contacts	20	Safety Valve	12
David Lawrence	12	Smoke Rings	13
Deaths	15	Shipping	22
Dorothy Dix	18	Society	19
Editorials	12	Sports	22, H1, H2, H3, H4
Financial	20	Veterans' News	27
Irvin Cobb	13	Want Ads	27, 28, 29
It Can't Happen Here	15	Women's Clubs	18

COMPARATIVE TEMPERATURES

	High	Low		High	Low
San Francisco	64	47	New York	42	30
Los Angeles	76	51	Chicago	42	30
Seattle	50	44	Denver	46	26
Honolulu	78	70	New Orleans	80	58

San Francisco Chronicle

THE CITY'S ONLY HOME-OWNED NEWSPAPER

Weather
Fair and Mild
Complete Weather Report on Page 37

FOUNDED 1865—VOL. CXLIX, NO. 148 CCCC* SAN FRANCISCO, CAL., THURSDAY, DECEMBER 10, 1936 DAILY 5 CENTS, SUNDAY 10 CENTS

EDWARD VIII ABDICATING TODAY; KING TRADES THRONE FOR LOVE; CABINET NOTIFIED OF DECISION

S. F. Ship Officers Reject Peace Pact Of Schooner Men

Vote 282 Against to 9 for Operators' Proposal; Similar Action Seen at Other Pacific Ports

Union masters, mates and pilots on the Pacific Coast voted overwhelmingly yesterday not to accept a set of proposals for a new working agreement submitted by operators of coastwise steam schooners.

The vote in San Francisco was 282 against, and 9 for.

It was said a similar ratio would exist in final tabulations at other coast ports.

Although the vote had the effect of cold water on persistent peace overtures, it was explained that it does not prevent further discussions among the negotiators, and it came at a time when a distinct step forward was being taken in another direction.

Assistant Secretary of Labor McGrady reached the point in his program of clearing the way for resumption of union and offshore conferences that he said there was "a bare possibility" that such a gathering may take place this evening.

He spent most of yesterday with members of the Coast committee

(Continued on Page 6, Col. 1)

EDITORIAL

A New Suggestion For Peace

The Shipping Merchants' Association comes out with a constructive suggestion for breaking the present stalemate in the maritime dispute.

It is that the principals themselves take it up directly with each other. The shippers point out that the negotiations between the present shipowners' committee and the leaders of the striking unions have reached a degree of bitterness which makes any agreement, as between them, seem impossible.

On the other hand, the very fine spirit in which Mr. Roger Lapham, president of the American - Hawaiian Steamship Company, was received at the Tuesday night mass meeting, demonstrated that the problem can be discussed rationally, by men disposed to do so.

The shippers, therefore, "after a careful study of the situation to date, and after conferring with all parties concerned," urge that the negotiations be transferred to "a closed meeting of only shipowners and the duly elected officers of the striking unions."

Thus, with a fresh personal and emotional approach, free from the atmosphere of recent controversy and taking advantage of the fine spirit shown on both sides at the great mass meeting, the prospects of an early, a sound and just solution of the problem would be greatly improved.

The shipping merchants have rendered a real public service in calling attention to this very important aspect of the situation and in suggesting a way to meet it.

In the same spirit, The Chronicle is glad to indorse the proposal and to express the hope that it will be adopted.

Richberg Resigns Government Post

WASHINGTON, Dec. 9 (AP)—Resignation of Donald Richberg, onetime NRA administrator, as a special Assistant Attorney General was announced today by Attorney General Cummings.

Richberg, who had been assigned to prosecute oil companies charged with having defrauded the Osage Indians, resigned as of November 30 when he formed a law partnership.

Ship Murder 'Confession' Put in Record

Defense Counsel Held in Contempt After Row Following Loss of 5-Day Battle

Resner, Conner Attorney, Hurls Charges of 'Unfair Trial'

By HARRY LERNER

A five-day battle to prevent admission of the confession of Frank J. Conner in the ship murder of Chief Engineer George Alberts failed yesterday.

In a turbulent court session climaxed by the contempt sentence of Conner's attorney, Herbert Resner, the confession was read into the record to link Conner, by his own statement, as the finger man in the engineer's stabbing last March.

COURT IN TURMOIL

Resner's futile last-ditch stand against the reading of the confession threw the Oakland courtroom into turmoil and ended only when Superior Judge Frank M. Ogden sentenced him to pay a fine of $50 or spe d 10 days in the County Jail "for contemptuous conduct."

The attorney said after the court's action that he'd "just as soon go to jail," but Judge Ogden indicated that he would not enforce the sentence until a later date.

Conner's confession (since repudiated), which the defense contended had been extorted from him through threats, intimidation and deception, recited this story:

That on Saturday, March 21, at Howard Terminal in Oakland, Ramsay (Ernest G. Ramsay, union patrolman, another defendant), appeared at the ship, accompanied by Wallace (George Wallace, union member and the fourth defendant), and by one Ben ("Wimpy") Sakovitz, fugitive, and discussed with Conner a plan to beat up the engineer.

POINTED OUT CABIN

That on the following day, Conner was going into the engine room when he saw Sakovitz and Wallace walking toward the starboard passageway.

That Conner emerged from the engine room and pointed out Alberts' cabin.

"I didn't know they were going to kill him," the confession asserted. "I only thought they were going to beat him up, else I wouldn't have taken any hand in it. But they used a knife and some other weapon."

Before the confession was admitted, Judge Ogden advised the jurors that it must be considered as binding only on Conner.

Resner accused the Judge of bias and prejudice, of denying the defendants a fair trial, and having made up his mind to admit the confession before hearing testimony concerning it. At this point, the Judge held him in contempt.

The testimony was concluded with statements by Drs. Benjamin W. Black and O. D. Hamlin, county physicians, denying Conner did not know what he was doing on the night he signed the document, and asserting he informed them Warren's aids had treated him "fine."

State Editor Charged With Libeling F. R.

Article Calling Nation's Chief a 'Hypocrite' Brings Order for Arrest

Mountain View Writer Claims Attempt to Muzzle Press

By STANLEY BAILEY
Chronicle Staff Writer

MOUNTAIN VIEW, Dec. 9—Quick smiling, slow speaking country editor P. Milton Smith sat in a big leather chair at his home here tonight and waited for the Sheriff to arrest him on a charge of libeling President Franklin D. Roosevelt.

The amazing complaint, sworn to in San Jose, was based on an editorial November 27 in which the 68-year-old silver-haired editor said "America went mad on November 3."

It was sworn to by Horace E. Beales, president of the Mountain View Patriotic League, who thinks the attack on the President was akin to "anarchy."

'SMILING HYPOCRITE'

Editor Smith termed the President "A man universally hated for a smiling hypocrite, a mountebank of the lowest order and the biggest 'false alarm' since the creation of man."

"That's not criminal libel," he told The Chronicle. "That is the expression of an opinion and I have a right to express my opinion of a public officer. It makes no criminal charge against the President."

"This charge is an attempt to muzzle me—to end the freedom of the press.

Picture of Publisher Smith on Page 1, Second Section

"Even though this is only a weekly newspaper, I have every right to publish my opinion as has the editor of any newspaper in the country," Smith declared, "and when they attempt to stop me they are interfering with my constitutionally guaranteed rights. I have no fear that they will be successful."

Although the warrant was issued by Justice of the Peace Grandin Miller at 11 a. m. today, it had not been served late tonight and Sheriff George W. Lyle indicated action would be delayed until tomorrow.

EDITOR FOR 32 YEARS

Accompanying Beales, an electrician, to swear out the criminal complaint were Clyde Redwine, Mountain View chairman of the Democratic County Central Committee, and John M. Burnett, San Jose, committee chairman.

For 32 years Editor Smith has controlled the weekly Register-Leader, founded by the late Frank Bacon, the renowned 'Lightnin'" actor.

During that long time he has fired his editorial guns as he willed.

He opposed the reelection of President Roosevelt and still thinks that 26,000,000 people can be wrong.

"MANNA FOR INDIGENTS"

The election, Editor Smith declared in his editorial, was no "mystery" to him. The problem, he finds

(Continued on Page 2, Col. 1)

U. S. Orders 8-Hour Day For Maritime Workers

WASHINGTON, Dec. 9 (AP)—New regulations governig the hours of seamen were issued today by the Bureau of Marine Inspection and Navigation.

Acting under provisions of recently enacted amendments to the seamen's act, the bureau prescribed an eight-hour day for licensed officers, sailors, coal passers, firemen, oilers and water tenders effective December 25.

The regulations do not apply to vessels of less than 100 gross tons, or to ships operating in inland waters other than the Great lakes. Fishing or whaling vessels, yachts, tugs and barges and salvage vessels also are excluded.

The regulations said that customs authorities and marine inspection and navigation field men would enforce the regulations. No provision was made for payment of wages for overtime work.

Officials explained the rules were designed to eliminate the necessity for overtime. If, however, an emergency should arise making overtime work necessary, they added, payment of wages for this would depend upon contractual relations between ship operators and seamen.

Monarch's Flight Hinted
York May Refuse Crown

Wally Offer Of Sacrifice Still Stands

Divorcee Slips Out, Motors Through Countryside

CANNES, Dec. 9 (AP)—Wallis Warfield Simpson's offer to withdraw from the life of Edward VIII "if it will solve the problem" still holds good, her spokesman, Lord Brownlow, said tonight.

Asked whether any development in London or elsewhere had altered Mrs. Simpson's stand, Brownlow said, "Her position remains the same."

MOTORS INTO COUNTRY

It was disclosed tonight that Mrs. Simpson enjoyed a half hour motor trip through the countryside accompanied by a bodyguard.

Despite earlier denials she had left the house, it was said reliably she "slipped out" for a short drive but had paid no visits to any of her friends or spoken with anyone during the ride.

Earlier Mrs. Simpson talked for long hours with the attorney who handled her divorce suit against Ernest A. Simpson.

What they discussed, however, was known only to the principals. The barrister, Theodore Goddard, said only he "couldn't discuss the affairs of a client."

Lord Brownlow, gentleman in waiting to King Edward and Mrs. Simpson's spokesman, said, however, they had talked of "disposition" of Mrs. Simpson's recently acquired London residence on Cumberland Terrace and "other matters" which he declined to define.

He said that Mrs. Simpson had "signed no documents," thus contraverting reports that financial matters had come up for consultation.

Goddard first visited Mrs. Simpson in the Riviera villa of her friends, Mr. and Mrs. Herman Rogers. After he left, his clerk, Sydney Baron, went to the home for a brief conference.

DOCTOR AVOIDS VI. LA

Goddard, Baron and Dr. W. Douglas Kirkwood arrived in Cannes the night before after a perilous airplane and taxi journey from Croydon Airport, near London.

Dr. Kirkwood, whose visit was said to have been purely on the request of his friend Goddard, and in no way whatever connected with Mrs. Simpson, left earlier in the day for Marseille. He did not go near the Rogers' villa.

Today's Features

Amusements	8, 9
Army, Navy News	9
Book Reviews	11
Chester Rowell	10
Comics	H6
Coming Events	27
Crossword Puzzle	28
Contract Contacts	12
David Lawrence	10
Deaths	13
Dorothy Dix	16
Editorials	10
Financial	18, 19, 20
Irvin Cobb	11
Labor News	9
Lichty	11
Mallon	15
Merry-Go-Round	11
Ninon Fashions	16
Passing Show	11
Radio	12
Safety Valve	10
Smoke Rings	.1
Shipping	27
Society	17
Sports	H1, 2, 3, 4, 5
The Vampire	27
Veterans' News	9
Want Ads	27, 28, 29
Women's Clubs	16

You Can't Do That To Our Nell

We Went Oversea Once; We'll Fight Now for Love

By PAUL C. SMITH

MAYBE it's already too late. I've been intending for days to rush into print with a bit of sage comment on this Wally-Edward affair. No news conscious editor with half a grain of professional pride would overlook deliberately an opportunity to set forth his own views on the most Ah-inspiring love story the dinner table chatters have had to chew on since Henry VIII crunched small chicken bones behind his beard.

But maybe it's already too late. Perhaps by the time this reaches the cold glare of black type on high cost newsprint, Edward will have tossed the throne to the Baldwins and run off to fetch the apple of his eye from the swirl of the Riviera, or perhaps Wally will have taken things into her own hands and, for Church and Empire, put a stop to the whole silly business by eloping to Constantinople or even Sofia with Lord Brownlow, Edward's man-in-waiting.

POINTS WITH ALARM

In any event, William Allen White and Mencken have had their say, and I've never suspected either of them of fully understanding the international complications underlying this Anglo-American love affair. In other words, I'm not sure they see beneath the Cecil B. DeMille scale of the scenery with sufficient clarity of vision to unveil mentally all the fundamentals involved. Or perhaps that fundamental stuff is just a hangover from the local maritime strike.

Anyway, it is high time someone pointed with alarm to the possibilities of war between Great Britain and America unless Edward makes up his mind pretty fast. It may be too late to stop it now, even if King Edward has decided in favor of our Wally.

The strained relations between the two countries might right now be at the point of open conflict were William Hale Thompson still Mayor of Chicago. Big Bill was always taking oratorical socks at King George just because he was King George and Big Bill was Big Bill. Think of what Bill would have to work on if he had control of Chicago's police sirens and radio stations at a time when King Edward was stalling around about a simple choice between an American product and a little old English empire!

WHERE'S OUR RED BLOOD

Who is the Mayor of Chicago now, anyway? What has happened to the red-blooded Americanism of a better day?

But to get back to the war. This whole l'affaire Wally is fraught with the possibilities

(Continued on Page 4, Col. 1)

General Denhardt Released on Bail

NEWCASTLE, Ky., Dec. 9 (AP)—Circuit Judge Charles C. Marshall today granted bail to Brigadier General Henry H. Denhardt, charged with the murder of Mrs. Verna Garr Taylor, his fiancee.

Princess Elizabeth's Accession Possible With Regency Council Setup

LONDON, Dec. 10 (Thursday) (UP)—Announcement this afternoon that King Edward has decided to abdicate the British throne for the love of Mrs. Wallis Warfield Simpson was confidently expected today by press, public and most members of the House of Commons.

Usually reliable sources of information told the United Press late last night that Prime Minister Stanley Baldwin had informed the Cabinet, in an emergency session, that the King would quit the throne. Word went out to churches throughout Great Britain to be prepared to offer prayers for a new ruler on Sunday.

Informed persons said only an eleventh-hour change of mind on the part of King Edward could keep him on the throne. Powerful forces, it was said, were working to persuade him to reconsider, but the United Press was informed as early as Tuesday night—by a source that has been correct on every development in the constitutional crisis—that the King's mind was made up and that his decision was abdication.

Racing With Red Dispatch Case

A dispatch rider, on a motorcycle, raced last night from No. 10 Downing street, official residence of Prime Minister Stanley Baldwin, to Fort Belvedere, Edward's country estate, where for six days the young monarch has pondered his momentous decision.

Many persons thought he was carrying papers pertaining to the King's abdication. Around 11 o'clock he sped out of the

Bobbies and Bets

(Copyright, 1936, by the Chicago Daily News, Inc.)

LONDON, Dec. 9—The London police were ordered tonight to take special precautions to prevent demonstrations in the vicinity of Buckingham Palace and Downing street following the statement in the House of Commons tomorrow by Prime Minister Baldwin. Bets are being made tonight that the King will not be in London when the announcement is made.

Fort Belvedere grounds and headed for London, 24 miles away, still carrying the official red dispatch case.

There were other flurries of activity at Fort Belvedere. The royal truck, which carries the King's baggage, rumbled out of the gates of the estate and turned toward London, its lights winking in the darkness.

Early editions of the London newspapers, even the more conservative papers, cautiously forecast abdication.

King Meets Mother and Sister

Edward met his mother, Queen Mary; his sister, the Princess Royal, and his cousin, the Earl of Athlone, at the family home, Windsor Castle, late yesterday—a meeting which may have been a farewell. He also saw his brothers, the Dukes of Kent and York, at Fort Belvedere.

Discussion in political quarters turned to the question of succession to the throne. The Duke of York, King Edward's

(Continued on Page 13, Col. 1)

WALLY FINAL DECREE MAY BE RUSHED

LONDON, Dec. 9 (UP)—The Communist Daily Worker said tonight that an action had been filed at the divorce registry in Somerset House for the purpose of making absolute Mrs. Wallis Simpson's decree nisi of divorce.

The decree nisi in Mrs. Simpson's divorce action against Ernest Simpson was issued at Ipswich October 27 and ordinarily would not become absolute until April 27.

The Daily Worker said an action was entered at the registry to "show cause why the decree nisi should not be made absolute by reason of the decree having been obtained by collusion or by reason of material facts not having been brought before the court."

AMID CRISIS, KING FRETS OVER A DOG

LONDON, Dec. 9 (AP)—King Edward, with the world waiting for his greatest decision, busied himself today with his dogs.

Seriously concerned over the leg injury of Labrador, a retriever, the royal master of Fort Belvedere visited his kennels the first thing today. Dissatisfied with his pet's progress, the King called a veterinary. When the latter arrived, bringing four Pekingese along, the two knit their brows over the problem. After the veterinary left, said advices from Belvedere, the King looked relieved—almost carefree—again.

A Newsreel of Disaster! ∴ ∴ ∴

FULL PAGE OF WIREPHOTOS ON PAGE B
A Moment-to-Moment Story of the Blast

COMPARATIVE TEMPERATURES	High	Low		High	Low
San Francisco	56	49	Denver	70	48
San Jose ...	68	46	New York ...	70	54
Los Angeles..	64	56	Chicago	58	44
Seattle	76	46	New Orleans.	84	66
Honolulu	76	42	Salt Lake ...	74	52

San Francisco Chronicle
THE CITY'S ONLY HOME-OWNED NEWSPAPER

Weather
Partly Cloudy
Complete Weather Report on Page 30

FOUNDED 1865—VOL. CL, NO. 112 CCCC* SAN FRANCISCO, CAL., FRIDAY, MAY 7, 1937 DAILY 5 CENTS, SUNDAY 10 CENTS: DAILY AND SUNDAY PER MONTH. $1.15

Hindenburg, World's Largest Zeppelin, Destroyed in Lakehurst Explosion; 33 Killed, 64 Miraculously Escape

Photo Made at Instant of Blast

At the exact moment the Hindenburg exploded at Lakehurst last night an Associated Press staff photographer had his camera focussed on the mammoth dirigible and captured one of the most remarkable news photos ever taken.

Here is that picture:

The Zeppelin exploded with a terrific roar over the airport as it neared the mooring mast after a transatlantic journey from Germany.

Murray Becker, an ace cameraman of the New York A. P. staff, had been assigned to cover the arrival and as the ship dropped her lines to be hauled in to the navy mooring mast, was snapping pictures. Thus his camera in a series of pictures, recorded one of the most shocking air disasters in recent years

Those pictures are on Page B—a full page!

Crowd Views Landing Field Catastrophe

LAKEHURST, N. J., May 6 (AP)—Germany's great silver Hindenburg, the world's largest dirigible, was ripped apart by an explosion tonight that sent her crumpling to the naval landing field a flaming wreck with horrible death to about a third of those aboard.

Exactly how many died was still in dispute, as the flames licked clean the twisted, telescoped skeleton of the airship that put out from Germany 76 hours before on its opening trip of the 1937 passenger season.

The American-Zeppelin Company, through its press representative, Harry Bruno, placed the death toll at 33 of the 97 aboard. The company listed 20 of the 36 passengers and 44 of the 61-man crew as the disaster's survivors.

These figures were at slight variance with unofficial estimates of the number dead.

In the crowded hospitals in the communities neighboring this hamlet in the pine covered New Jersey coastal plain, many of the survivors were in critical condition, a number suffering from excruciating burns. Some were so gravely injured, among them Captain Ernest Lehman, that the last rites of the Roman Catholic church were administered to them. Lehman, skipper of the ship's 1936 flights, made the ill-fated flight as an observer. Captain Max Pruss, the commander, was listed among the injured survivors.

Storms and buffeting headwinds had delayed the slim, graceful ship far behind her schedule for the maiden trip, and she nosed down in the early evening to keep the unexpected rendezvous with disaster.

She had been due to tie up at the mooring mast at 6 a. m. (E.S.T.) but radioed last night that the bad weather had retarded her speed so much that she would land around sunset.

IN FULL VIEW OF CROWD

After cruising down over New York's crowded streets in the afternoon, she hove into sight at the air station here at 3:12 p. m. but landing conditions were not favorable and she circled around idly in full view of the small crowd of spectators who had assembled for what was to be a routine hurry-up arrival and departure. A rainstorm came up and whipped across the field and Captain Pruss decided to ride it out to make sure of most favorable landing conditions.

Rain was still falling lightly when she headed into the mooring circle shortly after 6 o'clock, nosing down gracefully and with the nice precision that had marked so many of her arrivals last year.

The ground crew of sailors, soldiers and marines moved out onto the field to handle her landing ropes. Lower she nosed, her Diesel motors throttled down. Passengers, gayly waving at the crowd, lined the long lounge windows which showed like transparent slits in the great silver belly of the ship.

LANDING ROPES LET OUT

The spider-like web of landing ropes snaked down the little trap doors in the nose. Men of the ground crew grabbed them at the wooden crossbars.

It was 6:23.

Then came the terrific explosion, and red flames suddenly splashed out toward the stern and the rudder that bore the red-and-black Nazi swastika. The detonation tore the ship in half as if it were made of paper. The tail dropped earthward. The blunt nose bobbed up, hung a moment in the air and then crumpled toward the field, flames running along its sides and its fabric flaking off in big chunks.

Passengers and men of the crew were hurled through the walls of the Hindenburg to the sandy loam below. The crowd receded in a panicky surge to the shouts of "run for your lives." Navy men dashed into the flaming debris to make rescues.

Collapsing in a tangled mass of girders and aluminum beams, the ship was torn by a series of additional explosions, lesser in force than the first shattering blast. And the flames roared up in a red and yellow wall to envelope the ship that had seemed so durable and safe a few short minutes before.

The flames burned well into the night, despite the efforts to quench them.

Night came down. A steady stream of ambulances carried away the injured. Badly burned bodies were gathered in a hastily improvised morgue and the grim task of identification begun.

As this went on, passengers for the homeward trip of the Hindenburg, unaware of the destruction which had overtaken the ship, were arriving to embark. Many planned to attend the coronation and the Hindenburg, until tonight, represented the fastest way of getting there if one left at the last minute.

Stunned, they saw the burning wreckage.

Hours after the first terrific explosion, the ship was still licked by flames and its red hot rings and girders glowed in the dark.

An explosion of the No. 2 gas cell toward the stern of the ship was named as the cause of the disaster by State Aviation Commissioner Gill Robb Wilson, who called the blast "strange." The high-inflammable hydrogen gas billowed into fierce flame as the explosion plummeted the ship to the airfield.

Additional news of the catastrophe on pages A, B and 2.

The surviving passengers were so stunned they could not describe later what happened. Some jumped, along with members of the crew. Others seemed to have pitched from the careening sky liner as it made its death plunge.

The heat drove back would-be rescuers, so it could not be determined for how many the Hindenburg made a burning tomb. Fire departments from nearby communities

(Continued on Page A, Col. 7)

HITLER STUNNED BY TRAGEDY

BERLIN, May 7 (Friday) (U.P.)—Reichsfuehrer Hitler was called from his bed early today to receive news of the worst disaster to German air transportation in history—loss of the proud dirigible Hindenburg.

The dictator apparently was stunned by the news. He refused formal comment.

A report of the catastrophe was telephoned to the Chancellor and Propaganda Minister Joseph Goebbels. Later, DNB, official Nazi news agency, announced German Zeppelin traffic across the North Atlantic will continue "unabated."

A new dirigible, now building at Friedrichshafen, "will continue to carry the German flag across the Atlantic in the Hindenburg's place."

The statement emphasized the previous "safety of German Zeppelins."

FIESTA!
A City Goes Wild — Read About It!

San Francisco Chronicle

THE CITY'S ONLY HOME-OWNED NEWSPAPER

PICTURES
And Stories on Pages B, 1, 2, 3, 4, 5, 6, 7, 8, 9, 10

THE GOLDEN GATE BRIDGE ☆☆☆☆ **A THIRTY-FIVE MILLION DOLLAR STEEL HARP!**

TODAY In The Chronicle

San Francisco Chronicle

THE CITY'S ONLY HOME-OWNED NEWSPAPER

Chronicle Home Carrier Service — If for any reason your Chronicle is not received please call City Circulation Department, phone DOuglas 1414, before 10 a. m. daily and 11 a. m. Sunday, and your Chronicle will be delivered promptly.

Weather Rain — Complete Weather Report on Page 10

FOUNDED 1865—VOL. CLII, NO. 56 CCCC** SAN FRANCISCO, SATURDAY, MARCH 12, 1938 DAILY 5 CENTS, SUNDAY 10 CENTS: DAILY AND SUNDAY PER MONTH $1.30

HITLER RULES IN AUSTRIA; TROOPS MARCH ON VIENNA

THE HIDDEN peril lies in a reported mobilization of Czechoslovakian troops on the Austrian frontier.

If this is true, Hitler cannot escape ordering that mobilization to cease, as the frontier is as close to Vienna as San Mateo is to San Francisco. If he orders it stopped and is defied, Hitler must invade Czechoslovakia, and France has guaranteed Czech freedom, must act or lose her whole face in Europe.

There are several "ifs" there, but the brakes seem rather worn, and in the face of everything the Czechs repeated last night that they would fight if invaded.

The actual Austrian demarche is a mild sample of the German purpose in Europe. Confronted with a plebiscite which would have shown Austrian Nazis in the minority, German militia invaded Austrian soil to put that minority in the saddle. The old-fashioned coffee shop Austrian is no Prussian, and he was unable to bring himself to meet German force with force.

The result was a headlong dissolution of the Schuschnigg regime. First came an ultimatum from Hitler demanding cancellation of the Sunday plebiscite. It was canceled, Schuschnigg resigned and Hitler's man Seyss-Inquart succeeded, installed a Nazi Cabinet, hoisted the swastika flag over the chancellory.

Riotous scenes attended this upset. Jews stayed indoors. Fatherland Front men were still unwilling to resort to machine-guns. Goering was reported (doubtfully) in Vienna. The provinces aped Vienna. Berlin Nazis started the buildup, talking about "Bolshevist chaos." Chancellor Seyss-Inquart extended the fiction, appealing for Hitler troops to prevent bloodshed. There was a corps mobilization at Munich, and the regulars moved in.

Archtypical of the change, a Nazi censorship of news was clamped down in Vienna. Refugees tried to crowd into neighboring countries to escape Nazi fury.

What will the rest of Europe do? No one knows. Britain called an emergency Cabinet meeting. France protested, but is having Cabinet trouble. Italy has refused to aid France in protest, but is mum. Czechs alone have spoken up. They denied the mobilization, but feebly, saying they were strengthening frontier guards.

Washington is the most silent

(Continued on Page 2, Col. 1)

Assembly Votes Resolution For Mooney's Pardon

Lower House Reverses Stand After Freedom Advocates Win Fight for Reconsideration

By EARL C. BEHRENS

SACRAMENTO, March 12 (Saturday)—Reversing its action of yesterday, the Assembly early this morning voted, 41 to 29, in favor of a resolution granting a "full and complete pardon," by the Legislature to Thomas J. Mooney.

The forty-first vote was cast by Assemblyman Peyser, San Francisco, who said he was changing his vote from "no" to "aye" to save a sick colleague, Assemblyman Cronin from being brought from San Francisco to vote. Cronin favored the resolution in the past. Peyser was implored by the Mooney supporters to change his vote. Oddly, his decision was not announced until after Assemblyman Richie, father of the resolution, had stated his group wanted to bring Cronin to Sacramento by plane. The Assembly had been locked up under a call of the House for some time when Peyser made his change of vote.

The Mooney pardon resolution passed two years ago by a vote of 45 to 28, but was defeated in the Senate.

RECONSIDERATION VOTE

Earlier by a vote of 42 to 28, the Mooney resolution backers secured a reconsideration of Thursday's defeat vote.

A vote on the pardon resolution immediately followed at an early hour this morning. The Assembly stood 40 to 30 against and was locked up while efforts were being made to secure the additional vote needed to make the 41 majority required to pass the measure.

Two San Francisco members, Levey and Williamson, both expressing disbelief in the legality of the attempted legislative pardon move, joined with the Mooney group while one of the members, Crowley of Vallejo, changed from the "yes" column and voted "no."

NO PARDON POWER

Attorney General Webb and State Legislature Counsel Wood both have advised the Legislature it has no power to grant pardons.

The Mooney resolution vote followed closely upon the appearance before the Assembly of Captain Charles Goff of the San Francisco Police Department who spoke in refutation of statements made yesterday by Mooney here.

Captain Goff, branded Mooney's declarations as false and again expressed confidence in the guilt of the noted prisoner.

Mooney characterized Goff as "now generalissimo of the frame-up forces," before the Assembly Thursday.

Captain Goff, attached to the Preparedness day bombing detail after the 1916 affair, traced Mooney's early history and challenged the truthfulness of the Mooney testimony given before the Legislators. He concluded with charges that the Mooney defense organization had "influenced" witnesses to recant their testimony given at the time of the bombing trials of Mooney and Warren K. Billings, 20-odd years ago.

DENIES COACHING WITNESS

Goff denied that John MacDonald, a key prosecution witness, or other witnesses who had identified Mooney and Billings as having been either at 721 Market street or at Steuart and Market streets, the scene of the bomb explosion, "had been coached" or had been aided to make their identification. Mooney and Billings were identified "free from any pressure by the police," Goff declared.

Goff quoted from the trial and subsequent legal proceedings to substantiate his statements. He declared

Continued on Page 11, Col. 5

Lion Attacks School Bus, Slain by Boy

Maddened Beast's Charge Stopped With Penknife

Special to The Chronicle

MAXWELL (Colusa county), March 11—A hunger-maddened 300-pound mountain lion, which attacked a school bus containing seven children and a driver today, met his match when he was killed by an 18-year-old high school student, with only his pocket knife as a weapon.

The Maxwell Union High School bus had picked up seven children at Stony Ford, and was proceeding along a winding mountain road toward Lodoga. Roy Rice was at the wheel.

LEAPS UPON STAGE

Suddenly, out of the underbrush, the huge cat leaped at the front of the stage. It landed on the hood, scratched and clawed at the windshield and then fell to the road. The lion immediately returned to the attack and sank its teeth into one of the front tires.

The motion of the wheel threw the lion to the ground heavily, stunning it.

Herbert Calcaterra, 18, school senior, opened his pocket knife, leaped from the door, and sprang upon the lion. Holding the lion by the ears, Herbert slashed its throat before it regained consciousness.

300-POUND BEAST

Herbert proudly placed the lion's carcass in the bus, Rice picked up other students at Lodoga and delivered all, including the lion, at the high school here only a few minutes late for classes.

Farmers said that continued snow in the mountains and the lateness of the lambing season had driven the lion to desperation from lack of food.

The lion measured 7 feet from nose to tail and weighed nearly 300 pounds.

Young Calcaterra is eligible for a State bounty, payable by the State Fish and Game Commission.

Today's Features

Amusements	4, 5
Aviation News	26
Bookman	9
Chester Rowell	8
Church News	6, 7
Comics	16
Coming Events	23
Crossword Puzzle	24
Contract Contacts	9
David Lawrence	13
Deaths	11
Editorials	8
Financial	17, 18
Kate O'Connor	14
Labor Scene	11
Lichty	9
Merry-Go-Round	8
Ninon Fashions	14
Passing Show	9
Radio	10
Real Estate News	12
Safety Valve	8
Smoke Rings	9
Shipping	10
Society	15
Sports	H1, 2, 3, 4 and 22
The Boss	7
Want-Ads	23, 24, 25
Women's Clubs	14

F. R. Defied By Morgan At TVA Quiz

Stop Squabbling or Get Out, Board Members Told

WASHINGTON, March 11 (AP)—Dr. Arthur E. Morgan, chairman of TVA, bluntly defied President Roosevelt today and declared himself not a participant in a hearing called by the chief executive to determine "the facts" behind TVA's bitter internal squabble.

The inquiry was adjourned after an all day session to convene again at 11 a. m. next Friday.

After the hearing concluded, Mr. Roosevelt ade a final statement:

Huge Shortage Claim Refuted

WASHINGTON, March 11 (AP)—Senator McKellar (D., Tenn.), read to the Senate today a letter from acting Comptroller General Elliott denying the accounting office had reported a $10,000,000 shortage in TVA accounts. McKellar said Elliott's letter refuted charges made in the Senate by Senator Bridges (R., N. H.), that TVA accounts were short.

"Frankly, I am disappointed that Chairman Morgan has not answered by giving any factual answers to the questions which I have put, but I hope that in the course of the next week Chairman Morgan will realize that it is of the utmost importance to the continuation of the work that he should reply to very simple factual questions."

"MAKE UP OR RESIGN"

Stephen T. Early, secretary to the President, said Mr. Roosevelt, in closing today's session, asserted that the three directors owed it to the country to discontinue to jeopardize the public interest by their personal differences.

He added that the President told all three, including Directors Harcourt A. Morgan and David E. Lilienthal, that if they could not work together harmoniously those refusing to do so should resign.

Face to face with the President and in the presence of his opponents on the TVA board—Vice Chairman Morgan and Director Lilienthal—Chairman Morgan criticized the inquiry as "an alleged process of fact finding" and repeated his plea for an "impartial, comprehensive and complete" investigation by Congress.

CHARGES TRICKERY

He accused the President of withholding full co-operation in correcting what he considered grave conditions within TVA, asserted the other directors were given adequate advance information of what today's

Continued on Page 5, Col. 2

Polish Children Greet Hoover

CRAKOW, Poland, March 11 (AP)—Herbert Hoover, former President of the United States, was welcomed by throngs of children as he arrived here today on his way to Warsaw.

He placed a wreath on the Woodrow Wilson monument and laid flowers on the graves of two Polish heroes, Marshal Joseph Pilsudski and Brigadier - General Tadeusz Kosciuszko of American revolution fame.

Cyclone Kills 25 in India

CALCUTTA, India, March 11 (AP)—Twenty-five persons were killed and 45 injured today when a small cyclone struck a community of tea estate workers in the hilly Dibrugarh district.

THE WEATHER

"My corns say rain, but the barometer is up," growled the Weather Man.

"Well, if I got out a forecast, I'd go by the corns," said Gadget, the Weather Bureau mouse. "They never fail. How'd you get your corns?"

"Tight shoes," said the W. M., and then added: "During the Republican era."

"I guess you'll have to stick to the barometer, boss," Gadget said. The W. M. nodded sadly and made out the forecast as: "Rain as usual."

At 524 Twenty-eighth avenue William P. Mangin held up a finger moistened by rain.

"Squalls," he said. "Wind and rain from all directions."

Czechs Bolster Border; Tension Grips All Europe

Praha Denies Army Is Mobilizing, But Defies Invaders

PRAHA (Prague) Czechoslovakia March 12 (Saturday) (U.P.) — Czechoslovakia today reasserted that any attempt by Germany to encroach upon her borders would be met with armed resistance.

The Czech Cabinet was summoned into emergency session last night by President Edouard Benes, while the frontier guards were being strengthened and Austrian refugees fled across the border into Bratislava.

Before the session was over the following communique was issued:

"The Czechoslovakian government is following events in Austria with special attention and considers the situation coolly and calmly along the lines of Premier Milan Hodza's recent declaration."

(Premier Hodza said in a speech several days ago that Czechoslovakia would throw every resource of her armed might into resisting any attempt upon the country's independence.)

"Premier Hodza and Foreign Minister Kamil Krfota are in constant telephonic communication with Czechoslovakian diplomats in the main capitals."

DENY MOBILIZATION

The government official denied that the Czechoslovakia army was being mobilized, but admitted that the customs guards were being reinformed to prevent illegal infiltration of fugitives. Strict control of the frontiers also was ordered to prevent arms smuggling.

Reports in Berlin that weapons were being delivered to Austrian Marxists were described as "unsubstantiated inventions behind which dark propaganda aims are hidden." All quarters controlling production and trade in arms flatly denied the reports.

Hundreds of panic-stricken Austrians were arriving by night trains from Vienna. Numerous private automobiles crossed the Danube bridge into Bratislava.

POPULATION EXCITED

It was rumored that Guido Zernatto, former Chancellor Kurt Schuschnigg's deputy commander of the Austrian fatherland front, was among the arrivals.

The population was excited, but so far there have been no demonstrations.

Czechoslovakia has 3,500,000 Germans who are demanding a share in the government. Chancellor Adolf Hitler has sworn to "protect" them.

BAER BEATS TOM FARR IN 15 ROUNDS

NEW YORK, March 11—The clown prince of the prize ring, Merry Maxie Baer, hammered Tonypandy Tommy Farr into fistic oblivion by winning a 15-round decision over the British heavy weight champion before a sellout crowd of more than 18,000 at the Garden tonight. After dropping Farr in the second and third rounds and winning seven of the first nine rounds, with one even, Baer hung onto his lead gamely despite a closed left eye, and had just enough left to win.

Farr, though he staged a great rally and showed his usual gameness, was fairly beaten. He was dazed all through the opening rounds, following his knockdowns, and fought mostly by instinct.

Going into the ninth round Baer was on front by eight points.

(Further details in Sporting Green.)

European Situation at a Glance

(By Associated Press)

VIENNA — Germany Nazifies Austrian government, sending in troops and reorganizing Cabinet with Arthur Seyss-Inquart, personal friend of Hitler, as Chancellor. Kurt Schuschnigg driven from office by German ultimatum threatening invasion.

BERLIN—Nazification of Austria hailed as another triumph for Reichsfuehrer Adolf Hitler. The German Chancellor will issue a proclamation today detailing events leading to the swift change in the Austrian government.

LONDON — Diplomatic sources agreed Great Britain would do nothing about Hitler's bloodless coup beyond a joint protest with France to follow up separate warnings to Germany on "possible consequences" of the Fuehrer's action.

PARIS—An official Foreign Office announcement said use of coercive measures by Germany in Austria must bring "gravest reactions of which it was impossible to foretell the issue." Premier-Designate Leon Blum worked to organize a Cabinet by early Saturday to deal with events in Austria.

WASHINGTON — Officials studied developments in Austria and Central Europe anxiously, but took their lead from Secretary of State Cordell Hull and maintained a "hands off" attitude.

ROME—An official announcement said Rome was in contact with Berlin and keeping a close watch on the Austrian situation. Although the Fascist Grand Council had no comment, Hitler's suden move was believed to have occupied Friday night's meeting of Italy's highest policy forming body.

PRAHA, Czechoslovakia — The Cabinet, meeting in special session, was represented as viewing calmly developments in her neighboring state, Austria, but planned to resist invasion.

Berlin Sees Rebirth Of Greater Germany

BERLIN, March 12 (Saturday) (U.P.)—Nazification of Austria marks a rebirth of a "greater German Reich," Field Marshal Hermann Goering asserted today as German troops entered Austria.

Commenting through his newspaper, the Essen National Zeitung, Goering added:

"What generations of German people have dreamed of, what Bismarck prepared for but could not accomplish, has now been realized by the action of our fuehrer.

"The coming weeks and months of this spring will bring speedy solution of a decade and of century old problems."

While there was speculation on Hitler's future ambitions in Central Europe, it was revealed that Dr. Arthur Seyss-Inquart, Austria's new Nazi chancellor, urged Der Fuehrer to dispatch troops into the country "to avoid bloodshed."

At that time the semi-official DNB News Agency reported from Linz, violent pro-Nazi upper Austria city, that hob-nailed German troops were goose-stepping across the border. It said that a revolt by the Austrian army and police against former Chancellor Kurt Schuschnigg's attempted "plot" to gain control of the country by ordering a plebiscite was responsible for his downfall.

Goering's newspaper went on to say "This marks the beginning of a national Socialist assault in Austria. Every hour of the coming days will create new and irrevocable factors.

"According to our will National Socialism will win in Austria as legally, but also as uncheckably, as it did in the Reich in 1933. (The year that Hitler assumed power.)

"Frivolously and criminally did Schuschnigg precipitate a crisis of which he himself fell victim while Naitonal Socialism from this crisis will go on to a wholesale and definite cleansing in Austria for which German Austria and the Reich waited so long."

France, Rebuffed by Italy, Joins in Warning to Reich

PARIS, March 11 (AP)—France, without a government and rebuffed by Italy on a proposal for joint efforts to save Austria's independence, stood helpless tonight as Nazi Germany proceeded to take power in Vienna.

Foreign Office officials announced that the French and British Ambassadors in Berlin had made a joint protest to the German government over Nazi steps in Austria.

At the same time, Premier-Designate Leon Blum, confronted with a threat to the peace of Europe, let it be known he was confident of forming a national union government—of all parties from Communist to the extreme right.

Sources close to the Socialist leader said the cabinet would be organized by early tomorrow and would be ready to deal with events in Austria.

Blum hurried consultations with political leaders, striving quickly to rally support. Besides the critical situation in Central Europe, he was confronted with a difficult financial problem and labor unrest at home.

Although the people's front showed sgns of cracking under the strain of events in Austria, its three main components—Socialists, Communists, radical-Socialists—as well as Socialist-Republicans, all agreed to the national union.

If Blum succeeds, Communists will enter a French cabinet for the first time.

Britain Fires Swift Protest As Cabinet Plans Session

LONDON, March 11 (U.P.) — The British government tonight protested in the strongest terms to Adolf Hitler against the use in the Austrian situation of "coercion backed by force to create a situation incompatible with Austria's national independence."

The British Cabinet was summoned to meet tomorrow morning to discuss the Austrian situation.

"Such action," the protest declared, "is bound to produce the gravest reactions whereof it is impossible to foretell the issue."

Germany's reported movement of troops across the Austrian border came today after a strong warning from Britain against German military action in Austria.

Usually reliable persons saw a fundamental change in the international situation. It was said the British government feels convinced Premier Mussolini of Italy now is more than ever prepared to enter into an agreement with Britain because of Austro-German developments of the past 24 hours.

Britain, it was believed in reliable quarters, had given indications to Chancellor Kurt Schuschnigg of Austria which encouraged him to

Continued on Page 3, Col. 1

Swastika Flag Flies at Chancellory; Schuschnigg Resigns

By Associated Press

VIENNA, March 12 (Saturday)—German troops moved toward Vienna in the early morning hours today to back up nazification of the Austrian State, accomplished in bloodless revolution by Chancellor Schuschnigg's capitulation to Germany's Fuehrer Hitler.

The troops, numbering about 1000 men in trucks, expected to reach the capital at noon (6 a. m., E. S. T.). They carried several pieces of light artillery, the gendarmerie commandant at Schoerding on the Bavarian border told the Associated Press by telephone.

They met no resistance and were heading first for Linz, where Nazis prepared an enthusiastic welcome.

Speed On to Capitol

From there they were to proceed quickly to Vienna.

Faced by a German ultimatum threatening armed invasion unless the government were reorganized as Hitler wished, the government gave up its five-year fight against the German Fuehrer.

For Editorial Comment See Page 8

The bloodless revolution came after two days of violence throughout Austria. It was accomplished in eight hours.

Swept out of office by Germany's demands was Chancellor Kurt Schuschnigg, who had fought to preserve Austrian independence in the old course of Chancellor Engelbert Dollfuss, who was assassinated in a Nazi putsch July 25, 1934.

Succeeding him as Chancellor and Austria's man of the hour was Austria Nazi leader, Arthur Seyss-Inquart, political friend of Hitler.

Rushes New Cabinet

Seyss-Inquart immediately formed a new Cabinet, all but two of whom were Nazis.

Apparently Wilhelm Miklas was still President.

The government radio told Vienna and other Austrian cities—where Nazis went wild in jubilant demonstrations—that Seyss-Inquart had been appointed by Miklas.

But the President, who through his years in office had supported Schuschnigg, made no announcement to the Austrian people.

Also swept out of office was another leader of the old regime—Mayor Richard Schmitz of Vienna.

His city staged a demonstration that was probably without precedent.

Crowds who heard radio announcements that German troops were on their way into Austria stampeded through

Continued on Page 3, Col. 3

San Francisco Chronicle

THE CITY'S ONLY HOME-OWNED NEWSPAPER

Chronicle Home Carrier Service — If for any reason your Chronicle is not received please call City Circulation Department, phone DO uglas 1614, before 10 a. m. daily and 11 a. m. Sunday, and your Chronicle will be delivered promptly.

Weather: Partly Cloudy and Mild. Complete Weather Report on Page 33

FOUNDED 1865—VOL. CLIII, NO. 76 CCCC** SAN FRANCISCO, THURSDAY, SEPTEMBER 29, 1938 DAILY 5 CENTS, SUNDAY 10 CENTS: DAILY AND SUNDAY PER MONTH, $1.30

POWERS HALT NAZI MARCH! PEACE MEET STARTS TODAY

By ROYCE BRIER

IF THE astronomers had said a planet was headed this way, and then the darn thing veered off, you could hardly breathe easier.

A planet might do a little more thorough job with us, but it would be less of a strain. And so we breathe, and that is what it is, a breathing spell. Adolf Hitler's irresistible will has a slight rift, but there's a condition in Central Europe which cannot easily be cured, certainly not by any conspiracy of Hitler and Mussolini to jockey Britain and France into submission by destroying Czechoslovakia.

One hates to be a sour old man with all this optimism bouncing about Europe but one cannot blot out the past. Two ways of life will face each other in Munich today. All recent history indicates these ways of life are irreconcilable. Who can reconcile them is the greatest man of our time.

Chamberlain, Daladier, Hitler and Mussolini will meet to discuss the fate of Czechoslovakia. Chamberlain and Daladier have said Hitler can have Sudetenland. Manifestly they construed that cession as one permitting the Czechs to carry on their national life. Just as manifestly, Hitler construed it as one crippling if not destroying, Czechoslovakia.

Chamberlain and Daladier could not in conscience submit to Hitler's demand. The Czechs wouldn't submit to it. Hitler implied he would invade Czechoslovakia to enforce it, set a Saturday time limit, moved it up to Wednesday. Chamberlain and Daladier implied that if he marched they would fight. That made war a matter of hours, when the break came. That is the history of it, but oversimplified.

Hundreds of forces, big and little, criss-crossed through this paralyzing situation. Poland was yelping, threatening to march, too. Mussolini was sitting on the fence, loudly crying friendship for Hitler and his cause, knowing war would wreck Italy and Mussolini. The German Army cannot see Hitlerian power politics all the way. Russia was a mystery, showing its face occasionally and dimly. The Balkans were another mystery, feeble and poor but geographically vital. Mobilization mounted here, lagged there, and comparative figures drummed in

Continued on Page 2, Col. 1

War Philosophy Touches U. S., Hoover Warns

Roosevelt Not True Liberal Despite His Words, Says Ex-President in Kansas City

KANSAS CITY, Sept. 28 (AP)—Former President Herbert Hoover, in an address charging the present Democratic Administration is "politically immoral," warned tonight that the threat of war "which darkens the whole world grows from a philosophy from which our Nation has in some degree become infected."

"This world crisis today is in part a moral crisis," the Republican leader said.

"There are in the forces which have led to this situation today a tragic warning to America. We are faced with a national election of the highest importance six weeks hence.

PARTLY INFECTION

"Our issues are also in part moral issues. They are in part the infection which has spread over the whole world."

Hoover accused President Roosevelt of attempting to form a new political party under a false banner of liberalism and declared "If this sort of stuff is liberal, then George III, Hitler, Stalin and Boss Tweed are liberals."

"What President Roosevelt is leading is not liberalism; instead of bringing the past up to the present he is bringing the present back to the past," Hoover said in a prepared address, the first of three in which he will "explore this proposed party."

REJECTS DEFINITION

Tonight, addressing a rally sponsored by Missouri Republican Clubs, Hoover rejected President Roosevelt's definitions of liberal and conservative, and accused the New Deal of being shot through with "political immorality." October 17, at Hartford, Conn., he will accuse it of destroying "government of free men." November 5, at Spokane, Wash., he will discuss its economic consequences.

Expansion of the three addresses to one hour each represents the former President's most extensive activity on the speaking platform since 1935, a member of his entourage said.

Tonight, asserting the time has come "to take the gloves off," Hoover flung eight specific charges of "political immorality" at the administration of his successor.

He accused it of building up the "G. E. A.—Get Elected Anyhow, Any Way," by making 200,000 political appointments without civil service examinations so that "working for the Government becomes a racket, not a career."

Second, he charged that relief ad-

Continued on Page 4, Col. 1

'All Should Back U. S. Peace Plea'

KANSAS CITY, Sept. 28 (AP)—Herbert Hoover, food administrator during the World war and the leader of the Belgium refugee work, said tonight "the efforts of our Government to maintain peace deserve our full support."

"The President will find every Republican and every thinking person behind him in that effort," Hoover said. "In that there is no partisanship.

"The President has rightfully urged negotiations as the way out. There is no American who will not agree that the council table is the solution—not the battlefield.

"Perhaps more vividly than any living American," he said, "I can look back over the long road of the past 25 years and count each milestone of futility and misery from the great war. Every nation was the loser. It brought no peace to the world."

Margot Grahame Weds Canadian

Special to The Chronicle

RENO, Sept. 28—Margot Grahame, blonde British glamour girl of stage and screen, who believes in plunging "wholeheartedly in love," is the secret bride of Allen McMartin, wealthy Canadian, her friends revealed today.

The beautiful advocate of impetuous lovemaking married McMartin and his reputed income of $20,000 a week following her recent divorce from Francis Lister, English actor.

Grand Jury Frees Bill Robinson

LOS ANGELES, Sept. 28 (AP)—Bill Robinson, 61-year-old Negro tap dancer, today was cleared of assault charges by the County Grand Jury, which investigated a fight following a traffic accident involving him and Paul Moffat, a student at the University of California at Los Angeles. Moffat said Robinson struck him with a gun.

Helen Vinson Hurt in Crash

NEW YORK, Sept. 28 (AP)—Helen Vinson, motion picture actress and wife of the British tennis player, Fred Perry, was seriously injured today in a collision of three automobiles at a midtown intersection. Three others also were hurt.

Miss Vinson suffered a deep cut beneath the chin, requiring several stitches, and contusions of the back, legs and body.

Weather:

"You and your showers," said Anemometer, the Weather Bureau cat. "We didn't get enough rain in this area to make a chaser for a gnat's cocktail."

"Our per'spitation was one hundredth of an inch," snapped the Weather Man.

"Our what?"

"Our per'spitation . ." said the W. M.

"That's a new word to me," said Anemometer. The W. M. scowled.

"Did you ever wear false teeth?" he demanded.

"O. K., boss," said Anemometer. "How about 'cloudy and mild' for Thursday? That'll be easy on the teeth."

The Weather Man merely nodded. The less you gue when your teeth are loose the better off you are.

Munich Meet
It Will Be 'Hitler's Last Peace Effort'

BERLIN, Sept. 28 (AP)—The peace conference at Munich tomorrow to be attended by ranking statesmen of four leading European powers was semi-officially described tonight as Reichsfuehrer Hitler's "last effort to accomplish peaceful cession of Sudetenland."

Hitler and his "axis" partner, Premier Mussolini of Italy, will confer with British Prime Minister Chamberlain and French Premier Daladier in the forenoon to search for a method of avoiding a second World war.

No definite time nor exact place of meeting had been set.

Reliable sources said tonight Hitler would meet Mussolini, already en route to Munich, at Brenner pass, historic gateway between Italy and now German Austria, and then accompany Il Duce to Munich.

Announcement of the Munich meeting brought joy to the German public and hope Hitler would score a bloodless victory over Czechoslovakia. Hitler's demands for peaceful surrender of Sudetenland by the Prague Government had set Saturday as the deadline.

Word of the Munich get-together co-incided with a decline in talk of German mobilization. The official news agency, DNB, had flatly denied reports that 2 p. m. (5 a. m., P. S. T.) today was a new deadline for Czechoslovak capitulation under threat of German mobilization.

DUCE ASKED THE DELAY

(But in London, Chamberlain indicated Hitler had agreed to defer a 2 p. m. time limit. The British Prime Minister said Mussolini had telephoned the fuehrer an expression of hope "that Herr Hitler would see his way to postpone the action which the Chancellor had told Sir Horace Wilson was to be taken at 2 o'clock today."

(Sir Horace is Chamberlain's adviser and was emissary to the Reichsfuehrer.)

"It is hoped," semi-official circles said, "that even in the last hour this exchange of views will lead to an agreement over putting into immediate effect measures for cession of Sudetenland as promised by the Czechoslovak government."

Thus, comment on the four-power conference showed Hitler was as insistent as ever on cutting off from Czechoslovakia the area in which reside most of the 3,500,000 Sudeten German minority.

The task for the Munich conferees was to find a peaceful method to conduct the operation—apparently on the basis of a new Anglo-French plan.

GOEBBELS SEES PEACE

Propaganda Minister Paul Joseph Goebbels told a Berlin throng late today he foresaw a peaceful solution of the dispute "within a few days." Goebbels did not, however, mention the Munich gathering.

To a deafening chorus of "heils" in historic Lustgarten, Goebbels merely said:

"I, as a man in the know of

Continued on Page B, Col 2
See No. Two

Czechs Warn Powers:
'No International Army!'

Copyright, 1938, by United Press

PRAGUE, Sept. 29 (Thursday) (UP)—Government officials warned early today that any decision from the four-power meeting in Munich to send an "international army" into the Sudetenland would be vigorously resisted.

The government of Premier General Jan Syrovy received news of the Munich meeting with deep misgiving and complained that the leaders of Britain, France, Germany and Italy may jeopardize Czechoslovakia's actual existence as a republic by demanding more sacrifices from her.

The only note of optimism this war-derby capital in the midnight hours was the fact that Hitler had given Czechoslovakia a breathing space by inviting Premier Mussolini, Premier Daladier and Prime Minister Chamberlain to meet with him in Munich at noon today.

Even this optimism was offset by a general feeling the "last chance" meeting would prolong the suspense and give Germany time to bring more troops up to the Sudeten border for a smashing invasion.

Hitler and Mussolini, it was feared, may prevail upon Chamberlain and Daladier to step down from the determination of France and Britain to fight in defense of Czechoslovakia.

The government's experts studying Hitler's ultimatum calling for full surrender of the Sudetenland to him by Saturday, said the likely compromise of the Munich conferees probably would be some sort of an international militia to take over temporary control of the Sudeten areas.

When this prediction was conveyed to government leaders the latter replied any such proposal would be stubbornly opposed by the Czech nation.

Czechoslovakia, they said, is determined to settle any question of dismemberment by negotiation alone.

There can be no question of foreign armed forces intervening before a complete settlement is reached.

Summary Of the Day In Europe

By ALBION ROSS
Foreign Editor The Chronicle

Fuehrer Adolf Hitler has decided to see what he can get without war.

Today, in Munich, Herr Hitler, Signor Mussolini, Monsieur Daladier and Mr. Chamberlain will sit around a table to decide means and ways of giving the Sudeten portion of Czechoslovakia to Germany without Hitler being forced to take it by invasion.

Rome dispatches also suggest that a broader European peace settlement will be discussed.

Mussolini, who is cast in the role of mediator, is rumored to have ordered his volunteers home from Spain as a first step.

Not clear is whether aroused Czechoslovakia under its military headed Cabinet will yield even if the four powers do reach an agreement. If not, it will be left to face Herr Hitler alone.

Continued French mobilization indicated that Paris is still somewhat uncertain that Hitler's proposals will prove acceptable.

Here are the developments yesterday of one of the most dramatic days this generation is likely to experience:

1—Great Britain and President Roosevelt appealed almost simultaneously to Mussolini to intervene.

2—The Duce got on the phone to Hitler. The result of the conversation: Hitler telegraphed to Neville Chamberlain, Daladier and Mussolini himself to attend a conference at Munich today. All three immediately accepted.

3—The note was delivered to Chamberlain in the House of Commons during an address that seemed to be leading up to a request to Parliament to declare Britain would go to war if Czechoslovakia were attacked. Chamberlain revealed that Hitler had refused to wait.

The announcement by the Prime Minister of Hitler's invitation brought a tremendous demonstration of joy in the House which soon spread to the throngs outside the Houses of Parliament. The same enthusiastic relief found expression in Paris streets.

4—Britain and France will propose an international army to occupy disputed Czechoslovak territory, Paris dispatches say. "Token occupation" of limited Czechoslovak border territory by German troops will be suggested. Plebiscites under international auspices, as in the Saar, would decide the fate of at least part of the Sudeten region.

5—Mussolini left for Munich by train. Mussolini and Hitler may demand the resignation of President Eduard Benes of Czechoslovakia an article by Mussolini's mouthpiece, Virginio Gayda reveals. Mussolini ordered and then suspended mobilization.

6—Belligerent little Joseph Goebbels, Hitler's Propaganda Minister, delivers a very pacific speech in Berlin saying that a "settlement is imminent." Confines his belligerency to insulting remarks about Benes. German public relieved and hopeful.

7—Washington reveals that President Roosevelt had also appealed to Hitler's other ally, Japan, to intervene for peace. A Berlin government spokesman refers contemptuously to Roosevelt's second peace message to Hitler saying that it would probably not be answered or the exchange would never cease.

Dispatches do not make it clear whether Hitler has been bluffing till the last moment or whether Mussolini's appeal really changed his mind.

The fact reported from Rome that Mussolini had shown no signs of mobilizing and that even airplane factories were only working an eight-hour day suggests two possibilities:

First, Hitler never meant to go

Continued on Page 2, Col 4
See No. Three

A New Plan
3 Nations May Police The Sudetens

(Copyright, 1938, by United Press)

PARIS, Thursday, Sept. 29—An "international army" of Italian, British and French troops to occupy Czechoslovakia's Sudeten areas pending their actual surrender to Germany will be proposed to Fuehrer Adolf Hitler at today's four-power meeting in Munich, it was reliably understood.

Premier Edouard Daladier took off from Le Bourget airdrome at 8:45 a. m. (11:45 p. m. P. S. T.) today for the Munich conference.

Paris, London and Rome were said to be virtually in agreement already on the proposal for an international "police force." Although Hitler wants to occupy the Sudeten areas with his troops immediately, the powers believe the plan offers a promising basis for a compromise agreement.

"POLICE" WOULD MOVE IN

The Italian, British and French troops would occupy the predominantly German areas, which are marked in red on Hitler's map of demanded territory, while the Czechs methodically evacuate their troops, civilians, defense materials and factories.

President Eduard Benes of Czechoslovakia was said to have given Daladier of France virtual blanket authority to defend Prague's rights at Munich today.

Early Czech demands for the right to send a spokesman into the conference were understood to have been ruled out on the grounds that appearance of a Czech representative might banish all hopes of bringing Hitler around to a bartering frame of mind.

Praise for developing the Munich meeting was divided among Prime Minister Neville Chamberlain of Great Britain, President Roosevelt and Premier Mussolini.

PHONE CALL THE CLINCHER

Mussolini's last-minute telephone call to Berlin, asking Hitler to hold his armies in leash for at least 24 hours, was believed to have clinched der Fuehrer's decision to call the leaders of the four big powers into conference.

Chamberlain and Daladier, it was said, will take advantage of the meeting to try to lay the groundwork for some sort of general plan of appeasement.

Among these matters are the war in Spain, an air armaments limitation pact involving pledges against the aerial bombardment of civilian populations and the far-reaching and troublesome problems of economic differences.

High French officials said early today that they were confident Prague would accept any definite solution agreed to by the conferees.

FRENCH HALT MOBILIZATION

France had called up her eighth category of army reservists, bringing 2,000,000 troops under arms just before the four-power agreement halted the war preparations. The order was later rescinded.

The United States Embassy in Paris said no American observers would be present at Munich.

Premier Daladier last night in a radio broadcast thanked the French people for their "attitude replete with courage and dignity."

The premier, also war minister, had intended to deliver a strongly-worded speech to the world warning that France is ready to fight, with Britain at her side, if Hitler invades Czechoslovakia.

Then, when word came of Hitler's invitation, he tore up his speech and made only a brief statement saying that "on the eve of such an important negotiation it is my duty to postpone the explanations which it was my intention to give you."

Crisis Coverage

The text of Chamberlain's address before Parliament is on Page A together with an analysis of America's possible role in future international relations. On Page B, a graphic map showing what Czechoslovakia stands to lose at the Munich conference. Also on Page B, thumbnail biographies of the "four strong men"; an abstract of a "white paper" published by Great Britain revealing the correspondence between Hitler and Chamberlain at Godesberg; dateline stories out of Washington and Rome.

Hitler Defers War Plans After U. S., British Pleas

Mussolini Will Be Mediator At Parley by Request of Roosevelt and Chamberlain

Copyright, 1938, by United Press

LONDON, Sept. 28 (U.P.)—Adolf Hitler suddenly opened the door to peace today, at almost the exact hour he had set to send his armies smashing into Czechoslovakia, by acceding to requests that Europe's "big four" meet in Munich tomorrow for a showdown between the dictators and the democracies.

At the last moment the German Chancellor—who had been bluntly told that the British and

Text of Chamberlain's Address on Page A

French war machines were being mobilized to fight him—stepped down from the boldest and most defiant undertaking of armed force in modern history.

He gave Europe new hope of peace, at a moment when every nation was resigned to the inevitability of war, by agreeing to delay, at least 24 hours the march of his troops who were to have plunged across the Czech frontier at 2 p. m. (5 a. m. P. S. T.) today.

A Hunt for "the Way Out"

At Munich, where naziism was born in bloodshed 15 years ago, Hitler will sit down with Prime Minister Neville Chamberlain of Great Britain, Premier Benito Mussolini of Italy and Premier Edouard Daladier of France to seek a way out of the headlong plunge toward war.

The announcement of Hitler's abandonment of war plans today was made by Prime Minister Chamberlain in the House of Commons under conditions more sensational than anything that has occurred in the "Mother of Parliaments" in its six and a half centuries of existence.

On the Verge of War—Peace!

Chamberlain was speaking and preparing the nation for war when a messenger stumbled in, bearing word of Hitler's new offer.

His hand shaking, the 69-year-old Prime Minister read the message that held out an unexpected hope of peace—and then burst into tears.

Although he played no direct role in the 11th-hour development that pulled Europe back from the brink of war, President Roosevelt's name stood out tonight in connection with events leading up to it.

Mr. Roosevelt has sent two appeals to Hitler within a space of 24 hours, pleading for peace and suggesting an immediate conference of the interested powers. He sent another personal appeal to Mussolini just after Britain also had sought Il Duce's aid in finding a way out.

Mussolini immediately communicated with his brother-in-arms in Berlin, and to London flashed Hitler's decision to

Continued on Page B, Col 1. See No. One

Chamberlain Flies; 'Try, Try Again'

HESTON AIRDROME, London, Thursday, Sept. 29 (U.P.)—Prime Minister Neville Chamberlain and his party, bound for the momentous conference with heads of the German, French and Italian governments in Munich, left by airplane at 8:35 a. m. (11:35 p. m. P. S. T.) today.

Before entering the plane, the Prime Minister, who hopes to bring about a peaceful settlement of the German-Czech quarrel and save Europe from a general war, said:

"When I was a little boy I used to repeat, 'If at first you don't succeed, try, try, try again.' That is what I am doing. When I come back I hope I may be able to say, as Hotspur says in 'Henry IV,' 'Out of this nettle of danger plucked this flower safely'."

Inside You'll Find...

3 **Crime:** An ex-policeman kills brother's wife.
4 **Nation:** Witness says industrialists back Bund.
5 **New Bishop:** Dr. Block's consecration today.
6 **The Films:** Corrigan miffs glamour girls.
7 **Politics:** Party clashes may bare Olson financing.
8 **The Woman:** The stars predict decline of dictatorships.
The Social Day: Mrs. Conger Pratt welcomed here.
10 **Labor:** More warehouses shut down.
11 **Metropolis:** Herb Caen's column, and why people marry!
12 **Editorial:** Chester Rowell and David Lawrence comment.
13 **Passing Show:** An engineer analyzes Russia.
14 **Contract Contacts:** Oakland scores again.
15 **Financial:** Stocks rise as war fears abate.
22 **Comics:** Tears soften Bungle's case.
23 **Radio:** Daily log and short wave.
Shipping: European sea traffic demoralized.
26 **Exposition:** Season pass deadline near.
The Boss: He has a new polo coat.
Sporting Green: Cubs take National League lead.

THIS WORLD TODAY

San Francisco Chronicle

THE CITY'S ONLY HOME-OWNED NEWSPAPER

FOUNDED 1865—VOL. CLV, NO. 40 CCCC** SAN FRANCISCO, THURSDAY, AUGUST 24, 1939 DAILY 5 CENTS, SUNDAY 10 CENTS: DAILY AND SUNDAY PER MONTH, $1.30

COMPARATIVE TEMPERATURES

	High	Low		High	Low
San Francisco	63	56	Denver	92	60
San Jose	73	58	Salt Lake	94	67
Los Angeles	83	65	New York	88	70
Seattle	82	52	Chicago	79	58
Honolulu	84	74	New Orleans	88	74

See Below for Local Forecast

Complete Report on Page 23

Nazis, Soviet Sign Pact; Hitler Tells Britain It's 'Too Late' For Peace; All Europe Arms!

This World Today

By ROYCE BRIER

MOST STREET FIGHTS start when neither man will back down. Very few men care to go about with missing teeth, black eyes or even fractured skulls, but a great many men would rather bear the risk of such injuries than suffer their pride to be humbled.

So the old sequence of "one word leads to another," so conspicuous in all human relations, is, in the average street fight, sublimated until it becomes fury, when the resort to force is inevitable.

It may be that in this column the parallel between individual and national psyches has been too rigorously urged. But it is difficult to escape it in our consideration of Europe. In the individual field it is common observation. In the greater field we are handicapped by an infinite complexity of cultural and psychological forces which no man understands thoroughly.

But for all this complexity, the result in 1914, and the threatened result in 1939, appear to depend fairly upon processes which are quite familiar to us in everyday life. If this should be true, it may be that recognition of it will aid our understanding of the tragedy which looms darkly across our mother soil.

If you will go back to 1936, when Herr Hitler marched into the Rhineland, you will perceive this as the beginning of Teutonic action to recover from the humiliation of 1919. It was not, however, the beginning of the thought. That began as soon as the shock of defeat had worn off.

But Herr Hitler personified the recovery, and that largely accounts for his success with his people. It makes no difference that he imposed upon them a rigid and dehumanized despotism. Pride was the touchstone, not freedom.

Now, Herr Hitler by peculiar but not unprecedented gifts made a religious cult of German pride, and each coup he could flash before his people was accompanied by a pride having more and more the inner structure of religious frenzy, a mania which has deep-seated human causes, which can afflict whole peoples as well as groups and individuals. Indeed, this mania is present in all peoples actually at war. We have ourselves been afflicted with it, and laughed wryly at it later.

But there is in the British

Continued on Page 2, Col. 1

Waterfront Employers Renew Offer To Bargain

Following the refusal of the International Longshoremen and Warehousemen's Union to submit their proposed contract amendments to arbitration, the Waterfront Employers' Association yesterday offered to bargain collectively with the union at any time on amendments proposed by both groups.

In a letter to the union, F. P. Foisie, association head, cited three offers employers had made since negotiations for a new coastwise agreement were launched several weeks ago. The present contract expires September 30.

Foisie likewise urged the union to reconsider its stand regarding arbitration, which he described as highly preferable to any economic action which would result in a loss of wages to workers and a loss of business to shippers.

BRIDGES' COUNTER PLAN

Harry Bridges, ILWU district president, on Tuesday, rejected the proposed arbitration, and countered with a proposal that a new effort be made to reach an agreement by using as a basis for discussion only those amendments and clarifications already submitted by the union.

It is the employers' stand, however, that amendments offered by both groups must be considered in any collective bargaining action, otherwise the term of collective bargaining could not justifiably be applied.

Foisie's letter to the union of yesterday follows:

"Gentlemen — We acknowledge receipt of your letter of August 22 in which you reject our offer to submit all questions between us to arbitration by Dean Wayne L. Morse.

"You suggest that an effort be made to negotiate such differences based upon your proposed amendments only. That is not collective bargaining.

READY TO BARGAIN

"Collective bargaining consists of the consideration of proposals submitted by both parties and an effort to justify them by facts, figures and reasons. We are ready to collectively bargain with you at any time.

"We are impressed by the statement contained in your letter:

"'We have learned from past experience that no arguments, facts or reasons we can present to your association serve to convince the association without some other agency being utilized, such as arbitration or only after economic action of some form.'

"If you are convinced that such is the case, we urge upon you the acceptance of our offer of arbitration. Arbitration is highly preferable to economic action which means strikes, loss of wages and loss of business.

"We have offered:

"To renew the existing contract.

"To collectively bargain with respect to all differences between us.

"To promptly submit all such dif-

Continued on Page 12, Col. 3

64 Perish As Ship Sinks

BAHIA, Brazil, Aug. 23 (UP)—The National Telegraph Agency said today that 64 persons—46 passengers and 18 members of the crew—perished when the coastal steamer Itacare capsized in heavy seas and sank at the entrance to Ilheos harbor, south of Bahia.

LONDON: Der Fuehrer's Polish Stand Stuns British

LONDON, Aug. 24 (Thursday) (AP)—Already moving to place herself on a wartime footing, Great Britain viewed gloomily but grimly the German-Soviet Russian nonaggression pact signed early today in Moscow.

Diplomatic quarters said the pact was a blow to remaining British hopes that the crisis precipitated by Germany's demands on Poland might be solved peacefully by a firm British-French stand.

In particular, it was said, article two, apparently preventing either of the signatories from supporting in any way a third power engaged in war with the other was regarded as carrying unhappy implications for British-French determination to aid Poland if she goes to war over Germany's demands.

There had been some hope that the British-French front might procure a "benevolent neutrality" from Russia with access to supplies and possibly leeway for troop movements from the black sea. The Rus-

sian-German pact, however, it was said, seemed to remove this possibility.

The German Fuehrer's reported statement that Poland must either yield to his demands or be partitioned also came as a staggering blow to British hopes for a peaceful settlement.

The British government was said to have considered the message delivered to Hitler today by Sir Neville Henderson, British Ambassador to Berlin, as its ace card.

It had been hoped a clear statement that Britain would fight by Poland's side might cause Hitler to give serious thought before risking war.

Official circles received reports of the Hitler-Sir Neville talk in silence, but diplomats took the gravest possible view.

Parliament will meet in special session today to vote the government virtually dictatorial powers to deal with any emergency.

All officers and key men in antiaircraft batteries of the territorial army were called up, along with an undetermined number of reservists in the army, navy and air force.

The Home Office ordered air raid precaution forces to be ready, beginning last night for a nationwide blackout at a moment's notice. All telephones were ordered manned day and night to notify

Continued on Page 2, Col. 8

Poland Begins To Mobilize Her Reserve Troops

WARSAW, Aug. 24 (AP)—Poland **prepared today for any emergency by calling to the colors a large number of reserves, it was reliably reported.**

Additional defensive preparations were understood to be under way, including the possibility that still more men would be mobilized.

Delays in normal train schedules indicated either troop or reservist movements had taken available engines and rolling stock.

Important decisions also were reported in well informed circles to have been taken in a series of conferences of government leaders throughout yesterday and into the late hours of the night.

European Situation At a Glance

Yesterday in the international drama:

Europe, with 10,000,000 men under arms and laboring under the worst, and most protracted suspense since Munich, looked for a showdown with Germany within a few days, perhaps even as early as tomorrow, while:

1—Germany and Russia sign nonaggression pact at Moscow in presence of Josef Stalin.

2—Hitler raises demands against Poland. He now demands, in addition to Danzig, entire Corridor and all other territory acquired by Poland from both Germany and Austria after the World war. For the rest of Poland he plans a German protectorate, similar to the arrangement in what was Czecho-Slovakia.

British Ambassador to Germany tells Fuehrer that Chamberlain will stand by Poland, but is at the same time urging a peaceful solution on Warsaw, but Hitler is reported to have replied the assurances came too late.

3—Britain, dealt a staggering blow by announcement of Russian pact and "failure of urgent warnings to Hitler," is fast going on war footing. Reservists called up, air raid precautions perfected, Mediterranean fleet reinforced, ship sailings to German ports cancelled, King George rushes back to London from vacation, defense council meets. With the rest of the world, entire nation waits to hear from Chamberlain in Parliament today.

4—France orders partial mobilization of its huge army. Call for troops plastered on walls of public buildings throughout the nation.

5—Italy's Foreign Minister reported to have told Britain Rome's army will back Hitler if war comes. Garrison on French front held in readiness.

6—President Roosevelt is rushing back to Washington from vacation because of critical international situation. Hull confers at State Department. State and Treasury departments studying procedure to save business from upset in case of war. Warning from the United States starts general exodus of Americans from Europe.

7—War risk insurance on cargoes to Germany and Italy raised 20 times in New York. London firms also increase rates.

8—Spain's Franco reported to have denounced anticomintern pact as result of Hitler (Germany) signing non-aggression pact with Russia. Japanese paper declares treaty reduces anti-comintern treaty to "scrap of paper."

Japanese Land 6000 in Shanghai

SHANGHAI, Aug. 24 (AP)—Reliable foreign sources reported today that the Japanese army had landed 6000 troops in the Shanghai area preparatory to "some action against the International Settlement."

The Japanese were said to have been planning to occupy the Settlement, but to have postponed the action because of the Soviet Russian-German non-aggression pact negotiations, which left them uncertain of their position in the world lineup. (American, British, French and Italian troops totaling nearly 5000 are stationed in the Settlement.)

BERLIN: Germany Now Demands All Territory Lost to Warsaw, Protectorate Over Rest

By LOUIS P. LOCHNER

BERLIN, Aug. 23 (AP)—**Adolf Hitler appeared tonight once again to hold Europe's fate in his hands, adhering firmly to his demands upon Poland, which a reliable informant said now included acceptance by the Poles of a protectorate government.**

The demands, according to trustworthy information, were dispatched yesterday to most European capitals, as follows:

1—Unconditional return of Danzig.

2—Cession of those sections of Poland which were German before the World war (Posen-Poznan—Pomorze, or the so-called Polish corridor, and Polish Upper Silesia).

3—Acceptance of a protectorate for the area remaining, similar to that of Bohemia and Moravia, parts of former Czecho-Slovakia.

The British Ambassador, Sir Neville Henderson, was said to have restated Britain's pledge to aid Poland as an answer to these demands in a call at Hitler's Berchtesgarden home today. Sir Nevile landed at Tempelhof airport tonight and went at once to the Embassy.

The expose to other governments is said to have contained Hitler's two alternatives for a Polish settlement:

Either Poland accepts these terms and permits Germany peacefully to occupy the sections claimed, or Poland fights, with the result that Germany will see to it that her eastern adversary is partitioned once again as has been her fate in the past.

According to one version Sir Neville assured Hitler that Prime Minister Chamberlain was continuing his efforts on behalf of peace.

"Too late" was in effect the German dictator's reply, it was ascertained reliably.

Hitler, according to the official German news bureau, DNB, "left no doubt in the mind of the British Ambassador that the obligations assumed by the British government could not induce Germany to renounce her championship of national interests vital to the life of the Reich."

THREE QUESTIONS

Three questions were on everyone's lips as they met today on the streets, in restaurants or in society:

1—Will the Fuehrer strike on Friday, as it has generally been assumed by Germans in all walks of life as well as those in the foreign colonies of Berlin?

2—Might he even decide to press the button for a showdown with Poland tonight, in the hope of completing his coup before the British

Continued on Page 5, Col. 1

MOSCOW: Ten-Year Treaty Blasts Allies' Hopes of Signing Russia; Balance Shifts

MOSCOW, Aug. 24 (Thursday (AP)—**Nazi Germany and Communist Russia signed a 10-year nonaggression pact in the presence of Joseph Stalin here early today and remade the military and diplomatic picture of Europe.**

What hopes Britain and France may have held to align the Soviet in their bloc apparently were completely smashed.

In two meetings, both of which Stalin attended, the historic agreement was reached behind the huge walls of the Kremlin, with V. Molotoff, Soviet Premier and Commissar for Foreign Affairs, and Joachim von Ribbentrop, Nazi Foreign Minister, who flew here only yesterday in Chancellor Adolf Hitler's private airplane, as the principal negotiators.

Von Ribbentrop was expected to take off at 1 p. m. today (3 a. m. E. S. T.) to make a personal report to Chancellor Hitler, completing one of the speediest diplomatic flights in world history.

Russians, who learned only last night through a broadcast that Von Ribbentrop had arrived at 1 p. m. yesterday, read

For map, stories and pictures of Europe today, see pages 2, 3, 4, 5.

a Tass communique in Thursday morning papers that their country was now pledged not to fight the nation they had been taught to hate.

The amazing Nazi diplomatic stroke effected a tremendous shift in Europe's balance of power in one of her most critical times since the World war.

Diplomatic circles were convinced that article 4 of the agreement, which pledges either party not to associate itself with any group of powers "which directly or indirectly is aimed at the other party," served a death warrant on the military talks among Russia, Britain and France which had been in progress here since August 12.

(Russian official quarters, however, have insisted throughout that a defensive alliance with Britain and France was not incompatible with a nonaggression pact with Germany.)

Informed persons also considered article 3, providing for "consultation regarding questions of common interest" as especially significant in the light of the present conflict between Germany and Poland.

The nonaggression clauses bound each power to refrain

Continued on Page 2, Col. 6

The Treaty Text

By Associated Press

Following is the text of the German-Soviet nonaggression pact as announced in Berlin and Moscow by the two governments:

The German Reich's government and the Union of the Socialist Soviet Republics, moved by a desire to strengthen the state of peace between Germany and the U. S. S. R. and in the spirit of the provisions of the neutrality treaty of April, 1926, between Germany and the U. S. S. R., decided the following:

"ARTICLE ONE—The two contracting parties obligate themselves to refrain from every act of force, every aggressive action and every attack against one another, including any single action or that taken in conjunction with other powers.

"ARTICLE TWO—In case one of the parties of this treaty should become the object of warlike acts by a third power, the other party will in no way support this third power.

"ARTICLE THREE—The governments of the two contracting parties in the future will constantly remain in consultation with one another regarding questions of common interests.

"ARTICLE FOUR—Neither of the high contracting parties of this treaty will associate itself with any other grouping of powers which directly or indirectly is aimed at the other party.

"ARTICLE FIVE—In the event of a conflict between the contracting parties concerning any question, the two parties will adjust this difference or conflict exclusively by friendly exchange of opinions or, if necessary, by an arbitration commission.

"ARTICLE SIX—The present treaty will extend for a period of ten years, with the condition that if neither of the contracting parties announces its abrogation within one year of expiration of this period, it will continue in force automatically for another period of five years.

"ARTICLE SEVEN—The present treaty shall be ratified within the shortest possible time. The exchange of ratification documents shall take place in Berlin. The treaty becomes effective immediately upon signature.

"Drawn up in two languages, German and Russian.

"Moscow, 23d of August, 1939.

"(Signed)

"For the German government, Ribbentrop.

"In the name of the government of the U. S. S. R., Molotov."

German Army To March Today, Berlin Reports

By OTTO D. TOLISCHUS

Copyright, 1939, N. Y. Times Foreign Cable Service

BERLIN, Aug. 24 (Thursday)—Swift on the heels of the signing last midnight of the German-Russian non-aggression pact and Chancellor Hitler's rebuff of a British warning against precipitate action in Danzig, word spread throughout Berlin that the zero hour, which will set the German army on the march, will come today.

These rumors are supplemented with the additional details that the exact hour is 6 p. m., which might mean "contact with the enemy" some time tomorrow.

Furthermore, orders to postpone action, issued after Foreign Minister Joachim Von Ribbentrop's departure for Moscow, have been cancelled again. For, according to German expectations, Von Ribbentrop will be back in Berlin tonight.

The Embassies and Legations of all countries are preparing for the worst.

It is assumed that the American Embassy will be charged with representing British and French interests.

To Arms! 2,000,000 Mobilized by France

PARIS, Aug. 24 (Thursday) (AP)—Posters calling two French classes to arms were plastered on government buildings early today as France increased her empire forces to almost 2,000,000 men in a partial mobilization against a feared clash with Germany.

Announcement that a German-Soviet Russian nonaggression pact had been signed in Moscow caused deep pessimism in France.

Government sources had said prior to the Moscow announcement that signing of the pact would make it "almost impossible to avoid war over Germany's Danzig claims."

Requisitioned taxis early today in Paris carried "bucket brigades" to various government buildings where they pasted up the posters. Automobiles and trucks also were requisitioned.

The first to be posted were the requisition orders which read:

"The right of requisition is opened in the commune of Paris beginning Thursday the 24th of August, 1939, at zero hour."

Little knots of early morning home goers drearily read the posters. They winced, then made their way home darkly mindful of a pre-

Continued on Page 4, Col. 4

Roosevelt Will He 'Fire Another Shot For Peace?'

WASHINGTON, Aug. 23 (AP)—President Roosevelt hurried homeward from a suddenly curtailed vacation cruise today while Washington wondered if it was his intention—using his own phrase for it—to "fire another shot for peace" in Europe.

High officials of the State Department made arrangements to go into conference with the chief executive immediately upon his return—scheduled for midday tomorrow—and also to go over the situation at once with Secretary Hull. The State Department chief returned from his vacation today.

Meanwhile, State and Treasury department officers were meeting to discuss America's position in case war actually developed abroad. They were concerned with the grave questions of keeping domestic business on a steady keel, safeguarding the foreign value of the dollar, and the problem of removing thousands of American citizens from war-menaced regions.

Merchant ships will be relied upon to transport the majority of Americans from danger zones, officials explained, but they added that more than a score of naval vessels in the Atlantic squadron could help if necessary.

The President was aboard the

Continued on Page 3, Col. 6

Weather

The Weather Man felt very brisk as he stomped into the office, rummaged through the closet and came out with his golf bag. "Elmo," he said to the little Mexican jumping bean, "the time has come for you to take over. I am definitely through with predicting overcast weather."

Idly the W. M. ran a speculative eye over his mashie. "I will give you some friendly tips, Elmo. Showers are going to boom around the Sierra-Nevada region. There are light to moderate northwest winds off of the Pacific Coast. Multiply these by two and you'll get your forecast," he said, closing the door.

Indifferent Elmo hopped once, landed on a rubber stamp marked "**Cloudy Thursday, with morning fog.**" Then he went back to sleep.

Inside You'll Find . . .

CALIFORNIA (10)—Farmers seek "Grapes of Wrath" ban.
COMICS (16)—Superman is up to his usual tricks again.
CONVENTIONS (7)—Port officials of Coast open meet.
CRIME (11)—Boy, 14, confesses murder of 13-year-old.
DRAMA (6)—The perfect dodge—"Me no spikee English."
EDITORIAL (14)—Chester Rowell, David Lawrence comment.
EXPOSITION (10)—7,000,000th visitor at Fair.
FINANCE (17)—Traders pound the market down four points.
LABOR (7)—Laws will not solve troubles, says Woll.
PASSING SHOW (15)—The Capital Parade, Merry-Go-Round, Bookman, Labor Scene, New York Day by Day.
RADIO (23)—Here's what's on the air today.
SHIPPING (23)—Weather table, mail schedules.
SOCIAL DAY (8)—Box of candy tells story of romance.
SPORTING GREEN—Cobb speeds 368.85 m.p.h. to new record
THE WOMAN (9)—Dr. Alice Masaryk to speak here.

WAR EXTRA!

San Francisco Chronicle

THE CITY'S ONLY HOME-OWNED NEWSPAPER

FOUNDED 1865—VOL. CLV, NO. 48 CCCC*** SAN FRANCISCO, FRIDAY, SEPTEMBER 1, 1939 DAILY 5 CENTS, SUNDAY 10 CENTS: DAILY AND SUNDAY PER MONTH, $1.20

COMPARATIVE TEMPERATURES

	High	Low		High	Low
San Francisco	67	56	Denver	91	56
San Jose	76	53	Salt Lake	93	65
Los Angeles	89	65	New York	67	61
Seattle	69	56	Chicago	77	65
Honolulu	81	74	New Orleans	90	75

See Page 11 for Forecast
Complete Report on Page 27

Warsaw, 5 Cities Bombed! Hitler Says It's Finish Fight; Poles Call Nazis Aggressors; Allies Rush War Mobilization; Danzig Returns to the Reich!

By ROYCE BRIER

ROME, heir of Greece and all the ancients, struggled with the barbarians and won. Rome decayed and struggled with the barbarians again, and lost. The Church which followed after twilight, struggled with the semi-barbaric princes, and seemed to win, but did not destroy them. Charlemagne struggled with the Church and the petty princes, partly won.

France became great. But soon Spain became great, and the two struggled for dominance. The Church went on, still a great power. It struggled with Islam on Islam's ground, lost. The Moors came, really Islam striving with Christianity on Christianity's ground, and Islam lost. The Mongolians came, and were thrust back. Twice Europe had warded off engulfing cultures.

Then England became great, contesting with Spain and France in Europe, and for possession of the New World. Spain slowly declined, but France became greater, and the Holy Roman Empire, which was really South Germany, emerged, spread to Spain and Italy. But England and France were dominant now. Russia emerged from barbarism to join the eternal strife. North Germany appears for the first time. Austria declined. So it was England and France dominant, Prussia doubtful, Spain and Austria failing, Russia untried—struggling for Europa. Sometimes against the Turks, who were ever threatening from the southeast. Then France was shaken, the whole monarchal and social system, post-feudal, was shaken, but it emerged in more predatory form, and all combined against it and finally wrecked it. That was Napoleon.

Spain and Austria were out, North Germany and Russia were static, and England, spreading across the earth, was dominant. France became an adjunct of England as Germany congealed, and Austria long fought becoming an adjunct of congealing Germany. Then Germany struck France, and rivaled England.

The Anglo-German struggle was sly, but paramount in Europe, and eventuated in 1914. The German power overreached, and again England, with France as an adjunct, was dominant again. Save that a new great power from overseas had intervened, save that Japan was stirring to dominate Asia, save that

Continued on Page 2, Col. 1

LONDON AND PARIS

Britain, France on Full War Footing as Evacuation Starts

3,000,000 Will Be Moved Out of English Centers

LONDON, Sept. 1 (AP) It was officially reiterated today that Britain and France were determined to fulfill their obligations to Poland despite Adolf Hitler's Reichstag speech.

King George summoned the Privy Council to a meeting today and Parliament was called to meet this afternoon as German offensive against Poland became known here.

The Cabinet met at 11:30 a. m. and the Privy Council was to meet at noon (7 a. m., E. S. T.)

The Mass Evacuation of London Starts! For a story of the exodus, a map of the areas to be evacuated and a Wirephoto of London children being prepared for the flight, turn to Page 6.

The text of Hitler's 16 points—his final demands on Poland—will be found on Page 4.

Parliament was called to meet at 5 p. m. (9 a. m. P. S. T.)

A Reuters Dispatch from Warsaw said that towns in the Polish Corridor being attacked were Dzialdowo and Chojnice, and that the fighting in Upper Silesia was in the region of Czestochowa.

Great Britain, meanwhile, standing pat on her pledge to fight for Poland's independence, received the news of Germany's latest moves in the European crisis with the deepest gravity today as the nation moved swiftly toward a full war footing.

(Poland's charge of Nazi aggression (See Warsaw column 4), making British aid imperative, came just a week to the day after the

Continued on Page 6, Col. 1

Daladier Talks With Gamelin, Chief of Armies

PARIS, Sept. 1 (AP)—The French Cabinet, meeting with President Lebrun on an urgent summons this morning after outbreak of German-Polish hostilities, decreed general mobilization and a state of siege today and called Parliament for tomorrow.

It was stated through the Havas Agency that the German action would necessitate "new military measures" by France and Britain.

According to Havas reports, German troops began their offensive in two directions:

On the frontier of Eastern Prussia the attack was toward Mlawa, Dzialdowo and Chojnice;

In Southern Poland toward the Silesian frontier mining region.

The port of Gdynia also was bombarded this morning by German aviation, Havas said.

Upon receipt of word of the German operations, Premier Daladier rushed to the War Ministry and called Generalissimo Maurice Gustave Gamelin, supreme commander of land, sea and air forces, into consultation.

A little later Daladier summoned Foreign Minister Georges Bonnet.

The Polish Embassy said Germans had violated the Polish frontier at four points and at the same time it characterized German charges that Poles had crossed into Germany as "pure invention."

Havas, French News Agency, announced that "a German declaration of war against Poland probably will lead France and Great Britain to take new military measures."

Britain and France are committed to aid Poland in any

Continued on Page 5, Col. 3

WARSAW

Hostilities Started at Many Points

WARSAW, Sept. 1 (A.P.)—The Foreign Office said today that German planes had bombed Krakow, Katowice, Czestochowa, Tczew and Grudziadz early this morning.

Diplomatic dispatches received in Budapest, from Warsaw, said the outskirts of the Polish capital also had been bombed. There were no figures on casualties.

According to the United Press, the Foreign Office immediately charged Germany with aggression, announcing:

("Shortly after 7 a. m. Germans started military action at different points on the frontier. This undoubtedly is German aggression against Poland. Military action is now developing.")

The Budapest dispatches were supported by similar dispatches of Reuters, British news agency, and Havas, French news agency.

The Havas dispatches said air raid alarms were sounded in Warsaw three times before the German planes finally dropped bombs on the city at 9:30 a. m. Sounds of the raiding planes and anti-aircraft artillery were heard.

MANY DEAD, WOUNDED

Many were killed and injured when the Polish frontier town of Tczew, not far from the Danzig border, was bombed, Exchange Telegraph reported. This agency said the railroad station and other buildings were destroyed, and the bombing continued for at least an hour.

One air raid also was reported by Exchange Telegraph to have been carried out against a railway station and tunnel on the Krakow-Warsaw railway.

It was reported officially that German troops had attacked Polish defenses near Mlawa, bordering the southern part of East Prussia.

There was no announcement of the damage resulting from the bombing.

The Foreign Office also confirmed that fighting had started in Danzig.

(In Paris Havas News Agency said six Polish cities had been bombed

Continued on Page 8, Col. 5

BERLIN

First Casualties Roll Into Berlin After Artillery Fire Heard on Pole Border; Gdynia Port Blockaded

Der Fuehrer Warns Reich's Neighboring States Not to Interfere--'We'll Know What to Do!'

In a speech full of emotion, Adolf Hitler early today told the German Reichstag he would continue his war against Poland until Warsaw was ready to discuss with him the Danzig question, guarantee the rights of Germans and adjust the frontier of Germany.

He assured his cheering deputies, hurriedly called into session that he had pledges of neutrality from neighboring states—and that if any of them violated their pledges, Nazi Germany would know how to deal with them.

The Fuehrer placed the blame for the outbreak of hostilities on Poland. Polish troops fired on Germans, he declared and the Germans replied in kind. But though he explained he had instructed his air force to exercise all the care humanly possible, he said his troops would not be called off until he won satisfaction for "Germany long a sufferer at the hands of Poland."

The Fuehrer called on all German men and women to fulfill their duty in this, their crucial hour. But he added he had donned his own army uniform, that he was not asking others to do what he would not do himself. And, he added, should something happen to him—death or disability—that then his sceptre of power would go to Field Marshal Hermann Goering. Next in line he mentioned Rudolph Hess.

His explanation of the events preceding the last few days of the crisis was pretty much a repetition of his old complaint.

"We have all been suffering under the torture which the

Continued on Page 8, Col. 2

Foreigners Warned, Nazis Clear Neutral Shipping From Baltic; All German Schools Are Closed

BERLIN, Sept. 1 (AP)—Adolf Hitler took Danzig into Germany today and ordered his mighty army to "meet force with force" as a result of Polish "violations" of the German border.

Artillery fire was heard at Sleiwitz, Germany, near the Polish-Silesian frontier, and at 9:10 a. m. soldiers on stretchers arrived at the emergency hospital here. It could not be ascertained where the ambulance came from.

A short time after the army order was issued Albert Foerster, Nazi chief of state in Danzig, proclaimed the reunion of the Free City with Germany and notified Hitler of his action. Hitler accepted the Free City into the Reich.

His army was massed on Polish frontiers, but it was not known immediately whether it had orders to advance. Other developments:

A naval blockade of the Polish harbor of Gdynia was announced.

German warships started clearing neutral shipping from the Baltic.

Poland was declared dangerous territory for foreigners.

A warning was issued that neutral ships in the Baltic would enter Danzig or nearby harbors at their own peril.

(In Poland it was reported that five cities had been bombed by German planes.)

All schools in Germany were closed indefinitely.

East Germany was warned of possible attacks by Polish planes.

All but military flights across Germany were banned.

There was no suggestion yet, either officially or unofficially, of a declaration of war.

The order banning all but German military flights across Germany declared offending planes would be shot down.

Foerster notified Adolf Hitler, Fuehrer of Germany, of his anschluss decree by telegram.

Article one of the decree suspended the constitution of the Free City immediately.

(Under the city's League of Nations status its constitution was guaranteed by the league, and changes without its consent were declared illegal.)

Article 2 of the decree placed all legal and administrative power exclusively in the hands of the Chief of State, Foerster.

Foerster's telegram to Hitler read:

"My Fuehrer. I have just signed and then put into effect the following basic law, concerning the reunion of Danzig with the German Riech.

"The basic state law of the Free City of Danzig and the reunion of Danzig with the German Reich is effective September 2, 1939.

"To lift the immediate distress of the people and state of the

Continued on Page 8, Col. 6

Hitler's Proclamation To the German Troops

By United Press

Following is the text of Chancellor Adolf Hitler's proclamation to the German army early today:

"The Polish state rejected the peaceful regulation of neighborly relations which I sought. Instead, it called to arms.

"The Germans in Poland have been harried with bloody terror and driven from their homes and farms.

"The number of frontier violations, which are intolerable to a great power, show that Poland no longer has the will to respect the German Reich's frontiers.

"In order to put an end to this mad activity I have no other choice than to answer force with force from now on.

"The German armed forces will conduct battle for honor and the vital rights of the re-arisen German people with hard determination.

"I expect that every soldier will do his duty to the last in the spirit of the great tradition of the eternal German soldier.

"Be aware that in every situation that you are the representatives of the Nationalist Socialist Greater Germany.

"Long life our people and the Reich.

Berlin, September 1, 1939. "ADOLF HITLER."

FINAL MORNING EXTRA!

San Francisco Chronicle

THE CITY'S ONLY HOME-OWNED NEWSPAPER

FOUNDED 1865—VOL. CLV, NO. 50 CCCC**** SAN FRANCISCO, SUNDAY, SEPTEMBER 3, 1939 DAILY 5 CENTS, SUNDAY 10 CENTS: DAILY AND SUNDAY PER MONTH, $1.30

COMPARATIVE TEMPERATURES

	High	Low		High	Low
San Francisco	74	55	Denver	93	64
San Jose	83	48	Salt Lake	78	57
Los Angeles	80	61	New York	80	64
Seattle	62	54	Chicago	87	69
Honolulu	81	73	New Orleans	91	75

See Below for Local Forecast

Complete Report on Page 6C

GREAT BRITAIN DECLARES WAR

The Nippon Round-World Flyers Land At Oakland, Feted in S. F.

Just a week to the day from its take-off from Tokyo, the Japanese good will monoplane "Nippon" circled Treasure Island at 1 o'clock yesterday afternoon, then descended in a graceful spiral to Oakland Municipal Airport.

It had made the 737-mile trip from Seattle in exactly four hours after abandoning a plan to fly north and circle Vancouver, B. C. as a gesture of cordiality. Customs arrangements had not been made, and besides, the Nippon was already two days behind schedule on its 34,000-mile round-the-world voyage, owing to inclement weather.

AVOID BANNED ZONES

The Japanese scrupulously avoided flying over Fort Baker and other prohibited zones where the United States Government's authority reaches into the stratosphere.

A crowd of men, women and children—Japanese and Americans intermingled—rushed forward as the twin-motored ship settled to the field, its silver fuselage and wings glinting in the sunlight.

It carried on its wings the great red dot representing the Rising Sun of Japan, and above its blunt nose fluttered a stand of three flags—the American, the Japanese and the figured ensign of the two Nipponese newspapers sponsoring the flight (Osak Mainichi and the Tokyo Nichi Nichi).

EIGHT STEP OUT

Back surged the crowd as the sleek plane taxied toward Hangar 4 and was trundled inside. Out stepped eight men. The tallest, Sumitoshi Nakao, 36 years old, was the flight commander. For a Japanese, 5 feet 8 inches is tall.

Five others, all young men, were subordinate officers and members of the crew. The seventh and shortest (5 feet 1) spoke English quite well and with an American accent — Takeo Ohara, chief of the aviation departments of the two papers and designated as the "people's envoy."

FLEW OVER STORMS

"California weather," he said, "is the only good weather we've had during the entire trip so far."

The 2500-mile overseas hop to Nome was uneventful—"We flew above the storms. The wings were frozen some. We ran a little short of oxygen."

He did not know whether the Nippon would visit European capitals as originally planned. "We will have some time to learn what conditions will be there." The good will

Continued on Page 6, Col. 5

BERLIN AND WARSAW

Victories In Corridor, Silesia Claimed By Nazis; Warsaw Bombing Terrors Described

The Pomorze Pinched Off, Say Berlin Leaders

By MELVIN WHITELEATHER
Associated Press Staff Writer

BERLIN, Sept. 2 (AP)—Nazi troops moving swiftly but as effectively as a steamroller—according to high command communiques—tonight continued their advance over the lowlands and lakes of Pomorze (the Polish corridor) and hilly regions of Silesia.

At the same time the British and French Ambassadors awaited the reply to their goverments' final "warnings" delivered to the Foreign Office last night. Authoritative German sources said they did not know when Adolf Hitler's replies would be made.

Polish Envoy Leaves Berlin

Meanwhile, diplomatic relations with Poland were broken off in fact when Polish Ambassador Jozef Lipski left Berlin early today.

The German Ambassador to Warsaw, Hans von Moltke, has been in Berlin some time.

The supreme high command announced the corridor was practically pinched off, trapping Polish soldiers remaining in its extreme northern tip.

German Troops Near Contact

Troops advancing from West Prussia were north of Kulm, only a few miles from their comrades driving west from East Prussia.

(The corridor lies between East and West Prussia, separating East Prussia from Germany proper).

It was stated the West Prussian corps had reached the Vistula river at that point, leaving but a small gap to close.

Grudziadz, where the Polish cavalry schools are located in an old fortification on heights overlooking the Vistula, apparently still was held by the Poles.

The high command's communique stated naval aviators had bombed Gdynia, Poland's Baltic port, and the strong Polish fortifications on the peninsula of Hela in Danzig harbor.

It claimed Germany was in abso-

Continued on Page 3, Col. 1

Soviet War Mission In Berlin

BERLIN, Sept. 2 (AP)—Alexander Schkvartseff, new Soviet Ambassador to Germany, and seven members of a Soviet military mission landed at Templehof airdrome at 5:34 p. m. today.

A large crowd of officials gathered to meet the visitors and a brass band lined the runway. Baron von Doernberg, chief of protocol for the Foreign Office, greeted the new Ambassador as he stepped from the plane.

A number of army generals shook hands with their Soviet colleagues, all of whom were dressed in mufti and wearing soft hats.

The cordiality of a reawakened German-Russian friendship was underscored at the reception formalities.

The new Ambassador reviewed an honor guard. Previously, the honor company's commander reported to the Ambassador, saluting with drawn sabre.

The party then departed for the Soviet Embassy via Unter Den Linden. The Soviet auto caravan, flying small hammer and sickle flags, was wildly "heiled" as it passed Wilhelmstrasse and the Chancellory, where a large crowd had been milling all day.

Schkvarzeff will be received by Hitler tomorrow for presentation of his credentials. The Ambassador will be accompanied by the head of the Russian military commission, General Maxim Purkajev.

Poles Say Troops Have Entered Germany

WARSAW, Sept. 3—(Sunday)—(UP)—A semi-official source said today that counter-attacking Polish troops had entered Germany. The claim was made soon after an official communique charged that Germany had bombed "not less" than 24 Polish cities Saturday, killing and wounding 1500 persons, most of them civilians.

By LLOYD LEHRBAS
Associated Press Staff Writer

WARSAW, Sept. 2 (AP)—Twenty-one dead and over 30 wounded were counted tonight after German bombs had struck an apartment house in a Warsaw workingmen's quarter.

The bombs tore off the side of the apartment house as if it had been made of paper. Rescue workers still were clearing away the resultant pile of debris in a search for further casualties when I inspected it.

One of the bombs had dug a crater fully 20 feet in diameter, and the open ground was piled high with furniture and belongings.

DWELLING SHATTERED

In the center of a large park in the southern section of Warsaw, I saw where a bomb had struck a simple wooden dwelling, killing two persons and wounding one. In an open field near the Vistula river, where 10 light bombs apparently had been released simultaneously, they had dug craters in a 100-yard circle.

With me on this tour of inspection of damage done by the German

Continued on Page 4, Col. 1

Bendix Air Race

Frank Fuller First, Sets Record, Wins $12,500

CLEVELAND, Sept. 2 (AP)—Sportsman-Pilot Frank Fuller rode the crest of the Bendix transcontinetal air race to a smashing new record and $12,500 in cash prizes today.

Fuller gunned his powerful Seversky, a stripped-down military type plane, at an average speed of 282.098 miles an hour from Burbank, Calif., to Cleveland, for the opening of the National Air Races. A crowd of 15,000 greeted him.

The ruddy-faced San Francisco paint manufacturer negotiated the 2042 miles in seven hours, 14-19 minutes—40 minutes better than his record of 258 miles an hour, set in 1937.

Fuller then raced the extra 406 miles to Bendix, N. J., arriving with a coast-to-coast slapsed time of 8 hours, 58 minutes, 8:4 seconds, for another Bendix record, an average speed from Burbank of 273.14 miles an hour. His previous coast-to-coast mark was 9 hours, 35 minutes.

Miss Jacqueline Cochran, who won the 1938 Bendix with an average speed of 249.774 miles an hour, failed to start today's race. She said she feared to take off in foggy conditions with her plane so heavily loaded with gasoline.

Arthur Bussey of Royersford, Pa., followed Fuller into Cleveland with an elapsed time of eight hours, 21 minutes and eight seconds, averaging 244.486 miles an hour. The position won him $5,000 in prize money. Paul Mantz of Hollywood won the third place $3,000 by reaching Cleveland in eight hours, 41 minutes and 38 seconds, averaging 234.875 miles an hour.

Max Constant, Hollywood pilot, flying one of Miss Cochran's planes, was fourth with an average of 231.366 miles an hour. The place brought him $2,000.

Mrs. Arlene Davis, titan-haired Cleveland aviatrix, the only woman besides Miss Cochran to enter, finished fifth with an average speed of 196.842 miles an hour.

Dale Myers of Tulsa, Okla., flew with Mrs. Davis but said "she handled the controls all the way."

Inside *You'll Find...*

AUTO WORLD (6)—New York is enthused over the new cars.
CITY HALL (10)—A church gets a break.
CROSSWORD (6C).
CONVENTIONS (9)—Sigma Delta Chi holds symposium.
CALIFORNIA (5)—Court ruling for placing oil referendum on
EXPOSITION (10)—Jack Benny may perform a violin feat.
FINANCE (7, 8)—Stocks stage strong rise.
LABOR (4)—CIO prepares for Labor day parade.
SHIPPING (6C)—Weather report and mail schedules.
SPORTING GREEN—U. S. Davis cup team leads, 2-0.
TRAVELOGUE (4)—Go down and see Buenos Aires.

SPECIAL SECTIONS:
COLORGRAVURE—Labor day number.
COMICS—Judy "lands" Uncle Walt.
PEOPLE—Rushing isn't what it used to be.
THIS WEEK—Newest Chronicle Feature.
THIS WORLD—Will Italy march with Hitler?
RADIO—Log and programs, This World, Page 23.

REACTION

The English Are 'Fed Up' With Hitler

By JOHN GUNTHER
Released by North American Newspaper Alliance

LONDON, Sept. 2 (by wireless)—The second world war has begun.

All Europe is bracing itself for the shock of an unexampled catastrophe. But the British are calm and confident. There is not the eslightest sign of panic here, not the slightest nervouaness.

The chief British emotion is what I can only describe as "fed-up-ness." They are sick and tired of Hitler and his appalling recklessness to say nothing of his bad faith.

A few days ago it became clear that the British people the common, ordinary people—were in no mood to endure another crisis like this one. It has dislocated all normal activity, and exasperated folk in every walk of life. I have heard dozens of comments to the effect that "even war is better than the incessant assault on the nervous system in these crisis months."

THEY LOATHE WAR

The British do not like war. They are a civilized people and they loathe the idea of making war. But they are convinced that the sort of thing Hitler has been doing must absolutely be stopped. "We cannot go on this way," I have heard everybody say.

If anything were finally necessary to stiffen the British and remove any last trace of the feeling that negotiations were still possible, it was the manner of Hitler's behavior just before he struck at Poland. The British like good form. Perhaps, it was foolish to expect nice manners from Hitler, but it really seems that the British were almost more bothered by the way in which Hitler provoked the final crisis than by the effect of his behavior.

Hitler strung out the negotiations with the British, giving some faint hope that there might be a peaceful settlement. Then on Tuesday he informed the British that the Polish plenipotentiaries must be in Berlin by midnight Wednesday prepared to sign an agreement to cut their own throats.

INFORMED BY LONDON

He never had direct contact with the Poles at all. British Ambassador Henderson in Berlin informed London of the ultimatum and the British then told the Poles.

From 8 a. m. Thursday until 8 p. m., Polish Ambassador Lipski in Berlin asked for an opportunity to see German Foreign Minister Ribbentrop. The Germans asked him if he wanted an interview in his capacity as Ambassador or a plenipo-

Continued on Page 4, Col. 1

President Roosevelt will speak to the Nation at 6 o'clock tonight "to allay public anxiety and relieve suspense" as a result of the European war conditions. The broadcast will be heard in this area over KPO, KGO, KSFO and KFRC.

BULLETIN

LONDON, Sept. 3—Prime Minister Chamberlain announced this morning that England is at war with Germany because of Hitler's refusal to agree to withdraw troops from Poland at the deadline set at 11 a. m. (2 a. m. P.S.T.).

"That this country is at war," he said in a voice choked with emotion, "you can imagine what a bitter blow it is to me after all I have done to bring about a peaceful settlement of the problem."

The Prime Minister said he did not think anything further could be done.

"Up to the last," he declared, "it might have been possible for Hitler to make a peaceful and honorable settlement with Poland."

He added: "Yet he (Hitler) would not accept it."

There is no chance to expect that this man will ever stop unless he is stopped by force and England and France in fulfillment of our obligations to Poland will take our places.

May God bless you all and may he defend the right. . . . I am certain right will prevail.

The British Broadcasting Corporation announced today that Britain had given Germany until 10 a. m., Greenwich Mean Time (2 a. m., PST), to answer satisfactorily Britain's final warning.

It broadcast a communique from 10 Downing street saying that Sir Nevile Henderson, British Ambassador in Berlin, had told the German government that if assurances were not received by then "a state of war" would exist between Great Britain and Germany.

The announcement said Sir Nevile Henderson informed the German government at 8 a. m. (12 M., PST)

The answer demanded by Britain was to Prime Minister Chamberlain's "final warning" of September 1 that Germany cease her aggression against Poland and call off her troops from Polish soil.

The following is the text of the communique:

"On September 2 his majesty's ambassador in Berlin was instructed to inform the German government that unless they were prepared to give his majesty's government in the United Kingdom satisfactory assurances that the German government had suspended all aggressive action against Poland and were prepared promptly to withdraw their forces from Polish territory, his majesty's government in the United Kingdom would without hesitation fulfill their obligations to Poland.

"At 9 a. m. this morning (12 m. PST) his majesty's ambassador in Berlin informed the German government that unless not later than 11 a. m. (2 a. m. PST). British summer time, today, September 3, satisfactory assurances to the above effect had been given by the German government and had reached his majesty's government in London a state of war would exist between the two countries as from that hour.

Chamberlain said Saturday in the House of Commons that Britain and France would set a time limit during the night for a German reply.

Chamberlain told the House

Continued on Page 2, Col. 1

By TAYLOR HENRY
Associated Press Staff Correspondent

PARIS, Sept. 3 (Sunday) (AP)—France and Britain, through their highest spokesmen, declared definitely late last night that unless Adolf Hitler calls his troops out of Poland a general European war will commence.

It was understood generally a final and formal notice to that effect would be delivered to the German Fuehrer before dawn today.

The notice would require an immediate reply or at least one within a set time limit.

The British and French proposals were identical.

Daladier, before the French Chamber of Deputies, and British Foreign Secretary Lord Halifax, before the British House of Lords, yesterday said negotiations still were possible if German troops cease hostilities and withdraw from invaded Poland.

On the bare shred of hope that Hitler might accept this proposal seemed to hang the chances of peace.

Everyone here went on the assumption that he would not. In that case, it was agreed generally that France and Britain would have to start a war of assistance to Poland without much more delay.

President Albert Lebrun in a message read to Parliament said:

"The future of civilization is at stake."

Daladier, addressing the crowded Chamber of Deputies, said no Frenchman will go to war with hatred for Germans at heart but all will have the knowledge "the very existence" of their country was in the balance.

In a late joint French-British communique, issued shortly before midnight, the French and British governments spoke of war as a foregone conclusion.

They announced they had accepted President Roosevelt's appeal to refrain from bombing undefended cities and civilian populations and reiterated their promise not to use gas.

The London-Paris Allies also agreed not to use bacteria and not to attack commercial ships which conform to the rules of war.

Their statement, issued under

Continued on Page 2, Col. 7

ROME

Il Duce Works All Night on His Peace Plan

By REYNOLDS PACKARD
United Press Staff Correspondent

ROME, Sept. 3 (Sunday) (UP)—Premier Mussolini early today was described on high authority as working throughout the night at Chigi palace in an effort to formulate a final peace plan.

Lights were burning in all offices at the palace after Foreign Minister Count Galeazzo Ciano had talked with the British and French Ambassadors and then reported to the Premier.

The Press as usual reflecting government policy, praised Premier Mussolini's attempts to secure a peace and castigated Britain and France for "fomenting" war.

A less tense atmosphere was apparent among the people following Adolf Hitler's statement that Germany will not require the military aid of its Axis partner. Nevertheless, throngs gathered around loudspeakers for news bulletins and the people eagerly awaited word of the newest developments in London and Paris.

Mussolini conferred with the King for an hour yesterday and reported fully on the international situation. Precautionary defense measures which the government had been taking at the rate of three or four a day were absent.

Gruening Named Alaska Governor

WASHINGTON, Sept. 2 (UP)—President Roosevelt today appointed Ernest H. Gruening governor of Alaska. He succeeds John W. Troy who resigned effective October 15, because of illness.

Weather:

The Weather Man showed up in white flannels with a tennis racket under his arm.

"I'm leaving the hive for a week-end," he said.

"A sort of blackout, boss?" asked Gadget the mouse.

"Yes," said the W. M., "the worker is leaving. The drones can carry on."

"And who gets the honey?" asked Anemometer, the cat.

"You ought to know," said the W. M., "you're a Democrat."

And he slammed the door and left the staff to get out a nice fair forecast for the week-end.

Woman News Writer Vanishes

VIENNA, Sept. 2—Frau Elisabeth Thury, Vienna correspondent for the Havas News Agency, has disappeared under mysterious circumstances. The Vienna police seemed but slightly interested when first informed of her disappearance and no information has been forthcoming regarding her possible whereabouts.

Dies Gets a New Prober

WASHINGTON, Sept. 2 (AP)—Speaker Bankhead (D., Ala.) has appointed Representative Casey (D., Mass.) to the House committee investigating un-American activities, South Trimble, clerk of the House, announced tonight.

San Francisco Chronicle EXTRA

THE CITY'S ONLY HOME-OWNED NEWSPAPER

FOUNDED 1865—VOL. CLV, NO. 138 CCCC***** SAN FRANCISCO, THURSDAY, NOVEMBER 30, 1939 DAILY 5 CENTS, SUNDAY 10 CENTS: DAILY AND SUNDAY PER MONTH, $1.30

Russia Goes to War!

FINLAND IS INVADED

Capital Bombed; Ports Shelled!

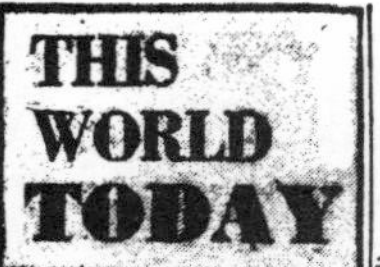

By ROYCE BRIER

ONCE there was a whale which went swimming around, as whales will, bunting into everything. But he was so big that every time he bunted into small fry, why, the small fry would say, "Beg pardon."

Even the other whales sometimes said, "Beg pardon."

So one day this whale turned his eyes down real close and spied a minnow swimming near him, but the minnow, being self-respecting and thinking the ocean was free, didn't say beg pardon when he saw the whale coming. So, the whale said to himself, what kind of minnow is this, that won't say beg pardon when he sees me coming? And he began to think this was a very bad minnow.

Then the whale looked around at the other whales, and said, "Look, this minnow is bunting me. I'm shaken from muzzle to flukes. I tremble from these villainous attacks—look!" And he trembled from muzzle to flukes.

So the whale became livid with anger to observe himself tremble thus, and made passes at the minnow with his flippers and opened his mouth at him. The minnow wanted to know why all the show of whalebone, and asked, but the only answer he got from the whale was that the minnow was bunting him, and planning to put out an eye, and maybe then tear him to pieces, or strand him on some lonely beach where he would only become a health department problem.

Well, the whale whipped himself into such a fury over this minnow, and thrashed around and churned the sea so violently, that the minnow was finally stunned, and had to quit menacing the whale, who could now go about his business, hoping to goodness he wouldn't encounter any more minnows to threaten his existence, at least this week.

The moral position of Soviet Russia in the Finn controversy is not its cardinal weakness. It's bad enough, but not so bad as its human position, lending itself to such offhand and perhaps awkward parables as that above.

If you will read Molotov's talk explaining why Russia broke diplomatic relations, you will be struck less by its coercive mood than by its absurdity in the circumstances. Coercion is common in diplomatic notes and so

Continued on Page 2, Col. 1

Bank of America
NATIONAL TRUST & SAVINGS ASSOCIATION
Member Federal Deposit Insurance Corporation
BAH!
HA!
FAIR

Waterfront

Public Gets Its First Look at a Stalemate

But Who Invited Rossi?

That Was the Big Question Before the Meeting; It Was—It Seems—a Misunderstanding

Picture on Page 5

A cross section of the general public was permitted a look yesterday inside the big tent where verbal acrobatics of the last 20 days have failed to settle the strike of waterfront ship clerks.

The public saw no change in the net result, the same being a continuation of the deadlock, but it did see what many pronounced the most entertaining show of the year.

In fact, it proved so interesting a study, Dr. Louis Bloch, member of the Maritime Labor Board, who presided, feared the SRO sign would have to be hung out today, so he declared this afternoon's session would return to the more prosaic surroundings of an executive conference.

Only Principals In Today's Cast

Dr. Bloch also indicated that the cast of actors for this afternoon's performance would be restricted to principals — negotiators for ship clerks and their employers—instead of continuing with a host of extras in supporting or atmospheric roles.

The latter were so numerous yesterday that they crowded to capacity the room set aside in the

Governor Olson says his committee is out to find the facts—and that's all. See Page 6.

Federal Reserve Bank building, where contract discussions have been held. Oddly, the "show" was more or less of an impromptu affair, having developed because of a misunderstanding.

The misunderstanding—for lack of a more explicit term—centered around Mayor Rossi and John E. O'Connor. O'Connor is a member of the United States Conciliation Service and was assigned to "do something" about the waterfront strike by Secretary of Labor Perkins.

The Mayor said O'Connor had invited him to the meeting. O'Connor said he had merely informed the Mayor the meeting was to be held. Each stuck by his story, although several hundreds of words were bandied in the sticking process.

The Mayor was under the impression that members of the Governor's

Continued on Page 5, Col. 1

Weather

Gadget, the Weather Bureau mouse, did a little forecasting on his own. He licked the end of his tail and held it to a crack in the window.

"Hum," he said, "a light and variable wind. That means generally fair and mild for Thursday with little change in temperature."

The Weather Man threw down his pencil.

"I give up," he said. "The Government gives me $10,000 worth of instruments to find out what the weather is going to be, and a three-inch mouse with a toothbrush moustache does the same thing with half an inch of wet tail. Bah!"

He clapped on his hat, kicked his waste-basket and went to lunch in a temper, which when you come right down to it, was the way he usually went to lunch.

Complete Report on Page 5H.

Kuhn

Jury Convicts Him of Bund Fund Thefts

NEW YORK, Nov. 29 (UP)—Fritz Kuhn, national leader of the German-American bund, was convicted tonight by a blue ribbon jury of grand larceny and forgery, on which he is liable to imprisonment for as many as 30 years.

The bundsfuehrer was found guilty on all five counts charged against him when the case was given to the jury at 1:30 this afternoon.

The jurors returned their verdict at 10 p. m., and Judge James G. Wallace directed that Kuhn be sentenced on December 5. He was locked up in the Tombs.

Kuhn, a chunky, bespectacled figure in a shiny gray suit, listened with ashen face but outthrust chin, heels together, to the verdict which convicted him of stealing $1217.02 of the bund's money.

His posture was that of a soldier at court-martial.

He swayed slightly as the foreman announced that the Bundsfuehrer, who contended that he was an all-powerful leader and so could not have stolen money which was tantamount to his property, was "guilty on all counts." His stolid features never changed expression.

Among the charges against Kuhn was that of spending $717.02 to transport the furniture of a blonde woman friend, Mrs. Florence Camp, from Los Angeles to New York and from New York to Cleveland. His romantic antics over Mrs. Camp, including some passionate love letters, were fully related during the three weeks trial, in which Kuhn originally was accused of stealing $5600. Judge Wallace dismissed five of the original 12 counts and two were not brought to trial.

In announcing continuance of sentence to December 5, Judge Wallace also announced that he would continue until then, or the next day, the question of his action regarding Kuhn's lawyer, Peter L. F. Sabbatino, who was accused of contempt of court during the trial.

When the verdict had been delivered and the jurors were dismissed, Kuhn, his chubby right hand resting on a Bible, was sworn, and testified that he was 43 years old, married, had both parents living, had no previous convictions and had spent nine days in jail while waiting for funds when his bail was raised from $5000 to $50,000. This is information preliminary to sentence.

Since he has not previously been convicted on any larceny or forgery charges, Kuhn may be sentenced below the minimum called for by his conviction, which would amount to 10 years.

Erich Rix

'It's Death If I Go Back,' He Tells Court

In a bare little hearing room in the United States Custom House a sober-faced ex-German seaman, Erich Rix, yesterday face a charge which may send him back to a German concentration camp. He was in such a camp once, and there was no doubt about his seriousness when he said:

"If they send me back, they write my death warrant."

His hope of escaping deportation lay entirely in the human interpretation of the immigration laws. And as he answered the simple questions put to him by Examining Inspector Patrick J. Farrelly, it was obvious that he was looking back 18 years to a Germany through which hunger and suffering stalked in the ruins of an unprecedented political and economic upheaval.

Death, for One Sack of Flour?

For back in 1921 Erich Rix possessed a small sack of flour in violation of the stringent food rationing laws. He got the flour in Hamburg. In his home town of Barmen his mother and two sisters were hungry.

Erich Rix took the flour home, but the sharp eyes of the police saw him. He was arrested and fined 4500 paper marks, about 50 cents. The matter was soon forgotten. It happened every day in Germany to scores of persons who were trying to get enough to eat.

At the end of the day it was announced that the hearing had been continued for 30 days to allow attorneys time to study German laws.

In 1936, Erich Rix entered the United States with the hope of becoming an American citizen. Questioned by immigration authorities then he neglected to tell about the time he was fined 50 cents for possessing the sack of flour. He just didn't remember it, he said.

'Someone Remembered' —And Then Came Jail

Recently someone did remember the incident. Rix was arrested in his home and taken to Angel Island. Later he was released on bail.

The United States immigration laws hold that if an immigrant neglects to tell of an arrest or fine when he applies for citizenship papers, he may be deported. And

Continued on Page 6, Col. 5

First Lady Buys Christmas Gifts

NEW YORK, Nov. 29 (AP)—Mrs. Franklin D. Roosevelt selected Christmas gifts today at two bazaars held for the benefit of Czecho-Slovakian and other Eastern European refugees.

Among other things, she purchased gilt necklaces and bracelets, leather novelties, linen sets and a toy penguin, which she described as "Fortunately slim enough for a stocking."

WPA to Advance Yule Pay Day

WASHINGTON, Nov. 29 (AP)—Colonel F. C. Harrington, WPA commissioner, today ordered that approximately 800,000 Work Projects employes receive pre-holiday pay checks totaling almost $20,000,000.

The Russo-Finnish War

Soviet War Machine Opens Onslaught From Land, Air and Sea; Attack Comes Without Warning; Capital Airfield Bombed

HELSINKI, Finland, Nov. 30 (Thursday) (U.P.)—Russia began an undeclared war on Finland today with simultaneous attacks from land, air and sea.

Russian troops crossed the Finnish border at Suojarvi, north of Lake Ladoga, and occupied a sector of Finnish territory after an artillery barrage.

Five bombs were dropped on the town of Viborg and three houses in the east part of town were burning.

The town of Tammelsuu in Karelia was shelled by warships from the Gulf of Finland.

An artillery battle now was under way at Kivena, on the Karelian border.

Russian airplanes bombed the Helsinki airport and dropped leaflets on the workers' quarters, printed in the Finnish language, reading: "You know we have bread; don't hunger."

The first warning the government had was when six Russian airplanes bombed the Helsinki airport at 9:25 a. m. (12:25 a. m. PST) and drove the people here to underground shelters. The bombs exploded on the field, causing no damage or casualties.

In a few minutes, reports from the frontiers disclosed that Russian artillery had started pounding the Finnish lines in Karelia, and in the far Northern Lapland, and that Russian ships had opened fire in the eastern part of the Gulf of Finland.

The Red Army Forces Cross Border on Karelian Isthmus

The sectors attacked by artillery were Suojarvi, north of Lake Ladoga in southeast Finland; Rabotchi and Kola in the far north, the sub-Arctic land where winter darkness now falls at 2 p. m. and the nights are 19 hours long.

(The Associated Press reported a Finnish Foreign Office spokesman announced at 9:20 a. m. (11:20 p. m., PST) that Red army forces had crossed the frontier on the Karelian isthmus and that Soviet warplanes were bombing Terijoki (300 miles south of Suojaervi), Finnish city near the frontier.

("The war is on," he said.

(The Karelian isthmus lies between the Gulf of Finland and Lake Ladoga, north of Leningrad.

(Reports in Copenhagen said the Soviet fleet had been sighted from the Helsinki water front and that Russian artillery was bombing Terijoki.

(The Exchange Telegraph, British news agency, said the first air alarm sounded in Helsinki 10 minutes after Red army troops started crossing the border at several points at 9:15 a. m. (4:15 p. m., PST.).

(It was reported in Copenhagen also that a bomb, apparently intended for a woodpulp factory, had struck a nearby hospital.

Air Raid Warnings Sends People Flying to Shelters

Objective of the Russian warships was not learned immediately, but presumably was one or more of the defenseless Finnish islands that Russia has demanded for naval bases.

The attacks came without warning less than 12 hours after the Soviet Premier-Foreign Minister, V. M. Molotov, had severed Russia's diplomatic relations with Finland on the grounds that the Finns were threatening to attack Russia "at the instigation of western imperialists."

The day had begun here as a normal one; the weather was

Continued on Page 4, Col. 6

Foreign Digest

Russia Tears Off the Veil At Last

By ALBION ROSS
Foreign Editor The Chronicle

Soviet Russia this morning flung aside the last veil which might have obscured from full public view the identity of her imperialistic policy with that of Czarist Russia, and began an undeclared war on her tiny Baltic neighbor, Finland.

This morning's onslaught against a smaller and helpless victim was reminiscent of that day in September when the Nazi war machine opened its campaign against Poland.

On that September day the Nazis handed the Polish Ambassador to Germany a list of demands, and, figuratively speaking, before the man could say "Jackrabbit," the German army was on the move.

Late last night, Russian officialdom had accused Finland of intransigeance, had denounced her for stubborness, etc., etc., and broke off relations with Helsinki. But she indicated she would resume negotiations if Finland would set up a new Ministry. However, before the full import of her words could be digested, the Russian war machine was on the move.

Russia had a non-aggression pact with Finland—a promise not to attack her—but Moscow denounced that Tuesday, and yesterday she broke off diplomatic relations with the Helsinki government.

Russian warplanes, according to the United Press, raided the Finnish capital, just as the Germans did the Polish capital. Russian artillery opened fire—and the long-threatened war on the Baltic was on—as yet undeclared.

What is the background of these new hostilities in Europe? A graphic description is presented with the map on page 4.

Entry of the immense Soviet empire into the world struggle for power, on the terms of submission or destruction which it offered Finland, indicates that the present generation on the European and Asiatic continents need hardly expect a return to peaceful progress.

What Is Nazi Role?

The German press continues to announce Germany's "sympathy" with the Russian policy. If Germany is really willing to go the whole way in a combined Russo-German policy of imperialism, this may be the turning point to a universal European and Asiatic war.

The two powers will increasingly indicate their determination not to tolerate genuinely sovereign states anywhere within the possible sphere of their military domination.

Four Canadian Flyers Killed

BELLEVILLE Ont, Nov. 29 (AP)—Four members of the Royal Canadian air force were killed today in the crash of a twin-engined Oxford bombing plane just north of the Trenton air base near here.

Moscow

Hostility Had Become 'Unbearable'

MOSCOW, Nov. 30 (Thursday) (AP)—Russia last night broke off diplomatic relations with Finland and ordered the red army and navy already concentrated along the Finnish land and sea frontiers to "be ready for all emergencies."

Premier and Foreign Commissar Vyacheslav M. Molotov, speaking to the 180,000,000 Russian people by radio at midnight, said that Finland's hostility "has become unbearable and the Soviet government can no longer stand it." (See page 2 for a partial text of Molotov's speech.)

Molotov demanded, in effect, the setting up of a new Finnish government in Helsinki as Russia's price of a resumption of diplomatic relations and a peaceful settlement.

Soviet Army Within Striking Distance

The Soviet forces already were concentrated within striking distance of Finland in overwhelming numbers, and, if necessary, Russia would be able to draw from a reservoir of 25,000,000 troops—the largest army in the world—against Finland's 800,000 or 900,000 poorly equipped conscripts.

Text of Finnish note and partial text of Molotov's radio speech severing diplomatic relations on Page 2. Map of Finland on Page 4.

The breaking off of diplomatic relations, the last act before the armed blow, was announced after Vice Commissar of Foreign Affairs Vladimir P. Potemkin had communicated Russia's decision to the Finnish Minister, Baron Arno A. Irjo-Koskinen, at 10:30 o'clock last night.

Red army troops moved up to the frontier north of Leningrad. Soviet warships and submarines were concentrated in the Gulf of Finland during the day and the press announced that Russia's "long patience is ended."

Russ Will Ignore U. S. Mediation Offer

Molotov also indicated that Russia would turn a deaf ear to the United States Government's offer late yesterday of its "good offices" for a peaceful settlement of the Soviet-Finnish crisis.

The crisis concerns only Finland and Russia, he said, and "others have no right to interfere since the Soviet government is not threatening any third power."

The diplomatic break came only 23 hours after Russia formally renounced her 1932 pact of non-aggression with Finland because of the latter's alleged "hostility" and refusal to withdraw its border troops.

Molotov's last previous radio speech was on Sunday, September

Continued on Page 4, Col. 3

Here's Where to Find It:

WAR

PAGE 3—The United States Navy takes a blimp out on the Atlantic to demonstrate rescue in air at sea.

PAGE 4—A comprehensive summary by the foreign editor; a map of Finland showing the crisis center.

GENERAL

CALIFORNIA (11)—Bonelli attacks Fitts over payoff quiz raids.

COMICS (6H)—Ryan's gallantry plus!

CONTRACT CONTACTS (25)—Maureen O'Brien's "Here's How."

CRIME (12)—Co-ed shoots football star.

DRAMA (10)—School use urged for historical films.

EDITORIAL (14)—Chester Rowell, David Lawrence comment.

FINANCE (17)—Stocks break one to five points.

HERE'S HOW (25) — Maureen O'Brien gives you the answer.

LABOR (6)—Court reverses verdict against union in damage suit.

METROPOLES (13)—Herb Caen's Memos to Himself.

PASSING SHOW (15)—Smoke Rings, Merry-Go-Round, Bookman, Labor Scene, The Capital Parade.

RADIO (25)—The daily log.

SHIPPING (5H)—Weather and mail schedules.

SOCIETY (8 and 9)—Another member of Oliver clan engaged.

SPORTING GREEN—Landis cracks down on big league clubs.

THE NATION (7)—Dies committee told that Communists instigated the auto industry sit-down strikes,

San Francisco Chronicle

THE CITY'S ONLY HOME-OWNED NEWSPAPER

FOUNDED 1865—VOL. CLV, NO. 168 CCCC*** SAN FRANCISCO, SATURDAY, DECEMBER 30, 1939 DAILY 5 CENTS, SUNDAY 10 CENTS: DAILY AND SUNDAY PER MONTH, $1.30

COMPARATIVE TEMPERATURES

	High	Low		High	Low
San Francisco	.60	51	Denver	.38	12
Los Angeles ...	72	53	New York	39	25
Seattle	54	42	Chicago	30	22
Honolulu	77	74	New Orleans ..	50	41
San Jose	62	44	Salt Lake	32	20

See below for local forecast

Complete Report on Page 17

Bridges Wins Deportation Case; Not a Communist, Landis Rules!

THE BRIDGES DECISION

Secretary Perkins Receives Findings Of Trial Examiner

CIO Leader Isn't Affiliated With Party, Harvard Dean Says in 75,000-Word Report

WASHINGTON, Dec. 29 (AP) — James M. Landis, Harvard Law School dean, acting as a special Labor Department examiner, submitted to Secretary Perkins today a finding that Harry Bridges, West Coast CIO leader, is neither a member nor affiliated with the Communist party.

Landis' finding was set forth in a letter to the Labor secretary transmitting his report on the deportation proceedings instituted by the department against Bridges, at which Landis presided.

He made no specific recommendation as to whether Bridges should be deported although his finding was negative on the principal grounds for deportation.

Landis informed the secretary that the evidence submitted "does not permit" a finding that the CIO leader has Communist affiliations.

Bridges has denied that he was a Communist.

Deportation Action Instituted in 1938

The deportation proceedings against Bridges were instituted in March, 1938, on the grounds that he was a member of an organization allegedly advocating overthrow of the Government by force and violence.

The 39-year-old CIO leader, who came into labor prominence during the 1934 maritime strikes on the West Coast, is a native of Australia. He came to the United States in 1920.

The hearing afforded Bridges an opportunity to show cause why he should not be deported and the Government was faced with the obligation of proving two essential points to win its case.

U. S. Had to Prove Two Specific Points

It was required to prove:

FIRST, that Bridges was a member of the party or affiliated with it at the time warrant was served upon his in March, 1938.

SECONDLY, the Government was required to prove that if Bridges was a member or was affiliated with the party, that organization advocated the overthrow of the Government by force and violence.

In his report to Secretary Perkins, Landis said he did not deem it necessary to make a finding as to whether the party "advocates, advises or teachers the overthrow of the Government of the Uninted States by force or violence . . ."

The next step in the case—ap-

Continued on Page 5, Col. 4

Statement of Harry Bridges

Harry Bridges made the following comment on the decision in his case:

"Naturally, I am very happy tonight to learn that after a fair hearing this constant charge of membership in the Communist party has been cleared up and that Dean Landis has not recommended deportation from a country I happen to want to live in just as much as most of those luckily born here.

"I intend to continue to do whatever I can to improve the condition of the working class in this country, and I hope that now this red herring has been worn out by its frequent dragging across the trail.

"Anyway, there is no more to say until I have had a chance to read the text of Dean Landis' report."

Fair in '40

PresidentMay Be Named On Tuesday

With the announcement of the appointment of a president and general manager expected Tuesday, officials of the 1940 Golden Gate International Exposition worked yesterday to bring about a more glorious Treasure Island for the new year.

George D. Smith, head of the group which raised the money needed to bring back the glories of the World's Fair next May, said he had been in constant conferences with other members of the G. G. I. E.'s executive committee of 15 men regarding announcement of the Fair's active managers.

While declining to discuss the identities of the men under consideration, Smith said the committee hopes to combine the offices of president and general manager in one man for the "Fair in '40."

Leland W. Cutler, president of the Exposition this year, once more issued a denial he had been "drafted" for 1940. He said he will assist the Fair in every means at his com-

Continued on Page 3, Col. 8

Windless Swells Batter L. A. Port

SAN PEDRO, Dec. 29 (AP)—Southern California's mysterious high waves, striking again in the absence of winds that might account for them, hammered at San Pedro and Long Beach ocean front areas today.

The great swells lashed over the Los Angeles harbor breakwater here. They breached the sea wall in several places on Alamitos bay peninsula, near Long Beach.

Waterfront

New Peace Meet Called For Today

The climax in San Francisco's latest waterfront strike ailment is due this morning.

Negotiators for the striking Ship Clerks' Association and the Waterfront Employers' Association will meet at 10 o'clock for the announced purpose of "negotiating a possible return to work."

Authorization for the conference was given last night by the union's strike committee. Employers shortly thereafter confirmed the joint session.

Will Be Submitted To Rank and File

Before the conferees will be a formula for putting the strikers back to work—as well as 4000 idle longshoremen blocked off by clerks' picket lines—and reopening the port. By the time the discussion is concluded, its phraseology will be in shape to submit to the rank and file of the union for approval or rejection at a special union membership meeting scheduled for 1:30 o'clock next Tuesday afternoon, unless a special session is summoned before that time.

Announcement of today's joint meeting ended a day of rapid-moving activities intensified by the silence of the preceding two days.

Details of the formula were not disclosed, but reports that it was a compromise between three previous sets of recommendations, augmented by unrevealed new suggestions received virtual confirmation when Harry Bridges, head of the ILWU, declared it represented a "combination" of previous proposals and "some new things."

Bridges did not amplify this description of the plan; his terse comment followed his presentation of it to members of the ship clerks' negotiating committee at a special session yesterday morning.

Proposal Stands As Combination

What little Bridges did say indicated to observers that the proposal as it now stands is a "combination," with additions or deletions, or both, of the "opinion" expressed by Governor Olson's fact-finding committee, the Governor's own amendment to that suggestion, and the "arbitrate all issues" recommendation of the Maritime Labor Board, made when the board had decided all other methods of settlement had been exhausted.

Bridges would not comment on a question as to whether the union's negotiating committee would submit a recommendation with submission of the plan to the membership.

The union previously had scheduled a special membership meeting for 1:30 p. m. Tuesday "to discuss the various phases of the strike." The call for the meeting had been issued December 26, according to the strikers' official bulletin, "Checkers."

Accordingly, after Bridges had emerged from his discussion with the union's negotiating committee, he said the proposition for getting the men back to work and reopening the port would be laid before them at that time.

Subsequently, reports circulated

Continued on Page 3, Col. 5

Turkey Quake

Thousands Homeless in Sub-ZeroCold

ISTANBUL, Turkey, Dec. 30 (Saturday) (U.P.) — Sensational accounts of the loss of life and property resulting from earthquakes in Eastern Turkey continued to pour in today over hastily repaired communication lines.

Relief expeditions made increasing progress in penetrating the devastated area of some 25,000 square miles in which 92 cities, towns and villages were reported partly or wholly in ruins.

The first report of earth shocks in the western part of Turkey were received today.

The shocks damaged the seacoast town of Dikili, 55 miles north of Smyrna. Floods followed yesterday's shocks, aggravating the damage and impeding relief.

Death Toll May Reach 100,000

Reports from an official inquiry mission which reached Erzincan, center of the devastated zone, indicated that the death toll might reach 100,000. Many more were injured and scores of thousands were homeless in a killing cold of 10 to 20 degrees below zero.

It was certain that an exact record of those killed would never be obtained. Fires were raging in many sections and bodies were being consumed before they could be removed from the debris of smashed buildings. It will be days before even an approximation of the extent of the disaster will be possible.

Villages Reported Obliterated

The lowest estimate of deaths in Erzincan alone was 5000. Other reports reaching the outside said as many as 42,000 had been killed in this city and that casualties throughout the province of the same name—populated by 180,000 people—ran equally high.

As soon as rail lines into Erzincan were restored other relief trains carrying more doctors and nurses, medical supplies, warm clothing and food left various Turkish cities for the region.

Some villages were reported to have disappeared almost without trace.

Continuous heavy snow and the bitter cold greatly hampered relief work. All military and governmental employes in Central and Eastern Anatolia were mobilized for rescue work.

An Earthquake Rocks Honduras

TEGUCIGALPA, Honduras, Dec. 29 (AP)—A three-minute earth shock which caused no great material damage was reported today at the town of Colomoncagua in the southwestern part of Honduras. The shock was described as unusually severe for that section.

CCC Director Seriously Ill

WASHINGTON, Dec. 29 (AP)—Robert Fechner, 63, director of the Civilian Conservation Corps, was in a serious condition at Walter Reed Hospital today as a result of a complication of arthritis, a lung congestion and heart trouble.

Weather

"Boss," said Anemometer, the Weather Bureau cat, "how come it rains when the barometer is up?"

"Oh," replied the Weather Man, "the barometer usually works a day or two ahead of the storm. Besides, you can't believe anything a Democratic barometer says anyway."

"What do you think a Republican barometer would do?" asked Anemometer.

"Specialize in indecision — tell you nothing."

"Well," said Anemometer, "as between the two I'd rather have a wet feather on a string. That doesn't tell you anything and you have no worries."

And he knocked off Saturday's forecast as "cloudy, unsettled, mild, light rain or drizzle possible at night."

WAR IN THE NORTH

10,000 Russians Hemmed in By Finn Ski Corps; Soviets Thrown Back on Six Fronts

Russia Bombs Own Troops, Helsinki Says

COPENHAGEN, Dec. 30 (Saturday) (AP)—Finnish ski scouts have cut off 10,000 Russian troops from communication with their base on the Central Finland border near Salla, reports from Kemijarvi indicated early today. The reports added that the Finns, under General Kurt Martti Wallenius, commander of the central-front army, were gathering a strong force to surround this group of invaders effectively and force them into a decisive action northeast of Kemijarvi.

By WEBB MILLER
United Press Staff Writer

HELSINKI, Dec. 29—The Finnish high command tonight announced that the Russians had been thrown back on six battle fronts on the Karelian Isthmus and northward along the eastern frontier where Soviet warplanes were alleged to have bombed and machine gunned their own troops, either by mistake or, possibly, to drive them into battle.

In two of the battles, at Kelva on the Karelian Isthmus and on the northern shore of Lake Ladoga around Syskyjaervi, the Russians left 900 dead on the field and the Finns captured much war material, the high command said.

Russ Hurl 100,000 At Mannerheim Line

The Russians, held at a virtual standstill on the Karelian Isthmus since December 6, launched the second month of war by throwing an army estimated at 100,000 men at the western end of the Finns' Mannerheim line today in an effort to strike a knockout blow.

The bulk of the 100,000 troops were astride the main Leningrad-Viipuri highway and everything indicated a massed surge toward Viipuri along the western side of the isthmus near the Gulf of Finland.

The shifting of the Russian attack to the western side of the isthmus appeared to be explained by tonight's communique which told of suicidal red army attempts yesterday to storm across Lake Suvanto at the eastern side and smash the left wing of the Mannerheim line.

In a fierce battle at Kalja, just south of the lake, beginning at 8 p. m. Tuesday and ending at noon Wednesday, the snowy bat-

Continued on Page 2, Col. 3

The Foreign Digest

Daladier Presents Plan For Postwar Europe

By ALBION ROSS
Foreign Editor The Chronicle

French Premier Eduard Daladier took the lead yesterday in presenting vaguely a program for a new Europe when the war ends. He told the French Senate that Europe must prepare for a "federal system" among the various European states.

The proposal is the first even mildly specific program advanced by the allies for settling Europe's problems and is a radical departure in the policy of the now intensely nationalistic French regime. It is also the first time in the last decade that one of the leading statesmen in power has asserted that the European states can only live together by surrendering to some extent their sovereignty.

Daladier pointed to the Franco-British alliance as the nucleus from which a reconstruction of Europe will start. He said:

"France and England are inseparably united even beyond victory."

There was in the speech no hint of compromise, however. Daladier said Britain and France must be victorious or must receive far-reaching concessions.

Passes War Budget

The French Senate passed the war budget, which is to be invested chiefly in completion of three 35,000-ton battleships, on aviation and tanks.

Holland gave evidence it has some reason to fear the worst by issuing a decree empowering the Queen to call up at any time every man from 18 to 59 years of age for emergency service. The decree was issued by Major General Reynders, commander in chief of the defense forces.

West Snowed In

Britain's Admiralty, meantime, acknowledged a battleship, said to be of the Queen Elizabeth class, had been damaged by a torpedo, but said it made port under its own power, with only four missing. Britain has only 11 real battleships.

The West Front was snowed in.

On the Finnish war front the Russian forces were reported to be fighting all about Salla without establishing any direct line of advance.

Paris estimates on the cost of the war to all European nations are now set, according to United Press, at roughly $150,000,000 a day. Germany is supposed to be spending $44,000,000 daily, and Britain is next with $33,600,000. Russia is supposedly spending only $22,400,000.

The service points out the French estimates for other countries are largely speculative.

British battleship's escape from sinking good news for London. See Summary, Page 2.

Hungry Nazis

They Plan to Make Fats From Coal

By HOWARD W. BLAKESLEE
Associated Press Science Editor

COLUMBUS, Ohio, Dec. 29—Germany is prepared to make edible fats from coal and shale. Quite literally, in a pinch she can make her butter from coal.

Details of this discovery were given to the American Association for the Advancement of Science today by a recently arrived German expatriate, Dr. Willy Lange, of the basic science research laboratory, University of Cincinnati.

Fats and copper are the two materials which informed scientists here said Germany was most likely to run short of in war. This month there have been news reports that Germany was progressing on the fat problem with new synthetic chemistry.

The coal fats, Dr. Lange said, are made by blowing steam through burning coal to produce carbon monoxide and hydrogen. This poisonous gas is the starting substance which, with subsequent chemical treatments, becomes first industrial fat and then edible fat.

Shale, of which Germany has a larger supply than of coal, is another starting material for butter substitutes. The shale is first converted into oil.

Chemists who heard Dr. Lange's paper said it appears that anything which produces a lot of carbon monoxide is good for making edible fats.

The cost, however, of making coal fats, Dr. Lange said, is nearly twice that of natural fat.

Cancer Award Announced

NEW HAVEN, Conn., Dec. 29 (AP)—Dr. John Graydon Kidd, 31, of the Rockefeller Institute, won the 1939 Eli Lilly award of $1000 and a bronze medal for his research work on animal cancer, it was announced tonight at the annual meeting of the Society of American Bacteriologists.

Dr. Kidd's investigations were described by leading bacteriologists as among the methods of approach to the cancer problem in human beings.

City of St. Francis

Civil War Struggle for State on Radio Tonight

Should California join the Union or the Confederacy?

That is the question which provoked such a hectic struggle as the clouds of the Civil War were gathering in 1858 and 1859.

And that is the struggle that will be dramatized in tonight's Chronicle-KGO-KPO presentation, "The City of St. Francis." The broadcast will be heard over both stations at 9:30 p. m.

There was a strong party working for the Confederacy at the time and plots to throw the State to the support of the South. In fact the political connivers hoped to create a vast new area in the far West and Southwest in support of slavery.

However, California remained with the North as an anti-slave State and this decision was due in large measure to the development of transportation and communication systems. The inauguration of the famous Overland Mail, a stage coach line connecting the East and West, followed by the romantic Pony Express and then the telegraph, all played important parts in the evolution of the California as we know it today.

Later came the railroad and in 1865 The San Francisco Chronicle was founded to give residents news of their city, the State, the country and the world. It will be chapter 7 in the story of "The City of St. Francis," and one of the most thrilling stories in the series.

Next Tuesday evening KGO and KPO, in cooperation with The Chronicle, will dramatize the Comstock Lode and the coming of the railroad, another vital chapter in a throbbing human story.

The Index

WAR

PAGE (2)—The U. S. Navy is savoring the idea of 65,000-ton battleships—see U. S. and War: Dr. Julian S. Huxley says belligerents are on a par with dinosaurs—see Science and War.

GENERAL

COMICS (10)—Charlie Chan shoots it out with Keeno's men.
CONTRACT CONTACTS (17)—There is something new under the bridge sun.
DRAMA (4)—Fidler knows all about Hollywood's publicity stunts.
EDITORIAL (8) — Chester Rowell, David Lawrence comment.
FINANCE (11)—"Failure of stock index to match upturn in production is mystifying."
NATION (3)—New food, drug law effective January 1.
PASSING SHOW (9)—Merry-Go-Round, Bookman, Labor Scene, The Capital Parade.
RADIO (17)—The daily log.
SHIPPING (17)—Weather and mail schedules.
SPORTING GREEN — Santa Anita race meet opens today.
METROPOLIS (7)—Chinese produce films at $1,995,000 less than Hollywood.
RELIGION (20)—Tomorrow's services in San Francisco churches.
SOCIAL DAY, WOMAN (6)—Jane Spieker makes her debut.

STATE RELIEF COSTS

Salaries Boosted $1,408,394

By EARL C. BEHRENS

California taxpayers had to contribute a million dollar increase for salaries of State Relief Administration officials this year, the Associated Press reported out of Sacramento yesterday.

The salary total of the SRA was boosted from $5,623,696 for the first 11 months of last year to $7,032,090 for the equivalent period in 1939, records of the State Controller's office disclosed.

Executive and other administrative expenses rose proportionately from $421,919 for the whole of 1938 to $559,090 for the 11 months of the present year.

The announcement of the big boost in the SRA salaries was an outstanding development yesterday in the State Relief Administration controversy which will come to a climax when the Legislature meets in special session January 29 to act upon a request of Governor Olson for additional funds for relief and for the consummation of his proposed production-for-use program.

The Governor scheduled a conference at Los Angeles with State SRA Administrator Walter Chambers, while State Senator John Phillips, head of a Senate interim committee of relief, conferred here with members of the Legislature and revealed SRA conditions as reported to him by investigators from the Edwin N. Atherton and associates organization and others.

Atherton's firm was employed through funds supplied by private individuals to conduct an inquiry into asserted waste, inefficiency, incompetency, radicalism and sundry other charges.

Phillips is compiling a survey of the reports submitted to him for presentation to the members of his committee when the Legislature meets. The committee has not yet held a meeting and Phillips has been delegated by his colleagues to whip the material placed before him in shape before the special session begins.

A legislative investigation of the entire SRA situation is imminent as a result of the recent disclosures and also because of the demand from many sources that the administration of relief be returned to the counties.

Controller Harry B. Riley's tabulation of the increase in SRA salaries was made in month by month form at request of members of the Legislature who asked for information to guide them in making relief appropriations at the special session.

The record showed a total relief outlay of $48,111,122 from January to November inclusive this year, compared with $40,180,742 in 1938 and $27,887,216 in 1937.

Cash doles accounted for $35,015,900 in 1939; $28,073,168 in 1938, and $20,682,839 in 1937.

The State Controller's figures showed that the SRA case load of jobless while fluctuating from month to month, averaged considerably higher than during the two preceding years. The case load in November, 1937, was 38,001; in 1938, 47,969 and last month 89,592. (**For stories on SRA probe charges and counter charges turn to Page 3.**)

1939—A YEAR IN REVIEW in Sunday's THIS WORLD

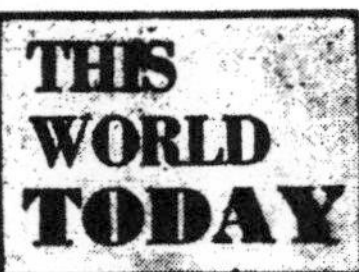

By ROYCE BRIER

LORD BEAVERBROOK, who runs a string of English newspapers which are not too consistent in policy, has come out editorially in the London *Evening Standard* for a house-cleaning.

The Baron beseeches Prime Minister Chamberlain to "clear away the deadwood, particularly the old stumps." He is quite candid about it, too, naming the "old stumps" as Stanley, Board of Trade head; Dorman-Smith, Agriculture; Morrison, Food; Wallace, Transport; Chatfield, Coordination of Defense.

They haven't the "caliber" for their jobs, Beaverbrook says.

These names don't mean much to us. We have our own appraisals for an Ickes or a Farley, but whether Sir Reginald Dorman-Smith and Baron Chatfield are geniuses or stuffed shirts, we have no means of knowing. Nor can we bank on the judgment of Beaverbrook, who is at outs with the Chamberlain government and has a hard time making up his mind. Last year he blistered Chamberlain for messing in the Czech affair, and this year he thinks Chamberlain moved too slowly in the Polish affair.

But whatever Beaverbrook's judgment here, he is sure to be partly right in general, and we will see changes in the war administration of England before the peace.

England defers to age, not altogether age in years (but one of the men named above is old), but age in ideas. The English go to extremes in this deferment, just as we nowadays may be going to extremes in our deferment to youth.

But age (in years) in England is exceedingly competent. It doesn't feel sorry for itself, and is quite unself-conscious, just plugging along at its job. As for age in ideas, even that is often competent in its curious fashion. Tradition means so much more there than it does here, that it is made to work, and in the long view sometimes subserves the very progress it is supposed to thwart, actualizing the fable of the Tortoise and the Hare.

So it is effective in the administration of a democracy under ordinary conditions.

But let this democracy be confronted by a war of profoundly subversive character, and this world of tradition undergoes strain. War today is so dynamic

Continued on Page 2, Col. 1

1940-1949

MAY 30, 1940
Allies Concede Defeat in Flanders

JUNE 14, 1940
Nazis Take Paris

DECEMBER 8, 1941
U.S. at War

DECEMBER 9, 1941
Japan Planes Near San Francisco; War Is Declared

FEBRUARY 4, 1942
U.S. to Move Aliens Inland

FEBRUARY 24, 1942
Sub Shells California

APRIL 10, 1942
Defeats in Bataan, Burma

MAY 6, 1942
Corregidor Surrenders

NOVEMBER 29, 1942
Fire Sweeps Boston Night Club

SEPTEMBER 3, 1943
Italy Invaded

JUNE 7, 1944
Allies Land in France

JULY 19, 1944
Port Chicago Disaster — Munitions Ships Explode at San Francisco Bay Port

NOVEMBER 8, 1944
FDR Leads in 24 States

MARCH 24, 1945
Third Army Storms Rhine

APRIL 13, 1945
FDR Dies

MAY 2, 1945
Hitler Killed

MAY 8, 1945
Victory Over Germany

JULY 29, 1945
Bomber Crashes Into Empire State Building

AUGUST 7, 1945
Atomic Bomb Blasts Japan

AUGUST 8, 1945
Flyers' Story of Atom Raid

AUGUST 9, 1945
USSR Declares War, Attacks Manchuria

AUGUST 15, 1945
Peace

AUGUST 18, 1945
First Photos of Atomic Bomb Test

SEPTEMBER 2, 1945
Japanese Surrender Signed

MAY 3, 1946
Armed Revolt on Alcatraz

OCTOBER 2, 1946
Nazi Leaders Convicted at Nuremberg

APRIL 17, 1947
1200 Killed in Texas Disaster

JANUARY 31, 1948
Gandhi Assassinated

MAY 15, 1948
Tel Aviv Bombed

NOVEMBER 3, 1948
Truman Holds Narrow Lead

MAY 12, 1949
Berlin Blockade Lifted

SEPTEMBER 24, 1949
Russian Atomic Disclosure

SEPTEMBER 30, 1949
Tokyo Rose Guilty

San Francisco Chronicle

THE CITY'S ONLY HOME-OWNED NEWSPAPER

FINAL Morning Edition

FOUNDED 1865—VOL. CL, NO. 136 CCCC**** SAN FRANCISCO, THURSDAY, MAY 30, 1940 DAILY 5 CENTS, SUNDAY 10 CENTS: DAILY AND SUNDAY PER MONTH, $1.30

By ROYCE BRIER

THE CAMPAIGN for Flanders is almost over, probably will be in a couple of days, and the war is about to enter a new stage.

The surrender of the Belgian army hastened the denouement, and served Germany well. It doubtless will result in the capture of several Allied divisions which would otherwise have been evacuated. The half million may dwindle to 100,000 if the disarmed Belgians are counted out, and the Germans can consolidate their territory and try to consolidate their ports.

The 36 hours following the Belgian collapse brought heavy German inroads. Without resistance, they moved from Bruges to Ostend and down to Dixmude, directly north of Ypres. They also entered Lille from east and west, surrounding an undetermined number of Allied troops north of Cambrai.

At this moment such Allied troops as have not been evacuated are in an area running roughly 30 miles southeast of Dunkerque. The French are opening the gates of the Yser canals, hoping for a day or two of delay.

The Allies have thus taken a thorough licking in this campaign for a complex of reasons having nothing to do with the combatant quality of Allied troops. History will discover and classify these reasons much better than we can, though some are already emergent. There was some bad generalship, but this alone could not account for it had the Allied command in the past eight months come even close to appraising the German driving power.

But that water is over the dam, and the question now is what the Allies will do about the next stage. It is likely to be even more volcanic than the last three weeks, but the Allies have had enough experience to bring their expectancy to a level with it.

The war has now passed two stages. Neither side was prepared at the opening for war in the west. Winter was coming and so the Germans prepared for this spring. They wrought well. Is it conceivable British Intelligence didn't get a smattering of what was going on? Or did London and Paris, from long habit, pooh-pooh Intelligence reports because they were so extraordinary?

The first stage, then, of eight months' duration, was to mount the attack, and to prepare to meet it, and the preparation was

Continued on Page 2, Col. 1

CARNAGE Lost Army Writes A Story in Blood

Mudstained, Walking as if Asleep, the Flanders Army Comes Home

By WALLACE CARROLL
United Press Staff Writer

LONDON, May 30 (Thursday)—Shattered remnants of the British expeditionary force—most of them wounded and the rest blood-stained, muddy, and walking like men asleep—began arriving in British ports early today.

They described a plain hell—constant, pitiless German bombing and strafing bombardment of the French ports from which Viscount Gort is attempting to save his trapped divisions.

Revealing that the shattered British forces were "sliding off a stretch of coast 30 miles long," they said that some of the men had to walk into the water to reach shallow draft ships. Others left the beaches in rowboats and small fishing craft, and were picked up at sea by Allied ships.

German bombs rained continually, even on hospital ships, they said. Quays and harbor works of the French ports were under terrific German air attack night and day as Allied warships and the Royal Air Force worked and fought like mad to aid the rescue of the battered, betrayed armies of Flanders whose fate was teetered on the channel's brink.

British naval engineers maintained quayside and harbor works as best they could under terrific enemy air attack, while long range British naval guns laid down a protecting curtain of fire.

Members of the returning vanguard were pitiful sights. None had shaved for many days and their beards were caked with mud and blood. Uniforms were tattered and grimy. Many boots were soleless. Some men had one shoe. Those able to walk staggered as if they were in a coma—evidence of the nightmare of fighting and marching and fighting again without sleep or respite for days on end.

The British wounded described the Germans' reckless expenditure of manpower, hurling and sacrificing thousands in mass attacks.

"They came on like automatons moving to certain death," a British soldier said. "They would be mowed down in hundreds and wiped out without gaining anything. Then we would counter-attack.

"Piles of German dead blocked the bridges. We had to use them as sandbags behind which we established machineguns."

A wounded German soldier brought out with the British survivors was quoted as saying from his hospital bed: "What can we do? We obey or die. We were brought up for this since we were children."

Everywhere youthful members of the B.E.F. gave vent to bitterness. One gunner said: "The wickedest trick of the Germans was to herd refugees, women and children in front of their advancing troops to make us hold fire."

Another British private said:

"I have never imagined anything like it even in my worst nightmares. It was just hell. I was near the German lines at the beginning of their big push. Throughout the fighting I saw very few German infantrymen—only tanks, bombs, flame-throwers and planes.

"One night I was sleeping on duckboards only a few kilometers from the German lines. As dawn came their planes came over and rained down shrieking explosive bombs for two hours. Then came their tanks.

"How I got back, God knows. It turned my hair white, but I didn't know that until the next day."

The Defense Drive:

FDR to Ask 750 Million More for Bigger, Better Anti-Tank and Plane Guns

General Marshall Tells House Army Also Needs Light Machine Gun; Tax Bill Readied for Today

WASHINGTON, May 29 (AP)—Military lessons learned from Germany's blitzkrieg led President Roosevelt today to rush preparation of a request that Congress add another large sum—probably $750,000,000—to the $1,182,000,000 extraordinary defense fund.

General George C. Marshall, army chief of staff, was reported to have told a House Appropriations Subcommittee that $750,000,000 would be necessary to buy more powerful anti-tank guns, a new type of light machine gun, additional mechanized equipment and other weapons.

Committee members said the General testified the relentless march of German troops already had demonstrated the comparative ineffectiveness of the 37 millimeter anti-tank guns.

"That's why the French were forced to use their 75 millimeter filed guns at point blank range," one legislator said. "We may have to develop a 90-millimeter weapon, the same size as our newest anti-aircraft guns, to meet the situation."

Members said the European war also had demonstrated the need for a light machine gun which soldiers could strap on and fire at any angle in front of them. One member mentioned a gun capable of firing 400 shots a minute.

A new anti-aircraft gun to combat the dive bombers also is being developed by the army, members said. This weapon was described as designed for use in synchronized batteries of 16 guns which would move on a half sphere and thus be capable of firing at 16 different angles at once so as to take care of bombers diving at

Continued on Page 3, Col. 1

Did Gamelin Kill Himself? A Rome Report

ROME, May 30 (Thursday) (AP)—Il Popolo D'Italia's correspondent in Bern, Switzerland, reported today that the French Generalissimo, Maurice Gustave Gamelin, is "understood to have killed himself following definite instructions of the French High Command."

General Corap, who commanded the French 9th army, which was overrun in the German break - through at Sedan, the correspondent said, had been executed.

Deportation

House Speeds Measure to Oust Bridges

WASHINGTON, May 29 (AP)—Legislation for the summary deportation of Harry Bridges, West Coast CIO leader, won the right-of-way to the House floor today by unanimous vote of the Rules Committee, and informed members predicted its speedy passage.

Majority Leader Rayburn (D., Texas) said, however, that no plans had been made yet to bring the measure up for debate. No such action has ever before been taken by Congress against an individual.

The Rules Committee approved the legislation in less than five minutes. It had heard earlier from Representative Allen (D., La.), author of the bill, that the House Immigration Committee was convinced that Bridges was an "undesirable" alien.

"Bridges is regarded by the framers of this bill as a menace to the interests of this country," the committee reported. "His close asso-

Continued on Page 10, Col. 3

Mme. Dollfuss to Live in Canada

OTTAWA, Ont., May 29 (AP)—Mme. Englebert Dollfuss, widow of the Catholic Chancellor of Austria who was slain in an attempted Nazi putsch in 1934, has been granted permission to enter Canada and intends to take refuge here, it was learned tonight.

Informed sources said she is likely to arrive in Canada shortly.

Actress' Wedding, Divorce Revealed

HOLLYWOOD, May 29 (AP)—Priscilla Lane, screen actress, was revealed by her mother today to have married Orin W. Haglund, assistant film director, at Yuma, Ariz., January 23, 1939, left him the following day and obtained a divorce last May 3.

Windsors Pay Visit to Riviera

NICE, France, May 29 (AP)—The Duke and Duchess of Windsor, traveling incognito, have arrived at their La Croe estate on the Riviera. They will stay for an indefinite period.

The Digest

Russia Kills British Hope For a Deal

By ALBION ROSS
Foreign Editor The Chronicle

Everything for the Allies now depends on how much mechanized equipment Germany has lost in the battle of Flanders, how exhausted its troops are and the practicability of the as yet only partially tested German theory that the British fleet can be paralyzed by bombers.

Equipment surrendered by King Leopold will probably immensely speed the process of German reorganization for a general attack on France.

Under the circumstances probably the most vital report of the day is the British claim they have 500,000 mechanized troops ready for immediate service out of the 1,500,000 under arms in the British Isles.

Russia Slaps Britain

British hopes of a quick agreement with Russia via trade negotiations collapsed yesterday. Official Soviet Tass news agency announced that the Moscow government will not deal with Sir Stafford Cripps, left wing member of Parliament, on his way to the Kremlin as a "special negotiator." London was informed that if it wants to negotiate on trade it should either send back to Moscow British Ambassador Sir William Seeds or name a new Ambassador.

The Tass declaration contained the significant rebuff:

"If the British government really desires to conduct trade relations between Britain and U. S. S. R. and not merely confine itself to talk about some nonexistent turn in relations between Britain and the U. S. S. R., it could do so through its Ambassador to Moscow."

Peace?

Rome had a report yesterday suggesting that there is something to the idea that the Rome-Berlin axis will make a major effort to get a separate peace with France.

Writing in the semi-monthly official Fascist review "Conquista di' Impero," Conquest of Empire, Nicola Marchitto claimed that the Italian attack will be made eastward and that Italy will assume a purely defensive position on the French frontier and the French North African frontier between Italian Lybia and Tunis.

Official German standpoint, as

Continued on Page 10, Col. 5

The British have succeeded in rescuing at least a part of the trapped BEF. See the Foreign Editor's summary, page 10.

Police Quell Panama 'Unrest'

PANAMA, Panama, May 29 (AP)—Police announced tonight that their forces had occupied the rebellious town of Laguna and suppressed pre-election unrest among residents.

Where to Find It . . .

WAR

PAGES 2, 3 and 10—War maps, the Summary, news and feature stories of the war and Wirephotos direct from the front.

GENERAL

COMICS (14)—An empty gas tank might save the day for Smitty and Blacky.

CONTRACT CONTACTS (24)—San Francisco Bay Area bridge experts corner the blue ribbon market.

CITY HALL (6)—Court upholds S. F. and the Howard street trolley.

CRIME (8)—'The Duchess' and her three aids will die in San Quentin gas chamber.

DRAMA (4, 5)—Jimmie Fidler gets out the little black book.

EDITORIAL (12)—Chester Rowell, David Lawrence comment.

FAIR (11)—Treasure Island to present special Memorial day ceremonies.

FINANCE (15)—Many corporations find their own bonds the best investment.

IN THE DISTRICTS (24)—Marina children will parade in style in a grand celebration at Funston Field.

LABOR (8)—Euclid Candy strikers may face a perjury investigation.

METROPOLIS (11) — San Francisco's program for Memorial day.

PASSING SHOW (13)—Merry-Go-Round, Smoke Rings, Labor View, the Capital Parade.

PHOTOGRAPHY (5)—Pets are good subjects to turn into prize-winning pictures.

POLITICS (9)—First new "ham and eggs" petitions filed for November ballot.

RADIO (21)—The Daily Log.

SHIPPING (24)—Weather report and mail schedules.

SPORTING GREEN—500-mile classic on Indianapolis Speedway today.

VITAL STATISTICS (9)—Births, marriages, deaths.

WOMEN'S WORLD (6-7)—A popular socialite remarries before her friends even knew she was divorced.

Allies Concede Defeat in Flanders

Nazis Claim Foe Again Cut in Two, Expect Surrender Soon; Suicide Squads Guard Rear

North, South Armies Meet, Capture Lille

By the Associated Press

BERLIN, May 29—Admittedly taking great losses themselves in a crunching drive against cornered British and French who were selling themselves dearly, the German army today nevertheless expected the capitulation at any moment of the half million troops fighting a suicide battle in Flanders.

The Germans were reported smashing furiously with hundreds—perhaps thousands—of dive bombers, tanks and massed artillery in an effort to ring down speedily the curtain on the Flanders carnage.

The British and French were cut apart in the general vicinity of Lille, the British to the north and the French to the south of the city, their predicament turned to disaster by the sudden surrender yesterday of 300,000 Belgians.

Only a miracle, Germans said, could prevent their annihilation or capitulation. The Nazis spoke of the desirability of a quick Allied surrender to end "this futile waste of blood."

Then, if wide speculation is borne out, there will be a tremendous rush on Paris—not England.

BRITISH FORCE CUT OFF FROM FRENCH

In the main part of the Allied triangle, pushed against the channel and blazing Dunkerque, are the men of the British expeditionary force which rushed in 19 days ago to resist the invasion of Belgium.

In the broken-off tip of the

Continued on Page 2, Col. 3

How Many Can Escape?

Britain's Expeditionary force of between 300,000 and 400,000 men—originally—struggled yesterday to escape from the narrow trap in French Flanders south of Dunkerque and stretching out for some 30 miles along the coast.

French forces south of Lille in a roughly 12-mile circle about Orchies had no escape left. The Germans west and east of Lille, according to last reports, had joined forces.

Early in the day German forces struck the British defense lines at all points where the Belgian surrender had let them through. Ostend was taken and in rapid succession, according to the German communiques, the line was driven up to Ypres and Armentieres. Lille, chief fortress in the region, was circled and stormed.

Meantime the Germans to the west of the trap moved up.

(See Page 2 for a detailed map of the fighting.)

The Latest Communique

PARIS, May 30 (AP)—The French High Command today reported "violent fighting" during the night on the Yser and in the region of Cassel.

The communique said:

"Various operations mentioned in yesterday evening's communique continued during the night. Violent fighting on the Yser (river) and in the region of Cassel. On the Somme and the remainder of the front no new developments."

Weather

The Weather Man's feet slipped off his desk with a bang and he awoke with a start.

"Doggone," he said. I wish I was back in the cavalry again. M'feet used to stay put in those days.

"Have you still got your spurs?" asked Anemometer, the cat.

"You bet," said the Weather Man. "And one of these days I'm gonna wear 'em to work and ride you all over the fifth floor of the Federal building.

"Gosh," said Anemometer, as he marked up "INCREASING CLOUDINESS WITH LIGHT RAIN" for Thursday. "I think he means that."

Complete report on page 24.

The British

A Half-Million Mechanized Troops Ready for Action

By DREW MIDDLETON
Associated Press Staff Writer

LONDON, May 29—Britain hurled her air force into mass battle tonight with waves of German fighters and bombers over the vital English channel port of Dunkerque—last back door to safety for the Allies' lost battalions in the Flanders death trap.

The fight for air mastery raged on into the twilight of an anxious day for England. These were the high lights:

1—In Flanders "die or surrender" triangle, Allied veterans, possibly numbering 500,000, under Lord Gort, commander in chief of the BEF, fought off repeated German thrusts with "stiff rear guard action" as they pushed doggedly down a narrowing corridor toward the coast.

2—Out of the million and a half men now actually under arms in Britain, half a million, especially equipped for modern mechanized warfare, are ready for action in France. They can join the French on the Somme river line in any gouge into German defenses to ease the pressure on their comrades in Flanders.

3—The War Ministry announced capture of the strategic Arctic iron ore port of Narvik, Norway, held by Germans through a month of fighting.

4—A second Royal Canadian Air Force contingent has reached England and will go into immediate training for coming battles.

An Air Ministry communique described the fight over Dunkerque as the latest of a recent wave of air attacks designed to ease the German pressure on the Flanders pocket and to shatter communications and bases behind the lines.

Twenty-two of the "large number" of German planes over Dunkerque were reported shot down. One British bomber failed to return.

Our Hearts Are With You, King Tells Troops

LONDON, May 29 (AP)—From their King today went words of encouragement—echoed by the entire nation—to the hard-pressed British Expeditionary Force in Flanders:

"The hearts of every one of us at home are with you and your magnificent troops in this hour of peril," King George VI said in a message to Lord Gort, commander in chief.

"All your countrymen have been following with pride and admiration the courageous resistance of the British Expeditionary Force during the continuous days of fighting of the last fortnight.

"Placed by circumstances outside their control in a position of extreme difficulty, they are displaying a gallantry that has never been surpassed in the annals of the British Army."

Lord Gort replied:

"The commander in chief with humble duty begs leave on behalf of all ranks of the British Expeditionary Forces to thank your majesty for your message.

"May I assure your majesty that the army is doing all in its power to live up to its proud tradition and is immensely encouraged at this critical moment by the words of your majesty's telegram."

Now, the Front Moves to the Somme, Aisne

By the Associated Press

PARIS, May 29—The Allies tonight gave up as lost the battle of Flanders and, in a great retreat, opened the flood sluices around Dunkerque to guard their last port of escape on the sea.

The bloody conflict in the north was all but over. The Germans, thus, were left substantially in control of France's northern industrial region and her northwest coast, across from England.

At least, however, the battle had given the Allies time to build a strong southern front along the Somme and Aisne rivers, for 200 miles across France.

AN INFERNO OF FIRE AND FLOOD

Across Flanders field, amid an inferno of fire and flood, the Allied armies, fighting at every step, pressed doggedly toward the English channel—not beaten by the fiercely-attacking Germans alone but by the surrender of the Belgians. King Leopold's defection had laid their flanks open and hastened the virtual collapse of their cause in Flanders.

The conflict has been transformed into a seething, flaming mass—a great whirlpool, which, before it has spun its course, may suck down to death hundreds of thousands of British, French and German youth.

Apart from the terrible ground fighting, with artillery pouring shells into massed men at close range, both Allied and German airforces were raining bombs into the enemies' ranks with appalling results. Military experts said it would not be surprising if the slaughter exceeds anything the world has known previously.

While the waters rose steadily in the vast system of streams on the plain of Dunkerque, French divisions fought across the tortured landscape to hold the rear while British troops defended points of the coast for the main forces seeking the coastline.

CANAL LOCKS OPENED TO COVER RETREAT

The Allies brought on the inundation by opening the locks southwest and northeast of Dunkerque, on the great canal that flows by the city and follows the coast for many miles.

In Dunkerque, the last Allied resistance was rallied under Vice Admiral Jean Marie Abrial, 61-year-old commander of the port. The Allied armies, navies and air forces fought together in an effort to save as much as possible from the wreckage of Flanders.

The retreat was harassed by heavy German fire. Some Belgian units, refusing to lay down their arms despite their King's order to capitulate, were reported still fighting beside the British and French.

A single French division which had been stationed with the Belgians as the backbone of their front tried to hold back the Nazi rush in the Nieuport-Dixmude sector, a World war battlefield on the coast northeast of Dunkerque.

Suicide squads also held out on the eastern and southern sides of the Allied path to the sea. Some Allied units had to fight through German columns.

Dunkerque, manned by French sailors, was the last island of solid Allied positions.

The rest of the battlefield was a

Continued on Page 10, Col. 4

Dispatches from Europe and the Far East are subject to censorship at the source.

San Francisco Chronicle

THE CITY'S ONLY HOME-OWNED NEWSPAPER

FINAL Morning Edition

FOUNDED 1865—VOL. CL, NO. 151 CCCC**** SAN FRANCISCO, FRIDAY, JUNE 14, 1940 DAILY 5 CENTS, SUNDAY 10 CENTS: DAILY AND SUNDAY PER MONTH, $1.20

NAZIS TAKE PARIS!

Government May Flee Again; Italy: French Attack Repulsed!

By ROYCE BRIER

GOD helps those who help themselves. In our childhood we thought that homily was a little hard for such an easy world, and then in the flow of the years we learned bitterly that the world is a little hard.

America, if it would, could not play God to a world which cannot help itself. America is vast and myriad-minded. No man can conceive the immense place of America in the future. But it is not an infinite force, and being myriad-minded, it cannot transcend time. The best we can say for it is that, given a little time, it can roll up such power as cannot be calculated by anyone whosoever.

Yesterday Premier Reynaud addressed a new and final appeal to America to help France. This appeal has come 20 months too late, and if you will count back you will come to—Munich.

Saying it is "too late" is a way of speaking. In each of the 20 months until the last, tangible and intangible obstacles of course barred such an appeal. So, saying it is "too late" is a way of saying that France, for reasons which it would ill become us to stigmatize, has not prepared for this incrowding darkness.

It is futile, these days, to be anything but as honest as we can be. Reynaud appeals for a people Americans admire and would wish to see unbeaten, nay, it is to America's urgent interest that France survive. But America, for all its immensity, all its good will, all its historic purpose and ego, cannot in days or hours stay the rush of eternal fate.

This little man Reynaud has the courage which has always instilled France in dark days.

He said, "France's soul is not broken. It is France's life which is at stake. I call to the world. I must tell them of the heroism of our soldiers—these soldiers who for six days and nights have been fighting, broken by marching and fatigue. But that is not the end of the war. It is not the end of our fatherland. Our cause will prevail. The day will come and must come. Our fight has no sense if we do not see far ahead the image of our victory.

"We know what a high place ideals hold in the life of the great American people. Will they hesitate yet to declare themselves against Nazi Germany?"

He wants "all legal aid—it is necessary that clouds of air-

Continued on Page 2, Col. 1

The Foreign Digest

As 'U. S. Hour of Decision Draws Near,' the Nazis Mock The Drive to 'Stop Hitler Now'

Japan Warns Belligerents to Withdraw All Forces From Orient—And Again Eyes the East Indies

By ALBION ROSS
Foreign Editor The Chronicle

America's hour of decision drew considerably nearer after Premier Reynaud in a radio address in effect called for the immediate aid of the American air force. German newspapers mocked the United States. Commenting on the stop Hitler movement here Berlin papers remarked, evidently with the customary official inspiration:

"That is easy to say several thousand kilometers from the Marne. Weygand would like to carry through, too, but he will not make it any more."

The French Premier added his promise to British Premier Churchill's that if the Allies are driven out of Europe and neighboring Africa his government will retreat to the French American possessions, presumably bringing their battle fleet with them.

The speech suggested, however, that France proper will surrender unless America openly declares war. Reynaud said:

"Our fight, each day more painful, has no further sense if in continuing we do not see even far away the hope of a common victory growing."

The appeal followed Reynaud's direct demand of the American people:

"Will they hesitate still to declare themselves against National Socialist Germany?"

Orient

In the Orient Japan gave new indications that she intends to expand her already immense empire toward the south. The Japanese army command in South China issued a statement announcing it is "no longer able to condone aid given Chiang Kai-shek by the authorities of French Indo-China who are unable to take cognizance of the new state of affairs in East Asia."

The United States, meantime, was again "protesting" the tortures to which the Chinese are being put. Secretary of State Hull at Washington said that the United States "condemns" such ruthless bombings as the systematic destruction of a great part of Chungking Wednesday and the slaughter of some 1500 civilians.

Uninterested in "condemnations," the Japanese had their puppet Wang Ching Wei regime at Nanking publish a declaration demanding all troops, warships and other armed forces of the European belligerent powers stationed in China be withdrawn.

Japan's spokesman for the naval ministry called in the correspondents and told them his country will not be responsive to any American offers of friendship **unless we "co-operate with Japan in constructing a new order in East Asia." The statement means that we can expect an unfriendly Japan unless we support and recognize the conquest of China.**

Japan still seemed to be hunting for a pretext to invade the Netherlands East Indies. Despite official denials of the East Indies government the Foreign Office announced it "regards with extreme gravity" the story floated in the Tokyo newspaper Nichi Nichi that 2000 British troops had landed in the Netherlands colonies. The East Indies government also flatly denied a Dutch patrol plane had fired on a Japanese fishing boat The report said the plane had been sighted "fishing" within 100 meters of the coast and had been merely warned away.

The Japanese Foreign Ministry indicated it has investigated the affair and has ascertained the vessel was fired on. Japan will protest formally.

Egypt

Egypt officially adopted the position of a non-belligerent granting the use of her territory for all military activities of the British army. The Egyptians will not send an expeditionary force against the Italians.

Alien Measure

House Passes Bill to Deport Harry Bridges

WASHINGTON, June 13 (AP)—The House approved 329 to 42 today a bill directing the Attorney General to deport Harry Bridges, CIO West Coast maritime leader, to Australia, immediately. The measure now goes to the Senate.

As originally introduced by Representative Allen (D., La.), the bill was aimed at possible deportation of Bridges as an undesirable alien, but provided for a hearing and trial.

At the last minute, however, Representative Van Zandt (R., Penn.) secured a revision providing for mandatory deportation of the Australian-born labor leader "whose presence in this country Congress deems hurtful." The phrase was taken from a Supreme Court decision dealing with the powers of Congress to enact legislation for the deportation of aliens.

When Van Zandt proposed the revision, Representative Michener (R., Mich.) arose to inquire what would happen if Australia refused to

Continued on Page 6, Col. 4

The Index

COMICS (20)—The Hawk leaves a clue behind after his latest crime.
CONTRACT CONTACTS (30)—Two teams tie for first place in Alcalde tourney.
DRAMA (8)—Movie fans need more comedy, less of war horror, says Jimmie Fidler.
EDITORIAL (18)—Chester Rowell, David Lawrence comment.
EXPOSITION (9)—Fair visitor No. 1,000,000 expected to arrive on the island tomorrow.
FINANCE (21)—The war sours the market, stocks drop to lower levels.
IN THE DISTRICTS (30)—New Southern Council Civic Club officers start work tomorrow night.
LABOR'S DAY (9)—Teamster parley expected today despite ultimatum.
METROPOLIS (17) — Roosevelt "edits" "America! Cavalcade of a Nation"; see Herb Caen.
POLITICS (7) — Former Olson aid will run for the Senate if recall is not speeded.
PASSING SHOW (19)—Merry-Go-Round, Smoke Rings, Bookman, Labor View, the Capital Parade.
RADIO (14)—The Daily Log.
SHIPPING (14) — Weather Report, Mail Schedules.
SPORTING GREEN — Arturo Godoy's fight plans startle even his manager.
STATE (6)—Governor Olson names 50 to the defense council.
VITAL STATISTICS (15)—Births, marriages, deaths.
WOMEN'S WORLD (10, 11, 12)—The P.-T. A. voices opposition to the proposed reduction in the city's school budget; Jane Friendly has a new recipe for homemade ice cream, see Page 12.

Rome's First Land Action; 2 Subs Claimed

ROME, June 14 (AP)—Italian troops have driven back a French attack on the Alpine frontier at Galisia hill, where there is a mountain pass into Italy, the Italian High Command communique announced today.

Fighting at Galisia hill, which is about 36 miles northwest of Turin, is the first land action so far reported in Italy's participation in the war.

The communique said two enemy submarines had been hit in the Mediterranean, and that one was seriously damaged.

An Analysis

Is France's Role in the War Ended?

By THE FOREIGN EDITOR

France has seemingly lost her war with Germany and disappears from the scene as **a major power,** at least for the duration of the present struggle.

Both flanks of Weygand's forces have broken. The vital drives have come on the Seine in the Rouen sector north of Paris, at Chateau Thierry on the Marne 40 miles east, and in the Reims sector 80 miles east.

Hitler's armies, according to the French communiques are pouring over the Seine between Rouen and Vernon heading toward Central France and the temporary capital at Tours 100 miles away.

Weygand's left wing can apparently only find a new line of defense by falling all the way back a hundred or more miles to the Loire, furiously pressed by the already victorious and speedier Germans.

RIGHT FLANK'S POSITION IS DESPERATE

The position of the right flank along the Marne is no less desperate. In the Reims sector the Germans have broken through southeast and are threatening the Maginot line from behind. France's only remaining important heavy industries region, Lorraine, may be taken within a few days.

The break through at Chateau Thierry means that the right and left wings will be fighting a hundred or so miles apart.

The surrender of Paris takes from the French the other third remaining industrial region besides Lorraine and the already occupied northeast. France's industrial sinews have been cut. Roughly half of all important French industries are gone.

Loss of Paris is likely to have the most disastrous effect on French morale besides shattering the French communications system. France more than any country in the world is centered on its capital.

NOT MUCH CHANCE OF BRITISH AID

Chances of British aid being effective have been severely reduced by the collapse of the French left wing along the Seine. French forces falling back to the Loire will be isolated from the channel ports and all British aid must arrive after a long sea detour.

With Le Havre likely to fall any time only one important port, Cherbourg, remains on the north coast of France and it is not equipped for mass traffic, being chiefly a port of call for liners that stay a few hours to discharge mail and passengers en route to other ports.

The French, in fact, seem perfectly aware, as Reynaud's speech indicated, that they have lost the "battle of France."

A Baby Comes to Mama, 12, Dad, 16

NEW ORLEANS, June 13 (AP)—A seven-and-a-half-pound boy was born here today to a 12-year-old French-speaking mother, wife of a 16-year-old Louisiana bayou fisherman. Charity Hospital physicians said the birth was normal.

Germans Take Over a 'Quiet' Capital

Premier's Plea for America to Rush Aid Hints France Might Give Up; London Pledges Support, Rushes Aid

'France Shall Stand Erect in Her Grandeur'

By the Associated Press

LONDON, June 14 (Friday)—Great Britain, drawing from forces reserved for defense of her own island in face of an expected Nazi invasion, rushed reinforcements to France today and renewed her pledge "to continue the struggle at all costs in France, in this island, upon the ocean and in the air wherever it may lead us."

This pledge was made shortly after Premier Reynaud in a dramatic **radio broadcast said there was** "no sense" in continued resistance unless there was a "common" democratic victory in sight, and had asked for "clouds" of airplanes from the United States to defend "wounded" France.

"Great Britain will continue to give the utmost aid in her power," said the British government's message to France.

"We shall never turn from the conflict until France stands safe and erect in all of her grandeur, until the wrong and the wronged and enslaved states and peoples have been liberated and until civilization is free from the nightmare of Nazism."

BATTLE LINES WILL AVOID PARIS

The British said they would share with France the costs of repairing the ravages of war.

A military spokesman said if the French were forced to retire further they would fight up to the outskirts of Paris on the north and then would form a continuous line immediately behind the city to prevent its being made a battle ground.

"All arrangements have been made to enable this maneuver to be carried out if decided upon," the spokesman said.

With every available fighting man, gun and tank pledged to a "death-or-victory" beside the weary French, military sources reported fresh British troops already are there—hurled into the Seine river line.

"Thousands" more, their numbers and route guarded closely, were on the way as the London press urged that even untrained divisions incompletely equipped be rushed to the continent.

With troops pouring out of England, 20,000 school children — the vanguard of 120,000 to be moved out of the capital in the next six days—said goodbye to bomb-conscious London and piled into trains en route to the safer west country, church bells were silenced except to warn of parachute invasion, and a government spokesman said some "danger areas" might have to be cleared entirely of civilians.

Press and public agreed that home defense must be left to the home guard. The army is needed in France:

To be saved is Paris, where the

Continued on Page 4, Col. 6

Craven Loses His Nullification Plea

LONDON, June 13 (AP)—The 22-year-old Earl of Craven today was denied nullification of his marriage to Gwendoline Irene Meyrick, 25, night club hostess, last May 3. The earl had pleaded he was suffering alcoholic poisoning at the time and was "unawares he was being married." The divorce court judge said evidence showed the earl married the then Miss Meyrick under his own volition and granted Lady Craven full restitution of her conjugal rights.

The Invaders' Drive on Both Sides of Paris Speeds Up; Retreat 'Orderly' French Say

TOURS, France, June 14 (Friday) (AP)—The French army abandoned Paris to the advancing Germans today, explaining that no worthwhile strategic aim would justify the devastation of the historic capital which would result from its defense.

(The United States Ambassador to France, William C. Bullitt, reported to the State Department at 7 o'clock last night Paris time—10 p. m. P. S. T.—that the German army was "inside the gates of Paris," and thus was the first to inform the world of the surrender.)

Unofficial sources said the Germans entered the capital by the Aubervilliers gate.

This gate is at the northeastern end of the capital on the **road from Senils, where the Germans had massed huge forces** and had been fighting hard for several days.

The French, although saying their withdrawals before the Germans were "in the greatest order," acknowledged two deep enemy thrusts southward from the Champagne region.

One of these, said today's High Command communique, appeared to be directed toward Romilly, which lies on the Seine 50 miles south of Reims and 65 miles east and slightly south of Paris.

(Editor's Note: The Associated Press staff here prepared to leave for Bordeaux during the day. The preparations were taken as indications the French government may be forced to move again to escape the advancing Germans.)

The High Command communique said:

"The enemy push on two sides of Paris still further was accentuated.

"Due to this advance, the troops protecting Paris have withdrawn from the city, conforming to orders.

"The French High Command, in renouncing direct defense of the capital, which now is an open city, wished to save it from the devastation that would result from such defense.

"It was considered that no

For the texts of Reynaud's two appeals, see Page 4.

worthwhile strategic result justified the sacrifice of Paris.

"On the Champagne front the enemy armies are progressing, fighting their way south. Their most advanced elements appear to be directed toward Romilly on one hand and Saint Dizier on the other.

"Our fighting and our movements continue in the greatest order."

Official German sources neither affirmed nor denied the surrender of Paris, but said significantly that "an official German announcement

For wirephotos, stories and maps of the course of World War II, see Pages 2, 3, 4, 5, 6 and 16.

is expected very soon."

France, through its Premier, called yesterday upon the United States for "clouds of airplanes" and challenged Americans to "declare themselves against Nazi Germany."

"We know what a high place ideals hold in the life of the great American people," Premier Paul Reynaud said in a broadcast to his country.

"Will they hesitate yet to declare themselves against Nazi Germany?"

He spoke of the French as "losing this battle," but declared that "despite our reverses the power of the democracies remains immense. We have a right to hope that the day is coming when all that power will be placed in force."

But he remarked pointedly that France's fight "has no further sense" if a growing hope of a "common" victory is not seen—"even far away."

In announcing his second plea to President Roosevelt for aid—the first, asking all aid short of an expeditionary force having been made public today—the Premier declared:

"It is necessary that clouds of airplanes come from across the Atlantic to crush the evil power that has descended over Europe."

Having already been promised the

Continued on Page 2, Col. 5

Berlin: Large French Units Collapsing

BERLIN, June 14 (AP) — Events of "the greatest magnitude," informed German sources said today, are shaping up in connection with the reported fall of Paris.

Reports this morning spoke of the collapse of large French units, they asserted.

Informed quarters said that news concerning Paris undoubtedly would have the most severe repercussions on other parts of the French army.

By SIGRID SCHULTZ
Copyright, 1940, Chicago Tribune Foreign Cable Service

BERLIN, June 13—Negotiations for surrender of Paris—if the Germans recognize the French capital as an open city—were carried on today between France and Germany and between two neutral countries, it was learned from a reliable source.

(This story was written before Bullitt reported to Washington that German troops had entered Paris.)

NAZIS ATTACK THE FRENCH WILL TO RESIST

Quite a number of Nazis hope that if Paris surrenders unconditionally, as demanded by the Germans, this will completely demoralize what is left of the French army and stir up the French population to such a degree that it will rise against its leaders.

The German radio is doing its best to further the feeling of panic in France. It floods France with appeals and warnings carefully written by Germany's propaganda experts. Neutral observers who believe that from a military viewpoint the French still can make a stand south of the Seine, meet with the serious disapproval of the Nazis who loudly claim that "the morale of the French population is not good enough to enable the French high command to continue resistance."

That German troops are pressing

Continued on Page 2, Col. 4

Dispatches from Europe and the Far East are subject to censorship at the source.

State Department

This Is How Bullitt Told Washington of the Surrender

By Associated Press

WASHINGTON, June 14—From beleaguered Paris Ambassador William C. Bullitt notified the State Department early today that German troops were "inside the gates" of the famous city which twice staved off their thrusts in the 1914-18 war.

The laconic message stated that "the city was quiet."

The message took almost 11 hours in transit from France. The State Department disclosed that Bullitt telephoned the word of the German entry to Anthony J. Drexel Biddle, United States Ambassador to the exiled Polish government now at Tours.

Biddle relayed the information by cable about 11 a. m. (P. S. T.) yesterday, but the cable did not reach Washington until nearly 1 a. m. today (10 p. m. P. S. T.)

It gave no details about the number of troops or the exact location which they had reached.

Yesterday Bullitt had cabled that he, with members of his staff, were remaining in Paris "as the representative of the diplomatic corps" in the hope of rendering "any assistance possible in seeing to it that the transfer of the government of the city takes place without loss of human life." (See the Washington story, Page 2, for details.)

Even before the German advance threatened Paris, Bullitt found his post one of danger. On June 3, during a German air raid on the city, a bomb hit the ceiling of a room where he was a luncheon guest, but it did not explode.

"God was with me," Bullitt said, describing the narrow escape to President Roosevelt by transatlantic telephone a little later.

Weather

"If I knew where I could borrow a good lie detector I'd slap it on the barometer," said the Weather Man. "It's getting so I can't believe a word it says."

"I could use a lie detector, too," said Anemometer, the cat. "The milk I got this morning tasted as if it came from a tin cow."

"Listen, you banjo-eyed ingrate," snapped the W. M., "the Government buys you the best grade A on the market."

"Then what was the Government doing with this can opener on this sink?" asked Anemometer.

"How do I know?" roared the Weather Man. "Maybe somebody's been opening a bid."

He seemed very irritated as he hung up the Friday forecast of **"FAIR AND MILD."**

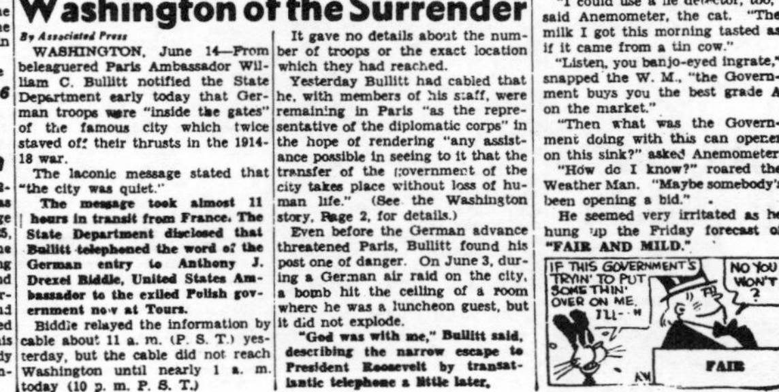

FINAL MORNING EXTRA

San Francisco Chronicle

THE CITY'S ONLY HOME-OWNED NEWSPAPER

COMPARATIVE TEMPERATURES	High	Low		High	Low
San Francisco	60	50	Denver	69	25
San Jose	61	39	New York	56	44
Los Angeles	79	56	Chicago	35	26
Seattle	—	—	New Orleans	61	52
Honolulu	77	70	Salt Lake	44	20

Local Forecast: Fair

Complete Report on Page 11

FOUNDED 1865—VOL. CLIII, NO. 146 CCCC***** SAN FRANCISCO, MONDAY, DECEMBER 8, 1941 DAILY 5 CENTS, SUNDAY 10 CENTS; DAILY AND SUNDAY PER MONTH, $1.30

U.S. AT WAR!

PARATROOPS LAND IN PHILIPPINES!

THIS WORLD TODAY

By ROYCE BRIER

NOW let us look at history, and let us look at it calmly, for we are the greatest people in history, and that imposes upon us a great responsibility.

And let us look at history in its wide and true sense in our time, as the chronicle of mankind. We need not as a people worry unduly about the Japanese. We will take care of these upstarts after awhile, and when we have they will be back in the murky feudalism from which they emerged 89 years ago.

But the chronicle of mankind is something else, a deep and mighty river forever flowing toward an unseen sea.

So in the beginning there lived not long ago in the great gray city of Vienna, a man, a John Wilkes Booth kind of crazy man, but not too crazy, brooding and hating in an apparently fathomless anonymity. Yet this man was a true son of our history.

In him, in his hate, his madness, his inborn treachery and tigerish bent, the history of our days strained convulsively, like the white-hot core of a volcano. For he was a revolutionary and an unexampled revolution was burning in many men, and after a certain number of years had passed in turmoil and confusion, then lo! the revolutionary and the revolution were one.

They were one by inner preordination from the beginning, but in the reaches of the deep and mighty river they did not find each other at first. When they did, most of us did not know it, and far across the earth millions upon millions of the unknowing were pitched abruptly into the abyss.

"And the war came - - -"

As in Abraham Lincoln's day, it came slowly and blunderingly and in false-face. But instead of striding across a continent it strode across a world. It moved a little east and a little west, a little north and a little south, this revolutionary war which was in motion through time as well as space. It struck and recoiled, struck and recoiled, but always it engulfed a little more time and a little more space, for this is the way of revolutions.

It did not want to show its face until it had to, for this is the way of revolutions, too, especially is it

Continued on Page 2, Col. 1

LLOYD GEORGE ACCEPTS BRITISH PREMIERSHIP . . . CONVICT WALKS OUT AT SAN QUENTIN . . . SEA-TO-SEA STEAMER LINE FINANCED TO CURB RATES . . . STREET CARS HERE CARRY MORE PASSENGERS THAN IN L. A.

* * *

America at War!

EDITORIAL

By the act of Japan, America is at war. The time for debate has passed and the time for action has come. That action must be united and unanimous. "Politics is adjourned," whether between parties, factions or economic groups. From now on America is an army with every man, woman and child a soldier in it, all joined to the one end of victory.

If war had to come, it is perhaps well that it came this way, wanton, unwarned, in fraud and bad faith, virtually under a flag of truce. For in war there can be only one side in action, and now there is only one side in thought or feeling. Its slogan is, "Americans unite, for victory and freedom."

We can not know how long this war will last, how wide it will range, nor what it will cost us, in toil, in sacrifice and in treasure. We do know that whatever the cost, we will pay it, and that our reward will be to hand down to our children the free America which our fathers bequeathed to us.

Americans, unite!

U. S. Faces War: Losses May Be Heavy, Nation Warned

WASHINGTON, Dec. 8 (Monday) (AP)—Bombs from Japan made war on the United States today and as death tolls mounted, President Roosevelt announced he would deliver in person today a special message to Congress.

In the background as the Commander-in-Chief went before the joint session of the House and Senate was a Government report of "heavy" navil and "large" losses to the Army.

Whether Mr. Roosevelt will ask for a formal declaration of war by this country, to match the action taken in Tokyo, was left uncertain after a hurriedly summoned meeting of his Cabinet and congressional leaders of both parties tonight at the White House. Also uncertain was whether that declaration might extend to Japan's Axis allies, Germany and Italy.

It was clear from a statement made by the participants, however, that Congress would be requested to adopt a resolution of some nature, and equally clear that it would quickly give its approval. A request for governmental power equivalent to that under a war declaration was expected as a minimum.

WAR CAME WHILE TALKS WERE CONTINUING

War came suddenly to the United States early yesterday afternoon. Without warning, and while Japanese diplomats were still conducting negotiations for peace, the Japanese Air Force struck at Honolulu, Pearl Harbor and Hickham Field, all in the Hawaiian islands. Soon afterward, Japanese bombs were raining upon Guam and, later, portions of the Philippines were attacked.

As quickly as word of the first bursting bomb was received, the President as commander-in-chief called upon the army and navy to repel the attack. Far in advance of any action which Congress may take today, the United States was fighting an attack.

Tokyo later announced its declaration of war on this country, and Great Britain as well. As was the case here, the British Parliament was called into special session for this afternoon to take action.

Quickly many of the discordant elements which have been bickering over foreign policy for months,

Continued on Page 6, Col. 1

Paul C. Smith Called to Active Service

Paul C. Smith, Editor and General Manager of The San Francisco Chronicle, has been called to active duty with the Navy.

He was ordered last night to report to the Navy Department, Washington, D. C., at once.

Smith is a Lieutenant Commander in the U. S. Naval Reserve. He leaves today.

Japs Bomb Hawaii, Invade Thailand

350 Slain----Then Tokyo Declares War on U. S., Britain; President Roosevelt Will Go Before Congress Today!

Pacific Coast Springs to Wartime Alert; Leaves Are Canceled, Guns Manned

The West Coast, from San Diego to the Canadian line, and the entire Western Continental United States were swinging to a wartime basis within a few hours of the air attack on Hawaii by Japan.

Air raid listening devices went into action. The fastest pursuit ships and bombers of the Army Air Corps were poised for any sign of raid by land, sea or air.

Leaves and furloughs of all officers and enlisted men of the 11th, 12th and 13th Naval districts were canceled and the men ordered back to their ships.

A roundup of Japanese aliens who have been under suspicion as possible subversive agents was ordered by the Attorney General of the United States. FBI agents here, as well as in other cities of the United States took a number of these Japanese into custody.

FACTORIES TIGHTEN WATCH FOR SABOTEURS

The outposts of the Nation's far-flung Pacific Coast defenses at Alaska and the Panama Canal were blacked out last night.

Leaves of all soldiers in the 9th Corps Area — California, Nevada, Utah, Idaho, Montana, Washington and Oregon—were summarily canceled by the War Department and all men were ordered to their posts.

The United States Coast Guard ordered all Pacific Coast craft into port, and the Customs Department canceled all departure permits. Movements of craft in harbors was restricted.

All enlisted men of Class M-2, Naval Reserve, were instructed by the navy to report today for mobilization orders.

OLSON CALLS FOR GUARD VOLUNTEERS

Governor Olson issued a statement at Sacramento proclaiming the State "the most vital natural objective of any attack which may be contemplated by air, sabotage or other means of destruction," and called for 10,000 volunteers to the State Guard.

Attorney General Earl Warren in a State-wide, all-points broadcast out of Los Angeles warned all law enforcement agencies and civilians to be on the alert against disorder, and urged that reason and calm judgment prevail.

He instructed citizens to call his office in the State building, San Francisco, "in the event of need of outside civilian assistance to prevent civilian disorder of any kind."

Under these circumstances, the nearest FBI office should also be called, he said.

Under orders from the War and Navy departments, industrial plants tightened their guard systems to forestall sabotage of defense industries.

Instructions from Major General J. L. Benedict, commanding General of the 9th Corps Area, closed all entrances to all army posts to civilians, excepting those on official business.

Military police details on guard duty were strengthened.

In the Bay Area, where a score of cargo ships are on the ways of shipbuilding plants, armed guards were called into immediate service to augment the patrols which have

Continued on Page H, Col. 5

INSIDE

You'll find full war coverage—news, background and pictures: See Pages A, B, C, D, E, F, G, H, 3, 4, 5 and 6. Other war news on pages 2, 7 and 11.

Hoover: Our Decision's Clear

By Associated Press

Former President Herbert Hoover last night called for an all-out fight against the Japanese, saying, "American soil has been treacherously attacked by Japan. Our decision is clear."

Wendell Willkie, Republican standard bearer in 1940, said: "I have not the slightest doubt as to what a united America should and will do."

FDR on Air

Network radio stations will carry President Roosevelt's address to the joint session of Congress this morning. Among them will be stations KGO, KPO and KSFO in San Francisco. Time here will be 9:30 a. m.

Raids Took a Heavy Toll, Hawaii Says

(This is the last uncensored Associated Press dispatch from Honolulu in the new war. Soon after this dispatch was telephoned a heavy censorship was imposed on dispatches from the Hawaiian islands. In Washington, some hours later, the War Department gave the White House a preliminary estimate that 104 were dead and more than 300 wounded in the army forces alone by the bombing.)

HONOLULU, Dec. 7 (AP)—War struck suddenly and without warning from the sky and sea today at the Hawaiian islands, and Japanese bombs took a heavy toll in American lives.

Cannonading offshore indicated a naval engagement in progress.

Wave after wave of planes streamed over Oahu in an attack which the army said started at 8:10 a. m., Honolulu time, and which ended at around 9:25, an hour and 15 minutes later.

Witnesses said they counted at least 50 planes in the initial attack.

The attack seemed to center against Hickam Field, huge army airport three miles northwest of Honolulu, and Honolulu, where the islands' heaviest fortifications are located.

The planes streamed through the sky from the southwest, their bombs shattering the morning calm. Most of the attackers flew high, but a few came low, five down to under a hundred feet elevation to attack Pearl harbor.

An oil tank there was seen blazing and smoking. An unconfirmed report said one ship in the harbor was on its side and four others burning.

Army officials said two Japanese planes had been shot down in the Honolulu area.

Planes which did not bomb Pearl

Continued on Page C, Col. 7

Raiders Fly From Hidden Aircraft Carrier; Guam Is 'Surrounded'; Wake Falls

NEW YORK, Dec. 8 (AP) -- Royal Arch Gunnison, broadcasting to WOR-Mutual from Manila, reported today that Japanese parachute troops had been landed in the Philippines.

He said native Japanese had seized control of some communities where they are thickly concentrated, but said that in other sections Filipino police were rounding up Japanese nationals and taking them to concentration camps.

Gunnison also reported, without detail, that "in the naval war the ABCD fleets under American command were appearing to be successful against Japanese air and sea invasions," WOR announced.

By the Associated Press

The Japanese bombed Pearl Harbor and Honolulu with murderous effect Sunday and proceeded today to assault or invade Thailand and United States and British possessions in the far reaches of the Pacific in the hasty prosecution of a war which the Japanese government declared only after it had been in deadly progress for three hours.

The Hawaiian bombing came at 7:35 a. m. (10:05 a. m., San Francisco time) Sunday.

The Japanese claimed among their successes the sinking of the U. S. battleship West Virginia and the setting afire of the battleship Oklahoma—grievious blows if true.

In general the first tidings told of heavy—"doubtless very heavy losses" — to the American

Continued on Page 11, Col. 1

FINAL MORNING EXTRA

San Francisco Chronicle
THE CITY'S ONLY HOME-OWNED NEWSPAPER
FOUNDED 1865—VOL. CLIII, NO. 147 CCCC°°°°°° SAN FRANCISCO, TUESDAY, DECEMBER 9, 1941 DAILY 5 CENTS, SUNDAY 10 CENTS: DAILY AND SUNDAY PER MONTH, $1.30

COMPARATIVE TEMPERATURES

	High	Low		High	Low
San Francisco	65	51	Denver	48	20
Los Angeles	81	56	New York	35	27
Seattle	51	37	Chicago	38	34
Honolulu	—	—	New Orleans	53	46
San Jose	—	—	Salt Lake City	43	25

Local Forecast: Cloudy
Complete Report on Page 29

JAPAN PLANES NEAR S. F.—4 RAID ALARMS

THIS WORLD TODAY

By ROYCE BRIER

IN THE WHOLE Pacific world, surprise will pile on surprise in the days to come.

For the past year, with mounting tempo up to the moment of execution Sunday morning, the Japanese have been charting both the tactical operations and the larger strategy of these days. The timing was Herr Hitler's, but the work must be done by his ally. Herr Hitler has his own work to do.

To lay out the work covering so immense a theater, requires a great deal of time. Such steps as the Japanese have taken this year, with the Indo-China incursion as a keystone, have been devised to underlie, and to articulate with, the final lunge at the Pacific power of the United States.

There is no strongpoint of the American power in the Pacific (and this applies as well to our allies throughout the area) for which the Japanese have not drawn up and matured a plan of armed assault. Some of these points are necessarily beyond Japanese attack immediately, but the Japanese hope the points will later be within reach. The Golden Gate Bridge would be one of these points for delayed action, or the Boeing plant in Seattle, or the Panama Canal.

But it is necessary for us to understand quite coolly that the plans for all these operations, running into hundreds, lie in type in the War Office in Tokyo, and that the orders for execution will be issued by the Japanese General Staff when and if it is the judgment of the Staff that the operation promises success.

But "success" in the Japanese sense, as in the Hitler sense, goes much beyond strict military definition. This is always true of under-baked peoples, who lean heavily on a big front and its corollary called face.

Let us explore the implication for a moment. Success in this revolution means, in addition to the military, a political, psychological or moral success. If one of these three sucesses can be clearly scored in a military operation, it may outweigh a tactical or even a considerable strategic failure.

Now, the very opening of the war, the thrust without warning at our primary blue ocean strongpoint, was an attempt to gain a psychological success,
Continued on Page 2, Col. 1

West Coast on Alert

All Bay Radios Are Ordered Silenced; A Night of Blackouts

At 4:50 a. m. today another preliminary (the fourth) precaution signal was flashed to police headquarters of the Bay Area from the Interceptor Command at the Presidio.

All radio stations of the Bay Area were ordered off the air early this morning as the third air raid warning forced the Bay Region into another general blackout.

At 1:59 a. m. reports that unidentified planes had been detected approaching the coast were flashed to police by the Fourth Interceptor Command at the Presidio.

At 2:06 a yellow "alert" message was sent out. That was 20 minutes after radio stations were ordered from the air until further notice.

A blackout was ordered at 2:31 a. m. and 19 minutes later came the "blue" stand-by signal that enemy planes were approaching.

Almost immediately the roar of planes were heard—particularly in Marin county, in Berkeley and in San Francisco.

Reports of dogfights proved however, to be without foundation, and at 3:30 the "all clear" signal was sounded through the streets.

The army later said there was a possibility that navy planes approaching the coast on patrol had caused the alarm, but Brigadier General William Ord Ryan of the Fourth Interceptor Command who earlier in the evening had reported the first apparent attempt by enemy planes to bomb the U. S. mainland, said:

"The controller at the board of the command detected planes about which we knew nothing. We had been informed there were no friendly planes in the air, so the alert was flashed to police according to arrangement with the Civilian Defense Council.

"We are supposed to know every friendly plane in the air and its exact location."

General Ryan repeated earlier declarations that his command had not sounded any alert or warning signals for practice drills.

"We are sounding warnings when the detection signals on our control board call for them.

"Our responsibility is to notify the San Francisco Police Department that enemy aircraft has been sighted in the vicinity and that a blackout should be established."

The blackout covered the entire Bay Area, including Oakland and Berkeley and extended as far as
Continued on Page 12, Col. 3

Rossi Lauds S. F. for Aid In Blackout

Mayor Rossi last night issued this statement following the blackout:

My congratulations to those loyal citizens who heeded tonight's emergency air raid alarm.

Shortly after dusk tonight I received word from the Naval Intelligence Officer at Treasure Island that unidentified airplanes were approaching San Francisco. This warning was quickly confirmed by high Army and Navy officials.

The report was personally confirmed to me by Lieutenant General John L. DeWitt, commanding General, 4th Army.

As rapidly as possible I completed by check with the United States Army Aircraft Warning Service Fourth Interceptor Command, and with the chief of staff of the Twelfth Naval District.

I was informed that a strong squadron of enemy planes, believed of enemy origin, was off the Golden Gate. I was further informed that all local radio stations had been ordered off the air in order that enemy aircraft might not be guided by radio beams.

At the urgent insistence of Army and Navy officials I ordered as complete a blackout as possible of the city. That blackout existed for approximately two and one half hours until I was personally assured by Brigadier General Ryan, U. S. Army Aircraft Warning Service, that all was clear. I then ordered the lights on.

This emergency which threatened to become a most serious one, convinces me of the necessity for immediate and more thorough control of neon lights, billboard illumination, theater marquees, and kindred illuminations. Steps will be taken tomorrow to remedy this situation so that in the event of another blackout a more complete result may be obtained in this vitally strategic defense city.

All hospitals in San Francisco tomorrow will be warned to prepare in the future for a complete blackout and the necessity of providing their own standby lighting service.

Once again my congratulations to those who heeded the sudden appeal to blackout.

The Weather

Humidity III, the Weather Bureau turtle, paced the floor nervously, an eye on the door.

"Trouble?" asked the Weather Man.

"Just watching for the mail man," said Humidity. "Expecting a call for service any time now. The Government needs every armored unit they can get, and that's me!"

And he filed the **CLOUDY** forecast for Tuesday in an absent-minded fashion.

Complete report on page 29.

ALL OUT FOR THE GOOD OLD U.S.A. EH, BOSS!

CLOUDY

THE PRESIDENT

A Cheer Greeted Him On the Capitol Steps

Briefly and solemnly, one of the master orators of our time yesterday asked the United States Congress to declare that a state of war existed between the United States and Japan. The Congress accepted his proposal within the hour. . . . President Roosevelt forecast "an inevitable triumph." and stated that "As Commander in Chief of the Army and Navy, I have directed that all measures be taken for our defense. . . . No matter how long it may take us to overcome this premeditated invasion, the American people in their righteous might will win through to absolute victory."

Tokyo: Japanese Claim Their Navy Now Holds The Mastery of the Pacific

By the Associated Press

TOKYO (Official Radio Pickup), Tuesday, Dec. 9—Japanese Imperial headquarters announced last night the sinking of two U. S. battleships and a mine sweeper, severe damage to four other American capital ships and four cruisers and the destruction of about 100 American planes in Japan's surprise blows at Hawai, the Philippines and Guam.

The official news agency Domei quickly interpreted "these magnificent early gains" as giving Japan naval mastery over the United States in the Pacific, and said that any force which the U. S. could muster now "would be regarded as utterly inadequate to accomplish any successful outcome in an encounter with the thus-far-intact Japanese fleet."

In addition "many enemy merchant ships were captured" in the Pacific, it was announced, and the communique listed an unconfirmed report that a Japanese submarine had sunk an American aircraft carrier off Honolulu.

"No Japanese ships were lost during the fighting," it added.

Japanese newspapers identified the two American battleships declared sunk Sunday at Pearl Harbor, Hawaii, as the 31,800-ton West Virginia, and the 29,000-ton Oklahoma.

(An Italian broadcast, however, quoted Domei as listing the Oklahoma and the 33,100-ton Pennsylvania as lost.

(In Berlin, DNB said in a Tokyo dispatch that an American transport carrying 350 men had been sunk off Manila.)

(Japanese radio broadcasts picked up by a listening post in San Francisco, as reported by the United Press, told the Japanese people that the United States fleet had been reduced to "two battleships, six cruisers and one aircraft carrier" as result of Japanese attacks. The broadcasts claimed the capture of Midway and
Continued on Page 7, Col. 1

Inside . . .

The Foreign Summary covers the Russian War, Page 2; a military analysis of Malayan peninsula fighting, Page 4; a map of the entire Pacific war area, Page 4; a map of Luzon, showing Manila bombing, Page 5; Page 11 is turned over to pictures of the day; "Spirit of the War Chronicle," a drawing by Howard Brodie, Page 12; Coastal defense news is on Pages 11, 12 and 13.

War Is Declared; the Fighting

Japanese Reported Capturing a Vital Isle Off Manila Harbor; U. S. Admits Heavy Navy Losses

Manila Blitz; Guam, Wake Fall Claimed

By the Associated Press

MANILA, P. I., Tuesday, Dec. 9—Japanese troops were reported today to have landed with the probable help of "fishermen" fifth columnists on Lubang island near the entrance to Manila bay as Japanese warplanes carried out widespread raids on military objectives throughout the Philippines, including moonlit assaults on Manila itself.

The report of the landing on Lubang, some 60 miles southwest of the big American naval base of Cavite was not confirmed officially, but enough credence was placed in it that defense officers were trying urgently to contact the provincial Governor.

Japanese fifth column activity also was reported unofficially from Davao, on the big southern island of Mindanao where 25,000 Japanese present a vital threat to Philippine security. One report said 3000 armed Japanese already were resisting.

The U. S. aircraft carrier Langley was reported attacked in Malalag bay near Davao in a series of daylight raids culminating in the raids early this morning on Manila. Other daylight objectives included Clark Field, a military airdrome 40 miles north of Manila where 200 casualties were reported unofficially.

At least 150 other casualties were reported outside the Manila area for a total of 350.

(An NBC report said it was officially stated that 10 Japanese bombers attacked Nichols field at Manila, killing one soldier and wounding 12, all Americans. One hangar was damaged, and one officers' quarters was burned. Other points were bombed with 100 dead and 100
Continued on Page 5, Col. 3

Home Guard Wounds S. F. Woman

A San Francisco woman was shot and seriously wounded near the First street ramp of the San Francisco-Oakland Bay Bridge last night by an armed member of the California Home Guard.

The woman, Mrs. Marie Sayre, 27, 3155 Octavia stret, was struck near the spine by a rifle bullet that ripped through the back of the automobile in which she was riding.

Police reported the sentry, Private Albert Rownd of Company L of the Home Guard, fired after his shouted order to halt the car was ignored.

The sentry said the car was proceeding toward the bridge with its lights on during last night's blackout. He was under instructions to halt cars and direct their operators to put out their lights.

Don Sayre, the woman's husband, driving the machine, told officers he did not hear the sentry's warning.

Mrs. Sayre was taken to San Francisco Hospital. Her condition was reported serious.

The President Will Explain The Hawaii Attack Tonight; Congress Votes Speedily

By the Associated Press

WASHINGTON, Dec. 8—America declared war on Japan today after that nation's air bombers had dealt the navy the severest blow in its history and inflicted losses which raised the harsh possibility that the Japanese fleet may now enjoy a temporary superiority in the Pacific.

Some details of the savage Japanese attack—which admittedly cost the navy a battleship, a destroyer, a number of smaller craft, and killed or wounded 3000—will be given to the Nation by President Roosevelt tomorrow night in a 10 o'clock (7 p. m., P. S. T., Tuesday) radio address.

Presidential Secretary Stephen Early announced that the chief executive would speak for half an hour and that the address would be carried by all networks.

The President's speech will supplement the brief message with which he asked Congress for a declaration of war today—a request both houses followed with action breathtakingly swift.

United by the shock of battle and aroused by startling losses to the American forces in the Pacific, Congress approved the declaration by an all but unanimous vote and did so in record time—less than an hour.

The Senate voted 82 to 0 and the House 388 to 1.

The solitary negative ballot was cast by Miss Jeannette Rankin (R., Mont.). She was roundly hissed by some of her colleagues. Others gathered about her imploring her to change her vote so that the action might be made unanimous. Miss Rankin, who in 1917 burst into tears as she voted against the declaration of war on Germany was obdurate. (See Wirephoto, Page 11.)

These developments came at the close of a day which saw this country not only declare war on Japan but also accuse
Continued on Page 11, Col. 1

List of Hawaiian Casualties

By Associated Press

The following is the list of members of United States armed forces killed in the war in the East, as disclosed by official advices to the next of kin:

FIRST LIEUTENANT HANS CHRISTIANSEN, 21, Woodland, Calif., marine aviator, at Pearl Harbor.

PRIVATE GEORGE G. LESLIE, 20, Arnold, Pa., army air corps, at Hawaii

ROBERT NIEDZWICKI, 22, Grand Rapids, Mich., at Hawaii.

LIEUTENANT JAMES DERTHICK, 22, Ravenna, Ohio, army air corps at Honolulu.

SECOND LIEUTENANT FORGE A. WHITEMAN, Sedalia, Mo., air corps, at Pearl Harbor. (Trained at Randolph and Kelly Fields, Texas.)

GORDON MITCHELL, Hoisington, Kas., air corps at Hawaii.

PRIVATE DONALD PLANT, 22, of Wausau, Wis., air corps, at Wheeler Field, Hawaii.

PRIVATE DEAN W. CEBERT of Galesburg, Ill., at Honolulu.

SERGEANT JAMES GUTHRIE, Republican Grove, Va., air corps engineer, in Hawaii.

THEO. F. BYRD, 20, Tampa, Fla., private first class, air corps, at Wheeler Field, Hawaii.

SERGEANT GEORGE R. SCHMERSAHL, 22, Bloomfield, N. J., air corps at Hawaii.

PRIVATE ROBERT SHATTUCK, 21, Blue River, Wis., at Hickam Field, Hawaii.

CORPORAL MALACHI J. CASHEN, Lamont, Iowa, at Pearl Harbor.

SERGEANT VINCENT M. MORAN, Stamford, Conn., at Honolulu.

THIS WORLD TODAY

By ROYCE BRIER

IT IS NOT impossible that the Russian winter offensive has spent the greater part of its force.

There is no sure sign of this, and the true situation is beyond our estimate. There are little, vague signs, such as the failure to clear the Crimea, after a good start, or to unhinge the extreme right of the German siege lines before Leningrad at Schusselburg.

These signs might easily constitute tactical details in the far-flung strategy of the battlelines, that is, the Russians are punching where the punching is best, and when some operation develops difficulties they turn to a more promising sector of the front. This is classic strategy, and the Germans have brought it to a high state in their European campaigns.

The successful Russian sectors at present lie south of Vyasma, where they are 100 miles from Smolensk, and east of the Dnieper bend. Without confirmation, they are reported 20 miles from the river.

Notwithstanding, the terrors of a winter offensive in the weather prevailing are inconceivable to us, and as the Russians slowly advance through blizzard and inhuman cold, their transport problems pile up.

They have about six weeks of winter until the thaw. When the thaw begins there is some doubt if they can advance farther. Neither can the Germans, but the thaw will lift the burden of cold from them, and permit an immobile recuperation. The thaw is thus a stone wall for both armies, many experts believe, and it lasts six or eight weeks.

The Russians are waiting the thaw. Herr Hitler said last week he is waiting the same thing, rather, waiting for the end of the thaw, especially in the south, when the roads would harden. Then he would go.

At any rate, the thaw is likely to create a stalemate, if one doesn't appear before then. There have been hints of rifts in German morale at the front, but nothing decisive, and Moscow has frowned on the use of the word "rout" to describe the German retirement. So far as we can learn, German rear guard operations have been stubborn, and the whole retirement orderly.

So if the Russians can reach a line roughly Lenigrad-Smolensk-Dnieper by the time the thaw begins, they will have done an

Continued on Page 2, Col. 1

U. S. Fleet: Offensive Patrol

Photo Story On Page 24

San Francisco Chronicle

THE CITY'S ONLY HOME-OWNED NEWSPAPER

FINAL Morning Edition

FOUNDED 1865—VOL. CLIV, NO. 20 CCCC*** SAN FRANCISCO, WEDNESDAY, FEBRUARY 4, 1942 DAILY 5 CENTS, SUNDAY 10 CENTS: DAILY AND SUNDAY PER MONTH, $1.50

NEW JAP PUSH TO THE SOUTH!

War in Far East

Huge Jap Convoy Moves On Indies, Burma; Marines; Navy Reinforce MacArthur

Grim Singapore Awaits Gigantic Frontal Assault

By C. YATES McDANIEL
Associated Press Staff Writer

SINGAPORE, Feb. 3—Invading Japanese columns, expanding by the hour as reinforcements poured down through Southern Malaya in an unceasing stream, still stood silent before Johore Strait tonight but the supreme hour of peril seemed near at hand.

Apparently heralding an imminent attempt to force the mile-wide water barrier by troops, enemy bombers rained fire and explosives on Singapore in violent, unending attacks, while British land defenses, forming a 70-mile perimeter, grimly endured the fourth day of siege—prepared for anything. Afield all was quiet save for intermittent artillery fire.

BURMA AWAITS HUGE JAP DRIVE

In Burma, too, little fighting was reported today but a determined Japanese drive to take Rangoon and cut the Burma road, China's highway of supply, was awaited.

Chinese information of huge Japanese troop movements southward in the Formosa strait—a single enemy convoy of 69 ships having been sighted off Amoy—suggested that the assailant was gambling high in an effort to quiet the rising menace of American and other reinforcements which have been hitting him hard in Indies waters and in the Burma-Thailand area.

Twenty-one ships of the convoy were transports, the Chinese spokesman said, and 41 were warships.

He said, too, that several Japanese divisions which had been moving south on the Tientsin-Pukow railroad on January 23 had been diverted at Tsinan to the North China port of Tsingtao and there embarked on waiting transports; and

Continued on Page 6, Col. 6

U. S. Torpedo Boat Sinks Jap In Manila Bay

By RICHARD L. TURNER
Associated Press Staff Writer

WASHINGTON, Feb. 3—A battalion of marines and bluejackets is fighting with General Douglas MacArthur's hard-pressed men on Bataan peninsula, the navy announced tonight, and an American motor torpedo boat has torpedoed a Japanese warship in Manila bay.

Making these disclosures, the navy also revealed that one of its tankers, the U. S. S. Neches, a 5400-ton craft, had been sunk in an undesignated area by an enemy submarine. Fifty-six men have not been accounted for, it said, but 126 are safe at an unnamed port.

TWO JAP ATTACKS ARE THROWN BACK

The department's statement followed the issuance of an army communique which revealed that MacArthur's fighting men repulsed two Jap attempts to land behind his lines on Bataan peninsula last night and that an American counter-attack had overrun three lines of enemy trenches.

The navy gave no details about the navy bluejackets and marines now fighting with MacArthur, simply stating that they had been organized into a battalion and were fighting the Japs. They presumably consist of several hundred men.

There was speculation that these forces may have been left behind MacArthur's lines when the navy withdrew from the Philippines.

Although the navy announced when its base at Cavite was abandoned that its personnel had been evacuated, it was recalled that MacArthur's original Bataan line encompassed the secondary naval station at Olongapo on Subic bay.

When the navy announced the formation of the battalion today,

Continued on Page 6, Col. 1

Jap Bombers Attack a Vital Dutch Naval Base on Java

By WITT HANCOCK
Associated Press Staff Writer

BATAVIA, Feb. 3—The Japanese invader broadened his offensive to planes at the most vital position of the United Nations in the East Indies, the Dutch naval base of Surabaya (Soerabaja) on Java.

Twenty-six Japanese bombers escorted by swarms of fighter planes rained explosives on the great base and its surrounding airdromes in an attempt to smash the Allied offensive power which apparently has kept a Japanese invasion armada bottled up in Macassar Strait more than 300 miles to the north.

The terrific assault, lasting more than two hours, caused extensive destruction from the heart of the city to outlying airdromes. It was in the area surrounding the air fields that the greatest number of dead and injured were counted. From the military establishments the Japanese headed for the center of the city and there they unloaded bomb after bomb on civilian establishments. Various shops, a hotel and a Chinese cemetery were hit.

(The fact that fighters as well as bombers appeared over Java indicated that the enemy had brought aircraft carriers into the Java sea, since the nearest known Japanese land base, at Balik Papan on Borneo some 500 miles to the north, is well beyond the effective range of ordinary fighter craft).

This first big air raid on Java came a day after United States bombers sank two and probably three more Japanese transports off Balik Papan, Eastern Borneo port.

Besides Surabaya, now vital to the United Nations as a naval base because of immobilization of besieged Singapore, the Japanese also attacked Rembang, Malang, Madioen and Magetan, all within a 125-mile radius of Surabaya.

Some naval establishments and a few aircraft lying in the eastern Java port were damaged, and some serious casualties were suffered, the Dutch communique said in preliminary reports.

The news agency Aneta said Surabaya's anti-aircraft batteries shot down one bomber and several fighter planes.

In describing the attack on Malang, the site of an important airfield 60 miles south of Surabaya, Aneta said the alert sounded at 1 a. m., followed 15 minutes later by the appearance of three Japanese fighter planes.

A few minutes later, four more fighters roared over, and only a single Allied craft arose when the Japanese bombers, flying at 10,000 feet, swept across the airport.

One grounded Allied plane was hit and set afire, but no other damage was done, it said.

(At Melbourne, meanwhile, it was learned Australia's volunteer defense corps will be vastly increased and schooled principally in guerrilla tactics to be employed when and if the Japanese attempt an invasion of the commonwealth mainland.)

SEE MAP ON PAGE 8.

OFFENSIVE PATROL IN THE PACIFIC—A navy patrol bomber soars past an aircraft carrier somewhere at sea. This Associated Press Wire-photo was made during an offensive patrol against the Japanese. For more pictures of the patrol at sea, see the picture page, 24.

Aliens in California: U. S. to Move Thousands Inland to Undisclosed Farm Colonies

Thousands of enemy aliens ordered out of California defense zones will be moved to inland farm colonies by the Federal Government.

This was revealed here yesterday by Tom Clark, alien coordinator for the Western defense command.

It was the first indication of Government plans for the mass evacuation of Japanese, German and Italian nationals from 86 forbidden zones in California. A few areas must be cleared by February 24, most by February 15.

In addition, he announced, the Department of Justice will establish other restricted areas into which enemy aliens will be admitted only by pass.

The evacuees, Clark promised, would be given every consideration during the move—but they will be moved, without exception.

Other developments yesterday included the following:

1—With many strategic defense zones "overlooked" by the first 86 proscribed areas, Washington officials predicted another batch of forbidden zones to be announced within 48 hours.

2—State authorities began a careful census of all alien farmers in the San Joaquin valley, including a check of the amounts of vegetable insecticides they had on hand.

3—Federal bureaus were mobilizing to aid in the resettlement of alien evacuees.

4—Enemy aliens were registering for new identification certificates, jamming photographers' shops for the required identification pictures.

5—Surveys showed the enforced evacuation will involve approximately 3000 in Pittsburg—approximately one-third of the city's population; 3000 in Monterey and 1600 from Alameda.

6—San Francisco Supervisors

Continued on Page 6, Col. 1

Navy May Take Over Stanford!

There is a strong possibility that the Navy will take over Stanford University as well as all Stanford sports facilities. For details see first page of the Sporting Green.

Mountain Blasted To Gain Copper

SILVER CITY, N. M., Feb. 3 (UP)—In a single giant blast of 90,000 pounds of powder the Nevada Consolidated Copper Corp. today shook down almost an entire mountain to expose 450,000 tons of copper ore for use in the national defense effort.

The huge blast was made at the Chino open-pit mine at Santa Rita, New Mexico.

Lombard Film Premiere Feb. 19

HOLLYWOOD, Feb. 3 (AP)—Carole Lombard's last picture, "To Be or Not To Be," will be released to theaters over the Nation March 6, United Artists announced tonight. It will be given a world premiere in three Los Angeles theaters February 19.

San Diego Has Two Hour Alert

SAN DIEGO, Feb. 3 (AP)—The Fourth Interceptor Command ordered an air raid alert in San Diego at 8:44 tonight. The all-clear was sounded at 10:38 p. m. Army interceptor officials gave no reason for the alarm. There was no blackout.

De Valera Wants Army of 500,000

DUBLIN, Feb. 3 (UP)—Premier Eamon De Valera said today that Eire must have 500,000 soldiers "trained to fight as well as any men on earth."

S. F. Laid Out For One-Way Street Traffic

A system of one-way streets throughout the downtown area has been mapped by city planning experts, it was reported yesterday.

The proposed pattern was submitted to Mayor Rossi, and represents a six-month study by city planners. George W. Melville, city planning engineer, said one-way streets would help solve traffic and transportation problems.

Traffic on Market street, under the plan, would flow only in a westerly direction. Only two sets of street car tracks would be required, thus allowing two additional street lanes for automobile traffic.

CRITICISMS OF THE PLAN WITHHELD

On Mission street, the flow would be easterly, with a "loop" connecting with Market street at the Embarcadero. The system would be extended to all streets in the area between Van Ness avenue and the Embarcadero and from Clay street to Towr d.

Mayor Rossi withheld any detailed criticisms of the plan, observing only that unification of

Continued on Page 8, Col. 5

Nation Still Has 4,200,000 Jobless

WASHINGTON, Feb. 3 (AP)—The WPA said today that despite the accelerated war porduction effort the number of unemployed had risen by 400,000 in January and now totaled 4,200,000.

Civilian Defense: Rossi Says Needs Are Critical, Urges $5,000,000 Bond Issue

San Francisco faced a showdown on wartime finances yesterday, with surpluses vanishing and a $5,000,000 bond issue suggested as a solution to civilian defense needs.

Mayor Rossi advanced the bond issue possibility after receipt of word from the Office of Civilian Defense that allocation of Federal equipment will fall far short of meeting the city's requirements for equipment.

APPROPRIATION WILL BUY FIRE EQUIPMENT

Auxiliary fire fighting equipment and gas masks will be purchased from the $100,000,000 civil defense appropriation made by Congress, OCD announced, and requisitions from San Francisco and other cities in "target areas" will not be needed.

However, Fire Chief Charles Brennan said the allotment of fire-fighting equipment would not meet San Francisco's needs. Allocations of gas masks have not yet been made public.

At the same time, Berkeley took steps for a charter amendment to raise additional funds and committees of the San Francisco Board of Supervisors authorized the Mayor to investigate all possible sources of revenue, even to the extent of recommending expenditures of the city's $3,000,000 cash reserve fund.

Mayor Rossi appeared before a joint meeting of the police and finance committees of the Board of Supervisors and said a bond election "in the neighborhood of $5,000,000 may be necessary."

Supervisor Green, member of the finance committee, asked Controller Harold J. Boyd: "Is there any fund of the city government that can be tapped to provide these necessary moneys?"

Boyd replied: "The answer is no."

His reply was seen as an indication that he would not agree to spending the reserve fund, which some observers say would be equivalent to bankrupting the city and would leave it without reserves in case of a disaster.

The Mayor's $300,000 emergency fund has been exhausted and recently the Board of Supervisors made $300,000 available from departmental surpluses.

USE OF CASH RESERVE FUND WAITS RULING

Later, Rossi said legality of use of the cash reserve fund may have to be decided by a court ruling. He stressed, however, that $65,000 is available in the budget for holding a special election if decision is

Continued on Page 11, Col. 1

Department of Crystal Gazing

LOS ANGELES, Feb. 3 (AP)—Mrs. Edna Gormley, 24, called it cruelty because her husband, Clayton, put more faith in the predictions of a fortune teller than in her, and won a divorce today.

"He accused me of going out with other men in the future," she testified.

Military Digest: The Far East, African and Russian Fronts

Singapore and Surabaya, the two great Allied naval bases in the Southwest Pacific, are entering a period of appalling air assault. The correspondents at the former city were not permitted to say how great the day's damage had been, but they were trying indirectly to indicate it was much more than the communique admits.' The RAF and perhaps U. S. flying fortress squadrons struck back at Jap bases at Kluang about 50 miles up the peninsula.

The Chinese heard that the Jap 16th Division had been cut to pieces in Malaya before the British retreat, and that a fleet of transports sufficient for another full division, with no less than 41 warships in escort, was moving down the coast. The German radio said the Japs were concentrating naval forces south of the island.

Singapore morale, terrible at the beginning of the war, may be on the upgrade, now that the hell of air bombardment has really begun. Governor Sir Shenton Thomas and Commanding General A. E. Percival worked in their shirtsleeves among the debris, side by side with coolies. The "pukka Sahibs" are evidently growing humble.

Dutch Indies

Surabaya, city of 350,000, is the only major naval base available to the Allies in the Southwest Pacific. Bad news is the Dutch admission that 26 bombers escorted by many fighters attacked it and its satellite airdromes, causing considerable damage. An Aneta (Dutch news agency) dispatch says at Malang airdrome only one Allied fighter went up after the Jap bombers, though there was plenty of warning.

The Jap fighters almost all belong to the navy, and though slow, outrange any others in the world. They are obviously operating from bases at Kuching, Sarawak; Balikpapan, Dutch Borneo, and perhaps Kendari, Celebes, or from carriers near these points.

U. S. Flying Fortresses sank two transports, and perhaps a third, in a raid of Balikpapan.

Burma

The Chungking spokesman said the Japs have already established several pontoon bridgeheads across the Salween river, but added that the Chinese forces will make contact with the Japs soon. Tokyo said Martaban, across the river mouth, was subjected to a "mass bombing," and that powerful forces are crossing the Salween for an attack on Rangoon, port of the Burma road.

The Philippines

General MacArthur reports repulse of another Jap landing attempt—this under naval escort—on the west (ocean) coast of Bataan Peninsula. U. S. night fighters spotted and machine-gunned the invaders, indicating a shadow air force is being maintaind. A battalion of bluejackets and marines, probably from Olongapo naval base, has been organized to fight with the USAFFE under MacArthur. Another torpedo boat may have sunk a Jap warship in night action inside Manila Bay. The ominous aspect to this is that any warship got past the guns of Corregidor. It may have sneaked in by night.

Libya

There were hints of a British counter-offensive, although Rome claims Cyrene, 110 miles beyond Bengasi has been by-passed.

Russia

Hitler was reported rushing up reinforcements to the Ukraine, where the Red Army is said to be within 20 miles of Dnieperopetrovsk. The march on Smolensk, in the north, continues, but there are no details.

COMPLETE COVERAGE ON TEACHERS' CONVENTION

San Francisco Chronicle

THE CITY'S ONLY HOME-OWNED NEWSPAPER

FINAL Morning Edition

FOUNDED 1865—VOL. CLIV, NO. 40 CCCC*** SAN FRANCISCO, TUESDAY, FEBRUARY 24, 1942 DAILY 5 CENTS, SUNDAY 12 CENTS: DAILY AND SUNDAY PER MONTH, $1.30

SUB SHELLS CALIFORNIA!

THIS WORLD TODAY

By ROYCE BRIER

WANDERING ALONG the Hooghli quay in Calcutta or through the cloth bazaar in Bombay, you might be aware of a vague mental discomfort, unrelated to the physical discomfort of the temperatures and the smells.

This discomfort could be characterized as a moral riddle. Now we all perpetually face moral riddles, and when we die we have licked some, and been licked by some, though often our final judgments on this are delusory. And history is full of such riddles, the black-and-white interpretation being unsubstantial and in defiance of the record.

So here is India, constituting one-fifth of mankind, and all the Indians you will ever see in a lifetime are incomprehensible beings. They are across an impassible abyss from you. Their souls are indescribably remote, and all you can see or feel is the land they live in, and a little of how they live, and a little of the people who rule them, and your deepest and most awful feeling about them is their countlessness.

Even in China you have not this inner sense, let us put it this way, a sense of biological anonymity, of smooth uniformity of mass. It is like a faraway sighing, a whispering rhythm induced by God for His own sufficient purpose.

Well, you know this is important to you, to your own world, for you suspect a fifth of your fellow men were not put there and left there for nothing. And that engenders the riddle, which has a hard-surfaced, pragmatic, political aspect, for you know this inscrutible myriad is directed by a few men of your own kind, men no better than you, and no worse, either.

Scene Offhand you might doubt this, wandering in Calcutta or Bombay or Madras, thinking the British raj wrong. But you, as an American, have the theory, though the practice may differ. It is no good to say, as Herr Hitler does, that the British took India long ago, because most of us decline to answer for the sins of our forebears, being answerable for enough right now.

So what is right about this India, and what is wrong? That's what makes you uncomfortable, aside from the humidity, for it is much more comfortable to dis-

Continued on Page 5, Col. 1

War Strikes California

Big Raider Fires on Oil Refinery 8 Miles North of Santa Barbara

Volley of Some 15 Shots From Deck Gun Does No Damage

Axis shells fell for the first time on California soil last night.

A big enemy submarine, presumably Japanese, surfaced half a mile from shore in the Santa Barbara channel, and hurled some 15 shells from its deck gun in an attack on an oil refinery near the town of Goleta, eight miles north of Santa Barbara.

There were no fires, no damage, no casualties, in this, the first and long expected attack on the United States mainland in this war.

The shelling appeared to be directed at the Bankline Oil Company refineries and derricks on the edge of the Ellwood oil field, one of America's big petroleum producing centers, 350 miles south of San Francisco.

The 11th Naval District in an official announcement, early today released an account of the shelling by F. W. Borden, superintendent of the Bankline refinery:

"At 7:10 p. m. (PWT) one large submarine came to the surface about one mile offshore and fired approximately 15 shells from a deck gun," Borden reported in the Navy statement.

"One direct hit was registered on a well, causing minor damage to the pumping unit and the derrick. There were several close misses on a crude oil storage tank and a gasoline plant.

"Apparently no damage was caused by these shells," Borden said. "A complete survey of the ground has not yet been made and there may be superficial damage. Whatever other damage is discovered will not be extensive.

"No fires were started as a result of the firing. No tanks were hit. From fragments of shell found and marks on the ground it is believed a four of five-inch gun was used. The firing was done leisurely, apparently only one gun being used. It required about 25 minutes to fire the approximately 15 shells."

Only last week President Roosevelt had warned, in a press conference, of the likelihood of enemy attacks on American soil.

The audacious attack occurred at about 7:15 p. m., just as President Roosevelt was delivering his radio address from Washington.

It appeared probable in some quarters that the submarine commander deliberately timed his attack to coincide with Mr. Roosevelt's speech.

All Japanese submarines carry

Continued on Page 4, Col. 6

BROADWAY DIMS

CHICAGO, Feb. 23 (AP)—The Wrigley gum sign on Times Square on Broadway, New York, will be dismantled beginning tomorrow to conserve electric power. The sign is one of the largest in the world. It consumes enough electricity to illuminate a city of 10,000. A block long and 10 stories high, the sign was completed in 1936.

Indies and Burma: Bali Invasion Fleet Destroyed; Rangoon Is in Peril

Enemy Loses 19 to 36 Ships In New Thrust

By the Associated Press

BANDOENG, Dutch East Indies, Feb. 23—The Japanese have overrun part of Bali and control the airport at Denpasar, on the southeast of the island near its only good harbor, but his entire invading fleet has been destroyed, damaged or dispersed and their landing troops are isolated, the Dutch announced tonight.

Thus was summed up the first phase of the invader's thrust at the near approaches to the Java keystone in the Allied arch—a thrust in which Japanese seapower suffered, under co-ordinated American-Dutch bomber and warship fire, its gravest wounds since the battle of Macassar strait off Borneo.

Again, the enemy had reached a limited objective, but this time at a cost proportionately greater even than the price he paid at Macassar.

(According to unofficial calcula-

Continued on Page 4, Col. 5

British Lines Wavering As Japs Smash On

By the Associated Press

LONDON, Feb. 23—All Burma was threatened gravely tonight as Japanese assault units, probably reinforced by troops from Singapore, were reported smashing against the swaying British lines between the Bilin and Sittang rivers.

British authorities admitted hopes of holding Rangoon were dwindling and that its fall probably would open the way to Japanese invasion of the whole Colony, the barrier to India and gateway to China.

The scant news of the Burma fighting came from Calcutta and Chungking, suggesting that the cable to Rangoon, at the mouth of

Continued on Page 4, Col. 4

Burlesque Bows Out of Manhattan

NEW YORK, Feb. 23 (AP)—Burlesque quietly bowed out of Manhattan tonight with the closing of Broadway's Gaiety Theater.

Landis Appoints OCD Assistant

WASHINGTON, Feb. 23 (AP)—James M. Landis, director of the Office of Civilian Defense, tonight appointed Jonathan Daniels, North Carolina editor, to be assistant director in charge of civilian mobilization.

This division will replace the voluntary participation division of which Mrs. Franklin D. Roosevelt, recently resigned, was the head.

Sedition Hearing

Noble Lauds Japs, Hitler; Jeers at FDR

Special to The Chronicle

LOS ANGELES, Feb. 23—Nazi sympathizers shocked their listeners from their seats today at an interim legislative committee hearing on American Legion charges of sedition and subversive activities.

The legislators hardly believing their ears, heard one of the witnesses uphold the Japanese' sneak attack upon Pearl harbor; heard him praise Hitler; heard him declare the Allies had already lost the war; heard him belittle the gallant defense of the Philippines by General MacArthur.

The witness was Robert Noble, pension movement leader and head of a new anti-war organization here called "Friends of Progress." As a result of his defiant admissions and other facts brought out at the hearing, the committee considered prompt action on an American Legion recommendation that they ask President Roosevelt to appoint a board to investigate enemy propaganda declared rampant in many parts of California.

The Legion charged the Federal sedition act is not being enforced in the State.

Noble and several other witnesses, including Ellis O. Jones, founder of the National Copperheads, were taken into custody by the FBI some

Continued on Page 13, Col. 1

California's alien coordinator says we need a custodian of alien property. Alien curfew goes into effect at 12 o'clock tonight. For details see Page 13.

Arrest Made in Attack Killing

CHICO, Feb. 23 (AP)—Officers, tracing an automobile abandoned near the body, today arrested Laurence "Larry" Fraser, 30, of Chico, in the killing of Mrs. Larue McGaha Dodd, 26-year-old divorcee from Altadena.

Mrs. Dodd's body was found on a river bank four miles west of town. She had been raped, beaten and her throat was cut.

District Attorney J. M. McPherson said Fraser had admitted he "picked up" a girl yesterday but that he was so drunk he recalled nothing more.

The President's Speech

U. S. Warned to Expect Further Setbacks Before Tide Turns

FDR TEXT

TEXT of President Roosevelt's speech to the Nation last night will be found on Page 8. Reference to the world map printed in yesterday morning's Chronicle will prove an invaluable aid in reading the text.

Thousands of U. S. Troops Already in Southwest Pacific

By the United Press

WASHINGTON, Feb. 23—President Roosevelt revealed tonight that "thousands" of American troops, as well as bomber and fighter planes, already are in action in the Southwest Pacific, and promised that American production would overwhelm the Axis on land, sea and in the air so that "we, not they, will make the final peace."

But he warned that the Nation must pull together, saying that "we can lose this war only if we slow up our efforts or if we waste our ammunition sniping at each other."

The President's report was in the form of a fireside chat, which was broadcast internationally. It was heard by millions of Americans in their homes and by other thousands gathered at George Washington dinners to liquidate Democratic party indebtedness.

HE CALLS FOR A THREEFOLD PURPOSE

He recommended three "high purposes" for all Americans as a means of combatting Axis attempts to "divide and conquer."

1—No work stoppages because of labor-management disputes until the war is won.

2—No special privileges or special gains for any group or occupation.

3—Cheerful sacrifices for the war effort.

In a war report to the Nation and the world, he said that Japan had a tremendous initial advantage at the start of the conflict because of her multitude of bases on the Pacific island stepping stones and the China, Indo-China, Thailand and Malay coasts, but he added:

"We knew that the war as a whole would have to be fought and won by a process of attrition against Japan itself. . . . Nothing in the past two months has caused us to revise this basic strategy."

PEOPLE WILL BE FULLY INFORMED

He renewed his promise to keep the people informed of the progress of the war, declaring the Government has unmistakable confidence in "your ability to hear the worst, without flinching or losing heart." But, he said they must in turn have "complete confidence" that the Government is withholding only information of value to the enemy."

He struck directly at reports that losses at Pearl Harbor had been worse than officially reported and at claims that the "sneak" attack

Continued on Page 5, Col. 8

Educators: Act Today to Insure Future, Spokesman Warns the Convention

By STANLEY BAILEY

American education has declared total war.

A solemn warning was given to the seventy-second annual convention of the American Association of School Administrators yesterday:

"What we here now and those back home do or fail to do this very day and in the strategic days that lie ahead may determine the course of mankind forever."

The message was delivered by Dr. Alexander J. Stoddard, superintendent of schools of Philadelphia, to some of the estimated 15,000 members of the association, affiliated organizations and California teachers gathered in the city and to all the people of the Nation.

Talk of war and how the schools can serve and what the educators should do ran all through the far-flung activities of the meeting—at technical group meetings, at hundreds of conferences in hotel rooms, in other speeches before general sessions.

Speakers stressed that what has happened to the country as a whole is happening to education. Permanent changes have been made. "Vast changes" must be made.

Many urged full teaching of the democratic concept, both as an inspiration for full effort to defeat dictatorship and as a full guide for the peace that is to follow.

"Any picture of what is involved for education in wartime, to be understandable, must be projected against the strategic background of the total national effort," declared John Lund, senior specialist in education of school administrators, United States Office of Education, in addressing an evening general session.

"The war and the peace must be won together. The line between war and peace is not going to be sharply and nicely drawn. We are not going to be at war one day and at peace the next. . .

"The will with which we fight, the knowledge with which we fight, the purpose for which we fight and the spirit in which we fight will determine the kind of a peace that we win. . .

"Now will and knowledge and purpose and spirit are not produced in factories. . . They are the products of that process of growth that goes on in every human individual," he said.

"We must fight the dictators and all their forces, not only with greater force, but with ideas and faith."

The schools and colleges of America, he added, "are in the midst of a conversion process every bit as significant and vital as the conversion of the factories in America. I wonder if we realize fully that all of this business of expansion and acceleration that occupies so much of our time and attention is not going to stop when the war is won."

Speaking of post-war problems, and the return of America's fighters, he added: "The planning job for education extends far into the future."

Lund said that to the usual lists of civil liberties, there be added the right to work, to fair pay, to

Continued on Page 9, Col. 3

Tallulah Rested, Leaves Hospital

NEW YORK, Feb. 23 (AP)—Tallulah Bankhead, stage and radio star, last night left Lenox Hospital, where she went Wednesday for a few days' rest. The actress suffered a weakening attack of influenza several weeks ago.

60,000 Work Hours Gone Forever!

200 Bay Defense Plants Shut Down on Washington's Birthday

One-third of a Flying Fortress . . .

One thousand hours of .50-caliber machine-gun fire . . .

One dozen anti-tank guns . . .

One of these three was lost to American soldiers yesterday as unions and employers in 200 small war industry plants in the San Francisco Bay Area were immobilized by a dispute over the overtime rate of pay for Washington's birthday.

Workers in the plants took a holiday and the man-hour loss was estimated between 60,000 and 100,000 hours. This despite a plea from Donald Nelson, U. S. production chief, that all plants continue to operate.

Two more such days would be the equivalent of one Flying Fortress or 60 badly needed military training planes.

War took no holiday in Java or in Burma—or on the shores of California. While guns roared in the Pacific, small machine shops, machine tool plants and small but vital foundries were silent during the day. More than half of the plants called by Chronicle reporters failed to answer the telephone, presumably shut for the day.

Less than half were working with skeleton crews.

These were the plants making parts on sub-contracts for planes, ships, guns, shells, tools. They repair heavy production machinery. They can foods. They produce electrical

Continued on Page 6, Col. 1

The Story of the Survey

Nation-wide attention turned to San Francisco yesterday as approximately 200 small war industry shops closed down for Washington's birthday. Estimates of man hours lost ran as high as 100,000. Two San Francisco Chronicle reporters, Stanton Delaplane and Robert O'Brien, made a telephone survey that showed approximately 60,000 hours lost. Though this number is small in relation to the total hours worked in the country, it assumes importance because Donald Nelson, U. S. production chief, specifically asked that all work continue, because while war goes on 24 hours a day, these production hours can never be regained.

THIS WORLD TODAY

A Page of Last Bataan Photos!

See Page 8

San Francisco Chronicle

THE CITY'S ONLY HOME-OWNED NEWSPAPER

FINAL Morning Edition

FOUNDED 1865—VOL. CLIV, NO. 85 CCCC*** SAN FRANCISCO, FRIDAY, APRIL 10, 1942 DAILY 5 CENTS, SUNDAY 12 CENTS: PER MONTH $1.40 DAILY AND SUNDAY

BATAAN'S STORY!

Exhaustion, Disease End Epic

THIS WORLD TODAY

By ROYCE BRIER

IN THESE long and solemn hours when we are giving an ever-growing share of thought to the fate of our country, now fairly entering the storm, we will give some time to Bataan.

It was a word having no meaning for us short weeks ago, and when we first saw it in print we were not sure how to spell it. It's only a reach of mountain and jungle far away, but as the storm gathered dark on the distant horizon, a man divined in Bataan a sanctuary from which the foe might be held off for awhile.

It was no accident that Bataan became a sanctuary, it was the insight of the man who knew war and the foe, who saw the storm gathering and knew what it would be like.

So into this reach of mountain and jungle he flung twoscore thousand, what he could salvage from the forlorn scramble in the broader valleys, a motley of Yankees and Filipinos with nothing but guns and guts, nothing in the air to speak of. And the foe had everything.

There was no way of getting much help to them. The foe owned the air and the sea, and for every ship we sent them, two were lost.

So that was it. They knew that was it, but they settled down in their fox-holes, and they stood the foe off. They never complained, though they knew there was no daylight for them, no streets where they would ever march to the cheers that ring for victors, nothing but a slow and hopeless struggle, and in the end for most of them capture and an unstinted misery.

For almost a hundred days they stood there.

Now, Americans have not been in a hole like this for many a year, not since they were backed up against the river in Shiloh's woods, not since they crouched in the trenches at Petersburg and beheld the last flickering of the Lost Cause.

Americans in your time and mine have fought hard and have fought well, but they have fought with hope, and with a consciousness of strength and in alliance with time and space, and they have won. But these men of Bataan found time and space standing pitiless against them, and there was no help for it.

So maybe we thought, as there stretched long years since we had fought a hopeless fight, that we wouldn't be so good at it. May-

Continued on Page 5, Col. 7

THE FOX HOLES OF BATAAN have been abandoned, but in the American imagination they have taken root as a battle cry nearly the equal of Pearl Harbor. It was from these fox holes—these sometimes hand-dug trenches—that American and Filipino troops carried on the resistance which enabled Bataan to hold out for three besieged months. This Associated Press Wirephoto shows four of those defenders huddled in a typical—if somewhat spacious—fox hole, while shrapnel from a Japanese battery bursts about them. A full page of the latest Bataan peninsula photos (that fill out the story released by the Army Signal Corps) will be found on Page 8.

Defeats in Bataan, Burma

36,853 of Wainwright's Men Dead or Face Capture; Japs Sink Two British Cruisers Near India

Japs Close To Burma Oil Fields

By the Associated Press

LONDON, April 9—The Japanese planes have blasted the British heavy cruisers Dorsetshire and Cornwall to the bottom of the Indian ocean, thus virtually opening the way for an invasion of India by way of the Ganges basin. Heavy enemy naval forces now aprowl in the Bay of Bengal remained opposed only by light British units.

Thus superior at sea, where he already had destroyed several Allied merchant ships, the enemy for the first time hurled his bombers at the British naval base of Trincomalee on Ceylon, working undetermined damage.

(A late British announcement disclosed that an enemy naval squadron had been assaulted by Allied bombers. It spoke of near misses scored against an enemy carrier, implying, although not specifically stated, that it had been damaged.

(The British say four Japanese fighters were shot down during the attack on the aircraft carrier, and that six more planes were bagged in defending Trincomalee. Six other aircraft were "probably destroyed," the communique said. "Some of our aircraft are missing," the communique added.)

NO CONFIRMATION OF BRITISH REINFORCEMENTS

While some London naval reporters speculated that one of the biggest naval battles of history was about to open in Bengal Bay, this could be made possible only by the arrival in those waters of large British naval units. Some hope was expressed that a British squadron described March 28 by the Italians as two battleships, two aircraft carriers, a cruiser and light forces

Continued on Page 2, Col. 1

Little Hope Is Held For Handful of Men Fighting on Corregidor

By the Associated Press

WASHINGTON, April 9—The heroic epic of Bataan Peninsula ended today with the Japanese victorious through the sheer overwhelming weight of hordes of fresh troops—and with most of the 36,853 American and Filipino soldiers slain or facing captivity.

Cut off from reinforcement, outnumbered by five, six, seven or even eight to one, tragically deficient in air power, and exhausted by short rations, disease and constant battle, a courageous band of fighting men was forced to a bitter but inevitable defeat.

Radio messages still were being relayed tonight to Corregidor, and other Manila bay fortresses were at last report still holding out, but there was only scant hope that they could long stand and no hope at all that the majority of the men of Bataan could ever find shelter there.

Bataan went down fighting, on its feet and never on its knees.

For days, the Japs had been attacking in waves, sending rank upon rank of fresh troops against sleepless and fatigue-ridden men.

Today, Lieutenant General Jonathan Wainwright, who took command when General Douglas MacArthur was transferred to Australia, reported the enemy had enveloped his eastern flank manned by his second corps. To relieve the situation he ordered the first corps to counter-attack.

Obeying to the last, the first corps staggered forward for the supreme and doomed effort—an effort, said a War Department communique, that "failed due to the complete physical exhaustion of the troops."

Wainwright's left had fallen, his center had fallen, his right had fallen, and from Washington President Roosevelt sent him word to make whatever decision that he felt must be made. This meant that the General was free to end resistance, if as appeared continued resistance would only mean a futile loss of more blood.

In view of these developments the War Department concluded and announced that "this situation indicates the probability that the defenses of Bataan have been overcome."

And to this, Secretary of War Stimson added at a press conference:

"Our troops, outnumbered and worn down by successive attacks by fresh troops, exhausted by insufficient rations and disease prevalent on that peninsula, finally had their lines broken and enveloped by the enemy.

"A long but gallant defense has been worn down and overthrown.

"We have nothing but praise and admiration for the commanders and the men who have conducted this epic chapter in American history."

But even as he sadly conceded a great reversal, Secretary

Continued on Page 6, Col. 1

OUR Fight For Freedom

". . . that we here highly resolve that these dead shall not have died in vain; that this Nation, under God, shall have a new birth of freedom, and that government of the people, by the people, and for the people, shall not perish from the earth."

—From Abraham Lincoln's Gettysburg Address, November 19, 1863.

Earl Warren Will Run for Governor

Attorney General Earl Warren will be a candidate for Governor.

Ending prolonged speculation, Warren announced his intent yesterday. He will seek the Republican nomination at the August 25 primary and indicated he will file also on the Democratic ticket to cut as deeply as possible into the voting strength Governor Olson will woo in an attempt to succeed himself.

Warren said he had been persuaded by urgings which have persisted "for the past year or more," promised a "vitally needed" nonpartisan administration if elected,

For comment, see the Editorial Page

and called for a cessation of petty politics in favor of all-out "protection of our homes, our lives and our property."

Only by indirection did the Attorney General recognize the unannounced but certain re-election candidacy of the present Governor.

In a prepared statement, he said civilian protection is "the most vital problem either presently with us or on our immediate horizon" and declared Californians are "crying out for the opportunity to serve," adding with oblique significance.

"If elected Governor, it would be my purpose to give encouragement and direction to this response in an all-out effort free from politics."

The cry of politics has been a familiar sound during the Olson administration.

Continued on Page 7, Col. 1

Roosevelt Given First Buddy Poppy

WASHINGTON, April 9 (AP)—The first Buddy Poppy of the 1942 sale, conducted by the Veterans of Foreign Wars to raise money for relief activities, was presented to President Roosevelt today by Geraldine Reynolds, 5.

Anna Lee Seeks U. S. Citizenship

LOS ANGELES, April 9 (AP)—Movie Actress Anna Lee applied today for American citizenship. In private life the wife of Robert Stevenson, film director, Miss Lee was born in Kent, England.

The India Dilemma: British, Hindu Agreement Reported; America's Influence Helps

By the Associated Press

NEW DELHI, India, April 9—Britain and the Hindu leaders of India were reported tonight to have come to terms on the delicate, danger-fraught question of independence for India. The influence of the United States appeared to have weighed heavily in the final bargaining.

Has Germany sufficient arms to carry out her spring drive? See Foreign News Fronts on page 4.

Apart from the still open question of adherence to the compromise plan by the Moslem League, there appeared to be lacking little more than the formalities of signature and promulgation to give India a national government now, guarantee her dominion status after the war, with a dominion's right of secession, and place her in the front as an Asiatic bulwark of the United Nations.

The successful formula compounded by Britain's negotiator-in-chief, Sir Stafford Cripps, and leaders of the dominant All-India Congress party, with the helpful influence of President Roosevelt's personal emissary to India, Louis Johnson, was reported to provide for a clear division of functions under the projected national government for India.

General Sir Archibald P. Wavell, British commander for India, it is said, would be supreme commander for conduct of war under an Indian War Cabinet whose Defense Minister would be an Indian.

Both Cripps and Johnson were believed to be eager that Pandit Jawaharlal Nehru, past president of the Congress party and one of its ranking leaders, take the defense portfolio.

Consolidation of Indian and British direction of India's war effort, as envisaged, was believed to have composed the sharpest difference between the Congress party and the British. The original plan carried by Cripps to New Delhi last month provided that responsibility for the Indian defense remain solely in British hands.

Late last week, amid signs of a breakdown over the British plan and the Congress party's rejection, John-

Continued on Page 2, Col. 3

Weather Man

The Weather Man tipped a bit of milk in the cat's saucer and put out some cheese for the mouse.

"Get your vitamins," he said. "We have to keep up our morale and health."

"Who says so?" said Anemometer, the cat, lapping his milk.

"Florence McAuliffe says so, that's who," said the W. M. "He's in charge of morale around here."

"What's morale, Boss?" said Gadget, the mouse.

"It's like a politician's promises," said the W. M. "It keeps your spirits up whether you get what he promised or not. Now do you know?"

"Sure," said the mouse, wiping the cheese from his whiskers, "just another name for bock beer."

Olson Says No Need to Worry About Guard

By STANLEY BAILEY

All's well with the State Guard—say the politicians.

Today California is giving inadequate protection to vital points—say the men who are out there trying to do a job in spite of every handicap.

Immediate action is essential—say the officers. Enlistments are falling off and confusion rules.

Two possible steps were urged to solve the situation—Federalization of the guard, or a special session of the State Legislature to repeal the atrocious bill passed in January and enact a measure which would permit organization of the guard along military lines.

Governor Olson won't (as yet) call the special session, saying it would be futile until the legis-

Continued on Page 14, Col. 7

Beaverbrook Visits Duke of Windsor

NASSAU, Bahamas, April 9 (AP)—Lord Beaverbrook, Britain's former Minister of War Production who had been on a mission in the United States, arrived here today. He called upon the Duke of Windsor, Governor of the Bahamas.

Plane Crash Kills Santa Clara Youth

BAKERSFIELD, April 9 (AP)—Two army flyers were killed when their training plane crashed near the edge of Minter Field yesterday.

The dead are Lieutenant William B. Raabe, 23, Seattle, and Aviation Cadet Iril W. Crowe, 22, Santa Clara. Crowe was a graduate of San Jose State College.

Military Digest: A Round-up of Action on War Fronts

By PETER D. WHITNEY

It appears that General Wainwright was trying to repeat General MacArthur's brilliant maneuver of January 24-25 when, his left flank threatened with a Japanese breakthrough, he audaciously counterattacked on his right where the Japs were weakest, and forced them to retreat in disorder. This time, however, the men of Bataan were too exhausted by sickness, short rations, and continual fighting, and the attempt failed. The right flank was enveloped, and the Japs by now undoubtedly control much of the road back to the Port of Mariveles on the tip of the peninsula. The evacuation of many troops back to Corregidor is unlikely. The fortress itself can probably not hold out long caught between the crossfire of Jap artillery from Cavite and Bataan.

Tokyo radio said 60,000 U. S.-Filipino troops "begged" to surrender.

The rainy season begins soon on Luzon, and tropic vegetation soon will cover fox-holes and shell-craters, and the cemetery mounds of Bataan. Monkey and macaw will chatter again, now that the artillery is silenced, and there will be a kind of peace.

Indian Ocean

The Japanese Navy appears to have won domination of the Indian ocean with a single stroke. The British admit loss of the heavy cruisers Dorsetshire and Cornwall to torpedo-plane attack. One of the Jap aircraft carriers has been spotted and suffered "near bomb misses," which may have severely damaged it. Trincomalee naval base was attacked by a "large force" of bombers and fighters, at least six of which were destroyed, and damage is admitted to airdrome and harbor.

The best hope for India, from the naval point of view, is now the one or two British aircraft carriers reported (in Axis broadcasts) to be steaming around Africa to the scene of battle. The American Navy, based on Perth, Australia, may be able to help. Otherwise, the main supply route to India and China—almost a billion Allied peoples—is hopelessly compromised.

Berlin insists a Jap landing force is marching toward India from the Burma border.

Burma

Good news from the Burma front is the reappearance of the AVG flyers, who shot down 10 and damaged two of a fleet of 20 Navy-Zero fighters last Wednesday. The AVG is now based in Yunnan, China, since devastating Japanese raids on their Burma airdromes March 21 and 22.

Descriptions of the April 3 raid on Mandalay have at last passed the censors, and it is revealed as one of the most wanton and destructive in modern warfare.

The Chinese are disclosed to have been resisting a four-day Jap attack on their sector of the land front, and there have been skirmishes on the Thai-Burma border. In China proper, the Japs have been ejected from Sutzekow, northeast of Nanchang, Kiangsi province.

Australia

A Jap air raid on the Florida island capital of Tuagi, administrative capital of the Solomon chain, stirred fears the Japs may be trying to establish bases perilously near the U. S. convoy route to Sidney, harassing rather than frontally attacking the Allied base in Australia for the duration of the Indian ocean battle.

Allied bombers destroyed "many" Jap planes at Rabaul, New Britain.

Libya

A British column of some strength is apparently fighting a skirmish with Axis armored forces in the desert no-man's land south of Tobruk. General Rommel's assault in force has not yet materialized.

In the Mediterranean, the British announce one of their subs has torpedoed and sunk one of Italy's last three crack 10,000-ton, eight-inch-gun cruisers—a type of ship more important for the Mediterranean fighting than the battleship.

Russia

The German communique itself is authority for the fact that the Russian winter offensive continues. "Continued powerful attacks" are admitted in the central and northern sectors, apparently referring to the capture, reported from neutral sources Wednesday, of a bridgehead over the upper Dnieper, isolating the German garrison in the Vyazma fortified area. The German radio admits a break-through some days ago north of Orel, but declares that the line has been restored. The Moscow communique again declares there are no "significant changes" in the front.

San Francisco Chronicle

THE CITY'S ONLY HOME-OWNED NEWSPAPER

FINAL Morning Edition

FOUNDED 1865—VOL. CLIV, NO. 111 CCCC**** SAN FRANCISCO, WEDNESDAY, MAY 6, 1942 DAILY 5 CENTS, SUNDAY 12 CENTS: DAILY AND SUNDAY PER MONTH, $1.6

CORREGIDOR SURRENDERS!

By ROYCE BRIER

THAT TIME it happened quick to the Axis boys.

Since 1935 they've been handing us all the fast ones, and we've been handing them all the legal arguments. It cloys. So now the Axis boys can think up some legal arguments. And don't think they won't. The agony of the cheater cheated is deafening.

The British moved in on Madagascar in the early hours. They landed on the northern beaches, apparently a naval expedition coming down from the Red Sea, or over from Tanganyika, which has rail connections with the Sudan. They may be landing at other points, the island having about the shoreline length of California. Primarily they are after a naval base.

There was a little fighting, but no detail. One vague report was that the British used paratroops. If they did, they could have come from Zanzibar, about 750 miles.

But the fighting should not be severe if the expedition is adequately prepared. The British apparently went to work when Laval showed, as such an attack would require about three weeks to mount. Most of the violence will probably run to cable charges, when the Axis really gets to brooding over the failure of enemy urbanity.

This indignation is already getting a touch in Berlin and Tokyo, and they could be pretty funny about it if in form, but the most elaborate pattern must be laid in Vichy, in the office of Pierre Laval. Indeed, M. Laval has already put out some preliminary reflections on the matter.

As the British moved, the Vichy Ambassador in Washington was handed a note:

"The President of the United States has been informed Madagascar has been occupied by British forces. This occupation has the full approval of the government of the United States.

"The government of the United States is at war with the Axis powers, and if it becomes necessary or desirable for American troops or ships to use Madagascar in the common cause, the United States will not hesitate to do so at any time."

The note added that the island will be restored to France after the war, or whenever it becomes unessential to the common cause, and says a "warlike act" permitted by Vichy will be considered an attack on all United Nations.

Continued on Page 4, Col. 7

Terms of Capitulation Being Arranged; 7000 Are In Japs' Power; Food and Bullets Exhausted

ALLIED HEADQUARTERS, Australia, May 6, (AP)—Corregidor and the other fortified islands in Manila harbor surrenndered today, it was officially announced.

Besides the fortified rock that is Corregidor, the United States forts which had held out in the entrance to Manila Bay are Fort Mills (on Corregidor), Fort Hughes, Fort Drum and Fort Frank.

The end came in the second day of the final Japanese assault, launched at midnight Tuesday, Manila time, with landings from Bataan peninsula after Corregidor particularly of the American forts had been pounded again and again by Japanese big guns and aerial bombs.

In Washington the War Department announced that terms were being arranged for the capitulation of the island forts in Manila bay.

The War Department's communique said:

"1—Philippine theater: The War Department has received a message from Corregidor advising that resistance of our troops has been overcome. Fighting has ceased and terms are being arranged covering the capitulation of the island forts in Manila bay.

"2—There is nothing to report from other areas."

Officials gave no indication of when the fighting ended.

A spokesman for General Douglas MacArthur, who led the brilliant defense of Bataan and the forts at the mouth of Manila bay until ordered to Australia, made this announcement at 4 p. m.:

"General Wainwright has surrendered Corregidor and the other fortified islands in Manila harbor."

There were believed to be about 7000 men and women altogether on Corregidor and the other fortified islands.

Besides the original garrisons, there was a naval detachment originally consisting of some 3500 Marines and Blue Jackets who were removed to Corregidor when fighting ceased April 9 on Bataan peninsula and a group of army nurses also reached the island.

Thus ended the 5-month-old battle of Luzon except for isolated guerrilla resistance. Manila bay, offering the best harbor in the Orient, is opened for use as a Japanese naval base.

The outcome was never in doubt after the invaders overwhelmed the defenders of Bataan peninsula April 9, but bands of American and Filipino troops are said still to be ranging areas of Luzon as well as other islands in the archipelago.

The Earlier Details:

By United Press

WASHINGTON, Wednesday, May 6—The War Department announced late yesterday that a Japanese assault upon Corregidor, including a landing attack, was in progress, and early today an absence of further news led to fears that the mighty island fortress in Manila bay might have fallen to the invader.

The desperate plight of an estimated 7000 to 8000 men, many of them probably weakened by disease, was revealed in a terse communique made public at 2 p. m. (P. W. T.) saying the Japanese attack began at midnight Tuesday Manila time.

(From Melbourne, General MacArthur's headquarters, announced today (Wednesday) that the Japanese attack was launched against the north beach of the island.)

The fort, one of the most bombed spots in the world, suffered terri-

Continued on Page 2, Col. 6

Keep Out of Debt

U. S. Stiffens Installment Buying Law

By the Associated Press

WASHINGTON, May 5—Stiff regulations controlling installment purchases of nearly every article in common use in the American home were promulgated tonight by the Federal Reserve Board which, in addition, decreed that ordinary charge accounts must be paid up relatively quickly.

The charge account rules, first ever issued governing this type of buying, provided that an article must be paid for by the tenth day of the second month following the purchase.

Effective at midnight tonight, the regulations were issued in compliance with President Roosevelt's recent request that people pay off their bills and stay out of debt as much as possible. Hitherto, the purchase on credit of a score of articles had been regulated, but tonight's rules lengthened the list to 46 classifications, and stiffened the requirements.

The new list of restricted articles included all civilian clothing, kitchen articles and dishes, linens, jewelry, auto accessories, all electrical appliances, luggage, umbrellas, sports equipment, used furniture and yard goods, in addition to the score of previously limited items such as furniture, radios, vacuum cleaners, bicycles and clocks.

Gas rationing may spread to areas beyond the East Coast States. See page 15.

The rules apply only to the 46 listed types of articles and no others. They provide:

1. **Cash purchases**—no restrictions.

2. **Charge accounts—must be paid by the 10th day of the second month following purchase, but no down payment required. For instance, a listed article bought any day up to the end of this month must be paid for by July 10. That date also is the deadline for charged articles on the list which were bought before today.**

3. Installment credit—any person buying a listed item on the installment must pay ⅓ down and the balance in 12 months, except that automobiles may be bought ⅓

Continued on Page 6, Col. 1

Bay Area Undergoes 18th Alert

Approach of an unidentified plane which later proved to be friendly, caused the Fourth Interceptor Command to place the San Francisco Bay Area on the alert at 9:18 o'clock last night. The all clear was ordered 27 minutes later.

At 9:22 the blue, or second warning was flashed in the East Bay and radios were ordered off the air.

The all-clear came at 9:45.

The alert was the 18th air raid warning since the war. There have been eight blackouts, the latest of which lasting 45 minutes, was ordered Sunday night when an unidentified "target," which later proved friendly, was reported approaching the area.

F. H. Meyer Named S. F. Traffic Czar

Frederick H. Meyer, San Francisco architect and transportation expert, yesterday was appointed Administrator of Defense Transportation. He was the choice of a five-man committee named by the Mayor to select a man for the job.

The fact that the position is set up with Federal backing means that Meyer will have unlimited authority in moves to settle the city's critical transportation problems.

The new "czar" of transportation elected to serve without pay . . a fact which caused some surprise at the City Hall, since E. G. Cahill, city manager of utilities and chairman of the Mayor's committee, acknowledged he had planned to recommend a salary of $10,000 a year.

"Mr. Meyer," said Cahill, "told me he wanted the job to be out of politics and did not desire a salary for his services. He did not want his name placed before the Board of Supervisors, which would have been required if the position was made a city-paid job."

It was learned that Ralph Koeber, research expert of the Chamber of Commerce, will be loaned by the

Continued on Page 12, Col. 5

Two Nazis Escape Prison in Canada

BOWMANVILLE, Ontario, May 5 (AP)—Two German war prisoners escaped tonight from their internment camp here.

British Behind Madagascar Naval Base

By DREW MIDDLETON
Associated Press Staff Writer

LONDON, May 5—British commandos, regular infantrymen and Royal Marines moved upon Madagascar's Diego Suarez naval base tonight in a swift incursion which struck from the reaching hand of the Axis a vital Indian ocean position and effected a major Allied coup in the world-wide struggle for mastery of the seas.

"Operations are proceeding and our casualties have so far been light," the Admiralty and War Office said in a brief joint communique at 10 o'clock. "It is understood that the Governor General of Madagascar has declared his intention to resist."

The landing forces, protected by warships and warplanes, dashed ashore at Courrier bay, 10 miles across the isthmus from Diego Suarez itself, at dawn

By nightfall they had broken the Vichy French coastal defenses, captured a battery which had shelled the landings and were smashing at the back door of the base through the hot tropical jungle.

Advices released by Vichy sources tonight said the British occupying forces, which the French estimated, perhaps excessively, at 20,000, had reached Andrakaka, four miles from the naval base. The same report put the French and Indian defenders at 7500.

Vichy reports said waves of parachutists had been landed at the outset of a double attack in which warships and squadrons of aircraft made a frontal thrust from the sea, timed with the overland assault on the rear by light armored units landed in Courrier bay.

The French said also that British naval forces consisted of two cruisers, four destroyers and two

Continued on Page 4, Col. 4

U. S. Ready To Move on Vichy, Too

By ERNEST BARCELLA
United Press Staff Writer

WASHINGTON, May 5—Secretary of State Cordell Hull reiterated today that U. S. warships and troops are ready to back up the British thrust into Madagascar, if necessary, and strongly intimated that United States would move in on Martinique or any other French possession if they are menaced by a Vichy sell-out to the Axis.

Asserting that relations with Vichy are on a day-to-day basis, he made it clear that this country is keeping a sharp watch for any Axis-inspired retaliation by Vichy. He added in this connection that the United States is giving close attention to Martinique, French Caribbean island, and to other French possessions.

While he did not say so directly, his reference to French possessions in general appeared broad enough to include the strategic West Afrifan base at Dakar—long coveted by the Axis as a base for depredations against Allied South Atlantic supply lines.

What retaliatory action—if any—would be taken by Vichy was conjectural. Senate Majority Leader Alben W. Barkley (D., Ky.) predicted after a White House conference that Vichy would protest in "military, naval or verbal form."

A few hours later, Vichy dispatches said pro-Nazi Pierre Laval, French chief of government, curtly rejected President Roosevent's warning that any warlike act against Britain or the United States would be considered a warlike act against all the United Nations.

Laval was quoted as saying that France will not take the initiative in any diplomatic break with the United States as a result of the Madagascar incident.

(For Laval's text and "blasts" from Petain and Darlan, see page 2.)

Informed diplomats here, evaluating the situation cautiously, generally believed the Madagascar episode would not precipitate war

Continued on Page 4, Col. 3

Bay Blast Reported

Reports of a violent explosion "somewhere down the peninsula" were being checked by peninsula police departments early this morning.

The reports came from as widely separated points as Woodside, San Mateo, Hillsborough and Brisbane. Some persons reported their homes had been violently shaken while others living within a couple of miles reported they had not been aware of any blast.

Navy and Army authorities asserted they had no information of guns having been fired.

Those who heard and felt the reported blast described it as being a "deep rumbling roar."

Military Digest: Laval Rejects U. S. Warning; Intervention Of French Fleet Likely

By PETER D. WHITNEY

Sordid Pierre Laval, who helped bring the world to its present pass by once trying to deliver free Ethiopia to Italy, brazenly played the injured innocent yesterday. He rejected the American memorandum warning that resistance to Britain's invasion of Madagascar will be considered an act of war against all the United Nations. He declared he will never initiate a break of relations with the U. S., however, and said:

"Let President Roosevelt realize that the consequences will fall on him."

It sounds like a threat. The people whom Laval saw yesterday morning were in this order: The U. S. Charge d'Affaires, the newly-arrived Japanese Ambassador, the German Consul General, the Vichy Secretary of Colonies, Commander-of-Armed Forces Admiral Darlan. Then a message was sent to Madagascar's Governor Annet, ordering resistance to an "odious aggression."

The two Japanese Admirals who had been making one of those Axis-style "courtesy calls" in Vichy flew away, like a couple of frustrated carrion crows to Berlin. Altogether, it looks as if the French fleet might openly fight for the Axis. In this connection Secretary Hull's warning that U. S. ships and men are ready to back up the Madagascar invasion, has sharp point.

The Invasion

Vichy is the most detailed source of news on the military aspect of the invasion. Apparently the British are using the most modern techniques. Upon expiration of the ultimatum at 7 a. m. yesterday, parachutists dropped on the peninsula behind the naval base at Diego Suares, which was itself attacked by bombers. A marine landing force went ashore at Courier bay, across the peninsula from Suarez, and is now reported proceeding with "light casualties" toward the base. A French submarine was reportedly sunk and two British planes downed.

The French General Guillemet is not expected to be able to resist very long.

Burma

The Madagascar affair is balanced by the news from Corregidor and the Tokyo announcement that Japanese army units have occupied the airdrome at Akyab, Bay of Bengal port only 350-odd miles from Calcutta. Akyab can become an important advance naval and air base for the invasion of India and the domination of the eastern half of the Indian ocean.

In Burma, the Japanese spearhead has crashed through to the Shweli river, which here is the border between Burma and Yunnan province of China. They have been repulsed in an initial attack on Chinese positions at the bridgehead of Wanting, but have made a two-mile penetration into Chinese territory. This is a technicality beside the fact that they are already in the hills above and fifty miles distant from Ghamo, only remaining Burma road terminus. Significantly, as escape seemed about to be cut, a Chungking spokesman pledged China's troops will not be withdrawn from Burma. On the other hand, the badly mauled British are reported to be retreating over the two-mile-high Patkai mountains to India. Final disaster of the Burma campaign would be fall of Myitkyina, northern terminus of the Burma railroad system and last important center in the Burma lowlands. After that, the Allies would have to fight from the hills, and the Japs would have an air base within 150 airline miles of Sadiya, which is to be the railhead for China's new lifeline, the Assam road now under tedious construction.

Chungking reports an amazing series of guerrilla raids since April 20 on 15 of China's greatest cities, now Japanese-occupied, including Shanghai, where huge fires and bomb explosions were set; Nan-

Continued on Page 2, Col. 4

Women Farmers May Help to Harvest

AWVS Proposes Vacation for Victory Plan

A standing army of 1500 women will be recruited by the American Women's Voluntary Services to help California farmers harvest their crops between July and October.

Mrs. Stanhope Nixon, State head of the AWVS, and Mrs. Nion Tucker, chairman of the San Francisco AWVS unit, said enrollment of women over 18 would be started about the middle of this month.

They estimate that between 8000 and 10,000 women must be enrolled to provide the standing army of 1500 needed.

They will be called upon only after farm areas have exhausted their local labor supply, it was stressed, but a few harvesters may be needed before the end of the month for picking cherries in Sonoma county.

Mrs. Tucker has assigned Mrs. George Bahm as State agricultural chairman to work out details of the enrollment. According to Mrs. Bahm, the U. S. employment service is to provide registration cards within a few days.

Under the AWVS "Vacations for Victory in Agriculture Plan," women registered will be certified to the U. S. employment service, and farmers will draw upon this registration for as many workers as they need.

Farmers in Sonoma, Napa, Lake and Mendocino counties have already agreed to provide suitable camp sites for the women agricultural workers, she said.

Women will furnish their own bedding and may purchase meals at cost from AWVS communal kitchens staffed by trained nutritionists.

Women who spend vacations in the harvest, she said, will be paid the basic farm wage, ranging from $4 to $8 a day.

As soon as details concerning transportation, housing, feeding and other phases of the program are worked out, enrollment will start at the local AWVS headquarters, 665 Market street. Simultaneous registration throughout the State would also begin then, she said.

As the registration progresses, mobile registration units will be established in banks, department stores, schools and other public places for the registration of housewives, business and professional women and college students.

When the first group of women are enrolled, cards will be certified to the U. S. Employment Service, and working schedules arranged to coincide with vacation schedules of the first group.

The first 1500 women will go into the fields about July 15, to be replaced by the end of July by the

Continued on Page 11, Col. 1

San Diego Rail Accident; 42 Hurt

SAN DIEGO, May 5 (AP)—Forty-two persons were injured, 12 seriously, in the rush-hour collision of two street cars in downtown San Diego late today.

Police said a track switch was thrown open accidentally, turning one street car into the path of the other, approaching from the opposite direction, at an intersection.

May Snowstorm Hits Nebraska

OMAHA, May 5 (AP)—The State Highway Department reported snow ranging from four to eight inches in Northwestern Nebraska as an unseasonal May storm swept into that portion of the State today.

A Ringside Seat at the Greatest Naval Battle in World's History

The Men of Guadalcanal Sat on the Beach and Watched the Holocaust Of November 13---Here Is What They Saw in All Its Dramatic, Heroic Detail

Here, by Ira Wolfert, a man outstanding among war correspondents of the world, is a truly eye-witness account of the biggest naval disaster in history. Wolfert viewed, without even needing field glasses, the rout of the Japanese naval forces in the Solomons during the battles of November 12, 13, 14 and 15. The American commander, Admiral William F. Halsey, has characterized this story by Wolfert as a great piece of description. When Wolfert was writing this, he kept insisting the Japanese losses must be larger than the very careful naval authorities yet would claim officially. Since then, Navy Secretary Knox has placed the enemy's losses in these battles as at least 28 ships certainly sunk and others damaged. Our Navy also has announced American losses at two light cruisers and seven destroyers sunk.

By IRA WOLFERT
North American Newspaper Alliance

FROM A BASE IN THE GUADALCANAL SECTOR, Nov. 15 (delayed)—The fifth battle of the Solomons, which in many ways proved a Japanese disaster unprecedented in the history of the world's great navies, began with a dispute over reinforcements of men and supplies for our embattled land forces on Guadalcanal.

Reconnaissance had revealed that the Japanese were building up an extensive force to retake the Solomons, but we threw the first punch, landing the initial wave of our reinforcements on November 11. We held the initiative that day, and on November 12 when the second wave landed.

The reinforcements were sufficient to make General Vandergrift of the marine corps remark to this reporter: "I now feel it is no longer possible for the Japs to land enough strength at any one time to take Guadalcanal away from us."

So the Japs had quite a target to shoot at, and they shot and shot again, and shot four times altogether, missing each time. As he was shooting, the Jap was hastily forming convoys behind his first line of fire, an invasion force estimated by intelligence here to be three divisions with full equipment.

The sea train formed consisted of eight transports, one an NYK liner which is the biggest the Japs have. The other seven ranged downward to 18,000 tons. Accompanying these troop ships were four cargo vessels of about 12,000 tons, carrying the raiment of the Emperor's divisions, while screening the array were at least four battleships, plus a complement of cruisers and destroyers.

On Friday, the 13th, this force, making up the bulk if not all of Japan's South Pacific fleet, moved toward the arena and wrested the initiative from us. This transformed the character of the dispute into a replica, only more so, of all the previous Solomons battles—a skillful, tenacious, heedlessly bloody attempt to reduce permanently our Guadalcanal salient by wiping out its sea armor and obliterating its garrisons, planes and men.

At 1:40 on Friday morning, United States forces here began fighting not for some future offensive with the Japs, but for their lives. The result of this desperate, completely reckless fight for life by the Americans was 28 Jap ships sunk, including two battleships, plus ten damaged.

This reporter, being less conservative than the U. S. Navy and more willing to trust the evidence to his own eyes, personally scores more than half of the ten "damaged" as being sunk. Our cost was seven destroyers and two light cruisers.

This unprecedented battle had many curious features which no doubt will be debated in naval academies for many years. Naval vessels fought in the night, airplanes fought in the day, both in the same arena.

To climax the battle, on the afternoon of November 14 Jap warships fled from the transport and cargo vessels they were supposed to guard, and left the Emperor's three divisions naked to the assaults of our planes which were based 20 minutes away.

These were all very novel tactics but even more novel, at least from the point of view of this eyewitness whose life was one of those immediately being fought for, was the fact that all the major actions of the battle took place within clear view of the naked eye. This is the first battle in the history of modern war that could be viewed in its entirety by a single man standing still.

The holocaust was unfolded to this reporter's front row seat like

Continued on Page 4, Col. 1

IRA WOLFERT
Before his eyes

The Signals
BLACKOUT— *Fluctuating sound, rising and falling, for two minutes on official sirens and Ferry building siren. Street lights go out.*
ALL CLEAR— *Continuous siren sound of one pitch and intensity for two minutes. Street lights go on.*

Chronicle Home Delivery Service
Federal war regulations to conserve rubber prohibit all special deliveries. If for any reason you do not receive your Chronicle, kindly telephone DOuglas 1414 or your local Chronicle Dealer before 10 a. m., so the delivery may be checked. We appreciate your co-operation in this emergency.

FOUNDED 1865—VOL. CLV, NO. 137 CCCCAAAB SAN FRANCISCO, SUNDAY, NOVEMBER 29, 1942 DAILY 5 CENTS, SUNDAY 15 CENTS: DAILY AND SUNDAY PER MONTH, $1.50

260 Killed, Scores Hurt as Fire Sweeps Boston Night Club! Russ Rip Nazi Lines at Moscow

Latest News on The Ration Front

Food, Gas Supplies Adequate---IF Buyers Don't Jam Markets

Eggs, Butter Scarce, but There's Plenty of Meat and Coffee; Gas For All If Stations Aren't Rushed

Here's the general week-end situation in rationed goods at a glance:

MEAT—There's plenty in all lines.
EGGS—Not so good and getting worse fast.
BUTTER—Hard to get.
COFFEE—Enough if customers don't jam the markets with their ration tickets the first couple of days.
GASOLINE—Good supply but a last minute run expected. Sunday and Monday might tie up available gasoline trucks.

The consumer today was faced with a plentiful supply in all lines of food and gasoline.

On the subject of coffee, there is a plentiful supply in all stores for the first day of [illegible] in that commodity. Officials of [illegible] OPA expressed a wish consumers would not rush to their markets to pick up their first month's quota because of the resulting difficulty in maintaining the local coffee traffic.

Gasoline company heads also insist they are ready for any increase in gasoline sales caused by motorists filling up their tanks today and Monday, prior to the rationing deadline which comes Monday at midnight.

Some parts of the country reported near-panic rushes to retail outlets over the week-end when false rumors spread the Government was planning to freeze the present gasoline and oil stocks.

This is NOT true, OPA officials said, and there will be plenty of gasoline if everyone does not rush the stations the last few hours on Monday.

Eggs were going fast in the markets yesterday and by noon many stores reported they had no more on their shelves. The local office of the OPA was at a loss to explain the rush and credited it to a panicky attitude of the consumer, displayed in the Bay Area during the past few weeks.

There was plenty of meat. The public has been eating turkey and other fowl for the last four days, giving the retailers a chance to stock up on all types of red meat.

Proprietors of meat markets proudly displayed their crammed refrigerators yesterday and said they could very well see the year

Continued on Page 13, Col. 1

S. F. Alert! It Lasted 45 Minutes

San Francisco Bay Area's 25th alert was given last night.

The alert period continued for 45 minutes between 10:38 p. m. and 11:23 p. m.

The alert was ordered by the San Francisco Air Defense Wing which later issued the following statement:

"A preliminary alert and radio silence in the San Francisco Bay Area was ordered tonight by the San Francisco Air Defense Wing. The all-clear was given when unidentified targets were identified as friendly. The preliminary or yellow alert was given at 10:38. Radio silence was ordered at 10:48. The all clear was given at 11:23."

The War Digest

Sinking of Axis Ships May Be Key to Toulon

By [illegible]VER D. WHITNEY

One of the keys to the African situation is the Admiralty announcement in London that British submarines have sunk nine and damaged three Axis vessels on their way with reinforcements or supplies for Tripoli and Tunisia. It is even possible that this kind of hamstring of his supply lines was what drove Hitler to make his desperate lunge for the French fleet.

The result is summed up in the War Department communique yesterday declaring the Axis is on the defensive all along the Tunisian front, with our troops pushing through Tebourba after shooting up 10 German tanks on Friday. Morocco radio yesterday had them but 14 miles from the capital. Correspondents' delayed dispatches from the vanguard say German defenses at Medjez-el-bab consisted only of deeply zoned machine-gun positions, self-propelled tank-buster guns, too heavy to be flown across from Sicily, will be the Germans' crying need.

De Gaulle may visit Washington to clear up l'affaire Darlan. See Foreign News Fronts, page 6.

There is no news at all from El Agheila, where the British Eighth Army is undoubtedly preparing to attack such positions as Rommel has arranged. U. S. and RAF bombers attacked the Italian-held island of Leros in the Aegean, and the Gerbini airdrome in Sicily.

War in Russia

The Russians issued a special communique yesterday announcing their four-day-old offensive on the so-called Kalinin-Moscow front. The German communiques have described this fighting for three days—fairly accurately, it now appears. The Russians claim to have cut the north-south railroad between the "hedgehog" fortress Rzhev and Vyazma, junction on the main Moscow-Minsk line. They claim also to have isolated the important junction of Velikie Luki, far to the west, driving spearheads between it and Nevel on the south, and Novo Sokolniki to the west. The town is important to the entire German communications system between Moscow and Leningrad.

The triumphant tone of the Moscow announcer in making the new offensive public underlines its critical importance in this turning point of the war. Swedish reports on the state of German morale say that last winter's

Continued on Page 6, Col. 4

Back Bay District Holocaust

Toll May Rise to 400; Trapped Victims Leap From the Roof

Service Men Carry Bodies From Gutted Coconut Grove; 1000 May Have Been in Building

BOSTON, Nov. 29 (Sunday) (AP)—Fire which flashed swiftly among Saturday night merrymakers in the Cocoanut Grove night club in the Back Bay district killed an estimated 260 and injured scores of others and some officials at the disordered scene estimated the death toll might rise to 400.

Newsmen counted 210 bodies at the city's southern mortuary, and 50 more at the northern mortuary.

A night club manager who was in the Cocoanut Grove when the fire broke out estimated there might have been as many as 1000 persons in the building at the time.

As officials tried desperately to gain a true estimate of the dead, an unofficial compilation made at police headquarters placed the dead at above 400. The possibility existed, however, that some of the bodies counted in hospitals might have been counted again at the morgues.

All bodies were believed removed from the one-and-a-half-story building by 1:15 a. m. (E.W.T.), three hours after the first alarm, which was followed by four others and calls for all available ambulances, police cars and physicians. Soldiers, sailors and Coast Guardsmen assisted in carrying out the dead.

Eyewitnesses said a cloud of smoke burst among the dancers just as the orchestra prepared to play the Star Spangled Banner, opening the floor show. Some said the blaze apparently originated in the kitchen, in the cellar, and spread swiftly to the Melody Room, a lounge also below street level.

Some of the trapped night clubbers leaped from the roof and

Continued on Page 13, Col. 3

It's Georgia In Rose Bowl

University of Georgia, winner of the Southeastern Conference football championship, last night was chosen to represent the East in the annual Rose Bowl game in Pasadena next New Year's Day. The West's representative will be chosen after December 12.

For details, see the Sporting Green.

Battle of Africa

Nine Axis Ships Sunk; Allies Gain in Tunis

By the Associated Press

LONDON, Nov. 28—Nine more Axis supply ships, including a tank carrier, have been sunk in the Mediterranean by British submarines fighting attempts to rush men and provisions to German and Italian troops now forced back within 15 miles of Tunis.

Announcement of this destruction of Axis ships and supplies urgently needed by the Nazi defenders of Tunis and Bizerta came from the British Admiralty at the same time enemy sources described the mounting scale of the Allied assault on the North African siege ports.

(The usually unreliable radio Morocco reported American troops, supported by French contingents, occupied an important position about 14 miles west of Tunis.)

In addition to the nine cargo vessels sunk, the British reported they had damaged three other supply ships and an Italian destroyer of the Trione class that was escorting the relief convoy. The date of the sinking was not given.

Texts of the communiques are on Page 9.

Among the ships sunk was a large twin-funneled passenger liner which was intercepted off the coast of Sicily Another was a small tanker laden with benzine. A second tanker which previously had been damaged by aircraft was found burning and was sunk by torpedoes, the Admiralty said.

The tank-landing craft, of medium size, might have been trying

Continued on Page 6, Col. 7

The Red Army's Winter Drive

Russ 90 Miles From Latvia, Kill 10,000, Take 300 Towns

Five German Divisions Routed; Soviet Pincers Are Near Closing Trap on Enemy at Stalingrad

By the Associated Press

MOSCOW, Nov. 29—The Russians announced today Sunday) that a surprise offensive on the Northwest front had killed 10,000 German troops, routed five divisions, "liberated more than 300 populated places" and broken wide gaps in German fortifications less than 90 miles from the old Latvian border.

A special communique issued by the Soviets said that the Red Army had broken through to a "strongly fortified defense zone of the enemy" and that in the area of the town of Velikie Luki, which is 90 miles from Latvia, "the German front has been broken over a distance (width) of 30 kilometers (about 20 miles).

The Russians have, in fact, pushed on to the west of Velikie Luki, for the communique said the rail line between Velikie Luki and Novosokolniki, 25 miles to the west of that city, had been broken, as well as the line from Velikie Luki to Nevel, 35 miles southeast of Velikie Luki.

The Red Army also continued going strong in its giant Stalingrad maneuver. Giving the enemy no respite, it hurled the last German forces back across the Don river west of Stalingrad and wheeled eastward in a mighty drive to smash the Nazi army before the besieged citadel.

RUSSIANS HAVE OPENED TWO FRONTS

(If they advance a few miles further, the Russians will have cut the main artery connecting German armies in the center and south with those in the north.

(London observers happily noted that Hitler could manage to attack on only one front last summer, but that Stalin, with winter upon him, has opened major offensives on at least two fronts.

(Meanwhile, the German radio today asserted Soviet forces were massing also near Voronezh, some 300 miles northwest of Stalingrad).

(The military correspond-

Continued on Page 2, Col. 3

French Navy Followed 1940 Orders

By Associated Press

LONDON, Nov. 28—An escaping French submarine arrived in Barcelona today as the lone known survivor of the home fleet at Toulon which was destroyed, according to a communique broadcast from Vichy tonight, on instructions issued at the time of the June, 1940, armistice.

There was no detail on the instructions, but it was assumed that they were probably meant to be put in operation when and if the Germans breached the armistice terms, as they did in overstepping the demarcation line last November 11 and in grabbing for the armistice-bound fleet yesterday.

The Vichy communique said scuttling of the warships was preferable to "letting them be taken over by any foreign power whatever."

The Vichy ministers were called into Pierre Laval's office and told of the German decision to occupy Toulon after the operation was in progress, it said.

Admiral Jean Darlan issued a proclamation in Algiers declaring that all the French fleet at Toulon had been "sunk or scuttled" and this was officially termed "welcome news" at Allied headquarters in North Africa. But hope was held out that some of the units got away, as did the submarine at Barcelona, and would join the Allies.

Lieutenant-General Dwight D.

Continued on Page 6, Col. 6

Kenny Ill in N. Y. Hospital

NEW YORK, Nov. 28 (AP)—State Senator Robert W. Kenny, Attorney General-elect of California, was hospitalized at the Harkness Pavilion today after becoming ill late yesterday.

The Senator and Mrs. Kenny had come to New York to attend a national executive board meeting of the National Lawyers' Guild, of which he is president. Kenny telephoned reporters he had a streptococcus infection, but hoped to leave for Washington Monday.

Hawaii Delegate Sworn Into Navy

WASHINGTON, Nov. 28 (AP)—Delegate King of Hawaii was sworn in today as Lieutenant Commander in the United States Naval Reserve.

King has been ordered to report to the chief of naval personnel here for duty January 4, following completion of his eighth year as delegate to Congress from Hawaii. His assignment was not disclosed.

Bauxite Deposit Found in Jamaica

Copyright, 1942, by the New York Times and The Chronicle

KINGSTON, Jamaica, Nov. 28—Bauxite has been found on a large property here and an engineering firm has been employed to work it. The Government took charge of the Bauxite today as State property.

Churchill On Air Today

Prime Minister Churchill will make a world-wide broadcast today (Sunday) on the eve of his 68th birthday.

The broadcast is scheduled for 1 p. m., San Francisco time.

All four major American networks announced they would carry the broadcast.

Solomons: Bombers Smash Japs' Bases; Ground Forces 'Mop Up'

By Associated Press

WASHINGTON, Nov. 28—American aircraft, striking heavily at Japanese bases in the Northwestern Solomons, were reported by the Navy today to have destroyed all buildings in the Munda area of New Georgia island and blasted the Kahili airdrome on the island of Bougainville.

Ground operations around American positions on Guadalcanal island were limited to local skirmishes. In a series of these actions our patrols killed 50 Japanese and captured a number of machine guns Friday about six miles west of the American airfield, a communique said.

Two enemy bombers made the third straight night nuisance raid on American positions on the island Friday night. They dropped bombs near the mouth of the Lunga river but caused no damage.

In contrast with this greatly curtailed enemy activity, the result of smashing blows dealt the Japs in the Solomons earlier this month, was a report made here today by a Marine combat engineer on the first two months of the American occupation of Guadalcanal.

Captain Walter K. Lyle said the airfield was repeatedly and accurately bombed while he was there, although damage was quickly repaired; that day and night aerial attacks and night naval bombardments were frequent and that the Japanese on land were constantly punching at the American lines so that the engineers completing and extending the airfield sometimes had to fight all night and then work all day.

Today's communique, like all others issued in the last two weeks, indicated that the Japanese have been entirely on the defensive, except for nuisance activity, since their greatest effort at reconquest of the southeastern Solomons was crushed by American air and naval power two weeks ago.

That they are collecting for an-

Continued on Page 5, Col. 1

San Francisco Chronicle

THE CITY'S ONLY HOME-OWNED NEWSPAPER

FINAL Morning Edition

FOUNDED 1865—VOL. CLVII, NO. 50 CCCCAAA SAN FRANCISCO, FRIDAY, SEPTEMBER 3, 1943 DAILY 5 CENTS, SUNDAY 15 CENTS: DAILY AND SUNDAY PER MONTH, $1.30

ITALY INVADED!

Allies Strike From Messina

A Foothold in Europe

British Eighth Spearheads the Landing on Mainland With Canadians Joining in Assault

RAF and American Flyers Form Air Umbrella in Dawn Advance; Blow Comes Less Than 3 Weeks After Fall of Sicily

By the Associated Press

ALLIED HEADQUARTERS IN NORTH AFRICA, Sept. 3—British and Canadian forces, under the command of General Dwight D. Eisenhower, swept across the Strait of Messina in today's dawning light and landed on the beaches of Italy.

Thus, the Allies had made good their promise to invade the European mainland.

The long-awaited and historic assault came on the fourth anniversary of the day that Great Britain declared war on Germany.

The invading forces of the American commander less than three weeks ago brought to a conclusion the victorious Sicilian campaign.

It was from footholds won in that 38-day campaign, from the eastern shore of Sicily, that the mainland invaders sprung.

From there, it was only a brief boat ride, 20 minutes or a half hour, to the mainland—and possibly another good step toward Berlin.

British and Canadian troops of the Eighth Army, famed for its fighting in North Africa and Sicily, made up the attacking force.

Allied naval units escorted the landing barges. Overhead, American and British airmen swept away the enemy.

(The American Seventh Army, which mopped up the greater part of the western half of Sicily, presumably was being held in reserve, for the time being at least.

(In a broadcast this morning from Algiers, John Daly, CBS correspondent, reported the invasion was preceded by a number of successful Commando and reconnaissance missions in the past few nights.

(Daly said these missions were successful in helping to knock out enemy coastal defenses, and at the same time, he said, they reported valuable information back to attack headquarters.

(This report recalled that the Italians said several days ago a Commando-type landing had been made in the region of Reggio Calabria. This was never confirmed.

(Daly said details were lacking as to exactly where the landings occurred, although in general they took place along the Calabrian peninsula. Daly said the Germans were believed to have done most of the initial fighting in the first phase against the invasion forces.)

The first landings were made at 4:30 a. m. (7:30 p. m., Thursday Pacific time) and were announced

Continued on Page 4, Col. 3

THE NEW FRONT: Invaders stream across the Straits of Messina and the toe of Italy now feels the heel of Allied might.

THIS WORLD TODAY

By ROYCE BRIER

THE MOSCOW magazine, *War and the Working Class*, which in our alphabetical civilization works out as WWC, said: "The neutrality of Turkey becomes increasingly more favorable and necessary to Germany." The article is entitled: "Who Gains from the Neutrality of Turkey?" and the author is N. Vasilev.

Now, none of these articles and editorials in *WWC, Pravda, Red Star* and such Russian publications are accidental. They do not result, as in the West, from a sudden brainstorm of the editor, who thinks to dash off a careless agglomeration of thoughts and prejudices, which will annoy any number of people and maybe find agreement only in his adoring family.

On the contrary, these pieces are cautiously worded, and in part and in whole articulated with Kremlin policy. They are actual reflections of that policy, published after actual consultation with the Kremlin authorities who know the purpose of Premier Stalin and the Politbureau. This is not our way of doing things, but it is Russia's right to do things its way, and we are benefited when we have a clear idea that this is the way things are done.

In that light, WWC's article is significant, in that it partly dispels a great deal of recent speculation regarding Soviet policy in Southeastern Europe. Furthermore, it hints strongly that pressure is about to be brought to bear on Turkey, or is already being brought to bear, to join the allies. And Turkey is more receptive to Soviet suggestion than it is to Western suggestion.

It means flatly that a southeastern front is likely and that Turkey may enter the war.

For a year Anglo-American forces and equipment have been assembling in the Near and Middle East. With headquarters in Cairo, the forces have spread in Palestine and Syria, and off across the desert to Teheran, the southern focus of lend-lease aid to Russia. They have an island outpost in Cyprus.

Since the clearing of the Mediterranean, the communications of these forces have been incalculably strengthened. It has been assumed the force is not there for nothing, but would ul-

Continued on Page 2, Col. 1

The Russian Victories Are Piling Up

By the Associated Press

LONDON, Friday, Sept 3—Russia announced early today that five Red Armies plunging westward had cut the Bryansk-Kiev railway 150 miles from Kiev, smashed German reinforcements in a six-mile gain on Smolensk, and rolled up Axis lines in a new 45-mile-wide spurt in the Donets basin.

Marshal Stalin's Thursday order of the day said the Ukraine citadel of Sumy, 90 miles northwest of Kharkov, had fallen to General Nikolai Vatutin's army, and a communique announced the capture of Krolevets and Yampol, two points on the vital Bryansk-Kiev railway linking the enemy's central and southern fronts.

LARGE SCALE RETREAT

Lisichansk, Voroshilovsk, Slavyanoserbsk, and other cities were seized in the Donets basin, while Budenovka, 20 miles from Mariupol, was taken in the push along the rim of the Sea of Azov, said the communique recorded by the Soviet monitor.

The swiftness of the Russian advances and the tone of the communique indicated the Germans were engaged in a large scale retreat toward the Dnieper river, particularly in the huge Donets Basin. The bulletin, however, emphasized that the Germans were fighting stubbornly all along the 600-mile front.

More than 9000 Germans were killed yesterday as the Red armies overran nearly 250 cities and villages, many of them strategic prizes.

Germany's 1941 invasion lines now have been cracked by the Russians in a 1943 offensive that has carried the Red Army more than half way along the comeback trail from historic Stalingrad to the Polish border.

The capture of Krolevets, 25 miles north of the rail junction of Konotop, put the Red Army 150 miles from Kiev after a 130-mile summer lunge from Kursk.

Moreover, Krolevets' fall further flanked Bryansk from the south and may force Germany's south-central armies to fall back on Kiev. Captured Yompol lies 32 miles northeast of Krolevets.

On the Smolensk front the Russians swept on six miles after toppling Yelnya and Dorogobuzh. German troops there were being reinforced by fresh reserves hurled into battle straight from the march, but the communique said:

"All attempts of the Hitlerites, however, to stem our attacking units met with failure."

(Further news of Russian fighting on Page 4.)

Rome Is Silent

LONDON, Sept. 3 (U.P.)—The Rome radio broadcast its regular 7 a.m. Newscast today without mentioning the landing of Allied troops in Southern Italy two and one-half hours earlier.

A Note to Fathers About Draft Letter

SACRAMENTO, Sept. 2—Thousand of pre-Pearl Harbor fathers have misunderstood a letter recently sent them by their local draft boards and are changing their employment when they don't have to, Lieutenant Colonel Kenneth H. Leitch, State Director of Selective Service, said today.

The letter calls upon the registrant to submit to the draft board certain information concerning himself.

"He should submit that information," Leitch said, "but should make no move at this time toward changing his employment because of the letter."

United States Employment Service offices are being besieged by fathers who are misinterpreting the letter, thinking they have only five days to change employment and enter a war essential or war production industry, Leitch explained.

The letter does not mean that at all, he declared. It merely wants the registrant to submit data on any change in his status from the last time he supplied the board with his family information, as, for instance, new babies, change in employment, other dependents incurred, etc.

The registrant has five days to submit this information. Later—the date depending upon his status as subsequently determined by the board after a review of new information—a letter may be sent him asking him to change jobs.

Language of the letter is being clarified, Leitch said, but already thousands have been sent out and "much damage has been done."

Salvage of Used Hose to End

WASHINGTON, Sept. 2 (AP)—Collection of used silk and Nylon stockings under the war-time salvage program will be discontinued after September 30, the War Production Board announced today.

Paul C. Cabot, director of WPB's salvage division, said the public response to the stocking salvage appeal has been "amazing."

Weather Man

The Weather Man wore his silk topper and best smile. "This is it," he beamed. "The morning of our secret snack."

Anemometer, Gadget, Humidity III, Mimi danced in delight. The table was laden with milk, cheese, raw hamburger and a big fly for Mimi.

The W. M. looked about. He also looked puzzled. "Where's everybody?" he asked, polishing off today's DIM-OUT WARNING: Sun sets at 7:38.

"Everybody who?" asked the cat, innocent-eyed.

"The 728,236.09 people I sent invites out to."

Anemometer took a sudden interest in his left forepaw.

Meat Points Cut

OPA Raises Ration-Stamp Price Of Butter and Frozen Foods

(Tables on Pages 8 and 19)

WASHINGTON, Sept. 2 (AP)—A hike in the ration-stamp price of creamery butter, frozen foods and some canned fruits coincided today with a reduction of a point or two in the value of 35 different cuts of meat.

All the changes—based on new surveys of what civilians want and what they can get—will go into effect Sunday.

The Office of Price Administration boosted creamery butter from 10 to 12 points, blaming local shortages and reports that production is running 5 per cent behind orignal estimates. It cut the value of country farm-churned butter from 10 points to six in an effort, it said, to get more of it to market.

FROZEN FOODS UP

Frozen foods and some canned fruits will go up in stamp value in an effort to discourage shoppers. The agency said the demand was running retail stocks low.

Expectations of 7 per cent more meat for civilians this month, OPA said, cleared the way for a cut in the stamp value of several types of beef roasts and steaks, lamb and bacon. OPA said the improved supply was not sufficient "to permit substantial reductions in all meats."

All lamb and mutton, with the exception of breast and flank and some variety meats, will be reduced one point. Most bacon cuts will go down two points and a few other types of pork will be cut a point. Beef rib cuts, roasts and steak and sirloin steaks will be lowered one point.

In processed foods—sold for blue ration stamps—OPA increased the value of 13 items and reduced eight others.

NEW POINT VALUES

Following are the new point values which will go into effect Sunday (there is no change in rationed items unlisted below):

Meats, butter, etc., with the point value per pound:

Beef—10-inch rib steaks, 10 points; seven-inch rib steaks, 11 points; sirloin steaks, 11 points; 10-inch cut, rib-standing roasts, nine points; seven-inch cut, rib-standing roasts, 10 points.

Lamb-mutton — Loin chops or roast, nine points; rib chops or roast, six points; leg chops and steaks, seven points; shoulder chops, blade or arm chops, six points; leg, six points; sirloin roast (bone in) six points; yoke (bone in) three points; yoke (boneless) five points; chuck or shoulder, square cut, four points; cross cut, three points; neck (bone in) two points; boneless neck, four points; shank, one point; lamb patties, five points.

Pork—Bellies, fresh and cured, four points; slab bacon (rind on), five points; slab bacon (rind off), six points; sliced bacon (rind off), six points; bacon ends, two points.

Variety Meats—Beef brains, one point, heart, three points; tongue, six points; veal brains, one point; heart, four points; sweetbreads, eight points; tongue, four points;

Continued on Page 8, Col. 1

FDR, Churchill Confer Day And Night

WASHINGTON, Sept. 2 (AP)—President Roosevelt and Prime Minister Churchill are back on a night and day schedule in their war talks, but no word is forthcoming from the White House on the subjects.

The chief executive and the Prime Minister talked until 1 o'clock this morning in Mr. Roosevelt's study and resumed their discussions during the day.

Mr. Roosevelt took time out, however, to meet Major General Eurico Gaspar Dutra, Brazil's War Minister, who is surveying the American war effort, and to preside at a meeting of his Cabinet.

Churchill meanwhile conferred with General George C. Marshall, chief of staff of the United States Army, and with British military leaders and chiefs of British missions in America.

Mrs. Roosevelt In Australia

CANBERRA, Australia, Sept. 3 (AP)—Mrs. Franklin D. Roosevelt, wife of the President, arrived today by plane (Friday).

(The dispatch did not state from where the plane came, but she previously had been in New Zealand.)

Japs' Madang Supply Base Blown Up

By the Associated Press

ALLIED HEADQUARTERS, Southwest Pacific, Friday, Sept. 3—Japanese army headquarters, fuel and ammunition stores have been blown up in the Madang, New Guinea sector above ground-menaced Salamaua by more than 206 tons of bombs dropped from fighter-escorted bombers, General Douglas MacArthur announced today.

Fires which erased warehouses and buildings sent their flames up for 1500 feet as the heavy and medium bombers spread ruin after the fashion of raids in early August which virtually levelled Salamaua.

TREE TOP HEIGHT

The raiders, sweeping down to tree-top height to pour 90,000 rounds of machine-gun and cannon fire on enemy installations, already plastered by bombs, struck at Madang, Amron Mission and Alexishafen.

"Widespread havoc and destruction was wrought in all three target areas with warehouses, buildings and headquarters sites left in ruins, fuel and ammunition dumps exploding and over 50 fires raging throughout the area," the communique said.

The big fires set could be seen for 30 miles. Not a Japanese plane was encountered in the air in the Madang area, which is just below

Continued on Page 3, Col. 1

THIS WORLD TODAY

By ROYCE BRIER

WHY ARE we on the beaches of France? Well, it's a long story. The story of what is happening there is your story. No one can tell you what it means to you, nor how it is going, nor what the end will be.

But there are things to remember. They are out of the past, and if we remember them it may not be vainly. It is all words can carry to you in such a time.

Along in the last century the somber forces which had been journeying down many centuries to make today, converged. They gathered to beget a struggle among Western men over the purpose and the fate of the civilization they had built. In this brief writing it makes little difference who was who. The age-old circumstance of Athens and Sparta faced mankind, as it had again and again, as it ever will, and there was nothing to do but fight it out.

It went on into our century, the peoples vaguely waiting and restless. Thirty years ago this month a wild young man in Sarajevo shot an Archduke. If you were at the age of reason then you hardly gave it a passing thought. Hate and violence for uncounted years had been the way of life in that part of the earth. So came the Great War.

To us for a time it was remote. Had we not made this country from nothing to escape such strife? But the struggle was not to avenge the life of an Archduke. The struggle was not to confirm a dying empire in its lust for a neighbor's soil. It was not to vindicate the noisy pretensions of an Emperor. The struggle was over the purpose and fate of the civilization, and in the end there was nothing to do but fight it out.

A man is little. He is given so little time to learn. Everything big strains his understanding. The riddle of love and life, the sway of peoples in the convulsions of history, the mystery of eternal nature—these bring him uncertainty.

This war was so big it covered men with confusion. It was not easy to see where wrong and right lay, where wisdom and folly. Voices of fear and doubt were a whispering chorus in the very air. The voice of conscience was often stilled, and the voice of the jungle, of self against man, spoke in a soft and endless drone. Men had to fall back on dim instinct, and in dim instinct

Continued on Page 4, Col. 1

INVASION EXTRA!

San Francisco Chronicle
THE CITY'S ONLY HOME-OWNED NEWSPAPER

FOUNDED 1865—VOL. CLVIII, NO. 144 CCCC SAN FRANCISCO, WEDNESDAY, JUNE 7, 1944 DAILY 5 CENTS, SUNDAY 15 CENTS: DAILY AND SUNDAY PER MONTH, $1.50

ALLIES WIDEN HOLD, RUSH MORE TROOPS!

Channel Weather Getting Rough

(AP) Wirephoto from Coast Guard Signal Corps Radio

ORDER OF THE DAY—Before H-Hour, General Eisenhower (left center) walked among his paratroopers. He talked to them of Kansas, of haircuts and the crops at home. Then, before they stopped into the waiting transport planes, he gave his orders—"Full victory—nothing else." A page of invasion radio photos are on Page 8.

Fighting Heavy, Says Berlin

Invaders Are Battling Inland on 100-Mile Front; New Sea Force Sighted Near Calais, Say Nazis

1000 Troop Carrying Aircraft Are Hurled Against French Coast; U. S. Battleship, Cruisers Aided in Assault

By the Associated Press

SUPREME HEADQUARTERS ALLIED EXPEDITIONARY FORCE, Wednesday, June 7---Masses of Allied air-borne troops which landed in France with little opposition were fighting their way inland early today along a 100-mile stretch of the Normandy coast between Cherbourg and Le Havre.

Heavy reinforcements, meanwhile, were being rushed across the channel in the face of a falling barometer.

In the second communique since the long-awaited invasion of Hitler's Europe began before daylight yesterday, the Allied High Command disclosed that more than 1000 troop-carrying aircraft, including gliders, participated in the air-borne phase of the gigantic operation with "unexpected success" and that two U. S. cruisers and the battle ship Nevada shelled the German defenses in support of the landings.

The bulletin said Allied naval casualties were regarded as "very light."

A British naval officer, who accompanied the task forces, said the Supreme Command was "still worried about the weather" and that there had been much seasickness among the invasion forces. The wind over the channel grew stronger during the night.

The German High Command in a special late communique declared that "fighting in the Cherbourg-Le Havre area is in full swing. South of Le Havre strong air-borne units have been annihilated. New enemy operations must be expected but have not taken shape yet. Fighting is extremely fierce everywhere as the Anglo-Americans are putting up a most tenacious resistance."

"It must be admitted," said the Nazi-controlled Vichy radio, "that the Allied beachhead area has been considerably widened and that Allied reinforcements are pouring in."

There were indications that the Germans were losing touch with their battle groups and that they were not sure where the main force of the Allied assault was striking.

At a late hour last night hundreds of Allied planes still were in the air, guarding the convoys and the beachheads and striking beyond the zone of operations to paralyze Nazi de-

Continued on Page 2, Col. 3

Churchill: Advance Steady, Losses Low

By Associated Press

LONDON, June 6 (AP) — Prime Minister Churchill announced today that Allied air-borne troops had captured several strategic bridges in France before they could be blown up and that "there is even fighting proceeding in the town of Caen."

"Air-borne troops are well established," Churchill reported in a second statement of the day to the House of Commons.

Allied troops had penetrated in some cases several miles inland after effective landings on the coast on a broad front, he said.

"Many dangers and difficulties which appeared at this time last night extremely formidable are behind us," the war leader reported.

"Passage of the sea has been made with far less loss than we apprehended.

"The resistance of batteries has been greatly weakened by bombing by the air force and the superior bombardment of our ships quickly reduced their power to dimensions which did not affect the problem."

DESCRIBES LANDINGS

Churchill, addressing the House of Commons after a visit to General Dwight D. Eisenhower's headquarters in company with King George, described the landing of airborne troops on the European continent as an outstanding feat "on a scale far larger than anything there has been so far in the world."

"These landings took place with extremely little loss and great accuracy."

Earlier, he told the cheering House that the Allied liberating assault was "proceeding according to plan—and what a plan."

"All this, of course, although very

Continued on Page 2, Col. 7

Latest Bulletins

By the Associated Press

A U. S. HEAVY BOMBER BASE IN SOVIET UNION, June 6 — Scores of United States heavy bombers—heavily escorted by fighters—took off from here today and roared over the Russian-German front, showering tons of high explosives and incendiary bombs on an airdrome at Galati, Rumania.

LONDON, June 6 (UP)—The Berlin radio said tonight that about 15 Allied cruisers and 50 to 60 destroyers were standing ready west of Le Havre, and late in the day a great number of landing craft were seen in the same area, apparently awaiting orders to hit the coast.

LONDON, June 6 (UP)—The German Transocean News Agency said tonight that the Allied "offensive area" had been extended to the entire Normandy peninsula.

Tokyo Radio Not Off Air

By United Press

The Office of War Information and National Broadcasting Company reported the Japanese - controlled Saigon (Indo-China) radio went off the air today. There was no immediate explanation, although Bangkok, capital of Thailand, northwest of Saigon, was bombed heavily yesterday.

Tokyo radio faded badly during mid-day, but the OWI said it did not stop broadcasting.

FDR: Two Destroyers Sunk---Air Toll Light

By United Press

WASHINGTON, June 6—President Roosevelt reported late today that the invasion of Europe is running "up to schedule."

He said that up to noon American naval losses in the operation comprised two destroyers and one escort ship.

He told a news conference that air losses were relatively light, amounting to about 1 per cent.

(In London it was announced that four heavy bombers and seven fighters were missing from three U. S. Eighth Air Force heavy bomber missions against more than 180 targets in German coastal defenses Tuesday.)

The President seemed openly pleased at the progress of the thrust into Hitler's fortress Europe.

Asked for his personal reaction to the operation, he said he found it was running "up to schedule." Then he added that that is saying a mouthful.

Mr. Roosevelt seemed particularly proud that naval losses up to noon had been limited to the two destroyers and the one landing ship. He said this information about naval losses had come to him in a dispatch from General Dwight D. Eisenhower, commanding the invasion.

Mr. Roosevelt again warned against too much overconfidence, however, saying that neither the invasion nor the war are by any means over.

He said the country had full reason to be thrilled, but he hoped this would not lead to overconfidence which would destroy the war effort.

The President said the decision to open the Western front was made in the December conferences at Teheran, where he met with Prime Minister Winston Churchill and Soviet Premier Joseph Stalin.

He explained that the opening of a front in Western Europe has been under discussion since the first conference of the joint chiefs of staff

Continued on Page 2, Col. 1

AND HERE . . .

Lights and shadows raced across the faces of the people of San Francisco yesterday in reaction to invasion news. For a detailed account of his observations read the story by J. Campbell Bruce on Page 6.

Exclusive Aerial Photos of the Disaster

San Francisco Chronicle

THE CITY'S ONLY HOME-OWNED NEWSPAPER

EXTRA

FOUNDED 1865—VOL. CLIX, NO. 4 CCCC SAN FRANCISCO, WEDNESDAY, JULY 19, 1944 DAILY 5 CENTS, SUNDAY 15 CENTS

BLAST DEATH TOLL NOW 377; 1000 INJURED!

Here is tangible evidence of the most disastrous explosion in the history of the Bay Area. This exclusive Chronicle aerial photo shows the tangled pilings; the twisted dock at the Navy's Port Chicago ammunition depot. Although taken only a few hours after the terrific blast, the picture indicates some restoration work.

Terrific Explosion In the Bay Region

Damage at Port Chicago Is Well Over Five Million; No Cause Has Been Found

The Army Brings Up Armored Car And Troops to Protect Property; Only a Few Bodies Are Recovered

Death toll resulting from the explosion Monday night at Port Chicago, on San Francisco Bay of tons of war munitions in the holds of two ships mounted to the 377 mark yesterday as semiofficial estimates were compiled.

Damage was estimated to be more than $5,000,000, excluding the cost of the munitions lost. The ships were valued at about $4,300,000.

Destruction of the huge Army arsenal at Benicia, only seven miles from the scene of the Port Chicago catastrophe was averted by miraculous chance. The blast, according to military officials, caused damaged there estimated at $150,000 to the arsenal facilities and injured six persons.

Reports from official sources gave this death roster:

KNOWN DEAD

250 Enlisted Navy personnel.
9 Navy officers.
70 United States Maritime Commission seamen.
5 Coast Guardsmen.
3 Civilian railroad workers.

337 TOTAL

To that total must be added, Navy spokesmen said, members of two armed guard crews of the two munition ships. Strength of a guard crew is restricted military information. Unofficial sources estimated their strength at 20 men each. With two crews missing, an estimated 40 more names might eventually be added to the known death list, bringing the total to at least 377 men.

Additional civilians and military personnel may have perished. No exact count of the "missing" (considered dead because no identifiable trace of the victims' bodies is expected to be found) is expected for several days. Merchant marine losses will be totaled after all crewmen alive report to the offices of the shipping lines operating the destroyed vessels.

Other stories and pictures of the blast are on Pages 7, 8, 9 and 11.

In addition to the two ammunition ships, three vessels were involved. They were two Coast Guard boats, one a crash boat, which is missing, and the other was a patrol boat, which was damaged. The fifth was the Red Line tanker, moored about 1000 yards from the disintegrated ship, which was damaged.

ESTIMATED INJURED

With the death toll high, there were an estimated thousand persons injured by the explosion. They suffered broken bones and face and body lacerations as the force of the detonation shattered window glass for miles around and sent

Continued on Page 4, Col. 5

Monty Boosted For Parliament

LONDON, July 18 (AP)—The London Daily Mirror boosted General Sir Bernard L. Montgomery as a possible candidate for Parliament after the war in its lead editorial today entitled "Monty, M. P.?"

"There is some ground for believing that the General does cherish political ambitions and we agree with those who are hoping that eventually he will stand for Parliament," the editorial said. "It is easy to imagine his becoming an outstanding figure in Commons."

A Town Dies Hard

Each Port Chicago Building Shows Struggle for Life

By CAROLYN ANSPACHER

PORT CHICAGO, July 18—The clock in the Port Chicago Hotel stopped last night at 10:19 o'clock.

Two red-coated horsemen riding lithographically to the hounds halted suddenly in their eternal quest and dipped drunkenly as the entire roof caved in.

That was how death came last night to Port Chicago . . . suddenly, drunkenly, on two devastating waves of thunder.

First came the sound and then, an instant later, the town rocked as if a titan had picked it up in a burst of fury and hurled it toward the sky. And then came darkness and the sort of silence that accompanies oblivion.

COMES THE DAWN

It is dawn now—a bitter cold dawn and nothing is left of Port Chicago. Nothing is left but the spirit of its 3000 inhabitants.

Every building is warped beyond recognition. Not a pane of glass remains intact.

Both men and cities die hard. Even little cities, like Port Chicago, fight for life.

Every building here shows signs of that struggle.

The Santa Fe depot where I am trying to write this story on the only typewriter in town that still functions is a mass of rubble.

Plate glass lies an inch thick on the littered floor. Bills of lading are whipped around like overgrown flakes of dirt-encrusted snow. Shredded green window shades wrestle valiantly with the north wind that beats through the building's skeleton.

Here is death. But here also there is resurrection.

THE AMMUNITION TRAIN

The station master already is back at work. Somewhere on one of the tracks outside there is an ammunition train. The station

Continued on Page 9, Col. 6

The Index

Comics	3H
Crossword	10
Contract Contacts	10
Drama	6
Editorials	14
Finance	4H
Lichty's Cartoon	13
Radio Log	3H
Ration Dates	13
Society	10
Vital Statistics	11
COLUMNS	
Bookman's Notebook	14
Will Connolly	1H
Bill Leiser	1H
Lyons Den	10
San Francisco	13
Washington Merry-Go-Round	14
Marquis Childs	5
Harry B. Smith	2H
Dorothy Thompson	14

Listen to The Chronicle-KYA Time-Clocked News—1260 on your dial—6 a. m. to midnight.

Armour to Take Pan-America Post

WASHINGTON, July 18 (AP)—The State Department announced today that Norman Armour, former Ambassador to Argentina, will head the department's office of American republic affairs, succeeding Lawrence Duggan who is leaving the Government shortly.

Armour is a career diplomat and has served in almost every European capital.

California Delegates For Wallace

By the Associated Press

CHICAGO, July 18—The California delegation to the Democratic national convention adopted by an overwhelming voice vote today a resolution indorsing Vice President Henry A. Wallace for renomination.

California has 52 votes in the convention. Twenty-seven of these previously had been claimed for Wallace.

The delegation's action amounted only to an expression of sentiment and did not bind the members to vote for Wallace.

This was the second big State to show Wallace strength today, and the CIO was driving sharply to renominate Wallace and to head off the candidacy of War Mobilization Director James F. Byrnes, who has exercised general control over wages.

CIO President Philip Murray, who forced a poll of the Pennsylvania delegation which disclosed 41 of its 72 votes were for Wallace, reputedly informed convention leaders that the labor organization would not stand for Byrnes' nomination.

WALLACE ON WAY

With the convention opening tomorrow, Wallace left Washington by train tonight for Chicago Democratic Convention battlegrounds, to inject new fervor into a

Continued on Page 11, Col. 4

Convention On the Air

Broadcasts of the Democratic convention will begin on all networks at 9 o'clock this morning, San Francisco time. Night session broadcast will begin at 6 p. m.

Weather Man

The Weather Man, en route to the beach on a Market St. car with his bureaubrats, was intrigued by the bearded gent in the seat ahead. "So you're on WPA?"

"And what," bridled the other, "is wrong with that?"

"Nothing, except there ain't no more WPA."

"Where'd you hear that?"

"I read it in the paper long ago."

"You believe what you read in the papers, eh?"

"Seems like a lotta people do, from the kicks we get," and Anemometer smirked as he handed the W. M. this note: **Cloudy in the morning.**

Horthy Vows End Of Jew Expulsion

BERN, Switzerland, July 18 (AP)—Admiral Nicholas Horthy, regent of Hungary, has promised the International Red Cross committee that no more Jews will be transported forcibly out of Hungary, it was learned today. He also authorized the committee to direct evacuation of Jewish children to countries willing to receive them.

Wife Tops Blood Gift of Governor

LOS ANGELES, July 18 (AP)—Governor Earl Warren gave his third pint of blood to the Red Cross today but Mrs. Warren went him four better. She gave her seventh.

The Governor's family is spending the summer here.

Tojo Is Fired As Japanese Army Chief

By the Associated Press

Premier General Hideki Tojo has been relieved as chief of the army general staff in the second sweeping shakeup of Japan's high command in two days in the face of what Tojo himself called "an unprecedentedly great national crisis." The changes were announced by Tokyo yesterday (Tuesday) in a series of broadcasts.

The navy, chief sufferer in recent heavy defeats in the Pacific, underwent a similar shakeup Monday, when the relatively obscure Admiral Naokuni Nomura replaced Admiral Shigetaro Shimada as Navy Minister.

Tojo's statement was read just after an imperial headquarters announcement told the Japanese people for the first time that all Japanese resistance at Saipan had come to an end; that the once-powerful Japanese garrison had been wiped out, and that among those slain were Vice Admiral Chuichi Nagumo, supreme commander in the Saipan area, and his chief aides, Lieutenant General Yoshitsugo Saito and Rear Admiral Takashia Tsujimira. Ad-

Continued on Page 2, Col. 5

Teddy Jr. Died on Eve of Promotion

GENERAL EISENHOWER'S ADVANCED COMMAND POST, July 18 (AP)—On the night that Brigadier General Theodore Roosevelt died in Normandy, General Dwight D. Eisenhower was preparing an order promoting him to Major General in command of a division.

Secretary Stimson disclosed this today and added that on his trip to Normandy "I was privileged to see the grave of my old friend, whose death was a very sad thing to me."

Great British Drive Splits Nazis at Caen

By the United Press

ALLIED SUPREME H. Q., London, July 18—Behind an 8000-ton aerial bombardment, the most concentrated in history the British Second Army burst the German line at Caen wide open today and raced in massed tank formation across the flat plain toward Paris—112 miles away—while American troops captured St. Lo in their toughest battle since D-Day.

The tremendous British break-through shattered the communications of 20 to 25 German divisions—perhaps 250,000 men—and left them, for the moment at least, in grave peril in what was called an Allied victory of "gigantic proportion."

WIDE NAZI RETREAT

After weeks of painstaking progress, Allied power exploded into a massive coordinated drive across the entire 120-mile French front that threw the Germans into retreat everywhere.

General Sir B. L. Montgomery's troops opened the great attack early today from the Orne bridgehead just above Caen, taking the Germans completely by surprise since they had massed to the south where the Tommies have been carrying out elaborate diversionary attacks.

Quickly blasting through the enemy's defenses, the British stormed into Vaucelles, Caen's southeastern suburb where the enemy held out after losing the main city, and began mopping up the last resistance, a dispatch from Montgomery's field headquarters said.

By afternoon the break-through was complete and "strong armored and mobile forces are operating in open country farther to the southeast and south," said the announce-

Continued on Page 2, Col. 4

ELECTION EXTRA!

San Francisco Chronicle
THE CITY'S ONLY HOME-OWNED NEWSPAPER

COMPARATIVE TEMPERATURES

	High	Low		High	Low
San Francisco	60	53	Salt Lake	51	41
Oakland	62	48	Chicago	50	30
Sacramento	..	45	New Orleans	75	..
Los Angeles	..	..	New York	44	35
Seattle	53	49	Washington	46	38

Forecast: Partly cloudy.

FOUNDED 1865—VOL. CLIX, NO. 116 CCCC SAN FRANCISCO, WEDNESDAY, NOVEMBER 8, 1944 DAILY 5 CENTS, SUNDAY 15 CENTS DAILY AND SUNDAY PER MONTH, $1.50

FDR PILING UP A LEAD IN 24 STATES!

Roosevelt Ahead in Pa., Illinois
Dewey Leads in 16; N.Y. Close!

By ROYCE BRIER

THIS KOISO is getting to be the worst chatterbox imaginable, and is in a fair way to talk himself out of work in the not distant future. It just goes to show you, war nowadays will make a gabby old woman of the best of them.

Like, you glance over the newspaper clippings of Mr. Koiso's past, and you find he was quite a fellow, one of the Kwantung Army plug-uglies and a flower of the Yamato race. He was governor-general of Korea for a time, and bowed to no man in the matter of beheading the helpless. A few years ago he landed home from the Manchurian front, and said those Russians couldn't fight for beans. Why, he said, we've got 'em trapped like rats if they so much as fire a cap pistol.

In those days, they said, he went around looking mean as dirt. In a grinning people this was considered a virtue, and who is to say it wasn't? At any rate, it was noteworthy. Not that Mr. Tojo was so amiable, all things considered. You will remember they called him "The Razor," not bad, so they called Mr. Koiso "The Tiger," not bad, either. You got to thinking of William Blake's poem, and it never would have occurred to you to mark Mr. Koiso down for a bargain day except for one little tip-off.

It was given in an unguarded moment by Tokyo Radio, which revealed a peccadillo in Mr. Koiso most disillusioning. He liked to sing. He liked to sing so much they had another nickname for him, to wit, "The Singing Frog." It was further disclosed to the palpitating Asiatics, not to mention the rest of us, that he was a two-bottle man in the sake department, and this was just too much for human flesh to bear.

For what have we here—a barber sharp chord expert posing as a world conqueror? Well, that's radio for you. Maybe Caesar twanged a ukulele, too, but he didn't have any waggish broadcaster to tip him off to the Gauls. If he had, history would have been a lot different, and maybe we wouldn't be here, which would have been terrible, you'll allow.

But to get back to Mr. Koiso, he took over that confining work last summer, and the first thing he did was make a speech. In that speech he said things were

Continued on Page 4, Col. 1

Total Kill: 440 Planes

Six Jap Ships Sunk, 24 Hit In Manila Fight

By the Associated Press

U. S. PACIFIC FLEET H. Q., Pearl Harbor, Nov. 7—Third Fleet carrier planes returned to the Manila area Sunday, destroying 240 Japanese planes to raise their two day toll to 440 and running their shipping score to 6 ships sunk and 24 damaged, with addition of 5 sunk and more than 5 damaged.

Admiral Chester W. Nimitz, announcing the continued neutralization of the Manila area in a communique today, reported additional "heavy damage" was inflicted on ground installations.

Three oil storage areas were set afire on the north strip at Clark Field and a tremendous explosion started another large fire in the northeast area of the same airdrome.

North of Malvar, a railway engine and five tanks cars were destroyed.

Five ships were sunk Sunday and five more, plus several cargo vessels, were damaged. One ship was sunk Saturday and five plus several cargo ships damaged.

These ships were sunk Sunday: Three cargo vessels, one oil tanker and one destroyer.

Damaged: Two destroyers, two destroyer escorts and one trawler and several cargo ships, bringing to 14 the two-day toll of these vessels.

Presence of many cargo ships in Manila harbor indicates the Japanese either have been able to slip one or more small convoys into the Philippines or were preparing to rush supplies to other Philippine islands.

Yanks Locked in Battle With Reinforced Enemy

GENERAL MACARTHUR'S H. Q., Philippines (Wednesday), Nov. 8 (AP)—The U. S. 24th Division is locked in a critical fight in Ormoc valley on Leyte, in the Philippines with elements of four Japanese divisions, including three rushed in as reinforcements, General Douglas MacArthur's headquarters reported today.

This was the crucial battle pre-

Continued on Page 2, Col. 1

Earl of Strathmore Dies in Scotland

LONDON, Nov. 7 (AP)—The Earl of Strathmore, 89, father of Queen Elizabeth of Great Britain, died today after a month's illness at Glamis Castle, his home at Forfarshire, Scotland.

His death brought the second bereavement to the British royal family in less than a fortnight. The court was due to go out of mourning Thursday for the death of Princess Beatrice, great aunt of King George VI and the last surviving child of Queen Victoria.

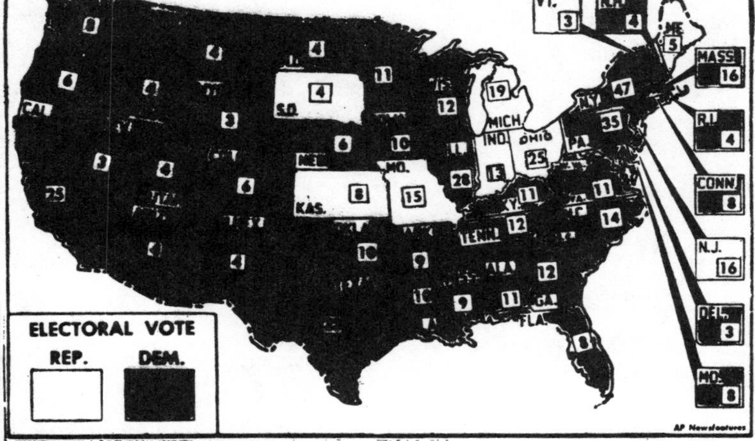

ELECTORAL VOTES OF THE NATION—This map shows the election trend so far in terms of the electoral college. There are 531 electoral votes, and 266 are necessary for election.

Philadelphia Victory for FDR Likely

By Associated Press

PHILADELPHIA, Nov. 7—A Roosevelt victory in Philadelphia was strongly indicated early tonight.

With returns missing from only 298 of the city's 1338 precincts, the count was 240,919 for Roosevelt and 265,498 for Dewey.

That represented a 75,421 lead for the President.

Roosevelt carried the city in 1940, polling 532,149 against Wendell Willkie's 354,878 for a majority of 177,271.

In Allegheny county, 51 precincts gave: Roosevelt 19,165, Dewey 13,456.

Polling places were jammed throughout Pennsylvania as voters in the pivotal keystone State made their choice for the presidency—and then waited for the count to learn whether the soldier vote would determine the issue.

Clear, cool weather helped to bring out the heavy vote which party headquarters estimated might equal or surpass the 1940 total when 82 per cent of the commonwealth's registered vote was cast.

An estimated 250,000 soldier votes to be counted November 22, was an undetermined but possibly decisive factor.

Election Bulletins

Associated Press returns from 7577 of the country's 130,826 voting units showed the popular vote:

ROOSEVELT	1,539,818
DEWEY	1,209,574
Total	2,729,392

WASHINGTON, Nov. 7 (UP)—Vice President Henry A. Wallace in effect claimed victory for President Roosevelt in a statement issued at 9:40 p. m. (EWT) tonight.

He issued the following statement:

"Roosevelt until 1948 means a country confident, moving with full steam ahead. The vote constitutes a mandate to Congress to prepare the way for 60,000,000 jobs. Corner apple selling disappeared under Roosevelt. The people have determined to lick the dole. Full employment means prosperity to farm and city alike. Plans will now go ahead for a permanent, enforceable peace."

(AP)—CALIFORNIA, 908 precincts of 14,841: Roosevelt, 82,846: Dewey, 55,912.

HYDE PARK, N. Y., Nov. 7 (UP)—President Roosevelt lost his home district of Hyde Park to Governor Dewey by approximately 375 votes, the election board reported tonight.

There was no complete tabulation available. The district usually goes Republican.

HARTFORD, Conn., Nov. 7 (UP)—Representative Clare Boothe Luce (R.), failed to carry the city of Stamford in the Fourth Congressional District by 524 votes. She took the city two years ago by 114 votes. Today the vote was:

Luce, 13,772; Connors (D.), 14,296.

ALBANY, N. Y., Nov. 7 (AP)—Representative Hamilton Fish, Republican candidate for re-election to a 13th term in the 29th Congressional District, led Augustus W. Bennet in first returns from five districts of Orange county tonight.

Totals were: Fish, Republican and Jeffersonian party, 1717; Bennet, Democratic, American Labor, Liberal and Good Government parties, 1136.

Orange is the only holdover county from the old 26th

Continued on Page 9, Col. 5

The New York Returns Are Nip-and-Tuck

NEW YORK, Nov. 7 (AP)—Governor Thomas E. Dewey forged slightly ahead of President Roosevelt in New Yor State tonight in early scattered returns.

In 297 election districts of 9121, Dewey polled 84,750 votes to 80,354 for the President. All but two of the districts were in predominantly Republican upstate.

In the U. S. Senate race, unofficial returns from 40 of 5421 upstate districts gave Secretary of State Thomas J. Curran, Republican candidate for U. S. Senator, 8481 votes to 6822 for the Democratic incumbent, Robert F. Wagner.

The presidential vote gave indications of approaching or exceeding the 1940 record of 6,301,000.

The State's voters included President Roosevelt, who came home to the normally Republican Dutchess county to cast his ballot, and Governor Dewey, who returned from Albany to Democratic New York City to do the same.

New York State, with 47 votes, was the No. 1 electoral prize.

In the first seven hours of the 15-hour polling period, approximately half of the vote was cast and the pace of the balloting continued. The polls closed at 9 p. m.

The vote was uniformly heavy in Democratic New York City and Republican upstate.

The Election

President Is Up Front in States With 324 Electoral Votes---Dewey With 152

California Voters Jam The Polls

By EARL C. BEHRENS

California voters in unprecedented numbers jammed the polls at yesterday's general election in all of the more heavily populated areas of the State.

Balloting for the Presidency, Vice Presidency, U. S. Senator, Congressional and legislative offices, and on the other items, was reported as orderly throughout the State in spite of the sharpness of the campaign during the recent months.

Democratic leaders predicted the heavy vote, particularly in the areas adjacent to war industries, meant the fourth term candidacy of President Roosevelt would score a sizeable margin over Governor Thomas E. Dewey, Republican nominee.

William F. Reichel, Dewey-Bricker manager in Northern California, held to the hope that the big turnout of voters would be a "protest" vote that would bring victory to his side.

If the Democratic claims are true, the Roosevelt margin could easily reach the 250,000 figure.

But the Republicans refused to concede a political inch and were out urging the voters to support the Dewey-Bricker ticket.

The voters went to the polls unusually early in many localities. San Diego reported a third of the voters had balloted in the first three hours.

HUGE TURNOUT

By 3 o'clock, Registrar Cameron H. King estimated that 51 per cent of the registered electorate, or 207,000, had voted. He predicted an 85 per cent vote would be cast.

The record was set in 1936, when 85.5 per cent of those registered went to the polls.

Women voters went to the polls here much earlier than usual. In many precincts long lines of citizens were awaiting the opening of the polls at 7 o'clock. Polls close in San Francisco at 8 p. m., instead of at 7 as in the remainder of the State.

The Registrar's office reported minor complaints of assistance given to voters by election officials, but on the whole both sides reported balloting progressing without incident.

ABSENTEE BALLOTS

Secretary of State Jordan estimated a total State vote of from 70 to 75 per cent. But the heavy balloting in the metropolitan areas seemed to indicate this figure would be exceeded.

In 1940 3,300,410 voted at the general election. President Roosevelt

Continued on Page 9, Col. 1

Downstate Illinois Gives Edge to GOP

By the Associated Press

Riding a groundswell of returns from vote-heavy pivotal States, President Roosevelt surged to the front by 10:45 p. m. (EWT) last night in States with 324 electoral votes —58 more than a winner needs.

At that hour, with millions of votes yet to be reported, Thomas E. Dewey trailed in his bid for the White House, holding a lead in 16 States with 152 electoral ballots.

The President was out ahead in early returns from such important States as New York, Pennsylvania and Illinois—the heaviest voters of them all.

Altogether, Roosevelt spurted into leads in 24 States by mid-evening. Eleven of them were in the normally "Solid South," which were giving a hearty indorsement to the fourth term.

WALLACE

Confidently, Vice President Henry Wallace telephoned the Associated Press in Washington that it's "Roosevelt until 1948." Wallace campaigned for the President, although Senator Truman of Missouri took his place on the ticket.

But it was nip and tuck in New York and upstate Republican legions again pushed Dewey out ahead within a short time. Only two New York city precincts had been counted and the bulk of the returns from the State as a whole were still missing.

Philadelphia apparently hung up a Roosevelt victory, but by a narrower margin than four years ago, and the President swung out front early in Pennsylvania as a whole.

IN ILLINOIS

The early returns from Illinois shoved Roosevelt ahead in that key State, but they were mostly from the Chicago precincts where that outcome was to be anticipated. Downstate, Dewey was leading.

The Republican nominee set the early pace in Ohio, home State of his running mate, Governor John W. Bricker. The greater part of the initial counts came from the rural districts where Dewey and Bricker looked for their heaviest backing.

Dewey also led in Michigan, New Jersey and Indiana—and in Missouri. That's Truman's home State. Missouri, however, had been wavering, jumping first into the Roosevelt column then picking up the Dewey banner as the vote-count proceeded.

In Michigan, the first tabulations came from outside industrial Detroit.

Maryland, a border State, turned

Continued on Page 9, Col. 4

San Francisco Chronicle

THE CITY'S ONLY HOME-OWNED NEWSPAPER

FOUNDED 1865—VOL. CLX, NO. 68 CCCCAA SAN FRANCISCO, SATURDAY, MARCH 24, 1945 DAILY 5 CENTS, SUNDAY 15 CENTS DAILY AND SUNDAY PER MONTH, $1.75

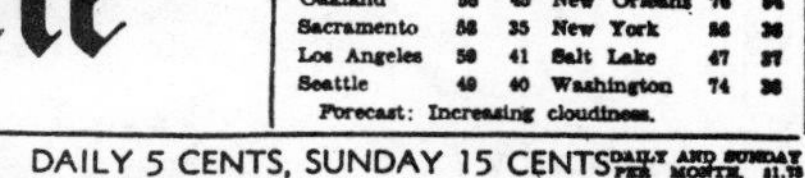

COMPARATIVE TEMPERATURES	High	Low		High	Low
San Francisco	54	46	Chicago	76	46
Oakland	55	45	New Orleans	76	64
Sacramento	58	35	New York	56	36
Los Angeles	50	41	Salt Lake	47	37
Seattle	49	40	Washington	74	36

Forecast: Increasing cloudiness.

THIS WORLD TODAY

By ROYCE BRIER

THE DISPATCH says: "By now the little man of Japan must be thoroughly perplexed." It is an interpretation of Tokyo broadcasts intercepted in San Francisco.

Mr. Togachi was what might be called a little man. In his youth he had been a fisherman in a village down on the Suwo Sea, but his oldest son, going to Kobe to work the docks, had persuaded him a better life was to be found in the great world of the cities. He was sixty now, and for twenty years he had been working in an armature factory in Osaka. Work had been irregular at first, but not for ten years. For four years it had been almost intolerably regular.

Mr. Togachi, however, was not a man to question fate. He accepted it wholly, and indeed he had been a contented man, at least until this perplexity came not long ago.

He had always known certain things to be true. He had known the Emperor, whom he had never thought of as a man with a name, was divine. He had known the great, who ruled in the nameless one's name, so to speak, were incapable of ruling unwisely. He had known his race was the greatest, the bravest and most honorable, his culture the only one worth calling a culture, his truth the only truth.

All people not his people were in fact evil, and striving to destroy the good, but he had always known they could not do it, because the good Japan was impregnable. He had not the shred of a dream the coming universal fatherhood of the Emperor could be thwarted, let alone that his own right and imperishable world could prove temporary, vulnerable, and in sum, could perish before his eyes.

Therefore, those events in history involving his people in recent years, could not induce in him the slightest effort at analysis. The invasion of China he had always heard was inevitable, for the Chinese were an evil people who must be subjected to the rule of good people at a time chosen because it was right.

Mr. Togachi thought of the Americans as a more dangerous and probably more evil people. He had seen a few while sojourning in Kobe briefly before coming to Osaka, and that was enough. There might be Japa-

Continued on Page 2, Col. 1

RHINE PONTOON BRIDGE—When the bridge captured by the U. S. First Army at Remagen collapsed, material continued to flow to Yanks on the east bank across this and other similar emergency spans. Rapid construction is possible when Army engineers float numerous pontoons into position, fasten them together side to side and lay down a road surface across them. Two spare pontoons and a section of road surface are in the right foreground. (AP Wirephoto from U. S. Army Signal Corps

East and West Fronts

Third Army Storms Over Rhine, Smashes East From Bridgehead; Oder Line Is Cracked, Berlin Says

90,000 Russian Troops Break Through East of Capital, Enemy Claims

By the United Press

LONDON, March 23—A Soviet force of 90,000 men broke through Berlin's immediate defenses and with strong tank and plane support drove to the outskirts of Golzow, six miles west of Kuestrin and only 32 miles from the imperiled Reich capital, German reports said tonight.

(Associated Press quoted a dispatch from Berlin to the German-controlled STB Agency in Stockholm saying:

"The major Russian offensive against Berlin is immediately at hand.")

Finding a weak spot in the Germans' Oder line after weeks of probing from bridgeheads in the Kuestrin vicinity, Marshal Gregory K. Zhukov's First White Russian Army exploited the situation with strong attacks southwest and northwest of the city, the Berlin reports indicated.

The Germans have reported Soviet bridgeheads at Genschmar, seven miles northwest of Kuestrin, and at Manschnow, three miles southwest.

BALTIC BREAKTHROUGH

The attack began after a shattering one and one-half hour barrage, the Germans said, and was spearheaded by more than 100 giant Joseph Stalin tanks and swarms of Stormovik dive-bombers.

Estimating the size of the Russian force at six rifle divisions—normally some 90,000 men, a German front reporter said "the enemy succeeded in breaking through our front owing to the great masses of war material employed and in reaching the outskirts of Golzow.

"He was then halted by our own counterattacks," the report said. "Our counterthrusts met with tenacious enemy resistance and a fluctuating battle continues."

Moscow's communique revealed only that Red Army troops mopping up in the Baltic sector had broken through to the sea between Danzig and Gdynia and captured the resort town of Zoppot.

STETTIN SHELLED

The Germans also reported that **Marshal Ivan S. Konev's First Ukrainian Army had extended its offensive across Upper Silesia into Czechoslovakia and was fighting on both sides of Hotzenplotz.**

Moscow dispatches said Russian forces at the Oder estuary opposite Stettin had unleashed a gigantic barrage against that vital Baltic port.

No less than 10 Russian armies were reported by Berlin to be assailing the last ramparts of Danzig and Gdynia and their tremendous pressure was admitted to have hammered the German garrisons into a constricted coastal pocket.

In Hungary, the Berlin communique said, the Germans had been forced back to a shortened line, but had prevented a breakthrough by strong Russian tank and infantry formations which had reached the area south of Komarom.

Nazis Taken by Surprise; None Killed in Crossing; Bombing Isolates Ruhr

By the Associated Press

PARIS, March 24—The U. S. Third Army swarmed in strength across the Rhine Thursday night in the war's greatest river crossing, overwhelmed the startled enemy and struck inland with lightning speed from a firm bridgehead on the shortest road to Berlin—265 miles ahead.

By Friday the Americans had seized a sizable strip of territory east of the river, for an official announcement referred to the position as a bridgehead, which in army terminology means the crossings are beyond enemy light artillery range. (That might mean they were as much as five miles beyond the Rhine.)

Three other Allied armies—the American Ninth, Canadian First and British Second—were poised at the northern end of the front for Rhine crossings which the Germans said were imminent.

NO BOMBARDMENT

Carrying out to perfection a coup rehearsed for months, Lieutenant General George S. Patton Jr. put the first American assault waves across at an undisclosed point on the east bank without the Germans firing a shot and without the loss of a man in the actual crossing.

The crossing, which the Germans said was made with amphibious tanks as well as assault boats, came without a preliminary bombardment which might have tipped off the enemy.

Patton was pressing home what might well prove a mortal blow without giving the enemy time to recuperate from the Nazi catastrophe west of the Rhine. The charging doughboys were talking in high spirits of beating the Russians to Berlin.

A STARTLED ENEMY

The enemy was so startled by this swift assault that some troops, resting from their defeat west of the river, were caught eating and not a single heavy shell was fired until two hours after the first troops touched the east bank in the moonlight of 10:25 p. m., Thursday.

Thus Patton showed his contempt for the Rhine, Germany's historic moat which never before had been stormed, although the U. S. First Army won the honor of being the first across by taking the Ludendorff bridge intact at Remagen more than two weeks ago.

The Germans, giving the first hint of the dazzling coup, said earlier in the day that Patton had crossed near Oppenheim, 10 miles south of the fallen city of Mainz.

THE GERMAN VERSION

The ease of the crossings and the swift push inland pointed up the tremendous victory which the Third and the U. S. Seventh Armies had won the west bank.

The German First and Seventh Armies, which might have been on the east bank for the defense of inner Germany, were destroyed—100,000 of their troops in prison cages and their tanks, armored vehicles, trucks and guns strewn by the thousands on the battlefield west of the Rhine.

If the Germans are correct in saying that Patton crossed at Oppenheim, then his forces are out of the Frankfurt plain on one of the best natural approaches to Berlin through the waist of Germany.

"WAVE ON WAVE"

There the Rhine is 500 yards wide, and a short distance north it turns into the narrow gorge that leads on to Coblenz.

That would place it about 85 air-line miles south of the First Army's east bank front, which is bursting out southward and is nearing the Rhine opposite Coblenz.

Oppenheim is 20 miles southeast of Frankfurt-on-the-Main, and is little more than 100 airline miles west of where the Russians are swinging westward.

Wave on wave of hard-hitting veterans crossed in what Associated Press Correspondent Edward D. Ball declared from the front was "the greatest over-water assault since the Normandy beaches."

The Germans then began pouring in some mortar and anti-tank fire and they were answered and silenced by thunderous salvos from American artillery drawn up along the river.

STRIKE INLAND

By dawn the first wave had pushed on inland and more and more men and supplies were landing on the bridgehead in assault boats. Ball said the beachhead by

Continued on Page 2, Col. 2

New Crossing ---First Hand

Only Correspondent With Third Tells of Storming the Rhine

Edward D. Ball of the Associated Press was the only correspondent to make the night crossing of the Rhine with the American Third Army and for the first 12 hours of the operation was the only correspondent eyewitness. He tells about it in the following remarkable dispatch.

In a message to his home office, Ball, 40, complained that his copy was held by censor until simultaneous announcement at all headquarters and added this lament: "On top of all that, all guts slashed out of my copy."

By EDWARD D. BALL
Associated Press Staff Writer

WITH THE U. S. THIRD ARMY EAST OF THE RHINE, March 23—The Third Army stormed across the Rhine at 10:25 p. m. last night without loss of a man and without drawing a single shot from the Germans until a good 20 minutes after the crossing was made good.

By dawn today a solid bridgehead was driven into Hitler's inner fortress against opposition that still was spotty and erratic despite some artillery and mortar fire.

At the first crack of day a couple of Messerschmitt 262 jet-propelled planes poked inquisitive noses over the bridgehead and promptly were knocked down.

Patton's men moved like lightning and the elated doughboys, who three weeks ago were urging the Russians on to Berlin, now nominated themselves for the job of taking the German capital.

HUNDREDS OF VEHICLES

I saw the doughboys on Omaha beach in Normandy last June 6 and I went across the Rhine with them last night.

The spirit was identical, and so was the overwhelming superiority in men and equipment.

The Rhineland never saw a more amazing sight than last night's. Probably it never will. For miles back the roads were lined with trucks and other vehicles struggling up the hills.

Hundreds of conveyances of all kinds which had pulled up just out of sight of the river during the day stood silent and shadowy in the moon-splashed fields and along the edges of woods near the Rhine. Engineers who had spent back-breaking months at home preparing for this show were on hand to help get the vehicles across.

A fleet of pint-sized artillery spotter planes, impressed into service as emergency one-man troop carriers, stood ready on a dozen uncharted wheat fields. The little cow pasture transport force was to shuttle across the river, putting down anywhere it could, if the doughboys storming the Rhine found more than they could handle. But the planes were not needed.

For months columns of trucks

Continued on Page 2, Col. 2

The S.F. Conference

Bretton Proposals Key Part of Security Plan, Says Acheson

By CHARLES RAUDEBAUGH

Assistant Secretary of State Dean Acheson yesterday told San Francisco that the Bretton Woods monetary proposals are an "absolutely essential counterpart" of the Dumbarton Oaks plan to be submitted to the United Nations at the forthcoming world conference here.

He took spirited issue with New York banker Leon Fraser, one-time director of the Bank for International Settlements, for telling a House committee on Thursday that the Bretton Woods world money fund would be "a grant in aid to England."

"I haven't read Mr. Fraser's testimony, but if I've talked with him in the past, and his particular form of expression is an extreme if not reckless way to talk about something as important as Bretton Woods," said the State Department official.

"If you go into his concept—what he has in mind is a very traditional and limited viewpoint which is not representative of the bankers."

(A local controversy between supporters and opponents of the Bretton Woods agreement appeared yesterday when it became known that a Chamber of Commerce sub-committee had voted in a meeting Wednesday to support the agreement. Charges were denied that the meeting was "secret and undercover." See Page 3.)

While Secretary Acheson was addressing a San Francisco audience, Australian Foreign-Minister H. V. Evatt was outlining to a Charter Day audience at the University of California his country's hopes that the proposed international organization to be drafted at the San Francisco Conference will include full employment and freedom from want among its goals.

Evatt declared the provisions of the Dumbarton Oaks proposal which deal with economic and social co-operation should be "clarified and tightened" to embrace specifically "some of the fundamental principles of the Atlantic Charter and the 1944 Philadelphia Declaration of the International Labor Organization."

"There is everything to be said for

Continued on Page 3, Col. 1

France, Australia Join Shipping Pool

WASHINGTON, March 23 (AP)—The War Shipping Administration today announced the addition of France and Australia to the United Maritime Authority. This raises to 10 the nations which will submit their shipping to Allied central control for at least six months after the war.

Berlin Ruin Urged As War Monument

LONDON, March 23 (AP)—Captain Sir William Bass, Conservative, suggested to Commons today that a badly bombed section of Berlin be preserved in its state of devastation as a reminder that Germany started the war. He said Prime Minister Churchill should incorporate the proposal in surrender terms.

No Sun for Palm Sunday, Says the WM

The green light was on for good weather over the week-end for a time yesterday but it changed to a bright red last night.

However, the Weather Man still holds hopes of doing better next week for Easter.

His forecast for today:

INCREASING CLOUDINESS, RAIN TONIGHT.

Warren's Tax Bill

Assembly Votes to Add 57 Million For Local Projects to Measure

By EARL C. BEHRENS
Political Editor The Chronicle

SACRAMENTO, March 23—Governor Warren's State tax cut program suffered a major setback in the Assembly today when $57,000,000 in post-war subsidies to cities and counties was written into the Fourt bill.

The administration defeat resulted from the defection of 11 Republicans who joined with the Democrats, who have been urging delay on State tax cuts. Eight Democrats voted with the Republicans to prevent what was characterized as "a political grab bag" amendment.

The amendment objected to by administration forces was approved 41 to 39 after a day of debate. However, Assemblyman Harrison W. Call, Redwood City, placed a block in the way of further immediate action before the week-end recess, by serving notice he will ask to reconsider the vote on Monday, which threatens the entire Warren legislative program.

Under the terms of the O'Day amendment, which the Democratic leadership supported with gusto, the League of California Cities, the County Supervisors and the Associated Contractors chalked up at least part of the score they hope to record at this session in the way of State subventions of local political subdivisions.

The $57,000,000 sum, which under the Governor's program would go into the State postwar fund, will now go into a reserve fund for local projects.

Each locality will have to scramble for its share of the pot when the legislators at a future session divvy up the funds.

Democratic minority leader Alfred Robertson urged support for the subsidy amendment on the grounds of "expediency."

Assemblyman Gardiner Johnson, one of the 11 Republicans who joined the 30 Democrats in supporting the subsidy proposal questioned the constitutionality of the bill. He is the author of League of Cities, County Supervisors and Associated General Contractors bill which would grant local political subdivisions a $100,000,000 in State subsidies. This bill would boost State taxes.

Last night, a Senate committee amended a similar proposal of the same groups to provide that 55 per cent of the $100,000,000 go to cities and cities and counties and 45 per cent to counties and to cities and counties. Thus San Francisco, being both a city and county, would fall into both classifications. Distribution of the funds would be on a basis of the 1940 population figures.

The Assembly amendment did not set up any yard-stick for distributing the $57,000,000 but would let each community fight it out in the legislature for its share.

THE TAX REQUIREMENT

If the money is allocated on a matching basis, then presumably, as pointed out by Assemblyman Armstrong, "cities and counties will have to raise taxes to match State funds." Armstrong opposed the amendment.

Assemblyman Walter J. Fourt, Ventura, who is handling the Governor's tax reduction program, said the amendment proposed a new departure in the State "that was put in the position "of raising money for local political subdivisions as such." He did not believe it was wise for the legislators to be "primarily concerned in raising funds for local officials to spend."

Assemblyman J. J. Hollibaugh, city councilman of Huntington Park, opposed the subsidy on the grounds that "city and county officials are going to the State government for more and more of their share of basic revenues." Assemblymen Thomas H. Werdell, Bakersfield, Thomas A. Maloney and John Pelletier, Los Angeles, also urged defeat of the subsidy proposal.

Home town officials are more careful in spending their neighbors' tax money than in expending funds received from the State or "other outside sources," Rolland A. Vandegrift, legislative auditor, told the Assembly in the open hearing held prior to the voting.

Vandegrift's testimony was really intended to develop his contentions that enactment of compulsory health insurance would result in a $100,000,000 annual deficit to the State. Supporters of compulsory health insurance bills deny the Vandegrift prediction.

THE WRONG ANSWER

Minority Leader Robertson wanted the Vandegrift testimony to buttress his own position that action on tax cuts should be delayed until the health insurance issue was decided. But Vandegrift gave another answer that did not fit into the Democrat leadership's moves. This was to the effect that more money goes to labor if expended by private capital.

Continued on Page 9, Col. 1

Patch Decorated For Invasion Plan

WASHINGTON, March 23 (UP)—Lieutenant General Alexander M. Patch, commander of the U. S. Seventh Army, was awarded the oak leaf cluster to the distinguished service medal today for his "masterly" skill in planning the invasion of Southern France.

The War Department citation said the Seventh Army's successes in storming the beaches of the French Mediterranean coast were due "largely to the careful planning and exceptional training" of the staff and units under Patch.

He Lived Through Shelling for This!

ARTESIA, N. M., March 23 (AP)—War Correspondent Kenneth L. Dixon dodged shells, bombs and small arms fire in Africa and Italy and on the Western Front for 18 months, came home on leave and today turned up with—the mumps.

Dixon, who plans to return to the war front soon, was ordered to bed for a week by his doctor.

"I'm O. K. Just tell folks not to laugh at me," he said tonight. "But," he added, "I can't help laughing myself."

U. S. Loses A Carrier

Jap Planes Destroy The 'Bismarck Sea' In Attack Off Iwo

By the Associated Press

GUAM, March 24—Japanese planes which counterattacked U. S. amphibious forces off Iwo Jima the night of February 21 sank the escort carrier U. S. S. Bismarck Sea, Admiral Chester W. Nimitz announced today (Saturday).

The Bismarck Sea, a 4000-ton vessel, was the eleventh U. S. carrier listed as lost in the war. Ten of the eleven have been lost in the Pacific. Six of the flattops were escorts, one was a light carrier and four were full carriers.

(In Washington, the Navy said the Bismarck Sea had a displacement of 10,200 tons. She was known as the Alikula Bay, when launched at Vancouver, Wash., by the Kaiser company. The name was changed when she was commissioned May 20, 1944.)

Nimitz said "most" of the Bismarck Sea's personnel—estimated at 1500—were rescued, but Captain John Lockwood Pratt, the skipper, in an interview told war correspondents "many" of his men were killed in explosions caused by Japanese aerial torpedoes and by the fires which followed. He said many others were killed in the water by Japanese pilots who returned to strafe survivors.

Coast Guard and other small craft rescued the survivors.

This was the first announcement of U. S. losses in the February 21 attack by some 800 craft.

Captain Pratt, of Milford, Del., and Coronado, Cal., made every effort to save the carrier, Nimitz reported, before ordering personnel to abandon ship. She sank a short time later.

The executive officer, Commander M. E. Born, Coronado, Calif., and Captain Pratt were picked up safely from the water by small boats of other U. S. warships.

(Other Pacific news on Page 3.)

Noose Tightened On Japs in Burma

CALCUTTA, March 23 (AP)—Indian armored forces, driving south from Mandalay at a 30-mile-a-day clip, have captured the towns of Pindale and Wundwin just short of Meiktila, further constricting the noose around thousands of Japanese troops cut off west of the Mandalay-Thazi rail line, Allied Headquarters announced.

Pindale is 19 miles north of Meiktila and Wundwin is 18 miles northeast, on the main north-south trunk road.

Lieutenant General Daniel I. Sultan's three-pronged drive in Central Burma made progress everywhere. A column pushing west from Lashio crossed the Nan Ma river after wiping out an enemy delaying party and was reported within 10 miles of a junction with the British 36th Division.

Allied planes lashed Japanese installations and communications over wide areas of Burma and Thailand.

Shipment Arrives From France

NEW YORK, March 23 (AP)—The first French cognac and perfume to arrive in this country for four and a half years was unloaded today at the East river.

It will take about three months to clear the rare, pre-war brandy through customs, price it with the help of the OPA, and distribute it among retailers.

Ten Millions in Gifts Sent to Italy

ROME, March 23 (AP)—A total of $10,830,500 was sent by United States residents to relatives in Italy in the nine months ended February 28, the Allied Commission announced today. Remittances numbered 215,713. The cash gifts were limited to $500 per household per month.

Your Blood Saved 4000 On Iwo Jima

This is a report to West Coast blood donors from the boys who were wounded in the Marine assault of Iwo Jima island:

The Marines are grateful. Nearly 4000 wounded owe their lives to whole blood transfusions.

From Navy headquarters on Guam, Sergeant Stanley Fink, Marine Corps combat correspondent, yesterday reported that 5600 pints of whole blood were used in Iwo beaches and fox holes.

Some Marines needed 10, 16 and even 18 pints of blood because their wounds were so severe, the sergeant said.

You can help save a Marine's life.

Make an appointment now at the Red Cross Blood Donor Center, 2415 Jones street, call GRaystone 9373.

Mickey Rooney Arrives in Paris

PARIS, March 23 (UP)—Mickey Rooney arrived in Paris today with 52 other Army entertainers after three months in the Roer river sector. After touring the city's monuments he said he hoped to revisit Paris after the war.

"I have performed in barns and bomb-ruined houses," Mickey told a reporter, "but what does it matter as long as the soldiers are happy?"

Manila's Traffic Rules Go Yankee

MANILA, P. I., March 23 (AP)—Manila's police chief today announced the Philippine Commonwealth decreed that effective April 1 everyone must drive on the right side.

The Chronicle Post-War Forum

State Senate Indorses Unity Program

Special to The Chronicle

SACRAMENTO, March 23—The Senate unanimously adopted a resolution by Senator John F. Shelley indorsing The Chronicle war and post-war forum to be held in the late summer.

The resolution was adopted last Thursday after Senator Shelley had expressed belief that great good would result from the meeting of representatives of every segment of Northern California life, including labor, industry and agriculture.

"We feel sure that out of such a forum there will come a unity of opinion on a program for the State as a whole, for all Northern California and for our own San Francisco Bay Area which will be of great aid in meeting the complex problems produced by the war and the post-war period following cessation of hostilities."

Senator Shelley said the forum suggestion had been indorsed by Governor Warren, Mayor Lapham, as well as officials of many Northern California communities, labor, business and spokesmen for every phase of activity in the State.

The resolution follows:

"WHEREAS, The San Francisco Chronicle has announced plans for a forum of representatives of the various groups and the various sections of California with a view to exploring the State's war and post-war problems and attaining a meeting of the minds of men of good will, who will place community service above the service of individuals or groups, and

"WHEREAS, Such a forum holds the possibility of unlimited good for all of California; now, therefore, be it

RESOLVED BY THE SENATE OF THE STATE OF CALIFORNIA, That this body hereby indorses the proposed forum of the San Francisco Chronicle and offers whatever support it can to the undertaking."

(Indorsements of Forum continue to pour in. See Page 4.)

The Chronicle Index

Barnaby	11	Society	6
Casualties	2	Vital Statistics	6
Churches	8	Weather	6
Comics	3H	COLUMNS	
Crossword Puzzle	6	Bookman's Notebook	12
Drama	10	San Francisco	11
Editorials	12	Washington Merry-Go-Round	12
Finance	4H	Bill Leiser	1H
Lichty's Cartoon	11	Will Connolly	1H
Marty Links' Cartoon	6	Harry B. Smith	2H
Radio Log	4H	Chester Rowell	12
Ration Dates	11	Lyons Den	7

EXTRA

San Francisco Chronicle

THE CITY'S ONLY HOME-OWNED NEWSPAPER

COMPARATIVE TEMPERATURES	High	Low		High	Low
San Francisco	56	46	Chicago	81	66
Oakland	65	38	New Orleans	—	63
Sacramento	66	43	New York	—	46
Los Angeles	—	—	Salt Lake	45	30
Seattle	—	37	Washington	70	54

Forecast: Clear, cool.

FOUNDED 1865—VOL. CLX, NO. 88 CCCC SAN FRANCISCO, FRIDAY, APRIL 13, 1945 DAILY 5 CENTS, SUNDAY 15 CENTS

F.D.R. DIES!

THIS WORLD TODAY

By ROYCE BRIER

THE CAIRO correspondent was probably a green man, good, but green. He probably stuffed the teletype into his pocket and went to the terrace of the Continental-Savoy, or to Shepheard's garden. After a few drinks he pulled out the dispatch and read it.

So it said the head of Nefertiti, the Egyptian Queen, had been found in the salt mine in Germany where the Americans stumbled on the money and some of the antiquities from the Berlin museums. Two hundred words, please, said the dispatch.

When the Cairo correspondent went back to his office, he obliged. He got it right that Queen Nefertiti was the mother-in-law of Tutankhamen, the famous King Tut. But when he got down to cases he decided the head had to be mummified, so that's the way he described it. That's the way the first dispatch came in Tuesday. There's a war on, and you haven't much time.

The head of Nefertiti, who was one of the great and beautiful women of all time, is a sandstone bust about a foot high, as originally found at Tel-el-Amarna, up-river from Cairo a couple of hundred miles, not many years ago. It retains its original tan tinting of feature, and the coloring of the necklace is as bright red and blue as though done yesterday. The bust had glass eyes, and one was missing. Also missing was a tall green headdress, which was restored.

Nefertiti is almost the only life-like portrait bust ever to be found in Egypt. In fact, very little was known of the Queen until the bust was found. The Britannica chronology does not mention her, but she was one of the wives of Akhenaton of the 18th Dynasty, about 1400-1350 B. C. She must have been a sort of Marie Antoinette with great political influence, for those were revolutionary times.

Akhenaton was perhaps the most extraordinary of all the pharaohs, a revolutionary. He established a new sun religion much more advanced than that of the preceding 2000 years, and at El-Amarna built a great and beautiful capital, and abandoned Thebes and Karnak. This was undoubtedly man's first social revolution, but it failed at Akhenaton's death, and El-Amarna

Continued on Page 2, Col. 1

War in The West

Tanks of Ninth Cross the Elbe; ---It's 57 Miles

By Associated Press

PARIS, April 12—Tanks of the U. S. Ninth Army swept across the Elbe river on a six-mile front, 57 miles from Berlin, today and awaited only orders from Lieutenant General William H Simpson to begin a dash on a wide open road that might put them by tomorrow into that capital of death and devastation.

A report attributed to French sources said Allied parachute troops had been dropped at Brandenburg, barely more than 20 miles from Greater Berlin, but this was wholly without official confirmation.

Germany appeared in her final hours of organized resistance in the west as all Allied armies cut loose.

Even No. 1 Nazi propogandist Paul Joseph Goebbels declared gloomily in his weekly newspaper that the war "cannot last much longer in my opinion."

TANKS RIP THROUGH

Three tank columns of the U. S. Third Army, ripping beyond the heart of Germany in dashes up to 46 miles of that overwhelmed Weimar—birthplace of the German republic—were 129 miles from the Russian lines, 40 miles from the Czech border and 109 miles from Berlin. The Ninth Army was within 115 miles of the Russian lines.

With the U. S. First Army, which was thundering eastward at the rate of 30 to 40 miles a day, the Third Army was closing on Leipzig, 75 miles southwest of Berlin and a communications city second only to the capital.

Advancing flank to flank, these two armies last were reported about 22 miles from Leipzig and a First Army field dispatch said the Yanks might be in the city by Friday.

So near did the two American armies appear to a junction with the Russians that liberated Soviet slave laborers turned eastward in their wake, believing they could get home quicker that way.

SCHWEINFURT FALLS

The U. S. Seventh Army, joining in the drive to cut Germany in half, smashed eastward to within 35 miles of the Munich-Berlin superhighway, most important north-south German road link, and was nearing Bamberg, 30 miles northwest of the Nazi shrine city of Nuernberg.

The Seventh Army captured Schweinfurt, a ballbearing manufacturing center of 42,000 population, while farther to the southwest the French First Army seized the Black Forest cities of Baden Baden and Rastatt.

On the northern end of the front, the British Second Army captured Celle, a German training center for gas warfare 50 miles south of Hamburg, and deepened its Aller river bridgehead thrust within 45 miles

Continued on Page 2, Col. 6

Spanish-Jap Rift Leaves U. S. Cool

WASHINGTON, April 12 (AP)—Secretary of State Stettinius said today that Spain's break in relations with Japan, announced yesterday, will have no effect upon United States relations with the Franco government.

The United States now has diplomatic relations with Spain and is represented in Madrid by Ambassador Norman Armour. However Washington has been critical of Spain's role during the European war and Stettinius' reply apparently was intended to emphasize that this attitude is unchanged by Spain's action toward Japan.

One Bright Thing In Berlin---the Sun

LONDON April 12 (UP)—A broadcast Berlin dispatch to Zurich, recorded by the BBC, said today that the only bright thing left for the Berliners was the spring sunshine.

FRANKLIN DELANO ROOSEVELT

Eastern Front

Great Battles Rage Along Oder—Final Berlin Drive Is Near

By United Press

LONDON, April 12—The Moscow Radio reported tonight that heavy battles were raging west of the Oder before Berlin, indicating that Marshal Gregory K. Zhukov had launched his final drive on she Reich capital in concert with Allied forces moving on the city from the west.

The Soviet High Command communique did not confirm the report, but said Russian armies had cut the last serviceable German escape lines from Vienna and had mopped up 60 blocks of the comparatively small area inside the Austrian capital, where German diehards are holding out. Berlin said the Russians' Danube flotilla had landed troops amid these last German positions.

The daily German communique failed to mention the Berlin sector, but Berlin commentators told of vast movements of troops and weapons along Zhukov's front from Stettin bay to the confluence of the Oder and Neisse rivers.

Marshal Rodion Y. Malinovsky's Second Ukrainian Army, outflanking Vienna from the north side of the Danube, cut the Vienna-Brno railroad and parallel highway by capturing the rail town of Elbesbrunn, six miles north of Vienna's trans-Danube suburb, Floridsdorf, the communique broadcast from Moscow said.

This left the Germans with only a line out of Vienna to the north-

Continued on Page 3, Col. 8

Franklin Delano Roosevelt (Editorial)

A newspaper is for news, but it is only half a newspaper unless it strives forever to express a sense of history.

We believe history will write the name of Franklin Delano Roosevelt indelibly on her role of high purpose and achievement.

All men born of woman pass through life doing right or wrong, doing wisely or unwisely. If they be historical men, leaders of men, history judges them and in good time hands down a verdict.

She discards the passions, the prejudices and the untruths in the day of judgment. She throws away the little things and looks to the big things, and her verdict is true

We believe history, looking to the big things, will judge Franklin Delano Roosevelt as a great American, a courageous fighter for civilization, a great citizen of the world.

We on The Chronicle have often taken issue with Mr. Roosevelt. We never doubted he sought to do good for the lowly, the struggling, the underdog. We disagreed with his method. We dissented often from his theory of governing men. We never dissented from, but supported, his interpretation of the right and wrong of history which has come in our time, and we are thankful to him that he saw the evil forces bearing down upon us, and that he fought them unswervingly even to the eleventh hour, the eve of triumph.

So we say hail and farewell to Franklin Delano Roosevelt, who died at the eleventh hour, with all before him, as some men must, for the ways of fate may never be known.

British to Cancel Upper Age Draft

LONDON, April 12 (AP)—Britain plans to discontinue conscription of men of 31 years and older for the armed forces after May 1, except where there is a need for specialists or other special factors, Labor Minister Ernest Bevin announced today.

New Cache of Art Found in Germany

PARIS, April 12 (AP)—Another hideaway of art treasures, believed to surpass any store of paintings and art works yet uncovered, has been found by American soldiers at Mercedes, South of Gotha, it was announced today.

The President

Cerebral Hemorrhage Cause Of Death at Warm Springs; Truman Is Sworn Into Office

Cabinet Will Be Retained

By the Associated Press

WASHINGTON, April 12—Harry S. Truman, who 11 years ago was a Missouri County Judge, became the thirty-seconly President of the United States at 7:09 p. m. (EWT) tonight ands olemnly pledged himself to the policies of Franklin Delano Roosevelt.

Sworn in 2 hours and 34 minutes after Mr. Roosevelt's death in Warm Springs, Ga., as a shocked capital sought to weigh the import of the sudden change, Truman announced in quick succession:

1—He will try to carry on as he believes President Roosevelt would have done.

2—The San Francisco United Nations Conference will go on as scheduled, April 25.

3—He has asked the Roosevelt Cabinet to stay on with him.

4—The war will be pressed to a "successful conclusion."

The new chief executive issued this statement:

"The world may be sure that we will prosecute the war on both fronts, East and West, with all the vigor we possess, to a successful conclusion."

A short time earlier Truman had announced that the Uniter Nations Confernece would open as scheduled on April 25 to draft a plan for a world organization.

Thus Truman acted immediately to carry out the twin objectives of winning the war and seeking a lasting peace.

Crowds stood silently outside the White House. Flags on Embassies and other public buildings dipped to half staff.

It was Mrs. Eleanor Roosevelt who summoned Mr. Truman from his Capitol office to

Continued on Page 3, Col. 1

S. F. Conference Will Go On, Says Truman

WASHINGTON, April 12 (AP)—President Truman announced tonight that the United Nations Congerence called for April 25 will go on as scheduled.

White House Secretary Jonathan Daniels said President Truman, who was sworn in late today had authorized Secretary of State Stettinius to make a statement that the United Nations meeting will be held as planned.

Several delegations already have arrived in this country.

President Roosevelt had intended to address the meeting

It was not known immediately whether President Truman will travel to San Francisco to speak.

Sudden Passing 2½ Hours After The First Attack

By the Associated Press

WARM SPRINGS, Ga., April 12 — President Franklin Delano Roosevelt died suddenly at 3:35 p. m., Central War Time, today of a cerebral hemorrhage.

Commander Howard Bruenn, naval physician, made this announcement to reporters shortly after White House Secretary William D. Hassett called a hurried news conference to announce the death of the Nation's only fourth-term chief executive

Mr. Roosevelt died in the little white

Sketch of Roosevelt career on page 6

house on top of Pine Mountain where he had come for a three-week rest. He was 63 years old.

Dr. Bruenn said he saw the President this morning and he was in excellent spirits at 9:30 a. m.

"At 1 o'clock," Bruenn added, "he was sitting in a chair while sketches were being made of him by an architect. He suddenly complained of a very severe occipital headache (back of the head).

"Within a very few minutes he lost consciousness. He was seen by me at 1:30 p. m., 15 minutes after the episode had started.

"He did not regain consciousness and he died at 3:35 p. m.

Only others present in the cottage were Commander George Fox, White House pharmacist and long an attendant on the President; Hassett, Miss Grace Tully, confidential secretary, and two cousins, Miss Laura Delano and Miss Margaret Suckley.

Bruenn said he called Vice Admiral Ross T. McIntyre, Navy Surgeon General and White House physician, in Washington, and that McIntyre in turn called Dr. James E. Paullin of Atlanta, an internal medicine practitioner and honorary consultant to the Navy Surgeon General.

Paullin was present when Bruenn gave the statement of the cause of death to reporters of the three national news services.

In response to a question, Dr. Bruenn said the President died without pain.

News of the President's death spread quickly and caused many a tear among the 125 infantile paralysis patients at the foundation here.

Mayor Frank W. Allcorn of Warm Springs was giving a barbecue at his mountain cabin this afternoon for the President and about 50 other guests. Allcorn was awaiting the President's arrival when reporters got word

Continued on Page 3, Col. 6

EXTRA

San Francisco Chronicle

THE CITY'S ONLY HOME-OWNED NEWSPAPER

FOUNDED 1865—VOL. CLX, NO. 107 CCCC SAN FRANCISCO, WEDNESDAY, MAY 2, 1945 DAILY 5 CENTS, SUNDAY 15 CENTS DAILY AND SUNDAY PER MONTH, $1.75

COMPARATIVE TEMPERATURES

	High	Low		High	Low
San Francisco	77	50	New York	62	50
Oakland	84	46	Chicago	50	40
Seattle	67	52	Salt Lake	76	45
Los Angeles	73	54	Washington	64	46
Sacramento	90	53	New Orleans	76	60

Forecast: Clear and cooler.

HITLER IS KILLED, NAZI RADIO SAYS

Doenitz Is Reported Successor

THIS WORLD TODAY

By ROYCE BRIER

IT IS of course impossible in the exceedingly loose hegemony of the United Nations that you can associate only with people who believe politically as you do.

For "you" are many different kinds of people. "You" are a Russian who believes in a socialized, or collective, State, and not in government responsible to periodical election. "You" are an American, who believes in republican forms, or in the blanket term, democracy, with tumultuous argument about everything, and public opinion the final arbiter. "You" are an Englishman, who sticks by old institutions like kingship, but still keeps a free and responsive society.

Those are the three big "yous," and there are many smaller ones, in various gradations of political form. Is Saudi Arabia a democracy? Why, bless you, democracy, whatever it is, is something very curious to the Islamic soul. Islam didn't invent it, we in the West invented it, and Islam is very chary of our inventions, as well Islam may be. Most of our Western inventions have not benefited Islam, no matter how blandly we tell them to take the nice medicine, which will brighten the eyes, tone up the muscles and cure all the known diseases.

So we are sitting out here in the Opera House, 49 different peoples, and about 490 sorts of political dogmas, and there's no such thing as "our" kind of people politically speaking. To expect it is to put a chameleon on plaid, which is said to make chameleons bust all to pieces.

Well, then—and this gets around to Argentina after a time—if we haven't any prevailing political belief, what are we going to use as a yardstick for admission to our team?

Mr. Molotov appears to feel that fascism is the yardstick. Fascism, true, is very hard to define. This doesn't mean that everybody who seeks a definition is weaseling, and secretly sympathetic with fascists or fascism. Neither does it mean that you have to accept "fascist" as an epithet, a form it has lately taken under the ministrations of some who run to epithet.

But in any case, fascism is not a good yardstick because the various peoples of the United Nations can't define it. Argentine fascism is in fact rather hard to define, and rather hard

Continued on Page 4, Col. 7

Charting Security

Political Flurry Over---Bigwigs May Leave Soon

By CHARLES RAUDEBAUGH

The San Francisco Conference of the United Nations moved swiftly yesterday toward its task of preparing the charter for a world security organization.

There were numerous indications that with the political pathway now cleared, many of the leading personalities would soon begin departing for their homes and leave the technical work in the hands of technicians.

Monday's dramatic forensics over Argentinean participation removed some of the political hurdles in the path of the Conference, and by yesterday was clearly apparent as a display which added stature and unity to the Big Four—America, Russia, China and Great Britain.

PRESSURE OF OTHER DUTIES

No departure dates for any of the Conference personalities have yet been set, but it was known that two of the big four—Soviet Foreign Commissar V. Molotov and British Foreign Secretary Anthony Eden—were under extreme pressure to return home because of the war developments.

Mr. Stettinius said yesterday that Mr. Molotov already has been away from Moscow more than a week, but made it clear the Soviet official would remain another few days until the commissions and committees get down to their serious work.

France is already plunged in an enormous reconstruction task, and Foreign Minister Georges Bidault was known to be considering an early departure as well. Others include Prime Minister Mackenzie King of Canada, who is facing an election shortly; New Zealands Prime Minister Peter Fraser, and Foreign Minister Jan Masaryk of Czechoslovakia.

SPOT FOR ARGENTINA

The executive and steering committees met yesterday morning and quickly approved assignments on various commissions and committees to all of the United Nations, including White Russia and the Ukraine, and kept open a spot which may possibly go to Argentina.

Great Britain politely stepped down from an assignment as rapporteur of the committee on enforcement arrangements under the commission on the security council, making way for France.

The Ukrainian Soviet Socialist Republic was given the chairmanship of the committee on preamble, purposes and principles of the new world organization, and the White Russian Soviet was assigned as a rapporteur of the committee on structure and procedures of the general assembly.

The spot reputedly held open for Argentina—although Secretary of State Edward Stettinius said Argentina had not been formally discussed by the steering committee for the post—was that of rapporteur to the commission on judicial organization.

In announcing the work of the

Continued on Page 9, Col. 3

Variety Is The Spice of ---Weather

There will be a variety of weather today.

The assortment is calculated to please every taste.

The Weatherman's forecast: "High fog in the morning. Sunshine in the afternoon."

Australians In Landing On Borneo

By the Associated Press

MANILA, May 2—Official Australian sources and the Japanese radio agreed today that Allied forces have invaded Dutch Borneo, and confirmation of the operation from the headquarters of General Douglas MacArthur was awaited.

At Canberra, Joseph B. Chifley, Australia's Treasury Minister, told the House of Representatives that a veteran Australian division, seasoned warriors from Middle East battlefields, was participating in an invasion of Borneo, one of the richest prizes seized by the Japanese in their blitz sweep through Asia more than three years ago.

Earlier, Radio Tokyo had reported that Allied assault forces hit the beaches near Tarakan, great oil shipping port immediately off Dutch Borneo's northeast coast.

FIERCE FIGHTING REPORTED

The Japanese claimed their Tarakan garrison was locked in fierce fighting with Allied amphibious forces. Tokyo said the invasion was accomplished Tuesday night, Borneo time, after a daylight attempt had been repulsed.

America's air power in the Southwest Pacific and the veteran Yank 41st Division have been paving the way for a Borneo invasion for several months. As ground forces squeezed in from the north and northeast on the island, a producer of great quantities of rubber and oil, flyers were softening up Japan's Borneo defenses.

The 41st doughboys, under Major General Jens A. Doe, have been headed for Borneo since they first entered Pacific action more than three years ago during which they won a trio of Presidential citations. Their campaign reached a climax in recent months. They invaded Palawan, Philippine Island, just north of Borneo last February. The next month they hopped to Zamboanga, in Mindanao, and on April 2 they

Continued on Page 2, Col. 5

'Next Year,' Ike Cables Mother

ABILENE, Kan., May 1 (AP)—The hope that he will be able to see her "before another year rolls around" was expressed by General Dwight D. Eisenhower in a birthday greeting to his mother, Mrs D. J. Eisenhower, who was 83 today.

Mrs. Eisenhower, named yesterday as the Kansas State Mother of 1945, observed her birthday quietly at her home. None of her five sons was able to be present, but all sent flowers and good wishes. Her husband died two years ago.

Bodies of Schiller, Goethe Rescued

WEIMAR, Germany, May 1 (AP)—Two German civilians were disclosed today to have stolen and hidden the bodies of Goethe and Schiller to foil a Nazi gauleiter's plan to destroy the remains of Germany's two greatest literary figures to keep "The American barbarians" from finding them.

The civilians, a doctor of philosophy and a lawyer, turned the caskets over to American military government officers in Jena and the bodies will be returned and reinterred in shrines here, where both Goethe and Schiller were born.

Battle Of Berlin

Chancellery Is Stormed; Baltic Port Captured

By the Associated Press

LONDON, May 1—The Germans, announcing the death of Adolf Hitler in Berlin, indicated tonight that the Russians had overwhelmed most of the die-hard remnants of the blazing capital's decimated garrison, storming the Reichschancellery, nerve-center of the enemy's tottering resistance.

Although there was no Allied confirmation that Hitler was in Berlin, it was possible that the Soviet High Command later might announce the finding of the German Fuehrer's body by Red Army soldiers.

Earlier, the Nazi High Command had said that the fanatical last-ditch defenders were huddled around Hitler in the underground fortress in the Tiergarten, which reportedly is linked to the Reichs-Chancellery.

CARPATHIAN VICTORIES

Premier Stalin, who issued three orders of the day, did not announce any new developments in the savage 11-day battle for Berlin, but his third order told of the capture of Bohumin, Velka-Bytca, Cadca, Grystat and Skocov in the Carpathian Zone of Czechoslovakia by General Andrei I. Yeremenko's Fourth Ukrainian Army.

Premier Stalin announced that Soviet tanks, maintaing a powerful 20-mile-a-day sweep across Germany's northern redoubt had captured the Baltic port of Stralsund, terminus for the main railroad ferry service to Malmo, Sweden, and surged within 33 miles of Rostock in a drive that won five major communications centers north of Berlin.

Marshal Konstantin K. Rokossovsky's Second White Russian Army tanks and cavalry, plunging across the Mecklenburg plains, captured Demmin, Grimmen, Malchin, Waren and Wessenberg in a drive that knifed within 63 miles of Field Marshal Bernard Montgomery's British Second Army on the lower Elbe.

BERLIN SUICIDES

Stralsund, a city of 43,600 persons, lies on an arm of the Baltic separating the German mainland from the German island naval base of Ruegen.

In Berlin, dozens of new suicides were reported by soviet war corre-

Continued on Page 3, Col. 5

Giant Photo Lens Is for Air Forces

ROCHESTER, N. Y. May 1 (AP)—Development of a giant 48-inch telephoto lens for the Army Air Forces was announced today by Eastman Kodak Company.

With the lens—three feet long and weighing about 100 pounds—twice the focal length of the customary 24-inch lens for aerial photography, the new equipment makes objects photographed at a given distance appear twice as large, the company said.

A Curbstone Consultant--- With a Formula for Security

The trouble with the Conference, says a real, live Man In The Street (captured by The Chronicle), is that the delegates haven't gotten around to throwing meringue pies yet. Yes, sir, Cab Driver Vince Rundle says the big-wigs are all clamming up and won't even talk to each other. Rundle tells you about it on page 10.

In a more vital vein, Military Analyst Max Werner today presents a synthesis of the Soviet's Conference attitude, which he says is a conciliatory one, yet has been widely misunderstood. Werner's article is on page 5.

Be sure to see Don Freeman's drawing—"The Visitor"—on page 4 today.

Hopeful London---Hopeless Reich

Germans Claim He 'Died a Hero' in Berlin; Churchill May Have 'Important News'

Prime Minister Avoids the Word Peace, but Asks Permission to Make 'Brief Announcement' Himself

By the Associated Press

LONDON, May 1—Prime Minister Churchill told the House of Commons today that he might have "information of importance" to impart before Saturday, but disappointed hopes that he would clarify immediately the prospects of peace in Europe.

Never once using the word "peace," Churchill told an expectant House that "should information of importance reach his majesty's government during the four days of our sitting this week as it might do—I will ask the speaker's permission to ask the indulgence of the House to interrupt the business and make a brief announcement."

Parliaments' normal weekly program ends Friday night.

(In Washington President Truman hinted at possible momentous news in the offing when he left his White House office late Tuesday. Newsmen, anxious over war developments, asked him: "Are we safe to go home for the night?" The President smiled and said he couldn't answer that. The previous night he had answered the same question in the affirmative.)

The fact that the Prime Minister did not divulge the progress of peace negotiations carried potential significance. Only a few hours earlier the Foreign Office had announced Churchill would have a statement to make when he appeared in Commons. In the interval he changed his plans.

BERNADOTTE RETURNS

Shortly before Churchill spoke Count Bernadotte, the Swedish intermediary who carried Heinrich Himmler's first surrender offer to the Allies, returned to Stockholm from Denmark, where it had been reported he had a fresh meeting with Himmler.

The Swedish Foreign Office, however, announced that "Count Bernadotte did not bring with him any new message to be handed over through the Foreign Office to the Allies."

Speaking with unusual hesitancy, obviously guarding against a premature disclosure in this delicate moment, Churchill told the packed Chamber the victory proclamation might come before the last pockets of Nazi resistance had surrendered.

For a while he appeared determined to stand on his terse but jocular summation of the war situation as "definitely more satisfactory" than it was five years ago. Then, as Britain's lawmakers clamored for additional information, he carefully offered a few details.

CABINET MEETING

Before going to Commons Churchill had an audience with the King. On his return from the House he called a Cabinet meeting that lasted into the night. There was no indication an announcement would be made of what was discussed.

To Commons Churchill made it clear that "the good news will not be delayed," but will be announced whether Parliament is in session or not. Then he added with a grin, "it will come from some authorized or unauthorized source; if the House is sitting I will take the liberty of coming down and informing them myself."

Churchill's high spirits were taken as a good omen.

"There is general belief that peace will be announced this week," said the British Press Association. "That is based on Mr. Churchill's rather smiling and happy demeanor during the question and answer interlude in the House today."

Broadcast Declares Fuehrer Fell At Chancellery Command Post; There Is No Hint of a Capitulation

By the United Press

LONDON, May 1—The German radio said tonight that Adolf Hitler was killed this afternoon in his Chancellery command post in Berlin and Grand Admiral Karl Doenitz, commander in chief of the navy, had succeeded him.

The reported death of the Fuehrer 12 years and three months after he established the Nazi Reich that was to have endured a thousand years, was not confirmed by the Allies.

Doenitz at once issued a proclamation announcing he had taken over as head of state and commander in chief of the fighting forces "to try to save the German people from bolshevism."

Each reference by the German radio and by Doenitz in his proclamation to Hitler's "heroic death" was interrupted by a ghost voice which shouted: "That's a lie!" and "he was the biggest fascist!" .. ...

NO PEACE TALK

Doenitz gave no hint that German capitulation was near. But by implication he invited the United States and British armies to stop fighting.

"My first task," he said, "is to save the German people from annihilation by the advancing bolshevist enemy. The military struggle will continue only with this aim. Inasmuch and as long as the attainment of this aim is being hindered by the British and Americans, we shall have to fight on against them."

He said he would try to create "bearable conditions" for the people and appealed for help, order and discipline to prevent collapse.

The German radio did not at once make plain the circumstances of Hitler's purported death.

"FIGHTING BOLSHEVISM"

After a 45-minute build-up—"Achtung!" warnings of an impending important announcement, interspersed with Wagnerian music—the German radio said:

"It is announced that our Fuehrer Adolf Hitler this afternoon at his command post in the Reich Chancellery, fighting till his last breath against bolshevism, fell for Germany.

"On April 30 the Fuehrer appointed Admiral of the Fleet Doenitz his successor."

Doenitz then personally read his own proclamation.

If the report of Hitler's death is true, he died three days after the terrible end of his Axis partner in crime, Benito Mussolini. Hitler modeled his Third Reich on Mussolini's fascist hierarchy, and then assumed the leadership and made Mussolini his jackal. Together the two dictators forced the world step by step, into its most terrible war.

There have been many warnings that Hitler might try to go underground—to lead German resistance in the last redoubt and then perhaps try to lose himself, leading his underground Nazis as a fugitive from world justice. For these reasons the German radio could not be accepted as an unquestionable authority.

DETAILS OMITTED

Also the German radio did not say how he died. The inference was left open that he had committed suicide, especially as he named Doenitz his successor—according to Berlin—only yesterday.

There had been reports that Hitler had never recovered from the attempt on his life last July 20, when a bomb wounded him; that he was going insane; that he had suffered a stroke.

According to some reports Heinrich Himmler, his home front leader and gestapo chief, had said in putting out peace feelers last week, that Hitler could not live 24 hours.

There had been suggestions that

Continued on Page 3, Col. 1

ADOLF HITLER
A ghost voice shouted: 'It's a Lie!'

How Germany Heard--- 'Adolf Hitler Has Fallen'

By the United Press

The text of the German radio report announcing Adolf Hitler's death:

"It is announced that our Fuehrer, Adolf Hitler, this afternoon at his command post in the Reichschancellory, fighting till his last breath against Bolshevism, fell for Germany.

"On April 30 the Fuehrer appointed Admiral of the Fleet Doenitz his successor. The Admiral and successor of the Fuehrer now speaks to the German people.

DOENITZ BROADCASTS

(Doenitz then personally broadcast the following message):

"German men, women and soldiers of the Wehrmacht:

"Our Fuehrer, Adolf Hitler has fallen.

"In deepest sorrow and reverence the German people bow.

"He recognized the terrible danger of Bolshevism at an early date, and dedicated his existence to this struggle.

"The end of this, his struggle and of his unswerving path of life is marked by his heroic death in the capital of the Reich.

"His life was one single service for Germany. His action in fighting against the spring flood of Bolshevism was waged beyond that for Europe and the entire civilized world.

"The Fuehrer has appointed me his successor.

"Conscious of this responsibility, I am taking over the leadership of the German people in this grave hour of destiny. My first task is to save the German people from annihilation by the advancing Bolshevist enemy. The military struggle continues only with this aim.

BRITISH AND U. S. ALSO

"Inasmuch and as long as the attainment of this aim is being hindered by the British and Americans, we shall have to continue to fight against them.

"The Anglo-Americans will then continue the war no longer for their

Continued on Page 3, Col. 3

San Francisco Chronicle EXTRA

THE CITY'S ONLY HOME-OWNED NEWSPAPER

FOUNDED 1865—VOL. CLX, NO. 113 CCCC SAN FRANCISCO, TUESDAY, MAY 8, 1945 DAILY 5 CENTS, SUNDAY 15 CENTS DAILY AND SUNDAY PER MONTH, $1.15

V-E DAY TUESDAY!

War Ends Officially at 6 A.M.

THIS WORLD TODAY

By ROYCE BRIER

MR. SHIGENORO TOGO, the Japanese Foreign Minister, is pretty disgusted over the European situation. He's had a nasty shock, as we say, at the hands of the Germans.

True, Mr. Togo is trailing events by a few days, and perhaps he is even more disillusioned now than he was, but his present remonstrance is plaintive enough to be satisfying.

You will recall that a week ago, though it seems much longer ago, Herr Himmler was cutting some ice. We haven't heard from him since (nothing temporary, we hope), but anyway, at the time he was reported to be flashing a surrender offer to the Americans and the British.

This, Mr. Togo has now picked up indignantly, and complains that the power offer was made without consulting Japan. He also doesn't like it that the offer was made to the United States and Great Britain, with whom Japan is notoriously at war, while implicit in it is continuance of war against Soviet Russia, with whom Japan is notoriously at peace. Or as Mr. Togo put it, "with whom Japan is striving to maintain neutrality."

Mr. Togo called this a "flagrant violation of the Tripartite Pact," and people called diplomatic observers, which may be anybody from a wandering Tokyo reporter to Mr. Togo himself talking off the record, say Japan must "re-examine all her relations with Germany." Tokyo newspapers, indeed, are demanding that Japan break off diplomatic relations with Germany.

This spectacle of Japan walking out of the Axis in a huff may resemble the medieval philosophers arguing about the whereabouts of nowhere, but you'll have to concede the Japanese some justifiable annoyance at the turn of affairs.

Now, seriously we all think this is awfully funny about the Japanese being mad at the Germans, and maybe breaking off diplomatic relations, but that's a dizzy Westerner for you!

Mr. Togo is painfully right when he complains the Germans have violated the Tripartite Pact by getting licked. The preamble of the Pact says flatly that the three powers, Germany, Italy and Japan, "have decided to stand by and co-operate with

Continued on Page 5, Col. 1

The Conference--- A Faster Tempo

Big Four in Agreement On All Major Amendments, Molotov Tells the Press

The United Principles Leave No Room for Fascist Nations, Soviet Foreign Minister Says

By CHARLES RAUDEBAUGH

Big Four unanimity on all major amendments to the Dumbarton Oaks plan for a world organization was announced yesterday by Soviet Foreign Commissar V. M. Molotov at a special press conference in the St. Francis Hotel.

With the end of the war in Europe stepping up the tempo of the San Francisco Conference of the United Nations, Mr. Molotov said that the first phase of the world meeting is now concluded. "As a result," he said, "a unanimity has been achieved which is essential to the success of the Conference."

While there was admission that the unanimity did not extend down to every phase, working accord was sufficient that some of the European Foreign Ministers announced their departures from San Francisco to attend to business at home. The technical work of the Conference will continue in the hands of subordinates.

SPAAK LEAVES CITY

Belgian Foreign Minister Paul Henri Spaak left the city Sunday night, and Norwegian Foreign Minister Trygve Lie departed last night. Problems at home resulting from the end of hostilities required their departure.

The Big Five—the United States, England, Russia, China and France—were in session most of the day at the Fairmont Hotel headquarters of Secretary of State Edward Stettinius.

POINTS OF AGREEMENT

Mr. Molotov went into considerable detail in his discussion of points of agreement among the Big Four sponsoring nations and declared that to these Soviet Union attached "greatest importance."

He enumerated these to include the observance of the principles of justice and international law, the principles of equality and self-determination of nations and for "encouragement of respect for human rights and fundamental freedoms for all without distinction as to race, language, creed or sex."

"Such a program is incompatible with the membership of Fascist countries in the organization of international security," the Soviet Foreign Commissar declared. "But then this is quite natural, for Fascist countries are known to be not only centers of sinister reaction, but of war as well, and so they cannot serve the cause of peace and security of nations."

Mr. Molotov disclosed that the Soviet delegation had submitted a "right to work and right to education" amendment to the other sponsoring Nations—America, England and China—but had not in-

Continued on Page 9, Col. 6

Production Green Light

Peace-Time Goods Expected on Market Within a Half-Year

By Associated Press

WASHINGTON, May 7—Most peacetime goods will be back on the market within six months of today's momentous victory in Europe, although quantities of some will be limited.

Within a year, by official War Production Board estimate, factories will be making consumer goods at the 1939 rate or higher.

But shortages of textiles, lumber and some other things will persist. One official was not being facetious when he said, "It may be easier to buy a refrigerator next fall than a shirt."

CURFEW END PROMISED

Immediately, it is promised, the "brown-out," the midnight curfew and the horse racing ban will be lifted.

Gasoline rations will be increased within 30 to 90 days, on the word of Interior Secretary Ickes. A jump from four to six miles of driving daily for A-card motorists is foreseen by Ickes, but OPA says the increase may be less. B-card drivers will get some increase also.

Other rationing programs will remain in force, with food supplies generally getting leaner before they are fatter.

More tires may be expected, but the rationing will continue indefinitely.

Stoves may come off rationing rather soon, passenger cars not until productions hits a volume of about 100,000 a month.

LONG WAIT EXPECTED

Months probably will pass, officials warn, before the effect is felt in appreciable replenishing of retail

Continued on Page 9, Col. 7

Medical Aid Sent To Starving Dutch

WASHINGTON, May 7 (UP)—The Foreign Economic Administration announced today that 16,000 pounds of amigen, a protein substance, have been flown from the United States in the past 10 days in an effort to prevent death of 80,000 persons in the Netherlands.

These persons are so near starvation that they are unable to digest ordinary food. Amigen solution is fed to them intravenously and by mouth.

Thousands of Dutch are dying of starvation, FEA said.

Parting Shots

Russians Take Breslau; Yanks Are in Prague

By the United Press

LONDON, May 7—Premier Joseph Stalin tonight announced capture of Breslau, last defended bastion in Germany, and General George S. Patton's American tanks were reported in revolt-torn Prague as the war in Europe swept to a close.

More than 40,000 Germans and their commander, General von Gnikow, were captured as Breslau, capital of lower Silesia, fell after a bloody 84-day siege—almost 10 times as long as Berlin held out—Stalin announced in an order of the day to Marshal Ivan S. Konev's First Ukrainian Army.

Other parting blows of battle were reported struck by Russian bombers on the Danish island of Bornholm, where a 28-year-old German Navy Captain named Von Kampy was said to have refused to capitulate under last Friday's surrender covering Denmark.

NAZI SHIPS BOMBED

A United Press dispatch telephoned to Stockholm from Copenhagen said that two waves of bombers attacked the Bornholm towns of Roenne and Nexoe at 12:50 and 2:10 p. m., killing at least six persons at Roenne where the harbor was filled with German naval vessels.

The Swedish home radio, quoting telephoned reports from Oslo, said that an Allied naval force of 48 ships had been sighted at Oslo fjord and were expected to land troops in Norway at any moment. Whether they were occupation or assault forces was not indicated.

The nightly Soviet communique, however, gave no hint of an approaching end of hostilities. It announced the capture of several towns west and southwest of Moravska-Ostrava, east of Prague, and said that Russian forces had reached the Elbe north and southeast of Magdeburg, completing the liquidation of a German pocket southwest of Berlin.

SITUATION IN PRAGUE

The exact situation in Prague was clouded by various and conflicting reports from underground sources and the German-controlled radio in the Prague area which insisted that Grand Admiral Karl Doenitz' capitulation announcement did not affect the German forces fighting the Russians in Bohemia and Moravia.

The Czechoslovakian government here, however, said that Patton's tanks had entered Prague while the last official operational report from Third Army headquarters — at 11 a. m. European time (6 a. m. EWT) placed American tank vanguards 48 miles southwest of the city.

The famed Fourth Armored Division had gone into the vanguard of the Prague drive and its lightning advances are usually cloaked in security silence until objectives have been reached.

Reports from Prague to American-

Continued on Page 9, Col. 7

France to Spain: We Want Laval

PARIS, May 7 (UP)—The French government has sent a new and strongly worded note to Spain requesting that Pierre Laval be surrendered to France immediately, authoritative sources said today.

The note asked that Laval, chief of government in the infamous Vichy regime, be expelled from Spain to France as "undesirable," thereby avoiding the necessity of extradition proceedings.

House Votes 'War Criminal' Bill

WASHINGTON, May 7 (UP)—The House today passed by voice vote and sent to the Senate a resolution to express Congressional determination that war criminals be punished even if they must be brought out of refuge in neutral countries.

Under the measure, authored by Representative Cecil R. King (D., Cal.), the United States would join with the Allies in bringing war criminals to trial and use whatever means necessary to ferret out those who sought refuge in neutral lands.

Victory Over Germany

The Enemy's Surrender Is Unconditional; Truman, Churchill to Make Announcement

President Plans to Hold Press Talk

By the United Press

WASHINGTON, May 7—The White House announced tonight that President Truman "confidently expects" to make a radio announcement to the Nation at 9 a. m., E. W. T. (6 a. m. P. W. T.) tomorrow—presumably the long-awaited proclamation that V-E day is here.

Press Secretary Jonathan Daniels said Mr. Truman's plans are based on "reports now received" and that the program will be carried through "unless unforseen developments" cause a change.

A White House press conference will be called at 8:30 a. m. (5:30 PWT) at which time the press and radio will be given in confidence the text of the President's radio remarks.

CONSISTENT REFUSAL

Earlier the President had revealed that arrangements have been made to announce V-E Day simultaneously in London, Washington and Moscow.

The White House had refused consistently to say in so many words when the announcement would come, although the British Ministry of Information in London had announced that tomorrow definitely would be V-E Day and that Prime Minister Winston Churchill would speak to the British people at 3 p. m., British time—6 a. m. (PWT) tomorrow.

At the time of the British announcement the President told newsmen in a formal statement that the announcement would come simultaneously and he added:

"Until then, there is nothing I can say or will say to you."

There were reports that an effort had been made to advance the time of the announcement but that the Russians opposed. As a result it was said, the President decided to go along with Russia.

TO MAKE SURE

Moscow was understood to have advised this Government that it had heard nothing from its representatives at the purported surrender meeting and reportedly wanted to wait and make certain that everything would be concluded satisfactorily.

Mr. Truman was described as de-

Continued on Page 4, Col. 5

French Great Dine With McAuliffe

INNSBRUCK, Austria, May 7 (AP)—Major General Anthony C. McAuliffe, famed nuts-to-the-Germans defender of Bastogne, had at dinner guests yesterday former French Premiers Edouard Daladier and Paul Reynaud and other notables, including Lieutenant John G. Winant Jr., son of the U. S. Ambassador to Britain, all just liberated from a Nazi prison.

The American meal, elegant in comparison with their fare in prison, pleased the French guests, but they hesitated over the American apertif.

It was whisky.

ORDER TO NAZIS IN NORWAY: 'CLENCH YOUR TEETH---OBEY'

LONDON, May 7 (AP) — Gen. Boehme, German commander in chief in Norway, broadcast an order of the day over the Oslo radio tonight commanding his troops to lay down their arms in obedience to Foreign Minister "Von Krosigk's announcement of unconditional surrender of all German fighting troops."

Boehme said the surrender order "hits us very hard because we are unbeaten and in full possession of our strength in Norway and no enemy has dared to attack us."

"In spite of all that," he added, "in the interests of all that is German we also shall have to obey the dictate of our enemies. We hope that in the future we shall have to deal with men on the other side who respects a soldier's honor . . . Clench your teeth and keep discipline and order. Obey your superiors. Remain what you have been up to now—decent German soldiers who love their people and homeland more than anything in the world."

He said he also "expected" that the Norwegian population "will keep discipline with respect to the Germans which the German soldiers in Norway always kept towards the Norwegians."

How the News Broke

The World Listened To Reims . . . as Allied Capitals Were Silent

PARIS, May 7 (AP)—A supreme headquarters order suspending filing facilities of the Associated Press in the European theater was lifted tonight except as it applied to Edward Kennedy, chief of the AP's Western front staff, who sent the Reims dispatch telling of Germany's unconditional surrender. The earlier order of supreme headquarters Public Relations Division had halted all AP filing from here for several hours.

By the Associated Press

The news for which the world had been waiting for days—that Germany had surrendered unconditionally and that Allied victory had come in Europe—came in an Associated Press dispatch from Reims, France, at 9:35 a. m., Eastern War Time (6:35 a. m., PWT), Monday.

Four hours later, the British Ministry of Information announced that tomorrow, Tuesday, May 8, would be treated as V-E Day, with Prime Minister Churchill making an official announcement at 9 a. m., Eastern War Time, and King George broadcasting to the empire at 3 p. m., Eastern War Time.

THE FIRST NEWS

Edward Kennedy, chief of the AP staff on the western front and a

Continued on Page 4, Col. 3

Son of Nimitz Wins Navy Cross

WASHINGTON, May 7 (AP)—Commander Chester W. Nimitz Jr., son of the Fleet Admiral, has been awarded the Navy Cross for his exploits as a submarine commander.

Announced today, the citation credits young Nimitz's submarine, on its seventh patrol, with sinking several Japanese warships and with sinking or damaging an additional 18,000 tons of merchant shipping in attacks on heavily escorted enemy convoys.

Nimitz's wife lives at 40 Carroll street, Vallejo, Cal.

Jubilant London

City Doesn't Wait For Official Message Before Going Wild

By the Associated Press

LONDON, May 7—War-scarred London burst into jubilant celebration of the end of the war in Europe today, its millions of happy citizens unable to wait for the government's formal V-E Day proclamation tomorrow.

When the news was flashed that final, unconditional surrender terms had been signed by the Nazis, millions surged into the streets, from Buckingham Palace to sedate East End.

Piccadilly Circus, the Whitehall and Westminster areas filled with a laughing, shouting throng. Some old-timers said the scenes eclipsed those of the 1918 armistice.

THE KING'S MESSAGE

The British Ministry of Information announced that tomorrow would be treated as V-E day in accordance "with arrangements between the three great powers." Prime Minister Churchill will make his formal announcement, at 3 p. m. (6 a. m. PWT) and King George will broadcast at 9 p. m. (12 noon PWT).

The King tonight congratulated Gen. Eisenhower and his armies on their "complete and crushing victory" in Europe.

"All the world now knows," he messaged the Allied supreme commander, "that after fierce and continuous warfare this force (the Allied armies) has accomplished its mission with a finality achieved by no other expedition in history."

Churchill, however, got the jump on his countrymen with a personal victory luncheon at No. 10 Downing street at noon today, the British Press Association reported. Members of his war cabinet and the British chiefs of staff were the guests.

IN MID-AFTERNOON

The news hit London town in mid-afternoon and the crowds swelled by the thousands. Many American soldiers helped lead the

Continued on Page 9, Col. 5

Submission Made to All Three Allies

By the Associated Press

LONDON, May 7—Germany surrendered unconditionally to the Allies today, completing the victory in the European phase of the Second World War—the most devastating in history.

Prime Minister Churchill will proclaim the historic conquest at 9 a. m. (Eastern War Time) tomorrow from 10 Downing street, and simultaneous announcements are expected from President Truman in Washington and Premier Marshal Stalin in Moscow. Late today the President announced that he expected to broadcast to the Nation at the same time, 9 a. m. (6 a. m. PWT).

Churchill will report directly to Commons and ask for adjournment to Westminster Abbey for a service of thanksgiving.

The whereabouts of such war criminals as Himmler, Goering, even Hitler himself, although he had been reported dead, were unknown or if they were known they had not been officially announced.

IN THE SCHOOLHOUSE

Germany's formal capitulation came at 2:41 a. m. (French time) (5.41 p. m. Sunday, PWT), in the big red Reims schoolhouse, headquarters of General Eisenhower, supreme commander of the Allies of the west.

The crowning triumph came just five years, eight months and seven days after Hitler invaded weak but proud Poland and struck the spark which set the world afire.

It marked the official end of war in Europe, but it did not silence all of the gun, for battles raged on in Czechoslovakia.

There, Nazi General Ferdinand Schoerner, who has been designated a war criminal, defied the orders of Grand Admiral Karl Doenitz, successor of the dead or missing Hitler, to lay down arms.

But this force—all that remains of what once was the mightiest military machine on earth—faced inevitable liquidation or surrender.

Presumably the victorious powers soon will label these troops guerrillas.

Continued on Page 3, Col. 1

The Chronicle's 'Surrender' Extra . . .

On the strength of an Associated Press dispatch announcing Germany's unconditional surrender, The Chronicle, in common with other newspapers went to press Monday morning with an extra headlined "Surrender."

When confirmation was not forthcoming, the presses were stopped. Thirty-five hundred copies of the edition had already reached the street, but were confined to the downtown area only.

No additional copies were run off.

San Francisco Faces Victory Day---Calmly

City Adopts an Attitude of 'Now for the Japanese'

"O. K., now let's finish the Jap!" That might have been the voice of San Francisco speaking through a giant megaphone.

For surrender of Germany yesterday found this war port city prepared by a week of piled up sensations to accept the news with a calmness and a sense of grim realization that something still remained to be done.

What celebrating is to be done will be done today and there was no indication last night that it will be the wild, unrestrained mass demonstration that officials had feared and had prepared for.

The city awaited the official announcement of V-E Day scheduled to be made at 6 a. m. today by President Truman, Prime Minister Churchill and Marshal Stalin.

In the meantime, saloons remained open. They will close today for a 24-hour period immediately following Truman's announcement of V-E Day, Commissioner George R. Reilly, member of the State Board of Equalization, has been assured.

"Grocery, drug and other stores which remain open," said Reilly, "are asked to close their liquor departments."

While there was no legal way of enforcing the closing order, Reilly said he was confident that observance would be general under an agreement reached several weeks ago.

Meanwhile, tongues were hanging out in Oakland from a two-day dry spell. Bars closed there yesterday, far in advance of the official time, when Police Chief Robert P. Tracey sent officers on the rounds to tell owners it was "time to close" on the basis of the Germany surrender report.

Thirsty Oaklanders were promised relief, however, tonight. Because they jumped the gun, Tracey said, bars will reopen at 7 p. m., immediately after polls in today's bond election close. This was the first publicly announced deviation from the general nationwide agreement to keep bars closed for 24 hours after the official V-E time of 6 a. m. today.

Yesterday's Oakland closings were under a voluntary agreement between authorities and the United Tavern Owners' Association of Alameda county, made effective by premature announcement of surrender. President Charles Tye of the association closed his own place and left for Stockton.

The closing agreement announced here by Reilly covers bars in his district—the counties of San Francisco, San Mateo, Santa Clara, Santa Cruz, San Benito, Monterey, and San Luis Obispo.

As word of the surrender was received Oakland and San Leandro ordered mobilization of police off

Continued on Page 2, Col. 3

Weatherman Can't Promise A Thing

The Weather Man is trying hard to coax the sun out today. He may manage it this afternoon.

His forecast for today:

"High fog in the morning: clearing in the afternoon; continued cool."

The Chronicle Index

Barnaby	3H
Casualties	2
Comics	3H
Contract Contacts	6
Crossword Puzzle	6
Drama	8
Editorials	12
Finance	4H
Marty Links	3H
Lichty's Cartoon	3H
Ration Dates	3H
Radio Log	3H
Society	6
Weather	3H
Vital Statistics	9

COLUMNS

San Francisco	1H
Harry B. Smith	1H
Washington Merry-Go-Round	12
Chester Rowell	12
Dorothy Thompson	12
Will Connolly	1H

Listen to The Chronicle-KYA Time-Clocked News — 1260 on your dial—6 a. m. to midnight.

Tune to KYA, 10:15 p. m., Monday through Friday, for "Reports to the Managing Editor," a Chronicle news conference.

Bomber Crashes Into Empire State Building, 13 Killed, Flaming Gas Spreads Destruction

NEW YORK, July 28—A twin-engined Army B-25 bomber, lost in a blinding fog, crashed into the Empire State building at a point 913 feet above the street level at 9:49 a. m. today. Thirteen persons, including all five occupants of the plane and eight persons at work within the building, were killed in the resulting catastrophe, and 15 others were injured.

The plane, en route from Bedford, Mass., to Newark on an undisclosed mission, had flown over LaGuardia Field a few minutes earlier, but its pilot declined to follow the advice given him by the control tower to land there. Instead, he asked for the weather at Newark airport, and headed in that direction.

Horror-stricken occupants of the building, alarmed by the roar of engines, ran to the windows just in time to see the plane loom out of the gray mists that swathed the upper floors of the world's tallest office building. It was banked at an angle of about 15 degrees as Lieutenant Colonel W. F. Smith, the pilot, swung it in a curve out of the northeast.

It crashed with a terrifying impact midway along the north, or Thirty-fourth street wall of the building. Its wings were sheared off by the shock, but the motors and fuselage ripped a hole 18 feet wide and 20 feet high in the brick wall of the seventy-eighth and seventy-ninth floors of the structure.

Brilliant orange flames shot as high as the observatory on the eighty-sixth floor of the building, 1050 feet above Fifth Avenue, as the gasoline tanks of the plane exploded. For a moment watchers in the street below saw the tower clearly illumined by the glare. Then it disappeared again into the gray murk and the smoke of the burning plane.

One of the plane's two motors hurtled clear across the seventy-eighth floor, tore a hole in the south wall of the building, and plummeted to the roof of the 12-story office building at 10 West Thirty-third street, where it started a fire that demolished a penthouse.

A propeller was imbedded in the wall of the building; the other motor and part of the landing gear crashed into an elevator shaft, where they fell to the sub-cellar 1000 feet below. Other sections of the fuselage were blown as high as the Eighty-sixth floor observatory. The steel girder at the seventy-ninth floor level was bent inward 18 inches by the shock.

Cascading torrents of flaming gasoline poured through the seventy-eighth and seventy-ninth floors, setting fire to everything that was combustible. The burning fuel ran down stairwells into hallways as far as the seventy-fifth floor, while choking fumes and smoke rose upwards to the observatory.

Between 15 and 20 persons, most of them girl clerical workers, were at their desks in the offices of the war relief service of the National Catholic Welfare Council, occupying the southwest section of the floor, when the flaming flood burst in upon them.

Most of them ran in terror for the doors. At least some of them, it was established tonight, safely reached the haven of the fireproof stair well, but several were overtaken by the raging flames as they ran, and burned to death. Three of them who had pathetically sought shelter in a separate office at the south side of the building were followed and killed there by the flames.

Paul Dearing, 37-year-old volunteer publicity man for the service, saw the flames approaching his desk near the west wall of the building and jumped from a nearby window. He struck a ledge outside the seventy-second floor and was instantly killed. He was identified by a police card showing he was formerly a reporter for the Buffalo Courier Express.

The bodies of the three occupants of the plane were hurled into the fiery inferno on the seventy-ninth floor, where, like those of the girl employes who were trapped there, they were burned beyond recognition. Two of the three were members of the crew of the plane, Colonel Smith and Staff Sergeant Christopher S. Domitrovich, 31, of Granite City, Ill.

An aviation machinist's mate, second class, in the Navy, who had apparently obtained a ride in the plane as a "hitch hiker" when it left Bedford, was the third occupant.

The seventy-eighth floor of the building was unoccupied, and was being used for the storage of various building supplies, which helped to keep the death toll down. However, one man, possibly a building employe, was trapped and burned to death there.

When the wreckage of the plane smashed into the north bank of elevators, it struck a girder between two elevator shafts weakening it and damaging some of the elevator cables. One car, which was empty, plunged immediately to the sub-cellar with a plane engine on top of it, but the other car figured in the most amazing of the many miraculous escapes of the day.

A girl elevator operator had opened the door of her car in another bank of elevators toward the south side of the building just as the explosion came. She was blown out of the car and painfully burned by flaming gasoline.

Roy Penzell, president of Air Cargo Transport Corporation, reported that just as another elevator door closed

Continued on Page 3, Col. 1

A Chronicle Man Watched Empire State Plane Crash

Read Milton Silverman's eyewitness account (phoned to San Francisco) and other stories, plus late Wirephotos, on

PAGE 8

San Francisco Chronicle

THE CITY'S ONLY HOME-OWNED NEWSPAPER

VOL. CLXI, NO. 14 CCCCAAA SAN FRANCISCO, SUNDAY, JULY 29, 1945 DAILY 5 CENTS, SUNDAY 15 CENTS DAILY AND SUNDAY PER MONTH $1.??

Jap Leader Calls Surrender Impossible---Carriers Attack, B-29s Fire Six Cities on List

The Pacific War at a Glance:

PEACE—Japanese publicity media shouted "on with the war" but there was nothing official yet on what the governing gang thought of the Potsdam ultimatum.

NIMITZ—American and British carrier planes completed neutralization of Japan's main battle fleet by sinking or damaging 15 more vessels includng 9 warships, while B-29s bombed six of the 11 cities earmarked for destruction in a pre-raid warning by leaflets. Also 150 planes were destroyed or damaged Saturday bringing the score of Halsey's offensive since July 10 to 1078 planes destroyed or damaged and 740 ships sunk or damaged, including 47 warships.

MacARTHUR—Bombers caught three Jap convoys and sank nine for sure and sank or damaged 62.

CHINA—Kweilin, the great former American airbase, was recaptured by the Chinese.

Sea-Air War

By the United Press

GUAM, July 29 (Sunday)—U. S. Third Fleet carrier planes ruling the skies over Japan sank or damaged 15 more ships, including nine warships, destroyed or damaged 150 planes and heaped new disaster on the enemy's shattered navy in yesterday's (Saturday) third day of destructive attacks on the Inland Sea.

The figures for Saturday's assault, still incomplete, raised Japanese losses to 1078 planes destroyed or damaged, and 740 ships sunk or damaged, including 47 warships, since Admiral William F. Halsey's fleet opened its air-sea bombardments of Japan July 10.

A few hours before Admiral Chester W. Nimitz announced the results of the third strike against the Inland Sea in five days by more than 1000 American and British carrier planes, 20th Air Force headquarters disclosed that 550 to 600 Superfortresses heaped 3500 tons of bombs on six Japanese cities early today (Sunday). All of the cities were on the 11-city "death list" issued by the American commanders less than 24 hours previously.

The cities hit were on Honshu. They were Tsu, Aomori, Ichinomiya, Ujiyanada and Ogachi.

All planes returned safely after starting raging fires in all cities as well as the Shimotsu oil refinery, 40 miles south of Osaka. Results were described as "good to excellent." All cities were bombed visually through broken clouds. Only 11 Superfortresses have been lost from approximately 5000 used this month on 14 major missions.

As the carrier planes and Superfortresses worked over the Japanese homeland in a continuation of a 20-day assault that has seen almost 40,000 tons of bombs and shells dropped, General Douglas MacArthur announced a crushing blow against the enemy's ocean supply lanes.

MacArthur's bombers caught three convoys near enemy shores on

Continued on Page 2, Col. 1

'Surrender . . . And Be Free'

By United Press

WASHINGTON, July 28—The United States told the Japanese people tonight that if they surrender now they will win "freedom they have never enjoyed under the domination their military oppressors."

Navy Captain E. M. Zacharias, official spokesman of the U. S. Government, said in an Office of War Information broadcast that "one simple decision" by the Japanese people will save their homeland for "a sovereign existence under a peacefully inclined and responsible government."

Tokyo's Reply

By the Associated Press

The president of Japan's powerful totalitarian political party declared Saturday his country would never accept the Allied surrender ultimatum, as Nippon awaited an address by Premier Suzuki on the war and the coming "battle of the streets."

While the Japanese government officially remained silent on the edict from Potsdam, and Tokyo's newspapers preached a common refrain of rejection, General Jiro Minami, president of the Political Association of Great Japan, gave the first reaction to the ultimatum by an acknowledged public figure.

Radio Tokyo quoted Minami as saying Japan would never quit and the "entire Japanese nation will remain absolutely unaffected in their resolute determination to save their country from national extermination."

NO ALTERNATIVE

The broadcast, recorded by the Federal Communications Commission, quoted Minami as describing the ultimatum terms as "contrary to what the Japanese people think are righteous peace conditions" and the natural conclusion would be that the Japanese had no alternative but to fight.

"These enemy leaders who signed their names to the Potsdam proclamation know full well that the Japanese nation would never surrender, even if their homeland should be thoroughly devastated and ravaged, and therefore it is impossible to win victory over Japan by military might," Minami declared.

The Japanese Domei Agency, which yesterday said it had "learned authoritatively" the government would spurn the quit-or-be-destroyed proclamation, summed up the editorial opinion of the various Tokyo newspapers.

PRESS COMMENT

The proclamation was conceived by the Allies, Domei said, to revitalize their own peoples' flagging war spirits by creating the opinion the war had to continue because Japan wouldn't accept the peace terms; Anglo-Americans were dissatisfied because the unconditional surrender terms carried out on Germany had brought heavy sacrifices; the ultimatum served as propaganda to "magnify" the military might of the Allies; it was merely propaganda aimed to impress the Japanese.

Terms such as "tomfoolery," "day dream" and "ridiculous" were applied to the proclamation by the publications.

Suzuki's expected address, his first to the people since he took office, was billed by Domei as a "speech expressing determination for sure victory and firm and unshakable measures to cope with the final decisive battle between Japan and America."

The speech was under the auspices of the Tokyo newspapers, which have had some difficulty explaining the shift of the war tide to the Japanese people, and the aircraft industry association, which has taken a battering from American air power.

Inside . . .

CABLE FROM ATTLEE
The new Prime Minister's exclusive report on the Principles of Labor Government . . . . . . Page 4

LET'S LOOK AT THE MAP
The Tokyo Bay Region is today's subject for discussion by Larry Fanning on KYA. The special map appears on . . . . Page 2

REPORT BY JACK FOISIE
First in a series on a Soldier's Return to Civilian Life . . . Page 5

REGULAR FEATURES

Aviation	6
Books	10TW
Casualties	2
Will Connolly	3H
Contract Contacts	6S
Crossword	3S
Drama	13TW
Events	18
Fashions	6S
Gardens	6
Bill Leiser	1H
Music	9TW
Pink's Pickups	9
Radio Log	19TW
Ration Dates	6
Vital Statistics	9
Weather	9

SPECIAL SECTIONS
Classified Section (C), Comics, Sporting Green (H), This World (TW), Women's World (S).

The Weather
CLEAR, EXCEPT HIGH FOG IN MORNING

Dreiser Seeks to Join Communists

Special to The Chronicle

NEW YORK, July 28—Theodore Dreiser, American novelist, has applied for membership in the Communist party of the United States, Communist Leader William Z. Foster announced today. In a letter to Foster, from Hollywood, Dreiser asserted "the name of Stalin is one beloved by the free peoples of the earth."

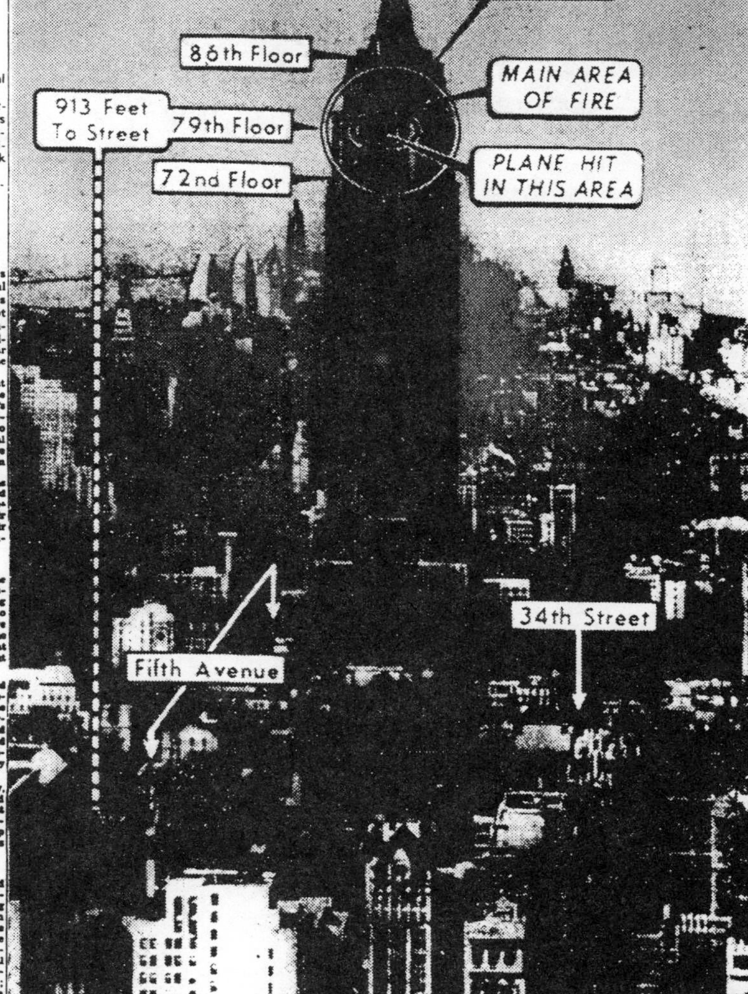

This is the scene of the bomber crash into New York's Empire State building, viewed from the RAC building. (AP) Wirephoto

Charter Ratified

Senate Vote Is 89-2; Shipstead, Langer Opposed

By EARL C. BEHRENS
Political Editor, The Chronicle

WASHINGTON, July 28—The Senate late today voted 89 to 2 to make the United States the first major power to ratify the San Francisco Charter of the United Nations.

With the galleries jammed by spectators, the Senate launched the United States on its new pathway of international co-operation to bring world security, and peace.

Two Senators only, Langer (R., N. D.) and Shipstead (R., Minn.) cast their votes against the ratification resolution.

California's Hiram W. Johnson, ill in the Naval Hospital here, did not vote. He would have voted "No" had he been in his seat, it was announced. Senator Downey (D., Cal.) voted for ratification.

The other absentee Senators were all in favor of ratification.

On motion of Democratic Majority Leader Barkley (Ky.), President Pro Tem of the Senate McKellar (D., Tenn.) immediately dispatched a message to President Truman at Potsdam telling him of today's action.

OVERWHELMING VOTE

The overwhelming vote of approval was a startling contrast to the results in the Senate 26 years ago when the League of Nations covenant, dream of Woodrow Wilson, was turned down.

As was the case in 1919, hundreds crowded the Capitol to hear the closing debate on the Charter. Many were unable to obtain admission to the galleries and the spectators were permitted to stand in the aisles for brief periods.

The negative votes of Langer and Shipstead have been predicted for days.

Senator Langer was the subject of a bitter Senate controversy five years ago, when fraud charges followed his election to Congress.

Ironically, one leader who supported Langer's position that his State had duly elected him was Senator Connally (D. Tex.), Foreign Relations Committee chairman, and the man who steered the Charter through the Senate.

THE OPPOSITION

Langer held off his speech denouncing the Charter until all the other formal speeches had been delivered and the Senators were preparing to vote. He insisted adoption of the Charter would "mean perpetual war, enslavement of poor people and one step toward compulsory peace-time conscription."

Just before the roll was called, Langer's colleague, Senator Young (R.) expressed regret that there was a division of belief in the North Dakota representation. He strongly supported the charter.

When Senator Johnson's name was called, Senator Wherry (Neb., GOP whip, arose and announced that were the Californian present he would vote "nay."

Johnson was the only member of

Continued on Page 3, Col. 4

The Memoirs of Paul Reynaud

by PAUL REYNAUD
Former Premier of France

STUDY OF FRANCE--NATION IN DECLINE

Who was guilty in the death of France? As the trial of Marshal Petain unravels, the story of the decline of the Third Republic is being pieced together. Among the leaders of France there were the venal, the helpless and the unwise. France fell for many reasons, not all of which have yet been told. In March, 1940, the nation called on Paul Reynaud. The long "phony war" was trying French nerves. Inaction, a growing defeatism and the massed forces of Hitler beyond the Maginot had spelled defeat for Premier Daladier. To take an uncertain helm and lead France to victory—that was the task the former Finance Minister faced. "I shall not fail," Reynaud promised—but France had already failed. Though Reynaud had himself propped up French economy, the foundations of the nation were no longer strong enough to match an enemy armed for conquest. France fell, Reynaud passed the reins of state to Petain and the four years of darkness settled down over the land of liberty, equality, fraternity. A prisoner of the Nazis, Reynaud wrote his memoirs, a study of the causes of France's humiliation, in a Pyrenees prison camp. This is the first of a series by the former Premier. A second article will appear in The Chronicle Monday.

France has experienced the greatest disaster of her history since the Hundred Years' war. She has been conquered, invaded, occupied, pillaged, mauled, trampled and humiliated.

For more than four years the world has been submerged in a flood of German-ordered lies about us.

Today it wants the truth; it must have the truth.

When, after destroying Czechoslovakia, Hitler invaded Poland on September 1, 1939, France sprang to arms by the side of Britain.

She went to war with firm resolution and a clear conscience. Was this French declaration of war on Germany an act of "criminal folly," inspired by the "war-mongers" in the government of that time—men such as Paul Reynaud, Georges Mandel, Champetier de Ribes and Cesar Campinchi—as the German press in Paris and Vichy claimed for four whole years?

Was our crime not rather that we had not prepared ourselves for this war, which had for years been gathering on the horizon?

A military alliance between France and Russia was the bogy of the German general staff. Why did we decline this when it was offered to us?

Why had we built up an army of defense instead of an army of attack, and why was this army of defense lacking even in those defensive weapons which the attackers had in such quantity?

And why up to the eve of war were we not able to cope with that economic crisis which was sapping the strength of France, splitting her up into factions and hampering her rearmament?

Where does the responsibility lie?

When disaster overtook us in Belgium in May 1940, why was it that I, as head of the government, called in Marshal Petain and General Weygand?

And when the battle of France had been lost, why did I want to go on fighting? Why was I overthrown, and why did France surrender on June 16 1940?

Are we crazy enough to believe, this time also, that the war through which we have just passed will be the last? We must examine these questions, recalling the epitaph Rudyard Kipling suggested for the graveyard of the British soldiers who fell in the battle of the Somme: "We lie here because our fathers lied." France must stand her trial, and I stand forward as a witness. I have to give an account of my

Continued on Page 4, Col. 7

Senator Hiram Johnson Is Dead

San Francisco Chronicle

THE CITY'S ONLY HOME-OWNED NEWSPAPER

FOUNDED 1865—VOL. CLXI, NO. 23 CCCC SAN FRANCISCO, TUESDAY, AUG. 7, 1945 DAILY 5 CENTS, SUNDAY 15 CENTS

COMPARATIVE TEMPERATURES

	High	Low		High	Low
San Francisco	61	54	Chicago	80	73
Oakland	65	56	New Orleans	90	78
Sacramento	91	56	New York	81	63
Los Angeles	85	65	Salt Lake	98	59
Seattle	84	56	Washington	81	64

Forecast: high fog night and morning, clear in afternoon.

THIS WORLD TODAY

By ROYCE BRIER

COMMANDER Herbert Agar, U. S. N. R., editor-on-leave and what may be described, for want of a better term, as a student of human affairs, on June 29 said: "If the war (European) had gone on for another six months, it is quite possible this planet would have ceased to exist, because it is probable some one would have learned to break the atom without controlling it."

This, of course, is the same approach, so to speak, to a *non sequitur* which prophets of doom have been using on us since the first recorded days in Egypt. That is, if the world is going to "end," it can't make much difference to any one who happens at the moment to be in it. Certainly it is nothing to worry about, as is one's own personal extinction.

One of the intense anxieties of one's own personal extinction is that one's enemies, some of them, and probably the worst ones, will survive. This is altogether more luck than they deserve, but there is nothing one can do about it. On the other hand, "the end of the world" cures this prospective injustice, and one can contemplate it philosophically.

True, the extinction of the planet, Earth, is a concept quite different from the end of the world, and probably a more cheerful concept. In the end of the world, it might be that another "world" would in time appear with some of the flaws of this one, whereas the end of the planet does not mean that another planet will appear to take the place of this one in the orbit. The solar system would simply have to scrape along with one less planet. If this would throw the whole thing out of kilter, let the astrophysicist have that headache.

Nor, if the planet, Earth, is to be—as Juliet hoped for Romeo—"cut . . . out in little stars," does it make much difference whether it is done by man, or by some cosmic body mooching around, or a drift of incandescent hydrogen. If man did it, there would be no one to stigmatize him, if stigma there be, though unhappily there would be no one to praise him, either, if the act in the long run turned out to be praiseworthy.

This is really a melancholy aspect of the affair, for undoubt-

Continued on Page 3, Col. 1

ATOMIC ENERGY UNLEASHED ---NEW BOMB BLASTS JAPAN

Multiply This by Two Thousand!

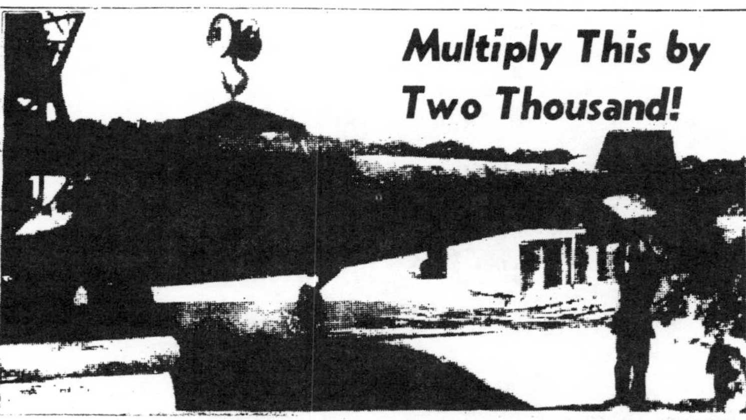

(A. P. Wirephoto)

20,000 TONS OF TNT—The easiest way for the imagination to grasp the meaning of the new atomic bomb's power is to compare it with other bombs. It packs a punch equivalent to 2000 of the monster British "grand slam" block-buster pictured above. The new bomb explodes with a greater force than 40,000,000 pounds of TNT. A single atomic bomb has the wallop equal to that of 2000 Superforts fully loaded with their present cargoes of destruction. Size of the new bomb has not been announced, except that "the explosive charge is exceedingly small."

New Epoch in Science, War

Enemy Faces 'Rain of Ruin'---Capitulation May Be Hastened; Test Burst Is Felt for 250 Miles

Results of Experiment---Steel Tower Vaporized, Fire Ball at 40,000 Feet

By the Associated Press

LOS ALAMOS, N. M., Aug. 6—The atomic bomb, dropped on Japan for the first time today, was previewed by scientists and military authorities in the New Mexico desert July 16 when a test sent a ball of fire, many times brighter than the mid-day sun, billowing skyward, and set off a blast which rattled windows more than 250 airline miles away.

The steel tower from which the test was detonated was vaporized. A huge sloping crater was left where the tower stood. Men outside the control center more than five miles away were knocked down by a heavy pressure wave.

Witnesses said a huge multicolored cloud was sent 40,000 feet into the stratosphere in five minutes.

SEEN IN CALIFORNIA

The blast at 5:30 a. m. at a remote location on the Alamogordo, N. M., Army Air Base, caused consternation throughout southwestern New Mexico and southern Arizona.

Windows rattled at Gallup, N. M., 250 miles northwest. An Army flyer reported on landing at Albuquerque that he saw the flash from the explosion at Needles.

Forest rangers 150 to 175 miles away thought there had been an earthquake and checked with the Smithsonian Observatory on Burro Mountain, southwestern New Mexico.

At Albuquesque, 120 miles away, a blind girl, when the flash of the test lighted the sky before the blast was heard, asked "What was that?"

SHOULD SHORTEN WAR

In a War Department release today, an Army General who witnessed the test said:

"As to the present war, there was a feeling that no matter what else might happen, we now had the means to insure its speedy conclusion and save thousands of American lives.

"As to the future, there has been brought into being something big and something new that would prove to be immeasurably more important than the discovery of electricity or any of the other great discoveries which have so affected our existence."

Scientists and military authorities said the test of their $2,000,000,000 experiment was successful beyond all hope.

A thunderstorm delayed the test an hour and a half and blotted out aerial observation.

OBSERVED FROM 10,000 YARDS

The nearest lookout point was set up 10,000 yards from the steel tower from which the experiment took place. Key figures in the experiment took their positions 17,000 yards away. They were ordered to lie down with their heads away from the blast tower.

Final assembly of the atomic bomb had begun the night of July 12 in an old ranch house. Various component parts were assembled from distant points and put together there.

One false move would have blasted the scientists and their efforts into eternity.

During final preliminary assembly, a bad few minutes developed when the assembly of an important sec-

Continued on Page 3, Col. 4

First Target Obscured By Cloud of Dust, Smoke; 'Basic Power of Universe'

By the Associated Press

WASHINGTON, Aug. 6—The most terrible destructive force ever harnessed by man—atomic energy—is now being turned on the islands of Japan by United States bombers. The Japanese face a threat of utter desolation, and their capitulation may be greatly speeded up.

Existence of the great new weapon was announced personally by President Truman in a statement issued through the White House at 8 a. m., Pacific war time. He said the first atomic bomb, invented and perfected in the United States, had been dropped on the Japanese army base of Hiroshima 16 hours before.

That one bomb alone carried a wallop more violent than 2000 B-29 Superfortresses normally could hand an enemy city, using old type TNT bombs.

DUST OBSCURES RESULTS

Tokyo raidio named the place and approximate time the atomic bomb hit the homeland but made no mention of the terrific destruction such a bomb would cause. The Japanese broadcast said only that Hiroshima, the southwestern Honshu target city of the atomic bomb, was raided by "a small number" of American B-29s with incendiaries and explosives at 8:20 a. m., Monday (Japanese time). That was about the hour President Truman said the bomb was dropped.

Secretary of War Stimson followed through with a report that the blast stirred a cloud of smoke and dust so impenetrable as to make immediate, accurate observation of results impossible. The power of the bomb, Stimson said, is such as to "stagger the imagination" and he asserted it would "prove a tremendous aid" in shortening the Japanese war.

Stimson's emphasis on this point renewed speculation all over again as to whether Japan may be completely crushed by air attack without invasion.

"RAIN OF RUIN"

Mr. Truman noted the Japanese rejected the Big Three surrender ultimatum from Potsdam, and that this had been intended to spare the Japanese people from "utter destruction."

Now, he said, with the new bomb, the Japanese "may expect a rain of ruin from the air, the like of which has never been seen on this earth."

The announcement heralded an Anglo-American victory at a cost of $2,000,000,000 in one of the grimmest battles of the war—the battle of the laboratories—to unlock the secrets of the atom and yoke its energies to military use.

The Germans were striving desperately to win this highly secret contest in the closing months of the European struggle.

Scientists agreed that a new epoch in both war and peace was probably at hand. Although much experimenting remains to be done, this newly controlled energy can doubtless also be used to drive rockets, planes, ships and trains for constructive as well as destructive purposes.

President Truman said the new bomb, which draws its energy from

Continued on Page 5, Col. 4

Maj. Bong, Top U. S. Ace, Killed In Jet Plane

BURBANK, Aug. 6 (UP)—Major Richard Bong, America's top air ace, with 40 victories over the enemy was killed today when an Army jet-fighter plane he was flying overshot the Lockheed Air Terminal here and crashed in a vacant field. The wreckage took fire and Bong's body was badly burned. The curly-haired 24-year-old Major from Poplar, Wis., died testing a P-80 plane, a duty he had been assigned to because the Army did not wish to risk losing him in an air clash. Bong, who held the Congressional Medal of Honor for his spectacular series of successes against the Japanese, had been here for the past few months on his new duty.

Fighter Planes Again Raid Tokyo Area

By the United Press

GUAM, Aug. 7 (Tuesday)—Waves of Mustang fighters, striking in the wake of a Superfortress raid which left fires visible 150 miles in four Japanese "death list" cities, bombed and strafed the Tokyo area yesterday, the enemy reported.

American dispatches, meanwhile, indicated that Admiral William F. Halsey's Third fleet might be preparing to deliver its heaviest air-sea blow of the war against the Japanese homeland.

General Douglas MacArthur's war bulletin reported that more than 400 Okinawa-based fighters and bombers on Sunday hammered the waterfront and factory areas of Tarumizu on the eastern shore of Kagoshima bay in Southern Kyushu. Rockets, incendiary and demolition bombs caused widespread destruction, leaving the entire target area engulfed in flames. Smoke billowed 12,000 feet.

TRANSPORTS SUNK

Night patrol bombers sank a large Japanese transport and a medium freighter-transport in the Tsushima strait between Korea and Japan. Army reconnaissance bombers and Seventh Fleet planes hit Gunzan, in Southern Korea, by night.

Tokyo reported that 130 Mustang fighters from Iwo hammered the Greater Tokyo area in two waves Monday morning, bombing and strafing airfields and transport. One fleet of 70 planes hit north of Tokyo and another of 60 struck points southeast, northeast and north of the capital. The enemy claimed seven planes shot down and three heavily damaged.

A Sunday dispatch from United Press War Correspondent Ernest Hoberecht aboard a Third Fleet warship speculated on the possibility of the fleet returning to action, after breaking off its devastating assaults on July 30 with a massive carrier plane blow against Central Honshu.

ALL PLACES AT ONCE

He said the Japanese would give a lot to know where the fleet was, adding that "we could be off Kyushu off Tokyo or steaming through the cold waters of Hokkaido. In fact we could be at all places at once."

"We may be on our way home and we may be rolling up our sleeves for the heaviest assault of the war," Hoberecht said.

Trolley Signup

85 Carmen Choose Runs—None Leaves His Old System

The seniority signup on the Municipal Railway which came so near to causing a strike, started at 4:30 a. m. yesterday, and was watched intently all day by the rival unions and the management.

The crucial question was: Would men now on runs of the old Market Street Railway use their seniority rights to sign up for runs on the original Municipal Railway lines?

After the 85 men scheduled to sign up yesterday had picked their runs, just one former Market Street Railway man had yet claimed an original Muni run. Nor had any original Muni man claimed a Market line run.

BASEBALL PLEA

But since about 2400 are to sign by September 8, the CIO Municipal Carmen's Union remained uncertain as to whether the AFL Carmen's Union members, recruited largely from the old Market lines, would all heed the plea on the handbills distributed by the CIO:

"Remember, when the pick starts on Monday, let the Market Street men pick on the former Market Street lines, and the Municipal men pick on the original Municipal lines."

Early yesterday William Grogan, international vice president of the CIO Transport Workers' Union, of which Henry Foley's Municipal Carmen's Union is now a part, said he was still awaiting a reply from Mayor Lapham to Grogan's plea for arbitration of the difficulty which almost led to a strike.

Later in the day the Mayor wired Grogan:

"Your wire of August 4 received this morning. Just to keep the record straight let me refresh your memory. Mr. Marshall Dill (chairman of Public Utilities Commission) and myself met with you last Friday evening in an informal conference at which were present, besides Mr. Dill, yourself, and myself, Mr. Foley, Mr. Sherry, and Mr. Daugherty (officers of the CIO Municipal Carmen's Union group).

"I asked to appear before your membership meeting to state directly to city employees involved the position of the Mayor and said I would appreciate it if the press were also invited to attend.

"You asked if the Mayor had anything to propose to the meeting. I replied only this, that if at any time within the next 48 hours or before Monday, August 6, the two factions mutually agreed to arbitrate the preference of runs issue and would stipulate in writing to be bound by arbitrator's decision, I felt certain the Public Utilities Commission would authorize postponement of the signing up date until the arbitrator made his decision.

"I again requested permission to appear before your group. You, with Mr. Foley, Mr. Sherry and Mr. Daugherty, left to ascertain whether your membership would hear me. After a short interval I was advised your membership did not care to hear me and Mr. Dill and myself departed.

ACCORDING TO PLAN

"The two factions having failed to agree before Monday, August 6, the signup is proceeding according to the plan outlined July 21 in the

Continued on Page 5, Col. 4

Weather

A Baltimore hotel believes it has built a better mouse trap—if it can get the mice into it. The trap is in the form of a wooden box complete with automatic lights, doors for entrance and exit, and a ramp over which the animal tries to escape—only to be electrocuted.

In San Francisco, where mice for the duration will have to get along on the old-fashioned spring traps, the Weatherman says:

HIGH MORNING FOG: OTHERWISE CLEAR.

Hiram Johnson

Dean of Senate Republicans Dies in Maryland at 78

Opponent of United Nations Succumbs After Two-Week Illness

By the Associated Press

WASHINGTON, Aug. 6—Senator Hiram W. Johnson, a leader in the Senate battle that defeated United States participation in the League of Nations 25 years ago, died today. He was 78. The silver-haired Californian, a descendant of French nobility and dean of Senate Republicans in service, died in a coma at 8:40 a. m. (EWT) in the Bethesda, Md., Naval hospital.

Captain Robert E. Duncan, USN, his physician, attributed his death to thrombosis of a cerebral artery. He had been confined to the hospital 2½ weeks.

SON EN ROUTE

Mrs. Johnson was with him when he died and a son, Lieutenant-Colonel Hiram W. Johnson Jr., was en route by plane from San Francisco.

Senator Johnson, Republican Governor of California in 1910-1916, was the vice presidential candidate in Theodore Roosevelt's "Bull Moose" campaign of 1912.

He recovered from a critical case of pneumonia two years ago to engage in a bitter but unsuccessful fight this spring against Senate ratification of the United States-Mexico water treaty.

ONLY NO VOTE

Ranking minority member of the Senate Foreign Relations Committee, Senator Johnson cast the only vote in committee against reporting the United Nations Charter to the Senate without reservation or change.

Illness prevented him from being present when the Senate cast its final vote for ratification, but again he was recorded against.

Unwavering in his belief that this country should remain aloof from foreign alliances, he was vocal in his 1941 opposition to repeal of the 1939 neutrality act's prohibition against arming of American merchant ships.

Barely a month before the Japanese attack on Pearl Harbor, he told the Senate repeal of this provision and permission for the ships to carry war supplies to Britain was tantamount to a declaration of war by the United States.

CAPPER LEADS

Johnson was outranked in Senate service only by Senator McKellar (D., Tenn.), the Senate President. Both were elected at the same time, but Johnson waited 12 days after the beginning of his term, March 4, 1917, to take office, desiring to complete some business as Governor of California.

His death leaves Senator Capper (R., Kas.) the ranking Senate Republican and ranking minority member of the Foreign Relations Committee. Capper was 80 years old last month.

Flags on the Capitol and the Senate office buildings were lowered to halfstaff this morning, as many of his Senate associates issued statements expressing regret at the loss of "a great public servant."

For further details of the life and work of Senator Hiram Johnson, see pg. 8

Another Senator Guns for Hirohito

WASHINGTON, Aug. 6 (AP)—Senator McClellan (D., Ark.), today joined the growing ranks of legislators demanding that Emperor Hirohito's power be destroyed when Japan is defeated.

"I regard him as no different from Hitler and Mussolini, and he should be dealt with accordingly as a war criminal," McClellan said in a statement.

Over the week end, Senator Lucas (D., Ill.), also called for destruction of Hirohito's power, saying it must be wiped out "if we are to uproot and destroy Fascism in Japan."

TR's Widow 84 Years Old

OYSTER BAY, N. Y., Aug. 6 (AP)—Mrs. Edith Kermit Roosevelt, widow of President Theodore Roosevelt, today quietly observed her eighty-fourth birthday with her family at Sagamore Hill, Cove Neck.

In the group was her only surviving son, Lieutenant Colonel Archibald Roosevelt, who recently was discharged from the army after more than three years' service in the Pacific area.

Swedish Prince To Marry in U. S.

STOCKHOLM, Aug. 6 (AP)—Prince Carl Johan, grandson of King Gustaf and youngest son of the Crown Prince, and his commoner fiancee, Kersten Wijkmark will marry in the United States this fall and have their honeymoon in Cuba, Aftonbladet reported today.

The 26-year-old Prince expects to fly to New York in September, it was reported. Mrs. Wijkmark plans to take a boat in late August. She is editor of a Swedish woman's weekly and the daughter of Henning Wijkmark, prominent Swedish doctor of theology. She was once married to Axel Johnson, head of a large Swedish paper mill.

Army Colonel Protests 'Discrimination'

Wounded Nisei Rejected by VFW Post

ROME, Aug. 6 (UP)—Colonel V. R. Miller of Winneconne, Wis., commander of a crack Nisei regiment, sought the aid of the War and Interior Departments today in combatting discrimination in the United States against Japanese-American war veterans.

Miller was roused to action by rejection of an application of PFC. Richard H. Naito of Spokane, Wash., a former member of his 442d Infantry Regiment, for membership in Post 51 of the Veterans of Foreign Wars in Spokane. Naito was wounded while fighting in Italy with the Fifth Army.

Miller sent bluntly-worded letters to U. S. Interior Secretary Harold Ickes and Assistant Secretary of War John McCloy protesting discrimination against Nisei servicemen.

Miller also sent a letter to Dean Helbig, commander of Post 51, asking him to "correct this grave injustice to an individual and to a great American tradition."

Miller's letter to Helbig, along with Naito's letter to the post and Fifth Army Commander Lieutenant General Lucian K. Truscott's recent praise for Japanese-American soldiers, were published across five columns at the bottom of page one of the Stars and Stripes today.

Naito's letter to the VFW said:

"Twelve months ago, on a hot day, I was lying in the fields near Pisa, my right leg shattered by a German bullet . . . That day I didn't know whether I would ever set foot again on American soil.

"Today, on American soil, thousands of miles from Pisa, I have been wounded again by another weapon—hypocrisy or prejudice, call it what you will. Little did I expect that upon my return home to the people for whom I fought and suffered I would be repudiated."

Miller wrote to Helbig:

"When supposedly reputable organizations such as yours violate the principles and ideals for which we fight, these young Japanese-Americans are not the only ones to wonder about our war aims.

"Millions in Europe and Asia, too, will learn of your action and question the sincerity of American policy and ideals."

(Spokane VFW post defends action on Nisei. See Page 2.)

The Index

Barnaby	9
Comics	3H
Contract Contacts	6
Crossword Puzzle	6
Drama	6
Editorials	10
Finance	16
Lichty's Cartoon	9
Radio Log	3H
Ration Dates	9
Women's World	6
Vital Statistics	7
COLUMNS	
San Francisco	9
Washington Merry-Go-Round	10
Will Connolly	1H
Chester Rowell	10

THIS WORLD TODAY

San Francisco Chronicle EXTRA

THE CITY'S ONLY HOME-OWNED NEWSPAPER

FOUNDED 1865—VOL. CLXI, NO. 24 CCCC SAN FRANCISCO, WEDNESDAY, AUG. 8, 1945 DAILY 5 CENTS, SUNDAY 15 CENTS; DAILY AND SUNDAY PER MONTH $1.15

FLYERS' STORY OF ATOM RAID

By ROYCE BRIER

THERE is something faintly Hollywoodish in the environment in which this atomic bomb news story was born, and is growing up. Not in the bomb itself nor the research—all that is real enough—nor in the implications of the achievement, which have a valid appeal to the imagination of thoughtful men.

The allusion is to the news story. Perhaps it is inevitable today that public pronouncements have a slight blush of orchid. The *Second Inaugural* of Abraham Lincoln didn't, but then, those were simple times. We are much more clever today. We are all psychologists, the common people as well as Hollywood people and the Washington people.

It is necessary to say that the President's announcement of the bomb was handed to him by some public relations board. He would not be expected to know, nor would you nor I, what to say about so technical a discovery. The announcement may have been written by one man, but many minds went into it, military and scientific civilian minds, weighing each phrase and word for effect.

Consequently it was an artifice, a synthesis, and this reveals itself textually. It was timed. It had to be timed to follow the first strike of the bomb, a military necessity, but secondarily it gives internal evidence of being timed politically. It follows very closely the July 26 ultimatum, refers to it, and is geared to it in a threat that we are "now prepared to obliterate"—and so forth.

The announcement therefore becomes a supplementary ultimatum, whether or not we follow it with a second formal ultimatum, as London conjectures. The smashed atom enters the world as a political instrument, whatever it may be as a sober military and scientific fact.

And as a political instrument, it could be that the smashed atom is still somewhat short of the foreboding which heavily burdens the official announcement and the mountains of unofficial comment and speculation. That is, the scientists may be excused for the zeal they exhibit for the atom achievement as a scientific reality, but they are as much at sea in politics as politicians are in technics.

In this relation there are two

Continued on Page 4, Col. 1

The Crisis In Food

OPA May Ease Rules on Extra Points for Cafes

Strong prospects the Office of Price Administration within the next few days may make it easier for restaurant men to receive extra ration points high lighted these developments yesterday in the San Francisco food situation:

1—Leon Bosch, national co-director of OPA's food rationing division, has been in San Francisco for three days on a quiet investigation of the local restaurant situation for OPA Director Chester Bowles, it was learned.

Bosch has authority to recommend modification of present regulations, and is expected to forward a report to Bowles within 24 hours.

2—Milton S. Maxwell, secretary-treasurer of the Butchers' Union, asked Attorney General Robert S. Kenny to inspect public frozen food lockers throughout the State, declaring he was convinced they make possible "the black market in meat."

SUPERVISORS' MEETING

3—A week postponement in the OPA order placing fresh and frozen fish under price control, which was to have taken effect yesterday, was announced in Washington. The postponement was necessary to distribute copies of the order throughout the trade.

4—Supervisor Dewey Mead prepared to give hearing to all interested groups at a City Hall session Friday of the Committee on County, State and National Affairs of the Board of Supervisors to discuss the entire food situation.

5—The strike of 15 Auburn restaurant men who closed their doors August 1 in a plea for more ration points reached a definite stalemate. The OPA withdrew its offer to supply extra amounts of unrationed food items on the ground that the restaurant owners were making no effort to reopen.

RELIEF RECOMMENDATION

The new move by the OPA in San Francisco is reported to be a modification of the present regulation which requires that a restaurant show a 20 per cent increase in the number of meals served before it can qualify for supplementary ration points.

San Francisco district and regional OPA offices have recommended to Washington the requirement be cut to showing only a 10 per cent increase, and if the national OPA acts it is expected to be in line with this recommendation.

The overall San Francisco restaurant picture is somewhat confused, and Bosch's investigation here has confined itself largely to determination of exactly what has happened to the various categories of the restaurant business—hotels, public eating houses, dairy lunches and commissaries.

FOOD LOCKERS

Bosch and other OPA officials have conferred with the San Francisco Hotel Employers' Association, the San Francisco Restaurant Association and other food-serving groups.

Maxwell declared that since the war the use of frozen food lockers in California has increased from 2000 to 5000.

He declared they offered a subterfuge for the diversion of meat from the normal marketing channels to the black market, and in a letter to Kenny submitted legal authority which he said would justify an inspection of all meat in public food lockers.

Brownell Visits Idaho GOP Chiefs

BOISE, Idaho, Aug. 7 (UP)—Herbert Brownell Jr., chairman of the National Republican Committee, arrived here today to confer with Idaho party leaders and bolster their enthusiasm for the 1946 Congressional elections.

"I'm here to organize a drive to elect two Republican Congressmen from Idaho next year," said Brownell as he stepped off the train on his arrival from North Idaho.

Madigan to Head SWPC Office Here

Edward P. "Slip" Madigan, former St. Mary's football coach, said yesterday that he had been appointed chief of the Smaller War Plants Corporation office in San Francisco. He said he was notified of his appointment by Pat McDonough a director, now in Washington. Madigan had been serving as a consultant to the offices.

Weather

Mrs. Lela Dobson of Rockford, Ill., a deaf mute, recently paid $14.50 for disturbing the peace when neighbors complained of her noisy quarrels with her husband.

The weatherman here, however, forecasts:

HIGH MORNING FOG; OTHERWISE CLEAR.

Sen. Johnson To Be Buried Here Monday

Hiram Warren Johnson will be buried Monday in San Francisco, where he launched the career that made him one of the outstanding statesmen of his time.

Arrangements were outlined yesterday by his widow, his son, and Nevada's Senator Pat McCarran in Washington, with the co-operation, locally, of his one-time law partner, Theodore J. Roche.

In accordance with the Senator's wishes, Puritan simplicity will mark the preliminary rites in the Nation's capital, but in keeping with his position, a degree of ceremony will be observed here.

Mrs. Johnson and Lieutenant Colonel Hiram W. Johnson Jr., accompanied by a senatorial delegation of honor, will leave Washington with the body in a special car, on Thursday night. At Chicago, the car will be attached to the Overland Limited, scheduled to arrive in San Francisco at 9:20 a. m. next Monday.

The funeral party will be accompanied from the Ferry building by a small military and police escort to the rotunda of the City Hall. There it will be met by Governor Warren, Mayor Lapham and other officials.

The body will lie in state in the rotunda, with the casket unopened, until approximately 2 p. m.

A simple ceremony will be conducted there. Governor Warren, Mayor Lapham, Senator McCarran, chairman of the Senate delegation; Archbishop Mitty, Father Charles A. Ramm, Bishop Carl Morgan Block and Rabbi Elliott Burstein will be present.

The funeral cortege will be escorted a short distance from the City Hall, then will proceed privately to Cypress Lawn.

SENATORS ACCOMPANY BODY

Senator McKellar (D., Tenn.), President pro tem of the Senate, has named the following colleagues, who, in addition to McKellar, will accompany the body west:

Senators Downey (D., Cal.), Barkley (D., Ky.), White Jr. (R., Me.), Capper (R., Kas.), Shipstead (R., Minn.), Wheeler (D., Mont.), La Follette (Prog., Wis.), Vandenberg (R., Mich.), Connally (D., Texas), McCarran (D., Nev.), Thomas (D., Utah), Reed (R., Kas.), Tobey (R., N. H.), Chandler (R., Ky.), Willis (R., Ind.), Wherry (R., Neb.) and Cordon (R., Or.).

Soong in Moscow To Resume Talks

MOSCOW, Aug. 7 (UP)—Chinese Premier T. V. Soong and Foreign Minister Wang Shih-Chieh arrived today to resume discussions with Premier Joseph Stalin, which were interrupted by the Potsdam conference.

The Trial Of Petain

Vichyite Tells Of Secret Deal With Halifax

By the United Press

PARIS, Aug. 7—Jacques Chevalier, Vichy Education Minister, unfolded today at the trial of Marshal Henri Philippe Petain the hitherto secret story of how his indirect dealings with Lord Halifax, then Britain's Foreign Secretary, produced in 1940-41 an alleged agreement between the two powers on France's fleet, colonies and seaborne trade.

The negotiations, the witness implied, had the aid of Admiral William Leahy, then U. S. envoy to Vichy, at some stages.

Chevalier said the dealings with Halifax leading to the agreement were on a personal basis, with Canadian Minister to Vichy Georges Dupuy as intermediary. Halifax was his classmate at Oxford University in 1904-05, Chevalier said, and his friend for many years. He said they were carried on while Vichy maintained a "pretence" of full collaboration with the Germans.

CANADIAN INTERMEDIARY

Other witnesses contributed bits of the story of the negotiations. The agreement reached provided that Vichy would not hand over her colonies or fleet to the Nazis, and that the British would relax the sea blockade of metropolitan France. The court and Petain listened intently as Chevalier talked.

Contacts between continental France and Britain had been broken after the French-German armistice of June, 1940. Chevalier said the first contact with Halifax came December 4, 1940, when Dupuy brought him messages expressing a desire for resumption of contacts. They were addressed to him as Halifax' "most intimate friend," Chevalier said.

Dupuy was able to act as intermediary because Canada at that time had not broken diplomatic relations with Vichy.

Chevalier, thin, bespectacled, and dressed in the sober black which befits his occupation as professor, told how he was able to carry on contacts with Halifax even after the Maquis seized him in 1944.

PETAIN APPROVED

Petain knew and approved of the negotiations, Chevalier and other witnesses asserted. The negotiations went on in such complete secrecy the Germans were fooled, and found no cause to interfere on the basis of Article 9 of the Franco-German armistice, which provided that France should do nothing detrimental to German interests.

"The next day, December 5, I saw Petain and told him of the proposals," Chevalier continued. "He accepted under the reservation that the phrase 'artificial tension' be changed to read 'artificial evidence.'

"The next day I saw Dupuy and gave him a definite project for agreement, replacing the words as suggested. As far as the fleet was concerned, the British were to give us full support if needed. The British radio was to cease attacking France, and gasoline was to be allowed to come through to us. The next day, Dupuy and I saw Petain and the Marshal agreed to every point."

19 Killed, Many Missing in Ontario Grain Elevator Blast

By Associated Press

PORT ARTHUR, Ont., Aug. 7—An explosion wrecked storage elevator No. 5 of the Saskatchewan Wheat Pool, Ltd., today, and officials said it may have killed from 20 to 35 men.

The elevator was one of the largest at the head of the Great lakes.

At least 19 men were known to have been killed. Many others were missing, including a number of soldiers on leave to work in the lakehead elevators.

The blast rocked the twin cities of Port Arthur and Fort William shortly after 10 a. m.

A number of injured received first aid treatment at the site of the explosion.

Seventy men were employed at the elevator, one of a group of giant storage elevators located on the waterfront about three miles from the center of Port Arthur.

Four of the bodies were found 200 feet from the elevator.

The cause of the explosion was not immediately known.

An accumulation of grain dust, a source of explosions in grain elevators, may have caused the blast.

The workmen killed and injured were employed in the elevator workhouse, where the grain is unloaded and cleaned before being placed in the storage annex, from where it is loaded into ships.

"It is the worst explosion we ever had," said John Burton of the Eastern Terminal Elevator Company, whose office is about 400 feet from the Saskatchewan Pool building.

"A sheet of flame 200 to 300 feet long swept from the workhouse at the instant of the explosion and the walls collapsed. Only the concrete beams are standing."

Reports on the First Assault

Japanese City May Have Ceased to Exist; Enemy Cabinet May Be Considering Crisis

Tokyo Calls It 'Diabolic,' 'Desperate'

By the Associated Press

The Japanese Cabinet was reported assembled in special session Tuesday, presumbaly to discuss the drastic turn of events prompted by the loosing of an atomic bomb on the homeland.

As enemy broadcasts warned the people to brace for renewed attacks by the superbombs, NBC in New York picked up a BBC broadcast quoting the Tokyo radio as saying the Cabinet had been called together.

BBC said the wording of the broadcast implied that Premier Suzuki had summoned his advisers to discuss the atomic bomb raid which ripped the big military base of Hiroshima Monday.

"DIABOLIC"

Throughout the day the Japanese had broadcast repeated accounts of the new bomb, carefully refraining from using the word "atomic" or admitting the breadth of destruction, but branding it a "diabolic weapon."

"Since it is presumed that the enemy planes will continue to use this new bomb," the Osaka radio said in a domestic broadcast, "the authorities will point out measures to cope with it immediately."

Japanese accounts said "several bombs" fell on the big military base Monday, coming from the bomb bays of only a few Superforts, and Osaka added: "Even if the enemy does raid with a small number of planes we must be careful not to look at the raids lightly."

CONSIDERABLY DAMAGED

Another broadcast beamed to the United States declared that the use of the atomic bomb branded "the enemy for ages to come as a destroyer of justice and mankind."

All train travel into Hiroshima—which the Japanese conceded was "considerably damaged"—was forbidden.

"The destructive power of the new weapon cannot be slighted," warned Domei Agency, which said "a few" of the annihilating bombs floated in over the military city by parachute and burst "before reaching the ground."

Apparently the Japanese could not believe that a single atomic bomb, which President Truman disclosed yesterday had hit Japan for the first time Monday (Tokyo time), could cause all that violence.

Both Domei and an imperial headquarters communique recorded by the Federal Communications Commission said more than one bomb struck.

A number of broadcasts reported investigations of the havoc still were under way 36 hours after the attack.

"WANTON ATTACKS"

"As a result of this wanton attack," added Domei, "a considerable number of houses in the city were demolished, while fires were caused to start at several points."

Domei declared the people must be prepared for new attacks by "this new bomb"—nowhere did the Japanese speak of atomic bombs—and that until authorities found means to combat it the only remedy was "to strengthen the present air defense structure."

The imperial communique claimed that this new terror from the skies was unloaded by Superforts, the first hint from any source of the type of plane that carried the atomic bomb. One Japanese broadcast said 20 Superforts staged the raid.

Domei speculated that the Americans hoped to bring Japan quickly to her knees by the use of the atomic bomb, but asserted "effective measures are being worked out" to combat this weapon new to history.

"SADISTIC, BESTIAL

"By employing the new weapon, designed to massacre innocent civilians," said Domei, "the Americans unveiled to the eyes of the entire world their sadistic nature.

"What caused the enemy to resort to such bestial tactics which revealed how thin is the veneer of civilization the enemy has boasted of, is impatience at the slow progress of the enemy's much-vaunted invasion of Japan's mainland.

"In these circumstances the enemy began to employ the barbaric method as a last and desperate resort."

Truman Back In U. S.—Heads For Washington

NEWPORT NEWS, Va., Aug. 7 (AP)—The U. S. S. Augusta, bearing President Truman and his party, returning from the Big Three Conference at Potsdam, docked at Hampton Roads port of embarkation here today at 5:25 p. m.

The President and his party, which included Admiral William D. Leahy and Secretary of State James F. Byrnes, left immediately by special train for Washington.

The Pacific War Fronts

300 Planes Raid Two Kyushu Cities With Fire Bombs

By the Associated Press

More than 300 Liberators, Mitchells and Invaders of the Far East Air Forces struck heavily at two Southern Kyushu cities Monday with fire bombs and jellied gasoline, producing great fires and explosions throughout the target area, General Douglas MacArthur announced today (Wednesday).

The manufacturing city of Kagoshima took the hardest impact as more than 200 Liberators and Mitchells of the Fifth and Seventh AAF's, escorted by Thunderbolt fighters, bombed and strafed its submarine assembly yards, oil storage depots and iron and sheet metal works.

The rail center of Miyakonojo was hit simultaneously by more than 100 Seventh AAF Invaders and Thunderbolts.

REPRISAL RAID

The enemy made a reprisal raid by sending four planes on a predawn attack on Okinawa Sunday. One raider was destroyed and one probably was downed by a Black Widow night fighter.

A night-flying Liberator sank a 3000-ton transport-freighter and damaged another Sunday in Tsushima straits, where less than 24 hours earlier a 10,000-ton transport and a 3000-ton freighter had been destroyed in a raid announced yesterday.

Other raids along the Asiatic coast from Korea to Indo-China and extending to Java, Borneo and New Guinea, inflicted heavy damage. Several ships were sunk and shore installations destroyed. Marine and New Zealand planes also attacked troop concentrations and supplies at Rabaul and on Bougainville.

While censorship shrouded details of the first atomic bombing of the Japanese homeland, Air Force headquarters at Guam announced that 125 Superforts, loaded with conventional high explosive bombs, spread ruin across the Toyokawa naval arsenal, 175 miles southwest of Tokyo, in a concentrated raid Tuesday.

LUZON TROOPS

Tokyo said that about the same time 40 Mustangs from Iwo Jima, in concert with "several British planes of unspecified category," bombed and strafed the Tokyo area for an hour. There has been no official report of a British land-based air raid on Japan.

Chungking, expressing belief that the atomic bomb would force Japan to surrender quickly, reported the capture of strategic Yuengkong, 125 miles southwest of Canton, cementing the Chinese grip on a 50-mile strip of the south coast for possible American landings.

American and Filipino forces on Northern Luzon were closing a pincers on 6000 Japanese troops cornered in the mountains, hoping that the trap would yield up, dead or alive, Lieutenant General Yamashita, arrogant conqueror of Singapore, who lost the battle of the Philippines.

In the mop-up of Southern Burma, Allied patrols tested enemy strength in thrusts across the old Sittang river channel 60 miles northeast of Rangoon, while the main force battled the mauled remnants of the all-but-liquidated Japanese 28th Army trapped west of the river.

Superfort Crew Describes Terrific Flash and Blast; 'A Mountain of Smoke'

GUAM, August 7 (AP)—America's new weapon, the atomic bomb, struck squarely in the center of the industrial city of Hiroshima August 6 (Tokyo Time) with a flash and concussion that brought an exclamation of "My God!" from a battle-hardened Superfortress crew 10 miles away.

The flyers' report gave reason to believe that the Jap city has ceased to exist.

PILOTS FEEL CONCUSSION

Crewmen who carried the awful new bomb which is declared to have an explosive power the equivalent of bombs that 2000 Superfortresses would have had to carry previously although they were far away, felt the concussion like a close explosion of antiaircraft fire.

Colonel Paul W. Tibbets Jr. of Miami, Fla., who piloted the Superfortress and Navy Captain William S. Parsons of Sante Fe, N. M., Navy ordnance expert, described the explosions as "tremendous and awe-inspiring."

Neither man could give an estimate of what damage the bomb had wrought but they declared it "must have been extensive."

There is good reason to believe, however, that this southern Honshu city of 343,000 no longer continues to exist.

"It was 0915 (9:15 a. m.) when we dropped our bomb and we turned the plane broadside to get the best view," said Captain Parson. "Then we made as much distance from the ball of fire as we could.

"We were at least 10 miles away and there was a visual impact even though every man wore colored glasses for protection. We had braced ourselves when the bomb was gone for the shock and Tibbets said 'close flak' and it was just like that—a close burst of anti-aircraft fire.

'MOST REVOLUTIONARY'

"The crew said 'My God!' and couldn't believe what had happened.

"A mountain of smoke was going up in a mushroom with the stem coming down. At the top was white smoke but up to 1000 feet from the ground there was swirling, boiling dust. Soon afterward small fires sprang up on the edge of town but the town was entirely obscured. We stayed around two or three minutes and by that time the smoke had risen to 40,000 feet. As we watched the top of the white cloud broke off and another soon formed."

Details of the bombing were disclosed at a press conference attended by General Carl Spaatz who termed the new bomb the "most revolutionary development in the history of the world."

Spaatz was obviously highly elated at the new bombing weapon. He said if he had had it in Europe "it would have shortened the war six to eight months."

Major General Curtis Lemay said that if this bomb had been available there would have been "no need to have had D-Day in Europe."

The full extent of the damage done to Hiroshima was not known, however. Photographs taken at the time of bombing showed only smoke. Photographs taken four hours later showed smoke still obscuring the city and rising to 40,000 feet.

SECRET MISSION

The Superfortress which carried the bomb took off from a Marianas base and only three men knew what they carried—Colonel Tibbets, Captain Parsons and the bombardier, Major Thomas W. Ferebee, Mocksville, N. C. Another crewman knew only that it was a highly secret, important mission.

Surrender Demand?

Experts Guess Atom Bomb Will Lead to Another Ultimatum

By the Associated Press

WASHINGTON, Aug. 7—The cataclysmic might of atomic bombs prompted Washington and London predictions tonight of a new surrender ultimatum to Japan.

How soon either an ultimatum or a Japanese decision might come was highly conjectural.

But one able military authority here said "inevitably" Japan will be told—quickly—that she must quit or face the onslaught of the most terrible weapon ever devised. And another declared the Japanese may be expected to make up their minds within six weeks whether to get out of the war or see their home islands devastated from the air.

LONDON'S GUESS

The London press spoke of an ultimatum—one newspaper said it would carry a 48-hour deadline for acceptance.

Yet there was a possibility that for the moment the Allies of the Pacific war would be content to capitalize on the tremendous propaganda value of the first atomic bomb strike Sunday on the army city of Hiroshima, and on the threat of repeat performances.

That would give Japan a chance to change its mind about accepting the "surrender now" decree already issued by Britain, China and the United States at the Potsdam Conference.

Certainly the OWI was busy at propaganda. It filled the air waves with information on how the atomic bomb rivals with reality the fantasy of some of junior's favorite comic strips.

BIGGER CITIES NEXT?

And the attack on Hiroshima appeared calculated to impress Japan's civilians as much as the military. Military authorities suggested other and bigger key cities might be the next to suffer the awful destruction of the super bombs.

There was some expectation that President Truman might see fit to emphasize in his forthcoming report to the Nation the futility of Japanese resistance.

Nevertheless, there were no indications that the armed forces had swerved in the slightest from their promise of ultimate invasion of the land of the setting sun.

But the loosening of the forces of nature itself against the enemy by release of the tremendous energy bound up in atoms reverberated around the world.

VATICAN REGRETS

There were attempts to appraise what it would mean in wartime and in peace.

The Vatican City newspaper L'Os-

Continued on Page 3, Col. 7

The Chronicle Index

Barnaby	9
Casualties	2
Comics	3H
Contract Contacts	3H
Crossword Puzzle	4
Drama	6 and 7
Editorials	10
Finance	16
Lichty's Cartoon	9
Radio Log	3H
Ration Dates	9
Vital Statistics	8
Women's World	8
COLUMNS	
San Francisco	9
Washington Merry-Go-Round	10
Bill Leiser	1H
Harry B. Smith	2H
Dorothy Thompson	10
Veterans' Guide	6

Listen to The Chronicle-KYA Time-Clocked News — 1260 on your dial—6 a. m. to midnight.

EXTRA

San Francisco Chronicle

THE CITY'S ONLY HOME-OWNED NEWSPAPER

FOUNDED 1865—VOL. CLXI, NO. 25 CCCC SAN FRANCISCO, THURSDAY, AUG. 9, 1945 DAILY 5 CENTS, SUNDAY 15 CENTS: DAILY AND SUNDAY PER MONTH, $1.75.

COMPARATIVE TEMPERATURES

	High	Low		High	Low
San Francisco	60	52	Chicago	72	62
Oakland	63	54	New Orleans	96	77
Sacramento	83	53	New York	79	63
Los Angeles	81	61	Salt Lake	85	63
Seattle	75	60	Washington	85	66

Forecast: Morning fog.

THIS WORLD TODAY

By ROYCE BRIER

IN THE course of the rise of the Western civilization over some six hundred years, it has many times been endangered by internal revolt, but only twice has it been challenged by an alien force.

The first time was in the Ottoman invasion of the seventeenth century, reaching high tide in the siege of Vienna in 1683. This was an exceedingly dangerous incursion, which might easily have demolished the civilization. Then, as later when faced with extreme peril, the Atlantic powers were confused and apathetic. It remained, in fact, for Slavs—Poles and Russians—to save the day, for it was the Pole, Sobieski, who raised the siege, and started the Turks back to their own lands.

The Turks were really a little late. Fifty years earlier Europe was exhausted by the Thirty Years War, the most devastating ever fought in proportion to the mass of the civilized organism in which it was fought. The Turks should have started about 1630.

A few years after Vienna was saved, Peter the Great came to power. The Russians in the seventeenth century were neither of the West nor of the East. They comprised a rude world suspended between the two civilizations. Peter the Great swung them toward the Western orbit. While retaining many of their Eastern characteristics and interests since, they have notwithstanding approached nearer to the Western orbit every decade since Peter the Great came to power.

This is not a reference to political form. Political form is but an encrustation on the deep movements of civilized experience and cultural trend, and the efforts of such as the correspondent, von Wiegand, to make Stalin out as "oriental" begs the question, when it isn't merely tawdry journalism designed to catch the unwary or ignorant.

The second alien attempt to demolish the Western civilization was made manifest December 7, 1941. Unlike the Turks, the Japanese struck at what appeared to be the most auspicious moment, when the West seemed to be so torn with internal disorders that it would be unable to defend itself.

Like the Turks, the Japanese had planned this assault for a long time. It was an inner feeling with them (and this had also been true with the Turks since the Crusades) that they must

Continued on Page 4, Col. 2

RED ARMY ATTACKS, MANCHURIA SAYS

THE NEW FRONT—This map, specially prepared by Chronicle staff artist G. B. Reesor, indicates how Soviet Pacific territory is an arrow aimed at the heart of Japan—with the great port of Vladivostok as the tip of the arrow. Lower on the map a small black arrow indicates Hiroshima, an important city on the Inland sea until it was hit by a single atomic bomb last Monday. Soviet bases bring the entire enemy homeland within close fighter plane range.

USSR Declares War

Ground and Air Assaults Reported by Enemy Radio

Moscow, Truman Announce the News; Speedy Surrender of Japs Anticipated

By the United Press

The Soviet Army suddenly launched an attack against Japanese forces on the Soviet-Manchukuo border shortly after midnight Wednesday, according to a Kwantung (Japanese) Army headquarters communique issued at Hsinking.

The Hsinking radio broadcast, recorded by United Press, said the Soviet Army attacked along the eastern border at 1 a. m. Thursday (Russian time).

The communique added that at the same time a small number of Soviet aircraft started bombing attacks on strategic points in Manchukuo territory.

Exact location of the attacks in Manchukuo (Manchuria) was not given.

Another Japanese broadcast simultaneously reported the Red Army had opened its attack along the Russian-Manchurian border but gave no other details.

WASHINGTON, Aug. 8 (AP)—Russia has declared war upon Japan.

The declaration, announced to the United States first by President Truman and followed by a report on the Moscow radio, became effective at 5 p. m., Eastern war time (midnight August 8-9 Russian time).

The first reaction in Washington, unanimous and unequivocal, was that Russia's entry, coupled with the atomic bomb, means an early end of the Japanese war. The President announced the Soviet action at a hurriedly summoned White House news conference.

The President used these words, on which he authorized direct quotation:

"I have only a simple announcement to make. I can't hold a regular press conference today but this announcement is so important I thought I would call you in. Russia has declared war on Japan. That is all."

A Government official in a position to know told newsmen that agreement for Russia's entry into the Japanese war was concluded at the Big Three meeting at Potsdam.

This official, who declined use of his name, recalled that the Russians were said authoritatively to have agreed at the Yalta Conference that they would enter the war in due course.

EARLY SURRENDER DUE

There was no decision at Yalta, however, it was said, on the timing.

Some surprise was expressed that the Russians had decided to fight the Japanese at such an early date. But there have been persistent reports, lacking official confirmation, that Russia would enter the Japanese war 90 days after the collapse of Germany. The Germans surrendered May 8.

Belief that Russia's war declaration could force an unconditional Japanese surrender in a few days, was expressed by some ranking military and naval authorities.

Piling one sensational development on another, these officials consider the Soviet action coming after the atomic bomb attack has

Continued on Page 3, Col. 5

The Atomic Bomb

'Practically All' Life in Hiroshima Snuffed Out

Too Many Dead To Be Counted, Tokyo Reports

By the Associated Press

Destruction of "practically all living things" in atom shattered Hiroshima, city of 343,000, was reported by Japan Wednesday in broadcasts picturing such confusion that a definite check on casualties was impossible.

Persons outdoors were "burned to death while those indoors were killed by the indescribable pressure and heat" generated by the atomic bomb dropped on the city in Monday's historic raid, one broadcast said.

While authorized quarters charged America with violation of international law in using the bomb, a special meeting of government officials considered a report on the "disastrous ruin" that befell Hiroshima.

"INDESCRIBABLE"

Tokyo's reports, monitored by the FCC, said of the stricken city:

"Practically all living things, human and animal, were literally seared to death" by the "new type bomb." Use of the term "atomic bomb" was carefully avoided in domestic broadcasts.

Houses and buildings were crushed and "all the dead and injured were burned beyond recognition."

"The dead are too numerous to be counted" and "authorities are having their hands full in giving every available relief possible under the circumstances."

"The destructive power of these bombs is indescribable."

Monitored Japanese domestic transmissions appeared more moderate and restrained, after yesterday's propaganda pattern of vivid accounts of destruction and charges of American atrocities.

Voice broadcasts and wireless transmissions aimed at North America and Europe meanwhile seemed to be trying to establish the propaganda point that the bombings should be stopped.

"HONOR" PROPAGANDA

One of these foreign emissions described the bombing as "useless cruelty" which "may have given

Continued on Page 2, Col. 7

Heart of City Was Demolished Photos Reveal

By the Associated Press

GUAM, Aug. 9—Japanese perished by uncounted thousands from the searing, crushing atomic blast that annihilated 60 per cent of the 343,000 population of the city of Hiroshima Monday, photographic and other evidence indicated today (Thursday).

Photographs showed that not even stout concrete structures in the heart of the city, presumed to have been air raid shelters, escaped. The structures still stood, but all their insides were apparently burned out.

Both General Carl Spaatz, who announced from his Strategic Air Force Headquarters here that 60 per cent of Hiroshima had been "completely destroyed," and Tokyo radio warned that more atomic bombings could be expected.

Spaatz declared other Superforts were ready to follow the B-29 "Enola Gay" which Colonel Paul W. Tibbets Jr., Miami, Fla., piloted over Hiroshima to drop war's newest and most devastating weapon.

HARBOR AREA ESCAPES

Tokyo radio, which referred to the bomb only as something new in its home broadcasts, urged the Japanese to keep their spirits firm, and predicted that a defense against the bombs would be developed. Tokyo referred to the bomb as "atomic" in its foreign broadcasts.

Spaatz announced reconnaissance photographs showed 4.1 square miles of Hiroshima's built-up area of 6.9 square miles were wiped out and that the destroyed area included five major industrial targets.

The photographs disclosed that

Continued on Page 2, Col. 8

Truman's Report

He'll Discuss Atom Power, Potsdam In Broadcast at 7 o'Clock Tonight

By United Press

WASHINGTON, Aug. 8—President Truman, preparing to report to the Nation at 10 p. m. (EWT) tomorrow (7 p. m. PWT) on recent momentous developments, today received latest information on the atomic bombing of Japan and then conferred lengthily with Secretary of State James F. Byrnes.

Secretary of War Henry L. Stimson's bombing report to Mr. Truman was interrupted by Undersecretary of State Joseph C. Grew, who hastened into the President's office with a small sheaf of papers, remained only long enough to deliver them and departed without comment.

Presidential Secretary Charles G. Ross had no explanation of the hurried visit.

LEGISLATURE CALL

Byrnes added to the mystery when he refused to tell reporters whether he and Mr. Truman had discussed the atomic bombing.

"Ask the President," he replied. "He's doing the talking now."

Meanwhile, Senator Harley M. Kilgore (D., W. Va.) predicted after a conference with the chief executive that Congress may be called into session before October 8, the scheduled date, if the new bomb speeds victory over Japan.

White House officials indicated there was nothing specific about recalling the legislators, but it was pointed out that Congress naturally would be reconvened if the Japanese surrender.

Ross said Mr. Truman would mention the atomic bomb in his 30-minute radio address to the Nation, but probably to no great extent. The speech, to be carried over all radio networks, will be devoted chiefly to the Big Three Conference at Potsdam. Ross said Mr. Truman would go into greater detail about the Conference than did last week's official communique.

BUSY DAY

The President's first day back at the White House was a busy one. Besides conferring with Stimson and Byrnes, he also:

1—Announced the Russian declaration of war against Japan.

2—Formally ratified this country's membership in the United Nations World Security Organization by signing an ornate instrument of ratification. He thus made the United States the first nation to put into force the Security Charter adopted June 26 by 50 United Nations.

3—Discussed with Kilgore the latter's proposal for Government-sponsored scientific research in the light of the new atomic bomb discovery and the need for additional reconversion legislation.

4—Conferred with Senator Carl Hatch (D., N. M.), who said later that Mr. Truman regards the atomic bomb as an effective instrument for maintaining peace rather than a destructive weapon of war.

5—Caught up on paper work, which had accumulated during his one-month absence abroad and put the finishing touches on his radio address—the longest one since he became chief executive.

6—Arranged to hold a press conference early next week, probably Monday or Tuesday.

Stimson told reporters he had given Mr. Truman a full report on the atomic bomb destruction of Hiroshima, Japanese quartermaster station and army base, but he added that "I can't tell you what the report said."

White House officials dismissed reports that Mr. Truman intended to take personal charge of the use of the atomic bomb and declined comment on reports that a new "surrender-or-else" ultimatum would be handed to the Japanese.

German Debt 80 Billions

BERLIN, Aug. 8 (UP)—The Red Army newspaper Taglische Rundschau said today that Germany's national debt exceeds 800,000,000,000 marks ($80,000,000,000).

The newspaper said it included 300,000,000,000 marks in war damage and 60,000,000,000 in currency in circulation.

Weather

Protests have been made in India that entrants to civil service in Jaipur are compelled to know Urdu. The San Francisco weatherman, who speaks Urdu like a native, persists in predicting:

HIGH MORNING FOG; CLEAR IN AFTERNOON.

Jap Puppet Princes Meet

CHUNGKING, Aug. 8 (UP)—Japanese-sponsored puppet princes in Mongolia held a three-day meeting last month to consider ways to protect themselves in the event of a Japanese defeat, the Chinese newspaper Takungpao reported today.

The meeting was held under the leadership of Prince Ter, the newspaper said. The Japanese, learning of the conference, ordered the princes to remove their families and belongings to Taonan on the borders of Inner Mongolia and Manchuria, the paper added.

Kunming Has a Chennault Road

CHUNGKING, Aug. 8 (UP)—A street in the crowded shopping center of Kunming, capital of Yunnan province, has been named Chennault road in appreciation of the protection Lieutenant General Claire L. Chennault afforded the city from air raids since 1942.

Chennault, former commander of the U. S. 14th Air Force in China, has just completed a 3000 mile tour of China. He will return to his Texas home for what his friends said would be a temporary rest.

French Election Set for October 21

PARIS, Aug. 8 (UP)—The government today announced that the general election and popular referendum on the new constitution will be held October 21.

Russ War on Japs, Truman Goal at Berlin

By ERNEST B. VACCARO

A. P. White House Reporter

WASHINGTON, Aug. 8—Final agreement upon Russian entrance into the war with Japan, it may now be disclosed, was the primary objective of President Truman's trip to the Big Three Conference in Berlin.

As vital as was, and is, his interest in bringing harmony to the European scene, the President repeatedly told newsmen (of whom the writer was one) en route with him to Europe aboard the cruiser Augusta that his main concern was to bring the Pacific war to a close "with the least possible cost in American lives."

TO SAVE YANK LIVES

A Soviet declaration of war, he reasoned, might save hundreds of thousands of Americans from injury or death.

Perhaps that was the reason Mr. Truman personally announced the war declaration at a brief news conference today.

Leaning against a rail of the Augusta, en route to Europe, the President frequently remarked upon the big job ahead at Potsdam.

He wanted more than anything else, he said, the use of Russian air bases with which to step up the assault on Japan and its conquered territories.

The results were evident in his demeanor on the way back. He couldn't confide in reporters but his pleasure was evident.

Mr. Truman's friends reported he preferred not to go to Berlin. They said he would rather have the State, War and Navy Departments conduct negotiations abroad with the British and the Russians.

WHY TRUMAN WENT

It was the hope that he could make a final agreement for Generalissimo Stalin to throw Russia's might into the Allied cause, friends report, that brought his decision to leave the country at a time when the war with Japan was at its height, the United Nations Charter was pending in the Senate and re-

Continued on Page 3, Col. 1

The Chronicle Index

Barnaby	8	Women's World	7
Casualties	2	COLUMNS	
Comics	3H	San Francisco	9
Contract Contacts	7	Washington Merry-Go-Round	10
Crossword Puzzle	8	Bill Leiser	1H
Drama	3H and 6	Harry B. Smith	2H
Editorials	10	Chester Rowell	10
Finance	16		
Lichty's Cartoon	8		
Radio Log	3H		
Ration Dates	8		
Vital Statistics	7		

Listen to The Chronicle-KYA Time-Clocked News—1260 on your dial—6 a. m. to midnight.

VICTORY EXTRA!

Chronicle Home Delivery Service
Federal war regulations to conserve rubber prohibit all special deliveries. If for any reason you do not receive your Chronicle, kindly telephone GArfield 1112 or your local Chronicle dealer before 10 a. m. so the delivery may be checked. We appreciate your co-operation in this emergency.

San Francisco Chronicle
THE CITY'S ONLY HOME-OWNED NEWSPAPER

COMPARATIVE TEMPERATURES

	High	Low		High	Low
San Francisco	62	52	New Orleans	90	78
Oakland	68	55	Chicago	88	69
Sacramento	88	57	New York	84	71
Los Angeles	86	60	Salt Lake	82	60
Seattle	75	56	Washington	86	70

Forecast: High fog.

FOUNDED 1865—VOL. CLXI, NO. 31 PAGE A SAN FRANCISCO, WEDNESDAY, AUGUST 15, 1945 DAILY 5 CENTS, SUNDAY 15 CENTS: DAILY AND SUNDAY PER MONTH, $1.75.

PEACE!

The Japs Give Up Unconditionally-- Allied Troops Told to Cease Firing; Enemy Gets Orders for Surrender

A City Goes Wild--- And Nobody Cares

Every Whistle Summons Crowds ---But the Church Bells Ring, Too

By CHARLES RAUDEBAUGH

The end of the long haul came at 4 o'clock yesterday afternoon in San Francisco—and the city went wild.

Split seconds after word of the war's end was flashed from the White House, the celebration started.

It swelled and surged and mounted through crescendo upon crescendo into a demonstration without parallel in the city's history.

MARKET STREET IS HUB

Market street was the center of the celebration, but there was hilarity and excitement and gratitude—and prayers—throughout the city.

The air raid sirens sounded first. Then automobile horns, factory whistles and ship's whistles—and church bells. Anything that could make a noise was blown, or pounded or beaten.

People surged from their homes into the streets and headed down town. The down town stores closed within a few minutes and sent their workers and customers out into the streets. Some of these people headed for home, but most of them stayed down town, willy-nilly.

By 4:15 o'clock, scarcely a street car could move on Market street. Automobile traffic was at the peril of unsolicited, laughing, shouting passengers, who climbed aboard fenders or perched themselves on roof tops.

TRAFFIC SNARLED

Traffic was hopelessly tied up on the city's main thoroughfare—both because of the density of the crowds and the pranks of the celebrants. Elated servicemen swarmed over the street cars, dismantled trolley poles, and stripped the stalled cars of their

Such traffic as could be diverted to secondary streets caused time-consuming jams along other routes.

A citizen's committee headed by Supervisor John J. Sullivan had figured out long in advance of the day of victory that the celebrants would need a band to lead them up Market street. Immediately on the announcement of victory the band was dispatched to the Ferry Building for the parade—but to all effect it was lost.

The people did not require a band to lead them. They formed their own parades, and there were probably a dozen all going at once—in different directions—the length of Market street. Anyone with a flag automatically found himself at the head of a line of march.

City and federal offices closed for the day without waiting to be told to do so. They may or may not be open today—no one was quite sure early last evening.

As a matter of fact, no one was quite sure of anything that would happen later in the evening, or today.

Liquor stores, bars, groceries and department stores will be closed today—but whether the banks are to be shut and whether other businesses also will observe a holiday was not clear early last night.

President Truman declared today and tomorrow to be legal national holidays. The state compliance was stalled somewhere in confusion over the state seal. Early last night the proclamation was being held up because no state seal was immediately available.

No one seemed to care, however, whether there was a proclamation issued, or a state seal. All that mattered was that the war had ended—and the days of "blood, sweat and tears" were over.

The churchbells rang for victory, too, and the houses of worship of all faiths were crowded by the devout.

But there was nothing irreverent in the more spectacular observance which went on in Market street.. Many who had lost brothers or husbands or sons in the war found that the void was somehow less if they joined in the parading and shouting.

San Francisco let go for the celebration with the same energy with which it had fought during the war. There is still a clamp of military security over the number of San Franciscans who were sent into battle by their draft boards, but

Continued on Page 2, Col. 1

Today and Tomorrow--- Legal Holidays

WASHINGTON, Aug. 14 (UP)—President Truman tonight officially declared Aug. 15 and 16—Wednesday and Thursday—legal holidays to permit payment of time and a half to essential workers who must stay on the job.

He said that since the National War Labor Board had permitted the payment of straight time wages for employes who are excused from working on those days, many employers had requested that employes who do work on those days should receive premium compensation.

Royce Brier's column on the peace is on page one.

Defeated Officers Will Bow to MacArthur; Hirohito and Suzuki Scheduled to Broadcast

Tokyo Radio Tells Nation To Stand By

By the United Press

SAN FRANCISCO, Aug. 14—Tokyo radio said Tuesday (S. F. time), Emperor Hirohito, breaking all tradition, personally would broadcast an important announcement to Japan and Japanese-occupied areas of Asia at 8 p. m., P. W. T., followed by Premier Baron Admiral Kantavo Suzuki.

It seemed apparent that the Emperor would tell his people, for the first time, that he had surrendered Nippon unconditionally to the Allies.

Text of an official Japanese Domei News Agency broadcast, recorded by United Press, here:

"His imperial majesty, the Emperor, will be graciously pleased to broadcast to the nation through the radio at 12 noon today (Wednesday).

"The radio broadcast by his gracious imperial majesty has no precedent in Japan's history. The Japan Broadcasting Corporation asked every member of the nation not to fail to listen to the imperial broadcast.

"Following his majesty's broadcast, Premier Baron Kantaro Suzuki will speak. Important announcements will also be made.

"All Tokyo morning papers postponed publication until 1300 (1 p. m.) today, in order to carry an important announcement after the personal broadcast of his majesty."

Attlee Gives The Big News To Britain

By the Associated Press

LONDON, Aug. 15—In calm tones Prime Minister Attlee told millions of war weary Britons in a midnight (4 p. m. PWT) broadcast that "Japan has today surrendered. The last of our enemies is laid low."

The Prime Minister, during his five-minute talk, quickly reviewed the Japanese war, paid tribute to "our fleets, armies and air forces that have fought so well in the arduous campaign against Japan," and said:

"Our gratitude goes out to all our splendid Allies, and above all to the United States without whose prodigious efforts this war in the East would still have many years to run."

Attlee said that Wednesday and Thursday would be holidays in Britain.

The fact that the Prime Minister was to broadcast at midnight was disclosed only a short time in advance, but listeners everywhere crowded around available radios and stood in hushed silence as the chimes of Big Ben tolled the hour of peace and then Attlee came on the air.

Moscow Announcement

LONDON, Aug. 15—The Moscow radio announced at midnight (4 p. m. PWT) the unconditional surrender of Japan.

Canadian V-J Today

OTTAWA, Aug. 14 (UP)—Prime Minister Mackenzie King said tonight that tomorrow will be V-J Day in Canada and that next Sunday will be a day of prayer and solemn thanksgiving for the victory over Japan and the ending of the war.

Inside

News and features in this special Victory edition of The Chronicle:

Page B—History of the war.

Pages 1 and 2—Latest dispatches on Japan's unconditional surrender.

Page 3—"Pacific Comeback," a picture story of the Pacific story

Page 4—News of Major William Knowland's appointment as successor to the late Senator Hiram Johnson.

Page 5—"Amphibious Operations," the picture and text story of our battle for the islands.

Pages 6 and 7—Drama and movie coverage.

Page 8—Late photos of San Francisco's celebration.

Page 9—Comics and Crossword.

Page 10—The Sporting Green.

Flags for Paris

PARIS, Aug. 14 (UP)—Andre Le Trocquer, President of the Paris Municipal Council, today issued a proclamation to Parisians to hang out theri flags in celebration of the war's end.

Petain Gets Death Sentence

LONDON, Wednesday, Aug. 15 (UP)—A Reuters dispatch from Paris said today that Marshal Petain had been convicted and sentenced to death.

The Potsdam Declaration Accepted, Truman Declares In an Official Statement

By ERNEST BARCELLA
United Press Staff Writer

WASHINGTON, Aug. 14—Peace came to the world tonight when President Truman announced that Japan has accepted unconditional surrender and that Allied forces have been ordered to cease firing.

General Douglas MacArthur, "the man who came back," was named Supreme Allied Commander to receive the formal Japanese surrender.

World War II—the bloodiest conflict in human history—was at an end, except for the formality of signing surrender documents.

V-J day will not be proclaimed until after the instruments of surrender are signed.

America's three allies in the Pacific war—Great Britain, Russia and China—will be represented at the signing by high-ranking officers.

Mr. Truman proclaimed the tidings (at 4 p. m. Pacific Wartime), shortly after he received Tokyo's formal reply to the Allied surrender terms.

Summoning reporters to his office, he read a statement which said:

"I deem this reply a full acceptance of the Potsdam Declaration which specified the unconditional surrender of Japan.

"In the reply there is no qualification."

Tokyo informed Mr. Truman that Emperor Hirohito is prepared "to authorize and ensure the signature by the Japanese government and the Im-

Continued on Page 2, Col. 4

TOKYO'S DELEGATION WILL LEAVE FOR MANILA SUNDAY

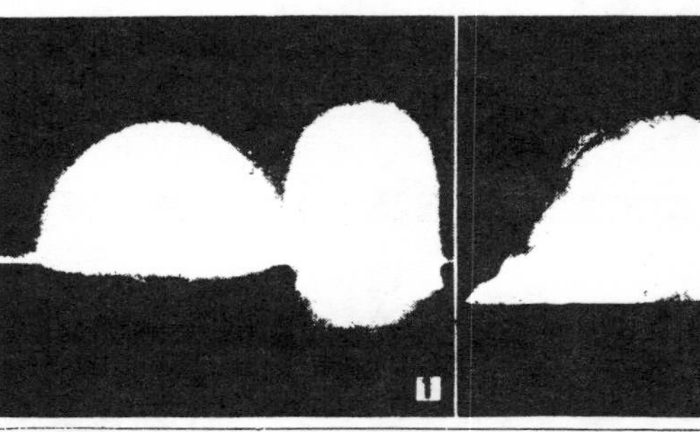

THIS WORLD TODAY

By ROYCE BRIER

YESTERDAY four United States photographic planes flew over the Tokyo area to take pictures. They were met by anti-aircraft fire and ten interceptor planes. Two of the interceptor planes were shot down. One of our planes was damaged.

A very interesting little war. It raises a question whether the Emperor's order to cease hostilities has reached the Tokyo area yet, or whether that is an outpost requiring several days to learn that the big war is over.

At any rate, there should be a way of ending the little war. Here is one suggestion: print some handbills right away, saying, "You attacked American photographic planes over Tokyo in defiance of your Emperor's orders. For that, we will send one hundred bombers over Tokyo in three hours. They will drop ten old-fashioned TNT bombs. If they are attacked by anti-aircraft fire or menaced by interceptors, they will drop one hundred bombs. Thereafter we will send four more photographic planes over Tokyo. If they are molested, we will give you warning of the reprisals we propose to carry out."

In "Message No. 5," Tokyo Radio appealed to General MacArthur in Manila to cause the Russians to halt their offensive operations in Manchuria, saying it was causing "great difficulties" to the Japanese in their effort to "cease hostilities."

Why? The way to "cease hostilities" is to lay down your arms. Then you won't be tempted to fight any more. In this connection the statement yesterday of Marshal Vasilevsky, the Soviet commander in Manchuria, seems eminently sensible. He said: "As soon as Japanese troops begin surrendering their arms, Soviet troops will discontinue war operations."

The Emperor has just formed a new government with Prince Higashi-Kuni, uncle of the Empress, as Premier. This gentleman was commander of home defense headquarters at the time of the Doolittle raid, April, 1942. It is reported that he threatened, or participated in, the execution of our captured flyers, which was actually announced about a month after he left office.

If he did, this man has blood on his hands that won't come off. Instead of dealing with him,

Continued on Page 2, Col. 2

San Francisco Chronicle
THE CITY'S ONLY HOME-OWNED NEWSPAPER
VOL. CLXI. NO. 34 CCCC SATURDAY, AUGUST 18, 1945 DAILY 5 CENTS, SUNDAY 15 CENTS

'Peace Rioting'

Grand Jury Will Get Report; New Patrol Set Up

San Francisco was busy yesterday cleaning up the debris—political and physical—left in the wake of three nights of "peace riots." Developments were:

1—District Attorney Edmund G. Brown announced he would present a full report on the rioting to the Grand Jury on Tuesday night. Brown was gathering statements of witnesses who saw specific acts of vandalism or misconduct.

2—The Army and Navy, Mayor Lapham, and Board of Equalization Member George R. Reilly got agreement from liquor stores that they would limit their package sales to the hours between 10 a. m. and 12 noon until V-J Day officially comes, and with the bars will then close down for two days.

3—The city police, shore patrol and the military police instituted a new and augmented patrol system along Market street last night as the city was placed "on limits" to servicemen again. All days off in the Police Department were canceled and the department alerted.

4—Directors of the Market Street Association — whose members' store windows were smashed and looted over the costly three-night celebration—expressed the hope that the city administration would be prepared for any future celebration "by giving the servicemen something to do instead of simply turning them loose on an empty street."

5—The National Maritime Union of the CIO stepped into the picture with a statement by its local port agent, James Drury, that the organization would not let the servicemen become the whipping boys to divert attention from the fact that civil and police authorities were unprepared to handle the celebration.

CASUALTY LIST

The casualty list remained unchanged yesterday—eleven persons dead and 1000 injured—but there still was no final figure on the property damage. It is estimated that replacement of 107 plate glass windows on central Market street alone will cost $25,000.

How far the Grand Jury will go into the matter will be up to the members of the jury, but District Attorney Brown was preparing a complete report. He also consulted with Presiding Superior Court Judge Robert McWilliams to determine the legal limits of the jury's action.

Both Mayor Lapham and Equalization Board Member Reilly said that the plan to restrict sale of bottled goods between now and the official V-J Day, and then close both off-sale establishments and bars for two days, originated with the Army and Navy.

Reilly still was on vacation in Pebble Beach, but transmitted the request—he has no authority to make it an order—to licensees through Don Marshall, local enforcement officer for the Board of Equalization.

LIQUOR DEALERS

Lapham also called a meeting of representatives of organized liquor dealers, cabarets, restaurants, hotels, bars and the bartenders' union. Unlike the star-chamber session Thursday when he first discussed the matter with civic leaders, yesterday's meeting was open to the press.

The fullest co-operation so far as possible in carrying out the new liquor sale plan was pledged, but some of the men present expressed fear that some individual dealers might not comply.

Lapham put the request to the meeting "as a straight business proposition."

"Apparently San Francisco was the prize of all the cities in the country," said the Mayor. "We were all in the mood to celebrate. I did, too—undercover."

"Looking at it in the broad way,

Continued on Page 5, Col. 1

Preparations for Surrender

Jap Delegates Leaving for Manila Sunday; 'Obey Emperor!' the New Premier Orders

Domei Says Allies Will Land 'Soon'

By the Associated Press

SAN FRANCISCO, Aug. 17—Japan's new Premier assumed his duties Friday with orders for strict observance of the imperial order to cease firing, but there were official and press hints of lingering Nipponese ambitions in East Asia.

Meanwhile the Japanese agency Domei said Allied occupation forces would land "soon" in the homeland and that the people would be required to "extend all accommodations." The broadcast asserted the Allies would not land as "combat units." It gave no authority for this statement.

General Prince Naruhiko Higashi-Kuni, first imperial prince to be Premier, announced a three-point basic policy of reconstruction, control of the military and enforcement of order, at his Cabinet's first meeting, said Domei.

First official act of Higashi-Kuni, who also holds the War Ministry portfolio, was to order the army to "strictly observe" Emperor Hirohito's rescript to quit fighting, Domei said in a broadcast.

RECONSTRUCTION

"If there should be any incident in violation of his majesty's command, we will lose the confidence of the world," the Prince said. "The new Cabinet must see that the work is carried out with great care.

"The second thing which we must bear in mind is that we must recover ourselves from the ravages of war and plunge into the work of reconstruction at the earliest possible moment."

The imperial rescript, after recounting three years and eight months of war against the United States and Britain, declared entrance of the Soviet Union into the war had endangered "the very foundation of the empire's existence."

"With that in mind and, although the fighting spirit of the Imperial Army and Navy is as high as ever, and with a view to maintaining and protecting our noble national policy, we are about to make peace."

CABINET MEETS

The portfolios of Foreign Minister and Minister for Great East Asia were given Mamoru Shigemitsu, Foreign Minister in two of Japan's war cabinets.

The Greater East Asia office during the war handled affairs of puppet regimes governing countries conquered by Japan. The Allied Potsdam declaration stripped Nippon of all territories overrun by her armies in nearly 50 years of aggression.

Domei said the Cabinet, which includes three members of the government of Premier Suzuki, which resigned Wednesday, held its first meeting for an hour and a half at Higashi-Kuni's residence. It was not indicated whether the meeting place was the Prince's palace, which was hit in the April 16 Superfort raid.

Tokyo broadcasts extolled Prince

Continued on Page 3, Col. 5

Another German Sub Surrenders

MAR DEL PLATA, Aug. 17 (AP)—A German submarine surrendered here today to Argentine naval authorities, 102 days after Germany surrendered.

The 600-ton craft carried the number U-977 and a complement of 32, including four officers, one of whom was Commander Heinz Schasser. The craft was similar to the U-530 which surrendered to Argentine authorities July 10.

A Battleship in Tokyo Bay Is Called the Logical Place For the Formal Ceremonies

By the Associated Press

MANILA, Aug. 18—Japan advised General MacArthur early today (Saturday) that its surrender delegation had been selected and would leave for Manila Sunday.

Prodded by a note from MacArthur to quit stalling, which had carried over two days, and get on with the peace negotiations, Tokyo acted without further delay.

MacArthur's headquarters announced at 2:45 a. m. (11:45 a. m. Pacific War Time Friday) that the desired information had been received from the enemy capital.

The Tokyo message was brief. It said the delegation could not leave until Sunday "due to necessary internal procedure" and promised further details would follow.

In Manila the Japanese delegation will hear what it must do before surrender articles are signed and Allied occupation forces move into Nippon.

SURRENDER SCENE?

Where that surrender might be signed still was conjectural. Details were being worked out.

An Associated Press dispatch from Guam, saying that Admiral Nimitz had been appointed by President Truman as a United States representative, suggested a battleship in Tokyo bay was the "logical scene."

The Supreme Commander's message also may have sped the departure from Tokyo of three Imperial parties carrying cease-fire orders to field commanders, who were expected to be told by the flying missions some time today that they must lay down arms.

They left for Manchuria, China and Indo-China by plane yesterday under safe conduct.

STILL FIRING

Only a few hours later 10 Japanese fighters and anti-aircraft fire greeted four unescorted U. S. heavy bombers on a photo mission over the same general area from which the enemy planes took off.

Two Japanese planes were believed destroyed, and one bomber was shot up although none of its crew was injured.

Two Lightning fighters on separate reconnaissance flights over the southern island of Kyushu also were fired upon by ground batteries the same day.

This sort of ing was trying Allied patience, coming close on Tokyo's report without apology to MacArthur that Japanese planes had attacked 12 Allied transports, probably inflicting some damage, when they approached "extremely near" the coast of the home island of Shikoku Thursday a few hours before the Emperor issued the cease-fire order.

The Japanese "earnestly requested" the Allies to avoid "approaching home waters of Japan proper" until cease-fire orders are "fully effectuated."

OTHER FRONTS

But slowly guns were falling silent on the Eastern Asia battle fields.

The Russians, who had given the Japanese until Monday to surrender in Manchuria and Korea, reported that 20,000 prisoners had been taken but that fighting continued.

Chinese Army commanders told the Japanese to cease hostilities.

The Tokyo radio claimed the Japanese commander-in-chief in China

Continued on Page 3, Col. 3

More Controls Go

Civilian Meat Supplies to Increase; All Sports Restrictions Are Lifted

By the United Press

WASHINGTON, Aug. 17—Another batch of wartime restrictions passed into history today amid official assurance of more meat soon and the prospect that meat rationing may end or be modified next month. As the Nation progressed with the happy job of adjusting itself to peacetime living, here's what happened:

1—Secretary of Agriculture Clinton P. Anderson said after a Cabinet meeting that meat set-asides for the armed forces may end by September 1 and that civilian supplies will increase. This does not mean that rationing will end at that time, he said, because a lot will depend on how much beef is moving to market. He added that he had his own ideas on when rationing should end but could not reveal them because agencies handling rationing have not reached agreement.

2—The Petroleum Administration for War ended its ban on the production of high-test gasoline for civilian motorists.

3—The restriction on congratulatory and greeting telegrams was removed and Western Union may even deliver singing telegrams.

4—All restrictions on sports were lifted, making the 1945 world series a certainty and permitting baseball, football and racing to return to a peacetime footing.

5—The Office of Defense Transportation announced that the 35-mile-an-hour speed limit for automobiles will be lifted soon. At the same time it removed restriction on organized group travel and on the sale of railway tickets to travel agencies.

6—The OPA suspended price controls over imported wines and spirits, not including whiskies. Brandy, rum and cordials are the major items affected. Scotch and other imported whiskies will remain under price control. Whisky production will return to normal soon.

7—The War Production Board lifted controls over the sale of plumbing, heating and cooking equipment. A WPB official said there is no immediate prospect of removing restrictions on newsprint.

8—Deputy Petroleum Administrator Ralph K. Davies predicted that the oil industry will be freed of Government control by the end of the year.

9—The National Housing Agency ordered regional offices to review low-rent projects interrupted by the war and to speed plans for building them.

10—The OPA announced plans to make available to civilians a large quantity of cotton and rayon piece goods originally slated for the armed forces.

11—Senator Elmer Thomas (D., Okla.) proposed that the Government spend $2,000,000,000 on public works during the next three years. He said this would boost employment and make needed improvements in roads, schools, flood control and reclamation.

Reconversion of war industry meanwhile proceeded apace. It was disclosed that Government agencies are ready with a program for speedy clearance of war plants so industry can get tooled up without delay for peacetime production.

A high-ranking WPB official said if any reconverting industry is impeded by delays in plant clearance, the WPB is ready to "nudge" the offending Governmetn agency.

The War Department intends to settle most terminated war contracts within four to six months after claims are submitted.

Weather

"A woman and four men have been appointed to solve Northern Ireland's housing problem," says a dispatch.

In San Francisco, where there's a feeling that carpenters will have to be appointed to solve such problems, the weatherman varies his prediction patter with:

SCATTERED CLOUDS; FOG NEAR OCEAN.

The Chronicle Index

		COLUMNS	
Barnaby	9	San Francisco	9
Casualties	2	Washington Merry-Go-Round	10
Churches	7	Harry B. Smith	2H
Comics	16	Will Connolly	1H
Crossword Puzzle	8	Bookman's Notebook	10
Drama	8	Bill Leiser	1H
Editorials	10	Chester Rowell	10
Finance	2H		
Lichty's Cartoon	9		
Ration Dates	8		
Radio	8		
Vital Statistics	7		
Weather	7		
Women's World	6		

Listen to The Chronicle-KYA Time-Clocked News — 1260 on your dial—6 a. m. to midnight.

Cuban Leftist Turn Predicted

NEW ORLEANS, Aug. 17 (AP)—The New Orleans item, in a copyrighted story, quoted General Fulgencio Batista, former President of Cuba, in an interview as saying today that Cubans would travel the "leftist" road if that proved the medium for better understanding between capital and labor.

Dr. Koo to Head World Group

LONDON, Aug. 17 (AP)—Dr. Wellington Koo of China was elected chairman of the executive committee of the United Nations Preparatory Commission today. He will serve two weeks, after which subsequent chairmen will be elected every fortnight until the committee completes preparation of the new world security organization.

(AP Wirephotos from U. S. Army)

First Photos of Atomic Bomb Test

History's greatest phenomenon of man-made power was tested in New Mexico last July 16. There, scientists set off the first atomic bomb, and the explosion rocked the earth as far as 200 miles away. These photos were taken by the Army, with an automatic newsreel camera six miles from the blast. They show: 1—A dome of intense light rises on the horizon. ("The whole country was lighted by a searing light with an intensity many times that of the mid-day sun," said observers 10 miles away.) 2—A great cloud billows up in the area of the first blinding flash. ("A huge multi-colored surging cloud boiled up.") 3—Smaller puffs roll out from the base of the cloud-dome. ("It was golden, purple, violet, gray and blue.") 4—The brilliant dome seems to expand. ("The cloud rose over 40,000 feet in five minutes.") 5—As the white cloud rises, the billowing puffs nearer the ground grow darker. ("There came a tremendous sustained roar and a heavy pressure wave that knocked men down.") 6—The white glare seems to become more diffuse. ("Soon the shifting sub-stratosphere winds dispersed the mass.") 7—The light almost fills the sky, and the smoke rises blacker and bigger. ("It was like the sun had come up and then suddenly gone down again.") 8—The horizon is completely obscured by heavy, dark masses of smoke. ("The steel tower that had held the bomb was entirely vaporized. Where it had stood was a huge, sloping crater.") The spots of light in the lower right-hand corner of some of the pictures are reflections of the camera's lense, caused by the terrific glare.

Norse Execute First 'Quisling'

LONDON, Aug. 17 (UP)—The Norwegian Information Service reported today a firing squad executed Raidar Haaland, the first Quisling war criminal sentenced to death by Norway's Supreme Court.

Nine Killed in Mexico Clash

VERACRUZ, Mexico, Aug. 17 (UP)—Nine persons were killed today when members of an armed farmers' organization clashed with Federal troops near here. Six of the dead were civilians, two were soldiers and one was the chief of the local military guard.

San Francisco Chronicle

THE CITY'S ONLY HOME-OWNED NEWSPAPER

FOUNDED 1865—VOL. CLXI, NO. 49 CCCCAAA SAN FRANCISCO, SUNDAY, SEPTEMBER 2, 1945 DAILY 5 CENTS, SUNDAY 15 CENTS

The Future---Death, or A Brave New World?

Hiroshima, No. 1 target of the atomic bomb, is mute testimony to the destructive power of the new force that man has unleashed for better or for worse. Below is the first ground view of the center of the blast area of that once prosperous Japanese city and army base of 345,000 people. All that remains is a Catholic church in the immediate foreground and an unidentified building (center). Not another building stands, no life exists, everything that had been built to endure has been dispersed by the power of universal energy, this Domei photo proves. That awful devastating power is a secret shared between the United States and Britain.

Former Secretary of State Stettinius, now American representative on the United Nations organization, said it has been proposed that the secret held by the two nations be turned over to the Security Council of the United Nations—to be shared by all those who seek to preserve the peace. He might have said, in the words of W. H. Auden, British war poet, "We must love one another as friends—or die." We are entering an era from which there is no retreat when Foreign Minister Mamoru Shigemitsu (below, right) signs the surrender terms, with General MacArthur at the left, Lieutenant General Richard K. Sutherland, chief of staff, in the center. This is tomorrow.

(AP Wirephoto from Army Signal Corps)

Japanese Surrender Is Signed; First Photos of Historic Day

This is Hiroshima, the first city in the world to know the full force of energy that man can wring from the universe.

This is Japanese Foreign Minister Shigemitsu (seated), who has just declared it to be in his country's interest to surrender.

Full Employment Bill

Bowles Supports Measure As Aid to Balanced Budget

By the Associated Press

WASHINGTON, Sept. 1—Price Administrator Chester Bowles asserted today that the so-called full employment bill and the program necessary to make it effective "provide the only practical hope of a balanced Federal budget."

"With a national production of 200 billion dollars worth of goods and services annually, a regularly balanced budget should be readily obtainable with relatively moderate taxes," Bowles said in a statement presented to the Senate Banking Committee.

"But who would assume," he asked, "that with a national production of, say, only 110 billion dollars and with 20 million men walking the streets in search of jobs, we could raise the necessary funds to meet our Federal commitments within the bounds of practical taxation?"

Asserting the bill merely states a national policy and calls for a program to achieve it, Bowles suggested such a program include:

1—A long-range tax program to encourage the maximum of private investment and enterprise, as soon as inflationary danger ends.

2—A Social Security program will cover all working groups.

3—A farm program which will develop into a national policy of maintenance of high farm income.

4—Dropping the controls developed during the war.

The committee closed its hearings on the measure with Bowles' statement and testimony from John W. Snyder, director of War Mobilization and Reconversion; Senator Sheridan Downey (D., Calif.), **(See page 7 for Downey's testimony)**, and Major General Philip B. Fleming, Federal Works Administrator.

Snyder declared the Federal government "must adopt measures which will, I believe, be the determining factor in whether or not we can reach and hold full employment."

Among such measures he listed tax policy, social security, foreign trade, housing and construction.

He stressed, however, that "we must rely on jobs in private business for the overwhelming majority of job opportunities."

The measure calls for an annual estimate of work in sight and of jobs needed, with the Federal government to take steps to make up any deficit, by encouragement of private investment and by public works if necessary.

Fleming testified that a construction volume of $15,000,000 "seems well within the realm of possibility." Such activity would give employment at construction sites to about 3,300,000 men, he said, and still a larger number would be employed in allied industries.

Cruiser San Diego Returning to S. F.

YOKOSUKA, Sept. 1 (UP)—The light cruiser San Diego, the first American vessel to dock at Japan, will lead a Navy vanguard home to San Francisco today. The ship leaves this afternoon for the Golden Gate.

Three Yanks From Atsugi

First to Come Back--They Flew In With A Load of Films

By STANTON DELAPLANE
Chronicle Staff Writer

FAIRFIELD AIR BASE, Sept. 1—At 5:30 this morning, a silver B-32 with black cloverleaf insignia circled Hamilton Field twice, feeling for a landing.

Then fog socked in over the field. The B-32 lifted and flew to Fairfield and let down in the sun.

The first three soldiers to hit the hard-baked ground had another first on their records. Six days ago they were the first three Americans to step onto the gravel taxi strip at Atsugi airdrome outside Tokyo.

The dust that showered off their shoes was the brown earth of battered Japan.

AHEAD OF SCHEDULE

The big bomber was two hours ahead of schedule. The "divine winds" of Japan boosted her from Okinawa to Kwajelein, Kwajelein to Pearl Harbor, Pearl Harbor to San Francisco. By the time reporters arrived for scheduled interviews at Hamilton Field, the three were breakfasting miles away at this Air Transport Command base.

The Army hustled out a bucket-seat transport and flew the interview party to Fairfield. There they met Colonel John H. Lackey, the Fifth Air Force troop carrier and airstrip expert; Lieutenant Benn F. Reyes and Captain Charles J. Russhon, who flew to Atsugi in the first ship with cameras.

The B-32 bulged with film, black and white and colored, motion pictures and still, a two-day record of Japan as she bowed in defeat before the occupation.

Lackey was pushed out of the picture for a time when news men found that one of his companions was Benny Reyes, now a Fifth Air Force Lieutenant. Reyes is best known here as the press agent who publicized Sally Rand, and her Nude Ranch at the 1939-40 World's Fair on Treasure Island.

FROM OKINAWA

The Colonel flew out of Atsugi the same day he landed. But Reyes and Russhon stayed in for two days to film the first sky-borne occupation.

"The recco party of 49 planes which was agreed to under the original terms took off from Okinawa at 2:30 on the morning of August 28," said Colonel Lackey.

"There were 16 planes in the first flight. We flew at 7000 feet and had radio contact with destroyers

Continued on Page 3, Col. 1

Russia's Role In the Peace --An Estimate

The Big Three—Russia, Great Britain and the United States—have pledged themselves to maintain the peace. Each of the powers has a stake in world security. What is Russia's strength, its limitations, its intentions? For a discussion of the Soviet Union in the new world, based on the map by Chronicle Staff Artist G. B. Reesor on Page 2, listen to "Let's Look at the Map" on KYA today at 12:10 p. m., with Larry Fanning, managing editor of The Chronicle.

Europe Faces A Serious Coal Famine

By the Associated Press

WASHINGTON, Sept. 1—The Office of War Information said today nothing can prevent a severe coal famine in Europe next winter and it could be drastic enough to destroy "all semblance of law and order."

In a detailed coal report to which five Government agencies and two economic missions contributed, the OWI concluded:

1—Even if maximum outside aid is forthcoming, liberated European nations—principally France, The Netherlands, Norway, Denmark, Belgium, Luxembourg, Greece and Italy—will fall at least 50,000,000 tons short of "normal requirements" for the "coal year," ending on next March 31.

2—If no imports are forthcoming, these countries will be 80,000,000 tons short of "normal needs," and about 30,000,000 tons below "minimum essential requirements" for sheer existence during the winter.

3—If the coal famine brings chaos in Europe, the entire world economy will be affected.

There is a world-wide shortage of coal, "the most critically scarce raw material needed by the European economy," the report said, with the United States and Russia affected along with Britain and the rest of Europe.

For the European shortage, the report listed two basic reasons:

1—Liberated countries never able to supply all their own needs will produce only 55,000,000 tons this year, compared with 92,000,000 in pre-war 1938.

2—They will get far less coal than

Continued on Page 4, Col. 5

The Chronicle Index

Weather—Clear, Morning Fog

Art	18TW
Books	14TW
Will Connolly	2H
Crossword	3S
Drama	9TW
Fashions	4S
Gardens	6
Music	13TW
Radio Log	19TW
Ration Dates	6
Harry B. Smith	3H
Society	3S
Weather	7
Vital Statistics	7

Aviation and Pink's Pickups are on page 4 of the Sporting Green. Bridge News and Report on Congress are on page 8 of the Classified Section.

Special Sections
CLASSIFIED SECTION
COMICS
SPORTING GREEN (H)
THIS WORLD (TW)
WOMEN'S WORLD (S)

Making History Aboard the Missouri

Formal Surrender Is Signed in Tokyo Bay; The President Proclaims Today V-J Day

Truman Broadcasts Over A World-Wide Network---Hopes for the Peace Era

By the Associated Press

WASHINGTON, Sept. 1—President Truman today proclaimed Sunday, September 2, V-J Day—for Japan a day of "retribution," for America and the world a day of the "victory of liberty over tyranny."

Mr. Truman spoke over a globe-girdling radio hookup that linked the White House with Tokyo, where aboard the battleship Missouri just off the enemy capital, Japan signed the terms of her surrender.

And to the occasion the President attributed a four-fold significance:

1—For this country—a day for "renewed consecration to the principles which have made us the strongest nation on earth and which, in this war, we have striven so mightily to preserve."

2—For Japan—and end of "power to destroy and kill."

3—For the world—a bright new era of hope for "peace and international good will and co-operation."

4—For history—"the day of formal surrender by Japan."

CABINET AT WHITE HOUSE

"We shall not forget Pearl Harbor," he said.

"The Japanese militarists will not forget the U. S. S. Missouri.

"The evil done by the Japanese war lords can never be repaired or forgotten. But their power to destroy and kill has been taken from them. Their armies and what is left of their navy are now impotent."

For this event of mingled solemnity and joy, Mr. Truman invited members of the Cabinet to sit with him in the broadcast room on the first floor of the White House—the White House where Japan once haughtily boasted she would dictate surrender terms. They listened to the ceremonies aboard the Missouri and, in the midst of them, the President spoke.

Then the all-network switched back to Tokyo Bay for addresses by General Douglas MacArthur, Supreme Allied Commander, and Admiral Chester W. Nimitz, Pacific Fleet Commander, American signers of the surrender documents.

OBLIGATION TO WAR DEAD

There was little of gloating or elation in the President's address. Rather there was sober emphasis on what victory has cost and what it will mean.

Our first thoughts now, the President said, are thoughts of grate-

Continued on Page 4, Col. 7

What They Said

V-J Day, a day of things ending and beginning, was made memorable by the word that men spoke to commemorate the things men had done. "We have a renewed faith and pride," President Truman said. "The guns are silent . . . let us pray for peace," General MacArthur declared. "We can be proud," Nimitz said. For text of the statements and the official surrender terms for Japan, see Page 6.

12 Signatures Affixed To the Document During Brief Historic Ceremony

By MURLIN SPENCER AND SPENCER DAVIS
Associated Press Staff Writers

U. S. S. MISSOURI, Tokyo Bay, Sept. 2—Two nervous Japanese formally and unconditionally surrendered all remnants of their smashed Empire to the Allies today (Sunday), restoring peace to a war-battered world.

Surrender hour was cool and cloudy, but the sun broke through the overcast 20 minutes later as General MacArthur intoned "these proceedings are closed."

Foreign Minister Mamoru Shigemitsu, who signed for the Japanese government, doffed his top hat and nervously fingered his fountain pen before he firmly signed the two copies of the surrender document—one for Japan, one for the Allies. Shigemitsu penned his name in English on one document.

MacARTHUR'S FIVE PENS

General Yoshijiro Umezu, for the imperial staff, also nervous, signed hurriedly; quickly stepped aside. A Japanese Colonel wiped his eyes. All of the Nipponese present were tense and drawn.

Then MacArthur signed, deliberately, using five pens. The first two—silver-plated especially for the occasion—he handed in turn to Lieutenant General Jonathan M. Wainwright and to British General Arthur Ernest Percival, who were forced to surrender Corregidor and Singapore, respectively, in the war's darkest hours.

Wainwright and Percival smiled; saluted snappily. They had been rescued only a few days ago from Japanese prisoner of war camps.

TRUMAN'S MESSAGE

"It is my earnest hope and indeed the hope of all mankind that from this solemn occasion a better world shall emerge out of the blood and carnage of the past," MacArthur said.

The historic signing took place on a long table on the gallery deck.

Minutes later, from the White House, where Japanese warlords once asserted they would dictate their own peace terms, President Truman broadcast:

"We shall not forget Pearl Harbor. The Japanese militarists will not forget the U. S. S. Missouri."

The 45,000-ton Missouri, which less than a month ago was blasting Japanese war industries with her 16-inch guns, had those rifles pointed skyward and her bow pointed toward the heart of Japan for the ceremony. Flags of the United States, the United Kingdom, China and Russia fluttered from the spic verandah deck.

SIGNING INCIDENT

Once there was a slight delay when it appeared someone had signed on the wrong line. Gen. Sir Thomas Blamey, representing Australia, signed the Japanese document first by error—then shrugged

Continued on Page 4, Col. 4

Hillman in London En Route to Paris

Copyright, 1945, by the New York Times and The Chronicle

LONDON, Sept. 1—Sidney Hillman, CIO leader and chairman of the Political Action Committee, arrived in Southampton last night aboard the Queen Mary en route to Paris to attend the World Trades Union Congress.

He is chairman of the American delegation.

Hillman traveled ahead of the remainder of the delegation in order to meet Sir Walter Citrine and other British labor leaders in London.

Italy Warned to Vote 'Peacefully'

MILAN, Sept. 1, (AP)—Premier Ferruccio Parri told delegates to the congress of Italy's six-party Committee of National Liberation today that he desired voting for the Constitutional Assembly as soon as possible but warned "I will cancel the elections if there is a threat of violence against the voters."

Parri declared, however, that the Constitutional Assembly could be revoked only by "A free people, not under armistice conditions."

The Premier said the government would try to alleviate unemployment by a program of public works

Flood Destroys Chinese Villages

CHUNGKING, Sept. 1 (UP)—Central News Agency said today that a Yangtze river dyke had broken 20 miles below Shasi in Hupeh province and flood waters had washed away hundreds of small villages.

San Francisco Chronicle

THE CITY'S ONLY HOME-OWNED NEWSPAPER

FOUNDED 1865—VOL. CLXII, NO. 108 CCCCAAB SAN FRANCISCO, FRIDAY, MAY 3, 1946 DAILY 5 CENTS, SUNDAY 15 CENTS DAILY AND SUNDAY PER MONTH $1.75

COMPARATIVE TEMPERATURES	High	Low		High	Low
San Francisco	58	48	New York	74	54
Oakland	59	49	Chicago	68	54
Los Angeles	69	56	New Orleans	83	68
Sacramento	71	46	Washington	69	61
Seattle	81	47	Salt Lake City	73	38
Reno	80	28	Pensacola	74	72

One Guard Killed, Nine Injured In Armed Revolt on Alcatraz; Photos of the Prison Rebellion

YOU ARE WATCHING the battle of Alcatraz from a boat only 100 yards off the island in San Francisco bay. The three men in the circles below are penitentiary guards who have just fired long-range through the barred cell block windows to smash the glass. Now the guards along the catwalk, half way up the wall, are crouching for momentary safety, then reaching on tiptoe to fire bullets and tear gas bombs through the jagged windows. The guard in circle No. 1 is in the act of firing through the bars at prisoners who are fighting back with everything they've got, including tommy guns and rifles. The desperadoes are in command of the center tier of the three-tier block from the northern end of the building to the seventh window, as shown by dotted line (No. 2). The guards' advance is in wartime fire-and-cover style.

By ROYCE BRIER

SENATOR ELLENDER of Louisiana is one of Huey Long's boys. He was a floor leader in Huey's personal legislature, and two years after the assassination he was still telling what a wonderful little guy Huey was, and singing the virtue of the Long kind of dictatorship.

Aside from that—which will place him for you in case you have forgotten—Ellender is just another run-of-the-mill Southern statesman of the Claghorne brand, not as obnoxious to sensible men as Bilbo, but without much to recommend him but his set of prejudices. These are pretty gaudy, being compounded of ignorance-of-the-subject, gallte-attack-it-anyway, isolationism and a full quota of sectional obsessions.

This man has proved in a hundred speeches that he knows very little history (excepting that of the Lower Mississippi, 1861-1946), very little about how and why peoples act in the mass, and very little of the problems besetting the modern world, particularly the problems besetting Europe. His speeches reveal that he follows a reactionary line at home, and abroad a vague anti-foreign line, which he and those of like mind find synonymous with "pro-American," a term they use repeatedly. Brooks of Illinois let it float on the breeze only yesterday.

But Ellender is a very important man in the affairs of the United States out in the world. As a member of your Senate, he has one-ninety-sixth of the say as to whether we will have a decent and stable future, or another and more massive dose of the chaos we have been enjoying for a third of a century. Consequently his words are worth weighing when he gets on his feet to face an issue like the proposed British loan.

Ellender is against the loan. That is his right, and is not particularly interesting. What is interesting is his reasoning or belief in the matter.

He says Britain is a "dead horse" which can't be revived, and that $3,750,000,000 would be only a "shot in the arm."

"To keep Britain in her trade position," he avers, "we will have to keep pouring money into London like pouring water into a rat-hole."

He went on to say Britain is past the point where the islands can maintain a large population by selling manufactured goods to

Continued on Page 4, Col. 1

Here's the Story of How It Happened - - -

By STANTON DELAPLANE

This was how it happened on Alcatraz:

About 3 o'clock, one of the toughest cons ever sent to the Big House overpowered a guard in the gun gallery catwalk and took his gun away from him.

This man is believed to be a Kentucky bank robber, doing 26 years the hard way. He was too tough for Atlanta Penitentiary. So they sent him to the Rock.

In the toughest stir, this man went crafty and tractable. That may have given him access to the catwalk where an armed guard, behind screen and locked doors can survey the whole cell block.

At gun point he drove the guard down to the guard's room, where he stuck up 20 or more guards getting ready to go on duty.

He gathered up all the guns he could carry. Then, driving the guards before him, he went back to the cell block, where he threw the master switch opening the cells.

"Come on boys. Let's go," he said.

Sixteen cons joined him and armed themselves.

At 3:30, motorists on the Golden Gate Bridge heard firing from the island. By 4 o'clock, patrol boats circled the island, guards outside opened fire and Alcatraz cell block D was under siege.

Warden Johnston tried to contact the cell block by an extension telephone, but no one answered.

Johnston threw a main switch, locking every cell in the prison.

The captured guards have not been seen. They may be tied up as hostages. They may be dead.

It was reported late last night that 16 hard case cons are still holding the cell block, pouring out a light volume of gun fire.

The remaining 200 prisoners

Continued on Page 7, Col. 8

Dead and Wounded

Dead and wounded in the Alcatraz revolt are:

DEAD:

Harold P. Stites, guard, shot through the back.

WOUNDED:

Fred J. Richberger, guard, wounded in calf of leg.

Harry Cochrane, guard, wounded badly in upper left arm near shoulder.

Robert Sutter, guard, slight nose wound.

Elmus Besk, shot in both legs.

Herschel R. Oldham, guard, shot in left arm, hand and other parts of the body.

Henry Winehold, captain of the watch, serious but undetermined injuries.

Joe Simpson, lieutenant of the watch, serious but undetermined injuries.

A man identified only as Miller. Two unidentified guards.

Battle Continues Ten Hours After Convict Captures Guns

By EDWARD V. McQUADE

Rioting desperadoes on Alcatraz island yesterday turned the Federal penitentiary there into an inferno of gunfire in one of the bloodiest prison uprisings in California history.

One guard was killed and at least nine guards and an undetermined number of convicts wounded in a pitched battle that still was raging early this morning, more than 10 hours after the rebellion broke out.

At midnight, however, the besieging guards had finally shot their way into the main western cell block, where the convicts were intrenched.

The barricaded prisoners were holding approximately 20, or more than half the normal complement of the island's guards as hostages. One of these escaped last night and reported two of the captive guards were wounded.

The dead guard was Harold P. Stites. He had been machine gunned in the back at close range, according to the Coroner's office here. It was believed he may have been a "grudge" victim, as some years ago he broke up an escape attempt by killing one convict, wounding another and capturing a third.

Associate Warden Edward P. Miller was reported among the wounded.

A "tough guy" convict, Bernard Paul Coy, Kentucky bank robber, precipitated the riot. Convict Coy's job was to clean up gun galleries. It was reported he overpowered a guard there, helped himself to weapons and made his way to the guards' dressing room, forced them at gunpoint into the cell block and threw a master switch opening all cells in the block. He asked the inmates to join him. Sixteen did.

Thousands of rounds of ammunition and tracer bullets split the night sky as thousands watched from hilltops and piers on both sides of bay.

The island was a ring of fire in the night, outlined harshly by searchlights and the blinking beacons of ceaselessly patrolling gunboats.

A determined attempt to storm a gun gallery held by the convicts was repulsed last night, Warden James A. Johnston reported, with two guards seriously wounded in the attack.

The most sustained burst of gunfire of the entire day came shortly after 9 o'clock and lasted 45 minutes.

At the same time heavy clouds of smoke poured out the windows of the entire cell block. Apparently a fire inside the cell block had been started by tracer bullets fired by the guards and by incendiary flares.

At 9:10 p. m. the police boat D. A. White, patrolling the island, had reported the firing as still "heavy and continuous."

Thirty Marines from Treasure Island, sent at the request of Warden James A. Johnston, were detailed to guarding about 150 prisoners not involved in the insurrection.

The Marines rounded up these men in the prison yard and held them there, impaled in the glare of giant searchlights. The Marines were armed with rifles, submachine guns, smoke and tear gas bombs.

A cordon of heavily armed Navy and Coast Guard planes and boats encircled the island. Picked San Francisco police marksmen also partolled the area in the police boat.

An unknown number of women, the wives of guards, nurses and clerical workers,

Continued on Page 7, Col. 5

Blood on An Island

Alcatraz was the Isle of Pelicans to the Spanish; now it is an island of steel and submachine guns. A history of Alcatraz and a description of its 1946 layout is on Page 9. On the same page is a picture of Harry Cochrane, guard who was wounded yesterday. Page 10 is a complete page of pictures of the uprising, a diagram of the island and an inside view of the cell block. Two Chronicle reporters, only 50 yards from the island aboard boats, give eyewitness accounts on Page 11 of the guards' first attack. Also on 11 are pictures of San Franciscans watching the battle from the Marina.

A SUMMARY OF THE NEWS INSIDE

At the Big Four foreign ministers' meeting, U. S. Secretary of State Byrnes demands a revision of the armistice terms for Axis satellite nations. He also warns Russia that America will not send relief money to defeated countries if the money is to wind up as reparations to Russia. Page 2

Protesting the report of the British-American committee on Jewish immigration to Palestine, Arabs warn Britain they will organize all their forces to resume the bloody battles of 1936. Page 2

Iran announces the withdrawal of Soviet troops from Azerbaijan is nearly complete. Page 3

The Chinese government news agency reports America's General Marshall has asked Chinese Communists to turn Changchun, Manchurian capital, over to the Chungking government. Page 4

President Truman indicates the Government intends to seize the coal mines, strike-bound for 32 days. Page 7

Harold L. Ickes appears at a stockholders' meeting of the Standard Oil Company of California, but the reason for his appearance—Ralph K. Davies—announces his resignation. Page 14

Petitioners for the recall of Mayor Lapham declare they can meet the deadline to get the issue on the June 4 ballot "if they want to." A citizens' group threatens a $60,000 damage suit. Page 7

Despite efforts of Mayor Bowron to bring disputants together, Los Angeles transit workers will go on strike at 4 a. m. today. Page 13

Representative Miller, of Oakland, announces President Truman may be asked to intervene in the Bay Area P. G. & E. dispute. Page 13

In an attempt to avoid a strike against O'Connor Moffatt, the Retailers' Council and the AFL Department Store Employes agree on a plan for negotiating a master contract. Page 13

COMPARATIVE TEMPERATURES					
For Tuesday, October 1					
	High	Low		High	Low
San Francisco	61	54	New York	64	46
Oakland	66	56	Chicago	65	38
Los Angeles	70	66	New Orleans	75	60
Sacramento	74	56	Salt Lake City	73	58
Seattle	64	48	Washington	58	46
Reno	56	46	Pensacola	76	58

Forecast for Wednesday: Cloudy
(FOR COMPLETE DETAILS SEE PAGE 13)

San Francisco Chronicle

THE CITY'S ONLY HOME-OWNED NEWSPAPER

FOUNDED 1865—VOL. CLXIII, NO. 79 CCCCAAB SAN FRANCISCO, WEDNESDAY, OCTOBER 2, 1946 DAILY 5 CENTS, SUNDAY 15 CENTS DAILY AND SUNDAY $1.50 PER MONTH

American Legion Rolls Out the Barrel

Parade Wows the City, But Why It Wound Up In Four Hours Is a Mystery

Blustery Winds Fail to Spoil the Pageantry, Music, Noise and Gags; Estimated 100,000 Watch the Event

By ALVIN D. HYMAN

The Legion marched yesterday.

And marched, and marched and marched.

It marched the length of Market from the Ferry building to the Civic Center and there, where the San Francisco's parades traditionally dissolve into a milling throng of footsore individuals, it swung left, and marched some more, out Tenth street to Seals Stadium.

It marched through blustery gusts which grabbed at flags and banners and sorely complicated the task of a thousand standard-bearers, and brought no comfort to the largest, comeliest, most proficient contingent of baton-twirling majorettes San Francisco has ever seen.

The Legion marched in numbers far below the pre-parade estimates in a big parade that ended in less than one-third of the 14 hours against which police had prepared. But while it was on the march it provided an estimated 100,000 watchers with pageantry music, noise and gags which ranked high in the appraisals of old-time parade watchers.

DURATION, FOUR HOURS

The first foot fell on the Market street pavement precisely at the appointed hour of 10 a. m.; the last one spurned the sod of Seals' Stadium, an hour's march, shortly before 2 p. m. while more than 300 planes—Army B-29s and Navy Corsairs and Hellcats—roared overhead.

What happened to condense the procession from an expected 14 hours to pass a given point to an actual four hours was not entirely clear. Edward Sharkey, general chairman of the convention, suggested that rigid adherence to schedule was responsible.

He pointed out that in prewar parades, many units were kept waiting at staging points three or four hours after the scheduled time of assembly. Many bands, drum corps and marching units, he said, relied on similar delays yesterday, arrived at assembly points late, and were frozen out when the units stepped off on precise schedule.

Another explanation was advanced by an unofficial Legion authority, who sized it up thus:

"Look at the delegations as they swing by. There isn't a handful of youngsters in any one of them—no World War II men at all, compared to the number of old boys from World War I. These youngsters did not fight a marching war; they rode everywhere. They don't know marching, and they don't like marching—and that goes for parades, too."

BAG OF TRICKS

The 25,000 to 30,000 who did fall in and make the long hike from the Ferry to Seals' Stadium knew and used all the tricks that make a parade memorable.

They made music. Behind tall, strutting, be-shakoed drum majors they played "Stars and Stripes," and "California Here I Come," and "Long, Long Trail," and "Hinky Dinky Parlez Vous."

They made noise. They fired cannon, and set off bombs, and rang bells, and pounded drums and whooped.

They wore extraordinary uniforms—gay creations compounded of

Continued on Page 2, Col. 1

Baby Flies Here From Japan For Operation

After a flight by Army ambulance plane from Japan, 2-year-old John Urban Jr. will undergo an emergency operation this morning at Children's Hospital.

The purpose: removal of a peanut he "swallowed the wrong way" at his birthday party in Tokyo. It went down a bronchial tube and lodged in his lung.

The little boy arrived here last night, accompanied by his parents, Lieutenant Colonel and Mrs. Urban, with a flight surgeon and air nurse administering penicillin en route to prevent complications.

The operation this morning will be performed by Dr. Lewis F. Morrison.

His maternal grandparents are Mr. and Mrs. C. E. Partridge, 219 Twenty - seventh avenue.

L. A. Bandit Gets $100,000 in Gems

LOS ANGELES, Oct. 1 (UP)—Dan Bennett, 35, diamond merchant, today was robbed of $100,000 worth of diamonds by a bandit who stuck a gun in his ribs as he stopped his car for a street signal.

Bennett, associated with Harry Winston, Inc., one of the Nation's largest diamond brokerage firms, said the robber escaped with a brief case containing 333 carats. The largest of the more than 100 gems weighed 2½ carats.

Japan Dissolves Three Big Trusts

TOKYO, Oct. 1 (UP)—Japan's three biggest Zaibatsu firms—Mitsui, Mitsubishi and Yasuda—went officially out of existence today in obedience to an Allied Headquarters directive. The companies were dissolved formally at a final general stockholders' meeting.

Their holdings of negotiable bonds, totaling 1,697,000,000 yen, soon will be transferred to the Zaibatsu Liquidation Commission.

Royce Brier is accompanying Paul C. Smith, Editor and General Manager of The Chronicle, on an air tour of Europe. Brier's column will be resumed upon his return.

The Index . . .

Barnaby	15
Comics	18
Crossword Puzzle	12
Drama	11
Editorials	12
Financial	17
Lichty Cartoon	14
Radio	16
Shipping News	16
Vital Statistics	18
Women's World	12
COLUMNS	
Bookman's Notebook	16
Herb Caen	11
Contract Contacts	16
Rip Tides	16
Washington Merry-Go-Round	16
Harry B. Smith	2H

Action Planned For Convention Session Today

There will be plenty of action at today's session of the American Legion convention.

General Omar Bradley will answer Commander John Stelle's attack on the handling of veterans' job training.

World War II veterans will take to the floor in their fight for creation of a new honor and fun society to rival the Forty and Eight of World War I veteran fame.

Notables to address the convention include Secretary of War Robert P. Patterson, Under Secretary of the Navy John L. Sullivan, Fleet Admiral William F. Halsey, General Carlos P. Romulo of the Philippine republic and Major General T. B. Larkin, Army Quartermaster General.

A full page of pictures of Legion events will be found on Page 8. Auxiliary activities are described in a roundup on Page 12. Other Legion news appears on Page 2, with the official program of today's convention events.

Film Strike Violence

Club-Swinging Police Halt Demonstration Led by Veterans

By the United Press

HOLLYWOOD, Oct. 1—A mass demonstration of film studio strikers led by hundreds of uniformed veterans was broken up by club-swinging officers today near Metro-Goldwyn-Mayer studios.

More than 1500 striking members of the Conference of Studio Unions, led by the Flag-carrying veterans, sought to block streets leading to the studio in Culver City.

Nearly 200 police and deputy Sheriffs, after ordering the demonstrators to disperse, charged into their ranks with night sticks swinging.

A violent battle raged for nearly 15 minutes as the strikers fought back, while sympathetic bystanders hurled rocks, striking officers and unionists alike.

When the melee ended 16 persons, nine of them Sheriff's deputies, were hospitalized while 13 strikers were arrested and carted off in waiting patrol cars.

The strikers then formed their parade again and circled the town's City Hall before breaking up their demonstration.

The parade began on the outskirts of Culver City and marched down the town's main thoroughfare.

It was headed by a band of World War II veterans wearing parts of sailors' and soldiers' uniforms and carrying American Flags and banners.

"This is what we fought for," read one sign.

"The street must be cleared for traffic—please move back to the curb," a voice called over the police loudspeaker.

Parade leaders shouted for their men to hold their lines, and one minute later deputies charged them, swinging their nightsticks.

Meanwhile the International Alliance of Theatrical Stage Employes, the non-striking rival union, announced it would pull its members out of independent studios unless they discharged conference members.

The IATSE declared conference members at the independent studios were financing the strike of their fellow unionists at the major studios.

Filipinos Report Jap Cannibalism

MANILA, Oct. 1 (AP)—Philippine military police today reported a patrol surprised seven starving, unsurrendered Japanese feasting on the flesh of a murdered Filipino woman at Malaybalay, Mindanao.

MP's killed six of the Japanese; the seventh escaped. They said this was the third recent cannibalism incident on the Bukidnon plateau and estimated 100 Japanese remain in the area.

Egypt's Premier To Try Again

CAIRO, Oct. 1 (AP)—The Egyptian Broadcasting System said tonight King Farouk asked Premier Ismail Sidky Pasha to form a new government.

The King's action came soon after his uncle, Sherif Sabry Pasha, an independent, announced failure of his attempts to form a four-party government.

Germans to Hang For Killing PW

Special to The Chronicle

WINNIPEG, Man., Oct. 1—Four German prisoners of war will be hanged in jail at Lethbridge, Alberta, early Wednesday morning. They were convicted of slaying Dr. Carl Lehman, doctor of philosophy, in a prisoner of war camp at Swift Current, Sas., eight months ago after prisoners had held trial on him, claiming he was anti-Nazi.

Traffic Death No. 92

The black flag flies today from The Chronicle tower for the first time since September 16. It marks the 92d traffic death in San Francisco this year. Drive carefully, and raise the white flag on the masthead. Watch yourself and watch the other fellow. (Story of the 92nd traffic death is on page 15.)

Ship Strike

U. S. Force Owners to Grant Union Demands

America's merchant marine was strikebound again yesterday.

Secretary of Labor Schwellenbach met with the Maritime Commission last night to work out a settlement formula after 36 hours of nearly continuous conciliation efforts with employers and unions had proved fruitless. The sessions continue today.

Through its ownership of 77 per cent of America's merchant fleet, the Maritime Commission was reported ready to force employers to grant union demands for preferential hiring and pay boosts.

The strike—second tieup of the industry in a month—was called at midnight Monday by the CIO Marine Engineers Beneficial Association. Pickets were placed along the waterfront at 9 a. m.

ILWU ALSO OUT

As a member union of the Committee for Maritime Unity, CIO longshoremen on the Pacific Coast joined the strike at the same time—although settlement was near in their own negotiations for a new contract.

The AFL Masters, Mates and Pilots, also in the midst of negotiations for a new contract, left their jobs under a policy of "no contract, no work."

Both the CIO engineers and the AFL deck officers placed responsibility for the new strike on West Coast employers. They said progress was being made in sessions with East and Gulf Coast operators, but that Pacific Coast shipping men had been the stumbling block.

Randolph Meriwether, West Coast business agent for the Marine Engineers, named the Matson Navigation Company and American Hawaiian Steamship Company as "the real obstructionists."

In a telegram to the San Francisco membership, he charged the two companies had threatened to return Government-owned ships to the Maritime Commission if the Government were to attempt to force a closed shop or preferential employment.

SHIPPERS' DENIALS

"We're not in the habit of delivering ultimatums to the United States Government," said an official of Matson, who denied any knowledge of such a threat.

"That goes double in spades for us," said Lewis Lapham, assistant to the president of American-Hawaiian.

Marion Plant, attorney for the Pacific American Shipowners' Association who was in Washington for the negotiating sessions, said West Coast employers would not compromise on the union demand for preferential hiring.

In addition to the demands for union security, the engineers were asking a 35 per cent pay increase and the deck officers a 30 per cent boost.

ILWU PACT NEAR

In San Francisco, Special Mediator Nathan P. Feinsinger was reported to have brought the CIO longshoremen and the Water Front Employers' Association into agreement on all major points for a new contract.

This was said to include a 15-cent-an-hour increase to $1.52 base pay, establishment of a Federal commission to study water front safety conditions, and CIO jurisdiction for walking bosses and check clerks on a Coast-wide basis.

Final negotiating sessions today are expected to resolve the single remaining issue, that of the month-old strike of 27 CIO office clerks

Continued on Page 3, Col. 6

Bob Hope to Adopt Two Babies

Chicago Sun News Service

CHICAGO, Oct. 1 — Mrs. Bob Hope, wife of the screen and radio comedian, appeared before County Judge Edmunds K. Jarecki today to obtain the court's approval for the adoption of two babies from The Cradle in Evanston.

The couple already have two adopted children, Linda, 7, and Anthony, 6, both from The Cradle.

Argentine Meat Plants Close

BUENOS AIRES, Oct. 1 (AP)—The Argentine meat packing industry closed down today after 18 days of a "slow down" in which workers and employers were unable to agree on a wage issue.

The action blocked all meat exports and made 58,000 persons idle.

Harriman Due In U. S. Today

LONDON, Oct. 1 (AP)—W. Averell Harriman left by plane today for the United States, where he will become Secretary of Commerce.

The Pan-American plane carrying him is due at La Guardia Field, New York, early tomorrow.

Cordell Hull Has Stroke, Is in Serious Condition

WASHINGTON, Oct. 2 (AP)—Cordell Hull, former Secretary of State, remained in serious condition early today (Wednesday)—his 75th birthday—in the United States Naval Hospital where he suffered a stroke Monday night.

"There has been no change in Mr. Hull's condition," said a hospital bulletin issued at midnight.

Two hours before the hospital, through the Navy Department, said the condition of the frail former Cabinet officer "remains serious. No improvement has been noted in his condition since the last bulletin."

Earlier at 7 p. m. the hospital said Hull's condition remained serious.

Hull took a turn for the worse during the day yesterday and close friends expressed grave concern.

The former Secretary of State, who retired from the Cabinet October 2, 1944, entered the hospital September 12 for a rest and checkup.

Previously, the hospital had described his illness as a "light stroke." Word of the attack reached the State Department only a few minutes after Undersecretary of State Dean Acheson, noting that today was Hull's birthday, opened his news conference with a high tribute to the former Secretary's contribution "to national and world affairs."

Hull, once acclaimed by President Roosevelt as "the father of the United Nations," has been engaged in preparing a massive work on events during his years in public service.

(Hull dramatically pleads for big power unity. See Page 6.)

Nazi Leaders Convicted at Nuernberg

12 to Hang, Seven Get Prison, Three Freed; Jackson, Soviet Judge Protest Acquittals

U. S. Prosecutor Regrets Failure To Declare General Staff Criminal

By the Associated Press

NUERNBERG, Oct. 1—Justice I. T. Nikitchenko, Soviet Judge on the international military tribunal, assailed today the acquittal of three high Nazi leaders and declared that the freeing of Financier Hjalmar Schacht was "in obvious contradiction to the evidence."

The acquittals also brought a statement of regret from Justice Robert H. Jackson, chief U. S. prosecutor. Jackson said he was in doubt concerning the effect of the decision on future trials of German militarists and industrialists.

Sir Hartley Shawcross, British chief prosecutor, said he had no comment.

Both Nikitchenko and Jackson expressed regret that the tribunal did not declare the criminality of the German General Staff.

The Soviet Justice also asserted that the court erred in not declaring that the Reich Cabinet and High Command were criminal organizations. And he declared Rudolph Hess should have been sentenced to death instead of life imprisonment.

CRIMINAL PLAN

The Russian Judge, a General in the Russian army, said it was not by chance that Hitler spared Schacht's life in the Nazi regime and that "Schacht's leading part in the preparation and execution of a common criminal plan is proved." He said Franz Von Papen "faithfully served Hitler up to the very end" and bore considerable responsibility for Nazi crimes, and that Hans Fritsche, in his last broadcast as a Nazi propaganda official, urged Germans to join the underground Nazi "Werewolf" bands.

Nikitchenko said Fritsche, as a radio propagandist, "had a most basic relation to the preparation and conduct of aggressive warfare."

The most detailed dissent was in the case of the German general staff and high command, of which Nikitchenko said:

"Without their advice and active co-operation, Hitler could not have solved (his) problems. In the majority of cases their opinion was decisive . . . the general staff issued most brutal decrees and orders for relentless measures against unarmed, peaceful population and prisoners of war."

Nikitchenko reviewed the various orders of the Reich Cabinet and asserted it was that activity "that brought on the war which took millions of lives."

Some members of the Allied prosecution staffs made it plain unofficially that they were not too happy about some of the verdicts.

The acquittal of Von Papen, smooth diplomat who led German intrigue in two wars, rankled most of them. One prosecutor, who may not be named, said on behalf of his delegation:

"Frankly, we are a little pained about Von Papen."

CRIMINAL GROUPS

The 100,000-word judgment declared that the court could not hold the Cabinet and General Staff and High Command as criminal organizations, because they were not organizations or groups as defined in the tribunal's charter.

The Russian protest was an-

Continued on Page 4, Col. 5

Goering Heads Death Sentence List; Von Papen, Schacht, Fritsche Free

By the Associated Press

NUERNBERG, Oct. 1—Hermann Goering and 11 other Nazi chiefs who helped Adolf Hitler plunge the world into the greatest war of all time were sentenced today to death by hanging. Seven other defendants, including Rudolf Hess, were sentenced to prison and three were acquitted by the four-power military tribunal in the first international war crimes trial.

The death sentences will be carried out in the Nuernberg jail, probably October 16. The prison terms will be served in a four-power jail in Berlin.

Concluding the 10-month trial, the international military tribunal announced the sentences after completing the reading of a 100,000-word, history-making judgment ruling that aggressive warfare "is the supreme crime."

THREE ACQUITTALS

Hans Fritsche, Franz Von Papen and Hjalmar Schacht were acquitted, with Russia dissenting.

Sentenced to hang, besides Goering, were Joachim von Ribbentrop, Field Marshal William Keitel, Ernst Kaltenbrunner, Alfred Rosenberg, Hans Frank, Wilhelm Frick, Fritz Sauckel, Julius Streicher, Colonel General Alfred Jodl, Arthur Seyss-Inquart and Martin Bormann (tried in absentia).

Sentenced to prison were Hess, Walter Funk and Grand Admiral Erich Raeder, life terms; Baldur von Schirach and Albert Speer, 20 years; Constantin von Neurath, 15 years, and Grand Admiral Karl Doenitz, 10 years.

Goering, whose guilt was declared by the court to be "unique in its enormity," put his head in his hands and appeared lost in thought, but his expression remained immobile as Chief Justice Sir Geoffrey Lawrence continued reading in a monotone.

FUNK AFFECTED

Hess dashed the earphones from his head and did not even hear sentence pronounced.

Keitel gulped, lowered his sharp Prussian chin and stared blankly into space.

The pudgy Funk alone appeared physically affected by the sentencing. His knees sagged as he walked out.

Frick, an old Nazi street fighter, bowed curtly to the court as he received his sentence of death.

And all the others reacted much in the same way that has characterized their demeanor in all the long trial.

Shortly after their acquittal Schacht, Von Papen and Fritsche strolled smilingly out of the jail and held a turbulent news conference at which Schacht was as cocky and belligerent as ever.

The financier of Hitler's war machine said that there used to be "laws and free opinion in Germany," but "there appeared to be neither laws nor free opinion now."

ANOTHER TRIAL

Their freedom may be shortlived, for they face possible trial before denazification boards. Dr. Wilhelm Hoegner, German Minister-President of Bavaria, said that any of the three who remained in the American zone would be hailed promptly before such boards, and added that "this certainly means several years at hard labor."

An American Army officer said the three would spend tonight in the same cells they had occupied during the 10-months trial.

Apparently it was impossible to arrange transport for them to their homes before tomorrow.

When the tribunal read its verdict acquitting Schacht, Goering turned in his seat in a rage and whispered something to Hess. Goering for many years had been a bitter enemy of the former Reichsbank president and apparently had hoped that Schacht would suffer the same fate as himself.

Funk, who served as Reichsbank president after Schacht and still had not heard his own sentence of life imprisonment read, turned excitedly in his seat and held up one finger, indicating one acquitted.

When Von Papen was acquitted,

Continued on Page 4, Col. 1

Twelve Will Hang

—EDITORIAL—

There was something almost pathetic in the way the men who had made a foul joke of human dignity in their days of power strove feebly to cling to the tatters of their own dignity when they heard their personal fates decreed at Nuernberg.

The effort was a miserable travesty. Goering, stripped of his beloved medals and braid, his clothes drooping formlessly over his pulp, strode off with all the impressiveness of a hog trying to walk like a man. Von Ribbentrop, the picture-book diplomat, went pale and limp; found, embarrassingly, that his feet wouldn't track, and had to be helped from the room. Kaltenbrunner of the Gestapo and Frick, the "protector" of Bohemia and Moravia, managed musical comedy bows. Hess, the addle-headed one, was too far gone even to bother listening to the sentence. One of the 10 to escape the noose, the clemency was patently lost on him . . .

The savage truth—and it is said reluctantly of those who once laid claim to parity, nay, superiority, as humans—is that those who heard the gallows prescribed for their crimes had become more animal than man. Perhaps this was inevitable considering the long conditioning process. It is hardly possible to conduct systematic and bestial war against the basic dignity of man without undergoing the metamorphosis which, in reverse, once elevated man above the beast. That process, once begun, is apparently self-perpetuating; the murder of a million Jews, to such as Hans Frank, differed only quantitatively from the murder of one Jew.

The lesson and the comfort from the Nuernberg example do not lie, then, in the mere fact of merited extermination—of destiny catching up. There is no more satisfaction to be gained from the hanging of these 12 than from the eradication of any other 12 jackals; likewise, the motive of vengeance is lost, because these 12, like their four-footed counterparts, are in a measure insensate.

The lesson to be drawn from Nuernberg is that the Hitler order, with its infinite record of the beast-and-prey relationship that existed between the Nazis and the exponents of decency, missed by the narrowest margin being the world order today. Reverse El Alamein and project the Dunquerque debacle across the English Channel and you have to grant a 1946 in which most of the world would have come under the lash of these 12 apostles of butchery, and their departed master.

The comfort of the Nuernberg example is the enactment there of the kind of justice we had hoped would prevail in a world in which free men had triumphed. It would have been easier simply to steal a page from the book of the man who killed Jews because they were Jews, and to have killed the Nazis because they were Nazis. Having resisted that human impulse, the Judges at Nuernberg placed an unbridgeable chasm between democracy and Nazism and left it there for all future generations to see. This is the kind of justice that befits the symbol of Justice we have conceived—blind to those distractions that make for prejudice, but alert to the principle of fairness.

It is also, we think, the kind of justice those millions of innocents, dead in their common ditches, would approve. They were not vengeful people, but gentle, and lovers of peace.

They would have agreed with the Judges at Nuernberg that those with blood on their hands should die because they had proved a thousandfold their unfitness for living. They would have agreed that the roots of the system that produced these creatures, that denied the existence of human dignity should be turned up and burned.

But they would also have agreed that the great effort should be toward a durable new order, built on the broad principles of humanity, of justice tempered with mercy and sternness with humility—the only kind of order worth the building. They would have seen the makings of that kind of new order at Nuernberg, where 12 will hang and seven be imprisoned, but three will go free. They would—and not for any love of those who escaped the noose—have said "Amen" to all of that.

Chocolate Will Cost You More

WASHINGTON, Oct. 1 (AP)—OPA today ordered a 27 per cent boost in manufacturers' ceiling prices for chocolate and cocoa, effective tomorrow.

Wholesalers and retailers will be allowed to pass the increase along as soon as they receive chocolate and cocoa at the higher rates.

The OPA also kicked chewing gum out from under price control today with the explanation it is not important to the cost of living.

OPA also raised ceiling prices of cloth for window shades, oil cloth and other coated and combined fabrics at manufacturers' levels as of tomorrow.

THE GREEN AT ST. LOUIS

Bobby Stevens, Sporting Green baseball writer, is the first West Coast reporter to reach the scene of the greatest climax games in major league history. He reports today of the St. Louis victory over Brooklyn, will stay with these teams until the play-off issue is decided, then cover the World Series. Turn to the Sporting Green today, and stay with the Sporting Green daily for top coverage in all fields. Wherever sports action is important you'll find a Sporting Green man doing first hand coverage for you.

Light Showers Fell Here; Snowstorms In Eastern States

San Francisco and the Bay Area had early morning showers yesterday, while snowstorms hit the northeastern States.

Locally the forecast was for increasing cloudiness today, with fresh westerly winds, and partly cloudy and slightly warmer tomorrow. Light rain in the extreme north portion of the State was predicted.

Light showers fell on San Francisco between 3:08 and 3:45 a. m. The recorded precipitation was .05 of an inch. Oakland received .10 of an inch between 2:30 and 4:50 a. m., with a heavier fall in the surrounding hills.

Los Angeles did better with .39 of an inch. Part of Pasadena was without lights for two hours when power lines failed.

In the eastern half of the country, meantime, temperatures fell rapidly under polar winds.

Heavy snow fell in areas along both sides of the Canadian border, and flurries of snow and rain were reported in Maine, Massachusetts and New Jersey.

German POW's Strike Near End

LIVORNO, Italy, Oct. 1 (AP)—A majority of several thousand German war prisoners who downed tools at U. S. Army installations here yesterday in protest at delays in their repatriation resumed their jobs today. Some 1500 who refused to end their strike were held in close confinement on reduced rations.

New Housing Delay Will Be Investigated

WASHINGTON, Oct. 1 (AP)—Senate War Investigating Committee agents are digging into reasons for the delays and hindrances to new home construction.

Senator Ferguson (R., Mich.), told reporters today he and Chairman Kilgore (D., W. Va.), had reached an understanding on the housing inquiry and investigators already are doing "spade work" preliminary to formal hearings later on.

"What we have got to do is find out what are the bottlenecks and what can be done to break them," Ferguson added. "The housing situation is the most serious problem of the country."

The Michigan Senator has been urging the committee to drop everything else, if necessary, and turn its attention to that problem.

Completing the preliminary inquiries may delay formal hearings several weeks. Also several members are preoccupied with election campaigns.

Esquire Theater Roof Burned

Five hundred patrons at Market street's Esquire Theater were herded out of the place with no panic or injuries last night when a two-alarm fire blazed up on the roof of the structure.

It was quickly controlled. Damage was estimated at $7500. Traffic was jammed for about half an hour at the Powell, Market and Fifth street intersections.

Inside News

THE WORLD

Archbishop Stepinac, accused by Marshal Tito's Yugoslav regime of collaborating with the Axis, implies he is not being given a fair trial. The head of the Roman Catholic church in Yugoslavia asserts he intends to publish his entire political position. **Page 6**

At the Paris Peace Conference, Yugoslavia issued a plea for a special position in the life of Trieste international zone, declaring that otherwise the zone is doomed to "stifle to death." This argument comes as Paris delegates are working against the clock to meet the Friday deadline for all committee work. **Page 5**

THE STATE

The State political picture is highlighted by a challenge issued to Will Rogers Jr. by former Democratic Assemblyman Seth Millington, who asks the candidate for U. S. Senator to state specifically whether he is for or against the foreign policy expounded by Henry Wallace. **Page 3**

Another political development stems from U. S. Attorney General Tom Clark's visit to San Francisco. He announces he personally will argue the Federal Government's suit against California for title to oil-bearing tidelands. And he says the State hasn't a legal leg to stand on. **Page 3**

THE CITY

Clark also participated in a solemn ceremony on Alcatraz, when he presented a citation honoring Howard P. Stites, the guard who lost his life in last May's attempted break, to his widow and two small sons. **Page 3**

THIS WORLD TODAY

San Francisco Chronicle

THE CITY'S ONLY HOME-OWNED NEWSPAPER

FINAL

FOUNDED 1865—VOL. CLXIV, NO. 92 CCCCAAA SAN FRANCISCO, THURSDAY, APRIL 17, 1947 GA 1112 DAILY 5 CENTS, SUNDAY 15 CENTS

TWO NEW BLASTS!

Eyewitness Report from Scene

By ROYCE BRIER

DR. T. V. SMITH, a distinguished University of Chicago educator, spoke here before the National Conference of Social Work on the education problem in the former enemy countries. Dr. Smith was formerly in charge of this work in the occupations, and was dealing with adult re-education, as well as with normal child education. He is not too hopeful of it, seems to think it is going better in Japan than in Germany and Italy.

This is the occasion for some thoughts here on the problem, based on observation, but confined to the child phase in Germany.

Of all the functions of the American Military Government in Germany, the re-education of German children (or reorientation as they prefer to say over there) has thus far been the least promising. General Clay conceded this last October, but not that the responsibility lies with his education division.

In fact, the educators we have sent to Germany have been conscientious and for the most part, energetic men. If any blame attaches to them, it has been in an over-optimism which has translated in the news dispatches as an American go-getter tradition of tearing in and extirpating Nazi ideas from little German heads. That was the way last year's news read, though that isn't what happened. But why it didn't happen is complicated and blame attaches to no small group of men, nor to any snide political prejudice.

At the base of the trouble was refusal of Congress to give Clay enough money to set up a real, driving reorientation organization. So there was superimposed on 26,000 screened, non-Nazi German teachers in the American zone, a group of 56 American supervisors and these were subject to the same rapid turnover disability which has afflicted our whole occupation authority.

These 26,000 teachers comprised about half the normal teaching force for the population in prewar Germany. They were mostly very young, so escaping the Nazi taint, or old ones whom the Nazis had fired. But in any case, 56 American supervisors wouldn't know what the teachers taught. They could—and they did—lay down a curriculum, but by and large they had to take it on faith that the curriculum was followed.

But there were other serious

Continued on Page 2, Col. 1

Texas Disaster

1200 Reported Killed; Many More Feared Hurt In the New Explosions

Survivors Flee From Flaming City

By the Associated Press

TEXAS CITY, Texas, April 17 — Two new explosions rocked this stricken city at 1 a. m., today (Thursday) injuring many persons who survived yesterday's disastrous blasts. There were no immediate reports of additional deaths.

A reporter for The Beaumont Enterprise, said another ship had blown up in the Texas City harbor. Earlier, the nitrate-loaded freighter, the High Flyer, was reported burning.

At nearby Lamarque, the state highway patrol said that one of the explosions was that of an oil tank on the Republic Oil Company's tank farm.

The patrolmen also reported that the freighter, The High Flyer, which was expected momentarily to explode, was still burning.

Yesterday's giant explosions smashed the industrial waterfront of this Gulf port, bringing death to hundreds and injury to thousands.

SURVIVORS FLEE

Survivors of yesterday morning's disaster fled the area of danger from further explosions or possible spread of poisonous gases.

Reports from Galveston said the two new explosions this morning shook buildings in Galveston, 15 miles from Texas City.

Yesterday's blast was touched off by the explosion of the French ship Grandcamp, killing its crew of some 40 men and many spectators lining the waterfront.

Estimates of the dead still ranged from the 1200 reported by State Highway Commission officials, down to 450. The American Red Cross said there were 500 known dead.

Father M. A. Record of Houston, who with other priests probed the wreckage to administer the last sacrament to the dead, said:

"There are hundreds of bodies still to be found."

General Jonathan M. Wainwright, hero of Bataan, visited the scene and said:

"I have never seen a greater tragedy in all my experiences. I have come here to offer this stricken community every facility that the Army can place at its disposal."

Wainwright now is commanding general of the Fourth Army.

SHIP BLOWS UP

Many of the fatalities occurred on the waterfront after the nitrate-loaded Grandcamp, an American-built Liberty ship, exploded, killing all of its crew of about 40 men. Sightseers flocked to the docks, to be caught by following blasts which demolished the $19,000,000 war-built plant of the Monsanto Chemical Company.

The plant was built in wartime to make styrene, an ingredient of synthetic rubber. Styrene, while not explosive, burns as rapidly as gasoline.

The Grandcamp explosion at 9:12 a. m. followed a fire that broke out at about 8:30 a. m. while it was being loaded with nitrate and, The Houston Post said, "possibly with small ammunition."

Mayor J. C. Trahan said he knew of 300 dead. G. B. Finley, State Highway Commission official, said at Austin that officials at the scene had indicated the toll would reach 1200. Houston Police Sergeant Wiley Whatley, at the disaster scene, estimated the death toll would be between 400 and 500.

A Houston Post report from State

Continued on Page 4, Col. 1

Reporter Writes From Blast Scene

By WILLIAM C. BARNARD
Associated Press Staff Writer

TEXAS CITY, April 16—This tonight is a city of flames, torn steel and smoking rubble, a city where the dead are uncounted and the living are too dazed and weary to cry.

Scores of bodies of explosion and fire dead are stacked on benches and tables in a brick mid-town garage and in the nearby high school gymnasium. Outside these places the people gather in silent, expressionless groups.

Dozens of embalmers are at work in the garage, and there the slow process of identification goes on.

When identification and embalming are completed, a body is wrapped in a rough brown blanket and a numbered ticket is wired to a toe.

An ambulance is then called out of the long line in front of the garage and the body is passed out on a stretcher and taken to the gymnasium.

50 ACRES WRECKED

A mile away black smoke from six roaring fires billows 5000 feet into the air and drifts southward out over the gulf. A 50-acre area of devastation marks the scene where the twin explosions of a ship and a chemical works wrought the greatest tragedy this area ever knew.

I stood in the City Hall and saw a woman find the name of her son on casualty list. Her shoulders sagged, her arms fell limp at her sides and her face twisted with grief. Her husband, his face a dazed mask, caught her under the arm and led her out.

In the light of the towering blazes a few hundred yards from the grotesque mountains of twisted steel, I talked to Philip Flores, young Army veteran.

"I was working in a warehouse 25 yards from the ship when it blew up," he told me. "The concussion knocked me down.

"I crawled over to some flour sacks and buried my head under them. Then a few seconds later the (Monsanto) chemical plant exploded. The roof and walls of the warehouse were coming down around me. I got up and ran for my life. Later I helped pull the bodies out of the wreckage. It was the most terrible thing I've ever seen.

"One man with a leg blown off was screaming with pain. I couldn't tell you how he looked because he didn't have much face left."

"Most of the bodies were mangled."

FAMILY VANISHES

Juan Torres lives in a house a quarter of a mile from the destroyed chemical plant. I found him sitting on a bed in the front room staring at the floor. In the back part of the house the walls had caved in and the place was in a shambles.

Torres was away at work when the explosions took place.

"I came home," he said, "and found my brother, my father and

Continued on Page 4, Col. 2

A pall of heavy black smoke hangs over explosion-torn Texas City. (For a full page of pictures, see page 12.)

Nazi Marshal Is Given Life

NUERNBERG, April 17 (UP)—Former Air Field Marshal Erhard Milch, Goering's wartime right-hand man, was sentenced today to life imprisonment for his part in the Nazi slave labor program by an American war crimes tribunal.

'Protection' Inquiry

Assembly Votes to Investigate Collins and Confidence in Him!

By EARL C. BEHRENS
Political Editor, The Chronicle

SACRAMENTO, April 16—The Assembly late today again voted to investigate accusations against Speaker Sam L. Collins . . . and then adopted a resolution which "expressed full confidence" in that official. An appropriation of $7500 was voted for the investigation. The two actions climaxed a day of many maneuvers over accusations against Collins by Appellate Judge William C. Doran of Los Angeles.

Collins himself took the floor to give a lengthy review of circumstances in connection with Doran's letter. He was given a big hand by his friends in the Assembly.

Not the least of the day's events was the appointment by Speaker Pro Tem Thomas A. Maloney of freshman Richard J. Dolwig, South San Francisco, as chairman of the special investigation committee set up this afternoon. Dolwig replaced Assemblyman C. Don Field, Glendale. Field asked that he be permitted to "disqualify himself as chairman and as a member" of the committee yesterday charged with the investigation.

GROSS INSULT

Collins in a letter written by Doran was declared to have introduced a bill "designed to protect the gambling interests." Doran said the bill accomplished this by taking "from parole officers the authority of peace officers."

In speaking to the Assembly, Collins said Doran's statement "that I am interested in or appear to be interested in gamblers is a gross insult and a deliberate falsehood."

"In my opinion," said Collins, "the Judge (Doran) who would read the law so loosely as to interpret this bill as being designed to aid gamblers has no learning in the law and apparently no conception of what evidence is or is not acceptable and satisfactory when he asks us to accept such rank hearsay testimony and, furthermore, is completely lacking in judicial temperament as evidenced by his intemperate letter of March 26."

Collins suggested the investigating committee give consideration to Doran's qualifications for the bench.

The speaker said the section of the penal code giving parole officers powers of peace officers was never intended to give them unlimited police powers. He cited a letter from former Assemblyman Walter J. Fourt to substantiate this statement. Fourt, a close personal friend of Collins, handled the bill which gave the parole officers police powers. Fourt wrote that the parole officers never were intended to have full police powers.

GAMBLING ANGLE

Doran in his letter said his son John C. Doran, State parole officer, had failed to receive co-operation of the Long Beach police chief in closing gambling joints allegedly frequented by parolees.

Collins said the police chief denied this.

As to the gambling charges at Santa Ana, where a parole officer

Continued on Page 7, Col. 1

The Chronicle Attacked

Assembly approves resolution attacking a Chronicle editorial calling on Speaker Collins to step down during investigation of the Doran charges. For details, see page 7.

Telephone Walkout

Union President Says the Workers Won't Give in

By the Associated Press

WASHINGTON, April 16—The leader of the striking telephone workers said tonight the countryside tieup will continue until the Bell System "gives in or until the workers are starved into submission."

Joseph A. Beirne, 36-year-old president of the National Federation of Telephone Workers, an independent union with 39 striking affiliates, made the statement in an ABC broadcast.

Beirne spoke in reply to Secretary of Labor Schwellenbach, who last night blasted both the union and the American Telephone and Telegraph Company for turning down his arbitration plan.

The union head said Schwellenbach's proposal "was rejected because it contained no wage increase offer and because it contained a thoroughly unworkable arbitration proposal."

Beirne continued:

"There are at least two ways in which the telephone strike can be settled . . . one of these methods would be for the AT&T company to forget all about arbitration, to take the strings off the companies they control, let the local bargaining committees sit down with our local bargaining committees and work out a settlement.

"The other way would be for the AT&T to sit down with the NFTW

Continued on Page 9, Col. 5

Greek-Turk Aid

After Fiery Debate, Senate Agrees To Vote on the Program Tuesday

By the United Press

WASHINGTON, April 16—The Senate agreed unanimously tonight to vote on President Truman's $400,000,000 Greek-Turkish aid bill next Tuesday.

The Senate established its vote deadline at an extraordinary night session after 8½ hours of continuous debate. Senate President Vandenberg (R., Mich.), in a fiery plea for speed, broke into the hot arguments to tell the Senate that the President's program may be the United States' last chance to halt Communist aggression short of war. He warned his colleagues they will bear a heavy responsibility for world peace if they hold up the program too long or reject it.

His demand for speedy action came as the House Foreign Affairs Committee finally approved an almost identical bill and prepared to send it to the House floor some time next week.

NIGHT AND DAY

The Senate had gone on a day-and-night schedule in an effort to get the aid bill out of the way as soon as possible. But Senate Republican Whip Kenneth Wherry of Nebraska said the vote agreement apparently would eliminate the need for a session tomorrow night.

Wherry first proposed that the Senate vote Monday on the measure but, when Senator Taylor (D., Idaho) objected, he modified the request.

The final four hours of debate on Tuesday will be equally divided between advocates and opponents.

Taylor first objected to any proposal that a definite time be set, declaring "public opinion is turning in favor" of a proposal that the entire relief matter be handed over to the United Nations.

Senator Johnson (D., Colo.), an opponent of the bill, high lighted tonight's session by warning the Senate that the proposed aid to Turkey would, if carried out, constitute an act of aggression.

"We'll have to admit this is a threat to Russia," he said.

Senator Brooks (R., Ill.) described the program as a "grave mistake" which might lead to "countless" Pearl Harbors and Bataans around the world.

CHALLENGE FORESEEN

Brooks told the Senate that the proposal to quarantine Communism in the Middle East and send $400,000,000 in relief and military supplies to Greece and Turkey will be challenged by other nations. Then, he said, this Nation must back up

Continued on Page 6, Col. 4

The Moscow Conference

Secretary Marshall's meeting with Prime Minister Stalin was understood yesterday to have solved no deadlocks in the Big Four Conference at Moscow. For details see page 6.

Garbage Collection Firm Reports $226,485 Profit

The Scavengers' Protective Association, one of the two garbage collection companies operating in San Francisco, yesterday reported gross income of $1,886,889 last calendar year.

The net profit amounted to $226,485.25. The income report was based largely on rates lower than those now being charged. An increase on collections made from residences and flats was voted by the people last November, but did not become effective until mid-December.

City Controller Harry Ross, to whom the report was submitted, said further financial statements must include a complete audit of accounts to permit him to recommend a possible reduction in rates to the Board of Supervisors. The requirement was written into the charter amendment raising the rates.

Rate increases amounted to 80 per cent in some categories.

Company representatives, arguing for submission of a ballot measure last year, stated an increase was necessary to pay higher wages to employees and for purchase of new equipment.

Ross said he had not received a financial report from the Sunset Scavenger Company.

Here's How You Can Place Classified Ads in Chronicle

Although dial phones are still functioning, you may also place your Classified ads in The Chronicle in any one of the following ways:

1—You can send your ad in by mail.

2—You can send your ad in by telegraph.

3—You can send your ad to The Chronicle main office at Fifth and Mission streets.

4—Or you can bring the ad to our branch office, Murray the Stationer, 1705 Fillmore street.

5—If you are in the East Bay, you can bring your ad to our Oakland office, 325 Eleventh street, Oakland.

6—On the Peninsula, in Marin county or other areas, contact your local Chronicle circulation dealer listed in the phone directory.

7—A trained representative will call at your home or office.

25 Years on the Airwaves!

Station KPO is 25 years old today. See Page 18 for Paul Speegle's column and a nostalgic picture.

The Index . . .

THE WEATHER
Fair

Comics	18
Contract Contacts	8
Crossword Puzzle	6H
Drama	10, 11
Editorial Page: "The Telephone Confusion"	16
Financial	17
Lichty's Cartoon	2
Radio Column and Log	18
Vital Statistics	13
Women's World	8
COLUMNS	
Herb Caen	15
Bill Leiser	1H
Bookman's Notebook	18
Washington Merry-Go-Round	18

San Francisco Chronicle
THE CITY'S ONLY HOME-OWNED NEWSPAPER

FOUNDED 1865—VOL. CLXVI, NO. 16 CCCCAAA SAN FRANCISCO, SATURDAY, JANUARY 31, 1948 GA 1-1112 DAILY 5 CENTS, SUNDAY 15 CENTS

Cal Cable Strike Authorized; Walkout Is Possible Tonight

Today's column by Royce Brier is the last in a series of three articles dealing with the German Foreign Office documents recently published by the American State Department.

By ROYCE BRIER

AFTER September, 1940, Germany and Russia fell into a stony fury with each other concealed by chilly smiles but increasingly hard to conceal from the world. It is doubtful if there is a more striking record anywhere of the corroding poison of mutual suspicion in power-motivated regimes, than is contained in the State Department's publication of the German archives covering German-Russian collaboration, 1939-1941.

This is the third and last discussion of the documents. We opened with the signing of the Moscow Pact, a week before Hitler invaded Poland, and went on to the small but gathering difficulties which marred this extraordinary "friendship." We have noted that Russia consolidated its power in Eastern Europe at periods when the Germans were preoccupied with such operations as Norway, France and the Battle of Britain.

Mr. Molotov was a hard customer, and showed an uncommon gift for squeeze plays. Herr Ribbentrop and his exalted boss had to take it and smile. Finally chronic difficulty arose over German meddling in Finland and Romania, which soon extended to Bulgaria when the British got a foothold in Greece. It is clear that in 1940, Russia's long-range, vital policy was domination of the Balkans. On the other hand, Hitler was doing the current dominating, and the Russians were not prepared to resist it except by wile.

Hitler's guaranty of Romanian independence (snide on its face) annoyed Russia no end. Molotov fussed about it perpetually to Count Schulenburg, the German Ambassador. Turkey's status also caused friction (and "back-door work by both powers) and then came the Tripartite Pact, a mutual assistance treaty between Germany, Italy and Japan, directed at the United States and specifically exempting Russia from its terms.

Molotov was most dour and finicky about Tripartite. The Russians were deep in calculations about the dangers of Japanese expansion while Russia was walking a home tight-rope and trying to pick up land, peoples and power which were the by-

Continued on Page 2, Col. 1

Sanction By AFL

Labor Council Backs Rejection Of Compromise

A special three-man AFL Labor Council committee last night was granted permission to give strike sanction to California Street Cable Car employees should no settlement be reached today.

The strike settlement deadline has been set for 40 minutes after midnight tonight.

The council approved unanimously the special committee's report turning down a company-suggested compromise.

Earlier in the day, S. Waldo Coleman, president of the California Street Cable Railroad Company, presented a plan which would require the co-operation of the city and the unions to keep the cars running.

THREE POINTS

The plan called for a reduction in service of the Sacramento street Municipal Railway bus line, which parallels the California cable; installation of traffic signals at California and Hyde streets to free two company-employed signalman, and acceptance by carmen of a 7 per cent wage cut for one month with the "good possibility" this would be repaid them in the following months.

Coleman's proposals were attacked in a report issued by the committee, composed of Council President John F. Shelley, Wendell Phillips and George Johns.

TEXT OF REPORT

It said:

"We feel Mr. Coleman is obviously using the 140 working men involved as pawns in his efforts to sell the railway to the city at a profit to himself . . . We have proposed arbitration of all issues in dispute as well as a 30 to 60-day breathing period wherein negotiations could be pursued.

"The only answer from the company has been a proposal assuring a seven per cent decrease in wages and a confused list of conditions for making up this decrease, most of which are beyond our control in that they depend upon action by the city.

"We therefore recommend that the Labor Council empower and instruct the committee to make all efforts to amicably adjust this matter by February 1, failing which the committee shall be empowered to release strike sanction to the union involved and in event of work stoppage shall advise, counsel and guide the situation until an adjustment is realized."

COMPROMISE EFFORT

The committee indicated hope for a meeting with management sometime today in an effort to effect a last minute compromise.

Coleman last night had no comment on the latest union action but said he was willing to meet with the committee today.

California Cable employees now receive $1.368 per hour. Under the "co-operation" plan proposed by Coleman yesterday they would receive $1.272 per hour during February.

With this "co-operation," Coleman said, his employees can be assured at least 93 per cent of the full scale now being paid would continue in February.

Utilities Manager James H. Turner declared it would be "impossible" to decrease bus service on the Sacramento street line. He said the city was not even giving the service demanded on the line now.

Under the plan Coleman hoped to keep the line running until the question of city purchase can be put on the ballot as was the case of the Market Street Railway.

The Labor Council Re-elects John Shelley

The San Francisco AFL Labor Council last night re-elected its president, John F. Shelley, and its secretary-treasurer, John O'Connell. Both were unopposed.

Shelley's new term will be his 12th in that post. He is also president of the State Federation of Labor. O'Connell first was elected secretary of the local AFL in 1912.

George W. Johns was elected vice president. Johns polled 203 votes to 188 for Thomas A. Rotell.

MOHANDAS K. GANDHI
In a world torn by strife, he struggled for peace

Death in New Delhi

Assassination of Gandhi Leads To Fear of New India Fighting; Crime Motive Called 'Political'

World Leaders Mourn a 'Tragic Loss,' Speculate On Rekindled Holy War

By the Associated Press

LONDON, Jan. 30 — Humble men and great, around the world, mourned tonight the assassination of Mohandas K. Gandhi, the little Hindu peacemaker who was shot as he walked to prayer.

They wondered, too, whether his sudden passing will rekindle the first of Hindu-Moslem religious war or cause an outbreak between Britain's two new dominions. Gandhi's simple fasting twice damped the fires of communal violence in less than half a year. But his death found them still smouldering, and the India-Pakistan dispute over Kashmir still before the United Nations.

Some thought the spirit of Gandhi's philosophy of nonviolence might prevail more permanently in his death than in his life.

Authoritative British government officials with long experience in India said Gandhi's death removed the most powerful moderating influence in India.

NEHRU STRONGER

They said Prime Minister Jawaharlal Nehru of India, who is inclined to the left politically, would now be in a stronger position. Although Gandhi had been losing influence, his restraint had compelled many of the younger and more exhuberant Congress party leaders to go slow. They may now feel they can make faster headway, especially on social and economic programs.

On the other hand the millionaire Sardar Vallabhai Patel, Deputy Prime Minister and representative of powerful industrialists, may find himself in a weaker position. In many ways Gandhi saw eye-to-eye with Patel.

Government officials noted one factor, however, which they said might make a settlement of the dispute over Kashmir easier. Some of these officials feel that Patel, outspoken in his attacks on Moslems, was behind the policy in Kashmir, and that Nehru might now be able to adopt a more accommodating course. Kashmir is the northern princely state where Indian forces have been fighting Moslem tribesmen. The state joined India but its population is mostly Moslem.

Prime Minister Attlee expressed Britain's official hopes in a broadcast tonight.

"The voice which pleaded for peace and the brotherhood had been silenced, but I am certain his spirit will continue to animate his fellow countrymen," Attlee said. Calling Gandhi India's "greatest citizen," Attlee said "he seems to belong to a different period of history."

'GREATEST BLOW'

Miss Doris Lester, co-founder of Kingsley Hall social center, where Gandhi lived while here on a visit in 1931, called the death "the greatest blow to the world since the atom bomb."

King George VI, who lost his Indian empire when Gandhi's dreams of independence came true, messaged Governor General Earl Mountbatten in New Delhi: "Will you please convey to the people of India our sincere sympathy in the irreparable loss which they and indeed mankind have suffered."

Winston Churchill, who predicted an "awful" civil war in India when he fought against the independence bill, said he was shocked at this wicked crime."

In the dark streets of London's squalid East End where Gandhi lived in 1931 the word passed from door to door:

"Gandhi's dead. They shot him. Poor old chap."

From elsewhere came the comment of sympathy and shock from many old enemies, Moslem and Hindu, the Eastern world and the Western.

George Bernard Shaw, long-time admirer of Gandhi, said the assassination "shows how dangerous it is to be too good."

Continued on Page 4, Col. 6

Slayer Jailed, Identified As Hindu Sect Member; Mahatma's Funeral Today

By G. MILTON KELLY
Associated Press Staff Writer

NEW DELHI, Jan. 31—An assassin killed Mohandas K. Gandhi, India's apostle of peace, at prayer last night.

The 78-year-old Mahatma, or great souled one, was cut down by the bullets of a young Hindu for what police called political reasons.

The news crossed India's troubled continent swiftly and bloody rioting broke out in Bombay, perhaps the forerunner of terrible conflict. Fifteen were reported killed and 54 injured in fighting between Hindus and Moslems.

By last midnight, however, an official statement there said:

"Full police and military precautions have been taken and the situation now is under control."

Gandhi, the little Hindu who for long led the struggle of India for independence, died soon after two bullets crashed into his body as he was about to start his evening prayer meeting. The shooting occurred in the gardens of spacious Birla House, home of a millionaire industrialist. One bullet struck him in the chest, the other in a leg.

The assailant was grabbed and beaten by Gandhi's worshippers. To police he gave several aliases, but he was booked under the name of Nathuram. He is 25. Police said the assassin was motivated by "political reasons."

EXTREME NATIONALISTS

(United Press said the murderer was fully identified late last night as Narayan Vinayak Gadse, a member of the Mahratta race of Indians. They are extreme Nationalists and almost all are Hindus like Gandhi himself. They object to Gandhi's creed of peace among all religious sects.)

Police said he tried to kill himself before his pistol was taken away. He was swiftly removed to a secret place to prevent a lynching.

All night long hundreds of Gandhi's faithful kept a vigil outside Birla mansion. Crowds jammed roads leading to it. Today (Saturday) they will follow the body on foot over the more than five miles it will be carried to a Hindu burning ground on the Jumna river for cremation on a huge pyre of logs according to the wish of Gandhi.

A five-wicked Hindu oil lamp lighted the space where the frail man lay in death. At midnight Jawaharlal Nehru, India's Prime Minister and foremost in the Indian dominion after Gandhi, appealed to the crowds to be calm.

'LIGHT HAS GONE OUT'

"The light has gone out of our lives," said Nehru.

There were shouts to bring the body out for view. Nehru asked the people to disperse, saying, "at least let the body be in peace."

His voice broke and he had to be led away.

Soon after the shooting the body was carried to the second floor of the Birla house where Gandhi was staying and where he died. The couch on which the body lay was tilted and floodlighted so that many could view the face.

(United Press, in its description of the historic scene, said that when night came and the wails of women and the grief-stricken cries of men echoed throughout the capital, the full-length windows of a balcony of the villa opened suddenly.

(Out of the windows stumbled a little group of Gandhi's followers. They carried in their arms the frail body of their leader.

CROWD GASPS

(As the crowd gasped and surged forward, the body, its blood-soaked garment covered by a white sheet, was put in a chair facing the crowd. A spotlight blazed on the wizened brown face, the eyes closed in repose.

(Little Manu Gandhi, 18 years old, one of Gandhi's nieces, folded her hands before the face in symbol of a last blessing by the leader to his people, and lovingly stroked his head.)

At Madras 200,000 milled about newspaper offices clamoring for more information of the assassination.

Widespread looting, arson and stabbing started in Bombay two

Continued on Page 4, Col. 8

Row Among Democrats

Fight Appears on Docket Over Choice Of State Delegates

By EARL C. BEHRENS
Political Editor, The Chronicle

Dissident Democrats are ready to start a fight today over the picking of a Truman slate of delegates at the Oakland meeting of the executive committee of the Democratic State organization.

Edwin W. Pauley, retiring national committeeman and close friend of the President, is being charged by the friends of State Chairman James Roosevelt with responsibility for the protests over delegation recommendations.

ROGERS PROTEST

"I think the delegation from Southern California should be widened to include pro-Truman groups," said Will Rogers Jr., last night.

"It is my hope we can arrive at a compromise and then go ahead and elect Truman. We can win California if Warren is not the Republican presidential nominee."

Unless peace is restored Rogers and Roosevelt will have a lively tilt at today's meeting.

Rogers is not a member of the executive committee but has been invited to speak before it, anyway, by Chairman Roosevelt.

Two years ago, Rogers led the bitter fight within the Democratic party to make Roosevelt State chairman.

SCULLY AND ROGERS

Thomas P. Scully, Los Angeles capitalist, who opposed Roosevelt for the chairmanship, is one of those left off the list of persons recommended for a place on the Truman slate for the June 1 primary. He organized the first Truman-for-President Club in Southern California last summer.

Rogers' name also is not on the list.

It is reported Rogers was not seeking a place for himself but for Charles E. Arnn, Los Angeles. Arnn was the leader of the Scully forces in the chairmanship contest.

Roosevelt forces declare the State chairman had nothing to do with leaving the name of Arnn off the slate delegation. Arnn is an executive of the Los Angeles Daily News.

They contend the blame, if any, belongs to Paul Weaver and Lillian Andrus, Sixteenth congressional leaders who canvassed their area and made recommendations based on sentiment in their district.

Among Northern Californians on the recommended list as delegates-at-large are San Francisco District Attorney Edmund G. Brown and John F. Shelley, president of the San Francisco Labor Council.

(For the complete list of recommended delegates from California, see Page 3.)

Repeal Urged For Special Taxes

WASHINGTON, Jan. 30 (AP) — Congress got a petition from more than 300 organizations today asking repeal of special taxes put on autos, trucks, tires and tubes, gasoline and oil during the war.

Orville Wright Dies at 76

By the Associated Press

DAYTON, Ohio, Jan. 30 — The co-inventor of the airplane, 76-year-old Orville Wright, died tonight in his sleep under an oxygen tent at Miami Valley Hospital.

The aged pioneer of modern aviation died of a lung congestion and a heart disease.

Death came at 10:40 p. m.

Four persons stood at his bedside at the end. They were Mr. and Mrs. Horace A. Wright, Mrs. H. S. Miller and Nurse Delyle Meyers. Horace Wright is a nephew and Mrs. Miller a niece of the dead inventor.

Dr. A. B. Brower, who brought Wright through his first heart attack October 10, 1947, last saw his famed patient at 7:30 p. m. With the doctor was one of Wright's closest personal friends, Colonel E. A. Deeds, Chairman of the Board of the National Cash Register Company.

The announcement of the death was made by Brower.

Brower said Wright took a turn for the worse last night, and sank slowly through the night.

Death resulted, said the doctor, from a lung congestion and coronary arteriosclerosis.

Brower said his patient, experiencing difficulty in breathing, asked to be placed back in an oxygen tent last night. He apparently still was being given oxygen at the time of his death.

Brower earlier said there had been no change between 6 a. m. and noon, but Wright sank slowly as the afternoon waned.

(Wright's other two relatives, his nephew, Milton Wright of Dayton, and his niece, Mrs. John H. Jamieson of Evanston, Ill., were notified of Wright's death, according to United Press.

(Funeral services will be held in Dayton, but the time has not been determined.

(General Joseph T. McNarney commanding general of the Air Materiel Command at Wright Field, Dayton, was the first to pay his respects to the veteran inventor "As representative of the Air Materiel Command, I desire to join the Nation in honoring one of its greatest men," he said. "Our great hope is that through the gift he gave the Nation, America will be empowered to maintain world peace.")

(For how world fame came to Orville Wright, who hated publicity, see page 9.)

Sabotage, Fight Open Winter Olympic Games

The winter Olympic Games opened in Switzerland yesterday in an atmosphere of such ill will and violence that the future of the entire program of international sports competition semed in peril.

The games, established on the premise that such events create international good will, yesterday produced:

1—A free-for-all fist fight during a hockey game, which made it uncertain whether other matches will be played today.

2—Sabotage of two U. S. bobsleds.

3—Much wrangling over official rulings for the various events.

(For details of what is described as "the wildest day in international sports history, see the Sporting Green.)

British Reply On Jewish, Arab Militias

By the Associated Press

LAKE SUCCESS, Jan. 30—Britain informed the United Nations late today no Jewish or Arab militias could be organized in Palestine while Britain maintained control.

There was no immediate comment from the U. N. Palestine Commission. Observers commented, however, that Britain's declaration appeared to raise obstacles which would make it difficult, if not impossible, for the commission to carry out the plan to partition the Holy Land.

Britain's declaration was made by Sir Alexander Cadogan before the Commission. In answer to questions he made these other assertions with regard to Britain's policy on partition:

1—Britain would not look with favor on any decision by the Commission to arrive in Palestine more than two weeks before termination of the British mandate. This is now scheduled for May 15.

2—Britain would not accept responsibility for safety of the Commission if it arrived earlier than the date specified by the British.

3—Britain could not comply with the General Assembly's recommendation that the administration of Palestine be turned over to the U. N. Commission piecemeal. Cadogan said the entire administration would be transferred on the day the mandate is ended.

(The Commission pointed out, according to United Press, that the Assembly asked Britain to turn over its administration "progressively" to the Commission. Cadogan

Continued on Page 4, Col. 6

Once Again— Fair Week End Is Forecast

The same old story was told last night by the Weather Bureau. The forecast was for continued fair weather today and tomorrow.

Twenty-three days have now passed without a drop of rain in the San Francisco Area. There were sprinkles yesterday over Del Norte and Humboldt counties.

The forecast for the Bay Region is for gentle variable winds becoming moderate northwesterly in the afternoon of today and tomorrow.

(For more about the weather, see Page 2.)

A Pair of Spirited Con Men Haven't a Ghost of a Chance

Two brothers from Detroit, who tried the extortion business in Oakland, blamed it on their late departed daddy yesterday.

It was a bum rap—a couple of bum raps on the spiritualistic table top that sent them into the racket, said Daniel and Howard Leonard, 22 and 33.

If it hadn't been for papa's pounding on the table, they told Oakland police inspectors, they would have stuck to their work in the Cosmo Group of Spiritualism, currently contacting the other world from an East Bay hall.

The Leonard boys were picked up after they made several financial passes at Francis M. Madsen, manager of a music store.

First they offered him a violin—a genuine Stradivarius, they said—for prices ranging from $10,000 down to a quick grand. Then they had a plan for making gasoline out of water.

HOWARD LEONARD
The raps they heard . . .

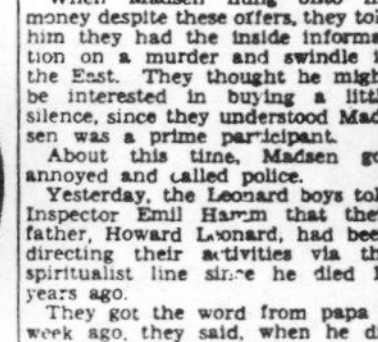

When Madsen hung onto his money despite these offers, they told him they had the inside information on a murder and swindle in the East. They thought he might be interested in buying a little silence, since they understood Madsen was a prime participant.

About this time, Madsen got annoyed and called police.

Yesterday, the Leonard boys told Inspector Emil Hamm that their father, Howard Leonard, had been directing their activities via the spiritualist line since he died 10 years ago.

They got the word from papa a week ago, they said, when he directed them by spirit writing to put the finger on Madsen. By spirit writing (with a modern ball point pen) they were told that Madsen had been involved in a swindle and murder of a man named Weaver in Pennsylvania.

DAN LEONARD
. . . were a judge's gavel

Details, wrote Howard from the spirit world, could be had from the files of the Philadelphia Herald, March 19, 1923. (That paper had printed its last edition 10 years earlier.)

The Leonard brothers sent airmail for the clippings. Meanwhile, they decided to put the bite on Madsen.

Father Howard's last message was delivered at 2:15 p. m. yesterday in the inspectors' bureau in Oakland when brother Daniel picked up a pen lightly by the top and implored papa to give him the word, or the name of a good defense lawyer.

In straggly letters, the pen wrote: "Let the inspectors see you write. They will believe you."

Papa was wrong. Inspectors threw Daniel and his brother back in the jug. So far as they knew, the police said, father has not come through with any better advice since.

The Index

Herb Caen	11
Comics	14
Crossword Puzzle	16
Drama	7
Editorial: "Gandhi—A Career of Ironies"	12
Finance	13, 14
Lichty's Cartoon	11
Radio	9
Vital Statistics	5
Women's World	6

THE WEATHER
Fair and Mild
(Details on Page 9)

Seals and Acorns Both Win — See Sports For Details

San Francisco Chronicle

THE CITY'S ONLY HOME-OWNED NEWSPAPER

FINAL

FOUNDED 1865—VOL. CLXVI, NO. 121 CCCCAAA SAN FRANCISCO, SATURDAY, MAY 15, 1948 GA 1-1112 DAILY 5 CENTS, SUNDAY 15 CENTS

TEL AVIV IS BOMBED; U. S. RECOGNIZES JEWISH STATE

THIS WORLD TODAY

By ROYCE BRIER

SECRETARY MARSHALL went before a class which has been undergoing training for consular and subordinate embassy service and told the men they should avoid exclusive contact with ruling groups abroad, and should cultivate acquaintance with peasants, workers and the people generally.

This is worthy advice, but most difficult to put into practice for several good reasons. Any national group in a foreign land tends to colonize, and by human nature cannot merge itself with an alien people. Furthermore, diplomatic and consular people are circumscribed by protocol. Some of this protocol is absurd, appealing to snobs and bureaucratic minds, and some is founded on common sense and international necessity. It may be modified by an intelligent representative, but not disregarded entirely.

Then, in a modern police state, indiscriminate contact of diplomatic employes with the masses of the host people is so discouraged as to be in effect proscribed. In London or Paris an American consular official may have such friends as will have him among the people. In Moscow or Belgrade this is quite out of the question.

Still, the Secretary's advice is salutary. There is a good deal of margin in many foreign lands between the traditional diplomatic or consular life, and a life which would tend to a sounder mutual understanding and more friendly relations between America and the peoples abroad. If this margin can be taken up in certain cases by chipping away a little protocol, nobody will be harmed but those bleak souls who live for protocol.

Then the Secretary said something interesting that his class might be presumed to know, in a way. He said the world is in a state of "social revolution."

During various cycles of history, the existence of great social cleavages was not known to the masses, and it is doubtful if the masses today note that existence more than vaguely. But students of diplomacy should see it and they should see something more. They are deadwood in diplomacy if they don't see something more.

Returning to the masses, a very brief glance at history reveals that in cleavage cycles they believe that the manifestations are peculiar to their generation.

Continued on Page 2, Col. 5

Hearings On Rents

Continued City Hotel Controls Recommended

The County, State and National Affairs Committee of the Board of Supervisors yesterday recommended continuance of rent controls for San Francisco's hotels until March 31, 1949.

That recommendation will go before the Board of Supervisors for action next Monday.

The committee, after a hearing in which hotel tenants and hotel operators presented their views, voted approval of a proposal to extend the life of the present control ordinance beyond its present expiration date of May 31.

It turned down a proposal that the present ordinance, allowing a 25 per cent boost over wartime OPA rentals, remain in effect until the end of 1948.

Hotel residents from Nob Hill, the waterfront and South of Market helped to fill the Board of Supervisors chambers in the City Hall, where the hearing was held. Operators of the hotels were there in force, too.

FIRST CHANCE

Tenants had first chance at yesterday's hearing.

First to speak was J. Oscar Goldstein, an attorney living at a downtown hotel. He would not state his monthly rent, but said it had increased 40 per cent since 1942.

"San Francisco is a hotel city," he declared. "Thousands of families live in hotels all their lives. If they are forced out—and they would be if ceilings were removed—they'd have no place to go."

Paul Combs, seaman living in at an Embarcadero hotel, said:

"I pay $4.50 a week. Before the war it would have been $2.50. You take off ceilings and you're going to have it like during the war."

Other witnesses told of their difficulty recently in finding permanent hotel rooms. One woman said she was turned down by 15 hotels before finding one on Post street.

Hotelmen said they couldn't understand that.

On the contrary, said Raymond Crummy, secretary of the San Francisco Hotel Association, hotels have many vacancies today.

Since last November, he said, the percentage of vacancies has increased from 11 to 17 per cent—and it's still growing.

"Business is bad," he declared. "Some of our members are even getting in a price-cutting war. No one is raising rents now—the competition is too keen."

At this point, the proceedings were interrupted by boos and laughter from the 250 tenants present. Crummy continued:

RISING COSTS

"Some costs have increased more than 100 per cent. We lose money on transient rooms rented under ceilings. All we want is to adjust those rents so they are equitable compared to costs."

David Monasch, member of the Mayor's Fair Rent Committee, urged continuance of controls. The committee has been administering the ordinance since October.

Only one hotel has come before the committee with a request for an increase in the ceiling on the basis of hardship, he said. That one case was decided against the hotel.

From that, Monasch drew the conclusion the hotels are not suffering generally under the ordinance.

Robert E. Burns, attorney for the Hotel Employers Association of San Francisco, representing 30 hotels, said there is no emergency now in the availability of hotel rooms.

"Costs are from 150 to 200 per cent higher now and the rates should be higher, too," he said.

"Why should hotel men have to any more than the grocery or the subsidize the high cost of living gas station?" he asked.

"The hotels were empty before the rate freeze, and the customer could name his own price."

Stock Market Takes Frenzied Upward Whirl

NEW YORK, May 14 (AP)—Stocks took a frenzied whirl upward today in the fastest trading in eight years.

Gains of $1 to $7 a share for principal issues boosted total market value of listed stocks by around $1,700,000,000.

Buying orders buried the exchange facilities under such an avalanche of business that high-speed quotation tickers couldn't keep up with them. For extended periods, including most of the final hour, the tape fell as much as 5 minutes behind actual transactions.

Brokers' wires hummed with out-of-town orders from all over the Nation, and local boardrooms were crowded as interests which have been out of the market for a long time put idle funds to work.

Back of the immediate reasons, of course, was a basic confidence engendered by recent expressions of many responsible leaders who see a steady and profitable future for business. This has been reflected by a consistent climb in prices of industrial shares. Sidney Allen's comment on Page 12.

Slayings—And Suicide

Killer of Youth, 18, Takes His Own Life; Wife Stabs Husband

Two persons were slain and a third committed suicide last night in the Hunters Point housing project district.

The dead were:

Burt Lauthern, 18, of 258 West Point road, killed by Edmund Blockwitz, 27, of 1151 Hearst avenue, who shot himself.

James C. Thomas, 34, of 217 East Point road, stabbed through heart by his wife, Mrs. Katherine Margaret Thomas, 39, who claimed self-defense.

The murder and suicide were the result of a quarrel between Lauthern's sister, Patricia, 21, and Blockwitz, police said.

The bodies of Lauthern and Blockwitz were found in the Lauthern home by the youth's mother and two sisters late yesterday.

RENO MARRIAGE

About a year ago, police learned, Patricia and Blockwitz reportedly went through a Reno marriage ceremony. Later they learned that his divorce was not final. After the final decree was granted, he refused to marry her, police said.

Several weeks ago she visited a sister in Colorado and when she returned to San Francisco Sunday, told him she would not marry him.

Blockwitz, police said, yesterday visited her at the Navy shipyard where she works and threatened her with a gun. He said if she would not elope to Reno with him for a valid marriage ceremony, he would kill her or "a member of your family."

She warned her brother and sister, Doris, 25, not to go home. The brother replied:

BODIES FOUND

"I'm old enough to take care of myself."

The two sisters went to meet their mother at the [illegible] when she returned from [illegible] their father, Claude Lauthern, a Navy veteran patient at the Oak Knoll hospital.

They found the bodies when they entered their home.

The youth had been shot in the head with a .25-caliber automatic pistol. Blockwitz was stretched on a bed, shot through the head. The gun lay on the floor near his hand.

Blockwitz, a Treasure island postal employee, is survived by his mother, Mrs. Margaret Blockwitz, of Lincoln, Neb.

Thomas was slain by his wife, police reported, as the climax of a domestic quarrel.

He was cuffing her, she told police, and she attempted to defend herself with a nine-inch butcher knife. The blade cut through his heart.

Israel Is Proclaimed; Arabs March

Truman Action Stuns Closing Session of U. N.; Battle in Jerusalem; Egypt Orders Invasion

Jews Said To Control Holy City

By the United Press

TEL AVIV, Israel, May 15—The Jews took sovereignty over their own state of Israel today (Saturday) and less than six hours later enemy planes dive-bombed Tel Aviv and Sarona, the capital.

As the Jews girded to defend their undefined frontiers against five Arab armies poised on Palestine's frontiers, two planes identified as bombers and two fighters swooped in over Tel Aviv.

Ten bombs were dropped. One Jew was killed, three were hospitalized. Fires glowed north of the city, but damage was believed slight.

EGYPT ANNOUNCEMENT

Egypt announced at 12:01 a. m. that its troops had been ordered to enter Palestine.

Armies of four other Arab nations were poised on the borders.

(It was reported from Amman that Arab armies moved from Trans-Jordan at 12:01 a. m. to "liberate the Holy Land from Zionism," an official communique announced.)

(The general secretariat of the Arab League proclaimed a state of war exists between the Arab League nations and Palestine Jewry, Associated Press reported.

(It was still not clear, however, whether the Arab armies would invade the Jewish section of Palestine. Previous dispatches have indicated the troops might merely confine themselves to protecting the areas now held by the Arabs.)

Egypt, Iraq and Syria declared martial law. Leganon proclaimed a state of emergency.

The Egyptian communique issued at 12:01 a. m. said:

"Orders have been given the Egyptian armed forces to enter Palestine with the object of restoring security and order in that country and putting an end to the massacres perpetrated by terrorist Zionist gangs against the Arabs and against humanity."

JERUSALEM BATTLE

There was heavy fighting in Jerusalem, where troops of the new Jewish army were reported to have seized effective control of the heart of the city.

It was reported also that Jews had captured Acre, the northern seaport earmarked for the Arabs under a United Nations partition plan.

Army Commander-in-Chief Israel Galilee, in his first order of the day, said:

"The enemy is threatening invasion. We are ready on all fronts. But the public must give its full support. Air raid shelters should be made ready without delay. I will not allow any large public gatherings in the streets."

Ben-Gurion Announces His Cabinet

By the United Press

TEL AVIV, Israel, May 15—After 2000 years as wanderers the Jews took sovereignty over their own state of Israel today (Saturday).

Proclaimed yesterday, the new nation entered officially into being at midnight when the British Palestine mandate expired.

A 4 p. m., in the three-story Tel Aviv Museum in Rothschild boulevard, Prime Minister David Ben-Gurion proclaimed the state of Israel to an audience of 400 men and women, who wept in happiness.

Some of them had attended the first Zionist Congress in Switzerland 50 years ago. Some had suffered in Russian pogroms. Some bore the scars of Nazi lashings, or the shameful tattoo marks of internment camps. Some had come to Israel from the United States and other free countries to be citizens of their own new country.

". . . We, the members of the National Council, representatives of the Jewish people of Palestine and the Zionist movement of the world, met together in solemn assembly today, the day of termination of the British mandate over Palestine, by virtue of the natural historic right of the Jewish people and of the resolution of the General Assembly of the United Nations, hereby proclaim the establishment of a Jewish state in Palestine, to be called Israel," the proclamation said.

"We hereby declare that as from the termination of the mandate at midnight this night of the 14th to 15th of May, 1948, and until the setting up of duly elected bodies of state in accordance with a constitution to be drawn up by a constituent assembly not later than the first day of October, 1948, the present National Council shall act as a provisional state council and its executive organ—the national administration—shall constitute the provisional government of the state of Israel."

OFFICIALS NAMED

Ben-Gurion announced Zwi Scharf would be Chief Secretary of the provisional government.

Ben-Gurion himself, 60-year-old Polish Jew, will serve as both Premier and War Minister.

Moshe Shertok will serve as Foreign Minister.

(Other Cabinet posts for the new state, as listed in an Associated Press dispatch from Jerusalem on April 26, included: Treasury, Eliezer Kaplan; Trade and Industry, Fritz Bernstein; Communications, David Remez; Interior, Isaac Gruenbaum; Minister for Jerusalem, Rabbi J. L. Fishman; Immigration, Moshe Shapiro; Agriculture, Aharon Zisling; Labor and Public Works, Isaac Bentov; Legal, Felix Rosenbluetn; Police and possibly Arab Affairs, A. Shitrit; I. W. Levin, unassigned.)

Scharf formerly was administrative secretary of the political department of the Jewish Agency.

There was one Communist among the 37 members of the new governmental general council, which had charge of the historic ceremony. He is Meir Wilmer, 30, leader of the Palestine Communist party.

The Israel government called upon Arabs living in the Jewish state "to return to ways of peace and play their part in development of the state, with full and equal citizenship."

"We offer peace and amity to all neighboring states," the proclamation said.

Palestine At a Glance

In the course of two days that will fill pages of history, there were these developments in Palestine Friday and Saturday:

1—The Jewish state of Israel was born at 12:01 a. m., one minute after Great Britain relinquished her Palestine mandate.

2—President Truman surprised the world by announcing the U. S. was recognizing the new state.

3—The United Nations special Palestine Assembly adjourned after approving one proposal—a U. N. mediator to be sent to the Holy Land.

4—Egypt announced her army had been ordered to enter Palestine, and other Arab nations went on a war footing.

The Stassen, Dewey Feud

New Yorker Snubs His Foe in Oregon; Debate Agreed On

By EARL C. BEHRENS

Political Editor, The Chronicle

KLAMATH FALLS, Ore., May 14—Harold E. Stassen and Thomas E. Dewey passed each other out on the old Oregon trail today on their hoped for journey to the White House.

But Dewey avoided a personal meeting with the ex-Minnesota Governor and his bus kept right on rolling through the little town of Cascade Locks, 48 miles east of Portland.

Stassen, who had made a brief stop, stood in the roadway as the New Yorker kept right on his way to Portland.

Stassen has agreed to meet Dewey Monday night on the latter's terms in a radio debate on Stassen's demand that the Communist party be outlawed.

The debate will be held in Portland. Both candidates for the Republican presidential nomination will alter the schedule of their campaign for Oregon's 12 delegates to the national convention to participate in the debate.

MAYOR IS PEEVED

The maddest man in Oregon is Mayor Russell H. Nichols of Cascade Locks, a town of 756 inhabitants. He also is a candidate for the Legislature.

This morning he breakfasted with Dewey at Columbia Gorge. The Mayor arranged to have Dewey stop in his community en route to Portland.

All the school kids were released from their classrooms and were down on the town's main street to greet Dewey.

James Travis, an Oregon editor and candidate on the Stassen ticket at the May 21 primary, got into town ahead of Dewey. He saw the kids, distributed Stassen buttons and cards.

When Stassen arrived in town he saw the kids, stopped to greet them.

Word was flashed that the Dewey party, which had been campaigning in the area now being traveled by Stassen, was coming down the highway.

Stassen was prepared to say, "Greetings, Tom."

Newsreel cameramen had moved

Continued on Page 8, Col. 8

The UNESCO Conference

Editor Says U. S. Is Ahead of Russia In the 'Cold War'

By CAROLYN ANSPACHER

America, although still a "half-dozing giant," is ahead in its cold war with Russia.

We are paying the bill for the recovery and unification of Western Europe.

We are re-arming, and in so doing, we are restoring the physical means of protecting the unification of the west and of keeping the peace.

These were the words last night of Erwin D. Canham, editor of the Christian Science Monitor and president of the American Society of Newspaper Editors.

He spoke at the second plenary session of the Pacific Regional Conference on UNESCO at the Opera House, which was crowded by 3000 delegates from seven Western States Alaska and Hawaii.

It is not Canham's belief that rearmament alone will attain a lasting peace. But he does hold that national strength is today the first, indispensable step along the road which can lead to peace.

'MANY THINGS WRONG'

There are many things wrong in our relationship with the Soviet Union, Canham said. But the remedy is neither appeasement nor weakness.

"We have had relatively good diplomatic relations with Russia when we have been strong; we had not had good diplomatic relations when our interests conflicted and we were weak," the editor said.

"We must not fall into the trap set for Neville Chamberlain in 1938 when he proclaimed 'Peace in Our Time.'

Intensity of American public opinion on the subject today is so provocative, Canham said, that the mistakes of 1914 and 1939 are not being repeated. Today, he said, there is no possibility that an aggressor can "deliberately push his expansion by means of a limited war.'

DANGER REDUCED

"War today cannot be limited. And there is no possibility that an aggressor today suddenly will wake up to find himself unexpectedly facing the United States. He faces the United States already.

"Thus the first war danger—a miscalculation on the part of an aggressor—has been reduced to the lowest possible point.

"Not only is American public opinion alert and outspoken, it is positively violent. I cannot think that for this brief period in world history it is a bad thing for the traditionally isolationist and pacific American people to give the impression of having itching trigger fingers."

For all this Canham does not hold to the popular belief that war is inevitable.

"There is a difference, he said, "between rejecting the idea of inevitable war and being willing to

Continued on Page 2, Col. 5

U. S. First To Concede Sovereignty

By JOHN M. HIGHTOWER

Associated Press Staff Writer

WASHINGTON, May 14—President Truman, in a move that surprised the world, tonight recognized the new Jewish state of Israel in Palestine a few minutes after it was proclaimed.

The news caused intense elation among the Zionists, stunned the Arabs and threw the United Nations into turmoil.

The action placed the great weight of American prestige behind the claim of the Jews to govern the homeland they have carved out for themselves in the Holy Land.

In 42 fateful words, Mr. Truman proclaimed:

"This Government has been informed that a Jewish State has been proclaimed in Palestine and recognition has been requested by the provisional government thereof.

"The United States recognizes the provisional government as the de facto authority of the new State of Israel."

(The use of the legalistic term "de facto authority" is common in such instances where a new government is in process of creation but is still provisional. It means simply that the United States recognizes that the government of Israel is in fact the ruling authority of the territory in question.

"De jure" recognition means recognition of a government as the legally constituted authority.)

SENSATION IN U. N.

The news of recognition created a sensation in the United Nations Assembly Hall in New York. It came while the U. N. was rejecting a U. S. proposal to set up a trusteeship-type for Jerusalem. The U. N. Assembly adjourned a few hours later. (See Page 2.)

Guatemala's delegate to the U. N. announced that his country had recognized Israel and thus became the second nation to do so.

Andrei A. Gromyko, Soviet delegate at the U. N., said in New York that his country recognizes Israel's existence. He did not announce formal diplomatic recognition.

The President's announcement immediately raised speculation here as to whether the American Government was also prepared to lift its embargo against arms shipments to the Middle East in order that the Jewish state might obtain weapons in the United States.

Diplomatic informants would say only that recognition did not automatically affect the embargo.

Along with the recognition announcement, the White House reaffirmed that the United States will continue to support efforts to obtain a truce in the Jewish-Arab fighting in the Holy Land and expressed the hope that the Jewish government would co-operate to that end.

A statement issued by Charles G. Ross, the President's press secretary, said:

"The desire of the United States to obtain a truce in Palestine will in no way be lessened by the proclamation of a Jewish state."

"We hope that the new Jewish state will join with the Security Council Truce Commission in redoubled efforts to bring an end to the fighting which has been throughout the United Nations consideration of Palestine a principal objective of this Government."

Steelworkers Give Murray a Raise

BOSTON, May 14 (AP)—The CIO steelworkers today gave President Philip Murray a $5000-a-year raise, bringing his salary to $25,000.

Father Flanagan Of Boy's Town Dies in Germany

BERLIN, May 15 (AP)—Msgr. Edward J. Frannigan, 61, the Nebraska priest who founded the internationally known Boy's Town near Omaha, died at an Army hospital today (Saturday) after suffering a heart attack.

(Story on Page 20).

The Index

Herb Caen	9
Comics	4H
Crossword Puzzle	7
Drama	5
Editorial: "Air Mail Has Achieved Youthful Maturity"	10
Lichty's Cartoon	4
Finance	12, 4H
Radio	20
Vital Statistics	7
Women's World	11

THE WEATHER

Fair and Mild

(Details on Page 7.)

Old Jail Term Bobs Up to Plague Judge in Cothran-San Jose Water Works Feud

By ALVIN D. HYMAN

Chronicle Staff Writer

SAN JOSE, May 14—Cothran against the San Jose Water Works, an expanding universe of litigation that has been whirring through the Santa Clara county courts for two generations, reacted to the law of relativity today and began bending back on itself.

Shelley R. Cothran, currently suing the company for $350,000 damages, threw a trial-stopping challenge at Superior Judge Raymond McIntosh, largely on grounds Judge McIntosh had thrown his brother, Ralph, into jail during one of the gaudier manifestations of the case back in 1937.

The challenge caught everybody but the Cothrans by surprise, because Judge McIntosh, who presides over the Sierra county court, was specially assigned to the Santa Clara county court and to "Cothran against the San Jose Water Works" by the State Judicial Council. That action became necessary last month when the Cothrans, who act as their own attorneys, disqualied five Judges at one lively session and cleared every bench within a day's journey of the jurisdiction.

In expressing dissatisfaction with Judge McIntosh, Cothran used language and put forth charges that did not please the Court.

Judge McIntosh looked darker and darker as Cothran read a long affidavit to disqualify. There was an edge on every word as Judge McIntosh abruptly stopped argument on the matter and said coldly:

"I deny the allegations and demand a hearing on the matter. My integrity, my reputation have been assailed in this affidavit. In justice to myself, I should be heard in the matter, and I so demand. I shall take the time allowed by law to file an answer, and will demand a trial."

Judge McIntosh has five days in which to reply to charges against him, after which the Judicial Council will assign a Judge and fix a date for a hearing.

But that hearing may run into technical difficulties of its own. Cothran was not at all reluctant to announce that if the Judicial Council assigns the disqualification hearing to a Judge unsatisfactory to him, he will challenge that Judge, too. The situation, he conceded, has unlimited possibilities.

Before reading the affidavit that got under the Judge's skin, Cothran read a prefatory statement in which he pleaded that everything he was about to set forth bore the mark of deference and respect. Then he started right in to point out that doubtless the Judges of the inquisition were honest and sincere, and maybe Pontious Pilate would have been fair enough if his prejudice and bias had not been "fanned by the money changers."

Then he got down to cases. He said first, that Judge McIntosh once sent his brother, Ralph, to jail "on a hypertechnicality," and "largely on the suggestion of water company counsel." He said this was "a frame up and crucifixion of Ralph Cothran, based on perjured affidavits." He added:

"The main issue of fact in the aforesaid proceedings was the attempt to take plaintiff's property by means of perjured affidavit. One of the issues in this case is the taking of plaintiff's property by means of force and fraud."

He said further that "affiant feels Your Honor has been politically intimate with learned counsel for the water company."

He talked at length about the alleged resentment and prejudice any lawyer feels for a layman who acts as his own attorney, and he tossed in this paragraph:

"In order to take plaintiff's property without compensation, counsel, with perfidious insincerity, have attempted to bind and gag justice, with the misapplied authorities and nefarious red tape."

With a bow toward his ancient enemy, the water company, as a group that "conspire while they respire to shield frauds, wrong and crime," he charged that Judge McIntosh's bias and prejudice would preclude him from "proceeding against those who are now violating the penal, health and water code of this State."

Bennett Leib and Robert Brown, counsel for the water company, showed signs of great surprise, though they insisted they have long since become proof against surprise from the Cothran quarter.

Leib accosted Cothran with a querulous inquiry. He patiently told the layman that one allegation against Judge McIntosh—that he was prejudiced against laymen acting as their own counsel purely because he was himself a lawyer—might equally be applied to any Judge in the State. Cothran looked down his nose and suggested:

"You may look for the answer to that in your lawbooks."

San Francisco Chronicle
THE CITY'S ONLY HOME-OWNED NEWSPAPER

FOUNDED 1865—VOL. CLXVII, NO. 111 CCCCAAAB SAN FRANCISCO, WEDNESDAY, NOVEMBER 3, 1948 GA 1-1112 DAILY 5 CENTS, SUNDAY 15 CENTS

TRUMAN HOLDS ON TO NARROW LEAD

Democrats Control Senate, Appear Certain of the House; Havenner Defeats Mailliard; School Bonds Win in the City

This World Today

By ROYCE BRIER

AN INTERREGNUM means literally a period when a throne is vacant between successive reigns. It may be used loosely to designate the period between a presidential election and the inauguration of a successor, when the President does not succeed himself.

While an interregnum might not occur in the current presidential election, the situation is not unusual, and a historical review of it may be pertinent.

It is a peculiar circumstance that most voters in the United States under the age of thirty have not been conscious of such a period, the last having occurred in the winter of 1932-33, in the changeover from President Hoover to President Roosevelt.

That interregnum lasted about four months, and so it has been in most of our history. Originally the inauguration of the President occurred on March 4 of the year following the election because the new Constitution went into effect on that day of 1789 (though Washington was not inaugurated until April 30). Subsequently the XII amendment (1804), which revised the electoral voting system, by indirection kept the March 4 inauguration date.

This was quite natural to the time, because in horse and stagecoach days, the assembling of electors and the ultimate transmission of the election result to the President of the Senate was a slow process. Tradition and inertia kept the March 4 date for much more than a century, and when in our generation sentiment arose for a shorter interim, it did not pivot on the President's term.

Rather, it resulted from the absurdity of those who had been defeated in election — "lame ducks"—going back to Congress in the January session and making laws until they were superseded in March. This resulted in what was popularly known as the Lame Duck Amendment (XX) to the Constitution, which went into effect in 1933.

Here for the first time we have a specific date. Section I of the Amendment reads: "The terms of the President and Vice President shall end at noon on the 20th day of January..."

That set the interregnum to two and a half months, and none of us thought that in ordinary circumstances this was too

Continued on Page 4, Col. 5

In the City and State

California Remains 'Doubtful,' May Be Key to U. S. Decision; Liquor Control Plans Are Beaten

The City Turns Down All the Bond Proposals (Except for Schools)

San Francisco voters yesterday approved a $49,890,000 bond issue for expansion and modernization of its public school system but rejected all other bond issue proposals on the ballot, on the basis of semiofficial returns from all 1204 precincts.

Vote on the school bonds was:

Yes 229,702
No 74,679

Changes in the charter provisions governing retirement of policemen and firemen were approved.

The vote on the police and fire department pension plan was:

Yes 179,616
No 92,488

The proposal for establishment of a Traffic Engineering Bureau and a Director of Traffic and abolishing the Traffic Advisory Board was approved by a narrow margin.

The vote was:

Yes 130,419
No 126,946

The airport bond issue, providing $8,600,000 for modernization and expansion of San Francisco International Airport, apparently was defeated. The proposal received more than a majority but failed to receive the required two-thirds vote. The vote was:

Yes 169,500
No 113,586

Commenting on defeat of the Airport Bonds, Chairman Edward Mills of the Citizens Campaign Committee said he believed the voters were confused because of the many propositions on the presidential ballot.

Both he and Airport Superintendent B. M. Doolin indicated that the proposition would be resubmitted to the voters at the earliest possible opportunity. Mills said he would be happy to serve as campaign committee chairman if a number of propositions were not presented with the airport proposal.

Without the funds for expansion and modernization of the airport, the city will have to operate the terminal as a "circus," said Doolin, without benefit of such facilities as an adequate administration building and terminal.

Voters turned down the $6,000,000 bond issue for construction of a modern Hall of Justice by about the same margin. The vote was:

Yes 147,044
No 135,153

The $15,000,000 bond proposal for construction of an elaborate Con-

Continued on Page 2, Col. 6

The Index

Herb Caen	17
Comics	4B
Contract Contacts	26
Crossword Puzzle	25
Drama	12, 13
Editorial: "The Scandinavian Dilemma"	18
Radio	15
Women's World	10, 11
Lichty's Cartoon	6
Vital Statistics	15

City Vote on Propositions

Following are the complete semi-official returns from all the 1204 precincts in San Francisco. Total vote was 348,156.

CITY AND COUNTY PROPOSITIONS

Proposition	YES	NO
PROP. A—School Bonds:	229,702	74,679
PROP. B—Airport Bonds:	169,500	113,586
PROP. C—Hall of Justice Bonds:	147,044	135,153
PROP. D—Convention Center Bonds:	134,574	146,170
PROP. E—Library Bonds:	154,168	106,918
PROP. F—Butano Forest Bonds:	169,669	89,858
PROP. G—Annual Vac. Employees:	139,865	104,794
PROP. H—Sale, Abandonment or Discontinuance of Use of Land Held for Park Purposes:	147,840	111,049
PROP. I—Municipal Court:		
PROP. J—Receipt, Custody, Deposit of Funds, Investment of Trust Funds:		
PROP. K—Suspension and Removal, Municipal Court Judges:		
PROP. L—Superior Court Appoint.:		
PROP. M—Bureau of Traffic Eng. Admin.: Dir. of Traffic; Chief of Inspectors, Police Dept.	130,419	126,946
PROP. N—Retirement Prov., Police and Fire Depts.:	179,616	92,488

Mrs. FDR Tells How She Voted

PARIS, Nov. 2 (AP)—Mrs. Franklin D. Roosevelt said today she had cast an absentee vote for President Truman.

Asked her plans in the event of a Republican administration after January 20, she smiled and said, "I've got to finish my work here." She is an American delegate to the United Nations.

Truman Wins in S. F.; Congressional Contests Are Close in the State

By EARL C. BEHRENS
Political Editor, The Chronicle

California continued early today to be a doubtful State in the presidential race.

Governor Thomas E. Dewey tenaciously held on to his slender lead over President Truman in the contest for the State's 25 electoral votes.

The Associated Press reporting 10,460 precincts, some complete and some incomplete out of 16,802 gave the following:

Dewey-Warren	682,392
Truman-Barkley	669,857
Wallace-Taylor	73,538

Shortly after 3 a. m. Governor Warren, Republican nominee for Vice President, talked with reporters. He had just previously had a telephone conversation with Governor Dewey, the party nominee for President.

Warren said he had decided to go to bed since he did not expect any "conclusive" results until later today.

RURAL VOTE

Oliver J. Carter of Redding, Democratic State chairman, issued a statement, declaring: "It is a very, very close race and will go right down to the wire. I am surprised how well the rural districts are holding up for Truman. Actually it is the back country, the votes are coming out of the mountains now, that will decide the contest."

"I am convinced that the Republican party will carry California by a margin of more than 100,000," Senator William F. Knowland declared early this morning.

As the national tabulations proceeded early today there was some possibility that California might again become the key State in the election of a President if the Republicans can pick up the strength in eastern and midwestern States claimed by Herbert Brownell, Republican national chairman.

NEW YORK STATEMENT

From New York City early this morning, Edward Jaeckel, former Empire State GOP chairman, insisted that the late returns from other States would assure a Republican victory.

Jaeckel, however, is counting upon California's 25 electoral votes.

In 1916, California by approximately 3700 votes turned the apparent election day tide from Charles Evans Hughes to Woodrow Wilson and sent the latter back to the White House for a second term. It was California's then 13 votes which gave Wilson his second victory.

Senator William F. Knowland last night said he believed a similar situation might prevail this year.

From New York, Jaeckel insisted that rural Republican votes would give the Dewey-Warren ticket Illinois, Indiana, Iowa, Michigan and other States in doubt early this morning.

Whether the Republicans can

Continued on Page 8, Col. 1

Bulletin

PARIS, Nov. 3 (AP)—Secretary of State George C. Marshall will resign next January 20 regardless of the outcome of the presidential election, an informed source in the American United Nations delegation said today. Marshall, the source said, plans to retire to his farm.

There was no confirmation of this statement from Marshall.

The Election At a Glance

ELECTORAL VOTES

Truman leading in 28 states with 282 electoral votes; Dewey in 16 with 211; Thurmond in four with 38, including capture of 28 in Alabama, Mississippi and South Carolina.

POPULAR VOTE

From 91,865 of the country's 135,367 voting units:

Dewey	15,286,030
Truman	16,580,771
Wallace	828,741
Thurmond	737,282
Total	33,423,435

SENATE

Republicans elected, 2; holdovers, 33; total, 35.

Democrats elected, 13; holdovers, 30; total, 43.

Contests undecided, 18.

HOUSE

Republicans elected, 71. (Present Congress, 243; vacancies, 3.)

Democrats elected, 170. (Present Congress, 185; vacancies, 2.)

Contests undecided, 193.

GOVERNORS

Republicans elected, 4; (Republican gains, none).

Democrats elected, 11; (Democratic gains, 3).

Contests undecided, 18.

Showers Expected All Today

Northern California voters were dampened yesterday while on their way to the polls. And there will be more rain today.

The Weather Bureau predicts intermittent showers all day.

Yesterday's rains brought more than half an inch of precipitation to San Francisco to boost the lagging seasonal total to .84 of an inch since July 1. Normal to date is 1.78 inches. Last year 2.44 inches had fallen by November 2.

Small craft warnings continued to fly along the Northern California coast as a trailing storm front moved over the area from a disturbance center in the Gulf of Alaska.

Farmers expressed their usual conflicting opinions about timeliness of the wet weather.

The storm brought little snow to California's mountains and the California State Automobile Association reported all major highways open. No chains were needed, they said.

San Joaquin cotton growers, for whom the next 45 days of picking and ginning are critical, wanted dry weather, while cattle and sheep men expressed concern over the dry ranges.

In the Nation

President Holds an Edge With More Than Half of the Votes In; GOP Still Expects a Victory

Democrats Are Ahead in All 'Crucial' Senate Races, Gain Strongly in House

By the Associated Press

WASHINGTON, Nov. 3—Barring upsets, Democrats won control of both branches of Congress in Tuesday's elections.

On the basis of unofficial returns, President Truman's party elected 16 Senators against 5 for the Republicans and 188 Representatives against 86 for the Republicans.

They had needed a net gain of only four Senate and 31 House seats for control.

Senate Democratic gains included seats now held by Republicans in Oklahoma, West Virginia, Iowa and Illinois. Their House gains included 36 Republican and one American-Labor seats. Only one House Democratic seat went to a Republican, and the GOP had captured no Democratic Senate seats.

THOSE IN DOUBT

Of the 12 Senate seats still in doubt, Democrats were leading in eight and Republicans in four. Democrats held margins in Minnesota, Kentucky and Wyoming, where seats now are held by Republicans.

Republicans were not ahead in any States where the Democrats are fighting to keep Senate seats already theirs.

Democrats lost both the House and Senate in 1946.

Democrats won senatorial contests in Tennessee and Colorado which were Democratic in the last Congress, but which Republicans had hoped to capture.

Democrats led in Montana and New Mexico for seats held by their own party.

In addition, Senator Dworshak, Idaho Republican, was trailing Democrat Bert H. Miller.

Democrats elected included Lyndon Johnson in Texas and J. Melville Broughton in North Carolina.

To add to the Republican woes, Democrats led incumbent Republican

Continued on Page A, Col. 1

Dewey Takes New York By 40,000

By the Associated Press

NEW YORK, Nov. 3—Governor Thomas E. Dewey early today (Wednesday) edged out President Truman in their hammer-and-tongs scrap for New York State's prized 47 electoral votes.

With 9929 of the State's 9856 election districts tabulated, the unofficial count was:

Dewey	2,833,175
Truman	2,792,975
Wallace	507,449

This included all of the votes in Democratic New York City. Only 20 upstate districts were missing. The upstate area as a whole gave Dewey a big margin.

Truman made a surprisingly close fight of it but failure of New York city to come through with its accustomed vote cost him the State.

He carried the metropolis by 469,087 as against the 771,213 margin it gave President Roosevelt over Dewey four years ago.

Upstate, with the 20 districts missing, Dewey had a margin of 551,387. The 20 districts were in the GOP counties of Ulster, Hamilton, Delaware, Jefferson and Oswego.

The more than half million votes piled up by Henry A. Wallace, Progressive party nominee, were a big factor in the Empire State.

He got 422,424 in New York City. Most observers believed the Wallace strength came from sources which otherwise would have been Democratic.

Democrats gained eight seats in New York State's 45-member Congressional delegation, returns indicated.

Seven of the victories were at the expense of the Republicans, and one was over an American Labor party Congressman in the Bronx, Leo Isacson.

Democrats picked up three seats in Queens in New York City, one in a joint Manhattan-Staten Island district, one in the Bronx and two in Erie county—all at the expense of the Republicans.

The other ALP Congressman in the State, Vito Marcantonio, won reelection for a seventh term in a close three-way contest with Democratic and Republican opposition.

Inside ...

Chronicle coverage of the election includes:

Map showing how each State voted, Page A.

Table of State-by-State Presidential returns, Page A.

Table of California counties' Presidential voting, Page A.

What happened in gubernatorial races, Page A.

Stories about the various headquarters, Page B.

Stories of how the counties voted, Page 4.

Account of Franck R. Havenner's victory, Page 5.

Table of U. S. Senatorial voting, Page 6.

State-by-State election returns story, Page 6.

Tables of county-by-county votes on key propositions; table of State vote on all propositions, Page 8.

Dewey Is Tops in Largest States, But Truman Clings to Smaller Ones

By the Associated Press

President Harry S. Truman, the man who wouldn't say die, led Governor Thomas E. Dewey today (Wednesday) in one of the most astounding presidential elections of U. S. history.

The contest was far from over, but the man from Missouri, whom the pollsters marked off as licked months ago, clung doggedly to a majority of the electoral votes.

At 3 a. m. (EST) Mr. Truman was leading in 28 States with 282 electoral votes, whereas Dewey was ahead in 16 States with 211. Needed for election: 266.

And the President's margin over Dewey in the popular tally was 1,294,741 with 33,433,435 ballots tabulated of an expected 50,000,000 or more.

Republican campaign managers toned down their victory predictions as the night wore on. But, after midnight, victory in New York State set off new GOP claims.

Herbert Brownell Jr., Dewey's campaign manager, repeated that the election of the Republican ticket was "assured."

But Senator J. Howard McGrath, Democratic National Committee chairman, reaffirmed at 2:25 a. m. his previously expressed conviction that President Truman would be re-elected.

Amazingly, the Democrats swept into position to control both Senate and House at the 81st Congress—provided they suffer no upsets in the tabulations yet to come. And at this point, the trend was for, not against, the Administration party.

They had captured four Republican Senate seats—all they needed for a bare majority. As for the House, they had thrown enough GOP members out of that chamber to regain control—if they lost none of their yet-to-be decided seats to the Republicans.

Neither the presidential struggle nor the congressional fight had been finally decided, but the mounting flood of the ballots had cast up enough surprises to keep the leaders of the experts wagging for months, if not years.

As expected, Dewey captured the massive electoral tallies of New York and Pennsylvania, but it was distinctly not expected Truman rolled into the lead in such States as Ohio, Massachusetts and Wisconsin.

Truman led Dewey by 67,797 votes in big Illinois with only 1763 precincts still unreported.

Of the 1763 missing precincts, 1273 were outside Chicago, territory that normally is Republican.

Returns from 7442 of the State's 9231 precincts gave Truman 1,610,[illegible] and Dewey, 1,552,880.

Truman led in Arizona, Arkansas, Colorado, Delaware, Florida, Georgia, Idaho, Illinois, Iowa, Kentucky, Massachusetts, Minnesota, Missouri, Montana, Nevada, New Mexico, North Carolina, Ohio, Oklahoma,

Continued on Page A, Col. 3

Seals Win By Shutout; Oaks Lose

SEE SPORTS

COMPARATIVE TEMPERATURES
For Wednesday, May 11, 1949

	High	Low		High	Low
San Francisco	58	50	New York	60	47
Oakland	66	52	Chicago	71	36
Los Angeles	75	54	Kansas City	75	43
Sacramento	86	51	Miami	86	69
Reno	81	35	Washington	53	48

Forecast for Today: HIGH FOG
(For Details and Weather Map, See Page 17)

San Francisco Chronicle
THE CITY'S ONLY HOME-OWNED NEWSPAPER

FINAL

FOUNDED 1865—VOL. CLXVIII, NO. 117 CCCCAAA SAN FRANCISCO, THURSDAY, MAY 12, 1949 GA 1-1112 DAILY 7 CENTS, SUNDAY 15 CENTS

TRAINS, CARS REACH BERLIN, BUT SOME DISCORD ARISES

The City Budget

$944,907 More Chopped Off by Committee

Another $944,907 was slashed from Mayor Robinson's record-breaking 1949-50 budget yesterday by the economy-minded three-man finance committee of the Board of Supervisors.

The Mayor has asked for $138,-585,000 to run city departments during the coming year.

But yesterday's finance committee action brought to $3,011,836 the amount cut to date from this figure.

A third round of budget slashing is scheduled by the committee for Monday morning. Monday afternoon, the budget bill will go before the board for approval.

RECOMMENDATIONS

Principal economies recommended yesterday by the committee concerned the Departments of Public Works and Public Health.

A total of $539,968 was cut from the proposed Public Works Department budget of $4,316,588. This money would have paid for new shops and yards, sewer improvements, street cleaning and certain repairs to public buildings.

In the proposed Public Health department budget of $9,860,487, committeemen made cuts of $344,-711. Largest items deleted were $66,982 for repairs to the Laguna Honda Home and $107,511 for maintenance and improvements at San Francisco Hospital.

The finance committee consists of Supervisors Dan Gallagher, chairman, Chester MacPhee and Don Fazackerley.

POLICE, FIRE FUNDS

Their economy-mindedness was further demonstrated yesterday in skirmishes with the Police and Fire Departments over recommendations for personnel increases for both departments.

An increase of 127 men in the Police Department is being sought in the new budget plus 143 new firemen.

Police Chief Michael Mitchell and Fire Chief Edward Walsh, flanked by members of their commissions, defended their requests for more men. Mitchell said additional personnel is required for the downtown traffic detail, protection of school children at street crossings and for policing parking meters.

Chief Walsh explained the fire department will open new houses in the Sunset and Lake Merced districts and personnel will be needed to man them.

REQUESTS CHALLENGED

Supervisors Chester MacPhee and Don Fazackerley, however, said they were not convinced the departments require all of the men requested.

Fazackerley said employment of the new policemen would represent a 12 per cent increase in the force. "If these men are really needed," he added, "there must be a manpower crisis in the department. I have received no evidence that such is the case."

Both Fazackerley and MacPhee indicated they would support a "compromise," but Chairman Dan Gallagher stated he would vote for the full increase requested.

The additional policemen and firemen would cost more than $1,000,000 in salaries next year.

The committee took no action on the police and fire budgets yesterday after hearing the chiefs.

TAXPAYERS' STAND

The San Francisco Municipal Conference, an organization of large taxpayers' groups, added its voice to demands upon the Supervisors that they allow only necessary expenditures to avoid a tax rate increase.

Arthur E. Wilkens, conference chairman, suggested the Fire and Police Departments be denied new employments until an organizational study can be made.

Royce Brier is on vacation. His column will be resumed upon his return.

More Fog This Morning, Clear In Afternoon

The Weather Bureau predicts more high fog this morning, clearing in the afternoon except near the ocean.

Temperatures will be lower with an estimated high of 60 in San Francisco, 66 in Oakland.

Winds will be moderate and westerly in the afternoon.

The interior is due for cooler weather and there will be some thunderstorms in the mountains.

(List of week-end events on page 12.)

Bay Area Job Drop

April Total Is 6800 Below A Year Ago

San Francisco Bay Area factory employment decreased in April, the fourth consecutive month showing a loss.

Despite seasonal increases in the canning industry, employment of production workers was down 600 from March and 6800 from April, 1948, State offices reported.

While statistics for the current month are incomplete, local indications of a possible continuing trend were not encouraging.

One South San Francisco machine plant, the Mutual Engineering Company, has laid off 37 boilermakers, machinists and helpers from its normal crew of 50, it was learned.

A neighboring plant of the Enterprise Engine and Foundry Company has cut work in its foundry operations to "three or four" days a week in what was said to be a temporary action.

The Ford Motor Company's Richmond assembly plant expects to run out of parts Monday because of the Detroit Ford strike. It will shut down temporarily and lay off 1700 production workers.

The area-wide factory employment decrease was disclosed in a joint statement by Paul Scharrenberg, State Director of Industrial Relations, and James G. Bryant, director of the California Department of Employment.

A total of 103,200 production workers were employed in Bay Area manufacturing establishments in April compared with 103,800 in March and 110,000 in April of last year, Scharrenberg said.

"Excluding canning there was a decrease of more than 2000 in factory employment between March and April," he added.

Significant month-to-month reductions were reported in the following industries: Apparel, iron and steel products, shipbuilding and machinery. A small rise was reported by the automobile industry.

Bryant reported a slight reduction during April in the number of Bay Area workers receiving unemployment insurance benefits.

Some 1000 less workers received insurance weekly during April than during the previous month. However, the April total of 50,600 was 20,800 over that for the same period last year.

Yesterday's reductions followed announcement of drastic cutbacks by the Navy which plans to eliminate 1862 Bay Area shipyard jobs and 10,000 such workers throughout the Nation.

Earlier the Veterans' Administration announced it is laying off 8000 employees—416 from Northern California.

Three steel companies in South San Francisco have also announced that some of their operations have been cut back from five to four days due to lower demands for steel.

Tanker Afire In the Atlantic

NEW YORK, May 12 (UP)—The 9,083-ton Swedish tanker Atalanta is on fire in the North Atlantic, Coast Guard headquarters here reported early today (Thursday). The ship's position was given as 330 miles northeast of the Barbados. All crew members, except for the captain and radio operator, have taken to the lifeboats, the Atalanta reported.

Doctors vs. Red Cross

Dispute Over Blood Banks Out in Open

By MILTON SILVERMAN
Science Writer, The Chronicle

LOS ANGELES, May 11—A long-standing feud between California doctors and the National Red Cross flared into the open here today.

It concerns the life-and-death problem of blood and blood banks.

At concluding meetings of the California Medical Association, Dr. John R. Upton of San Francisco, chairman of the CMA's Blood Bank Commission, made these charges:

1—California doctors now are getting barely half the blood needed for optimum treatment of their patients.

2—Red Cross blood banks are unable to fill medical needs and yet the Red Cross is blocking the establishment of community non-profit banks.

3—In addition, a number of small, "jealous hospitals" which operate their own banks, often to their financial profit, are refusing to make blood available to other hospitals.

4—Several small commercial laboratories, buying blood for $4 a pint and selling it for $17.50, are likewise blocking development of non-profit banks.

'THE TIME HAS COME'

"We do not want to fight with the Red Cross," he said. "We want to co-operate. But the time has come to tell the truth as we see it."

The Red Cross, he added, can "have the publicity if we can render the service."

With the official support of the CMA, Dr. Upton and his fellow commission members urged the establishment of a co-ordinated, non-profit blood bank system to provide complete coverage for California.

These banks, he said, should be directed by local medical societies and operated at cost for the benefit of patients.

Patients receiving blood from such banks have two obligations. First, if they can afford it, they should pay the processing costs of the blood—from $6 to $7.50 a pint. Second, they should replace it with blood donated by a relative or friend.

FOUR BANKS

Four such banks now are operating in San Francisco, Alameda, San Mateo and Sacramento.

The Red Cross opposes this system. It advocates "free blood to all," getting its donors by public appeal. In California, the Red Cross operates three banks in Stockton, San Jose and Los Angeles, and participates in a fourth in San Diego.

"But their basic idea is all wrong," Dr. Upton claimed. "There is no such thing as free blood—or free anything else. Somebody always pays for it. We feel the patient who gets the blood should pay the processing costs if he can."

He said a patient is no more entitled to free blood than to free penicillin, free bandages or free bubble-gum. Furthermore, he declared, donors will gladly give their blood during a war, but in peacetime they won't keep giving for strangers.

'THE PROOF'

"The proof of this," he said, "is

Continued on Page 16, Col. 7

Lifting of Barriers Cheered

Russians Turn Back Some German Trucks; Acheson Indicates U.S. Will Be Firm at Paris

Secretary Is Against Compromise

By JOHN M. HIGHTOWER
Associated Press Diplomatic Writer

WASHINGTON, May 11—Secretary of State Acheson said today the success of the forthcoming Big Four meeting on Germany is up to the Russians.

Whether a solution of German problems can be reached at the Paris meeting of Foreign Ministers he said, depends "on the willingness of the Russians to make or consider proposals which will not retard in any way whatsoever the great progress" which the Western powers have made in dealing with German issues.

The conference starts May 23. The United States, Russia, Britain and France will take part.

Acheson's statement appeared to be a virtual declaration of no compromise on any of the basic principles and plans which the Western nations already have laid down for Germany.

He suggested, in effect, that if the Russians want to go along with those principles and plans the Paris meeting will be a success but if they try to block them it will fail to produce an agreement on Germany.

CIVIL RIGHTS

Responding to questions at a news conference, he declared that any four power arrangements for unifying and governing Germany must provide adequate guarantees for civil rights and personal freedom for the German people.

He steered away from any extreme optimism about the prospects for a quick or easy solution of the

For editorial comment see page 20

German problem. On the contrary, he said that "perhaps over a long period of time we can move forward to a solution."

The scheduled end of the Soviet blockade of Berlin gave a lift to Acheson's news conference. The Secretary hailed this development as a victory for the pilots who flew the Berlin air lift for the past 10 months with "great morale, great discipline and superb courage."

However, he added:

"While we are delighted that their efforts have brought the end of the blockade, we must not regard that fact alone as having solved the German problem."

ILLEGAL MEASURE

Actually, he continued, the ending of the restrictions on travel and commerce between the Western zones of Germany and the city of Berlin "puts us again in the situation in which we were before the blockade was imposed."

"It was an arbitrary, and in our view, an illegal measure," he said.

"It has failed because they (the Russians) have indicated it was unsuccessful and because the counter measures (taken by the United States, Britain and France) reduced their effect."

Thus the net result as he saw it was simply the removal of an obstacle which had stood in the way of East-West negotiations for a settlement of Germany's future.

At the moment American officials are by no means certain how far the Russians will go at the Paris meeting in proposing police state measures for Germany.

However, Acheson made it clear that it is one of the issues on which he does not intend to compromise.

(Other news of the blockade's end, pictures and map—Pages 4 and 5.)

Air Lift to Continue For at Least 30 Days

BERLIN, May 12 (AP)—The air life planes roared on today (Thursday), ignoring the blockade-lifting order just as they did snow, ice, rain and wind to supply the city.

Lieutenant General John K. Cannon, commander of U. S. Air Forces in Europe, said: "The lift will continue as at present until an adequate stockpile is available and we are certain that surface transportation can meet all the requirements of Berlin. The future only can determine an exact date when the lift will end."

American pilots said they had received instructions to keep the air lift going full blast for another 30 days, until the Western powers measure the intentions of Soviet Russia.

A force of 60,000 men runs the giant show. By the end of March, the United States had spent more than $150,000,000 on it. British expenditures ran to about $50,000,000 more. Fifty-one lives were lost in crashes that cost $8,000,000 in equipment.

Air lift has carried a total of 1,583,686 tons of supplies—food, coal and machinery—in 195,530 flights in the last 48 weeks. British Air Minister Arthur Henderson announced in London that one-fourth of the job was done by the British Royal Air Force and the remainder by the Americans.

Lieutenant Robert R. Keller, Sibley, Iowa, said there would be no slackening for about another month and then the Air Force might cut back the 24-hour schedule to 16 hours daily.

A Protest From West Is Likely

By WES GALLAGHER
Associated Press Staff Writer

BERLIN, May 12 — The 327-day Soviet blockade of Berlin ended today (Thursday) with Western power trains and motor cars pouring passengers and food into Berlin.

The first automobiles crossed the Soviet zone into Berlin at 1:45 a. m. Berlin time (3:45 p. m. Pacific Standard Time, Wednesday), ending Berlin's isolation from the West by road.

A slow moving special train from the West severed the last rail blockade link at 5:08 a. m. when it reached the city limits after a 100-mile run from Helmstedt.

There were two discordant notes in the rising of the curtain across Germany.

Soviet measures indicated the Russians would seek to block West sector Germans from sending anything from Berlin to the West without Russian permission. Soviet check points turned back German trucks trying to leave the city, saying they needed licenses from the Soviet-controlled East German administration or the Soviet military government.

This Russian action seemed certain to bring a sharp protest from the British, Americans and French.

PREVIOUS CLASH

This was one of the same restrictions which the Russians sought to clamp on last year. The Western powers maintained that anything shipped from their sectors to the West required only their approval and refused to accept the Russian demand. This was one of the clashes that led to the Soviet blockade.

Technically the Russians are not required by the four-power agreement of May 4 to lift their order concerning Soviet permission for shipments from Berlin. The original order dates from January, 1948—although not enforced until much later—while the agreement of May 4 calls for lifting only the restrictions clamped on since March 1, 1948.

Another potential dispute arose in Helmstedt on the British zone border when the Russians insisted that Western trains be pulled by Soviet locomotives while in the Russian zone. Western officials acceded to this demand, made at the last minute, and Russian locomotives were attached to the trains waiting at the border.

SOLUTION EXPECTED

It was understood that General Lucius D. Clay and Sir Brian Robertson, American and British Military Governors, had given orders to accede to the demand.

Sir Robert Inglis, British-American Transport Chief, suggested the demand might not represent high-level Soviet policy and "everything should come out in the wash" later today.

Elsewhere, the blockade-lifting ran smoothly with Soviet officials,

Continued on Page 4, Col. 7

Eisler Flight Is Reported

Polish Ship Says Stowaway by His Name Is Aboard

By the Associated Press

NEW YORK, May 11—**The Polish liner Batory reported at sea today that a stowaway aboard had identified himself as Gerhard Eisler, the name of a man described as a top alien Communist in this country.**

Eisler, 53, facing two possible jail sentences in the United States and awaiting deportation proceedings, could not be located in New York.

The Justice Department said it was investigating the report.

The Batory, of the Gdynia-America Shipping Lines, Ltd., sailed from New York last Friday. Her destination is Gdynia, with stops scheduled for Southampton, England, May 14 and Copenhagen, Denmark, May 15.

The line flies the Polish flag but is owned partly by Danish interests.

A spokesman said a radio message from the Batory on May 9 reported discovery of a stowaway who then paid first-class passage.

The line's office here reported the matter to immigration officials in a routine manner, the spokesman said. Then the Batory was asked for "the full name, nationality and port of debarkation" of the stowaway.

This ship answered this request of yesterday with a message received here today. It read in part: "Stowaway, Gerhardt Eisler, German, disembarking Gdynia."

Scotland Yard has been alerted and has been asked to hold the stowaway, the department said.

Eisler, an acknowledged former German Communist, has been fighting to avoid two jail terms. One of his appeals has been pending before the Supreme Court for several months.

Less than a month ago the Court of Appeals here refused to throw out his conviction on a charge of hiding Communist connections when he sought a permit to leave the country. He faces a one to three year sentence on that charge.

The appeal taken to the Supreme Court was from a conviction on a charge of contempt of Congress growing out of his refusal to be sworn as a witness before the House Un-American Activities Committee. He was sentenced to serve one year and pay a $1000 fine on that charge. He was at liberty on $24,500 bail.

Israel Now In the U. N.

Nation Is Admitted By 37 to 12 Vote; Arab Bloc Protests

By the Associated Press

NEW YORK, May 11—**Israel was admitted to the United Nations tonight as the 59th member. The Arab bloc walked out of the General Assembly in bitter protest but a few hours later ended their brief boycott of the U. N.**

The vote admitting Israel was 37 to 12. Nine countries abstained. None of the 58 members was absent.

Egypt, Syria, Saudi Arabia, Yemen and Lebanon walked out promptly.

Later, single delegates of Egypt and Yemen returned to a night meeting of the Assembly. This indicated the other Arab nations would resume their seats at later sessions.

The United States, Russia, China and France, voted to admit Israel. Britain abstained, along with Belgium, Brazil, Denmark, El Salvador, Greece, Siam, Sweden, and Turkey.

It was the second walk-out by the Arabs. They left the Assembly hall angrily on November 29, 1947, when the Assembly voted 33 to 13 to partition Palestine into Jewish and Arab States.

Amidst loud cheering over the vote, Australia's Dr. Herbert V. Evatt, Assembly President, called Israeli Foreign Minister Moshe Sharett to the rostrum to be accepted as Israel's representative here.

The resolution approved by the Assembly said the Assembly decides Israel is a "peace-loving State which accepts the obligations contained in the charter and is able and willing to carry out those obligations."

Sharett said at the start of his maiden speech in the Assembly that the State of Israel claims no allegiance from Jews in other lands. He said it rests on the loyalty of its own citizens.

Typist Foils Break Attempt By Three San Quentin Lifers

The keen eye of a San Quentin typist thwarted an attempted break by three lifers yesterday.

Marguerite Barbera of the prison's Guidance Center discovered a cell bar sawed in two in the south corner of the east cell block as she was on her way to lunch.

After a quick double-take, Mrs. Barbera reported the damage to guards.

Rounded up in the block were brothers Herbert, 28, and Wilbur Stuart, 26, and John McNamara, 28.

McNamara admitted he had stolen several hack saw blades from the prison print shop during the past two months.

Yesterday when other prisoners were taken out of the cell block to lunch, the trio hid and waited until they were locked in alone. Then they went to work.

They were not surprised when they were discovered, however, McNamara said, because they saw Mrs. Barbera's reaction to the metalwork on the cell bar.

The three men had parallel records. All three were committed for robbery or burglary. They were all separately transfered to Chino in 1948 and escaped within a few months.

After an outbreak of additional robberies, they were all recaptured—the Stuart brothers after a short, fierce gunbattle with San Leandro police and McNamara in Los Angeles. They were recommitted for terms ranging up to life.

After the attempted break was discovered, their careers continued to be similar. All three were placed in solitary confinement.

Two Die in Oakland Fire

Two men were burned to death last night when fire destroyed a shed in the rear of 914 Fifth street, Oakland.

The men were identified as Pete Sotello, 52, a laborer who lived at the Fifth street address but sometimes slept in the shed, and Ramon Ramirez, 50, a section hand.

Lorenzo Lopez, Sotello's son-in-law, said Sotello and Ramirez had been drinking in the shed during the day. Police surmised the fire may have been caused by candles, which were the shed's sole means of illumination.

The Index

Herb Caen 19
Comics 4H
Contract Contacts 9
Cross word 27
Drama 14, 15
Editorial: "The Offensive Changes Hands" 20
Financial 22, 23
Lichty's Cartoon 16
Radio 21
Vital Statistics 17
Women's World 9, 10, 11

Cat Assists in Painting of Acclaimed British Modernist

LOUGHBOROUGH, England, May 11 (AP)—Artist Thomas Warbis does not take a lot of trouble over his paintings.

He splashes them—dozens of them—with a bold brush . . . or his bare finger . . . or an old stick with a chewed end.

He lets his cat, Jill, pad over the fresh paint, sit on it and swish her tail over it.

And while turning out his masterpiece, "Figure 8: Skegness," he spilled a saucer of paint on it by accident, smudged it, tried erasing, muttered, "Oh shucks," and let it ride.

But sponsors of a local art show thought "Figure 8: Skegness," was good enough to hang.

Critics praised it. Said the Leicester Mail: "A fine specimen of modernism by the Barrow-on-Soar artist, Thomas Warbis."

They found later that Artist Warbis is six years old.

Tommy's father, Alfred, a commercial artist, said he found Tommy's venture in modern art while looking for packing paper to send his own pictures to the exhibit.

"I sent the picture as a joke and a test of people's knowledge of art," he moaned. "And to think I've been trying for 40 years to get somewhere in art."

Thomas D. Pearce, the organizer, wasn't blushing.

"It's no worse than a lot of stuff which poses as modern art," he said.

When Tommy himself turned up at the exhibit, a caretaker threatened to bounce him.

He tried to stand on his head in a corner.

Pacific Swamps Loyola 52-0

See Sports For Details

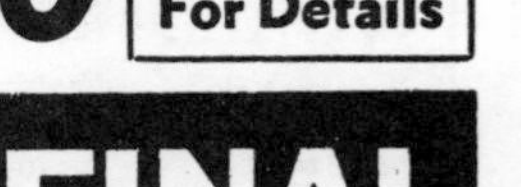

San Francisco Chronicle

THE CITY'S ONLY HOME-OWNED NEWSPAPER

FINAL

FOUNDED 1865—VOL. CLXIX, NO. 71 CCCCAAA SAN FRANCISCO, SATURDAY, SEPTEMBER 24, 1949 GA 1-1112 DAILY 7 CENTS, SUNDAY 15 CENTS

RUSS ATOM DISCLOSURE STIRS CONTROL DEMAND

THIS WORLD TODAY

By ROYCE BRIER

THE NEWS that the Russians have exploded an atom bomb is nothing for the West to get excited about.

It is naturally interesting, and warrants some of the discussion which was carried on about it yesterday. It re-emphasizes the certain and simple truth that technological achievement is not the unique gift of one people, or of a kind of people.

This fatuous concept has been advanced for four years by some unthinking and blatant elements in the West, attended by the implication that there was an atomic fission "secret" to be kept by the Americans. Under this implication, secrecy was made a fetish, heavily colored with a rare combination of chauvinism and xenophobia, hatred of foreigners.

There was never any secret about atomic fission. There was a series of secrets—a layman couldn't know how many, or have more than a superficial knowledge of their nature—about how to make an atomic bomb. We possessed this series for some time, but the Russians have now discovered some of them. Some we yet retain. The Russians will learn some of them by further experiment—by technological achievement. Whether they will learn all (we will continue to learn new secrets by experiment) in one year or fifty years, it is futile to conjecture.

All we can say now is that a non-American atomic bomb was inevitable. Given the will and the resources, any people can make one. All we can concede now is that there are differing rates of technological achievement in differing peoples. The Russian rate has always been slower than some Western rates. It may or may not remain slower for any visible future. The Russians undoubtedly had the help of captive German technical knowledge and skill in making and detonating a bomb.

And still, all this has no determinable bearing on the potential of the Russian accomplishment on the present structure of human relations. There is no historical evidence to support such a determination, whatever it might be to one or another observer, and so no rational cause for perturbation.

You have often heard it said, and you will hear more of it now, that when Russia gets the bomb (or a sufficient stockpile) she will be prepared to make an armed conquest of the West. But

Continued on Page 2, Col. 3

Football Rears Two Ugly Heads

Odd phenomena doubtless related to the 1949 football season popped up in the East Bay yesterday.

The big C. on the hills above the University of California campus, turned red overnight and sophomore students were buying up yellow paint to reconvert it.

Hiram Jacobs, University of California student, showed up with his head shaved bald, except for a hirsute outcropping in the form of the letter "S." As a companion piece, Bob Mires, fellow student, appeared with a shaved head adorned with an "M" in native hair.

Both said their hair-do's were acquired on the St. Mary's campus shortly after midnight.

Warren on Lobbyists

Luncheon Club Told of Formula To Curb Corruption

By EARL C. BEHRENS
Political Editor, The Chronicle

Governor Earl Warren yesterday laid before the Commonwealth Club a program for ridding California of "organized racketeers" and of curbing "sinister lobbyist" evils at Sacramento.

The Governor's suggestions were made at the Palace Hotel luncheon meeting as the closing remarks of his prepared speech on "California and Its Future."

Warren spoke extemporaneously on the organized crime and lobbyist subjects, which he pointed out had been occupying much attention in the newspapers and magazines.

The Governor said he believed "a few conspiracy trials of higher-ups" would clean out the organized racketeers, hoodlums and their ilk "who have given all law enforcement agencies a black eye in California."

Warren said some of the criticism of law enforcement was "deserved in some instances, undeserved in others." He paid tribute to the character and work of the "majority" of law enforcement officers.

"We do have organized criminals in California connected up with organized criminals in other parts of the country," said the Governor.

GAMBLING TIE-IN

He said that as long as "gambling and other lucrative rackets are permitted to operate," California would have "gang warfare, hoodlums, and killings."

Warren said he had asked creation of the Governor's Commission on Organized Crime in 1947 and its continuance in 1949 because of the "organized" crime in the State.

He stressed the fact that he did not have any law enforcement powers nor did the Commission on Organized Crime.

On the lobbyist issue, the Governor said it was up to the businessmen and organizations such as the Commonwealth Club to help see to

Continued on Page 8, Col. 4

Cal Cable Accord

Strike Settled; Service Will Resume Monday

The California street cable car strike was settled yesterday—with the help of a loan from the striking employees.

The company announced service will be restored Monday morning.

AFL carmen, who shut down the transit system on September 1 in a wage dispute, ratified the back-to-work agreement last night.

The settlement made it certain a charter amendment to provide for city purchase of the cable car lines would be placed on the November 8 ballot.

SETTLEMENT BASIS

Federal Conciliator Andrew J. Gallagher said the basis of settlement was an hourly wage rate of $1.506 payable "as of now" and to continue until the State Legislature ratifies the charter amendment.

The company's 148 crewmen walked out when directors announced wages would be cut from $1.484 to $1.36 because of falling revenue. The union had been negotiating for a raise to $1.506, which is the rate paid Municipal Railway carmen.

Gallagher said the settlement did not include retroactivity to July 1, when the former contract expired.

Both company officials and union officers were confident voters will approve the $150,000 purchase price.

This confidence was reflected in the fact the employees of the line dipped into a company-sponsored welfare fund to lend money to the management to finance the wage increase pending the November 8 election.

Whether the fund is large enough to continue supplying the wage increase until the Legislature meets next March was not disclosed by Theodore J. Roche, attorney for the company. In any event, the company will have gilt-edged credit once electors authorize the purchase.

Roche said the five employee-trustees of the welfare fund voted unanimously to finance operations until the election. The fund was set up by the company "a number of years ago" for the general welfare and financial security of employees, the attorney explained.

CRITICAL OF ESTIMATE

The directors were sharply critical of an estimate by City Controller Harry Ross that municipal operation of the system will cost $206,897 per year.

A spokesman said this estimate was "about $200,000 too high," and obviously had been based on figures supplied by the city's Public Utilities Commission, which is opposed to acquisition of the lines.

The spokesman said the difference between the $1.36 wage rate which could be met by revenues, and the $1.506 Municipal Railway rate, was only $4000 per month.

Ross's estimate was based on operations of the Powell street cable lines, which have an annual deficit of $185,000.

Ross prepared his figures under a charter provision which requires him to inform voters on financial aspects of all ballot propositions.

Eastern Daylight Time Ends Sunday

NEW YORK, Sept. 23 (AP)—Daylight saving timers get a 60-minute sleep dividend this Sunday.

Daylight saving for some 50,000,000 Americans in the Eastern time zone ends at 2 a. m. (EDT) Sunday when the clock is set back one hour earlier.

Truman Announces Soviet Explosion

It Occurred in Recent Weeks, the President Says; Scientists, Statesmen Cite Need for Curbs

Comment By Public Leaders

By the Associated Press

WASHINGTON, Sept. 23—An anxious clamor for international control of the vast destructive force of the atom arose tonight after President Truman indicated the Russians have broken the American A-bomb monopoly.

President Truman, Senators, scientists and many others joined in calling for agreement between Russia and non-Communist nations to clamp down effective curbs. So far all attempts at agreement have failed.

Mr. Truman's disclosure, though long anticipated, hit with a terrific impact in world capitals. Major international repercussions, with possibly a sharp change in the atmosphere of the East-West "cold war," were seen as inevitable.

But U. S. policymakers predicted it would not mean World War III. For one thing the United States has a four-year head start on atom bomb making.

BRADLEY'S ADVICE

The country's top military man, General Omar N. Bradley, counseled everybody to keep his head:

"The calmer the American people take this matter the better," said the chairman of the Joint Chiefs of Staff.

"We have anticipated it for four years and it calls for no change in our basic plan."

Bradley, as if to show he himself was not worried, spent part of the day playing golf.

On Capitol Hill, Senator Bryan McMahon (Dem-Conn.), chairman of the Senate-House Atomic Energy Committee, and several other members of Congress suggested anew that the vital hour has arrived for President Truman to meet with Premier Stalin.

McMahon suggested Mr. Truman might even go to Moscow for such a meeting, if that is the only place

Continued on Page 4, Col. 4

Rajk, 2 Others Sentenced to Die

BUDAPEST, Sept. 24 (AP)—Former Interior Minister Laszlo Rajk and two of his seven co-defendants in Hungary's treason trial were sentenced to death today (Saturday) by a people's court.

The other two sentenced to die were Dr. Tibor Szoenyi, former Member of Parliament and a Communist party official, and Andras Szalai, a party official.

Lazar Branko, counsel of the Yugoslav Embassy, was accused of treason and trying to overthrow the Government. He was sentenced to life imprisonment.

Brother Found After 27 Years

Frances Norton, 33, of 860 Waller street, was reunited in New York last night with a brother she had not seen for 27 years.

The brother, Associated Press dispatches said, is Abraham Cohen, 29, a linotype operator of Staunton, Va.

Probably A Bomb, Say Experts

By MILTON SILVERMAN
Chronicle Staff Writer

NEW YORK, Sept. 23—American and British scientists tonight greeted the announcement of a Russian atomic explosion with this grim verdict:

"We told you so."

Most of them had predicted in 1945, after the attack on Hiroshima, that the Russians would have the secret of atomic explosives "within three to 20 years."

President Truman's statement in Washington this morning that an atomic explosion had occurred in Russia "within recent weeks" was generally accepted as proof that the Russians had solved the atomic puzzle in four years.

PROBABLY A BOMB

It also appeared obvious that:

1—The detonation was that of an atomic bomb, and not the accidental explosion of a Russian atomic pile.

2—The Russians have at least one factory for full-scale production of more atomic bombs.

3—The United States, with or without British aid, has surrounded Russia and Siberia with a ring of strategically located detecting stations.

4—Any American political strategy based on a theory that "we have a monopoly on the bomb" is a dead duck.

Here and in Washington, however, atomic scientists and governmental officials claimed actual American policy has been based on the supposition that the Russians would get the bomb sooner or later. Now they have it sooner.

LITTLE SURPRISE

With but two exceptions, nobody indicated any surprise at this development.

One exception was the general public.

The other was Russian Foreign Minister Andrei Vishinsky. When the news reached the United Nations meeting at Flushing today, Vishinsky indicated that this was all a surprise to him.

In Atlantic City, Dr. Linus Pauling of the California Institute of Technology and President of the American Chemical Society told reporters the Russians had probably obtained the bomb secrets by their own research, without stealing them from this country.

"No espionage would have been necessary," he said.

THREE SOURCES

He declared the Russians had all the "secrets" they needed from three easily accessible sources:

1—The standard scientific journals which, as early as 1939, reported that atomic fission was possible.

2—The Hiroshima explosion, which proved that large-scale fission was effective, and that an atomic bomb would work.

3—The famous Smyth report, released by the United States Army, which indicated roughly how uranium and plutonium were prepared in the U. S. atomic bomb project.

But he and other experts scoffed

Continued on Page 4, Col. 2

Atom Story in Brief

WASHINGTON, Sept. 23 (AP)—Here is today's big atomic story in brief:

President Truman announced evidence that an atomic explosion occurred in Russia within recent weeks. Secretary of State Dean Acheson called it an atomic weapon.

This excited the world because the news (1) came sooner than the West had been led to expect and (2) men fear an atomic war would ruin the world.

What does it mean?

Probably that America no longer has the awful power of the bomb to itself. But she is years ahead of the Russians in developing it.

How about war?

State Department officials generally felt that evidence of one atomic bomb neither increased nor decreased this prospect.

What can be done?

Officials and Congressmen immediately chorused that international agreement on atomic energy control is the real solution. Efforts to reach accord with Russia have fallen flat in the past.

President Truman said the news emphasizes the necessity for "enforceable" world controls.

Secretary General Trygve Lie of the United Nations said that if Russia has the bomb, international agreement is "indispensable."

How did we learn about the Russian bomb?

Mr. Truman didn't even hint. Maybe it was espionage. But scientists have radiation-detection instruments which spot rays. It's barely possible that earthquake recorders may have picked up such evidence.

Sept. 23, 1949, takes its place among key dates in the atomic era. Others include:

July 16, 1945. First test explosion, set off in New Mexico.

Aug. 6, 1945. First use in warfare, on Hiroshima, Japan.

May 17, 1948. United Nations atomic commission announces deadlock on control plans after two years of work.

Vishinsky's Speech

Other Powers Skeptical of His Address to U. N.

By the United Press

FLUSHING, N. Y., Sept. 23—Soviet Foreign Minister Andrei Y. Vishinsky told the United Nations today Russia was not thinking of attacking anyone, and ignored President Truman's announcement of an atomic explosion in Russia.

Instead, Vishinsky called on the Big Five powers to negotiate a new pact "for strengthening of peace."

(Associated Press reported the other big powers were immediately skeptical of Russian sincerity.

(American Delegate Warren R. Austin issued a two-sentence statement to the press:

("It is the same propaganda as before. As for the proposal for a five-power pact, I must have more information of its substance before commenting."

(Britain, France and China were equally skeptical.)

In a major policy speech before the U. N. Assembly, the Russian spokesman condemned "preparations for a new war being conducted in a number of countries, particularly the United States and the United Kingdom."

RUSSIA IS READY

Although the Soviet Union is ready to answer "blow for blow," he said, it is not thinking of threatening or attacking anyone and is desirous of bringing about a peace pact between Russia, the United States, Britain, France and China.

Vishinsky spoke for 30 minutes and not once did he refer to the Washington announcement about the atomic bomb. He had said previously he might mention it if

Continued on Page 5, Col. 3

U. S.-British Union

State Department Exploring the Need For Closer Bonds

By CARROLL KILPATRICK
Washington Correspondent, The Chronicle

WASHINGTON, Sept. 23—A closer-knit organization of the English-speaking world than has ever before been thought possible is being seriously discussed and debated in high official quarters, it was learned today.

department's policy planning staff,

George F. Kennan, State Department counselor and chief of the is one of the officials here who believe closer relations must be established, particularly between the United States, Canada and Great Britain.

Kennan is the leading apostle and strategist of the post-war containment policy against Russia.

While no definite plans have been worked out, Kennan is understood to believe that the force of events will require officials in Washington, Ottawa and London to examine the practical aspects of the problem within the near future.

THE DIFFICULTIES

Some officials in the department are by no means as optimistic as Kennan that some form of union is possible, but they recognize that in many fields unity of operation is desirable and even inevitable if the Western world is to survive.

Kennan is understood to be fully aware of the enormous practical difficulties, but he is said to believe that the alternative to a stronger economic, political and military alliance represents the more hazardous course to follow.

Already this month two Anglo-American-Canadian conferences of far-reaching importance have been held here.

The first was the economic con-

Continued on Page 4, Col. 1

American Monopoly At an End

By the Associated Press

WASHINGTON, Sept. 23—An atomic explosion has occurred in Russia—a fateful portent that the Soviets have broken the American A-bomb monopoly on which the non-Communist world depended so heavily.

The historic news, comparable only in significance to the announcement of the Hiroshima blast of Aug. 6, 1945, was given to the world today by President Truman in these words:

"We have evidence that within recent weeks an atomic explosion occurred in the USSR."

Probably a Bomb

He did not say it was an atom bomb that exploded somewhere in the vast reaches behind the iron curtain. But Secretary of State Acheson said he assumed the blast was that of an atomic weapon—and there was every indication that the United States no longer is the sole possessor of the dread secret.

As matter of fact, a high U. S. Security official told a reporter tonight:

"There's no question about it. It was an atomic bomb. But so far as we know Russia has made only one bomb. They'll never catch up with us."

Need for Control

Acheson said the news came as no shock and it would not change the United States-sponsored plan for international control of atomic energy.

The formal statement from the White House was couched in calm tones.

"Ever since atomic energy was first released by man, the eventual development of this new force by other nations was to be expected," the President said. "This probability has always been taken into account by us."

The statement, released after the Chief Executive had called his Cabinet into an hour-long secret session, went on to say:

"This recent development emphasizes once again, if indeed such emphasis were needed, the necessity for that truly enforceable international control of atomic energy which this Government and the large majority of the members of the United Nations support."

Russia's Plan

Russia and her satellite nations have balked at the American plan for control of the A-bomb.

Russia has urged a plan of

Continued on Page 4, Col. 2

The Fog Is Back---People Are Wearing Coats Again

A sharp drop in the temperature yesterday ended San Francisco's six-day heat wave.

The hot spell which brought with it sizzling days, warm nights and frayed tempers started to break up Thursday evening with the weather "situation normal" by early yesterday.

Starting last Saturday temperatures steadily rose to a peak of 89 Thursday, the second hottest day of 1949, exceeded only by the 92 of June 2.

At noon yesterday the thermometer read 59, an even 30 degrees off the previous day's high. Morning fog paid a delayed visit to the city, followed by strong westerly winds in the afternoon. The temperature was not expected to rise above 68, exactly San Francisco's average temperature.

(Hour-by-hour chart of Thursday and Friday temperatures on Page 8.)

The break in the heat wave was caused by the moving eastward of a high-pressure system which has been covering Northern California, Oregon, Washington, Northern Nevada and Southern Idaho.

The clear, hot days were caused by the pressure system blocking off the strong, cooling westerly winds normal to this coast.

Absence of the winds, blowing from the sea and bringing to the land either cool or warm air, eliminated the temperature differences which caused fog.

The cooling weather spread over the Bay Area and is expected to extend into the Sacramento, Salinas and San Joaquin valleys by today, San Francisco District Forecaster R. C. Counts said.

In Oakland the warmest temperature recorded at the airport was 67 compared with 96 Thursday.

The Walnut Creek firehouse, where the thermometer hit 108 Thursday, recorded 89 yesterday.

Brentwood dropped off 6 degrees from Thursday's 100 and Antioch dropped from 94 to 88.

Meanwhile, Los Angeles was suffering from a record September 23 temperature of 102. The Indian summer there also is caused by a high-pressure system. Worst of the L. A. situation is not in the high temperature, but in the eye-stinging smog, limiting visibility in many sections to a few blocks, which has settled on the city for the sixth successive day.

Over the rest of the Nation the weather was seasonal with some exceptions.

East and Middle Atlantic States had some showers and storm warnings were hoisted in Gulf States because of rain squalls.

The Index

Herb Caen	9
Comics	11
Crossword Puzzle	17
Drama	6
Editorial:	
"Inevitable as Tomorrow"	10
Finance	12, 17
Lichty	2
Radio	11
Vital Statistics	7
Women's World	8

Bums Win Pair, Regain Lead

San Francisco Chronicle

THE CITY'S ONLY HOME-OWNED NEWSPAPER

FINAL

FOUNDED 1865—VOL. CLXIX, NO. 77 CCCCAAA SAN FRANCISCO, FRIDAY, SEPTEMBER 30, 1949 GA 1-1112 DAILY 7 CENTS, SUNDAY 15 CENTS

TOKYO ROSE GUILTY

Bookie Slain Here, Gang-Style

THIS WORLD TODAY

By ROYCE BRIER

TAEGLICHE RUNDSCHAU, the Red Army newspaper in Berlin, carries an article of advice to Germans on the status of women.

Embedded in it are a few entertaining bits of malarkey, as you would expect, but these should not blind us to the fact the piece is provocative, and perhaps even instructive.

It addresses the German woman directly, saying her husband "confines you to the household and to childbearing. Your place is certainly by your husband . . . but also in factories, offices and in public life."

"Many German men still appear to want their wives all to themselves. This is egotistic, and betrays a capitalistic-feudalistic tradition."

Now in Russia women are happier "because they enjoy equal privileges, not only in marriage, but also in public life." Russian women, says the article, have so much energy for public life, because there isn't much else to do. "Russia is so highly industrialized that practically all food is offered in a prepared form. This reduces cooking to a mere mechanical affair of half an hour. . ."

German women are advised that "even in capitalistic countries many married women have jobs of their own. But they are not independent, and they are forced to work, as their husbands do not earn enough to support the family."

Well, for years it has been noted by writers and sociologists that German women stick in the house, and German men have long been accused of being autocrats in their households.

There may be considerable reality to the underprivileged status of German women in our time. But writers and sociologists are mostly urban fellows. They hang around hotel suites and get a lot of their stuff by traipsing around city streets and in government bureaus.

And it is certainly true that German women have never taken much part in German public life.

But it is also a truth, known to casual travelers in Germany, that German country women are privileged to work in the fields. They sow turnips and harvest turnips, according to the season. They pitch hay and they plow. This is also true of Soviet women, tens of millions of them. It is true of the whole

Continued on Page 2, Col. 5

Test Vote In Britain

Laborites Win, 350-212, Against Censure Move

By the United Press

LONDON, Sept. 29 — The House of Commons tonight gave the Labor government a vote of confidence on its devaluation of the British pound sterling.

The vote for the government motion was 342 to 5. The Conservatives and Liberals abstained.

The negative votes were cast by Communists and independent laborites.

But the result, which was a certainty because of the big Labor majority in the House, did not quell the growing reports that the government will call a snap general election this autumn.

THREE-DAY DEBATE

The expected vote came after a hectic and bitter three-day "electioneering" debate during which the Labor government rejected opposition demands for early elections and suggested that Conservative Leader Winston Churchill "retire from public life."

The government motion gave approval to devaluation, to the agreements reached at the Washington conference and to the Socialist government's policy of maintaining full employment and the social services.

Churchill's motion of "no confidence" was defeated 350 to 212. That was the real test of strength. It would have placed full blame for devaluation on "four years financial mismanagement" by the Laborites.

RECORD OPPOSITION

The 212 votes in support of Churchill's motion equaled the record opposition vote established during the lifetime of the Parliament. The previous vote of 212 against the government came last December 17 on the bill to nationalize the iron and steel industry.

Although the debate was called to discuss the complicated devaluation problem, its consequences and "the very grave crisis" created by the action, most of the debaters used their time for what both sides charged was "electioneering."

(Attlee says Churchill is "always wrong." See Page 4.)

At Least 2 Die In C-82 Crash

McCLEARY, Wash., Sept. 29 (U.P.)—An Army C-82 "Flying Boxcar" crashed and burned four miles northwest of here tonight, killing at least two of the three crewmen aboard. A third man is still missing.

The plane, based at McChord Field, Wash., sheared off treetops for 1000 feet. A small brush fire was started.

The plane apparently attempted an emergency landing on the McCleary airstrip, an unlighted emergency field.

INSIDE THE CHRONICLE

A Big Week End---and The Sporting Green

Both major leagues are experiencing their wildest finishes in years. In the National, the Brooklyn Dodgers won two yesterday, while the St. Louis Cards were dropping a single game rocketing the Dodgers into first place. In the American League, the New York Yankees and the Boston Red Sox were still all tied up moving into the climatic week end. . . . The Chronicle Sporting Green gives you a box seat at these and other big events of one of sport's busiest week ends. Bill Leiser previews the national game-of-the-week (Michigan-Stanford) and picks Stanford by one point. . . . California's Golden Bears are favored over Oregon State by 14 points. Will Connolly will report the game in Sunday's Chronicle . . . Art Rosenbaum does some speculating about tonight's Loyola-USF game.

IT'S ALL IN THE SPORTING GREEN TODAY AND EVERY DAY

Labor News— A strike in "Big Steel" seems inevitable at Friday midnight . . . and there's more violence in the coal tie-up. Page 2.

Skid Road— "Credit is easy, but when do we eat?" Kevin Wallace's story and Howard Brodie's sketches of the men at the end of the road. On Page 7.

Shooting In Street

Marty Breslauer Led From Auto, Shot to Death

Martin D. (Marty) Breslauer, 61, a San Francisco bookie for three decades, was slugged to his knees and then shot through the heart on a Daly City street at dusk last night.

His two killers assisted him to the sidewalk, calmly walked back to their automobile, and were driven away by a third man.

The cold-blooded murder sent San Francisco and San Mateo county authorities into action to determine whether Breslauer was the victim of a gang war, or was killed by a personal enemy.

There was evidence to support either theory.

BROWN COMMENTS

Police pointedly refrained from favoring either one, but San Francisco District Attorney Edmund G. Brown commented:

"And people think this bookie business isn't serious."

Breslauer's widow gave officers the name of one suspect, and search was begun for a tenderloin character known as "Camel Joe."

Witnesses to the killing were so agape at the casual maner in which it was carried out that none obtained the license number of the gunmen's car.

All agreed on this sequence:

A few minutes after 6 p. m. a late-model blue, four-door sedan, stopped at the corner of Los Banos and San Diego streets, two blocks west of Mission street and about seven blocks over the San Francisco county line.

Breslauer, in the back seat with two other men, got out and started to walk to his own automobile, parked at the curb since 10 a. m. The two other men accompanied Breslauer.

As the three turned the rear of the blue sedan, one man slugged Breslauer, who sank to his knees with a cry for help.

TWO SHOTS FIRED

The other man fired two shots at the kneeling Breslauer with an automatic pistol.

The standing men then lifted Breslauer under the arms and took him to the sidewalk.

As they returned to the car and were driven away, Breslauer staggered into the doorway of a market at 198 Los Banos avenue.

"They robbed me and shot me," he gasped. Then he collapsed. He was dead on arrival at Junipero Serra Hospital.

The two men who got out of the car with Breslauer both wore tan hats. One had a tan jacket and the other a plaid jacket. One man was about 34 years old.

Mrs. Blanche Button, 28, 27 Wil-

Continued on Page 10, Col. 3

IVA TOGURI D'AQUINO

After hearing the verdict

(More pictures, page 5)

'Orphans of Pacific'

Jury Decides Toyko Rose Committed Treason in Her Broadcast on Leyte Gulf

Foreman Had Stood Firm in Favor Of Acquittal During Four Days of Debate---Was Last One to Give in

By STANTON DELAPLANE

Iva Toguri d'Aquino, stony-faced and silent, heard herself judged a traitor to her native United States at 6 o'clock last night.

Such was the end for Tokyo Rose of three months trial and four days of jury debate.

The jury stood evenly divided at 6-6 on its first ballot Monday. Foreman John Mann yesterday was the last man to give in. He had stood for acquittal throughout.

Tokyo Rose was found guilty on only one count of the eight acts charged against her by the United States:

"That on a day in October, 1944, the exact date being to the Grand Jurors unknown . . . she did broadcast into a microphone in the city of Tokyo in Japan concerning the loss of ships."

This was the famed broadcast testified to by a number of Japanese witnesses and war correspondents, that Tokyo Rose speaking of the Battle of Leyte Gulf, broke into her nostalgic recordings to tell South Pacific GIs:

"Orphans of the Pacific, you really are orphans now. How will you get home now that all your ships are sunk?"

MASS OF TESTIMONY

It was the testimony of War Correspondent Clark Lee, of Radio Tokyo's American-born handyman Ken Oki, of San Francisco's George Mitsushio that clamped the apple cart of Tokyo Rose.

"It was the mass of evidence," said one juror who clung to the acquittal side until the eleventh hour.

That was when the jury stood 9-3 for conviction.

The verdict came suddenly and unexpectedly to a courtroom thinned of spectators by boredom and the dinner hour. Judge Michael J. Roche had just suggested that the jury go to dinner.

They had asked for a clarification of certain of his instructions.

AFTER FEW MINUTES

But within five minutes they were back. This time it was the verdict which had eluded them through four days of debate.

Court Clerk James Welsh handed it to the Judge who read and without change of expression handed it back. Then Welsh read in a loud voice:

"Guilty!"

From the 40-odd spectators left in the courtroom there was an audible "Oh!"

It is an interesting point that most of the regular spectators who sat through 13 long weeks had concluded the 33-year-old Los Angeles girl was not guilty.

(The press table on a trial's-end ballot voted 9-1 for acquittal on all eight counts.)

Clerk Welsh read down the list of the acts charged:

"Do you find the act as charged in the indictment correct and true?"

In each case he read the answer: "No."

Until he came to No. 6. Then he read: "Yes."

This was enough to find Tokyo Rose guilty as charged.

It brought her the name of "traitor," a sentence of not less than five

Continued on Page 4, Col. 5

Gate Bridge Crash

20 Persons Hurt When Bus and Lumber Trucks Collide in Fog

A flat tire stalled an automobile on the Golden Gate bridge early yesterday under conditions of weather and traffic that created the worst series of accidents in the 12-year history of the span.

Twenty persons were hurt, two perhaps fatally, and nine sufficiently to require hospital treatment.

A Greyhound bus was mashed between two heavily laden trucks and its 43 passengers were hurled to the floor, pinned between twisted seats, and battered by flying scantlings.

At least a dozen automobiles piled up in a series of crashes.

At one time five of the bridge's six lanes were blocked; heavy southbound traffic was backed up for miles and did not resume normal flow until almost three hours after the first crash.

The most serious crash involved the bus, San Francisco bound from Mill Valley, and two tractor-semitrailer-trailer rigs, southbound from Willits with loads of two-by-fours and other heavy lumber.

The first truck, driven by Charles Buletti of Willits, had drawn to a halt in the outside southbound lane; slightly behind it, and in the adjoining or middle southbound lane, the bus was also halted.

In the outer lane, behind the stopped truck, feeling its way through the heavy fog at a speed estimated at no more than 5 miles an hour, was a passenger car driven by Ralph Akers of Bakersfield.

And behind Akers, also in the outer lane, was a second tractor-semitrailer-trailer rig, driven by William Wooley of Willits. Akers told highway patrolmen:

"I saw the stalled truck ahead of me. I heard brakes screetch behind me. In my rear view mirror, I saw a second truck bearing down on me; it swung into the second lane and ploughed into the rear end of the bus. It pushed the bus forward 15 or 20 feet, and sent it veering off to the right so that part of its front end was telescoped by the rear end of the truck-trailer ahead. Then flying lumber buried my car and I couldn't see anything more."

Subsequent examination showed that the rear end of the bus was battered in for a distance of three feet. The impact was so great that the entire lumber load of the trailer shifted forward eight or nine feet and carried the tractor cab with it.

The driver, Wooley, was crushed beneath the lumber that wiped off the cab and then spilled onto Akers' car. His condition was critical late yesterday.

Also in serious condition was Mrs. Louise McIntire of Mill Valley, who suffered broken ribs and a possible fracture of the back. She was riding in the forward section of the bus that was telescoped against the rear end of the first lumber truck.

Richard Sellman of Mill Valley, a bus passenger, told this story:

"I was in the last seat. The way I figure it, there was a truckload of lumber up ahead of us, and it was stopped, so the bus stopped. Somebody yelled 'Look out' and the first thing I knew a truck ploughed into us from behind.

"Everybody was down on the floor. I was caught between two seats and couldn't move. People from outside came in with two-by-fours and pried

Continued on Page 15, Col. 1

45-Mile Limit Goes in Effect On Gate Bridge

A speed limit of 45 miles per hour will be put in effect on the Golden Gate Bridge following yesterday's multiple crash.

The speed limit goes into effect tomorrow and the Highway Patrol has announced it will be rigidly enforced.

For pictures on yesterday's crash and safety measures being considered to prevent future wrecks, as well as a diagram of how the big crash occurred, see Pages 9 and 15.

Three-Way House Race

Cosgrove, Garry, Shelley Qualify for Fifth District Post

By EARL C. BEHRENS
Political Editor, The Chronicle

San Francisco's Fifth District congressional race yesterday became a three-candidate affair certain to attract national notice at the special November 8 election.

The three candidates will be Lloyd J. Cosgrove, attorney; Charles R. Garry, attorney, and John F. Shelley, State AFL president and Labor Council secretary.

Shelley has already qualified for a ballot place with 10,653 valid signatures out of the 12,771 he filed with Registrar Thomas A. Toomey Wednesday.

To qualify required 9469 valid signatures.

Cosgrove, accompanied by members of his family and Garrett Welch, Sonoma county rancher and son of the late Congressman Richard J. Welch, visited the Registrar yesterday and filed his petitions. They contained 13,479 signatures. He seeks election to the place of the late Representative Welch, which will be filled at the special election.

A test of the names on the Cosgrove petitions showed he would have sufficient signatures to qualify.

Shortly after Cosgrove filed, Garry arrived with additional petitions. He said a total of 18,000 signatures were on his petitions.

A spot check of the Garry names showed that 6591 out of the first 8340 filed were valid.

Garry was accompanied by Mrs. Garry, Benjamin Dreyfus, treasurer of his campaign, and his law partner, Julius Keller.

Yesterday was the deadline for filing petitions for those seeking to qualify for the November 8 Congressional election ballot.

Registrar Toomey expected to have all of the petitions checked immediately, since next Tuesday is the last date upon which they can be certified to the Secretary of State.

Toomey will send one of his deputies to Sacramento with the certifications Tuesday.

(Candidates' statements and pictures, Page 18.)

Quiet Reigns In The Dalles

Police Keep Pickets Away From 'Hot' Pineapple Dock

Special to The Chronicle

THE DALLES, Ore., Sept. 29—This quiet Columbia river grain port was tense today following yesterday's raid by CIO longshore pickets on a barge-load of "hot" Hawaiian pineapple.

State police carrying riot guns, with fixed bayonets, cleared pickets from the waterfront area where they had injured six truck drivers and damaged unloading equipment in yesterday's outburst.

All persons without special permits were ordered out of the dock district.

Fearful of further clashes, The Dalles Dock Commission asked the Hawaiian Pineapple Co. to take their barge out of the port.

The request was made, the commission said, in order "to protect the community from further violence and for the protection of property."

There was no immediate reply from the company.

In Portland, police armed with tommy guns were dispatched to the Northern Pacific Railroad yards after two truck drivers had been beaten.

The drivers had brought Hawaiian pineapple from Tillamook where it was quietly unloaded from a barge Tuesday.

Automobiles loaded with long-shore reinforcements began arriving here during the morning.

The dock workers poured into town from Portland and other downriver ports despite an injunction prohibiting further picketing of the "hot" pineapple barge.

Some 18 local nonunion workers were unloading the barge before pickets disrupted operations.

Local men, many in 10-gallon cowboy hats and high-heeled boots, warily eyed longshoremen as they circulated through downtown The Dalles handing out pamphlets which blamed the "pineapple kings of Hawaii," and the "dictators of Hawaii" for yesterday's violence.

Pickets ousted from the docks stared sullenly over a narrow strip of "no man's land" near the terminal where 35 blue-uniformed State police stood guard.

Continued on Page 2, Col. 6

Two Transports To Dock Today

The Army troop transports will arrive this morning from the Orient.

The General A. W. Brewster, with 852 military and 69 civilian passengers from Yokohama, will dock at 8 a. m., Pier 2 West, Fort Mason.

The General W. F. Hase, carrying 974 military and civilian passengers from Yokohama, Guam and Manila, will tie up at 10 a. m. at Pier 2 East, Fort Mason.

Foreign Aid Bill Passes Both Houses

WASHINGTON, Sept. 29 (AP)—The Senate tonight passed a $5,809,990,000 bill for foreign economic aid, already approved by the House, and sent it to the White House.

Senate approval of the huge aid measure was by voice vote. The House had passed the bill earlier in the day with little more than token opposition.

(For details, see Page 4.)

The Index

Herb Caen	21
Comics	18
Chess by Mail	29
Crossword Puzzle	29
Drama	16, 17
Editorial: "Question Mark Remains in Pink Tag Party"	22
Finance	24, 25
Liebly	19
Radio	23
Vital Statistics	19
Women's World	12, 13, 14

The Right Key

When Mrs. M. Yepez, 836 Webster street, wanted to sell a leather bar and a pair of stools, she turned to the Bargain Counter. "We sold the bar on the first day," says Mrs. Yepez, pleased with the results, "and call that pretty fast work. Other methods just didn't pull for us."

Opening doors and bringing the seller's message to buyers is The Chronicle Bargain Counter's specialty. Satisfied users have found that the Bargain Counter brings results, reaches prospects for those spare household items.

Turn your unwanted household items into extra cash. It's easy and inexpensive when you use the Bargain Counter. Just call GA 1-1112 and an experienced ad-taker will assist you.

Clergy Candidates Must Take Mental Tests

By CAROLYN ANSPACHER

A resolution requiring that psychiatric or psychological examinations, or both, be given all postulants and candidates for holy orders was unanimously adopted yesterday by the House of Bishops of the Protestant Episcopal Church.

The action was taken during the church's triennial general convention at the Civic Auditorium on motion of Bishops Benjamin M. Washburn of Newark, N. J., and Henry W. Hobson of Southern Ohio.

The matter now comes before the House of Deputies for concurrence.

The resolution emphasizes that church canons already provide that the examination of an applicant shall cover mental and nervous, as well as physical condition, and adds:

"A man's intellectual and spiritual capacity will fit him for the exercise of a useful ministry only if it is accompanied by a mental and nervous stability."

The Bishops drafting the resolution explained that in many dioceses standard psychiatric examinations already are being given applicants.

So far, the Bishops declared, there has been unanimous testimony from dioceses as to the importance and value of such examinations.

In at least ten of the dioceses questioned, the Rorschach test is being used with good results. Others mentioned use of the Minnesota-Multiphasic Personality Inventory, Goodenough, Szondi, Wechsler-Bellevue Intelligence Scale and the Strong Vocational Tests.

"Ultimate decision as to the admission of a postulant quite properly rests solely with the Bishop of a diocese," the Bishops' statement said. "It is neither desirable nor proper that we should be relieved of our responsibility. The responsibility is grave. For its right discharge there are certain areas in which each of us needs expert counsel and advice from those well qualified to give it."

1950-1959

FEBRUARY 1, 1950
Super Bomb Started

JUNE 28, 1950
Seoul Captured by Reds

JUNE 29, 1950
MacArthur in Korea

JULY 1, 1950
Yank Troops Move to Front

AUGUST 27, 1950
18 Dead in Ship Disaster

NOVEMBER 2, 1950
Plot to Shoot Truman Fails

APRIL 11, 1951
General MacArthur Fired

APRIL 18, 1951
Thousands Cheer MacArthur

JANUARY 16, 1952
Streamliner 'City of San Francisco' Snowbound at Yuba Gap

FEBRUARY 6, 1952
King George Dead — Elizabeth Is Queen

APRIL 9, 1952
U.S. Seizes Steel — Strike Is Off

JUNE 3, 1952
Steel Shut Down — Seizure Ended

JULY 22, 1952
Tehachapi Quake Kills 11

NOVEMBER 5, 1952
It's Ike — Landslide for GOP

MARCH 6, 1953
Stalin Dead

JUNE 2, 1953
British Expedition Conquers Mount Everest; Queen Elizabeth Crowned

JUNE 20, 1953
Rosenbergs Die at Sing Sing

JULY 27, 1953
War Is Over — Armistice in Korea

MAY 8, 1954
Dien Bien Phu Captured

MAY 18, 1954
Court Bans Segregated Schools

JULY 21, 1954
Indo-China Peace Signed — Vietnam Split Approved

APRIL 14, 1955
Olson Floors Maxim Twice

OCTOBER 1, 1955
Crash Kills James Dean

JULY 26, 1956
Andrea Doria Hits Big Liner

OCTOBER 25, 1956
Hungary Revolt Spreads

OCTOBER 30, 1956
Egypt, Israel Clash Near Suez

NOVEMBER 7, 1956
Ike Landslide; French, British Seize Suez

SEPTEMBER 25, 1957
Ike Sends Army to Little Rock; H-Bomb Test by Russia

OCTOBER 5, 1957
Russian Satellite Sighted Over S.F.

JULY 1, 1958
Alaska Statehood

MARCH 13, 1959
Hawaii Statehood

THIS WORLD TODAY

San Francisco Chronicle

THE CITY'S ONLY HOME-OWNED NEWSPAPER

FINAL

FOUNDED 1865—VOL. CLXX, NO. 17 CCCCAAA SAN FRANCISCO, WEDNESDAY, FEBRUARY 1, 1950 GA 1-1112 DAILY 7 CENTS, SUNDAY 15 CENTS

WORK ON THE SUPER-BOMB STARTED, PRESIDENT HINTS

'Expendable' in Global War?

By ROYCE BRIER

U. S. News and World Report carries a page of Washington gossip, not frivolous gossip, but brief reports about serious affairs. It is called "Whispers."

About a month ago "Whispers" contained the following item:

"Under the new concepts of national defense, formulated by the dominating group of military planners, the West Coast is considered 'expendable,' while attention is centered on the East Coast and on Europe.

"Russia is concentrating much of her growing naval power in the Pacific, while U. S. is forced to disperse its dwindling power at sea, so that there isn't enough to go around."

You will remember Thermopylae. It is the most famous case in all history of the most famous animal strategy of all natural history, for, the little foxes pursue it when need be, as well as men.

But just in case it has slipped your mind, there was the great Xerxes coming down into Greece in 480 B.C. with his horde, and the little Greeks were out to stop him. The Spartan King Leonidas put forth with a few thousand men with that purpose.

The Joint Chiefs

Now the ephors, a sort of Joint Chiefs of Staff, were rather luke-warm about Leonidas's strategy, and wanted to make a stand somewhere else, but Leonidas chose the Pass of Thermopylae, a trail about fifty feet wide between the mountain and the sea.

Leonidas had only 300 men in the clutch, and still for most of a day he was doing all right, axing down the Persians as fast as they clambered up the trail.

Then a shoddy fellow named Ephialtes went over to Xerxes, and showed one of the Persian captains a roundabout mountain path which brought a force in behind Leonidas. That did it. Leonidas and all his men, taken in reverse as we say, were exterminated.

And ever since, (and before, of

Continued on Page 2, Col. 1

Storm Is Moving In

Short Respite Expected From the Cold Wave

A storm of moderate intensity moved toward San Francisco from the Pacific yesterday.

The forecaster said it was expected to reach here by nightfall, bringing rain locally and snow in Northern California foothills and mountains, and with slightly warmer temperatures everywhere. But after Thursday, another icy chill was in prospect, he added.

"There is yet no definite indication of a break in the steady flow of cold air down from the north which has persisted for a month," said Forecaster R. C. Counts.

Recent rains were blamed by authorities for a landslide that closed the Niles canyon road for several hours early yesterday.

Tons of boulders and earth and scrub oaks roared down onto the narrow, twisting road about midway between Niles and Sunol.

John Adams, 35, of Kilgore Woods near Sunol, was driving down the canyon about 5 a. m. when he noticed a few rocks tumble off the hillside onto the road ahead. When the rocks turned to boulder-size, Adams slammed on the brakes, shoved his car into reverse and backed out of the danger zone.

Other trucks and cars blocked by the slide had to back out of the canyon. Highway crews cleared the obstruction in a few hours.

Icy conditions on highways over the Sierra and the Siskiyous made tire chains necessary, the California State Automobile Association reported.

Snow was 96 inches deep at Soda Springs.

Missouri Still Stuck in Mud

Fourth Refloating Effort Fails; Rock May Be Holding Ship

Picture on Page 12

By the United Press

NORFOLK, Va., Jan. 31—Three thousand men and 14 tugs made a fourth, but futile, attempt today to dislodge the battleship Missouri from a Hampton Roads mudbank and one official voiced fear the giant was fast "on a rock."

Meantime, a Navy tug and merchantman, the 7465-ton U. S. Lines freighter Steel Navigator, also ran aground during the thick fog that cloaked the tremendous push-and-pull dislodging operation.

The tug worked itself free after repeated efforts, and a commercial tug went to the aid of the freighter which was fast about three miles from the grounded Missouri on the opposite side of the channel.

The herculean effort to refloat the Missouri was billed as a "dress rehearsal" for another all-out attempt Thursday when the tide will be at its highest since the ship ran aground January 17.

Rear Admiral Homer N. Wallin, commandant of the Norfolk shipyard, said he believed the Missouri had plowed into a huge rock when it settled in the shoal.

He said Navy divers have been unable to burrow far enough under the hull to find out what is holding the ship.

Another "dress rehearsal" for the all-out effort will be held tomorrow.

But officials made clear they were pinning their faith on Thursday's operation, although they were "hopeful" of success tomorrow.

If both efforts fail, three destroyers will be sent at high speed close to the battleship to throw up heavy waves which might rock the big dreadnaught and possibly help the tugs free her.

Two Children Die In Salinas Fire

Special to The Chronicle

SALINAS, Jan. 31—Daniel Romero, 4 and his sister, Mary, 3, died tonight in a fire which swept through one room of their home.

The mother, Mrs. Lupe Romero, told police she was eating at a nearby restaurant when the fire broke out.

The little girl was dead by the time firemen reached her. The boy died a short time after he was carried unconscious from the burning house.

Track Down Lost Articles

It's not easy to recover lost property in a big city like San Francisco. When you use Chronicle Want Ads, however, you reach a wide audience and your chances of finding lost articles are greatly improved.

When Miss D. M. Fowler, 161 Battery street, lost her purse near the Ferry Building, there was no identification in it, and she had little hope of getting it back. An ad in The Chronicle, which ran three days, brought a call from the finder and the return of the purse. Happy to have found it, Miss Fowler gratefully thanks Chronicle Want Ads for her success.

Recover your lost valuables through the Lost and Found columns of The Chronicle. The cost is small for reaching a large, diversified audience when you use Chronicle Want Ads.

Truman Acts In Coal Strike

President Calls for 'Normal' Work and Talks on Contract

By the United Press

WASHINGTON, Jan. 31—President Truman proposed today that John L. Lewis and the coal operators resume "normal production" Monday while they negotiate their contract dispute, or that they agree to a fact-finding board outside the Taft-Hartley law.

His settlement formula held the implied threat that he will invoke the politically distasteful Labor-Management Act if his plan is turned down.

He set noon (EST) Saturday as the deadline for a reply on his first suggestion. If this is rejected, he said, he wants to know by 5 p. m. (EST) the same day whether the miners will return to the pits for 70 days while a fact-finding board investigates.

VOLUNTARY METHODS

The President underscored it is "national policy" to try to settle such disputes by voluntary methods. But then he added:

"The Government can no longer stand by, however, and permit the continuance of conditions which now have come to have such a serious effect upon the public interest."

Mr. Truman deliberately did not define "normal production," but aides said he would be satisfied with the three-day work week imposed by Lewis last December.

General Counsel Robert N. Denham of the National Labor Relations Board is scheduled to ask the Federal courts tomorrow for an injunction against the short work week as an unfair labor practice.

A JOB FOR LEWIS

Acceptance of the President's proposal would confront Lewis with the task of persuading more than 105,000 rebellious coal miners to end their "wildcat" walkout. They have ignored his "suggestion" that they resume the three-day week.

The President outlined his proposal in telegrams to Lewis and leading Southern, Northern and Western soft coal producers.

Taft-Hartley fact-finding boards are limited to a mere statement of the facts and can not suggest a settlement.

Marine Museum Talks Today

Plans for the development of Aquatic Park as a maritime museum will be discussed today at the first meeting of a citizens' committee recently appointed by Mayor Elmer E. Robinson.

Edward Harms, operating manager of Pope & Talbot Co., chairman of the committee, said the group would organize and prepare its plans for the acquisition of a number of sailing vessels, which would be presented to the city and installed at the park for a permanent display.

The Trial Of Bridges

Robert Kenny Spars With Prosecution

By ALVIN D. HYMAN

Robert W. Kenny, former Attorney General and Democratic candidate for Governor of California, spoke three short words in defense of Harry Bridges yesterday.

Asked for his opinion of Bridges' reputation for truth, honesty and integrity, he testified in the Court of Federal Judge George B. Harris: "It is good."

Then, taken over for cross-examination by F. Joseph Donohue, chief prosecutor, Kenny used several thousand more words, larded with such names as Franklin D. Roosevelt, Dean Acheson, Justice Wiley Rutledge, Wendell Willkie, Culbert Olsen, John Gunther and Frank Sinatra, to defend his use of the adjective "good."

His testimony served to enliven the 44th court day in the trial of Bridges, Henry Schmidt and J. R. Robertson on charges of perjury and conspiracy that grew out of Bridges' naturalization in 1945. The Government charges that Bridges lied by denying that he was ever a member of the Communist party.

SCHMIDT BACK

When Kenny stepped down after his hard-swinging verbal joust with Donohue, the defendant Schmidt resumed the witness stand to undergo a dogged cross-examination. For the rest of the day, Donohue chipped away at Schmidt's direct testimony in an attempt to show that this defendant conspired with Bridges to hide the alleged Communist membership.

At day's end Donohue estimated that another hour or two would end his concern over Schmidt—an estimate indicating that the defendant Robertson may be called to the stand today, and that Bridges, himself, may be on the witness stand before the week is over.

It was Kenny, the veteran lawyer, bank director and oil man, the former Superior Judge and former State Senator, who stole yesterday's courtroom show.

SCHNEIDERMAN CASE

Donohue wanted to know just who had ever discussed Bridges' "good reputation" with Kenny, and Kenny mentioned Justice Rutledge of the U. S. Supreme Court, Governor Olsen, and John Gunther.

Donohue suggested that Kenny had once defended William Schneiderman, Communist party leader, in a naturalization case; Kenny said yes, he and Wendell Willkie were attorneys for Schneiderman, and won their case in the U. S. Supreme Court.

Donohue said Kenny, as a State Senator, had fought legislation to outlaw the Communist party in California and Kenny said, yes, so he had—and the State Supreme Court later upheld his contention that the legislation was unconstitutional.

Donohue asked about Kenny's speeches before the American Youth for Democracy — successor to the Young Communist League — and Kenny said he appeared there with General Evan Carlson of the Marines. "Now deceased?" asked Donohue. "Yes," said Kenny, "and also a speaker was Frank Sinatra, now alive."

Donohue let the jury of eight men and four women know that Kenny

Continued on Page 2, Col. 1

Good Will Head In S. F. Dies

Monroe H. Hess, executive director of Good Will Industries' San Francisco unit, died last night at Stanford Hospital after a long illness. He was 56.

Mr. Hess was a member of the Official Board of Temple Methodist Church and a trustee of the California Annual Conference of the Methodist Church.

He leaves his widow, Elma Hess, and a son, Monroe Jr.

Funeral services will be held Friday at 1:30 p. m. from Nat C. Maneely Mortuary, 1363 Divisadero street.

S. F. Widow Gives $50,000 To the Shriners' Hospital

A gift of $50,000 by Annunziata Sanguinetti of 1100 Union street to the Shriners' Hospital for Crippled Children was announced yesterday.

It is the largest cash contribution ever received by that institution from a living person.

Mrs. Sanguinetti said the presentation was made in memory of her husband, Joseph, and her late sons, Louis and Attilio, who were members of the Islam Temple of Shriners.

The late Mr. Sanguinetti came to San Francisco in 1876 and opened a restaurant and grocery store at 1 Vallejo street, later transferring his business to the North Beach district.

The San Francisco hospital is one of 16 orthopedic institutions maintained by the Shriners for care of crippled children unable to pay for treatment, regardless of color, race or religion.

Dread New Hydrogen Weapon

Truman Tells the AEC to Continue Research On 'All Forms' of Nuclear Explosives

British and French Are Approving

By the United Press

LONDON, Jan. 31—President Truman's announcement that the United States was working on the hydrogen bomb hit war-fearful Europe tonight with an explosive force of its own.

Political and diplomatic leaders foresaw a terrible race between America and Soviet Russia for development of weapons of destructive power almost beyond human conception.

A British scientific leader and a French Parliament member were first to greet the President's announcement as right.

The British Communist party and the "Red" Dean of Canterbury were first to criticize it.

Newspapers bannerlined the news and radios blared it in all European capitals. Some radio newscasts were devoted entirely to the President's announcement.

(The announcement was broadcast in a score of languages to foreign listeners by the "Voice of America" radio. State Department officials said the development was reported on a straight news basis much as it was handled by the American press and radio.)

BRITISH SCIENTIST

"Only a half-wit would believe the H-bomb could be banned," said Professor A. M. Low, president of the British Institute of Engineering. "You might as well try to ban influenza."

"President Truman's decision was wise and sensible. It is his duty to defend the United States. Therefore, if he can get a bomb that will blow everyone to hell he's obviously right.

"There can be no doubt that Russia knows something about the theory of the H-bomb. But I don't think the Russians are as far ahead in hydrogen bomb development."

Dr. C. J. Bakker, Professor of Experimental Physics at the University of Amsterdam, said the United States might well have its first hydrogen bomb within one year.

FRENCH VIEW

Marcel Anxionna, formerly chairman of the army committee of the French National Assembly, said in Parliament in Paris tonight:

"It is high time Mr. Truman facilitated development of the H-bomb. After Russia's recognition of the rebel government in Indo-China it is certainly time Mr. Truman made such a move."

Harry Pollitt, secretary of the British Communist party, called the President's announcement "the logical outcome of American war policy," adding:

"If the aim is to intimidate peace-loving nations it will fail in the same manner that the supposed monopoly of the atomic bomb failed."

But, pointing to speculation that atomic weapons might destroy the world, Pollitt continued:

"People must be roused to demand abolition of the atom bomb, prohibition of the manufacture of the hydrogen bomb, withdrawal of American bombers and Air Force from Britain and the signing of a peace pact between Britain, America, France, China and Russia."

The Very Rev. Hewlett Johnson, "Red" Dean of Canterbury, said, when informed of the President's announcement:

"I regret to hear it."

More Atomic Developments

Most scientists approve President Truman's go-ahead order on the hydrogen super-bomb, but all are not sure of the weapon's practicability.

The New York Times science writer, William L. Laurence says the newest bomb is a T-bomb, not an H-bomb—T for Triton.

Bernard Baruch hails the decision as "necessary to the peace of the world" until Russia agrees to effective international atomic control and inspection.

Atomic Energy Commission's semi-annual report to Congress says atom bomb development and stockpiling continued at a growing pace last year.

For details, see Page 4.

Surplus Potatoes

It Looks As If U. S. Will Destroy 50 Million Bushels

By the Associated Press

WASHINGTON, Jan. 31—Unless Congress orders otherwise, the Government is going to throw away 50,000,000 bushels of surplus potatoes acquired under the farm price support program.

The potatoes cost the Government an average of about $2.25 a bushel. Counting the throwaway and other potato operations on which it took losses, the Government stands to lose a total of $80,000,000 to $100,000,000 on last year's spud crop.

It lost nearly $250,000,000 on the 1948 crop, however.

(A spokesman for the State Production and Market Authority in Berkeley said no potatoes are being dumped in California. PMA is the agency which buys crops under the Government price support program.)

Secretary of Agriculture Charles F. Brannan broke the bad news today to the Senate Agriculture Committee. Chairman Harold D. Cooley (Dem-N.C.) of the House Agriculture Committee sat in. So did Republican Senators Owen Brewster and Margaret Smith from potato growing Maine.

The Department of Agriculture has been trying to get shut of the surplus by giving them away for school lunches, to local and overseas relief agencies, and by diverting them for livestock feed and the manufacture of alcohol and starch.

Even so, Brannan figures he's going to have close to 50,000,000 bushels left.

The cheapest way to get rid of them, he advised Congress, is to dump them where raised. He didn't go into details, but this could mean piling them up in fields to rot, or burning them, or spraying dye on them so they could not be diverted into the market.

Senator Clinton P. Anderson (Dem-N. M.), who preceded Brannan as Secretary of Agriculture, said Congress ought to do one of two things: Let the department control production by limiting the number of bushels that could be grown, or simply drop the whole potato price support program.

As the law now stands, the department has to support potatoes at not less than 60 per cent of parity which is a legal standard for measuring farm prices designed to give farmers the same purchasing power they enjoyed in past years.

The department has called for a 6 per cent reduction in potato acreage this year. The problem is complicated by the fact that per capita consumption by Americans has hit an all-time low of 106 pounds. Americans were eating 138 pounds a year in 1934.

Quirino to Leave Hospital Today

BALTIMORE, Jan. 31 (AP)—President Elpidio Quirino of the Philippines plans to leave Johns Hopkins tomorrow morning after two weeks of convalescence. The President was operated on January 16 for removal of a kidney stone.

The Index

Chess by Mail	3
Comics	4H
Bill Leiser	1H
Contract Contacts	5
Crossword Puzzle	22
Bob de Roos	13
Drama	8, 9
Editorial: "Walrus and the Carpenter"	12
Finance	18, 21
Lichty's Cartoon	15
Radio	21
Vital Statistics	11
Weather Map	11
Woman's World	6, 7

Congress Reaction Is Varied

By the Associated Press

WASHINGTON, Jan. 31—"I pray God that we may never have to use it."

That fervently spoken comment by Senate Majority Leader Scott Lucas of Illinois summed up congressional reaction today to President Truman's announcement that the United States is going to try to make the world's most devastating weapon—the hydrogen bomb.

"The free peoples of the world know that this country will not use a bomb of this kind—or any other bomb—unless we are attacked by an aggressor," Lucas said. "I am confident that the potentiality of destruction that is involved in the hydrogen bomb will ultimately be the instrument which will bring mankind to its senses."

As the news of Mr. Truman's go-ahead order spread over Capitol Hill, other Senators and Representatives added their words of sober comment, mostly in approval, but with a few dissenters.

UNANIMOUS APPROVAL

Senator Brien McMahon (Dem-Conn.), chairman of the Joint Congressional Atomic Energy Committee, told reporters the White House decision met with the "unanimous approval" of the 18-member committee.

But Representative W. Sterling Cole (Rep-N. Y.), a committee member, said later that he does not approve of Mr. Truman's action, which he declared was a "usurpation of congressional authority."

"This epochal decision goes beyond the security of the United States," Cole said. "The security of mankind is also at stake."

The New Yorker's statement said the President has assumed individual responsibility "in a matter involving military, social and moral consequences of such profound and permanent implications that only the people of this Nation should determine after a full understanding of the factors involved."

ONLY COURSE

But Senator Millard Tydings (Dem-Md.), chairman of the Senate Armed Services Committee, said he thinks the President has taken "the only course possible under the existing circumstances."

Tydings, who also is a member of the Joint Congressional Atomic Energy Committee, added:

"All of us wish that atomic control with proper inspection would make it unnecessary to proceed with the hydrogen bomb. So long as that control and that inspection can't be maintained, we have no alternative except to keep America strong where no nation can attack us without fear of equal or more potent attack."

Chairman Carl Vinson (Dem-Ga.) of the House Armed Services Committee likewise observed that the President "has done the right and proper thing."

But Senator Arthur V. Watkins (Rep-Utah) declared "the whole country ought to be consulted about a decision like this." He said "Congress as a whole hasn't been given sufficient information from which to make any intelligent decision on the President's action."

On the other side of the Capitol there was a scattering of applause when Representative Chet Holifield (Dem-Calif.) interrupted House debate on a cotton acreage bill to break the news.

"In my opinion," he said, "it is the most important announcement of our time."

Measure Called Vital To Defense

By the Associated Press

WASHINGTON, Jan. 31—President Truman today gave the fateful order for development of the hydrogen super-bomb so that the United States may defend itself "against any possible aggressor."

Mr. Truman indicated that the Nation's atomic scientists may already have started tackling the problem of creating a weapon far surpassing the destructive fury of the A-bomb.

The President said:

"I have directed the Atomic Energy Commission to continue its work on all forms of atomic weapons, including the so-called hydrogen or superbomb.

"Like all other work in the field of atomic weapons, it is being and will be carried forward on a basis consistent with the over-all objectives of our program for peace and security."

MONTHS OF DEBATE

Reputedly five to 1000 times more devastating than the atomic bombs dropped on Japan during World War II, the H-bomb has been the subject of behind-the-scenes debate for at least four months.

The cost of producing the new superweapon has been variously estimated at $100,000,000 to $4,000,000,000.

Mr. Truman said he gave the historic order because "it is part of my responsibility as Commander in Chief of our Armed Forces to see that our country is able to defend itself against any attack."

He said he has directed the AEC to press forward with the development of atomic weapons, including the H-bomb, "until a satisfactory plan for international control of atomic energy is achieved."

WAYS AND MEANS

Within two hours after Mr. Truman's announcement, the Senate-House Atomic Committee set to work with the Atomic Energy Commission (AEC) to chart "ways and means and plans" for building the H-bomb.

Chairman Brien McMahon (Dem-Conn.) told newsmen "the utmost speed is necessary," but he did not explain why.

Mr. Truman's announcement clearly took committee members by surprise. The President had said last week that he alone had the power of decision—a statement which ruffled some lawmakers—and there were indications today that the committee had not expected a presidential announcement before next week.

The committee had been expected to make its own recommendation in a few days, and there were suggestions that Mr. Truman had "jumped the gun."

ARMAMENT RACES

McMahon also declared there should be "a nation-wide discussion"—not on the merits of building the H-bomb itself, but on armament races "and how they can be halted in the interests of the peace of the world."

Asked if he favored a new approach to Russia, which so far has blocked the American plan for international atomic control and inspection, McMahon replied:

"Wait and see."

He said he would have more to say along that line in the Senate later this week.

Mr. Truman's statement gave no hint of a possible attempt to renew atomic negotiations with Russia. But he did say:

As Bricklayers, Much Underpaid

Street Repairmen Win $4000 Back Pay

The District Court of Appeals yesterday awarded two municipal street repairmen more than $2000 each in back pay—and Internal Revenue Collector James G. Smyth stepped in line ahead of them for his share of back income taxes.

Winners of the award were William G. Randall and Hugh McGill, both city pavers. Their duties required them to replace the bricks and cobble stones on such streets as California and Powell.

They contended they were not pavers, who were getting $13.50 a day in 1947 when they filed their suit for more money, but bricklayers who then got $18 a day.

They had cards in the AFL bricklayers' union to prove it. They based their suit on the charter provisions that require city employees be paid the same rate as private industry workers performing comparable duties.

The suit went through the courts and finally ended yesterday. Now the rate for bricklayers, according to Secretary William Henderson of the municipal service commission, is $34 a day.

"The men will have about $2000 each coming in back pay under the ruling," Henderson said.

Smyth added:

"We'll collect our share, figuring the wage each year and applying the appropriate tax rate."

Henderson commented that the decision, which he does not think will be appealed to the State Supreme Court, may encourage other workers to join unions and demand higher pay.

Seals and Oaks Both Win

See Sports

San Francisco Chronicle
THE CITY'S ONLY HOME-OWNED NEWSPAPER
FINAL

FOUNDED 1865—VOL. CLXX. NO. 164 CCCCAAA—CP SAN FRANCISCO, WEDNESDAY, JUNE 28, 1950 GA 1-1112 DAILY 7 CENTS, SUNDAY 15 CENTS

CAPTURE OF SEOUL CLAIMED BY REDS

THIS WORLD TODAY

Brief Treatise On a D-Day

By ROYCE BRIER

ON A SLIGHTLY GRIM DAY, perhaps another touch of the same will do no great harm.

It has news in it, too, though not much history, in case you are tired of that. All around the country the papers are printing items about it, and literally millions of people are talking about it, and living it in a glassy-eyed kind of way. It got into the doughty New York Times the other day, on the editorial page, a whimsical piece about the summer camp.

The present treatise will not be too whimsical, one hopes. You can only bounce back from this or that experience with the passage of time. In our youth the summer camp was not an experience, being undreamed. You went camping, the family or some groups, but without the automobile you didn't go far, unless you took a train to a lake country. In rugged land boys went hiking.

This was a Yankee practice. The European kids have never done it, unless perhaps some half-hearted English and German boating and tramping trips. Just so, the organizational summer camp is a Yankee practice of the past quarter-century. It has got big, an industry. It has got into advertisements and merchandising. It requires year-round secretaries, skeleton camp maintenance in winter, screening and training senior and junior counselors of both sexes.

Business Opportunity

It requires the laying in, washed, pressed, folded and stamped, of at least twenty million pairs of shorts.

Never mind Editor Greeley's advice to go West. Just get into the shorts business. The summer camp is the most perfect economic consumption machine yet devised by man. It consumes *all* the shorts fed into it in any given year. There is no sur-

Continued on Page 2, Col. 1

The Weather Will Go On As Usual

Another amiable day is forecast for San Francisco today by the weather bureau.

Skies will remain fair—except, of course, for morning fog along the coast—but the temperature will probably not exceed a high of 62 here. Yesterday's high was 63 at Civic Center.

Northern California weather will continue fair and warm, with brisk breezes off the coast.

Socialized Medicine

New AMA Chief Says Issue Is Key To All U. S. Freedom

By MILTON SILVERMAN
Science Writer, The Chronicle

The man who last night became America's number one doctor claimed the fight over socialized medicine will determine the future of all freedom in this country.

Dr. Elmer Lee Henderson of Louisville, Ky., installed here as president of the American Medical Association, told his fellow doctors and a nation-wide radio audience:

"Men of little faith in the American people propose to place all our people—doctors and patients alike—under a shabby, Government-dictated medical system which they call compulsory health insurance."

This is socialized medicine, he said, regardless of how strenuously the label may be denied.

"But it is not just socialized medicine which they seek," he declared. "That is only their first goal. Their real objective is to gain control over all fields of human endeavor . . . to strip the American people of self-determination and self-government.

Behind the drive for socialized medicine, he charged, are "the little men whose lust for power is far out of proportion to their intellectual capacity, their spiritual understanding, their economic realism and their political honesty."

In his inaugural speech at the Palace Hotel, Dr. Henderson paid tribute to the American press for its stand.

"If it were not for leadership of the American press in defending our fundamental liberties," he said,

Continued on Page 4, Col. 5

80 Killed in Syrian Blast

DAMASCUS, Syria, June 27 (AP)—Eighty persons were killed and 300 seriously injured in an explosion today at a big fuel depot near Homs, 100 miles north of Damascus.

Giannini Served

B. of A. Head Faces Charge Of Contempt

By SIDNEY P. ALLEN
Financial Editor, The Chronicle

L. M. Giannini, president of Bank of America, and Sam H. Husbands, president of Transamerica Corp., yesterday were ordered to show cause why they should not be held in criminal and civil contempt of court.

The U. S. Circuit Court of Appeals made the order returnable Friday at 2 p. m. The two financial institutions also are named in the order.

The contempt charge came as a result of Bank of America's action Monday in opening new branches at the identical locations of 22 banks acquired from Transamerica Corp. despite a court order prohibiting acquisition of the banks.

The order was requested by J. Leonard Townsend, counsel for the Federal Reserve Board. The court named Townsend to represent it in the criminal proceedings.

CIVIL PROCEEDINGS

He instituted the civil proceedings for the Reserve Board.

Maximum penalty for a criminal contempt finding is six months in prison and $1000 fine. The Court has the power to set the penalty for civil contempt.

Townsend said "it is not unusual for defendants to be committed until they comply with the Court's order."

The Court on Friday had issued a temporary restraining order against acquisition of the banks. And at an extraordinary session on Saturday the Court issued a permanent injunction against the acquisition until conclusion of the Federal Reserve Board antimonopoly action against Transamerica.

The initial order was petitioned by Counsel Townsend, acting for the Reserve Board.

Bank of America, in opening the new branches, contended that the deal had already been concluded, and that the order couldn't apply to an action already consummated. It further maintained that with the issuance of branch permits from the Comptroller of the Currency and the order of sale of the State banks by the California State Superintendent of Banks it was "obligated" to open the branches.

STATEMENTS ISSUED

Giannini and Husbands issued statements yesterday shortly after they were served with the contempt show cause orders. Giannini said:

"We have repeatedly stated our position and there is little more to say until the facts are presented to the Court. I am advised by counsel and am personally confident that when the Court is presented with the true and complete facts it will be convinced that we have fully complied with the Court's orders and have acted in the only manner possible consistent with the law and the public interest."

Husbands said: "Neither I nor Transamerica Corp. have taken any affirmative action in connection with the acquisition of assets referred to in the Court's restraining order since receipt of the restrain-

Continued on Page 2, Col. 6

Erickson Begins Prison Term

NEW YORK, June 27 (UP)—Kingpin gambler Frank Erickson went to Rikers Island Prison today to begin his two-year sentence for bookmaking. Slightly nervous, Erickson left the Manhattan Tombs Prison handcuffed to a thief.

Harriman Flying To Washington

PARIS, June 27 (AP)—W. Averell Harriman, President Truman's new special adviser on foreign affairs, left by plane today for Washington.

Truman Orders Defense of the Far East

Radio Says Communists Occupy Entire Capital; U.S. Planes Bomb and Strafe Invaders' Lines

Tokyo Hears Broadcast on Seoul's Fall

By the United Press

TOKYO, June 28 — The Communist North Korean radio today (Wednesday) claimed the capture of Seoul, capital of the American-backed South Korean republic.

The North Korean Pyong Yang radio, monitored in Tokyo, asserted Seoul fell to the Red invaders at 11:30 a. m. (6:30 p. m. PDT Tuesday). A South Korean Seoul radio broadcast heard here said the capital was captured at 1:30 p. m.

Only a few hours before the broadcasts, American jet fighter planes and assault bombers returned from what were described as successful bombing and strafing missions of the Red positions and General Douglas MacArthur announced that the South Korean troops were holding the invaders.

MacArthur noted, however, that a concentration of Russian-made armored vehicles, "possibly 40 in number," were reported several miles north of the capital.

EMBASSY 'LIBERATED'

The Seoul broadcast, apparently made by Reds, said the Communist forces had "liberated" government offices, the U. S. Embassy, the radio station and newspapers.

No mention was made of U. S. Ambassador John J. Muccio, Dr. Syngman Rhee or other South Korean government officials.

The Korean Red radio broadcast reported troops entered the city at 3:30 a. m. and had completely occupied it eight hours later. It appealed to all residents to return to their homes and remain calm.

The South Korean mission here expressed surprise at the report, but admitted it had had no late word from Seoul.

An Air Force spokesman at the Itazuki Air Base, new advanced general headquarters for Korean operations, said the fighter and bomber missions were "successfully carried out against a variety of targets." Targets presumably included artillery, tank and troop concentrations, bridges and other ground installations. (For an eye-witness dispatch from Itazuki, see Page 8.)

The aerial attackers—F-80 Shooting Star fighters armed with rockets and 50-caliber machine-guns and A-26 bombers laden with 500-pound bombs—restricted operations to below the 38th parallel between South and North Korea.

ON TRUMAN ORDERS

The planes took off this morning from Itazuki Air Base to bring shooting aid to the embattled South Korean Republic under direct orders from President Truman.

Somewhere along South Korea's sea frontiers the U. S. naval units

Continued on Page 8, Col. 1

The Index

City Notices 21
Chess-by-Mail 20
Contract Contacts 34
Comics 31
Crossword Puzzle 32
De Roos 23
Drama 16, 17
Editorial: "The Cold War (Delete Cold)" 24
Finance 25, 26
Leiser 1H
Lichty's Cartoon 2
Lyons Den 2
Radio and Television 18
Vital Statistics 21
Weather Map 21
Women's World 13, 14, 15

This Is the Policy---in Brief

WASHINGTON, June 27 (AP)—Key points in the Far Pacific policy announced today by President Truman:

1—U. S. air and sea forces to give the Korean government troops cover and support;

2—The 7th Fleet to prevent any attack on Formosa;

3—The Chinese government on Formosa to cease air and sea operations against the mainland;

4—U. S. forces in the Philippines to be strengthened and military aid speeded up;

5—Military aid for France and the associated states in Indo-China to be stepped up and a military mission to be sent to work with the Indo-China forces;

6—The United States will continue to uphold the rule of law.

—(AP) Wirephoto map

FIGHTING ZONE—Korean invaders from the north and defenders from the south are fighting seesaw engagements along the heavy black line (see white arrows). A late broadcast from Seoul carried a claim by the North Koreans that they had captured this South Korea capital.

Top U. S. Officials Believe Russia Will Not Fight

By CARROLL KILPATRICK
Washington Correspondent, The Chronicle

WASHINGTON, June 27—Top Administration officials, who recommended the far-reaching and challenging decision announced today by President Truman, believe Soviet Russia will not fight.

But they concede that if Russia wants war now, all bridges have been burned by the historic White House announcement committing American forces to the defense of South Korea.

President Truman's military and diplomatic advisers, it was said officially, were in agreement in urging the decision he made. But it was understood that some of the military advisers were more cautious than the diplomatic advisers.

Political leaders on Capitol Hill were virtually unanimous in praise of what many people here regard as the boldest action an American President has taken in time of peace.

The military officials, it was said, recognized the risk that this country is running in throwing down the challenge to Russia at this time. But it was said that in the end they saw no alternative to the President's decision.

The weight of the President's advice was that the risk of no action was greater than the risk of bold action. The diplomatic advisers pointed out to the President that abandonment of South Korea to the Communists would mean the loss of American prestige all over the world and the loss of many allies, who no longer would have much confidence in the word of this country.

"If the Russians want war," one official explained, "then our action will mean that war will come now. If the Russians want war and we

Continued on Page 8, Col. 4

INSIDE

Truman's decision doesn't mean we have declared war. Page 6.
Yanks evacuated from battle area. Page 7.
Congress goes all-out to back Truman. Page 8
U. S. military action is defensive. Page 9.
No alerts sounded for our armed forces in Bay Area. Page 10.
The steps leading to U. S. decision to act. Page 11.

U.N. Council Backs U.S. Call for Aid

By the United Press

LAKE SUCCESS, N. Y., June 27—The Soviet-boycotted United Nations Security Council today called on all U. N. members to join the United States in sending arms to hurl back the Communist invasion of South Korea.

It was the first time in history that a world organization has imposed military sanctions against an aggressor.

The vote was 7 to 1 in favor of the resolution. Yugoslavia abstained. Egypt and India did not take part in the voting because they had not received instructions from their governments. Russia, of course, was absent.

The affirmative votes were cast by the U. S., Britain, France, (Nationalist) China, Ecuador, Norway and Cuba.

MALIK SEES GROSS

Prior to opening of the Council session, Russian U. N. Delegate Jakob Malik had luncheon with Ernest Gross, America's No. 2 U. N. delegate.

(Associated Press said that Malik insisted that Sunday's Council demand for a cessation of hostilities in Korea was illegal. He laughed and said "nyet" (no) when asked by Secretary-General Trygve Lie if he would not go along to the Council meeting from the lunch.

(Malik will leave on vacation soon and there is considerable speculation here about Russia's future in the U. N. now. The Russians are certain to declare today's resolution illegal.)

The key clause of the American-proposed Council resolution "recommends that the members of the U. N. furnish such assistance to the Republic of Korea as many be necessary to repel the armed attack and to restore international peace and security in the area."

The closest the League of Nations ever came to taking such extreme measures to keep the peace was in voting economic sanctions against Italy for invading Ethiopia in 1935.

MEDIATION REJECTED

Immediately after approval of military sanctions against Communist Korea, the Council defeated Yugoslavia's alternative resolution to renew Sunday's cease-fire order, initiate mediation proceedings, and invite a North Korean representative here to represent his regime.

Only Yugoslavia voted for its own resolution. It was opposed by the same seven nations which put over the sanctions vote. Again, India and Egypt did not participate.

The sanctions resolution was placed before the Council by Ambassador Warren R. Austin, chief U. S. Delegate, shortly after the mid-afternoon opening of the historic Council session.

The meeting was recessed after two hours and met again at 10:25.

Before Austin took the floor to make this country's proposal, Council Chairman Sir Benegal Rau of India made an oblique proposal that President Truman and Premier Josef Stalin meet face to face in an effort to halt the dangerous worsening of world tension.

"The people of the world are weary of war and rumors and we must try our best not to fail them," he said.

(Text of U. N. Resolution on Page 11.)

President Bars Attack On Formosa

By the United Press

WASHINGTON, June 27—President Truman today threw U. S. combat planes and warships into the battle to save Red-invaded South Korea and, in another challenge to world Communism, ordered the Navy to block any Communist attack on Chinese Formosa.

To protect further the vital U. S. defense line in the Pacific, he ordered more U. S. troops rushed to the Philippines and more aid for Communist-menaced Indo-China.

After the President's orders had gone out the State Department dispatched a note to the Russian Government urging it to use its influence to stop the war at once and tacitly warning Moscow not to help the North Korean invaders.

(In the first Russian reaction to President Truman's orders, Pravda, official Communist party organ, said the U. S. had committed a "direct act of aggression." See page 6.)

The President moved swiftly and dramatically under last Sunday's United Nations mandate to all U. N. members to come to the rescue of South Korea if Russian-controlled North Korean troops refused to pull back behind their own border.

For editorial comment see page 24

"This they have not done, but on the contrary have pressed the attack," Mr. Truman said in a bluntly-phrased, 400-word statement. "In these circumstances I have ordered United States air and sea forces to give the Korean Government troops cover and support."

He said he took the far-reaching action because "Communism has passed beyond the use of subversion to conquer independent nations and will now use armed invasion and war."

The President's momentous decisions—which committed U. S. forces to action on a major scale for the first time since World War II—were announced after an emergency White House meeting with his top military and State Department officials.

The President ordered the Seventh Fleet not only to protect Formosa from invasion because occupation by the Chinese Communists "would be a direct threat to the security of the Pacific Area," but also to prevent Generalissimo Chiang Kai-shek's Nationalist forces on Formosa from attacking the Chinese mainland.

(For text of President Truman's statement and more on U. S. note to Moscow, see Page 6.)

Stocks Dive, Commodities Close Higher

NEW YORK, June 27 (AP)—The stock market touched bottom this afternoon after a two-day plunge.

But on the commodity market rubber, tin and pepper futures closed higher as prices followed an erratic pattern in response to new developments in Korea.

Losses on the stock market ranged to around $5 a share, and in a few cases more, before a stand was made. For details, see Financial, Page 25.

THIS WORLD TODAY

Oakland Wins; Seals Lose

See Sports

San Francisco Chronicle
THE CITY'S ONLY HOME-OWNED NEWSPAPER
FINAL
FOUNDED 1865—VOL. CLXX, NO. 165 CCCCAAA SAN FRANCISCO, THURSDAY, JUNE 29, 1950 GA 1-1112 DAILY 7 CENTS, SUNDAY 15 CENTS

MACARTHUR IS IN KOREA

B-29s Bomb Kimpo Airfield

Korean Problem In Its Setting

By ROYCE BRIER

THE possibility pervades this day in the American time that the Korean situation will explode into a great war for survival between the United States and Soviet Russia.

We can do no less than acknowledge this possibility, meditate the forms of action it could take, and find in ourselves again the national integrity, the iron determination, the calm intelligence and the willful energy which have made us a great people.

The probability, however, is that there will be no such culmination, that there will be no war between the United States and Soviet Russia over Korea.

But should the probable occur, the burden will not be lifted from us. The cold war will go on. The conflict of belief and interest between the United States and Soviet Russia will go on. The burden will be a different kind of burden, but it will be as formidable as war itself, and perhaps tax the American character even more than war itself.

It will be a burden of understanding — understanding ourselves and the world and history and the human struggle, and of finding our directions accordingly, and of sticking to those directions, no matter what the cost.

The Reasoning

The reasons for conjecturing there will be no immediate war are fairly simple, and are mainly three:

1—We have no direct evidence, but good circumstantial evidence that the Soviet Union is not now prepared for all-out war with the United States and such of the Western peoples as will help. The Soviet empire faces dangerous and unresolved problems within itself — geographical, ethnic, political and economic-industrial.

2—The authoritarian-aggressive, politico-military organism, when determined to make a seizure, reacts instantly to very

Continued on Page 2, Col. 4

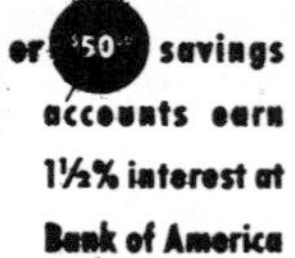

School Raises

Clish, Teachers Given Increases By the Board

Dr. Herbert C. Clish was granted a new four-year contract as superintendent of San Francisco schools and a pay increase from $18,000 to $20,000 a year by the Board of Education last night.

In a surprise compromise move, the board also voted six to one to grant 3300 San Francisco teachers a $300 a year cost of living bonus for the year beginning next Saturday.

Dr. Clish's present four-year contract had one more year to run when it was superseded by the new one.

The unprecedented action of the board—taken by a 5-2 vote—was opposed by Board Members George W. Johns and Joseph L. Alioto.

"I don't agree that the Superintendent should be given a new contract and the reason is because of his recent action in opposing pay raises for teachers," Johns said.

This opposition Johns called "a poor and reprehensible act."

The contract renewal was brought up as the first order of business at the meeting in a surprise move by Board Chairman Bert W. Levit. Arguing for the motion, he declared:

"I don't think it's a healthy thing for the school district always to be changing its top man. Clish has proved himself an able and efficient superintendent of schools. The schools have made progress under his supervision, even though we have not reached a state of perfection.

"We should know where we're going to go in the future and Dr. Clish should known where he's going to go in the future," he added.

The favorable vote was taken after Alioto tried vainly to defer action until August. He said he was willing to grant Clish a $2000 a year pay raise but thought the contract renewal should follow a full-dress policy discussion on philosophy and methods of education.

Alioto praised Clish personally, but added:

"I fear the men who head the elementary and secondary departments are dedicated to what has been called 'progressive education'—this philosophy that does not stress basic skills."

This was an obvious reference to Dr. Harold Spears, brought here by Clish to be superintendent of elementary education, and Dr. Edward Redford, superintendent of secondary education.

Clish, who is the fourth San Francisco superintendent of schools in 16 years, thanked the board for its action and indicated he is not at-

Continued on Page 13, Col. 4

Patten Jury Locked Up For the Night

Grand theft charges against C. (for Cash) Thomas Patten, Oakland evangelist, were given to a jury yesterday after the longest trial in the history of Alameda county. The jury retired at 2:45 p. m., and at 10:25 p. m. was locked up for the night. (See Page 2 for details.)

Treatment of Atom Victims

Problems in Event of A-Bomb Disaster Considered by AMA

By ALVIN D. HYMAN

If an atom bomb falls ——

The medical profession, military and civilian, considered that dire possibility yesterday, and in scientific papers read before a session on Military Medicine and Surgery of the American Medical Association, voiced these views:

Rear Admiral Joel T. Boone, general inspector of Medical Department Activities of the U. S. Navy:

"In this age of warfare which is carried to civilian populations and not, as in former eras, limited to military camps, the civilian populace as a whole must be given the benefit of military knowledge in coping with dangers it faces, by what methods it may be attacked, how it can be protected, and, if a war casualty, what therapeutic measures must be applied."

General James P. Cooney, chief of the radiological branch, military application division of the Atomic Energy Commission:

"The grave uncertainty in today's international situation has imposed a unique, unprecedentedly heavy responsibility on the American doctor. He is being called upon by planning groups throughout the nation to assist in making realistic preparations, should atomic bombing of our cities occur."

FIRST AID SUPPLIES

Dr. Norvin C. Kiefer, director Health Resources division, National Security Resources Board (in a paper prepared jointly with and read by Dr. Robert H. Flinn, emergency medical services consultant for the board):

"Consumable supplies for first aid treatment of casualties would constitute one of our most severe shortages. Following a major wartime civilian disaster, our Nation's existing supplies would be consumed within a few hours.

"First aid and surgical supplies for the first week following an atomic bomb disaster comparable to Hiroshima would fill 200 railroad boxcars. The cost of 200 carloads of supplies would be about $3,000,000."

Dr. Everett I. Evans, professor of surgery, Medical College of Virginia: Obviously the medical profession is confronted with a gigantic, complex task in planning for the care of mass burn casualties. Lest we be overwhelmed and thrown into despair, search for the best

Continued on Page 12, Col. 3

The Weather Will Stay Summery

It will be shirt-sleeved weather in most of the Bay Area today. But on the coast there will be the usual summer fog.

The Weather Bureau promises little change in temperature and westerly winds of 15-to-25 miles per hour in the afternoon.

Queuille Will Try To Form Regime

PARIS, June 28 (UP) — Henri Queuille, onetime Premier, agreed today to try to form a "government of national unity." Queuille had earlier refused the call, but accepted after Georges Bidault also refused the task.

Battle Rages for Key Base of Suwon

Some U. S. Ground Troops Alerted for Action; Truman Renews His Pledge to Periled Lands

President Denounces Communism

By the Associated Press

WASHINGTON, June 28—President Truman declared today the "unprovoked invasion" of Korea is an example of the danger Communism presents to all undeveloped areas.

"We must and we shall give every possible assistance to people who are determined to maintain their independence," he said. "We must counteract the Communist weapon of fear."

The President addressed the annual convention of the CIO American Newspaper Guild.

It was his second speech of the day which touched on Tuesday's momentous decision to use American planes and warships against the Communist invaders of Korea.

HOPE EXPRESSED

To the Reserve Officers' Assn., he said earlier that "we face a serious situation" but expressed hope that the U. S. challenge to the onward march of Communism will mean "peace in the world."

Much of his address to the Guild was concerned with his so-called Point Four program of American aid for the development of backward areas of the world.

He said the Communists are attempting to turn the "honest dissatisfaction" of peoples in undeveloped areas into support of "Communist efforts to dominate their nation."

WEAPON OF FEAR

He continued:

"In addition to these attempts of persuasion, the Communists use the weapon of fear. They constantly threaten internal violence and aggression.

"The recent unprovoked invasion of the republic of Korea by Communist armies is an example of the danger to which underdeveloped areas particularly are exposed.

"It is essential that we do everything that we can to prevent such aggression and to enforce the principles of the United Nations Charter."

The President went on to say "we must not be misled into thinking that our only task is to create defenses against aggression."

"Our whole purpose in creating a strong defense is to permit us to carry on the great constructive tasks of peace. Behind the shield of a strong defense, we must continue to work to bring about better living conditions in the free nations."

CHATTY TALK

Mr. Truman's talk to the Reserve Association was off the cuff, without benefit of prepared manuscript.

In chatty vein, he spoke for several minutes without mention of

Continued on Page 6, Col. 5

The Index

Chess by Mall 6H
Contract Contacts 28
Comics 25
Crossword Puzzle 26
De Roos 15
Drama 10, 11
Editorial:
"What We Face in Korea" 16
Finance 17, 18
Fun With Words 25
Leiser 1H
Lichty's Cartoon 2
Lyons Den 2
Radio and Television 6H
Vital Statistics 13
Women's World 9

Korean War at a Glance

By Associated Press

Tokyo—General Douglas MacArthur arrives in Korea; authoritative source says American combat troops have been alerted for action in South Korea "at a moment's notice." Fighting moves 20 miles southward. B-29s are in action with other U. S. planes.

London—Britain orders naval forces in Japanese waters—22 or 23 ships including an aircraft carrier—to support American action in Korea.

Washington—President Truman declares the "unprovoked invasion" of Southern Korea was an example of the threat Communism presents to all undeveloped areas. Expresses hope peace will result from U. S. action to help Korea.

Moscow—Russia declares U. N. resolution calling for aid to South Korea has no legal force.

—(AP) Wirephoto map

BATTLEGROUND—The fighting in Korea is indicated as it was reported Wednesday. North Korean forces (solid arrow) moved southward as South Koreans attempted to establish a defense line (sawtooth line and open arrows) about Suwon. U. S. planes bombed tanks, troops and a railway yard at Munsan. The temporary South Korean capital was established at Taejon. In broadcasts North Korea claimed the capture of Utchin and Yongwal (broken arrows) and a landing at Pohangdong followed by a drive at Taegu. B-29s bombed Kimpo airfield.

Russia Replies to the U. N., 'No Legal Force' to Action

By the Associated Press

LONDON, June 29—Russia declared today (Thursday) that the United Nations Security Council resolution calling on U. N. members to help South Korea has no legal force.

The Soviet news agency Tass made public the Soviet reply to the resolution. The reply was broadcast by the Moscow radio.

Pravda calls U. S. action aggression. Text of editorial on Page 6.

The Security Council voted 7-1 Tuesday night at Lake Success to ask all member nations to apply military sanctions against the North Koreans.

The Soviet Union boycotted the meeting as she has all U. N. meetings since the first of the year, because of the presence of Chinese Nationalist representatives.

Russia said the Nationalist Chinese delegate who cast the seventh vote in favor of the resolution had "no lawful right" to take part in the proceedings. The resolution was offered by the United States.

Seven affirmative votes are required to pass a resolution in the Security Council.

The Russians also maintained that the U. N. charter specifies that all five permanent members of the council—the United States, Britain, France, Russia and China — must vote in favor of a resolution to make it legal.

The text of the Soviet reply:

To the Secretary General of the United Nations organization, Mr. Trygve Lie, in New York:

The Soviet government has re-

Continued on Page 7, Col. 2

Location of South Army Unknown

By VANCE JOHNSON
Washington Correspondent, The Chronicle

WASHINGTON, June 28—Hours or days yet must pass before there is any indication whether American military intervention in Korea is going to be enough to save the young republic from its Communist invaders.

It appeared altogether possible—although not necessarily probable—tonight that the South Korean army is teetering on the brink of disaster and that no amount of American military activity short of committing ground forces would be of avail.

The big question late today was what had happened to the South Korean divisions which had been committed to the unsuccessful defense of Seoul, the capital, which fell to the Communists late yesterday afternoon.

An Army spokesman declared these troops "decidedly are not retreating in disorder," but it was evident that his statement was based on an absence of information to this effect rather than positive confirmation.

MORALE GOOD

Army officials were unable after a teletype conversation with General Douglas MacArthur's headquarters to state the whereabouts of the defenders of Seoul. This was so even though a spokesman declared, with an air of assurance, that morale among the South Korean troops "is extremely good and very much improved as a result of the action taken by the President yesterday."

Three divisions—the Headquarters, less one regiment, the Second and Seventh—were in position in the immediate environs of Seoul at the outbreak of war on Sunday, two others, drawn up from the south, since have been thrown into the battle for the capitol city.

If these South Korean forces—which constitute more than half of the South Korean army—were "scattered and chewed up" by the tank-led Communist forces, as an Associated Press dispatch from Tokyo said today, the chances of stemming the invaders' southward advance would appear to be slim indeed.

"BULGE" PARALLEL

On the other hand, if these forces were able to withdraw in order and should be able to reform quickly and take up defensive positions south of Seoul then it would be possible to bring the full weight of American air support to bear.

Army spokesmen expressed confidence if this can be done that the tide of the Korean war can be turned against the Communists.

The situation at present is described as closely paralleling that of the Battle for the Bulge in December, 1944, when the trapped American 101st air-borne division was badly mauled until weather opened up and the air force could come to their support.

Weather over Korea was described by an Army spokesman as "foul" all day Wednesday, limiting visability and in general hampering air operations and at dawn Thursday it was described as cloudy to overcast.

United States planes were in ac-

Continued on Page 4, Col. 7

Truman Sets News Conference

WASHINGTON, June 28 (AP)—President Truman will hold his regular weekly news conference tomorrow at 3 p. m.

Commander To 'See for Myself'

By the Associated Press

TOKYO, June 29—General MacArthur flew to the South Korean war front in an unarmed transport plane today (Thursday) and U. S. B-29 bombers went into action against the North Korean invaders.

The commander of American forces in the Far East arrived in the Communist-invaded little republic with several of his top officers "to see for myself" the turn of battle that was going against the South Korean Army. (See page 4.)

Shortly after MacArthur's plane landed Far East Air Force headquarters in Tokyo announced the big Boeing Superfortresses had bombed Red-captured Seoul's Kimpo Airfield this morning.

'GOOD RESULTS'

The big B-29s bombed Kimpo Airfield, 16 miles west-northwest of Red-captured Seoul, this morning with "good results," the FEAF announcement said. The number of planes in action was not disclosed but all returned, headquarters said.

After the B-29 raid, the Korean military mission here reported a renewal of the fighting for Seoul. It said Republican troops were pushing back the Reds' heavy concentration of Russian-made tanks in the western sector of the city that had fallen to the invaders yesterday.

Fierce fighting, the mission said, was continuing at Kimpo airfield, and at Uijongbu, a Red-held city 12 miles north of the capital.

South Korean headquarters has moved back to Shihung, between Seoul and Suwon, 20 miles south, the announcement said.

The headquarters withdrew from Seoul to Shihung yesterday and moved south to Suwon this morning.

COMBAT TROOP ALERT

As MacArthur left Tokyo's Haneda Airport, the South Korean defense position was reported so grim that authoritative sources in Japan said some U. S. combat troops had been placed on the alert for possible immediate movement to the war zone.

The source declared the deteriorating military situation in the Communist-invaded half of the country may force the United States to commit ground soldiers to the battle.

The authoritative source said a decision on whether the combat troops would be sent into action might be made today.

So far no U. S. combat troops have been sent to South Korea.

It is known that top-level American authorities believe such a move cannot be delayed much longer if the Reds are to be kept from overrunning the Peninsula.

(Britain has placed her naval forces in Asiatic waters at the disposal of the United States. See page 6.

(The Australian Royal Navy

Continued on Page 8, Col. 1

INSIDE

British give U. S. control over their Far East naval forces. Page 6
Pravda says U. S. actions are "aggression." Page 6
Formosa still China, Nationalists stress. Page 5
Congress votes extension of the draft for a year. Page 13
Acheson says Korea is a test of the U. N. Page 6
Local naval bases are closed to visitors. Page 7

Mathias Sets Decathlon Record

See Sports

COMPARATIVE TEMPERATURES
For Friday, June 30, 1950

	High	Low		High	Low
San Francisco	71	55	New York....	83	66
Oakland.....	90	59	Chicago	74	58
Sacramento	108	69	Kansas City.	87	66
Los Angeles..	91	64	Pensacola ..	85	75
Portland	82	57	New Orleans	95	75
Seattle	77	57	Washington..	86	66

Forecast for Today: FAIR AND WARM
(For Details, See Page 7)

San Francisco Chronicle
THE CITY'S ONLY HOME-OWNED NEWSPAPER

FINAL

FOUNDED 1865—VOL. CLXX, NO. 167 CCCCAAA SAN FRANCISCO, SATURDAY, JULY 1, 1950 GA 1-1112 DAILY 7 CENTS, SUNDAY 15 CENTS

YANK TROOPS MOVE TO FRONT

South Korean Army Is Quitting

Disputed Fare Slash

40-Cent Gate Bridge Toll On Private Cars in Effect ---Commutes Unchanged

Truck Rates Slashed by Board, Directors in Heated Argument Over First Cuts in 13 Years

Toll reductions involving everybody but commuters were ordered in effect on the Golden Gate Bridge at 11 p. m. last night despite the heated protests of three members of the bridge's board of directors.

At a meeting yesterday afternoon the board voted 9 to 3 to go ahead with the toll cuts originally proposed May 26.

Royce Brier is out of the city. His column "This World Today" will be resumed upon his return.

The action sliced 10 cents off the basic passenger car toll, bringing it to 40 cents per crossing, and reduced truck rates through eliminating weighing and instead establishing charges of 50 cents for two-axle trucks and 50 cents for each additional axle.

The cuts—bitterly fought by commuter organizations as well as by Supervisors of both Marin county and San Francisco—will reduce the income of the Golden Gate Bridge an estimated $574,000. However, some of the loss will be made up by the anticipated increase in truck and casual passenger traffic.

Bridge Director Philipps S. Davies, San Francisco banker, led yesterday's fight against the proposed toll cuts. He was supported in the final vote by Directors Leland S. Murphy and M. A. Graham of Marin county.

Davies said he felt more time for study of the proposed new tolls was needed, to see if the commuter should not be first in line for any benefits.

He suggested that, first of all, the five cents additional charge for every extra passenger in the commuter's car should be eliminated. He also proposed, "for study," the outright reduction of the commute fare from the present 40 tickets for $8 to 50 tickets for $8.

Davies also thought the bus commuter might eventually benefit with a lower fare if the bridge cut the Greyhound toll from $1.25 to $1.15 a bus. The latter is the charge for buses crossing the much longer SF-Oakland Bay Bridge.

The finance committee's recommendations were supported by Committee Chairman William D. Hadeler, who said the toll matter had been studied for "years" before the proposal was made.

The reduction from 50 to 40 cents in the one-way auto fare is the first basic toll reduction since the Golden Gate Bridge was opened 13 years ago.

The directors meantime announced the bridge in the fiscal year ended last night had gross revenues of $4,517,000—the highest in history. Last year's income totaled $4,186,815.

Delaplane in Las Vegas

Bulletin for Delaplane Postcard addicts: The Chronicle's Pulitzer Prize winner is investigating glamorous Las Vegas. His first two reports involve glittering casinos, charcoal-broiled steaks, sun-tanned starlets and atomic bathing suits. Anyone interested see tomorrow's and Monday's Chronicle.

Final Action By the AMA

Attendance Record Set as Doctors Close Convention

By MILTON SILVERMAN
Science Writer, The Chronicle

The American Medical Association closed its annual convention here yesterday, after smashing all its attendance records for a Western meeting.

The five-day session drew more than 22,250 registrants, including some 10,200 doctors.

Before their adjournment the doctors took these actions:

1—They named Dr. John Cline, Stanford surgeon, president-elect, to take office in 1951.

2—They prepared to launch a new $1,100,000 educational campaign against compulsory health insurance.

OCTOBER DRIVE

The drive is scheduled to start early in October, a month before the November elections. In most quarters, it was frankly admitted that the campaign will be directed toward unseating the Truman Administration.

In final scientific sessions, the doctors heard promising reports on "quick-cure" treatments of early syphilis.

From the University of Maryland, Drs. Harry M. Robinson and Harry M. Robinson Jr., announced in a preliminary report that some of the new antibiotics can make a patient non-infectious in a few hours, and apparently cure all sores in a few days.

Aureomycin, they said, gets rid of all surface germs in 18 to 72 hours, and cleans up lesions of early syphilis in 7 to 14 days.

TERRAMYCIN EFFECTIVE

Terramycin, they added, "caused the surface syphilis organisms to disappear in 24 hours and the lesions to heal in seven days."

Curative results were also re-

Continued on Page 6, Col. 3

U. N. Building Contract Signed

LAKE SUCCESS, June 30 (AP) — Secretary-General Trygve Lie today signed an $11,000,000 contract for construction of the General Assembly building on the site of the permanent United Nations headquarters in New York.

Truman Extends American Intervention

Infantry Battalion Flown Into Fight From Japan; 33 Nations Back U. N. Action; Egypt Dissents

Support for U. S. Position In the U. N.

By the Associated Press

LAKE SUCCESS, June 30 —Thirty-three countries have lined up in support of American-led military measures under United Nations auspices to save South Korea, the Security Council was advised today.

There was one day in the otherwise solid line-up of non-Communist nations offering material and moral support.

Egypt told the Council she would not accept the Council's resolution of Tuesday night endorsing American intervention in Korea and asking other nations to contribute their support.

Egyptian Delegate Mahmoud Fawzi Bey said his government regarded the Korean conflict as just one more divergence between the East and the West.

He also told the Council it had not acted in the past to stop territorial grabs or aggression against peoples. This was an apparent reference to the Council actions on the Palestine war, which the Council ended with cease-fire orders and truce negotiations.

THE 33 BACKERS

The 33 countries joining the fight are the 21 American republics which made their decision in the Council of the organization of American States in Washington; Britain, Nationalist China, India, Belgium, the Netherlands, New Zealand, Canada, Australia, South Africa, the Philippines, Turkey and Pakistan.

Against this array were protests from Russia, Czechoslovakia and North Korea that the Council moves are illegal because Russia and Red China did not participate in making them.

Council members privately discussed arrangement for co-ordinating the war effort outside the range of on-the-spot decision being made by General Douglas MacArthur.

The Council adjourned after a brief session today.

AUSTIN SPEAKS

American Chief Delegate Warren R. Austin told the Council of President Truman's authorization for use of U. S. ground forces in Korea and the President's announcement of a Korean coastal blockade by Navy vessels and the air attacks on North Korea. Austin also said the United States will give every assistance to the U. N. Commission for Korea toward resuming its functions in the south.

Sir Benegal Rau of India, Council president for this month, told the Council his government accepted the resolution because the halting of aggression and quick restoration of peaceful conditions are essential preludes to a satisfactory settlement.

Bombing of North Zone Ordered

By the United Press

WASHINGTON, June 30—President Truman today ordered American combat ground troops thrown into the Korean war.

He also directed the Air Force to bomb military targets in enemy territory and ordered the Navy to blockade the entire Korean coast—a maneuver that would smash any amphibious operation from Russian-controlled North Korea.

The Air Force apparently was in action over North Korea. The North Koreans claimed 27 American B-29's bombed their capital, Pyongyang, Thursday night.

The orders apparently were given General Douglas MacArthur late Thursday after the Supreme Allied Commander in Tokyo reported on his flying inspection tour of the war zone.

Mr. Truman was "briefed" early today by the U. S. Joint Chiefs of Staff. Then, before issuing his announcement, he called in his Cabinet and Republican and Democratic congressional leaders and told them of his decisions.

The White House announcement said MacArthur was authorized to use "certain supporting ground units"—a phrase which Army Secretary Frank Pace Jr., said was decided upon after careful consideration.

FOUR DIVISIONS

MacArthur has in his Far East Command an Army strength of 123,500 men. This includes four divisions. They are the First Cavalry Division—an infantry division despite its name; the Seventh Infantry Division, the 24th Infantry Division and the 25th Infantry Division.

The U. S. ground troops are stationed in Japan, Okinawa and other islands of the Ryukyu chain, and the Philippines.

Following the White House announcement, an Army spokesman said that all of the Army troops in the Far East Command have been alerted. The Army also has an additional 8000 men in Hawaii.

Secretary of Defense Louis Johnson was asked about Nationalist China's offer to send 30,000 troops to Korea. He said such offers had been received from "everybody" and that the Government is considering them all, but doesn't want to announce a decision yet.

Mr. Truman began his day with the 9 a. m. briefing by the U. S. Joint Chiefs of Staff, Secretary of State Dean Acheson and Johnson. W. Averell Harriman, his new assistant on foreign affairs, also was present. Then he summoned his civilian leaders and members of Congress.

Korean War At a Glance

TAEJON—First battalion of U. S. Infantry flies to Korea as South Korean Army collapses. American headquarters and vital airfield at Suwon abandoned. Taejon, 70 miles south of Suwon, becomes temporary Korean capital.

WASHINGTON — President Truman orders American ground troops into Korean fighting and directs MacArthur to bomb military targets in North Korea. Navy ordered to blockade to be thrown around entire Korean coastline. Congress generally approves orders.

LAKE SUCCESS — Egypt tells United Nations she will not support American-led action against North Korea. But 33 other countries are now behind the action, Security Council is advised.

Senate Votes Arms Aid

Tally Is 66 to 0 for $1,222,500,000 Bill; House Action Next

By Associated Press

WASHINGTON, June 30—In a rare display of unanimity the Senate today approved, 66 to 0, a $1,222,500,000 program to arm nations resisting Communism, including South Korea.

Republicans who have heatedly assailed Administration methods of defending the free world against aggression suddenly closed ranks behind the bill, impelled by the Korean crisis.

The legislation now goes to the House. It is an authorization measure which requires separate action to finance it.

Although the bulk of the funds, $1,000,000,000, would go to strengthen North Atlantic Treaty Allies, Senator Tom Connally (Dem - Texas), chairman of the Senate Foreign Relations Committee, said the bill's $16,000,000 earmarked for Korea and the Philippines could be increased at any time by a shift of funds.

The bill represents the second year of arms aid. Besides $1,000,000,000 cash, the Atlantic nations would get $250,000,000 in equipment. The bill also carries $131,500,000 for Turkey, Greece and Iran, and $75,000,000 for the general area of China. There is provision for sale or donation of arms to other nations whose security the President considers vital to American defense.

Senator Robert Taft of Ohio, Republican policy leader who had opposed the Truman arms aid program, told the Senate he was voting for the bill although he is against the general idea of arming foreign nations at heavy expense.

Yank Retreat From Suwon Described

By PETER KALISCHER
United Press Staff Writer

TAEJON, July 1 — Some 280 wet and exhausted American soldiers arrived in Taejon this (Saturday) morning after a 10-hour retreat from Suwon.

"We are not going any farther back," Brigadier General John H. Church vowed as he set up his headquarters here. The soldiers, members of the American Advisory Mission, agreed.

It was their second retreat in the Korean war. First from Seoul, where they retrieved some of their possessions. Then from Suwon. They drove all night and arrived in Taejon with nothing but the clothes on their backs.

When the planned defense of Suwon was given up as impracticable and under-armed South Korean fighters "melted away" under the fire of Communist armor, the Americans were given ten minutes to evacuate.

The order was given about 9 p. m. Friday.

ANY VEHICLE

When the men arrived here some of them collapsed on the floor, and rolled up in soggy blankets. Others cooked breakfast. Others silently watched a movie on the wall of a clubhouse.

Disposition of troops was a military secret. But officers, men and State Department civilians roiled out of Suwon in trucks, jeeps, weapons carriers — anything that held promise of getting them over 95 miles of bad Korean roads, turned into quagmire by driving rain.

Military Police Corporal George F. Miller, 21, Burrowsville, Okla., broke his ankle at the start of the evacuation when he jumped over an embankment to get in his jeep.

He drove four hours with a broken bone before the pain forced him to quit. Miller was among those who escaped across the Han river early Wednesday morning, partly by rowboat and partly by wading.

JEEP WRECK

Corporal John J. Maroudetz, 22, Rib Lake, Wis., fell asleep at the wheel of his jeep and ran into a ditch, spilling out his three com-

Continued on Page 2, Col. 1

Two Transports Due Here Today

Two military transport ships are scheduled to arrive at Fort Mason today.

The General D. E. Aultman will dock at Pier 3 East at 3 p. m. with 956 military and civilian passengers from Yokohama.

The General E. T. Collins will arrive at Pier 2 West at 1 p. m. with 495 military and civilian passengers from Okinawa and Guam.

North Tanks Sweep on Southward

By the Associated Press

TOKYO, July 1—A battalion of the U. S. 24th Infantry Division has been flown into South Korea. The South Korean army has collapsed and virtually quit fighting against fast-rushing North Korean Communist tanks.

The North Koreans have lost Suwon and its strategic air strip. Dispatches from the Far South today indicated the Northern invaders already are nearly 40 miles south of that position.

The 290-man American field headquarters had to flee Suwon by jeep and truck.

Brig. Gen. John H. Church, commanding the headquarters, told AP Correspondent Tom Lambert in Taejon today that the first battalion would be flown to Pusan, southern port, and taken by train to defend bridges 25 to 30 miles north of Taejon.

That temporary South Korean capital is 70 miles south of Suwon, where the defense previously had been aligned.

(United Press reported that the battalion moved by truck and train from Pusan to a base town and then went on to the front. It said the rest of the division is due by ship.

(American staff members patrolled to the town of Suwon Saturday and returned to say they saw no Communists in it. The staff men disclosed that air observation of 50 truckloads of Communist troops approaching in a threat to flank the Suwon air strip, had caused the retreat Friday, United Press said.

(The United Press also reported that a new South Korean defense line was being formed along the Kum river, 60 miles south of Kuwon.)

General Church said at least one full American division would go into combat in the south and would—with South Korean help—undertake to drive the Northerners back north o. the 38th parallel boundary.

(A full strength battalion numbers between 900 and 1000 men. It is impossible to say if the present battalion is of normal strength or whether is has additional components to strengthen it. A division may run anywhere from 10,000 to 20,000 depending upon the number of attached units.)

Asked by Lambert what would happen if the Russians came to the northereners' aid, Church replied: "If the Russkies come down, we'll fight the Russkies too."

Lambert reported the South Koreans, hard pressed ever since the Northern Reds invaded last Sunday, had virtually quit fighting by 6 p. m. Friday (1 a. m. Friday, Pacific Daylight Time).

The Reds were officially reported to have gotten 40 to 50 armored vehicles across the broad Han river, crossing at several points south of

Continued on Page 2, Col. 4

Holiday Weather Will Be Hot---Traffic's Sizzling, Too

Coastal fog was forecast as the only exception to an otherwise entirely fair pre-Fourth of July week end.

Inland weather will be cooler, the Weather Bureau said.

The transportation business will be hot, however, with near-capacity reservations and extra sections scheduled by all major bus, railway and air lines.

The highways will be kept hot by "over a million" cars in California, according to the California State Automobile Association, and 34,000,000 cars throughout the country, according to the National Safety Council.

The council said it expects "the worst traffic jam in history" between 6 o'clock last night and midnight Tuesday.

It added that it expects the traffic jam to kill at least 385 people.

Drownings, firecracker fatalities and miscellaneous violent deaths are expected to add to the holiday toll.

All agencies broadcast the usual warnings:

Don't drive after drinking; watch out for other drivers; don't crowd; don't swim in unfamiliar ponds; don't kill yourself, and try not to kill too many other people, please.

Governor Warren came up with a novel pre-Independence Day suggestion. He told Californians they ought to eat turkey on the Fourth of July. (To help California turkey growers sell their crop.)

The Weather Bureau said it doesn't expect new heat records to match the anticipated travel records. Pleasanton, in Alameda county, registered 106 degrees yesterday, a high for the year, but elsewhere readings were down from Thursday's record heat.

Walnut Creek, for instance, was down from 112 to 106; Oakland was down from 91 to 87; San Francisco was down from 76 to 71.

Through the central valleys most towns registered temperatures over a hundred and Los Angeles hit 91 for the second straight day.

In El Centro, where the mercury climbed to 118, the death of Mrs. Della L. Nevins, 39, was attributed to the heat.

The East Bay Municipal Utility District reported its customers tapped their greatest day's supply of water in history Thursday—160,000,000 gallons of the cool stuff, about 50,000,000 gallons more than usual.

For the survivors of the highway rush—building up to the biggest ever recorded for the date last night on Golden Gate Bridge—scores of Northern California communities were planning week end and July Fourth celebrations, rodeos, festivals and fairs.

The Index

Comics 11
Crossword Puzzle 4H
Drama 5
Editorial:
"The U. N. Stake in Korea"... 10
Finance 12, 4H
Leiser 1H
Lichty's Cartoon 9
Lyons Den.................. 2
Radio and Television......... 3H
Vital Statistics 7
Women's World 6

By Chronicle Photographer Ken McLaughlin

GREEN PACIFIC SWELLS—So coldly lethal the night before—rippled gently yesterday over the Benevolence and over the dead, if any, trapped below. Waves broke into bubbling surf against the sunken hospital ship, and water only inches deep flowed glass-like over the freshly-painted red cross on her white hull. The Benevolence floundered on her side in 75 feet of water outside the Golden Gate (far background). Two lifeboats still tied to the ship jutted out of the water like grave-markers over the dead at sea. A hundred yards beyond, the Coast Guard buoy-tender Magnolia stood to warn vessels of the wreck, now become a menace to navigation.

FOUNDED 1865—VOL. CLXXII, NO. 43 CCCCAAA SAN FRANCISCO, SUNDAY, AUGUST 27, 1950 GA 1-1112 DAILY 7 CENTS, SUNDAY 15 CENTS

Korea---Losses, but Optimism

Enemy Takes Town in the East; Allies More Confident, Anyway

South Koreans Fall Back From Kigye, Near Pohang

By the Associated Press

TOKYO, Aug. 27—North Korean Communists gained two miles last night (Saturday) on the northeast end of the Korean war front, 65 air miles north of the United Nations' lifeline port of Pusan.

On the southern end, 35 air miles west of Pusan, advance elements of 15,000 tank-supported Communists forced back a U. S. 25th Division outpost today in a continuation of attacks possibly presaging a full-scale offensive.

The Communist push on the northeast, in the Pohang-Kigye sector:

1—Overran the town of Kigye.

2—Drove South Korean Capitol division troops eight miles south of positions they had held on August 24.

3—Prompted the U. S. Eighth Army commander to fly to the sector for a look at the situation.

The Capitol Division, after yielding Kigye, nine miles northwest of Pohang, withdrew two miles to a road junction to the southeast.

On the Capitol Division's right flank, the South Korean Third Division, which had advanced past coastal Hunghae, was pushed back Saturday night two miles to a position one-half mile south of the town. Hunghae is eight miles north of Pohang, best United Nations port in Korea outside of Pusan.

ALLIED BOMBARDMENT

These reverses were suffered by the defenders despite a supporting bombardment of 1100 rounds of heavy shells poured into Communist positions over a 24-hour period, starting Friday morning, by American warships.

The new Red coastal punches were dealt on a front some 35 to 45 miles east-northeast of Taegu. The North Koreans had shifted their main forces eastward since 50,000 Reds had failed in seven days of fierce fighting to capture Taegu.

American officers, analyzing the Red defeat before Taegu, said it meant the United Nations' forces have passed the crisis and will hold although minor withdrawals still are to be expected.

THE SITUATION

This was the situation along the 120-mile battle perimeter, beginning at Pohang and curving west and south:

Pohang—Lieutenant General Walton H. Walker, commander of the U. S. Eighth Army, and Lieutenant General Earl Partridge, commander of the Fifth Air Force, rushed to the sector to study the South Korean reverses north of Pohang and south of Kigye. The Red drive, which American officers had been expecting, menaced not only the port city of Pohang, but a near-by airfield used by supply planes.

Taegu Area—Near Chongno, 24

Continued on Page 4, Col. 3

Reds Have Shot Bolt, U. S. Leaders Believe

By HOMER BIGART

Exclusive to The Chronicle from the New York Herald Tribune (Copyright, 1950)

WITH U. S. TROOPS IN KOREA, Aug. 26—Troops of the First South Korean division advancing against very slight opposition retook the village of Chonpyong this afternoon and straightened out a vulnerable salient in the Allied line north of Taegu.

Success of this action was further evidence that North Korean Communists no longer were capable of maintaining continuous pressure on the United Nations bridgehead.

In fact some of the line officers were of the opinion that the Red divisions (3d, 13th and 15th) massed for assault against Taegu were now so badly mauled and depleted that it was necessary for the enemy to withdraw most of his infantry back beyond range of American artillery to reorganize.

Mounting confidence was reflected in diplomatic as well as military circles. American Ambassador John J. Muccio, visiting Taegu today, said the tide of battle had definitely turned and that the North Koreans had failed completely in their attempts to propagandize the occupied areas of South Korea.

General officers guessed that it would be victory by Thanksgiving. About three more weeks might be needed for the Allied buildup and meanwhile the enemy would be capable of only limited action against the bridgehead.

There was the tantalizing prospect that the Reds would collapse suddenly once Americans swung into an offensive. But a more likely possibility was that the Communists would fight ferociously even with their army organization de-

Continued on Page 5, Col. 1

Shoppers

Most of San Francisco's leading downtown stores will remain open tomorrow until 9 P. M.

The Index

Music And Art	19TW	Leiser	3H
Automobiles	7L	J. P. McEvoy	14
Books	19TW	Msgr. Sheen	8WA
Chess	8L	Puzzles	8L
Clubs	15SS	Radio and Television	21TW
Contract Contacts	18	Society	14S
Crossword Puzzle	8L	Travel	4L
Drama	14TW	Vital Statistics	8WA
Fashions	1S	Want Ads (WA); Leisure (L);	
Gardens	2L	This World (TW); Women's	
Homes	3L	World (S); Sporting Green (H).	

5 Die, 30 Hurt in Welsh Rail Crash

CONWAY, Wales, Aug. 27 (AP)—At least five persons were killed and an undetermined number injured when the crack Irish Mail collided with a light engine and overturned near here early today (Sunday).

A spokesman for the British Railways said that five passengers were known to have perished "and there may be more." Thirty persons have been rushed to hospitals with serious injuries, he added.

Matthews Rebuked

Acheson Says 'Preventive War' Talk Not Official

By the Associated Press

WASHINGTON, Aug. 26—Secretary of State Dean Acheson, with an assist from President Truman, cracked down on Navy Secretary Francis P. Matthews today for saying the United States should be willing to institute a war "to compel co-operation for peace."

The action not only precipitated the first wide open Cabinet split on foreign policy since the row between James F. Byrnes and Henry A. Wallace in September, 1946—it also seemed to make inevitable a public debate on a preventive war with Russia.

Matthews expressed his view in a speech at the Boston Navy Yard last night. Today the State Department was asked whether what he said represented Government policy—or was some sort of policy-making trial balloon.

"NOT CLEARED"

Press Officer Roger Tubby, in a statement initiated by Acheson and reportedly okayed by the President, asserted:

"The speech was not cleared by the Department of State. Mr. Matthews' remarks about instituting a war for peace do not represent United States policy. The United States Government does not favor instituting a war of any kind." The White House press office added that the Matthews speech was not cleared by the White House.

Tubby told reporters that ever since the Wallace-Byrnes incident, there has been a firmly established policy on clearance of speeches on foreign affairs. Any speech by Government officials which goes beyond the established lines of foreign policy (as laid down by the President) should be cleared with the State Department, Tubby explained.

Wallace was fired by Mr. Truman in 1946 after making a speech advocating a softer policy toward Russia. The President at the time laid down orders that no official should

Continued on Page 7, Col. 1

As for Weather, No News Is . . . etc.

Another foggy morning and fair afternoon were forecast for today by the Weather Bureau.

While valley temperatures hit the 100 mark and sat there, San Francisco was promised "little temperature change," which meant the mercury would hover in the low 60's.

Westerly winds from 10 to 20 miles an hour are due this afternoon.

18 Dead in Ship Disaster

Navy and Coast Guard Inquiries Begun on Collision Off the Gate

492 Rescued From Ocean; 13 Believed Still Missing

CAPTAIN B. E. BACON
Acting captain of sunken ship

The Navy and the Coast Guard opened formal inquiry yesterday into the offshore crash that ripped open the hospital ship Benevolence at dusk on Friday and sent her to the bottom within 30 minutes.

They sought to fix the blame for the loss of at least 18 lives when the freighter Mary Luckenbach sliced into the Navy craft, spilled more than 500 persons into the cold seas and produced the worst marine disaster in these waters since the Rio de Janeiro carried 128 to death in 1901.

As a formal board of inquiry convened on Treasure Island, as a Coast Guard board surveyed the damaged freighter, and as divers peered at the sunken hospital ship as she lay in 12 fathoms, less than two miles off the Cliff House, the Navy announced these statistics:

Eighteen persons died, all from injury and exposure suffered in the cold waters into which they slid or jumped as the ripped-open Benevolence went to the bottom.

Four hundred and ninety-two persons were rescued by small craft that converged on the fog-shrouded scene and milled about in the darkness in such numbers that one of the rescued exclaimed: "It looked like Fifth and Market at 5 p. m."

Of the 492 blue-lipped and shivering survivors that passed through Letterman, Marine and Oak Knoll Hospitals, only three were found to be in serious condition; all the rest were discharged by late yesterday.

These—plus the 18 whose bodies were recovered—are believed to account for almost all persons who were aboard the Benevolence as she steamed out of this port at 2 p. m. Friday for the shakedown run that ended in tragedy.

Navy spokesmen said an estimated 13 persons remained unaccounted for.

In a search for their bodies or for unlikely survivors, surface craft crisscrossed the area of the crash all day yesterday and helicopters surveyed the beaches and inlets along the coast on both sides of the Golden Gate.

The Coast Guard, which had closed the port to shipping at 10:29 p. m. Friday to protect the small armada of rescue craft and the survivors it sought, opened up the lanes again at 7 a. m. yesterday.

The Coast Guard cutter Gresham, after an all-night tour of the seas outside the heads put into port shortly before noon with the last group of survivors—thirty-one who had been pulled to safety shortly after the Benevolence sank but spent the night at sea.

In all discussions of the collision,

Continued on Page A, Col. 5

More News and Pictures Of Shipwreck Are Inside

There are two pages of pictures and numerous stories of the crash in the fog and the sinking of the hospital ship on inside pages of today's Chronicle.

PAGE A—Drawings of the tragic collision by Chronicle Artist Frank Rinna; the story of the officers of the Benevolence.

A map of the area in which the collision occurred, showing the ship channel.

PAGE B—A full page of pictures of the disaster and rescue work.

PAGE 2—List of the survivors; list of the identified dead.

A report of the first inspection of the sunken hulk of the Benevolence by Navy divers.

PAGE 3—Reports on the last survivors brought ashore, 20 hours after the collision, and on the harbor pilot who was among the dead. Pictures include one of the damaged freighter Mary Luckenbach.

A report of the work of the Red Cross in the catastrophe.

A picture of one of the many distressed relatives who hunted at hospitals and piers for survivors during the terrible night.

PAGE 10—Stories of the search work of a Coast Guard picket boat, and the crowds at Ocean Beach, with more pictures.

A report that the Navy has already begun to activate another ship to replace the sunken Benevolence.

PAGE 11—Pictures of the Navy nurses who were rescued after the Benevolence sank, and a story of their experiences after the Navy hospital ship went down.

PAGE 12—A full page of pictures taken by the radio operator of the Mary Luckenbach after the collision, showing how the rescue work was done.

The story of the fisherman who rescued 24 of the survivors.

George Bernard Shaw Dies at 94

COMPARATIVE TEMPERATURES For Wednesday, November 1, 1950	High	Low		High	Low
San Francisco	69	57	New York	83	58
Oakland	72	54	Chicago	81	64
Sacramento	68	55	Kansas City	71	58
Los Angeles	83	55	New Orleans	83	59
Portland	56	44	Miami	80	69
Seattle	50	42	Washington	85	57

Forecast for Today: Fair, Morning Fog
(For Details See Page 15)

San Francisco Chronicle
THE CITY'S ONLY HOME-OWNED NEWSPAPER
FINAL

FOUNDED 1865—VOL. CLXXII, NO. 110 CCCCAAA—CP SAN FRANCISCO, THURSDAY, NOVEMBER 2, 1950 GA 1-1112 DAILY 7 CENTS, SUNDAY 15¢

After the Attack

(AP) Wirephoto

AFTER SHOOTING—President Truman wore a sober look as he stood beside British Ambassador Sir Oliver Franks at Arlington Cemetery shortly after the attempt on the President's life yesterday afternoon.

PLOT TO SHOOT TRUMAN FAILS

(AP) Wirephoto

FALLEN ASSASSIN—With blood streaming from head wounds, one of the gunmen who tried to assassinate President Truman yesterday lay on the steps of Blair House after the gunplay had died down. He was Oscar Collazo of the Bronx. A bullet from a Secret Service agent's gun had brought him down, but had not killed him.

Blair House Gunfight

Two Puerto Rican Rebels Shot Down---One Dead; One Guard Slain, Two Hurt

Battle Wakens President From Nap; Assassin Says Plot Is Aimed at Winning Freedom for Puerto Rico

By the United Press

WASHINGTON, Nov. 1—President Truman escaped assassination by minutes today when two Puerto Rican extremists were shot down in a wild gun battle on the President's Blair House doorstep.

One of the assassins and a White House guard were killed in the shooting. The other assailant was wounded but was expected to live.

Two other guards were wounded in the battle, but both were expected to live. The wounded Puerto Rican, Oscar Collazo, 37, of New York, was under heavy police guard at a local hospital after being booked on a murder charge.

Killed in the attempt to storm the doors of the President's home was Collazo's friend and fellow New Yorker, Griselio Torresola, alias Lorenzo Angelina Torresola. Both were members of the anti-United States Puerto Rican Nationalist party.

Secret Service Chief U. E. Baughman quoted Collazo as saying that he and Torresola were alone in deciding to "kill the President and start a revolution in this country and win independence for Puerto Rico." Baughman said the pair conceived the plan in New York Monday and immediately left for the capital.

White House Guard Leslie Coffelt died while undergoing emergency surgery for bullet wounds in the chest and stomach.

Guard Joseph Downs was in critical condition with a bullet wound in the neck, and Guard Donald T. Birdzell was in fair condition with wounds in both legs. But Brigadier General Wallace Graham, the President's personal physician who supervised their treatment, said both "are going to pull through."

Mr. Truman was rudely awakened from an after-lunch nap when the gun battle broke out under his second-floor bedroom window about 2:15 p. m. Later, apparently unruffled by the first direct attempt on his life, he kept a scheduled appointment at an outdoor memorial service in Arlington National Cemtery. Later in the afternoon the President kept an appointment with Democratic National Chairman William M. Boyle, and returned to Blair House about 5 o'clock.

JUST BEFORE TRIP

Torresola and Collazo rushed at the Blair House entrance on Pennsylvania avenue with blazing pistols just a few minutes before the President had been expected to leave for the Arlington trip.

Police speculated that the two gunmen knew of the President's impending trip, and had timed their bold raid in hopes of meeting him at or near the door. If that was the plot, their timing was only several minutes off.

Leader of Puerto Rican revolt arrested. Wife of assassin arraigned for conspiracy; two other suspects hunted. For these stories and more pictures, see Page 12. Other stories of the plot on Page 13.

On Torresola's body, police found letters signed by Puerto Rican Nationalist leader Pedro Albizu Campos urging him to further "the movement" without "hesitation of any kind."

The Nationalists, a small but active splinter group, demand immediate independence for Puerto Rico. They staged a bloody uprising in the U. S. island territory earlier this week. The Blair House attack occurred almost simultaneously with an ineffective bombing of the Puerto Rico government offices in New York.

MIXING WITH TOURISTS

Collazo and Torresola approached Blair House from opposite directions, mingling with Government workers returning to their jobs after lunch and with tourists strolling in the unseasonably warm afternoon sunshine.

Blair House is across Pennsyl-

Continued on Page 13, Col. 1

Teachers Must Sign Oath Today

The San Francisco Board of Education last night recommended that all school employees who do not sign the State loyalty oath by the midnight deadline tonight be immediately suspended.

The action was the first formal position on the controversial oath taken by any school board in the State.

The vote on the recommendation, which was passed in the form of a resolution - directive to Superintendent Herbert Clish, was unanimous. Two board members, Louise Nason and Dr. Karl Schaupp, were absent.

Clish announced following passage of the resolution that he would confer with the Board's attorney, Irving G. Breyer, today on what final action to take.

However, he said, in view of the board's directive, teachers not signing the oath will not be allowed to teach Friday or thereafter.

41 NONSIGNERS

A total of 41 school employees who have so far not signed the oath will be affected by the order, Clish said.

Among these 41 are ten teachers, two child care center employees and one clerk who refuse to sign. There are 11 other employees who are "considering" but have not definitely refused and 17 others who have not signed and have declared no intention of signing or refusing to sign.

Earlier yesterday the disputed loyalty oath won its first constitutional test in Superior Court challenges by a number of nonsigners. (For details on the court action see Page 2.)

Despite yesterday's court test, however, the constitutionality of last night's school board action was heatedly questioned by representatives of the nonsigners.

ATTORNEY'S CHARGE

Attorney Wayne Collins, of the American Civil Liberties Union, said the law violates the tradition of allowing the Appellate Courts to resolve such questions.

He said he was confident the law would be found unconstitutional eventually even if it is necessary to appeal to the U. S. Supreme Court.

He said that if the law is found unconstitutional, the board's suspension of the nonsigners will have been a "subversion of the State and U. S. Constitutions."

He urged the board to allow the nonsigners to continue teaching, even without compensation if necessary, until the law is finally tested.

George Johns, labor member of the Board of Education, expressed the common view of the board members when he said:

"I don't like this law. But when the Legislature passes a law, we have to live with it whether we like it or not."

The Korean War

American Regiment Is Encircled As Chinese Reds Join Fighting

By the Associated Press

SEOUL, Nov. 2—Rocket-firing Chinese and North Korean troops today (Thursday) pressed attacks which have encircled an American regiment and forced other units to retreat in Northwestern Korea.

Utilizing a new weapon—82 millimeter rockets—the revitalized Reds struck on the left flank of an American armored column which pushed up the west coast to within 15 air miles of the Manchurian border. This was a four-mile advance since yesterday.

A U. S. 1st Army Corps spokesman called the situation serious. The attacks put U. S. 1st Cavalry elements and four South Korean divisions—the 1st, 6th, 7th and 8th—on the defensive. One thousand Reds on horseback were in the attacking forces.

For the first time, a U. S. 1st Corps spokesman admitted that "Chinese troops" were attacking in the northwest.

Corps officers cautiously added they were "not sure whether Chinese troops form the bulk of enemy forces which have thrown the United Nations off balance for the moment."

High American officers previously had acknowledged a Chinese Red regiment was in action in Northeastern Korea. South Korean officers have insisted at least two Chinese Red divisions were in battle there.

The surrounded American regiment, a unit of the U. S. 1st Cavalry Division, was in the Unsan area on the east flank of a U. S. 24th Division armored spearhead which drove west 17 miles yesterday to within 15 air miles of the Manchurian border.

Other 1st Cavalry elements moved up to the aid of the encircled regiment.

The advancing column of the 24th Division thrust beyond Charyongwan to a point 15 air miles southeast of the border at its nearest point and 18 air miles southeast of Sinuiju. Sinuiju is just across the Yalu river from the Manchurian city of Antung, where the Chinese Reds maintain a large air base.

Meanwhile, Russian-made jet fighter planes made their debut in support of Red forces. Six jet planes fought inconclusively with slower, propeller-driven Mustangs, then broke off the engagement near Charyongwan.

Fair, Warmer Today, Says the Weatherman

Northern California's weather settled into its usual November rut yesterday after being jounced around by the windiest, wettest October in years.

The last remnants of rain-bearing clouds vanished and the Weather Bureau got out the standard forecast: "Fair except for local fog in the morning."

It will be slightly warmer, with the temperature climbing to a predicted high of 73. Low today is forecast as between 46 and 51. Light westerly winds of 10 to 15 m.p.h. will blow in the afternoon.

Pope Pius Proclaims New Dogma

By the Associated Press

VATICAN CITY, Nov. 1—The ancient Roman Catholic belief that the Virgin Mary was taken into heaven in body as well as in spirit became an article of the church's creed by proclamation of Pope Pius XII in a spectacular ceremony today.

A multitude regarded here as the greatest assembly of its kind since the start of Christendom prayed and cheered under the eyes of the Pope in St. Peter's Square. Vatican sources estimated the crowd numbered more than 500,000. Church bells pealed throughout Rome.

As night came on around the world, Catholics lit up their churches and homes in rejoicing. Millions of lights flamed. The celebration with lights had been suggested to Bishops by the Holy Year Central Committee. As the rites progressed in Rome, other ceremonies were held throughout the world, in cathedrals, churches and even in missionary huts in jungle clearings.

This All Saints Day had witnessed the crowning event of the Catholic 1950 Holy Year Jubilee. It

Continued on Page 5, Col. 4

Liner Not to Be a Transport

WASHINGTON, Nov. 1 (AP)—The Government tonight dropped plans to turn the superliner United States into a troop ship.

The Index

City Notices 15
Chess by Mail 9
Comics 19
Contract Contacts 14
Crossword Puzzles 26
Delaplane 17
Drama 12, 13
Editorial:
"The Solid Warren Record" 18
Finance 20, 25
Bill Leiser 1H
Lichty 23
Lyons Den 2
Radio and Television 25
Women's World 10, 11

Royce Brier's column, THIS WORLD TODAY, is on the Editorial Page.

G. B. SHAW
Almost a century

G. B. Shaw, Dramatist, Dies at 94

By the Associated Press

AYOT ST. LAWRENCE, England, Nov. 2—George Bernard Shaw, one of the modern age's greatest dramatists and its most caustic critic, died today (Thursday) at the age of 94.

The white-bearded Irish-born sage, whose wit was renowned throughout the world for a half century, succumbed at 4:59 a. m. (8:59 p. m. Wednesday, Pacific time).

Shaw's death was announced to newsmen by his housekeeper, Alice Laden.

Shaw lapsed into his final coma yesterday morning at 3 a. m. (10 p. m., Tuesday, Eastern Standard Time) and never regained consciousness. Operated on seven weeks ago for a broken thigh, suffered when he slipped and fell in his garden, Shaw grew steadily weaker. A bladder ailment aggravated his condition.

(For the story of Shaw's life, see Page 3.

Kaiser Steel Settles Debt With the RFC

By SIDNEY P. ALLEN
Financial Editor, The Chronicle

Henry J. Kaiser yesterday handed a check for **$91,185,990** to the Reconstruction Finance Corp. in full payment of loans on Kaiser Steel Corp.'s plant at Fontana.

Payment was made at a ceremony at the Chase National Bank in New York city. It consummated the largest single industrial financing by private funds in the history of the Western States.

Kaiser Steel previously had repaid $32,119,110 in principal on the RFC loans. In addition $22,944,604 had been paid in interest on the loans.

REFINANCING PROGRAM

Yesterday's repayment marked completion of a $125,000,000 financing deal by Kaiser Steel whereby it raised private money to pay off Uncle Sam and undertake another major expansion.

The company has given an immediate go-ahead order for a $24,545,000 expansion at its plant. This will increase its steel capacity by 150,000 tons a year. The company also will construct a tin plate mill with a capacity of 200,000 tons a year.

The expansion will boost Kaiser Steel capacity to 1,380,000 tons. This contrasts with a capacity of 450,000 tons in 1943, first year of production.

SUPPLY FOR WEST

The tin plate mill will help supply the West's concentration of can manufacturing and food canning plants. Studies have shown the seven Western States last year consumed 700,000 tons of tin plate, yet there is only one tin-plate mill west of the Mississippi river.

Following the ceremony, Kaiser told a New York news conference that if the economy remains free, and is not curbed by credit controls, he believes the Nation should have an annual capacity of 130,000,000 tons of steel "as quickly as it can be built."

EXTRA

San Francisco Chronicle

FINAL

THE CITY'S ONLY HOME-OWNED NEWSPAPER

FOUNDED 1865—VOL. CLXXIII, NO. 86 CCCCAAA SAN FRANCISCO, WEDNESDAY, APRIL 11, 1951 GA 1-1112 DAILY 7 CENTS, SUNDAY 15¢

COMPARATIVE TEMPERATURES
For Tuesday, April 10, 1951

	High	Low		High	Low
San Francisco	56	48	New York	56	49
Oakland	69	49	Chicago	51	41
Sacramento	92	54	Kansas City	49	42
Los Angeles	64	56	New Orleans	74	55
Portland	67	41	Miami	72	61
Seattle	64	39	Washington	58	47

Forecast for Today: FAIR
(For Details See Page 27)

MACARTHUR FIRED

Truman Ousts Him From All Jobs ---Tokyo HQ Stunned by the News

Sterling Hayden Says He Was a Communist

Film Actor Admits He Joined Party In 1946, but Soon Quit in Disgust

Exclusive to The Chronicle From the New York Herald Tribune

WASHINGTON, April 10 — Sterling Hayden, motion picture actor, told the House Un-American Activities Committee today how he joined a Hollywood Communist cell in 1946, but resigned six months later in revulsion against totalitarian ways.

Hayden, who was a marine captain during World War II and served behind the German lines in the Balkans, told the committee today he had joined the Communist party because he became enthused about the spirit of the Yugoslav partisans.

"It was the stupidest, most ignorant thing I have ever done," Hayden told the committee. "I had a very emotional, unsound approach."

Hayden said he decided to leave the party "because of the manner in which everything is predetermined." Although he had "become a victim of the idea they had the

A top Navy explosives expert—and his wife, a State Department employee — are suspended. See Page 5.

form of democracy," he said, "it only took a couple of months for me to realize that they think they have the key to everything by some occult power."

Unlike Larry Parks, another Hollywood actor who admitted former Communist membership to the committee, Hayden had no compunction about mentioning the names of others he said were Communists. The only Hollywood personality of any note whom he named, however, was Actress Karen Morley, whose connection with Communist front groups has caused comment for several years.

(Associated Press reported Hayden said he didn't know any big-name Hollywood personalities who are or had been connected with the party. While he originally had the impression that a number of name actors were Reds, he said, he later learned there weren't enough actors in the party to form their own group.)

Hayden urged the committee to recommend legislation "so people in the same position can get this thing off their chests." He declared: "I have heard there are many, very many — thousands — of ex-Communists who don't know what to do about it."

Hayden said that in his own case he wrote FBI Director J. Edgar Hoover within a month after the start of the Korean war to confess his former ties. He said he wanted to clear himself for possible military service in case the fighting spread.

In rapid, intense tones, Hayden

Continued on Page 5, Col. 1

Remmer Gives Up

Gambler Posts Bail on Charge Of Tax Evasion

Elmer F. (Bones) Remmer, San Francisco and Nevada gambler, surrendered in Reno yesterday on a Federal Grand Jury indictment charging him with evading $160,687.64 in income taxes for the years 1944-46.

The chubby gambler, released on a $15,800 property bond after being fingerprinted at first refused to discuss the charge, but his attorney attributed it to "politics."

"There is no criminal case," said John R. Golden, Remmer's San Francisco lawyer who flew to Reno to conduct the surrender. "Pressure created by the California Crime Commission and the Kefauver Committee, putting the Internal Revenue Bureau on the spot, precipitated this thing."

Remmer was angry when he later talked to reporters:

'If I am guilty of tax evasion, so is every other businessman in the country.

"I filed my returns honestly, the same as they do. Anything more than that I will tell in court."

The indictment, returned by a Federal Grand Jury at Carson City on Monday, was taken off the secret file after Remmer's surrender. It specified six counts on which Remmer "wilfully and knowingly attempted to defeat the purpose of

Continued on Page 17, Col. 1

Mao Tze-Tung Reported Sick

HONG KONG, Wednesday, April 11 (UP)—The Chinese Communist Government has announced privately that Mao Tze-tung, Red China's No. 1 leader, is ill and that his duties have been taken over temporarily by Liu Shao-chi, Communist Party secretary, an official of the Indonesian Embassy in Peiping revealed yesterday.

The Index

Royce Brier	20
Chess Column	14
Comics	21
Contract Contacts	14
Crossword Puzzle	17
Delaplane	19
Drama	14, 15
Editorial: "Fact and Fancy in Crisis"	20
Finance	22, 4H
Horoscope	29
Leonard Lyons	2
Lichty	16
Radio and Television	30
Vital Statistics	17
Women's World	12, 13

The President's Historic Decision

General Ridgway Is Given Far East Commands ---MacArthur Receives His Ouster in Silence

'He Had No Advance Warning'

By RUSSELL BRINES
Associated Press Staff Writer

TOKYO, April 11—A small brown envelope with "flash" printed on it in red carried to General Douglas MacArthur today (Wednesday) the news that he had been fired from his commands by President Truman.

It was delivered to the five-star general by a senior aide, Colonel Sid Huff.

Huff said MacArthur received the news without comment. He indicated the general had no forewarning that he was being relieved.

The general said he would have no statement immediately.

(United Press reported MacArthur took the news "magnificently," according to his military secretary.

(The general "never turned a hair," Major General Courtney Whitney said.

("His soldierly qualities were never more pronounced," Whitney said. "I think this has been his finest hour.")

The message came as a Signal Corps communication about the time the Army radio announced MacArthur was finished as commander.

MacArthur got the news while at lunch with his wife, Senator Warren Magnuson (Dem-Wash.) and William Sterns of Northwest Airlines. He was joined a few minutes later by his 13-year-old son, Arthur.

MacArthur returned to his headquarters in the Dai Ichi Building at 5:20 p. m. accompanied by Major General Courtney Whitney, his military secretary.

The American Embassy got the news and reporters relayed it to General MacArthur's honor guard. Guardsmen

Continued on Page 17, Col. 2

GENERAL DOUGLAS MacARTHUR
He is relieved of all commands, "effective at once"

GOP Incensed

McCarthy: 'A Victory for Reds'; Knowland: 'Step Toward a Munich'

WASHINGTON, April 11 (UP)—Republican supporters of General Douglas MacArthur were violently critical today (Wednesday) of the President's action in firing the Far East commander.

Senator Joseph R. McCarthy (Rep-Wis.) one of Mr. Truman's consistent critics, said it is "perhaps the greatest victory the Communists have ever won."

Senator William F. Knowland (Rep-Calif.) said:

"By his action the President has yielded to British and American critics of General MacArthur. Our position in Japan and the whole Far East is placed in jeopardy by an action which most observers will interpret as a preliminary step to a Far Eastern Munich.

"It is also a great victory for Acheson and his Far Eastern policies. When General MacArthur arrives home the American people will have the opportunity to demonstrate to the world and to the President the high regard they have for MacArthur and his service to his country."

McCarthy said "If MacArthur had been enough of a traitor and gone along with 'Operation Acheson' of letting our Allies fall without having it appear that we shoved them' he wouldn't have been replaced."

He said the "shoved" quotation was from Owen Lattimore, whom McCarthy has accused of being a chief architect of State Department Far Eastern policy.

Republican House Leader Joseph

Continued on Page 4, Col. 5

'He Has Proven Himself Unable to Co-operate With United Nations Policy'

By the United Press

WASHINGTON, April 11—President Truman today (Wednesday) relieved General Douglas MacArthur of all his Far Eastern commands because of his inability to give "his whole-hearted support" to the policies of the United States Government.

The President designated Lieutenant General Matthew B. Ridgway, now commander of the Eighth Army in Korea, to succeed MacArthur.

Announcement of the President's decision followed days of international controversy over the General's endorsement of policies, particularly relating to

The text of Mr. Truman's statement on General MacArthur, the text of the President's order relieving the general, and the texts of hitherto secret documents pertaining to the policy controversy—are on Page 8.

Meanwhile, the British have proposed that we give Formosa to the Chinese Reds and let the Peiping regime represent China on the Japanese peace treaty. See Page 17.

the use of Chinese Nationalist troops, in conflict with the announced policies of the President.

Mr. Truman discharged MacArthur from his commands with this statement:

"With deep regret I have concluded that General of the Army Douglas MacArthur is unable to give his whole-hearted support to the policies of the United States Government and of the United Nations in matters pertaining to his official duties."

The President added that in view of his responsibilities under the United States Constitution and the United Nations, "I have decided that I must make a change of command in the Far East."

"I have, therefore, relieved General MacArthur of his commands and have designated Lieutenant General Matthew B. Ridgway as his successor," the President said.

Lieutenant General James A. van Fleet was named to succeed Ridgway in command of the Eighth Army in Korea.

White House release of the announcement at 1 a. m. today (10 p. m. San Francisco time) was timed with delivery of the President's orders to MacArthur in Tokyo. The orders were transmitted through regular military channels.

In addition to the brief orders to MacArthur and Ridgway, the White House released a hitherto secret file of communications between the Joint Chiefs of Staff and MacArthur which, according to Press Secretary Joseph Short, proved that MacArthur on several instances . . . recently made statements publicly and privately which made it "questionable" in the President's mind whether MacArthur was in full sympathy with the policies of this Government.

The President, in a brief statement accompanying his action, said he regretted having to relieve MacArthur because the general's place in history "as one of our greatest commanders is fully established."

"The Nation owes him a debt of gratitude for the distinguished and exceptional service which he has rendered his country in posts of great responsibility" the President said.

"For that reason I repeat my regret at the necessity for the action I feel compelled to take in his case."

Mr. Truman supported the idea of "full and vigorous

Continued on Page 4, Col. 1

Veterans' Affairs Leader Leaps to Death

Alfred G. Boss, 57, haberdasher and former president of the 91st Division Assn., yesterday leaped to his death from the Bay Bridge.

The jump was witnessed by California Highway Patrolman Claude Harmon and Luther Riley, of 107 N. Ridge road, San Francisco, who reached the bridge railing seconds after Boss went over the side at 8 a. m.

In the cash register of his store at 650 Market street, Boss left a note to his wife, Ann, saying he had been "slipping lately" and that the doctor would substantiate his view.

'I believe all is in order and there is enough for you to have those wonderful trips. Think of me. The stars are looking down on you from heaven," the note said.

It was signed "your Al."

The jump took place near the first bridge pier east of Yerba Buena island.

Highway Patrolman Harmon said he saw Boss driving slowly east and pulled up alongside his automobile thinking something was wrong.

"He smiled and waved me on," Harmon said, "but a minute later I looked back and saw him leaving his car and running toward the rail."

Riley, who was driving directly behind Boss' car, stopped and rushed out to try and prevent the jump. He was too late.

He said Boss took off his coat and threw it down on the pavement just before hurdling the rail.

"It sounded like a pistol shot when he hit the water. I saw it," Riley said.

The Coast Guard recovered Boss' body after a 45-minute search and identification was made at the San Francisco's Coroner's office by William Duffy, a clerk in the Boss store.

The firm was started at the same location 50 years ago by Boss' father, the late George Boss.

Boss and his wife lived at 7613 A street, Hayward. They have no children.

Besides his wife he is survived by a sister, Charlotte Wolff.

During World War I, Boss served with the 363d Infantry Regiment in the 91st Division. He was active in veterans affairs and served as commander of Post 4?5 of the American Legion.

He was a member of the Legion, the 40 and 8 Society and the Shrine.

He also was a member of General Jacob Smith Post No. 83, VFW.

Funeral services will be held Friday at 1 p. m. at Halsted's, 1123 Sutter street, under auspices of King Solomon Lodge No. 260, F. & A. M. Officers and members of the various military groups in which he was active, will hold services at 8 p. m. tomorrow (Thursday).

Valley Towns Roasted as Mercury Soars

Record heat began giving California's interior valleys a presummer baking yesterday.

Some temperatures were up to 100, and the Weather Bureau said the heat spell would continue today.

San Francisco had a typical "summer" day with a high of 56—fair with afternoon fog rolling over Twin Peaks on a chill westerly wind. The same sort of thing was forecast for today.

MACARTHUR IS HERE

San Francisco Chronicle
THE CITY'S ONLY HOME-OWNED NEWSPAPER
VOL. CLXXIII, NO. 93 CCCCAAA SAN FRANCISCO, WEDNESDAY, APRIL 18, 1951 7 CENTS, SUNDAY 15c

FINAL

Hundreds of Thousands Wait, Cheer General; New Ceremonies Today

Crowds Go Wild at Airport---Schedule Is Thrown Aside

By ALVIN D. HYMAN

General Douglas MacArthur came home last night to San Francisco's wildest welcome.

He came home a five-star General of the Army without a command, and the city gave him a tumultuous greeting that frequently lapsed into near riot.

How many hundreds of thousands turned out to glimpse the soldier who defended Bataan, and reconquered the Philippines, and ruled a conquered empire of 90,000,000, was anybody's guess.

Some said a half million and some said three quarters of a million—but they thronged and milled about General MacArthur in numbers that disrupted the carefully planned formalities and threw the triumphal procession from San Francisco airport to the St. Francis Hotel entirely out of schedule, and brought repeated emergency calls for police squads to untangle traffic knots and let the motorcade proceed.

THE BIGGEST EVER

Police who struggled with other crowds that crowd-loving San Francisco has put forth—crowds celebrating the arrival of Presidents and ocean-jumping flyers and greeting heads of foreign states, crowds opening bridges and crowds inaugurating world's fairs—tossed up their hands at last night's outpouring and said flatly: "The town has never seen anything like THIS."

It began when the general first stepped briskly out of his four-engined transport, "Bataan," shortly after 8:30 p. m. It progressed through a half dozen almost immovable traffic jams that clotted at intervals along the route of the procession and frequently brought it to a dead halt.

It reached its full flower around Union Square, as thousands pressed against other thousands and tempers sometimes flared and fists occasionally swung in the long wait for the homecoming party to reach the Hotel St. Francis.

A LONG WAIT

A trip expected to take some 30 minutes, from airport to hotel, lengthened to an hour, and another half hour, and yet another 15 minutes, so impenetrable were the throngs that came out to shout "Welcome Home Doug" and "Glad to see you, Mac."

More than 5000 of them closed in on San Francisco's international airport to catch an early glimpse of the returning hero of Bataan.

They usurped all parking space around the Pan-American terminal at least two hours before the estimated time of arrival. Then they began parking on shoulders and in the broad fields along both sides of the approach road. Then they spread out in both directions along the old Bayshore highway, leaving their parked cars as far as four miles from the airport, and hiked in.

Meanwhile, more hundreds of thousands were taking up vantage points along the pre-announced route. They came so early and sat so tight that Mayor Elmer Robinson, on arriving at the airport a full hour before the general's arrival, estimated a quarter million were already lined up and waiting.

Expected to touch the local airport at 8 p. m. on the 2400-mile hop from Hawaii that began at 11:30 a. m., the "Bataan" lagged back a half hour.

An announcement spotted her position as off the Farallones at 8:20. Her running lights, blinking red and green, were spotted from the airport on a southward run eight minutes later. The throng set up a cheer as her landing lights went on and she came in for her landing at 8:29 p. m.

Some 200 military police were drawn stiffly to attention in a cordon around the area. An honor

Continued on Page A, Col. 1

And on the Inside . . .

A full page of pictures of the general's reception at the airport on Page D.

A big picture of the big crowd in Union Square is on Page B.

Other stories and pictures of the welcome party are on Pages A, C, 3, 4 and 5.

A map of the route for today's parade is on Page 2.

Latest reports on the Nation-wide political controversy over the general's dismissal are on Page 6.

Civic Tribute This Morning at 10:45, At the City Hall

Today will be woven into San Francisco's history as another memorable day:

General Douglas MacArthur Day.

By proclamation of Mayor Robinson the added significance was bestowed on this day so that the citizens of San Francisco may honor the soldier who "has given the American people over 50 years of devoted, diligent, and distinguished service."

To observe it—to accord the Liberator of the Philippines "the finest tribute of welcome the people can possibly extend"—the Mayor called upon all San Franciscans to attend civic ceremonies at the City Hall this morning, or to express greetings along the route that will carry the general from his hotel to the reviewing stand.

The procession is scheduled to leave the St. Francis Hotel at 9:45 a. m. and arrive at City Hall by 10:45 a. m.

GLIMPSE OF GENERAL

Thousands jamming Union Square will get a glimpse of the general.

It will move the short distance down Powell from the hotel entrance and swing into Geary, down Geary to Stockton, up Stockton to Post.

It will pass into Post and down Post to Market, thence to California. It will turn back on California to Montgomery, along this financial canyon to Market, and out Market to the City Hall via Fulton, Larkin, McAllister and Polk streets.

Mayor Elmer Robinson and Governor Earl Warren will occupy the leading car with the distinguished warrior, behind an escort of motorcycle police.

Scenes reminiscent of great days in the past when heroes have come home from the wars, or when processions up Market street have commemorated notable events, will be enacted. A paper blizzard swirling in Montgomery street, throngs filling the sidewalks, other thousands waving from skyscraper windows, flags flying, traffic at a standstill.

The biggest crowd in years is expected to cover the flagstones, the benches and probably the flower beds of Civic Center—men and women of every station in life, taking a recess from work; delegations of school children, and on the reviewing stand the dignitaries of city, county and State.

The citizens' reception committee, the ranking military officers of the Bay Area, the visiting public officials will all be gathered at the stand. John Francis Neylan and Henry Boyen, co-chairman of the committee, will introduce the Governor and the Mayor. They will deliver addresses of welcome.

A BRIEF RESPONSE

General MacArthur will respond briefly. This will be an informal response and will not touch upon the politico-military matters that led to his abrupt dismissal from all commands in the Far East and his return home. It will require, his aides say, no more than two minutes.

From these ceremonies, due to end at 11:30 a. m., the general's party will speed directly to the airport, over a route along Polk and Tenth streets to Potrero avenue, and thence to Bayshore boulevard.

Indications are that the party will board the Bataan—the general's plane—and take off for Washington by 1:30 p. m.

The Other News . . .

The Chinese Reds are pulling back to evoid fighting Allied tank columns probing deep beyond the 38th parallel. See Page 5

President Truman names W. Stuart Symington to be the one-man boss of the RFC. See Page 7

Organized labor wins a recommendation for a wage stabilization board, but industry objects and Eric Johnston says the plan is illegal. See Page 7

Captain Barton E. Bacon Jr., skipper of the ill-fated hospital ship Benevolence, will be court-martialed. See Page 11

Accordionist Dick Contino is reported found in a Los Angeles sanitarium and the FBI here charges him with being a draft dodger. See Page 18

Cloudy Early, Sunny Later

A cloudy morning and a sunny afternoon is the Weather Bureau forecast for the Bay Area today. Temperatures should be about the same.

Clouds are expected to hover over the rest of Northern California for most of the day. No rain is in sight, the forecaster said.

The Index

Royce Brier ... 20
Chess Column ... 21
Comics ... 18
Contract Contacts ... 21
Crossword Puzzle ... 19
Delaplane ... 19
Drama ... 14, 15
Editorial: "Another Phoney Peace Feeler" ... 20
Finance ... 22, 4H
Lichty ... 18
Radio and Television ... 10
Vital Statistics ... 17
Women's World ... 12, 13

Thousands of San Franciscans flocked to the International Airport last night to greet General MacArthur. Above, left to right, John Francis Neylan, Lt. Col. Anthony Storey (the pilot), Mayor Elmer E. Robinson, Supervisor John J. Sullivan, the General, and Henry Boyen. Neylan and Boyen were members of the reception committee. In foreground are Mrs. Douglas MacArthur and son, Arthur, 13. On all sides, newsmen, radio men, TV men and just plain people were there.

Democrats Block GOP On Inquiry

By VANCE JOHNSON
Washington Correspondent, The Chronicle

WASHINGTON, April 17 — Senate Democrats today blocked a Republican move for a full-scale investigation into President Truman's foreign and military policies but announced they will start one of their own.

Chairman Richard B. Russell (Dem-Ga.), of the Senate Armed Services Committee, who will direct the inquiry, said he plans "a very careful and exhaustive" study of the entire range of controversy.

The investigation, to be conducted jointly by the Armed Services and Foreign Relations Committees, will get under way next week. Russell said General Douglas MacArthur may be the first witness.

Russell's plan—which is to conduct the hearings largely behind closed doors, in order to delve more deeply into military and diplomatic secrets — apparently has White House blessings.

White House officials yesterday

Continued on Page 2, Col. 1

Welcome for MacArthur

EDITORIAL

A heartfelt welcome awaits General Douglas MacArthur, a welcome richly deserved.

Regardless of the political circumstances that determined the time of the return, regardless of the violent clashing of opinions of individuals and political groups on the rights and wrongs of these political matters, the people of San Francisco, of the State, and of the Nation will be unanimous in paying tribute to MacArthur the soldier and MacArthur the living American legend.

The fourteen years of the general's absence from his homeland have been years of unprecedented impact upon the world's history, and it has been given to General MacArthur as it has been given to few men to exert great force in the shaping of that history. How ably he seized his opportunities is indelibly in the record. He fought superbly, and he fought with a dramatic flair that endeared him to the people and inspired them, and this was all part of the substance with which victory was gained. The corncob pipe, the cavalier cap cocked jauntily above the hawk-like nose, the dramatic phrase, dramatically timed — these were symbols not only of MacArthur, but of the very struggle in which the Nation was desperately engaged. They became part of the MacArthur legend, and so they remain.

For his substantial part in the Pacific victory, for his able stewardship of Japan in the postwar years, for his courage in the face of overwhelming odds in the early days of Korea, his audacious coup at Inchon, and the manner in which he turned the tide in our favor, MacArthur deserves the welcome reserved for those of the top category of distinction. And as an American of high integrity and long experience in the complex situation in the Far East, he deserves, when the celebration has ended, the respectful attention of the Nation as he presents his viewpoint on current matters.

He is, in the last analysis, brought back as the result of his profound and unswervable devotion to a viewpoint on the most compelling issue before the world today. All free men must be prepared in the end to face this issue, for it involves their very destiny.

British Sub On Bottom; 75 Aboard

By the United Press

PORTSMOUTH, England, April 18 — Hope faded today (Wednesday) for the 75 men and officers aboard the submarine Affray found mired in the mud of the English channel 198 feet below the surface.

Dawn passed without any of the men surfacing through the submarine's escape apparatus although rescue vessels in response to faint tapping from the disabled vessel informed the crew they were in position to pick them up.

The submarine, missing near the Isle of Wight off the south coast of England since Monday night, was discovered shortly after midnight and rescue vessels ringed the area. The men had oxygen enough for only 40 hours and that deadline had passed.

The Admiralty which made the first announcement that other submarines were in contact with the Affray planned to send divers down to investigate if the men aboard did not leave it at dawn through

Continued on Page 11, Col. 3

EXCLUSIVE STORY FROM THE TRAIN

Copyright, 1952, by The Chronicle Publishing Co.

By ART HOPPE
Chronicle Staff Writer

ABOARD THE CITY OF SAN FRANCISCO MAROONED IN THE HIGH SIERRA, Jan. 15—We made it through to this snowbound train at 4:30 this afternoon, in a wild, howling blizzard.

This dispatch is being written by the light of an emergency lantern in the cold, damp interior of the train. The lantern's rays glint on a 20-foot wall of snow that presses against our windows and cuts off all sight of the outside world.

I hope to get this report out by Sno-cat, which is the only vehicle that can move through the wild and frightening weather.

Chronicle Photographer Kenneth McLaughlin and I reached the train after two and a half hours on skis—150 minutes of slipping, stumbling and crawling around boulders festooned with icicles and the buried wrecks of snowplows.

The train is intact. Its passengers are on short rations, but they're bundled up against the cold, their morale is high and they are not complaining about the prospect of still another night before rescue.

McLaughlin and I left the Yuba Gap maintenance camp, a mile and a half from the train, at 2 p. m. Earlier today we tried to get a ride on a snow weasel, but the weasel couldn't get through, and we decided to try it on rented skis.

I've used skis about five times before, two years ago. This was McLaughlin's second time on the boards.

But Mac slung his camera in a canvas bag over his shoulder and I carried a few supplies, and we took off. Both of us had warm clothes.

The wind was blowing the snow almost horizontally, and the drifts were piling up ahead of us. We were more than a little scared.

It was downhill almost all the way, but we couldn't slide because the snow was so powdery. We sank down a foot with every push of our skis.

We slogged about a mile down Highway 40 with a terrific wind behind us. Then we reached the railroad underpass, crossed it, and headed along the tracks for another half mile to the train.

The double-track roadbed along this stretch lies half-way up a steep slope, terraced in against the hill. But drifts have obliterated the terracing, and at times we had to use our ski poles to cut a tiny ledge of flat snow for a path.

Huge boulders lie above and below the tracks, great chunks of glacier-smoothed rocks that are piled high with snow and sheathed in ice.

As we fought our way forward we could hardly see more than a few feet. The blizzard backlashed off the rocks and into our faces. Whipping winds howled down the hillside against us.

We passed the wrecks of three rotary snowplows, half buried in snow. On their lee sides were crazy clusters of wind-twisted icicles.

You can look through a hole in the snow to the cab of one of the plows that is lying on its side. That is where they dragged out the dead body of the engineer on Monday.

We found the train 200 feet beyond a short tunnel. The engine is buried in the snow and the cars stand like some permanent, strung-out settlement of buried cabins.

A single dark tunnel in the snow marked the entrance to the baggage car and as we entered a musty, sour odor of stale breath, heating fumes and cold food hit us. It was dark in the tunnel, dark in the first baggage car, and dark in the other baggage cars beyond. Only an occasional red lantern glimmered as we groped toward the passenger cars.

The cars all tilted sharply in toward the mountain, and in the strangely still interior we clawed for balance against the train's dank walls.

In the first coach, we found the passengers, their feet wrapped in torn sheets, huddled on facing seats.

The passengers told us of their

Continued on Page 10, Col. 5

COMPARATIVE RAINFALL
FORECAST: SHOWERS
(For details, see Page 21.)

	Last 24 Hrs.	Seas'l To Dt.	Nrml. To Dt.	To Dt. Lst. Yr.	Seas'l Nrml.
San Francisco	.75	19.31	9.70	15.37	22.02
S. F. Airport	.89	15.87	7.53	11.08	18.91
Sacramento Airport	1.02	14.49	7.78	13.24	17.95
Oakland Airport	.44	17.39	8.24	13.21	18.76
Stockton	.10	10.04	6.01	11.61	14.31
Fresno	.45	5.57	3.99	6.02	9.38
Los Angeles	.42	10.46	5.77	3.20	15.33

Precipitation data to 4:30 p. m., Tuesday; inches and hundredths.

FOUNDED 1865—VOL. CLXXV, NO. 1 CCCCAAA SAN FRANCISCO, WEDNESDAY, JANUARY 16, 1952 GA 1-1112 DAILY 7c, SUNDAY 15c In San Luis Obispo, Kern, Tulare, Inyo and all counties to south—Daily 10c;

Rescuers Blocked---Third Night for 221 Aboard Streamliner; 27 Sick

Doctor, Nurses Save 60 Stricken by Gas Fumes; Blizzard Bogs Relief Teams

By EDD JOHNSON

The grimy, bone-chilled passengers and crew of the stricken streamliner City of San Francisco have passed another miserable night—their third—aboard the snowbound train in the High Sierra.

There are 221 persons aboard, many of them sick. They have been held prisoner of the century's worst blizzard on a mountainside near Yuba Gap since their train stalled in mountainous snowdrifts Sunday noon.

Last night, the passengers and crewmen heard the news that all rescue attempts had bogged down, short of their goal, and that the best they could expect—a problematic best—was that they might be freed "some time after daylight."

It befell a Chronicle reporter, the only newsman to reach the scene of the tragic mishap, to tell those aboard that the blizzard was still master of the High Sierra, despite the utmost efforts of men and machines.

The news was hardest to take for 27 of the passengers, stricken by gas fumes and saved from asphyxiation by the heroic efforts of a civilian physician and five Armed Forces nurses earlier in the day. All of them were bed-ridden, vomiting, and subject to severe gastric pains.

For those not stricken by the gas fumes, conditions of life were grim but not yet critical.

"They are sitting there, wearing all their clothing," Art Hoppe, of The Chronicle reported from the train. "Somehow, they manage to keep up their spirits. They've had two meals today and the dining car steward says he has enough eggs and milk to give them breakfast tomorrow. But they're a pretty sad looking bunch, and very cold."

Hoppe, and Kenneth McLaughlin, Chronicle photographer, reached the train by skis from Yuba Gap Highway Camp at 4:30 p. m. yesterday. They were the only newspapermen to get through the mountainous drifts to reach the train. They brought the first eyewitness account of how the passengers were faring.

"The air aboard the train is foul," Hoppe reported. "There is great difficulty in keeping even minimum ventilation because the snow has to be shovelled away from the windows before they can be opened. In addition, the plumbing has frozen and the toilets and drains aren't working."

Hoppe verified earlier reports

Continued on Page 11, Col. 1

Snow Still Piling Up In the Sierra

By DAVID PERLMAN

The high spine of the Sierra Nevada lay isolated from the world this morning, covered by snows that fell throughout the night in a wind-whipped blizzard.

The snowpack ran to 15 feet in many mountain hamlets, and drifts piled 30 feet or higher over roads and across rooftops.

Hundreds of mountain residents tunneled for air from their windows and gave up hope of seeing beyond their own walls for days.

Within most snowbound communities citizens laid plans over telephone party lines for rescue posses and evacuation attempts should the snow outlast meager fuel supplies.

But throughout the chilled, blinded and darkening area there was plenty of food and few critical emergencies.

The major shortage was fuel for heating and cooking; the major inconvenience was darkness when power lines snapped in the snow and wind.

Skiers who had passed last week end at resorts were reconciled to days more of enforced vacations. At most resorts they were guests of the management; at some, where supplies ran short, they were evacuated to better-stocked points.

TAHOE SNOWBOUND

Around the southern shore of Lake Tahoe 1200 people were snowbound in their homes. Neighbors within 50 yards of each other might just as well have been separated by 50 miles.

The area is served by the Tallac telephone exchange, and a survey by The Chronicle, with the help of Doris Arntzen, a telephone operator at Richardson's Camp, disclosed no serious emergencies.

The tiny telephone building where Mrs. Arntzen, her husband, Chick, and another operator were at work was buried under snow.

But their phone line got through to the town of Bijou, on blockaded U. S. Highway 50, where a rescue posse was being organized to evacuate families in the area who were running out of fuel.

Eldorado County Supervisor Andrew Robertson was in charge of the 70-man team.

"As far as we know we're all O. K. up here," Robertson reported. "The kids are getting sick of canned milk and dried staples, but there's no illness and nothing to be alarmed about yet.

SNOWSHOE HAUL

"From a fuel standpoint most homes can last about four more days, but we may have to try evacuating some places in the next day or so."

Before darkness fell last night Robertson's crew accomplished one perilous mission. Four men on

Continued on Page 11, Col. 4

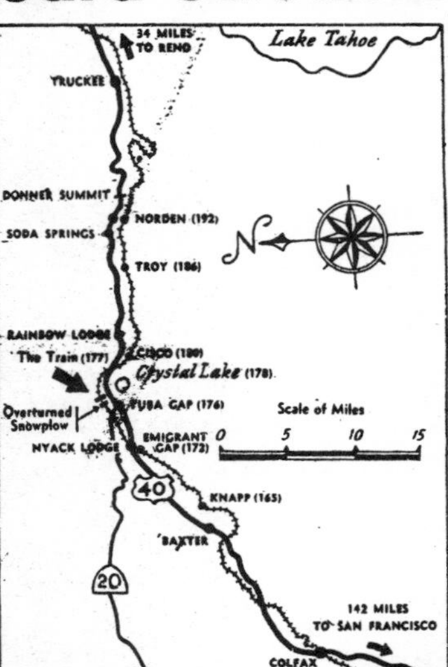

SNOWBOUND—This map shows where rescuers are battling mountainous snow drifts to reach the 221 persons trapped aboard the City of San Francisco near Yuba Gap. Parenthetical figures are mileages from San Francisco. Rescue teams converging on the stranded train by rail from Reno and from Colfax and by road from Nyack Lodge bogged down last night in the blizzard. More stories and pictures of the violent storm on Pages 8, 10 and 11. Editorial comment, Page 14.

Brace Yourself: More Rain and More Snow Due

By ALVIN D. HYMAN

Northern California, battered for four days by violent storms that soused lowlands with record rains and buried the Sierra under record snows, surveyed its hurts yesterday and braced itself for possible further punishment by wind, rain and snow.

"Frequent rains" are in store today for all valley areas between the Oregon line and Los Angeles, the Weather Bureau forecast; the Sierra Nevada will continue to pile up snow.

All this new precipitation, the forecaster said, will come from the storm that first roared into this region on Sunday night; a storm whose center has remained almost stationary off the Washington coast, while sending a front through California.

The storm front was sloshing rain over Southern California yesterday, so generously that it left more than three inches in 24 hours in the San Luis Obispo area.

Northern California still was getting intermittent downpours and blustery winds, as the storm center showed no inclination to move eastward. Some hope was expressed by meteorologists that a spell of "clearing" weather may set in by tomorrow—but, they warned, another storm is brewing off the Alaskan coast and may move south and east in time to slash new downpours over this region.

Brief violent hail storms clattered over the city at intervals last night. The squalls lasted for only minutes but they layered streets and buildings with white. Ice from

Continued on Page 8, Col. 1

Killer Cons Face Trial for Murder

D. A. to Seek Indictment Of Quentin Guard-Slayers; Warden Tells Escape Plot

San Quentin was back on routine yesterday after a brief, violent escape attempt that left two guards dead, two critically hurt and one convict hospitalized.

District Attorney Richard M. Sims said he will ask the Marin County Grand Jury to vote murder indictments against the two convicts—one of them a San Francisco "bad boy"—accused of slaying the guards in the abortive break on Monday night.

The slain guards were Charles D. Wiget, 31, of Petaluma, employed at the prison since 1947, and Vern A. Mackin, 38, of San Rafael, nearly four years on the job.

Hospitalized with skull fractures were Guards Virgil E. Stewart, 43, of Woodacre, and Ralph E. Dascombe, 36, of San Rafael, a sergeant.

The convicts charged with the murderous break attempt are James Alonzo Rogers, 22 — who staged a spectacular gun battle with cops in the Mission district here shortly before he went to San Quentin in October—and Eugene Burwell, 24, a Los Angeles robber.

Convict Charles Bragg, who swapped cells and identification cards with Rogers, enabling the latter to participate in the plot, was in solitary confinement yesterday, as was his pal. Convict Burwell was in the prison hospital with a serious stab wound.

Warden Harley O. Teets, who succeeded Clinton Duffy only three weeks ago, said the escape plot was hatched three months ago.

Teets told newsmen Burwell related this story:

He began laying plans for the escape three months ago, and in time collected a double-edged hatchet, a 12-inch scissors blade and a six-inch knife. When Rogers entered the prison in October Burwell took him on as an accomplice.

Rogers, a newcomer, was ineligible to attend night school in the prison. So he changed cells—and identification cards—with Bragg, 24, a bad check passer. They are "look alikes."

Rogers then began attending night classes, as a ruse, for they had planned their escape for nighttime—to get over the wall at a dark spot.

Instead of going to class Monday evening, Rogers slipped into the library where he lay in wait with Burwell. They knew that Rogers' failure to answer at class roll call would send a guard on the hunt.

They were right. Guard Wiget came in shortly.

Instantly fists flew and scissor blades flashed. Once Wiget wrested a knife from his assailants and plunged it into Burwell's right lung. Rogers got a leg hold on the guard and threw him. Burwell stabbed Wiget—and left the blade in the back of his neck.

When Wiget died the convicts dragged his body into a closet, then bound and gagged Joseph E. Wolfe, 22, a Los Angeles burglar and inmate librarian, who had witnessed the struggle.

This took time, and they figured another guard would be showing up, looking for Guard Wiget. They

Continued on Page 3, Col. 1

GOP Clash Due on Delegations

By EARL C. BEHRENS
Political Editor, The Chronicle

California may face a stiff fight before the Republican National Committee to retain her tentatively allotted 70-member delegation to the Chicago presidential nominating convention.

Big Eastern States which are due to lose congressional seats under the 1950 Federal census are ready to make a fight to retain larger delegations at the July Republican National Convention.

Under the plan of tentative allocation of delegates to the national convention, the Republican National Committee proposes to recognize the 1950 census figures and give California, Arizona and Oregon, as well as several other States, greater representation at the July convention.

FIRST CLASH TODAY

The first brush on the delegation matter will come up this afternoon at a meeting of the "committee on the convention call," according to McIntyre Faries, California's GOP national committee member.

New York, Pennsylvania and some of the other States are demanding more votes in the convention.

Faries and Majorie Benedict, national committeewoman, will be on hand at the meeting to represent California.

Roy Dunn, Minnesota member of the national committee, is chairman of the "convention call" committee.

WASHINGTON PLEA

Mrs. Meal Tourtellotte, national committee woman from Washington, said yesterday her State would put up a fight to obtain six more delegates under the "bonus" system which awards States that elect Republicans for Governor and Senator additional seats in the national convention.

Mrs. Tourtellotte said an "ambiguity" in the "bonus provision in the national committee's rules robs Washington of an additional six delegates.

The tentative program gives Washington 18 delegates and Mrs. Tourtellotte will ask for a total of 24.

She said she had the support of various committee members, including Ezra Whitla of Idaho.

The Washington spokesman cited the rules which give a "bonus" to States voting Republican for President in 1948 or electing a Republican U. S. Senator or Governor in 1950.

Washington elected Governor Arthur B. Langlie in 1950 but did not elect a U. S. Senator, that office going to a Democrat.

1200 DELEGATES

The tentative apportionment calls for approximately 1200 delegates to the 1952 convention.

New York, which has been allotted 96, now wants four more, according to word from the Southern Pacific's weather-delayed City of San Francisco.

That train is bringing National Chairman Guy Gabrielson and many of the national committee members to the three-day sessions of the national committee due to begin at the Fairmont Hotel tomorrow.

Gabrielson and his party expect to arrive here early this morning.

The final allocation of the number of delegates each State, territory

Continued on Page 2, Col. 5

Ex-Senator Shortridge Dies at 90 in Atherton

Samuel M. Shortridge, United States Senator from California from 1920 to 1932, died in his sleep in his Atherton home yesterday. He was 91. One of the most colorful and controversial pesonalities ever to serve California in Washington, Senator Shortridge was a native of Iowa and a lawyer by profession.

Samuel Shortridge

In a Chronicle interview five years ago, the aging statesman described himself as the last of the "100 per cent Abraham Lincoln Republicans" and declared:

"For reasons which are obvious, I will not remain here much longer. It is given to few men to achieve four score and six years."

But, added the man who had engaged fearlessly in many of the hottest political battles of his lifetime, "I hate no one, for the man who has hate in his heart harbors a nest of vipers."

Samuel Morgan Shortridge was born Aug. 3, 1861, in Mt. Pleasant, Iowa, the son of a minister. The family moved to Oregon in 1874, and a year later to San Jose, where the future Senator went to work as the town lamplighter and a newspaper bundle wrapper.

He went to high school in San Jose, then studied and taught at various schools in Northern California, emphasizing law in his studies, and in 1884, passing the State Bar.

Soon after starting practice in San Francisco, he began to be known as a quick thinker and a lively speaker.

He joined his brother, the former State Senator Charles W. Shortridge, in legal partnership and together they acted as counsel in many celebrated cases of the day. At one time the two brothers were publishers of the San Jose Mercury-Herald.

Senator Shortridge entered politics in 1888, becoming an elector that year for President Benjamin Harrison.

But it was not until 1920, when he was 59 years old, that he achieved a lifelong ambition—election to the United States Senate. In that first campaign, he defeated Democratic Senator James D. Phelan.

During his career in the Senate,

Continued on Page 12, Col. 4

Narriman Does It---Has a Boy

CAIRO, Jan. 16 (UP)—Queen Narriman, gave birth today (Wednesday) to a boy, it was announced officially.

The child, which was named Ahmed Fuad, was born at 8:30 a. m. Both the Queen and son were reported well.

The Queen, the former Narriman Sadek, and King Farouk were married May 7, 1951. She was 17 at the time.

Thick Fog Halts N. Y. Air Traffic

NEW YORK, Jan. 15 (AP)—Thick fog stopped air operations in the New York Metropolitan area today. Harbor traffic continued to operate, but at a much slower pace.

Four Possible Routes to Save Stricken Passengers

There are four possible escape routes for the striken passengers aboard the City of San Francisco, snowbound in the High Sierra. They are:

1—From the west, a Southern Pacific snowplow engine is inching toward Emigrant Gap, six miles from the train. Behind it will come a freight, carrying weasels, which can navigate heavy snow, and a passenger train, with bunks made up. When the track is clear up to Emigrant Gap, an attempt will be made to take the passengers from Yuba Pass, a half mile from the train, by highway to Emigrant Gap. The train cannot get through to the City of San Francisco from the west because the right-of-way is blocked by overturned snowplows.

2—From the East. A fully equipped train was assembled and brought to Norden, but attempts to reach the stranded "City" were called off when it appeared certain the train from Colfax would get through first.

3—By highway all the way. A rotary snowplow from Colfax passed Emigrant Gap last night, but the blizzard was closing the highway behind it.

4—By helicopter. In Colfax, a half hour's flight away, a Coast Guard plane, able to carry six litter passengers, waited for clearing weather in the hope it might be able to take off the more seriously ill passengers.

The Index

Chess	21
Comics	15
Contract Contests	21
Crossword	11
Delaplane	13
Drama	9
Editorial: "U. S. Lifeline in Jeopardy"	14
Finance	16, 4H
Horoscope	23
Dean Jennings	2
Lichty	5
Radio and Television	3H
Vital Statistics	11
Women's World	6, 7

COMPARATIVE TEMPERATURES
For Tuesday, February 5, 1952

	High	Low		High	Low
San Francisco	63	45	New York ...	49	42
Oakland	64	42	Chicago	38	34
Sacramento .	58	39	Kansas City..	49	34
Los Angeles..	81	51	New Orleans.	60	44
Portland	..	42	Miami	74	60
Seattle	49	33	Washington..	48	42

Forecast for Today: MORNING FOG
(For details, see Page 18.)

San Francisco Chronicle
THE CITY'S ONLY HOME-OWNED NEWSPAPER

VOL. CLXXV, NO. 22 CCCCAAAB SAN FRANCISCO CHRONICLE, WEDNESDAY, FEB. 6, 1952 GA 1-1112 DAILY 7c, SUNDAY 15c

KING GEORGE DEAD
ELIZABETH IS QUEEN

Two Cops Accused of S. F. Thefts

Picture on Page 17

Police Chief Michael A. Gaffey ordered the suspension of two police officers as suspected thieves yesterday.

He said they are under suspicion in connection with about 20 thefts during the past three months in the Taraval district, which is their patrol territory.

The suspected officers frequently investigated their own alleged thefts, Gaffey said.

Suspended at 4 p. m. yesterday and held for questioning were:

Richard A. Urbais, 28, of 430 Head street, who joined the force on July 5, 1950. He is married and had been a photographer previously.

Earl Prater, 28, of 540 Easterby street, Sausalito, a limited tenure officer appointed July 16, 1951. He formerly was a policeman in Sausalito, is married and is the father of two children.

BOTH BOOKED

Urbais was booked at City Prison last night on suspicion of burglary and Prater was booked on suspicion of grand theft.

Urbais confessed entering buildings to steal, Gaffey declared, and Prater admitted only taking plywood sheets from a Stoneson project near Lake Merced.

This plywood led to the implication of the two officers, their superiors said. Engler said the wood was sold to a Sausalito cabinet maker and his checks in payment were traced to the patrolmen.

Both of the officers were assigned to Taraval station in the southwestern section of the city and served most of their time in the department in that district.

Their suspensions followed a month's investigation by Captain John Engler, director of personnel, and Captain Leo Tackney, in charge of Taraval District.

Two other officers were questioned last night:

William J. Stathes, 2333 Filbert street, on the force for four and a half years.

Richard LaFountain, 2707 40th avenue, who joined the department the same day as Urbais, July 5, 1950. He is married and has one child.

Stathes and LaFountain denied any connection with the thefts and no stolen property was found in their homes.

"We found nothing to implicate them," said their chief.

Gaffey said the suspicion of top officers in the department was aroused by a series of unsolved burglaries, following the same pattern and in the same district of Taraval, bounded by 19th avenue and the beach and Sloat boulevard to the county line.

PATTERN CRIMES

The crimes were all committed at night; they involved thefts of thousands of dollars worth of tools and building supplies from construction projects and some goods from large commercial establishments; some were investigated by the suspected officers; and no arrests were made.

Of Urbais and Prater, Engler said: "We worked out a pattern on the last 14 burglary jobs and found that in all except two cases either one officer or the other was on duty in the area at the time. They don't admit to all 14. . ."

The captain said he became doubly suspicious when inspectors from the burglary detail were assigned to some of the Taraval cases and the thefts suddenly ceased.

Gaffey said the two patrolmen were involved in three night-time burglaries at the San Francisco State College Science Building under construction in the 3800 block of 19th avenue.

Other items stolen in the wave of burglaries included an automatic dishwasher and a 500-pound table saw.

Prater, who drew $285 a month for his police job, said he stole to pay his family's doctor bills, according to Engler.

Urbais, a civil service appointee, is paid $295 a month.

The Index

Chess 15
Comics 4H
Contract Contacts 15
Crossword 15
Delaplane 17
Drama 12, 13
Editorial: "Saar Basin Full of Woe" 18
Finance 19, 20
"I Led Three Lives" 4
Dean Jennings 2
Radio and Television 14
Women's World 11

Judge Fee Rebuffs Smyth Defense

Court to Decide on Hearing

By DAVID PERLMAN

James G. Smyth, former collector of internal revenue, lost a legal round yesterday in his fight against an indictment charging him with conspiracy to defraud the Government.

In a two-hour court session, U. S. District Judge James Alger Fee took these steps:

1—He canceled all 18 subpoenas which Smyth's attorneys had served on prospective witnesses.

2—He impounded the affidavits and briefs in which Smyth charged that a Federal Grand Jury had been tampered with and illegally influenced when it indicted him and three other defendants.

3—He rebuked Smyth's attorneys in strong but precisely legal terms for attempting to violate the secrecy of Grand Jury proceedings and for attempting to set up a formal hearing without Judge Fee's sanction.

What he left to Smyth and his fellow-defendants were the bare bones of a motion to dismiss the indictments, and the opportunity to argue for an open hearing on that motion.

Smyth's attorneys promptly took advantage of that opportunity. And, under prodding by Judge Fee, Government counsel marshaled their arguments to oppose the hearing.

What happened yesterday was a debate on whether or not Smyth is entitled to an open hearing, complete with witnesses, on his claim that he was illegally indicted.

The next step, if Judge Fee orders it, would be the hearing itself, where Smyth's charges of jury tampering could be aired. If the hearing proves tampering, Fee may quash the indictments; if not, Smyth and his fellow defendants must stand trial for conspiracy.

The morning session, which started out in a courtroom crowded by former grand jurors, FBI agents and others under subpoena, developed quickly into a sharp debate.

Judge Fee, with swift and punctilious interruptions, barred all references to alleged jury tampering from the floor of his ornate, old-fashioned courtroom in the Federal Building at Seventh and Mission streets.

And he took the occasion to warn attorneys not to speculate on the

Continued on Page 6, Col. 4

Two-for-One Special Offered in Action Ads

The San Francisco Chronicle is offering classified advertisers double their money's worth this week in observance of Action Ad Week.

You can buy a two-line Chronicle Action Ad for as little as $1.20 daily or $1.50 on Sunday. During this week, any person who orders an Action Ad for one day will be given one additional day without extra charge! He may order for two days and get two days, or up to seven days and get seven days without extra charge. A two-for-one value!

So, take advantage of Action Ad Week to convert your used articles into cash.

King Group Told of Tax Back-Dating

By CHARLES RAUDEBAUGH

Ace T-man William E. Frank told the King Congressional Committee here yesterday that the backdating of tax documents was the "principal thing" he has found wrong in the San Francisco office of Internal Revenue.

Recounting his four months' scrutiny of tax bureau personnel as the first public witness to be heard by the Congressional investigators, Frank said a total of "approximately eight" cases of backdating have been uncovered with a total loss to the Government of some $40,000.

"It was done for friendship, political favors and motives of that kind rather than for money," he testified. "It was not done for bribes." Of the total $40,000 in taxes lost to the Government, $38,000 is accounted for in the backdating of estate tax returns, cited in the indictments voted last December against Former Revenue Collector James G. Smyth and three other men, Frank said.

He disclosed that John Malone, suspended tax bureau official and a brother of William M. Malone, local Democratic leader, is involved in a backdating case still under Grand Jury investigation. Frank said the back-dating involved approximately $800 for cosmetic taxes from the drug store of Dr. Thomas E. Shumate, one-time San Francisco Police Commissioner.

Frank's testimony also included the declaration he had found "very little substantiation" to most of the charges in the so-called "bill of particulars" which launched the Grand Jury inquiry of the tax bureau last year. And of the specific charges against Smyth personally in the bill of particulars, he found nothing true, he said.

SESSION TODAY

The short, chunky Treasury agent will be on the witness stand again when the committee resumes its public sessions at 10 o'clock this morning. The committee, headed by Congressman Cecil R. King (Dem-Los Angeles), is meeting in the courtroom ordinarily occupied by Federal Judge George B. Harris in the Post Office Building at Seventh and Mission streets.

Veteran of 28 years with the Treasury Department, Frank told the five committee members that a foolproof system to prevent backdating would probably be too cumbersome, and declared it was better for the Bureau to "take a calculated risk on it."

Taxpayers who file late returns can save themselves 25 per cent penalty and 6 per cent interest on the tax due when they can persuade a bureau employee to date the returns as of the proper date.

FURTADO CASE

Most of the back-dating related by Frank to the committee revolved around the activities of Edwin Furtado, a former audit chief in the Bureau's wage and excise tax division. Furtado, now serving a 10-year term on McNeil Island for embezzling some $20,000, is scheduled to be brought here Friday for a Grand Jury appearance.

Frank spoke the name of Malone with reluctance. He said Malone's activities are now under Grand Jury investigation "and I don't know what the jury will do."

Congressman Eugene Keogh, (Dem., N. Y.) protested at the

Continued on Page 7, Col. 1

Britain's Wartime Ruler

KING GEORGE VI
Death came unexpectedly

Ruler Passes at 56; New Monarch Abroad

Lung Removed Last Fall Had Caused Concern for The British Sovereign

SANDRINGHAM, England, Feb. 6 (AP)—King George VI died peacefully in his sleep today. His 25-year-old daughter, Elizabeth, immediately became Britain's Quen.

An official announcement said death came at his country residence here in the farm country of Norfolk.

The King, 56, underwent a serious lung operation last September 23. Recently he had appeared haggard but yesterday he seemed in good health.

He appeared to be in his usual health when he retired last night.

The 56-year-old ruler of the British Commonwealth and Empire became King on Dec. 11, 1936.

He led Britain through the perilous years of World War II and the economic and political crisis that followed.

King George had been plagued by poor health since he ascended the throne on the abdication of his brother, King Edward VIII, the present Duke of Windsor.

The King's elder daughter, Princess Elizabeth—first in line of succession—now becomes Queen and ruler of millions of British subjects around the world.

The King had been in ill health frequently over the last four years.

He was operated on last summer for removal of all or part of one lung under circumstances which indicated he might have cancer.

The reason for the operation was never officially announced, however.

Fears for his health had been expressed with increasing frequency lately.

Recent pictures of the King have shown a haggard and tired man, with deep circles under his eyes.

But the monarch apparently had felt himself on the road to full recovery.

Just before his daughter and heir, Princess Elizabeth, and the Duke of Edinburgh left on a trip to Africa and Australia and New Zealand last week the King joined them in a visit to the theater.

He accompanied them to the airport to see them off.

The new Queen and her husband now are in Kenya, an East African colony.

At the time of departure Elizabeth looked with deep seriousness at her father's lined face.

The King who was 56 last December 14 was out yesterday both in the morning and in the afternoon at Sandringham.

Queen Elizabeth and Princess Margaret are at Sandringham.

They went cruising on the inland streams of the Norfolk Broads yesterday.

Princess Elizabeth, now at her shooting lodge at Nyeri, Kenya—a wedding gift from the people of Kenya—was scheduled to leave tomorrow for Mombasa and catch a ship for Ceylon.

Their son and the new heir to Britain's throne, tiny Prince Charles, also is at Sandringham. He is just over three years old, born on Nov. 14, 1948.

It is the first time in history that a sovereign has acceded to Britain's throne while abroad in the Commonwealth.

King George came to the throne on Dec. 11, 1936, upon the abdication of his brother, King Edward VIII.

The quiet family man who put royal duty above personal pleasure quickly endeared himself to his millions of subjects around the world.

The monarch led Britain through her worst ordeal when the island kingdom faced the victory-flushed German armies alone. His words of comfort, his prayers, his encouragement helped Britons meet and turn back the foe's blitzkreig. With his Prime Minister Winston Churchill, King George will be long remembered for his part in "Britain's finest hour."

WIDE TRAVELED

The monarch was better known both to his own subjects and to foreigners than any other modern king. His radio addresses were heard around the world. He traveled extensively despite poor health which plagued him from the time he ascended the throne.

George VI was the first ruling British king to visit the United States. Some 600,000 roared out a welcome in Washington to the King and Queen and Elizabeth in June, 1939, when the royal couple arrived by train for a state visit with President and Mrs. Roosevelt. They were introduced to many American novelties including hot dogs at a Hyde Park picnic.

After World War II the King and Queen with their charming Princesses visited South Africa. The trip, to cement the bonds of the British Commonwealth was pronounced a success in London. A planned visit to Australia and New Zealand in 1948 had to be postponed because of the King's health and Elizabeth and her husband went instead.

Continued on Page A, Col. 8

Dog Track Boss Killed by Auto Bomb

Tom Keen, wealthy Peninsula manufacturer of racetrack "tote" boards and a national figure in dog-racing circles, was blasted to death yesterday in a typical gangland slaying.

He was blown to bits when he pushed the starter button on his Fleetwood Cadillac sedan in the garage of his fashionable home in 105 Hayward street, corner of Palm drive, San Mateo.

About 9:30 a. m. a friend—Edwin J. Cox of 421 Fairfax street, San Mateo, operator of a San Francisco department store restaurant—called at Keen's home to pick up several dozen eggs just sent in from the Keen farm at Newark, in Alameda county. They talked for about 20 minutes.

Keen then went into the house, said goodbye to his wife Emma, donned his topcoat and went out to the garage. Their housekeeper, Mrs. C. A. Rogers, was in the front of the house. Mrs. Keen went to the rear to wave another goodby to her husband. She watched him enter the detached garage and then, in as many moments as it would take to climb in the car, get settled and push the starter—the garage came apart at the seams, with a loud whoosh.

The overhead doors at the far end of the garage were up, and the force of the blast went out there—and smashed windows in the house across the street.

The blast scattered fragments of garage and car over a wide area. Ronald Erickson, who lives down

Continued on Page 8, Col. 1

Mrs. Morris Sticks Grimly To Her Story

By EDD JOHNSON

"Yes," Mrs. Gertrude DiBernardi Morris said yesterday.

"Yes," she said, she did shoot and kill her husband, Milton. "Yes," she killed him with malice aforethought.

"Yes, yes, yes," she told Norman Elkington, chief assistant district attorney, and the jury of nine women and three men in the courtroom of Superior Judge Harry J. Neubarth.

"That's right, keep it up," J. W. Ehrlich, the defense attorney, jeered at Elkington. "She'll say 'yes' to anything you ask her."

THE ONLY WITNESS

But by that time, Elkington was about through. He had the testimony of the only witness to the killing that the act was premeditated, and done with malice aforethought—thus murder in the first degree. No prosecutor ever had a tidier confession.

The jury, by now aware that Mrs. Morris has frequently tried to kill herself and, failing that, has tried to plead guilty of first degree murder so that she might be sent to the gas chamber, listened in-

Continued on Page 12, Col. 1

Demos to Spend $2,800,000

WASHINGTON, Feb. 5 (AP)—The executive committee of the Democratic National Committee today approved a 1952 campaign budget of $2,800,000.

Seal Rally Fails--The Oaks Win

See Sports

COMPARATIVE TEMPERATURES
For Tuesday, April 8, 1952

	High	Low		High	Low
San Francisco	60	48	New York	57	42
Oakland	61	51	Chicago	60	34
Sacramento	69	59	Kansas City	81	54
Los Angeles	64	48	New Orleans	76	52
Portland	53	37	Miami	69	59
Seattle	55	29	Washington	51	36

Forecast for Today: Partly Cloudy
(For Details See Page 17)

San Francisco Chronicle
THE CITY'S ONLY HOME-OWNED NEWSPAPER

FINAL

FOUNDED 1865—VOL. CLXXV, NO. 85 CCCCAAA SAN FRANCISCO, WEDNESDAY, APRIL 9, 1952 GA 1-1112 DAILY 7c, SUNDAY 15c 50 MILES OUTSIDE S. F. SINGLE COPIES, DAILY 10c, SUNDAY 20c

U.S. SEIZES STEEL ---STRIKE IS OFF

Taft Wins Huge Victory in Illinois

Ike Write-In Small; Kefauver Wins

Stassen Second in GOP Race; Stevenson Draws Heavy Vote for Governor

CHICAGO, April 8 (AP)—Senator Robert A. Taft of Ohio swept to an impressive victory tonight in the Illinois GOP primary on a tide of votes that swamped a write-in effort for General Dwight D. Eisenhower.

Taft ran far ahead of both Eisenhower and Harold E. Stassen of Minnesota in a race that never was in doubt from the start.

With more than half of the State's 9610 precincts counted, Taft was leading Stassen 6 to 1 and Eisenhower—in third place—by more than 7 to 1.

Taft and Stassen were on the GOP ballot, while the General's votes were write-ins.

In the Democratic primary, Senator Estes Kefauver of Tennessee piled up a huge vote in his uncontested preferential race for President.

There had been expectations that write-in drives would develop strength for Eisenhower in the GOP race and for Illinois Gov. Adlai Stevenson on the Democratic ballot.

But a comparatively small percentage of Illinois voters appeared to have taken the trouble to write in their votes.

On the basis of returns from more than half of the State's 9610 pre-poll an ultimate total of 721,000 votes, Stassen 119,000, to 101,000 for Eisenhower.

Incomplete returns indicate that Taft men may win almost all the 50 GOP national convention delegate posts.

But Kefauver—despite his showing in the primary—could not count on any of the 50 elected Democratic delegates. The State Democratic organization is expected to give the delegate vote to Stevenson in case he enters the presidential race.

The elected delegates—and the 10 others to be named later by each party convention — are not bound by the results of the presidential popularity contest.

The vote totals from 7076 of 9610 precincts showed:

Republicans—Taft, 477,674; Stassen, 83,436; Eisenhower, 70,300.

Democrats—(5595 precincts) Kefauver 313,625.

At this point Stevenson had 4937 write-in votes with only a small portion of Cook county (Chicago) write-ins counted.

Among the GOP presidential hopefuls, Taft had in an early calculation 75 per cent of the vote, Stassen 12.5 per cent and Eisenhower 9.97 per cent. Kefauver piled up around 99 per cent of the reported Democratic vote.

The voting for Stevenson as Governor was running ahead of the voting for Kefauver (for President) in 3441 precincts. The returns showed about 40 per cent more Democrats voted for Stevenson for Governor than voted for Kefauver on the presidential slate.

Supervisors Are Cool on Fare Hike

San Francisco's Supervisors were not exactly happy yesterday with the Public Utilities Commission's proposal for a straight 15-cent Municipal Railway fare.

What made them especially unhappy was the accompanying financial breakdown, which told them that even with a 50 per cent fare raise, the Muni still will need a $1,600,000 subsidy from property taxes.

"This fare raise is just a smoke screen," said Supervisor John J. Ferdon. "Something must be done to meet the problems that brought it about."

And Supervisor George Christopher declared:

"I'm so mad I can't see straight. A 50 per cent increase in fares and we still lose money. I may look around for somebody to buy the system."

NO CHANGE POSSIBLE

The Supervisors, who have 30 days to consider the proposal, began their deliberations with a deep sense of frustration stemming from a Charter provision which prevents them from making any changes in the plan proposed by the PUC.

They can approve it—with a vote of at least eight of the 11 members—or they can reject it or they can simply ignore it, in which case it will go into effect automatically on June 1.

It was clear yesterday that some of the Supervisors wished heartily that they could make some changes in the proposal.

Ferdon and Edward Mancuso voiced support for a fare of 15 cents straight, two tokens for 25 cents.

A two-for-a-quarter fare structure would result in an operating deficit of $4,219,594, but the Supervisors said they believed operating economies could be accomplished to reduce the loss.

Ferdon and other members suggested that the commission eliminate costly parallel transit lines and propose Charter changes regarding wages and working conditions of the operators.

CHARTER CHANGES URGED

The Down Town Association—which favors a 15-cent, two tokens for a quarter fare—has proposed these specific money-saving steps: Repeal of the two-man streetcar ordinance; repeal of the eight-hours-within-ten Charter provision; modification of the present wage formula, which is based on the average of the two highest wages paid in the State, and elimination of duplicate lines and services and overtime for employees.

Conductors, motormen and bus operators are due for a wage increase of at least 14 cents an hour on July 1. Revised working schedules for a basic eight-hour work day in a spread of ten hours have resulted from a recent court ruling.

Together, these wage increases and improved working conditions will cost the railway $2,000,000 in the next fiscal year.

Dewey Mead, chairman of the board, and Supervisor Francis McCarty view the commission's proposal more calmly.

"It looks like we are caught in the middle," said Mead. "If we don't vote for the 15-cent fare we will have to vote for a huge property tax subsidy."

City Hall fiscal experts agree continuance of the dime fare will result in an operating deficit of more than $7,000,000. This would force a 70-cent increase in the $6.19 tax rate.

McCarty said a fare increase "seems necessary," but added he would study the problem more closely before voting for the 15-cent plan.

Mead announced the board would schedule hearings next week on the fare recommendation.

President Blasts Industry's Position; Companies Go to Court on Seizure

Murray Orders Union: 'Stay on Job'

By the Associated Press

NEW YORK, April 9—CIO President Philip Murray bowed to President Truman's steel industry seizure last night and called off a midnight strike of 650,000 steelworkers.

But two major steel companies filed suit early today (Wednesday) challenging the legality of the President's seizure order.

Attorneys for Republic Steel Corp. and Youngstown Sheet and Tube Co. filed papers with District Judge Walter M. Bastian early today asking for an injunction to block the seizure.

The attorneys, John Gall and John T. Wilson, went before the Judge in his home only a few hours after the President's order and presented a complaint against the Government's action, a supporting affidavit and a motion for a temporary restraining order.

HEARING SET

Judge Bastian reviewed the documents and directed that attorneys for the Government appear at 11:30 a. m. to answer the companies' attack.

Murray, president of both the CIO and the United Steelworkers, announced his "no-strike" decision slightly more than one hour before the walkout deadline, as tens of thousands of his members already were streaming from the Nation's mills.

Murray said in his statement of compliance:

"The President of the United States tonight announced that the Government had seized the steel plants involved in our dispute. In so doing, the President requested that the members of our organization continue to work without interruption.

"As patriotic Americans, the United Steelworkers will comply with the President's request and continue to work for their Government."

Murray said the following message was sent to all steel unions, poised for their first Nationwide walkout in three years:

"The Government having seized the steel plants, you are hereby directed to comply with the request of the President of the United States and to continue to work."

LAST MINUTE TALKS

Murray and the steel industry had engaged in hectic last-minute bargaining sessions during the day without reaching any truce in their bitter wage deadlock.

These talks came to an end about

Continued on Page 8, Col. 6

The Strike Box Score

The current wave of labor disputes has affected thousands of Bay Area workers. This was the situation yesterday:

STEEL—CIO steelworkers, including thousands in the Bay Area, reported for work on the midnight shift after President Truman seized the industry. Some were sent home again because the plants had cut operations in preparation for a strike, but company officials said full crews should be on the job within 24 hours.

TELEPHONE—The walkout of 7000 CIO communications workers in Northern California was spreading. The union accused the PT&T of a "lockout" and the company denied the charge. Operators may join the two-day old walkout. Some 51,000 on strike nationally.

TELEGRAPH — Nation-wide strike against Western Union was in its seventh day. Some 30,000 members of the AFL Commercial Telegraphers' Union involved, including 1300 in the Bay Area. Peace meetings planned in New York.

WESTERN ELECTRIC—More than 16,000 members of the same CIO union, including 900 in the Bay Area, on strike throughout the Nation for second day. Negotiations conducted in the East.

CARPENTERS — Negotiations collapsed in the strike of 12,000 AFL carpenters in four Bay Area counties. Contractors withdrew a 15-cent wage increase offer after the union rejected it as an "ultimatum." Strike went through its eighth day. All major construction halted.

GREYHOUND — Some 2900 members of the AFL Motor Coach Employees had been on strike against Pacific Greyhound's seven-State system for 38 days. Local negotiations continuing.

PILE DRIVERS—Strike of 600 AFL pile drivers and bridge builders in Northern California was in its second day.

PT&T Denies Lockout Charge

Phone Tie-Up Spreading; Operators May Join Strike

By PETER TRIMBLE

Northern California CIO Communications Workers started spreading their strike to all units of Pacific Telephone and Telegraph Co. yesterday in retaliation for what they charged was a "lockout."

The action was ordered as the two-pronged nation-wide telephone strike went through its second day and the equally widespread Western Union walkout went through its seventh day with no peace in sight.

Union officials here said the Northern California phone strike was spread after the company announced nonstriking workers who respect picket lines would be assigned work only on a day-to-day basis.

Roy N. Buell, San Francisco division manager of the company, denied the lockout charge.

"In doing our best to maintain service we are assigning those people who want to work and are willing to continue working without interruption to locations where they are required," Buell said.

"Those employees who do not want to continue working without interruption are being assigned work on a day-to-day basis," he said, "but only if there is work available."

While there are only some 7000 mechanical employees of PT&T officially on strike, the union said, the "lockout" could spread the work stoppage to affect some 25,000 nonstriking employees of the company, including operators, commercial and accounting units.

San Francisco telephone installations were blanketed with pickets yesterday but picketing in other cities was described as "not quite as general" as on Monday.

Pickets were out in 56 of the approximately 100 towns served by PT&T, in contrast to 79 towns in which there was picketing Monday.

Only urgent long distance calls were being accepted by operators and only the patient subscriber could get an operator.

Most of the 56 picketed installations were able to handle almost all calls. Exceptions came in Marin county, where exchanges in Mill Valley and San Rafael were said to be handling a majority of calls. The Sausalito exchange was accepting only urgent calls.

Telephone traffic employees, including operators, met here last night to discuss joining the picket lines because of the "lockout."

Representatives of the telephone company met with union officials for two hours yesterday but no progress toward settlement was announced.

Federal Conciliators Omar Hoskins and William Foley said they would bring both parties together at 3 p. m. today in a continuation of peace efforts.

(United Press reported last night from Detroit that E. Marvin Sconyers, a top Federal labor mediator, had arrived to attempt a settlement of the Michigan Bell Telephone Co. strike.

(Talks between Michigan Bell and the CIO Communications Workers have been said to hold the key to Bell System strikes elsewhere.

(The United Press reported the Michigan strike picture "the brightest it had been since the beginning of the telephone strike Monday morning.")

The union has demanded a 23-cent hourly increase. The company has offered 10 cents.

The telephone strike was called System companies in five States. A total of some 51,000 telephone workers are involved.

At the same time some 16,000 members of the same union, including 900 in Northern California, struck Western Electric Co. plants throughout the Nation. WE manufactures and installs central office equipment for the phone companies.

Already out at the time and still on strike are 30,000 employees of Western Union who belong to the AFL Commercial Telegraphers Union. They struck from Coast-to-Coast eight days ago because the company refuses to give them any wage increase.

35 Elections Are Held in The Bay Area

Four Bay Area counties held 35 hotly contested municipal elections yesterday.

In the 35 communities, elections to the City Council were of primary interest.

In San Mateo county, 12 cities voted on city offices and propositions.

Contra Costa county held elections in ten of its cities.

There were also elections in eight municipalities in Marin county and five in Alameda.

(For details see Page 2.)

Truman, in Broadcast, Calls Price Demands Outrageous; He Uses 'Inherent' Powers

By the United Press

WASHINGTON, April 8—The Government headed off a steel strike 90 minutes before the midnight deadline tonight by seizing the industry.

President Truman ordered the seizure in a dramatic test of his constitutional powers, and CIO President Philip Murray immediately ordered steel workers to stay on the job.

Mr. Truman issued his order in a hastily arranged radio and television talk to the Nation, in which he bitterly assailed the steel companies, saying they demanded outrageous price increases in return for wage boosts recommended by the Government.

Confronted with the collapse of negotiations in New York, Mr. Truman ordered Secretary of Commerce Charles W. Sawyer to assume control of the industry to head off what he termed a "grave danger" to national security which even increased the risk of war.

Two of the 86 companies affected immediately asked the U. S. District Court for a temporary restraining order—and Federal Judge Walter M. Bastian ordered Government attorneys to answer. (See column 4.)

Acting Mobilization Director John R. Steelman invited representatives of the six big steel companies and Murray to meet with him in Washington at 3 p. m. in a renewed effort to hammer out a contract that would end Government operation of the mills.

Mr. Truman blasted the industry for refusing to agree to what he called a "fair and reasonable" settlement proposal recommended by the Wage Stabilization Board.

Noting that the steel companies have demanded a price increase far above that permitted under Government stabilization rules, Mr. Truman said grimly:

"The companies have said, in short, that unless they can have what they want, the steel industry will shut down. That is the plain unvarnished fact of the matter."

The President said he would have been derelict in his duty if he had failed to seize the mills and prevent a strike because "our soldiers at the front in Korea" would have stopped getting the shells and bombs they need to fight the Communists.

He said the "immediate" effect of a strike would have been to "delay" the Atomic Energy program and halt plane production. But he saw even more far-reaching effects if a prolonged walkout had been permitted to cut down the overall defense program.

"I have no doubt that if our defense program fails, the danger of war, the possibility of hostile attack, grows that much greater," he said.

"Our national security and our chances for peace depend on our defense production. Our defense production depends on steel.

"Therefore, I am taking two actions tonight.

"First, I am directing the Secre-

Continued on Page 8, Col. 7

Carpenters' Strike Talks Collapse

Efforts to settle the four-county strike of AFL carpenters collapsed yesterday.

Contractors represented by eight associations withdrew their offer of a 15-cent hourly wage increase and announced no further peace meetings were scheduled.

The action was announced after the carpenters' district council rejected the wage increase as an "ultimatum" and said employer "stubbornness" was responsible for the strike.

Some 12,000 carpenters struck eight days ago and started mass picketing of building projects on Monday. The walkout and picket lines have halted most construction activity in San Francisco, Alameda, San Mateo and Marin counties.

The announcement withdrawing the employers' wage offer was made by John I. Hennessy, executive vice president of the Associated Home Builders of the East Bay.

"It is regretable that the carpenters' representatives did not see fit to submit the employers' offer to their members," he said.

"The arbitrary rejection of the offer has evidently been made in a manner not in keeping with traditional bargaining processes."

C. R. Bartalini, secretary of the Joint Council of AFL Carpenters, said the proposal was unanimously rejected by delegates of 30 carpenter locals.

He said the union contract provided for an interim increase in wages, yet the employers "repeatedly insisted" on reopening the entire contract and making a one-year agreement.

An important factor in the union's rejection of the employer plan, Bartalini said, was the contractors' rejection of union demands for a welfare plan and retention of interim negotiations for wage increases.

Contractors have been further restricted by a strike of 600 Northern California AFL pile drivers and bridge builders. They walked off their jobs Monday, demanding a 15-cent increase.

Today's Forecast: A Few Clouds

The Bay Area's slightly clouded version of spring weather will continue today with temperature about the same as yesterday—and the usual night and morning coastal fog.

The Index

Royce Brier 20
Chess 20
Comics 16
Contract Contests 17
Crossword 17
Delaplane 19
Drama 14, 15
Editorial: "A Straight 15 Cents First" 20
Finance 21, 22
Horoscope .... [illegible]
Dean Jennings 2
Lupton Goldquest .... [illegible]
Radio and Television .... [illegible]
Woman's World 11, 12, 13

Listen to KNBC Tonight (See Page 24 For Details)

Complete Election Coverage

Read Tomorrow's Chronicle For Final Primary Results

COMPARATIVE TEMPERATURES For Monday, June 2, 1952	High	Low		High	Low
San Francisco	62	50	New York	81	60
Oakland	70	52	Chicago	82	53
Sacramento	88	50	Kansas City	92	68
Los Angeles	72	55	New Orleans	90	67
Portland	78	47	Miami	83	74
Seattle	72	47	Washington	79	60

Forecast for Today: HIGH FOG (For Details See Page 18)

San Francisco Chronicle
THE CITY'S ONLY HOME-OWNED NEWSPAPER
FINAL
FOUNDED 1865—VOL. CLXXV, NO. 140 CCCCAAA SAN FRANCISCO, TUESDAY, JUNE 3, 1952 GA 1-1112 DAILY 7c, SUNDAY 15c 50 MILES OUTSIDE S. F. SINGLE COPIES, DAILY 10c, SUNDAY 20c

STEEL SHUT DOWN ---SEIZURE ENDED

'Unconstitutional,' Says Highest Court

Truman Promptly Returns Mills to Their Owners; Civilian Deliveries Halted

By VANCE JOHNSON
Washington Correspondent, The Chronicle

WASHINGTON, June 2—The Supreme Court ruled today that Government seizure of the steel industry to prevent a strike was unconstitutional. President Truman promptly returned the mills to their private owners.

Philip Murray, president of the United Steelworkers (CIO), ordered his men out on strike once more. At the same time he called on the steel companies to resume negotiations. They replied they were willing to start talks "without delay."

Late today, the Government ordered an immediate halt to all deliveries of steel for civilian projects in an effort to conserve supplies for vital defense needs.

(In the San Francisco Bay Area, some 8000 steelworkers started walking off their jobs in seven plants at 10:30 a. m. Strikers were tapping furnaces in an orderly shutdown, company spokesmen said, and all plants were expected to be closed this morning.

(Plants affected were Bethlehem-Pacific in South San Francisco and Alameda, U. S. Steel's Columbia-Geneva division plant in Pittsburg, U. S. Steel Products, Alameda; California Wire Cloth, South San Francisco and Oakland, and Armco, Berkeley. Pickets were posted at all of the plants.)

Other News of Steel Dispute

The full text of the Supreme Court decision and more details of the steel situation are on Page 7.
For editorial comment, see Page 14.

MAJORITY'S VIEW

The majority of the Supreme Court—which split 6 to 3—held that Congress may, if it sees fit, "authorize the taking of private property for public use" in a situation such as that presented by the steel strike. It declared, however, that only Congress has this power—and the President does not possess "inherent powers" to accomplish that which Congress fails to accomplish by legislation.

It ruled that the President's order of April 8 seizing the steel mills was in the nature of legislation, and therefore and encroachment on the constitutional prerogatives of the law-making branch.

"In the framework of our Constitution," wrote Justice Hugo Black, speaking for the majority, "the President's power to see that the laws are faithfully executed refutes the idea that he is to be a lawmaker. The Constitution limits his functions in the law-making process to the recommending of laws he thinks wise and the vetoing of laws he thinks bad."

DIVISION OF COURT

Black was joined in the majority opinion by Justices Felix Frankfurter, William O. Douglas, Robert H. Jackson, Harold H. Burton and Tom C. Clark—each of whom wrote concurring opinions elaborating their individual interpretations of the issues.

The decision upheld an April 29 ruling by District Judge David A. Pine. The case was taken to the Su-

Continued on Page 7, Col. 3

U. S. Rests, Smyth Asks Acquittal

By DAVID PERLMAN

The Government rested its tax fraud case against James G. Smyth yesterday, after its final witness leveled a series of damaging blows at the former Internal Revenue Collector's defense.

Smyth's attorneys promptly asked Federal Judge James Alger Fee to direct a verdict of acquittal, claiming that the nine prosecution witnesses who have testified during the four days of the trial failed to show Smyth committed any crime.

Judge Fee will hear more arguments on the defense motion when court convenes this morning.

The prosecution's last witness yesterday was Richard Nickell, gruff, white-haired, and a stickler for detail He is assistant collector of internal revenue here, and a veteran of 19 years in the tax office.

Nickell, the highest-ranking man in the parade of tax bureau officials who have testified against Smyth, made these points about revenue office procedure:

1—That taxpayers are always required to submit excuses when they file their income tax returns late and wish to avoid penalties for delinquency.

2—That bureau regulations insist that all income tax returns be date-stamped on the date they are received in the office, regardless of why they are filed late.

3—That the date of March 15, 1946, stamped on the returns of Smyth and his wife, led the bureau's auditors to believe the returns were filed on time and thus to assess no penalties for lateness.

KEY WITNESS

Smyth is accused of fraudulently back-dating his returns to evade $402.20 in penalties and interest.

Over repeated objections by Defense Attorney Harold Faulkner, Nickell produced a manual of instructions for tax bureau employees and Prosecutor Irvin Goldstein succeeded in introducing the manual as Government evidence.

When returns are filed late, Nickell said, the tax bureau's audit section immediately assesses penalties for late filing unless the taxpayer submits a written excuse.

"If the taxpayer objected to the penalty," Nickell continued, "he was offered the opportunity of filing a statement or an affidavit to explain the lateness."

MANUAL OF INSTRUCTIONS

The Government contends Smyth never filed such a statement, but instead circumvented the requirements by back-dating his 1945 returns when he finally filed them in May of 1947. Smyth insists his late returns were filed as duplicates of ones that were lost in the bureau after he filed them on time.

Nickell's manual of instructions, from which Goldstein read, provided that excuses for late filing must "clearly establish" that there was no wilful failure, and listed eight acceptable excuses.

These included such technical points as: Delays in the mail, illness or death in the taxpayer's family, unavoidable absence of the taxpayer, or destruction by fire of the taxpayer's business records.

"Was the mere assertion by the taxpayer, without supporting evidence, that his return was timely, acceptable as reasonable grounds to abate a delinquency penalty?" Goldstein asked.

"A mere statement would not

Continued on Page 8, Col. 5

Two Transports Due Today

Two troopships of the Military Sea Transportation Service are due at Fort Mason this morning with 4387 combat veterans from the Far East.

The USNS General D. I. Sultan, carrying 1333 Army and Navy men returning from duty in Korea, is scheduled to dock at 7:30 a. m. The USNS General E. T. Collins, carrying 3054 Army troops also returning under the combat rotation program, will dock at 8:30.

Vote in the Primary!

Editorial

In any presidential year a primary election is important. It is especially important, however, in a wide-open presidential situation such as the American people face this year. Having the second largest delegations at both party conventions, California inevitably will throw a great deal of weight into the choice of both presidential candidates. All these obvious considerations add to the urgency of the decisions which individual registered voters will make today.

The first decision any voter makes is the most important. It is to decide whether or not to go to the polls. If you participate in today's primary, you participate in determining the future direction and character of the Government of the United States. If you do not participate, your individual influence goes for nothing.

In any American election a distressingly high percentage of voters stays away from the polls and lets the decision of the ballot go by default. That is not the way to make democracy work better. The essential first step in the process of making American democracy stronger is to get out to the polls today and vote.

Lurline Home, Joins Fleet of Struck Ships

By PETER TRIMBLE

The passenger liner Lurline steamed into San Francisco Bay from Honolulu yesterday to join the fleet of dock-bound West Coast ships that have been struck by AFL sailors.

The Lurline tied up at Pier 35 at 9 a. m. and was allowed to discharge 653 passengers, baggage, mail, a few autos and some frozen cargo.

Six striking members of the Sailors' Union of the Pacific posted themselves in front of the dock as pickets at 5 p. m.

Caught behind picket lines at the same pier was the freighter Hawaiian Farmer. Both ships are operated by Matson Navigation Co.

The seven-day sailors' strike so far has tied up 32 ships in West Coast ports, including nine in the Bay.

And no settlement was in sight.

Directors of Pacific Maritime Association—representing 25 major ship owners—met throughout the morning in a search for a way out of the labor dispute, then adjourned with no comment and no further meetings scheduled.

The Sailors' Union has demanded a 5 per cent pay raise, overtime pay for Saturdays at sea and retention of current contract provisions that allow it to cancel its contract on 60-day notice.

The shipowners want a one-year contract or a similar long-term agreement.

Federal Conciliator Omar Hoskins continued his attempts yesterday to arrange for a resumption of joint negotiations, but announced no progress after meeting with PMA negotiators and Harry Lundeberg, head of the union.

Pickets at Pier 35, headed by William Duncan, said they would allow the Lurline's crew members to cross their line but would attempt to keep longshoremen off the dock so the vessel could not be provisioned for her next voyage.

The Lurline is scheduled to sail for the islands at 4 p. m. tomorrow with 723 passengers.

Matson officials expected to make her tie-up official late today if no settlement of the waterfront dispute is reached by then.

Meanwhile, a majority of 16,000 West Coast longshoremen ratified a new long-term agreement with PMA during balloting up and down the coast.

The agreement grants them a 17-cent hourly pay raise and additional welfare fund benefits.

Ike Gives Up His Pay; Asks To Retire

By the United Press

WASHINGTON, June 2—General Dwight D. Eisenhower has asked for his formal Army retirement and surrendered his $19,541 retirement pay so he can take an active part in the pre-convention GOP political campaign, it was disclosed today.

In a letter to Defense Secretary Robert A. Lovett, Eisenhower said he wanted to be put on the retired list so he could "feel free" to meet delegates to the Republican National Convention "without any possible interpretation that I might be violating or embarrassing the Government or the Army in any way."

He said in view of the "special circumstances" of his case—"My name is directly involved in the national political campaign" — he would waive his Army pay.

BAN IS BROAD

Eisenhower evidently sought to avoid any possible clash with Army regulations which prohibit officers on active duty from engaging in political campaigns. Retired officers are exempt, but those merely on "inactive status" are subject to recall to active duty.

The ban on political activity is so broad it even bars any attempt to influence a convention. Eisenhower plans to confer individually with Republican delegates at Abilene, New York and Denver, Colo., before his party's convention next month.

The Defense Department made public the text of the five-star general's request to be placed on the retired list effective last Saturday. However Eisenhower will not consider himself officially retired until he receives his retirement orders at a Pentagon ceremony tomorrow.

LAST MINUTE CONFERENCES

The announcement came as the former head of Atlantic Pact Forces was winding up his military career with a round of last-minute conferences, and receiving his final tribute as a general — a Distinguished Service Medal pinned on his chest by President Truman.

Following another strictly military schedule tomorrow, he will take off from Washington National Airport at 6 p. m. for Abilene, Kan., where he will make his first public address as a private citizen and Republican presidential candidate at a homecoming celebration Wednesday.

State Votes Today; Top Turnout Due

By EARL C. BEHRENS
Political Editor, The Chronicle

This is election day.

The polls open at 7 a. m. and close at 7 p. m. in all counties except San Francisco. Voting hours in San Francisco are from 7 a. m. until 8 p. m.

Voting machines will be in use in each of the 1309 precincts in this city.

The count of the ballot is expected to be a slow one because of the large number of candidates.

National political interest is focused on California's presidential primary balloting.

It's Earl Warren against what he has termed a "phantom delegation," nominally pledged to Congressman Thomas H. Werdel. This latter group appears to be a Taft-MacArthur slate which has been disavowed by Senator Robert A. Taft.

EXPENDITURES QUESTIONED

Last night Warren, in urging the Republicans to go to the polls today, questioned the "huge" expenditures of his opponents in the presidential primary. (For further details on Warren's charges about campaign expenditures, see Page 5.)

State election officials at Sacramento said there were indications the expenditures of the anti-Warren group would hit the $1,000,000 mark, a sum unprecedented in California's primaries.

Television spot announcements by the Werdel forces alone were said to cost $150 a minute in local stations. Prodigious sums were being spent for radio, newspaper ads, "throwaway" sheets and campaign literature.

The money spent by the Warren managers was a puny sum in comparison, according to State election officers.

On the Democratic side, there is Senator Estes Kefauver, an actual candidate, and Attorney General Edmund G. Brown, to whom the original Truman delegation, with a few changes, has been nominally pledged.

NO WRITE-INS

Write-in voting for presidential candidates is not permitted in California.

Eisenhower's Volunteers in California, since the general's name is not on the ballot today, are urging all Eisenhower backers to vote for the Warren delegation.

The anti-Warren forces appeared to be trying to spread confusion.

Nominal candidate Werdel in TV announcements said those who favor Taft, MacArthur, Stassen or Eisenhower, none of whose names are on the ballot, should vote for him.

Huge newspaper ads declared the

Continued on Page 4, Col. 3

Banks to Close, Some Offices

Today, election day in California, there will be business as usual at most commercial establishments and in Federal offices and courts. However: City and State offices and courts will be closed all day.

Banks will be closed today.

A few insurance offices will close.

And bars and liquor stores will not open until the polls close—8 p. m. in San Francisco, 7 p. m. in all other counties.

THE CHRONICLE Recommends:

For the guidance of inquiring voters, The Chronicle offers the following as its judgment on candidates and ballot measures at the consolidated primary election Tuesday:

FOR PRESIDENT (Republican Ballot)
Earl Warren

(Candidates The Chronicle recommends for all offices below have cross-filed, with the exception of the judges who run on a nonpartisan basis.)

FOR U. S. SENATOR
William F. Knowland

CONGRESS—Fourth District
William S. Mailliard for Republican nomination
Franck R. Havenner for Democratic nomination

Fifth District
John F. Shelley

Sixth District (Contra Costa & Solano counties)
John F. Baldwin Jr.

Seventh District (Alameda County)
John J. Allen Jr.

Eighth District (Alameda County)
Charles C. McGonegal

Ninth District (San Mateo County)
J. Arthur Younger

MEMBERS OF THE ASSEMBLY
Nineteenth District—Charles T. Travers
Twentieth District—Thomas A. Maloney
Twenty-first District—Caspar W. Weinberger
Twenty-second District—Frank J. O'Brien
Twenty-third District—George T. Alvers
Twenty-fourth District—Samuel W. Wicklow

SUPERIOR JUDGE (Office No. 7)
Judge John B. Molinari

(Judge George W. Schonfeld for Office No. 3, and Judges Herman A. Van der Zee, Thomas M. Foley, Melvyn I. Cronin, William F. Traverso and Robert McWilliams, who are unopposed.)

CITY BALLOT PROPOSITIONS

Prop.		VOTE
"A"	(Police and Firemen Pay)	Yes
"B"	(Leasing of City Lands)	No
"C"	(Legion of Honor Palace Trustees)	Yes
"D"	(Zoning Appeals)	Yes
"E"	(Abandonment Portion McLaren Park)	Yes

(Republican County Committee recommendations on Page 4.)

Maybe an Encore?

Judge Drops Curtain On Crown Terrace Scene

Grace Perego's war to open up Crown terrace for access to her near-by apartment house has been long and it has been bitter.

High mark came last April when Crown terrace residents dragged her car off the little Twin Peaks lane with an angry Mrs. Perego clutching the steering wheel.

Then the residents put up a chain and Mrs. Perego filed suit. Among other things ($91,000) she wanted an injunction ordering that chain taken down.

Yesterday Superior Judge William T. Sweigert issued the following decision on the request for an injunction:

SCENE IS SET

"High upon the eastern slope of San Francisco's Twin Peaks lies Crown terrace. There have lived these many years a score of families, secluded and serene, in comfortable homes that command a thrilling view of San Francisco and its bay.

"In all this great city it would have been difficult to find a place less likely to become the scene of stirring events. Yet, it must be recorded that here, on the 28th day of April, a day that will long enliven and enrich the already colorful annals of San Francisco, occurred the strange Battle of Crown Terrace.

"Without finally determining, at this point, the legal status of Crown terrace, this much can be said:

REALLY A LANE

"Only smilingly can Crown terrace be called a street. Whatever the maps may show, it is really an irregular, narrow lane, only partly improved to meet the needs of the quiet little neighborhood. The section whereon these homes front has been crudely paved to a width of 17 feet at the expense of the residents themselves. For, the city's Bureau of Works has never deigned to notice, much less accept, this rustic way as a full-grown street. This section has all it can do to accommodate its snugly parked cars and the romping of a large number of playful youngsters—with their equally playful dogs—and a strewn array of tricycles, toy wagons and other paraphernalia of childhood.

WELL-CUT PATH

"The more southerly section of Crown terrace, beyond the row of homes, has never received even the modest acknowledgment of a paved surface. It is little more than a well-cut path that climbs and turns, narrowing to 12 feet, until it reaches a crest whereon modern enterprise has constructed with marvelous ingenuity an apartment house known, impressively, as One Twenty Graystone, a corporation.

"Never in the past has Crown terrace been a thoroughfare for vehicular intrusion. Frankly, the judicial mind contemplates with a feeling akin to horror the spectacle of automobiles crunching down the steep path and crowding through this once happy lane. Nature has not formed, nor has the hand of man yet adapted, Crown terrace for the burdens of such traffic. It should not be so used, unless upon great necessity and under strict conditions.

NECESSITY NOT PROVEN

"No showing of necessity has been made. The apartment dwellers—12 tenants in all, each with a family car—are not dependent upon Crown terrace for their means of communication with the outer world. They are not marooned, awaiting rescue by the judicial arm. Not at all. They have their own, specially constructed, well-surfaced Burnett street access which directly connects them with the main Twin Peaks boulevard only a few hundred feet away. This Burnett street

Continued on Page 2, Col. 1

High Fog May Last All Day

The Weather Bureau got out of its rut yesterday. Today's forecast is NOT "morning fog along the coast and fair inland."

It is: "All-day fog along the coast and fair inland."

The fog will be a high one, the Weather Bureau said. Bay Area temperatures will range from 55 degrees in San Francisco to 75 in San Rafael.

Thunderstorms and rising temperatures were forecast for the High Sierra.

The Index

Bayes' Brier 34
Chess 18
Comics 28
Contract Contests 20
Crossword 28
Deaths 18
Drama 8, 9
Editorial "Pacific Coast Table, Science and Engine..." 14
Finance 16, 17
Horoscope 20
Lively 19
Panorama 28
Radio and Television 24
Vital Statistics 18
Women's World 10, 11

Congress and U. S. Salaries

Steel Verdict May Get Postmen Paid

WASHINGTON, June 2 (UP)—The Supreme Court decision declaring seizure of the steel mills unconstitutional may have cleared the way for more than 400,000 postal workers to get their pay.

(About 8500 Bay Area postal workers are affected.)

A $968,000,000 deficiency appropriations bill carrying funds to pay postal and many other Federal workers has been stalled in a House-Senate Conference Committee for weeks as a result of the steel issue.

The Senate attached a rider to the bill barring use of any of the money to pay any Federal employee engaged in the operation of the Government-seized mills. A deadlock ensued when House spokesmen refused to accept the Senate provision.

After the Supreme Court declared the steel seizure unconstitutional, Chairman Clarence Cannon (Dem-Mo.) of the House Appropriations Committee said an agreement may be reached quickly on the appropriations bill.

The bill, carrying about $968,000,000 in deficiency appropriations for the current fiscal year, provides nearly $375,000,000 to meet the pay rolls of most civilian agencies of the Government through June 30.

THE QUAKE IN PICTURES

COMPARATIVE TEMPERATURES
For Monday, July 21, 1952

	High	Low		High	Low
San Francisco	62	53	New York	88	76
Oakland	69	58	Chicago	94	78
Sacramento	88	54	Kansas City	95	80
Los Angeles	86	59	New Orleans	91	73
Portland	67	53	Miami	88	75
Seattle	69	49	Washington	98	76

Forecast for Today: Morning Fog, Fair
(For Details See Page 11)

San Francisco Chronicle
THE CITY'S ONLY HOME-OWNED NEWSPAPER

FINAL

FOUNDED 1865—VOL. CLXXVI, NO. 7 CCCCAAA SAN FRANCISCO, TUESDAY, JULY 22, 1952 GA 1-1112 DAILY 10c, SUNDAY 20c

BIG SWING ON TO STEVENSON

Tehachapi Quake Kills 11

Where Four Children Died

This furniture store on Tehachapi's main street crumbled in rubble, crushing a car and killing four children in an apartment in the store

(AP) Wirephoto

At Least 25 Injured, Millions in Damage

Railroad Tunnels Collapse; Town Is Left in Ruins by Worst Temblor Since 1906

At 4:53 a. m. yesterday, as the blackness of a moonless night faded into the graying of a midsummer's dawn, there occurred a violent convulsion in the earth's crust.

It was a painful, twisting convulsion, of almost unprecedented strength—second only in intensity to the great San Francisco earthquake of 1906.

For ten minutes the fury lasted. It ripped open an ancient scar in the earth's crust—the Garloch fault—which geologists believed had healed millions of years ago. That rupture sent sympathetic tremors rumbling down the infamous old San Andreas fault, which lies lengthwise of California.

By the Grace of a Benevolent Providence, the epicenter of the disturbance came in one of the most sparsely settled parts of the long jittery fault areas on the Pacific slope.

Stories and pictures on the quake on Pages A, B, 2 and 3.

The little mountain town of Tehachapi (population 1700) in the uplands above the Mojave desert, bore the brunt of the resultant disaster.

Eleven persons lost their lives beneath the falling walls and tumbling masonry of Tehachapi, and at least 25 others were injured sufficiently to require hospitalization. The center of the town was ruined.

Ranging both ways from Tehachapi, toward the prosperous cities of the San Joaquin Valley, and the densely populated areas of Los Angeles county, the property damage was far greater. It will run to millions of dollars—millions as yet uncounted and unestimated.

Yet, for such a cataclysm, it was a mercifully small toll.

A suggestion of what might-have-been could be seen in the great earth slides along the highway arterials between Fresno and Los Angeles.

It could be seen in the way the mountains moved, as the convulsions continued, and the railroad tunnels, hewn through solid rock, collapsed like hollow straws.

It could be seen in the minor panics which occurred in Long Beach and Santa Barbara—cities which have known real earthquakes, and now were getting only the spent waves of this big one.

There was uneasiness and minor damage all along the tender fault

Continued on Page 2, Col. 3

The Index

Royce Brier	14
Chess	12
Comics	18
Crossword	11
Drama	8, 9
Editorial: "'Great Debate' Rends Demos"	14
Finance	16, 17
Horoscope	25
Dean Jennings	2
Lichty	15
Panorama	15
Radio and Television	26
Vital Statistics	11
Women's World	8

The Weather
Fair, Coast fog

Two Families: One Broken, One Spared

By DAVID PERLMAN
Chronicle Staff Writer

TEHACHAPI (Kern county), July 21—This is the story of two families: the family of Pete Quintana, which was broken when the earth trembled this morning, and the family of Ira Davis, which was miraculously spared.

Quintana came here last night from New Mexico with his wife Blanche and his nine children. At 4:53 a. m., his wife and four of his children were killed in their beds.

"We hoped that God would smile on us here in California," Quintana said this morning. "Now we have come to a broken land and my family is broken . . . broken . . . broken . . ."

When they arrived here last night, the Quintana family found a tiny two-room house on "G" street, the city's main street.

Bobby, 5, Gloria, 13, Nicola, 16, and Joe, 11, climbed into a single bed in one room and Quintana, who is 40, his wife, Blanche, 36, and the five other children, settled down in the other room.

A brother, Mike, and sister, Felipe, also found room in the little house.

When the quake came, a furniture store next door collapsed. The brick walls crumbled and the ceiling beams knifed into the room where the four children slept. Another beam struck and killed Mrs. Quintana, but missed her husband and the other five children.

Screaming in Spanish, Quintana ran into the smashed room and tried to claw his way to the bodies of his wife and children. A handful of volunteers, also wakened by the quake, tried to help him lift the heavy beams. Then they saw that the effort was futile.

Quintana, a dark, stocky man who came to California to work in the vineyards near here, collapsed in the street and began to mutter: "Madre de Dios"—Mother of God.

All through the day, Quintana ran back and forth between the shattered apartment where his wife and four children had died to the Red Cross tent in the town park where the five children who had been spared were being cared for. He continued his visits to the place where his family had been broken even after the bodies had been removed to the fire house and then

Continued on Page 11, Col. 1

X marks the heart of the disaster

Barkley Quits the Presidential Race; Delegate 'Loyalty Oath' Rule Approved

Southerners Overridden

By VANCE JOHNSON
Chronicle Staff Writer

CHICAGO, July 22 — Rejecting Southern warnings that it would imperil Democratic party candidates in November, the Democratic National convention early today (Tuesday) voted to require delegates to subscribe to a modified "loyalty pledge."

As finally adopted by voice vote, the resolution would prevent the seating of any delegate who fails to "give assurance" that he will "exert every honorable means available to him" to see that the names of Democratic candidates appear on the November ballot.

The resolution provided that the pledge would not be binding "upon those delegates who shall so signify to the Credentials Committee prior to its report to this convention."

The convention was told, however, that any delegate who would not agree to abide by the pledge would not be allowed to take his seat in the convention.

Southern spokesmen warned that delegations from six States—Texas, Mississippi, Louisiana, Georgia, South Carolina and Virginia—could not remain in the convention if the resolution was approved.

Indications were, however, that the Southerners would not walk out of the convention but would wait for the Credentials Committee to refuse them a permanent seat.

If the Southerners stick by their announced resolve, it may result in a repetition of the Dixiecrat efforts ment of 1948 and concerted efforts south of the Mason and Dixon line to put names of others than Democrats on the ballot in the columns usually reserved for the Democratic party.

Senator A. Willis Robertson of Virginia predicted that Senator Richard B. Russell of Georgia would feel compelled to withdraw from the Presidential race as a result of the vote.

Proponents of the resolution rejected all of these contentions — declaring it will not affect the outcome of the election in November and denying it was intended to throw anybody out of the convention.

Northern and Southern Demo-

Continued on Page 4, Col. 1

Big U. S. Day at Olympics

American track and field forces had a big day in the Olympic Games at Helsinki yesterday as they walked off with four gold medals, with a sweep of the first three places in the shot-put.

Lindy Remigino of New York won the 100-meter dash in a photo finish; Charlie Moore of Cornell took the 400 meter hurdles; Jerome Biffle of Denver won the broad jump; and USC's Parry O'Brien won the shot-put followed by United States teammates Darrow Hooper of Texas A & M and Jim Fuchs, formerly of Yale.

(See Sporting Green for Staff Writer Art Rosenbaum's story.)

Veep's Delegates Expected To Go Over to the Illinoisan

By EARL C. BEHRENS
Political Editor, The Chronicle

CHICAGO, July 21—Vice President Alben Barkley announced tonight his withdrawal from the race for the Democratic presidential nomination—apparently clearing the way for the certain nomination of Governor Adlai Stevenson as a "draftee" of the Democratic National Convention.

Barkley's withdrawal came partly as a result of a notice from the CIO and AFL that they would not support him and because of a lack of support which Barkley's friends had expected he might receive from President Truman.

(Associated Press reported there were rumors President Truman is getting set to support Stevenson. Officials with White House connections predicted that Truman will come out for Stevenson tomorrow afternoon or tomorrow night. (For details, see Page 4.)

Barkley announced his withdrawal with an angry blast at "self-anointed political labor leaders" who considered him too old for the race. (For Barkley's statement, see Page 5.)

It was predicted that Stevenson, despite his reluctance to run for the Presidency, would win the nomination on an early ballot.

But the other leading candidates, Senators Estes Kefauver, Richard Russell and Robert Kerr, refused to concede defeat tonight.

Stevenson's popularity with the delegates was apparent this morning when he received a six-minute ovation when he rose to deliver an official welcoming speech to the convention on behalf of the State of Illinois.

It was the delegates who did the welcoming. They stood, cheered, waved their State standards and indicated that despite the Governor's disinclination to have his name presented to the convention as candidate, it will be proposed anyhow.

Aside from the backstage maneuvering, the main event on the program tonight was a thundering keynote address by Governor Paul A. Dever of Massachusetts who denounced the Republicans as "selfish opportunists" and demanded the

Continued on Page 4, Col. 6

Inside . . .

There's a lot of convention news on the inside pages this morning.

Sources close to the Administration hint that Mr. Truman is going to support Governor Stevenson for the nomination. See Page 4

Kefauver turns up on the convention floor, an unusual thing for a candidate at this stage. For that and a view from Eisenhower's camp. See Page 5

Labor leaders demand a strong platform. See Page 6

And for the color of the whole, great show. See Page 10

FINAL ELECTION EXTRA

COMPARATIVE TEMPERATURES
For Tuesday, November 4, 1952

	High	Low		High	Low
San Francisco	77	56	New York	50	42
Oakland	77	47	Chicago	61	34
Sacramento	76	41	Detroit	50	31
Los Angeles	88	62	New Orleans	68	53
Portland	57	36	Miami	79	69
Seattle	55	50	Washington	51	40

FORCAST FOR TODAY: Cloudy, Cooler
(For details see Page 15)

San Francisco Chronicle
THE CITY'S ONLY HOME-OWNED NEWSPAPER

FOUNDED 1865—VOL. CLXXVI, NO. 113 CCCCAAAA SAN FRANCISCO, WEDNESDAY, NOVEMBER 5, 1952 GA 1-1112 DAILY 10c, SUNDAY 20c

IT'S IKE

Eisenhower: 442
Stevenson: 89

Here (at left) is how the nominees stand in the contest for electoral votes on the basis of the latest—but incomplete—returns across the Nation. The table below shows the State standings. A star (★) indicates the candidate has clinched the electoral vote in that State. A ball (●) indicates the party is leading for that State's electoral vote—but the final outcome is in doubt. To be elected, a candidate must have 266 electoral votes.

STATE	Electoral Vote	REP.	DEM.	STATE	Electoral Vote	REP.	DEM.	STATE	Electoral Vote	REP.	DEM.
Alabama	(11)		★	Maine	(5)	★		Ohio	(25)	★	
Arizona	(4)	★		Maryland	(9)	★		Oklahoma	(8)	★	
Arkansas	(8)		★	Mass.	(16)	★		Oregon	(6)	★	
California	(32)	★		Michigan	(20)	★		Penn.	(32)	★	
Colorado	(6)	★		Minnesota	(11)	★		Rhode Is.	(4)	★	
Conn.	(8)	★		Mississippi	(8)		★	So. Car.	(8)		★
Delaware	(3)	★		Missouri	(13)	★		So. Dakota	(4)	★	
Florida	(10)	★		Montana	(4)	★		Tennessee	(11)	●	
Georgia	(12)		★	Nebraska	(6)	★		Texas	(24)	●	
Idaho	(4)	★		Nevada	(3)	★		Utah	(4)	★	
Illinois	(27)	★		N. Hamp.	(4)	★		Vermont	(3)	★	
Indiana	(13)	★		N.J.	(16)	★		Virginia	(12)	★	
Iowa	(10)	★		New Mex.	(4)	★		Wash.	(9)	●	
Kansas	(8)	★		New York	(45)	★		W.Virginia	(6)		●
Kentucky	(10)		★	No. Car.	(14)		★	Wisconsin	(12)	★	
Louisiana	(10)		●	No. Dakota	(4)	★		Wyoming	(3)	★	

Landslide for GOP; Mailliard Is Elected; Proposition 3 Ahead

After 20 Years---Democratic Reign Ends

Molinari Is Winner; City Votes Firehouse Bonds; Muni Plan Loses; Congress Lineup Still Close

Propositions: Muni Bond Plan Loses

San Francisco voters approved a $4,750,000 bond issue for new firehouses yesterday but failed to give the necessary two-thirds majority to a $6,620,000 Municipal Railway improvement program.

Returns from the city's 1306 precincts gave an affirmative vote of 212,010 for the firehouse bonds and 76,729 against them.

The Municipal Railway Bond proposal received a substantial plurality—158,025 Yes to 95,007 No—but lacked about 10,000 votes for the two-thirds majority required by the charter for bond issues. Although there is a record-breaking total of 16,117 absentee ballots yet to be counted, it was considered unlikely that the required figure could be reached.

While turning down the Muni railway bonds, the voters expressed, by 192,595 to 78,371, a willingness to contribute $100,000 toward the purchase of Butano redwood forest as a park.

In another declaration of policy, San Franciscans favored city acquisition of Angel island for recreational purposes by a vote of 136,790 to 107,181.

They turned down a suggestion that the city contribute its share toward the cost of building a model of San Francisco bay for the study of bridge routes and water control. The vote was 172,305 No to 98,617 Yes.

San Franciscans cast big majorities for the two State bond proposals on the ballot. Proposition No. 1, authorizing $150,000,000 in Veterans Farm and Home bonds, was approved 238,616 to 46,732.

State Proposition No. 24, calling for a bond issue of $185,000,000 for construction of new schools, carried the city by 202,053 to 50,755.

San Franciscans gave an even larger majority to State Proposition No. 2, which would increase State payments to local school districts. The vote was 211,724 Yes to 77,148 in opposition.

State Proposition No. 3, to extend tax exemption to private non-profit schools, was endorsed 173,299 to 137,127 in San Francisco balloting.

State Propositions Nos. 5 and 6, dealing respectively with subversives and a new loyalty oath for all public workers, had almost identical tallies. No. 5 received a Yes vote of 172,965 to 100,636 No. No. 6 received 172,355 Yes votes to 100,872 No.

McLAIN'S PLAN

Pension Promoter George McLain's latest scheme, on the ballot as Proposition No. 11, was rejected 166,321 to 113,866.

Proposition No. 13, to prohibit cross-filing in elections was rejected 138,330 to 122,066.

Voters clearly supported the al-

Continued on Page 2, Col. 4

S. F. Vote on Congress And Judges

Complete semi-official returns from all 1306 precincts in San Francisco give:

Representative in Congress
(Fourth District)

Mailliard (Rep.)	96,110
Havenner (Dem.)	79,398

Member of Assembly
20TH DISTRICT

Maloney (R-D)	25,641
Paolinelli (IPP)	4,084

21ST DISTRICT

Blake (Dem.)	18,720
Weinberger (Rep.)	33,202

24TH DISTRICT

Collins (Dem.)	21,713
Wicklow (Rep.)	18,141

Superior Court, Office No. 7

Molinari	157,709
McMahon	119,813

The Local Candidates: Mailliard Wins

William S. Mailliard, youthful San Francisco Republican, swept veteran Congressman Franck R. Havenner out of office yesterday.

The 35-year-old Mailliard won overwhelmingly from his Democratic opponent—an opponent twice his age who had served in Congress for six terms.

Mailliard scored his triumph in the Fourth Congressional district, an area that was redrawn last year and in which—before the South of Market precincts were lopped off—Havenner had defeated Mailliard by 4800 votes in 1948.

THE GOP TIDE

With final returns in from all the city's 1306 precincts, the unexpectedly strong Republican tide gave Mailliard 96,110 votes to 79,398 for Havenner.

The tide was vividly evident in other races, too.

General Dwight D. Eisenhower pulled San Francisco into the GOP column with 177,476 votes to 160,881 for his defeated opponent, Adlai E. Stevenson.

In the non-partisan contest for Superior Judge, Municipal Judge John B. Molinari piled up 157,709 votes to 119,813 for his opponent and fellow-member of the Municipal bench, John J. McMahon.

In the 21st Assembly district Caspar W. Weinberger, 34-year-old Republican lawyer, trounced William C. Blake, Democratic busi-

Continued on Page 2, Col. 1

The Senate Could End In a Tie

By VANCE JOHNSON
Washington Correspondent, The Chronicle

WASHINGTON, Nov. 5—Incomplete returns early today (Wednesday) indicated the Republicans will just barely be able to organize the new Congress when it convenes in January.

Apparently the most the GOP could hope for in the Senate was a two-vote margin, and as dawn approached across half of the country thre still was a possibility (if not a probability) of a tie.

While returns from congressional races still were so incomplete at this hour that a firm picture of the new membership was impossible, it began to appear that earlier assumptions of a large Republican majority in the House may have been unjustified.

Neither the Senate nor House races were following the pattern of the immense Eisenhower vote. The General's vistory was enough to pull through several Republican Senators who had been in serious trouble and to unseat four Democratic incumbents—including the present Democratic leader, Ernest W. McFarland of Arizona. Put other Republican candidates were falling by the wayside in States which Eisenhower won handily.

This is how the picture shaped up at 5 a. m.

SENATE—The Republicans had won 17 seats—which, with 25 holdovers, assures them 42 seats. The Democrats had won 11 seats—which, with 35 holdovers, would give them 43 seats. Republicans, were leading in six other races—and if trends of the early returns should be sustained this would bring the GOP total to 48 seats. Democrats were leading in three contests and if these trends likewise should be sustained, they would wind up with a total of 46 seats, but they presumably could count on the Senate's new Independent, Wayne C. Morse of Oregon, to vote with them on organization—thus giving them 47.

One nip-and-tuck race—between Major General Patrick J. Hurley, Republican, and Democratic Senator Dennis Chavez in New Mexico—well might decide whether the Republicans wind up with a definite majority or whether the Senate is equally divided between the GOP and the Democrats, plus Morse.

If Hurley wins, the Republicans presumably would wind up with 49 votes to 46 Democrats and Morse.

This, incidentally, would exactly reverse the present Senate lineup, which now is 49 Democrats and 47 Republicans.)

House—At 3 a. m. (PST) 163 Democrats and 170 Republicans had been elected, with 102 seats still undecided. The Republicans had gained a net of one seat each in North Carolina, Arizona, Indiana,

Continued on Page 14, Col. 3

State GOP Boosts Edge In House

By EARL C. BEHRENS
Political Editor, The Chronicle

General Dwight D. Eisenhower and his running mate, Senator Richard M. Nixon, won California's 32 electoral votes for President and Vice President in a smashing victory yesterday.

The Eisenhower-Nixon decision ended a 20-year drought in presidential elections for the Republican party in this State.

Associated Press tabulations for 11,685 precincts out of 20,755 in the State early this morning gave:

Eisenhower-Nixon (Rep)	1,241,395
Stevenson-Sparkman (Dem)	970,469

The Republicans increased their control of both the State Senate and the Assembly.

HOUSE MARGIN

From the available returns, it was indicated that the Republicans would increase their margin in the House.

Yesterday, California elected 30 members to the House of Representatives. It was the first election under the new apportionment—under which the State gained seven additional seats in the House.

U. S. Senator William F. Knowland had only token opposition for re-election to a second six-year term. He won both the Republican and Democratic nominations at the primaries.

PROPOSITION 3

Tabulation returns from all parts of the State early this morning indicated that the voters had approved Proposition No. 3, the hotly contested law which would grant tax exemption to nonprofit, private schools, mostly parochial.

The belated returns also indicated that No. 7, providing that candidates designate their party affiliation on the ballot at primary election was being approved. But No. 13, the measure seeking to abolish the 41-year-old cross filing for political nominations law was being defeated.

Should both pass the measure receiving the higher vote would be the law.

Both of the measures sponsored by Pension Promoter George H.

Continued on Page 6, Col. 1

The Index

Chess	19
Comics	20
Crossword	15
Delaplane	17
Dean Jennings	5
Drama	12, 13
Editorial: "The High Cost of Trade Walls"	18
Horoscope	27
Lichty	18
Radio and Television	19
Vital Statistics	15
Women's World	10, 11

The Victory

Editorial

The American people voted a change of national leadership yesterday.

It was a momentous change, carried out at a critical moment of the world's history. And yet it was accomplished, as has always been true in this democracy of ours, without imposing any dangerous strain upon the Republic, without any perceptible rocking of the Ship of State.

We congratulate Dwight D. Eisenhower—President-elect Eisenhower—for ably and honorably winning the highest honor the American people can bestow. He has shown that he will wear that honor humbly, and with full regard for the responsibility it carries.

We congratulate the Republican party for returning, undaunted, to the struggle and regaining the national leadership after 20 years. It is a victory all the more remarkable because during that 20 years successive Democratic Administrations had built a remarkable edifice of political power, and laid a broad and solid foundation for that structure. A regime in charge of a payroll approaching 3,000,000 persons, and a spending program approaching the $100,000,000,000-a-year mark, has formidable staying power. It took a solid jolt to bowl it over.

We congratulate Governor Adlai Stevenson for waging one of the most remarkable campaigns within our memory, remarkable for its quality, its good humor and its adherence to high principle. This was a contest between two good men, and the antics of certain lesser lights in the ranks of each candidate did not persuade the people otherwise.

And we congratulate the American people. They moved into this campaign as we have never known them to move into any other. They studied the issues and they followed the candidates with great care. They perceived the need for change, in the face of one of the most vigorous and artful propaganda campaigns in history, aimed at persuading them that such a change would work to their eternal detriment. History will record few more impressive examples of an alert, informed followership doing its duty conscientiously.

From all these signs, the democracy is in good hands, and the Nation can move confidently into the future under the guidance of a great soldier who has also proved himself a great statesman.

U. S. Vote at a Glance

By Associated Press

The Nation's election picture at 6:30 a. m., Wednesday:

Dwight Eisenhower elected President in landslide. His popular vote was 25,144,752 to 20,627,243 for Adlai Stevenson in 105,395 of 146,347 precincts.

Eisenhower led in 40 states with 442 electorial votes; Stevenson in eight with 89.

Senate: 35 races: Democrats elected 6, holdovers 35, total 41. Republicans elected 17, holdovers 26, total 42. Needed to control 49. Democrats leading in six and Republicans in 6 undecided races.

House: 435 races: Democrats elected 163. Republicans 170. Needed to control 218.

Governors: 30 races: Democrats elected six. Republicans 11.

S. F. Returns for President

Complete semi-official returns from all 1306 precincts in San Francisco give:

Eisenhower-Nixon (Rep.)	177,476
Stevenson-Sparkman (Dem.)	160,881
Hallinan-Bass (Prog.)	3,149
Hamblen-Holtwick (Proh.)	763

Eisenhower Even Cracks The South

By the Associated Press

General Dwight D. Eisenhower won the Presidency by a landslide early today (Wednesday) and brought to a crashing end the 20-year era of Democratic political reign.

Down to defeat went Governor Adlai E. Stevenson of Illinois. The Democratic nominee conceded it was all over at 1:44 a. m. (10:44 p. m., PST).

"My fellow citizens have made their choice . . . and I gladly accept it," Stevenson said.

To a wildly cheering throng at his New York headquarters, Eisenhower declared this was a "day of dedication rather than triumph."

He promised the American people he would never give "short weight" to his great new responsibilities.

The popular vote at 6:30 a. m.: Eisenhower 25,144,752; Stevenson 20,627,243.

Eisenhower had won 442 electoral votes and Stevenson 89.

A GREAT VICTORY

At one mighty blow Eisenhower had demolished political ramparts which had securely sheltered Franklin D. Roosevelt and Harry S. Truman while they built their "New Deal" and "Fair Deal."

For Eisenhower, a professional soldier whose name became almost legend in his lifetime, the victory, in its way, was as great and overwhelming as any he ever carved out on the battlefields of Europe.

Never before had General "Ike" tried for public office. Then in a single effort he vaulted all the way to the White House. In politics, the man with the magic smile, the cry that it was time for a change, the promise to go to Korea, started at the pinnacle.

NIXON IS VEEP

Eisenhower carried with him to victory youthful Richard M. Nixon, California Senator and exposer of Alger Hiss. Nixon beat out Senator John Sparkman of Alabama for the Vice Presidency.

Eisenhower started his victory sweep by capturing traditionally Democratic Virginia and going on to win Florida and Oklahoma while piling up leads in Texas and Tennessee.

Border State Maryland swung into line.

Then the vital big-population States enrolled in the Eisenhower column—New York, New Jersey, Ohio, even Stevenson's own Illinois. The general forged ahead also in Michigan and Pennsylvania.

The Farm States moved in the same direction—the same Midwestern region that gave President Truman his victory in 1948.

Then, California Democrats conceded their State's 32 electoral votes to Eisenhower.

To Eisenhower, his own campaign was a "great crusade"—

Continued on Page 8, Col. 4

STALIN DEAD

San Francisco Chronicle
THE CITY'S ONLY HOME-OWNED NEWSPAPER
VOL. CLXXVII. NO. 50 CCCCAAA FRIDAY, MARCH 6, 1953 GA 1-1112 DAILY 10c, SUNDAY 20c

Pictures, Story of His Long Career

STRONG HINT ON SUCCESSOR

Stricken Leader Dies After 4 Days

Highest Officials Jointly Announce Death---Body to Lie in State in Moscow

By the United Press

MOSCOW, March 6—Joseph Stalin, 73, died last night (Thursday) at 9:50 p. m. (10:50 a. m. PST).

The Soviet Premier had been unconscious and paralyzed since Sunday when his fatal illness began with a massive brain hemorrhage. Thursday morning he suffered a major heart attack.

"The heart of Comrade Stalin has stopped beating," an official announcement said.

At his bedside were his family and closest associates in the Presidium and Central Committee.

The announcement was withheld from the outside world for six hours. It was not until eight hours after death that the news was announced to the Russian people.

At 6:05 a. m. today (Friday) (7:05 p. m. Thursday, PST) they were told that Stalin, successor to V. I. Lenin as head of the Soviet Union and the International Communist party, was dead.

Stalin's body will lie in state in the Hall of Columns of the House of Unions.

OFFICIAL ANNOUNCEMENT

The announcement of Stalin's death came from the Central Committee of the Communist party of the Soviet Union, the USSR Council of Ministers and the Presidium of the Supreme Soviet (parliament) of the USSR.

It called on all workers of the nation to pursue the policies mapped by Stalin and the Communist party.

The official announcement said the party was "in every way strengthening the Soviet Army, Navy and intelligence organs with a view to constantly raising our preparedness for decisive rebuff to any aggressor."

"The foreign policy of the Communist party and the government of the Soviet Union has always been and always is a policy of maintaining peace, the struggle against preparation and unleashing of another war, a policy of international collaboration, and the development of businesslike relations with all countries," the announcement said.

UNITY APPEAL

It added that "in these sorrowful days, all peoples of our country are rallying ever closer in the great fraternal family under the tested leadership of the Communist party."

(Communist leaders from around the world were being summoned to Moscow. Foreign Minister Andrei Vishinsky, who has been representing Russia in the United Nations in New York, is leaving immediately. French Communist leader Jacques Duclos was another of those summoned.)

Eight hours and 15 minutes after Stalin's death occurred, the Moscow home radio service broadcast the chimes of the Kremlin and then the Soviet national anthem. Then the senior Moscow announcer began reading the full statement issued by the government and the Communist party.

DOCTORS BULLETIN

The nine doctors under the direction of Minister of Health A. I. Tretyakov who had fought desperately to save Stalin, issued their fourth and final bulletin shortly after news of his death.

It reviewed the fatal attack from its first onslaught Sunday night and said that on his last day Stalin suffered repeated heart attacks.

For the Russian people, his passing was a climax to a period of shock followed by intense anxiety.

They did not learn of the attack until 48 hours after it occurred.

For those who had grown up in the period since the 1917 revolu-

Continued on Page 2, Col. 5

Full Report Of Stalin Story

Page A—Biography of the Russian Premier. Pictures of his children and birthplace.
Page B—A full page of pictures showing his rise to power.
Page 2—Official text of the Moscow announcement of Stalin's death. Full medical details are given.
Page 3—A dramatic picture of Stalin and his probable successor. Analyses of the Russian political future.

Van Fleet: I Didn't Get Men, Ammo

By the Associated Press

WASHINGTON, March 5. General James A. Van Fleet told Congress today American troops in Korea have been handicapped by a "serious shortage" of ammunition.

Senator Harry F. Byrd (Dem-Va.) promptly dispatched an urgent message to Secretary of Defense Charles E. Wilson demanding that the Pentagon punish officials responsible for what he termed "this criminal inefficiency."

The Virginia Senator's outburst came after Van Fleet had testified at a public hearing of the Senate Armed Services Committee that Pentagon not only failed to fulfill promises to increase U. S. armed forces in Korea, but at times left him critically short of ammunition.

Later, at a closed-door session, Senators quoted the former commander of U. N. forces in Korea as saying he had been assured on his return to this country that the ammunition situation has improved "and will be better."

A CONTRADICTION

His testimony about ammunition shortages was in seeming conflict with testimony he gave yesterday that there are "no shortages of a serious nature" in supplies for troops in Korea. There was no explanation of the apparent contradiction.

Defense Secretary Wilson's office said he has already been giving "urgent attention" to the reported serious shortage of ammunition in Korea.

A defense spokesman said Wilson received Byrd's letter late this afternoon. The spokesman said the letter "will be looked into thoroughly and a factual reply will be made."

In reporting the ammunition shortage, Van Fleet particularly mentioned hand grenades.

Major General Floyd Parks, Army Chief of Information, told newsmen later today that he had checked Pentagon records and he declared:

"I find no immediate evidence of a shortage of hand grenades in Far East Command depot stocks since the beginning of the Korean war. No doubt there have been

Continued on Page 4, Col. 4

Pravda Mentions Malenkov's Name

Reference Is Believed Significant

By the United Press

LONDON, March 5—Russia hinted broadly today that Joseph Stalin's policy would be carried on "under the tried leadership of the party" and that Georgi M. Malenkov might be its head man.

A front page editorial in the Communist party's official organ, Pravda, written before the announcement of Stalin's death, said:

"Plans which determine the prospects and ways of our progress are based on the laws of the national economy, on the science of the Communist society structure, which have been evolved by Comrade Stalin."

It attributed that pronouncement to Malenkov, bracketing him with Stalin and V. I. Lenin, the father of Communism, as the only three men mentioned by name.

The other two reported candidates, V. M. Molotov and L. P. Beria, were not mentioned by Pravda.

Molotov now is sitting at the head of the Council of Ministers as Senior Vice Premier, but Malenkov, a Vice Premier, is head of the Communist party.

Previous to the Pravda statement, there had been speculation that Malenkov, Molotov and Secret Police Chief Lavrenty Beria might form a triumvirate to guide Russia for a considerable period of time.

(In Washington members of the Senate Foreign Relations Committee said Undersecretary of State Walter Bedell Smith, who testified before them Thursday, believes Malenkov is Stalin's most likely successor.)

Pravda's mention of Malenkov, Secretary of the party and a highly regarded prospect for Stalin's mantle, seemed significant to those familiar with Soviet indirection and innuendo.

The forward-looking policy of which he spoke at the 19th party congress in Moscow last October was one of peaceful co-existence with the capitalist world, on the theory that capitalism finally would fall apart on its own.

The statement dwelt throughout on the identity of interests of the party and the Russian people. It

Continued on Page 3, Col. 4

Ike Sends 'Official Condolences'

By the Associated Press

WASHINGTON, March 5 President Eisenhower tonight instructed the Secretary of State to transmit the "official condolences" of the United States Government on the death of Premier Stalin of Russia.

The President directed John Foster Dulles to send this message to the American Embassy in Moscow for transmission to the government of the USSR:

"The Government of the United States tenders its official condolences to the government of the Union of Soviet Socialist Republics on the death of Generalissimo Joseph Stalin, Prime Minister of the Soviet Union."

It was noted immediately that the message, which spoke only of "official condolences," omitted the usual words of sympathetic tribute which are almost a part of protocol when the leader of any other nation dies.

The message was sent directly to Jacob D. Beam, charge d'affaires at the American Embassy in Russia,

Prior to announcement of Stalin's death, Eisenhower took a position of alert watchfulness toward Russia while expressing willingness to meet a successor to Stalin half way in the interests of world peace.

But Eisenhower declared, at a morning news conference, that he was unable at that point to say what the effect of Stalin's incapacity would have on the struggle between the free and the Communist worlds.

Regardless of personalities involved, the President told a news conference, the goal of peace must be pursued seriously.

Was his feeling one of "misgiving or optimism?" a reporter inquired.

Pausing in the middle of his answer and weighing his words, the Chief Executive said it is one of very definite watchfulness.

Did his remark of last week that he would go halfway to Moscow to meet Stalin in the cause of peace hold good for a successor?

So far as he can tell at this moment, yes, the President replied. If there is any way to promote the cause of world peace, he said, he can think of no personal inconvenience or sacrifice he would not make.

It was Eisenhower's third news conference and it produced a third packed house. The President volunteered at the start some remarks on the Russian situation, Government reorganization and price controls, but left most of

Continued on Page 4, Col. 3

Tibet Quake: 55 Reported Killed

HONG KONG, March 5 (Reuters)—First details of an earthquake in Tibet said to have killed 55 persons and destroyed 870 buildings, were revealed today, six months after it happened.

The Communist New China News Agency reported that the Central Government of Communist China sent relief to the victims and the destroyed buildings have been rebuilt. The wrecked area was 100 miles north of Lhasa.

Quake in L. A. Beach Areas

LOS ANGELES, March 5 (AP)—A rolling earthquake was felt in the beach areas west of here early this morning.

Some residents of Palos Verdes, Redondo Beach, Hermosa Beach and Westwood said they were awakened by a sharp, rolling shock. There were no reports of damage, police said.

Madge Meredith Signs for Movie

HOLLYWOOD, March 5 (AP)—Actress Madge Meredith was signed today for her first role since Governor Earl Warren commuted her prison sentence in July, 1951.

Universal-International said she will play a featured part in an outdoor adventure story.

Your Chronicle Index

The News That Matters—plus a Big Entertainment Section

Royce Brier	14	Horoscope	23
A Bookman's Notebook	15	Dean Jennings	16
Bobby Sox	16	Lichty Cartoon	14
Bridge	18	O'Flaherty	18
Chess	18	Panorama	15
Comic Page	23	Drew Pearson	15
Crossword Puzzle	23	The Silver Chalice	15
Delaplane's Postcard	13	Sporting Green	1H-4H
Dennis the Menace	5	TV, Radio Logs	18
Drama Pages	16, 17	Vital Statistics	24
Editorial Page	14	Weather	24
Finance	9, 10	Women's News	6, 7, 8

PREMIER JOSEPH V. STALIN
A drawing by Chronicle Staff Artist Hubert Buel

Marcus to Solitary; Cohn To Agnew

The names of Paul (Bouquet) Cohn and Bernard (Madman) Marcus were scratched yesterday from the list of five codefendants scheduled to go on trial next Monday for kidnaping and extortion.

With two principals out of the running, even temporarily, it was probable that the trial itself would not get under way as planned.

Cohn, wealthy cigar store and tavern owner, and ex-bookie, was adjudged "mentally ill" in Fresno yesterday and committed to Agnew State Hospital.

Marcus, ex-salesman and alleged operator of a Tenderloin "Cash-or Clobber Collection Agency," bidded for similar committment by smashing his fists through a San Francisco Hospital window, mangling his index fingers, and winning solitary confinement in a psycopathic ward.

This left only ex-boxer Grant Butcher, his brother Terrell and their associate, James Eberhardt, mentally unruffled enough to meet the Superior Court appointment set for them by District Attorney Thomas A. Lynch.

CONTINUANCE SOUGHT

Lynch thought they were scarcely worth it, and said "We'll ask for continuance and see if the others suddenly get sane, once their psychiatric reports are on the record."

Police expressed lay opinions to the effect that Marcus is mentally ill like a fox, and is putting on an act to dodge prosecution.

But two court-appointed psychiatrists declared such was not the case with Cohn. He is "not feigning," they agreed.

Cohn came to their attention February 25, after he was arrested 20 miles south of Fresno, at Kingsburg, for making his way toward Santa Anita race track at a clip of 110 miles an hour, driving on the wrong side of Highway 99, passing on the wrong side, passing through a red light, ignoring a police siren and, for good measure, sporting dual straight pipes on his flashy '52 Chrysler.

Deposited in Fresno county hospital's psycopathic ward for observation, he was visited "several" times by Dr. V. S. Briden and deigned to talk to him once, and was visited five times by Dr. Max Levishon, and talked to him on three of these occasions.

The two psychiatrists testified at yesterday's lunacy hearing in the

Continued on Page 5, Col. 6

Robber Put on Wanted List

WASHINGTON, March 5 (AP)—Fred William Bowerman, 60-year-old specialist in armed robbery, was added today to the FBI's list of "10 most wanted men."

More Fair Weather

Farmers Face a Crisis In Continuing Drought

Fair and warm, fair and warm.

Yesterday, today and tomorrow.

A sweet refrain for city dwellers, a swelling dirge for the farmer, particularly the rancher and dairy farmer to whom moist, green grass through the winter is life itself.

San Franciscans basked happily in sunshine that pushed the mercury to 71.7 degrees at 1:50 p. m. yesterday, a temperature that matched the season's previous high of February 13.

Although some morning fog is forecast for today, it will be only slightly cooler. Bay Area farmers' representatives sounded warnings that the pleasant weather carried anything but pleasant implications.

"Unless we have some good rain and growing weather, preferably windless, within ten days to two weeks, we may have to start shipping cattle in every direction like we did in 1948," J. Edga Dick, secretary of the California Cattlemen's Association, said yesterday.

FARM ADVISER

"We don't want to be alarmists," he declared. "If we get the rain, we'll get by. But we need it and need it badly."

And Sheldon Jackson, Marin county farm adviser, said that many livestock and dairy farm pastures are "getting on the borderline."

"It's not a crisis yet, but if there's no rain in the next ten days, it will be one," Jackson declared. "Marin, Sonoma and Napa counties are all in the same boat, and it's a risky one. The pastures are getting drier every day."

The Weather Bureau promised no relief. Yesterday, it reported, was the 44th consecutive day without measurable rain, the longest winter dry spell in San Francisco's 104-year-old weather history.

The only note of cheer for any farmers in yesterday's news came from Willows, Glenn county, where the U. S. Forest Service reported that the snow pack at 6300 feet holds more water than usual despite its lack of depth.

Dick's note of warning to the cattle industry came in a report prepared for the association's newsletter:

"California ranges are drying rapidly with some areas experiencing the longest midwinter period without rain in many years," it said. "In the Central Coast counties, Santa Clara and San Benito particularly, cattlemen are beginning to look for range or irrigated pastures in other parts of the State."

The report also told cattlemen that the association is working with the State Agricultural Extension Service to locate irrigation

Continued on Page 5, Col. 2

Appliances, Cars, Bread Decontrolled

The fifth price decontrol order since President Eisenhower took over on January 20 was issued by his price chief, Joseph H. Freehill, yesterday. The order removed ceilings from bread and all other bakery products, the major household appliances, new cars and postwar used autos, parts and accessories; and such services as laundry, dry cleaning, linen and diaper supply. Freehill estimated the items affected by the order represent an annual volume of $25,000,000,000. All remaining ceilings are due to expire April 30 unless renewed before then. (For full details see Page 4.)

Population In '52 Grew 2,698,000

WASHINGTON, March 5 (AP)—The Census Bureau estimated today that the population of the United States on January 1, this year, was about 158,468,000.

This was an increase of 2,698,000 in 1952—the biggest jump of any year in the Nation's history.

Queen Mary Slightly Better

LONDON, March 5 (Reuters)—The ailing Dowager Queen Mary, 85, had a "very good night," it was announced today.

She has been confined to bed for a week with an unspecified stomach disorder. An announcement from her home, Marlborough House, said a slight improvement in her condition reported yesterday was continuing.

Dutch Flood Toll Now 1783

THE HAGUE, March 5 (UP)—Dutch Red Cross authorities announced today the total death toll of last month's flood disaster now stands at 1783.

COMPARATIVE TEMPERATURES For Monday, June 1, 1953	High	Low		High	Low
S. Francisco	58	51	New York	75	54
Oakland	61	52	Chicago	69	53
Sacramento	69	49	Kansas City	84	68
Los Angeles	64	54	New Orleans	95	72
Portland	64	47	Miami	..	76
Seattle	59	45	Washington	61	55

Forecast for Today: Generally Fair
(For Details See Page 24)

San Francisco Chronicle
THE CITY'S ONLY HOME-OWNED NEWSPAPER

FOUNDED 1865—VOL. CLXXVII, NO. 138 CCCCAAA SAN FRANCISCO, TUESDAY, JUNE 2, 1953 GA 1-1112 DAILY 10c, SUNDAY 20c

British Expedition Finally Conquers Mount Everest

Hillary and Bhutia Plant Union Jack on Summit As 'Gift' for the Queen

By the Associated Press

LONDON, June 1—A British expedition has climbed hitherto unscaled Mt. Everest, the world's highest peak, planting the Union Jack on the summit as a Coronation "gift" for Queen Elizabeth II, Buckingham Palace announced tonight.

Word that the party had reached their goal in a third attempt within a month reached the palace tonight, a spokesman said.

The Queen was awakened and informed of the "gift" a few hours before she was scheduled to arise for her Coronation. She retired again after hearing the news.

The conquering party of mountain climbers, who succeeded where ten previous expeditions had failed, was headed by Colonel John Hunt.

Reports reaching London from Hunt said two men of his party—New Zealander E. P. Hillary and a famous Sherpa tribesman guide Tensing Bhutia—had reached the more than 29,000-foot-high summit May 29.

Hunt's message said "All is well." It gave no details.

These few words bade well for the great events of today, and added to the jubilant mood in London.

The news that Everest had been conquered spread rapidly through the streets of London where the crowds were waiting for the Coronation procession.

"We did it, we did it," shouted many, slapping each other on the back.

"What a Coronation Day gift for the Queen," was the joyous comment of many.

Reliable but unconfirmed reports from Katmandu, Nepal, reaching London via New Delhi, India, earlier today said the British party had failed in two attempts in late May to climb the mist-shrouded peak.

Earlier reports had said that if the Britons succeeded in another try, word of their success would be withheld until Coronation Eve.

New Zealand Premier S. G. Holland, here for the Coronation, said: "Naturally, I am extremely proud that a New Zealand member of the team has been the first Britisher to conquer Everest."

Holland added the hope that "this terrific example of tenacity" would be a Coronation year symbol "that there are no heights or difficulties which the British people cannot overcome."

(Climbers won race against monsoon season. See Page 12.)

Witnesses Take On the Keating Probe

Two ex-U. S. Attorneys, accused by former Grand Jurors of obstructing justice, finally got their innings yesterday before a Congressional subcommittee hearing here. A third called the proceeding "exceedingly unfair" when Congressman Kenneth B. Keating adjourned before he could testify.

All three called testimony by the jurors and others either misleading or deliberately untrue. For details see Page 5.

Judges Clash With Keating Probers

Goodman Refuses to Testify On Judicial Affairs Here

By CHARLES RAUDEBAUGH

A House Judiciary subcommittee investigating the administration of Federal justice here clashed head-on yesterday with U. S. District Judge Louis E. Goodman and, in lesser degree, with his colleagues on the Federal bench.

As perhaps the first Federal Judge ever to be summoned before a congressional investigating committee, Judge Goodman refused to testify about any judicial matters or about the handling of Grand Juries.

His position, backed by a statement signed by his six fellow Federal jurists, was somewhat weakened when two of them — Senior Judge Michael J. Roche and Judge Edward P. Murphy — later appeared before the committee and testified.

Judge Goodman

Congressman Kenneth B. Keating (Rep-N. Y.), chairman of the subcommittee, declared as the group left for Washington last night that "further consideration" would be given to Judge Goodman's adamant refusal to answer questions.

"Further consideration" could mean contempt of Congress proceedings, impeachment or "further investigation," he said.

The Judges testified before a standing-room-only audience in the carved wood chambers of the Board of Supervisors at the City Hall. The spectators broke into applause at two points, for the first time in the three days of the committee's hearings, and were admonished by Chairman Keating that such expressions were not permitted.

Goodman based his refusal to testify on the statement signed by all the members of the local Federal District bench, declaring the legislative branch of Government cannot compel the judicial branch to talk about judicial matters.

"The separation (of the judicial, legislative and executive functions) is founded on the historic concept that no one of these branches may dominate or unlawfully interfere with the others," the statement said.

"The Constitution does not contemplate that judicial proceedings be reviewed by the legislative branch, but only by the appropriate appellate tribunals. The integrity of the Federal Courts, upon which liberty and life depends, requires that such courts be maintained inviolate against the changing moods of public opinion."

A second statement signed by the Judges said that none of them had "directed or author-

Continued on Page 6, Col. 1

The Index

A Bookman's Notebook	15
Bridge, Chess	18
Comic Page	23
Delaplane's Postcard	13
Dennis the Menace	11
Drama Pages	16, 17
Editorial Page	14
Finance	10, 11
Abe Mellinkoff	15
Panorama	15
Drew Pearson	15
Sporting Green	1H-4H
TV and Radio	18
Marjorie Trumbull	15
Vital Statistics	24
Women's News	8, 9

This Is Clue No. 3

Here's a tricky clue to ponder
Digging here and digging yonder
Leave all private lands alone
And seek the treasure 'neath a stone.

For additional information guiding you to the $1000 treasure, see the Dividend Clue which appears today with Pinkney Gage's column, "Buried Treasure," in the Classified Action Ads.

So you will know what you are digging for, the actual chest and medallion found in the San Francisco treasure hunt will be displayed today at Hale Bros., Washington at 11th, Oakland. They will be shown later at other stores in the East Bay until the treasure is found.

More Details on Page 16

Queen Elizabeth II

The Queen was painted last summer by Margaret Lindsay Williams, Britain's most famous living portrait painter. The ribbon and star are those of the Order of the Garter, Britain's highest order of chivalry. The 27-year-old Queen's gown is blue and gold embossed brocade on an off-white background, her jewels diamonds.

Delaplane and Anspacher Report---Pages 2 and 13
Coronation Features on Editorial, Panorama Pages

POWS' RECAPTURE DEMANDED BY REDS

Bobo Wins U. S. Title

See Sports

San Francisco Chronicle

THE CITY'S ONLY HOME-OWNED NEWSPAPER

FINAL

VOL. CLXXVII, NO. 156 CCCCAAA · SAN FRANCISCO, SATURDAY, JUNE 20, 1953 · GA 1-1112 DAILY 10c, SUNDAY 20c

Hopes for Quick Truce Dwindle

Communists Deliver Hot Protest

By the United Press

TOKYO, June 20—Hopes for an early truce vanished today (Saturday) as the Communists demanded the recapture of 26,000 war prisoners freed by President Syngman Rhee and assurances that the South Korean Army will abide by a truce.

The Communist delegation made its demand in a strongly worded protest to General Mark Clark, U. N. Supreme Commander, delivered to the Allies' full-dress truce team in Panmunjom. The Reds declared the U. N. command must bear the responsibility for Rhee's action.

The Communist note called the prisoner escapes "deliberately contrived" and said the act casts doubts the U. N. could carry out the terms of an armistice.

The session was brief—only 25 minutes — and then the plenary session recessed indefinitely at Communist request to give the U. N. time to come up with answers to the series of questions asked by the Reds.

The formal protest was signed by North Korean Marshal Kim Il Sung and Chinese General Peng Teh-huai — the men who would sign an armistice if one can be achieved. It said Clark's command "deliberately connived" in the mass prison breaks and "must bear the serious responsibility."

Then the Red commanders

Continued on Page 2, Col. 2

Clark Says Rhee Broke His Word

By the Associated Press

TOKYO, June 20 — A stinging letter from General Mark W. Clark, U. N. Supreme Commander, accusing South Korean President Syngman Rhee of breaking his personal word in the "shocking" release of Korean war prisoners, was made public by Clark's headquarters today.

He said that on several occasions "in recent weeks" Rhee had assured both Clark and U. S. Ambassador to South Korea Ellis O. Briggs that he would not take unilateral action until after full discussion with Clark.

Only a few hours earlier Acting South Korean Prime Minister Pyun Yung Tae had defiantly announced that the South Koreans will not recapture the prisoners, as the Red truce delegates demanded, and issued a letter he had written Clark telling him not to do anything that might "provoke the passions of the masses."

Pyun also bluntly demanded that the U. N. release all the escaped POWs who have been recaptured. He declared that these and all other anti-Communist prisoners must be liberated.

"I ask you," Pyun said in his letter to Clark, "to turn them over to us to be released by our hands. We must liberate them all, preferably, if possible, in a manner least likely to cause trouble."

CLARK'S LETTER

Soon afterward Clark's headquarters released the letter Clark wrote Rhee Thursday, after the first release of prisoners by South Korean forces on Rhee's orders.

Clark recalled that in the summer of 1950, when the United States and other nations responded to Rhee's appeal to the United Nations to repel the attack from North Korea, the United Nations received from Rhee a message giving the U. N. command over all forces of the Republic of Korea.

"Notwithstanding," Clark said, "and in clear violation of my authority, certain officers and men of the Republic of Korea Army willfully permitted the escape of many thousands of lawfully detained prisoners of war . . .

'PROFOUND SHOCK'

"I must inform you with all the sincerity which I possess that I am profoundly shocked by this unilateral abrogation of your personal commitment, which was so freely and voluntarily given at the time."

Clark added, "On several occasions in recent weeks you have personally assured both Ambassador Briggs and me that you would not take unilateral action with reference to ROK forces under my control until after full and frank discussion with me. Your actions today have clearly abrogated these assurances.

"I cannot at this time estimate the ultimate consequences of this precipitous and shocking action on your part, nor can its effect on the common cause for which we have sacrificed so much during these past several years be forecast at this time."

THE ROSENBERGS DIE AT SING SING

Are YOU the Unknown Heir?

Northern Californians have sums coming to them totaling more than

$100,000

Today's Chronicle begins publishing their names. Perhaps you'll recognize one of them. Perhaps it'll be yours! Turn to Page 13 of The Chronicle

Today

Southern Span Hearing Set In Washington

Governor Warren, members of the Toll Bridge Authority, and a delegation of San Francisco city officials have been invited to appear before a House subcommittee in Washington Tuesday for questioning in the dispute over construction of a southern crossing of San Francisco Bay.

The invitation was extended by Representative Harry MacGregor of Ohio, chairman of the Subcommittee on Roads of the general Committee on Public Works.

WARREN'S PLANS

Governor Warren, who announced yesterday he would ask the California Toll Bridge Authority on July 1 to apply immediately for a Federal permit to construct a southern crossing, said in Sacramento he had not heard of such invitation, and had made no plans to fly to Washington for the hearing.

In San Francisco, however, it was announced that Acting Mayor Marvin E. Lewis, City Administrator Thomas Brooks and San Francisco's Washington lobbyist, Francis V. Keesling Jr. will fly to the capital tomorrow night.

ALL-OUT SUPPORT

Warren pledged all-out support of a southern crossing, and added the State will not hold up action pending outcome of the current congressional controversy over continuance of tolls on the present bay bridge to finance additional crossings.

A section of the 1931 congressional bill authorizing construction of the Bay Bridge provides that when the bonded indebtedness is paid up, the span should become toll free. Amendment to this section is being sought.

"We will move forward with dispatch," the Governor told a press conference, "on the things within our jurisdiction in an effort to carry into effect the policy of the State as determined by the Legislature."

Warren turned one provision

Continued on Page 3, Col. 1

Weather Will Be Foggy, Then Fair

Prevailing fair weather, with some morning fog, will continue today, with little change in temperature, the Weather Bureau said yesterday.

The Index

Churches	12
Comic Page	18
Crossword Puzzle	18
Dennis the Menace	14
Drama Page	11
Editorial Page	10
Fashion Plate Diet	5
Finance	6, 7
Horoscope	18
Lichty's Cartoon	2
The Owl	8
Drew Pearson	9
TV and Radio	14
Vital Statistics	13
Weather	13
Women's News	5

Tax Office Probe Here Described

By CHARLES RAUDEBAUGH
Chronicle Staff Writer

WASHINGTON, June 19—An intelligence agent from the Bureau of Internal Revenue testified here today that he found no evidence of illegalities during an investigation into the filing of tax returns in the San Francisco revenue office two years ago.

The agent was Ray Weaver, head of the Tax Fraud Branch of the Intelligence Unit, and he told his story before the House Judiciary Subcommittee investigating the Department of Justice.

DATE STAMP

Weaver told the committee he did find a date-stamping "machine" in the office of James G. Smyth, former Collector of Internal Revenue in San Francisco, but that he did not discover any indication that the device had been used improperly.

Weaver's statement that there was a date-stamping device in Smyth's office brought sarcastic comment from Congressman Patrick J. Hillings (Rep-Arcadia) and from Congressman Kenneth B. Keating (Rep-N. Y.), chairman of the subcommittee.

"This is the first time I ever heard of a Collector of Internal Revenue maintaining his own machine," Hillings said. "In view of what we have heard about the San Francisco tax office, it gives rise to considerable suspicion how the machine was used. He could sit there with his handy-dandy machine and stamp returns for individuals who might have some influence."

(The device in question is the common type of rubber stamp with a changeable date. All incoming returns are stamped with them by hand.)

MANY MACHINES

Weaver noted there were many such date stamps in the Tax Bureau in San Francisco; that the one in the Collector's office was actually in his secretary's anteroom; that many people had access to it for handling incoming returns, and that there was no evidence that anyone used it to backdate returns.

The agent was on the stand here all this morning. He said he was, in effect, detached from his regular duties with the In-

Continued on Page 7, Col. 6

Moore Machinery President Dies

Charles E. Moore, president of the Moore Machinery Company of San Francisco, San Jose and Los Angeles, died of a heart attack last night on a trail ride with the San Mateo county Sheriff's posse near La Honda. He was 59 and lived on Overlook road, Los Gatos.

End to Long Fight for Life

All Last Minute Appeals Rejected in Atom Spy Case

Ike, Court Refuse to Save Pair

By the United Press

WASHINGTON, June 19 — Julius and Ethel Rosenberg lost their dogged two-year fight for life today when both President Eisenhower and the Nation's highest court spurned their last-chance pleas to escape execution for espionage conspiracy.

In a drama-packed session, the Supreme Court ruled that the husband-wife spy team had received a full measure of justice in the lower courts and in the nine times their case had come before the high tribunal. It said no question remained unanswered.

Mr. Eisenhower, who once before had refused to intervene, was equally adamant. He said the Rosenbergs had brought the possibility of atomic war closer by conspiring to slip atomic secrets to Russia.

Six Justices joined in rejecting the Rosenbergs. Only two —William O. Douglas, whose stay of execution was overthrown by the full court, and Hugo L. Black, who joined Douglas today in dissent — favored a further review. Justice Felix Frankfurter wanted more time.

Despite the decisions by the court and Mr. Eisenhower, attorneys for the Rosenbergs battled up to the last minute in a desperate attempt to save the couple whose case attracted world-wide attention.

WHITE HOUSE TRIP

Chief defense attorney Emanuel Bloch appealed personally to Justices Harold H. Burton and Robert H. Jackson for a last-minute stay of execution. Rebuffed there, he went to the White House to try to persuade the President to change his mind.

Bloch carried with him a letter from Ethel Rosenberg. It appealed to the President as an "affectionate grandfather" and a "devoutly religious man" to spare herself and her husband.

Previously, Bloch himself had sent a telegram to the President seeking clemency. The White House said it was turned over to the Justice Department.

APPEALS COURT

Shortly after 5 p. m., less than three hours before the Rosenbergs died, Judges Jerome N. Frank and Thomas W. Swan

Continued on Page 3, Col. 7

ETHEL ROSENBERG JULIUS ROSENBERG

First U. S. civilians to die for espionage

How Rosenbergs Died

Eyewitness Report of Death House Scene

By RELMAN MORIN
Associated Press Staff Writer

OSSINING, N. Y., June 19 — Julius and Ethel Rosenberg died in the electric chair tonight, silent and without emotion.

Julius, treading firmly and unsupported by guards, entered the Sing Sing death chamber first, at 8:04 p. m. (EDT), as a chaplain intoned the 23d Psalm by his side. Two and three-quarters minutes later he was pronounced dead.

His wife was then led in, at 8:11, and she was dead at 8:16, just 15 minutes before the last rays of the setting sun betokened the start of the Hebrew Sabbath.

At 8 p. m. the voice of Rabbi Irving Koslow could be heard in the corridor leading to the death chamber.

He was intoning the 23d Psalm, "The Lord is my shepherd, I shall not want . . .

"Though I walk through the valley of the shadow of death, I shall fear no evil."

The Rabbi was in his rabbinical robe.

Rosenberg, wearing dark brown trousers and a white undershirt and slipper - like shoes, followed him.

BLANK STARE

Without his glasses, his eyes seemed to be staring blankly, without recognizing anything in the room.

The leather mask covering his face, the helmet over his head and the electrodes to his right leg were then attached. He sat quietly.

In an alcove off to the side of the death chamber, Joseph Francell, the executioner, awaited the signal.

When it came, there was a rattle and a hum in the otherwise deathly still room.

Rosenberg's chest strained hard against the straps that held him. His fist clenched.

His neck and chest turned red. Then he slumped.

The first shock lasted three seconds. The two following lasted 57 seconds each.

Each time the straps were strained as his body pressed hard against them.

Then the strange sound, a blend of humming and buzzing, ceased in the room.

DOCTORS EXAMINE

Two doctors, Dr. H. W. Kipp and Dr. George McCracken, stepped forward.

They tore the undershirt covering Rosenberg's chest.

The two physicians applied stethoscopes and Dr. Kipp said: "I pronounce this man dead."

In death, Rosenberg's face had the same staring, wondering expression that he had worn when he walked into the chamber.

His body was placed on a white, wheeled hospital table and quickly removed.

Again the room was silent. There were 10 witnesses present.

Continued on Page 4, Col. 1

The Decisions And Reactions

European crowds reacted angrily to the Rosenbergs' death, parading and shouting anti-American slogans. See Page 2.

Texts of the Supreme Court decisions which sealed the Rosenbergs' fate—and of Justice Hugo Black's dissent — are on Page 4.

Husband Goes First To the Chair

By the United Press

SING SING PRISON, N. Y., June 19 — Julius and Ethel Rosenberg were electrocuted tonight for conspiracy to commit atomic espionage.

Their deaths ended a day of suspense in which nine appeals were made to Judges in Washington, New York and New Haven, in which the U. S. Supreme Court denied their final appeals and in which President Eisenhower again refused them clemency.

Rosenberg, 35, died first in Sing Sing Prison's death chamber. He was placed in the chair at 8:04 p. m. and was pronounced dead at 8:06½ p. m., after receiving three shocks of electricity.

He was followed by his wife, Ethel, 37, who was placed in the chair at 8:11½ p. m. She was pronounced dead at 8:16 p. m.

JEWISH SABBATH

The execution was moved up from the customary hour of 11 p. m. because the Jewish sabbath began at sundown, 8:30 p. m.

The couple thus became the first American civilians ever to die for spying against their country.

Both the Rosenbergs' lives reportedly could have been spared, if they had chosen to talk. Until the moment the electricity was turned on the judge who sent them to their deaths, Federal Judge Irving R. Kaufman, sat in his chambers in the Federal Court House in New York City. He was available for any last-minute motions in the Rosenbergs' behalf. He also was ready to act if the couple made a last-minute decision to talk.

NO CONFESSION

President Eisenhower and Attorney General Herbert Brownell both "stood by" in Washington.

There were reports that Federal officials had made it clear

Continued on Page 3, Col. 6

Inside

The Western representatives in Berlin sent another protest yesterday to the Soviet occupying authorities over their martial rule in East Berlin since riots broke out there Wednesday. See Page 2.

In Hawaii a Federal Court jury convicted seven individuals, including longshore union leader Jack W. Hall, of Communist conspiracy to overthrow the Government. Immediately longshoremen walked off all Hawaiian docks. See Page 3.

Sirens Scream Today

Air raid warning sirens here will scream in a special Civil Defense test at 10 a. m. today.

The public is not expected to take part in the tests which will send an estimated 1000 Civil Defense workers to their posts in San Francisco for day-long exercises in a simulated bombing. (Story on Page 2.)

FINAL TRUCE EXTRA

YESTERDAY'S TEMPERATURES

	High	Low		High	Low
San Francisco	66	51	Fresno	96	61
Oakland	69	51	Los Angeles	83	64
San Rafael	82	50	New York	83	63
Redwood City	82	49	St. Louis	98	73
San Jose	79	51	Portland	73	48
Sacramento	94	56	Washington	85	63

FORECAST: FAIR, COASTAL FOG
(For Details See Page 22)

San Francisco Chronicle
THE CITY'S ONLY HOME-OWNED NEWSPAPER

See Page 13

FOUNDED 1865—VOL. CLXXVIII, NO. 12 CCCCAAA SAN FRANCISCO, MONDAY, JULY 27, 1953 GA 1-1112 DAILY 10c, SUNDAY 20c.

WAR IS OVER

Full Key Strike Effect Due Today

Bay Area Braces for Jam In Traffic; Talks on Tieup Halted; Deadlock Remains

Today the Bay Area will begin to find out how much the struck Key System means to its daily life and commerce.

Authorities on both sides of the Bay agree that the full impact of the strike of the System's 1500 operating employees—which began at 12:01 a. m. Friday—will be felt for the first time both in the East Bay and in San Francisco's congested downtown traffic.

The week end was almost without incident. The few who found it necessary to commute apparently did so without difficulty, or else stayed near their jobs. One way or another, the usual Saturday shoppers got to Oakland's downtown stores and kept sales levels about normal.

Even the taxicab companies, looking forward to a bonanza, reported only small increases in their business.

Today, however, was expected to be a different story. About 27,000 commuters from the East Bay must get to jobs in San Francisco. Most of the 100,000 passengers who ride the Key System daily in the East Bay will probably find it necessary to resume their usual rounds.

Police were braced for extra traffic loads, expecting that cars usually left at home would increase the normal congestion in downtown areas on both sides of the Bay Bridge. Bridge patrolmen were also set for added traffic, issuing warnings to motorists to make sure they have enough gas before they make the trip.

Oakland has 29 extra policemen assigned to handle its problems. San Francisco has 42 extra officers to help break up jams and steer vehicles to special free emergency parking areas at Columbia Square, the Southern Pacific freight yards and the space under the Bayshore freeway ramp near Vermont and 15th street.

Apparently, an incidental effect of the strike was a wave of auto thefts in Oakland over the week end, jumping the usual number of three to 15.

Only one aspect of the strike appeared likely to remain unchanged today—the status of negotiations between the Key System management and the striking employees.

Vern Stambaugh, president of the striking AFL Carmen's Union Local 38, reported he had heard nothing from either the Key System management or Federal Conciliator Fred Ferguson since the final futile meeting a few hours before the strike began.

He said he was willing to discuss matters with either at any time in order to put the System back in operation, but said no meetings are now scheduled.

Management spokesmen said they knew of no new developments either, nor any to be ex-

Continued on Page 7, Col. 5

Most Stores Will Stay Open

Most of San Francisco's downtown department stores will be open this evening, for the convenience of after-dinner shoppers.

For the exact hours at each major store, see its advertisement in this copy of The Chronicle.

News On the Inside

The San Francisco Fair Rent Committee has received 300 tenant and landlord complaints. For the story of the committee's job and some typical complaints, see Page 6.

Barney Gould still is battling to keep the SS Fort Sutter at Aquatic Park. Story on Page 7.

San Francisco's flying jeweler, Peter Gluckmann, modestly accepts a gala welcome after his trans-Atlantic hops. See Page 7.

Law officers staged a massive raid on Short Creek, Ariz., the community on the Utah border where it is believed that several wives are better than one. For the story of the crackdown on polygamy. See Page 10.

3 Inspectors Face Charges In Hijacking

Charges of neglect of duty probably will be filed Wednesday against three police inspectors being investigated in the hijacking of the winners of a $79,000 Tenderloin dice game, Police Chief Michael Gaffey said yesterday.

The inspectors are Frank Lucey, former head of the police general works detail, and his former assistants, Jesse Ayer and Van P. Denike.

They will make their third appearance tonight before the Grand Jury.

"If nothing new develops from that hearing," Gaffey said, "we probably will file charges Wednesday morning. I'm not going to premit this thing to drag on and on."

The basis of the charges, Gaffey said, will be that they failed to file a report of the fact that at 2 a. m. on June 6—the night of the big dice game—they went to the Wilkins apartment in response to a phone call from Mrs. Wilkins who said she and her husband had been "robbed."

He said he had been waiting the outcome of the Grand Jury

Continued on Page 7, Col. 7

Hamburg Mourns Bomb Victims

HAMBURG, July 26 (AP)—Hamburg, West Germany's largest city, mourned today its 55,000 victims of 213 World War II Allied air raids.

Armistice in Korea; Fighting Ends Today

History at Panmunjom

U. N., Reds Settle Three-Year War In Brief Ceremony

(Compiled from dispatches of the Associated Press and United Press)

PANMUNJOM, Korea, July 27—The armistice ending the Korean war was signed here today (Monday).

The historic signing ceremony began at 10:01 a. m. (6:01 p. m. Sunday, Pacific Daylight Time) and was finished ten minutes later.

All shooting along the 155-mile battle front was to stop 12 hours from the time of the signing at Panmunjom.

Pyongyang radio announced at 11 a. m. that the Chinese and North Korean commanders had ordered their troops to cease fighting as of 10 p. m. (6 a. m., PDT). It said the Chinese and North Korean Armies also had been ordered to withdraw to "non-fighting areas" within 72 hours.

Allies Plan for Swift Withdrawal

An Eighth Army staff officer said some Allied front-line units may start withdrawing to new positions the moment the cease-fire order goes into effect.

Lieutenant General William K. Harrison Jr. signed for the U. N. command. North Korean General Nam Il signed for the North Koreans and Chinese Communists.

Three hours after the negotiators had signed the agreement U. N. Supreme Commander Mark W. Clark put his signature to the documents at Munsan. They were then dispatched to Panmunjom to be taken into Communist territory for signing by North Korean Marshal Kim Il Sung and Chinese General Peng Teh-huai.

The signing went like clockwork, in contrast to the more than two years of bitter debate that led up to it.

South Korea Not Represented

The Republic of Korea, which opposes a truce that leaves Korea divided, with Chinese Communist troops in the north, was not represented at the signing. The armistice was signed in a pagoda-like structure built by the Communists in this wide place in the road near the 38th Parallel.

It was that parallel which the North Korean Communist army crossed at dawn on June 25, 1950, in a surprise assault aimed at unifying Korea by force.

Today it was humid, hot and overcast when General Harrison arrived by helicopter at the truce site at 9:30 a. m.

The Communist delegates had arrived five minutes earlier.

Harrison was accompanied by Rear Admiral John C. Daniel. As they left their helicopter they saluted a United Nations command honor guard, resplendent in their multi-colored uniforms and representing the armed might of the U. N.

Exactly at 10 a. m., Harrison walked into the ceremony hall. He sat down and immediately signed the first copy of the bulky truce document.

Communist copies of the agreement were bound in dark brown leather. The U. N. copies were covered simply by a light blue paper. The documents lay on two green-covered tables near the center of the armistice hall.

Between the U. N. and Communist tables was a third table for the actual signing.

The Allied table was [illegible]

Continued on Page A, Col. 2

The highpoints of three years of war—up and down Korea

AP Wirephoto map

Your Chronicle Index

Ad News and Notes	22	Panorama	13
A Bookman's Notebook	13	Sporting Green	1H-4H
Bridge	16	TV, Radio Logs	16
Royce Brier	12	TV and Radio Column	16
Chess	16	Marjorie Trumbull	13
Comic Page	21	Vital Statistics	22
Crossword Puzzle	21	Women's News	8, 9
Dennis the Menace	5		
Editorial Page	12		
Drama Pages	14, 15		
Dick Friendlich	11		
Horoscope	21		
Lichty Cartoon	12		
Lyons Den	11		
Abe Mellinkoff	13		

THE WEATHER: Fair With Coastal Fog

Ike Speaks to the Nation, Appeals for World Peace

WASHINGTON, July 26 (AP)—President Eisenhower called on all nations tonight to "use the wisdom" of the newly-signed Korean armistice and settle their differences without more "brutal" strife.

He voiced a renewed hope for world peace in a Nation-wide radio and television speech carried by all the networks less than an hour after the truce was signed in Panmunjom.

He offered "prayers of thanksgiving" that the long, bloody struggle in Korea was at last to cease, but he also warned that "an armistice on a single battleground" is not "peace in the world."

The President, sober and serious, spoke from the White House broadcasting room. He was followed on the air by Secretary of State John Foster Dulles, who underscored Mr. Eisenhower's warning that America must keep its guard up. (See Page 2.)

The President said the Communists can now show their "good faith" in the campaign for peace by the "swift return" of the United Nations troops who are being held as prisoners of war.

He said fighting men of 16 Allied nations under the U. N. banner had met the Communist challenge "with deeds, not words." He paid special tribute to the "valorous" army of South Korea whose president came close to wrecking the truce.

Mr. Eisenhower's radio-TV appearance capped an eventful day which began at the Quantico, Va., Marine Base where the Nation's top military leaders have been in conference.

The President concluded his

Continued on Page A, Col. 8

The Truce Coverage

The Chronicle brings you complete coverage of the truce signing in Korea yesterday plus a review of events that have led up to it, reports of reaction here and elsewhere and a full page of pictures. See pages A, B, 2, 3 and 4.

ANOTHER U.S. BOOKIE RAID SURPRISES POLICE HERE

$3000-a-Day Setup

Tax Men Smash 'Clearing House'

Seven Internal Revenue Service agents, unaccompanied by police, raided Apartment 203 at 585 Turk street yesterday and broke up what they described as a $3000-a-day bookie operation. They arrested Jerry Karakashian, 36, chauffeur, of 3649 18th street for failing to register or buy Federal wagering tax stamps.

The raid recalled the furor that occurred on Lincoln's Birthday when 25 Federal officers raided four bookie joints here and pointedly ignored local police in the cleanup.

Agent Jack Wilks said the operation, working as a clearing house for 25 outside bookies, had done $2500 business yesterday up to the time of the raid at 4:40 p. m.

In the next hour and a half, Agent George Wilson answered the phone and accepted another $100 in bets.

FIRST DAY

The agents said they have been following the operation from address to address for three weeks, and nabbed it yesterday in the first day of its operation in new quarters. Local police were not notified of the raid plan and were not invited to participate.

Glen T. Jamison, District Director of Internal Revenue here, said, "We are not required to notify the local police every time we make a raid.

"We had a tip on this particular place and for several days we've been trying to catch up on it. We finally got it located and moved in on it."

Asked for comment on the raid, Police Chief Michael Gaffey said, "As far as I know, we knew nothing about it. These things operating in apartments are impossible to find without a tip and evidently the Treasury men had a tip."

He said he will call for a report from Captain Edward Greene, head of the Northern police district in which the raid occurred. Greene could not be reached for comment.

Informed by the press of the raid, Captain Harry Nelson, head of the special services bureau, said, "Oh, no. Gee, my men knew nothing about it.

"That isn't the only one going, you know. We've done pretty well. We arrested two or three of the same type this month and four or five last month."

PROMPTED PROBE

It was independent action by Federal authorities last February that caused the San Francisco Police Department to investigate itself.

In the Lincoln's Birthday raid, one of the biggest of its kind in a long time, the revenue agents arrested seven persons and charged them with failing to obtain gambling tax stamps. They took the names of 116 horse racing followers in four wide open betting parlors and confiscated thousands of dollars in cash.

The local police reaction was immediate and embarrassed. It ended in a police commission investigation, a shakeup of precinct captains, creation of the "super vice-squad" and a shutdown of the town that nearly starved the Tenderloin.

United States Commissioner Joseph Karesh set bail for Karakashian at $2500 and set Thursday as the date for a preliminary hearing.

The bail was posted by Charles Puccinelli, a bail bond broker.

Santo Mob Guilty; Harriet Gets Life

Special to The Chronicle

QUINCY, May 7—The Mountain Murder Mob was convicted today of the bloody massacre of a Chester grocer and three small children.

Jack Santo and Emmett Perkins were found guilty by the jury in a verdict that meant the death penalty.

Harriet Henson, Santo's sullen mistress, who turned against him under the urging of State agents, was saved from the gas chamber when the jurors recommended she be sent to prison for life.

Superior Judge Ben V. Curler set May 24 for sentencing.

The jury's verdict ended a trial that began last March 29 and a mystery that began when the bludgeoned bodies of Guard Young and the children were found stuffed in Young's car on a lonely mountain road October 10, 1952.

It was the most shocking crime in recent California history, and many months elapsed before the clues began to point toward Santo and Perkins.

Those two, even if they die,

Continued on Page 8, Col. 5

San Francisco Chronicle
THE VOICE OF THE WEST
FINAL
No. 32,430 CCCCAAAB GArfield 1-1112 SATURDAY, MAY 8, 1954 10 CENTS WEATHER: HIGH CLOUDS

Dien Bien Phu General Captured, Rebels Say

Treasure Hunters Get Warmer

(Picture on Page 3)

The treasure hunters were getting warmer and warmer yesterday.

From his vantage point, the Emperor Norton surveyed the sight of San Franciscans bending to their shovels and said:

"That group there is mighty close, mighty close."

Which group did he mean? The Gracious Emperor would not vouchsafe so much as a wave of his hand.

"Someone has been studying the clues," was all he said, "and the studious shall be rewarded with my Imperial Largesse."

The largesse, of course, is the Norton Treasure — a wooden casket containing a golden medallion which, if turned in at The Chronicle's offices before June 30, will entitle the discoverer to 1000 silver dollars.

The Emperor had some important advice for his digging subjects yesterday.

The treasure, he said, will NOT be found in Golden Gate Park. It is not buried anywhere in the park, it never has been, and all the Emperor's subjects should stop digging there. Nowhere in Golden Gate Park is the treasure. Nowhere.

Likewise it is NOT in ANY cultivated park or playground area. And NOT in Corona Heights recreation area.

Also, said the Emperor, the treasure is NOT around the Navy's electronic installation at Twin Peaks and the Great Highway. It is not there and the Emperor's subjects are advised not to dig there, as an electric cable buried near the Navy station might give someone a bad shock if it were hit with a shovel.

Other than that, said his Majesty, dig anywhere you like except on private property, cultivated grounds, the Presidio or on school campuses.

There are no limits on who may participate in this clue-by-clue search for the treasure, except that employees of The Chronicle and KRON-TV and their families, as well as last year's winners, are barred.

This Is Clue No. 14

The Emperor's own alphabet
Somehow omitted the Z,
He also remarked on a gap
That lay 'twixt the U and the V.

So you will know what you are looking for, duplicates of the Buried Medallion are on display at J. C. Penney; Sears Roebuck, Mission Branch, and Sears Roebuck, Geary and Masonic Branch.

For the dividend clue see the Classified Ads Section

Clouds Today, Maybe Showers Tomorrow

Considerable cloudiness will prevail over the week end in the Bay Area with the possibility of showers tomorrow, the Weather Bureau forecast yesterday.

There will be little change in temperature and the wind will stay in the 10 to 20-mile range, the forecaster said. The same weather will hold over most of Northern California.

Kidnaper Lear Collapses 'From Fear'

By HENRY PALM

Joseph W. Lear, facing death in the gas chamber for the kidnaping of Leonard Moskovitz, collapsed in the county jail exercise yard yesterday morning, apparently from fright.

Lear, found guilty and given a death sentence by a jury Thursday afternoon along with Harold Jackson, was taken unconscious by police ambulance to Mission Emergency Hospital for treatment.

Dr. William Ashley, physician for the County Jail, said Lear was suffering from catatonic schizophrenia, hysteria or an overdose of drugs.

At the hospital, Dr. Thomas Albers, superintendent, had Lear's stomach pumped out and said there were no drugs. He ordered that Lear be held at the hospital under guard 24 hours for observation.

The 43-year-old Lear had become progressively more excited since the guilty verdict was read late Thursday afternoon, and had been weeping often, Dr. Ashley said.

Lear got up early yesterday and began talking to reporters at 7:30 a. m., complaining he could "hardly keep my eyes open," which Dr. Ashley later said was a symptom of the approaching collapse.

In mid-morning, he was let into the exercise yard. Other prisoners reported he sagged to the ground, his eyes glazed, and apparently unconscious. He was dragged back to his cell.

Captain Frank Smith, superintendent of the jail, said, "It looks like fear." Other prisoners defined it in convict terms, "the second-day shakes."

One of Lear's attorneys, Frances Carr, arrived shortly after the collapse. She intended to ask if Lear would be allowed to see his parents, Mr. and Mrs. James Lear, who were scheduled

Continued on Page 8, Col. 3

Boy, 3, Dies After Surgery

Three-year-old John B. Day, son of Mr. and Mrs. Byron K. Day, of 858 Via Morella, San Lorenzo Village, died early yesterday at Hayward Hospital, following surgery on his fingers, which he cut in an accident with his father's power saw.

Coroner Berhard Bungarz made an autopsy, but said the cause of death could not be determined until laboratory tests are concluded.

A Red Victory---and U. S. Reaction

Dulles Says We May Have to Fight To Save Asia From Communism

'Seventeen Companies Captured'

By the Associated Press

SAIGON, Indo-China, May 8—Dien Bien Phu has fallen.

The French command said today (Saturday) the battered garrison was overrun last night after 57 days of terrible struggle.

(Hong Kong reported that the Communist Vietminh radio in Indo-China announced tonight that the French commander of Dien Bien Phu and about 17 companies of French Union troops were taken prisoner when the fortress fell.

(The broadcast did not mention Brigadier General Christian de Castries by name, but said the commander of Dien Bien Phu was a prisoner.

(The Red radio claimed "a complete victory" and said all French union forces have surrendered.)

The French command here said de Castries telephoned from his dug-in command post at 4:45 p. m. yesterday (1:45 a. m. P.D.T. Friday) that the whole central redoubt of his stronghold was about to be submerged by the Vietminh tide.

After sending this last message he destroyed his radio equipment.

"Since then there has been no word from General de Castries," the French command said.

After the fall of the main camp, the isolated southern resistance point of Isabelle continued in contact with headquarters in Hanoi. But the Vietminh masses turned on it at about midnight.

ISABELLE CONTACT

At 1:50 a. m. today (10:50 a. m., P.D.T. Friday) the Isabelle radio reported: "I can no longer communicate with you."

(United Press reported from Hanoi Saturday that remnants of the 2000-man French force at outpost "Isabelle" hurled a counterattack at the enemy at 3 a. m. The official announcement was believed to have come from French pilots flying over the Dien Bien Phu area.)

Vietminh General Vo Nguyen Giap hurled the greater part of his effectives—four infantry divisions supported by a heavy artillery division—into the last great assault that brought them the long-denied victory.

The attack began just before Thursday midnight and was directed at first against three sides of the central redoubt where de Castries had his headquarters.

Inside the remnants of 12 French Union battalions, the cream of Indo-China's fighting men, braced themselves.

In uninterrupted fighting that

Continued on Page 7, Col. 5

And Then Silence From Dien Bien Phu

PARIS, May 7 (AP)—"They're a few meters away . . . Theyre infiltrating everywhete . . ."

Those were the last telephoned words of Brigadier General Christian de Castries before the fall of Dien Bien Phu, the French news agency reported today.

After that, the agency said, there was silence.

McCarthy-Army Hearing

New Brownell Ruling On FBI 'Letter' Asked

By the Associated Press

WASHINGTON, May 7—Senate investigators sent a new query to Attorney General Herbert Brownell tonight about using a controversial "letter"—based in part on a secret FBI report—in the McCarthy-Army hearings.

The query avoided for the moment a showdown between Brownell and Senator Joseph R. McCarthy (Rep-Wis.) on whether material in security-loyalty cases can be made public.

Senator Karl Mundt (Rep-S. D.) said he was asking Brownell to say whether any portions of the McCarthy-produced document can be used as evidence in the public airing of McCarthy's dispute with Army officials.

Mundt is acting chairman of the Senate Investigations Subcommittee investigating the dispute, but Senator John McClellan (Dem-Ark.), senior Democratic member, said the new request to Brownell "is not a committee action, it's the action of the chairman."

Brownell said yesterday publication of the "letter" in full "would be contrary to the public interest," but McCarthy countered that "I don't intend to" keep such material secret unless FBI Director J. Edgar

Continued on Page 7, Col. 7

Tomorrow: The Story of FBI's Hoover

The story of J. Edgar Hoover, for 30 years director of the Federal Bureau of Investigation and one of America's best known and most influential figures, will appear in the Sunday Chronicle. Written by Don Whitehead, Associated Press Pulitzer Prize winner, it is a definitive study of Hoover's work in the FBI, of his private life and his basic philosophy. Watch for it tomorrow—in your Sunday Chronicle.

Secretary of State Urges 'United Front'---Rules Out Use of American Troops Now

By the Associated Press

WASHINGTON, May 7—Secretary of State John Foster Dulles tonight ruled out use of American armed forces in Indo-China at this time but declared saving Southeast Asia from Communism may yet demand "serious" military commitments by free world nations.

"Free peoples will never remain free unless they are willing to fight for their vital interests," Dulles asserted in a radio-TV report to the American people.

He expressed firm confidence that collective action by anti-Communist powers will be able to block a Communist drive for the rich resources of Southeast Asia.

"I feel confident that unity of purpose persists, and that such a tragic event as the fall of Dien Bien Phu will harden, not weaken, our purpose to stay united," Dulles declared.

FORTRESS SIEGE

He delivered his 30-minute report on the Asiatic crisis within hours after Indo-China Reds overwhelmed French Union defenders at Dien Bien Phu after a 57-day struggle.

If the Geneva conference fails to yield an Indo-China armistice "on honorable terms and under proper safeguards," Dulles declared, the need will be "even more urgent" for united action to defend the area. But, he added:

"In making commitments which might involve the use of armed force, the Congress is a full partner. Only the Congress can declare war."

In ruling out any armed intervention in Indo-China now, Dulles said "present conditions

Continued on Page 2, Col. 1

First Decline In Unemployed Since October

Compiled from dispatches of the New York Herald-Tribune and Associated Press

WASHINGTON, May 7—Unemployment declined in April for the first time since the current recession began last year, the Government reported today, but the drop of 260,000 was termed mostly seasonal.

In addition, the number of factory jobs continued downward, dropping by 250,000 between March and April.

A combined Labor-Commerce Department survey of the job situation showed April employment up nearly half a million from March, to 60,600,000. Unemployment declined from 3,725,000 in March to 3,465,000 in April.

When the recession began to affect unemployment, in October, the total jobless was at a postwar low of 1,162,000, and in April, 1953, the total was 1,582,000.

Secretary of Labor James Mitchell and Secretary of Commerce Sinclair Weeks said in their joint statement the changes were largely seasonal but they represented the first sizable improvement since "the start of the employment downturn last summer.

The number of jobs increased in April in farming, trade, construction and other seasonal activities, but continued declining among factory workers and miners.

This worried some Government experts, who said it indicated business uncertainty and unwillingness to accumulate inventories of durable goods or the materials to make them.

The Index

Churches 12
Classified 15-17
Comics 14
Crossword Puzzle 13
Death Notices 13
Dennis the Menace ... 3
Drama 11
Editorial: "Fall of the Fortress" 10
Finance 6, 7
Hedda Hopper 11
Horoscope 17
Lichty 10
The Owl 4
Real Estate 18
Short Story 10
Sports ...... Week-Ender
TV, Radio Logs 13
Vital Statistics 13
Women's News 5

Yesterday's Temperatures

	High	Low
San Francisco	60	49
Oakland Airport	62	51
Hamilton Field	68	47
Redwood City	72	56
San Jose	69	58
Sacramento Airport	81	46
Fresno	90	55
Los Angeles	68	54
Portland	81	47
Chicago	51	38
New York	63	48
Washington	64	52

(Weather details, Page 13.)

Seals Win Fifth Straight, 15-7

See Sports

YESTERDAY'S TEMPERATURES

	High	Low		High	Low
San Francisco	63	50	Fresno	95	61
Oakland	72	52	Los Angeles	72	56
San Rafael	80	49	Portland	86	46
Redwood City	68	54	New York	73	63
San Jose	83	53	Chicago	62	51
Sacramento	93	54	Washington	77	60

Weather Details, Page 6

San Francisco Chronicle

THE VOICE OF THE WEST

FINAL

No. 32,440 CCCCAAA GArfield 1-1112 TUESDAY, MAY 18, 1954 10 CENTS WEATHER: FAIR

RUSS ARMS IN GUATEMALA

Court Bans Segregated Schools

A Week---or More

Ike's Order Stalls McCarthy Hearing

WASHINGTON, May 17 (AP)—The McCarthy-Army hearings bumped into a presidential order today and the result was that they came to an unexpected halt—for a week at least, and maybe forever.

Taking a personal hand, President Eisenhower issued a directive forbidding Army witnesses to testify about the role of White House officials and other top executive aides in the controversy between Senator Joseph McCarthy (Rep-Wis.) and Army chiefs.

McCarthy cried "iron curtain!" Democrats raised a protest of "whitewash." And in the end the Senate Investigations Subcommittee voted to recess the public inquiry until next Monday to see if Mr. Eisenhower would withdraw or modify his secrecy order.

Acting Chairman Karl Mundt (Rep-S. D.) said there is nothing about the recess which "even remotely implies a discontinuation of these hearings" for good. The Democrats, however, said it looked to them as if the hearings may well have blown sky high—unless the President changes his mind.

REVERSAL UNLIKELY

The chances of Mr. Eisenhower doing this appeared pretty slim.

The President said, in today's secrecy order issued to Secretary of Defense Charles E. Wilson, that his stand was taken "to maintain the proper separation of powers between the executive and legislative branches of the Government in accordance with my responsibilities and duties under the Constitution."

And he said, too, in language that left little if any room for backtracking:

"This separation is vital to preclude the exercise of arbitrary power by any branch of the Government."

And so ended—for the time being, at least—18 days of unprecedented, televised hearings that brought day after day of testimony from Secretary of the Army Robert T. Stevens and Army counsel John G. Adams—but only brief, incidental trips to the witness stand by their main antagonists, McCarthy and his chief counsel, Roy M. Cohn.

The uproar at today's session, first over the Presidential directive and then over the recess motion, almost drowned out another important development—the refusal of Attorney General Herbert Brownell Jr. to agree to publication of any part of the so-called "FBI letter" produced earlier in the hearing by McCarthy.

ADAMS GAGGED

Specifically, Mr. Eisenhower's order forbade Adams—who was still on the witness stand when the breakup came—to give any further details of a January 21 meeting of White House and other top-level officials that led to the Army's head-on collision with McCarthy.

At the January 21 meeting,

Continued on Page 8, Col. 1

The Index

A Bookman's Notebook	19
Bridge	19
Royce Brier	18
Bennett Cerf	19
Chess	19
Classified	29-31
Comic Page	22
Crossword Puzzle	19
Death Notices	29
Delaplane	17
Dennis the Menace	5
Drama	20, 21
Editorial: "Equal Rights Are for All"	18
Finance	27, 28
Dick Friendlich	17
Hedda Hopper	21
Horoscope	31
Lichty	18
Lively Arts	19
Terrence O'Flaherty	20
Panorama	19
Drew Pearson	19
Sporting Green	1H-4H
Marjorie Trumbull	19
TV, Radio Logs	20
Vital Statistics	29
Weather	6
Women's News	12, 13

Big Arms Shipment From Poland

By the Associated Press

WASHINGTON, May 17. The State Department announced today that an "important shipment of arms" from Soviet-controlled territory is now being unloaded in Guatemala.

The department, which has repeatedly charged that the Guatemalan government is "playing the Communist game," said it considers this a "development of gravity."

The department's announcement came in a period of mounting concern among American authorities over indications of increasing Communist activity to promote strife in various Central American countries.

A wildcat strike, now ending its first week, is continuing to paralyze the entire northern sector of Guatemala's southern neighbor, Honduras. Secretary of State John Foster Dulles suggested last week that Guatemalan diplomatic agents may have triggered the unprecedented walkout.

On January 29 the Guatemalan government charged it had uncovered a plot to invade Guatemala by land, sea, and air. It said Nicaraguan President Anastasio Somoza was preparing the invasion with support from El Salvador, the Dominican Republic, Venezuela and "the Government of the North," meaning the United States.

Several weeks ago the Nicaraguan government announced discovery of a cache of 40 rifles, two submachine guns, 20 hand

Continued on Page 4, Col. 6

Board Pledges Funds to Fix City Hospital

Faced with City Hall protests over drastic cuts in the Health Department's hospital budget, the Board of Supervisors promised yesterday that the institution will get the modernization money it needs, either by bond issue or special appropriation.

The Supervisors refused to reopen the budget, which was voted Saturday, but questioned Health Director Ellis Sox and Chief Administrative Officer Thomas A. Brooks at length during an afternoon session.

The hospital budget had been slashed to $187,300 for the coming fiscal year—a cut of $963,100 from the figure recommended by Sox, Brooks and Mayor Elmer Robinson.

But Supervisor Francis McCarty, acting as spokesman for the budget cutters, said the amount of nearly $1,000,000 was merely being deferred.

If the voters approve bond issues in November for modernizing the hospital and Laguna Honda Home, then the money will come from that source, McCarty said. But if the bonds—probably totaling nearly $9,000,000—are turned down, McCarty promised that the board will vote the funds year-by-year.

A motion by Supervisor James Leo Halley to reopen the budget—presumably to restore the cuts—died at the meeting yesterday because no one would second it.

The Supervisors said there is

Continued on Page 15, Col. 1

Miss Golden Gate

World Trade Week in the Bay Area opened yesterday with the crowning of Betty Jardine, 23, as "Miss Golden Gate" to rule over the week-long celebration. For a full review of the Bay's importance in the world's commerce and pictures and stories on the activities of its several ports, see the special World Trade Section with today's Chronicle. Details of week's activities, Page 3.

AFL Loses Steward Vote, 1287 to 743

By LEONARD GROSS

West Coast ship's cooks and stewards have refused to accept either of the two unions offered them in a Government-supervised representation election, it was announced yesterday.

By a clear majority, they have placed their marks instead in the "neither union" square of a National Labor Relations Board ballot.

That "neither" vote had been advocated by Harry Bridges as an endorsement of his longshore union, after that union was barred from participation in the election.

HOW VOTING WENT

The tally, following a count yesterday morning at the Appraiser's Building, was:

AFL Marine Cooks and Stewards, 743; National Union of Marine Cooks and Stewards, 14; neither, 1287.

The International Longshoremen's and Warehousemen's Union announced soon after the result that it would "move immediately to negotiate the long-overdue contract for steward's department employees."

Such a move would place the Pacific Maritime Association, shipowner's bargaining repre-

Continued on Page 2, Col. 7

Racial Inequality Declared Unconstitutional, 9-0 Vote

Warren Writes Decision

Compiled from dispatches of United Press and Associated Press

WASHINGTON, May 17. The Supreme Court ruled unanimously today that segregation of Negro and white children in public schools is unconstitutional.

The court put off steps to carry out its historic racial rights decision, however, because of their far-reaching nature and the "great variety" of local conditions that must be considered.

It scheduled fresh arguments this fall on how the ruling should be carried out, and whether it has power to ease the impact of its decision by "an effective gradual adjustment."

Thus the court's 9 to 0 decision requires no immediate changes in segregated schools systems prescribed by law in 17 Southern States and the District of Columbia.

Today's epochal 12-page decision, written by Chief Justice Earl Warren, held that racial segregation in public schools is a "denial of the equal protection

Text of the ruling is on Page 14. For editorial comment, see Page 18.

of the laws," and therefore violates the 14th Amendment to the Constitution.

In its decision, the high court struck down the long-standing "separate but equal" doctrine first laid down by the Supreme Court in 1896 when it maintained segregation was all right if equal facilities were made available for Negroes and whites.

The nine-member court ruled to a man that "separate educational facilities are inherently unequal."

Here is the heart of today's decision:

"We come then to the question presented: Does segregation of children in public schools solely on the basis of race, even though the physical facilities and other 'tangible' factors may be equal, deprive the children of the minority group of equal education opportunities?

"We believe that it does."

The high bench said the op-

Continued on Page 11, Col. 4

SEGREGATION

Required

Permitted

AP Wirephoto map

Map shows how much of the Nation is affected by the anti-segregation ruling

Dixie Leaders Comment

Many Southerners Bitter ---Others Urge Caution

Compiled from Dispatches of United Press and Associated Press

White political leaders in the Deep South reacted all the way from bitter criticism and near-defiance through milder anger and on to quiet caution yesterday when the United States Supreme Court outlawed the area's traditional segregation of races in public schools.

Officials in Georgia, South Carolina, Mississippi and Louisiana expressed firm and sometimes bitter opposition to the Supreme Court decision.

Kansas, Oklahoma, Texas and Maryland officials said they would obey the ruling.

Most Southern members of Congress called the Supreme Court ruling an invasion of States' rights.

PRAISE FROM NORTH

Many Northern Congressmen, on the other hand, commended the Court's action as a sound one that advanced the interests of social justice in the United States.

The National Association for the Advancement of Colored People hailed the court decision as "vindication" of a 45-year fight.

Negro leaders from several fields joined with NAACP leaders in a jubilant news conference in New York after the court's announcement. The chief points they made were:

1—The actual end of segregation in public schools may not be accomplished for five or six years.

2—There is no way for States to get around the decision.

3—The ruling "gives the lie to the Communist propaganda that American democracy is decadent" and will have "a great effect on American relations and prestige throughout the world."

4—The effect of the ruling will be spread into fields beyond the campus by ending segregation on school buses and in activities connected with schools.

NO COMMENT NOW

James C. Hagerty, presidential press secretary, told a Washington news conference the White House would have no comment at this time. He noted that the

Continued on Page 11, Col. 1

Shovels Ready In East Bay Treasure Hunt

The golden hills, the gladsome dells, the fertile plains and sandy strands of the great East Bay stood firm yesterday, waiting the onslaught of Emperor Norton's East Bay Treasure Hunters.

The great new search for the famous oak-casketed plaque, worth $1000, was just getting under way.

There were still no signs of diggers in Alameda and Contra Costa counties. But then the clues, printed daily on The Chronicle's front page and in its classified section, hadn't yet told much more than this: The buried treasure is on neither planted nor private property.

As more clues come in to be analyzed by searchers, the shovels will get busy.

The rhymed, cryptic clues in the present Treasure Hunt refer to geographic features of the East Bay, and standard maps of the two counties will be indispensable to unraveling them.

As in the previous Emperor Norton $1000 Treasure Hunts, anyone at all is eligible to join in — except employees of The Chronicle and KRON-TV and members of their families and previous Treasure Hunt winners.

This Is Clue No. 3

On the ground

Where it was laid

You'll dig around

In dappled shade.

TODAY'S CLUE! $1000 EMPEROR NORTON Buried Treasure

So you will know what you are looking for, duplicates of the buried medallion are on display at The Chronicle Classified offices, 377 15th St., Oakland; Macy's, Richmond; J. C. Penney Co., Walnut Creek; Roos Bros, Berkeley.

See Classified Section for Dividend Clue

Pennsylvanians To Vote Today

PHILADELPHIA, May 17 (AP). Pennsylvania voters pick candidates for six statewide offices, including Governor tomorrow.

Key System In the Black, Berkeley Told

Berkeley City Manager John D. Phillips reported yesterday that Key System is making money.

Key now has an application for a fare increase pending before the Public Utilities Commission. It states it has been losing money.

Phillips' report was made public at the same time an Assembly interim subcommittee on transit opened hearings in Oakland. The first three witnesses told the Assemblymen that "the only solution to the mass transportation problem in the East Bay is public ownership."

PHILLIPS' REPORT

Phillips said in his report which is to be presented to the Berkeley City Council this morning, that "the Key System has been operating successfully from a financial point of view and can continue to do so."

He said the company had lost only $30,161 last year, despite the 76-day strike. He said it had also lost money in January and February of this year, but had made enough in March to show a $13,793 profit for the first quarter of the year.

He said that although Key passenger volume was half of what it was during the peak war year of 1943 it was still 18 per cent above the 1940 figures.

"The company is making

Continued on Page 2, Col. 1

Clear and Balmy Days Are Ahead

Thanks to a high pressure system off the coast, the Bay Area will enjoy balmy summer weather for the next few days.

And so today, said the district forecaster, will be clear and warm—except for morning fog.

Summer's heat has already come to the interior, with Redding reporting 101 and Red Bluff 100 degrees Sunday.

'Police Payoffs' Enter Vice Inquiry

YESTERDAY'S TEMPERATURES

	High	Low		High	Low
San Francisco	63	52	Fresno	94	61
Oakland	67	55	Los Angeles	83	68
San Rafael	80	50	Portland	60	54
Redwood City	77	50	Chicago	98	71
San Jose	76	53	New York	91	71
Sacramento	89	53	Washington	93	72

Weather Details, Page 6

San Francisco Chronicle
THE VOICE OF THE WEST

No. 32,504 CCCCAAAB GArfield 1-1112 WEDNESDAY, JULY 21, 1954 10 CENTS WEATHER: MORNING FOG

INDO-CHINA PEACE SIGNED

Cease-Fire Date Is Not Set Yet

Vice Inquiry Spreads

'Police Payoffs' on Call Girls Charged

The District Attorney's investigation of vice operations here, stemming from the raid last March on the alleged call house of Mabel Malotte has spread to include possible police payoffs, it was learned yesterday.

"I don't believe any madam could operate in San Francisco for 25 years without a payoff of some kind to police and politicians," said Chief Assistant District Attorney Norman Elkington.

"There has to be, from the nature of the business."

"By 'a payoff of some kind' you mean money payoffs?" he was asked.

"Yes, of course."

The investigation of payoffs came to light when it was learned that a brunette prostitute, who testified before the Grand Jury Monday night that she had worked for Mrs. Malotte, was questioned about her knowledge of protection payments.

KNOWLEDGE DENIED

The girl said she knew nothing about the matter and denied also that she had ever seen any police officers in or about any of the places she plied her trade in San Francisco.

The fact that she was asked the questions, however, was the tipoff that the investigation has expanded. This was subsequently confirmed by Elkington.

The prostitute, whose name has not been made public, was one of 23 arrested by State agents in their big July Fourth raids at Pismo Beach. Homicide Chief Frank J. Ahern — who headed the short-lived super vice squad that shut down Mabel Malotte's place—learned in questioning the girl at the San Luis Obispo County Jail that she had worked in San Francisco, and subpoenaed her to appear before the Grand Jury.

DIFFERENCE OF OPINION

The Chronicle disclosed exclusively yesterday that a difference of opinion between the District Attorney's office and Chief of Police Michael Gaffey had almost blocked the interrogation of the Pismo Beach prostitutes by San Francisco officers.

Elkington wanted to send Inspector Jack Cruickshank, a member of the defunct super vice squad, to Pismo Beach after the State Attorney General's office said it had learned some of the girls had been hired through San Francisco pimps.

Gaffey denied yesterday there was any difference of opinion with Elkington, but agreed that he had declined to send Cruickshank alone. Gaffey wanted Cruickshank accompanied by a member of the department's regular vice squad, which in turn was unacceptable to the District Attorney's office.

IMPASSE RESOLVED

The impasse was finally resolved when Ahern himself became available to make the trip, and took Cruickshank with him.

Cruickshank was one of three officers to receive an award of merit from the United States Secret Service yesterday for their roles in breaking up a ring which allegedly dealt in stolen Treasury Department checks.

Cruickshank, and Inspectors John McNamara and Frank Van Dervort, were cited by the Treasury Department for developing information that led to identification and apprehension of the members of the ring in Los Angeles.

The Index

A Bookman's Notebook	17
Bridge	17
Royce Brier	16
Chess	17
Classified	25-27
Comic Page	20
Crossword Puzzles	17, 26
Death Notices	25
Dennis the Menace	17
Drama	18-19
Editorial	16
Finance	12, 13
Dick Friendlich	15
Horoscope	27
Lichty	16
Abe Mellinkoff	16
Terrence O'Flaherty	18
Panorama	17
Drew Pearson	17
Sporting Green	1H-4H
TV, Radio Logs	18
Vital Statistics	25
Weather	6
Women's News	9-11

(AP) Wirephoto

Time to Retire

A SEAL drowsed peacefully on a rock in the Scilly Isles off England, yesterday, apparently undisturbed by the automobile tire around his neck. Nobody knew how he acquired the strange collar, but the Royal Society for Prevention of Cruelty to Animals has been trying for three weeks to catch him and take it off. San Franciscans who may be reminded of a similar incident on Seal Rocks in 1948 will be sorry to hear that the local sea lion, who wore a toilet seat, has never been heard from since. That is, unless he changed collars and swam to England.

B. of A. Names Tapp Vice Chairman

Jesse W. Tapp, executive vice president of Bank of America, has been advanced to vice chairman of the board of directors and will transfer his activities to the Los Angeles headquarters of the bank about September 1.

Announcement of the advancement was made yesterday by S. Clark Beise, president of the bank, following a meeting of the board of directors.

It is assumed in banking circles that Tapp is slated to succeed Alfred J. Gock, board chairman of the bank, due for retirement later this year.

Jesse W. Tapp

Tapp is currently president of the San Francisco Chamber of Commerce and is expected to resign from that position. What procedure the chamber will follow in naming a successor has not been announced.

BRAUNSCHWEIGER POST

Gock has served as president of the Los Angeles Chamber of Commerce, the only San Franciscan to hold that position.

Beise also announced that Walter J. Braunschweiger will continue his state-wide activities as executive vice president with headquarters in Los Angeles.

A member of the bank's managing committee, Tapp is also a member of the finance committee and is adviser to the bank on agricultural financing policies. He has served on the advisory council of the board of directors and on the executive committee.

TAPP'S U. S. JOBS

Prior to his affiliation with the bank in 1939, Tapp occupied a number of positions with the United States Department of Agriculture. A native of Kentucky, he is a graduate of the College of Agriculture of the University of Kentucky and has done graduate work in economics at Harvard and the University of Wisconsin.

The bank's board of directors also declared two regular dividends of 40 cents each, the first payable August 31 to holders of record August 10; the second payable November 30 to holders of record November 9.

S. F. Uranium Stock Boom Investigated

A rags-to-riches boom in uranium stocks on the San Francisco Mining Exchange is under investigation by the Securities Exchange Commission, The Chronicle learned yesterday.

Staff members of the Federal agency are in the midst of a confidential inquiry into a recent rash of transactions on the Exchange here—a series of hectic dealings in which volume has soared and values of some shares have jumped from three to 25 times within a few days.

The investigators are out to see whether there were any violations of stock trading laws during the past two months of frantic activity, and the State Division of Corporations is also looking into the boom.

IT STARTED IN MAY

The spurt in prices began last May after several old-time California gold mining companies announced that they had acquired claims or interests in potential uranium-bearing land in the Sierra or in Nevada or Utah.

William Orrick, regional administrator of the Securities Exchange Commission here, told The Chronicle yesterday:

"The reason we are investigating the Mining Exchange and some of the companies listed is because of abnormal activity in uranium stock. We want to know why there has been this tremendous activity. The activity became quite marked in May, but it has now settled down a good deal.

"The investigation and the

Continued on Page 2, Col. 4

McCarthy Lets Cohn Resign

By the Associated Press

WASHINGTON, July 20—Senator Joseph McCarthy (Rep-Wis.) today reluctantly accepted the resignation of Roy Cohn as chief counsel of the Senate Investigations Subcommittee and transferred Donald A. Surine, another subcommittee aide who has been under fire, to his personal staff.

McCarthy moved in advance of a showdown session of the subcommittee, a majority of whose members had demanded a "housecleaning" of the staff.

Surine was one of two subcommittee assistants who have been refused clearance by the Defense Department to handle secret matters. The other, Thomas LaVenia, was kept in his post, at least temporarily.

McCarhy's maneuver beat to the punch the members of the Investigations Subcommittee who were bent on a staff shake-up. But because only six of the seven subcommittee members met today there was nothing that could be done about firing Cohn or Surine.

A decision on Lavenia was put off until a report comes in from the Defense Department regarding its refusal to grant him security clearance for handling secret correspondence.

The subcommittee will meet before July 31 to decide on LaVenia. If the group takes no action before that date he will be discharged automatically.

CLEARANCE REFUSED

McCarthy confirmed to reporters that both Surine and LaVenia have been refused security clearance. He said he has asked Secretary of Defense Charles E. Wilson for the reasons why the two men were not cleared. He added that he plans to seek Surine's return to the subcommittee staff when a reply comes in.

However, a spokesman at the Pentagon said the Defense Department would not give McCarthy any reasons for denying the clearances. The spokesman said Wilson has written McCarthy a letter explaining that the Defense Department's stand is based on confidential information.

Aside from Cohn, Surine and LaVenia, all of the other 22 men and women on the staff were confirmed in their jobs by the subcommittee, including Chief of Staff Francis P. Carr.

HEARING PRINCIPALS

Cohn, McCarthy and Carr were the principals in the recent hearings into McCarthy's fight with the Army. The Army principals were Secretary of the Army Robert Stevens and Counselor John Adams. During the hearings it was proposed that both Cohn and Adams resign.

Secretary Wilson said today

Continued on Page 4, Col. 6

Cambodia, Laos Reds to Withdraw

Vietnam Split Approved; Hanoi, Delta Area Lost

Air, Naval Bases Saved For France

Compiled from Dispatches of Associated Press and United Press

GENEVA, July 21—France and the Communists signed a cease-fire agreement for Vietnam and Laos early today (Wednesday) to end nearly eight years of war in Indo-China.

A similar truce agreement for Cambodia, the third Indo-Chinese state, was to have been signed at the same time, but it was held up by last-minute technicalities and the signing was delayed until this afternoon.

The date on which the cease-fire will go into effect has not yet been disclosed. Commanders in the field will have to sign the documents first.

NEAR DEADLINE

French Premier Pierre Mendes-France missed his midnight deadline for "peace with honor" by only two hours, but he missed it by so little that he was not expected to carry out his threat to resign.

A spokesman said the cease-fire agreements come into force with the signing, but he was uncertain as to when the fighting would formally come to an end. Presumably the end would come as soon as word could be relayed to the troops in the field, a matter of three days in the Red River Delta and up to two weeks in isolated districts.

For France, the achievement of peace was costly.

VIETNAM PARTITION

France agreed to the partitioning of strife-torn Vietnam near the 17th Parallel, gave up the rich and teeming Red River Delta area with its great cities of Hanoi and Haiphong and turned over more than 12,000,000 natives to the Communists.

But Mendes-France, in his headlong rush to end hostilities within a month, salvaged the great Tourane air and naval base and the ancient Annamese capital of Hue, well below the cease-fire line across the 40-mile narrow waist of Vietnam.

STATES NEUTRALIZED

The armistice agreements with Laos and Cambodia will leave their French-sponsored governments in control. However, they are to be neutralized, with their armed forces limited to those necessary for self-defense.

These provisions will prevent the United States from supplying military instructors or equipment, and their only real protection will be the realization by the Communists that an armed attack may precipitate American intervention

In addition, Laos and Cambodia bind themselves to remain out of any Western-backed Southeast Asia Treaty Organi-

Continued on Page 6, Col. 5

Churchill Refuses Germany Details

LONDON, July 20 (AP)—Prime Minister Winston Churchill turned down a request in Commons for details of the British-American plan to speed West German sovereignty.

Talks between Britons and Americans recently produced a draft proposal to separate the Bonn convention—the sovereignty agreement—from the European Defense Community Treaty with which it is closely linked.

(AP) Wirephoto

CEASE-FIRE LINE — The heavy black line across the narrow waist of Vietnam is the truce line finally drawn yesterday in Geneva. The entire shaded area to the north goes to the Communist Vietminh, including the Red River Delta areas still held by the French. The French keep Highway No. 9, which runs partway across the peninsula.

Peace Terms Approved

U. S. to 'Accept' Pact On Indo-China Treaty

Exclusive to The Chronicle From the New York Times

WASHINGTON, July 20—The United States Government will issue a unilateral statement tomorrow accepting in principle the terms of the Indo-China cease-fire agreement and announcing its "ability to respect" such terms under the United Nations Charter, diplomatic officials disclosed tonight.

The decision to state this Government's position on the agreement, probably by President Eisenhower at his regular news conference, was disclosed after diplomatic intelligence sources established that the terms contain a clause permitting a free exchange of populations between Northern and Southern Vietnam.

FREE MOVEMENT

For a period of one year, according to this understanding, no effort will be made to prevent movement between the two areas.

Diplomatic officials attach great importance to this clause, which they believe will avert the swallowing of the anti-Communist and predominantly Catholic population of Northern Vietnam by the Red regime.

Of only slightly less importance is a provision in the agreement whereby the right of the free portion of the partitioned Indo-China states to receive foreign military assistance will be interrupted only temporarily, so that no interference with their sovereignty will be entailed.

'DISENGAGEMENT' PERIOD

It was understood the temporary restriction on the receipt of military assistance from the U. S. and other free nations will end after a period of "disengagement" during which Communist and anti-Communist forces will be withdrawn from existing front-line areas.

Diplomatic officials familiar with its terms hold that the cease-fire generally comes within the terms of the seven prin-

Continued on Page 6, Col. 3

Sneak Thief Gets Henry Fonda's Movie Cameras

A sneak thief made off with about $400 worth of Henry Fonda's photographic gear at Tarantino's restaurant on Fisherman's Wharf yesterday.

The famous actor, his wife and three children, went to the crowded restaurant for lunch at 2 p. m.

Halfway through his meal, Fonda suddenly remembered he'd left his gadget bag on the floor of the restaurant's lounge. When he went back to retrieve it, it was gone. Stolen were a 35-millimeter camera, a 16-millimeter movie camera, a light meter and two rolls of film.

And Fonda was understandably upset about the loss. He and his family are leaving for a Hawaii vacation today aboard the Lurline.

Ike to Give Polio Data to World

YESTERDAY'S TEMPERATURES	High	Low		High	Low
San Francisco	58	50	Fresno	77	42
Oakland	59	48	Los Angeles	84	59
San Rafael	66	46	Portland	48	40
Redwood City	70	40	New York	—	41
San Jose	66	42	Chicago	71	60
Sacramento	69	42	Washington	55	46

Weather Details, Page 32

San Francisco Chronicle
THE VOICE OF THE WEST

FINAL

No. 32,771 CCCCAAA GArfield 1-1112 THURSDAY, APRIL 14, 1955 10 CENTS WEATHER: PARTLY CLOUDY

OLSON FLOORS MAXIM TWICE IN EASY WIN

Fight on Polio

U. S. to Give Salk Report to World

By the Associated Press

WASHINGTON, April 13—President Eisenhower, in an international gesture of good will, decided today to send latest information on the Salk polio preventive to nations around the globe, including Russia and other Red countries.

Secretary of State John Foster Dulles announced tonight he will do this at the President's direction. Dulles said he also will consult with other Government officials to see how far the United States can go in making the vaccine itself available for export.

Only a few hours before, the Commerce Department clamped export controls on the newly approved vaccine. Officials said at the time it might be possible to meet world-wide demands for the long-sought weapon against the dreaded disease in 1957.

Senator Lister Hill (Dem-Ala.) proposed, meanwhile, that Mr. Eisenhower call a nationwide conference to choke off any "black market" that might spring up in the vaccine—officially described as safe and effective in preventing paralytic polio.

State Department officials said Dulles will get tomorrow from the National Foundation for Infantile Paralysis a copy of yesterday's report by Dr. Thomas Francis Jr., which gave a favorable evaluation of Dr. Jonas Salk's vaccine.

Dulles then will send copies

Continued on Page 4, Col. 6

Pupils Get Polio Shot Consent Slips

Children in the first and second grades of San Francisco's public, parochial and private schools were given consent slips yesterday in preparation for next week's mass injections of Salk polio vaccine.

The vaccine is to be given free to children in those two grades if their parents want them to get it.

Each child was told to take his slip home so that his parents could sign it. The signed slips, authorizing the injection of the vaccine, are to be returned to school by tomorrow.

Parents of children who forgot their slips or lost them are asked to get in touch with authorities at their children's schools.

Meanwhile, the schedule of how shots will be administered remained in some doubt yesterday.

Officials of the National Foundation for Infantile Paralysis were meeting in New York to study whether the original plan of three shots in a five-week span is to be allowed. Dr. Jonas E. Salk, developer of the vaccine, reported Tuesday he believed only two shots should be administered in the first several weeks.

The third shot, he added,

Continued on Page 4, Col. 4

Downtown Store Backs Garage Plan

By TOM MATHEWS

Spring thaw hit the frozen parking program yesterday in two important areas.

The Parking Authority asked the Board of Supervisors to designate a $2,000,000 piece of property on the southeast corner of Fifth and Mission streets as a parking project.

The authority acted after hearing a spokesman for the Emporium Capwell Co. confidently predict a merchants' association will be formed to build a three-level, 1200-stall garage on the site.

The authority also approved in principle a large fringe parking experiment on a block of land underneath the Bayshore Freeway at Sixth and Bryant streets. Rates would be 40 cents a day, including a round trip to the downtown area by Muni bus.

675 FEET LONG

The Mission street site approved by the authority lies between Mission and Minna streets and stretches from Fifth street 675 feet to the east.

The estimated $2,000,000 purchase price is already covered by money still left in the authority's 1947 bond fund.

Originally the plans called for removing the buildings and operating a surfaced parking lot until new bond funds could be obtained to build a garage.

However, the entrance of Emporium Capwell into the picture will probably mean that a garage construction can start as soon as the site is purchased, according to the authority's general manager, Vining T. Fisher.

EMPORIUM OFFICIAL

The enthusiasm of the company was expressed by Reginald H. Biggs, vice president. "This is an extraordinarily good site," he told the authority. "One third of the downtown re-

Continued on Page 6, Col. 5

Rain Falls Short Of Bay Area---Clouds Due Today

Light to moderate rain swept the Northern California coast from Fort Bragg northward yesterday, but not even a drizzle reached San Francisco—and none is expected today.

A few more showers may fall north of Ukiah and Red Bluff today, Forecaster E. H. Quinn said, but elsewhere in Central and Northern California the forecast is partly cloudy today, generally fair Friday.

In San Francisco there will be variable cloudiness, with skies clearing completely by tonight. Temperatures will remain about the same.

Uranium-Loaded Rock a Mystery

Special to The Chronicle

STOCKTON, April 13 — A piece of rock that has lain forgotten in an ore drawer at an assay office here for more than a decade has tested out at 8.61 per cent uranium—worth a fabulous $1500 a ton—a pair of chemists said today.

The chemists do not know where the rock is from, or even who it was that brought it to their office for testing.

"It was after the fall of Singapore, and everyone was looking for tin," said D. K. Proffitt, local assay chemist. "A man brought it in and wanted to know if it was tin. It wasn't. He paid us and left."

Singapore fell in February of 1942, cutting off the Allies' tin supply.

The sample, about the size of a man's fist, was tossed into a drawer of various ore samples, and was forgotten until a few days ago.

Roger Loh, Proffitt's partner, said a friend brought in a Geiger counter for testing. It was put near the ore drawer and the needle swung to the end of the scale.

"It tested out as pitchblende containing 8.64 per cent uranium," said Loh.

"Whoever it was that brought the rock in, has sure missed a fortune. It is the highest testing uranium we've ever seen. We've never seen anything higher than 2 per cent. The Government is happy if the ore is only .15 of 1 per cent."

Loh said he is inclined to think that the piece of pitchblende came from outside California—maybe Arizona or Colorado.

"But we can't even remember what the man looked like," said Loh.

$4365 Robbery at Noon

'Skid Roader' Holds Up Bank on Market Street

A poor speller turned robber got $4365 in a noontime holdup of the Market-New Montgomery branch of the Bank of America yesterday. And last night, with the robber still at large, 20 police inspectors and 20 FBI agents combed the city's Skid Road in the hope of finding him.

They had a description of the robber as a "Skid Road type," and they had his hat, lost as he ran away. They also had an idea that the same man staged the $1500 holdup of the Bank of America's Day and Night branch on March 3.

Yesterday's holdup came at about 12:30 p. m. A man described as between 50 and 60 stepped up to the window of teller John McCallister and placed a note on the counter.

The note, with letters printed on lined paper, read:

"Hold Up.

"Keep Quite. No buttons.

"No Gaurd. 5's, 10's, 20's, 50's."

After reading the note, McCallister took a second look in disbelief at the robber who returned the look by jamming his hands farther down into the pockets of a black overcoat.

"I thought he had a gun," McCallister said. "I took all the loose fives, tens and 20s in my cash drawer and put them on the counter.

"He grabbed them, stuffed them into his overcoat pockets and went away."

As soon as the bandit had turned his back, McCallister yelled "hold up" to assistant chief of operations Louis Ferrigno, who turned in the alarm.

The bank has entrances on both Market and New Montgomery streets. McCallister said he did not know by which door the bandit left.

It was believed by bank officials, police and the FBI, however, that he went out the door on New Montgomery and fled east on Stevenson street directly behind the bank.

This belief was built on the

Continued on Page 5, Col. 6

PG&E Failure Blacks Out Fight Reports

One of three lines of a 110,000-volt transformer bank in Pacific Gas and Electric Co.'s Martin substation at Visitacion Valley burned out a 7:52 o'clock last night and:

Caused a "dip" or flicker of lights all over town, including the Cow Palace, where patrons were waiting for the start of the tenth and last round of the Olson-Maxim fight.

Blacked out TV picture transmission of the fight by KPIX—which was for network but not local broadcast — for four minutes.

Silenced KCBS radio and KPIX-TV network sound transmission from the Cow Palace for 50 seconds.

Blacked out lights of all types in parts of Visitacion Valley and in western Sunset District areas served by neighborhood substations at 35th avenue and Taraval street, at 35th avenue and Sloat boulevard and at 46th avenue and Noriega street for periods ranging from 28 minutes to, in a few areas, an hour and four minutes.

Service was restored by rerouting power through alternate circuits.

Gen. Fields Named AEC Manager

WASHINGTON, April 13 (AP)—Brigadier General Kenneth E. Fields, a key figure in nuclear weapons development, tonight was named general manager of the Atomic Energy Commission.

Commission chairman Lewis L. Strauss said Fields would replace Major General Kenneth D. Nichols on May 1.

Nichols previously had announced his resignation as of the end of this month to become an engineering consultant in Washington.

Provoo Treason Case Appealed

BALTIMORE, Md., April 13 (AP)—The Government filed notice today that it will ask the Supreme Court to reinstate treason charges against former Army Sergeant John David Provoo.

Ike Approves Trading Atom Data in NATO

Exclusive to The Chronicle
From the New York Herald Tribune

AUGUSTA, Ga., April 13—President Eisenhower approved today a far-reaching agreement for the transfer of military atomic information — but not atomic weapons themselves nor plans for making them—to the North Atlantic Treaty Organization.

Under the agreement, the other 13 member nations also would give NATO such similar atomic information as they possess.

America's contribution would be atomic information necessary to:

1—Development of defense plans.

2—Training of personnel in the use of and the defense against atomic weapons.

3—The evaluation of the capabilities of potential enemies in atomic warfare.

While NATO will get no American atomic weapons under the agreement, the way is opened for it to receive information about the external characteristics of these weapons, including their size, weight and shape, their yields and effects and the means of using them and delivering them to a target.

"The North Atlantic Council strongly endorsed the proposed agreement, and I consider it to be a great stride forward in the strengthening of our common defense," the President said in a letter today to Senator Clinton P. Anderson (Dem-N. M.), chairman of the Joint Committee on Atomic Energy.

White House Press Secretary James D. Hagerty said the terms of the agreement were in strict accordance with the amendments to the Atomic Energy Act which Congress passed last year specifically to permit the United States to share some of its atomic secrets with NATO.

High Winds Again Delay Atom Shot

LAS VEGAS, Nev., April 13 (AP)—Atomic testers again have postponed the firing of a large nuclear shot designed to test weapons and supplies.

Atomic Energy Commission scientists said today that a forecast of continuing high winds aloft makes weather conditions unacceptable for any test tomorrow.

Mail Truck Lost Awhile---Driver Couldn't'Recall

A two-ton mail truck was lost for seven hours here yesterday, and it took the best efforts of police and postal authorities to find it.

The truck, carrying six registered parcels and other mail, failed to return to the Rincon Annex post office at 4 p. m. and a search failed to turn it up.

The driver, Jack R. Sullivan, was found at his home at 1848 29th avenue minus truck. He couldn't remember very much, even where he had left the truck, according to Postmaster John F. Fixa.

Shortly after 11 p. m. the truck was found, parked on 11th street between Mission and Market. All the mail was intact, Fixa said.

"We'll be talking to the driver again in the morning," the Postmaster added.

S. F.'s Champ Goes Up in Class

By Barney Peterson, The Chronicle

Champion of the middleweights, Carl (Bobo) Olson of San Francisco last night showed he was ready for the best of the light-heavyweights. Olson floored former light-heavyweight champ Joey Maxim in the second and ninth rounds on his way to an easy Cow Palace decision. In this fifth-round action, Olson punished Maxim with a hard right. For details see Sporting Green.

State Launches Drive for Student Farm Workers

State Employment Director William A. Burkett announced yesterday a campaign to put young people to work in the State's fields during the summer vacation.

An AFL Agricultural Union official immediately criticized the plan however, as not meeting the problem of replacing imported Mexican agricultural workers.

Burkett told a meeting in San Jose that high school youths will be urged to work on farms during their summer vacation to reduce the need for importing Mexican agricultural workers.

Predicting that more than 50,000 youths will work on farms this summer, Burkett said: "The program is part of our policy of eliminating the need for foreign labor in California."

Ernesto Galarza, international representative of the AFL National Agricultural Workers Union, said this latest plan is in keeping with "the unrealistic operation of the Department of Employment."

Galarza said the problem is not in finding "school-kid" replacements for the Mexican nationals now imported to work in the fields.

"There are plenty of American agricultural workers who are available to work wherever and whenever fair wages and working conditions are offered," the union official said.

He charged that "employment of school children is part of the thinking that brought cheap foreign workers into California to displace American field workers."

"As usual," he said, "there is no mention of the wages to be paid these school kids and the conditions they'll work under. It's another cheap substitute—as are Mexican nationals—for experienced, American agricultural workers."

U. S. Population Is 164,367,000

WASHINGTON, April 13 (AP)—The U. S. population, including members of the armed forces stationed overseas, was approximately 164,367,000 on March 1, the Census Bureau estimated today.

INDEX

Bridge 31
Chess 31
Comics 26
Crossword Puzzles 23, 35
Death Notices 31
Drama 24, 25
Editorial Page 22
Financial Pages 18, 19
Food Pages 11-14
Hedda Hopper 25
Horoscope 35
David Hulburd 36
Panorama 23
TV, Radio Logs 24
Vital Statistics 31
Weather 32
Women's World ... 15-17

YESTERDAY'S TEMPERATURES	High	Low		High	Low
San Francisco	59	50	Fresno	88	49
Oakland	63	49	Los Angeles	74	52
San Rafael	79	43	Portland	67	44
Redwood City	74	45	Chicago	62	50
San Jose	77	50	New York	70	62
Sacramento	85	47	Washington	73	64

Weather Details, Page 12

San Francisco Chronicle

THE VOICE OF THE WEST

FINAL

No. 32,941 CCCCAAA GArfield 1-1112 SATURDAY, OCTOBER 1, 1955 10 CENTS WEATHER: FAIR

THEORIES ON BLAST TOLD

Crash Kills Film Star James Dean

Many Ideas, No Proof

Explosion Angles Baffle the Experts

The big blast that rocked San Francisco at 7:23 p. m. Thursday remained a baffler yesterday.

The question was what blew up?

What blew up, for sure, appeared to be every rational theory advanced to explain the big boom and its window-breaking, house-rocking, panic-making concussion.

Only the irrational theories—involving Moscow rockets and Mars saucers—remained unchallenged, inasmuch as they couldn't be checked.

WAS IT JET?

The closest rational explanation was that a supersonic jet plane changed direction overhead, inflicting the noisy and little-understood phenomenon of a "ring-shape vortex" shock wave on the city.

This aerial theory would account for the blast's source being reported east of the beach, north of Daly City and north of Parnassus Heights, south of the Presidio and west of downtown — without any earthly trace of the blast itself within these boundaries.

The troubles with the theory were two.

First, Samuel Schaaf, an associate professor of mechanical engineering at the University of California, researching supersonic phenomena for the Air Force at the Richmond field station, said the jet plane's shock wave would have been concentrated in a small area — not spread all over town.

Second, none of the Navy or Air Force operators of jet aircraft admitted to having a plane capable of supersonic speeds over the city at the time.

Nor did the Mount Tamalpais Air Force radar station have a plane in its scope over the city then.

Nor did Fort Miley's volunteer aircraft spotter station in the Richmond district hear any planes—or, for that matter, rockets or saucers—overhead at that time.

The next best rational the-

Continued on Page 2, Col. 6

France Walks Out of U. N. in Algeria Row

From Associated Press and New York Herald Tribune

UNITED NATIONS, N.Y., Sept. 30 — French Foreign Minister Antoine Pinay and the entire French delegation walked out of the United Nations General Assembly today after that body had voted to take up the Algerian question.

By a margin of one vote, the Assembly rejected the recommendation of its 15-nation Steering Committee that the Assembly skip the issue for this session.

The vote was 28-27 to reject the recommendation.

U. S. BACKS FRANCE

The United States and Britain sided with France. There were five abstentions.

Pinay immediately took the floor and said France would regard any action taken by the Assembly on Algeria as null and void.

The French delegation then rose and left.

The Arab-Asian bloc had called for debate on the Algerian question because of riots and disorder in recent months.

'PART OF FRANCE'

Pinay reminded the Assembly that he had warned of the "consequences" of such a U. N. decision. He reported that the French National Assembly will review tomorrow "relations between France and the U. N." and he said he did not know what the consequences of that review will be.

Pinay argued that Algeria has been, since 1930, an "integral part of France" and therefore is not a matter for U. N. consideration.

All of the North Atlantic Alliance nations joined France in opposing debate on Algeria.

Ike Signs Papers---First Official Job

From Associated Press and United Press

DENVER, Sept. 30—President Eisenhower tonight took the first small but momentous step in a long March back toward active command of the Government by signing two Federal documents.

The action, taken by the President from his hospital bed after another day of encouraging progress in recuperation from his heart attack, came at 8:27 p. m. (MST)—a few hours short of a week from the time he was stricken.

The President's first official move occurred after medical reports this morning for the first time used the word "excellent" in describing his condition.

The signing of the documents, providing for promotion of State Department Foreign Service officers, was the first business transacted by the Chief Executive since last Friday, the eve of his attack.

FULL SIGNATURE

Originally the White House officials had said Mr. Eisenhower merely would initial the two papers. Instead, using a pen from his desk at the temporary White House here, he wrote his full name on each.

His motorized bed was elevated slightly to permit him to write.

As the President's personal physician, General Howard M. Snyder handed the President the lists, he tried to explain to the President how to sign them.

"Howard," the President said, "I know more how to do this than you do."

SPECIALIST RETURNING

These other developments marked the President's day:

1—The hospital announced that Dr. Paul Dudley White, the eminent heart specialist who examined Mr. Eisenhower shortly after he suffered the attack, has agreed to return to Denver.

The purpose of the return visit, said White House Press Secretary James C. Hagerty, is to consult with other physicians on the case with respect to the President's condition at the time.

2—President's assistant, Sherman Adams, flew here from Washington tonight, to take charge of the Denver White House.

(For details on the President's health, see Page 6).

Red Guns Shell 2 Chiang Islands

TAIPEI, Formosa, Sept. 30 (AP)—Communist Chinese guns on Amoy Island fired more than 100 shells at Nationalist-held Little Quemoy and Chuyu islands today.

JAMES DEAN
A star in "East of Eden"

Young Actor Dies Driving Sports Car

From Associated Press and United Press

PASO ROBLES, Sept. 30 —James Dean, rising young film actor, was killed early tonight in a head-on collision about 25 miles east of here.

Dean, 24, a racing car enthusiast, was killed when his German-built Porsche sports car collided with another vehicle at a highway intersection near Cholame, Paso Robles War Memorial Hospital authorities said.

Dean, and his seriously injured mechanic, identified as Rolph Wuetherich, were on their way to road races in Salinas.

An attending physician said Dean suffered a broken neck, numerous broken bones, lacerations over the entire body and was terribly "battered" by the impact of the crash. He was killed instantly.

The California Highway Patrol said the fatal accident occurred at the intersection of Highways 41 and 460. Dean's car and one driven by Donald Turnupseed of Tulare collided head-on. Turnupseed suffered minor injuries.

Dean shot into film prominence in the leading role in John Steinbeck's "East of Eden."

Dean had been working for several months on "Giant," film version of Edna Ferber's novel about Texas. Work on the picture had not been completed.

George Stevens, director of "Giant," said tonight that Dean's death was a "great tragedy . . . he had extraordinary talent."

Dean was born at Marion, Ind., Feb. 8, 1931. He was raised on a farm at Fairmount, Ind., was graduated from the high school there and came to California. He attended UCLA for a time and studied drama and then went to New York, where he got a part in a play "The Immoralist."

Warners signed him, and he became an immed[illegible] star.

His father, W[illegible] Dean of Los Angeles, [illegible]

Fog Closes Airports

The San Francisco and Oakland International Airports were socked in for more than two hours yesterday morning by a heavy ground fog that cut visibility to less than 350 feet.

Airliners at both airports were forced to wait for the fog to lift and one Qantas plane from Australia, unable to land, was sent to Sacramento.

There may be fog along the coast today but skies will be clear otherwise, the weatherman said.

The morning fog, which settled in parts of the Bay Area about 4:30 a. m., closed all airports in the area except Travis Air Force Base at Fairfield.

The Oakland Airport shut down at 5:20 a. m. and did not reopen until 7:45 a. m.

At the San Francisco International Airport operations were halted at 4:49 a. m. and reopened at 7:26 a. m.

Ship Rescues Plane, Crew Down at Sea

A crippled Catalina flying boat was forced to land on the ocean 500 miles southwest of San Francisco yesterday. And within minutes, the plane and its four-man crew were safe aboard a freighter.

The PBY-5A was bound from Guam to Oakland via Honolulu. It was 1000 miles from its destination when one engine conked out.

The aircraft flew another 500 miles on its single engine as two rescue planes dispatched from the Bay Area winged toward it.

Then, because gas was running low, it decided to land at sea. Radio guidance from the Coast Guard here sent the disabled plane toward the Lykkes Brothers freighter Harvey Culbreath.

The aircraft first radioed its distress call at 9 a. m. yesterday. It reached the freighter at 1:55 p. m., and landed beside the vessel at 2:04 p. m.

A nine-foot swell was running, but the freighter's crew had a lifeboat already in the water as the plane came down, and the four crewmen were speedily transferred to safety.

The freighter then swung a cargo boom over the side and hoisted the plane out of the water. The craft was

Continued on Page 2, Col. 3

$100,000 Hypnosis Stunt on TV

Picture on Page 5

HOLLYWOOD, Sept. 30 (IP)—A 19-year-old coed was hypnotized tonight as part of a national television stunt that may earn her the biggest video jackpot to date—$100,000.

Patricia Morris, a freshman at the University of Southern California, was given a post-hypnotic suggestion that she will be unable to return next week to the NBC "Truth or Consequences" show and pick up the cash.

The girl was chosen before tonight's program from the studio audience.

She was one of several contestants hypnotist Arthur Allen attempted to put in a trance. Of eight candidates, Patricia was the most easily induced into hypnotic sleep.

By showtime, Patricia could be put into a trance at the snap of Allen's fingers. While she was mesmerized, Allen frequently repeated "Pat, you will be unable to accept $100,000 from anyone at anytime within the next ten days unless I clap my hands."

Patricia was then taken out of her trance and brought before the cameras. She told master of ceremonies Jack Bailey she would return next week to try to outwit Allen and his hypnotic spell when the 100 grand is placed before her.

Patricia will be accompanied to classes this week by a special chaperon who will also spend the nights with her in a hotel room.

"That's to keep her from being worked on by other hypnotists or psychologists who might break the spell," Allen explained.

Reunion in Grief

Marcus Benedicto consoled his wife after she fell at his feet and pleaded for his help in making authorities "understand" her kidnaping of the Marcus baby. They met in the police show-up room.

UC's May Dies

Funeral services were held in New York city yesterday for Professor Samuel C. May, internationally renowned political scientist of the University of California. He died en route to Italy. For the details of career see Page 6.

Dodgers Win; Larsen vs. Erskine Today

BROOKLYN, Sept. 30 (AP)—The Brooklyn Dodgers got back into the World Series today by defeating the New York Yankee 8-3 at Ebbets Field.

The Yanks won the first two games.

The series resumes tomorrow with Carl Erskine scheduled to pitch for Brooklyn and Don Larsen for New York.

(For all the details and photographs, see the Sporting Green.)

Kidnap Arraignment Delayed

Mrs. Benedicto Screams Guilt in Court, Faints

By Carolyn Anspacher

Betty Jean Benedicto, her pudgy face blotched, sobbed a confession of guilt yesterday in the crowded courtroom of Municipal Judge Alvin E. Weinberger.

Rocking back and forth, as if in pain, she screamed she had taken baby Robert Marcus and tried hysterically to forestall the court's appointment of an attorney to represent her.

"I don't want none," she wailed. "I took baby Mark. I don't want no lawyer. I done it, you hear—I done it."

FALLS IN FAINT

A few minutes later she fell in a dead faint in a Hall of Justice corridor.

Mrs. Benedicto, already charged with kidnaping and held on bail of $100,000 cash or $200,000 bond, was brought to the Hall of Justice from San Francisco Hospital, where she had been under psychiatric observation since Wednesday night.

Her shattering experience did not end there. At 4 p. m., she was half-carried into a police showup room. Five of 13 Mt. Zion Hospital employees who saw her before and after the September 19 kidnaping identified her postiviely as the kidnaper.

It was a little after 10 a. m. when Mrs. Benedicto shuffled into court—her straw blonde hair tied back with strips of hospital gauze, her flabby body shrouded by a loose blue gabardine coat. Supporting her were Inspectors George Dyer and Frank Gibeau and Policewoman Margaret Dillon.

Her appearance before Judge Weinberger was mercifully brief.

He looked closely at her puffy face, her swollen eyes, her gaping mouth and ordered

Continued on Page 5, Col. 1

Freed Yank Flyer Due Here Today

Lawrence Robert Buol, the Stockton civilian flyer recently released from a Red China prison, will arrive at 10:45 a. m. today at San Francisco International Airport, en route home.

INDEX

Churches	12
Comics	16
Crossword Puzzles	10, 26
Death Notices	22
Drama	15
Finance	8, 9
Hedda Hopper	15
Horoscope	26
David Hulburd	11
The Owl	7
Drew Pearson	11
TV, Radio Logs	14
Real Estate	10
Vital Statistics	22
Women's News	13

EXTRA

BIG LINERS CRASH ...'ABANDON SHIP!'

WEATHER FORECAST
Bay Area: High fog near ocean extending inland morning and evening, but mostly fair otherwise. High temperatures Thursday, 62 in city, 76 in San Rafael; low 53 to 57.
Full Report on Page 25

San Francisco Chronicle
THE VOICE OF THE WEST

FINAL

92nd YEAR No. 208 | CCCCAAA | THURSDAY, JULY 26, 1956 | 10 CENTS | GArfield 1-1112

Attack on Hall

Stassen Reveals Anti-Nixon Plans

By Don Whitehead
New York Herald Tribune Service

WASHINGTON, July 25—Presidential aide Harold E. Stassen said today he will drop his one-man "dump Nixon" drive in the event President Eisenhower says in unmistakable terms that he wants Vice President Richard M. Nixon as his running mate.

Stassen made this statement to reporters at the end of a politically stormy day during which:

1—He bluntly accused **Republican National Chairman** Leonard W. Hall of trying to bar the door to the vice presi**dential nomination to all ex**cept Nixon.

2—He declared that Nixon, in confidential polls of public sentiment taken during the last four weeks, had emerged as the weakest of eight potential Republican candidates for the vice presidency.

3—He hinted broadly that prior to the Republican convention in San Francisco next month the President "will make his position clear." The statement implied that Stassen clung to a hope of support from the President although most politicos here regarded it as "whistling in the dark."

Stassen indicated that until Mr. Eisenhower spoke out more strongly for Nixon than he already has, then his anti-Nixon drive would continue despite the fact that not a single well-known political leader has come to his support.

Thus it appeared that Stas-
Continued on Page 7, Col. 2

3.7 Billion in Aid, Tito Ban Agreed Upon

WASHINGTON, July 25 (AP) — **Senate-House conferees, agreeing to split the difference on foreign aid funds, today approved an appropriation of $3,766,570,000 for this year's program.**

The conferees also accepted the Senate's ban on the use of any of the money for military aid to Yugoslavia.

The compromise figure on the appropriation for fiscal 1957 is $344,350,000 less than the Senate voted yesterday and $341,120,000 more than the House approved July 11—almost an even split.

It is also more than one billion dollars less than President Eisenhower originally requested to carry on his mutual security program through **the 12 months beginning July 1. He had asked for $4,859,000,000 in new funds.**

Disaster Off East Coast

Luxury Vessel Sinking --All Passengers Saved

The Andrea Doria was carrying 1134 passengers and 500 crewmen

'Andrea Doria' Carrying 1634 Hits 'Stockholm'

BOSTON, (Thursday), July 26 (AP)—All passengers aboard the Italian liner Andrea Doria, which collided with the Swedish motorship Stockholm, were rescued, the Coast Guard reported at 5 a. m. (EDT) this morning.

BOSTON, Mass., (Thursday) July 26 (AP) Two big ocean liners, the Andrea Doria and the Stockholm, collided in a dense Atlantic fog off the New England coast last night.

In a gigantic many-ship **rescue operation, at least** 875 passengers **had been rescued from the stricken** Andrea Doria before daylight.

At 2:30 a. m. (EDT)—**three hours after the col**lision—the Andrea Doria **had radioed the Coast Guard** it had "begun to abandon **ship.**"

Less than five minutes later, one of the rescue ships that raced to the scene radioed it had taken the first lifeboat load of survivors aboard. The vessel was the Cape Ann, a fruit ship.

There were no indication **as to casualties.**

Five hours after the collision, the Coast Guard disclosed 425 survivors of the Andrea Doria had beer picked up by the Stockholm, itself badly damaged.

The French liner Ile de France, one of the first ships to reach the area, had rescued

List of those known to be aboard vessels is on Page 5

200 survivors; the Cape Ann 200 persons, and the Army Transport Thomas 50.

A Coast Guard official said he thought survivors would be taken to New York.

The scene of the collision was 45 miles southeast of Nantucket Island off Massachusetts.

The Andrea Doria carried 1134 passengers and about 500 crewmen. The number on the Stockholm was not known, but it has a capacity of 364 passengers.

The passengers reportedly
Continued on Page 4, Col. 4

The Stockholm can carry 364 passengers

Steel Pact Near

New York Times Service

NEW YORK, Thursday, July 26—Industry and union negotiators worked into the early hours today to clear the way for the end of the nationwide steel strike this afternoon.

Continuing good progress indicated a three-year contract would be ready for approval of the United Steelworkers' Wage Policy Committee at 2 p. m. (EDT).

Industry sources anticipated steel price rises of from $8 to $10 a ton or more as the result of new package wage increases.

McKeon Case ---Drunk Test Results Told

By Robert S. Bird
New York Herald Tribune Service

PARRIS ISLAND, S. C., July 25 — A medical test on Staff Sergeant Matthew C. McKeon three-and-a-half hours after he had led a night march into a tidal stream where six recruits drowned showed a measurable quantity of alcohol present in his blood, a Navy Medical Corpsman testified today.

The sergeant admitted in a statement he made after his arrest that he may have had up to four drinks of vodka on the afternoon be-
Continued on Page 13, Col. 5

Treasurer Retreats in Knight Feud

By Jackson Doyle

SACRAMENTO, July 25 — State Treasurer **Charles G. Johnson backtracked considerably today on his charges that** Governor Goodwin J. **Knight had injected politics into the handling of State bank deposits.**

Johnson conceded that one of his claims, made in statements to reporters June 21, was wrong. He added he was sorry his other accusations were published and had embarrassed the Governor—but he didn't deny them.

At the same time, the 75-year-old Treasury head confirmed reports, first published by The Chronicle, that, for reasons of health, he will not appear at tomorrow's legislative hearing into his charges, which have been vehemently denied by the Governor.

Senator Ben Hulse (Rep-El Centro), chairman of the Joint Legislative Budget Committee which is investigating the controversy at Knight's request, said the hearing will go on as scheduled. And Knight's office said the Governor still wants the investigation.

Knight will testify, along with his finance director, John M. Peirce, and State Controller Robert C. Kirkwood.

Johnson, who has been ab-
Continued on Page 13, Col. 6

State Told It Was 'Robbed' On Road Aid

The State Highway Commission learned ruefully yesterday how California, apparently a sheep among political wolves, had been sheared of a good percentage of expected Federal highway aid.

The story came from Robert E. Reed, the commission's chief legal aide, at its meeting here yesterday.

Reed was explaining why California's share of the new Federal highway aid bill was 6.9 per cent based on population, 5.23 per cent based on area, but only 2.127 per cent based on post roads.

It is upon a combination of these three factors—population, area and post road mileage—that total Federal aid is computed.

Reed, who followed the bill through Congress in Washington last month, told of his
Continued on Page 13, Col. 4

House Bans Liquor on Airliners

WASHINGTON, July 25 (AP) The House of Representatives voted today to outlaw the airborne cocktail.

It passed by voice vote and sent to the Senate a bill forbidding airlines to "sell or otherwise furnish" alcoholic beverages to passengers on domestic flights.

Pact OK'd In Strike of Embalmers

An apparent settlement of the 64-day-old embalmers' strike was reached last night.

The agreement, reached last night by a secret session of the negotiating committees for the S. F. Funeral Directors' Association and the union, is to be submitted to their respective memberships today.

Its terms were not disclosed pending ratification.

The principal unsettled issue had been over the number of embalmings a year
Continued on Page 4, Col. 4

INDEX

Bridge	25
Chess	25
Comics	20
Crossword Puzzles	17, 29
Death Notices	13
Editorial Page	16
Finance, Business	11, 12
Food	8, 9
Movies, Drama	18, 19
Stocks (Up 0.96)	12
TV, Radio Logs	25
Weather	25
Women's News	10

REVOLT SPREADS OVER HUNGARY

WEATHER FORECAST

Bay Area: Fair, with clouds increasing tomorrow. Low temperatures Thursday, 44 to 47 degrees; high, 65 to 72.

Full Report, Page 35

San Francisco Chronicle

THE VOICE OF THE WEST

FINAL

92nd YEAR No. 299 CCCCAAA THURSDAY, OCTOBER 25, 1956 10 CENTS  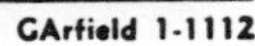 GArfield 1-1112

Turmoil in Red Satellites

Hungary Revolt Spreads, But Russ Are in Control

The Battle of Budapest Moves to Provinces--- Soviets Use Troops, Tanks

From Associated Press and New York Times

VIENNA, Oct. 25—Hungary's bloody rebellion against Soviet domination and Budapest's Communist leadership blazed through its second night and spread to the provinces today.

The government claimed early today to have "almost liquidated" the rebellion, but Budapest Radio acknowledged that fighting had raged into its third day despite the overpowering advantage of Soviet military might on the side of the Hungarian government.

The Interior Ministry appealed to the population to surrender all arms and ammunition "illegally" in its possession.

There were indications the fighting was spreading to the provinces but the Budapest regime—throwing Soviet tanks, planes and troops into the battle against workers and students—claimed the rebels were being systematically vanquished.

Moscow and East Berlin broadcasts also said the rebels were beaten.

Budapest was cut off entirely from the West. No direct telephone contact had been made since Tuesday.

Eye-witnesses returning to Austria from Hungary reported that hundreds have been killed in battle. Some said the dead might reach 350.

Austrian businessmen returning from Hungary told

Continued on Page 8, Col. 3

GOP Deceit Is Charged By Stevenson

NEW YORK, Oct. 24 (AP)—Adlai E. Stevenson said tonight the Republicans were waging "a campaign of deceit unmatched in United States politics."

"The Republicans have been treating the American people like so many children who can be put to sleep with a lullaby," the Democratic presidential nominee told a party rally at White Plains in neighboring Westchester county.

Stevenson said the Democrats have been partisan in the American political tradition, "but we haven't tried to deceive the people on the issues—on matters of life and death and of war and peace. The Republicans have."

Stevenson said the Democrats "told the people for the first time of the danger to us and to our children in continued H-bomb tests."

He said Republicans had

Continued on Page 6, Col. 2

Ike, Dulles Confer on Red Unrest

WASHINGTON, Oct. 24 (AP) President Eisenhower and Secretary of State John Foster Dulles discussed the unrest in Poland and Hungary and the Suez Canal situation in an hour-long conference today.

Dulles gave newsmen that information as he left the White House, but he declined to provide any detail or answer any questions.

Dulles said the session was "part of the normal kind of talks I have with the President almost every day." He added:

"We were particularly interested today in Poland and Hungary."

Women Quiz President on Draft, Bomb

WASHINGTON, Oct. 24 (AP)—President Eisenhower today called the hydrogen bomb a great deterrent to war—a weapon, he said, which tells any potential enemy it would be "suicidal" to attack America.

The President set forth his views in responding to questions put by seven women on a nation-wide TV-radio program sponsored by the Republican Congressional Campaign Committee.

The committee said the women it chose to appear on the program were "representative of all walks of life and various sections of the country."

In discussing the H-bomb, Mr. Eisenhower did not touch on the proposal by Adlai

Continued on Page 6, Col. 4

New Polish Outbreak Is Quelled

From United Press and New York Times

WARSAW, Poland, Oct. 24—Thousands of young people demonstrated in the streets of Warsaw tonight in an outburst of feeling against the Soviet Union and of sympathy with the Hungarians trying to throw off the Soviet yoke.

For a while it appeared that the demonstrations might get out of hand. But swift handling of the situation by Polish internal security troops prevented an explosion of violence.

For about two hours the youngsters marched around the center of Warsaw shouting "Rokossovsky to Moscow" and other anti-Soviet slogans.

The demonstrators were mostly students but they appeared to include some young workers as well.

PARTY HEADQUARTERS

At one point, several hundred of them pushed into the headquarters building of the Polish United Workers (Communist) party chanting against Marshal Konstantin Rokossovsky and for Wladyslaw Gomulka, the party's new First Secretary.

Gomulka defied Soviet demands to keep Rokossovsky on the Polish politburo in last Sunday's Central Committee election. He is still Defense Minister, a post to which he was assigned by Josef Stalin in 1949.

Earlier Gomulka told the Polish people that Soviet troops would stay in Poland as long as there are North Atlantic Treaty Organization bases in West Germany. He addressed a crowd of 200,000 outside the Palace of Culture.

Both Gomulka and Premier Josef Cyrankiewicz insisted the Russian soldiers would be

Continued on Page 8, Col. 1

Near-Record Bay Chill; Low in S. F. Was 49

Wintry weather laid a heavy hand on most of Northern California yesterday, sending themometers to the lowest points in Weather Bureau history for this time of year.

San Francisco had one of the chilliest October 24 mornings on record yesterday. Low point, just before dawn, was 49 one degree above the all-time low for the day set in 1881 and tied in 1949.

The lowest October 24 on record was reported yesterday in Redwood City, where the mercury dipped to 36. Woodacre in Marin county chalked up an early morning 29 degrees, which officials said was "not too unusual."

Oakland had an all-time low of 40 and in Orinda the temperature dropped to 30 degrees. Touches of frost were reported throughout the East Bay.

Temperatures are expected to rise slightly today.

Reno reported a low of 19 degrees yesterday; Susanville had 21 and Mt. Shasta, 27.

Crackdown On Skid Row Liquor Sales

Frank Fullenwider, area administrator of the State liquor department, announced yesterday tough, new enforcement policy against the sale of liquor to drunks on Skid Row.

The policy is also being extended, he said, to two so-called problem areas at 16th and Mission streets and on the Embarcadero between Howard and Mission streets.

State agents have just completed a week-long investigation in Skid Row, and in these two districts, Fullenwider said, and 13 arrests have been made for sales to "obviously intoxicated" persons by bartenders and package store operators.

15-DAY SUSPENSION

Accusations are now being filed against the offenders, he added. The penalty is a 15-day license suspension for proven first offenders, he said.

Fullenwider noted that no new liquor licenses have been issued for the Third and Howard street district (Skid Row) for a year and a half.

Now, he said, he is going to recommend against issuing any licenses in the two new problem areas.

The local liquor chief said the action by his department was part of a three-pronged attack on the Skid Row problem in San Francisco.

POLICE ACTION

He declared the crackdown on sales to intoxicated patrons and the halting of liquor licenses in "problem areas" will implement Police Chief Frank Ahern's policy of sending drunks to the County Jail.

"The police department, the courts and the rehabilitation commission are doing their

Continued on Page 4, Col. 1

2 Planes Hit Over Homes; Seven Killed

MIDLAND, Texas, Oct. 24 (AP)—An Air Force jet exploded and plunged into a Midland home today after colliding with a civilian plane.

The bodies of seven persons—two from the jet and five from the private plane—dropped from the skies with the debris of the planes. No one was injured on the ground.

The jet wreckage plunged into the home of a family that was not at home.

The engine of the civilian plane crashed into the unoccupied kitchen of another home.

The body of one occupant of the private plane crashed through the roof of another home and lodged in the bathtub.

Webb Air Force Base reported that one of the airmen in the T-33 ejected himself from the plane, but his chute failed to open.

Babies in Polio Test

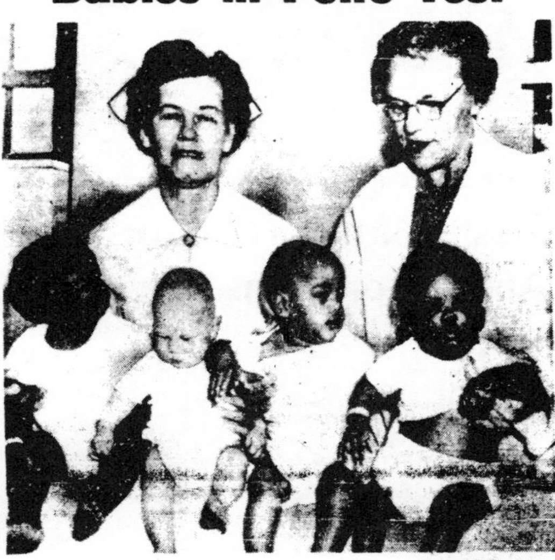

A. P. Wirephoto

Supervising nurse Florence Darlson and Dr. Agnes Flack, with four of the babies being fed live polio virus in a test at New Jersey State Reformatory for Women

Feud Out In Open as Bakers Meet

By Jack Howard

The 25th annual convention of the Bakery and Confectionery Workers' Union opened here yesterday and promptly became involved in the bitterness that has marked preconvention sessions.

Everyone, from the priest who gave the invocation to the knots of policemen on duty in the hallways, attested to the factional feud that promises to wrack the convention.

In his opening address President James Cross touched briefly on the "unfortunate incident" that resulted in criminal charges against him and three of his aides.

His remarks brought one of his accusers, Joseph Kane, of New York, to his feet in an attempt to get a "point of special privilege" over to the delegates.

He was gavelled and booed into silence.

ELECTION CHANGE

All the convention's afternoon session was taken up with one of its most controversial issues.

After two hours of impassioned debate, delegates on a roll call vote of 4966 to 560 amended the constitution to eliminate election of officers by membership referendum.

Effective with the election tomorrow, new officers will be elected to five-year terms by majority vote of the 649 delegates, rather than by a vote of the 185,000 members.

Former President Harry S. Truman will speak to the convention at 11:30 a. m. today.

Continued on Page 4, Col. 6

Prison Experiment

Live Polio Virus Fed to Infants

CLINTON, N. J., Oct. 24 (AP)—Newborn infants are being fed live polio virus in their bottles at the State Reformatory for Women here to trace their hereditary resistance to the crippling disease.

The tests, the first ever given children under 6 months of age, are being conducted on children of inmates by the Lederle Laboratories of the American Cyanamid Co.

None of the children has contracted the disease.

Some 34 mothers volunteered their children to be given the live virus, mixed in their formula by an eyedropper.

The studies are trying to determine the active antibody response of infants while still possessing immunity inherited from their mothers.

Lederle announced that it has given live virus to 800 volunteers over the last six years. Lederle is trying to

Continued on Page 4, Col. 5

Capt. English Again Sick, May Retire

Police Captain James English, demoted as chief of inspectors last week, was ordered to bed by his doctor yesterday.

The physician, Dr. Emil D. Torres, said Captain English was suffering from pectoral neuritis.

Word of Captain English's illness lent fuel to rumors that he plans to seek retirement.

These reports have been common since Police Chief Frank Ahern ousted English from command of the detective division of the department and banished him to the command of remote Taraval station.

AHERN 'DISSATISFIED'

Chief Ahern said he was "dissatisfied" with the Bureau of Inspectors, which English had commanded for seven years.

Captain English could not be reached for comment on the retirement reports.

His wife said that he was in bed under doctor's orders and could not answer the telephone.

Captain English suffered a heart attack on June 25 and

Continued on Page 4, Col. 4

INDEX

Bridge 26
Chess 26
Comics 6H
Crossword Puzzles .. 25, 39
Death Notices 35
Editorial Page 24
Finance, Business .. 19-21
Food 13-18
Horoscope 39
Hulburd 40
Movies, Drama ... 26, 27
Panorama 25
Shipping News 35
Stocks (Down 2.38) 20
TV, Radio Logs 28
Vital Statistics 35
Weather 35
Women's News 9-12

WEATHER FORECAST
Bay Area: Rain today, slackening tonight and tomorrow. Winds to 45 m.p.h. this morning, decreasing in afternoon. Low temperature Tuesday, 50 to 55; high, near 60.
Full Report on Page 37

92nd YEAR No. 304 CCCCAAA TUESDAY, OCTOBER 30, 1956 10 CENTS GArfield 1-1112

BIG EGYPT BATTLE

Cairo Reports Israelis In Clash Near Suez

Attack Sets Off Wide War Scare

From United Press and Associated Press

JERUSALEM, Israeli sector, (Tuesday) Oct. 30—Israeli forces lunged across Egypt's Sinai desert today and were reported within 12 miles of the Suez canal. Egyptian Army headquarters in Cairo declared the invaders were being "liquidated."

The Cairo announcement said Egyptian troops inflicted "heavy casualties" on the Israeli forces. It gave no casualty figures in what it reported was night-long fighting.

Israeli troops struck into Egypt yesterday and swept about 120 miles, according to Israeli reports.

The swift attack set off a world-wide war scare.

An Israeli communique said the raiders attacked the bases of Egyptian "suicide commandos" in their sweep through the Sinai desert along the edge of the Et Tih plateau. It said the forces jumped off from the border near the Egyptian town of El Kuntilla.

The Israeli communique said the invading force had dug in west of the major road junction of Nekhl, half way to Suez.

The Cairo announcement was the first indication from the Egyptian side that fighting had taken place. Earlier, military spokesmen admitted Israelis had crossed the fron-

Continued on Page 6, Col. 4

Adlai: Attack Belies Ike's 'Good News'

BOSTON, Oct. 29 (AP)—Adlai Stevenson said tonight that developments in the Israeli-Egyptian conflict show that President Eisenhower's reports of "good news" from that area "have been tragically less than the truth."

In a speech at Mechanics Hall, which was broadcast and telecast nationally, Stevenson said it was hard "to speak about today's ominous and confusing developments in the Middle East."

"But I must say this," Stevenson said, "and it is only to repeat what I have been saying throughout the campaign:

"The Government in Washington has been telling us that all is well in the world, that there is peace, that there is—as the President announced only a few days ago—'good news' from the Middle East.

"These reassurances — as today's news confirms—have

Continued on Page 10, Col. 6

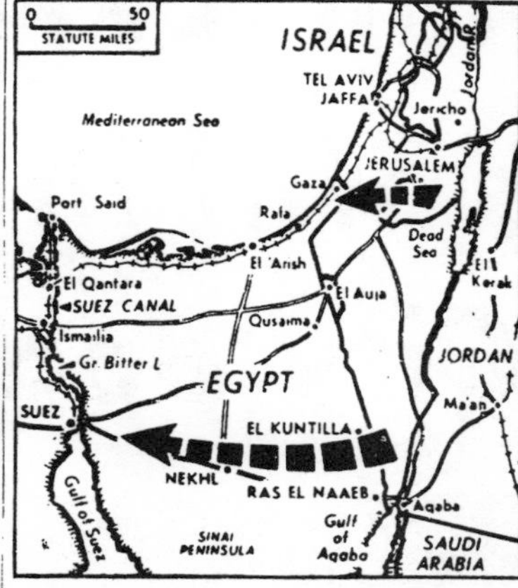

A. P. Wirephoto

Large arrow shows advance of Israeli troops. Arrow to north shows where fighting flared on Gaza Strip.

Ike Pledges U. S. Role in New Crisis

From Associated Press and New York Herald Tribune

WASHINGTON, Oct. 29 President Eisenhower, in a statement on the Israeli invasion of Egypt, tonight said that the United States would live up to its pledge to assist the victim of any aggression in the Middle East.

The statement, coming after a high-level conference at the White House tonight, said:

"The question of whether and when the President will call a special session of Congress will be decided in the light of developing events."

The President said the U. S., acting under the tri-

Continued on Page 6, Col. 1

Ike Carries Campaign Into South

New York Herald Tribune Service

WASHINGTON, Oct. 29 President Eisenhower, fighting to crack the "solid South" again, made a one-day foray into Florida and Virginia today and, in Miami, appealed for "intelligent understanding" of the problems of desegregation.

The President nowhere mentioned the Supreme Court's decision banning racial segregation in the public schools. He discussed the civil rights question only in passing and only in the broadest terms. He urged that it be handled justly and in a nonpartisan spirit and to the greatest extent possible by State and local governments instead of by the Federal Government.

In his speeches at the airports in Miami, Jacksonville and Richmond he based his appeal for Southern votes chiefly on the administration's record of ending the Korean war, keeping the

Continued on Page 20, Col. 5

4 Airmen Die in Carrier Training

WASHINGTON, Oct. 29 (AP) The Navy today reported the deaths of four airmen in the crash of an aircraft operating from the carrier Randolph off the coast of Greece Saturday night.

A. P. Wirephoto

JAMES HAGERTY AND PRESIDENT EISENHOWER
Press secretary told President of Israeli push into Egypt

Mayor Says He Okayed Cop Shakeup in Advance

By Charles Raudebaugh

Police Chief Frank Ahern's demotion of Captain James L. English as chief of inspectors had the approval in advance of Mayor George Christopher, it was learned yesterday.

"The Chief said he wanted to transfer English and asked if I had any objection," Christopher, vacationing in Honolulu, declared.

"I told him my policy was to appoint the chief and let him run the Police Department. If he, as chief, thought English should be removed, that was up to him."

The Mayor said that English's transfer, and the subsequent reorganization of the bureau of inspectors under Captain Daniel McKlem, "all meets with my approval."

"If I'm going to have a Chief of Police, I'm not going to tie his hands and say he can't remove or transfer any

Continued on Page 14, Col. 1

Russ Troops Pulling Out Of Budapest

VIENNA, Oct. 29 (AP)—The Hungarian army high command announced tonight that Russian troops have begun to withdraw from Budapest.

The battle of Budapest appeared to be ending, but rebellion still blazed in the countryside.

About 100 Hungarian rebels and some army deserters held out against Russian tanks in a maze of tenements in Budapest's poorest district.

They were the last rebels still fighting in Budapest on the seventh day of the revolt.

Budapest radio carried an announcement by the Hungarian army command saying the defiant young rebels in the capital will surrender their arms by 9 a.m. tomorrow as the Russians carry out their evacuation.

This followed earlier word from Premier Imre Nagy's government that the rebels had agreed to turn in their arms and the Russians would leave within 24 hours.

TROOPS REPLACED

But the high command announcement said Hungarian troops were already replacing Russian troops in the industrial section of Southern Budapest.

The high command added that replacement of Soviet troops by Hungarians and "unmolested withdrawal from Budapest" of the Russians were conditions for additional evacuation of Russian forces.

"Withdrawal of Soviet troops will be continued throughout tomorrow in agreement with the pact with the rebels," the high command declared.

Revolutionaries in control of the countryside urged that the rebels disregard the agreement in Budapest.

Nagy's shaky regime was trying desperately to restore order and get some control over the country.

Nagy was being assailed by the rebel radio at Gyoer, a stronghold in Northwest Hungary, as "a tool of the

Continued on Page 4, Col. 1

Storm Moves In; More Rain Due

A storm moved in on San Francisco from the Gulf of Alaska yesterday, bringing rain and winds expected to last through tonight.

In the Bay Area, the rains are expected to taper off to scattered showers tonight and tomorrow, and little change in temperature is expected.

The Chronicle Recommends:

For the guidance of inquiring voters, The Chronicle offers the following as its judgment on candidates and propositions at the November 6 election:

PRESIDENT AND VICE PRESIDENT
Dwight D. Eisenhower* **Richard M. Nixon***

U. S. SENATOR
Thomas H. Kuchel*

U. S. REPRESENTATIVE
Fourth District—**William S. Mailliard***
Fifth District—**John F. Shelley*** **(unopposed)**

MEMBER OF THE ASSEMBLY
Nineteenth District—**William Ebert**
Twentieth District—**Thomas A. Maloney***
Twenty-first District—**Caspar W. Weinberger*** **(unopposed)**
Twenty-second District—**John A. Busterud**
Twenty-fourth District—**Irv Shore**

SUPERIOR JUDGE
Raymond J. Arata*
(Give a "Yes" vote to State Supreme Court Justice Marshall F. McComb, Appellate Justice Herbert C. Kaufman, San Francisco Board of Education members Mrs. Lawrence Draper Jr. and Joseph A. Moore Jr.)

STATE PROPOSITIONS

		Vote
No. 1	(Veterans Loan Bonds)	Yes
No. 2	(State School Bonds)	Yes
No. 3	(State Building Bonds)	Yes
No. 4	(Oil and Gas Conservation)	Yes
No. 5	(Eliminate Food in Bars)	Yes
No. 6	(Church Parking Lot Exemption)	Yes
No. 7	(Change the name Assemblyman to Representative)	No
No. 8	(Budget Sessions)	No
No. 9	(County Boroughs)	No
No. 10	(Employment of Private Architects and Engineers	No
No. 11	(County Charters)	Yes
No. 12	(State Indebtedness)	No
No. 13	(Repeal Alien Land Act)	Yes
No. 14	(Legislative Employees)	Yes
No. 15	(Mutual Water Companies)	Yes
No. 16	(Civil & Criminal Appeals)	Yes
No. 17	(Judiciary)	Yes
No. 18	(Non-Lawyer Judges)	No
No. 19	(State Boundaries)	Yes

CITY PROPOSITIONS

A	(School Bonds)	Yes
B	(Airport Bonds)	Yes
C	(Expenditures by Chief of Police)	Yes
D	($25 Increase in Pension Allowances)	Yes
E	(5-Day Week for Carmen)	Yes
F	(Increased Fire Department Pensions)	Yes
G	(Budget Improvements on Deficit Utilities)	Yes
H	(25 Additional Police Inspectors)	Yes

* **Indicates incumbent.**
(For Recommendations on other Candidates for Congress and the Legislature, see Page 2.)

Donald Cameron Quits PUC in Huff

One of the long-time Public Utilities commissioners whom Mayor George Christopher failed to root out of City Hall earlier this year resigned yesterday in an evident huff.

Donald A. Cameron's sudden departure will give Mayor Christopher majority control of the city's most important policy-making commission for the first time.

Cameron, a real estate and insurance man, was among three members of the five-man commission serving out terms to which they were appointed by former Mayor Elmer E. Robinson.

Mayor Christopher told The Chronicle by telephone from Honolulu where he is vacationing that "perhaps Mr. Cameron presumed he would not be reappointed."

"In this presumption," the Mayor said, "he was correct. But I don't know why he chose this inopportune time—while I am out of the city—to resign.

"The purpose of my admin-

Continued on Page 2, Col. 4

INDEX

Bridge	30
Chess	30
Comics	6H
Crossword Puzzles	27, 41
Death Notices	37
Editorial Page	26
Finance	21-23
Horoscope	41
Hulburd	42
Movies, Drama	29
Shipping News	37
Stocks (Up 0.85)	22
TV, Radio Logs	30
Weather	37
Women's News	19, 20

FINAL ELECTION EXTRA

WEATHER FORECAST
Bay Area: Clear today and tomorrow except for local morning fog. Little temperature change. High Wednesday, 68 to 74; low, 44 to 50.
Full Report on Page 29

San Francisco Chronicle
THE VOICE OF THE WEST

Chronicle Want Ads
Will Sell Anything
GA 1-1112

92nd YEAR No. 312 CCCCAAA WEDNESDAY, NOVEMBER 7, 1956 10 CENTS GArfield 1-1112

IKE LANDSLIDE

Proposition 4 Trounced; Congress Still in Doubt; Kuchel, City Bonds Win

Middle East Crisis

French, British Seize Suez, Then Order Cease-Fire

LONDON, (Wednesday), Nov. 7 (AP) — The British and French seized control of the Suez Canal zone today and ordered their troops to cease fire in the advanced positions they have won.

Just before the deadline the Allied Command announced the capture of Ismailia.

It is the midway control city on the 103-mile Canal and sight of great British military installations of the former occupation era.

The cease-fire was declared in effect by the British and French at 2 a. m. Egyptian time (midnight London, 4 p.m. Tuesday (PST).

The cease-fire hour set by Britain and France passed without official word from Cairo that Egypt had accepted.

CAIRO BROADCAST

Cairo radio broadcast the U. N. announcement that Britain and France had agreed to end the fighting. It noted Egypt had accepted the first U. N. order for a cease-fire on certain conditions.

Egyption officials would not say if their forces in the field had stopped fighting, but gave indications of fighting on, apparently in the belief that all the conditions would not be met.

The capture of Ismailia gave British and French forces the northern half of the waterway after two days of battle.

Port Said, the northern terminal, was overrun yesterday.

The French said the cease-fire was possible because the British and French have Continued on Page 11, Col. 3

State Joins Ike Parade; Kuchel Wins

By Earl C. Behrens
Political Editor

President Eisenhower won California in yesterday's general election by a margin which is mounting as additional returns poured in early this morning from all parts of the State.

U. S. Senator Thomas H. Kuchel, Republican, who succeeded Vice President Richard M. Nixon in the Senate in 1952, was increasing his lead over Democratic State Senator Richard Richards of Los Angeles as additional returns were tabulated.

The Eisenhower margin over Stevenson was greatly Continued on Page D, Col. 1

PRESIDENT EISENHOWER AND VICE PRESIDENT NIXON
Shoulder to shoulder, they answered a victory ovation

Late U. S. Returns

President Wins In 41 States

Associated Press returns from 104,250 of the country's 154,844 voting units showed the popular vote:

Eisenhower 25,076,662

Stevenson 18,341,406

Eisenhower was leading in 41 States with 457 electoral votes.

Stevenson was leading in 7 States with 74 electoral votes.

☆ ☆ ☆

By Associated Press

Dwight D. Eisenhower won re-election to the presidency early today by the massive, overwhelming vote of a Nation that heard and heeded his pledge of peace and prosperity.

Beneath an avalanche of Eisenhower victory votes were buried the presidential ambitions of Democratic presidential nominee Adlai E. Stevenson — now and probably for all time.

Stevenson conceded at 1:20 A. M. (EST) a defeat that had been obvious and inevitable from the moment the ballot counting from yesterday's election got under way.

Congress Still in Doubt

Control of Congress, now in Democratic hands, still dangled in tantalizing doubt.

But for President Eisenhower that was a clear-cut, resounding vote of confidence from the American electorate—and one of the most crushing landslide victories in the Nation's political history.

The soldier President became the first Republican to win a second term since William McKinley did it in 1900—56 years ago.

This was the box score at 1:55 a. m., with returns in from 76,373 of the Nation's 154,844 polling places:

Eisenhower 19,000,368 votes; leading in 42 States Continued on Page B, Co. 5

State Demos May Gain 3 in House

By David Perlman

California Democrats piled up surprising strength in Congressional races throughout the State early this morning, and threatened to capture at least three Republican seats.

The race for a fourth House post was so close that it may be up for grabs until the last vote is counted.

Democrats held what appeared to be commanding leads in the Sixth and Eleventh Districts; they were moving well ahead in the Twenty-ninth, and fought over the thinnest of edges in the First.

San Francisco's only Congressional contest, however, was an overwhelming victory Continued on Page D, Col. 4

Prop. 4 Rejected by 3-1 Margin

Proposition 4, the oil conservation act, was swamped by a margin of more than three to one yesterday.

A big "no" vote started piling up in the very first returns, and the trend never changed.

Early this morning the count stood at 701,055 votes against the proposition and only 217,655 for it, with nearly half the State's precincts reporting.

The voters whipped the measure after six months of bitter propaganda from both sides and after the most fantastically expensive State ballot campaign in California history.

Warring factions in the oil industry spent a total of Continued on Page 8, Col. 1

How S. F. Voted

- San Francisco voters gave President Eisenhower a majority of approximately 10,000 votes over Stevenson.
- The $27 million school bond issue, which needed only a two-thirds vote, was passed by better than five to one.
- The $25 million airport bond issue passed better than four to one.
- The five-day week for Municipal Railway Employees was approved almost three to one.
- Municipal Judge Raymond Arata overwhelmed Municipal Judge Alvin E. Weinberger for Superior Court No. 9.
- Republican Thomas Kuchel lead Democrat Richard Richards for the U. S. Senate by less than 10,000 votes.
- Representative William S. Mailliard (Rep) defeated Democratic challenger James Quigley.
- Democratic Incumbent Charles Meyers won handily over William Ebert in the 19th Assembly District.
- Republican Incumbent Thomas Maloney appeared defeated in the 20th Assembly District by Phillip Burton.
- Republican John A. Busterud won over Democratic Incumbent Bernard R. Brady in the 22nd Assembly District.
- Democratic Incumbent Edward M. Gaffney beat Irv Shore in the 24th Assembly District by a big majority.

Demos Have Small Lead In Congress

New York Herald Tribune Service

Democrats took the narrowest of leads late Tuesday night in the contest for control of the Senate, but the impact of President Eisenhower's landslide held the issue in doubt.

In the House, Republicans, scored surprising gains in widely scattered areas, but there, too, the final outcome could not be safely forecast.

In 16 nip-and-tuck Senate races, Democrats led in Ohio, Illinois, Pennsylvania, Idaho and South Dakota, seats now held by Republicans. Republicans led in the contest for one Kentucky seat, in West Virginia and Nevada, all now Democratic.

But the Democrats, who Continued on Page 6, Col. 1

THE CHRONICLE INDEX

Bridge	22	Hulburd	34
Chess	22	Movies, Drama	20, 21
Comics	6H	Panorama	19
Crossword Puzzles	19, 33	Shipping News	29
Death Notices	29	TV, Radio Logs	22
Editorial Page	18	Vital Statistics	29
Horoscope	33	Women's News	13, 15

U.S. PARATROOPS TAKE SCHOOL

WEATHER FORECAST
Bay Area: Fair today and Thursday, with morning fog. High temperatures Wednesday, 68 to 76; low, 52 to 57. Afternoon winds.
Full Report on Page 31

San Francisco Chronicle
THE VOICE OF THE WEST

FINAL

93d YEAR No. 268 CCCCAAA WEDNESDAY, SEPTEMBER 25, 1957 10 CENTS GArfield 1-1112

U.N. Puts Off Red China Decision

UNITED NATIONS, N. Y., Sept. 24 (AP)—The United Nations General Assembly decided tonight to shelve for another year the question of seating Red China in the United Nations.

By a vote of 47 in favor, 27 against and seven abstentions, the Assembly adopted a United States proposal.

Voting against shelving the question were the Soviet bloc, India, the Scandinavians, and several Asian and Middle East nations, including Syria and Egypt.

Egypt Seizes Israeli Vessel

PORT SAID, Egypt, Sept. 24 (Reuters)—Egyptian Coastguards today captured an Israeli fishing boat

Living Cost In Nation At New High

The cost of living climbed to a record high throughout the Nation in August, the Government reported in Washington yesterday.

Nationally it was the 12th consecutive monthly advance, but in San Francisco the average level of food prices remained stable.

Locally the U. S. Department of Labor's Bureau of Labor Statistics announced that its index of food prices for August was 118.2, the same as in June and July.

Max D. Kossoris, Western regional director of the bureau, said, however, that this level is still the highest ever recorded for the city—3 per cent higher than a year ago and a little more than 17 per cent above the mid-1950 index.

ALL-TIME HIGH

In Washington the Labor Department announced its consumer price index — a monthly sampling of prices for 300 goods and services across the Nation—stood at an all-time high of 121, 3.6 per cent higher than a year ago.

Food prices rose four-tenths of 1 per cent during the month; housing costs were up two-tenths of 1 per cent, but the prices of non-food com-

See Page 6, Col. 7

AEC Reports H-Bomb Test By Russia

New York Times Service

WASHINGTON, Sept. 24 — The Atomic Energy Commission announced today that the Soviet Union set off a large nuclear explosion late last month north of the Arctic Circle.

The AEC said the force of the explosion was measured in megatons — or millions of tons of TNT. While not stated by the AEC, the strength would indicate a hydrogen bomb.

The yield of hydrogen bombs is measured in megatons, while that of atomic bombs is customarily measured in kilotons, or thousands of tons of TNT.

The location of the explosion raised the possibility that the test was conducted in connection with Soviet naval maneuvers in the Barents sea.

The AEC announcement was issued shortly after the Soviet news agency Tass said over Radio Moscow that, as part of the training of Soviet military forces, atomic and hydrogen weapons had been exploded in the Soviet Union.

The Russian explosion was the first to be announced by the AEC as taking place "north of the Arctic Circle."

The latest detonation was the third in the Soviet Union since August 22 to be announced by the AEC.

Ike Tells Why Army Sent To Little Rock

Negroes May Return to School Today

From Associated Press and United Press

LITTLE ROCK, Ark., Sept. 24 — Armed paratroopers equipped with live ammunition rolled into Little Rock tonight representing President Eisenhower's historic decision to back a Federal Court integration order with force.

Hundreds of Little Rock citizens watched quietly as the force of about 500 men of the famed 101st Airborne Division split, one group going to the Central High School grounds and another to the National Guard Armory.

NEGRO TROOPS

A number of Negroes were among the paratroopers.

Late tonight a second group of 500 paratroopers arrived at Little Rock Air Force Base. The new arrivals also separated into two groups and proceeded to the school and the armory.

With the arrival of the Federal troops it appeared that the nine Negro students would try to return to Central High again tomorrow.

The paratroops arrived by plane from Fort Campbell, Ky. An officer called the City Hall and asked for permission to enter the city, which was granted.

MOBILIZATION

A few minutes later Adjutant General Sherman T.

See Page 5, Col. 1

WHO
will build Arkansas
if her own people do not?

A.P. Wirephoto

Armed paratroops, called to enforce integration in Little Rock, rolled to the strife-torn city past a "public service" question to the people of Arkansas.

Guard Federalized; City Told to Obey

The Crisis in Brief

- **President Eisenhower sent U. S. troops into Little Rock and ordered the Arkansas National Guard into Federal service.**
- **He told the Nation on television and radio that "extremists" had brought Little Rock close to "anarchy."**
- **A thousand paratroopers of the 101st Airborne Division arrived in Little Rock and took up "battle stations" around Central High School.**
- **The nine Negro students are expected to attempt to attend classes again Wednesday.**

☆ ☆ ☆

From Associated Press and United Press

WASHINGTON, Sept. 24—President Eisenhower ordered 1000 Federal troops into Little Rock today to force compliance with court-ordered integration of the city's Central High School.

Mr. Eisenhower authorized use of the regular Army troops in an order that also called the Arkansas National Guard into Federal service to quell further riotous obstructions of the school desegregation order handed down by Federal Judge Ronald Davies at Little Rock.

The President, telling the Nation why he sped Federal troops to Little Rock, said tonight that "mob rule" there menaced the very safety of the United States and the free world.

That is so, he said in a TV-radio broadcast from the White House, because "gloating" Communists abroad are using the school integration riots to misrepresent the U. S., and undermine its prestige and influence around the globe.

For the Eisenhower text, see Page 9

Solemnly, he called upon Arkansas citizens to help bring an end to all interference with legal processes, because:

"Mob rule cannot be allowed to override the decisions of the courts."

U. S. TROOPS

Even as he spoke, the first of 1000 troops of the 101st Airborne Division were entering Little Rock, but the President pledged:

"If resistance to the Federal Court orders ceases at once, the further presence of Federal troops will be unnecessary . . ."

The president stressed that the troops were not sent to relieve local authorities of their duty to preserve order, nor to act as school administrators. Their only purpose, he said, is to prevent further interference with Judge Davies' order that Negroes be

See Page 4, Col. 1

New Hoffa Challenge By Senators

WASHINGTON, Sept. 24 (AP)—Senate investigators today challenged the credentials of James R. Hoffa and 29 other delegates to the forthcoming Teamsters Union convention at which Hoffa hopes to win the post of president.

The challenge came from Robert F. Kennedy, chief counsel of the special Senate Rackets Committee, and Senator Karl Mundt (Rep-S.D.), a member of the committee.

Kennedy and Mundt contended the election of Hoffa, Midwest chief of the teamsters, and other delegates from Locals 299 and 337 in Detroit, was not conducted in accordance with the union's constitution.

This brought an angry pro-

See Page 6, Col. 5

INDEX

Bridge	24
Comics	6H
Crossword Puzzles	21, 35
Death Notices	24
Editorial Page	20
Finance, Business	15 to 17
Movies, Drama	22 to 24
Shipping News	31
TV, Radio Logs	17
Weather	31
Women's News	12 to 14

Flu Knocks Out Half of High School

Nearly half the students in the Pleasant Hill High School near Walnut Creek were home ill yesterday as an outbreak of what was believed to be Asian flu swept through the Mt. Diablo Unified School District in Contra Costa county.

Principal Arthur C. Bloom said 720 of the 1522 students at Pleasant Hill High were absent yesterday. The school's Friday night football game with St. Mary's High of Berkeley was postponed and the school play called off.

At Mt. Diablo High near Concord, 877 of the 2500 students were out, while at Pacifica High in West Pittsburg, 180 of the 600 students were home ill.

While the absentee list was running about 41 per cent of the enrollment in the district's high schools, only 18 per cent of the junior high students and 9 per cent of the elementary grade pupils were not in school.

Asian flu also hit the University of California.

Eighty students were in bed at Cowell Memorial Hospital in Berkeley and an even larger number were being treated in residences.

In San Jose an outbreak of an illness as yet undiagnosed hit more than 1000 junior and senior high students.

Cities League Hears Blasts At Freeways

By James Benet

A temporary halt to all freeway construction in metropolitan areas was proposed yesterday, capping widespread criticism of the freeway program at the meeting of the League of California Cities here.

The proposal was made by John S. Burd Jr., a member of the Berkeley City Planning Commission, who declared:

"The State Highway Commission, having run out of immediate projects, is eyeing our tree-shaded streets.

"If politicians knew how the people feel, I seriously doubt that they would continue to support the present freeway program."

At another of the panel sessions which the league conducted yesterday, San Francisco Park Department Manager Max G. Funke called

See Page 6, Col. 6

Sixth Survivor Of Ship Found

From Associated Press and United Press

The Coast Guard announced in New York yesterday that a sixth survivor from the hurricane-wrecked German sailing ship Pamir was rescued from a drifting lifeboat.

Davis Accused of Helping Chessman Smuggle Book

George T. Davis, Caryl Chessman's lawyer, was accused yesterday of conniving in the mysterious process by which the convicted rapist's newest book was smuggled out of San Quentin prison.

The first public allegation that Davis had a role in the affair was made in Marin county Superior Court by District Attorney William O. Weissich.

He also said Davis is to receive a total of up to $50,000 —paid largely out of royalties on the book—for defending Chessman in his current Los Angeles attempt to escape the gas chamber.

Weissich made his accusation during a court hearing over the refusal of Rosalie

See Page 2, Col. 2

Judge of NRA Fame Dies

RUTHERFORD, N. J., Sept. 24 (AP)—Retired U. S. District Court Judge Guy L. Fake, who declared the National Recovery Act (NRA) unconstitutional in 1935, died last night at his home. He was 77.

Argentine Unions Set Big Strike

BUENOS AIRES, Sept. 24 (UP)—Sixty-two unions today set a general strike for Friday.

RUSS SATELLITE SIGHTED OVER S.F.

San Francisco Chronicle
THE VOICE OF THE WEST
FINAL EXTRA
93d YEAR No. 278 CCCCAAA SATURDAY, OCTOBER 5, 1957 10 CENTS

GArfield 1-1112

Russ 'Moon' Circling Globe--18,000 mph

Teamsters' Convention

Hoffa Is Elected; Probers Subpoena Union's Records

MIAMI BEACH, Fla., Oct. 4 (UP)—James R. Hoffa won the presidency of the Teamsters Union today in a landslide victory that immediately drew an official investigation by a Senate committee and threat of expulsion from the AFL-CIO.

Hoffa polled 1208 votes in his first ballot victory. William A. Lee had 313 and Thomas J. Haggerty 140 in the race for leadership of the 1.4 million-member union.

Before the final ballots were counted, the Senate Labor Rackets Committee stepped in with a subpoena.

The committee, charging that more than 50 per cent of the 1758 convention delegates were seated illegally, demanded the minutes and records of the Teamsters Credential Committee.

Frank Brewster, president of the 375,000-member Western Conference of Teamsters, was defeated as a vice president of the international union. He was replaced by George E. Mock, a Hoffa-backed candidate.

Brewster told the convention "it's a little rough" after 37 years in the union to withdraw, but "I can't beat the machine."

In Washington, AFL-CIO officials said the teamsters had voted themselves right out of the Federation by electing Hoffa their chief. The officials said they were confident the AFL-CIO Executive Council would recommend expulsion of the Teamsters at an October 24 meeting in New York.

AFL-CIO DEFIED

But Teamsters Secretary-Treasurer John F. English, who nominated Hoffa, mounted the stage immediately afterward to defy the AFL-CIO. The 68-year-old official said the Teamsters would ask for a one-year period to clean up the union instead of the 30 days they were granted by the federation.

"If they don't like that, we

See Page 4, Col. 7

Surviving Quints Have First Food

TOULON, France, Oct. 4 (UP) The two survivors of quintuplets born Wednesday took their first nourishment today —a bit of sugar and water. They also moved their arms and legs for the first time.

As the hours passed, doctors were more optimistic about chances for the two, Roland and Michele Christofle. They weighed about two pounds each at birth. A boy and two other girls died within 12 hours of birth.

Egypt Vessel's Seizure Reported

ATHENS, Oct. 4 (UP)—The Israel navy has seized a 1000-ton Egyptian freighter which entered Israeli waters, reliable reports from Tel Aviv said today.

Some Facts About That Satellite

MOSCOW, Oct. 4 (UP)—Facts and figures of the Soviet satellite:

SIZE: 22 inches in diameter.

WEIGHT: 184 pounds.

SPEED: 18,000 miles per hour.

ESTIMATED LIFE: Not more than three weeks.

ALTITUDE OF ORBIT: 560 miles.

SIGNALS: Two radio transmitters sending on 20.005 and 40.002 megacycles, strong enough to be picked up by ham operators.

VISIBILITY: Best at sundown and sunset with the naked eye.

ROTATION: Circles earth once every one hour and 35 minutes.

Thousands Battle Police In Warsaw

WARSAW, Oct. 4 (UP)—Thousands of Poles rioted tonight, battling police and militiamen in central Warsaw. Many of the rioters shouted for the downfall of Communist party chief Wladyslaw Gomulka.

Two separate clashes left a number injured, including some women. It was the second straight night of rioting in the Polish capital.

Students surged into the streets and were joined by other demonstrators. About 1000 steel-helmeted police and "workers militia" charged with clubs and fired tear gas bombs to try to break up the demonstration. Another demonstration promptly started in another district.

The rioters fought with their fists. The police and militiamen swung their clubs. The fighting flared for three hours.

It was nearly 11 p. m. before the streets were clear and the buses and streetcars were operating normally. Police and militiamen continued to patrol the streets in trucks and radio cars.

Police reportedly made at

See Page 2, Col. 3

Watchers In Midwest Sight It

By United Press

The Russian satellite was seen speeding over various parts of the United States tonight.

The first report came from Columbus, Ohio, where Moonwatcher Larry Ochs saw the satellite. At almost the same time, it was spotted in Terre Haute, Ind.

The satellite turned up later in other areas of the country. It was reported as far west as San Francisco.

Ochs, stationed at one of the 150 Moonwatch stations set up throughout the world in connection with the International Geophysical Year, said he was sighting through a refractor telescope. He described the "moon" as "sort of yellowish in color."

He said, "It was too small to tell any shape."

Slightly over an hour and a half after Ochs' sighting, another Moonwatcher reported the satellite sailing over Columbus again.

Ochs said a steady light took 24 seconds to cross his telescope. His report was received here at 11:48 p. m. (EDT).

Ochs said he spotted the brilliant flow at 10:28:51 and that it flashed across his lens in an easterly direction.

He estimated the light to be of the sixth magnitude and said it was traveling from

See Page 5, Col. 6

Jury Chosen For Spy Trial

NEW YORK, Oct. 4 (UP)—Selection of the jurors in the espionage trial of Colonel Rudolf Ivanovitch Abel was completed today after four alternates were chosen.

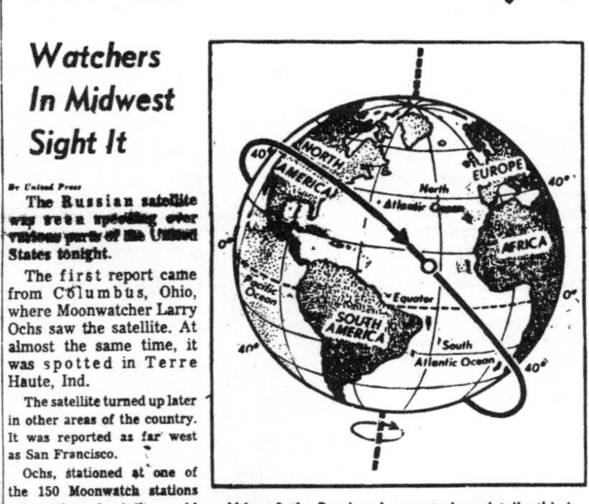

Although the Russians have not given details, this is a rough estimate of the path of their satellite.

Satellite Reported Seen Over S. F.

Russia's earth satellite, clearly heard by radio here, possibly was sighted over San Francisco last night.

Alfred Jensen, captain of a Moonwatch team atop the California Academy of Sciences, notified the Smithsonian Institution he saw what may have been the satellite at 8:55:30 p. m. PST.

"It looked like a slow moving star or meteor, but it was going in the right direction at the right time to be the satellite," he declared.

"It was white, and had a steady light equal to a star of the fifth magnitude or more. I just spotted it by chance."

Jensen said the "object" cut the corner of the field of view of his telescope in a west-to-east direction, on a course angled toward the equator at about 60 degrees.

The telescope next to Jensen's overlapped his field of view, but there was no observer at the eyepiece to confirm his sighting.

Jensen said the Smithsonian Institution told him the satellite is "self-illuminated,"

See Page 5, Col. 4

Christopher Reports on City's Year

Mayor George Christopher, in his annual message to the Board of Supervisors, marked parking space and the Ferry Park for special attention during the coming year.

He asked the Board to consider submitting a bond issue to the voters in June to finance the waterfront park, calling it essential to the ultimate development of the lower Market street area.

And he asked the Board to find new funds for the Parking Authority to continue its program. The Authority, he said, will exhaust its resources when it has finished financing the Sutter-Stockton Garage.

The Mayor did not put a price on the Ferry Park bond

See Page 2, Col. 4

Weather Delays Last A-Blast

LAS VEGAS, Nev., Oct. 4 (UP)—Adverse weather conditions today forced the Atomic Energy Commission to call a 24-hour postponement in the firing of the final nuclear shot of the 1957 test series.

Labor Leaders Gunning For Me, Knowland Says

By Earl C. Behrens
Political Editor

Senator William F. Knowland told a gathering at the Hotel Leamington in Oakland last night that he had been "marked for political liquidation by some of the National and State leaders of labor and by some public officials associated with them."

Knowland spoke at a homecoming dinner attended by a capacity audience of more than 850 persons. He declared he would continue to discuss the labor issues which had resulted in the "threats."

Senator Knowland, candidate for Governor of California in 1958, outlined his eight-

See Page 4, Col. 1

Tiny Satellite

Reds Beat U. S.--- First Into Space

By United Press

Russia Friday night announced the first successful launching of an earth satellite.

Hours after the announcement, the tiny "moon" was seen hurtling through the sky in various parts of the United States.

Soviet scientists hurled the satellite into space earlier Friday and sent it spinning around the earth at a speed of 18,000 miles an hour and at an altitude of 560 miles, the announcement said.

The sphere-shaped man-made "moon" was equipped with a radio transmitter sending signals to earth stations.

Stations Pick Up Signals

Within a few hours radio receiving stations began picking up the satellite's signal. Radio Corporation of America Communications Division reported hearing it in New York and the British Broadcasting System caught the tiny pulsating signal in London.

The Naval Research Laboratory at Washington announced that it recorded three passes of the "moon" over the United States.

The launching beat the United States by at least several months in the program to hurl an artificial moon into space during the current International Geophysical Year.

A Big Step Toward Space

The artificial moon project was the most imaginative venture of the IGY and one of man's biggest steps toward solving the mysteries of space. It was also the first stage in Russia's declared plan to send space ships to earth's moon, Mars and Venus.

The Soviet announcement made by the Tass News Agency called the launching a "tremendous contribution to the treasure house of world science and culture."

In Washington some of America's most distinguished scientists agreed that the satellite opened "a new era in science." They showed no rancor at being beaten into space by the Soviet engineers, and, as one of them put it. "We are all elated that it is up there."

The Russians said their satellite is 22 inches in diameter, or about twice the size of a basketball. It

See Page 5, Col. 7

The Chronicle Index

Building Review	9	Movies, Drama	13
Churches	10	The Owl	7
Comics	19	Shipping News	20
Crossword Puzzles	11, 24	TV, Radio Logs	12
Death Notices	20	Vital Statistics	20
Finance, Business	8, 9	Weather	20
Horoscope	24	Women's News	6

Scattered showers are forecast for the Bay Area Saturday and tomorrow.

ALASKA MAKES IT

Giambra Upsets Giardello

See Sports For Details

WEATHER FORECAST
Bay Area: Fair today and Wednesday except morning overcast. Cooler today. Low this morning, 50-55; high today, San Francisco 62, Oakland 68, San Mateo 70, San Rafael 72.
Full Report, Page 34

San Francisco Chronicle FINAL
THE VOICE OF THE WEST
94th YEAR No. 182 CCCCAAA TUESDAY, JULY 1, 1958 10 CENTS GArfield 1-1111

High Court Ruling

State Loyalty Oath on Tax Exemption Killed

California's law requiring a loyalty oath for property-tax exemption was declared unconstitutional by the United States Supreme Court today.

In a 7-to-1 decision the court ruled that the present oath requirement violates the "due process" clause of the U. S. Constitution.

The tribunal's ruling does not affect a provision in the California constitution that bars tax exemptions for subversive individuals and organizations.

But the decision did strike down a law implementing the constitutional provision — a law that forced everyone applying for a tax exemption to sign a loyalty oath.

The Supreme Court held, in effect, that if the State wants to deny anyone a tax exemption it must bear the burden of proving that the person is actually subversive.

The tribunal ruled yesterday on four California cases. Two involved Northern California veterans, and two involved Southern California churches.

The veterans were Lawrence Speiser of San Mateo, an attorney, and Daniel Prince, a San Francisco business executive.

The religious organizations were the First Unitarian Church of Los Angeles and the People's Church of San Fernando Valley.

The veterans and the
See Page 6, Col. 1

Russ Agree To Start Talks Today

New York Times Service

GENEVA, Switzerland, June 30 — The Soviet Union, in a reversal of its past position, agreed today to enter into technical talks with the West on ways of detecting atomic weapons tests.

As a result, talks between scientists of four Western and four Communist nations will begin here tomorrow afternoon in a conference room in the old League of Nations headquarters.

The Soviet agreement was announced by Dr. Y. K. Federov, head of the Soviet delegation of scientists, following a two-hour conference with Dr. James B. Fisk, chairman of the western scientific group.

Federov told reporters that it had been agreed that talks would begin tomorrow and that discussions would be
See Page 9, Col. 4

Ike Signs Bill On Excise Taxes

WASHINGTON, June 30 (UPI)—President Eisenhower today signed a bill repealing the 3 per cent Federal tax on freight shipments and extending for one year all other corporate and excise levies.

The measure also ended a tax of 4 cents a ton on transportation of coal and 4½ per cent on pipeline shipments of oil and gas.

Pacifist Yacht Nears H-Test Zone

HONOLULU, June 30 (AP)—The yacht Phoenix headed for the American H-bomb test area today and its pacifist skipper told the Coast Guard he intended to sail into the forbidden zone.

Navy headquarters here reported the skipper, Erle L. Reynolds, declared his intention to a Coast Guard cutter which hailed his yacht 100 miles east of the danger area and warned him against entering.

The latest report by the Navy placed the 50-foot Phoenix about one day's sailing time away from the prohibited area.

The Navy said the Phoenix is under surveillance but gave no hint what action it plans.

Cuba Rebels Kidnap More Americans

HAVANA, June 30 (UPI) Cuban rebels seized two more Americans and one Canadian today, increasing the number of hostages in their hands to at least 42 Americans and three Canadians.

The new abductions dimmed hopes for an early release of the prisoners.

The United States Embassy here was advised that the rebels, followers of Fidel Castro, snatched Sherman Avery White of New York city, manager of the U. S. Government-owned Nicaro nickel plant, and his assistant, J. Andrew Toll of Grand Rapids, Mich., at the plant this forenoon.

A few hours later, a spokesman for the Cuban sugar industry announced that Richard Sargeant, Canadian manager of a sugar mill near Guantanamo, was conducted by the rebels Thursday.

Unconfirmed reports from Santiago said still three more Americans had been kidnaped by Castro's rebels. The three Americans were said to be executives of the Ermita sugar mill, some 25 miles northwest of the U. S. Naval Base at Guantanamo.

Most of the rebels' victims
See Page 9, Col. 3

Strange 'Raid' ---Feds Seize Firecrackers

By Charles Raudebaugh

Federal narcotics agents confiscated eight cartons of firecrackers in a raid on a Chinatown shop last week, it came to light yesterday.

"We were on a narcotics investigation but we knew the firecrackers are illegal here in San Francisco so we picked them up," said John Trainor, assistant chief of the Federal Narcotics Bureau here.

One of the cartons was turned over to the Police Department and the others were kept at the narcotics bureau office except for one "which we destroyed," the officer said.

How was it destroyed, he was asked.

"We destroyed it," he said with a chuckle.

'NO AUTHORITY'

Ernest Besig, Northern California director of the American Civil Liberties Union, was astonished when he heard of the seizure.

"So far as I know, no Federal law was being violated," said Besig. "They seized, without any court authority, firecrackers which didn't belong to them.

"This is a very curious way of enforcing the law, a sort of private way of doing things. I've never heard of such a thing."

The firecrackers were taken June 24 from Ti Lung Hang and Co., 846 Grant avenue. Tse Shut Chi, manager of the store, said they were worth about $500.

Neither Tse, nor the two clerks in the place, were arrested, nor were they implicated in the narcotics investigation.

Trainor said that the matter of arrests was up to the
See Page 2, Col. 5

Anita Ekberg Enters Hospital

LONDON, June 30 (AP)—Swedish actress Anita Ekberg went into a London hospital today to have her appendix removed.

She has just finished work on a movie. She suffered an attack of appendicitis soon after the film unit returned here from Spain.

Wife's Heavy Spending Tips Cops to a 'Tax' Case

A free-drinking, free-spending young woman got her husband fingered for possible income tax evasion in Oakland yesterday.

And the couple left Oakland police flabbergasted with tales of a month-long binge financed by a roll of $500 and $100 bills that should have gone for tax payments.

The spree first came to the attention of Oakland authorities early yesterday.

Police said a woman who identified herself as Lola Sturgill, 29, at 2 a. m. hailed a cab driven by Glen O. Longacre, 1603 142nd avenue, San Leandro.

Wearing Bermuda shorts and a shirt, the woman got into Longacre's cab outside an Oakland motel and demanded that she be taken to another motel.

En route, the shoeless, coatless, hatless woman decided she wanted a drink, and the
See Page 4, Col. 6

Senate Puts Final OK On Alaska as State

A New Old Glory

A. P. Wirephotos

Since 1918, a Federal law has required that the Flag of the United States contain 13 red and white stripes. The Congress did not fix the number nor the arrangement of the stars.

Almost everybody else has had a crack at it, however.

Although a new design hasn't been necessary since 1912, plenty are ready. Some are shown above.

At upper left is the simplest—seven rows of seven stars. Its main disadvantage is that it would have to be completely redesigned if Hawaii is admitted as the 50th State.

Below it is a star of stars, superimposed on the 13 stripes. It has room for a 50th star.

The two designs on the right are really looking ahead — they contain 50 stars each.

Whichever one is adopted, it cannot become official for another year. **The flag law states that a new design becomes effective on the 4th of July following the State's admission.**

Admission Due This Winter

From New York Herald Tribune and A. P. and UPI

WASHINGTON, June 30 — Alaska was voted into the United States tonight.

Alaskan statehood, which first came before Congress in 1916, won final approval from the Senate, 64 to 20. The bill now goes to President Eisenhower, who is certain to sign it. It already had been passed by the House.

Alaskans must still approve the terms of statehood, but this is equally certain, and the 49th State is expected to be in the Union this winter— in time for its two Senators and one Representative to take their seats in Congress in January.

The Senate mustered heavy votes tonight to beat down a series of desperate attempts by Southerners to block Alaska's admission.

In rapid succession the Senators defeated:

- An amendment by Senator Strom Thurmond (Dem-S. C.) to reduce the size of Alaska. It would have eliminated the area from which the President can withdraw lands for national defense. This provision was one of the most controversial points of the bill.
- A second proposal by Thurmond which would have required congressional concurrence in any such move by the President.
- A proposal by Senator John Stennis (Dem-Miss.) to send the bill back to committee.
- A point of order raised by Senator James O. Eastland (Dem-Miss.), which would have declared parts of the bill unconstitutional.

After this was defeated, Eastland, leader of the Southern block, dropped his efforts to halt Statehood.

Southerners have led the
See Page 8, Col. 3

MacPhee on Job as Brooks' Successor

By Jack Burby

Chester R. MacPhee, 53-year-old real estate man and former Supervisor, was sworn in and put right to work yesterday as San Francisco's chief administrative officer.

With Mayor George Christopher's office packed with family, friends and officeholders, MacPhee took his oath at 10 a.m.

Confessing that appointment to the job was his fondest wish, MacPhee promised in a brief speech to "do my level best to live up to the job."

BROOKS RETIRES

His predecessor, Thomas A. Brooks, retired yesterday with fond tributes at the age of 72.

In 17 years, he served through four city administrations, winning what Christopher called a reputation as "a faithful servant, a dedicated and able man."

Brooks joined MacPhee in Christopher's office and beamed as his successor took office.

"And now," said the Mayor
See Page 11, Col. 5

Fox Says He'll Sue Adams For a Million

New York Herald Tribune Service

WASHINGTON, June 30. — Fireworks burst all over Washington in the Fox - Goldfine - Adams case today, and gaudiest of all was an announcement by John Fox that he was suing Sherman Adams for $1 million for libel.

Fox's announcement that he was bringing suit not
See Page 12, Col. 1

Pharmacists Give Brown New Chance

A half-hearted invitation was extended yesterday to Attorney General Edmund G. Brown to put in a make-up appearance at the California Pharmaceutical Association convention.

But the pharmacists made it clear Brown's failure to deliver the keynote address Sunday at the Sheraton-Palace Hotel was a bitter pill.

Brown immediately accepted the new invitation. The Democratic candidate for Governor told George A. Sargenti of Salinas, the CPA president, that "perhaps, together, we can compound a nostrum to solve the whole headache."

Brown will make his address at 9:45 this morning.

The tempest began Wednesday, when Brown informed Cecil A. Stewart, CPA executive secretary, that he
See Page 12, Col. 6

INDEX

Bridge	34
Caen	17
Chess	34
Comics	6H
Crossword Puzzles	28, 31
Death Notices	18
Delaplane	29
Editorial Page	30
Finance, Business	13-15
Horoscope	28
Movies, Drama	32, 33
O'Flaherty	29
Panorama	31
Shipping	18
TV, Radio Logs	34
Want Ads	18
Weather	34
Women's News	35

MAYS IS INJURED

Leg Cut in Slide---35 Stitches

WEATHER FORECAST
Bay Area: Fair today and Saturday, except for morning high fog. Slightly cooler today. Low Friday, 46-51. High Friday, 65-69. Westerly wind 8 to 16 miles an hour.
Full Report, Page 16

San Francisco Chronicle
THE VOICE OF THE WEST
FINAL

95th YEAR No. 72 CCCCAAA FRIDAY, MARCH 13, 1959 10 CENTS  GArfield 1-1111

Hawaii Statehood Wins Final Vote

Southern Protest Fails In 323-to-89 Approval ---Ike's Signature Next

From New York Times and New York Herald Tribune

WASHINGTON, March 12—The territory of Hawaii was voted into the Union as the 50th State today.

The House of Representatives gave final Congressional approval by a vote of 323 to 89.

The bill, which cleared the Senate 76-15 yesterday, probably will go to the White House tomorrow for President Eisenhower's certain approval.

To qualify fully for statehood, the Islands' voters must approve the step in an election that will also pick two Senators, a Representative and the Islands' first elected Governor. The process probably will not be completed before August.

THE ROLL CALL

There was an air of inevitability about the House proceedings which wound up Hawaii's 40-year fight for admission to the Union.

With House galleries jammed with spectators, the House started its long roll call in midafternoon. Among the spectators was the Governor of Hawaii, William Quinn. When the roll call began he quietly left the gallery and went to the office—just off the House floor—of Sam Rayburn (Dem-Tex.), Speaker of the House.

Governor Quinn put in a call to Acting Governor Edward Johnston in Honolulu and asked him to hold the line. Representative John Saylor (Rep-Pa.) had been counting the "Aye" votes. When he reached 219—the

See Page 6, Col. 6

In Hawaii, They Say Hah-vy-ee

HONOLULU, March 12 (AP) If you're a Hawaiian, you can pronounce it HAH-VY-EE.

Almost everyone else pronounces it HAH-WY-EE.

Scholars of Polynesian lore have long debated the origin of the word. They agree that Polynesians used it in one form or another to designate the place to which they migrated. It means "homeland."

40-Year Fight Ends In Holiday

HONOLULU, March 12 (UPI)—**News of Hawaii's acceptance into the Union swept through the islands like a tidal wave today—but a wave that left shouting and joy in its wake.**

The sound of horns, bells, sirens and firecrackers erupting in celebration of the long-awaited event gave an almost visible pulse to the news that went rumbling through the islands, spilling people into the streets to join the wild festivities.

Within 15 minutes the whole town of Honolulu went crazy. Schools, shops and offices were closed. Traffic was virtually halted by the dancing and kissing in the streets. Statehood was an accomplished fact and Hawaii's citizens were in a frenzy of joy.

Almost all work was suspended except in newspapers, radio stations and a few key spots.

Acting Governor Edward Johnston immediately declared a two-day territory-wide holiday. It was merely an official move that was hardly necessary. The citizens were going to "holiday" anyway.

In fact the celebration jumped the gun. At 10 a. m. (HST) (3 p. m. EST), some four minutes before actual

See Page 7, Col. 3

Cosmic Ray Safety Find Told by UC

By David Perlman

A mysterious "safety plateau" in the heavy cosmic rays that flash through outer space may make the radiation hazards of an interplanetary voyage less lethal than anyone thought.

This qualified assurance came yesterday from a team of University of California researchers as they disclosed a wealth of new findings in cosmic ray investigations.

The researchers announced:

1—That they have successfully used an atom smasher to fire beams composed of the hearts of atoms as heavy as argon—the heaviest nuclear particles ever made.

2—That they have thus recreated in their earth-bound laboratory the effects of the heavy cosmic radiation that constantly batters the outer shell of the earth's atmosphere.

3—That despite the biological dangers of this radiation to those who venture out beyond the atmosphere's protective armor, there seems to be a plateau, or leveling-off of destructiveness. Cosmic rays particles get more lethal as they get heavier—but only

See Page 8, Col. 6

Job Hassel; L. A. Makes Him Sick

SACRAMENTO, March 12 (AP) — A State electrician who said a transfer to Los Angeles left him depressed and mentally confused is gaining in his fight to retain his job.

The Third District Court of Appeals ordered a new hearing for John A. Wallace.

Wallace, who was fired for refusing to return to Los Angeles, complained that the move from Sacramento in 1955 caused him extreme depression, severe headaches, fatigue, muscle tension, insomnia, loss of weight and mental confusion. His wife blamed the traffic and smog.

Deputy Attorney General Willard A. Shank, representing the State, appeared to sympathize with Wallace.

"I get kind of sick when I have to go down there myself." he said.

Willie Dives Into Trouble

UPI Telephoto

Willie Mays of the San Francisco Giants tore mightily into home plate and disaster yesterday. Bolting all the way from second base on an infield roller during a training game at Scottsdale, Ariz., Mays dipped into his slide and hooked safely across the plate. But Boston Red Sox catcher Sammy White raised his shinguard and the collision sliced a gash in Mays' right leg that required 35 stitches to close. He will be out at least a week. Waving Mays in is Andre Rodgers. For details see the Sporting Green.

Fugitive From Parole

Ding Dong Daddy Quits 17th Wife

FRANCIS VAN WIE
Champion marrier

Special to The Chronicle

SACRAMENTO, March 12 — Francis H. Van Wie, famed "Ding Dong Daddy of the 'D' Car Line," has backed out of another marriage—his 17th—it was learned here today.

Van Wie, now a portly and sentimental 72, was sued for divorce by 73-year-old June Puckett Van Wie of 3821 Rio Linda boulevard, who charged him with mental cruelty.

Her attorney, however, said she may amend the complaint and ask for an annulment, charging the former San Francisco trolley conductor and lion tamer with fraud.

"I would say in view of Mr. Van Wie's past record, there is ample evidence," the lawyer said.

Mrs. Van Wie's modest complaint, on file in Supe-

See Page 4, Col. 4

Expectant Mother Hurt By Hit-Run

A pretty young housewife, expecting her first child in June, was struck and seriously injured by a hit-run car in the Outer Mission district yesterday.

Doctors said they were not sure they could save the baby.

Police sought a 20-year-old man for investigation of hit-run driving.

The victim was Marlene Busch, 19, the wife of Garry Busch, 25, a clerk of 5505 Mission street.

She was struck by the car as she crossed Mission at Foote avenue at 5 p. m. while returning home after a shopping trip.

Although the car was going only about 10 miles an hour, Mrs. Busch was thrown 24 feet by the impact.

Two witnesses saw the car speed off and they gave

See Page 4, Col. 4

Fine Weather Will Continue

There should be more of the same balmy, sunny weather — possibly a little cooler—in the Bay Area, the Weather Bureau said yesterday.

Most of the California coast continued to bask in good weather produced by a high-pressure system 900 miles west of San Francisco and no change appeared in sight.

Yesterday's high was 69 —reached at 12:40 p. m.

Child at Youth Center

Mother Sues City To Get Baby Back

A young divorced mother went to court yesterday to demand that the city give up her brown-eyed baby girl.

In her $10,000 lawsuit filed in Superior Court, Marion DeVaul charged that the city has "wrongfully and unlawfully" kept her daughter from her for four days.

And it appears she won't get her baby back till April 3.

Named as defendants in the action, along with the city, were the Youth Guidance Center and the Welfare Department.

Superior Judge Melvyn I. Cronin of the Juvenile Court

See Page 2, Col. 4

Mrs. Duncan Rages at Prosecutor

By Tom Mathews

VENTURA, March 12 The Mother Duncan defense hauled out its biggest guns today and peppered away at the People's case.

The firing began after District Attorney Roy Gustafson had closed his argument at noon with a burst of invective that blew Elizabeth Duncan out of her chair, shaking with rage and sibilant with profanity.

Gustafson showed the jury a picture of Olga Duncan, the 54 - year - old defendant's daughter-in-law.

"There she is—by every standard a lovely, sweet, wonderful girl," he said.

He held up a picture of Olga's grave, opened December 21 when officers were

See Page 4, Col. 1

INDEX

Bridge 10
Caen 13
Chess 10
Comics 33
Crossword Puzzles . 26, 29
Dear Abby 29
Death Notices 32
Delaplane 27
Editorial Page 28
Finance, Business . . 14-16
Horoscope 26
Movies 30, 31
O'Flaherty 27
Panorama 29
Shipping 32
Theaters 30, 31
TV, Radio Logs 32
Vital Statistics 32
Want Ads 16
Weather 16
Women's News . . . 10, 11

1960-1969

MAY 3, 1960
Chessman Dies in Gas Chamber

MAY 6, 1960
Russians Down Secret U.S. Jet

NOVEMBER 9, 1960
Kennedy Wins

JANUARY 4, 1961
U.S.-Cuba Break

APRIL 12, 1961
Russian Astronaut Orbits Earth

APRIL 18, 1961
Wild Reports on Cuban War

MAY 6, 1961
Shepard's Report from Spaceship; Kennedy Weighs Sending Troops to Vietnam

FEBRUARY 21, 1962
Glenn in Fine Shape After 81,000 Mile Trip

SEPTEMBER 30, 1962
U.S. Troops in Mississippi Crisis

OCTOBER 4, 1962
Pennant for Giants

OCTOBER 23, 1962
Navy Guns Ring Cuba

AUGUST 29, 1963
200,000 March for Rights in Washington

NOVEMBER 23, 1963
Murder of the President

NOVEMBER 25, 1963
Oswald Slain

MARCH 29, 1964
Four Alaskan Cities Ravaged by Quake

AUGUST 5, 1964
Raid on North Vietnamese

OCTOBER 16, 1964
Khrushchev Out — Brezhnev and Kosygin Take Over

MARCH 7, 1965
Marines to Vietnam

AUGUST 13, 1965
Rioting in L.A.

NOVEMBER 9, 1966
Big Reagan Majority — Brown Concedes Defeat

APRIL 5, 1968
Dr. King Murdered

APRIL 6, 1968
U.S. Racial Crises — Looting, Fires in Capital

JUNE 5, 1968
Robert Kennedy Shot

AUGUST 21, 1968
Soviet Armies Invade Czechs

NOVEMBER 6, 1968
Nixon Electoral Victory Is Near

OCTOBER 16, 1969
Massive Anti-War Protest

JULY 21, 1969
Men on Moon

McCormick Blanks Braves

See Sports

WEATHER FORECAST
Bay Area: Light rain beginning around noon Tuesday, scattered showers tonight, fair tomorrow. Little change in temperature. Chances for rain: 8 in 10. Winds to 29 miles an hour (25 knots).
Full Report, Page 30

San Francisco Chronicle **FINAL**
THE VOICE OF THE WEST

96th YEAR No. 124 CCCCAAA TUESDAY, MAY 3, 1960 10 CENTS GArfield 1-1111

SLIP COST CARYL LAST STAY

Speech to Nation

Ike Stresses Role Of Foreign Aid, Hits Fund Parers

From UPI and New York Times Service

WASHINGTON, May 2—President Eisenhower appealed directly to the people tonight to protect his $4,175,000,000 foreign aid program from congressional groups bent on cutting it by 25 per cent.

In an address broadcast by national television and radio networks, the President warned that any substantial whittling of his request for the Mutual Security Program would mean "a crushing defeat in today's struggle between Communist imperialism and a freedom founded in faith and justice."

The President's unusually sharp attack was aimed at "groups strategically situated in Congress," who he said sought to slash the appropriation request by $1 billion or more.

HEALTH PLAN

Simultaneously, the White House announced that Mr. Eisenhower will send a

See Page 9, Col. 1

Besieged Killer Is Found Dead

CHALON - SUR - SAONE, France, May 2 (Reuters)—A 35-year-old bricklayer, besieged by 100 policemen in his house here after he had killed one policeman, was found dead today.

Crash Closes Bay Bridge--- Driver Killed

An East Bay business executive was killed and four other persons were injured—two critically—in a head-on collision on the upper deck of the San Francisco - Oakland Bay Bridge yesterday.

Police arrested the woman driver of one of the two cars, Wanda Boren, on suspicion of manslaughter and suspicion of driving while under the influence of narcotics.

A third automobile rammed the wreckage immediately after the collision at 3:05 p.m. All traffic on the deck was halted for 35 minutes as State Highway patrolmen issued a Sigalert broadcast so they could rush in ambulances and unsnarl the traffic.

The crash took place between the second and third towers about midway between San Francisco and Yerba Buena island.

Thomas A. Hopkins, 43, the driver of one car in the head-on crash, was pronounced dead on arrival at Mission Emergency Hospital.

See Page 2, Col. 3

'Nixon Wants Rockefeller On Ticket'

By Robert J. Donovan
New York Herald Tribune Service

WASHINGTON, May 2 Vice President Nixon, **it can be said on high authority, definitely wants New York Governor Nelson A. Rockefeller as his running-mate this year.**

On the assumption that he himself will be nominated for President, Nixon is prepared to wait until the last minute at the Republican national convention in July to give the New York Governor a chance to make a final judgment on accepting the vice presidential nomination.

The Governor has said unequivocally that he would not "entertain any thought of accepting nomination to the vice presidency."

Nixon believes that as of this moment Rockefeller means it. He does not want the Republican party to try to force him to take it. Not until Rockefeller has been given every possible chance to reconsider at the convention will the Nixon forces turn to another candidate.

While there are some Republicans in high places who would like to see the vice-presidential nomination go to a conservative like Senator Barry Goldwater, of Arizona, or Republican Charles A. Halleck, of Indiana, Nixon is convinced that a majority of the party leaders want Rockefeller for the second place on the ticket.

New Stand By Mayor on Water Sales

Special to The Chronicle

SACRAMENTO, May 2 Mayor George Christopher backed off today from San Francisco's firm stand against competition from the State for some of the city's water customers on the lower Peninsula.

If the State's water service is not helped with a tax subsidy, and is cheaper, and is "in the best interests of the Bay Area," said the Mayor, "then certainly San Francisco has no objection."

Mayor Christopher expressed his view in a prepared statement at a conference of representatives of San Francisco, Alameda, Contra Costa, Santa Clara

See Page 2, Col. 4

Rain Likely at Game Today

The Weather Bureau came up last night with disheartening news for today's second encounter of the Giants with the Milwaukee Braves at Candlestick Park.

"Generally light rain beginning around noon," was the forecast. The forecaster's odds on that were 8 to 2.

The Question Man
Should bars be open between 2 and 6 a.m.?
See Page 18

By Joe Rosenthal

The clock told the story as Rosalie Asher and George Davis left court with Chronicle reporter Dale Champion (right). It was 10:05 and Chessman was dying

Judge's Plea for 'Hour' Too Late

By Carolyn Anspacher

Death overtook Caryl Whittier Chessman yesterday morning.

Eight times in the last dozen years the 38-year-old Chessman had held off the executioner. Yesterday, even as the apple-green walls of San Quentin's gas chamber were closing tighter, time became Chessman's enemy and defeated him.

Sodium cyanide pellets rippled into a sulphuric acid bath and began emitting their deadly perfume at the same moment a San Francisco Federal Judge was trying desperately to halt the execution.

Mischance in Final Minutes

In his chamber of extermination Chessman was remote from the legal tumult that attended his last hours on earth and died ignorant of the grim mischance that denied him at least another 60 minutes of life.

Two of Chessman's attorneys, George T. Davis and Rosalie Asher, whose last two appeals to the State Supreme Court had been rejected yesterday morning, turned to Federal Judge Louis E. Goodman for a writ that would stay the 10 o'clock execution.

The two lawyers dashed out of the State Building here at 9:50 a.m., an instant after the court had denied a stay. A car was waiting outside. They arrived at the Federal Courthouse a few blocks away three minutes later and were in Judge Goodman's chambers at 9:55 a.m.

What the two attorneys sought was a brief delay of the execution—just enough time to present arguments on whether the United States Supreme Court could be petitioned for a writ of review of the State court's decision.

An Error and a Delay

Judge Goodman listened for two minutes.

It was at that point, in the noise and tensions gripping everyone in Judge Goodman's chambers, that a half minute was lost.

Judge Goodman asked Davis for San Quentin's telephone number. Davis replied—GLenwood 4-1460. The Judge transmitted it orally to his chief clerk, Edward Evensen.

He hurried into an outer office and, again orally gave the number to Celeste Hickey, Judge Goodman's secretary, and asked her to call the warden.

Miss Hickey heard only four digits and midway in her dialing, questioned reporters about the prison phone number.

She waited an instant and then dialed again, this time the correct number.

Judge Goodman estimated the entire interlude took perhaps 20 seconds. Others in the room said 30 seconds were lost before Judge Goodman reached Associate Warden Louis Nelson.

By this time it was some seconds after 10:03. No one remembers precisely how many.

At 10:03.15 the deadly

See Page 13, Col. 1

Allen Drury, 'Fiorello' Win Pulitzers

NEW YORK, May 2 (AP) Allen Drury, a Washington newspaper correspondent for 17 years, today won the 1960 Pulitzer Prize in fiction with his first novel, "Advise and Consent." It is a story of politics in the Nation's capital.

The award for drama went to "Fiorello!" the first musical to gain Pulitzer recognition since "South Pacific" in 1950. The book is by Jerome Weidman and George Abbott, with music and lyrics by Jerry Bock and Sheldon Harnick. It stars Tom Bosley and Patricia Wilson.

The Pulitzer Prize for international reporting went to A. M. Rosenthal of the New York Times for his reporting

See Page 16, Col. 3

This is How He Quietly Died

By Tom Mathews

SAN QUENTIN PRISON, May 2 — Caryl Chessman died here today supported by the same intellectual discipline that he used to fight for his life.

He had said self-knowledge would enable him to accept death stoically. It did.

He turned to one of the sea-green glass windows of the gas chamber and carefully enunciated his last words. They were directed to a friend he had invited to see him go.

"It's all right," he said.

This reassurance to another human being was his final conscious act. For hours before he behaved in much the same way, prohibiting himself pity. He directed his mind to his defense and to the persons to whom he wished to make a final comment should that defense fail.

A procession of visitors called at his holding cell from early evening until past midnight. He discussed his will with one of his attorneys, Rosalie Asher. He talked philosophy with the Catholic chaplain, the Rev. Edward Dingberg.

He absolved his keepers of wrongdoing in a talk with Warden Fred Dickson. He waved away offers of fried chicken, the dish most favored by the executed, and ate hamburger.

At about 1 a.m. he began to compose letters on a writing ledge, the only furniture in the cell in addition to mattresses and a seatless toilet.

Through the night hours

See Page 12, Col. 5

INDEX

Bridge	32
Caen	17
Chess	32
Comics	44
Count Marco	15
Crosswords	26, 29
Dear Abby	29
Death Notices	33
Delaplane	27
Editorial Page	28
Finance, Business	40-43
Hoppe	28
Horoscope	26
Movies	30, 31
O'Flaherty	27
Panorama	29
Shipping	40
Sports	35-40
Theaters	30, 31
TV, Radio Logs	32
Want Ads	18
Weather	30
Women's World	14-16

Top of the Day's News

The World

Soviet Premier Nikita Khrushchev announced Russian forces had shot down a U. S. plane. Washington said it is believed to be a weather jet carrying only one man. Page 1.

Huge crowds assembled along the route by which Britain's Princess Margaret will travel to Westminster Abbey today for her wedding with Antony Armstrong-Jones. Page 1.

Turkey's Premier Adnan Menderes was booed and jostled when he attempted to address Ankara student demonstrators calling for his resignation. Page 6.

Soviet Premier Khrushchev announced that Russia will abolish almost all income taxes over the next five years, and convert the ruble to equal the U. S. dollar. Page 1.

The Nation

Tornadoes swept across communities in Oklahoma, and at least 23 persons were reported dead. Twisters also struck in Kansas and Alabama. Page 1.

Republican Governor Rockefeller of New York came out against subsidy financing in President Eisenhower's scheme for medical care for the aged. Page 4.

An elephant handler was stepped on and crushed by one of his charges, then was pulled away alive — though gravely injured — by another elephant, at Newark, N. J. Page 30.

The American Medical Association assailed the Eisenhower health care plan for the elderly. Page 4.

San Francisco and the West

A tall, dignified, white-haired old man tried to rob the Wells Fargo-American Trust Bank in Hayward by personally delivered message, but failed. Page 1.

Chancellor Glenn Seaborg, of UC, sternly warned student leaders to rescind their support of an Illinois professor fired for his tolerant views on premarital sex. Page 1.

A crowd of 300 spectators, some on horseback, interfered with firefighters at a Goleta Valley blaze in Santa Barbara county. One buff even seized a firehose and began using it. Page 5.

Big-name opera-singers who were under contract to the Cosmopolitan Opera Company for next season who, the company shut down asked to be paid their fees in full. Page 2.

A computer with 100 billion parts in a space as big as a couple of sugar lumps was proposed at the Western Joint Computer Conference here. Page 6.

Democratic and Republican prospective candidates for the presidency were invited to debate their cause here by the Junior Chamber of Commerce. Page 6.

The Sutter - Stockton parking garage is expected to be opened by October 1 — a month early — Parking Authority manager Ving T. Fisher announced. Page 24.

People and Places

Harvey S. Firestone III, crippled 32-year-old heir to the Firestone rubber fortune, plunged to his death from the 20th story of a swank hotel in Havana, Cuba. Page 1.

A 37-year-old Richmond high school coach announced he is planning to marry a 17-year-old student at the school. The romance blossomed on the gridiron. Page 3.

The former wife of Caryl Chessman denied the report he was the father of a 17-year-old daughter living in Northern California. Page 5.

Sports

The Cincinnati Redlegs swept their two-game series with the Giants by winning 4-3, behind the solid pitching of Bob Purkey and Bill Henry. Page 33.

A pair of young outsiders, Don Whitt and Dave Ragan, tied for the lead in the Las Vegas $45,000 golf tournament with five-under-par 67s. Page 33.

Weather Forecast

Bay Area: Fair today and tomorrow except morning overcast. Little change in temperature. High Friday, 62; low, 47 to 57. Full report, Page 31.

San Francisco Chronicle

THE VOICE OF THE WEST

96th YEAR No. 127 FINAL HOME EDITION ★★ FRIDAY, MAY 6, 1960 10 CENTS GArfield 1-1111

Russ Down Secret U.S. Jet; Nikita Charges 'Aggression'

Suicide Ruling

Firestone Heir Falls 17 Stories At Havana Hotel

HAVANA, May 5 (AP)—Harvey S. Firestone III, 32-year-old heir to one of America's great fortunes, fell or jumped to his death tonight from the 20th floor of the Havana Hilton Hotel.

A spastic, Firestone had been crippled from birth and was confined to a wheelchair. Havana police said a cousin, David M. Firestone, 29, of Sarasota, Fla., told them Harvey had tried to commit suicide two months ago in Florida.

Cuban police, who ruled the death a suicide, gave this account:

Firestone had been lying on a couch while his attendant, William J. Didas of St. Petersburg, Fla., was taking a bath. Clad only in white shorts, Firestone about 8 p.m. crawled to the balcony of his suite and from a chair top either fell or jumped over a 3½-foot-high aluminum barrier.

He was killed instantly **when he struck a third-story parapet above the main entrance to the 25-story skyscraper in the heart of the Cuban capital's fashionable Vedado district.**

The dead man was the only son of Harvey S. Firestone Jr. of Akron, Ohio, chairman of the board and chief executive officer of the Firestone Tire and Rubber Co. and the son of the founder of the company. The elder Firestone is in Paris to lay the cornerstone for a new tire plant on May 12.

The younger Firestone made his home in St. Petersburg, Fla., where his wife and 20-month-old daughter live.

Havana police said Harvey and David Firestone and Didas registered at the hotel today and said they planned to stay three days.

Two uncles of Firestone said tonight they believed

See Page 4, Col. 4

A. P. Wirephoto via radio

PRINCESS MARGARET
She was all smiles

All London Wild Over Wedding

LONDON (Friday), May 6 (UPI) — **Thousands of persons streamed into the city today in hopes of catching a glimpse of petite Princess Margaret Rose as she rode to Westminster Abbey for her royal wedding this noon to commoner Antony Armstrong-Jones.**

The crowd, estimated at 500,000, lined the route from Clarence House to the abbey, pushing its way against the railed barriers along the flower-strewn Pall Mall.

About 100,000 visitors were estimated to have swelled the ranks of London citizenry to see the procession.

Queen Elizabeth II took a back seat to her sister and became just a relative of the bride. The crowd along the route vied for positions to look at Margaret riding in a fairyland glass coach to her wedding.

"It's her day," newspapers headlined.

Teen-aged girls and women carrying thermos jugs, bedding and sandwiches and men sitting propped against trees and street lamps crushed against one another trying to catch a glimpse of Margaret.

Autos jammed the center of the city, bringing traffic conditions the Royal Automobile Club described as "the worst London has ever known."

Yesterday, while the celebrating swirled on unabated

See Page C, Col. 4

A Gentle Man Quietly Tries To Rob Bank

By Denne Petitclerc

The tall, dignified old man walked into the Wells Fargo-American Trust Bank in Hayward yesterday and quietly set in motion a transaction "to cure my financial difficulties."

He was distinguished looking in well-groomed sports clothes, his hair and neatly trimmed mustache as white as snow.

He sat down before the desk of assistant manager Harry B. O'Brien, 58, of 2831 Oakes street and gently handed him a typewritten note. Then he sat back with an old man's dignity and waited.

O'Brien smiled and opened the note.

The note, typewritten on fine - quality white paper, said:

"To whom it may concern: "This letter will serve to

See Page 3, Col. 1

State Dept. Launches Inquiry

WASHINGTON, May 5 (UPI)—**The United States lodged an immediate "inquiry" with Russia today to determine whether a U. S. plane shot down by Soviet forces Sunday was an unarmed weather craft with an unconscious civilian pilot at the controls.**

Acting on President Eisenhower's orders, the State Department instructed the U. S. Ambassador to Moscow, Llewellyn E. Thompson, to ask the Soviet government about the incident, "with particular reference to the fate of the pilot."

WEATHER PLANE

The plane was a oneman weather reconnaissance Lockheed U-2 jet operated by the National Aeronautics and Space Administration. It disappeared in the Turkish frontier area after the pilot reported he was having trouble with his oxygen equipment.

In Burbank, Calif., Lockheed officials identified the civilian pilot as Francis G. Powers, 30, Albany, Ga.

The State Department said the plane might have violated the Russian border accidentally after the pilot

See Page 8, Col. 5

Map:

A. P. Wirephoto Map

Premier Khrushchev said U. S. planes violated Soviet territory near Lake Van (left) on May 1 and near the Afghanistan border (right) on April 9

Crackdown On Student Chiefs at UC

Student leaders at the University of California were sternly warned yesterday to rescind their support of an Illinois professor fired for his outspoken views on premarital sex.

Chancellor Glenn Seaborg said the executive committee of the Associated Students exceeded its authority by interfering in an off-campus matter.

He ordered student body president Dave Armor not to mail the statement to the University of Illinois, but Armor said the directive came too late — the letter is on its way.

Armor added that he and other members of the student committee resent "vague threats" that they say, have accompanied the Administration demands.

Coming out of a special

See Page 2, Col. 4

Reston Reports

But What Did U. S. Expect to Happen?

By James B. Reston

Copyright, 1960 by the New York Times

WASHINGTON, May 5 Every time an American plane is shot down over or near the Communist empire, it is useful to recall certain basic facts about the Cold War.

It is a war, much as we'd like to forget it. The forces of two hostile coalitions face each other across half the world, and they are constantly watching each other from the skies and probing each other's lines.

Moreover, the disposition of these forces is spread along the whole vast periphery of the Eurasian continent from the north cape of Norway through the heart of Europe to the Middle East and thence into South Asia and the Far East.

The preponderance of ground power and rocket fire may lie with the Russians and the Chinese, but it is the United States that has military and air bases close to the Soviet and Chinese borders and not the other way round.

These are the unpopular facts which are seldom mentioned in this part of the world, but they help explain Soviet Premier Nikita S. Khrushchev's melodramatic and bad-mannered outburst over the American plane today.

There is a tendency here to dismiss Khrushchev's tantrum as part of the usual Soviet tactics just before a summit meeting with President Eisenhower, President Charles

See Page 8, Col. 1

Tornadoes Race Across Oklahoma---23 Killed

From AP and UPI

Killer tornadoes sliced through eastern Oklahoma last night. At least 23 were reported dead, scores were injured and property damage was heavy.

Other twisters raced across parts of Kansas and Alabama.

The tornadoes were the second outbreak of the day in Oklahoma. They flattened homes, a church, farm buildings and house trailers.

At least 11 persons were killed when a tornado lashed the town of Wilburton, Okla.'s site of eastern Oklahoma A&M college. The college apparently was untouched.

An estimated 50 persons were taken to hospitals, some of them badly injured.

Elsewhere in Oklahoma, three were reported killed in Sapulpa, two in Keota, five in the Roland-Moffett area, and two in Bristow.

Other "heavy casualties" also were believed to have occurred just outside, Moffett, where the victims were

See Page 4, Col. 5

Russ Boost Ruble Value, Alter Taxes

From Associated Press and New York Times

MOSCOW, May 5—Premier Nikita S. Khrushchev announced today that the Soviet Union will abolish almost all income taxes by the end of 1965.

He said this will boost Soviet workers' take-home pay by 74 million rubles.

Khrushchev also announced a revaluation of the ruble, effective January 1, 1961, to make it worth as much as the U. S. dollar.

CONSUMER GOODS

The greater take - home pay, the Premier said, will be matched by increased stocks of consumer goods in stores.

He promised a great new drive for production of consumer goods once his current ambitious seven-year economic plan is fulfilled.

Khrushchev told a joint session of the Supreme Soviet, the Parliament of the USSR, that workers would be progressively exempted from income tax over the coming five years.

After that, he said, the tax will be abolished for all factory and office workers earning less than 2000 rubles a month.

PAY CUTS, TOO

Workers making more will also have their income taxes abolished, but their pay will be cut accordingly. Income taxes also will be wiped out for single persons and those with small families, regardless of the amount of their pay, Khrushchev added.

The Premier said the cash wages of 50 million persons

See Page 8, Col. 8

Plane Was Lost From Turkey

MOSCOW, May 5 (UPI) Premier Nikita S. Khrushchev said today a United States plane had been shot down over the Soviet Union, and in one of his bitterest attacks said Russia wanted peace but the U. S. should realize it "could also suffer retaliatory blows" with rockets.

Khrushchev said there now it "little hope" for success at the Summit conference and charged that the downed plane was sent in by aggressive U. S. circles to "impress and frighten" Russia before the Paris meeting May 16.

Khrushchev did not actually threaten to send rockets or planes over American territory "because that might signify war," but he repeated an old Russian saying that "he who comes to us with the sword shall perish by it."

The Soviet Premier did not say what type of plane was involved. He said it flew in from Turkey and although the markings had been painted over it was established the plane was American.

Khrushchev reacted angrily to President Eisenhower's recent statement that he might be able to spend only a week at the summit conference in Paris and would have Vice President Richard M. Nixon serve as his deputy if necessary.

Khrushchev said this

See Page 8, Col. 1

INDEX

Bridge	14
Caen	14
Chess	14
Comics	40
Count Marco	11
Crosswords	23, 27
Dear Abby	27
Death Notices	31
Delaplane	29
Editorial Page	28
Finance, Business	37-39
Hoppe	26
Horoscope	23
Movies	28, 29
O'Flaherty	29
Panorama	27
Shipping	37
Sports	33-37
Theaters	28, 29
TV, Radio Logs	30
Vital Statistics	31
Want Ads	15
Weather	31
Women's World	9-13

The Question Man

Should guests help with the dishes?

See Page 14

WEATHER FORECAST
Bay Area: Fair today, except local morning fog or low clouds. Little change in temperature. Low, 40 to 50; Wednesday, 62 to 67.
Full Report, Page 16

San Francisco Chronicle
THE VOICE OF THE WEST

FINAL

96th YEAR No. 314 CCCCAAABC WEDNESDAY, NOVEMBER 9, 1960 10 CENTS GArfield 1-1111

KENNEDY WINS

But His Margin Is Razor-Thin As Nixon Cuts Into Early Lead; Prop. 1 Trails--Prop. 15 Loses

Kennedy Keeps Thin State Lead

By Earl C. Behrens
Political Editor

Democratic presidential nominee John F. Kennedy early today clung to a narrow lead over Republican Vice President Richard M. Nixon in the contest for California's 32 electoral votes.

Vice President Nixon refused to concede the State to Senator Kennedy up to an early hour this morning. The Senator went to bed in his Massachusetts home without claiming a California victory.

Kennedy's supporters, however, held victory celebrations last night.

Returns from 16,250 out of 30,682 gave

Kennedy 1,467,934.
Nixon 1,371,425.

Kennedy lead had dropped at one time this morning to less than 70,000 and then rose to nearly 90,000.

S. F. GOES DEMO

More than 50,000 of the Kennedy lead came from San Francisco. Many precincts in Los Angeles and a considerable number in San Diego county were yet to be

See Page D, Col. 5

Karesh Victory

United States Commissioner Joseph Karesh apparently won election to the Superior Court bench yesterday, defeating Municipal Judge Lenore Underwood.

Complete returns from the city's 1286 precincts gave 124,253 votes to 115,813 for Judge Underwood.

Although 18,371 absentee ballots were issued, their tally Monday was not expected to change the outcome.

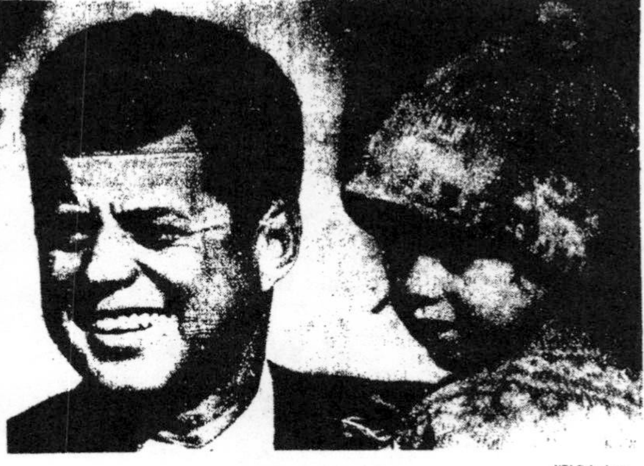

THE PRESIDENT-ELECT OF THE UNITED STATES
A jubilant John Kennedy held daughter Caroline in his arms

UPI Telephoto

Prop. 1 Falls Behind ---Prop. 15 Beaten

By David Perlman

A tide of "No" votes pushed California's mammoth water bond program out of an early lead today — but the final result may well hinge on the State's absentee ballots.

The referendum measure to reapportion the State Senate was defeated, however, and the lopsided margin of defeat was running heavier than two-to-one.

Proposition 1, to launch a $1.75 billion construction program for water projects, held a narrowing lead during last night's early counting, but dropped behind this morning after 13,165 of the State's 30,682 precincts had been tallied.

The early-morning count on Proposition 1:

Yes—751,502.
No—796,876.

But this abrupt change from the bond issue's earlier lead may have been partly a freak.

Los Angeles county, where the measure was running strong, stopped counting bal-

See Page 2, Col. 3

Mailliard, Shelley Romp To Victory

By Michael Harris

All 14 Northern California Congressmen appeared to have won re-election yesterday — though Representative Clem Miller (Dem-First District) led by only a shaky margin.

Changes in Southern

See Page 8, Col. 1

Democrats Keep Control Of Congress

WASHINGTON, Nov. 9 (Wednesday) (AP) — **Democrats easily retained control of Congress in slowly mounting returns early today.**

With 32 of the 34 Senate contests decided, the Democrats had won 20 seats to give them a total of 63. They needed 51 to keep the control they had since 1955.

Democratic leaders, claiming an early presidential victory for Senator John F. Kennedy, went ahead with plans to install Senator Mike Mansfield of Montana as the new Senate leader to succeed Lyndon B. Johnson, the Vice President-elect.

In the House, the Republicans made slight inroads into the big Democratic majority of the last session, but were unable to mount a serious

See Page 9, Col. 3

Presidential Race

Nixon Reduces Foe's Early Lead

WASHINGTON (Wednesday), Nov. 9 (AP)—Senator John F. Kennedy early today had the electoral votes necessary for election as the 35th President of the United States, but all was not absolutely certain.

At 2 a. m. (PST), the 43-year-old Massachusetts Senator had a popular vote margin over Republican Vice President Richard M. Nixon of less than 51 per cent.

And the fate of eight States — including the keys to victory or defeat, California (32 electoral votes), Illinois (27) and Minnesota (11) — remained in doubt. Kennedy led in these three States.

With 269 electoral votes needed for victory, Kennedy had definitely won 258. He had won or was leading in a total of 23 States with 331 electoral votes.

Nixon's Total 192

Nixon had taken or was ahead in 26 States with 192 votes.

Kennedy, although trailing in the total number of States in his column by 26-23, had piled up his margin in the populous industrial cities.

At 2:30 a.m. (PST), Kennedy's popular vote was 27,956,222. Nixon had 27,192,815.

Kennedy's percentage was 50.7; Nixon's 49.3.

The Massachusetts Senator went to bed without knowing whether he had actually been elected.

Nixon clutched at hopes that belated tallies in

See Page 1-B, Col. 4

THE INDEX

For complete election coverage, see Pages A, B, C, D and Pages 2 through 14 inside today's Chronicle.

Books	27	Dr. Molner	12	Movies	28-30
Boyd	36	Editorials	26	O'Flaherty	25
Bridge	31	Fashions	11, 12	Pearson	27
Brier	26	Hedda	29	Question Man	16
Caen	15	Hoppe	26	Rosenbaum	33
Chess	31	Jumble	21	Shipping	16
Comics	38	Leiser	34	Sports	33-37
Count Marco	13	Letters	26	TV, Radio	31
Crossword	23, 27	Lively Arts	27	Theaters	28-30
Dear Abby	27	McCabe	27	Want Ads	16
Deaths	16	Millie's Col.	10	Weather	16
Delaplane	25	Mellinkoff	26	Women	10-13

No financial section—Markets closed for election.

Election In Brief

PRESIDENT

Senator Kennedy held a close lead. The popular vote early today showed:

Kennedy 28,443,163
Nixon .. 27,698,452

Kennedy led in 23 States with 331 electoral votes. Nixon led in 26 States with 192. (A total of 269 is needed for election.)

PROPOSITION 1

Proposition 1, the $1.75 billion water bonds measure, was trailing according to returns from 13,165 of California's 30,682 precincts.

Yes 751,502
No 796,876

PROPOSITION 15

Proposition 15, the State reapportionment measure, was defeated, according to returns from 12,621 precincts.

Yes 393,006
No 860,582

THE SENATE

Democrats, with 43 holdovers, had elected 20 Senators and were leading in one race.

Republicans, with 23 holdovers, had elected 12 and were leading in one race.

THE HOUSE

At an early hour this morning, with all 437 seats up for election:

Democrats had elected 206, and were leading in 44.

Republicans had elected 98, and were leading in 63.

GOVERNORS

In races for 27 governorships (now held by 14 Democrats and 13 Republicans):

Democrats had won 12 and were leading in 3.

Republicans had won 9 and were leading in 3.

U. S., CUBA BREAK

Quakes Jolt S.F., Coast Area

WEATHER FORECAST
Bay Area: Fair today and tomorrow, except for morning fog. High temperature Wednesday 45 to 52; low, 28 to 36, except 40 in San Francisco and Oakland.
Full Report, Page 33

San Francisco Chronicle
THE VOICE OF THE WEST

FINAL

97th YEAR No. 4 CCCCAAA WEDNESDAY, JANUARY 4, 1961 10 CENTS GArfield 1-1111

No New Taxes

Brown Offers His Program for 1961 Legislature

By Earl C. Behrens, Political Editor

SACRAMENTO, Jan. 3 — Governor Edmund G. Brown submitted to the Legislature today a sweeping program aimed at carrying forward his policy of what he called "responsible liberalism."

The program, organized in ten broad fields, would require no new taxes, he said.

His biennial message to a joint session of the Legislature was more than 6000 words in length and took 50 minutes to deliver.

It immediately evoked praise from most Democrats and sharp criticism from Republican leaders.

The Governor's program covered the fields of education, administration of justice, social welfare, public health, election law reforms, reorganization of State government, labor-management legislation, natural resources, problems of State growth and the necessity of facing demands for fiscal responsibility.

GOP Minority leader Joseph C. Shell said the Governor's message would frighten business away from California.

Assemblyman William A. Munnell of Montebello, the Democratic majority leader, said, however, that the Governor had presented "a comprehensive program that meets the needs of our State without being overly ambitious."

In many instances, the Governor made no specific recommendations but "commended" to the lawmakers the study of certain reports

See Page 10, Col. 3

The Warmup

By Barney Peterson

GOVERNOR BROWN ON THE ROSTRUM
As joint session of Legislature applauded in welcome

A Question of Self-Respect

U. S. Breaks With Cuba In Fight Over Envoys

Ike's Statement Omits Navy Base's Future; 'Kennedy Aides Upset'

WASHINGTON, Jan. 3 (AP)—The United States tonight broke off diplomatic relations with the Cuban government of Fidel Castro.

President Eisenhower issued a statement at 8:30 p.m. EST saying "There is a limit to what the United States in self-respect can endure. That limit has now been reached."

Mr. Eisenhower gave as his reason for severance of relations the ultimatum delivered by Cuba this morning which ordered the U.S. to cut the personnel in its embassy and consulate in Havana to 11 persons within 48 hours.

James C. Hagerty, White House press secretary, declined to answer any questions about what the U.S. intends to do with the naval base it operates in Guantanamo, Cuba, which it leased from Cuba by a treaty dating back to 1903, and renewed in 1934.

Hagerty was asked whether the U.S. still intends to defend the base by force if necessary against any attack by Castro. He also was asked whether the U.S. intended

See Page 13, Col. 5

UPI Telephoto

Cuba---a diplomatic crisis near Florida

First Day For 87th Congress

From AP and UPI

WASHINGTON, Jan. 3 The Democratic-controlled 87th Congress convened today for a session that must grapple with a wide range of domestic and cold-war problems.

The highlight of the day was maneuvering in the Senate to change the rules on filibustering.

This weapon of marathon speechmaking has been used most frequently by Southerners against civil rights legislation, although it has also been employed by Senators from other areas in a variety of situations.

Action on the issue was blocked at least until tomorrow by an objection from Senator Richard B. Russell (Dem-Ga.), unofficial leader of the Southern bloc.

A rules-change effort also was under way in the House as Democratic congressional leaders sought to smooth the way for some of President-elect Kennedy's more controversial proposals during his first two years in the White House.

The struggle was being waged against the backdrop of the usual opening-day ceremonies and exchanges—the warm handclasps, the applause for new members and the election of officers.

All the elections went according to form. Senator Mike Mansfield of Montana, as expected, was elected Senate Democratic leader to succeed Senator Lyndon B. Johnson of Texas, who will

See Page 8, Col. 1

Soviet Airlift

U. S. 'Has Proof' Of Russ in Laos

From AP, UPI, Reuters and New York Herald Tribune

The United States Government formally presented proof yesterday of its assertions that Russia was airlifting weapons and North Vietnamese troops to aid pro-Communist rebels fighting the pro-Western government of Laos.

The State Department, for the first time, claimed "hard evidence . . . absolutely authentic information" of no fewer than 218 Russian-flown sorties into Laos.

At the same time, efforts to solve the acute Laotian crisis by diplomatic means, rather than military, began to take shape here and abroad in these developments:

- The State Department disclosed it was discussing revival of the three-power International Conciliation Commission for Laos, as demanded by the Soviet Union, Communist China and India, to deal with the Laotian crisis.
- In Bangkok, Thailand, Secretary General Pote Sarasin of the Southeast Asia Treaty Organization declared

See Page 12, Col. 1

Cuba Consul Here Under Police Guard

A round-the-clock police guard was ordered last night for Rodrigo Parajon, Cuba's Consul General in San Francisco.

The action came swiftly in the wake of shattered diplomatic relations between Cuba and the United States.

There were no reports of threats against Parajon's life, but State Department offi-

See Page 13, Col. 1

Ike Plans Farewell TV Talk

New York Times Service

WASHINGTON, Jan. 3 President Eisenhower is planning on making a farewell radio-TV address to the Nation and the world before leaving office on January 20, the White House disclosed today.

While the plan is still tentative, the White House indicated that Mr. Eisenhower had all but made up his mind to give the speech as one of the final acts of his Administration.

In disclosing the plan, James C. Hagerty, White House press secretary, said the speech would be a "talk to the people of the United States and, I assume, to the people of the world."

The President will send his final state of the Union message in writing to Congress on January 12.

Hagerty said the message was expected to be shorter than usual and amount to a review of the President's

See Page 7, Col. 1

Quake at Hollister Nudges S. F.

San Francisco was gently shaken by an earthquake yesterday.

The tremor was the second of two, 90 minutes apart, that centered in the Hollister area of San Benito county.

The first, at 3 p.m., went unnoticed here and registered 3.25 on the Richter scale at the University of California seismological laboratory.

A larger shock, the one felt here, was recorded at 4:30 p.m. and had a Richter reading of 4.

No damage was reported.

Light fixtures swayed in San Francisco and residents reported a distinct jar.

Even in S. F.

Winter Coats Bay Roads With Ice

Winter took an icy hold on the Bay Area yesterday.

For the first time in memory, a San Francisco street — Arguello boulevard, in its steep stretch below the University of California Hospital — had to be closed to traffic because of icy hazards.

Two women were drowned when their car skidded on heavy ice and crashed through a guard rail into the Napa river.

Another frosty morning, with high fog and a fair midday, was forecast for today.

The busy Altamont Pass on U. S. Highway 50 was closed when 15 vehicles became involved in five accidents.

Temperatures plunged into the low twenties—21 at

See Page 4, Col. 7

The Phone Company vs. The H-Bomb

New York Times Service

NEW YORK, Jan. 3— International Telephone and Telegraph Corporation said here today that it has had "encouraging promise from a low-cost nuclear fusion process" it has been experimenting with "for a number of years."

If the experiments should prove successful, it would mean that the thermonuclear reaction will have been controlled. This is tantamount to har-

See Page 8, Col. 4

A Foggy Bird Count

Special to The Chronicle

SACRAMENTO, Jan. 3— The Sacramento Audubon Society said today its annual bird count was seriously hampered by fog.

The mist yesterday was so soupy that eagle-eyed birdwatchers tallied only 46,515 birds in the Sacramento area.

Last year they counted 133,625.

Nevertheless, said their leader, Burgess Heacox, there was great excitement as the birdwatchers set new records of discovery. They spotted four ferruginous hawks, 17 lesser yellowlegs, 13 Anna's hummingbirds.

3 Dead in Big French Storm

PARIS, Jan. 3 (P)—Lashing winds and rain caused heavy property damage in wide areas of France last night and today, and indirectly caused three deaths.

Winds of up to 75 miles an hour were recorded atop the Eiffel Tower

THE INDEX

Allen	39	Editorials	28	Panorama	29
Books	29	Fashions	16	Pearson	29
Boyd	37	Finance	38-41	Question Man	20
Bridge	32	Food	17	Rosenbaum	35
Brier	28	Hedda	31	Shipping	33
Caen	19	Hoppe	28	Sports	35-38
Chess	32	Horoscope	25	Sylvia Porter	40
Comics	42	Jumble	22	TV, Radio	32
Count Marco	17	Letters	28	Theaters	30, 31
Crossword	25,29	Lively Arts	29	Vital Stats	33
Dear Abby	29	McCabe	29	Want Ads	20
Deaths	33	Mellinkoff	28	Weather	33
Delaplane	27	Movies	30, 31	What's Law?	23
Dr. Molner	15	O'Flaherty	27	Women	13-17

EXTRA

WEATHER FORECAST
Bay Area: Cloudy with possible rain afternoon or evening. Clearing tonight and tomorrow. West to southwest winds 14 to 29 miles per hour (12 to 25 knots). Chances for rain: 5 in 10.
Full Report, Page 24

San Francisco Chronicle
THE VOICE OF THE WEST

FINAL

97th YEAR No. 102 CCCCAAA WEDNESDAY, APRIL 12, 1961 10 CENTS GArfield 1-1111

MAN IN SPACE! HE'S BACK--ALIVE

Israel Disputes Eichmann Plea

By Homer Bigart
Copyright 1961 by the New York Times and The Chronicle

Adolf Eichmann sat stonily impassive in a Jerusalem courtroom Tuesday as his defense counsel debated with his prosecutor whether a special Israeli tribunal has the authority to try him for mass murder.

The state's ripping attack into the defense challenge of the court's authority continued as the trial began its second day Wednesday.

Before the second argument began, the judge formally extended Eichmann's arrest for the duration of the trial.

At Tuesday's opening session, Eichmann spoke only twice from the time he entered the courtroom — to stand for 70 minutes in his bulletproof glass cage to listen to the 15-count indictment—until the end of the

See Page 11, Col. 1

Giants Back; Same Old 'Next Year'

By Donovan McClure

To the everlasting credit of 41,423 Giant baseball fans who attended Candlestick Park yesterday, they accepted the sting of excruciating, last-minute defeat with the stoic grace of experienced sufferers.

No seat cushions were thrown. No scorecards shredded to the winds. No lasting epithets hurled at the great god Misfortune.

The silent throng filed toward the exits a mass of shrugged shoulders, but the pain was artfully concealed.

"It was still a fine ballgame, dammit," was the consoling cry.

The score was Pittsburgh 8, San Francisco 7.

There was further misery for those who fled gamely to the plush new Stadium Club, hopeful of assuaging their grief through bubbly. The joint was packed to its elegant, brand-new rafters, leaving hundreds dry and unassuaged outside.

The season's opening day had begun so auspiciously.

The weather was warm, the skies sunny. By noon, an hour before game time, the ballpark was almost filled.

Down in the Giant dugout, comedian Danny Kaye gave playful prophecy of dreadful occurrences to come. Run-

See Page 4, Col. 1

Is This His Ship?

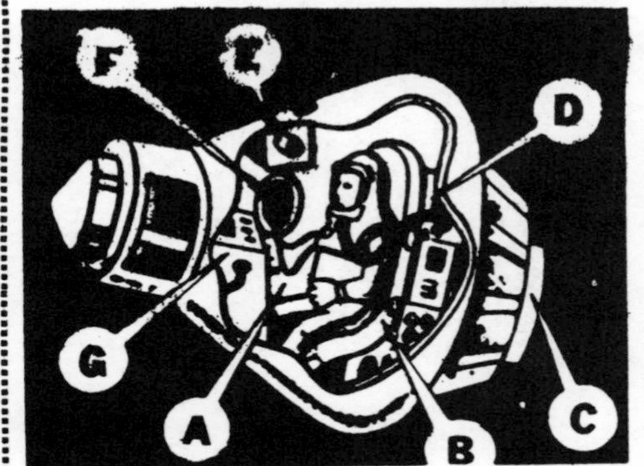

UPI Telephoto

Under the banner headline "The First Man in Space," The London Daily Worker printed this sketch. It was identified as "an artist's impression of the Soviet space capsule." Although the design appears somewhat similar to that of the United States' Project Mercury ballistic capsule, and items of equipment were located on the sketch, there was no information about its source. The Worker said the letters identify "(A) a pressurized cabin, (B) foam-padded seat to relieve pressure on take-off, (C) parachutes to slow speed of capsule on descent, (D) air supply, (E) television cameras, microphone, (F) porthole, (G) instrument panel."

It's Official

Russ Astronaut Orbits the Earth

From UPI and AP

LONDON, April 12—The Soviet Union announced it had brought a spaceman back to earth alive after an historic flight around the earth.

After the Russians announced they had won the race to put a man in space, the Tass news agency reported its first space navigator had "landed safely in the pre-arranged area of the U.S.S.R."

Moscow Radio said the first space navigator was sent up today in a five-ton spaceship that orbited the earth.

The space man applied a "brake device" which returned the ship to earth, Moscow Radio said.

The spaceman landed at 10:55 a. m. Moscow time (11:55 p. m. PST, Tuesday) and said he was well and had "no injuries or bruises," Tass reported.

Tass quoted him as saying:

"Please report to the party and government and personally to Nikita Sergeyevich Khrushchev that the landing was normal. I feel well, have no injuries or bruises."

The Big Descent

According to the announcement, the ship circled the earth, passing over South Africa and South America before beginning the descent from an orbit that ranged from about 109 to 187 miles above the earth.

A Moscow Radio announcer broke into a radio program at 10 a. m. (11 p. m. PST Tuesday) and said:

"Russia has successfully launched a man into space. His name is Yuri Gagarin. He was launched in a Sputnik named Vostok, which means east."

The radio announcer said the sputnik reached a minimum altitude of 175 kilometers (109½ miles) and a maximum altitude of 302 kilometers (187¾ miles).

The announcer said the weight of the sputnik

See Page 7, Col. 1

'Get Grant Out of Civil War'

CHARLESTON, S. C., April 11 (AP)—New Jersey accused the Civil War Centennial Commission of "pathetic mismanagement" tonight and angrily asked that President Kennedy remove Ulysses S. Grant III as chairman.

Joe Dempsey, vice chairman of the N. J. Centennial Commission, made the remark after Grant had turned down New Jersey's request for time to refute a South Carolina banquet speaker who had criticized its civil rights practices.

Grant and chairman Donald Flamm engaged in an impromptu debate in the banquet room at the Charleston Naval Base. To applause, Grant insisted that New Jersey bring the matter up at

See Page 22, Col. 3

8th Fatal Heart Attack

Candlestick Park's steep pedestrian ramp — the so-called "cardiac walk"—claimed its first fatal heart attack of 1961 yesterday, and its eighth since the stadium opened.

Donald Durbin, 45, wine and spirits sales manager for the Hudson Bay Co. in Los Angeles, complained of chest pains as he climbed the ramp prior to yesterday's baseball opener.

He collapsed in the new Stadium Club bar and doctors could not revive him.

Political Charges

Brown Will Probe 10 Per Cent Lobby

Governor Edmund G. Brown said yesterday he "certainly will get to the bottom" of charges that a Los Angeles trust deed corporation paid $20,000 to a lobbyist to take State pressure off the firm.

The story of the $20,000 came from Robert A. Manley, an official of two "10 per cent" mortgage firms, in testimony at a bankruptcy hearing in Los Angeles,

He named as the lobbyist Fred Zweiback, former administrative assistant to Lieutenant Governor Glenn Anderson, and a onetime vice president of the California Democratic Council, an organization of political volunteers.

Manley, president of the Western Certificate Fund and a vice president of the Western Trust Deed Corp., testified Zweiback told him the $20,000 would "get the State Commissioner of Corporations off the companies' back."

"I don't actually know that this money went anywhere other than into Zweiback's briefcase," said Manley.

He added, however, that he got no apparent results from the money. Instead, the situation got worse.

Corporation commissioner John G. Sobieski, attending

See Page 8, Col. 1

'Object' Up There, U. S. Confirms

WASHINGTON, April 12 (UPI) — The White House announced today American tracking stations have confirmed that Russia has launched "an object into space."

White House Press Secretary Pierre Salinger said "American tracking stations confirm the Soviet Union has launched an object into space. It is now orbiting the earth."

He said there would be no further comment from the White House for now.

James Webb, administrator of the National Aeronautics and Space Agency, said, "I think this is a splendid achievement.

"It is a significant event in terms of the Soviet timetable."

THE INDEX

Alton	49	Dr. Molner	18	Movies	38, 39
Animals	41	Editorials	36	O'Flaherty	35
Books	37	Fashions	16	Panorama	37
Boyd	46	Finance	48-52	Pearson	37
Bridge	40	Food	20, 21	Question Man	24
Brier	36	Hedda	39	Sports	43-48
Caen	23	Hoppe	36	Sylvia Porter	50
Chess	40	Horoscope	33	TV, Radio	40
Comics	41	Jumble	31	Theaters	38, 39
Count Marco	19	Letters	36	Vital Statistics	24
Crossword	33, 37	Lively Arts	37	Want Ads	25
Dear Abby	37	McCabe	37	Weather	24
Deaths	24	Mellinkoff	36	What's Law	30
Delaplane	25	Millie's Col.	17	Women	15-19

Liz Wins Oscar, Nearly Faints

WEATHER FORECAST
Bay Area: Variable cloudiness today, fair Wednesday. High temperature Tuesday, 57 to 63; low, 45 to 50. Small craft warnings, northwest wind to 40 m.p.h. (35 knots).
Full Report, Page 19

San Francisco Chronicle
THE VOICE OF THE WEST

FINAL

97th YEAR No. 108 CCCCAAAB TUESDAY, APRIL 18, 1961 10 CENTS GArfield 1-1111

WILD REPORTS ON CUBAN WAR

Tourist Promotion

S. F. Hotel Tax Is Voted 6-5; Halley Switches

By Mel Wax

Supervisor James Leo Halley, long an opponent of a hotel tax, switched sides yesterday with the explanation: "If you can't lick 'em, join 'em."

It meant the controversial 3 per cent tax on transient hotel rooms, expected to raise more than $1 million a year for tourist and convention promotion, won a 6-5 endorsement from the Board of Supervisors.

The bait was a promise the city would investigate buying the Fox Theater, and would use some of the hotel tax money for it if the Market street landmark is found to be "needed and necessary."

Defeated was a Halley proposal that only $400,000 be allocated for tourist business and that all the rest go to the Fox.

"I want to make my position clear," said Mayor George Christopher, in a rare appearance before the Board. "As much as I want the tax, I will be compelled to veto the bill if it comes to me in the present form — and I shall veto it."

Supervisor Harold S. Dobbs carried the ball for the tax with an eloquent, hour-long oration.

But it was Christopher's offer to compromise that finally paid off.

"I'd like to go along with you," Christopher said. "Why not consider the tax and the Fox on their merits, and have separate resolutions on each?"

"I have a flexible mind, and I'm in a pleasant mood," said Halley.

"Why not insert a provision saying we'll give 'due

See Page 2, Col. 1

Potrero Hill Freeway Link Approved

A route through Potrero Hill for the southern freeway was approved, 7 to 4, by the Board of Supervisors yesterday.

The $40 million route will connect the southern freeway at Evans avenue to the Embarcadero Freeway at Howard street.

Voting for that route were Supervisors William C. Blake, Harold S. Dobbs, John Jay Ferdon, James Leo Halley, J. Joseph Sullivan, Peter Tamaras and Alfonso J. Zirpoli. Against were Supervisors Joseph M. Casey, Charles A. Ertola, Clarissa S. McMahon, and Joseph E. Tinney.

The action followed by a few hours a plea by four Potrero women to Mayor Christopher to delay any decision.

They came up with an alternate plan, dropping the southern freeway from the east slope of the hill down to a double-decked route along Third street, with a bridge over Islais creek at Fourth.

The trouble with that

See Page 2, Col. 3

Oscars Go to Liz, Burt, 'Apartment'

By Bob Thomas

SANTA MONICA, April 17 (AP)—Elizabeth Taylor, near death two months ago, reached the peak of her career tonight by winning the award as best actress of 1960 from the Motion Picture Academy.

Burt Lancaster was acclaimed best actor for his role as the shady revivalist of "Elmer Gantry."

"The Apartment" won as best picture, and for best direction by Billy Wilder.

Shirely Jones of "Elmer Gantry" and Peter Ustinov of "Spartacus" won the top supporting roles.

DRAMATIC MOMENT

Miss Taylor's victory, for her role as the ill-starred wanton of "Butterfield 8," was one of the most dramatic moments in Oscar's 33 years, climaxed when she nearly fainted.

When she heard her name called as winner by Yul Brynner, Miss Taylor clapped both hands over her mouth and stared in apparent astonishment. Then she turned to husband Eddie Fisher, and he helped her to her feet.

Still weakened by her bout with double pneumonia, she was helped to the stage of Civic Auditorium, walking slowly and uncertainly.

'THANK YOU'

She stood there trembling before the audience of 2500, plus TV onlookers nationwide, and finally said in hushed tones:

"I don't really know how to express my gratitude. All I can say is thank you very much."

Liz looked radiant when she arrived on Fisher's arm, clad in a flowing gown with mint-green chiffon bodice and long white sheath skirt of Dior design. It was her fourth nomination for an Oscar.

As a mob of photographers closed in, however, her smile faded and she seemed to grow faint. Instead going to her seat she went to the lounge and rested 15 minutes. Then, walking unsteadily, she entered the auditorium.

After winning, Miss Taylor

See Page 4, Col. 1

Death Row Cons List Demands

San Quentin's Death Row hunger strikers broke silence yesterday and listed 24 ways to improve their diet.

And they vowed they would cheat the gas chamber by dying of hunger—unless their menus took on a more epicurean flavor.

In a letter to Warden Fred R. Dickson, with copies dispatched to Governor Edmund G. Brown and Director of

See Page 8, Col. 1

Gulf of Mexico
FLORIDA
Key West
Nassau
Andros Island
BAHAMA ISLANDS
MILES
Matanzas Province
Las Villas Province
HAVANA
CABANAS
Jaguey La Grande
Cienaga Oriental
Cienfuegos
Camaguey Province
Oriente Province
Isle of Pines
CUBA
BARACOA
Guantanamo
SANTIAGO
Caribbean Sea

AP Wirephoto map

The big arrow indicates major landing area on the Cuban south coast. Small arrow points to invasion site in Oriente province.

The News at a Glance

- Anti-Castro forces said there had been two confirmed landings and that one rebel force had penerated to Cuba's main east-west highway.
- In the U. N., Cuban Foreign Minister Roa claimed that jets from a U.S. carrier and Guantanamo forces were helping the rebels.
- In Washington, Secretary of State Rusk, while stating American sympathy for the anti-Castro forces, said there would be no intervention by U. S. forces.
- In Moscow, the Soviet Union said the Communist world was "prepared to help and support" the Castro regime.
- Leftist students staged pro-Castro demonstrations in 10 Latin American countries.
- Cuban exile sources said two top leaders of the rebel movement were en route to Cuba to land if their troops are successful.

Eichmann Told of More Atrocities

JERUSALEM, April 18 (Tuesday) (AP) — Israeli attorney-general Gideon Hausner renewed his harrowing review of Nazi atrocities as the trial of Adolf Eichmann for crimes against the Jewish people continued today.

Hausner, who recounted horrors the Nazis inflicted on the Jews in eastern Europe yesterday, turned today to western Europe and to Holland in particular.

Hausner said a special department was established by the Nazis in Amsterdam to "mark down Jews for extermination."

A series of laws passed to deal with Jews were worked out "in cooperation with Adolf Eichmann," Hausner said.

Among these were statutes banning Jews from attending movies and other entertainments, forbidding Jews from using telephones, subjecting Jews to an evening

See Page 12, Col. 4

'U. S. for Rebels, But No Armed Aid'

By James B. Reston
New York Times Service

WASHINGTON, April 17—Secretary of State Dean Rusk expressed the sympathy of the American people for the anti-Castro invaders of Cuba today but emphasized "there is not and will not be any intervention there by United States forces."

The Administration did not deny that it is giving material support to the raiding parties, but this aid is undoubtedly on a much smaller scale than originally planned here, and the landings in Cuba are much smaller than excited reports of "invasion" suggest.

No more than 200-300 men were involved in the week-end landings on the vast coastline of Cuba, according to reliable information reaching here.

In fact, the landings of the last 48 hours were not designed to get a lot of fighting men on the ground but to provide supplies for the anti-Castro underground already operating there as a result of at least six other landings that have taken place over the past few months.

Rusk was extremely cautious in his remarks on the

See Page 10, Col. 5

Russ Pledge Castro Aid, Accuse U. S.

MOSCOW, April 18 (Tuesday) (UPI)—The Soviet Union officially accused the United States today of preparing and starting the invasion of Cuba.

It warned of possible Russian aid to Fidel Castro's regime "should armed intervention not cease."

The official Soviet government statement was broadcast over Moscow radio. In

See Page 10, Col. 5

The Invasion

Castro, Rebels Claim Victories

From AP and UPI

Prime Minister Fidel Castro announced early today (Tuesday) that his government troops were continuing "to fight heroically" to repel an invasion force.

A spokesman for the invaders said late last night in Miami that the anti-Castro forces had penetrated to Cuba's main east-west highway. He added that "the most important contingents of our forces have not yet gone into Cuba."

Castro's announcement was broadcast over a hastily assembled nationwide radio network. It spoke of the heroic action of his troops in "southwest Las Villas province where mercenaries disembarked with imperialist support."

The statement said that "the successes of the Castro army, air force and militia will be announced to the people in the next few hours."

UNCLEAR

Castro's announcement and the statement by the exile spokesman in Miami did not make clear the size and scope of the military operation in Cuba.

The exile spokesman indicated the "invasion" was not yet of major proportions. This was supported by an announcement in New York yesterday by the Cuban Revolutionary Council that the week-end forays were primarily to land military supplies and equipment for resistance fighters already there.

The New York headquarters of the anti-Castro movement said that the "principal battle of the Cuba revolt will be fought in the next few hours."

It said the action Monday was largely of a supply and support effort to forces "mo-

See Page 8, Col. 1

Roa Charges U. S. Carrier Helps Rebels

UNITED NATIONS, N. Y., April 17 (AP)—Cuba charged here tonight that U. S. carrier-based jet planes were taking part in the invasion attempt aimed at toppling Prime Minister Fidel Castro from power.

Cuba further charged that regular United States forces from Guantanamo Naval Base had entered the fight in Oriente province.

In Washington a Navy spokesman said "there is nothing" to either story.

"We don't even have a carrier in that vicinity," he added.

The new charges followed earlier accusations that Cuba had been invaded from both Florida and Guatemala in an act of undeclared war by the U. S.

Cuban Foreign Minister Raul Roa delivered the charges before the U. N. Political Committee, and denials came from U. S. chief delegate Adlai E. Stevenson.

Meanwhile, the Soviet bloc laid before the committee a formal demand for an end to

See Page 10, Col. 3

THE INDEX

Allen 43
Animals 35
Books 31
Boyd 40
Bridge 34
Brier 30
Coen 17
Chess 34
Comics 35
Connolly 38
Count Marco 15
Crossword 27,31
Dear Abby...31
Deaths 16
Delaplane ...29
Dr. Molner ...15
Editorials 30
Fashions 14
Finance .. 42-46
Hedda 33
Hoppe 30
Jumble 25
Letters 30
Lively Arts ...31
McCabe 31
Mellinkoff ...30
Millie's Col. ..14
Movies ...32,33
O'Flaherty ...29
Pearson 31
Question Man 18
Rosenbaum ..37
Shipping 19
Sports ... 37-42
Sylvia Porter .44
TV, Radio ...34
Theaters . 32,33
Vital Stats. ..19
Want Ads ...19
Weather 19
What's Law ..34
Women ..13-15

Close-Up Photos of the Flight

WEATHER FORECAST
Bay Area: Occasional rain today. Clearing tonight, and fair tomorrow. Low temperature 48 to 52; high, Saturday, San Francisco 58, Oakland 63, San Mateo 65, San Rafael 65.
Full Report, Page 16

San Francisco Chronicle
THE VOICE OF THE WEST

FINAL

97th YEAR No. 126 — CCCCAAA — SATURDAY, MAY 6, 1961 — 10 CENTS — GArfield 1-1111

SHEP'S REPORT FROM SPACESHIP

South Vietnam

Kennedy Weighs Sending Troops

From UPI and AP

WASHINGTON, May 5—President Kennedy said today he is considering the possibility of using U. S. troops if necessary to save South Vietnam from Communist conquest. The President said no decision had been reached as yet.

Mr. Kennedy said Vice President Lyndon B. Johnson would discuss the question of bolstering South Vietnam against a mounting "barrage" of Communist terror and sabotage during his forthcoming special mission to Southeast Asia.

The President told his news conference it would be helpful to put off a decision until Johnson had consulted with the pro-Western South Vietnam government "as to what further steps could most usefully be taken."

The Chief Executive said he was consulting with the National Security Council and other government groups on the possibility of dispatching U. S. troops or other steps to block Red domination of South Vietnam.

Mr. Kennedy did not men-

See Page 9, Col. 3

Nixon Appeal To President: 'A New Start'

New York Times Service

CHICAGO, May 5 — Former Vice President Richard Nixon urged President Kennedy today to rally the American people for a new start in American foreign policy.

In his first loyal opposition speech, Nixon called for a "searching reappraisal of the free world's ability, particularly America's, to deal with, and end, the aggression in which Communists are now engaging."

Nixon said the United States must be prepared to go it alone in order to seek swift action while collective action machinery was being set up.

And, in a tone that was half censure and half sympathy, Nixon said this was the lesson of Cuba and Laos:

"We must never talk big-

See Page 4, Col. 5

UPI Telephoto

Spaceman Shepard beside capsule as copter began to hoist him aboard

Shepard 'Feels Fine' After Trip

New York Times Service

CAPE CANAVERAL, Fla., May 5 — A slim, impressively calm Navy test pilot named Alan B. Shepard Jr. was rocketed 115 miles into space today, the first American space explorer.

He landed safely 302 miles out at sea only 15 minutes later and was almost immediately lifted aboard a Marine helicopter.

"Boy, what a ride," he said, as he was flown to the carrier Lake Champlain.

The almost-perfect flight represented the United States' first major step in the race to explore space with manned spacecraft.

It was only a modest leap compared with the once-

See Page 5, Col. 1

The Ride--- Second By Second

By Associated Press

As he hurtled through space yesterday, Alan B. Shepard talked to his control center in the calm, precise tones of a veteran pilot making a routine test.

With no trace of fear or uncertainty in the voice, he reported on the progress of his space craft, as he has reported on the performances of numerous hot experimental planes he has tested in the past.

His voice became strained only during the time, in acceleration and again in descent, when he was submitted to crushing pressures.

Voices from the ground

See Page 7, Col. 1

Teamsters Move in on Farm Labor

By Kirk Smith
Chronicle Labor Writer

The Teamsters Union—without a single strike, or a court order—announced yesterday it had signed a farm labor contract with one of the State's biggest growers and was dickering with 110 more.

The contract with Bud Antle, Inc., of Salinas will immediately put hundreds of field hands into the Teamsters and will add many hundreds more throughout the year, the company said.

It is the first time in California that the nation's biggest labor union has accepted field workers, and it means a severe setback for the two AFL-CIO farm unions in the fields.

While the Packinghouse Workers and the Agricultural Workers Organizing Committee have been trying hard to organize the workers themselves, the Teamsters have apparently been busy organizing the growers.

The Council of California Growers quickly cautioned that the Antle agreement did not mean "a major swing of

See Page 2, Col. 5

THE INDEX

Alien	32	Graham	11	Shipping	16
Animals	34	Hedda	15	Sports	29-33
Churches	11	Jumble	20	Theaters	15
Comics	34	Movies	15	TV, Radio	14
Connolly	29	Owl	8, 9	Vital Stat.	16
Crossword	13, 25	Pearson	13	Want Ads	17-26
Deaths	16	Question Man	13	Weather	16
Fashions	10	Reston	13	Women	10
Finance	31-33	Rosenbaum	29	What's Law?	22

MAY 6, 1961

FIRST PHOTOS OF GLENN'S RETURN

WEATHER FORECAST
Bay Area: Variable cloudiness today and tomorrow; possible scattered showers today. Low, 37 to 45; high Wednesday, near 57. Chances for rain: 4 in 10 today.
Full Report, Page 43

San Francisco Chronicle
THE VOICE OF THE WEST

98th YEAR No. 52 | CCCCAAA | WEDNESDAY, FEBRUARY 21, 1962 | 10 CENTS | GArfield 1-1111

'A Real Fireball Ride'--He Beat Trouble Twice

Glenn in Fine Shape After 81,000-Mile Trip ---The Nation's New Hero

From A.P. & U.P. Dispatches

Cape Canaveral, Fla.

Astronaut John H. Glenn Jr. flew America's Friendship VII space capsule three times around the world yesterday.

In his flight of 4 hours and 56 minutes the 40-year-old Marine lieutenant colonel became the third human being to orbit the earth and the first American to do so.

Glenn's Project Mercury spacecraft splashed into the Atlantic ocean right on schedule after an exultantly successful trip that saw the pilot coolly take over manual control of the capsule when automatic devices malfunctioned.

'In Excellent Condition'

The U. S destroyer Noa scooped Glenn's capsule from the water at 3:01 p. m. (EST), and 19 minutes later the astronaut climbed out "in excellent condition." His only "injury" was a scraped knuckle.

A helicopter transferred him to the carrier Randolph at dusk; and after triumphal greetings, a medical exam, a de-briefing, and a filet mignon dinner, he was flown to Grand Turk island in the Bahamas for a two-day stay.

President Kennedy, who had watched the three-orbit mission on TV, hailed Glenn's achievement and planned a hero's parade for him in Washington next week.

As all the world knew, two Soviet "cosmonauts" had preceded Glenn into orbital flight; and two Americans had already flown Mercury capsules to the threshold of space.

A Spur Into Space

But Glenn's triumph was a tremendous spur to America's space program, and told the entire world this nation is now fighting successfully toward space leadership.

The world watched yesterday's flight intently, with expectation drummed high by all the disappointing delays of the past two months.

Millions of Americans were up before dawn to follow the flight second-by-second on all three TV networks. Radio broadcasts carried the news throughout every nation. The Russians noted Glenn's achievement briefly and punctiliously.

But the 400,000 citizens of Perth, Australia, sent tangible evidence of their good wishes: as the

See Page 1A, Col. 3

Down to Earth Again

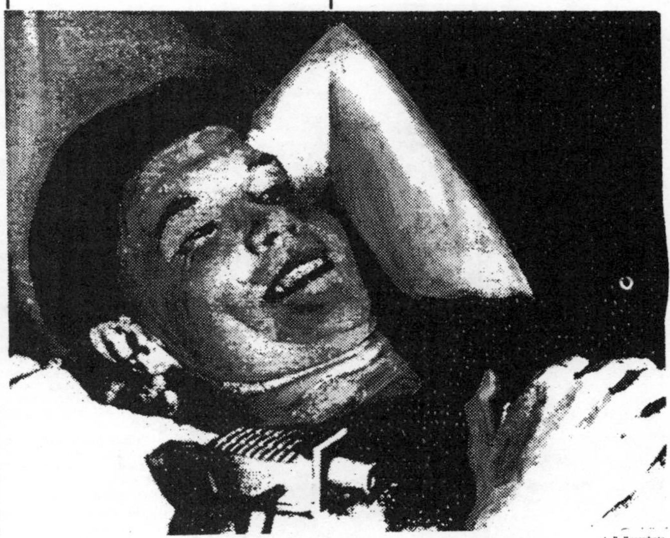

U. P. Wirephoto

Glenn, relaxed and smiling, waited for a physical on the U.S.S. Noa

'A Long, Interesting Day'

Glenn Relaxing At Bahamas Base

Associated Press

Grand Turk, The Bahamas

Brimming with delight, astronaut John H. Glenn Jr., reached this tiny Atlantic island a few hours after sunset—the fourth sunset he had seen yesterday—to rest and tell the story of his fabulous space ride.

Fellow astronaut M. Scott Carpenter helped him out of his plane and playfully butted him in the chest.

Glenn declared. "I feel wonderful, and I couldn't feel better."

'HOWDY'

He said "howdy" to his crowd of well-wishers and added, "It's been a long day and a very interesting one, too, I might add."

He had suffered a minor injury on his flight. As he left the space craft in Bahama water, he skinned his knuckles. He arrived aboard the aircraft carrier Randolph, wearing two little adhesive bandages on his right hand.

The American who zoomed through space at five miles per second arrived from the Randolph in a Navy anti-submarine patrol plane with a top speed of about 175 miles per hour.

Glenn walked with some

See Page 1A, Col. 5

A Tactical Defeat for Urban Plan

U.P. & A.P.

Washington

The Senate yesterday defeated 58 to 43 an Administration move to make certain both houses of Congress would have to go on record for or against President Kennedy's plan to set up a Department of Urban Affairs.

It did so by refusing to force out of the Government Operations Committee a resolution of

See Page 16, Col. 4

Talks With French

Algeria Rebels OK Peace Pact

Tunis

The Algerian nationalist provisional government yesterday gave full approval to the peace accords negotiated with the French.

One Algerian said afterward: "All 12 members of the government are in unanimous agreement." This was a reference to the five ministers who are prisoners in France, as well as the four who negotiated the agreement, and the three ministers who remained in Tunis during the secret talks last week on the French-Swiss border.

The next hurdle on the Nationalist side is the National Council of the Algerian Revolution, the "parliament" of the rebel movement, which will meet in Tripoli tomorrow.

CONFIDENCE

The ministers were confident they would obtain the four-fifths majority necessary for ratification. Only the National Council, a partly secret organization with a reported membership of 55 Nationalists, can order a ceasefire and end the seven-year-old war for independence.

The French administration hopes that the nationalist network will prove efficient and moderate enough when a cease-fire is announced to restrain the Moslem population from violence.

Ominously, extremist Secret Army Organization commandos yesterday continued building up a civil war arsenal by raiding army installations.

Unofficial indications are that another negotiating session with the French — this time a formal one — will be necessary before promulgation of a ceasefire.

QUESTIONS

Questions still to be settled, it is reported, concern transitional institutions, the executive body that is to rule Algeria between the ceasefire and a self-determination referendum.

The negotiators were Belkacem Krim, Mohammed Yazid, Saad Dahlab and Lakhdar Ben Tobbal. They met here yesterday with Premier Ben Youssef Ben Khedda, Abdel Hafid Boussouf and Mohammedi Said.

New York Times

Plaza Hotel Sold in Land Deal

The historic Plaza Hotel on Union Square and four adjacent properties have just changed hands in a $5 million deal, it was announced here yesterday.

Purchaser is American Factors, Ltd., of Honolulu. Company officials said they bought the San Francisco landmark strictly for trading purposes.

Seller was the Prudential Insurance Company of America, which bought the 36,000-square foot parcel in 1958, then announced plans to raze the Plaza and erect a new regional headquarters building.

"That plan was dropped

See Page 16, Col. 1

Supervisors' 'Bonanza' for City Workers

The Judiciary Committee of the Board of Supervisors was in the process late last night of approving an estimated $3.4 million pay raise for about 10,000 Civil Service employees in San Francisco.

George Grubb, the city's general manager of personnel, said the raises were being approved at a rate $1 million over the $2.4 million recommended by the Civil Service commission.

"That extra $1 million," said Grubb, "will add an extra 8.5 cents to the tax rate."

Supervisors Joseph Tinney,

See Page 8, Col. 5

Slides Peril Telegraph Hill Homes

Scores of persons were evacuated early today as persistent landslides threatened to undermine their homes perched on the brink of a 200-foot cliff on the east side of Telegraph Hill.

The slides, which crashed about five tons of rock onto a chemical plant below, were centered beneath the $100,000 home of Dr. Hans Klussmann.

The Klussmann home juts

See Page 13, Col. 1

Higher Cab Fares?

A Board of Supervisors' committee yesterday recommended taxi-fare increases of five cents for the first mile and 10 cents for each succeeding mile traveled.

The Police Committee unanimously recommended a rate of 85 cents for the first mile. This will be five cents more than the existing rate but 2½ cents less than what the Yellow Cab Co. had proposed.

The rates will affect all of the city's cabs, of which Yellow operates 68 per cent. If approved by the full Board

See Page 16, Col. 2

THE INDEX

Allen	51	Dr. Molner	21	Movies	40, 41
Animals	54	Dr. Nason	44	O'Flaherty	37
Art's Gallery	31	Editorials	38	Panorama	39
Books	39	Fashions	22	Pearson	39
Bridge	42	Finance	50-53	Question Man	42
Brier	38	Food	17-20	Rosenbaum	46
Caen	25	Hedda	41	Shipping	43
Chess	42	Hoppe	39	Sports	45-49
Comics	54	Horoscope	35	Sylvia Porter	52
Count Marco	21	Jumble	29	TV, Radio	42
Crossword	35, 39	Leiser	46	Theaters	40, 41
Dear Abby	39	Letters	38	Vital Stats.	43
Deaths	43	Lively Arts	39	Want Ads	26
Debbie Drake	23	McCabe	45	Weather	43
Delaplane	37	Mellinkoff	38	What's Law	27
Dreams	34	Millie	23	Women	20-23

San Francisco
Sunday Chronicle

98th YEAR No. 273 FINAL EDITION ★★ SUNDAY, SEPTEMBER 30, 1962 25 CENTS GArfield 1-1111

U. S. Calls Up Troops In Mississippi Crisis

Both Reach S. F.

Tanker Loaded With Gas Rams Freighter in Fog

The American supertanker Titan, heavily laden with potentially explosive high test gasoline, collided with a 338-foot Colombian cargo ship yesterday 20 miles south of the Golden Gate in a fog "so thick you couldn't see your shoelaces."

The impact shivered through the two ships in the pre-dawn darkness and for several minutes they were welded together.

When they managed to part, a gaping 20-by-20 foot hole had been cut in the Colombian freighter, Rio Magdalena, running from the main deck to below the waterline.

NO INJURIES

On the bridge of the Titan, the master, James Mardikos, 38, of New York, ordered damage crews to the bow. He had been on the bridge, his company said later, long before the two ships collided:

"He had sighted the Rio Magdalena on his radar miles away and the two ships were on course to pass port to port — when suddenly the other ship veered and crossed the bow of the Titan. He ordered full astern and made every effort to avoid the collision . . . but it was impossible."

There were no injuries, the Coast Guard reported.

Crewman of the 2123-ton Magdalena manned the lifeboats and the huge 735-foot Titan, which had thrown 18,423 tons into the smaller vessel, radioed other ships to stay clear of the collision area," because of the danger of explosion."

In the tense moments of the growing dawn the two ships drifted, all lights blazing in the thick fog, and assayed damage.

SOS

The Titan's first SOS went out to San Francisco at 4:50 a. m. By 6:45 a. m., two hours later, the 35 crewmen of the Magdalena were reported still standing by the

See Page 21, Col. 1

Clear Skies

Fair weather returned to the Bay Area yesterday after two drizzly days.

Clear skies and warmer temperatures are forecast for today.

Low temperatures expected today will be 47 to 53 degrees.

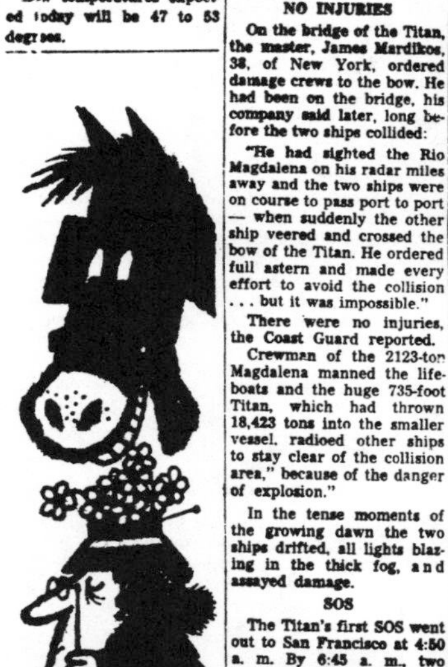

Sunset Special

By Gordon Peters

This ghostly white cloud danced over the Pacific horizon at sunset yesterday, prompting hundreds of telephone calls to police and newspapers.

The cloud — seen here from the Golden Gate Bridge—turned out to be the vapor trail left by a jet.

It was about 100 miles out and 1500 feet high when the trail ended because of atmospheric conditions, officials said.

Kennedy TV Speech Today ---State Guard Federalized

Army Setting Up a Camp Near Ole Miss---Other Units Sent to Memphis

A.P. & U.P.

Washington

President Kennedy last night ordered Army troops assembled at Memphis, Tenn., 50 miles from the campus of the University of Mississippi.

He authorized the Secretary of Defense to take any other measure he deemed necessary to carry out Federal court orders.

Then the President announced he will make a television and radio address to the nation tonight to explain the action being taken in the desegregation crisis.

The Pentagon announced early today that it is sending Army engineers into Mississippi to establish a tent camp for U. S. marshals involved in the integration crisis.

They will set up camp near Oxford.

In the hours before midnight and early today Mr. Kennedy took two more major steps.

CONFERENCES

The White House reported:

"The President talked today with the governor of Mississippi on three separate occasions. The President was unable to receive from Governor Barnett satisfactory assurances that law and order could or would be maintained at Oxford, Miss., during the coming week.

"The President is, therefore, federalizing the units of Mississippi's National Guard, army and air, in case they are needed to enforce the orders of the Federal Court."

HOPE

High officials still hoped that emergency use of Federal troops would not be necessary.

"One thing is certain," one said last night, "there is no room for compromise. It is basic that the Constitution as interpreted by the Federal court must be enforced."

In effect, the 7100-man guard was removed from

See Page 20, Col. 5

TV Times

President Kennedy's address to the Nation on the Mississippi integration crisis will be carried on all local TV and radio network stations at 4:30 p.m. today.

Re-broadcasts are scheduled on KRON-TV (Channel 4) at 11 p.m. and KPIX (Channel 5) at 7:30 p.m. No re-broadcast times have been set by KGO-TV and KNBC and KCBS-radio.

Mississippi Crisis

Lt. Governor Is Held in Contempt

Associated Press

New Orleans

The Federal Appeals Court declared Mississippi Lieutenant Governor Paul B. Johnson in contempt of court yesterday for his part in blocking James H. Meredith, a Negro, from the University of Mississippi.

The three-judge panel of the Fifth United States Circuit Court of Appeals ordered Johnson fined $5000 a day unless he shows by 11 a.m. Tuesday that he intends to cooperate with Federal court orders prohibiting interference with Meredith's enrollment.

The same court, with eight judges sitting, convicted Governor Ross Barnett of contempt Friday for stopping Meredith. It ordered him fined $10,000 a day and taken into custody if he fails to purge himself of contempt by 11 a. m. Tuesday.

The court did not order Johnson taken into custody.

ALTERNATE

But it did say that if the Lieutenant Governor acts in place of the Governor in violation of court orders he would be committed to cus-

See Page 20, Col. 3

Bobby Chides Lawyers on Dixie Crisis

Attorney General Robert F. Kennedy told a San Francisco audience last night he is disappointed that neither the American Bar Association nor the lawyers of Mississippi have supported the Federal courts in the Mississippi segregation dispute.

His message was delivered over the telephone from his Washington, D. C., home to a distinguished black-tie gathering of judges, lawyers, political leaders and alumni of the University of San Francisco gathered at the Fairmont Hotel.

Kennedy had planned to be here in person for the banquet, held as part of the dedication of the new USF law school building, Kendrick Hall.

PREVENTED

But the situation at the University of Mississippi prevented his trip.

Kennedy said that lawyers have a continuing responsibility to uphold "the fundamental of justice from which the law cannot depart."

The he turned to his present problems and said:

"One of my great disap-

See Page 12, Col. 6

Candid Views of A Visiting Prelate

By Donovan Bess

Dr. Geoffrey Fisher flew into town yesterday for a six-day visit, and almost immediately began a candid discussion about bookies, prostitutes, adultery and homosexuality.

The merry-faced, recently retired Archbishop of Canterbury—former spiritual leader of 45 million Protestants — also permitted himself a bit of boasting about his success in getting fraternization between top Anglican and Roman Catholic prelates.

He is the man who crowned Queen Elizabeth II, but he may go down in history primarily as the first Archbishop of Canterbury to meet with a Pope since the beginning of the Reformation in the 15th Century.

His Grace, as the English and the Episcopalians call him, is 75 years old. But he teems with interest in the world around him.

BOOKIES

He is the Earl of Lambeth and has a palace and a seat in the House of Lords. But he is by no means lordly. For instance, he thinks betting

See Page 26, Col. 1

Nixon Assails Brown's 'Double-Talk' on Farms

By Earl C. Behrens
Political Editor

Yuba City, Sutter county

Richard M. Nixon accused Governor Edmund G. Brown yesterday of attempting to double-talk California farmers on the State issues of the minimum wage and use of Mexican nationals.

He said the Governor had unsuccessfully backed a proposal before the Legislature for a minimum wage for farm laborers and frequently has opposed use of the "bracero program"—the employment of Mexican nationals in California.

But now in an election year, said Nixon, the Governor has been talking "out of both sides of his mouth" by suddenly changing positions on both sides.

"I am opposed to a California minimum wage for farm workers," declared the Republican candidate for

See Page 18, Col. 1

West Weighs U. N. Role in Berlin Crisis

By William R. Frye
Chronicle Correspondent

United Nations

What useful role, if any, can the United Nations play in solving the Berlin problem?

This question dominates private Western strategy sessions here today in the wake of a proposal by Britain that the U. N. tell Russia to "stop artificially creating crises" in the prewar German capital.

The proposal was made informally in a speech Thursday by Lord Home, British Foreign Secretary. Home was replying to Soviet Foreign Minister Andrei A. Gromyko, who had asked the U. N. to sanction the Berlin wall. Home did not ask for a formal vote.

Key questions being posed

See Page 15, Col. 3

THE INDEX

Art	TW	Fashions	WW	Puzzles	B
Autos	36	Finance	45, 46	QuestionMan	28
Books	TW	Gallup Poll	28	Radio	D
Boyd	42	Gardens	B, 34	Real Estate	34
Bridge	B	Food	B	Rhythm	TW
Caen	27	Hoppe	28	Rosenbaum	40
Chess	B, 32	Leiser	42	Rovere	29
Crossword	B	Marco	WW	Shipping	37
Dear Abby	WW	Millie	WW	Society	WW
Deaths	37	Movie Times	D	Sports	39-44
Dr. Brothers	23	Music	TW	Stamps	36
Dr. Fine	26	Pearson	28	Theaters	D
Dr. Molner	WW	Pets	36	Travel	30-33
Editorials	28	Photography	34	Weather	37

Bonanza (B), Datebook (D), Classified (C), This World (TW), Women's World (WW)

Pennant for Giants

THE CITY FLIPS

THE WEATHER
Bay Area: Fair and slightly warmer. High Thursday, 70-76; low, 48-53. Westerly winds 10 to 20 miles an hour. See Page 22.

San Francisco Chronicle
THE VOICE OF THE WEST

98th YEAR No. 277 CCCCAAA THURSDAY, OCTOBER 4, 1962 10 CENTS GArfield 1-1111

Six Orbits

Perfect Flight By Astronaut---Exact Landing

Associated Press

Cape Canaveral

Walter M. Schirra Jr., America's third and record-breaking orbital astronaut, went about his task yesterday in a brisk and businesslike manner.

He made a safe and successful journey to advance America's space technology immeasurably and won the plaudits of fellow astronauts and scientists of his performance.

Launched in his Sigma 7 space capsule here at 7:15 a.m. (EST), Schirra whirled around the earth six times [illegible] exactly nine hours and 13 minutes later.

Schirra completed America's longest and highest space flight, a journey of 160,000 miles, flying around the world at a speed of [illegible] miles at its highest point, 100 at his lowest.

In the most precise space flight yet engineered by Project Mercury scientists, the 39-year-old Navy Commander came down with pinpoint accuracy about 275 miles northeast of Midway Island.

His capsule passed through the 3000-degree heat of the atmosphere and dropped into Pacific waters only 4¼ miles from the aircraft carrier Kearsarge, the re-

See Page 10, Col. 1

Mob Scene at Airport-- No Joy in Mudville

How L. A. Took Day Of Despair

By Denne Petitclerc
Chronicle Correspondent

Los Angeles

Early Tuesday morning, as the jet from San Francisco landed at Los Angeles International Airport, the smog was so thick you could not see the sleek control tower through the tarnish of yellow haze.

"How long will you be staying?" Miss Evans, the smiling Hertz girl, asked us.

"That depends — if the Dodgers lose . . ."

"Oh," she brightened. "I'll put you down for two days."

FROWN

The smile turned to a shapely frown.

"Personally, I think those Dodgers deserve to lose—imagine, after having it already won . . ."

"Lady," said a man standing in line, "you said a mouthful."

But there was still the game to be played that Tuesday afternoon at Chavez Ravine. And there was a false note in all the sullenness.

From Pershing Square downtown to Hollywood's chic Chasen's Restaurant, it was the same. It was as if the whole condemned town was walking the last few steps up the scaffold, with one eye on the rope and the other on the telephone.

ACCIDENT

It was past noon when we drove the freeway out to Hollywood. Naturally, there was an accident.

Two cars collided some distance ahead, and by the time we reached the scene both wrecks had been pulled off to the side.

But the game had started on the radio. So help me, driving slowly past the wreck of the first sedan, I saw the driver sitting on the ruined fender with a transistor radio plugged into his right ear. Dodger fans are

See Page 14, Col. 5

Americas Condemn Cuba Threat

A.P. & U.P.

Washington

Inter-American foreign ministers unanimously denounced Sino-Soviet intervention in Cuba last night as "an attempt to convert the island into an armed base for Communist penetration of the Americas" and they called for new economic and security measures to meet the threat.

Brazil, Chile and Mexico—three countries which oppose tough measures—endorsed the general terms of the communique but forced the inclusion of a provision saying that no measures taken should violate the policy of nonintervention in internal affairs.

In the statement issued at the end of a two-day conference, the 20-nation group declared that Russia's arms build-up in Cuba "threatens the unity of the Americas and of its Democratic institutions."

Secretary of State Dean Rusk said after the six-hour 45-minute final session that "we had a good meeting. We are going to move now."

Officials said the lengthy

See Page 23, Col. 7

Typhoon Hits China Coast

Hong Kong

Typhoon Dinah hit the China coast with 115-mile-an-hour winds last night just south of the port city of Swatow about 130 miles northeast of Hong Kong.

Associated Press

BRING ON THOSE YANKEES!

Herb Caen's Guide for Yankees

By Herb Caen

DEAR, kind New York Yankees, from whom few blessings flow:

Welcome to San Francisco, where anything can happen — even a flag for the Giants. The welcome mat is out, with a banana skin on it. We offer you the key to the city, booby-trapped. We wish you no harm, no runs, and no hits. When somebody offers you a drink in a saloon, watch out for the kind of Mickey that doesn't have Mantle for a second name.

You'll like San Francisco. Everybody who isn't named Walter O'Malley likes San Francisco, and since nobody likes Walter O'Malley anyway, this cancels out.

It's a warm city. Sleep with your windows open. Wear Bermuda shorts and take a walk across the Golden Gate Bridge: we'll meet you halfway and ask you to lean over—juuuust a little bit more—to drink in the view. Literally. And don't miss Muir Woods. You could drive over there today, at about 11:30 a. m., and be back in plenty of time for the game. Believe me.

★ ★ ★

I KNOW THERE ARE A LOT of things you'd like to do besides play baseball, since you've never been here before, and we want you to do them. You're probably as sick of baseball as baseball is sick of—but no; politeness at all cost.

The swimming at balmy Fleishhacker

See Page 23, Col. 1

Delirium, Champagne In the City

By Ron Fimrite

San Francisco's long-suffering baseball faithful stopped holding their breath yesterday.

And what came out—from the Embarcadero to the Mission, from Twin Peaks to North Beach, from Montgomery street to the Sunset—was something like "Yowiiiii!"

BELIEVERS

Or, as Bill Manheim put it in the Ambassador Health Club on Post street, "Wow-eeeee!"

The Giants, cursed and cradled by fans who have grown to accept defeat as part of our heritage, made believers of everyone with their crazy 6-to-4 ninth-inning win over the Dodgers.

And on through the evening, Market street continued to bear every aspect of New Year's Eve—horn-blowing and streamer-streaming automobiles, cheering, laughing, sometimes wobbling pedestrians, mixing in a merry pandemonium.

"I've been cynical about the Giants all year," said stockbroker John Dalton, whooping it up with the crowd down at Ray's on Columbus avenue. "But not any more. Not after that game."

PHONE BOOKS

Believers and converts alike pitched telephone directories out windows onto Market street, kissed and hugged each other like French field marshals, fell off bar stools, climbed onto bar stools and generally forgot about such pedestrian matters as home and job.

Sam Cohen, owner of Sam's Lane Club on Maiden Lane and a one-share Giant stockholder, rolled out of his chic bistro after Willie Mays clutched the last out and dumped a bottle of Paul

See Page 23, Col. 2

Castro Foes Set To Strike Again

Miami, Fla.

Alpha 66, the secret anti-Castro action group, says it has 66 men ready to strike again.

A spokesman said the exile band, which damaged three ships in a foray off Cuba's coast three weeks ago, is set for a bigger operation, budgeted at $12,000.

Associated Press

Giants' Arrival

75,000 Fans ---And Chaos

San Franciscans burst into the streets by the thousands and down to the airport last night—happily and noisily celebrating the gala return of the victorious Giants.

The singing, shouting and completely unmanageable throng at San Francisco International Airport swelled to 75,000 before the Giants touched the runway shortly before 9 p.m.

The joy was complete.

Strangers shook hands and gave each other bear hugs.

Hundreds of fans wandered happily along downtown Market street, grinning happily and not saying anything.

STREAMERS

Cars with orange and black paper streamers wheeled past Market and Powell streets, with passengers and drivers shouting greetings.

Everywhere, the celebrating throngs ignored police suggestions that it was time to go home.

Finally, when the noise showed no sign of abating at

See Page 14, Col. 1

POW Negotiator Arrives in Cuba

Havana

New York attorney James B. Donovan arrived here yesterday to resume negotiations with Premier Fidel Castro for the release of 1113 Cuban invasion prisoners.

Donovan was welcomed by Mrs. Berta Barreto of the Cuban Families Commission which is coordinating efforts to free the men captured in April, 1961.

United Press

Starting Time--- 12 Noon

The first game of the 1962 World Series starts at noon today in Candlestick Park.

All reserved seats are sold out. Bleacher seats go on sale at 8 a. m. at the stadium.

For those who have tickets, the Municipal Railway is starting special express bus service at 9:30 a.m.

The game will be televised in color on KRON-TV (Channel 4) and KTVU (Channel (2). Identical telecasts on both stations will start at 11:25 a.m.

Radio coverage will start at 11:30 a.m. on KSFO and KNBC.

Odds on the Series in the Nevada gambling palaces were against the Giants: 8-5 in Reno; 15-to-14 in Las Vegas.

Billy O'Dell will pitch for the Giants and Whitey Ford will pitch for the Yankees.

THE INDEX

Allen	49	Delaplane	33	Movies	37-39
Animals	10E	Dreams	31	O'Flaherty	33
Art's Gallery	28	Dr. Molner	17	Panorama	35
Books	35	Editorials	34	Pearson	35
Bud Boyd	44	Fashions	19	Question Man	34
Bridge	7E	Finance	48-51	Shipping	22
Brier	34	Gleason	37	Sports	41-48
Caen	21	Hedda	39	Sylvia Porter	50
Chess	7E	Hoppe	35	Theaters	37-39
Comics	10E	Jumble	26	TV, Radio	36
Count Marco	17	Letters	34	Vital Stats.	22
Crossword	32, 35	Martin	44	Want Ads	23
Datebook	37	McCabe	41	Weather	22
Dear Abby	35	Mellinkoff	34	What's Law	26
Deaths	22	Millie	19	Women	16-19

FINAL EXTRA

THE WEATHER
Bay Area: Hazy sunshine after night and morning fog today and tomorrow. High temperatures Tuesday, 66 to 72 degrees; lows, 48 to 54. Variable winds 5 to 15 miles an hour. **See Page 22.**

San Francisco Chronicle
THE VOICE OF THE WEST

★ ★ ★ ★ FINAL

98th YEAR No. 296 CCCCAAA TUESDAY, OCTOBER 23, 1962 10 CENTS GArfield 1-1111

BLOCKADE IS ON

Navy Guns Ring Cuba --'Russ Ship en Route'

Day of Crisis In Brief

• **President Kennedy warned the nation that the Soviet arms build-up in Cuba now directly threatened the United States and ordered a "quarantine" on all ships carrying arms to Fidel Castro's regime.**

• **The Defense Department announced that the U.S. is ready to sink any ships headed for Cuba that refuse to stop and be searched.**

• **The U. S. Navy sailed a mighty armada into the Caribbean to enforce the blockade.**

• **The President canceled his scheduled political trips, including one for this weekend to California.**

• **Some critics viewed the Administration's move as "political" and thought the Democrats would gain at the polls in November.**

• **West Germany was the first Allied nation to approve the quarantine, Britain was cautious, Cuba called it an act of war and mobilized, Moscow was silent.**

• **United Nations observers expected Russia to counter the American action by coupling the Cuban crisis with that in Berlin.**

Vessels Will Be Told: Halt for Searching Or We'll Sink You

Associated Press

Washington

The United States is ready to sink every Communist bloc ship headed for Cuba that refuses to stop and be searched, a Defense Department spokesman said last night.

He said this country's blockade fleet, now being deployed, will order any ship of any nation obviously bound for Cuban ports to stop and undergo search by a boarding party.

A spokesman, in answer to questions, made it clear that force would be used if necessary.

The spokesman said Soviet vessels are en route to Cuba now. The first of the ships might be intercepted by U.S. warships in a day or two.

The Defense Department spokesman outlined the blockade procedure this way:

INTERCEPTION

Air and sea patrols will be watching vessels moving toward Cuba. Their positions will be reported by observation planes and ships. Warships will move in to intercept. They will hail the Cuban-bound ship. If it stops, a boarding party will be sent to look over the manifest.

If offensive weapons or long-range missiles or strategic-type aircraft, for instance, are found, the captain of the ship will be told he can head for any port other than Cuba.

If he refuses to change his course, "we will use force to compel him." Force also will be used if a ship refuses to stop for search.

VIGILANCE

A reporter asked the spokesman, "Are you prepared to sink Soviet ships?" The spokesman replied with one word:

"Yes."

A Pentagon spokesman also said the United States has ordered the Strategic Air Command and other military forces on a more vig-

See Page 2, Col. 8

Military Mobilization In Cuba

Associated Press

Key West, Fla.

All of Cuba's military forces have been mobilized as a result "of the news from the United States," Havana Radio said today.

The broadcast said the order was issued by Prime Minister Fidel Castro who will address the nation later today.

"Our combat units rapidly placed themselves on a fighting basis," said the radio.

The announcement, monitored in Key West, came a few hours after President Kennedy proclaimed a naval blockade against Cuba.

"Hundreds of thousands of men were mobilized in the

See Page 1-A, Col. 6

U.P. Wirephoto

The nuclear-powered carrier Enterprise was "somewhere off the Carolinas" and other U. S. ships and subs were heading for sea

Kennedy Says Red Missiles Peril U. S., Warns Soviet of War

U.P. & A.P.

Washington

President Kennedy put into effect a United States naval blockade against Cuba last night, saying the Soviets have started to turn Cuba into an offensive military base capable of raining nuclear destruction on all the Americas.

Speaking grimly to the Nation in a radio-TV broadcast, Mr. Kennedy said the United States would bring to bear "a full retaliatory response upon the Soviet Union" if any nuclear missile is fired on any nation in this hemisphere.

The President reported that within the past week the U.S. has received "unmistakable evidence" that—contrary to Soviet assurances—nuclear-type long-range missile sites are being established in Cuba and jet bombers capable of an atomic attack were being brought onto the island.

Climaxing secret feverish activity at the highest

The text of the President's speech is on page 1-A

echelons in the U.S. Government, Mr. Kennedy went on the air to announce a tough seven-point program of military and diplomatic action:

1—The U.S., "to halt this offensive buildup" in Cuba, is imposing "a strict quarantine on all offensive military equipment under shipment to Cuba."

All ships of any kind bound for Cuba are to be turned back if they are found to contain cargoes of offensive weapons. This embargo also will be extended to "other carriers" if need be—meaning airplanes.

2—Surveillance of Cuba and its military buildup will be stepped up, and the U.S. Armed Forces have been ordered "to prepare for any eventualities."

3—U.S. policy will be to regard any nuclear missile launched from Cuba against any nation in the Western hemisphere as an attack by Russia on the U.S. requiring full retaliation against the Soviet Union.

4—The U.S. Naval base at Guatanamo, on the eastern tip of Cuba, has been reinforced, U.S. dependents there have been evacuated and additional

See Page 2, Col. 1

Airliner Down at Sea ---102 Safe

Associated Press

Sitka, Alaska

A swift, skillful rescue at sea yesterday saved 102 persons aboard a military-chartered airliner that ditched in the ocean off this southeast Alaska city.

The Northwestern Airlines DC-7C with a crew of seven and 95 passengers — including men, women and children — came down with propeller trouble at 12:58 p.m. PST off the entrance of Sitka Sound.

The airline said six passengers were injured.

"The whole ship was evacuated in 2½ to 3 minutes," said the pilot, Captain Vinton Hanson of Bellevue, Wash.

The ditching was so smooth that the plane stayed afloat 22 minutes, while those aboard climbed into five 25-man liferafts.

"Apparently there was no panic," said Jim Jaqua of KSA-TV, who reached the scene before the plane sank.

"It looked to me like the pilot did a beautiful job. The top of the wings were just starting to be awash when I

See Page 16, Col. 6

$500,000 Demo Suit

By Michael Harris

Roger Kent, Northern California chairman of the Democratic Party, filed a $500,000 damage suit yesterday against recently formed "Committee for the Preservation of the Democratic Party in California."

The group, he charged, had sent out a heavy mailing of post cards containing "false, misleading and scurrilous statements" against Democratic candidates.

Then Kent promptly began a fresh attack on pro-Nixon forces, accusing them of using faked photographs in an effort to discredit Governor

See Page 12, Col. 1

U.S. Armada Heads for Caribbean

United Press

Miami

Military bases in the Southeast geared to wartime activity last night as ships, planes, munitions and troops were massed to back up the United States blockade of Cuba.

Even before President Kennedy announced the blockade, the Navy dispatched to the Caribbean an armada of warships from East Coast ports

See Page 2, Col. 1

Peiping's Third Front

Nehru Gears India For a Long Siege

U.P. & A.P.

New Delhi

Prime Minister Nehru declared last night that the independence of India was threatened by Chinese Communist attack.

If necessary, everything else must be sacrificed to meet the threat to the freedom of the Indian people, Nehru said in a broadcast.

He said India is facing a "powerful and unscrupulous enemy."

He spoke at the end of the third day of a Chinese offensive into Northeastern and Northwestern India.

OFFENSIVE

Early today Peiping announced still another offensive in the undeclared border war with India.

The Chinese Communists opened a third front at the extreme eastern end of the frontier and sent tanks rumbling toward an important Indian air base in Ladakh at the extreme western end at the frontier.

A Peiping broadcast conceded that the Chinese had launched a fourth major offensive in the northwesternmost part of Ladakh on the border of China's Sinkiang province. It said that the assault was near the source of the Karakash (Qaraqash) river. This is near K2, or

See Page 16, Col. 3

The U.N. Battle on Red China

Associated Press

United Nations

United States Ambassador Adlai E. Stevenson yesterday accused Communist China of premeditated naked military aggression against India in open scorn of United Nations principles.

Stevenson cited the India-Chinese border warfare in replying to a Soviet demand in the 109-nation General Assembly

See Page 16, Col. 1

THE INDEX

Allen	48	Delaplane	33	Movies	37-39
Animals	32	Dreams	30	O'Flaherty	33
Art's Gallery	27	Dr. Molner	19	Panorama	35
Books	35	Editorials	34	Pearson	35
Bud Boyd	42	Fashions	18	Question Man	34
Bridge	36	Finance	47-50	Rosenbaum	42
Brier	34	Gleason	37	Shipping	22
Caen	21	Hedda	39	Sports	41-47
Chess	36	Hoppe	35	Sylvia Porter	49
Comics	32	Jumble	25	Theaters	37-39
Count Marco	19	Letters	34	TV, Radio	36
Crossword	31, 35	McCabe	41	Vital Stats	22
Datebook	37	Mellinkoff	34	Want Ads	22
Dear Abby	35	Millie	17	Weather	22
Deaths	22	Monique	18	What's Law	25
				Women	16-19

A Day in History

THE MASSIVE MARCH

THE WEATHER
Bay Area: Fair except for high morning fog near ocean and extending inland. High temperature Thursday, 65 to 80; low, 52 to 57. Westerly afternoon winds. **See Page 25.**

San Francisco Chronicle
THE VOICE OF THE WEST

★ ★ ★ ★
FINAL

99th YEAR No. 241 | CCCCAAA | THURSDAY, AUGUST 29, 1963 | 10 CENTS  GArfield 1-1111

Hope Fading

Two Rescued ---5 Still Alive In Utah Mine

Associated Press

Moab, Utah

Seven desperate men who built makeshift barricades against deadly gases were found alive yesterday in a 3200-foot-deep potash mine where 25 miners were trapped Tuesday.

Rescuers brought up two of the men 17 hours after an explosion wracked the mine, and said five others were then still alive in the pit.

Late last night, however, crews reported they had been unable to rescue the other five who survived the initial blast.

Eight bodies were found. But the fate of the other ten men was not known.

Rescue efforts have been painfully slow, being plagued by gas, water, debris and mechanical trouble. One team was trapped in the lift bucket for more than an hour.

And last night there was a report that the water level in the tunnel was rising rapidly.

The main shaft of the mine is 2712 feet deep but the trapped men are farther down — caught in two lateral

See Page 6, Col. 2

Fellin's Story Of Weird 'Visions'

(David Fellin, one of the two men buried for 14 days by the Hazleton, Pa., mine cave-in, told this story of a life underground that few men have shared.)

★ ★ ★

By David Fellin
(As told to the Associated Press)

Hazleton, Pa.

Now they're trying to tell me those things were hallucinations, that we imagined it all.

We didn't. Our minds weren't playing tricks on us. I've been a practical, hardheaded coal miner all my life. My mind was clear down there in the mine. It's still clear.

We saw what we saw. These things happened. I can't explain them. I'm almost afraid to think what might be the explanation.

For example, on the fourth or fifth day, we saw this door although we had no light from above or from our helmets. The door was covered in bright blue light. It was very clear, better than sunlight.

Two men, ordinary looking men, not miners, opened the door. We could see beautiful marble steps on the other side. We saw this for some time and then we didn't see it.

We saw other things I can't explain.

One thing I was always

See Page 4, Col. 1

Inside Pages

For complete coverage of the rights demonstrations in Washington, San Francisco and elsewhere, see Pages 1A, 1B, 12, 14 and 15.

200,000 March for Rights in Washington

A. Philip Randolph—"A new beginning for all Americans"

A Powerful Appeal For Negro Equality---Eloquent, Orderly

By Richard Reston
Chronicle Bureau

Washington

The call for freedom that has been heard in Birmingham and Jackson and throughout the North and the South struck the heart of the Nation yesterday.

Negroes and whites—200,000 strong—delivered a dignified but powerful appeal for racial equality in a historic march on Washington.

They gathered quietly in front of the Lincoln Memorial, the very symbol of the freedom they were seeking.

There they asked the Nation to extend to Negroes the same basic rights the country's white population enjoys—a chance for decent housing, fair treatment from the police, the opportunity to get better jobs and a good education for their children.

The march route from the Washington Monument to the Lincoln Memorial was lined with hundreds of soldiers and local police, but at no time was force used to keep the massive crowd in check.

The day will be remembered in American history, perhaps most of all for its human element. Most of these people had ridden all night or even all week in buses, cars and trains to get to Washington for a ten-block walk and a two-hour ceremony of speeches. Last night they went back the same way they came, their mission filled and their message delivered.

It was exactly this sense of personal sacrifice and discipline that made the demonstration the

See Page 14, Col. 1

Arbitration Law

Congress Blocks Railroad Walkout

United Press

Washington

Congress overwhelmingly but reluctantly voted binding arbitration of the railroad labor dispute yesterday.

President Kennedy signed the measure into law less than six hours before a crippling nationwide rail walkout was scheduled to begin.

It was the first time in memory that Congress had ordered arbitration of a peacetime labor dispute. The legislation eliminates the threat of a rail strike for at least another six months.

The President, signing the legislation 90 minutes after final Congressional approval in the House, said it reaffirms "the essential priority of the public interest over any narrower interest." He said free collective bargaining is preserved.

'BACKWARD'

The American Association of Railroads hailed the move, but union leaders called it "regrettable and a backward step" that could change the course of labor - management relations.

One member of the House called it "the beginning of the end" of collective bargaining. But Congressmen generally felt the measure was the only way out of the

See Page 9, Col. 1

Four Swept Off Powell Cable Car

Four men were swept from the step of a Powell street cable car and injured yesterday when it scraped across the rear of a taxicab halted in the Sutter street intersection.

One of the passengers suffered a broken foot, another a possible foot fracture and the others cuts and bruises.

Police Accident Investigation Officer Richard Hallock said Yellow Cab driver Roy Riccetti, 43, of 2 Elsie street was making a left turn from Powel into Sutter about 1:20 p.m. and was forced to stop quickly for jammed up traffic at a Pacific Gas & Electric Company construction project.

Gripman Philip M. Boyd, 27, of 907 Divisadero street was unable to halt his cable car in time, Hallock said, and the four men, clinging

See Page 4, Col. 6

The Earth's Mixed-Up Magnetism

By David Perlman
Science Correspondent

The evidence from magnetism and fossils in ancient rocks is uncovering a fascinating theoretical picture of an earth in constant change.

A million and a half years ago, for example, a compass anywhere on earth would have pointed toward the south pole, not the north.

A billion and a half years ago Los Angeles was almost at the north pole, and 200 million years ago San Francisco was on the equator.

These theories, based on a swiftly emerging branch of science called paleomagnetism, were described yester-

See Page 6, Col. 5

Sergeant York Out of Hospital

Nashville, Tenn.

Sergeant Alvin York, 75, World War I hero and Medal of Honor winner, was discharged from Veterans Hospital yesterday after several weeks of treatment

Associated Press

Diem Calls U.S. Critics 'Unjust'

A.P. and Reuters

Saigon, Vietnam

President Ngo Dinh Diem's regime yesterday accused the U. S. Government of being off base in denouncing the military crackdown on his Buddhist opponents.

The American criticism was said to show "a profoundly unjust doubt in the government of (South) Vietnam, based on totally erroneous information."

A Saigon note charged that a declaration the State Department issued with President Kennedy's approval August 21 was "prejudicial to the honor and prestige of Vietnam, which has never broken its word to whomever it made promises."

Assured of continued U. S. military aid in the war against the Viet Cong, the government responded briskly to American criticism of the raids last week on Buddhist pagodas and the arrest of more than 1000 monks and nuns.

The State Department had

See Page 9, Col. 3

Kennedy Says U.S. Can Be Proud

Associated Press

Washington

President Kennedy said yesterday that "the cause of 20 million Negroes has been advanced" by the civil rights march on Washington.

Mr. Kennedy said the civil rights demonstration has been "conducted so appropriately before the shrine to the Great Emancipator," Abraham Lincoln.

The President issued a 400-word statement on the march immediately following a 75-minute meeting with ten leaders of the organizations that sponsored the huge demonstration in behalf of Administration - sponsored legislation.

"We have witnessed today in Washington," Mr. Kennedy said, "tens of thousands—both Negroes and whites—exercising their right to assemble peaceably and to direct the widest possible attention to a great national issue."

He said that efforts to obtan equal opportunity for

See Page 12, Col. 3

The Index

Bridge	40
Chess	40
Comics	24
Crossword	35, 39
Death Notices	25
Editorials	38
Entertainment	41-43
Finance	49-52
Lippmann	1A
Shipping	25
Sports	45-49
TV, Radio	40
Want Ads	25
Weather	25
Women	16-21

MURDER OF THE PRESIDENT

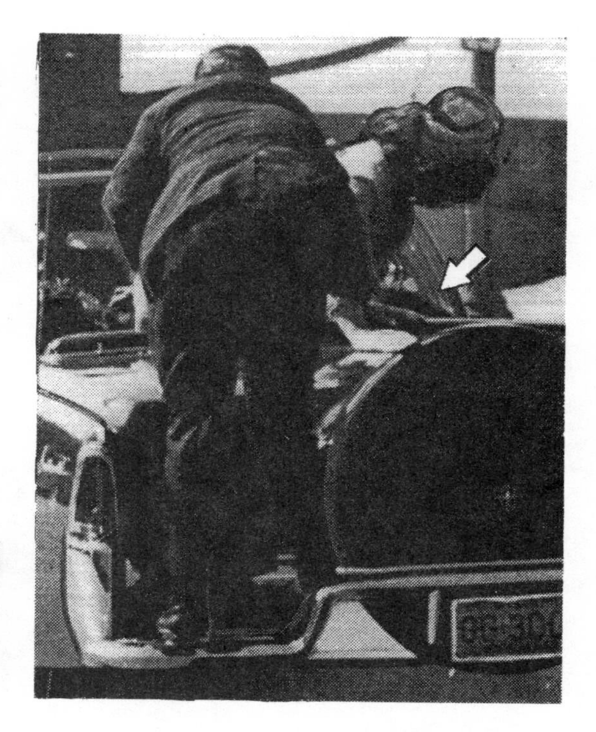

A moment after President Kennedy had been fatally shot in Dallas he slumped in the limousine and his wife, Jacqueline, cradled his head (arrow)

THE WEATHER

Bay Area: Occasional light rain today. Variable cloudiness tonight. Low, 47 to 52 degrees; high, 56 to 62. Chances for rain today: 7 in 10. **See Page 39.**

San Francisco Chronicle

THE VOICE OF THE WEST

★★★★ FINAL

99th YEAR No. 327 CCCCAAA SATURDAY, NOVEMBER 23, 1963 10 CENTS GArfield 1-1111

No Confession

Texan Charged With Murder

U.P. & A.P.

Dallas

Little more than 11 hours after a gunman assassinated President Kennedy from ambush, police charged a 24-year-old Texan with his murder.

Lee Harvey Oswald, a former Marine who once tried to renounce his American citizenship and live in the Soviet Union, made no confession.

"I did not kill the President. I did not kill anyone," Oswald told newsmen. "This is not justice. I might as well be in Russia."

POLICEMAN

He had first been arrested on a charge of slaying a policeman who stopped him for questioning.

His case will probably go to a grand jury next week. Dallas District Attorney Henry Wade said there is still additional information to be gathered. He would not discuss the question of fingerprints on the murder weapon.

Police said it was established that at the time of the assassination Oswald was in a building a block from the presidential car where a .765 Mauser rifle was found on a fifth floor landing. Oswald was employed as a clerk in the building.

FIGHT

Manacled, his face battered in a fight with the police who subdued him in a movie theater less than four miles from the assassination scene, Oswald was taken before Justice of the Peace David Johnson for arraignment.

After the formal charges were filed, Oswald was brought before newsmen.

See Page 6, Col. 1

Under Arrest

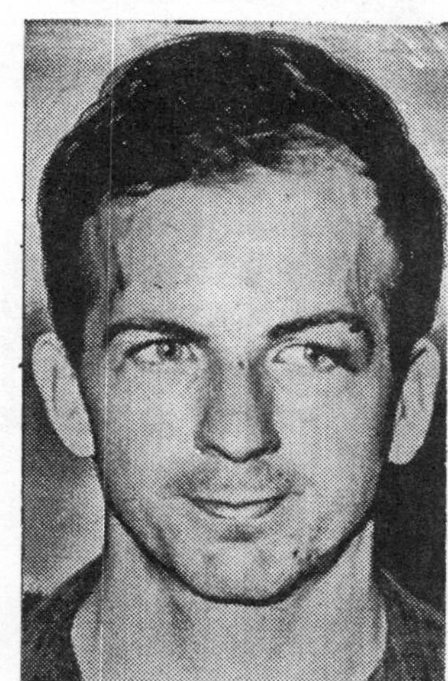

LEE HARVEY OSWALD

The accused assassin

John F. Kennedy, President

EDITORIAL

THE YOUNG PRESIDENT whom we lost yesterday gave at all times his best to the Nation. In the spirit of his Inaugural Address, he asked only what he could do for his country, and did it.

It is the country he served which somehow failed him. For in their shock and sorrow, the American people must feel troubled and ashamed that in this 176th year of their democracy they still have not learned to protect the life and safety of their highest servant.

No act can be more sordid and disgraceful than a political assassination. Who are we Americans, who claim the leadership of the Free World, that we should have allowed this kind of violent and insensate thing to happen to our national leaders four times within a century? The question

See Page 4, Col. 1

Hector Escobosa Is Dead at 56

Hector Escobosa, the president of I. Magnin & Co., died of a heart attack last night in Williamsburg, Va. Mr. Escobosa, who was 56, was a leader in the fashion industry. (For details, see Page 39).

Kennedy Is Slain By Texas Sniper

Gov. Connally Hit---
Jackie in Same Car

A.P. & U.P.

Dallas, Tex.

The President of the United States was assassinated here yesterday.

John Fitzgerald Kennedy, 35th President, was gunned down by a sniper armed with a high-powered rifle at 12:30 p. m. CST (10:30 a. m. PST).

Mr. Kennedy was shot through the head and neck as he rode beside his wife in a triumphal motorcade through downtown Dallas.

Three shots cracked. Blood sprang from the President's face and he fell face down in the back seat of the presidential limousine.

He died in a Dallas hospital half an hour later.

Governor John B. Connally of Texas, riding in the limousine with the President, was shot in the back.

Police seized as prime suspect a 24-year-old former Marine who once sought Russian citizenship. He was identified as Lee H. Oswald of Dallas, chairman of a Fair Play for Cuba Committee.

Late last night he was charged with the murder of the President.

The 46-year-old President died at 1 p. m. in Parkland Hospital after emergency transfusions and a tracheotomy.

Vice President Lyndon B. Johnson was sworn in as 36th President of the United States aboard the presidential plane shortly before it left Dallas for Washington with Mr. Kennedy's body. Mr. Johnson and the President's widow, Jacqueline Kennedy accompanied the body.

Johnson was in the cavalcade with Mr. Kennedy yesterday, but two cars behind him. He was not hurt.

Connally, sitting across from Mr. Kennedy in the

See Page 4, Col. 1

PRESIDENT JOHNSON IN DALLAS

Moments after taking the oath

Johnson Becomes 36th President

United Press

Washington

Lyndon B. Johnson took up the great burdens of the Presidency last night in Washington only hours after President Kennedy had been shot down in Dallas.

Mr. Kennedy's Vice President had taken the oath of his high office yesterday afternoon in the presidential plane which returned him, Mrs. Kennedy and the body of the President to Washington.

At the age of 55, Mr. Johnson thus became the nation's 36th President. Of all the Presidents who have taken office on the death of a predecessor, he will serve the shortest term — about 14 months.

Mr. Kennedy was pronounced dead at Parkland Hospital at 1 p. m. An hour and a half later, Mr. Johnson stood before Federal Judge Sarah T. Hughes and re-

See Page 2, Col. 1

The Index

Churches	30, 31
Comics	40
Crossword	24, 25
Death Notices	39
Entertainment	26, 27
Finance	36-38
Movies	26, 27
Obituaries	39
Owl	28-30
Shipping	39
Sports	33-36
TV, Radio	30
Vital Statistics	39
Want Ads	14
Weather	39
Women	10, 11

OSWALD IS SLAIN IN TEXAS JAIL

A Day of Tribute to The Dead President

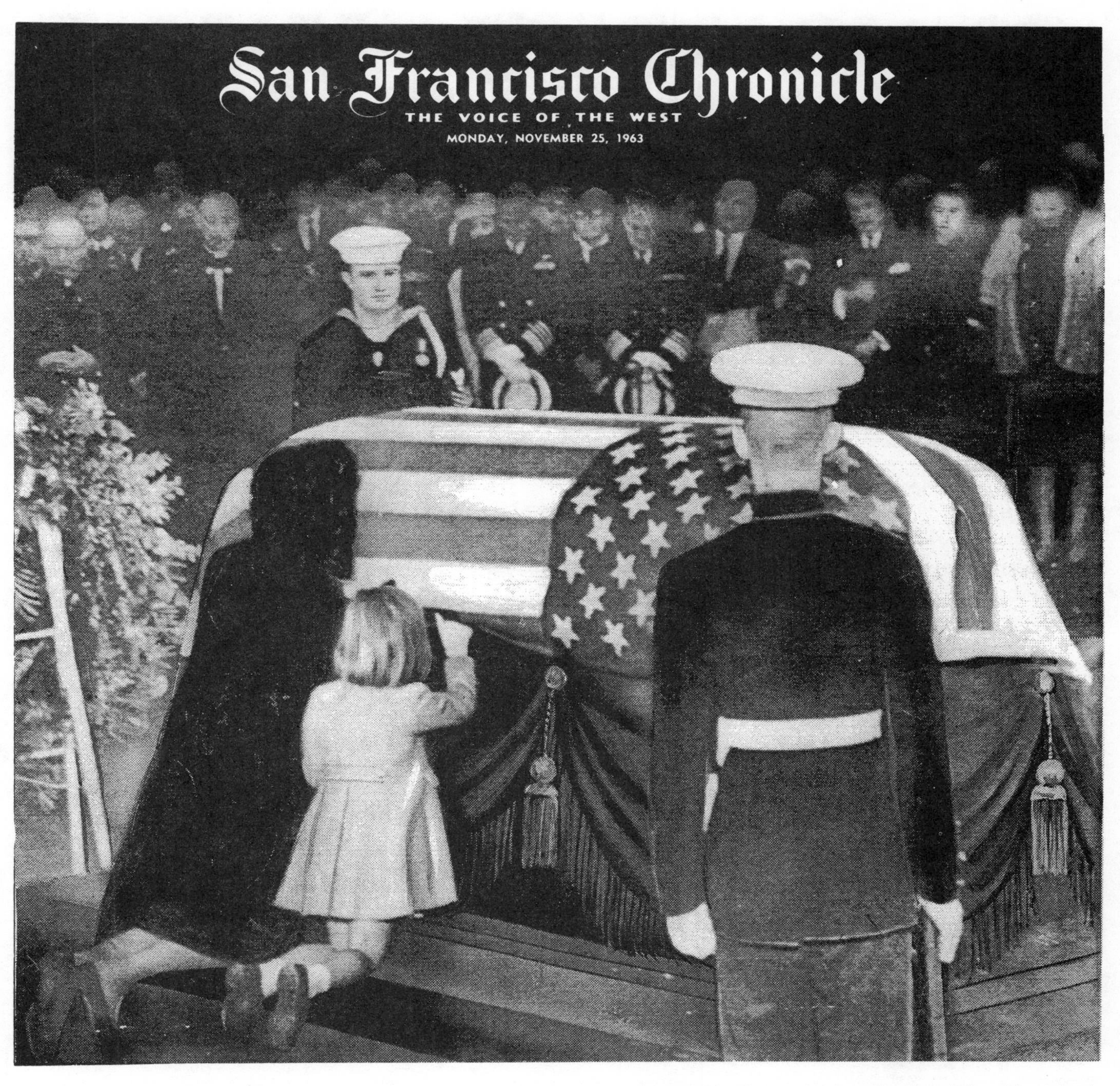

As President Kennedy's widow and daughter knelt in prayer before his flag-draped bier in the Capitol Rotunda yesterday, Jacqueline Kennedy leaned forward and kissed the casket and Caroline reached up and touched the flag

CCCCAAA PAGE 1A

San Francisco
Sunday Chronicle

100th YEAR No. 89 | FINAL EDITION ★ | SUNDAY, MARCH 29, 1964 | 25 CENTS | GArfield 1-1111

On-the-Scene Photos

TERRIBLE STORY OF QUAKE, WAVE

56 Blocks Gone

Crescent City Smashed Flat

By Elmont Waite
Chronicle Correspondent

Crescent City, Del Norte county

A mighty tidal wave roared out of the Pacific over this sleeping lumber and fishing town early yesterday with catastrophic results.

Ten persons were known dead, but authorities fear that at least two others may have been killed in the tidal wave.

Fifteen townspeople were missing, scores required hospitalization, and the remaining 3000 residents fled for their lives.

Governor Edmund G. Brown declared the town a disaster area.

A 56-block area was either knocked flat or severely damaged with losses estimated as high as $50 million.

FIRES

Power poles snapped and their falling wires touched off fires which firemen could not reach through the swirling waters.

One blaze caused four big storage tanks at the Texaco Company fuel storage yard to explode. Another fire

See Page 1D, Col. 1

Some Rain Forecast For Easter

Bay Area citizens would be advised to include a raincoat in their Easter Sunday wardrobe today the weatherman warned.

At the very least it will be foggy in the morning and cloudy in the afternoon. And there is, according to forecasters, a 7 in 10 chance that it will rain tonight.

There will also be wind up to 25 miles an hour, the weatherman forecast.

Rain or shine, thousands of San Franciscans looked forward to their annual dawn trek to the summit of Mount Davidson for sunrise services being held there for the 42nd year.

There were dozens of other

See Page 18, Col. 6

Buildings in downtown Anchorage sank into huge cracks

A Frantic Ride Past the Rubble

By Martin Ridner
Anchorage Daily Times

Anchorage

There were about 30 of us in the supermarket when the first tremor hit. The store manager shouted at us to slow down and not to panic. Within 15 seconds we were all out in a world gone crazy.

Outside, we watched the two-story brick building buckle under the quake. Plate glass cracked and showered down onto the sidewalk.

I dashed for my car and bricks fell on the hood as I pulled away from the crumbling building.

When I arrived home, my daughter Debra was screaming. Robin, our 2-year-old, wasn't scared.

Our house had been heavily damaged, but was still on its foundation.

We decided to go downtown and the two-mile drive was a terrible revelation. Every building more than one-story high in the Spenard's Shopping Center was smashed.

Romig Hills road was blocked by a buckled area eight feet wide. Detouring around that, we saw the Hillside apartments—six stories of devastation.

Further on downtown, we reached the center of damage. A pile of rubble was all that was left of the eight-story Four Seasons apartments. Firemen and several hundred people were gathered around the destruction.

It was getting dark as we drove on, and our car suddenly bumped into a four-foot-deep ditch. Beyond that was another hole, at least 20 feet deep and in some places 200 feet wide. Houses had

See Page 1C, Col. 5

Many Dead, Hurt

Four Alaskan Cities Ravaged

U.P. & A.P.

Anchorage, Alaska

Ravaged by one of the greatest earthquakes of modern times, Alaskans struggled yesterday to restore vital services and dig through the widespread wreckage in search of uncounted dead and injured.

The Governor's office said early in the day that the death toll from Friday night's shock might reach 600. But a statement last night indicated that the toll might not exceed 50.

"Casualties are less than we ever dreamed they could be," said Hugh Wade, lieutenant governor and secretary of state.

"The total won't be much over 50 dead, not counting the natives."

State officials said that 48 persons were dead and 26 missing in four communities on the mainland part of the hard-hit 800-mile coast of southern Alaska.

KODIAK

Reports from the island of Kodiak were conflicting. The office of Governor William Egan in Juneau said 30 persons in Kodiak city were dead and 50 others were missing. The Navy command on Kodiak later said, however, that there had been no casualties.

The mighty quake—which measured up to 8.6 on the Richter scale—sent seismic sea waves crashing on Pacific shores thousands of miles away, taking lives and wrecking property from Canada almost to Mexico.

The initial massive shock at 5:45 p.m. (7:45 p.m. PST) Friday was followed by numerous aftershocks. The sharpest, at 10:36 a.m. yesterday, registered 7 on the Richter scale. There were no reports of damage, however.

RESCUE

President Johnson declared the state of Alaska a disaster area, and Federal agencies mounted a huge rescue mission.

The official casualty list from the earthquake itself was surprisingly low. It included 16 dead in Anchorage, 28 dead in Valdez, 3 dead and 26 missing in Seward, and 1 dead in Cordova.

The Coast Guard counted one man lost in the tidal wave near Cordova. There were no other reports of

See Page 1C, Col. 6

Havoc at Bay Area Yacht Docks

The tidal wave unleashed by the Alaskan earthquake rippled harmlessly onto Ocean Beach here, but inside the Golden Gate it created havoc in small craft harbors.

Damage at San Rafael's swank Loch Lomond Yacht Harbor, hardest hit, was estimated at more than $1 million.

There the seismic wave rushed in like a flood-swollen torrent and ripped loose a pier with 30 boats attached to it. The waters swept the pier and the boats to an inlet 30 feet away, made a complete turn, swung them around the edge of a breakwater and deposited the pier—boats and all—against the bank of another channel.

Only one boat was seriously damaged in that freakish incident.

PIER

Another pier, with 33 boats tied up, broke loose and smashed against an adjacent pier. Several boats sank.

Virtually all of the 310 craft berthed at the harbor suffered damage ranging from scratches to sinking.

See Page 2, Col. 5

Index On Page 1A

DIXIE GRAVE -- 3 BODIES

THE WEATHER
Bay Area: Fair today except for patches of morning fog. High temperature Wednesday, 68 to 85 degrees; low, 52 to 58. Westerly winds. **See Page 24.**

San Francisco Chronicle
THE VOICE OF THE WEST

100th YEAR No. 218 | CCCCAAAB | WEDNESDAY, AUGUST 5, 1964 | 10 CENTS | GArfield 1-1111

Raid on North Viets

U.S. PLANES HIT BACK

Discovery in Dixie Grave

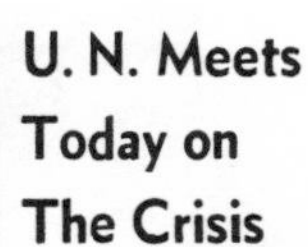

Michael Schwerner James Chaney Andrew Goodman

FBI Is 'Fairly Sure' Of Identification

Times-Post & A.P.

Philadelphia, Miss.

FBI agents last night found three bodies buried within several feet of one another in a low area of a creek southwest of Philadelphia, where three civil rights workers vanished six weeks ago.

Roy Moore, chief of the FBI office in Jackson, said that his agency is "fairly certain" that the bodies are those of the missing men, but that he cannot be positive until laboratory tests are completed.

The Neshoba county coroner made a preliminary examination at the grave. The bodies were then taken by car to the University of Mississippi medical center at Jackson, 70 miles away.

The three civil rights workers—Andrew Goodman, James Chaney and Michael Schwerner—have been missing since June 21.

The FBI search for them began June 22. The following day their 1963 station wagon was found abandoned and burned on a dirt road off Route 21, about 13 miles northeast of Philadelphia.

The scene of the discovery yesterday was a few hundred yards off Highway 21, but 20 miles southwest of where the station wagon was found.

When searchers first combed the farm area, thick wood and brush, they found what seemed to be a fresh earth dam thrown up to catch water.

Later it was noticed that the dam had collected no water, despite several showers in the area.

An excavation was or-

See Page 11, Col. 1

U. N. Meets Today on The Crisis

New York Times

United Nations

The United States asked last night for a Security Council meeting this morning on the attacks on U. S. Navy vessels off the coast of North Vietnam.

A spokesman said Adlai E. Stevenson, the chief U. S. delegate, had called for the meeting as soon as possible. The council president ordered the meeting scheduled for 9:30 a. m.

Stevenson was flown to New York last night by a U. S. Air Force plane from a vacation in Maine.

On his arrival, Stevenson presented the U. S. request to Sivert A. Nielsen of Norway, who is President of the Security Council this month.

The U.S. letter to the council president said:

"On behalf of the United States, I request that you convene an urgent meeting of the Security Council to consider the serious situation created by deliberate attacks of the Hanoi regime on United States naval vessels in international waters."

Although Stevenson's letter made no mention of the retaliatory U.S. action which President Johnson announced, a spokesman said one of the reasons for asking the council meeting was to inform it of what was going on.

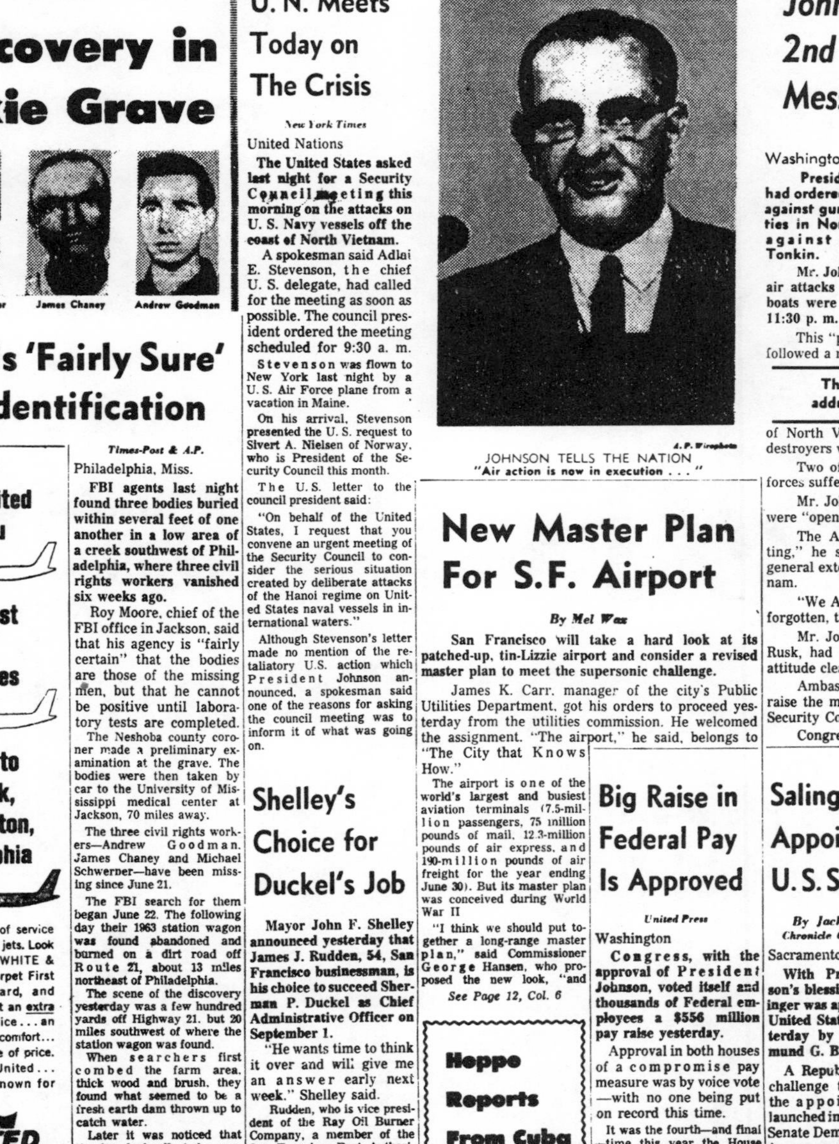

JOHNSON TELLS THE NATION
"Air action is now in execution . . ."

A. P. Wirephoto

New Master Plan For S.F. Airport

By Mel Wax

San Francisco will take a hard look at its patched-up, tin-Lizzie airport and consider a revised master plan to meet the supersonic challenge.

James K. Carr, manager of the city's Public Utilities Department, got his orders to proceed yesterday from the utilities commission. He welcomed the assignment. "The airport," he said, belongs to "The City that Knows How."

The airport is one of the world's largest and busiest aviation terminals (7.5-million passengers, 75 million pounds of mail, 12.3-million pounds of air express, and 190-million pounds of air freight for the year ending June 30). But its master plan was conceived during World War II

"I think we should put together a long-range master plan," said Commissioner George Hansen, who proposed the new look, "and

See Page 12, Col. 6

Shelley's Choice for Duckel's Job

Mayor John F. Shelley announced yesterday that James J. Rudden, 54, San Francisco businessman, is his choice to succeed Sherman P. Duckel as Chief Administrative Officer on September 1.

"He wants time to think it over and will give me an answer early next week." Shelley said.

Rudden, who is vice president of the Ray Oil Burner Company, a member of the San Francisco Port Authority, and a director of several corporations, said he wants to discuss the proffered ap-

See Page 12, Col. 3

Heppe Reports From Cuba

See Page 39

Big Raise in Federal Pay Is Approved

United Press

Washington

Congress, with the approval of President Johnson, voted itself and thousands of Federal employees a $556 million pay raise yesterday.

Approval in both houses of a compromise pay measure was by voice vote —with no one being put on record this time.

It was the fourth—and final —time this year the House had to vote on the potentially explosive election year bill that carries a $7500-per-year

See Page 12, Col. 1

Johnson Reply to 2nd Raid on Ships--- Message to Nation

New York Times

Washington

President Johnson said last night that he had ordered U. S. forces to take retaliatory action against gunboats and "certain supporting facilities in North Vietnam," after renewed attacks against American destroyers in the Gulf of Tonkin.

Mr. Johnson said in a television address that the air attacks on the North Vietnamese facilities and boats were taking place as he spoke, shortly after 11:30 p. m. EDT.

This "positive reply," as the President called it, followed a naval battle yesterday in which a number of North Vietnamese gunboats attacked two U. S. destroyers with torpedoes.

The text of President Johnson's address to the nation is on Page 6.

Two of the gunboats were sunk, but the U. S. forces suffered no damage and no loss of lives.

Mr. Johnson said the North Vietnamese attacks were "open aggression on the high seas."

The American response was "limited and fitting," he said, and his Administration sought no general extension of the guerrilla war in South Vietnam.

"We Americans know," he said, "if others have forgotten, the risks of spreading conflict."

Mr. Johnson said the Secretary of State, Dean Rusk, had been instructed to make this American attitude clear to all nations.

Ambassador Adlai Stevenson, he said, would raise the matter immediately in the United Nations Security Council.

Congressional leaders of both parties, he said, had assured him of speedy and overwhelming passage of a resolution "making clear that our Government is united in its determination to take all necessary measures in support of freedom and defense of peace in Southeast Asia."

He also had had assurances of backing, he said, from his presidential opponent, Senator Barry M. Goldwater.

Mr. Johnson closed with a

See Page 6, Col. 1

Salinger Appointed U.S. Senator

By Jackson Doyle
Chronicle Correspondent

Sacramento

With President Johnson's blessing, Pierre Salinger was appointed to the United States Senate yesterday by Governor Edmund G. Brown.

A Republican move to challenge the legality of the appointment was launched immediately, but Senate Democrats promptly prepared to counter it.

Senate Democratic leader Mike Mansfield of Montana

See Page 9, Col. 1

U. P. Wirephoto map

The Gulf of Tonkin where the attacks took place

Carrier Planes Hit PT Bases

U.P. & A.P.

Washington

Carrier-based American aircraft attacked PT boat bases in North Vietnam early today in retaliation for yesterday's new raid on U. S. destroyers in the Gulf of Tonkin.

President Johnson announced that the air strikes against selected targets in North Vietnam were under way last night, and Secretary of Defense Robert McNamara said they were continuing today.

In a Pentagon news conference following the President's nationwide address, McNamara also disclosed that a military buildup is under way in Southeast Asia.

(A U. S. spokesman in Saigon said today that U. S. Air Force F-102 jet fighters are being rushed to South Vietnam for defense against pos-

See Page 6, Col. 4

THE INDEX

Bridge	40	Movies	41-43
Chess	40	Obituaries	24
Comics	54	Shipping	24
Crossword	36, 39	Sports	45-50
Deaths	24	TV-Radio	40
Editorials	38	Vital Statistics	24
Entertainment	41-43	Weather	24
Finance	50-53	Want Ads	25
Food	20, 21	Women	16-19

Two New Top Men

KHRUSHCHEV IS OUT

THE WEATHER
Bay Area: Fair today. High Friday, 72 to 82; low, 48 to 56. Westerly afternoon winds to 25 m.p.h. **See Page 27.**

San Francisco Chronicle
THE VOICE OF THE WEST

100th YEAR No. 290 | CCCCAAA | FRIDAY, OCTOBER 16, 1964 | 10 CENTS | GArfield 1-1111

Brezhnev and Kosygin Take Over Government

New Government

Slim Labor Victory in British Vote

Times-Post Service

London

Britain's Labor party appeared certain this morning to have broken the 13-year rule of the Conservative party by a narrow margin in yesterday's general election.

But the probable accession of Harold Wilson as the new Prime Minister, succeeding Sir Alec Douglas-Home, was tinged with forebodings because of the extraordinarily thin Labor lead.

When counting was suspended at 4 o'clock this morning, Labor had definitely won 247 seats in the 630-member House of Commons. The Conservatives had 180 seats and the Liberals 2.

SWING

These figures from 429 of the constituencies reflected a 4.1 per cent swing to Labor in predominantly urban and industrial areas.

If this percentage is sustained in returns from rural areas later today, it will give Labor a 17-seat margin over the Conservatives.

But such a lead would not take account of additional seats that the Liberals may win. Whether Labor will have sufficient margin for a stable government is still in doubt.

On the basis of present projections, the 61-year-old Home will call at Buckingham Palace this afternoon to submit his resignation and Queen Elizabeth will then call upon Wilson, 48, to form a new government.

Labor's apparent victory, however, has been alloyed by the emergence of a strong racial factor in several of the constituency results, with evidence that Labor has been punished by a "white backlash" for having opposed restrictions on colored immigration from the Commonwealth countries.

Patrick Gordon Walker, who had represented Smethwick since 1945, and would have become Foreign Secretary in the Labor cabinet, lost his seat to Conservative Peter Griffiths. Contrary to the national Tory policy, Grif-

See Page 13, Col. 1

Composer Cole Porter Dies at 71

Cole Porter, one of the nation's great popular composers and lyricists, died at St. John's Hospital in Santa Monica last night. He was 71.

Porter, whose last years were filled with a variety of ailments, underwent surgery on Tuesday night for removal of a kidney stone. For details, see Page 15.

NIKITA KHRUSHCHEV
For ten years, he was the leader

Official Reasons: Age, Health

Associated Press

Moscow

The ten-year era of Nikita Khrushchev ended in the Soviet Union yesterday with the official announcement that he has been released from his posts as Premier and first secretary of the Communist party.

The announcement by the Tass news agency said Khrushchev had requested retirement because of deteriorating health and his age. He is 70.

He was also removed from the all-powerful 12-man Communist Party Presidium. There was no indication of his present whereabouts.

JOBS

His jobs were divided among two lieutenants he had long trusted. Leonid Brezhnev is taking the key post of party first secretary and Alexei Kosygin became premier.

A few short hours afterward the Soviet government apparently undertook to insure the world that its change of government meant no change in Khrushchev's policies of seeking a peaceful arrangement with the West.

The party newspaper Pravda indicated this morning that the new Brezhnev-Kosygin regime would continue to follow Khrushchev's post-1956 de-Stalinization policies and his plans to improve the economic conditions of the Russian people.

"RELEASE"

The announcement said Khrushchev's "release" — this was Tass' word — was granted this week. The Party Central Committee met Wednesday to take up his request for retirement, it added.

His release as first secre-

See Page 1 A, Col. 1

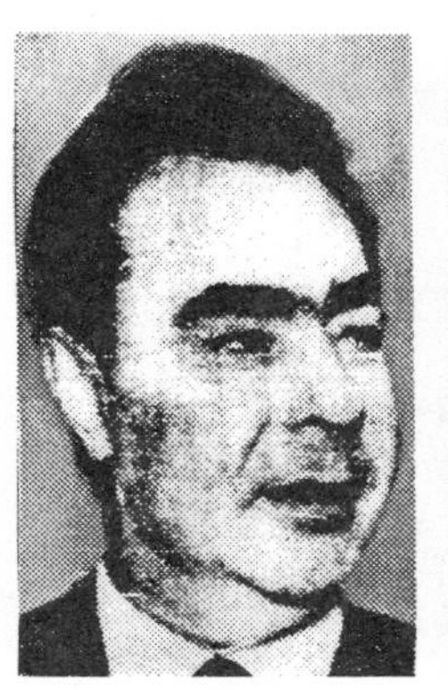

LEONID BREZHNEV
New first secretary

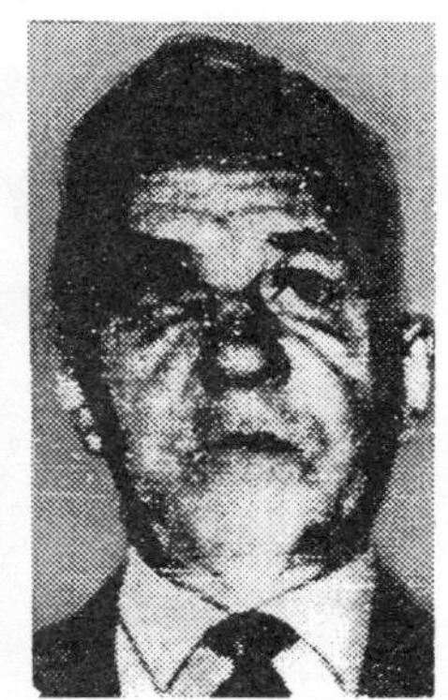

A. P. Wirephotos

ALEXEI KOSYGIN
The premier

Big Security Furor Over Jenkins Case

FBI and Secret Service Knew of 1959 Arrest

Times-Post Service

Washington

Both the FBI and the Secret Service knew in 1961 that Walter W. Jenkins, the resigned White House aide, had been arrested by District of Columbia police in 1959.

But what they did not know, apparently because of a failure to check police records, was that a morals charge was involved.

This was learned yesterday as a storm continued to build over the sudden fall from power—following another arrest on a morals charge last week—of Jenkins, the man in the White House closest to President Johnson.

The President made his first public comment on the Jenkins' call last night on his return to Washington from campaigning in New York. "Until late yesterday," he said, "no information or report of any kind to me had ever raised a question with respect to his personal conduct."

FBI Director J. Edgar Hoover announced yesterday that the President had ordered him to make a comprehensive inquiry and report promptly.

Mr. Johnson's statement also said that "no man I know has given more personal dedication, devotion and tireless labor."

"On this case, as in any such case," he said, "the

See Page 18, Col. 2

Market's Reaction

Stock prices plunged violently in very active trading yesterday following the first reports that Soviet Premier Nikita Khrushchev had been ousted.

Some prices fell as much as $7 per share but after half an hour the worst of the decline was over and prices began to come up from their lows.

Altogether the Dow-Jones industrial averages fell 6.74 points for the day to 868.44.

For details see Page 54

The Index

Bridges	42
Chess	42
Comics	26
Crossword	38, 41
Deaths	27
Editorials	40
Entertainment	43-46
Finance	53-56
Movies	43-46
Obituaries	15
Shipping	27
TV-Radio	42
Vital Statistics	27
Want Ads	27
Weather	27
Women	19-23

UC Speech Dispute

Students Accept Kerr's Peace Bid

A threatened outbreak of student revolt on the Berkeley campus of the University of California was headed off by president Clark Kerr yesterday.

Two compromises offered by Kerr were enthusiastically accepted by the students' Free Speech Movement, which had earlier planned a protest demonstration at today's meeting of the University Regents in Davis.

"We think we have won a very big victory," said Art Goldberg, one of the student leaders.

"We thank the administration for listening to our demands, and for acting in good faith and living up to the agreement of Otcober 2."

HOT WORDS

The protesting students had been circulating hotly worded pamphlets declaring Kerr had "betrayed our trust" be-

See Page 11, Col. 2

Realtor's Frank Talk On Bias in Housing

The leader of San Francisco's 3500 realtors expressed the opinion yesterday that most Negroes and whites prefer to live "with or near people like themselves."

Richard E. Horberg, president of the San Francisco Real Estate Board, told State Senate fact-finders various fears are at the root of discrimination against Negroes.

A major fear, he testified is that the man next door will be too different from himself.

"Man, as a social animal, does expect a degree of con-

See Page 11, Col. 1

How Washington Took The Soviet Shakeup

By Max Frankel
New York Times

Washington

The Administration was surprised but not alarmed by the change of leadership in Moscow yesterday.

Analysts of Soviet affairs were almost unanimous in the view that Premier Nikita Khrushchev had been forced to step down by his colleagues for reasons of personality and policy and not merely age and health.

But the survival and promotion of Khrushchev

See Page 1 A, Col. 1

San Francisco

Sunday Chronicle

101st YEAR No. 66 FINAL EDITION ★★ SUNDAY, MARCH 7, 1965 25 CENTS GArfield 1-1111

'Guard Duty'

MARINES TO VIETNAM

Uruguay Mystery

European Tip Leads to a Body ---Ex-Nazi Killer

United Press

Montevideo, Uruguay

The body of a man tentatively identified as Nazi war criminal Albert Cukurs was found here yesterday in a bullet-riddled trunk, the apparent victim of "Jewish revenge."

Police found the body after a news agency received a tip in Bonn, West Germany, from a group calling itself "Those Who Can Never Forget." In a typewritten note, the group said they had killed Cukurs and gave the address where the body was found.

Commissioner Santana Washington Cabria, security chief of the Uruguayan police, said the 64-year-old Cu-

See Page 21, Col. 1

California Demos Pick Ann Alanson

By Earl C. Behrens
Political Editor

Sacramento

The executive committee of the Democratic State organization yesterday unanimously selected Ann Alanson of San Francisco as the new Democratic national committeewoman.

They brushed aside a demand by 23 Democratic congressmen that the elec-

See Page 19, Col. 1

Wrong Bee Under The Bonnet

Arcadia, Calif.

Charles Ognibene's sports car was stolen last September. It was recovered a few days later, but the engine was missing.

Last week, Ognibene was driving along when another car passed him. Under its hood, Ognibene told police, he heard the smooth purring of his long-lost sports car motor. He took the car's license number.

Indulgent detectives checked the car's owner, who had just purchased the motor from a junkyard, which acquired it from a youth who admitted the theft of Ognibene's car.

"I told you so," the sharp-eared Ognibene said. Detectives, the car owner, the junkyard man—and the young thief—were at a loss for words.

Associated Press

Gun Blast Ends a Trail Of Murder

From Our Correspondent

Corning,
Tehama county

A manhunt for the killer of a woman and two children—all relatives of his estranged wife—ended in a shotgun blast in the tall grass of an olive orchard near here yesterday.

The suspect, a 38-year-old box factory worker, killed himself with the shotgun as a dozen officers were closing in on him, the Tehama county sheriff's office said.

Paul Lucero was identified as the killer by his wife, Alberta, 38, who was herself struck down by a blow on the head with a rifle stock.

RAMPAGE

Deputies said that Lucero on two previous occasions had attempted suicide. Before he finally took his own life in the olive orchard, he went on a grisly rampage in which:

He shot to death his wife's daughter-in-law, son and grandson.

He beat the daughter-in-law's two infant children with a skillet and left them lying in a pool of blood.

And he struck his wife so hard with a rifle stock that the wooden stock was shattered.

Found dead in a farm house near this olive-growing community 130 miles north of San Francisco were Dolores F. Gifford, 21; her son, Everett Ray, 3; and Terry Lee Gifford, 13.

Deputies said Lucero apparently shot them with a rifle about 9 p.m. Friday.

Mrs. Lucero, a waitress,

See Page 21, Col. 3

London Raider

U.P. Bitephoto

Goldie the wayward eagle finally ended its fast Friday and gobbled up a duck—to the relief of the small-dog owners of London.

The giant bird from Finland had declined food offered by zoo keepers trying to lure him back into the cage from which he fled eight days ago.

But hunger prevailed and Goldie swooped down in Regent's Park and scooped up a Muscovy duck almost as big as a goose.

Twice in recent days Goldie had swooped down on small dogs being walked in the park but was driven off.

Priest Criticizes Bay Birth Clinic

Oakland's plan for two family planning—or birth control—clinics was assailed yesterday by a Catholic priest at a workshop conference of the city's Economic Development Council.

The Rev. Clarence Howard, pastor of St. Patrick's Church in Oakland and a member of the council, said he was concerned that the people on welfare might feel obliged to use the services of the

See Page 17, Col. 5

Clear Skies for Sunday

The scattered rain of the last two days will give way today to clear skies, the Weather Bureau reported.

Clouds will clear away this morning and temperatures will range from a low of 40 to a high of 63 degrees in the Bay Area. Northwest winds of 10 to 20 miles an hour were forecast.

Snow flurries were forecast in the Sierra.

S. F. Rainfall
(Inches)

Storm to 8 p.m.	.25
Season to date	16.50
Normal to date	16.19
Last year to date	9.64
Seasonal normal	20.78

(July 1 to June 30)

Baboon Who Was a Goat's Best Friend

Associated Press

Okahandja,
South West Africa

Ahla, the baboon who did a job better than many humans, is missing. After intensive searches, her owner fears she is dead.

Ahla was trained to be a full-time goatherd. She was made widely known by South Africa's Professor Raymond Dart, anthropologist and joint author of "Adventures With the Missing Link."

According to Dart, Ahla's owner employed Ahla as a goatherd for years after she found human herders were not as efficient or as understanding.

Ahla took 80 goats to graze every morning and brought them back at night. She used a rallying "ho-ho-ho" cry, rounded up strays and collected new-born kids and carried them home.

Professor Dart once said Ahla's urge to bring together mother and kid when they became separated amounted to care-fanaticism. Often the goats' owner took one kid from a goat that had given birth to three, to have it

See Page 21, Col. 1

'Saigon Request'

3500 Troops For Security at Big Air Base

New York Times

Washington

The Pentagon announced last night that two battalions of Marines—approximately 3500 men—will be sent to South Vietnam at the request of the government in Saigon.

From the timing of the announcement the Marines' arrival in South Vietnam appeared imminent.

They will be the first United States ground combat troops committed to help the Republic of South Vietnam fight the Viet Cong Communist insurgency.

SECURITY

The Marines will be deployed to the vicinity of Da Nang to strengthen the security in that area. Da Nang is the site of a major jet bomber base used in recent raids against North Vietnam.

(United Press reported that advance elements of the Marine contingent arrived at Da Nang today.

(The U.P. report said a U.S. Marine Corps task element headquarters was already established there, and that the bulk of the Marines was expected either later today or Monday.)

The Marine battalions, each reinforced beyond the usual strength of 1200 to 1400 men in such units, will total more than 3500 men, defense sources said.

The Marines' deployment will bring to more than 28,000 the number of U.S. military personnel in South Vietnam.

ADVISERS

Most of the U.S. forces in the country, numbering about 23,500 men, serve as advisers to the South Vietnamese army, navy and air force.

They also operate helicopters in support of the South Vietnamese forces, perform escort missions for them on

See Page 17, Col. 2

How Johnson Explains War To Congress

Times-Post Service

Washington

President Johnson has warned Congress that the campaign to halt Communist aggression in Southeast Asia could be gravely jeopardized if America displays any sign of vacillation or discloses its future strategy.

In secret White House seminars for members of the House and Senate, the President has stressed repeatedly that the United States must not repeat in Vietnam the mistakes which compounded its difficulties in Korea in the early 1950s.

Mr. Johnson has declared that the struggle in South Vietnam could end in disaster if the U.S. Government wavers from its commitment to protect the freedom of that nation.

He also has contended that it would be dangerously unwise for him or other Admin-

See Page 18, Col. 1

THE INDEX

Art	TW, B	Finance	38-40	Radio	D
Autos	T	Gardens	T, B	Real Estate	T
Books	TW	Gilliam	TW	Rhythm	TW
Bridge	B	Homes	B	Rovere	28
Chess	T, B	Horoscope	B	Shipping	40
Crossword	B	Movie Times	D	Sports	31-38
Dear Abby	WW	Music	TW	Stamps	T
Deaths	22WA	Obituaries	26, 22WA	Theaters	D
Editorials	24			TV	D
Dr. Molner	WW	Photography	T	Travel	ST
Fashions	WW	Puzzles	B	Weather	26

Bonanza (B), Classified (WA), Datebook (D), Travel (ST), Real Estate (T), This World (TW), Women's World (WW)

Army of Cops

MORE RIOTING IN L. A.

THE WEATHER
Bay Area: Fair today except for high fog near the ocean. High temperature Friday, 70 to 82 degrees; Low, 50 to 58. Westerly wind 10 to 20 miles an hour in afternoon. **See Page 14.**

San Francisco Chronicle
THE VOICE OF THE WEST

101st YEAR No. 225 | CCCCAAAB | FRIDAY, AUGUST 13, 1965 | 10 CENTS | GArfield 1-1111

Police Fired on

Flying Wedge Disperses New Rioting in L.A.

A.P. & U.P.

Los Angeles

Police moved in force into a Negro section late last night and brought under control an eight-block "no man's land" where Negro youths had rioted for two consecutive nights.

The mob had raged through the Watts area for four hours last night before a flying wedge of police stormed on foot up the main thoroughfare and dispersed the throng, which numbered about 6000 at one time.

Police moved into the Avalon Boulevard sector after rioters began firing on patrol cars. They said at least five patrol cars were the targets of snipers. Highway patrolman Robert Mitchell was shot in the thigh.

Just after midnight, Inspector John Powers said: "The entire riot zone is under control."

GUNFIRE

Police later reported that about 500 persons gathered early today at Central and Imperial Highway, some of them throwing rocks.

Police added extra men to cope with any new outbreak in the highly volatile situation. The total available force reached 640 officers with additional police, sheriff's deputies and highway patrolmen.

At least 39 persons were injured last night, including four policemen and one fire-

See Page 7. Col. 1

Precision Escape at Quentin

By Charlotte Risnik and Keith Power

The telephone rang in the lonely gunpost on San Quentin's northwest wall and the guard answered it. There was no one on the line.

But in those brief moments of distraction, carefully plotted and finely timed, two nimble convicts broke into 30 feet of open ground, scaled the 20-foot wall on a 21-foot hook and jumped to freedom.

That was the escape story pieced together by prison officials yesterday as a statewide hunt was organized for the two fugitives who were

See Page 11. Col. 1

Arlo Acton's winning sculpture 'Idome'

Pat It, Poke It, Kick It in the Tank

By Ron Fimrite

There is a kind of cork on top of it which can be unplugged and dropped into the funnel-like thing on the right side of the jet tank.

Its arm can be twisted into amusing shapes. You can fiddle with its handle.

And when you rock it, it rolls. And rocks. And rolls.

It's "Idome" (Id of me—my id), $1300 worth of aircraft parts, kindling, and talent, the top prize winning sculpture at the 84th annual exhibition of the San Francisco Art Institute, which opened

See Page 7. Col. 1

Wolden Gives in--- Jury to Get Files

By Charles Raudebaugh

Assessor Russell L. Wolden surrendered yesterday to the Grand Jury's demand that he divulge the records of 62 firms under investigation in the tax-kickback scandal.

But it seemed unlikely that his last-minute capitulation would save him from appearing in criminal court this morning to show cause why he should not be held in contempt of court.

"While Mr. Wolden has notified me that he will produce the records, the matter of contempt is now out of my hands," said District Attorney John Jay Ferdon.

"The matter of the records and how and when they shall be produced now lies between Mr. Wolden and Presiding Judge Harry J. Neubarth of the criminal division of the Superior Court."

Wolden, who refused to comply with a Grand Jury subpoena to produce the records two weeks ago on the grounds they were inviolate under State law, announced at noon yesterday that he was changing his position because he had been overruled by the City Attorney.

"With my apology to the individual taxpayers for doing so, I shall make the records available," said Wolden.

"My desire has been and is to co-operate in the present investigation, and my refusal to open the records and work

Status Quo To Reign at Civic Center

By Charles Howe

Civic Center Plaza's backless benches, torpid fountains and sunbathing mendicants will not be changed by so much as a millimeter, the Recreation and Park Commission voted yesterday.

By a 3-2 vote, the Commissioners rejected a $10,000 proposal to bring two Parisian architects here to build models, based upon their prize-winning sketch, which would have transformed the plaza into a series of low terraces.

"Now I know the meaning

See Page 10, Col. 1

Enter Hero In Mime War With State

By Robert Graham

The Atheneum Foundation, in the heroic tradition of a Renaissance patron, yesterday cast its lot—and the fate of its Summer Festival of the Arts—with the San Francisco Mime Troupe.

The foundation announced, in the face of a warning from the State, that it will present the Mime Troupe's bawdy commedia dell'arte production of "Il Candelaio" tomorrow at the Mount Tamalpais amphitheater "as originally scheduled."

Earlier in the day, the

See Page 20. Col. 3

Sharp Rise In Fares for Greyhound

By Jerry Burns

Sweeping increases in Greyhound bus fares for Bay Area commuters were ordered yesterday by the State Public Utilities Commission.

The new rates, effective August 27, will affect all bus-riding commuters except those in Marin and Sonoma counties.

In addition, all Bay Area single and round-trip fares will be increased.

Commuters from Contra Costa county will pay 20 per cent more for service to points in Oakland and San Francisco, while Peninsula commuters will pay an additional $2 for 20-ride commute ticket books. The cost of the books varies depending on the distance traveled.

INCREASE

Ticket books for South San Francisco commuters, who travel approximately 11 miles to the city, will be raised in price from the present $4.50 to $6.50. The San Jose ticket book will be raised from $10 to $12 for 20 tickets for the 50-mile trip.

The only exception on the Peninsula will be commuters from Daly City, Colma and

See Page 20. Col. 4

Viet Cong Lifts Siege Of Duc Co

New York Times

Saigon

Viet Cong troops who earlier this week launched one of the biggest battles of the Vietnamese war at Duc Co temporarily broke off the fight yesterday after thousands of Americans and South Vietnam government reinforcements reached the area.

The six-week siege of Duc Co, in the highlands near Cambodia, 220 miles northeast of Saigon, was virtually lifted until early this morning after the

See Page 12, Col. 6

Johnson's Remark On Lodge Story

New York Times

Washington

President Johnson added his comment yesterday to the controversy on whether Henry Cabot Lodge told Senators that the United States would keep its forces in South Vietnam even if a government there requested their withdrawal.

Mr. Johnson said he and Lodge fully agree that the U.S. would not undertake sacrifices in Vietnam "if its

See Page 12, Col. 4

East Bay Protest

Battle Over Train --GIs Go Through

By California Photo Service—Norm Fisher

Demonstrator Ann Hallatt got aboard the engine—and an officer (left) tried to get her off. After riding several blocks she was finally knocked off the train.

Cops Use Clubs--- Two Held

By Paul Avery

Five hundred peace demonstrators made a dramatic and dangerous—but unsuccessful—bid again to stop a troop train traveling through Albany and Berkeley yesterday.

But other hundreds of persons lined street intersections and back yards bordering the railway right-of-way and cheered as the soldiers passed through the East Bay communities.

Dozens of the demonstrators leaped up and grabbed steel hand grips on the cars of the Santa Fe special as it rumbled slowly by, holding on with determination while police pulled, pushed and clubbed them.

One woman slipped and fell between two cars, and only the fact that she fell backwards instead of onto the tracks prevented a fatality during the protest against U.S. military action in Vietnam.

HANDHOLD

Another young woman who gained a handhold on the diesel engine itself was pulled off twice. The third time she managed to ride almost a mile before a policeman—striking her with a nightstick—knocked her to the ground.

A University of California student who jumped aboard between two cars was arrested for allegedly tampering with the train's air brakes.

A 16-year-old boy was taken into custody for allegedly hitting a policeman.

Those were the only ar-

See Page 10, Col 5

Civil Rights 'Ended'

Dr. King's Letters On Viet Peace

New York Times

Birmingham, Ala.

Nobel Peace Prize Winner Dr. Martin Luther King Jr. said yesterday that he was planning to appeal to President Johnson, president Ho Chi Minh of North Vietnam, the Viet Cong, and the Saigon government to halt the war in Southeast Asia.

Similar appeals will be sent in the next few weeks to the Government leaders of Red China and to premier Alexei Kosygin of the Soviet Union, King said.

Addressing a mass rally of the Christian Leadership Conference at its annual convention here, King called last night for "unconditional and unambiguous" statements from Mr. Johnson of this Nation's willingness to negotiate with the Viet Cong. He also asked the Johnson administration to "consider halting

See Page 12, Col. 1

The Index

Bridge 40
Chess 40
Comics 54
Crosswords 35, 39
Deaths 22
Editorials 38
Entertainment 41-44
Finance 50-53
McCabe 20
Movies 41-44
Obituaries 14
Shipping 22
Sports 45-50
TV-Radio 40
Vital Statistics 14
Want Ads 22
Weather 14
Women 15-19

ELECTION EXTRA

BIG REAGAN MAJORITY

THE WEATHER

Bay Area: Fair with some high cloudiness and slightly warmer. High Wednesday, 65 to 70; low, 37 to 47. Variable winds to 15 m.p.h. See Page 43.

San Francisco Chronicle
THE VOICE OF THE WEST

102nd Year No. 313 CCCCAAABC WEDNESDAY, NOVEMBER 9, 1966 10 CENTS GArfield 1-1111

Goldberg Plans Asia 'Peace Trip'

New York Times

United Nations

United States Ambassador Arthur J. Goldberg will visit South Vietnam, other countries in southeast Asia and "other areas" in search of a settlement of the Vietnam war, the U. S. mission to the United Nations announced yesterday.

The trip "in pursuit of peace" will be made at the request of President Johnson and Secretary of State Dean Rusk.

The reference to other areas in the announcement indicates, informed sources said, the probability that the tour may be extended to India, Pakistan and Indonesia, where governmental views on the way to end the war differ from those of the U.S.

BURMA

Goldberg may also visit Burma. The government of Burma maintains friendly relations with the North Vietnamese regime. In the past Burma has been used by Secretary General U Thant and others to convey their views on peace talks to Hanoi.

The ambassador told President Johnson Monday that he had detected "very faint, very indirect" signals from countries that formerly were strongly opposed to any set-

See Page 7, Col. 2

GIs Smash Viet Cong Human Wave

New York Times

Cha Ko

An outnumbered battalion of the United States First Infantry Division yesterday repulsed Viet Cong attacks and, with massive artillery barrages and air strikes, inflicted one of the heaviest defeats of the war on the Communists.

Lieutenant Colonel Jack Whitted, battlefield commander of the 475-man American battalion, said troops conducting sweeps around his defense perimeter 65 miles northwest of Saigon had reported counting 258 enemy dead after a four-hour battle.

He described U.S. casualties as "extremely light" in the battle on the southern edge of War Zone C, a 900-square mile forest area near the Cambodian border, 60 miles northwest of Saigon, which has been a major rebel sanctuary since the French Indo-China war.

The attack by at least 1000 Viet Cong main force soldiers — elements of the Dong Nghia regiment and a battalion of the 272d regiment of

See Page 7, Col. 3

The Results

GOVERNOR

BROWN	REAGAN
1,829,110	2,483,358

LT. GOVERNOR

ANDERSON	FINCH
488,027	616,864

SEC'Y OF STATE

JORDAN	SCHLEI
666,126	544,107

CONTROLLER

CRANSTON	FLOURNOY
684,733	544,455

TREASURER

BETTS	PRIEST
632,134	579,709

ATTORNEY GENERAL

LYNCH	WILLIAMS
696,788	510,858

STATE PROPS.

1-A (Legislative Salaries)

YES	NO
624,292	240,769

2 (College Bonds)

YES	NO
387,005	304,745

16 (CLEAN)

YES	NO
343,422	515,000

S. F. PROPS.

A (Airport Bonds)

YES	NO
156,802	81,527

Defeated, lacked two-thirds

B (Muni Bonds)

YES	NO
135,077	101,086

Defeated, lacked two-thirds

THE SENATE

The Democrats maintained their big majority, but the Republicans gained three seats. Among the winners were Hatfield in Oregon, Percy in Illinois and Brooke in Massachusetts.

THE HOUSE

The net Republican gain will be about 40 seats. This was more than anticipated. It may jeopardize presidential legislation.

GOVERNORSHIPS

The Republicans apparently may gain a net of six State Houses. Among the winners were Rockefeller in New York and Romney in Michigan.

CLEAN Amendment Loses in Big Upset

Proposition 16, the so-called anti-obscenity amendment, apparently was defeated by California voters yesterday in an astounding upset.

The measure had been seen as a sure winner, despite strong opposition by church groups and district attorneys, and equally strong legal doubts about its constitutionality.

What caused the voters to turn it down at the polls yes-

See Page D, Col. 7

Brown Concedes Defeat--- Republican Gains in U. S.

National Democratic Setback

New York Times

New York

A Republican National resurgence stronger than expected, an impressive group of new Republican faces, and further Republican inroads in the once solid South resulted from yesterday's midterm elections.

Although Republican gains were not substantial enough to signal a real repudiation of the Johnson Administration, the Democrats could take little comfort from anything but upset victories for the governorships of Maine and Kansas.

The Republicans won virtually all the nationally publicized races.

In Congressional races, the Republicans gained three Senate seats — in Illinois, Tennessee and Oregon — and about 40 seats in the House.

STRONG

As returns continued to pour in after midnight it appeared that the Republicans had picked up a net of six governorships, despite the loss of Maine and Kansas.

In the South, they elected Governors in Florida and Arkansas — the first elected in the old Confederacy since Alfred A. Taylor in Tennessee in 1921 — picked up a Senate seat in Tennessee, and had a strong chance to win in the Cliff-Hanger race for Governor of Georgia.

House returns showed Republicans taking 23 seats from the Democrats but losing three for a net gain of 20. By the time all the 435 districts had been heard from, the gain was expected to approach 40.

These were the major Senate results:

ILLINOIS — Charles H. Percy, the 47-year-old industrialist, defeated the veteran Democrat, Senator Paul H. Douglas, 74. The victory made Percy a national Republican figure.

TENNESSEE — Howard Baker Jr., the Republican son-in-law of Senator Everett McKinley Dirksen, scored the upset of the day by defeating Governor Frank G Clement, Democrat, for a Tennessee Senate seat. He became the first Republican ever to be elected to the Senate from that state

MASSACHUSETTS — Attorney General Edward W. Brooke, Republican, beat former Governor Endicott Peabody, Democrat, to become

See Page 1B, Col 1

UPI Telephoto

THE REAGANS AT HOME YESTERDAY EVENING IN PACIFIC PALISADES
Victory was apparent from the beginning

Finch Is Lieutenant Governor

By Michael Harris

Ronald Reagan was elected Governor of California last night.

The 55-year-old actor, who was ahead from the moment the counting started, racked up a huge majority. At 10:15 p.m. Governor Edmund G. Brown conceded defeat.

"I want to do everything within my power to see that the new Governor can keep the State moving ahead," Brown said in a statement to his supporters at the Ambassador Hotel in Los Angeles.

With returns in from 21,694 of the State's 28,573 precincts, the vote was:

Reagan—2,483,358
Brown—1,829,110

With a much smaller percentage of the vote counted in his race, Lieutenant Governor Glenn M. Anderson conceded defeat to Republican Robert H. Finch shortly after 10:30 p.m.

"It was a nationwide trend, and we're part of that trend," Anderson declared.

STATE

Republican Secretary of State Frank M. Jordan was leading Democrat Norbert A. Schlei by 37,153 to 20,226.

Controller Alan Cranston was leading his Republican challenger, Houston I. Flournoy, after trailing in early returns.

Attorney General Thomas C. Lynch was ahead of his Republican opponent, Spencer Williams, and Treasurer Bert Betts held a lead over Republican Ivy Baker Priest.

The races were by no

See Page 1B, Col. 5

EDITORIAL

To the Winner

WE CONGRATULATE Ronald Reagan on his election as the next governor of California.

The Chronicle did not endorse Mr. Reagan because it felt his lack of experience would be too much of a handicap in dealing with the many problems facing our vast and complex State.

We would be delighted to be proved wrong.

Reagan's Impact On Nation

By Earl C. Behrens
Political Editor

Republican Ronald Reagan's victory yesterday over Democratic Governor Edmund G. Brown will have national, as well as statewide, political repercussions.

The 55-year-old actor-rancher will emerge as a national figure and at the same time will bring about a drastic reshuffling of key positions in his new State administration at Sacramento.

Discounting the "Confederate South" with its special political climate Reagan was the only major Republican victor from the conservative or right wing of the party to win yesterday.

Throughout the rest of the Nation, Republican moderates were winner as Governors and U.S. Senators. It was evident they will be running with Reagan and his allies for control of the party nationally.

In turning back Brown's bid for a third term, Reagan will also precipitate a power

See Page D, Col. 1

GOP Victories in Governor Races

Times-Post Service

New York

The Republicans gained a net of six governorships in yesterday's elections, winning eight from the Democrats and losing two to them.

The GOP swept the State houses in the five most populous states and scored two stunning upsets in the old Confederacy.

Their most telling blow was the capture of the biggest prize, the California State House.

At the same time, the GOP held onto the governorships in New York, Pennsylvania, Michigan and Ohio.

Rated an almost sure loser as late as September, Governor Nelson A. Rockefeller made a surprising comeback to pile up a substantial majority over Democrat Ed-

See Page 17, Col. 1

Election news on Pages 1A, 1B, 1C, 1D, 8, 9, 10, 11, 12, 13, 14.

The Index

Bridge 48
Chess 48
Comics 60
Crossword 47, 60
Datebook 49
Deaths 43
Editorials 46
Entertainment 49-52
Jumble 28
Movies 50-52
Obituaries 43
Shipping 43
Sports 53-59
TV-Radio 48
Want Ads 30
Weather 43
Women's World 19-23

Special Sections

Teacher Protest 1E
Madrid Letter 4E

Food News 1-4W

Red Guards 15
Thai Goddesses 55

Memphis Ambush

DR. KING MURDERED

The Weather
Bay Area: Clearing. Warmer. Gusty winds. High temperature, 55-60. Chances for rain: 1 in 10.
See Page 42

San Francisco Chronicle

104th Year No. 88 ★★★★ FRIDAY, APRIL 5, 1968 10 CENTS GArfield 1-1111

Viet Strategy

The President Delays Flight To Honolulu

Times-Post Service

Washington

President Johnson, revising his plans because of the murder of the Rev. Martin Luther King Jr., postponed his trip to Hawaii for Vietnam strategy talks at least until today, the White House said last night.

The President had planned to leave Washington at about midnight last night for Southern California en route to Honolulu. The hour at which he will now leave was not announced.

The White House did not indicate whether Mr. Johnson would change an earlier plan to meet at March Air Force Base, Calif., to talk with former President Eisenhower.

The President's somber announcement came after a busy day in which he flew to New York for the investiture of Roman Catholic Archbishop Terence J. Cooke and conferred with United Nations Secretary General U Thant.

TALKS

He returned to Washington to talk with Ambassador Averell Harriman and Llewellyn Thompson, his newly named Vietnam negotiator.

He canceled an appearance at a Democratic fund-raising dinner after he learned of the murder of Dr. King.

The President was described as in an ebullient mood earlier, cheered by Hanoi's offer to meet with American officials for talks and by the applause for his latest peace effort.

But Washington officials cautioned against any undue optimism that Hanoi's offer to talk with American officials indicated a Vietnamese war peace settlement was imminent.

Responding to the President's peace talks proposal, North Vietnam has said it is willing to talk with American representatives about ending the bombing of North Vietnam.

After that issue is "decid-

See Back Page

The second article on the secret search for peace begins on Page 18.

Hanoi Claims U.S. Bombed Far North

New York Times

Washington

North Vietnam charged in a broadcast yesterday that United States planes had bombed a "populated area" in northwestern Vietnam — far north of the 20th Parallel.

The Defense Department said it knew of no such raid but was investigating.

President Johnson has ordered that there be no attacks on North Vietnam north of the 20th parallel as one step toward de-escalation.

REPORT

Hanoi radio, in a broadcast monitored and translated here, said three waves of U.S. planes dropped more than 50 bombs on a "populated area" about 30 miles west of the provincial capital of Lai Chau.

The nearest town to that point apparently would be Quang Lam, which is about 190 miles northwest of Hanoi, about 140 miles north of the 20th parallel and only about 10 miles from the ill-defined Loatian border. No casualties were mentioned by Hanoi radio.

MOUNTAINS

Quang Lam lies in sparsely populated mountain country. It is opposite the northernmost part of Laos, where North Vietnamese supply routes run into the Loatian province of Phong Saly to supply pro-Communist Pathet Lao guerrilla forces.

Loatian air force planes have carried out raids against these supply routes in the past. The U.S. Central Intelligence Agency, working with Meo tribesmen, has also carried out extensive anti-guerrilla operation in this part of Laos.

Although the area Hanoi radio said had been tatacked is far north of the northernmost limit that American bombing planes are now supposed to observe, Administration officials did not seem to

See Back Page

A Confident McCarthy-- 'No Deals'

By Michael Harris

Senator Eugene J. McCarthy, fresh from toppling President Johnson in Wisconsin, launched a new wave of attacks yesterday against a fresh trio — the CIA, the FBI and "the draft boards under General Hershey."

For perhaps the first time since he declared himself for the Presidency, the quiet, gray McCarthy found in his challenge to the draft boards an issue that stirred his audience to wild cheers.

The applause was tremendous, as might have been expected, when he attacked General Lewis B. Hershey in a talk to 10,000 students at the University of California.

But it was not until he spoke to an audience composed largely of parents of college-age children at the Hilton Hotel last night that he drew a standing ovation for his criticism of the draft.

His supporters, who had received him with something close to compassion when he was here in January, seemed ready to believe that the Minnesota Democrat might win in California's June 4 primary.

"I will not withdraw," he said. "There has never been any collusion between me and Senator Kennedy, and there will not be any. I made no concession to him. There will be no accommodations."

On his visit to the Berkeley campus, McCarthy reminded the students who packed the Greek Theater that it was there that, less than six months ago, he suggested the time had come for Secretary of State Dean Rusk to resign.

He also urged then that someone—he was not yet quite ready to specify himself—should challenge President Johnson for the Demo-

See Back Page

Dr. King Slain by Sniper--- Massive Search for Killer

UPI Telephoto

DR. MARTIN LUTHER KING
His last public appearance in Memphis Wednesday

Violence in Memphis-- The National Guard Called by Governor

New York Times

Memphis

The Rev. Martin Luther King Jr., who preached non-violence and brotherhood, was shot and killed here last night by a sniper who escaped.

The 39-year-old Negro civil rights leader was shot while he leaned over a second-floor railing outside his room at the Lorraine Motel.

He suffered "a gaping wound" in the neck and was pronounced dead at a hospital about an hour later.

The assassin might have been a white man who was "50 to 100 yards away in a flophouse," according to Police Director Frank Holloman. He added that police have no definite lead.

Paul Hess, assistant administrator at St. Joseph's Hospital, where Dr. King died despite emergency surgery, said the minister "received a gunshot wound on the right side of the neck, at the root of the neck, a gaping wound."

"He was pronounced dead at 7:05 p.m. Central Standard Time by staff doctors," Hess said. "They did everything humanly possible."

Four thousand National Guard troops were ordered into Memphis by Governor Buford Ellington after Dr. King died.

A curfew was imposed on this shocked city of 550,000 inhabitants, 40 per cent of whom are Negro.

Dr. King's mourning associates sought to calm the people they met by recalling his messages of peace, but there was widespread concern by law enforcement officers here and elsewhere over potential reactions.

Within minutes of the murder, angry Negroes ran wild in Memphis streets, looting stores and exchanging shots with the police.

Assistant Police Chief U. T. Bartholomew said early this morning that it was impossible to estimate the number of injured.

Bartholomew said unidentified persons firing from rooftops and windows had shot at policemen eight or 10 times during the night.

Bullets shattered the windshield of a police car, wounding two officers with flying glass.

Bartholomew said the rioting had been brought "under control" with the help of reinforcements from the National Guard, the Tennessee Highway Patrol the Arkansas Highway patrol and the Memphis sheriff's office.

Early this morning, the city's central and south sides were quiet.

The police issued an alarm seeking a young white man reported to have rushed out

See Back Page

More Dr. King news on Pages 12-14

Johnson's Words of Mourning

New York Times

Washington

President Johnson last night deplored the "brutal slaying" of the Rev. Martin Luther King Jr.

He asked "every citizen to reject the violence that him down."

The shock of Dr. King's **death was reflected on the President's face as he made a brief television address to the nation.**

Mr. Johnson said he and Mrs. Johnson had conveyed their sympathy to Mrs. King.

See Back Page

Wave of Violence Follows the Killing

Associated Press

New York

Sporadic incidents of violence were reported in a number of cities across the country last night following the assassination of the Rev. Martin Luther King Jr.

Memphis, where Dr. King was slain, was the scene of the first disorders.

Outbreaks of arson, looting and rock throwing then spread across the South — Raleigh, N. C., Jackson, Miss.; Birmingham, Ala.: Winston-Salem, Charlotte and Durham, N. C.; Miami, Tampa and Tallahassee, Fla.

Similar incidents were reported in New York, Boston and Washington, D.C.

ARSON

Cases of arson, looting and rock throwing were reported in most of New York City's Negro neighborhoods.

Police ordered 7000 men, due to go off duty at midnight, to remain on the city's streets.

Mayor John V. Lindsay and top police officials set up a command post on Harlem's 125th Street where the first disturbances broke out short-

See Back Page

Sabotage on Peninsula-- Tower Felled

By Jack Viets

A huge bulldozer toppled a 90-foot PG&E transmission tower in the hills above Redwood City early yesterday in the latest incident in a mysterious wave of sabotage against Bay Area utilities.

The massive blade of the dozer sliced into the big tower at 12:11 a.m., plunging portions of ten Peninsula communities into complete darkness.

"This was not a prank," said Captain Eugene Stewart of the San Mateo county Sheriff's Office. "It was a deliberate act of sabotage — and I expect there will be more of them."

And he is "convinced," the captain said, that the destruction of the Peninsula tower was "tied in with inci-

See Back Page

Crime Syndicate Linked to Fake Art

By Michael Grieg

A link between organized crime and the California traffic in fake art has been established by the State attorney general's office on fake art, The Chronicle learned yesterday.

The connection between phony Old Masters and old master criminals was turned up by the agency's newly organized crime unit, now investigating the role of the Mafia in California.

Chief Deputy Attorney General Charles A. O'Brien told The Chronicle that the mobster link may have widespread ramifications, including the bankrolling of galleries — notorious as business risks — at exorbitant interest rates.

The disclosure is a major result of the State's year-long art fraud probe, headed by O'Brien, which has enlisted the cooperation of reputable collectors, ethical dealers and museum officials.

"MUSCLE"

So far, O'Brien said, the investigation has shown the main thrust of mobster activity occurs when a shady business operator asks for "some national muscle" to ruin a competitor or to help "settle" a labor problem.

The shady businessman pays a substantial sum — as much as $100,000 — for the so-called favor. And, in addition to the favor, the mob fix-

See Back Page

Hughes Files a Claim In the Comstock Lode

Virginia City, Nev.

Billionaire Howard Hughes has staked a claim in the historic Comstock Lode country south of here, but this former bonanza town is far from stampede fever.

Hughes shifted his attention from the gambling casinos in Las Vegas with a deal to buy more than 400 acres and four gold and silver mines in the American Flat about five miles away.

The transaction came to light when it was recorded at Lyon County Court House. No closed, although one report placed it at $225,000.

The Hughes move into the Comstock Lode — source of old silver fortunes — followed an announcement that Union Pacific Railroad had leased claims near Virginia City and planned to start a large exploration program.

Virginia City residents were surprised by the Hughes purchase, but they are not about to dash out of town with pick and shovel.

The Hughes Tool Company arranged the purchase of the property from George Von Tobel of Las Vegas, a member of the Nevada Gaming Control Board, and the mines from E. L. Cleveland, also of La Vegas.

The mining claims are the Red Jacket, the Delaware, Pacific Lode and Southeast Lode.

Since the mysterious Hughes abruptly showed up in Las Vegas 15 months ago, he has invested more than $100 million in hotels and casinos on the strip.

Our Correspondent

Guerrilla Battle In Colombia

Bogota, Colombia

Ten guerrillas were killed yesterday in a clash with an army patrol in the Department of Meta in the western part of Colombia, the government announced.

Four soldiers also were slain and seven wounded in the encounter, the most serious between leftists and government forces in recent months.

Associated Press

Index

Comics	64
Deaths	42
Entertainment	47
Finance	59
TV-Radio	46
Vital Statistics	52
Weather	42
Women's News	23

Troops in Capitol

U.S. RACIAL CRISIS

The Weather
Bay Area: Fair, warmer. High temperatures in the 60s. Decreasing northwesterly winds.
See Page 27

San Francisco Chronicle

104th Year No. 89 ★★★★ SATURDAY, APRIL 6, 1968 10 CENTS GArfield 1-1111

A Proclamation

AS MAYOR of San Francisco I must give free voice to my heart tonight. And, as I do so I am speaking for every San Franciscan—man, woman and child.

The sentiments which are hereby expressed shall constitute a proclamation of the City of San Francisco. It is a proclamation not of material substance but spiritual in content. It concerns the souls of men, not their treasure they have laid up for themselves on this earth.

Slightly more than one day ago our nation suffered the loss by violence of one of the truly great Americans of this age. Dr. Martin Luther King had dedicated his work to non-violence. The role he played in the pageant of mankind was to assist his fellow citizens find richer lives.

He wished no man harm.

He wished no man misfortune.

He wished no man the agony of loneliness or the horror of hate.

Dr. King sought no selfish rewards for himself, no self glorification nor applause from the multitude.

His life was one of compassion toward his fellow man. He obviously was deeply moved by the teachings of our city's own patron Saint—Francis of Assisi—whose warm and gentle life fashioned so deeply the spirit of our citizens. The entire world knows the philosophy of non-violence that so characterized the spirit of this remarkable man.

Therefore, as Mayor of San Francisco, I am taking upon myself the opportunity of expressing the shock and numbness that has befallen our entire city caused by the loss of the Reverend Dr. Martin Luther King.

Martin Luther King carried forward his crusade for brotherhood and peace among all men. Let us pray together that his country—and ours—will harvest a reward of non-violence—the concept for which this humble and great American gave his life.

Given by my hand,
Friday, April 5, 1968

Joseph L. Alioto
Mayor

Thousands at City Hall Tribute

By George Draper

A most solemn ceremony honoring the memory of the martyred Dr. Martin Luther King was held in bright sunshine at Civic Center Plaza yesterday while City Hall flags flew at half staff.

Possibly the most moving tribute to the fallen civil rights leader came near the end of the hour-long program when some 7000 black and whites held hands and sang "We Shall Overcome."

The huge, grief-stricken audience, representing persons from all walks of life, had come quietly to the Polk street side of City Hall from all parts of the city.

There were housewives from Hunters Point, men in working clothes from BART projects, young secretaries from the nearby State and Federal Buildings, and many young students.

Directly behind the speakers' platform, according to Mayor Joseph L. Alioto, stood representatives of such youth groups as Youth for Service and Young Men of Action and two contingents of girls from Woodrow Wilson High School and Jefferson High in Daly City.

Mayor Alioto, who was the eighth speaker of the day, noted that Dr. King, like the late President John F. Kennedy, was brought up in the Judeo-Christian philosophy "that every human being is sacred."

Four years ago, the Mayor said, President Kennedy was shot by an insane white man

See Back Page

President Acts to Avert A National 'Catastrophe'

Session of Congress Requested

New York Times

Washington

President Johnson yesterday asked to address a joint session of Congress no later than Monday evening to propose "constructive action instead of destructive action in this hour of national need."

Gravely imploring American to "stand their ground to deny violence its victory" in the reaction to the murder of Dr. Martin Luther King, the President set out to arouse the Nation's conscience and to win quick action on long-stalled major items in his domestic program.

To deal with the divisiveness that he said was "tearing this nation apart," Mr. Johnson spent almost the entire day working "to avoid catastrophe."

MEETINGS

He met with moderate Negro leaders, members of Congress and of his Administration to find ways of containing the violence, arson and looting that threatened many big cities and which spread here to within a few blocks of the White House.

The President's Negro visitors told him that prompt action is needed to bring hope to the black inhabitants of urban ghettos if the nonviolent Negro majority is to reject the leadership of the violent few.

Mr. Johnson told them that Dr. King's murder could lead either to catastrophe or to final passage of legislation that has been waiting too long and to the rooting out of every trace of racism from white men's hearts.

EFFORT

He said he knew what Dr. King would have wanted, and left the impression that he would mount an extraordinary effort to pass the civil rights bill, including open housing; his anti-crime program; the model cities and poverty appropriations; measures to limit the sales of firearms and to begin massive construction of low-cost housing, and a tax increase to meet the costs.

"We must move with urgency and with resolve and with new energy," Mr. Johnson declared in a nationwide television and radio statement after he and his advisers returned from a memorial service for Dr. King at Washington National Cathedral.

"No words of ours and no

See Back Page

UPI Telephoto

Army troops manned a machinegun yesterday on the steps of the National capitol

'Arrest Near' In Murder Of Dr. King

United Press

Memphis, Tenn.

Attorney General Ramsey Clark said yesterday evidence indicates the assassination of Dr. Martin Luther King was "perpetrated by one man" and that authorities are "very close" to making an arrest.

"The investigation has spread some several hundred miles from the borders of Tennessee at this time," said Clark, who flew here on orders from President Johnson.

Clark said FBI agents are pursuing the investigation "in several sections of the country," and that "large numbers" of items of evidence have been uncovered, adn a number of out-of-state leads have been developed."

He did not elaborate on the out-of-state leads, except to say that while no positive identification had yet been made of the assasin, he is

See Back Page

Looting, Fires in Capital --6000 Troops on Scene

Times-Post Service

Washington

Six thousand armed troops were rushed into the streets of Washington last night to combat widespread burning and looting.

At least five persons were dead from the rioting.

Acting in the wake of the slaying of Dr. Martin Luther King, marauding bands of Negroes burned and plundered scores of commercial establishments in the capital.

There was a similar situation in Chicago, where three persons were shot to death by snipers and National Guard troops were patrolling the streets.

Guardsmen also were sent into Detroit. One looter was accidently shot to death.

New York City was the scene of a large protest march and it was followed by an outburst of looting and violence.

Philadelphia declared a limited state of emergency and National Guard troops were alerted for possible duty in Boston.

By evening, racial disorders were reported in 46 cities.

Washington police said two looters — one of them a 13-year-old boy — were killed by police bullets. Another man died when a wall collapsed. The other death occurred early yesterday, when a white man was stabbed fatally at a mid-city gas station.

Troops ordered into the riot-torn capital included a brigade of paratroopers of the 82nd Airborne Division from Fort Bragg, N.C., which arrived at Andrews Air Force base shortly after midnight.

At 1:10 a.m. today Mayor Walter E. Washington said the fires appeared to be contained and "we hope the situation is settling down."

However, the mayor said a curfew imposed last night would be imposed again tonight and no liquor or gasoline would be sold in the city. He said emergency centers were being set up to help persons in need of food and shelter.

Former Deputy Defense Secretary Cyrus R. Vance, acting as Federal "coordinator" or anti-riot strategy, said he agreed with the mayor's assessment and that in the hard-hit areas "the situation appeared to be under control."

A Pentagon spokesman said at least 350 persons had been treated for injuries at local hospitals, including six firemen and seven policemen.

He said that as of 10 p.m.

See Back Page

More on racial crisis: Pages 4-11

Index

Comics	16
Deaths	28
Entertainment	31
Finance	42
TV-Radio	36
Vital Statistics	28
Weather	27
Women's News	12

EXTRA EXTRA EXTRA EXTRA

The Weather
Bay Area: Drizzle becoming partly cloudy, then clearing tomorrow night. Fair Thursday.
See Page 37

San Francisco Chronicle

104th Year No. 149 ★★★★** WEDNESDAY, JUNE 5, 1968 10 CENTS GArfield 1-1111

KENNEDY IS SHOT

Brain Surgeons Operate --Attacker Seized in L.A.

PG&E Bomber Back Again

After a month's silence, the East Bay utility saboteur went at it again early yesterday, toppling with explosives three power towers in the Oakland hills.

The almost simultaneous blasts, near Round Top Regional Park, rocked homes in the Oakland-Berkeley hill area at 4:40 a.m. and cut off power to some 30,000 Pacific Gas and Electric Co. customers.

Power was restored by 6:02 a.m.

The loss of power delayed the opening of about 50 polling places from 15 to 30 minutes, accord-

See Back Page

Israeli Jets Hit At Jordan Guns

New York Times

Jerusalem

Israeli and Jordanian forces fought a day-long battle across the Jordan River with artillery and aircraft yesterday — the eve of the Middle East six-day war.

Israeli jet fighters pounded artillery positions on the East Bank of the river and struck at long-range gun emplacements near Irbed, an Arab town about 12 miles east of the cease-fire line.

It was the first time planes had been called into action in nearly four months along the truce frontier.

Three Israeli farmers were killed, and six civilians and one border policeman were wounded during the fighting, which flared intermittently during the morning and escalated into a major exchange in the afternoon.

(In Amman, a Jordan government communique reported casualties on both sides as 32 Jordanian civilians and three soldiers killed, 52 Jordanian civilians and 10 soldiers wounded and an estimated 45 Israeli soldiers killed or wounded, according to the Associated Press.

(The Amman communique also said Jordanian fire destroyed four Israeli tanks, six armored cars and three artillery positions.

According to the Israeli military spokesmen, the Jordanians poured artillery shells into eight settlements along the West Bank of the

See Back Page

Big Fire in Oakland

A general alarm fire badly damaged several businesses in an industrial area of East Oakland early today.

More than 100 firemen were called out to fight a spectacular blaze at Reed's Home Furnishers, 680 Hegenberger road, near the Oakland Airport.

The blaze, which broke out at 2:41 a.m., quickly spread next door to the F-B Truck Line Company, 690 Hegenberger road.

The French Strikers Keep It Up

New York Times

Paris

France went through the 17th day of economic paralysis yesterday.

The nationwide strike continued with only scattered breaks.

Despite recent appeals and warnings by President Charles de Gaulle, Premier Georges Pompidou and other governmental leaders, nearly nine million workers remained out.

A majority of 750,000 workers on the automobile, machinery and metal trade industries of the Paris region voted to stay off their jobs and, in some cases, to keep their factories occupied.

This group included the nationalized Renault factory which employs 35,000 workers in suburban Boulogne-Billancourt.

Union officials there called the factory management offer "ridiculous" because it

See Back Page

4 Die in Navy Plane Crash

Rota, Spain

A United States Navy plane crashed on a farm shortly after taking off from the joint U.S.-Spanish naval base here yesterday, killing four crewmen and injuring two others, American officials reported. *Associated Press*

Bobby Has Firm Lead In Primary

By Michael Harris

Senator Robert F. Kennedy swept into a commanding lead over Senator Eugene J. McCarthy only moments before he was shot leaving the podium of a ballroom of the Ambassador Hotel in Los Angeles early today.

The tragedy came after a day of double triumph for the young New York Senator—a smashing victory first in South Dakota and then a California triumph after his campaign had appeared to be sagging.

But with a comeback in California, Kennedy promptly challenged Vice President Hubert H. Humphrey to meet him "in dialogue or debate" to discuss in what direction the country should go.

SPEECH

He spoke of his distress at the violence and ill feeling that had marred the United States for the last few years.

"We are a great country. an unselfish country and a compassionate country." Kennedy said. "I intend to make that the basis of my campaign."

With 10,646 of the State's 21,301 precincts counted — about half the vote — the Democratic preidential vote was:

Kennedy 675,753.(46.Pct.)

McCarthy 623,071.(42.Pct.)

Lynch ... 183,611.(12.Pct.)

Both the lead and Kennedy's percentage were expected to grow as counting continued — according to the Columbia Broadcasting System, to 50 per cent or more for Kennedy.

In the Republican primary, Governor Ronald Reagan, running unopposed as a favorite son, got 100 per cent of his party's presidential primary vote. With 27 per cent of the Republican ballots counted, Reagan had 316,164 votes.

Prior to the shooting, McCarthy had acknowledged he had lost a hard-fought campaign in California.

The Minnesota Senator said he would not quit the campaign that he had promised to wage to the finish. He told his followers he would

See Back Page

More election news on Pages 2, 3, 4, 15A, 15B

UPI Telephoto

Clutching a rosary, Kennedy lay on the hotel floor

Rafferty Gaining On Kuchel

By George Draper

U.S. Senator Thomas H. Kuchel was holding an ever diminishing lead over Max Rafferty early this morning for the Republican senatorial nomination.

Returns from 8625 precincts out of 21,301 gave Kuchel 374,923 votes to 332,085 for Rafferty.

In the Democratic senatorial primary, former State controller Alan Cranston won handily over State Senator Anthony C. Beilenson.

Returns from 10,552 precints gave Cranston 783,464 votes to 279,663 for Beilenson.

Returns from 6106 precincts out of 21,301 gave Kuchel 258,161 votes to 196,824 for Rafferty.

The Kuchel-Rafferty race was projected by television network computers as headed for a hairline finish.

Kuchel started out with a substantial lead, percentage-wise, due to early returns from the northern portion of the State.

The veteran of 15 years in the Senate predicted victory at 11:30 p.m. last night, telling campaign workers in Los Angeles, "We're going to win."

Half an hour later, howev-

See Back Page

President

Democratic

KENNEDY	675,753
McCARTHY	623,071
LYNCH	183,611

Senator

Republican

KUCHEL	374,923
RAFFERTY	332,083

Democratic

CRANSTON	783,464
BEILENSON	279,663

Prop. A

YES	77,906
NO	34,562

S.F. Voters Rescue Market St.

San Francisco voters yesterday approved Proposition A, the $24.5 million bond issue to renovate Market street, and Proposition D, a $17.5 million measure to modernize the city's ancient sewers.

At the same time, voters defeated Proposition C— a $5.7 million measure to acquire the Cliff House and the Sutro Baths site as a park.

They also refused to approve Proposition B, which was a $14.8 million park and recreation bond issue to finance 28 separate recreation and park projects.

In the voting on Proposition E, voters gave strong assent to Mayor Joseph L. Alioto's plan to suspend for five years a charter provision prohibiting the city from

See Back Page

Others Injured in Wild Attack at Ambassador Hotel

A.P. & U.P.

Los Angeles

Senator Robert F. Kennedy was shot in the head early today by a gunman who turned a victory celebration into a scene of terror.

Six neurosurgeons began a delicate operation to try to remove a bullet in the brain and save his life.

Kennedy was hit twice by a slender young man who sprayed an Ambassador Hotel passageway with bullets.

One superficial wound was in the shoulder but the other bullet pierced his right mastoid bone, passed into the brain and lodged near the midline of the skull.

'CRITICAL'

Kennedy's press secretary. Frank Mankewiecz, described his condition as "very critical," but said his heartbeat and breathing were good.

At 4:45 a.m., two hours after the operation began. Press Secretary Mankiewicz announced that the surgical effort to remove the bullet from Senator Kennedy's brain would continue for at least another hour, and perhaps two.

It was obviously a critically delicate operation, since the bullet lodged in the brain raises the possibility of tissue destruction. Paralysis or damage to sensory and thought processes could result, although brain surgery of this type has often been accomplished with no permanent damage.

Mankiewicz said that while the Senator was still in surgery, with a team of six neurosurgeons attending him, his "life signs remain good." Respiration, heartbeat and blood pressure were all described as satisfactory.

Mrs. Kennedy and Senator Ted Kennedy, the candidate's brother. were waiting in the hospital for the long operation to end.

Although reports were conflicting, it appeared that four other men were slightly wounded in the shooting, which took place at about 12:15 a.m. today. A woman fell in the scuffle with the gunman and cut her hand. She too was hospitalized.

Seized immediately as he brandished a small pistol was a curly-haired man about 25 years old.

SHOUTS

Several eyewitnesses agreed they heard the man shout "I did it for my country! I love my country!" as he was seized after the shooting.

Police Chief Thomas Reddin later said the suspect has

See Page 1A

Johnson Asks Russia To Pitch In

Times-Post Service

Glassboro, N.J.

President Johnson called yesterday for co-operation between the United States and the Soviet Union to help solve the world's conflicts in Vietnam and the Middle East and to reach a new disarmament agreement.

Returning to this college campus where he conferred for two days last June with Soviet Premier Alexei Kosygin, the President said that the road to peace "is far less rocky" when America and Russia "are willing to travel part way together."

Mr. Johnson claimed, in a commencement address at Glassboro State College, that "we have made some progress" in the last year since his meetings here with the Soviet leader.

"In this day when some are not too hopeful, I am optimistic." the President said.

To the conferees in Paris, Mr. Johnson said that he would not give in to Hanoi's demand for a total halt in the bombing in North Vietnam until there are "some gestures on the other side toward peace."

"Until the men in Hanoi face the real problems of ending the war," he said,

See Back Page

Index

Comics	28
Deaths	38
Entertainment	44
Finance	55
TV-Radio	42
Weather	37
Women's News	18

EXTRA EXTRA EXTRA EXTRA

The Weather
Bay Area: Chance of early showers today, then fair. Low, mid 50s; high, mid 60s to mid 70s.
See Page 41

San Francisco Chronicle

104th Year No. 226 ★★★★• WEDNESDAY, AUGUST 21, 1968 10 CENTS GArfield 1-1111

RUSS INVADE CZECHS

Soviet Armies Take Over In Swift, Surprise Move

Ike's Condition Still Critical

A.P. & U.P.

Washington

Former President Eisenhower continued to have brief periods of irregular heart beat last night and his condition rmained critical.

This was the essence of a 10:30 p.m. medical bulletin issued by Mr. Eisenhower's doctors at Walter Reed Army Hospital. They said the 77-year-old five-star general was comfortable.

The text of the brief announcement by doctors said:

"General Eisenhower's condition remains essentially unchanged. He continues to have brief

See Back Page

Plan for City Tax On All Paychecks

By Michael Harris

A chance that San Francisco may impose a 1 per cent payroll tax on residents and commuters alike—but with special credits for those who live in the city—was acknowledged yesterday by Mayor Joseph L. Alioto.

The Mayor said he is considering alternative plans in case suburban boards of supervisors succeed in their suit to block San Francisco from taxing the 187,000 commuters who earn their livings in the city.

"If we lose the court case we would work out a plan for taxing everybody," Alioto said. "But what we would do is give some exemptions to those paying property taxes in the city.

"Most likely there would be an offsetting tax credit."

BERKELEY

The mayor discussed his alternate plan after learning that the Berkeley City Council had voted to invite spokesmen from other communities and school districts to discuss ways to free themselves from heavy dependence on property taxes.

Assistant city manager William Hunrick Jr. told the council that a 1 per cent payroll tax on everybody working in Berkeley, residents and non-residents alike, would yield $7.6 million a year.

That would be more than enough, he said, to eliminate the city property tax, which is currently producing $5.9 million annually.

TIME

"The time has come for a period of discussion rather than retaliatory action," declared Councilman Margaret Gordon, one of three members of a committee looking for new sources of city revenue.

The committee reported that in 10 years the property tax rate paid by Berkeley residents had climbed to $[illegible] per $100 assessed valuation, of which $2.80 was for city taxes, with most of the rest for school and county charges. In [illegible] the total rate was $7.38.

In other words, taxes on a house with a market value of

See Back Page

Watching Evolution In Action

New York Times

Tokyo

The development of the first method of observing evolution under artificial conditions was reported here today by a leading authority on chemical genetics from the University of Illinois.

The achievement not only is of great theoretical value in understanding the underlying chemical mechanisms of heredity, but also suggests a new approach to curing viral diseases such as cancer by rending the viruses incapable of infecting cells.

The Illinois scientist, Dr. Sol Spiegelman, described the development and its implications to an overflow audience of geneticists on the opening day of the 12th International Congress of Genetics.

His lecture stirred wide comment at the gathering and was hailed by many as an important new milestone in genetic studies. Dr. George W. Beadle, Nobel-prize winning geneticist and honorary president of the congress, termed the report "very exciting."

Others said it opened the possibility of "test tube evolution," allowing scientists to observe, and control, the molecular events associated with evolutionary change under controlled laboratory

See Back Page

Johnson's High-Level Meeting

New York Times

Washington

President Johnson met with the National Security Council in an emergency session last night to discuss developments in Czechoslovakia.

The meeting was called after he received a personal visit from the Soviet ambassador who informed him that Russian troops had moved into that country.

Ambassador Anatoly Dobrynin delivered the news in an aide-memoire, an official communication between governments, after the Russian troops had already crossed the border into Czechoslovakia.

MEETING

The council meeting, which was held in the cabinet room in the White House, began at 10:15 p.m. and lasted for 55 minutes. It was followed by a 15-minute meeting at the State Department between Dobrynin and Secretary of State Dean Rusk.

There was no indication after either of the meetings of what course the United States would take in the crisis, which clearly came as a stunning surprise here.

The White House press secretary, George Christian, said Dobrynin had asked for the meeting with the President, which took place about 9:15 p.m. Christian refused to disclose the nature of their talk, other than to concede that it covered events in Czechoslovakia.

TALK

Christian also refused to discuss the Rusk-Dobrynin meeting except to say that Mr. Johnson had asked the secretary to invite the ambassador in for a talk.

At the State Department, Dobrynin avoided all contact with newsmen and department officials refused to disclose what he and Rusk discussed. The ambassador arrived by chauffeured car at the department's basement entrance, took a private elevator directly to Rusk's seventh-floor offices, and departed in the same manner.

REPORT

Dobrynin arrived at the White House about 9:15 p.m. at about the same time, news tickers were beginning to carry the first reports of troop movements.

Christian declined to say whether the President had learned of the movements

See Back Page

Berlin
EAST GERMANY
POLAND
Vistula
Warsaw
Breslau
Krakow
0 200 Miles
U.S.S.R.
Lwow
WEST GERMANY
Prague
CZECHOSLOVAKIA
Vienna
AUSTRIA
Budapest
HUNGARY
ROMANIA
ITALY

Reston Reports

What Czech Crisis Means

By James Reston
New York Times

New York

The Soviet invasion of Czechoslovakia has transformed world and American politics.

It took place in the middle of the American presidential election just as the Soviet invasion of Hungary took place during the Eisenhower-Stevenson presidential election of 1956.

The Soviets moved on Prague while the United States was preoccupied in Vietnam, as they moved on Budapest in 1956 while the British and French were preoccupied with the invasion of Suez.

And the latest move by Moscow startled Washington just as officials there were convening on new moves

See Back Page

A Move by Democrats For 'Coalition of Doves'

New York Times

Washington

Supporters of the late Senator Robert F. Kennedy circulated in the Democratic platform committee yesterday a compromise "dove" plank on Vietnam that calls for a bombing halt, a cease-fire, and negotiations between the Saigon government and the National Liberation front.

Mississippi delegation ousted
See Page 8

In the bitter fight developing within the platform committee, the proposed plank is designed to provide a common front for supporters of Senator Eugene J. McCarthy, Senator George S. McGovern and the late Robert Kennedy.

For the moment, however, difficulty is being encountered in winning the approval of some McCarthy partisans, who are holding out for a tougher plank that would be more critical of the administration.

As the doves began to mount a concerted attack on the administration's Vietnam policy, Secretary of State Dean Rusk was brought in to defend the administration position.

Rusk, who originally had not been scheduled to appear before the platform committee, testified at a special evening session arranged by Republican Hale Boggs of Louisiana, the committee chairman, as a concession to doves demanding a fuller airing of the Vietnam issue.

Obviously seeking to counter dove suggestions for a bombing halt or the formation of a coalition government, Rusk advised the committee not to "outline tactics or strategy" in the party platform but to stick to statement of objectives.

What is needed, he said, is

See Back Page

National Guard Called To Protect Convention

Chicago

Governor Samuel Shapiro called up the National Guard yesterday to keep order during the Democratic national convention.

At the request of Mayor Richard Daley, the Governor ordered 5649 Illinois National Guardsmen to round-the-clock duty in Chicago beginning Friday to head off threats of "tumult, riot or mob disorder."

Meanwhile, an Army spokesman in Washington confirmed that about 6000 regular Army troops had received rigorous riot-control training at Fort Hood, Tex., last week as a precautionary measure.

Three units of the National Guard will report for duty in Chicago at 8 a.m. Friday. Sixteen more will check into armories here 24 hours later.

Details of the National Guard callup on Page 11.

New York Times

Prague Protests, but Rules Out Resistance --Some Deaths Reported

New York Times

Prague

Czechoslovakia was occupied early today by troops of the Soviet Union and her Warsaw Pact allies in a series of swift land and airborne movements.

Unconfirmed reports said two Czechoslovak soldiers and a woman were killed by Bulgarian tank fire in an affray in front of Radio Prague building shortly before the station finally was captured and went off the air.

Before its dramatic farewell to the Czechoslovaks, Radio Prague had reported "several clashes" in the city and the erection of barricades at several points.

CALM

The station, which all night had urged calm and insisted on the legality of Czechoslovakia's progressive Communist government, signed off at 7:30 a.m. with the playing of the national anthem.

A few moments earlier a woman announcer had said "we are still here but when you hear our Czechoslovak anthem it will be the end."

Then the station played a few bars of the composer Smetana's Vltava suite. Tnere was a pause of a few seconds, then the national anthem, and then silence.

TROOPS

The city was completely occupied by Soviet troops composed of tank, paratroop and infantry units as well as by the forces of the other Warsaw pact countries participating in the invasion, East Germany, Poland, Bulgaria and Hungary.

All the strategic points were surrounded by the occupation troops. Aircraft, including a communications plane, circled over this beautiful but sad city as it awoke to a gray morning.

Earlier, at 5 a.m., while it was still in the hands of adherents of the Communist liberals, Radio Prague broadcast a dramatic appeal to the population in the name of Alexander Dubcek, the first secretary of the Communist Party, to go normally to work this morning.

The radio also urged the populace to offer no resistance to the invading forces.

COMMAND

"Our army, security corps and people's militia have not received a command to defend the country," the radio said.

"The Czechoslovak Communist party's Central Committee's Presidium regards this act (the invasion) as contrary not only to the fun-

See Back Page

Russia's Explanation For Action

United Press

Moscow

The Soviet Union said today that "party and government leaders" in Prague asked for armed intervention in Czechoslovakia to save the country from "counterrevolutionary forces."

The Tass news agency carried the Soviet explanation of its actions in Czechoslovakia.

Tass said the armed forces would "immediately withdraw" as soon as the threat to Communism is eliminated "and the lawful authorities find that further presence of these armed units there is no longer necessary."

The communique said the Czech leaders asked for aid including "assistance with armed forces." The Czechs who asked for aid were not identified.

They asked for help, Tass said, to meet "the threat which has arisen to the Socialist system . . . from counterrevolutionary forces which have entered into a collusion with foreign forces hostile to Communism."

The Soviet press has been denouncing the liberalized Czech regime of Communist party First Secretary Alexander Dubcek and has accused it of flirting with the

See Back Page

Index

Comics	30
Deaths	41
Entertainment	47
Finance	56
TV-Radio	46
Vital Statistics	40
Weather	41
Women's News	18

EXTRA EXTRA EXTRA EXTRA

The Weather
Bay Area: Fair today, patchy morning cloudiness. Low, near 50. High, near 60. Gentle winds.
See Page 37

San Francisco Chronicle

104th Year No. 303 ★★★★ WEDNESDAY, NOVEMBER 6, 1968 10 CENTS GArfield 1-1111

ALMOST SURE FOR NIXON

At a Glance

PRESIDENT

HUMPHREY	NIXON	WALLACE
27,478,307	27,800,526	8,768,527

Humphrey has carried 14 states with 191 electoral votes; Nixon has won 27 states with 235 electoral votes and is leading in three more with 55 electoral votes. Wallace has picked up five states with 45 electoral votes. Five states remained in doubt. (Needed for election: 270 electoral votes.)

U. S. SENATOR

CRANSTON	RAFFERTY
2,971,374	2,609,152

Alan Cranston was elected.

THE SENATE

The Democrats won or were leading in 17 races, which, with 40 holdovers, would give them control with 57 seats. The Republicans were ahead in 16 races. With their 26 holdovers, the GOP seemed likely to have at least 42 seats.

THE HOUSE

The Democrats retained control by winning 227 seats and leading for 16 others, for a total of at least 243. The Republicans won 180 seats and were leading for 12 others, for a total of 192.

PROPOSITIONS

With a substantial vote tallied, State Proposition 9 was defeated while Proposition 1-A was winning easily. San Francisco Propositions B and C, the port control measures, both won handily.

Electoral Victory is Near; Cranston Wins Senate Seat

Rafferty Fails in Senate Bid

By Michael Harris

Democrat Alan Cranston was elected to the United States Senate early today.

With 81 per cent of the vote counted, Cranston had a lead of more than 360,000 votes over Republican Max Rafferty.

Results from Southern California were excruciatingly slow in coming in, but finally the tide turned strongly Cranston's way when the votes were counted in Los Angelesm

TOTALS

With returns in from 17,733 of California's 21,580 precincts, the totals for the two front-runners and the Peace and Freedom Party nominee Paul Jacobs were:

Cranston	2,971,374
Rafferty	2,609,152
Jacobs	74,855

Cranston's lead grew steadily through the night, but the first returns were largely from counties Cranston had been expected to carry.

As late as 2 a.m., for example, only 99 of Orange county's 1302 precincts had reported in, Rafferty stood to carry the county by a margin of perhaps 130,000.

L.A.

Early in the campaign, Cranston acknowledged all he could hope to do in the most southerly part of the State was to hold his losses to a minimum. He hoped to offset them with gains from the north and win the election in Los Angeles county.

With 2222 of Los Angeles

See Back Page

AP Wirephoto

HUBERT HUMPHREY
'A donnybrook'

AP Wirephoto

RICHARD NIXON
It's nearly certain

Reston Looks Ahead

By James Reston
New York Times

New York

Nobody won the election early this morning — certainly not the nation. For the voting was not only close but, as Vice President Humphrey said at 3:35 a.m., it "was a donnybrook."

One thing was fairly clear: The Next President of the United States will go to the White House with less than 50 per cent of the votes on his side, and if it is the Republican nominee, Richard Nixon, he will have both houses of the Congress in opposition hands as well.

So close was the balloting that at

See Back Page

Humphrey's Surge Loses Momentum--Wallace Drive Fails

New York Times

New York

Richard M. Nixon forged ahead in another hair-raising Presidential election finish early today as he wrested California and New Jersey from Vice President Hubert H. Humphrey.

He also was making a strong finish in Ohio. Thus it seemed increasingly likely that Nixon would be elected.

Final results from Ohio and Illinois will not be known until later in the day, so the outcome remains inconclusive and it is still possible that neither candidate will emerge with the 270 electoral vote needed for victory.

Such a deadlock would be due to the votes drained away from the two major-party candidates by George C. Wallace, who nevertheless did not run nearly as well as expected.

If Nixon's late lead does hold up and puts him in the White House, however, he will possess a most bewildering mandate because of the nearly dead heat in which the popular voting resulted.

SEE-SAW

In a tight race reminiscent of the Nixon-Kennedy cliff-hanger of 1960 and the Truman Dewey thriller of 1948, Nixon and Humphrey seesawed in the popular vote. Nixon held a tiny edge in the electoral vote.

With 83 per cent of the popular vote counted, the totals were:

Nixon	26,312,438	43%
Humphrey	26,006,060	43%
Wallace	8,357,775	14%

The electoral vote was:

Nixon	231	28 states
Humphrey	191	14 states
Wallace	45	5 states

If the final returns should give neither Nixon nor Humphrey 270, a delay of weeks at least might ensue before the identities of the new president and vice president are known.

ELECTORS

The issue might be decided when the presidential electors — the electoral college —vote on Dec. 16, if enough of the Wallace electors should shift either way to give Humphrey or Nixon 270 votes.

But if the Wallace electors should stick with their candidate, preserving the deadlock, the House of Representatives next January would have to choose a president for the first time since 1825. The Senate would choose the vice president. The two could be of different parties.

All along the route of this archaic selection process, however, there might be law-

See Back Page

Demos Keep Control of Both Houses

Associated Press

Washington

The Democrats kept control of the Senate despite losses in several states yesterday and also headed for continued control of the House.

In the House, which may have to pick the president if neither Democrat Hubert H. Humphrey nor Republican Richard M. Nixon wins a majority of the electoral vote, it appeared that there would be little change in the lineup which now favors the Democrats.

Among the major Senate races, Republican Everett Dirksen of Illinois was re-elected but Wayne Morse went down to defeat in Oregon.

Democrats J. W. Fulbright of Arkansas, Frank Church of Idaho, Birch Bayh of Indiana and Alan Bible of Nevada held their seats.

Republican New York Senator Jacob Javits defeated Democratic dove Paul O'Dwyer and Conservative James Buckley.

Republican hawk Barry Goldwater won handily in Arizona.

In the House, peace candidate Allard Lowenstein won in New York, as did former Congressman Adam Clayton Powell. Speaker John McCormack of Massachusetts

See Back Page

Index

Comics	56
Deaths	37
Entertainment	45
TV-Radio	42
Weather	37
Women's News	19

NLF Urges Go-Ahead

Peace Talk Delay --Saigon Still Key

New York Times

Paris

The first meeting of the expanded Vietnam peace talks, originally planned for today, was postponed at American initiative yesterday because of the South Vietnamese government's refusal to attend. No new date was set.

Reliable informants said the North Vietnamese had proposed that the United States, North Vietnam and the National Liberation Front go ahead without Saigon, but the United States refused.

In a private informal meeting yesterday, American negotiators were reported to have suggested a token meeting of American and North Vietnamese negotiators today to maintain the diplomatic momentum generated by the bombing halt. But the North Vietnamese rejected this suggestion.

Mrs. Nguyen Thi Binh, the chief of the National Liberation Front's delegation, told a news conference that the front is ready for tripartite talks. American negotiators, she suggested, could represent the "American government and the government of Saigon."

But American officials said this approach was unacceptable. "There can be no conference on the future of South Vietnam without the presence of the government of South Vietnam," an American spokesman declared emphatically.

The American side was reported to have told the North Vietnamese that the scheduled meeting, first announced by President Johnson last Thursday night, would have to be postponed because the "allied side" was not ready.

William J. Jorden, the American spokesman, announced the postponement of the planned session and indicated that Washington was pressing Saigon to send a negotiating team.

He said the United States is "hopeful" that the South Vietnamese negotiators would arrive "in the near future." But informed diplomatic sources saw little

See Back Page

Tax Relief Plans --Prop. 9 Defeated

By Elmont Waite

Proposition 9, which would have cut property taxes in California in half within five years — but provided no other sources of governmental revenue went down to defeat yesterday.

Proposition 1-A, an alternative proposed by the legislature drew a convincing margin of victory.

The returns showed that 14,203 of the state's 21,590 precincts gave Proposition 1-A 2,332,401 Yes votes and 1,985,844 No votes.

With 14,560 precincts reporting, Proposition 9 got 1,373,642 Yes votes and 2,-881,930 No votes.

As the two measures were presented on the ballot, the one that got the biggest yes vote would become law. This was 1-A.

Under its provisions:

- This year, every home owner will get a $70 payment from the State to help him with his property tax burden.
- In suceeding years, each home owner will have the assessed valuation of his

See Back Page

The S.F. Vote Count --Another Disaster

By Jerry Burns

New errors arose last night to bedevil once again San Francisco's election counting process.

For the third consecutive election — and the second involving the city's expensive bank of computers — errors delayed results for hours.

Officials who thought they had planned with military precision discovered shortly after the polls closed at 8 p.m. that mistakes were creating uncomfortable delays.

By 9:17 p.m., the results from just two city precincts were reported by the computers. But by 10 p.m., Tuolumne county, in the Mother Lode, was completely counted.

It was nearly another hour — 10:11 p.m. — before the to-

See Back Page

Nixon Has Key Victory In California

By David Perlman

Richard M. Nixon captured California's crucial 40 electoral votes last night in a narrow victory that may prove the key to the White House.

Late figures released by Secretary of State Frank Jordan early this morning gave the Republican Presidential candidate 46.9 per cent of the State's popular vote, with more than half the precincts counted.

Vice President Hubert Humphrey was behind with an even 46 percent of the vote — but the margin, slim as it looked was apparently unbeatable because of Nixon's strength throughout

See Back Page

Election news on the following 10 pages and Page 16.

Front Page

Americans in unprecedented numbers took part in anti-war demonstrations and observances across the nation.

Peaceful demonstrations were staged throughout the Bay Area urging that the Vietnam War be brought to an end.

Thousands upon thousands of Bay Area college students braved the rain to demand an end to the Vietnam War.

The threatened citywide school strike was called off by San Francisco teachers in a vote at Nourse Auditorium.

No evidence of criminal activity — but some of negligence — was found in the Police Department's investigation of Southern Station patrolmen suspected of being burglars.

President Nixon's popularity has declined 8 percentage points since late July, Dr. George Gallup reported, to the lowest point since he took office.

U.S. Senator George Murphy announced he is running for re-election.

Inside

Seven paintings from the Grover Magnin estate brought nearly $2 million at a New York art auction. Page 3.

Health, Education and Welfare Secretary Finch was severely criticized during House proceedings in the Administration's welfare reform proposals. Page 15.

TOP OF THE NEWS

A "hot spot" found on Mount Rainier indicates the sleeping giant may have bad news for its neighbors in Washington State. Page 4.

Fresno State College faculty voted to back their president in his decision not to hire a Black Muslim. Page 4.

The Civil Service Association in San Francisco has refused to go to the statewide convention of city employee groups. Page 2.

Bishop Fulton Sheen, famous in the 1950s for his television programs, resigned his position. Page 2.

Several thousand San Franciscans participated in peaceful protests throughout the city as part of Vietnam Moratorium Day. Page 8.

In the largest Bay Area observance of Vietnam Moratorium, more than 8000 persons listened to anti-war speeches at Stanford University. Page 12.

About 200 rain-soaked war protesters blew bubbles for peace on the steps of the Stock Exchange. Page 8.

Leaders of yesterday's moratorium here were pleased about the turnout and predicted an even larger one in November. Page 12.

A handful of American soldiers in Vietnam joined the war protest by wearing black armbands while on patrol. Page 11.

More than 50,000 anti-war demonstrators led by Coretta King walked in silent procession to the White House. Page 9.

Congress approved a new Eisenhower dollar, but Senate and House differed on the metal to be used. Page 14.

Reformer Alexander Dubcek lost his last position of political power in Czechoslovakia. Page 16.

The president of Somali was shot to death by a policeman. Page 18.

The Russian cosmonauts made further movements that suggested that they aren't apt to put together a space station at this time. Page 18.

Sports

The Mets are within one game of turning New York into bedlam after beating Baltimore, 2-1, and taking a 3-1 World Series advantage. Page 53.

George Archer, top pro golfer, has developed "tennis elbow" and will be out of action indefinitely. Page 53.

The Boston Bruins, led by Bobby Orr, scored six times in the last two periods to hand the Seals a 6-0 NHL defeat. Page 53.

Weather

Bay Area: Partly cloudy today with chance of showers tonight. High, in 60s; low, in 50s. Chance of rain: 4 in 10. Page 41.

San Francisco Chronicle

★★★★ FINAL

105th Year No. 289 ★★★★ THURSDAY, OCTOBER 16, 1969 10 CENTS GArfield 1-1111

Massive U.S. Anti-War Protest --Rallies, Marches in Bay Area

There's More Rain Ahead For Bay Area

The demonstration-soaking rain that washed away the last traces of a beautiful Northern California summer yesterday is supposed to let up today—but not for long.

The weatherman predicts the trailing edge of the slow-moving storm that moved into the Bay Area late Tuesday should pass through with more rain some time tonight.

The durable storm — which packed a powerfully wet punch — gave the Bay Area its first major rain of the season, which began July 1.

MEASURE

San Francisco got more than two inches of rain in the first 24 hours; Oakland got 1.12 inches; Redwood City, .56; San Rafael, 3.25; Concord, .50 and San Jose, .31. The rain gauge atop Mount Tamalpais collected 4.25 inches of water.

The storm was more partial to some others. While San Francisco was lashed fairly steadily all day long, San Jose had only light sprinkles.

In addition to making things miserable for the thousands of anti-war demonstrators yesterday, the rain was blamed for scores of minor auto collisions throughout the Bay Area.

FREEWAYS

The Highway Patrol reported numerous accidents on the slick freeways, although no one was seriously injured. AC Transit said its morning commute buses were delayed as much as 30 minutes by freeway snarls in the East Bay.

Power lines shorted out in Orinda and left some 1000 homes without electricity in that community and in nearby Lafayette shortly after ten p.m. Telephone service was also affected.

Richmond's Kaiser Hospital lost telephone communications early in the afternoon and expected phones to remain dead until this morning.

In Marin county, some 800 San Anselmo families were without lights for period in the afternoon because of a power failure but Pacific Gas & Electric spokesmen said the storm posed no particular problems.

In Pleasanton, however, the wetness short-circuited the city's three fire alarms at 6:45 a.m., setting off ten-minute shrieks that roused sleepers and alarmed householders.

The rain sent the snow line shrinking up toward the 8000-foot elevation but the weatherman expects cooler weather to bring it back down to the 5000-foot mark again before long.

S. F. Rainfall

(in inches)

Storm to date	2.20
Season to date	2.63
Normal to date	.61
To date last year	.47
Seasonal normal	20.78

(Season: July 1 to June 30)

Teachers Call Off Strike

By Dick Meister
Labor Correspondent

San Francisco teachers voted overwhelmingly yesterday to call of a citywide school strike that had been threatened today by the Teachers Union.

About 1000 teachers jammed into Nourse Auditorium to shout out — with no more than 25 or 30 voicing dissents — their agreement with a recommendation of union officers against the walkout.

They were ready to strike a week ago but voted at a similar meeting to withhold action while the Board of Education considered their demands.

And on Monday night, the

See Back Page

Sobel Firm Fined in Politics Case

Max Sobel Wholesale Liquors, Inc., was fined $10,000 in Federal court here yesterday for unlawfully contributing money in a Federal election and then hiding the contributions in its tax returns.

The sentence by Judge George B. Harris against the largest Northern California liquor wholesaler was the first in Northern California under the Corrupt Practices Act.

This act prohibits corporations from making contributions to political campaigns of persons running for National offices, such as elections for President, Senator or Congressman.

The political candidates who received the contributions were not revealed.

COUNTS

The charges against the firm were two counts of unlawful expenditure in Federal elections and two counts of falsely burying those expenditures in their income tax returns.

Judge Harris yesterday fined the company $2500 on each count, for a total of $10,000 after allowing the firm to plea no contest.

"I am very sorry this happened," Stanton Sobel, president of the company and son of founder Max Sobel, said somberly to Judge Harris before sentencing. "We have entered our plea and will stand by it."

CORPORATION ONLY

The charges were leveled against the corporation itself, not its officers, and concerned activities of the company when Max Sobel headed the firm. Sobel died on Christmas day, 1965.

The indictments alleged

See Back Page

Bay Killer's Shrinking Timetable

By Keith Power

The bragging, psychotic killer who wants to be known as "Zodiac" appears to follow a compulsive timetable of his own and the periodic, murderous outbursts are drawing closer together.

This ominous pattern emerged yesterday as police, working on the assumption that one man is responsible for five Bay Area killings, chased down scores of leads.

Investigators also noted that the murder of San Francisco cab driver Paul Stine occurred on a weekend — as have all the other killings that "Zodiac" claims.

The dates of the murders are December 20 (1968) in the Vallejo area (two victims), July 5 in the Vallejo area, September 27 at Lake Berryessa near Napa and October 11 in San Francisco.

Almost seven months elapsed between the first and second murders; not quite three between the second and third attacks; two weeks between the third and the killing of Stine in San Francisco.

Captain Marty Lee, chief of inspectors, said: "It doesn't make us any happier that they are getting closer together."

The killing of Stine in his

See Back Page

Chief Cahill's Report on Probe of Cops

A 10-week investigation into allegations that some Southern Station patrolmen were burglarizing businesses in the district turned up no evidence warranting criminal charges, Police Chief Thomas Cahill announced yesterday.

But, Chief Cahill added, the probe did turn up evidence of neglect of duty on the part of two sergeants and unofficer-like conduct on the part of a patrolman who will have to answer to the departmental charges before the Police Commission.

At a Hall of Justice news conference, Chief Cahill identified the three as Sergeants William Tregoning and Richard Willette and Patrolman Mark Hurley,

QUESTIONS

During questioning of the sergeants, Cahill said, it was discovered that on one occasion Tregoning and Willette had left their patrol cars to investigate a possible burglary without notifying communications of their whereabouts.

The probe also turned up the fact, Cahill said, that Pa-

See Back Page

Big Crowds Despite The Rain

By Charles Raudebaugh

Thousands upon thousands of Bay Area demonstrators asked in one way or another yesterday that the Vietnam war be brought immediately to an end.

The main body of most of the demonstrations were young people, although there was a strong representation of older citizens.

Drenching rain failed to quench the ardor of the demonstrators, although it was conceded that the rain reduced their number.

NONVIOLENT

It was a day without violence.

The most popular form of demonstration was a short parade and rally, such as that which brought about 3000 persons to the Federal Building plaza in San Francisco at noon.

There were the usual anti-war placards, with here and there a new one: "Would You Die to Save Nixon's Face?" and "Destroy Nixon in Order to Save Him."

"We say—damn the guns, let 'em rot, let 'em corrode," cried Jake Jacobs, oil workers union official, in a fiery address. "Pile 'em in a junk heap to commemorate all the soldiers who have died in that unjust war!"

By far the largest demonstration was on the Stanford University campus, where more than 8000 persons heard talks last night by two congressmen, among other figures.

The crowds were shuttled between Memorial Church and Memorial Auditorium which were filled to overflowing. In the main quad-

See Back Page

Four marchers carried a peace sign along rainy Bush street

Gigantic Turnout By Bay Students

By Ron Moskowitz
Education Correspondent

More than 25,000 Bay Area college and university students sloshed through a day-long storm yesterday to demand the war in Vietnam be stopped.

Acting as the core of Moratorium Day activism, the students picketed, chanted, sang, argued, handed out leaflets, marched and even boarded commuter trains to focus opinion against the war.

Promising non-violent protests, the students attracted thousands more older and younger citizens to their ranks.

The promise was kept. There was no violence. Two Stanford students were arrested for jaywalking while distributing leaflets in Palo Alto. Other than that, there were no incidents.

Considering the bad weather, the response was enormous. Nowhere was it greater than at Stanford University, where officials described moratorium events as "the largest outpouring of voluntary support for organized political activity in university history."

The climax came last night, when more than 8000 students, faculty members and local residents jampacked two halls and overflowed into 3400 wooden seats set up in the main quadrangle. All of these temporary seats were filled in spite of rain.

The speakers included Representative Paul McCloskey (Rep-San Mateo), who told his Stanford audiences the time has come to downplay violence in demonstrations in favor of persuasion tactics aimed at the White House and the Congress.

During the morning, more

See Back Page

Murphy Declares -- Gets Tough

By Earl C. Behrens
Political Editor

Los Angeles

U.S. Senator George Murphy scotched talk he might not seek re-election in 1970 by bluntly stating here last night, "I am running now."

The 67-year-old Republican was no less blunt in remarks he made criticizing Vietnam Moratorium demonstrators and supporting President Nixon's strategy to end the war.

Murphy even suggested that President Nixon consider resuming bombing North Vietnam as a way of hurrying the Hanoi regime to meaningful negotiations at the Paris peace talks.

"It might be very helpful," Murphy told newsmen.

DINNER

Murphy announcement of candidacy came at a $200-a-plate dinner which raised $300,000 for his campaign warchest. Two other fund-raising dinners for Murphy — $100-a-plate affairs — were held at the same time in Fresno and San Diego.

The senior California senator made a strong plea for

See Back Page

Poll Shows Nixon's Popularity Lowest Yet

By George Gallup

Princeton, N.J.

President Nixon's popularity rating has declined a total of 8 percentage points over four successive surveys since late July and now stands at 57 per cent approval.

His latest rating, recorded in a survey compiled prior to yesterday's Vietnam Moratorium, compares closely with an early July survey, taken prior to the July 20 moon landing, which showed the President with an approval rating of 58 percent.

Following the moon landing, the President's popularity rose to 65 per cent (one of four high points recorded for Mr. Nixon), but then started to decline steadily, to 57 per cent today.

A total of 1539 adults were interviewed in person in the latest survey which was conducted in more than 300 scientifically-selected localities across the Nation. This ques-

See Back Page

National Outpouring For Peace

New York Times

New York

Demonstrations ranging from noisy street rallies to silent-prayer vigils that involved a broad spectrum of the population were held across the Nation yesterday in a display of deep and growing public opposition to the war in Vietnam.

The Vietnam Moratorium—which began as a national protest by college students and spilled over to include such groups as the United Automobile Workers Union and the Pittsburgh City Council — was called an overwhelming success by its planners, the youthful members of the Vietnam Moratorium Committee.

And it also demonstrated the great divisions in American society that have been worsened, if not created, by the prolonged American involvement in Southeast Asia.

The demonstrations spawned counter-protests in

More Vietnam Moratorium news on Pages 5 through 13.

some areas and some supporters of the war who had been quiet for months spoke out in anger.

The emotional climax to the long day of protest was a candlelight procession around the White House by an estimated 50,000 persons following a rally at the Washington Monument that was addressed by Coretta King, the widow of Dr. Martin Luther King.

Altogether, the day's events were the largest public protest of the many that have been held against the Vietnam war, and historians in the Library of Congress said that as a nationally coordinated anti-war demonstration it was unique.

Only scattered incidents of violence marred the outpourings of small and vast crowds in which the black armband was the standard symbol.

There was no way to esti-

See Back Page

Index

Comics	42
Deaths	41
Entertainment	48
Finance	61
TV-Radio	46
Vital Statistics	41
Weather	41
Women's News	22

EXTRA EXTRA EXTRA EXTRA

The Weather
Bay Area: Fair today except for morning cloudiness. High: mid-80s; low: 60s. Afternoon winds.
See Page 51

San Francisco Chronicle

★★★★ FINAL

105th Year No. 201 ★★★★** N MONDAY, JULY 21, 1969 10 CENTS GArfield 1-1111

MEN ON MOON

Man Makes a Lunar Landing --Astronauts Walk on Surface

The first men on the moon, Neil Armstrong and Edwin Aldrin, planted a plastic American flag in the lunar soil

Historic Moment

Spacemen Scout The Landscape

Times-Post Service

Houston

Man stepped out onto the moon last night for the first time in his two-million-year history.

"That's one small step for man— one giant leap for mankind," declared astronaut Neil Armstrong at 7:56 p.m. (PDT) as he began his lunar exploration about 3½ hours earlier than originally scheduled.

Just after that historic moment in man's quest for his origins, Armstrong walked on the dead planet and found the surface very powdery, littered with fine grains of black dust.

Just after 8 p.m. (PDT) astronaut Edwin (Buzz) Aldrin joined Armstrong on the lunar surface and put on a show for a worldwide television audience that will long be remembered as a truly beautiful experience.

The two men walked easily, talked easily, even ran

More Apollo news
Pages 1A through 7

and jumped happily, so it seemed. They picked up rocks and talked at length of what they saw.

They planted an American flag, saluted it and talked by radiophone with the President of the United States in the White House and then faced the camera and saluted Mr. Nixon.

"The surface is fine and powdery," Armstrong said. "I can kick it up loosely with my toe.

"It adheres like powdered charcoal to the boot," he went on, "but I only go in a small fraction of an inch. I can see my footprints in the moon like fine grainy particles."

Armstrong found he had such little trouble walking on the moon that he began talking almost as if he didn't want to leave it.

"It has a stark beauty all its own," Armstrong said. "It's like the desert in the southwestern United States. It's very pretty out here."

Armstrong shared his first incredible moments on the moon with the whole world, as a television camera on the outside of the wingless Eagle landing craft sent back an amazingly clear picture of

See Page A, Col. 1

Eagle Lands Close to Target Area

Times-Post Service

Houston

In a spacecraft called Eagle, two Americans landed on the lifeless moon yesterday — the first humans in history to touch down on another heavenly body.

The majestic moment for astronauts Neil Armstrong and Edwin (Buzz) Aldrin came at 1:17 p.m. (PDT) when they set their four-legged wingless landing craft down in the moon's Sea of Tranquillity.

"Tranquillity Base, here," Armstrong announced to a breathless world. "The Eagle has landed."

'BEAUTIFUL'

"You did a beautiful job," astronaut Charles Duke said from Houston's Manned Spacecraft Center. "Be advised there's lots of smiling faces down here."

"There's two of 'em up here," Armstrong replied.

"And don't forget one up here," said astronaut Mi-

See Back Page

Index

Comics	34
Deaths	33
Entertainment	39
Finance	50
TV-Radio	38
Weather	51
Women's News	15

Air War Erupts In the Mideast

New York Times

Full-scale ground and aerial warfare erupted between Israel and the United Arab Republic yesterday in a four-battle along the Suez Canal.

Israeli fighter-bombers struck in successive waves at Egyptian military positions along the canal in the first assault since the Six-Day War in 1967. Egyptian aircraft followed with attacks on Israeli radar stations and anti-aircraft missile sites in the Sinai Peninsula.

Spokesmen in Jerusalem said Israeli jets bombed and strafed Egyptian SAM ground-to-air missiles bases, antiaircraft positions and artillery installations between Kantara and Port Said.

The Israeli attack began in reply to almost routine artillery fire and continued almost without opposition for two hours, when Egyptian jets were sent aloft.

Cairo reported at nightfall that its ground gunners and pilots had shot down 19 Israeli aircraft.

The Egyptian fighters came in low over the entire length of the canal. Three Israeli soldiers were reported injured in the Egyptian straf-

See Back Page

Chief Says Kennedy to Be Charged

New York Times

Edgartown, Mass.

The police chief of this small resort town on Martha's Vineyard sent Senator Edward M. Kennedy formal notice yesterday that he is seeking his prosecution for leaving the scene of an accident.

Penalties for those found guilty of such a misdemeanor range from two months to two years in jail. But Dukes county officials said that convictions for leaving the scene of an accident normally result in suspended sentences.

The notice, Chief Dominick

See Back Page

What Spacemen Found-- Moon's Unusual Rocks

By David Perlman
Science Correspondent

Houston

Two men and a space ship began to rewrite the science of the solar system last night.

Within minutes of their landing on the moon, in an exploration televised for all the earth to watch, they found unexpected rocks, collected uncontaminated nuclear particles from the sun, and examined craters of curious shapes and sizes.

The rocks may well prove the existence of volcanic activity on the moon — perhaps eons ago, perhaps very recently.

They may indicate that water has existed in the lunar matter — water whose atoms have now entered the crystalline structure of shiny moon minerals.

The first Apollo moon mission has already proven as valuable as the world's scientists had any right to hope for.

Astroanuts Neil Armstrong and Edwin Aldrin began making close-up scientific observations from their very first steps on the lunar surface — just as they had already done from lunar orbit earlier.

Even before he stepped on the moon, Armstrong kicked the soil with one foot while he still clung to the ladder of the lunar module. He kicked it and reported to Mission Control on earth how the "moon dust" collects in fine layers "like powdered charcoal to the sole and sides of my boot."

Examining the disc-shaped footpads on the spacecraft he reported how surprisingly little they had dented the soil on landing — little more than an inch or two, he said.

Soon he scooped up the first "contingency sample" of lunar material. The surface was soft, he said, and he scrabbled into it with a long-handled rod to which a

See Back Page

1970-1979

MAY 5, 1970
Four Students Killed by Ohio Troops

JANUARY 19, 1971
Standard Oil Tankers Collide Under Golden Gate

JANUARY 26, 1971
Manson Trial Defendants Guilty

FEBRUARY 10, 1971
L.A. Earthquakes

OCTOBER 26, 1971
U.N. Votes to Admit Peking

MAY 9, 1972
U.S. Mines Red Ports

MAY 16, 1972
Wallace Shot at Rally in Maryland

SEPTEMBER 6, 1972
Battle at Munich Airport

NOVEMBER 8, 1972
Huge Nixon Victory; Death Penalty Wins

MAY 1, 1973
Top White House Aides Quit

AUGUST 30, 1973
Judge Orders Tapes; Nixon Won't Comply

OCTOBER 11, 1973
Agnew Resigns

FEBRUARY 6, 1974
Hearst Daughter Abducted

MAY 18, 1974
Fiery Deaths for SLA

AUGUST 9, 1974
Nixon Resigns

SEPTEMBER 9, 1974
Ford Pardons Nixon

APRIL 30, 1975
South Vietnam Surrenders

SEPTEMBER 19, 1975
Patty Hearst Found

SEPTEMBER 23, 1975
Woman Shoots at Ford in S.F. Street

SEPTEMBER 9, 1976
Chairman Mao Dies at 82

MARCH 28, 1977
Jumbo Jets Collide — More Than 550 Die

AUGUST 17, 1977
Elvis Presley Dies of Heart Attack

AUGUST 7, 1978
Pope Dies

NOVEMBER 20, 1978
Jonestown 'Mass Suicide'

NOVEMBER 21, 1978
Jonestown Mass Poisoning — 400 Stood in Line to Die

NOVEMBER 28, 1978
Moscone, Milk Slain

DECEMBER 16, 1978
U.S. to Recognize China

MARCH 29, 1979
A-Plant Accident Leaks Radiation

MAY 22, 1979
Verdict on Dan White

MAY 26, 1979
Worst U.S. Air Disaster

NOVEMBER 5, 1979
Iranian Students Seize U.S. Embassy in Tehran

Front Page

Four students were shot and killed by National Guardsmen in a clash at Kent State University in Ohio.

The Pentagon said it has terminated the resumption of bombing of North Vietnam after three massive strikes.

Soviet Premier Kosygin condemned U.S. military operations in Cambodia and said President Nixon has betrayed the American people.

U.S. and South Vietnamese troops launched a new offensive into Cambodia.

Flurries of nighttime violence followed the burning of a U.S. Army truck by demonstrators at UC Berkeley.

Stanford University was "virtually at a standstill" as faculty and students raged against President Nixon's war decision.

Police forced 1500 antiwar demonstrators out of City Hall. Nine persons were arrested.

Inside

American troops in Cambodia are faced with new problems of mud and how to tell friend from foe. Page 1A.

Four student newsmen were injured at San Jose State College when police waded into a group of peaceful demonstrators. Page 3.

The Senate Foreign Relations Committee accused the President of usurping the warmaking powers of Congress. Page 4.

Three California Democratic office-seekers, in separate statements, denounced the invasion of Cambodia. Page 5.

TOP OF THE NEWS

There were indications in Paris that North Vietnamese negotiators may be about ready to pull out of the peace talks. Page 6.

U.S. officials in South Vietnam are beginning to scale down their definitions of success in the Cambodian sweep. Page 6.

The Supreme Court upheld the tax exemption on property used exclusively for religious purposes. Page 7.

The free-lance reporter who revealed the details of the My Lai incident was one of the winners of the Pulitzer Prize. Page 7.

The Labor Department said it found no link between the United Mine Workers' election and the Joseph Yablonski murders. Page 10.

Moshe Dayan, Israeli defense minister, made a surprise offer of a cease-fire to Egypt. Page 10.

A surprise witness in the Alioto-Look magazine libel trial testified the Mayor had a cordial meeting in his law offices here with an alleged Mafia killer. Page 12.

Teamster pickets cut off most of the taxi, bus and limousine service to the airport but removed the pickets later. Page 12.

Attorney Charles Garry said he will try to halt the Seale trial on grounds Black Panthers are "prisoners of war." Page 12.

Thirteen Air Force men were killed when their transport plane crashed into a fog-covered Sonoma county hillside. Page 15.

The Board of Education will not investigate charges that Superintendent Jenkins might be involved in a conflict of interest. Page 15.

Will California follow Hawaii's lead and leave the decision concerning abortion up to a woman and her doctor? Page 18.

San Francisco socialites are pitching in to get the city's brand-new Community Ecology Center off the ground. Page 16.

Conservationists held out little hope for rescuing the Lake Tahoe area from massive urbanization. Page 42.

The Santa Barbara Supervisors, hooted at by dissidents, declined to pass an anti-loitering law for Isla Vista. Page 42.

Sports

The Giants go on the road tonight to face Montreal, while the Athletics come home to host the Yankees. Page 43.

Howard Mudd, former 49er guard with the Chicago Bears, underwent another knee operation but is expected to be ready to start the 1970 season. Page 43.

The New York Knicks, with injured Willis Reed missing from the early minutes on, rallied to beat the Lakers, 107-100, and take a 3-2 lead in the NBA playoffs. Page 43.

Weather

Bay Area: Low morning cloudiness, otherwise mostly fair today. Lows in the 40s; highs, to upper 60s. Page 33.

San Francisco Chronicle

★★★★ FINAL

106th Year No. 125 ★★★★ TUESDAY, MAY 5, 1970 10 CENTS GArfield 1-1111

Kent State Tragedy

4 Students Killed By Ohio Troops

More News On Crisis

More coverage on the Indochina crisis appears on the following seven pages.

They contain news reports, photographs and analyses of events in Washington, Cambodia and on the U.S. scene.

Kosygin's Reaction to Cambodia

U.S. Halts Big-Scale Bombing of North

Guardsmen Open Fire On Rock Throwers-- Two Girls, Two Boys Die

United Press

Kent, Ohio

Four students were shot to death on the Kent State University campus yesterday when National Guardsmen, claiming they were attacked by a sniper, fired on a group of young persons demonstrating against the extension of the Indochina war.

At least 11 other students were wounded in the brief volley of gunfire which cracked along the tree-lined campus shortly before noon.

Students and the head of Ohio's National Guard differed in their versions of how the shooting began.

In Columbus, S. T. Del Corso, the state adjutant general, said that "a sniper opened fire against the guardsmen from a nearby rooftop."

Brigadier General Robert Canterbury, the commander of Guard troops on the campus, said no warning was given to the students that the troops would shoot.

Student eye-witnesses said

See Page 1B, Col. 1

Flareup of Violence At Berkeley

Flurries of nighttime violence followed the overturning and burning of a U.S. Army truck by anti-war demonstrators on the Berkeley campus of the University of California yesterday.

Some 200 demonstrators broke windows and started fires between 9 and 10 o'clock last night.

They failed in an attempt to burn the steam generator plant for the university but set fire to an automobile parked in front of it.

Windows were broken in campus buildings and trash cans were piled on Bancroft way and Telegraph avenue then set on fire.

Two persons were arrested in the violence which grew from a People's Coalition rally near Haste and Dana streets.

Roger H. Jackson, 18, a UC student of 2650 Haste street, was booked for assault with a deadly weapon and disturbing the peace. I. Robert Hubbard, 20, a non-student, of 896 Mead avenue, Oakland, was charged with possession of a firebomb.

While Berkeley police gradually accelerated patrols near the campus to disperse the demonstrators, campus police fired tear gas to scatter the militants from the generator plant which adjoins Callaghan Hall, headquarters for Navy ROTC.

During the day, demonstrators set fire to the Army truck, burned an American flag, smashed windows and barged into classroom buildings urging students to join them in a university strike

See Back Page

Stanford Campus at 'Standstill'

Stanford University remained virtually closed yesterday as faculty and students raged against President Nixon for the widening war in Southeast Asia.

Not even the administration could estimate how many of Stanford's 11,000 students and 1000 faculty members were heeding appeals to shut the university down.

But one university spokesman went so far as to say that the campus was "virtually at a standstill."

For the most part, faculty and students talked with bitter anger about the war at scores of teach-ins around the campus and discussed what they can do to end it.

There was no indication from anyone how long the student strike will last, probably because there is no single organization in charge.

Students and faculty in some departments were saying they will boycott classes

See Back Page

Anti-war protesters in City Hall before police forced them out

Anti-War Protesters Forced Out of City Hall

Some 1500 chanting, singing anti-war demonstrators were forced out of City Hall by police yesterday.

The demonstrators had swept into the building in a shoulder-to-shoulder phalanx after a noon-time rally in front of the Federal Office Building that ended with an exhortation that President Nixon be impeached.

There was sporadic rock and bottle throwing by the crowd in front of the City Hall, and nine persons were arrested.

Three persons, one of them a police photographer, were treated at Central Emergency Hospital for injuries suffered in the encounter.

Goal of the demonstrators was to present a resolution to the Board of Supervisors calling for cessation of American military involvement in Indochina.

It also asked the Supervisors to declare that no San Franciscan could be compelled to serve in Cambodia and Vietnam, and to initiate impeachment of the President.

The mass of demonstrators, led by attorney Terence Hallinan, chairman of the New Mobilization Committee to End the War in Vietnam, found a line of Tactical Squad officers at the entrance to the Board of Supervisors' chambers.

Deputy Police Chief Don Scott told Hallinan he could present his petition, but that the crowd that accompanied him would have to leave the building.

There was a tense moment of confrontation, and then Hallinan, clearly in view of the demonstrators as he stood at the top of the grand stairway in the City Hall rotunda, asked his followers to leave.

There were shouts of

See Back Page

Russ Chief Assails Invasion

New York Times

Moscow

Soviet Premier Alexei Kosygin assailed President Nixon yesterday for sending American forces into Cambodia.

He warned that the action might lead to a "further complication" in the international scene and a worsening of Soviet-American relations.

Reading from a prepared statement at the start of his first news conference in more than five years in office, Kosygin said the Cambodia intervention raised doubts about Mr. Nixon's sincerity in seeking an "era of negotiation" to settle issues.

"Is it possible to speak seriously about the desire of the United States President for fruitful negotiations to solve pressing international

See Back Page

New U.S. Drive Into Cambodia

Associated Press

Saigon

Thousands of American and South Vietnamese troops launched a new offensive into northeast Cambodia today, seeking to smash more North Vietnamese base camps and sanctuaries, the U.S. Command announced.

The American command said the operation kicked off in the Se San base area, about 50 miles west of Pleiku, in the central highlands.

A spokesman said troops of the U.S. Fourth Infantry Division and the South Vietnamese 22nd Infantry Division are participating in the operation.

The new operation is taking place in rugged, mountainous jungle 160 miles north-northeast of the Fishhook area where another task force of more than 8000 Americans launched the first U.S. offensive into Cambodia

See Back Page

A Report On Raids, Targets

New York Times

Washington

The Defense Depart-partment announced yesterday it has "terminated" large-scale air raids flown in recent days against three areas of North Vietnam.

For the first time, the Pentagon acknowledged that the raids had been larger in scope than any since the halt in the bombing of the North in November, 1968.

It also said that air defense "logistics support" facilities had been attacked in addition to antiaircraft gun and missile sites.

PLANES

The department said that from 50 to more than 100 planes had been employed in each of the attacks near Barthelemy Pass, Ban Karai Pass and in an area immediately north of the demilitarized zone.

All three areas, officials said, are key conduits for the flow of men and materiel to enemy military units throughout Indochina, and especially in South Vietnam.

But the official statements left unresolved the question of whether supply depots, unrelated to air defense sites, had also been targets.

TARGETS

When pressed repeatedly on this question, Daniel Z. Henkin, assistant secretary of defense for public affairs, reiterated: "The targets were antiaircraft facilites and associated logistics support."

"Logistic support" apparently refers to such things as stocks of antiaircraft ammunition and missiles, radar, power generators and other

See Back Page

Market Has Biggest Loss In Six Years

New York

The stock market, reacting to the expanding war in Southeast Asia, reeled to its biggest daily loss in more than six years yesterday.

The drop all but crushed hopes that the market might soon be able to pull out of its long slump, Wall Street analysts said.

The Dow Jones average of 30 industrials plummeted to 19.07 points, or 2.59 per cent, to 714.56, closing at its lowest level of the session.

This was its biggest drop since falling 21.16 points on Nov. 22, 1963, the day President Kennedy was assassinated. *Associated Press*

Details on Page 50.

Index

Comics	54
Deaths	33
Entertainment	39
Finance	50
TV-Radio	38
Vital Statistics	33
Weather	33
Women's News	16

Front Page

At least a half million gallons of oil were dumped into the bay after two tankers collided off the Golden Gate Bridge.

The Pentagon said the U.S. will use all its air-combat power in Cambodia against enemy troops that might threaten Vietnam.

The United States imposed economic sanctions on Ecuador in retaliation for the seizure of American fishing boats.

Bethlehem Steel agreed to a partial rollback of a price increase that had drawn the fire of President Nixon.

The dense fog that blinded airport traffic yesterday was expected to roll in again this morning.

The elderly proprietors of a grocery store on Russian Hill were killed during an apparent robbery attempt.

Inside

Mission district residents will get a chance to air their criticisms of government at a public hearing. Page 2.

A number of things happened to members of the Good Earth in court—none of them good. Page 2.

Police said motorists and pedestrians ignored their pleas for assistance as they were battling a gun-wielding suspect. Page 2.

New York police union leaders said patrolmen will go back to work today but the officers apparently had other ideas. Page 2.

Two UC professors said salaries had fallen so low it will be hard to recruit new faculty. Page 3.

TOP OF THE NEWS

Everyone tried to beat the expected last-minute rush to see the Van Gogh exhibit — creating an early crush. Page 3.

Hippies — and everyone else— can sit on Carmel lawns and sidewalks, the State Supreme Court ruled. Page 4.

The big San Francisco Bay oil spill was taking its toll among the bay's waterfowl. Page 5.

The question as to whether childbirth is obscene was raised by a sculpture on display at the M. H. de Young Museum. Page 6.

Industries that release wastes into the city's sewer system will have to pay fees for sewage treatment. Page 6.

An ordinance requiring all taxi cabs in San Francisco to have bulletproof shields was repealed. Page 6.

Another major milk company has begun using an easily understood dating system on its cartons. Page 7.

Forty per cent of Californians describe themselves as conservative, 25 per cent middle-road and 25 per cent liberal. Page 8.

A legislative committee recommended putting unemployed aerospace employees to work on environmental problems. Page 8.

Senator McGovern made his announcement that he is a candidate for the Presidency in the 1972 race. Page 9.

The Supreme Court agreed to decide whether a worker can take Sundays off, pleading religious grounds. Page 9.

Senator Muskie returned from abroad and said he was having second thoughts about a U.S. troop cutback in Europe. Page 9.

The court-martial of Lieutenant Calley was recessed indefinitely to allow psychiatric examination of the My Lai defendant. Page 10.

Details of the Army's project to spy on civilians began to emerge from interviews by the New York Times. Page 11.

Massive projects are under way in North Vietnam in an apparent attempt to shift to development of the home front. Page 13.

Sports

The Super Bowl aftermath has produced two substantial rumors involving quarterbacks. Page 39.

California athletic director Paul Brechler has taken himself out of contention for a similar position at Arizona State. Page 39.

NBC-TV was still savoring the tremendous viewing audience for its Sunday Crosby golf-Super Bowl doubleheader. Page 39.

Weather

Bay Area: Cloudy today, morning fog. High, in the 60s; low, mid-50s. Light winds. See Page 29.

San Francisco Chronicle

★★★★ FINAL

107th Year No. 19 ★★★★ TUESDAY, JANUARY 19, 1971 15 CENTS GArfield 1-1111

Pentagon Statement

U.S. Airpower To Aid Allies in Cambodia War

N.Y. Times Service

Washington

The Defense Department said yesterday that the United States intends to employ the full range of its air-combat power throughout Cambodia against enemy troops and supplies that "ultimately" might threaten American military men in South Vietnam.

A Pentagon spokesman, Jerry W. Friedheim, said this includes the use of American-flown helicopters to ferry South Vietnamese troops into combat — even under hostile ground fire.

The only things ruled out, he said, are the use of American ground troops or military advisers. He conceded that American air crews might sometimes leave their craft while on the ground in Cambodia in the course of moving supplies or troops to support South Vietnamese forces there.

But he denied a report from Saigon that American air liaison officers might have operated from Cambodian soil. South Vietnamese and Cambodian liaison officers are aboard some American spotter planes to help coordinate American fire support, he said.

FERRYING

A few troop-ferrying missions were flown over the weekend, Friedheim said, in support of troops fighting to open Highway 4, connecting the Cambodian capital of Phnom Penh with its major seaport to the south, Kompong Som.

A high P[illegible] official conceded yesterday that Secretary of Defense Melvin R. Laird, before he left on his tour of Southeast Asia, had turned down a request for similar authority to ferry troops and ammunition to a major South Vietnamese operation north of Phnom Penh, near Kompong Cham, on Highway 7.

The official said the request to authorize such activity in the current offensive south of the capital was considered and approved by Laird during his recent trip.

Laird and Admiral Thomas H. Moorer, the chairman of the Joint Chiefs of Staff, briefed President Nixon and the National Security Council yesterday on their findings during their visits to South Vietnam, Thailand and Cambodia.

WITHDRAWALS

Their report was described as generally optimistic about the prospects for continued, and possibly accelerated, troop withdrawals from Vietnam.

A Pentagon official said that while there had been two or three previous instances in which American helicopters had returned a South Vietnamese commander to his troops in the field in Cambodia or moved a squad

See Back Page

U.S. Punishes Ecuador for Seizing Boats

Associated Press

Washington

The United States imposed a 12-month ban on aircraft sales and ship-repair credits for Ecuador yesterday in retaliation for that country's seizure of American fishing vessels on what the U.S. considers to be the high seas.

Secretary of State William P. Rogers summoned Ecuadorian Ambassador Carlos Mantilla to his office to inform him of the action.

Press officer Robert J. McCloskey told a news conference four ships had been seized by Ecuador this month. Later he said fishing industry sources reported the seizure of five more with two others being pursued, evidently by Ecuadorian government vessels.

Rogers also threatened ac-

See Back Page

Fog Hides Airports --More Today

The thick tule fog that enveloped the Bay Area for hours yesterday, blotting out airport traffic, will be replaced this morning by dense fog rolling in from the ocean.

The tule fog—thickest of the season — kept incoming flights from San Francisco International Airport from 3 a.m. until noon, forcing diversions to Los Angeles, Las Vegas and Reno.

The Federal Aviation Agency said 46 aircraft were held over San Francisco for more than 30 minutes, and one of the commercial flights was stacked up for two hours and 30 minutes.

Traffic into Oakland and

See Back Page

Fugitives Afloat

By Stan Creighton

Seals fleeing the massive oil slick found refuge on a buoy off the Belvedere shore

Big Oily Mess in the Bay After 2 Tankers Collide

Slick Smears Beaches --May Be Bigger Than The Santa Barbara Spill

By George Murphy

Two Standard Oil Co. tankers collided off the Golden Gate Bridge early yesterday and floated into the bay, one of them dumping at least a half-million gallons of heavy, gooey bunker oil into the bay—the biggest recorded spill in its history.

Black, green and shiny, the oil reflected yesterday's brilliant sunshine as it moved inexorably onto beaches at Fort Baker, Ayala Cove on Angel Island, and into the shallow waters off Bridgeway in Sausalito.

The Coast Guard called it "a major spill," and estimated final figures could show as much as 1.9 million gallons dumped into the already ecologically precarious bay waters.

CONCENTRATIONS

Last night, the Coast Guard said the heaviest oil concentrations were in the vicinity of Alcatraz and the south side of Angel Island.

But, said a Coast Guard spokesman, there was oil "all around the Golden Gate" and traces in Raccoon Strait and in the Bay Bridge area.

Cleanup operations continued through the night. An aerial check will be made this morning.

ANCHORED

The Oregon Standard, the tanker from which the oil spilled, was anchored a half-mile west of Angel Island yesterday morning.

Around her scurried the Coast Guard cutter Point Barrow, her gleaming white hull oil-smeared as much as one and one-half feet above the waterline, two patrol boats and a Coast Guard hovercraft. Four barges were also standing by, ready to take aboard the remnant of the tanker's 100,000-barrel cargo, and three tugboats.

The tanker had been rammed by her sister ship, the Arizona Standard, shortly after 2 a.m. west of the Golden Gate Bridge.

Aboard a press boat, William Schill, general manager of Standard Oil's U.S. flag fleet — which runs tankers mostly coastwise — said there was at the moment "no idea" how the collision, in a dense fog, could have occurred.

AMOUNT

The spill, when final figures are determined — Schill said they would not be available "until all the gauges and records have been checked" — could be larger than the amount of oil released in the Santa Barbara

See Back Page

Bethlehem Cuts Back Price Boost

Associated Press

Washington

President Nixon achieved a partial rollback of a steel-price increase yesterday and launched a move to stem the wage-price spiral in the construction industry.

In a day dominated by economic developments, major interest rates continued to decline, and the Government reported that the Nation's "real" gross national product — output of goods and services—in the 1970 final quarter took its sharpest quarterly decline in 11 years.

Under pressure from the White House along with competitive reasons, Bethlehem Steel Corp. reduced to 6.8 per cent a previously announced 12.5 per cent boost in prices for steel used in construction.

THREAT

U.S. Steel had come out with a 6.8 per cent increase last Saturday after Mr. Nixon called Bethlehem's increase enormous and raised the threat of permitting more steel imports.

On the construction front, Mr. Nixon called on the industry's labor and management leaders to take "early action to attack the wage and price spiral."

The President called the problem "a crisis situation"

See Back Page

Russian Hill Grocer and Wife Slain

An elderly couple were brutally slain in their small Russian Hill grocery store last night during an apparent robbery attempt.

Police said residents around the Leavenworth Market at 176 Leavenworth street at Vallejo heard about five shots shortly after 9 p.m., just before the store was to close.

When officers reached the store they found the bodies of the proprietor, Cheuck Lee, 64, and his wife, Gim, 62, in the rear of the store.

Officer Douglas Rowell said the husband had been shot three times in the chest and his wife once in the head.

Both bodies were found near a rear rest area in the store, but Rowell said it appeared Lee was shot down near an open cash register toward the front of the grocery.

He apparently stumbled toward the rear of the store, where his wife was, in a desperate attempt to get help.

The bodies were found by a son, Thompson Lee, 26, who lives in a flat above the store at 1760 Leavenworth. Lee said he heard an argument and then the shots.

Police said that although the cash register was open it still contained some money. They were not immediately

See Back Page

Index

Comics	20
Deaths	29
Entertainment	36
Finance	44
TV-Radio	34
Vital Statistics	35
Weather	29
Women's News	14

Front Page

Charles Manson and three of his women followers were found guilty on all 27 counts in the seven Tate-La Bianca murders.

The Cambodian government toughened the curfew in Phnom Penh as enemy attacks tested the city's defense perimeter.

The captain of the Arizona Standard showed a Coast Guard hearing how his ship collided with another tanker last week.

Supervisors approved an ordinance to give San Francisco police some control over motion picture theaters.

Middle-class school children picketed the A. P. Giannini school to keep a black vice principal from being transferred.

The Supreme Court ruled that a company may not have one hiring policy for mothers with preschool children and another for fathers.

Army dissidents in Uganda claimed to have overthrown President Milton Obote, who was out of the country.

Inside

Several State and Federal agencies formed a task force to assess damage caused by the big bay oil slick. Page 2.

Interns at San Francisco General Hospital returned to work after being promised changes in its operation. Page 3.

The FTC moved to require water-pollution warnings in ads and on labels of phosphate detergents. Page 3.

The Nation's surgeon general, in a new report, suggested how cigarette smoking increases the risks of heart attack. Page 3.

The University of California at Berkeley, named the Nation's top graduate center, faced a crippling financial bind. Page 4.

Mayor Alioto supported a modest city pay raise but opposed an increase in the school taxing power. Page 4.

Work on Candlestick Park renovation continued despite some picketing by blacks. Page 4.

Tate trial jurors danced, lost weight, watched movies and walked a lot the past seven months. Page 5.

The Sierra Club said Interior Secretary-designate Morton is neither a distinguished, nor a committed conservationist. Page 6.

State Democratic leaders took a cautious tack in evaluating the performances of three presidential hopefuls. Page 6.

Ronald Reagan said he will not run for President next year but left open the possibility of a Senate race in 1974. Page 6.

A satellite capable of handling 9000 simultaneous telephone calls was sent toward an outpost over the Atlantic. Page 6.

The Supreme Court upheld a California law making it an offense to wilfully obstruct a policeman in his duties. Page 7.

The U.S. may send a military team to Cambodia to check on how that country is using American military equipment. Page 11.

Fifty-eight of 92 persons condemned in the aftermath of an abortive invasion of Guinea were hanged. Page 13.

The Chinese New Year will come to Hong Kong without a firecracker bang. Page 13.

American fashion buyers in Paris were shocked to find that designers were once again baring knees. Page 15.

Child support battles give an outlet to ex-marital partners' hostility but the children suffer. Page 16.

'Swinging'—casual sex encounters with strangers—has become the pastime of a growing number of middle-class couples. Page 17.

Sports

USC displaced UCLA, which lost its first game of the season, as the Nation's No. 1 college basketball team. Page 39.

The Cassius Clay-Joe Frazier heavyweight championship fight scheduled for March 8 already has a live gate sellout. Page 39.

Stanford will meet Missouri in the football season opener in 1971 at Columbia, Mo. Page 39.

Weather

Bay Area: Mostly fair today except for low clouds. High, in the 50s; lows, mid-30s to mid-40s. Light winds. Page 29.

San Francisco Chronicle

★★★★ FINAL

107th Year No. 26 ★★★★ TUESDAY, JANUARY 26, 1971 15 CENTS GArfield 1-1111

Manson Trial Defendants Found Guilty on All Counts

UPI Telephoto

Seven deputies escorted Manson from the courtroom, which was under the tightest security to date

1st Degree Murder and Conspiracy

Times-Post Service

Los Angeles

Charles Manson and three of his women followers were convicted yesterday on all 27 counts of first-degree murder and conspiracy to murder in the seven Tate-La Bianca killings 18 months ago.

The long-haired, bearded Manson and the three denim-clad young women had sat quietly, seemingly without tension, as the court clerk took 20 minutes to read the jury's 27 verdicts.

Co-prosecutor Stephen Kay said that as Manson was being led from the courtroom the defendant muttered to Los Angeles County Superior Court Judge Charles H. Older, "You won't live to see that day."

PANEL

The seven men and five women in the regular jury panel filed into the courtroom at 11:42 a.m. after nearly 43 hours of deliberation over nine days.

"Mr. Tubick, has the jury reached a verdict?" Older asked Herman C. Tubick, the foreman.

"Yes, you honor, we have," the mortician replied.

The verdict amounted to this:

Manson, 36, Susan Atkins, 22, and Patricia Krenwinkel, 23: guilty of first-degree murder and conspiracy to murder in the deaths of Sharon Tate, Abigail Folger, Voiteck Frokowski, Thomas John (Jay) Sebring, Steven Earle Parent and Leon and Rosemary La Bianca on Aug. 9-10, 1969.

Leslie van Houten, 21, guilty of first-degree murder and conspiracv to murder in the killings of the La Biancas.

As the jurors filed out of the room, Miss Van Houten leaned over to Miss Krenwinkel and said, "Look how sad they all look."

Heavy security was im-

See Back Page

Oil Spill Probe

Captain Says Radar 'Lost' Other Tanker

By Dale Champion

Moving with slow, inexorable deliberation, the captain of the Arizona Standard yesterday maneuvered two tiny gray ship models over a chart of the Golden Gate—and carefully shoved the bow of one into the other's side.

The terrible task—before a three-man Coast Guard Marine Board of Investigation probing the tanker collision that caused the Bay Area's disastrous oil spill—took the balding skipper a full minute.

There was only silence in the crowded courtroom on the 17th floor of the Federal building as more than 100 conservationists, oil and insurance company representatives, and Coast Guard and Government officials watched.

"When we came together, it wasn't the tremendous blow you'd expect," said Captain Harry H. Parnell of Alameda.

"In fact, it was rather soft."

Seconds before, the 46-year-old captain of the Arizona Standard said, "he had seen a red running light suddenly emerge from a thick tule fog just outside the Golden Gate Bridge.

"I knew immediately what it was," he told the investigating board. "I just saw the red light and the glow of the after house.

"It was one or two points off the starboard bow.

"I came hard left to take the collision on the bow. That was when we struck."

BLOW

He testified that the bow of his 17,000-ton tanker "went in quite a way" into the side of her sister ship, the Oregon Standard, outbound from Standard's Richmond refinery for British Columbia with a cargo of 106,000 barrels of thick bunker oil.

The two oil-laden tankers, "locked together," Captain Parnell said, began to drift on the flood tide back under the bridge toward Angel Island.

He quickly radioed the Coast Guard's Harbor Advisory Radar facility to report the collision, he said, "and

See Back Page

S.F. to Put Controls on Sexy Films

By Jerry Burns

An ordinance to give San Francisco police some measure of control over motion picture theaters—particularly the porno movie houses—won unanimous approval yesterday from the Board of Supervisors.

Not even a question was raised as the board adopted a law that will require the owners and operators of all theaters in the city to obtain $100 permits from the police chief.

RULES

The 13-page ordinance allows the chief to refuse to issue a permit only if the applicant has been convicted of showing an obscene production, is a registered sex offender or has been convicted of a felony involving force and violence.

It also says the chief may only revoke a permit if the applicant has not compiled with all building, health, zoning and fire laws or has been convicted of any of the same crimes.

The measure must be approved by the board again next Monday at its final reading. It will then go into effect 30 days after it is signed by Mayor Joseph Alioto.

Other sections of the ordinance allow the chief of police to require soundproofing of a loud theater and to limit the words and pictures on

See Back Page

Reds Probe Defenses of Phnom Penh

Associated Press

Phnom Penh

North Vietnamese and Viet Cong soldiers launched attacks last night against the outer defense perimeter of Phnom Penh, tense Cambodian capital under dawn-to-dusk curfew because of spreading terror in the streets.

A Cambodian high command spokesman said the major battle was fought at the village of Phnom Prey Khiev, 24 miles northwest of the capital, where an enemy force of 500 struck half an hour after darkness. The other battles were at Saang, 18 miles south of the capital, and Lovea Sar Kandal, 28 miles to the southeast.

All three enemy assaults were driven back by air strikes at midnight, he said.

CURFEW

The curfew order in Phnom Penh followed an attempt to bomb the South Vietnamese Embassy on a main boulevard and new attacks on the city's outer edges and the airport, already severely damaged by an enemy raid last Friday.

A Viet Cong cease-fire went into effect in South Vietnam for the four-day Tet lunar new year, but the holiday is not observed in Cambodia except by minority populations of Vietnamese and Chinese.

In fact, many residents of Phnom Penh fear a heavy attack on the city during Tet.

Since the airport raid the capital has been jittery, and explosions are heard through the night. Some are the result of grenades thrown into rivers by Cambodian soldiers trying to keep enemy frogmen from blowing up bridges.

A dusk-to-dawn curfew was imposed Saturday on a few main thoroughfares that are the addresses of foreign embassies and government buildings. Traffic was allowed on other streets.

Apparently the new enemy attacks, the attempt on the South Vietnamese embassy and the prospect of continued terrorism elsewhere prompted the government of Premier Lon Nol to extend the curfew to the rest of the capital.

Shortly before the curfew

See Back Page

Kids Picket To Retain a 'Good Man'

By Ralph Craib

Several hundred students at the predominantly white A. P. Giannini Junior High School protested yesterday because a popular black vice principal is being transferred—and then cut school for the rest of the sunny day.

Vice Principal Bennett Fonsworth was, according to Principal James Hannon, "assigned to get the kids involved." And, Hannon added, "he has really succeeded."

The protesting adolescents come from the neat row and tunnel-entrance houses of the Sunset district which surround the big school. In an enrollment of some 1370,

See Back Page

Mothers' Equal Right to Jobs

N.Y. Times Service

Washington

Employers cannot refuse to hire women solely because they have small children unless fathers of small children are also denied jobs, the Supreme Court ruled yesterday.

In its first sex discrimination decision under the equal employment provision of the 1964 Civil Rights Act, the court held unanimously that the law forbids "one hiring policy for women and another for men" when both are parents of pre-school-age children.

Yesterday's decision on sex bias in employment was only a partial victory for the women's liberation forces who had supported the litigation as a major test case.

The justices did reject the "sex plus" theory of employment, under which the lower courts had upheld the Martin Marietta Corporation's refusal to hire a mother of seven children as an assembly line trainee at a plant in Orlando, Fla. The woman, Mrs. Ida Phillips, was told that the company had a rule against hiring mothers of young children.

A Federal District Court and the United States Court of Appeals for the fifth circuit upheld this rule, on the theory she was not barred because of her sex but because of her sex plus the fact that she was a parent of young children.

Feminists complained that this opened a vast loophole in the anti-bias law, as factors such as marital status and size of family could always be cited as reasons for not hiring women.

EXCEPTION

Yesterday's unsigned opinion labeled the "sex plus" theory "erroneous," but it sent the matter back to the trial court for hearings as to whether Mrs. Phillips might be denied a job under special exception to the equal employment law.

This exception says that it is not illegal for an employer to refuse to hire any applicant because of his or her sex, religion or national origin where such trait is a

See Back Page

Army Claims A Takeover In Uganda

Associated Press

Kampala, Uganda

Army dissidents claimed to have overthrown the government of President Milton Obote yesterday as he was heading home from the Commonwealth summit meeting in Singapore.

A few hours after Radio Uganda announced the takeover, Obote arrived in Nairobi, Kenya, and associates said he had established radio contact with Kampala.

"The army takes over power and warns all foreign countries to keep noses out of Uganda's internal affairs," said the Uganda broadcast.

FIGHTING

It made the victory claim after 12 hours of fighting with a rival faction of the armed forces in which an undetermined number of persons were reported killed.

The broadcast said the revolt was led by Brigadier General Idi Amin, commander of Uganda's armed forces, and William Oryema, inspector-general of police.

Both leaders appealed for calm and urged the people to go back to work today.

The broadcast said all political prisoners will be set

See Back Page

What It Means to Be a Homosexual--II

By Merle Miller
N.Y. Times Service

A homosexual friend of mine has said, "Straights don't want to know for sure, and they can never forgive you for telling them. They prefer to think it doesn't exist, but if it does, at least keep quiet about it."

And one Joseph Epstein said in Harper's only last September: ". . . however wide the public tolerance for it, it is no more acceptable privately than it ever was . . . private acceptance of homosexuality, in my experience, is not to be found, even among the most liberal-minded, sophisticated, and liberated people . . . Nobody says, or at least I have never heard anyone say, 'Some of my best friends are homosexual.' People do say—I say—'fag' and 'queer' without hesitation—and these words, no matter who is uttering them, are put-down words, in intent every bit as vicious as 'kike' or 'nigger.'"

Is it true? Is that the way it is? Have my heterosexual friends, people I thought were my heterosexual friends, been going through an elaborate charade all these years?

I can never be sure, of course, will never be sure. I know it shouldn't bother me. That's what everybody says, but it does bother me. It bothers me every time I enter a room in which there is anyone else. Friend or foe? Is there a difference?

I was afraid I would never get into the Army, but after the psychiatrist tapped me on the knee with a little hammer and asked how I felt about girls, before I really had a chance to answer, he said, "Next," and I was

See Page 10, Col. 1.

Index

Comics	30
Deaths	29
Entertainment	35
Finance	44
TV-Radio	34
Vital Statistics	29
Weather	29
Women's News	14

Front Page

A major earthquake shook Southern California, killing at least 35 persons and injuring hundreds.

A perfect splashdown in the South Pacific climaxed the Apollo 14 mission, the United States' most successful moon flight.

South Vietnamese troops pressed deeper into Laos, pursuing enemy troops that retreated under U.S. air attack.

Susan Atkins confessed that she personally killed Sharon Tate.

Inside

A new $23.5 million hospital was declared a total loss after being shaken to the ground by the earthquake. Page 1A.

Medical disaster planning paid off in a smooth rescue operation for scores of injured. Page 1A

A veterans hospital that collapsed at Sylmar was a scene of devastation and heartbreak. Page 1B.

Thousands of residents were evacuated after cracks developed in the Van Norman dam in the San Fernando valley. Page 3.

The skyscrapers of Los Angeles passed their first earthquake test in good condition. Page 4.

One Los Angeles resident, awakened when the quake banged his bed against a wall, found his house in a shambles. Page 4.

The Los Angeles disaster may provide knowledge that will save lives in the Bay Area. Page 6.

TOP OF THE NEWS

Governor Ronald Reagan toured the Los Angeles earthquake area and promised state and federal aid to victims. Page 6.

A quarter of a million California children still attend class in buildings ruled unsafe in the event of an earthquake. Page 7.

A four-month-old baby died of a respiratory ailment after being refused admission to S.F. General Hospital. Page 8.

The State's free school lunch program is to be expanded to cover an additional 350,000 children. Page 8.

A militant Chinatown group accused police of harassment and threatened reprisal "by any means necessary." Page 9.

The State readied a massive, unprecedented crackdown on upstream polluters of the San Francisco Bay. Page 10.

As Teutonic influence grows in the eastern part of the country, jittery France is having identity problems. Page 12.

A land mine killed five civilians and brought Northern Ireland's death toll in the past week's violence to 11. Page 13.

Four out-of-work aerospace scientists tuned out the Apollo splashdown and tuned in on social consciousness. Page 14.

Scientists and space officials agree that Apollo 14 was the most scientifically successful lunar landing mission. Page 14.

Congress heard that the drives in Laos and Cambodia would speed the end of the U.S. ground-combat role in Vietnam. Page 15.

A column accusing Senator Fulbright of wanting the Laos incursion to fail was mailed to 600 writers by the White House. Page 15.

Anti-war protestors at Stanford voted to call a "roving" general strike. Page 16.

Israeli Premier Golda Meir proposed that both Israel and Egypt reduce troop strength along the Suez Canal. Page 17.

Neither earthquake nor fog kept art buffs from flying to Los Angeles for the annual Airlift for Art. Page 18.

Funds for more day care centers for children will not come this year, Assemblyman Loren Greene said. Page 20.

Sports

The San Francisco Warriors will play tonight's game against the Seattle Super Sonics at the Cow Palace. Page 51.

Satchel Paige was elected to a spot in baseball's Hall of Fame, although under a special rule and to a special section. Page 51.

Giants' third baseman Jim Ray Hart will remain in San Francisco undergoing treatment when spring training opens. Page 51.

Weather

Bay Area: Fair today; night and morning fog. High, 50s to low 60s; low, in the 40s. Light winds. Page 39.

San Francisco Chronicle

★★★★ FINAL

107th Year No. 41 ★★★★ WEDNESDAY, FEBRUARY 10, 1971 15 CENTS GArfield 1-1111

10 Pages of Quake Photos, Spot Reports

The L.A. Earthquake-- Death Toll Is Climbing

AP Wirephoto

At least 19 people were killed and many were trapped in the collapse of a Veterans hospital in Sylmar.

35 Known Dead, Damage Figure Over One Billion Dollars

N.Y. Times Service

Los Angeles

A major earthquake rumbled through southern California early yesterday, killing at least 35 persons, injuring hundreds and causing more than a billion dollars in damage to homes, businesses and roadways in Los Angeles and surrounding areas.

The death toll was expected to exceed 50 as rescue workers dug through the rubble of two hospitals and dozens of other collapsed buildings.

More than 850 persons were treated for injuries in the quake zone, according to the sheriff's office.

Powerful aftershocks continued early today to shake a dam at the head of the San Fernando valley and the police ordered the evacuation of more than 80,000 people who live below the reservoir.

The worst disaster was at a Veterans Administration hospital in Sylmar, a community about 25 miles from downtown Los Angeles and about ten miles from the quake's center in the town of Newhall. About 80 persons were trapped when two hospital buildings collapsed. Twenty-five were rescued. 19 were known dead and about 30 were missing.

Strongest

The tremor struck only seconds after 6 a.m. and lasted for close to a minute. It registered 6.5 on the Richter scale of 10, making it the strongest quake to hit Los Angeles since 1933. The famous San Francisco quake of 1906 would have registered about 8.3 if the scale had been in use at that time.

Centered near Newhall, 40 miles north of Los Angeles, the quake was felt in Fresno, 200 miles to the north; at the Mexican border, 130 miles to the south, and in Las Vegas, 225 miles to the northeast.

The shock waves were so powerful that they knocked out the seismographic instruments at the California Institute of Technology in Pasadena.

Victims

The time of the quake undoubtedly saved many lives. Most people were in bed, out of the way of falling debris. An hour or two later, and the freeways and business district would have been jammed with potential victims.

A sense of danger continued to hover over the city throughout the day. The Van Norman lakes, a series of reservoirs in the hills above the San Fernando valley, the area's main residential area, were badly shaken by the tremor. The cement facing of

See Back Page

Apollo 14's Splashdown-- 'Smack-Dab on Target'

Reuters, U.P. & A.P.

Aboard USS New Orleans

The Apollo 14 astronauts splashed down safely right on target in the South Pacific and were brought aboard this carrier yesterday after completing man's most successful moon mission.

Astronauts Alan B. Shepard Jr., Stuart A. Roosa and Edgar D. Mitchell dropped into the South Pacific at 1:05 p.m. PST, ending a nine-day, 1.15-million-mile voyage.

"We're all fine in here," said Shepard, seconds after the Apollo command ship splashed into the choppy water.

"Welcome home," the carrier radioed.

"Thank you, sir," came a quick reply.

The splashdown was one of the most accurate ever achieved.

"It seems like you broke the record without much doubt," Admiral Thomas B. Hayward, commander of the recovery force, told the astronauts. "You were smack-dab on the target."

Scientists were delighted with the mission. During the 33½-hour stay on the moon, Shepard and Mitchell collected rocks that may be 4.6 billion years old and set up an atomic-powered science station already working smoothly and providing valuable information.

White-suited sailors lining the deck of this prime recovery ship cheered loudly after two subdued sonic booms first announced that the spacecraft was coming down nearby.

Moments later, the spacecraft was sighted dragging two small white parachutes. These were followed by three

See Back Page

Confession In Tate Murders

Times-Post Service

Los Angeles

Pale, dark-haired Susan Atkins confessed to killing actress Sharon Tate and musician Gary Hinman yesterday in the penalty-phase of the Tate-La Bianca murder trial.

The story of the seven Tate-La Bianca murders told from the witness stand by the 22-year-old defendant closely resembled the testimony of the state's key witness, Linda Kasabian, except that in Miss Atkins' version:

• Charles Manson had

See Back Page

Weather Slows Invasion of Laos

Associated Press

Saigon

South Vietnamese troops and tanks pressed westward across branches of the Ho Chi Minh trail in southern Laos yesterday behind enemy forces retreating under U.S. air attacks.

In the second day of the operation, the main column reportedly had proceeded about 12 miles inside Laos along Highway 9.

The advance was slowed by U.S. bomb craters in the road and bad weather that closed in suddenly. The Saigon troops also were halting to seize munitions caches.

Ahead of the South Vietnamese, 25 miles deep into Laos, lay Sepone, heavily bombed and almost deserted. It is a main transshipment point on the trail and a North Vietnamese operating base.

Operating in front of the South Vietnamese, U.S. helicopter Cobras attacked enemy supply depots 15 miles inside Laos. Reports said the gunships hit at least one oil dump and an ammunition storage area, causing large fires and some explosions.

Field dispatches said the

See Back Page

Index

Comics	30	Vital Statistics	39
Deaths	39	Weather	39
Entertainment	46	Women's News	18
Finance	58		
TV-Radio	44		

Inside

Walt Disney World in Florida was officially dedicated amidst so many celebrities they often got snubbed. Page 2.

Mayoral candidate Harold Dobbs accused Mayor Alioto of lying about Dobbs' stand on strengthening the police force. Page 2.

The police hit-run detail investigated its first hit-run case involving bathtubs. Page 3.

A representative of San Francisco Tomorrow said waterfront development plans "could destroy many parts of our city." Page 4.

A battle is brewing in Marin county over plans to build a Sonoma-Marin aqueduct. Page 4.

TOP OF THE NEWS

Some delegates at the California Federation of Teachers convention accused the organization of internal racism. Page 5.

UC's amazing Joel Hildebrand, almost 90, worked on his latest chemical research project. Page 6.

The chairman of the board of Planned Parenthood-World Population issued a gloomy warning on population control. Page 6.

UC's new Berkeley chancellor has decided to intervene in the controversy over the campus psychiatric clinic. Page 6.

Labor's George Meany said the Nixon administration has injected politics into the Bureau of Labor Statistics. Page 8.

A Bakersfield man has been held in a Mexican prison for nearly four years although he has never been sentenced. Page 8.

James Farmer urged blacks to form their own political organization to deal with major parties at primary time. Page 9.

Pouring rain washed out the opening of an anti-war rally in Washington, D.C. Page 10.

Pakistan said 147 persons were killed in new fighting along the East Pakistan-India border. Page 11.

Military police kept a group of Vietnam Veterans for Peace from holding a memorial service at the Presidio cemetery. Page 12.

British troops put down a riot at a Northern Ireland prison camp where suspected Irish guerrillas are confined. Page 14.

After the great hemline debate, many American designers have settled down to classic styles. Page 19.

A seemingly-harmless classified ad for convention hostesses turned out to be more complex than it seemed. Page 21.

Weather

Bay Area: Fair Tuesday, becoming partly cloudy at night. Highs, 60s to 70s; lows, in the 40s. Light wind. Page 33.

The U.N. Vote--What It Means

See Below

San Francisco Chronicle

★★★★ FINAL

107th Year No. 299 ★★★★ TUESDAY, OCTOBER 26, 1971 GArfield 1-1111 15 CENTS

U.N. Votes to Admit Peking --Nationalist China Ousted

A Big Defeat for U.S. --Taiwan Delegates Walk Out on Assembly

Washington Post Service

United Nations

The General Assembly voted overwhelmingly last night to admit Communist China to the U.N. and expel the Nationalist Chinese of Taiwan.

The vote was 76 to 35 with 17 abstentions. Just before it was taken the Taiwan delegates walked out of the chamber and said they were quitting the organization.

The United States thus lost the battle it had been waging since 1949 with the supporters of Peking over Chinese representation at the United Nations.

The conflict was essentially the same this year despite the dramatic switch in American policy.

CRUX

The United States called for the seating of Peking for the first time but made the expulsion of Taiwan the crux of the matter.

Peking's supporters, led by Albania, moved to "restore the lawful rights of the Peoples' Republic of China" and expel the "representatives of Chiang Kai-shek."

The Assembly first defeated the U.S. resolution to declare the expulsion of Taiwan an important question requiring a two-thirds majority. The vote was 59 to 55 with 15 abstentions.

That was the key vote and the United States had predicted victory. Its loss started a landslide that gave the Albanian resolution a majority approaching the two-thirds it no longer needed.

'INFAMY'

U. S. Ambassador George Bush, looking weary, told newsmen, "I hope the U.N. will not relive this moment of infamy." He said that he would have predicted victory just before the vote was taken, and said he was "terribly disappointed" that "some firm commitments" were not kept. Bush added, "Obviously, I did not do a good job."

Bush said the U.N. vote

See Back Page

Liu Chieh (right foreground), Taiwan's U.N. representative, led his delegation from the chamber before the vote

UPI Telephoto

Robbers Strike in Wet Suits

The Trident restaurant on Sausalito's waterfront was robbed early yesterday by three armed men dressed in skin divers' wet suits who took an estimated $31,000 to $32,000.

"We think they came in off the water," said Lou Ganapoler, the Trident's manager.

Patrick Pendleton and Thomas Ribar, the only Trident employees on duty during the robbery, told Sausalito police that the men — each carrying a pistol — entered the kitchen at 3:30 a.m.

The two maintenance employees said the gunmen told them they would not be hurt if they obeyed orders. They said they were handcuffed, blindfolded with towels and forced to lie on the washroon floor.

Pendleton said he was

See Back Page

Canners Ask More U.S. Controls

Washington

Industry asked the government yesterday to impose tighter federal controls on food canneries to prevent a recurrence of last summer's incidence of botulism in canned soup.

Both Dr. Ira I. Somers, research director of the National Canners Association, and Sam D. Fine, associate commissioner of the Food and Drug Administration, said they could recall no previous instance of food processors seeking stricter Federal regulation of their own plants.

"We just don't think the canning industry can tolerate any more bad publicity," Somers said. "From a statistical standpoint our record is good but we want to tighten every screw we can."

The Canners Association petition asked the FDA to adopt 48 pages of regulations aimed primarily at insuring that canned foods are sealed and sterilized properly.

The proposed rules also would empower the FDA to bar a suspect cannery from shipping food. Somers said the FDA could adopt the regulations under provisions of the Food, Drug and Cosmetic Act never before used.

Somers said the proposed regulations were copied largely from Calilfornia cannery rules in force since 1925.

Fine said the FDA welcomed the proposals and would publish them in the Federal register for public comment.

The Canning Association 550 member firms produce about 90 per cent of the Nation's annual output of 29 billion cans and jars of food products.

United Press

Brezhnev in Paris--Quick Agreement

N.Y. Times Service

Paris

President Georges Pompidou and Leonid Brezhnev, secretary general of the Soviet Communist Party, reached quick agreement yesterday to begin active preparation for a European security conference.

The Soviet leader was received here with the honors of a chief of state and only a few minor discordant notes marred the generally friendly atmosphere of Brezhnev's first visit to a Western country since he became party leader in 1964.

In toasts at a state banquet in Versailles that marked the end of the first day of Brezhnev's six-day visit, both men spoke in similar terms of the need to end hostile blocs.

BLOCS

Brezhnev said France and the Soviet Union are close "on a fundamental problem — that of ending the division of the world into politico-military blocs."

Pompidou declared that such blocs carried within them "the certainty of permanent affrontment and the threat of a conflict that would be a final cataclysm."

The President said there is nothing to prevent the opening "in the shortest time" of the multilateral phase of preparation for a security conference in Helsinki. Both men upheld the principles of inviolability of frontiers, and of non-interference in the affairs of other nations and Pompidou pointedly added:

"We respect everyone's independence and we are determined to have our own respected and to give ourselves the political, economic and, why not say it, military means."

SECURITY

Some of the tightest security precautions ever taken here surrounded Brezhnev's visit. Approximately 8000 policemen and paramilitary forces were concentrated in the capital as anti-Soviet groups threatened demonstrations. As a precaution, 58 members of the extensive east European colony in Par-

See Back Page

80-Car Pileup Injures 44

Castelmadama, Italy

Forty-four persons were injured Sunday in a chain-reaction pileup involving 80 cars and trucks on a main highway seven miles outside Rome.

Polie said the pileup began when one car tried to go around another one in a no passing zone and one of them crashed into a guard rail. The pileup stretched more than one mile on the highway between Laquila and Rome.

United Press

Jumbo Jet Hijacked To Cuba

United Press

Miami

An American Airlines Boeing 747 with 221 passengers — including three sky marshals and an FBI agent — was hijacked to Cuba last night during a flight from New York to Puerto Rico.

The giant plane, second of its kind to be hijacked to Cuba, landed safely at Havana at 6:58 p.m. PDT.

At 11:30 p.m., the plane was still on the ground at Havana and Cuban authorities had failed to respond to inquiries about it.

A Federal Aviation Administration spokesman in New York said a man armed with a gun took a stewardess hostage in the first class lounge about an hour after the jet, Flight No. 98, left Kennedy International Airport in New York at 3:45 p.m. PDT, bound for San Juan.

The pilot, O.R. Selmela, notified American Airlines and the FAA "by prearranged signal, not voice communications," when the plane was over North Carolina, the FAA said.

In Washington, FAA spokesman David Gelfan

See Back Page

Some Tough Testimony On Reform of Prisons

By Tim Findley

A Congressional subcommittee expected to draft legislation aimed at national standards for prison reform began a search for solutions in an all-day hearing here yesterday.

"Extremists on both sides of the question ought to just shut up," State Department of Corrections director Raymond Procunier told the subcommittee of the House Committee on the Judiciary at one point.

Procunier, like virtually all of the dozen witnesses who testified at the Federal building, said he recognized need for reform, but insisted California is making progress faster than other jurisdictions.

COUNSEL

But attorney Faye Stender, a controversial leader of some reformists and counsel to many inmates, replied: "I'm always interested in hearing Mr. Procunier — he sounds so good, and yet it just isn't like that in prison, it just isn't true."

The hearing, which assembled a wide spectrum of witnesses — many of them admitted bitter political enemies — began with a flat assumption by nearly all those involved that prisons as they are currently functioning are a failure.

"I think the time is due — long past due — for us to begin those changes which will make out correctional system based on respect for the human being — whether he wears the inmate's denims or the officers's uniform," Committee Chairman Robert Kastenmeier (Dem.-Wis.) said in opening the hearing.

TOURING

Kastenmeier and the other eight members of the committee spent the weekend touring San Quentin and Soledad prisons and Alameda county's Santa Rita Rehabilitation Center.

Witnesses who testified before them yesterday generally divided themselves into two main groups.

State prison officials for the most part conceded the need for reform but appealed for more money and alluded sharply to outside pressure from such groups as lawyers and political organizations.

Reform-minded attorneys,

See Back Page

Profit Motive Is Ruining Ecosystem, Douglas Says

By Ralph Craib

Supreme Court Justice William O. Douglas said here yesterday that "technology and the profit motive have carried us far down the road to disaster."

"It is indeed," he said, "a desperate race to institute preventive controls that will save the ecosystem."

Justice Douglas, a crusading conservationist for all of his adult life, was the keynote speaker as the 54th national conference of the American Institute of Planners got under way at the Hilton Hotel.

He urged that planning be undertaken on a statewide basis throughout the nation

See Back Page

The World Impact of The Action

By Max Frankel
N.Y. Times Service

Washington

With the vote at the United Nations last night, China burst fully and finally from the isolation first imposed on it by the United States a generation ago and periodically preferred by its own Communist government.

Although Washington was calm or simply asleep at the symbolic moment, its rear-guard effort to save Taiwan in the world organization only heightened the drama of Peking's entry onto the world stage and deepened some of the resentments in conservative circles here.

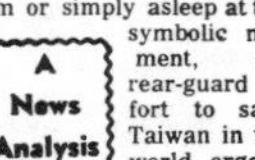

President Nixon undoubtedly will show some sympathy for those resentments. He considers his projected journey to China as far more significant than most actions of the U.N. and he sincerely hoped that his gesture would win a more gentle handling for the Nationalist Chinese.

But there was obviously a pent-up desire among many nations to make whole and unambiguous this final reversal of American policy. This will complicate the President's task in defending his new China policy and the irritations are bound to be reflected in Washington's rela-

See Back Page

An Earthquake In Philippines

Manila

The Weather Bureau's geophysical division recorded an earthquake off the northeastern coast of Mindanao, southern Philippines, early yesterday.

A spokesman reported the epicenter was traced to about 125 miles east-northeast of Surigao Province. He said the tremor was caused by slipping of the earth's crust.

Associated Press

Index

Comics	52
Deaths	33
Entertainment	40
Finance	48
People	14
TV-Radio	38
Weather	33

EXTRA EXTRA EXTRA EXTRA

San Francisco Chronicle

★★★★ FINAL

108th Year No. 130 ★★★★* TUESDAY, MAY 9, 1972 GArfield 1-1111 15 CENTS

U.S. MINES RED PORTS

President Orders the North Sealed Off From Arms Flow

Nixon Says Both Sea And Land Routes Will Be Severed

N.Y. Times Service

Washington

President Nixon announced last night that he has ordered the mining of all North Vietnamese ports and taken other measures to prevent the flow of arms and other military supplies to the enemy.

Mr. Nixon told a nationwide television and radio audience that his orders were being executed as he spoke.

From the President's somber and stern speech and from explanations by other Administration officials, the following picture of the American action emerged:

- All major North Vietnamese ports will be mined. Ships of other countries in the harbors, most of which are Russian, will have three "daylight periods" in which to leave. After that the mines will become active and ships coming or going will move at their own peril.
- U.S. naval vessels will not search or seize ships of other countries entering or leaving North Vietnamese ports, thus avoiding a direct clash with the Russians.
- American and South Vietnamese ships and planes will take "appropriate measures" to stop North Vietnam from unloading material on beaches from unmined waters.
- U.S. and South Vietnamese forces will interdict (halt) presumably by bombing, the movement of material in North Vietnam over rail lines originating in China.

Complete Nixon message on Page 8B

The President's speech also appealed to the Soviet Union not to let its support of North Vietnam lead it to a crisis with the U.S. over his decision to try to cut off supplies to North Vietnam.

CONFUSION

There was much confusion here last night about whether the U.S. and South Vietnam had proclaimed a blockade. The President did not use the word and Pentagon spokesmen denied that a blockade existed in the technical sense. But some observers felt that the practical effect on North Vietnam of the President's actions would be the same as a blockade.

Mr. Nixon said the mining, the attacks on the rail lines within North Vietnam, and the efforts to halt the movement of supplies by

See Back Page

U.S. Navy Planes Lay 1st Mines

Associated Press

Saigon

United States Navy planes today began carrying out President Nixon's order to mine the entrances to North Vietnam's ports.

The U.S. command said they shot down one MIG interceptor during the initial operation.

"The initial phases of the mining operation have been successfully accomplished," said a statement from the command, and "all planes have returned safely."

UNKNOWN

The statement gave no further details, and there was no information from other sources on which harbors were mined or what types of mines were dropped.

Presumably, however, Haiphong, North Vietnam's chief port, and Vinh were among the targets.

Since President Nixon in his broadcast announcement of the new intensification of the war said foreign ships in the North Vietnamese harbors had "three daylight periods" to leave them, it appeared likely that the mines contained a timing device that armed them after 60 or 72 hours.

SEVENTH

The North Vietnamese MIG reported downed was the seventh enemy jet claimed by American pilots since Saturday. Three MIGs were reported shot down yesterday when U.S. planes returned to the Hanoi area for the first time in three weeks to attack targets the U.S. command said "are helping to support the Communist invasion" of South Vietnam.

All American planes were said to have returned safely

See Back Page

NORTH VIETNAM'S PORTS AND LAND SUPPLY ROUTESJ
President Nixon said both water and land lines will be sealed off

UPI Telephoto

Mining Impact on War May Not Be Immediate

By William Beecher
N.Y. Times Service

Washington

Pentagon analysts say the mining of Haiphong and other harbors of North Vietnam, ordered last night by President Nixon, may have a negligible effect on the war over the short run, but substantial impact over the long run.

Over the short term, the analysts concede, even effective denial of outside war supplies probably would not cripple enemy offensive abilities in the south for several weeks.

To be really effective, they note, mining probably should be accompanied by a persistent bombing campaign to cut traffic over the two rail lines and eight roads from China.

DENIAL

But over the longer term, these analysts believe, denial of large quantities of gasoline, artillery, ammunition and tanks would make it quite difficult for North Vietnamese counteroffensives aimed at driving the enemy from captured territory.

Well-placed military sources said the B-52 raid on the Haiphong area about three weeks ago so disrupted unloading and storage facilities that in recent days North Vietnam has diverted freighters en route from Canton and Hong Kong for Haiphong to the secondary port of Hon Gay, about 20 miles north.

At the time of the mining operation, defense sources say, about 37 freighters and oil tankers were in Haiphong harbor and its estuary. Most were from the Soviet bloc and Cuba; about eight to ten were from Hong Kong and Britain.

Another 30 ships appeared to be en route to North Vietnam.

In his televised address to the nation, Mr. Nixon said the mining operation was under way as he spoke, but that the mines would not be activated until three "daylight periods" had elapsed in order to allow ships now in port to leave.

Thereafter, he said, any ships entering or leaving any of the ports of North Vietnam would so so "at their own peril."

Military sources said these four types of mines are available for dropping by naval aircraft to block

See Back Page

Sights and Sounds Of War in Hanoi

By Joel Henri
Agence France-Presse

Hanoi

Houses in central Hanoi shook under the impact of bombs dropped by American aircraft yesterday in what appeared to be a violent attack on areas around the capital.

The rumble of a long series of explosions could be heard even by people who had sought refuge in underground shelters.

From outdoor observation posts, the explosions — wave after wave at five-minute intervals for 35 minutes — could be heard very clearly.

Still unconfirmed reports said the targets included the small commune of Phe Xuyen some 20 miles from Hanoi.

I spent the previous night at Phu Xuyen. Nothing in the locality except perhaps a small rail and road bridge could constitute a military target.

Phu Xuyen was a target of the United States Air Force several times during the Johnson administration.

Other unconfirmed reports said the Hoa Binh region 25 miles west of Hanoi also was attacked.

Some explosions seemed to have occurred much closer. Rumors which could not immediately be checked said U. S. aircraft dropped

See Back Page

Phantom Jets Collide--2 Killed

Avon Park, Fla.

Two U.S. Air Force crewmen were killed yesterday when two F-4 Phantom jet fighter-bombers collided during a training mission and crashed on the Avon Park gunnery range.

Two other crewmen escaped serious injury.

Associated Press

Fires Set

War Rampage In Berkeley

Hundreds of shouting, rock-throwing demonstrators surged through the streets of Berkeley last night, smashing windows and setting trash fires in protest against President Nixon's new war measures in Vietnam.

At least one police car was overturned and burned. Windows were broken in dozens of business places.

Trash cans were overturned and set afire in the streets in many places.

There were reports early today that one or two buildings had been set afire, but they could not be confirmed.

Estimates of the number of demonstrators ranged from several hundred to more than a thousand.

MARCH

They started congregating shortly after 9 p.m. at Willard Park — sometimes called Ho Chi Minh Park — on Telegraph avenue. The demonstration started as a relatively quiet march along Telegraph, with many of the demonstrators raced from one street to another, from the University of California campus to downtown Berkeley, dodging police who tried to head them off from business areas vulnerable to "trashing."

By early today, the throng had broken up into smaller groups, but the violence showed no signs of abating.

There were sporadic reports of explosions and what sounded like gunfire, but police said they knew of no injuries and no arrests. 3

The heaviest damage was reported along Shattuck avenue, where rocks were tossed through numerous plate glass windows despite efforts of police to keep the protesters away from business places there.

Police seemed generally restrained in their response when rocks and bottles were thrown at them, but a few were observed swinging clubs as they chased protesters, and police cars with sirens screaming were driven onto sidewalks in some places as officers tried to disperse crowds.

An unoccupied squad car was tipped over and set afire, and a rock smashed a window of another police car full of helmeted officers, but none of them were injured, a Berkeley police spokesman said.

A section of the fence around People's Park at Bowditch and Haste streets, scene of a bloody battle between police and demonstrators in 1969, was torn down.

Meanwhile, there were nonviolent protests at other campuses.

STANFORD

At Stanford University, some 400 students marched on the campus residence of university president Richard W. Lyman, but dispersed after about an hour. Lyman refused to come out and talk to them in response to demands. Stanford students announced a mass protest rally would be held at noon today in White Plaza.

At Santa Barbara, the sheriff's office mobilized its forces to try to head off some 1500 students who were reported on the march from their Isla Vista housing area early today with the announced intention of blocking U.S. 101.

Students at the University of California at Santa Cruz and at Sonoma State College also announced plans for protests rallies today.

Arabs Hijack Jet, Hold Passengers

Associated Press

Tel Aviv

Armed Arab guerrillas seized a Belgian jetliner with 101 persons aboard yesterday despite a tipoff and security search, landed it in Tel Aviv and demanded freedom for 300 Palestinian guerrilla prisoners as the price of the passengers' lives.

As negotiations were carried on by radio between the grounded Boeing 707 and Israeli officials, the pilot said the plane was unfit to take off. The hijackers demanded that it be made ready to leave for Cairo by 8:30 p.m. yesterday PDT — or they would blow it up with the passengers aboard.

But the deadline passed with Israel's national radio station asserting that an emphasis was being placed on negotiations.

Airport officials said there was no indication that the guerrillas intended to carry out the threat, at least for the time being.

The gunmen also demanded to talk with an International Red Cross representative.

"I want to talk to the Red Cross man," a voice barked over the jet's radio. "I will only deal with a Red Cross man."

Israeli officials said a Red Cross representative was on his way from Jerusalem.

A senior Israeli army offi-

See Back Page

Demo-GOP Reaction-- A Big Split

Washington Post Service

Washington

Democratic war critics last night attacked President Nixon's latest move on Vietnam in the most scorching language heard on Capitol Hill since the Cambodia crisis two years ago, but Republicans rallied to Mr. Nixon's support.

In Lincoln, Neb., Democratic presidential candidate George S. McGovern said:

"This new escalation is reckless, unnecessary and unworkable. It is a flirtation with World War III. It will not save American lives, it will claim more American lives: it will not release American prisoners, it only tightens the locks on their cells . . . the ony purpose of this dangerous new course is to keep General Thieu in power a little longer, and perhaps to save Mr. Nixon's face a little longer."

In Omaha, Neb., Senator Hubert H. Humphrey (Dem-Minn.), another leading Democratic presidential candidate, suspended all further campaigning to return to Washington for consultations with congressional leaders on how to counteract the President's new policies.

"I cannot and do not sup-

See Back Page

Index

Comics 54
Deaths 33
Entertainment 39
Finance 48
People 12
TV-Radio 38
Vital Statistics 32
Weather 32

Full Photo Story

THE WALLACE SHOOTING

San Francisco Chronicle ★★★★ FINAL

108th Year No. 137 ★★★★ TUESDAY, MAY 16, 1972 GArfield 1-1111 15 CENTS

Shooting Scene

Governor Badly Wounded-- Young Suspect Is Seized

Wallace Shot at Rally In Maryland--5 Hours Of Exploratory Surgery

Washington Post Service

Washington

Governor George C. Wallace of Alabama, campaigning across Maryland for the Presidency, was shot and seriously wounded yesterday by a young assailant dressed in red, white and blue.

The 52-year-old Governor, in his second presidential campaign, was shot at close range following his speech at a Laurel, Md., shopping center, in the suburbs of the Nation's capital. Wounded in the chest and stomach, Wallace was reportedly paralyzed by "spinal complications."

A spokesman at Holy Cross Hospital in Silver Spring, Md., said the Governor's condition is "stable in that there is no immediate danger of his expiring."

Three persons traveling with Wallace were also wounded in the shooting. Police immediately arrested a crew-cut blond-haired young man who was identified as Arthur Bremer, 21, of Milwaukee, Wis. The man was in the rally audience—dressed in a red, white and blue shirt and socks, wearing a Wallace campaign button. He had been seen earlier in the day at a Wallace rally in Washington, D.C.

The suspect was described by acquaintances as a loner with a penchant for pornography.

Paralysis Confirmed

A doctor who was inside the hospital but not in the operating room said that Wallace "felt no sensaion from the waist down." A second doctor who works on the staff of Holy Cross Hospital confirmed that Wallace was indeed paralyzed when he was taken into surgery.

George Magnum, a Wallace campaign aide, said the 52-year-old Governor was taken into the recovery room shortly after 10:30 p.m. EDT following about five hours of exploratory surgery.

A doctor who assisted in the surgery said Wallace was struck by five bullets, two of which caused serious wounds. Magnum said one bullet was removed but another, near the spine, was left in place for the time being.

Just before midnight, one of the six doctors who performed the surgery said "we expect a good recovery" and that the Governor might "be able to go home in five to ten days."

But Dr. Joseph Schanno, a vascular surgeon, also cautioned that "there is some paralysis at this time from the hips down" and "it is difficult to predict what the spinal problem will be."

At a briefing early today, Schanno said Wallace was awake, alert, resting comfortably and making progress "as well as we can expect."

Reaction of Rivals

Governor Wallace's rivals expressed horror at the shooting, the fourth prominent American political figure to be gunned down in a decade. President Nixon swiftly ordered extra security precautions, dispatching Secret Service agents to guard Representative Shirley Chisholm, a previously unprotected candidate, and Senator Edward M. Kennedy, a non-candidate whose brothers both died by assassination.

Wallace was cut down about 4 p.m. EDT in the parking lot of the Laurel Shopping Center, about 30

See Back Page

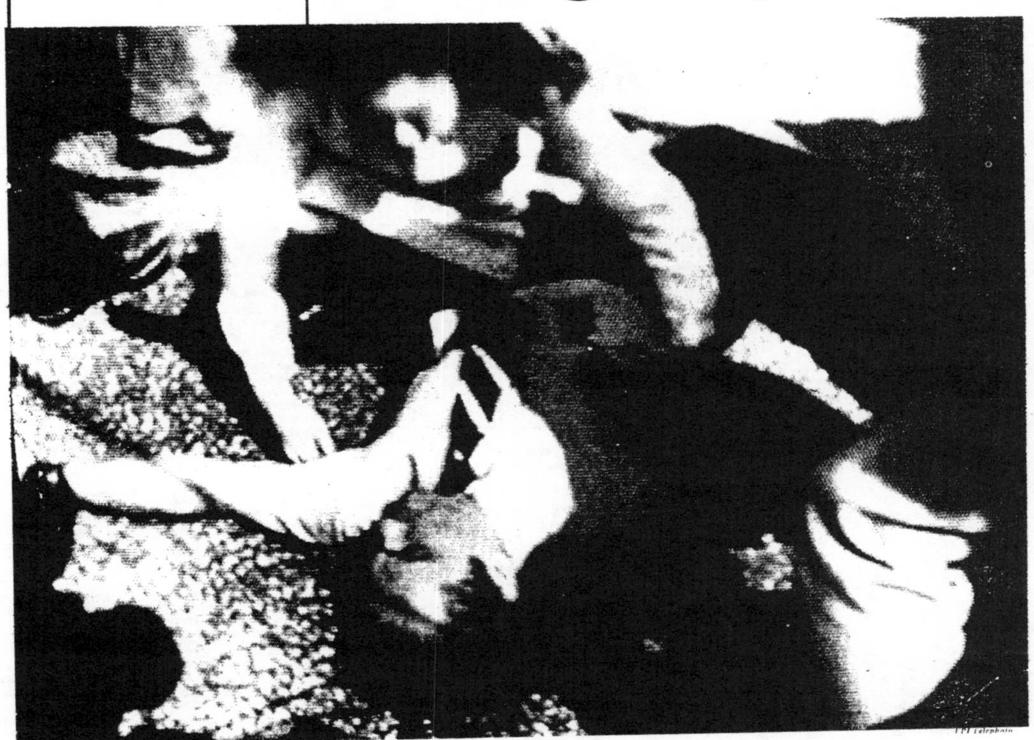

UPI Telephoto

Cornelia Wallace knelt beside her fallen husband seconds after he was shot in a Maryland shopping center

Red-Held Base Is Recaptured

Associated Press

Saigon

South Vietnamese infantrymen recaptured artillery base Bastogne yesterday in the second phase of an effort to head off an expected North Vietnamese attack on Hue.

The surprise reconquest of Bastogne, which had been abandoned under enemy attack 18 days ago, came as renewed fighting was reported in the central highlands. Communist troops also cut two key highways by destroying culverts.

The 6½-week siege of An Loc continued as enemy forces fired another 2500 rounds of artillery, rocket and mortar fire into the ravaged provincial capital 60 miles north of Saigon.

The U.S. command disclosed the loss of three more planes in raids over North Vietnam with all six crewmen listed as missing. This raised to 142 Americans reported killed or missing in Indochina air losses since Hanoi's general offensive began March 30.

At Bastogne, field reports said, a platoon of volunteers riding six South Vietnamese helicopters assaulted the base in midafternoon. They quickly secured it for ground forces which moved westward along Route 547 behind a shield of U.S. air attacks.

The attackers encountered only light resistance, the reports said, indicating North Vietnamese forces around Bastogne may have been surprised by the attack.

At nightfall the South Vietnamese First Division was reported to have full control of the base. But some troops still were reported trying to

See Back Page

Supervisors Approve S.F. Budget

By Jerry Burns

The Board of Supervisors unanimously approved the record annual budget for San Francisco last night, including a controversial helicopter program for the Police Department.

The budget for the 1972-1973 fiscal year, which begins July 1, will be $567,112,613 — an increase of $7.5 million over the budget for city services in the present year, but $5.7 million less than the budget proposed by Mayor Joseph L. Alioto.

"If there's no increase in the budget for schools, which hasn't been adopted yet, we have a good shot at avoiding an increase in the property tax rate," said Supervisor Robert Mendelsohn, chairman of the Board's Fi-

See Back Page

Dock Union OKs Pay Board's Cuts

By Jackson Rannells

The West Coast longshoremen's union announced yesterday—with face saving reservations—that it has accepted Pay Board cuts in its strike settlement and has dropped its threats of a renewed walkout.

The action is expected to free payment of $4.5 million in back wages and to activate a number of fringe benefit improvements in the contract for 13,000 dock workers.

Some factors in the move were the union members, desire to "get something" out of their 134-day strike, the difficulty of renewing the walkout with war flaring in Southest Asia and the short time remaining on the contract.

Harry Bridges, president of the International Longshoremen's and Warehousemen's Union, had talked of further strike action and a refusal to cooperate with the Pay Board since it rejected the contract's 72-cent hourly pay raise (16 per cent) and said it would approve only 42 cents (10 per cent).

Spokesmen for the ILWU insisted yesterday that their new announcement was not a reversal. They cited two points:

- Only Pacific Maritime Association, the 122-member employers group, will submit the revised and seemingly acceptable contract for formal approval. The union and PMA jointly filed the original pact.
- The new contract permits the union to cancel it on 60 days notice if wage or price controls are terminated on or before November 30, 1972, and on 24 hours no-

See Back Page

$200,000 Bail Set For Suspect

Reuters

Baltimore

A federal magistrate ordered Arthur Herman Bremer, 21, of Milwaukee, Wis., held on $200,000 bail last night on charges of shooting Governor George Wallace of Alabama and a Secret Service agent.

Bremer, a 21-year-old, five-foot, six-inch blond, was ordered held for a hearing a week from tomorrow on two federal counts: Interfering with a Secret Service agent—Nick Zarvos of Atlanta, who was also wounded — and interfering with Wallace by force and violating his civil rights as a political candidate.

U. S. Magistrate Clarence E. Goetz appointed Benjajim Lipsitz of Baltimore to act as Bremer's attorney.

See Back Page

Index

Comics	58	TV-Radio	44
Deaths	40	Vital Statistics	45
Entertainment	46	Weather	40
Finance	54		
People	25		

Terror at Olympics

ALL HOSTAGES SLAIN

San Francisco Chronicle

★★★★ FINAL

The Largest Daily Circulation in Northern California

108th Year No. 250 ★★★★• WEDNESDAY, SEPTEMBER 6, 1972 GArfield 1-1111 15 CENTS

Helicopter Death Trap

11 Israelis, 5 Arabs Dead --Battle at Munich Airport

AP Wirephoto

The burned-out helicopter (left) in which Israeli hostages were reported to have been killed

Terrorists Gun Down Captives

Washington Post Service

Munich

Arab terrorists turned the 1972 Olympic Games into a scene of political murder yesterday that began with a pre-dawn attack on Israeli athletes in the Olympic Village and ended 20 hours later in a bloody airfield shootout.

When it was over, 11 Israelis, 5 Arab terrorists and one West German policeman were dead.

The band of Arab guerrillas invaded the Israeli team's quarters at the Olympic grounds before dawn yesterday and shot and killed two Israelis.

They held nine others hostage through a day of tense negotiations that ended when captors and hostages were taken by helicopter to the airport and a plane that was to fly them to Cairo.

SHOOTING

Police sharpshooters opened fire on the Arabs when the helicopters landed, but missed some of them because of the darkness. The guerrillas who escaped the first shots turned their guns on the helicopters with the helpless Israelis inside, authorities said.

Five of the Palestinian commandos were killed and three were captured, police said. One policeman was reported killed and a helicopter pilot was seriously wounded.

Bavarian Interior Minister Bruno Merck said the Israeli hostages had agreed to go with the Arabs to Cairo. But the German authorities felt "this would have been a certain death sentence for them . . . We had to take a chance and attempt to free the hostages."

Merck said the wreckage

See Back Page

UPI Telephoto

Guerrillas climbed fence to get in; this athlete climbed gate to get out and away from danger area

How Guerrillas Got Into Village

Washington Post Service

Munich

The night-shift workers at the Olympic Village post office merely nudged each other and pointed to the fence-climbers outside, in the dim light of the early dawn.

No great to-do about that scene. Happened all the time in the Village, those agile Olympic athletes scaling the eight-foot fence to bypass the gate keepers and sneak back to their dorms after violating curfew.

You couldn't tell a dark Arab from a blond Scandinavian in the half light of 4 a.m., especially if he was dressed in those long sweat suits favored in Olympic Village.

This time not just a couple of kids sneaking home. There were five of them, "and they all were carrying those big adidas or puma bags," a postal worker said later.

A common sight in the Village, these carry-all bags. Big enough to conceal a snub-nosed machine gun, if necessary.

As for getting over the fences, "There's never any trouble about that," said another athlete, a cyclist from Holland.

"Two nights ago my friend and I slung our bikes over the same fence before we crawled over and got back to the dorms," he said.

The first shots rang out at 4:30 a.m. in Building 31. That's where the Israeli team was living, on the first

See Back Page

Nixon Visits S.F., Pushes Bay Park

By George Murphy

President Nixon took a brief ferryboat ride on San Francisco Bay on a windy, sunny day yesterday, posed for pictures on the top deck with the Golden Gate Bridge in the background, and said with a grin:

"I'll never have a better backdrop."

The President later held a press briefing on the lower deck of the motor vessel Golden Gate (the Sausalito ferry) to urge swifter congressional action on the proposed Golden Gate National Recreation Area.

DELAY

"There is no excuse for further congressional delay" on not only the Golden Gate proposal (known informally as "Gateway West"), but on other environmental bills, Mr. Nixon said.

The President said the Gateway West bill has received some action in the House, "because of the very strong support for it by Congressman (William S.) Mailliard," the San Francisco Republican.

CO-AUTHOR

The President did not mention the bills other co-author (with Mailliard), Congressman Phillip Burton—a Democrat.

Mr. Nixon said the bill is now "stalled in the Senate."

But Interior Secretary Rogers C. B. Morton, in a

See Back Page

14-Cent Cut In S.F. Tax Rate Is OKd

By Jerry Burns

A property tax rate of $12.59 was set by the San Francisco Board of Supervisors last night after a long and bitter debate.

The rate, imposed per $100 of assessed value, is a reduction of 23 cents from the 1970-71 rate.

It was set by unanimous vote, but only after a debate and parliamentary wrangle that spread over nearly five hours.

The discussion bogged down in a stalemate after the first 90 minutes—but a two-hour break for dinner and relaxing libations led to eventual agreement.

The new tax rate will mean a saving of about $8.75 for the owner of a typical home with a cash value of

See Back Page

Two-Year Sentence for Berrigan

Washington Post Service

Harrisburg, Pa.

The Rev. Phillip Berrigan was sentenced to two years in prison yesterday for smuggling four contraband letters out of the Lewisburg, Pa., federal penitentiary while he was an inmate there in 1970.

The sentence is to run concurrently with another that he is already serving.

His co-defendant, Sister Elizabeth McAlister, was sentenced to one year for smuggling three letters in to Father Berrigan during the same period.

Immediately after United States District Judge R. Dixon Herman handed down the sentences, the justice department dismissed all pending conspiracy charges against Father Berrigan, Sister Elizabeth and six other anti-war activists.

DELIBERATION

After 60 hours of deliberation here last April a federal court jury convicted the two key defendants of seven charges of smuggling contraband in and out of prison but reported that it was hopelessly deadlocked on charges that the eight had conspired to kidnap presidential adviser Henry Kissinger, to bomb tunnels un-

See Back Page

Confusion Added To the Tragedy

N.Y. Times Service

New York

Contradictory reports about the fate of the Israeli hostages seized by Arab terrorists in the Olympic Village threw the public into confusion all over the world.

During the day, millions of viewers throughout the world watched the drama on television, which was employing circuits that had been intended for the games.

But in the evening, when the events reached their climax, viewers could get no definitive word for hours on how the hostages fared.

At first the German government's official spokesman, Conrad Ahlers, announced that the intervention of German police and army at the airport had led to the escape of the hostages unharmed.

BRUNDAGE

This was confirmed by Avery Brundage, retiring president of the International Olympic Committee, who later said: "All our Israeli athletes are saved. It is a tremendous achievement."

Then there was silence, while police reports dealt with the number of terrorists killed or still at large. There was some speculation about how the hostages had escaped.

The next phase was the expression of doubt by the Munich police. A telephone call to the Munich police headquarters by the New York Times brought the ad-

See Back Page

AP Wirephoto

BRUNO MERCK
He confirmed bad news

Mostly Fair Skies Forecast

Fair skies were forecast for the Bay Area today, with the exception of some patchy clouds and morning coastal fog.

High temperatures will range from 60 degrees near the coastal to the upper 70s inland, according to the National Weather Service.

Index

Comics	52
Deaths	42
Entertainment	48
Finance	59
People	18
TV-Radio	46
Vital Statistics	41
Weather	41

Election Extra

HUGE NIXON VICTORY

San Francisco Chronicle

★★★★ FINAL

The Largest Daily Circulation in Northern California

108th Year No. 313 ★★★★• WEDNESDAY, NOVEMBER 8, 1972 GArfield 1-1111 15 CENTS

The President Triumphs--Demos Control Congress

The Death Penalty Wins

Californians voted overwhelmingly yesterday for Proposition 17, which will restore the death penalty in the state, and Proposition 21, which will prohibit the assignment of children to schools on the basis of their race.

But Proposition 18, the anti-smut measure, and Proposition 19, to legalize personal use of marijuana, failed.

So did the Watson Amendment, Proposition 14. If it had passed, it would have switched all welfare and most education costs from property taxes to other forms of taxation.

Proposition 2, the $156 million health sciences bond issue for the University of California, and Proposition 20, designed to protect the ecology of the California coastline, both seemed headed for voter approval.

The controversial farm workers initiative, Proposition 22, seemed to be narrowly defeated but the vote was close enough so that final returns might change the picture in that race.

Details on Page 5D

Mailliard Wins --Stark Trailing

By George Murphy

Congressman William S. Mailliard of San Francisco won election to his 11th term in the House of Representatives last night, defeating his Democratic challenger, San Francisco Supervisor Roger Boas.

Boas conceded shortly before midnight.

Nearly complete figures early today showed:

Mailliard: 110,420
Boas: 101,781

In a surprising turn of events, Fortney H. (Pete) Stark, the Democratic nominee for Congress from the Eighth District in the East Bay was trailing the virtually unknown Republican attorney Lew Warden, 30,890 to 28,728 early today.

Statewide, the Democrats increased their majority in the California delegation by at least two seats.

In Los Angeles, Assemblywoman Yvonne Brathwaite, a Democrat, became the first black woman elected to the House of Representatives from California.

RYAN

And in San Mateo County, Assemblyman Leo J. Ryan, a Democrat, handily won election to the seat vacated by Congressman Paul N. McCloskey, a Republican, when McCloskey opted to run in the newly-formed 17th District, which includes parts of San Mateo and Santa Clara counties.

In the 17th, McCloskey won a surprisingly easy victory over Democratic attorney James Stewart in a race that had been considered to be a close one.

San Francisco's Democratic Congressman Phillip Burton won in a landslide over Republican Edlo Powell in the Fifth District.

In Alameda County, Congressman Ron Dellums (Dem-Oakland) apparently was defeating his Republi-

See Back Page

S.F. Passes Both Bonds And Prop. K

Bond issues to finance improvement of the city's water and sewer systems —A and B on the ballot—were approved yesterday by San Francisco voters.

The measures authorize spending $39 million on water facilities and $25 million for sewer work.

The water bonds had been opposed by some conservationists who argued that passage of the measure would encourage population growth on the San Mateo county coast. Proponents disagreed.

Proposition K, calling for the re-opening of Park and Potrero police stations, was narrowly approved, despite strong opposition from police officials.

Voters turned down Proposition C, a proposal that would have dropped two city officials—the chief administrative officer and the utilities manager—from the planning commission and also defeated "L"—providing for a primary election for the office of mayor.

Details on Page 5C

Inside

Detailed coverage of the election appears on the following ten pages.

Senate, House Contests

N.Y. Times Service

New York

The Democratic party withstood the Nixon landslide yesterday to retain control of both Houses of Congress.

With voters in all parts of the Nation splitting their tickets in unprecedented numbers, the Democrats brought off a series of startling upsets in the Senate contests to gain at least one seat, just as they did in the face of the Eisenhower sweep of 1956.

The Democrats captured previously Republican seats in five states — Delaware, Iowa, Kentucky, Maine and South Dakota.

Those pickups more than offset Republican gains in two South-western states, Oklahoma and New Mexico, and two Southern states, Virginia and North Carolina.

The figures for the House were far less complete, but the Republicans were not making the gains they needed to take control. It appeared that they would pick up somewhere in the neighborhood of a dozen seats; they had already gained seven.

At present, the Senate lineup is 54 Democrats, 45 Republicans, one Conservative-Republican and one Independent who votes with the Democrats. In the House it is 255 Democrats, 177 Republicans and three vacancies.

IOWA

Perhaps the most dramatic example of the cross-tide at work came in Iowa, a traditionally Republican state that gave Mr. Nixon a traditionally heavy majority this year. But in the senate race, Senator Jack Miller, a relatively colorless Republican moderate who had served two terms, was beaten by

See Back Page

AP Wirephoto

PAT NIXON GAVE THE PRESIDENT A VICTORY KISS
They appeared at Republican headquarters in Washington

State Legislature --Marks Re-Elected

By Jerry Carroll

State Senator Milton Marks defeated San Francisco Supervisor Ron Pelosi yesterday in a race Marks called "the most bitter" he has ever had.

And it appeared that the Republicans may have captured control of the State Senate by winning a race in the north of the state by a razor-thin margin.

With 1309 of 1351 precincts reporting, Marks had 164,498 votes to 110,942 for Pelosi.

Marks once again convincingly demonstrated that a Republican who is liberal enough can win office and hold it in a city with an overwhelming edge in Democratic voters.

Beforehand, the race was expected to be one of the closest contests of the 100 races for state legislative office in California.

But in the final weeks of the campaign, Marks — with solid labor support — easily pulled away from the personable Democratic president of the Board of Supervisors.

In all, there were 80 As-

See Back Page

The Rain Should End Today

An erratic little weather front brought rain and gusty winds to the Bay Area yesterday morning, but by early afternoon skies had cleared, and today promises to be fair.

The rains started before 3 a.m. and .15 of an inch had fallen by 1 p.m., bringing the seasonal total to 7.12, about 5½ inches more than normal. At this time last year, San Francisco had had less than a half-inch of rain.

It snowed most of the night in the Sierra, and tire chains were required over the summits on Interstate Route 80 and U.S. Highway 50.

California Gives Nixon Big Margin

By Michael Harris

President Nixon capped his nationwide landslide last night with a victory that seemed sure to top a million votes in his native California.

His total vote approached the record set by President Lyndon B. Johnson, who defeated Barry Goldwater in 1964 by a statewide margin of nearly 1.4 million votes.

The count came in slowly last night and early this morning, however, and complete returns were not expected until after daylight.

But this was the total with 46 per cent of the California vote tabulated in the race between Mr. Nixon and Senator George S. McGovern:

Nixon 2,097,134
McGovern 1,575,834

San Francisco was one of the few exceptions to Mr. Nixon's statewide victory pattern. McGovern carried the city decisively.

Elsewhere, the President

See Back Page

Hotel Collapses --Seven Killed

Bangkok

A newly built three-story hotel collapsed in the provincial capital of Nakhon Sawan north of here yesterday, killing at least seven people.

Others were feared buried under the brick and concrete debris.

Reuters

Nixon Sweeps Nation In Popular Vote--Electoral Landslide

N.Y. Times Service

Washington

President Nixon won re-election by a huge majority yesterday, perhaps the largest ever given a president.

Mr. Nixon scored a stunning personal triumph in all sections of the country, sweeping erstwhile Democratic bastions from coast to coast.

He was gathering more than 60 per cent of the popular vote and won 521 electoral votes. He lost only Massachusetts and the District of Columbia, a total of 17 electoral votes, in a victory reminiscent of the landslide triumphs of Frankin D. Roosevelt in 1936 and Lyndon B. Johnson in 1964.

Despite this drubbing of Senator George McGovern, the Democratic challenger, the voters split their tickets in record numbers to leave the Democrats in control of both houses of Congress and a majority of the nation's governorships.

★ ★ ★

With 81 per cent of the vote counted, the totals were:

Nixon: 38,816,064 62 per cent
McGovern: 23,422,335 37

The President seemed certain to claim a clear mandate for his policies of gradual disengagement from Vietnam, continued strong spending on defense, opposition to busing to integrate the schools and a slowdown in federal spending for social programs—the issues which he had stressed through the campaign.

Vindication

The 59-year-old Mr. Nixon—who will be 60 before inauguration on January 20—could also claim a resounding personal vindication against the strong charges of corruption brought against him personally by the opposition. By coincidence the greatest triumph of his 26 years in national politics came on the tenth anniversary of his defeat for governor of California—the night he told newsmen they would not have Nixon to kick around anymore.

McGovern, 50, conceded defeat before midnight in the East with a telegram of support for the President if he leads the Nation to peace abroad and justice at home.

The President responded in a brief address from the White House, expressing appreciation to his supporters and respect for the supporters of McGovern, whose name he pronounced for the first time in months. He promised rapid progress toward peace and prosperity.

Agnew

Mr. Nixon carried into office again his running mate, Vice President Spiro T. Agnew, who will now be regarded as a formidable candidate for the Republican presidential nomination four years hence. His opponent, Robert Sargent Shriver Jr., has left many with the impression that he, too, will seek to lead his party.

Unlike four years ago, when he became the 37th President by the slenderest of margins, Mr. Nixon did not suffer even a moment's suspense yesterday. As

See Back Page

Index

Comics 30
Deaths 41
Entertainment 48
People 15
TV-Radio 46
Weather 40

Inside

Investigators picked their way past unexploded bombs to find the cause of the massive Roseville explosion. Page 2.

Indians held a wake for a militant who was shot to death in a gun battle with federal marshals at Wounded Knee. Page 2.

Marin Municipal Water District directors imposed an immediate two-week moratorium on new water connections. Page 2.

The Delancey Street Foundation received a one-month delay of the order to halt boarding-house use of two Pacific Heights mansions. Page 2.

San Quentin officials have tightened security to stop stabbings that are apparently related to the drug trade. Page 3.

The administration proposed tax reforms that would go after

TOP OF THE NEWS

large, sheltered incomes and make filing easier. Page 4.

The administration will soon introduce national health insurance legislation, Caspar Weinberger said. Page 4.

The Commission on Civil Rights said segregation in housing grows out of official action by federal, state and local governments. Page 4.

Watergate is taking its place in history along with Teapot Dome and the Grant scandals of the last century. Page 5.

Comment on Watergate developments by various officials here ranged from restrained approval to "It's about time." Page 6.

Members of Congress joined in praise for President Nixon's shakeup, but there was also talk of impeachment. Page 6.

The U.S. ambassador to Britain wrote a letter praising Mr. Nixon's policies at the bidding of a close Nixon aide. Page 8.

In a possibly significant Mideast development, jets from other Arab nations are reportedly visiting Egyptian bases. Page 10.

Libya's Colonel Khadafy banned all foreign travelers except those with Arabic-language passports. Page 10.

Henry Kissinger will fly to Moscow Friday for talks with Soviet Communist party leader Leonid Brezhnev. Page 11.

Paul F. Lawrence was relieved as regional commissioner of education here and reassigned to Washington. Page 12.

Electric acupuncture used in Hong Kong apparently has cured drug addicts, a Cupertino physician reported. Page 15.

Stag-hunting with hounds has become a corporate venture in France. Page 17.

West Coast longshoremen's president Harry Bridges called for a strike strategy against unfair wage controls. Page 52.

Weather

Bay Area: Fair and warmer Tuesday, but some coastal low cloudiness. High in the 70s except 60s near the ocean; low, in the 40s. Page 32.

Nixon's TV Talk on Watergate

See Below

San Francisco Chronicle

★★★★ FINAL

The Largest Daily Circulation in Northern California

109th Year No. 121 ★★★★ TUESDAY, MAY 1, 1973 GArfield 1-1111 15 CENTS

Top White House Aides Quit---President Explains

Haldeman, Ehrlichman Both Out

Washington Post Service

Washington

President Nixon accepted the resignations yesterday of his chief White House advisers, H. R. Haldeman and John D. Ehrlichman, and of Attorney General Richard G. Kleindienst.

He also announced that he had fired his counsel, John W. Dean III, who thus became a casualty of the very scandal the President had charged him to investigate.

The dramatic news of the dismantling of the White House command staff that served Mr. Nixon through his first four years in the presidency was the most devastating impact that the Watergate scandal has yet made on the administration.

REPLACE

The President immediately set into motion a major reshuffling of top administration personnel to replace the Watergate casualties.

Defense Secretary Elliot L. Richardson was appointed to replace Kleindienst and to take over responsibility for "uncovering the whole truth" about the Watergate scandal.

As temporary successor to Dean, the President chose his special consultant, Leonard Garment. Mr. Nixon said Garment "will represent the White House in all matters relating to the Watergate investigation and will report directly to me."

The immediate reaction to the White House announcement was a mixture of re-

See Back Page

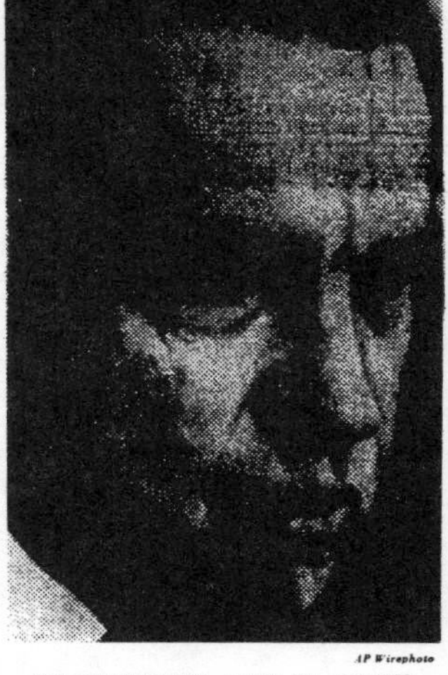

AP Wirephoto

PRESIDENT NIXON AFTER TV ADDRESS
He brushed away tears and said, 'It wasn't easy'

A Subdued Nixon Visits the Press

Washington

Moments after he completed his television speech tonight, President Nixon walked into the room where the White House briefings are held each morning.

With no Secret Service agents or aides accompanying him, he stepped behind the podium where Ronald Ziegler, his press secretary, usually answers reporters' questions. The lights in that part of the room were out. He stood in the shadows.

Then the President looked out to a group of 15 reporters and photographers who were standing there chatting. His voice was low; he appeared shaken.

"Ladies and gentlemen of the press," Mr. Nixon said, "we have had our differences in the past, and I hope you give me hell every time you think I'm wrong. I hope I'm worthy of your trust."

Then he turned and walked back toward the presidential living quarters upstairs.

N.Y. Times Service

Nixon Calls for Truth--Accepts Responsibility For Watergate Affair

N.Y. Times Service

Washington

President Nixon told the nation last night he had no knowledge of political espionage or attempts to cover it up in the Watergate case but that he would accept full responsibility for what happened.

The President went on television and radio to explain his feelings after he received the resignations of three top staff members who have been implicated in the case—H. R. Haldeman, John D. Ehrlichman and John W. Dean III. He also accepted the resignation of Attorney General Richard G. Kleindienst.

Last night Mr. Nixon was tense and grave. At the start of the speech he stumbled several times as he shuffled the pages from which he read. Afterward, technicians in the room said the President brushed tears from his eyes and said, "It wasn't easy."

COVERUP

As the President accepted the responsibility and pledged every effort to achieve justice in the case, he alleged wrongdoing or coverup attempts on the part of those he had delegated to run his 1972 presidential campaign and those he appointed to investigate the matter during the campaign. And he implied that his own election officials, in the Watergate espionage, were attempting to stop wrongdoing by the Democrats.

Mr. Nixon also said that hereafter the investigation of the Watergate matters would be delegated to his new attorney general, Elliott L. Richardson, while he, the President, turned his attention to grave foreign and domestic matters.

The speech, which came after weeks of growing tension at the White House as developments in the Watergate scandals implicated administration figures, was an emotional appeal to save the integrity of the presidency for the 1481 days — Mr. Nixon's count — remaining in his term.

PRAYERS

"Tonight I ask for your prayers to help me in everything that I do," Mr. Nixon said at the end. "God bless America, and God bless each and every one of you."

He gave the country the explanation that American leaders had been urging him to do for months.

First, he sought to estab-

See Back Page

UPI Telephoto

ELLIOT RICHARDSON
New attorney general

Ellsberg Demands Testimony on Link

Associated Press

Los Angeles

Daniel Ellsberg's chief attorney asked yesterday that 11 present and former government officials be ordered here to tell what they know about links between Watergate conspirators and an alleged burglary of an office containing Ellsberg's psychiatric records.

Attorney Leonard Boudin said he wants to find out whether the Pentagon Papers indictment was part of "political espionage" plot.

U.S. District Judge Matt Byrne took the request under submission but said affidavits probably would have to be taken from the men before they were called to testify at the trial.

The witnesses Boudin wants to call to a special hearing include former Attorney General John N. Mitchell, just - resigned Attorney General Richard G. Kleindienst, resigned White House aide John Ehrlichman, former acting FBI Director L. Patrick Gray and convicted Watergate conspirators E. Howard Hunt and G. Gordon Liddy.

Boudin also named former special presidential counsel Charles W. Colson; John W. Dean III, ousted yesterday as presidential counsel;

See Back Page

Rogers Gives Legal Case For Bombing

N.Y. Times Service

Washington

Secretary of State William P. Rogers said yesterday that the continued American bombing in Cambodia is legally justified by the Constitution and is "a meaningful interim action" to force the Communists to agree to a cease-fire there.

Testifying before the Senate Foreign Relations Committee, Rogers presented the administration's long-awaited legal justification for the Cambodia bombing — an issue that has aroused considerable criticism from members of the committee, including its chairman J. W. Fulbright (Dem-Ark.).

They have argued that President Nixon had no legal basis for the bombing now that all American troops have been withdrawn from South Vietnam.

SWAY

Although the committee members generally treated Rogers in a friendly fashion, his arguments, both in his comments to the committee, and in his 13-page legal

See Back Page

Doctors Who OKd Kemper

By Rick Carroll
Chronicle Correspondent

Santa Cruz

Edmund Emil Kemper III had already killed three of his victims in the Bay Area and Santa Cruz when two psychiatrists examined the hulking young man and declared him no danger to society, authorities said here yesterday.

Only three days after he killed and dismembered a 15-year-old Berkeley girl, they said, Kemper was given a clean bill of mental health by the court-appointed psychiatrists in a juvenile court proceeding in Fresno, they said.

Details of the psychiatric examination came to light at a press conference held before the arraignment of Kemper here on charges of murdering six young women

See Back Page

2nd Step Today

S.F. Board OKs Yerba Proposal

By Jerry Burns

A proposed settlement of the Yerba Buena controversy — guaranteeing construction of low-cost housing for persons forced to move by the $385 million convention center project — was approved yesterday by the Board of Supervisors.

The amended plan for the center was passed, 10 to 1, in an effort to end the suit that has blocked the project for more than four years.

It will be presented today to the Redevelopment Agency, which is expected to also approve it.

The proposed settlement, which still has a number of legal steps to mount before the suit is actually dismissed, calls for the city to allocate about $500,000 a year from hotel taxes for construction of low-cost housing on the edges of the south-of-Market project area.

SUIT

"The beauty of the settlement is that it will settle this 4½-year lawsuit without an increase in the hotel tax or in the property tax," said Supervisor Robert Mendelsohn.

He said that one-half cent of the hotel tax (now six cents on the dollar) will be used for rehousing persons forced to move by the Yerba Buena project, plus $100,-000-per-year from surpluses in the hotel tax fund.

Robert Rumsey, executive director of the Redevelopment Agency, said that approval of the proposed agreement by the five-member Agency board will allow his staff to approach residents of the project area to discuss moving out of the way of the convention center, sports arena and parking complex.

For the last several years, Agency staff members have been barred from discussing relocation by order of the federal court.

Rumsey and Anthony Kline, attorney for Tenants and Owners Opposed to Redevelopment, said after the supervisors' meeting that several additional steps are necessary before TOOR's suit is actually dismissed.

The supervisors had adopted a plan last week which would have allocated $400,000 from hotel taxes for the low cost housing, but they had to increase the amount to about a half a million dollars yesterday because Kline and his clients refused the first amount.

Still to come are actions by the Redevelopment Agency and the supervisors to amend the Yerba Buena plan to include an estimated 400 units of low-cost housing, paid for by hotel taxes, and another vote by the supervisors to re-allocate the hotel tax funds in accord with the agreement.

The only vote cast in opposition came from Supervisor Quentin Kopp, who argued that the vote was premature.

He said that, since the supervisors must hold another hearing and vote on amending the Yerba Buena plan, the vote on the proposed settlement should come later.

Controls Extended Another Year

Washington

With the reluctant support of the Administration, both houses of Congress approved yesterday and sent to the White House a compromise bill extending for another year President Nixon's authority to regulate wages and prices.

Mr. Nixon signed the bill into law later. The existing law was to have expired at midnight.

The vote in the House was 267 to 115, a larger margin for passage than appeared likely before the Easter recess. The voice vote in the Senate was unrecorded.

Mr. Nixon had sought a simple one-year extension of the act, but with the public's frustration over sharp price increases in recent months, proponents of stiffer controls and relief for low-income families managed to include in the bill several provisions initially opposed by the Administration.

One such provision increased to 25.2 million from 16.3 million the number of workers exempt from the government's standards for noninflationary pay increases. The bill did so by raising the maximum wage for such exemption to $3.50 an hour from $2.75.

Another provision disliked by the Administration requires public disclosure of some information on costs and profits by big corporations that raise prices by more than 1.5 per cent a year.

The measure was the version reported by a joint conference committee April 18 following initial passage in the two chambers of disparate bills.

Administration strategists, fearful that the basic authority might expire, recommended adoption despite the disliked provisions.

L.A. Times Service

Index

Comics	56
Deaths	32
Entertainment	38
Finance	49
People	16
TV-Radio	36
Vital Statistics	32
Weather	32

Inside

Harvey Rose, San Francisco's budget analyst, will go to Sacramento as the new auditor general of the state. Page 2.

Labor Day weekend offers a cornucopia of fun-filled activities for stay-at-homes in the delightful Bay Area. Page 3.

The 84th Fighter Interceptor Squadron left Hamilton and ended a chapter in Bay Area military history. Page 5.

The Delta jet that crashed in Boston, killing 88, had a history of electronics problems, investigators said. Page 5.

PG&E warned of an "electrical energy crisis" unless it gets permission to convert some facilities from natural gas to oil. Page 7.

An emergency appeals court gave the Cost of Living Council the go-ahead to impose price ceilings on gasoline Saturday. Page 10.

Spiro Agnew dropped to a tie with Ronald Reagan in a Gallup poll of GOP preference for the 1976 presidential nomination. Page 12.

West Point has rewritten its regulations, and the new cadet code now emphasizes self-discipline. Page 13.

The FBI's new chief disclosed what he is doing to improve the bureau's efficiency, techniques and public relations. Page 14.

A big rescue effort has begun to save two Britons trapped in a tiny submarine deep in the Atlantic off Ireland. Page 15.

Susan Agnew, the vice president's daughter, flew home from Brazil after threats on her life were reported. Page 17.

The CIA is reportedly trying to sell its controlling interest in a charter airline. Page 18.

Cambodian President Lon Nol held a rare press conference, but answered only previously submitted questions. Page 19.

Couture fashions are no longer front page news, and the press has become irreverent about the subject. Page 22.

The French think Mr. Nixon is trying to force Agnew to resign, according to former JFK aide Pierre Salinger. Page 23.

Debutantes have gone a step beyond the traditional curtsey—now it's Debs on Ice. Page 26.

Despite a lack of good news, the stock market made a broad gain on the heaviest trading in a month. Page 57.

Weather

Bay Area: Fair Thursday, cloudiness night and morning. Highs near 60 on coast to 80s inland; lows, 50s. Page 45.

How to Have a Big Weekend

See Page 3

San Francisco Chronicle

★★★★ FINAL

The Largest Daily Circulation in Northern California

109th Year No. 242 ★★★★ THURSDAY, AUGUST 30, 1973 GArfield 1-1111 15 CENTS

Mideast Merger

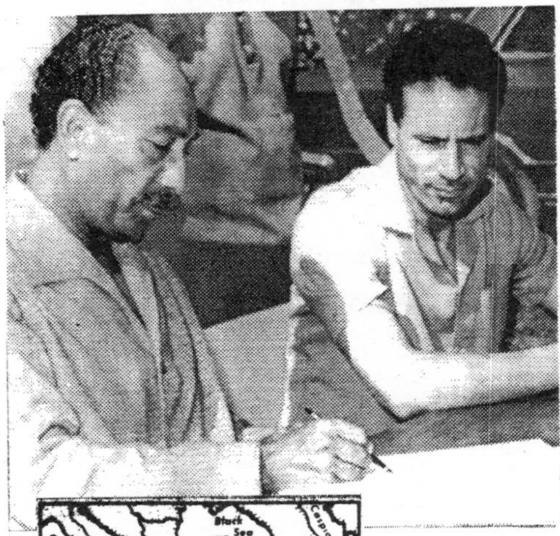

AP Wirephotos

President Sadat and Khadafy (top) signed the agreement that will merge their two nations.

A Gradual Union of Egypt, Libya

By Jim Hoagland
Washington Post

Cairo

Egypt announced last night details of a gradual merger with Libya.

The plan indicates that Libyan President Moammar Khadafy has finally agreed to a step-by-step union of the two Arab states instead of an immediate merger.

While awarding the rhetorical points to Khadafy, who had insisted on immediate merger in order to create a new Arab nation to confront Israel, the announcement over Cairo Radio at the end of two days of talks between Egyptian President Anwar Sadat and the Libyan president outlined the need for further delays and more study of the merger.

Khadafy was reported by official sources to have left Cairo for Libya late yesterday after signing the merger agreement with Sadat.

FEATURES

The main features of the 13-point communique that began by announcing "the birth of the unified Arab nation" of Libya and Egypt were:

● Referendums will be held in both countries to choose a president and endorse a constitution for the unified state. But no specific date was set for the referendum, which Khadafy had demanded should be held Saturday.

● A Constituent Assembly composed of 50 members from each country will oversee the referendum and act as a "founding assembly" for the unified state. It will draft the constitution and nominate candidates for

Back Page Col. 8

Mao, Chou Win China Policy Fight

Hong Kong

Delegates representing more than 28 million Chinese Communist party members met in Peking August 24-28 in the tenth National Congress and reaffirmed the leadership and policies of Chairman Mao Tse-tung and Premier Chou En-lai, according to a communique broadcast yesterday by Peking radio.

The 1249 delegates, in effect, endorsed the Mao-Chou program aimed at improving relations with the United States while at the same time denouncing "the hegemonism of the two superpowers: The U.S. and the USSR."

The initial reports on the congress indicated that Mao and Chou had successfully repulsed a counter-attack by pro-Soviet radical elements during recent weeks.

CHEERS

UPI correspondent Sylvana Foa reported from Peking last night that fireworks lit the sky and cheering workers celebrated in the streets as news of the conclusion of the congress spread through the Chinese capital.

Communist party functionaries scurried across the city spreading the news, calling workers and functionaries out of their homes and factories, she said.

Thousands of people marched through the city, beating drums and clanging cymbals carrying portraits of Mao and chanting, "Long live chairman Mao."

All public buildings were brightly lit and streets filled

Back Page Col. 6

10-Cent Letter Possible Soon

Los Angeles

Postmaster General E. T. Klassen said yesterday a 10-cent stamp for first class mail was possible in the near future and a 15-cent stamp may not be far behind.

The only way postage rates could be held down would be for congress to increase subsidies to the U.S. Postal Service, Klassen said.

United Press

Bitter Clash Over Reagan Tax Initiative

Sacramento

Legislative analyst A. Alan Post bitterly denounced Governor Ronald Reagan's tax ceiling plan as "a terrible thing" yesterday and recommended $786 million in major state spending cuts if voters approve the ceiling.

The cuts involved such things as slashing compensatory and early childhood education, charging tuition at community colleges, forcing local governments to take over some road building and highway patrol functions, eliminating state aid for county fairs, abolishing renter tax breaks and reducing property tax exemptions for senior citizens.

The legislature's nonpartisan fiscal adviser told the Assembly Ways and Means Committee during an unusually angry hearing that these cuts would be "impractical" but necessary if Reagan's tax initiative passes at a special election November 6.

ASSERTIONS

Post said 25 per cent of current state services either would have be be eliminated, shifted to local governments or turned over to the private sector.

He asserted that Reagan's proposal would force a $620 million cutback in state spending during the next fiscal year compared to what otherwise would be appropriated, and this would increase to nearly $1.4 billion by the 1977-78 fiscal year.

Post's contentions were fiercely disputed by the spokesman for Reagan at the hearing, chief deputy state finance director Kenneth F. Hall. But Hall said the administration would not have its own figures until October 1.

"It is very easy to criticize someone else's analysis if you haven't made one yourself," snapped a Republican committee member, Assemblyman Gordon Duffy of Hanford.

The administration renewed its attempt launched by Reagan Tuesday to discredit Post as a political puppet of Assembly Speaker

Back Page Col. 6

Judge Orders Tapes--Nixon Won't Comply

Sirica Wants to Hear Them Before Ruling On Confidentiality

Washington

President Nixon was ordered yesterday by Judge John J. Sirica to make tape recordings of White House conversations involving the Watergate case available to him for a decision on their use by a grand jury.

Presidential aides announced, however, that Mr. Nixon "will not comply with the order."

A White House statement said the President's lawyers were considering appealing the decision by Judge Sirica, who is chief judge of the U.S. District Court here, but it also hinted that they might find some other method of sustaining the President's legal position.

APPEAL

Faced with a refusal by Mr. Nixon to accept the court's ruling or to challenge it by an appeal, Archibald Cox, the special prosecutor, might initiate contempt proceedings or begin an appeal of his own, based on the court's refusal to give him the tapes directly.

It was only the second time in the nation's history that a court had required a President, against his will, to produce his private records as evidence, and the decision was certain to have serious political, governmental and legal consequences, both immediate and long-range.

Sirica said he was "simply unable" to decide whether the President's refusal to release the tapes and related documents was valid without inspecting the recordings himself. He upheld the authority of the court to take such action.

EVIDENCE

If he finds evidence relating to criminal activity in the tapes and it can be successfully separated from the privileged statements dealing with the President's official duties, the judge said, he will extract it and pass it along to the Watergate grand jury over which Archibald Cox, the special prosecutor, is presiding.

"If privileged and unprivileged evidence are so inextricably connected that separation becomes impossible," he continued, "the whole must be privileged and no disclosure made to the grand jury."

Only once before, in 1807, has a federal court ordered

Back Page Col. 1

AP Wirephoto

JUDGE JOHN SIRICA.
Hands full of Watergate

Court Hears Another Tape Plea

Washington

The White House asked a federal judge yesterday to refuse the Ervin committee's demand for President Nixon's Watergate tapes, charging the committee had exceeded its authority by conducting a "criminal investigation and trial."

The Senate committee promptly countered with a request that chief U.S. District Judge John J. Sirica issue a summary judgment — without further deliberation — for immediate release of the disputed tapes, which could yield conclusive evidence of who is telling the truth about the scandal.

The court exchange came a few hours before Sirica ruled on a similar demand for the tapes by special Wat-

Back Page Col. 1

AP Wirephoto

THE DISASTER IN RIO BLANCO
Residents dug through the rubble of their homes

Mexico Counts Its Quake Dead

Mexico City

Hampered by torrential rains, relief workers slogged through muddy rubble yesterday in search of victims entombed by the massive earthquake that jolted much of Central America early Tuesday.

Official figures put the death toll at 575 and the count was rising steadily as new reports sifted in to the capital from remote towns and villages.

Injuries were officially said to number 1000 or more in the devastated mountain area extending from Puebla, 80 miles southeast of here, almost 200 miles toward the Gulf Coast at Vera Cruz. Uncounted thousands were driven from their shattered homes.

FLOODS

The earthquake struck as vast areas of the nation were reeling from the effects of severe flooding in the wake of Hurricane Brenda.

Rivers were still on the rise as the death toll from widespread floods approached 100. Damage to rich farm and cattle land was extensive.

President Luis Echeverria Alvarez, who spent much of last week in an on-the-spot assessment of flood damage, flew into the quake region yesterday.

Accompanied by half-

Back Page Col. 5

Smallpox Wiped Out in Western Hemisphere

Atlanta

Smallpox has been declared officially dead in the Western Hemisphere.

A five-man commission concluded last week that Brazil, the last stronghold of smallpox in the Americas, has eradicated the disease.

"There is none left in the Western Hemisphere," Dr. Joseph Millar, one of the commissioners, said Tuesday.

Millar, director of the Bureau of State Services at the National Center for Disease Control here, said he and doctors from Canada, Venezuela, Portugal and Brazil checked medical records and performed spot examinations for two weeks ending last weekend.

Brazil began its eradication program in the late 1960s as part of the United Nations World Health Organization's international attack on the serious skin disease.

Associated Press

Index

Comics	60
Deaths	40
Entertainment	46
Finance	56
People	22
TV-Radio	44
Vital Statistics	40
Weather	45

Inside

Some questions still exist, but there is a formal procedure for filling a vacancy in the vice presidency. Page 3.

Governor Reagan was about the only California politician who wouldn't speculate on a successor to Vice President Agnew. Page 4.

The new war is forcing the Israeli public to revise its preconceived notions of Arab military inferiority. Page 10.

Iraq confirmed its full-scale entry into the war against Israel, and Jordan seemed likely to follow suit. Page 10.

Negotiators reported that an agreement may be near on a big price increase in crude oil. Page 11.

TOP OF THE NEWS

Fighting continues on the Golan Heights around the bodies of soldiers killed in the fierce battles for the heights. Page 12.

The financial plight of a San Rafael institution for the handicapped caused an angry reaction at a state hearing. Page 13.

A youthful spy for the Republicans told how easy it was for him to infiltrate Democratic camps in 1972. Page 14.

The Senate gave final approval to a bill limiting presidential powers to wage war. Page 15.

Acupuncture is used in less than half the operations in China and will never become more common than hypnosis in U.S. hospitals, anesthesiologists said. Page 15.

A letter found near two Monterey county murder victims was signed by the group that said it shot down an Oakland police helicopter. Page 20.

Rate increases of about 18 per cent were requested by the city's two garbage collection firms. Page 21.

BART has announced a three-pronged effort to solve its safety problems. Page 23.

Bay Area campuses today are quieter than they were in the '60s but students say that doesn't mean a return to the '50s. Page 26.

Now it's fashionable for women of all ages to look, well, terrible. Page 27.

The past five years have seen a boom in requests for sterilizations from single persons. Page 29.

The resignation of Vice President Agnew ignited a sharp burst of selling on the New York Stock Exchange. Page 60.

Weather

Bay Area: Cloudy Thursday. Highs, mid-60s to mid-70s; lows, 40s to low 50s. Afternoon winds up to 20 m.p.h. Page 43.

A's Lose; Mets Win Pennant

See Sports

San Francisco Chronicle

★★★★ **FINAL**

The Largest Daily Circulation in Northern California

109th Year No. 284 ★★★★ THURSDAY, OCTOBER 11, 1973 GArfield 1-1111 15 CENT

Agnew Resigns--Court Fines Him in Tax Case

U. S. Thinks Soviets Flying Arms to Arabs

Washington

Administration officials said yesterday there are indications that the Soviet Union is flying military equipment to resupply Egyptian and Syrian forces.

The Defense Department refused to confirm or deny reports that Israel is flying military supplies from the U.S., and from American bases in Britain and West Germany.

State Department spokesman Robert J. McCloskey said that if the Soviets are engaged in a massive resupply effort, this would put a "new face" on the Middle East conflict. But McCloskey said he is "not in a position to confirm that any of this is taking place at this time."

Other officials, apparently acting upon instructions laid down by the State Department, volunteered information about the reported Soviet airlift. These officials were providing "background" for newsmen and therefore cannot be identified.

Until yesterday, U.S. officials had been extremely reluctant to discuss any details of the Middle East

Back Page Col. 5

He Pleads No Contest-- Justice Dept. Reveals Evidence, Closes Case

By Eugene V. Risher
United Press

Washington

Spiro T. Agnew resigned as Vice President of the United States "in the best interest of the nation" yesterday, and pleaded no contest in U.S. District Court in Baltimore to a single count of income tax evasion in 1967.

The Justice Department at the same time dropped its criminal investigation of Agnew, and made public in court its evidence that Agnew was receiving cash payments from Maryand contractors as late as December, 1972.

Agnew, 54, who was fined $10,000 and placed on three years' probation, was the second Vice President in history to resign and the first to quit office under fire.

Nixon

Expressing a "great sense of personal loss," President Nixon said he would begin prompt consultations with national leaders of both parties on selecting a new Vice President, who must be confirmed by a majority vote of the House and Senate.

The White House said Mr. Nixon, who learned of the surprise decision during a 40-minute meeting with Agnew Tuesday night, played "no direct role" in the legal arrangement for his Vice President to resign and—in effect—plead guilty to a lesser charge.

Agnew left office less than two weeks after he declared in Los Angeles that he would "stay and fight" and would not resign even if indicted. But yesterday, he appeared unexpectedly before U.S. District Judge Walter E. Hoffman in Baltimore and, speaking in a low, firm voice, ended irrevocably his once-meteoric political career.

Interview

In an interview later, Agnew said he would address the nation within the next few days.

"The reason that I have changed my decision . . . is because I believe it would be against the national interest and have a brutalizing effect on my family to go through a long, two-to-three-year struggle in this matter," he told reporters outside the federal courthouse.

"I categorically and flatly deny the assertions that were made by the prosecutors with regard to their contentions of bribery and extortion on my part," said Agnew, who apparently could still face

Back Page Col. 1

Out of Office

SPIRO AGNEW OUTSIDE COURTHOUSE IN BALTIMORE
He said he was acting 'in the best interest of the nation'

Israel Says Its Troops Raided Across the Canal

By Charles Mohr
New York Times

Tel Aviv

Israeli ground troops struck across the Suez Canal early today for the first time in the fourth Arab-Israeli war and attacked Egyptian convoys, the Israeli command said.

Israeli commandos crossed the 200-foot-wide canal in its southern sector and returned without casualties after attacking "convoys and rear echelons of the enemy," the command said at dawn today.

Yesterday, the intensity of fighting in the Middle East war dwindled, but Israel prepared for a possible attack by Jordan and warned that nation not to join Egypt and Syria in the conflict.

Israel claimed to have driven the Syrian army out of the Golan Heights and back to the 1967 cease-fire line.

However, the Israeli forces clearly seemed to have suspended a counterattack aimed at ejecting Egyptian forces occupying the eastern bank of the Suez Canal.

A highly informed source said Israel now estimates the Egyptian invasion force at five divisions, which could be close to 75,000 men. The force, he said, crossed with about 800 tanks, and from 300 to 400 of these may still be operational.

"It was a very uneventful day," said an authoritative source. "There were small skirmishes on both fronts but no serious offensives."

The Iraqi command announced that its air and ground forces had joined the war against Israel and were taking "an active part" in the fighting on both fronts.

BOMBING

The Israeli air force bombed two airfields in the Nile delta area of Egypt, and a naval headquarters, fuel installation and power plant in Syria. But even in the air the intensity of operations slackened.

Prime Minister Golda Meir took the unusual step of broadcasting an address to the nation on the religious holiday of Succoth, the Feast of the Tabernacles, and said she had no doubt that the war would end in victory. She added, however, that the victory was not yet complete and that "it may take more than six days.

"But I am glad," she said,

Back Page Col. 7

Firsthand Look at War in the Sinai

By Henry Tanner
New York Times

In the Sinai Peninsula

Egyptian soldiers, tanks and equipment are continuing to pour across the Suez Canal, a group of Western correspondents confirmed from the battle area yesterday.

On a 3½ hour tour into the Sinai peninsula, this correspondent also saw evidence that Egyptian forces had reached positions ten miles or more east of the canal in some parts of the sector.

In the air war the Egyptians said they had shot down six more Israeli planes. Egyptian aircraft were said to have attacked Israeli command headquarters, combat units and administrative installations on the northern Sinai coast.

The Egyptian soldiers were in high spirits and seemed oblivious to Israeli shells bursting near them.

"Don't worry, God is with us" one of three young soldiers shouted laughingly to correspondents who had ducked for cover when a shell burst too close for comfort.

Trucks interspersed with antiaircraft guns were lined up in open country on the west bank waiting visibly without fear of air attack for their turn to cross.

They were waved onto the

Back Page Col. 5

Nixon's Search For a New No. 2

By Rudy Abramson
Los Angeles Times

Washington

Vice President Agnew's resignation yesterday came like a thunderbolt, threatening Republican party unity and setting the spark for yet another struggle between President Nixon and the Democratic-controlled Congress.

Speculation on a successor — who will be nominated by the President and who must be approved by both houses of Congress — was instantaneous.

The President set about his task immediately. He canvassed Republican congressional leaders at a late-afternoon meeting and Speaker Carl Albert (Dem-Okla.) and Senate Majority Leader Mike Mansfield (Dem-Mont.) in early evening.

GOP Chairman George Bush wired all members of the Republican national committee for their recommendations while White House chief of staff Alexander Haig sent telegrams to the 19 Republican governors for their suggestions.

ENVELOPES

Senate minority leader Hugh Scott (Rep-Pa.) told Republican senators to submit up to three names in sealed envelopes by this afternoon. "The envelopes I deliver will not be shown to anyone," Scott said.

Both Scott and Mansfield said they anticipated a presidential decision before the end of the week. 'There will not be any undue delays," Scott said. "The country will not be in suspense for too long."

Mansfield said he proposed two names and that Albert added another. While declining to name them, Mansfield said none is a potential 1976 GOP presidential candidate but that all would be confirmed by both houses with no trouble.

CRITERIA

Scott said Mr. Nixon asked them to help him make the decision, commenting, "the President has an open mind. He has simple criteria — a man or a

Back Page Col. 1

Agnew May Face More Tax Trouble

Washington

Former Vice President Spiro Agnew's plea of "no contest" yesterday in the income tax evasion case against him may mark only the beginning of difficulties for him with the Internal Revenue Service.

An official spokesman for Internal Revenue said that so far as the agency was aware, there was nothing in the agreement that led to Agnew's resignation that would prohibit Internal Revenue from attempting to collect taxes on every payment to Agnew that can be documented as having been made but not reported on his tax returns.

The charge of tax evasion, to which Agnew pleaded "nolo contendere," involved $29,500. But a document released by the Justice Department detailing the evidence against the former

Back Page Col. 8

500th Gate Bridge Suicide

The Golden Gate Bridge yesterday claimed its 500th known suicide victim since the bridge was opened in 1937.

The dead man is Stephen Houg, 26, a blood technician at Franklin Hospital in San Francisco. He jumped from the east side of the north tower at 6:35 p.m.

A note found in his car, parked at Vista Point, gave his identity and said the vehicle belongs to his brother, William C. Houg, who lives in Windsor, Sonoma county.

Deputy Coroner Bill Thomas of Marin county said the victim had been living in a commune at 1126 Haight street.

Index

Comics	64
Deaths	44
Entertainment	50
Finance	59
People	26
TV-Radio	48
Vital Statistics	44
Weather	43

Inside

A clash between Nazis and Marxists was averted at a Board of Education meeting also attended by a lot of policemen. Page 2.

Angry citizens filled the State Building auditorium to protest proposed PG&E rate increases. Page 2.

A little boy kidnaped more than a year ago was found alive and well living with a couple only three miles away. Page 3.

The firm that planned to barge tons of Bay Area garbage through the Suisun Marsh has a new plan —move it by rail. Page 3.

Patricia Hearst, the kidnaped girl, is called enthusiastic and independent by friends. Page 4.

TOP OF THE NEWS

A subdued Mayor Alioto said his wife's adventure would not deter him from running for governor. Page 5.

Leaders of the black community called for continuing cooperation with the police to solve the street killings. Page 5.

A freeze on fuel prices at truck stops ordered by President Nixon failed to effect an end to the truckers' strike. Page 6.

Oregon Governor Tom McCall has a plan to swap his state's hydroelectric power for California's gasoline. Page 6.

President Nixon has reportedly refused to comply with a request by Leon Jaworski for tape recordings and other evidence. Page 7.

The House Judiciary Committee could find it necessary to subpoena the President to appear in person in its inquiry. Page 7.

An actuarial firm said that California's legislative retirement plan needs an immediate $13.4 million appropriation this year. Page 7.

The United States hopes to conclude a new treaty with Panama this year. Page 8.

British coal miners will start an all-out national strike on Sunday Page 9.

A woman candidate for president of Colombia has a good chance and she may lead the country to socialism. Page 10.

Tired of hitchhiking? A new ride center matches drivers and riders who want to travel cheaply. Page 13.

New York's Chemical Bank — sixth largest in the U.S.—lowered its prime lending rate to 9¼%. Page 53.

Weather

Bay Area: Fair Wednesday and Thursday. Lows Wednesday in 30s and 40s; highs to mid 60s. Page 36.

Mrs. Alioto's Own Story

See Below

San Francisco Chronicle

★★★★ FINAL

The Largest Daily Circulation in Northern California

110th Year No. 37 ★★★★ WEDNESDAY, FEBRUARY 6, 1974 GArfield 1-1111 15 CENTS

She's Jealous

By Larry Tiscornia

MAYOR ALIOTO AND WIFE ANGELINA
She loved him, but wanted to punish him

Hearst Daughter Abducted By 3 Armed 'Commandos'

Kidnapers Burst Into Berkeley Apartment-- Her Fiance Is Beaten

By Charles Raudebaugh

Patricia Hearst, 19, one of the five daughters of newspaper executive Randolph A. Hearst, was abducted in Berkeley Monday night by an armed kidnap team of two black men and a white woman, all in their 20s.

The FBI officially entered the search for the kidnapers last night. The passage of 24 hours without any major clue to the fate of the girl gave the FBI jurisdiction on the legal assumption that she may have been taken across a state line.

There has been no announced contact between the kidnapers and the girl's parents, and the Berkeley police admitted they lack any solid pieces of evidence.

"At this time we have no basis for speculation in any way whatsoever," said Lieutenant Henry Sanders, spokesman for the Berkeley police department.

The Hearsts last night issued a public appeal to the kidnapers not to harm their daughter.

They noted that the kidnapers "could have eliminated all witnesses" but had not done so, and that this indicated a measure of compassion.

"We want our daughter back unharmed," said Hearst. "If she is released, we will not seek to imprison her abductors.

"We plead with them to communicate with us direct or through the press."

The kidnapers, described as "acting like commandos," fired at least four rifle and pistol shots at witnesses as they carried Miss Hearst, blindfolded and screaming, from the apartment of her fiance at 2603 Benvenue avenue.

Her fiance, Steven A. Weed, 26, had been beaten and kicked almost into unconsciousness by the kidnapers. A neighbor who heard the commotion and looked into help was also beaten.

Miss Hearst's parents were in Washington, D.C. but returned at once to their Hillsborough home in the hope of hearing from the abductors.

Miss Hearst is a granddaughter of the late William Randolph Hearst, a colorful figure in the history of American journalism. Her father is president and editor of the San Francisco Examiner and chairman of the board of the Hearst Corp.

The mother of the kidnaped girl, Catherine Campbell Hearst, is a member of the Board of Regents of the University of California.

The engagement of Miss Hearst and Weed was announced in December and they plan to marry in early summer. They had met at the University of California, where Miss Hearst is a sophomore majoring in art history and Weed is a graduate student in philosophy.

Weed, a Princeton grad-

Back Page Col. 1

PATRICIA HEARST AND FIANCE, STEVEN WEED
The kidnap victim is the daughter of Randolph A. Hearst

Mayor's Wife Blames Politics

Angelina's Angry Return

By Carolyn Anspacher

Angelina Alioto angrily and defiantly told a huge press conference yesterday that she dropped from sight nearly three weeks ago in Palm Springs because of jealousy and to punish her husband.

The 58-year-old blonde wife of San Francisco Mayor Joseph Alioto stepped boldly into the shoes of Martha Mitchell less than 12 hours after she returned to her palatial Presidio Terrace home from Santa Cruz.

As Mrs. Mitchell had hysterically inveighed against the political activities of her husband, former Attorney General John Mitchell, so Mrs. Alioto said she was "frustrated" over being cast into the background of the mayor's blossoming gubernatorial campaign.

Apparently, the climax of the frustration that plunged her, she said, into "anguish" came the night of January 18 when she, her husband, and their son and daughter-in-law, the Lawrence Aliotos, attended a banquet of the Italian American Golf Tournament in Palm Springs.

The mayor, sitting beside his wife at the press conference, almost apologetically said that he had been guest of honor at the function.

"He," said Mrs. Alioto, "was on cloud 101."

She darted a swift, venomous glance at the mayor.

"My son and his wife and I were stepchildren at the dinner. I thought we would be the assets and he seemed to be trying to hide us . . ." she said.

The mayor, unnaturally pale, held tight to his wife's heavily ringed hand.

It was after the banquet, Mrs. Alioto said, that she "skipped."

The mayor flew back to San Francisco to fulfill his Saturday commitments. "And I left my son and his Anne who should have been on their second honeymoon," Mrs. Alioto said.

"He left me with anguish and I took off."

The mayor's office, during the morning, issued a tidy summary of Mrs. Alioto's 18-day hegira in a rented white Ford. Traveling as "Angelina DiPuma" (her late grandmother's name) she drove that night to nearby Indian Wells Inn.

Then she made a pilgrimage to the California missions, visiting all of the missions outside the Bay Area except those at San Fernando and San Gabriel.

"I have no regrets whatever about taking off," she said. "I now feel better edu-

Back Page Col. 5

N.Y. Doctor

'Mercy Killing' Acquittal

Mineola, N.Y.

Dr. Vincent A. Montemarano, 34, was found not guilty yesterday in the "mercy killing" death of Eugene Bauer, a terminally ill cancer patient.

It took a Nassau county jury of eight men and four women only 55 minutes to arrive at the verdict, which caused pandemonium in the crowded courtroom when it was announced.

District Attorney William Cahn, the prosecutor, smiled faintly, and then congratulated J. Russell Clune and James O'Brien, the defense lawyers.

Cahn had prosecuted the case himself, something he had not done before in his 11 years as district attorney.

There had been national interest in the trial, in part because only one other physician had ever been tried in the U.S. in a "mercy killing."

In that case, 24 years ago, the physician had been accused of having killed a woman dying of cancer by injecting air into her veins.

He was acquitted.

Dr. Montemarano was ac-

Back Page Col. 5

Oil Firm's Papers Reveal Plan to Cut Output

By William Moore
Chronicle Correspondent

Washington

Officials of Standard Oil of California, one of the nation's five largest petroleum firms, made extensive plans to reduce existing crude oil production by 1972-73, according to copies of 1968 company documents now in the possession of Senate investigators.

Copies of inner-office reports and memos, obtained by The Chronicle, revealed that planners for the San Francisco-based firm were far more worried about how an oversupply of oil could affect their markets, rather than a scarcity.

The communications appeared to confirm, in part, a copyrighted story in The Chronicle, Saturday, which quoted a highly reliable source as saying that Senate investigators had evidence to prove that America's major petroleum companies deliberately worked to limit oil production in the late 1960s.

The object, this source said, was to drive up prices — and profits.

But the plans of the companies, operating through a maze of joint ventures and subsidiaries, were reportedly torpedoed by the Arab oil nations, beginning in 1970.

The Arabs, to no one's surprise today, discovered that they, too, had gained the power to limit production and drive up prices, and they could do it better.

Because the oil companies had already kept their spare crude capacity precariously low — "right down to the wire," as The Chronicle's source put it — the Arab ac-

Back Page Col. 1

Index

Comics	56
Deaths	35
Entertainment	42
Finance	52
People	10
TV-Radio	40
Vital Statistics	35
Weather	36

Shootout in L.A.

FIERY DEATHS FOR SLA

Weapon-wielding officers crouched near the surrounded Symbionese Liberation Army hideout as flames almost totally engulfed it

110th Year No. 138 ★★★★• SATURDAY, MAY 18, 1974 GArfield 1-1111 15 CENTS

5 Died in These Flames

When the front wall of the besieged house collapsed (more on shootout — 1A, 1B and 12)

Cinque Reported Among Victims

Police Trap Terrorists In Second L.A. Hideout

By Paul Avery
Chronicle Correspondent

Los Angeles

Donald DeFreeze, the gun-crazy escaped convict who called himself General Field Marshal Cinque of the Symbionese Liberation Army, died with four other persons in a savage gunbattle here with police and the FBI last night, law officials at the scene said.

Two of the dead they said were women members of the SLA, the terrorist group that murdered Marcus Foster, Oakland school superintendent, and abducted Patricia Hearst, daughter of San Francisco newspaper editor Randolph A. Hearst.

There was no immediate identification of the remaining two bodies, but both were women and this raised the grim possibility that the young kidnap victim may have been slain with her abductors.

The identified dead, police said, were Nancy Ling Perry, 26, the one-time Santa Rosa high school cheerleader who called herself Fahizah and was a theoretician of the SLA, and Camilla (Candy) Hall, 29, the social worker who was converted to the SLA by a lesbian lover.

The hour-long gunbattle, witnessed on live television by millions, ended when the stucco house in which DeFreeze had holed up was set afire by

Back Page Col. 1

India Joins The Atomic Powers

New Delhi

India has exploded a nuclear device, its atomic energy commission announced today.

India is only the sixth country to explode a nuclear weapon. The others are the United States, the Soviet Union, China, Britain and France.

Reuters

Index

Comics	46
Deaths	14
Entertainment	31
Finance	43
People	10
TV-Radio	30
Vital Statistics	14
Weather	14

Top of the News is on Page 12

Historic Speech

NIXON RESIGNS

San Francisco Chronicle

★★★★ FINAL

The Largest Daily Circulation in Northern California

110th Year No. 221 ★★★★ FRIDAY, AUGUST 9, 1974 GArfield 1-1111 15 CENTS

Ford to Be Sworn In As President Today

'Leadership of America Will Be in Good Hands,' Nixon Tells the Nation

Washington

Richard Milhous Nixon announced his resignation last night as President of the United States, the first chief executive to resign in the Republic's 198-year history.

Gerald Rudolph Ford, vice president since Dec. 7, 1973, will take the oath of office at noon today to become the nation's 38th President, the first ever to take office without having been elected by the people to either the presidency or vice presidency.

In a 15-minute television speech to the nation, Mr. Nixon, his face drawn and expression somber, said he no longer had "a strong enough political base in the Congress" to warrant continuing his fight against impeachment.

Mr. Nixon, who faced certain conviction in the Senate had he continued to fight, said he was leaving the presidency today in "sadness" but with satisfaction that with Ford as the new President "leadership in America will be in good hands."

The President said he had "never been a quitter" and that resigning was "abhorrent to every instinct of my body."

But to have continued the fight, he said, would have "totally absorbed" his time during the months ahead when the nation would need "a full-time President."

Mr. Nixon stopped short of acknowledging any guilt in the Watergate coverup, a principal charge against him in the impeachment proceedings, but admitted that he had made mistakes in the handling of the Watergate scandal.

By resigning, Mr. Nixon said, "I hope that I will have hastened the start of that process of healing which is so desperately needed in America. I regret deeply any injuries that may have been done in the course of the events that led to this decision. I would say only that if some of my judgments were wrong — and some were wrong — they were made in what I believed at the time to be the best interests of the nation.

Wearing an American flag pin in his lapel as he always does, the 61-year-old President read slowly and deliberately from his prepared speech, occasionally glancing up with a faint smile as he spoke of his hopes that the nation would unite behind Ford and continue to strive for the goals of peace and international understanding fostered by the Nixon administration.

He noted that his family—a dejected group that took his decision hard and remained secluded — had unanimously opposed his resignation. But he said he thought the best interests of the nation demanded it.

He expressed gratitude to those who had stood by him during his long ordeal and added, "I leave with no bitterness toward those who have opposed me."

In tone and content, Mr. Nixon's address was in sharp contrast to his frequently combative language of the past, especially his first "farewell" appearance—that of 1962 when he announced he was retiring from politics after losing the California governor's race and said the media would not have "Nixon to kick around" anymore.

Speaking of his accomplishments in ending American involvement in the Vietnam War and in helping settle the Mideast War, he said he was confident that

Back Page Col. 5

Top of the News on Page 20

It's All Over

AP Wirephoto

President Nixon hugged his daughter, Julie, after telling his family Wednesday night that he had decided to resign. Story on Page 5B.

AP Wirephoto

GERALD FORD RETURNED HOME TO WATCH PRESIDENT ON TV
He is expected to speak to the nation today

Nixon Made No Immunity Deals, Jaworski Says

Washington

Watergate Special Prosecutor Leon Jaworski stated after President Nixon's resignation speech last night that no deals had been either made or offered that would have given the President immunity from prosecution after he leaves office.

"There has been no agreement or understanding of any sort between the President or his representatives and the special prosecutor relating in any way to the President's resignation," Jaworski said in a statement issued by his office.

Jaworski's words, combined with the fact that Mr. Nixon made no mention of the immunity issue in his address to the nation, left unresolved, at least for the moment, the prospect that Mr. Nixon might be indicted and stand trial for crimes stemming from the Watergate scandals.

Mr. Nixon did not ask for any assurances of immunity from Jaworski before his speech, and Jaworski offered none.

"Although I was informed of the president's decision this afternoon," Jaworski's statement said, "my office did not participate in any way in the President's decision to resign."

Jaworski met with General Alexander M. Haig Jr., the White House chief of staff, earlier yesterday, but that session was said to have been merely for the purpose of informing the special prosecutor of what Mr. Nixon would be doing later on in the evening.

Earlier yesterday there were moves in both houses of Congress to grant Mr. Nixon immunity from prosecution, but they failed for lack of support.

Senator Edward W. Brooke (Rep-Mass.) and Representative John Buchanan (Rep-Ala.) introduced resolutions that would have had Congress express the "sense" that Mr. Nixon should not be subject to prosecution on leaving office today.

Many members took the position that on resignation Mr. Nixon should be liable for prosecution, just as any other citizen, and leave it to the courts to decide the legal issues.

There was the additional sentiment of, as it was phrased by one Democratic senator, "How can I recon-

Back Page Col. 1

Ford Praises Nixon for His 'Personal Sacrifices'

Washington

Vice president Gerald Ford praised President Nixon last night for "one of the greatest personal sacrifices for the country and one of the finest personal decisions on behalf of all of us as Americans."

Ford vowed to continue the President's foreign policy and announced that Secretary of State Henry Kissinger has agreed to stay on during the new administration.

"I pledged to you tonight, as I will pledge to you tomorrow and in the future, my best efforts in cooperation, leadership and dedication to what's good for America and good for the world," he said.

After watching Mr. Nixon on television with his family, the vice president stepped outside into a slight drizzle at his suburban split-level home in Alexandria, Va., to face television cameras and photographers assembled in the street and about 100 cheering neighbors.

Speaking without notes or a prepared text, Ford pledged to continue the Nixon foreign policy and called the sceretary of state "a very great man" whom he has known for many years.

On domestic policy he said that he had been "very fortunate in my lifetime" to have adversaries in the Congress but said that he did not think he had "a single enemy" there.

President Nixon had cited in his resignation address his lack of support in the Congress as one of the major reasons for his resignation.

"The net result is that I think tomorrow I can start out working with Democrats and with Republicans in the House as well as in the Senate to work on the problems — serious ones — which we have at home."

Ford began his remarks with no jubilation or pride

Back Page Col. 1

Index

Comics	36
Deaths	22
Entertainment	42
Finance	57
People	16
TV-Radio	40
Vital Statistics	22
Weather	22

EVEL KNIEVEL FLIGHT PHOTOS

San Francisco Chronicle

The Largest Daily Circulation in Northern California

★★★★ FINAL

110th Year No. 252 ★★★★ MONDAY, SEPTEMBER 9, 1974 GArfield 1-1111 20 CENTS

FORD PARDONS NIXON

Ex-President Is Excused Of Any Federal Crimes'

High Drama

AP Wirephoto

Evel Knievel's rocket-cycle bumped into the canyon wall as he floated down

Jump Fails But Evel's OK

Twin Falls, Idaho

Stuntman Evel Knievel parachuted in his mini-rocket into the Snake river canyon without serious injury yesterday in a futile but lucrative attempt to soar across the quarter-mile gorge.

John Branker, executive producer for Top Rank, Inc., which promoted the space-age stunt, said the parachute cover accidentally flew off at blastoff, preventing successful completion of the flight. He said the same thing happened during one of the two previous test flights.

Knievel said Robert Truax, the rocket's designer, and his crew performed their job well.

"They designed the 'skycycle' so that, if there was an unforeseen malfunction I had a chance to live," the stuntman said in a statement. "There was no Truax failure, no team failure, no Knievel Failure. There was a metal failure."

He indicated he might have released the "deadman stick" after the drag chute spurted from the craft and it began to roll.

Knievel emerged from the dented "Skycycle X-2" waving to the throngs that lined the runs of the treacherous, lava-walled canyon. He then was whisked by helicopter back to the launch site.

The blastoff came at 2:35 p.m., and the red, white and blue rocket rose from the launch pad for 8.7 seconds. Then the drag parachute popped from the tail, pulling out the main chute.

The rocket floated 600 feet to the rugged canyon floor alongside the swirling waters of the river.

"The shot almost knocked me out," Knievel

Back Page Col. 6

Party-Line Reaction in Congress

Washington

Congressional reaction to President Ford's pardon of Richard M. Nixon split sharply along party lines yesterday.

Most Republicans praised Mr. Ford for taking a courageous step, while Democrats criticized the pardon as "premature" and "an outrage."

Virtually all agreed it was a controversial act.

At the White House, switchboard operators said "angry calls, heavy and constant," began jamming their boards soon after Mr. Ford's announcement.

Vice President-designate Nelson Rockefeller called the pardon "an act of conscience, compassion and courage, undoubtedly controversial in the short run, but promising in the long run in that it will speed the healing of our nation."

The pardon drew criticism from one Republican, Senator Edward W. Brooke of Massachusetts, who said: "President Ford's blanket pardon without Mr. Nixon's full confession of his involvement in Watergate is, in my judgment, a serious mistake."

Senator Barry Goldwater, (Rep-Ariz.), said Ford's decision "was the only decent and prudent course for him to follow." He noted that special prosecutor Leon Jaworski "has made it clear that he doubted that former President Nixon could get a fair trial and I certainly agree with him on that."

Senator Edmund S. Muskie, (Dem-Me.) said that pardons normally are not granted "until the accused is in jeopardy of punishment."

Muskie, a lawyer, was interviewed on NBC-TV's "Meet the Press" and was asked whether he agreed with Mr. Ford's statement that it would be a long time before Mr. Nixon would be able to get a fair court trial. "No, I don't," he said. "I don't believe it's necessary to reach that judgment at this point."

Representatives of both parties said granting a pardon to Mr. Nixon raised serious questions of fairness in light of the many others who have been charged for Watergate offenses conducted in the former President's name, some of whom have gone to prison.

Many of the major figures

Back Page Col. 5

UPI Telephoto

President Ford waited with aides, including (third from left) White House chief of staff Alexandar Haig, for the first telephone comments on his action

Secret Maneuvers Behind the Decision

By Gaylord Shaw
Associated Press

Washington

Ten days of intense secret negotiations and maneuvering preceded President Ford's granting of a full pardon yesterday to former President Richard Nixon for his role in the Watergate scandal.

Mr. Ford enlisted a criminal lawyer, described by friends as looking like "a TV sleuth . . . a very tough cop," to handle the face-to-face meetings with Mr. Nixon.

And he called upon another long-time lawyer friend, white-haired, soft-spoken Philip Buchen, to coordinate preparations for his bombshell announcement.

According to reconstruction based on comments of official and unofficial sources, Mr. Ford made a tentative decision the middle of last week to grant the pardon, but did not reach a final decision until Saturday.

The reconstruction disclosed this chronology of events:

On Friday, August 30, Mr. Ford called Buchen, his White House counsel, to a private meeting and told him to research historic and legal precedents for the granting of a presidential pardon to an individual before his indictment or conviction.

Buchen worked into the night, and then throughout the Labor Day weekend on the assignment while Mr. Ford took his family for the first time to Camp David presidential retreat in the Maryland mountains.

After receiving Buchen's report of the legal and constitutional requirements for such an act, Mr. Ford called upon another friend, Washington lawyer Benton Becker. He asked Becker

Back Page Col. 1

Threat to Void Lease

Aliotos May Sue Port

By Larry Liebert

The shipping firm recently acquired by the Alioto family has threatened to void its 30-year lease and to challenge its $1.7 million debt to the Port of San Francisco, Mayor Joseph Alioto has told The Chronicle.

And, it was learned, former port director Miriam Wolff claims she quit this past July partly to avoid becoming "a patsy" in just such a maneuver.

In a weekend interview, Alioto complained th

berths were not dredged deep enough and that potholes line roadways at Pier 96, the cargo facility leased to Pacific Far East Line for $2.1 million a year.

He claimed those "de-

Back Page Col. 5

Back Page Col. 7

Amnesty Is 'Full, Free, Absolute'

Washington

President Ford yesterday granted former President Nixon a "full, free and absolute pardon" for any federal crimes Mr. Nixon "committed or may have committed" during his terms in the White House.

Mr. Nixon promptly issued a statement from his home in California, accepting the pardon and admitting he had made mistakes but not acknowledging any crimes.

Mr. Nixon had not been formally charged with any federal crime, but Philip W. Buchen, Mr. Ford's counselor, told reporters at the White House it was "very likely" the former President would have been indicted without yesterday's action.

He noted that one federal grand jury named Mr. Nixon an unindicted co-conspirator in the Watergate coverup months ago, when he was still the President and at a time when there was less evidence of his involvement than is available today.

Mr. Ford, in his formal proclamation of pardon, said he took the controversial step because "the tranquility to which this nation has been restored by the events of recent weeks could be irreparably lost by the prospects of bringing to trial a former President of the United States," a process he said would take a year or more and "cause prolonged and divisive debate" all across the country.

And "finally," Mr. Ford added in a statement delivered rather grimly before television cameras and a small pool of reporters in the Oval Office, "I feel that Richard Nixon and his loved ones have suffered enough, and will continue to suffer no matter what I do."

Mr. Ford had said himself, during his vice presidential confirmation hearings last November, that "I don't think the public would stand for it" if one President resigned and his successor then took steps to quash his possible prosecution. Yesterday he said simply that many decisions in the White House "do not look at all the same as the hypothetical questions that I have answered freely and perhaps too fast on previous occasions."

Mr. Nixon, in the statement issued in San Clem-

Back Page Col. 1

TerHorst Resigns In Protest

Washington

Jerald F. terHorst, close friend and adviser to President Ford, resigned as White House press secretary yesterday to protest the pardon Mr. Ford granted to former President Richard M. Nixon.

"The President acted in good conscience and I also found it necessary to resign in good conscience," terHorst said.

A few hours later, Mr. Ford issued a statement through a press aide saying "I deeply regret" the resignation but "I understand his position."

"I appreciated the fact that good people will differ with me on this difficult decision," Ford added. "However, it is my judgment that it is in the best interest of

Back Page Col. 4

Jet Crash In Greece --88 Lost

Athens

A TWA Boeing 707 jetliner crashed into the stormy Ionian Sea off Greece yesterday, and Greek aviation officials said all 88 persons aboard were believed killed.

Airline officials said 17 Americans, including an infant, were aboard the plane.

TWA headquarters in New York ruled out sabotage, despite a claim by a telephone caller in Beirut that a Palestinian organization called the Nationalist Youth for the Liberation of Palestine had sabotaged the plane.

In Beirut, the Palestinian

Back Page Col. 6

Index

Comics 54
Deaths 22
Entertainment 42
Finance 52
People 15
TV-Radio 38
Weather 34

★ ★ ★

Top of the News On Back Page

Inside

The University of California announced a major curtailment of its health sciences building program. Page 2.

Salaries of California's judges will jump ahead of their federal counterparts as of September 1. Page 2.

The budget of the controversial K&B Guard Service was slashed at a meeting of the Redevelopment Agency. Page 3.

A committee to set minimum graduation standards for city schools expressed some doubts about its project. Page 4.

Two English women are in the Bay Area to raise funds to help the children of violence-torn Northern Ireland. Page 5.

TOP OF THE NEWS

Tension and laughter, pessimism and hope filled the hours as President Ford ordered the Vietnam evacuation. Page 6.

The first of what is expected to be a massive group of Vietnamese refugees arrived at Camp Pendleton. Page 8.

The wife of former Vietnamese premier Nguyen Cao Ky was believed in San Francisco. Page 9.

Scores of South Vietnamese airplanes flew to Thailand, Hong Kong or U.S. ships, carrying thousands of refugees. Page 10.

The federal government turned down a grant request that Governor Brown personally rewrote to shorten it. Page 11.

Apollo astronauts returned from the first visit by Americans to the Soviet cosmodrome at Baikonur. Page 12.

Social rituals have grown up around cocaine, the latest of the fashionable drugs among pop music millionaires. Page 1C.

Maggie Kuhn, 70-year-old cofounder of the Gray Panthers, has become the Gloria Steinem of the geriatric set. Page 16.

Heroes with flaws and frailties have made Marvel Comics publisher Stan Lee a hot property on the college lecture circuit. Page 17.

General Motors reported its first quarter earnings fell 51 per cent to a 29-year low. Page 57.

Profits for the nation's two top steel producers doubled during the first quarter. Page 57.

Weather

Bay Area: Fair Wednesday, low clouds at night. Highs, low 70s; lows, mid-40s. Page 30.

Little Slugs Witness

See Below

San Francisco Chronicle

The Largest Daily Circulation in Northern California

★★★★ **FINAL**

111th Year No. 120 ★★★★ **WEDNESDAY, APRIL 30, 1975** **GArfield 1-1111** **20 CENTS**

South Vietnam Surrenders---Americans Gone

UPI Telephoto

A crewman helped evacuees one by one into a helicopter poised on a rooftop, one of many liftoff sites in downtown Saigon

Years of Fighting End--U.S. Flag Comes Down As Yanks Fly Away

Saigon

South Vietnam surrendered today to the Viet Cong.

The collapse came 2½ hours after the United States pulled down the Stars and Stripes and left the country it had spent 14 years trying to keep out of Communist hands.

President Duong Van (Big) Minh announced the surrender in a 60-second address to his people. He told his soldiers to stop fighting and said he was ready to meet Viet Cong leaders "to discuss the turnover of the administration, both civilian and military."

Columns of South Vietnamese troops pulled out of their defensive positions in the city and marched to central points to turn in their weapons.

Thirty minutes later, 20 Communist tanks loaded with soldiers and flying the red and blue, gold-starred Viet Cong flag rolled into downtown Saigon and onto the grounds of the presidential palace.

Viet Cong forces entered the palace and soon an explosion was heard. The cause was not immediately determined.

Other tanks and some trucks with North Vietnamese troops moved into the city and witnesses said some had opened fire. Government troops did not return the fire.

In Paris, the Viet Cong said it would accept the surrender only after fulfillment of one remaining condition: that U.S. ships leave Vietnamese waters. That was expected shortly.

The surrender ended 35 years of fighting in Vietnam, starting with the Japanese takeover in 1940. The United States invested 14 years, $150 billion and more than 50,000 lives in its efforts to block the communists.

America gave up yesterday.

President Ford approved "Option 4" — a massive and swift helicopter evacuation — and scores of helicopters swept into Saigon to pick up all Americans who wanted to leave, about 900 persons, and transported them to ships and carriers waiting in the south China Sea.

U.S. Ambassador Graham Martin, weary and drawn, stepped from a helicopter and onto the deck of the amphibious command ship Blue Ridge.

He symbolized the pullout that saw the Americans leave with Vietnamese screams of "Please take me! Please take me!" still echoing in their ears.

Gunshots resounded in the streets, and flames licked at the abandoned U.S. Embassy that Vietnamese first looted and then set afire. As mortar rounds pounded the city's outskirts, Minh

Back Page Col. 4

'Automatic' PG&E Rate Rises Halted

By Michael Taylor

The California Public Utilities Commission put an indefinite stop yesterday to the customary requests for higher rates made quarterly by utilities companies to meet the increases in the cost of oil and gas they use to generate electricity.

At the same time, the five commissioners delayed for another month any action on the most recent of such requests by Pacific Gas and Electric Co. The company had asked for $103 million but later reduced that to $73 million.

The unprecedented move halting the quarterly requests came after several hours of debate among the commissioners as they took up the "fuel offset" controversy that has been swirling

Little Punches, Chokes Witness in Murder Trial

By George Draper
Chronicle Correspondent

Sacramento

The Marcus Foster murder trial exploded in violence yesterday when Russell Little, one of the two defendants, attacked a prosecution witness with his fists.

A woman spectator in the rear of the courtroom screamed, "Kill him!" as Little threw a savage combination of rights and lefts at Christopher Thompson, the witness.

Before bailiffs could stop him, the 25-year-old Little got behind the witness stand and locked his arm around Thompson's throat.

The seven women and five men in the jury box gasped as the struggle erupted only four or five feet away from them.

Little, a philosophy graduate standing five feet nine overpowered by bailiffs Roy Swehla and John Pendleton.

They carried him out of the court on their shoulders and down to the basement holding cell where he has watched much of the trial on TV.

Thompson is one of the "enemies of the people," marked for death last spring by the Symbionese Liberation Army. He was also a key witness for the Alameda county grand jury that indicted Little and Joseph Remiro.

Thompson appeared more shaken than badly hurt in the brief scuffle. His glasses were knocked-off and he appeared to have a slight cut on the side of his head.

Remiro, Little's co-defendant, remained seated at the defense table while Little was slugging Thompson on the face and belly.

Defense Attorneys James placed restraining hands on Remiro although Remiro made no move to join the fight.

Little and Remiro almost overpowered two jailers in the Alameda county jail on March 1 in an abortive escape attempt.

At that time, Little jammed a pencil five inches into the throat of one deputy while Remiro all but gouged out the eye of another.

There was no immediate explanation why Little was allowed to move so close to the witness Thompson.

He had been granted the right by Superior Court Judge Elvin Sheehy to cross-examine witnesses and it was in his capacity of amateur lawyer defending himself that he approached the witness stand.

Thompson, a tall, articulate black militant, had

A Swarm of Copters to The Rescue

Aboard the Blue Ridge off South Vietnam

Two helicopters collided and another crashed into the main deck of the Blue Ridge as South Vietnamese refugees including babies, sobbing women and three-star generals flew to this American ship yesterday in the evacuation from Saigon.

In the rush of helicopter flights, several of the craft had to be pushed into the sea after landing in order to make room for other helicopters reaching the ship loaded with frightened evacuees.

Others were deliberately ditched by their South Vietnamese pilots after they unloaded their passengers to leave space for other craft arriving.

The Blue Ridge is the command and communications vessel of the 40-ship

Ford Urges U.S. 'To Close Ranks'

Washington

The United States completed the month-long evacuation of more than 6000 Americans and about 56,000 South Vietnamese from Saigon yesterday as President Ford called on the nation "to close ranks, to avoid recrimination about the past."

When word was flashed to the White House that Ambassador Graham Martin and the last evacuees had been airlifted from South Vietnam, Mr. Ford declared: "This action closes a chapter in the American experience."

Some 6500 persons were rescued on the last day, about 1000 of them Americans. Mr. Ford said it was now time "to look ahead to the many goals we share and to work together on the great tasks that remain to be accomplished."

Delays blamed on bad weather, pilot fatigue and stretched out the day's withdrawal, which marked the end of U.S. involvement in the Vietnam war — a war that Secretary of State Henry A. Kissinger acknowledged did not meet U.S. objectives.

But, sharing the President's sentiments, Kissinger said, "It is a time to heal wounds, to look to our international obligations and to remember that peace and progress in the world has depended importantly on American commitment and American conviction. . . ."

White House press secretary Ron Nessen said the operation was extended several hours because "a lot more Vietnamese were taken out than had been planned."

He said other reasons were occasional bad weather and pilot weariness. In addition, only two helicopters could go in at one time

Index

Comics	82
Deaths	30
Entertainment	46
Finance	57
People	13
TV-Radio	44
Vital Statistics	45
Weather	30

Inside

Bill and Emily Harris were described as a nice couple by their neighbors. Page 2.

The Senate voted to limit federal pay increases to five per cent as asked by President Ford. Page 7.

Big business in oil-producing Middle East nations often involves entire families. Page 8.

Jordan rejected terms set for the sale of Hawk antiaircraft missiles as "insulting to national dignity." Page 9.

Christian-Moslem fighting increased in intensity in Lebanon, and a government call for a cease-fire was ignored. Page 9.

The Postal Service moved to raise the cost of a first-class stamp from ten to 13 cents. Page 10.

TOP OF THE NEWS

Nobel laureate Linus Pauling and 12 others were presented the highest U.S. scientific award by President Ford. Page 10.

Air Force Sergeant Leonard Matlovich's record proves he can handle the stress of being a homosexual, a medical expert testified. Page 11.

A Spanish court sentenced three men and two women to death for the murder of a policeman. Page 11.

Berkeley policemen helped firemen fight a fire and rescue three invalid women from adjacent homes. Page 15.

Senate investigators were told the Army carried out mock poison and germ attacks on the New York subway and government installations. Page 17.

The United Farm Workers Union won a state ruling and 12 farm elections in the Salinas Valley. Page 19.

The rock group Labelle has made it from the chitlin circuit all the way up to the big time with a hot sex image. Page 20.

A survey contended that the state's family planning services were inadequate to serve the poor. Page 43.

Under pressure from the Federal Reserve, Bank-America Corp. found a buyer for 127 small loan company offices. Page 68.

Bargain hunters got into the stock market and the Dow Jones average went up 15.56 points. Page 58.

A high government council attacked the steel industry's plans to raise prices. Page 58.

Weather

Bay Area: Mostly fair Friday but overcast on coast extending inland night and morning. Slightly warmer. Highs, 60s to 80s; lows, 50s. Page 27.

Parents, Patricia Reunion

See Below

San Francisco Chronicle

★★★★ FINAL

The Largest Daily Circulation in Northern California

111th Year No. 262 ★★★★ • FRIDAY, SEPT. 19, 1975 GArfield 1-1111 20 CENTS

PATTY HEARST FOUND

Heiress, Three Others Are Captured in S.F.

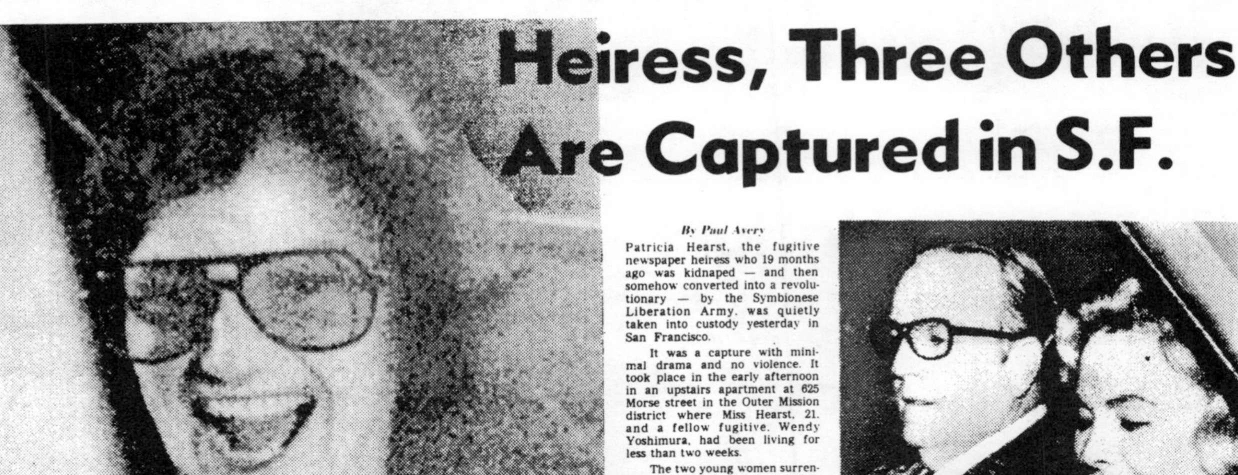

PATRICIA HEARST LEFT THE FEDERAL BUILDING IN A MARSHAL'S CAR

Her bond was set at $1,050,000 during her arraignment before a magistrate

AP Photo

By Paul Avery

Patricia Hearst, the fugitive newspaper heiress who 19 months ago was kidnaped — and then somehow converted into a revolutionary — by the Symbionese Liberation Army, was quietly taken into custody yesterday in San Francisco.

It was a capture with minimal drama and no violence. It took place in the early afternoon in an upstairs apartment at 625 Morse street in the Outer Mission district where Miss Hearst, 21, and a fellow fugitive, Wendy Yoshimura, had been living for less than two weeks.

The two young women surrendered to FBI agents and a San Francisco police officer -- Inspector Timothy Casey — who knocked on the apartment door at 2:25p.m.

One hour and ten minutes earlier, FBI agents had arrested SLA members William and Emily Harris as they were strolling down a sidewalk in the Bernal Heights district, apparently about to go jogging judging from their attire.

The end to one of the biggest manhunts ever conducted by the FBI apparently resulted from a tip from an unidentified source who became suspicious that the couple living at 288 Precita avenue might be the Harrises.

The FBI wasn't saying much last night, but sources told The Chronicle that in following up that lead agents were able to make a connection to the Morse street address.

Inspector Casey and FBI agents weren't sure who or what they might find there when Casey rapped on the door.

The knock was answered by Miss Yoshimura, a onetime Berkeley artist sought since 1972 on an Alameda county charge involving explosives.

Standing a few feet behind the 30-year-old Japanese-American was Tania of the SLA, Patricia Hearst.

"Patty," was all that Casey could say in that first moment. Then he barked out: "Don't make a move!"

"Patty replied 'all right,' and that was it," Casey said.

"I tried to ask her a few

Back Page Col. 1

AP Photo

The Hearsts as they left the airport to visit Patricia

Hearsts Visit Patty in Jail for 'Happy Reunion'

By George Snyder

Randolph and Catherine Hearst visited their captured daughter in San Mateo county jail early today and described the occasion as "a happy reunion."

"She's terribly thin, but otherwise looking well," Mrs. Hearst said of her daughter, Patty. "We told her that we loved her and we hugged and kissed her."

"She was happy to see us and she's perfectly willing to come home," added Randolph Hearst, who went with his wife and two daughters under police escort directly from the airport to the jail in Redwood City.

Both the Hearsts said they refrained from discussing Patty's role in the SLA or her days as a fugitive and kept the conversation strictly to "family matters."

Hearst described his daughter as calm. Mrs. Hearst said she was nervous.

"She's just nervous and thin and wants to come home," Mrs. Hearst said.

While the couple met briefly with the press at 1 a.m., their daughters Vickie and Ann remained in Patricia's cell to continue the discussion.

The family met Hearst when he arrived at San Francisco International Airport at 11:40 p.m. on a flight from New York. Mrs. Hearst carried a bouquet of yellow roses into the jail with her 25 minutes later, but it was not known whether her daughter accepted them.

The reunion was said to have lasted between a half hour and an hour.

Asked whether they would

Back Page Col. 1

U.S. Count of Viet Cong 'A Monument of Deceit'

Washington

A former CIA intelligence analyst testified yesterday that the 1968 Vietnam Tet attacks caught U.S. forces by surprise because top officials contrived phony enemy strength figures "to fool the American press, the public and the Congress."

The analyst, Samuel A. Adams, said U.S. forces were unprepared for the Communist offensive that took 3895 American lives because officials ordered false figures to indicate the Viet Cong was running out of men.

Testifying before the House Intelligence Committee, Adams released cables from former U.S. Ambassador Ellsworth Bunker and the deputy U.S. commander in Vietnam at that time, General Creighton Abrams, to support his assertion.

The cables showed both Bunker and Abrams wanted official estimates of the Viet Cong force kept below 300,000 — despite intelligence estimates of 600,000 — to show, in Bunker's words, that U.S. forces were "grinding down the enemy."

Adams said he was a CIA analyst for ten years and its only analyst on Viet Cong strength figures during the two years preceeding the Tet offensive. He said he resigned the day of the Tet offensive, calling the Viet Cong strength estimate in his resignation memorandum "a monument of deceit."

But he said U.S. intelligence officials started using the false figures.

"Although our aim was to fool the American press, the public and the Congress," Adams testified, "we in intelligence succeeded best in fooling ourselves."

Adams contended the falsified intelligence was typical of what he called "very haphazard, slip-

Back Page Col. 5

NFL Strike Is Off

The threat that Sunday's opening games of the National Football League season would be canceled because of a players' strike evaporated yesterday.

The five striking teams agreed to go back to work after their union signed a two-week no-strike pledge. The owners, for their part, agreed to come up with a new contract offer on Monday.

(Details in the Sporting Green.)

AP and KGO-TV

WILLIAM HARRIS

He surrendered quickly

Guns in Harris' Flat

The second-floor flat on Precita avenue where William and Emily Harris had been living was loaded with weapons, ammunition and explosive powder.

Inspector Gary Kern of the San Francisco police department's robbery detail listed some of the items found yesterday at 288 Precita avenue:

- Three 30-caliber, semi-automatic M-1 carbines.
- Two automatic shotguns.
- Two handguns.
- Forty pounds of black

Back Page Col. 5

Index

Comics	50
Deaths	26
Entertainment	44
Finance	58
People	20
TV-Radio	42
Vital Statistics	27
Weather	27

WOMAN SHOOTS AT FORD IN S.F. STREET

By Gary Fong

Seconds after the shot, Secret Service agents pushed Mr. Ford down behind the bullet-proof car and then bundled him into the auto

111th Year No. 265 ★★★★ TUESDAY, SEPT. 23, 1975 GArfield 1-1111 20 CENTS

President Unhurt—Suspect Arrested

UPI photo

The scene on Post street just after the shot: The assailant fired from the point marked # 1 on the map. The President was standing at the point marked # 2 in front of the St. Francis Hotel

Ford Is Rushed To Airport

By George Murphy and Jerry Carroll

A shot that missed was fired at President Ford from a crowd lining a street outside the St. Francis Hotel yesterday in the second alleged assassination attempt in 17 days against the nation's chief executive. Although badly shaken, Mr. Ford was unhurt.

Police said Sara Jane Moore, 45, was taking aim for a second shot when a disabled former Marine hit her arm, giving a policeman standing just six feet away time to reach her side and grab the .38-caliber chrome-plated revolver still in her hand.

Miss Moore, who had been identified by federal computers as a possible threat to the President's life, had been questioned Sunday by Secret Service agents and later in the day by San Francisco police. They confiscated a .44-caliber pistol found in Miss Moore's purse and cited her for carrying a concealed weapon.

When she was being interrogated in the hotel after the incident, Miss Moore said that if she'd had the .44-caliber pistol she would have hit the President. She was arraigned last night on a felony charge of assault on a president.

A short time after the arraignment, the President appeared on television in Washington to vow that he will not cower or capitulate to would-be assassins. He said the American people are entitled to see him and shake his hand.

"The American people are good people," he said. "And under no circumstances will I—and I hope no others—capitulate to those who want to undercut what's good in America."

The shooting came at 3:30 p.m. as Mr. Ford was leaving the Union Square hotel's Post street entrance after a luncheon speech before the World Affairs Council and a later televised interview.

The President stepped out of an elevator in the lobby, said, "Hi, fellows, how are you?" to a group there and then stepped out into the sunlight on the street. He raised his arms to wave at some 2000 onlookers outside when the

Back Page Col. 4

Berkeley Barb photo by Janet Fries

SARA JANE MOORE
She said she was a 'go-between'

Suspect's Story of Shooting

By Carolyn Anspacher and Paul Avery

Sara Jane Moore had a double worry yesterday as she sped from her home on Guerrero street to the St. Francis Hotel for her dark rendezvous with President Ford.

Questioned by Secret Service agents in the Hotel St. Francis' Borgia m room, the plump, gray-haired woman said she was "driving fast down the freeway, loading her .38-caliber revolver at the same time, and hoping she would be stopped for speeding."

And at the same time, she told her interrogators, she was worried about being able to fulfill her mission and still be on time to pick up her 9-year-old son at his

Back Page Col. 1

Ford, in Talk Here, Proposes A Huge Energy Corporation

By George Murphy

President Ford, declaring "the time has come for energy independence," yesterday called for a $100 billion government corporation aimed at giving the United States enough energy to sustain itself "in ten years or less."

Speaking to the national convention of the AFL-CIO Building and Construction Trades Council at the Hyatt Union Square Hotel, Mr. Ford said:

"This Energy Independence Authority will have the power to take any appropriate financial action—to borrow and to lend—in order to get energy action.

"It will serve as a catalyst and a stimulant, working through — not in place of — American industry."

White House officials explained later the $100 billion would be raised through a combination of government-backed bonds and through public selling stock.

Although no final financing program has been worked out, White House spokesmen said the administration is considering raising $25 billion through stock and $75 billion through a long-range program of federal government-guaranteed bonds.

Mr. Ford, looking refreshed and natty in a blue suit, was warmly received by 600 delegates to the council, in convention here preliminary to the national AFL-CIO convention in October.

Their warmth was in contrast to that of AFL-CIO president George Meany's occasional cool comments on the President's policies.

The delegates' applause interrupted Mr. Ford's speech six times, most loudly when he stated and varied the theme, "American jobs for Americans."

The President said his energy proposal, if adopted by the Congress, will have the following effects:

- "It can stimulate economic growth.
- "It can create new jobs.
- "It can give us control over our own destiny.
- "It can end runaway energy

Back Page Col. 6

Top of News On Page 24

Ex-Marine Probably Saved Ford

By William Cooney

A battle-taut ex-Marine stood 2 ½ hours in a crowd yesterday to see the President of the United States — and very likely saved President Ford's life.

"The President came out of the St. Francis Hotel, right across the street from me, and started to wave," said Oliver Sipple, who is 33 years old.

"I started to applaud and then, right in front of me, I saw the chrome revolver. I saw it pointed out there and I grabbed for it.

"I grabbed for the arm, to pull it down. I lunged and grabbed the woman's arm and the gun went off.

"A policeman told me I probably saved the President's life. He said that," and Sipple, still shak-

Back Page Col. 1

Index

Comics	26
Deaths	27
Entertainment	41
Finance	51
People	19
TV-Radio	40
Vital Statistics	27
Weather	27

Inside

The FDA decided to let ten drugs used in a cold remedies be sold without prescriptions. Page 2.

A Muni driver accused of taking his passengers on a wild ride along Market street was suspended without pay for 15 days. Page 2.

The Port Commission agreed to arrange financing of a new roadway in front of Warren Simmons' proposed waterfront complex. Page 2.

Mayor Moscone formally nominated Rudy Nothenberg to fill the post of chief administrative officer. Page 3.

Sworn statements by 65 cadets asserted that nearly 70% of their West Point colleagues violated the honor code. Page 4.

TOP OF THE NEWS

Thousands of young blacks in the Bay Area are ready for jobs that can't be found for them. Page 5.

A former Gulf Corp. lobbyist repudiated his earlier statement that he gave Senator Robert Dole $2000 in 1970. Page 10.

A filibuster threat has caused the Senate to drop a bill allowing a consortium headed by Bechtel to control uranium output. Page 12.

Fifteen congressmen will move to block a reported plan to sell U.S. missiles to Saudi Arabia. Page 12.

In a day of primary elections in four states, Arizona Representative Sam Steiger won a race marked by charges of religious bigotry. Page 14.

Congressional conferees agreed on tax legislation that would increase taxes on wealthy individuals. Page 14.

Palestinians claimed that Israeli troops have occupied five villages in Lebanon. Page 15.

South Africa will not bend to U.S. pressure to ease its racial separation policies, Prime Minister John Vorster indicated. Page 16.

The U.S. must now make "a major effort" to let blacks peacefully take power from whites in Africa, Mr. Ford said. Page 16.

An activist lawyer in Bolinas has fought both sides of environmental questions. Page 23.

Thanks to two women who came out from behind the venetian blinds, Belfast residents may give peace a chance. Page 24.

A plan for $1.5 billion to compensate whites in Rhodesia has won the backing of South Africa's Vorster. Page 26.

Weather

Bay Area: Fair Thursday, slightly cooler. Highs, 80s along the coast, 90s, to 102 inland, lows mid 50s to low 60s. Page 28.

Football Draft Ruled Illegal

See Sports

San Francisco Chronicle

The Largest Daily Circulation in Northern California

112th Year No. 204 ★★★★ THURSDAY, SEPTEMBER 9, 1976 777-1111   20 CENTS

Another Sizzler

Sweltering, smoggy weather that afflicted the Bay Area yesterday will continue today, only slightly abated.

San Francisco temperatures topped at 91 degrees at 2 p.m., then dropped to 88 degrees an hour later.

The record September 8 temperature in the city, 101, was set in 1904.

The Bay Area Air Pollution Control District reported "significant" amounts of pollution at San Francisco, Oakland, San Jose and in Marin county.

Chairman Mao of China Dies at 82

Tokyo

Mao Tse-tung died today, the official Chinese news agency Hsinhua announced.

Hsinhua said the chairman of the Chinese Communist party died about 16 hours before the announcement, at 12:10 a.m. Peking time (9:10 p.m. PDT Wednesday).

He was 82 and had been in failing health for many months.

Hsinhua said Mao's death was due to "the worsening of his illness and despite all treatment, although meticulous medical care was given him in every way after he fell ill."

The nature of Mao's final illness was not announced. He stopped receiving visiting foreigners in June although Chinese officials continued to say that he remained busy with affairs of state.

Only last week Hsinhua said a conference of earthquake relief workers was held in Peking under his "attention."

His death was expected to intensify the power struggle that has been under way in Peking for years and that has been waged with new intensity in the eight months since Premier Cho En-lai died.

There has been no indication of who would succeed the ac" knowledged supreme leader of the People's Republic of China since it was founded on Oct. 1, 1949.

Apparently the next man in line is Premier Hua Kuoa "feng, who was named both premier and first vice chairman of the Communist party only five months ago.

That development came in the latest of Mao's many batB tles against opponents of his policy of continual revolution to do away with all vestiges of capitalism and the bourgeois class in China.

Hua was elevated over First Vice Premier Teng Hsiao-ping, who foreign observers had considered certain to succeed Chou. Instead, he was fired -" by Mao, according to Peking's official announcements -" and accused of trying to restore capitalism in China.

The last foreign leader to see Mao was Pakistan Prime Minister Zulfikar Ali Bhutto.

He told reporters after their meeting on May 29 that Mao was suffering from a bad cold and was frail but "was very quick on the uptake and grasped everything."

Associated Press

By Peter Breinig

Christo Javacheff's Running Fence meandered through the Sonoma town of Valley Ford, which is bisected by the string of nylon panels

Ford-Carter Debate Rules Established

Washington

The League of Women Voters announced yesterday that the first Ford-Carter debate on September 23 will be held in Philadelphia. The league also disclosed ground rules designed to encourage complete answers by the candidates.

The site selected is the Walnut Street Theater, which has been open since 1809 and is said to be the oldest theater in continuous use in the country. It is in downtown Philadelphia, not far from Independence Hall, which league sources said had been considered but rejected as not large enough.

The league is committed to having an audience in the theater for all four scheduled debates—three between the presidential candidates and one between the vice presidential candidates of the two major parties.

The ground rules set by the league provide for questions by a panel of three journalists to be asked of Mr. Ford and Carter on an alternating basis, with a response of up to three minutes permitted.

Then, an optional follow-up question may be asked, with the answer limited to two minutes. Afterward the candidate to whom the question has not been directed may make a comment of up to two minutes. Before the end of the 90-minute discussion, each candidate will be given up to three minutes to make a closing statement, but there will be no opening statements.

Ground rules approved by both sides bar the use of scripts, and prohibit each candidate from bringing notes into the theater with him. However, the candidates will be permitted to make notes in the course of the debate.

The league also announced that live television coverage will be provided by all three major networks and by the Public Broadcasting System, and radio coverage by the Mutual Broadcasting System and National Public Radio. The first debate is scheduled to start at 6:30 p.m. PDT.

The Federal Communications Commission earlier cleared the way for the debates by exempting them from FCC provisions requiring the granting of equal time to other candidates.

Two of these, former Senator Eugene J. McCarthy, running as an independent, and former Governor Lester Maddox of Georgia, nominee of the American Independent party, have indicated they will challenge the ruling.

A third group, the American party, yesterday filed suit in U.S. District Court to block the Ford-Carter debates, charging that "the so-called debates are a political event staged for the media and are not bona fide news events, eligible for exemptions from the equal-time requirement of the FCC act."

Civil Service Ends Loyalty Questions

New York

The United States Civil Service Commission has ordered elimination of all political loyalty questions on the standard application for federal jobs.

One of these questions is whether a job-seeker has belonged to the Communist party or any group advocating forcible overthrow of the government.

Instructions to delete the questions are going out to all 105 field examining offices. A spokesman in Washington said that the commission decided on the action last month because of federal court rulings that "the questions were so overboard that they encroach on rights protected by the First Amendment," which guarantees free speech.

The federal move was disclosed by the American Civil Liberties Union whose legal director, Melvin L. Wulf, and national staff counsel, Joel M. Gore, in a statement hailed "the long overdue abolition of these relics of McCarthyism."

The late Senator Joseph R. McCarthy, a Wisconsin Republican, waged campaigns to dust Communists from government jobs.

The commission said that its questions on the job forms derived

How S.F. Bus Strike Hit the Schools

A drivers' strike — which showed signs of being a long one — shut down school bus service for more than half of San Francisco's elementary school students and most of its handicapped students yesterday.

School officials said 24,761 children attended elementary schools yesterday of the 33,044 anticipated, an attendance drop of 25 per cent. But they hoped the absenteeism will be lower tomorrow, when school resumes after the Admission Day holiday today.

Thousands of students affected by the bus shutdown made it to class anyway yesterday, officials reported, by riding the Muni or getting lifts from family or friends.

Federal mediator Robert Crall said he was attempting to hold the two sides, United Transportation Union Local 1741 and the Associated Charter Bus Co., in round-the-clock negotiations.

"We've got a long way to go," said Crall, who was called into the talks Tuesday. There are far more unresolved issues than union and company spokesmen had indicated publicly, he said.

Company spokesman James

Back Page Col. 1

Wallace Admits His Wife Secretly Tapped His Phone

Montgomery, Ala.

Governor George C. Wallace admitted yesterday that his wife had secretly ordered his bedroom telephone tapped.

He called it "a purely domestic matter" and refused to explain it.

"There were some tapes and a device" found in the governor's mansion, Wallace told a hastily called news conference. He said the "There were no politics involved at all," Wallace said. "No one has been hurt. No one has been harmed."

Wallace's attractive wife, Cornelia, who has said she may run for governor when Wallace steps down, was not at the news conference.

Wallace refused to explain the "domestic matter" that brought the

The Giant Fence Is Up And Running

By Charles Petit

Bulgarian artist Christo Javacheff's audacious 24-mile Running Fence crept slowly through the shimmering heat waves of Sonoma and Marin county cow country yesterday, drawing mixed reviews from bystanders all along the way.

Hot weather slowed the labors of more than 300 student workers as they strung the 2000 18-foot-high panels of nylon to steel poles meandering through hills, hollows and pastures from the sea to Highway 101, just south off Cotati.

Legal hurdles thrown in the way of the fence were crossed at the last minute, a complication resulting from Christo's lack of a permit from the California Coastal Commission for the last 1000 yards of glistening white fabric as it enters the ocean north of Dillon Beach.

Two suits were heard by Marin county Presiding Superior Court Judge David Menary. He refused to sign a temporary restraining order sought by the state attorney general's office for immediate dismantling of the last 1000 yards of fence.

Menary set October 14 for a hearing date, well after the scheduled September 21 destruction of the fence by its builders. Christo,

Index

Comics..........56
Deaths..........28
Entertainment..........43
Finance..........52
People..........22
TV-People..........42
Weather..........28

Inside

A group of cyclists staged a "bike-in" to protest the closing to bikers of a section of freeway. Page 2.

Tenderloin bar operators expressed surprise over indictments charging policemen with taking payoffs. Page 2.

A new sight appeared in North Beach — a 1918 coffee roaster in the Caffe Trieste. Page 3.

A man in Marin has come up with a system for earning a more than comfortable living while working fewer hours. Page 4.

The International Hookers Film Festival, scheduled to open today, has run into trouble from a home owners association. Page 4.

TOP OF THE NEWS

A letter written by the man executed for the Lindbergh kidnap-murder has turned up in a warden's papers. Page 5.

Eleanor Roosevelt blamed herself for her husband's affair with another woman, according to her son. Page 5.

The new, tough code of campaign ethics will finally go into effect this week, after two years of debate. Page 6.

President Carter is expected to ask for a tax on disposable bottles and cans in his environmental message. Page 6.

Vietnam insists the U.S. supply economic aid if it expects cooperation in finding missing servicemen. Page 7.

The job outlook may brighten in the next few months, a survey of business executives reported. Page 7.

A political prisoner described life inside a Bombay prison. Page 8.

The Arab League approved an extension of the Arab League peacekeeping force in Lebanon. Page 9.

A Rhodesian bishop called for an immediate referendum to replace Prime Minister Ian Smith. Page 10.

Katangan forces have reportedly overrun an important rail and road town 60 miles from the copper center of Kolwezi. Page 11.

A family of three got by on five gallons of water a day in the wilds of Alaska. Page 16.

The pool hall is, according to one regular, "just like life." Page 17.

Weather

Bay Area: Fair and slightly cooler Monday. Lows, 30s to lower 40s; highs, 50s to low 60s. Gale warnings for northwest winds, 20 to 40 m.p.h. Page 24.

San Francisco Chronicle

The Largest Daily Circulation in Northern California

113th Year No. 61 ★★★★ MONDAY, MARCH 28, 1977 777-1111 20 CENTS

Jumbo Jets Collide— More Than 550 Die

A fireman played water on the steaming wreckage of one of the jets. Map shows crash site.

Canary Islands Horror

Santa Cruz de Tenerife, Spain

A Dutch jet plowed into a packed Pan American jumbo jet on a foggy runway in the Canary Islands yesterday, and the two Boeing 747s erupted into flames.

Officials said more than 550 persons were killed in the worst disaster in aviation history.

The national news agency Cifra quoted Santa Cruz airport officials as saying 570 persons died.

Eight hours after the crash, police, soldiers and firemen had recovered 522 bodies, an airport spokesman said. Spokesmen for the island's hospitals said at least 84 persons survived, but some were critically injured.

There were reported to be 655 persons aboard the two planes. In Amsterdam, KLM Royal Dutch Airlines said all 235 passengers and 14 crew members aboard its 747 died. All of them were Dutch citizens.

The Spanish air ministry said at least 240 persons were killed and 40 injured on the American plane, which was struck broadside by the Dutch jet. One survivor aboard the Pan Am 747 — an official of Royal Cruise Lines, the San Francisco travel firm that chartered the craft — said it carried 381 passengers and 25 crew members.

Three hundred four were Californians, he said.

Television stations in the islands broadcast a statement at 10 p.m., more than five hours after the collision, quoting provincial Governor Antonio Oyarzabal as saying he feared there might be 560 dead.

The crash was the biggest disaster in aviation history. The worst previous tragedy was the crash of a Turkish DC-10 near Paris on March 3, 1974, that killed 346 people.

King Juan Carlos sent mes-

Back Page Col. 1

Crash Victims' Stories

Los Angeles

"Oh, God, I couldn't believe it," a Cupertino, Calif., man said from Santa Cruz de Tenerife in the Canary Islands as he waited for word on his seriously injured wife.

"Within five minutes, the whole plane was ashes."

Jim Naik, 37, and — he prayed — his wife Elsie were among the survivors of a chartered Pan American jumbo jet that was demolished when it was struck by another Boeing 747 on the fog-shrouded runway at Santa Cruz.

Several hours after the crash, Naik told the Los Angeles Times by telephone from the Hospital Generale Clinico Santa Cruz de Tenerife,

Back Page Col. 2

Worst Plane Disaster In History

New York

The collision of two 747 jumbo jets that killed hundreds of persons at Tenerife in the Canary Islands yesterday was the worst plane collision in history.

The worst previous single-plane crash was on March 3, 1974, when a Turkish DC-10 jet crashed in Ermenonville, France, near Paris, killing 346 persons.

The previous worst collision between two aircraft occurred near Zagreb, Yugoslavia, on Sept. 10, 1976. All 176 persons aboard a British Airways Trident and a chartered Yugoslav airliner were killed.

Yesterday's collision was the second major air disaster at Santa Cruz De Tenerife. On Dec. 3, 1972, a chartered Spanish airliner carrying tourists home to Munich, West Germany, exploded and burst into flames on takeoff from Los Rodeos

Back Page Col. 2

Gen. Brown's Alleged Slap At Congress

Chicago

General George Brown, chairman of the Joint Chiefs of Staff, told high-ranking military officers and government officials last year that Congress has meddled and behaved irresponsibly in defense and foreign aid, the Chicago Sun-Times reported yesterday.

In a story by syndicated cartoonist and political analyst Ranan Lurie, Brown was quoted as saying that Congress "seems very much to me like the man who is kibitzing a chess game and occasionally reaches in and moves a piece and thereby screws it all up."

Brown also was reported to have said:

- With respect to dissent over government surveillance, "If any citizen of this country is so concerned about his mail being read or is concerned about his presence in a meeting being noted, I'd say we ought to read his mail and we ought to know what the hell he has done."
- Israel's armored ground forces are stronger than those of the United States.
- He favors selling advanced weaponry to Egypt, particularly F-5 fighter planes, but "Congress just wouldn't face up to it."

GENERAL BROWN
New candid comments

Brown's outspokenness got him into trouble in 1974 after he contended that Jews have an undue influence on U.S. banks and newspapers and again last year when he said Israel is a defense burden to the United States.

White House press secretary Jody Powell was asked in a television interview about President Carter's reaction to Brown's remarks. Powell said the remarks came during a previous administration

Back Page Col. 6

Vance Says He Won't See Soviet Dissidents

Moscow

U.S. Secretary of State Cyrus Vance said yesterday he turned down a request for meetings with Soviet dissidents so he could devote all his time to nuclear arms control talks with Kremlin leaders.

Vance arrived in the Soviet capital Saturday night carrying a proposal for a comprehensive arms control agreement, under which the United States and the Soviet Union would make "deep cuts" in their strategic arsenals.

The secretary told reporters on the eve of today's first session talks that he hopes "to make real progress" toward establishing a framework for future negotiations on a second strategic arms limitation treaty.

Other topics expected to be discussed before Vance's departure Thursday include bilateral trade, the Middle East and Africa, the secretary said.

Asked by reporters if he would meet with dissidents while in Moscow, Vance said no. But he revealed that a dissident group which he did not identify had sought such a meeting.

"My reply was I was going to devote all of my time in the period that I was here working on the matters that I came to discuss," Vance said.

Checks with major dissident spokesmen, including Andrei Sakharov, failed to turn up anyone who acknowledged seeking a meeting with Vance.

Soviet officials have warned

Back Page Col. 5

Carter Activism Hasn't Hurt His Popularity, Poll Finds

By George Gallup

Princeton, N.J.

President Jimmy Carter's strong activist role in both domestic and international affairs has apparently had no adverse effect on his popularity with the American public.

Despite criticism from some quarters concerning his actions and statements, 70 per cent of Americans continue to endorse his handling of the presidency. Only nine per cent disapprove, while 21 per cent are undecided.

The latest rating represents virtually no change since the previous rating, obtained two weeks ago, when 71 per cent approved, nine per cent disapproved, and 20 per cent were undecided.

Analysis of the President's job rating by region reveals this inter-

Back Page Col. 6

Index

Comics....44
Deaths....24
Entertainment....41
Finance....52
People....16
TV-Radio....40
Weather....24

Inside

An enraged truck driver smashed three police cars and sideswiped at least 20 other vehicles in a gun-blazing chase. Page 2.

The Big Sur fire slowed its advance but was still burning out of control over 153,000 acres. Page 2.

A congressman charged that lack of a proper respirator contributed to the death of a woman at the Oakland Naval Medical Center. Page 3.

A manufacturer announced the development of a light bulb that may reduce electricity consumption by 60 per cent. Page 5.

A police group has expressed fears of a "military takeover" in California if a reorganization plan is approved. Page 6.

TOP OF THE NEWS

Governor Brown's bill to put a ceiling on hospital costs got an unfriendly reception in an Assembly panel. Page 6.

Congressman Pete McCloskey is seriously considering whether to remain in politics as he approaches 50. Page 6.

The governor of Ohio was hit in the face by a cream pie as he opened the state fair. Page 7.

Former President Ford endorsed the proposed new Panama Canal treaties. Page 7.

The oil industry said the House-passed energy bill would boost gasoline prices to a $1 a gallon. Page 8.

The Pentagon launched its last search for about 1000 men still missing in action in Vietnam. Page 8.

West Germany announced that it will not seek or arrest escaped Nazi war criminal Herbert Kappler. Page 9.

Indira Gandhi's three closest political aides have been accused of misappropriating party funds. Page 9.

Leonid Brezhnev, replying to President Carter, said Russia will "willingly look" for solutions to problems existing with the U.S. Page 11.

A young woman who advertised for a male roommate said most men thought she really was auditioning lovers. Page 14.

Gerald R. Ford confirmed that he never attends social functions where Richard Nixon might show up. Page 14.

David Berkowitz' attorneys entered innocent pleas to murder and assault charges against the man accused of being Son of Sam. Page 26.

This year may be a better one for housing than economists had expected. Page 57.

Weather

Bay Area: Mostly cloudy Wednesday with a chance of thundershowers. Highs, 60s to mid-80s; lows, in 50s. Chances for rain: 3 in 10. Page 28.

Son of Sam —His Day In Court

See Page 26

San Francisco Chronicle

The Largest Daily Circulation in Northern California

113th Year No. 183 ★★★★ WEDNESDAY, AUGUST 17, 1977 777-1111 20 CENTS

Carter's FBI Choice Reported

Washington

President Carter today will name U.S. District Judge Frank M. Johnson Jr. of Montgomery, Ala., as FBI director, The Los Angeles Times learned yesterday.

Informed sources said Attorney General Griffin B. Bell, rejecting the candidates proposed by a presidentially appointed selection committee, has turned to Johnson, 58, a Republican who is considered among the leading civil rights activists on the federal bench.

White House Press Secretary Jody Powell would neither confirm nor deny that Johnson was Carter's choice.

Johnson turned down the job last December when then President-elect Carter first discussed it with him at a meeting in Atlanta. He cited financial and family reasons, the same grounds he used when he later rejected Bell's offer to become deputy attorney general.

Bell is understood to have persuaded Johnson by arguing that the post will be among the most important appointments Carter makes during his Presidency and that the men proposed by the FBI search committee lacked the experience and stature Carter is seeking.

Johnson could not be reached yesterday. His brother, Jimmy, said he thought the judge had "gone fishing."

Bell was questioned as recently as two weeks ago about the possibility of turning to Johnson. At that time, he merely noted that Johnson had rejected the job twice.

But it was learned that Bell, dissatisfied with the candidates advanced by the selection committee and with a present FBI official that he had considered, decided to make still another approach to Johnson, whom he is known to regard as a man of unimpeachable integrity and repute.

An Administration source said last night that Johnson's stature is considered great enough to offset any criticism directed at the Administration on grounds that the search committee had failed to come up with worthy candidates for the job.

Johnson, named to the federal judiciary by President Dwight D. Eisenhower in 1955, pioneered in ordering the integration of Southern schools. He has clashed often with Alabama Governor George C. Wallace, and through his judicial orders he put the federal government in charge of such state functions as schools, the electoral process, mental hospitals and hiring state troopers.

Johnson, stern on the bench.

• *Back Page Col. 3*

Bus Blows Up —15 Die, 20 Hurt

Tunja, Colombia

Fifteen persons were killed and 20 injured when the gas tank of a bus exploded 30 miles south of this northeastern provincial capital, police said yesterday.

They said 20 escaped unhurt from last night's blaze. A gasoline leak in the engine was blamed for the explosion.

Reuters

Exclusive Interview

Elvis' Secret Drug Habit

Singer Dies of Heart Attack At Age 42

Memphis, Tenn.

Elvis Presley, the Mississippi boy whose rock 'n' roll guitar and gyrating hips changed American music styles, died yesterday afternoon of heart failure. He was 42.

Dr. Jerry Francisco, medical examiner for Shelby county, said the cause of death was "cardiac arrythmia," an irregular heartbeat. He said "that's just another name for a form of heart attack."

Francisco said the three-hour autopsy uncovered no sign of other diseases, and there was no sign of any drug abuse.

Presley was declared dead at 3:30 p.m. at Baptist Hospital, where he had been taken by a fire department ambulance after being found unconscious at his Graceland mansion.

Dr. George Nichopoulos, Presley's personal physician, said Presley was last seen alive shortly after 9 a.m.

Presley was discovered unconscious at his white-columned mansion by Joe Esposito, his road manager. A girlfriend, Ginger Alden, 20, was at the mansion, Nichopoulos said.

A Baptist Hospital spokesman said Esposito began resuscitation efforts and called for Nichopoulos and an ambulance.

Emergency medical technicians in the ambulance continued cardio-pulmonary resuscitation efforts on the way to the hospital.

Hundreds of people gathered outside the hospital and at his mansion.

Presley had been a frequent patient at the hospital over the past few years.

When he was rumored to be suffering from various incurable diseases, his physicians blamed his hospitalizations on eye trouble, a twisted colon and exhaustion.

Earlier this year, he canceled several performances in Louisiana and returned to Memphis where he was hospitalized for what physicians said was exhaustion.

He had seldom been seen in public recently, and

Back Page Col. 2

Elvis Presley's early style as shown at a concert in Oakland in 1956

Ex-Guard Tells of Final Days

By Bob Greene

Chicago

"Sometimes I couldn't believe it. Elvis would be sitting there, his eyes closed, his head hanging down, his mouth open — and he couldn't even manage to get his eyes open. He was on pills all day long, and he would give himself shots in the arm or the leg with those little plastic syringes. He would have us give him shots in the rear end. We prayed for this man many times. His drug habit is so severe that I'm convinced he is in danger of losing his life."

The speaker is Delbert (Sonny) West, for 16 years a confidant and bodyguard to singer Elvis Presley. Tuesday — only hours before Presley's death, in the first newspaper interview on the subject even given by a member of Presley's entourage — West outlined a startling list of particulars about the Presley lifestyle, a list that bore out repeated rumors of Presley's deteriorating physical and mental well-being. As the interview was being typed, news of Presley's death was reported by the wire services.

Among the areas touched on in the interview, West said:

- Presley's drug habit was so severe that he had to take pills to get up in the morning, to go to the bathroom, to stop going to the bathroom, to perform, and to go to sleep.
- Presley believed that he was a "supernatural power" put on Earth as a kind of modern-day Jesus, and felt that he had psychic healing powers.
- Presley enjoyed taking friends to funeral homes and mortuaries to examine embalmed bodies.
- Presley lived in mortal fear of assassination, and had instructed his bodyguards to "rip the eyeballs out" of any Presley assassin before the assassin could be brought to trial.
- Presley had ordered his bodyguards to kill the man who took his wife from him, and, on one occasion, ordered his bodyguards to produce a drug-pusher for Presley himself to execute.
- Presley had a fascination with firearms, and once bought 32 handguns in one month. He owned a Thompson submachine gun and

Back Page Col. 1

Guyana Mission

Peoples Temple Exodus Speeding Up

By Marshall Kilduff

Controversial Peoples Temple has stepped up the pace of its exodus from San Francisco to the point where it appears unlikely the church will maintain its powerful political and social base here.

Investigators from the district attorney's office, who have been looking into the church's activities, estimated yesterday that more than 400 church members have left the city aboard temple buses for Miami, where they board flights for Guyana.

That South American country has become the new home for the secretive chapel and its leader, Rev. Jim Jones, according to a half dozen interviews conducted by The Chronicle with former members.

Signs of the church's shift to Guyana include reports of late-night departures of temple buses from the rear parking lot of the temple at 1859 Geary boulevard, stories of chapel members abruptly quitting their jobs and special preparations being made to ship belongings overseas.

Such developments lend credence to earlier reports that the embattled Fillmore district church was considering such a departure.

Jones, a Disciples of Christ minister who has strong political connections with state and local liberal politicians, has been the focus of a series of bizarre charges.

In a New West magazine story published last month, Jones was charged with beating his followers to maintain discipline, faking medical healings to win new recruits and acquiring large sums of money and property from members.

Though such notoriety may be a factor in a stepped-up pace of the church's departure, former members indicated that Jones started the move to Guyana about six months ago.

At that time, vehicles with two or three families and a rental trailer filled with suitcases were dispatched from San Francisco to Miami.

The families were told to stay in cheap motels, often sneaking eight or ten people in a room, until church officials made arrangements for flights and boat trips to the church's agricultural mission.

The numbers involved in such a movement have grown to the point where a representative of Dutch Antillean Airlines confirmed yesterday that 35 members of the church took a flight to Guyana last Saturday.

There also were small bits of personal evidence that the exodus was under way. LaFlora Towne, a chambermaid for 15 years at the Carlton Hotel at 1075 Sutter street,

Back Page Col. 5

Index

Comics 50
Deaths 28
Entertainment 46
Finance 57
Food 18
People 14
TV-Radio 44
Weather 28

Inside

Opening and recapping "childproof" aspirin bottles are giving a lot of people headaches these days. Page 2.

A feminist and a corporate lawyer are giving San Francisco attorneys a real choice for a State Bar post. Page 2.

Crown-Zellerbach paper mills in three states were shut down by 5000 striking workers. Page 2.

Two-thirds of those interviewed say extra-marital sex is "always wrong," the Gallup Poll shows. Page 4.

A Victorian mansion housing a day-care center in Oakland has been renovated to bring out its classical details. Page 4.

TOP OF THE NEWS

The embattled head of the S.F. Housing Authority, Walter L. Scott II, is a veteran bureaucrat. Page 5.

Pope Paul will be remembered for bring a new openness to the papacy while maintaining papal authority. Page 6.

Plans for a mourning period and his funeral began within minutes after the death of Pope Paul VI. Page 8.

Three Italians and three non-Italians are considered the leading candidates to succeed Pope Paul. Page 8.

Blacks and Hispanics are expanding their political clout in California. Page 10.

Senator Abourezk said there could be no serious Mideast peace talks as long as Menachem Begin is in power. Page 11.

Senator Kennedy said he will not challenge President Carter in 1980, but felt other Democrats may do so. Page 12.

Three passengers and a stewardess successfully overpowered a Dutch hijacker shortly after take-off from Amsterdam. Page 13.

New research links the use of marijuana with harmful effects on human reproduction and the brain. Page 14.

"Hedonism" is a word Easterners favor when talking about laid-back California. Page 15.

A "tourist" lost in San Francisco found a lot of polite localites who were a bit fuzzy on directions. Page 17.

Although airline overbooking gets the emphasis, hotel overbooking also is a problem for travelers. Page 54.

Weather

Bay Area; Fair Monday with coastal fog morning and night. Winds from west, 15-30 m.p.h. Lows, mid 50s. Highs, 60s to low 70s. Page 20.

Pope Paul — Activist in a Troubled Age

See Page 6

San Francisco Chronicle

The Largest Daily Circulation in Northern California

114th Year No. 169 ★★★★ MONDAY, AUGUST 7, 1978 777-1111 20 CENTS

Stricken at Summer Residence

The Pope Dies — Heart Attack

POPE PAUL VI AT CASTEL GRANDOLFO LAST SEPTEMBER
The 262nd pontiff of the Roman Catholic Church reigned 15 years

Pontiff Was 80 Years Old

Rome

Pope Paul VI, the 262nd occupant of the throne of St. Peter, died last night after a heart attack in his summer residence at Castel Gandolfo, a small town 15 miles southeast of here.

The death of the pontiff, who would have been 81 years old September 26, was announced at the Vatican by Don Pier Franco Pastore, the acting head of the press service.

"With profound anxiety and emotion I must inform you that Pope Paul VI passed away at 21:40 (9:40 p.m.) this evening, Aug. 6, 1978," Pastore told correspondents gathered in the briefing hall of the Vatican press center.

At Castel Gandolfo, the bells of St. Thomas of Aquinas, the Pope's church, rang the death knell.

Outside the Pope's residence a crowd of tourists and local citizens had been waiting through the early evening. When the bells rang, many of them fell to their knees in prayer.

The lights in the square were turned off for a few minutes. Jean Cardinal Villot, the secretary of state of the Vatican, assumed the temporal and juridical but not spiritual powers of the pontificate upon Paul's death. The interregnum will last until the coronation of the new pontiff.

Villot will summon the conclave of cardinals which will elect the new pontiff. One hundred-sixteen cardinals will be entitled to cast their ballots under a new rule instituted by Pope Paul under which voting rights are limited to prelates less than 80 years old.

Fourteen cardinals are over 80. The conclave will begin 15 to 18 days from now.

The election may take several weeks.

The first indication of a serious deterioration in the Pope's health

Back Page Col. 1

World Praise For His Reign

Rome

Religious leaders yesterday praised Pope Paul VI for his efforts to promote world peace and his sensitivity to the troubles that wracked his church during his reign as leader of the world's Roman Catholics.

Evangelist Billy Graham said, "Pope Paul presided over the Roman Catholic Church when it was going through one of the most critical periods in its history. In one sense, he witnessed a revolution within the Roman Catholic world that has developed for several decades. In another sense, he sought to give that revolution direction and guidance. I believe history may show he was one of the most significant popes in modern times."

Dr. Donald Coggan, Archbishop of Canterbury and primate of the Anglican Church, said in London that Pope Paul's death "brings to an end a period which held within it great difficulty for the leader of the Roman Catholic Church."

"Pope Paul met these difficulties and faced these problems with a total devotion to the truth, as he saw it, and the church over which he presided," he added.

Robert J. Marshall, president of the Lutheran Church in America — the nation's largest branch of Lutherans — said, "It is a time for remembering the heavy responsibilities he carried and the long hours of prayer and work that he

Back Page Col. 1

159 Are Arrested in Diablo Canyon Protest

By Marcie Rasmussen
Chronicle Correspondent

Avila Beach
San Luis Obispo County

One hundred fifty-nine "pretty passive" anti-nuclear demonstrators were arrested for trespassing yesterday after they stormed the sturdy fences and coastal hills surrounding a nearly complete nuclear power plant at Diablo Canyon, sheriff's officers said.

Protesters with the "Abalone Alliance" vowed to return early this morning to try to block workers from entering the gates of the 735-acre Pacific Gas and Electric Co. property near San Luis Obispo.

During yesterday's anti-nuclear protest, one of several nationwide on the 33rd anniversary of the bombing of Hiroshima, demonstrators decried the prospects that Diablo Canyon's twin reactors will reactors will soon go into operation.

The demonstration began as a festive beach party, attended by what Sheriff George Whiting estimated as 3000 to 3500 demonstrators and 135 law officers assigned to protect the plant. (Other officials estimated that the crowd swelled to 10,000 during the afternoon.)

In bathing suits and cutoffs, the demonstrators looked at exhibits of solar panels and windmills and heard a musical group do such numbers as "Radiation Bluegrass."

Then teams of "occupiers," laden with backpacks and ladders, began waves of orderly assaults on the PG&E land, despite a temporary court order the utility won earlier in the work to bar the protest.

One group was reported to have sailed from the Port San Luis harbor in the Greenpeace ship Sea Witch and officers said 24, including a photojournalist were arrested at noon.

The next group of occupiers entered by land, bypassing the PG&E gates, some seven miles from the reactors, and scrambled up the

Back Page Col. 5

How Ex-POWs Got Healthier in Vietnam

San Diego

The rice and vegetable diet of Vietnamese prison camps may explain why returned American prisoners of war are healthier now than their military contemporaries who escaped capture.

A study in progress under the auspices of the Navy's Center for Prisoner of War Studies in San Diego suggests that the low-cholesterol, low-fat diet of imprisoned Navy pilots contributed to their long-term physical health.

John A. Plag, former director of the center, who directed the study, said he compared 78 former prisoners with non-prisoner pilots who had flown in Vietnam during the same period.

"Each of the pilots in the control group was matched with a returned prisoner of war, according to such variables as rank, marital status, years of schooling and number of flight hours," Plag

Back Page Col. 5

Vance, Begin Call Their Talks Useful

Jerusalem

Secretary of State Cyrus Vance and Prime Minister Menachem Begin of Israel yesterday held more than four hours of what both sides termed "serious, good and useful" talks, but a decision on reviving stalled Middle East peace negotiations awaits Vance's meeting with President Anwar Sadat in Egypt today and tomorrow.

Begin, clearly pleased that currently it is Sadat who is being perceived in the West as the one responsible for the breakdown in negotiations, said that if the atmosphere is as good in Alexandria when Vance confers with Sadat as it was in Jerusalem "there will be a success" and the negotiations can resume.

Talking to reporters at the end of the day, Begin, however, seemed to stand firm on Israel's previous proposals that had led Sadat to break off direct talks and to cancel a planned foreign ministers' meeting. And he said that Vance had not asked him to change his position.

"We were not approached to change," Begin said. "The whole problem is President Sadat's agreement to the tripartite meeting."

He said he had told Vance that Israel remained ready to participate in the Egyptian-Israeli-Ameri-

Back Page Col. 2

Rape Is Called Nation's Most Unreported Crime

Washington

Only one rape complaint in four results in an arrest and only one in 60 in a conviction, according to a government-financed report released yesterday.

Of even more concern to federal investigators, however, was the report's estimate that 250,000 rapes are comitted each year but only about 56,000 are reported to police.

"It is the most under-reported crime in the country," said Donna Schram, who directed the study.

"If we improve the way victims are treated it seems likely that more women will report."

The study was conducted by a private research organization, the Battelle Law and Justice Study Center of Seattle, under a $600,000 grant from the Justice Department's Law Enforcement Assistance Administration.

The report said that of 29 interviewed rape victims who did not report the crimes more than half said they feared the sort of treatment they might receive from

Back Page Col. 4

Report That Israeli Tip Led To Sadat's Peace Initiative

New York

A tip from Israeli intelligence sources to Egyptian President Anwar Sadat that Arab extremists were plotting to overthrow several moderate Arab governments — including his own — apparently led to his peace overture to Israel, Time magazine said yesterday.

According to Time, Israeli Prime Minister Menachem Begin relayed the secret information to Egypt that the extremists, trained in Libya, were plotting to overthrow governments in Egypt, Sudan and Saudi Arabia.

Time said that after he received the tip, Sadat launched heavy commando raids against Libya on July 22, 1977, setting off the brief border war.

Sadat, according to Time, then said: "Egypt is ready to sign a peace treaty with Israel that will guarantee Israel her place in the area."

This led Israeli Foreign Minister Moshe Dayan to visit several Moslem capitals in search of a peace formula.

Dayan's trip was followed by

Back Page Col. 4

Index

Comics....36
Deaths....20
Entertainment....41
Finance....54
People....14
TV-Radio....40
Weather....20

Jonestown 'Mass Suicide'

'400 DEAD IN GUYANA'

San Francisco Chronicle
The Largest Daily Circulation in Northern California
114th Year No. 259 ★★★★• MONDAY, NOVEMBER 20, 1978 777-1111 20 CENTS

Reporter's Exclusive Story

I Was in the Airport Ambush

Guyana Says 400 Bodies In Jonestown

By Keith Power
Chronicle Correspondent

Georgetown, Guyana

The Guyana Ministry of Information reported early today that military troops airlifted into Jonestown found "300 to 400 dead bodies" at the jungle settlement, apparently the victims of a mass suicide.

"No living persons were found," said a ministry spokeswoman, who said troops were "going through the bodies seeking to identify the dead."

There was no other immediate confirmation of this report from any other government agency here.

The spokesman said initial reports indicated the dead "appeared to have taken poison," but that this was uncertain, and medical personnel would be sent to the scene today to determine the cause of the deaths.

Guyana police and army troops were sent to the remote Peoples' Temple agricultural mission yesterday after Congressman Leo Ryan and four others were murdered as they attempted to escort fearful and disillusioned settlers out of the jungle.

One report said that eight men and one woman were arrested shortly after the Guyana forces arrived near Jonestown, the compound named after the Rev. Jim Jones, leader of the religious sect.

A government spokesman identified one suspect as Larry John Layton, an American.

The Guyanan government expressed official regret over the incident and pledged to make "every possible effort" to arrest the persons who cut down Ryan (Dem-San Mateo) and the others.

It also said that no Guyanese were involved in the Saturday massacre, which took place at an airfield at Port Kaituma, the nearest landing place to the temple's remote outpost.

Eyewitnesses said the unprovoked, surprise attack came from Americans who were living at the mission.

The vicious assault with pistols, rifles and a shotgun taken from a Guyanese policeman, killed Congressman Ryan and four others, including three newsmen.

The other dead were identified as Gregory Robinson, 27, a photographer for the San Francisco Examiner; NBC news correspondent Don Harris, 41, and NBC cameraman Bob Brown, 36, both of Los Angeles, and Patricia Parks who was identified as a member of the temple community who was seeking her freedom with Ryan's help.

Ryan and his party — accompanied by several People's Temple followers who wanted to leave

Back Page Col. 1

NBC cameraman Robert Brown got this picture of a man jumping off a trailer and beginning to shoot

Begin Rejects Egyptian Proposal

Tel Aviv

Israeli Prime Minister Menachem Begin said yesterday that Israel could not accept new Egyptian proposals for a peace agreement because they were not in accordance with agreements reached at the Camp David summit meeting.

Begin told the central committee of his Herut party that he would ask the cabinet to reject the latest Egyptian proposals when it meets again tomorrow to discuss them.

The cabinet, meeting yesterday in Jerusalem on the first anniversary of President Anwar Sadat's historic visit there, spent five hours discussing the new proposals but reached no decision.

After the cabinet meeting, Begin came to Tel Aviv for the meeting of Herut, the nucleus of the Likud alliance which heads the coalition government.

He had been expected to make a lengthy address but spoke only a few minutes.

He said that he could not go into great detail because the cabinet was still considering the new Egyptian proposals and a compromise formula suggested by the United States.

But Begin said that he would ask the cabinet to reject the Egyptian proposals for a timetable for the institution of local autonomy in the Gaza Strip. The strip was under Egyptian administration from 1948, when Egypt captured it, until 1967 when it was occupied by Israel.

Begin said that Israel was ready to sign a peace treaty with Egypt and negotiate the institution of local autonomy for the West Bank and Gaza Strip on three conditions:

- That the Israeli army would remain in the West Bank as agreed in the Camp David accord.
- That the security of Israel would be maintained.
- That Jewish settlement activity would continue.

The prime minister said he would suggest to the cabinet that Israel accept the draft treaty as contained in the U.S. compromise proposals of November 11.

He also said Israel and Egypt should agree to withdraw two proposals each side had made since then. But he did not elaborate on the nature of the extra proposals made subsequently by the two sides.

Begin and other Herut cabinet ministers were pelted with eggs when they arrived at party headquarters. Demonstrators, many from the ultra-nationalist Gush Emunim (Faith Bloc) movement that has tried to establish unauthorized settlements in the West Bank, chanted "Begin is a Traitor."

The cabinet debated Egypt's proposals for five hours before postponing decision on the Egyptian proposals.

Reuters

How Rep. Ryan, 4 Others Died

Chronicle reporter Ron Javers was a survivor of the Jonestown attack that killed Congressmam Leo J. Ryan and four others. He gave this account from Puerto Rico during a refueling of the U.S. military hospital plane carrying Javers and other wounded to Andrews Air Force Base outside Washington.

By Ron Javers
Chronicle Correspondent
Copyright 1978, Chronicle Publishing Co.

Jonestown is every evil thing that everybody thought — and worse.

We knew that before the shooting started.

All of us who had gone into the People's Temple colony in Jonestown on Friday with Congressman Leo J. Ryan felt lucky to be out of there alive.

Ryan seemed especially lucky. He had been attacked just before we left the jungle settlement and his shirt was stained by his attacker's blood.

Now, at 4:20 p.m. Saturday we could see two airplanes waiting for us on the nearby airstrip, and the ordeal seemed nearly over.

One plane was the twin-engine craft that had brought us to Port Kaituma, seven miles outside Jonestown, on Friday, and was ready to take us back. A small, single-engine plane was for refugees from the colony.

I was standing between Bob Brown and Don Harris, the two NBC men who were to be killed moments later by gunmen charging out of a nearby tractor-and-trailer parked on the edge of the airstrip.

The NBC crew and I became close friends in the course of our stay.

The firing erupted from guns close by. I was hit first. I was knocked to the ground by a slug in the left shoulder, apparently from a .38-caliber weapon.

I crawled behind the right wheel of the plane.

Bob Brown stayed on his feet and kept filming what was happening even as the attackers advanced on him with their guns.

He was incredibly tenacious.

While I was trying to decide whether to stay where I was or risk the 100-yard dash across the close-cropped grass field to the jungle, I saw Brown go down.

Then I saw one of the attackers stick a shotgun right into Brown's face — inches away, if that.

Bob's brain was blown out of his head. It spattered the blue NBC minicam.

I'll never forget that sight as long as I live.

I ran, and then I dived head-first into the brush.

I got up and scrambled as far into the swamp as I could. I was about 150 yards from the airstrip and up to my waist in water.

I pushed through the rain forest, walking parallel

Back Page Col. 4

Index

Comics 30
Deaths 31
Entertainment 51
Finance 63
People 20
TV-Radio 50
Weather 31

INSIDE JONESTOWN CAMP -- THE MASS POISONING

San Francisco Chronicle

The Largest Daily Circulation in Northern California

114th Year No. 260 ★★★★ TUESDAY, NOVEMBER 21, 1978 777-1111   20 CENTS

Rev. Jones Found Dead

400 Stood in Line to Die

The Temple's Rehearsals for Mass Suicide

By Ron Javers
Chronicle Correspondent

Andrews Air Force Base, Md.

When we were waiting in hopes of being rescued from Port Kaituma Saturday after the death of Congressman Leo J. Ryan and four others in our group, we were told that a mass suicide was about to occur at Jonestown.

And we were also told it was to be only the first chapter in a terrible reign of carnage.

The members of the People's Temple cult who survived the attack at the air strip with us described how they had once gone through a week-long "rehearsal" of their mass suicide.

And they were informed, they said, that not everyone would die.

Jim Jones, they said, was supposed to stay alive, and so were his security troops.

This chosen group of survivors was then to escape from Guyana and smuggle themselves back into the United States.

And then they would seek out their enemies one by one — and kill them.

But Jones' planned role in this horrible scenario ended, of course, with his death.

And now the authorities face the difficult task of screening the survivors — seeing which ones are genuine fugitives from Jonestown and which are bent on perpetuating the killing.

The identities of at least four members of the elite guard are known to authorities. They are the three gunmen who staged Saturday's attack at the Port Kaituma air strip, and also the driver of the tractor and flatbed trailer that served as the base of the assault.

All four are Americans, whose names are known by the FBI, and also by several other federal agen-

Page 8, Col. 1

FBI Probing Temple After Death Threats

By George Draper

The FBI reported yesterday it is checking out "some very heavy rumors" concerning the People's Temple crisis, including several purported death threats.

One of the death threats, it was learned, was directed against the son of Joe Holsinger, administrative assistant to Congressman Leo Ryan, who was gunned down in Guyana on Saturday.

Will Holsinger, 27, the son, nas been on the congressman's payroll for the past two months investigating People's Temple in the Bay Area.

His telephone rang Saturday night, a few hours after the first radio report of the Guyana shootings. Young Holsinger's wife answered the phone and heard a man's voice saying:

"Your husband's meal ticket had his head blown off and he (your husband) might be next."

The Holsingers notified authorities and moved to another San

Back Page Col. 6

AP Wirephoto

The 'throne' used by the Rev. Jim Jones, leader of People's Temple

Hundreds Fled Into the Jungle

By Keith Power
Chronicle Correspondent

Georgetown, Guyana

The death toll at Jonestown grew to 405 last night from the mass suicides and killings that began Saturday when the babies at the People's Temple settlement were lined up and given cups of purple Kool-Aid laced with cyanide.

Then the older children and adults took their turn, marching past the big soup kettle to receive their fatal doses.

It took the victims five minutes to die, one of the three survivors at the scene reported.

Most went to an altar at the end of the open-air pavilion where the Rev. Jim Jones had summoned his flock to tell them that the plan to kill not only Congressman Leo J. Ryan but also the visiting newsmen and relatives had failed.

The bodies of the dead were clustered so tightly it wasn't possible to see the ground near the altar.

Jones was one of only three who died by gunshot. He was shot in the right temple, apparently a suicide.

Jones' wife, Marceline, and their three children were also dead.

Apparently about 400 managed to flee into the jungle, escaping a fusillade of shots fired by guards stationed outside the central area of the colony.

Earlier estimates that Jonestown had a population of 1200 were scaled down when it was discovered that there were only 800 passports in Jones' office.

The first reporters to reach the scene found the dazed survivors.

One was Grover Davis, 79, who had been able to run away and hide in the brush. Another was Hyacinth Prash a white-haired woman who stayed in her dormitory bed because she was too ill to get up and attend the ghastly ceremonies.

The third survivor was Odell Rhodes, 36, a former teacher, who said he had been asked by the camp's doctor, Lawrence Schact, to bring him a stethoscope after Schact and the colony's nurses had completed making their cyanide brew.

Rhodes left on the errand as requested — and he didn't return.

Instead, he found a nearby refuge in the jungle, where he could view and hear the terrible scene.

It took five minutes for the convulsions that came from drinking the poison to result in death, Rhodes said — time enough for families to reunite with arms closed about one another before falling.

There was supposed to be a radioed signal as well, Rhodes said, with the words "White Knight," ordering People's Temple members in San Francisco, Los Angeles and Georgetown to kill themselves in Jones' name.

But the signal never went out.

Rhodes told reporters what the original attack plan

Back Page Col. 2

Experts Look at Cults and Suicides

By Charles Petit
Science Correspondent

What leads seemingly ordinary, rational persons to surrender their entire being — their material possessions, their critical faculties and even their lives — to charismatic cult leaders?

In the wake of the tragedy in Guyana, specialists in human behavior reviewed the little that science knows about cult psychology and the forces that could lead to the greatest possible act of devotion to a leader — mass suicide.

"Cults appeal to people who are not well socially integrated in the first place," said Dr. William Simmons, a professor of anthropology at the University of California in Berkeley. "They are people who are seeking an alternative to society."

"There are cults of many different kinds," said Dr. Margaret Singer, a UC Berkeley psychologist. "And they're not all religious. They can be political, even psychological."

What such cults offer to "lonely, depressed, unattached persons" is "love, instant companionship, and group belonging," Singer said.

The mass suicide in Guyana disturbed and surprised Singer, but she noted that "many persons who have been studying cults over the past few years have been aware of the tremendous power they have over their members."

By definition, she said, cults have "self-appointed, charismatic leaders who say they have been given a special mission by some source greater than themselves."

Such leaders, she said — like People's Temple founder, the Rev. Jim Jones — "must have a tremendously centered urge that they are going to succeed. Their minds congeal on the fact they have been appointed to succeed, that they are absolutely right. They have a self-assurance that gives them an aura of leadership and sureness some people just can't resist."

"Their lives get completely devoted to the movenent," said Charles Glock, a sociologist at UC Berkeley and editor of a recent study of California cults, including Hare Krishna, Synanon, Children of God, and the Church of Satanism (but not People's Temple).

One element common to such groups, Glock said, is that they produce "a magic transformation of self, so that

Back Page Col. 1

Index

Comics 30
Deaths 33
Entertainment 52
Finance 25
People 21
TV-Radio 50
Weather 33

City Hall Murders

MOSCONE, MILK SLAIN --DAN WHITE IS HELD

San Francisco Chronicle

The Largest Daily Circulation in Northern California

114th Year No. 266 ★★★★ TUESDAY, NOVEMBER 28, 1978 777-1111 20 CENTS

By John Storey/Copyright 1978, Chronicle Publishing Co.

FORMER SUPERVISOR DAN WHITE (LEFT) AND INSPECTOR HOWARD BAILEY
White was hustled into the Hall of Justice for interrogation by detectives

Mayor Was Hit 4 Times

By George Draper

Mayor George Moscone and Supervisor Harvey Milk were murdered in their City Hall offices yesterday morning. Former Supervisor Dan White turned himself in and surrendered his .38-caliber revolver to police about a half hour after the shooting deaths.

White, 32, a tough-on-crime conservative, was questioned briefly by homicide inspectors before being booked into City Prison on two counts of murder.

San Francisco Coroner Boyd Stephens released the preliminary autopsy report last night and found that Moscone was shot four times — twice in the right side of his head and twice in the chest-abdomen area.

The coroner said Milk had been shot five times — two bullet wounds to the back of the head, and three in the chest-stomach area. Milk was also wounded in the right wrist and left arm by bullets that passed through his body.

Stephens said the head wounds caused massive brain damage in both victims and caused "instantaneous death."

GEORGE MOSCONE
The slain mayor

The double assassination left San Francisco's liberal political scene without two of its leaders. Moscone, 49, was a socially concerned and liberal Democrat, and Milk, 48, was the city's first avowed homosexual to win elective office.

With the death of Moscone, Dianne Feinstein immediately assumed the post of mayor under a provision of the City Charter that requires the president of the supervisors to serve as mayor until a new chief executive can be selected by the full board.

Apparently, yesterday's violence was politically motivated. It seems to have stemmed from White's futile efforts to regain the Eighth District supervisor's seat he had resigned on November 10, explaining at the time that the $9600-a-year salary was

Back Page Col. 1

HARVEY MILK
S.F. supervisor

Feinstein Becomes the Mayor

By Jerry Burns
Political Correspondent

Dianne Feinstein, president of the Board of Supervisors, became mayor of San Francisco yesterday at the moment Mayor George Moscone was shot to death.

She assumed the tragically vacated job under a section of the City Charter that spells out the process for filling a vacancy in the mayor's office.

Under the law, Feinstein will be mayor until the Board of Supervisors chooses a permanent successor to Moscone.

At the same time, a spokesman for City Attorney George Agnost said yesterday, she will continue to be president of the Board of Supervisors.

Fighting to control her emotions, Feinstein's first official act yesterday was to announce to reporters that Moscone and Supervisor Harvey Milk had both been shot to death.

Two hours later, still near tears, Feinstein presided over a Board of Supervisors meeting that lasted only long enough for her to urge the public to "go into a state of very deep and meaningful mourning and to express its sorrow with a dignity and an inner examination

Describing the events as "an unparalleled time" in the history of the city, she said, "We need to be

Back Page Col. 1

Index

Comics 56
Deaths 31
Entertainment 48
Finance 21
People 28
TV-Radio 46
Weather 31

Inside

The State Department failed to warn Leo Ryan of reports that Peoples Temple had 170 guns in Jonestown. Page 2.

A Peoples Temple delegation once lobbied on Capitol Hill against State Department intervention in Jonestown affairs. Page 2.

Jackie Speier, Leo Ryan's legislative counsel, is considering running for the late congressman's seat. Page 2.

Several airlines have begun operating new routes from San Francisco, Oakland and San Jose airports. Page 3.

An inexplicable glow was detected on the dark side of Venus as the Pioneer exploration project climaxed. Page 4.

TOP OF THE NEWS

Mayor Feinstein has a list of 25 persons as possible successors to slain Supervisor Harvey Milk. Page 4.

Lord Snowdon, who married Princess Margaret in Westminster Abbey, wed his second wife in a register office. Page 5.

Norton Simon, charging "pork barreling," resigned as chairman of the state Transportation Commission. Page 7.

The nation's money chief denied that the U.S. has used most of its $30 billion war chest to support the dollar. Page 8.

Saudi Arabia lobbied for a moderate oil price increase on the eve of the OPEC meeting. Page 10.

Its chairman told how the TVA is inducing homeowners in seven states to conserve energy. Page 10.

The U.S. has moved to avert a major war between the South American countries of Chile and Argentina. Page 11.

The opposition announced an all-out economic war aimed at toppling the Shah of Iran. Page 12.

U.S. investigators have found no evidence linking any foreign nation to the smuggling of helicopters to Rhodesia. Page 12.

Meals on Wheels, the lifeline for many elderly shut-ins, has its eighth birthday in San Francisco tomorrow. Page 15.

The stock market dropped more than seven points as investors wondered about the mysterious Carter TV announcement. Page 48.

Industrial production increased at a solid rate indicating a steady economy. Page 48.

Weather

Bay Area: Fair and hazy with occasional high clouds. Chance of rain Saturday night: four in ten. Highs, upper 50s and 60s; lows, mid 30s to 40s. Light winds. Page 18.

$8 Million Temple Fund 'Missing'

See Below

San Francisco Chronicle

The Largest Daily Circulation in Northern California

114th Year No. 282 ★★★★ SATURDAY, DECEMBER 16, 1978 777-1111 20 CENTS

A Break With Taiwan

U.S. to Recognize China

President's Historic Message

Washington

Here is the text of President Carter's speech last night:

Good evening. I would like to read a joint communique which is being simultaneously issued in Peking at this moment by the leaders of the People's Republic of China:

"Joint Communique on the Establishment of Diplomatic Relations Between The United States of America and the People's Republic of China — Jan. 1, 1979.

The United States of America and the People's Republic of China have agreed to recognize each other and to establish diplomatic relations as of Jan. 1, 1979.

The United States of America recognizes the government of the People's Republic of China as the sole legal government of China. Within this context, the people of the United States will maintain cultural, commerical, and other unofficial relations with the people of Taiwan.

The United States of America and the People's Republic of China reaffirm the principles agreed on

Page 6, Col. 4

UPI Telephoto

President Carter just before last night's TV speech

New Policy To Begin January 1

Washington

President Carter announced last night that the United States and the People's Republic of China will establish diplomatic relations on January 1 and that Teng Hsiao-ping, the powerful deputy premier of China, will visit this country later that month.

It will be the first such visit by a high-level Chinese official since the Communists took power on the mainland in 1949.

In a dramatic, nationally televised speech, Carter also announced that the United States will terminate diplomatic relations with the Republic of China on Taiwan as well as the mutual defense treaty with Taiwan.

The United States will also withdraw its remaining military personnel from Taiwan in four months, the President said.

"We do not undertake this important step for transient, tactical reasons," Carter said. "In recognizing that the government of the People's Republic of China is the single government of China, we are recognizing simple reality."

"Normalization — and the expanded commercial and cultural relations it will bring with it — will contribute to the well-being of our own nation and will enhance stability in Asia," the president said.

Addressing the people of Taiwan, Carter told them he had taken care in reaching the agreement to make sure that the normalization of relations with the mainland "will not jeopardize the well-being of the people of Taiwan."

"We will continue to have an interest in the peaceful resolution of the Taiwan issue," Carter said. He added that the United States would maintain "our current commercial, cultural and other relations with Taiwan through non-governmental means."

Teng's visit, Carter said, "will give our governments the opportunity to consult with each other on global issues and to begin working together to enhance the cause of world peace."

The President made special

Back Page Col. 2

Reaction From U.S. Leaders

Washington

While conservatives protested, political leaders from Gerald Ford to Edward Kennedy endorsed President Carter's decision to extend U.S. diplomatic recognition to Peking and break with Taiwan.

Senator Barry Goldwater, R-Ariz., keynoted the bitter response from the right last night by accusing Carter of a cowardly act and threatening to challenge him in court.

Bill Brock, chairman of the Republican National Committee, was equally outspoken, calling Carter's move a "disgraceful" way to treat Taiwan.

"I am heartsick at the prospect

Back Page Col. 4

Cleveland Fails to Meet Loan Deadline

Cleveland

The city of Cleveland failed to meet a midnight deadline set by three banks for payment of $15.5 million in short-term notes, throwing the nation's 17th largest city into default that could lead to bankruptcy.

Mayor Dennis Kucinich and the City Council held an 11th hour meeting but failed to come up with a plan to pay the $15.5 million in notes held by six banks.

Three banks had set the midnight deadline and the Cleveland Trust Co. — holder of a $5 million note — had said it would remain open until midnight in case the city came up with a payment plan.

But the day-long bickering between Kucinich and council continued during the special meeting.

Officials had said that even though the city entered default, services would continue at a near normal level through the use of general revenue funds. But when the funds run out in February, the city would face bankruptcy — the first such collapse of a major American city since the Great Depression.

But at the council meeting, Kucinich said, "If Cleveland is to go into default, at least we will not

Back Page Col. 5

High Court Bans Crosses On City Halls

By Robert Bartlett

A huge, illuminated cross on the Los Angeles City Hall, displayed on Christmas and Easter, violates the state constitution's ban of governmental support of religion, the California Supreme Court ruled yesterday.

The decision may jeopardize similar, municipally sponsored religious observances — such as the Christmas illumination of the cross on top of Mt. Davidson in San Francisco — throughout the state.

Associate Justice Frank Newman wrote the majority decision. Justices Frank Richardson and William Clark wrote separate, dissenting opinions.

The lawsuit was originally filed in Los Angeles Superior Court on Dec. 23, 1975, by S. Dorothy Metzger Fox, a Los Angeles lawyer.

Yesterday's decision came 14 months and 12 days after the Supreme Court heard all arguments. Los Angeles City Attorney Burt Pines represented that city in the lawsuit.

Fox's attorney, Alexandra Leichter of Los Angeles, said she had

Back Page Col. 4

Israel Flatly Turns Down Treaty Proposals by Egypt

Jerusalem

Israel's government yesterday unanimously rejected the latest American-endorsed Egyptian proposals for a peace treaty and the "attitude and interpretation" of the United States regarding them.

At the end of a special four-hour meeting of the cabinet, Prime Minister Menachem Begin, who looked grim, told reporters: "The consultations, the negotiations will resume — we cannot say when."

Yesterday's endorsement by the full cabinet of Begin's unyielding stand in his talks with Secretary of State Cyrus R. Vance here on Wednesday and Thursday quashed any hopes that the proposed Egyptian-Israeli peace treaty might be signed by the December 17 deadline. The cabinet's refusal to share the U.S. view that the new proposals of President Anwar Sadat of Egypt are reasonable marked a low in American-Israeli relations.

Ever since Vance arrived on Wednesday with the Sadat proposals, government members and other politicians, newspaper editorials and broadcasts have alleged that Washington is no longer evenhanded in the disputes between Egypt and Israel, but has tilted toward Sadat and is trying to pressure Israel into acceptance of his terms, disregarding its security requirements.

With a tone of bitterness, Begin said after the cabinet session he hopes the government, Congress and public opinion of the United States will come to realize that it is in the "real interest of the free world to strengthen Israel, and not to weaken Israel."

Begin received support from the leader of the opposition, Shimon Peres, who in a statement said he agreed with the government in the rejection of the Egyptian proposals. However, Peres declared

Back Page Col. 1

Swiss Bank Reports Cult's Account Emptied

Washington

A government official said yesterday that a bank in Zurich had informed the Justice Department that the Peoples Temple assets, estimated at as much as $8 million, had been removed. The name of the bank could not be learned.

However, there were conflicting reports from different government agencies about the disposal of the assets.

After queries to the U.S. Embassy in Bern, the Swiss capital, an embassy spokesman said late yesterday: "We have taken appropriate steps to protect United States interests." The other official, in Washington, said yesterday evening: "The Swiss checked the accounts and they had been emptied."

A Justice Department spokesman said lawyer Mark Lane and Terri Buford, formerly a business manager for the Jonestown Peoples Temple commune, reportedly had gone to Switzerland to remove the secret Zurich assets.

The spokesman, Robert Havel, said that early yesterday the United States authorities here were in-

Back Page Col. 5

2 on Death Row Win Utah Review

Salt Lake City

The Utah Supreme Court agreed yesterday to consider a request for stay of execution for convicted killers Gypsy Codianna and Craig Marvell.

The men are scheduled to die by firing squad at the Utah State Prison January 3 for the slaying of a fellow motorcycle gang member.

Associated Press

Index

Comics 34
Deaths 18
Entertainment 38
Finance 48
People 15
TV-Radio 37
Weather 18

Inside

An overwhelming majority in the latest Chronicle Poll favors banning of movies about youth gang violence. Page 2.

San Francisco was ordered to amend its suit against the developer of Pier 39 within 15 days or have the case thrown out of court. Page 2.

A truck full of antique Chinese objects destined for the Treasures of the Orient exhibit was stolen on Russian Hill. Page 3.

A nuclear power plant near Sacramento has had several "minor leaks", but nothing as serious as the Pennsylvania accident. Page 4.

Governor Brown's political strategy is explored in detail by Chronicle political writer Larry Liebert. Page 6.

TOP OF THE NEWS

Mario Obledo defended California's mental hospital system. Page 7.

The Justice Department intervened to oppose a suit seeking to block extension of the ERA ratification deadline. Page 12.

Leaders of both parties in the Assembly unveiled plans for financing schools under Prop. 13. Page 13.

The House approved compromise legislation establishing a new U.S. relationship with Taiwan. Page 14.

A Soviet citizen with a bomb strapped to his body apparently blew himself up in the U.S. Embassy in Moscow. Page 15.

The U.S. has held informal discussions with Iran about buying back some U.S. aircraft and missiles. Page 16.

A real-life emergency room drama unfolded at a San Francisco hospital when a man entered with a gun, threatening suicide. Page 21.

The Gallup Poll reports on the outlook of Americans toward the nation and toward their own lives. Page 24.

Tanzanian forces closed within artillery range of Kampala and were reported to have shelled the Ugandan capital. Page 25.

The United States trade deficit during February was reported to the smallest in 21 months. Page 29.

The conservative new governor of Massachusetts is being called "wild and crazy, out of touch with reality." Page 36.

A Rockefeller by marriage is getting a divorce to pursue a show-biz career, with her husband's "blessing." Page 37.

Weather

Bay Area: Partly cloudy Thursday. Lows upper 30s to low 40s; highs in the upper 50s to mid 60s. Northwest winds to 20 m.p.h. Page 41.

Ivie Over McCovey On First

See Sports

San Francisco Chronicle

The Largest Daily Circulation in Northern California

115th Year No. 62 ★★★★ THURSDAY, MARCH 29, 1979 777-1111 20 CENTS

Appeals Court

Curb Appoints Judge — Brown Rejects Him

By John Balzar
Chronicle Correspondent

Sacramento

Lieutenant Governor Mike Curb, in his first independent deed as acting governor, announced the appointment of an important Court of Appeal justice yesterday — but Governor Brown ordered the appointment withdrawn almost instantly.

And last night the governor announced his own choice for the job.

The confrontation broke a three-month political truce agreed upon by the Republican lieutenant governor and the Democratic governor.

And it appeared to cast some legal shadow over the Court of Appeal vacancy.

Until yesterday, Brown and Curb had vowed a "spirit of cooperation" in governing California, even though they represented different political parties. They mostly adhered to that promise except for some occasional verbal sniping by Curb.

But then Curb abruptly charted an independent path, nominating Los Angeles Superior Court Judge Armand Arabian to be presiding justice of the Court of Appeal in Los Angeles. The appointment was announced publicly yesterday, but actually was executed on Tuesday.

Curb filled the three-month-old vacancy using his power as acting governor of California while Brown was out of the state, testifying before Congress.

Never before had Curb made such a significant appointment, and his previous actions as stand-in governor were cleared with Brown or his office ahead of time.

Recently, however, Curb said that he is under increasing pressure to act independently while Brown ventures out of California in his unannounced quest for the presidency. And yesterday's appointment is a strong signal of the home-state troubles the governor may face with such a campaign.

"I say good for Mike Curb," declared Assembly GOP leader Paul Priolo of Malibu.

"I think it is clear Mike Curb has sent a message that if Governor Brown wants to travel around the country in pursuit of the presidency, then the lieutenant governor intends to fill the vacuum and govern the state."

Brown returned to California in the pre-dawn hours yesterday. Immediately after Curb's announcement, he said the appoint-

Back Page Col. 2

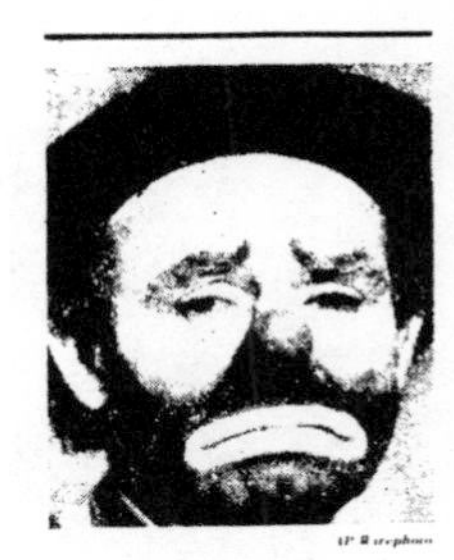

AP Wirephoto

Emmett Kelly Dies

Emmett Kelly, 80, the clown who as Weary Willie made millions smile, died of a heart attack. **Story on Page 41.**

Arabs Split On Sanctions Against Egypt

Baghdad

Three militant delegations stalked out of the Arab foreign ministers conference here yesterday, throwing into disarray the meeting called to take political and economic sanctions against Egypt.

The Palestine Liberation Organization, Syria, and Libya walked out after accusing their fellow Arab delegates of not acting strongly enough against Egypt for signing the peace treaty with Israel.

The Palestinians reportedly also wanted the conference to institute a boycott against the United States as punishment for President Carter's role in bringing the two Middle East antagonists to a peace settlement.

It was not immediately clear whether the walkout of the three Arab militants among the 20 delegations attending was merely a tactic to put pressure on the other Arab countries, or was a sign of a significant breach.

The closed-door meeting of the foreign ministers broke up early today without any apparent success at reconciling the widely divergent points of view among the Arab countries.

The Palestinians, led by PLO

Back Page Col. 5

Mishap In the East

A-Plant Accident Leaks Radiation

UPI Telephoto

Arrow points to building housing reactor core, where the accident occurred. Cooling towers are in the background.

Long-Term Effects Are Feared

Harrisburg, Pa.

A nuclear power station's cooling system malfunctioned yesterday, releasing radioactive steam and radiation that was detected at low levels 16 miles away. Power company officials said there was a radiation leak that lasted several hours.

There were no reports of injuries, but officials were concerned about long-term effects on the thousands of people who live near the plant at Three Mile Island in the Susquehanna river ten miles southeast of Harrisburg.

The accident triggered an automatic shutdown of the atomic plant.

Workers were ordered from the plant immediately, but Don Curry, spokesman for Metropolitan Edison Co., operator and part owner of the power station, said in Reading, Pa., that the company did not believe anyone was contaminated. He said a minimum shift was on duty at the time. Other owners of the plant are Pennsylvania Electric Co. and Jersey Central Power and Light Co.

The incident apparently involved a pump that pushes cooling water into the power station's 900-megawatt No. 2 reactor.

Curry said the pump malfunctioned and automatically caused the shutdown of the turbine inside the reactor. At the same time, the reactor itself was shut down, he said.

Curry said radioactive steam built up because the turbine was not moving and a valve released the steam onto the floor of the reactor room.

The NewYork Times reported that James Deddens, an engineer with Babcock & Wilcox, which built the reactor, said in Lynchburg, Va., that the mishap was not caused by valves, or pumps, or even pipes, but something else. He refused to elaborate on that point, but added that the coolant system had other pieces of equipment, such as control mechanisms.

NRC experts were at the plant monitoring radiation levels. The NRC said the plant would remain closed during an investigation into the cause of the incident.

About 13,000 persons live in the

Back Page Col. 1

Britain's Labor Government Falls — Defeated by 1 Vote

London

Britain's Labor party government was toppled from power by one vote last night in a cliff-hanging parliamentary ballot that launched the country into an early general election.

Prime Minister James Callaghan's three years of shaky rule ended when the House of Commons voted 311 to 310 for an opposition no-confidence motion. The vote was on Conservative party leader Margaret Thatcher's censure motion.

Callaghan immediately announced he would recommend to Queen Elizabeth that Parliament be dissolved and an election held. The date was expected to be May 3 or May 10.

The result followed one of the most exciting votes in British history. Conservative members of Parliament greeted it by throwing their arms in the air and waving agenda papers. Labor politicians reacted by singing "The Red Flag."

The outcome was decided by the illness of Labor party member of the House of Commons Alfred Broughton, who was too sick to be brought by ambulance to the voting lobby. Broughton's presence, and vote against the motion, would have saved the government.

Thatcher will go into the election campaign as a firm favorite to become Europe's first woman prime minister. Her party has a 13 percent lead in the latest opinion polls.

A grocer's daughter who was trained as a pharmacist and lawyer, she has been called the "Iron Maiden" by Moscow because of her tough warnings about Soviet militarism.

She made a low-key speech at the start of yesterday's rowdy

Back Page Col. 5

Beards OKd for Uniformed S.F. Cops

By Stephen Hall

After a clean-cut hiatus of about half a century, San Francisco's uniformed policemen will again be allowed to wear beards and goatees on duty.

The specifics — the allowable length for goatees and the "curly" factor in beards — have yet to be worked out, but the Police Commission approved "the concept" of facial hair for on-duty officers by a 4-to-1 vote last night.

The favorable vote — with only Commission President Richard J. Siggins dissenting — came despite a prediction by Police Chief Charles Gain that such permissiveness would make the SFPD "the laughing stock of the country."

"Our sole concern is appearance," said Gain, dismissing the notion that well-groomed beards and goatees might be safety hazards to the officers. "It simply does not enhance the appearance of police officers in uniform to have beards."

Gain, however, did not vigorously object when Commissioner Jane M. Murphy insisted on a motion giving general approval to

Back Page Col. 1

Index

Comics 54
Deaths 41
Entertainment 60
Finance 29
People 36
TV-Radio 54
Weather 41

VERDICT ON DAN WHITE

San Francisco Chronicle
The Largest Daily Circulation in Northern California
115th Year No. 108 ★★★★· TUESDAY, MAY 22, 1979 777-1111  20 CENTS

It's Voluntary Manslaughter — Maximum Penalty 8 Years

Four police cars went up in flames in front of City Hall during last night's rampage following the Dan White verdict

Several Jurors Weep in Court

By Duffy Jennings

Dan White was convicted by a jury of two counts of voluntary manslaughter yesterday for the killings of San Francisco Mayor George Moscone and Supervisor Harvey Milk in City Hall last November 27.

White, 32, who faced a possible death sentence if convicted of first-degree murder, could now receive a total maximum prison term of seven years and eight months for the manslaughter convictions and related charges.

DAN WHITE
Ex-supervisor

With good behavior, he could be eligible for parole in about five years.

The former city supervisor, fireman and policeman dropped his head and rubbed his eyes as the verdicts were read in a packed, emotion-charged courtroom at the Hall of Justice at 5:28 p.m.

Several jurors — many of whom had cried listening to White's anguished taped confession on the third day of the trial May 3 — wept openly while court clerk Anne Barrett read the verdicts.

White's wife, Mary Ann, cried with joy and embraced White's sister, Nancy Bickel, as Superior Court Judge Walter F. Calcagno polled each juror individually to confirm the verdicts.

It was the climax of six days of jury deliberation that began last Wednesday following an 11-day trial.

Defense lawyer Douglas R. Schmidt who called five mental health experts to testify that White was mentally ill from severe depression, reacted to his major victory with subdued elation.

"There's nothing I can say that will help the families of the victims, but the verdict is just," Schmidt said in a Hall of Justice corridor that was jammed with reporters and television equipment minutes after the verdicts were announced.

"It was a tragedy," Schmidt said of the shootings that stunned San Francisco nearly six months ago. "Now it's behind us.'

He said White, who walked expressionlessly out of the courtroom to return to his jail cell after the verdicts, was "guilt-ridden and filled with remorse."

"He's in very bad condition at the moment," Schmidt said.

A stern-faced District Attorney Joseph Freitas said the jury's conclusions were "somewhat of a tragedy."

"I don't think justice was carried out," Freitas said. "I'm very, very disappointed. There were two charges of first-degree murder and the evidence was there to

Back Page Col. 1

City Officials Shocked by The Verdict

By Marshall Kilduff and Eugene Robinson

News of the voluntary manslaughter verdict in the Dan White trial went through City Hall yesterday like an electric shock, bringing gasps of astonishnent and furious denunciations of the jury.

Mayor Dianne Feinstein, her eyes glistening with tears, reacted to the verdict with "disbelief."

"As far as I'm concerned, these were two murders," she said 15 minutes after the jury announced its decision. "This raises the question of who gets what kind of penalty and why."

Feinstein, who discovered the bullet-riddled body of Supervisor Harvey Milk on the day of the killings, issued a call for unity in the city.

"I think it's important that this town pull itself together again," she said. "We've gone through a physical bloodbath and now we are going through a mental one."

The mayor was asked if the verdict appeared to her to be a

Back Page Col. 5

A Bloody Protest at City Hall

Some enraged demonstrators smashed the doors at City Hall

Verdict Angers Gays

By Katy Butler

In a long night of looting, burning and chants for vengeance, more than five thousand demonstrators, many of them gay, rampaged through Civic Center and nearby neighborhoods last night in a violent protest of the manslaughter verdict against Dan White.

It began as a quiet march of shocked and grieved gays from Castro and Market Street at about 7 p.m. But the mood quickly became disorganized and chaotic as demonstrators arrived at City Hall and night fell.

For four hours, Civic Center Plaza was a virtual battlefield, lit by the eerie, smoky fires of trash barrels. Waves of police, dressed in riot gear and swinging batons, tried again and again to drive demonstrators away from the besiened City Hall and out of the plaza.

They finally succeeded shortly after midnight, driving bands of looters and demonstrators north

Back Page Col. 1

Index

Comics 50
Deaths 20
Entertainment 38
Finance 46
People 15
TV-Radio 36
Weather 37

Inside

A former Death Row inmate was sentenced to death in the murder of a San Francisco merchant. Page 2.

A sentimental crowd mourned the closing of Breens, a landmark San Francisco saloon. Page 2.

The Environmental Protection Agency announced tough new air quality standards for coal-fired power plants. Page 2.

Ed Zelinksy could care less about the gas shortage — his 1910 Rauch and Lang coupe runs electrically. Page 3.

The weather and gasoline outlook was brighter for the Memorial Day weekend in Northern California. Page 3.

TOP OF THE NEWS

Two Trinity County women, who have had miscarriages, filed suit against the Forest Service for its spraying of herbicides. Page 5.

The Army Corps of Engineers promised in writing to hold back on filling the New Melones reservoir. Page 5.

Governor Brown proposed 13 safety measures to deal with any possible nuclear plant accident in California. Page 5.

Supervisor Quentin Kopp's plan to require a review of all city job openings was rejected by the board. Page 5.

An eyewitness described the execution in Florida of John Spenkelink. Page 6.

Inflation continued at double-digit rates last month due to rising gas, housing and food costs. Page 8.

Iranian gunmen shot and wounded a moslem leade. who is reputed to be a key man in the new regime. Page 10.

Egypt and Israel, began trying to bridge the gap on the Palestinian issue. Page 10.

The California Supreme Court ruled that parents of minors may not consent to some police searches of their children's property. Page 11.

Diva Beverly Sills has been cheerful and energetic all her life, beginning with her very Jewish mother. Page 13.

Scandal is nothing new for the dignified wife of England's former Liberal Party leader, charged with conspiracy to murder a homosexual. Page 13.

Exxon Corp. offered to pay $1.165 billion to acquire a company developing a device that would cut power consumption in electric motors. Page 45.

Weather

Bay Area: Coastal fog and low clouds becoming fair in the afternoon. Highs, upper 50s to mid 70s; lows, 50s. Westerly winds 15 to 30 mph. Page 12.

Giants Hit 4 Homers, Beat Braves

See Sports

San Francisco Chronicle

The Largest Daily Circulation in Northern California

115th Year No. 112 ★★★★ SATURDAY, MAY 26, 1979 777-1111 20 CENTS

Worst U.S. Air Disaster — 270 Killed in Chicago

AP Wirephoto

Wreckage, including a piece of the landing gear (foreground), was still burning when this photo was taken shortly after the crash

Jetliner Has No Survivors

Chicago

A Los Angeles-bound American Airlines DC-10 jetliner jammed with 257 Memorial Day holiday travelers and 13 crew members crashed and burned shortly after takeoff from busy O'Hare International Airport yesterday. There were no survivors, authorities said.

It was the worst disaster in U.S. aviation history.

At least two persons on the ground were injured when the wide-bodied jumbo jet — which dropped its left engine onto the runway as it lifted off — plunged nose first into a vacant field about a mile north of the airport shortly after 3 p.m.(CDT).

Witnesses said the aircraft erupted into flames and a pillar of smoke rose nearly 200 feet into the air. Black smoke continued to billow over the crash site for several hours, as rescue teams pored over the rubble — at first looking for survivors, later marking the locations of bodies with flag-topped stakes they drove into the ground.

The plane went down in an unincorporated area of Cook County, narrowly missing three large mobile home parks and a large complex of oil storage tanks. Authorities said at least five mobile homes were damaged by debris from the aircraft.

"It looks like a Vietnam battlefield after napalm has been dropped," said Warren Baird, a firefighter with the suburban Hoffman Estates fire department, as he walked through the crash site. He was one of hundreds of law enforcement personnel from several jurisdictions who responded to the emergency.

Ben Flapen, manager of one of the mobile home parks, said he was just getting into his car when "I heard an explosion. I looked up into the air and saw a tremendous fire overhead. The ground was shaking, and I saw flames shooting all over."

Flapen said at least one trailer in his park caught fire when struck by flaming wreckage, and at least

Back Page Col. 1

First U.S. Execution In More Than 2 Years

Starke, Fla.

The state of Florida strapped John Arthur Spenkelink into the electric chair yesterday morning, dropped a black blindfold over his face and electrocuted him.

"He simply looked at us and he looked terrified," said Kris Rebillot, a television reporter who was a witness to the execution.

The first surge of electricity, 2500 volts, was administered at 10:12 a.m. Spenkelink jerked in the chair. A doctor unbuttoned his white shirt, pulled up the T-shirt underneath and placed a stethoscope to his chest.

The doctor stepped back and another surge of electricity was sent through the body.

There was another stethoscope check, another surge, the third, and the doctor checked for pulse, lifted the mask, flashed his penlight into either eye and nodded to the warden that Spenkelink was dead.

The execution was the first since Gary Mark Gilmore voluntarily faced a Utah firing squad on Jan. 19, 1977, and the first since 1967 in which the condemned was put to death against his will.

Spenkelink made no final statement; the prison authorities said that was his wish.

The Rev. Tom Feamster, an Episcopal priest who was the last to speak with him, said Spenkelink had told him, "Man is what he chooses to be; he chooses that for himself."

"But," the burly, six-foot-six minister said, "the last thing that he said to me was that he loved me, and the last thing I said to him was that I loved him."

He also quoted Spenkelink as saying, "If this comes down, I hope that some good will come of it."

The 10 a.m. execution hour was

Back Page Col. 5

Marin Mother Convicted of Killing Baby

By Jack Viets

A Marin mother was convicted of second-degree murder yesterday for the bizarre poisoning death of one of her foster baby daughters from Korea.

Priscilla Phillips, 33, of Terra Linda, a widely-respected County of Marin social worker, sobbed uncontrollably in the arms of her husband, Steve, when the jury's verdict was read.

"I didn't do it. I didn't do it," she screamed after Justice Louis H. Burke had polled and dismissed her murder jury of four men and eight women.

"God, I didn't do it."

The courtroom was hurriedly closed, but her screams pierced the closed doors. Groups of her friends

Back Page Col. 3

DA Probing a Claim Of White Juror's Bias

By Michael Harris

The district attorney's office is investigating reports from witnesses who claim one juror in the Dan White case told friends about a strong bias in favor of White even before the former supervisor's murder trial began.

District Attorney Joseph Freitas Jr., confirming information received by The Chronicle, said statements about possible favoritism toward White by one of the jurors had reached his office.

Freitas said he has asked state Attorney General George Deukmejian to take over the investigation — but it seemed likely late yesterday that Deukmejian would conclude that the charges are purely a local matter that Freitas himself should pursue them.

"The only thing I can tell you is that there have been allegations made following the verdict that a juror in the Dan White case may not have disclosed possible bias in the course of being selected as a juror," Freitas said.

Under the law it took the unanimous vote of all 12 jurors to reach a verdict. The juror under investigation as well as the other 11 all agreed on voluntary manslaughter. And whatever the outcome of the current investigation, it would not affect that trial verdict.

While being questioned before they were chosen to hear the case, all the jurors said under oath that they would hear the evidence without bias. Making a false statement under oath can lead to criminal prosecution.

"I want to make it very clear that the investigation is limited to

Back Page Col. 5

Index

Comics 48
Deaths 16
Entertainment 34
Finance 45
People 13
TV-Radio 33
Weather 12

Inside

The war games in Marin County featured a helicopter assault and more smoke bombs than a Kiss concert. Page 2.

Candidates for mayor in San Francisco went the campaigning rounds as election day nears. Page 3.

Art collectives that have sprung up in S.F. warehouses are a special problem to the Planning Commission. Page 4.

A report contends 75 percent of breast cancers can be found by physical examination and mammography. Page 5.

Tiburon and the SP face a challenge in using 38 acres, architecture critic Allan Temko said. Page 7.

TOP OF THE NEWS

George Bush scored a surprising upset over Senator Howard Baker in a Maine straw poll. Page 8.

The report on the Three Mile Island accident found there had been a decision not to release bad news. Page 8.

A panel of prominent Americans has recommended that the U.S. conduct "informal contacts" with the PLO. Page 10.

Prime Minister Begin reprimanded a cabinet aide for suggesting Israel might talk to the PLO. Page 10.

Massive sales of U.S. arms to Iran were said to be a major cause of the revolution that unseated the shah. Page 12.

A refugee camp somewhere along the Thai-Cambodian border contains 80,000 "free" Cambodians. Page 14.

Henry Kissinger, while teaching at Harvard in 1953, offered to provide information to the FBI. Page 19.

The S.F. supervisors are being asked to make good on a promise to add more city employees to the pension system. Page 21.

Calvin Klein and Perry Ellis are two New York designers who create realistic clothing for women. Page 23.

Dolly Parton, trimmed down by 35 pounds, will star with Jane Fonda in a new movie. Page 24.

Several factors combined to push oil industry profits this year to all-time highs. Page 62.

Michael Dingman is scoring ecological points and making money turning refuse into energy. Page 62.

Weather

Bay Area: Showers likely today and tonight. Highs, 55 to 65; lows, 45 to 55. Southerly winds to 20 mph. Chances for rain: 6 in 10. Page 21.

Fumbling 49ers Lose To Raiders

See Sports

San Francisco Chronicle

The Largest Daily Circulation in Northern California

115th Year No. 251 ★★★★• MONDAY, NOVEMBER 5, 1979 777-1111  20 CENTS

Deep Concern In Washington

Iranian Students Seize U.S. Embassy in Tehran

A Moslem revolutionary posted a picture of the Ayatollah Ruhollah Khomeini on the wall of the U.S. Embassy in Tehran

UPI Telephoto

They Vow to Hold Hostages Until U.S. Returns the Shah

By Nicholas Cumming-Bruce
Washington Post

Tehran

Several hundred Iranian students stormed and occupied the U.S. embassy yesterday, taking up to 100 hostages, including diplomatic staff, Marine guards and local Iranian employees in an assault that appears to have left the government temporarily paralyzed.

The students, mostly in their early 20s, said in a press conference hours after the occupation that they will continue to hold the embassy staff until the U.S. government agrees to send the shah back to Iran.

Spokesmen for the students appeared to have no clue about what they will do if the U.S. government refuses to send him.

The spokesmen said the students seized 90 American men, women and children and another ten Iranians. However, the State Department in Washington said there are probably only 59 American hostages, but "we can't be precise."

The brief assault on the embassy came at about midday after hundreds of thousands marched through the capital in demonstrations commemorating students shot dead by the shah's troops on Tehran University's campus this time last year.

About 400 students forced the gates of the embassy and scaled the compound walls in what was largely a non-violent occupation.

The attacking force included a small group who were heavily armed, according to Iranian eyewitnesses, but no weapons were carried by the students, who later controlled the embassy compound, many wearing large pictures of revolutionary leader Ayatollah Ruhollah Khomeini pinned to their chests.

A small group of U.S. Marine guards fired tear gas at the students as they broke into the compound but failed to stop them as they rushed the embassy buildings.

Embassy officials destroyed sensitive files during the attack, according to the students, who produced frames containing the charred remains of documents for inspection by the press.

They said they had found other documents relating to events in Kurdestan and oil-rich Khuzestan, two provinces in which there has been bitter fighting since the revolution between security forces and dissident ethnic minority groups. But they declined to identify the contents of the documents.

The attack was completed quickly but, throughout the day and late into the night, hundreds stood outside the embassy compound chanting anti-U.S. slogans.

"Khomeini struggles, Carter trembles," they shouted along with more familiar cries of "Death to America" and "America is the No. 1 enemy."

A mock gallows was produced from which dangled a poster saying "For the shah," while other

Back Page Col. 5

State Dept. Reaction

Dubious Assurances From Iran

Washington

The United States said yesterday it has received assurances from the Iranian government that it will do its best to free the Americans being held hostage in the U.S. Embassy in Tehran, but officials in Washington expressed uncertainty that the Iranian government can fulfill its pledge.

The takeover of the embassy by Iranian students caused a major scramble in Washington.

Top officials were roused in the predawn hours by the State Department's Operation Center and a special task force, headed by Harold H. Saunders, assistant secretary for Near East and South Asian affairs, was set up.

The State Department said later that no Americans had been injured and that the takeover was relatively peaceful. A few tear gas shells had been fired initially by the Marine Corps security contingent of 14 members, but officials denied that there had been "a battle" for the embassy as stated in some reports from Tehran.

Secretary of State Cyrus Vance, who had just returned from South Korea where he at tended the funeral of President Park Chung Hee, spent several hours at the State Department, and President Carter was kept informed at Camp David, Md.

The problem facing the Carter administration — deeply concerned over the safety of the Americans in the embassy — was that the takeover was another example of the disorder and disunity that has plagued Iran since the fall of Shah Mohammed Reza Pahlavi. There has been no

Page 11 Col. 3

A Rash of Gun Slayings In Stockton

By George Williamson

Stockton

Seven separate incidents of fiercely wild gunplay rocked this San Joaquin city over a 13-hour period that ended early yesterday with four men dead, three people wounded — one very seriously — and at least two houses ventilated by machine-gun-like attacks.

Police Lieutenant Don Garibaldi seemed to speak for the entirety of a shaken city of almost 120,000

Back Page Col. 5

Protesters in Bolivia Flee Jets' Gunfire

La Paz, Bolivia

Two Bolivian air force jet fighters roared over downtown La Paz yesterday with their guns blazing, scattering students and workers who had gathered in a central plaza to protest the four-day-old military regime.

The attack followed a night of bloody clashes between soldiers and civilians in which Red Cross and hospital officials said at least 20 civilians were killed and 40 wounded.

A communique broadcast by the new military administration of Colonel Alberto Natusch Busch, who led a coup against the civilian

Back Page Col. 1

Behind the Killings at the Anti-Klan Rally

Greensboro, N.C.

All four persons shot to death Saturday at the anti-Klan demonstration here were members of an organization that claimed responsibility for bursting into a Ku Klux Klan rally July 8, tearing down the Confederate flag and burning it.

The Klan had promised vengeance for the raid on the Community Center in China Grove, a small North Carolina community about 70 miles from here, by members of the Workers Viewpoints Organization.

Yesterday, 12 men described by the police as members of one or more violent Ku Klux Klan splinter groups were charged with first-degree murder in the slaying of the four members of the self-professed Communist action group, which sponsored the well-advertised "Death to the Klan" demonstration.

Police arrested a 13th suspect late yesterday and charged him with conspiracy to commit murder. Rayford Milano Caudle, 37, of Winston-Salem, surrendered to police in Winston-Salem. Unlike the 12 whites arrested Saturday, Caudle was not charged with first-degree murder.

A statewide search for the remaining person believed to have fled the scene was under way.

Eight persons were wounded Saturday in the brief but intense fusillade from shotguns and a semiautomatic rifle that laced into the anti-Klan demonstrators in a black neighborhood here. A fifth member of the action group was in critical condition yesterday and doctors said he had little chance to live.

Two others remained hospitalized in serious condition.

There were no signs yesterday that Greensboro was having other than a peaceful day. No extra police were in the streets, and people went to church and about

Back Page Col. 1

Index

Bridge	25
Business World	61
Chess	25
Comics	50
Deaths	28
Entertainment	48
People	22
TV-Radio	46
Weather	21

1980-1988

APRIL 25, 1980
Hostage Rescue Fails

MAY 19, 1980
Volcano Blows Up;
Miami Riot Grows

NOVEMBER 5, 1980
Reagan Sweep

DECEMBER 9, 1980
John Lennon Slain

MARCH 31, 1981
Reagan O.K. — Bullet Removed from Lung

APRIL 15, 1981
Shuttle's Triumph

MAY 14, 1981
Pope Survives Shooting

OCTOBER 7, 1981
Sadat Assassinated

JUNE 15, 1982
Argentina Surrenders — Britain
Recaptures Falkland Islands

NOVEMBER 11, 1982
Brezhnev Dies

SEPTEMBER 2, 1983
How Russian Missile Shot Down Airliner

OCTOBER 24, 1983
161 Marines Dead in Beirut

OCTOBER 26, 1983
U.S. Invades Grenada

OCTOBER 31, 1984
Assassins Kill Indira Gandhi

NOVEMBER 7, 1984
Reagan Landslide

JANUARY 21, 1985
49ers Win Super Bowl

JANUARY 29, 1986
Seven Killed in Shuttle Explosion

FEBRUARY 26, 1986
U.S. Flies Marcos to Guam

APRIL 15, 1986
U.S. Bombers Attack Libya

APRIL 29, 1986
Big Nuclear Accident in Russia

DECEMBER 24, 1986
Voyager Sets New Flight Record

MAY 19, 1987
Frigate's 'Ghastly Error' Left 28 Dead

SEPTEMBER 18, 1987
Pope's Dramatic Day in S.F.

OCTOBER 20, 1987
Financial Meltdown — Dow Falls 508

DECEMBER 8, 1987
S.F.-Bound Jet Crashes;
Gorbachev Arrives

JULY 4, 1988
U.S. Downs Iran Airliner

HOSTAGE RESCUE FAILS —U.S. PLANES CRASH

San Francisco Chronicle

The Largest Daily Circulation in Northern California

116th Year No. 86 ★★★★• FRIDAY, APRIL 25, 1980 777-1111  20 CENTS

8 Americans Die In Iran Operation

The hostages early in their captivity

The Official Announcement

Washington

Here is the text of the White House statement on the rescue attempt in Iran:

"The president has ordered the cancellation of an operation in Iran that was under way to prepare for a rescue of our hostages.

"The mission was terminated because of equipment failure. During the subsequent withdrawal, there was a collision between our aircraft on the ground at a remote desert location. There were no military hostilities but the president deeply regrets that eight American crewmen of the two aircraft were killed and others were injured in the accident.

"Americans involved in the operation have now airlifted from Iran and those who were injured are being given medical treatment and are expected to recover.

"This mission was not motivated by hostility toward Iran or the Iranian people and there were no Iranian casualties.

"Preparations for this rescue mission were ordered for humanitarian reasons to protect the national interests of this country and to alleviate international tensions.

"The president accepts full responsibility for the decision to attempt the rescue.

"The nation is deeply grateful to the brave men who were preparing to rescue the hostages.

"The United States continues to hold the government of Iran responsible for the safety of the American hostages. The United States remains determined to obtain their safe release at the earliest possible date."

United Press

Engine Trouble Blamed

Washington

A dramatic U.S. military operation to rescue 53 American hostages in Tehran was aborted because of an aircraft engine failure, and eight American servicemen died in the collision of a C-130 transport plane and a rescue helicopter on a remote Iran desert, officials said early today.

White House Press Secretary Jody Powell said there was no military clash with Iranian forces and no Iranians were injured in the effort to free the hostages, now in their 174th day of captivity at U.S. Embassy in Tehran.

He said the surviving Americans were immediately flown out of Iran and a number of others injured in the accident "are being given medical treatment and are expected to recover."

Senator Charles Percy, R-Ill., said he was informed by the State Department after midnight in Washington of the operation.

His information suggested that the United States attempted to set up a staging base using land-based transport planes and helicopters some distance from Tehran for a quick commando-like raid on the embassy.

An Israeli radio report said the night mission was launched from Egypt and involved a stop in the Persian Gulf nation of Bahrain. However, ABC News reported that some elements of the mission started from Pakistan and that the crash occurred in Iran near the Pakistani border.

Percy said the would-be rescuers encountered trouble "as they went in and it was decided to abandon the mission."

A White House source said the failure of an aircraft engine was the source of the initial trouble.

Percy said after President Carter had decided to cancel the mission, a lumbering C-130 transport — a four-engine turboprop craft that can carry up to 92 troops — collided with a helicopter on

Back Page Col. 3

It was a long night for the president — White House lights blazed until morning

Wild Rush From Cuba — Warnings Ignored

By Ward Sinclair
Washington Post

Key West, Fla.

With go-to-hell defiance for both Washington and Havana, the refugee boatlift from Fidel Castro's Cuba continued to wash into this tropical port yesterday.

The two-day total is more than 1300 refugees, and there are thousands more reportedly waiting in Cuba for vessels to bring them here.

The human tide that began to come in Sunday showed no signs of abating. It has this mellow vacation resort standing on its head. Motels are jammed, city streets carnival-like at 4 a.m.

Fishing boat captains, laughing off threats of prosecution by Washington, were leasing space on their vessels for $1000 or more per person to take exiles on the 90-mile cruise to pick up relatives at a port near Havana.

Cubans swarmed around the city's docks through the night and all day yesterday haggling over charter prices, while others clogged the waterways through the Florida keys, towing all sizes of pleasure boats for private missions.

Always sensitive to a dollar in the off-season, some local boatmen were offering their vessels for sale. A boat that changed hands Wednesday for $10,000 sank, with no loss of life, just after its new owners left port for Cuba.

In Miami, Coast Guard spokesman Mike Kelley said his office has been besieged with calls from boat owners asking how they could make the run to Cuba legally. "We tell them it's against the law, but some of them have been taking off (anyway) in 23-foot pleasure boats — the kind you water-ski with."

As a result, Kelly said, the

Back Page Col. 2

Anderson Starts New Campaign

Washington

John B. Anderson entered the 1980 race for the presidency as an independent candidate yesterday, promising to attract millions of new voters into the political process and raise issues that the major party contenders would avoid.

By dropping out of the Republican competition, and proposing a well-financed national campaign on his own, Anderson injected a new unpredictable element into the anticipated contest between President Carter and Ronald Reagan, the leading candidates of their parties.

Even if Anderson does not reach his goal of carrying enough states to win the election, he could

Back Page Col. 4

Hostages' Relatives Are Shocked, Shaken

Washington

Shock, bewilderment, confusion. Those were the reactions of hostages' relatives, as well as official and unofficial Washington early this morning as they groped to learn more details of the aborted rescue attempt in Iran that left eight Americans dead.

Sara Rosen, mother of hostage Barry Rosen, accused President Carter of "trying to kill" the Americans being held in the U.S. Embassy in Tehran.

"I've heard already," she sobbed when a reporter called her Brooklyn apartment. "It's a terrible thing."

"He (Carter) had no business doing it. He should have waited a little bit longer until it simmered" in Tehran. "He's trying to kill them."

She predicted the militants holding the hostages "are going to take it out" on them.

"I'm very upset," she sobbed, then hung up.

In San Diego, Dorothea Morefield, whose husband is a hostage, said:

"We had so hoped the entire situation would end without any death. Now we have eight dead and they are just as important as the hostages. We just hope it doesn't lead to anything worse."

Asked if she supported Carter's decision to try to rescue the hostages, she replied:

"Only he has all the information and he has to make these decisions. We have to accept them if he thought this was best and if he thought the hostages were endangered. We have to get them out without anymore lives being lost."

She said she is worried about her husband and the other hostages, adding, "I don't think anyone knows what reprisals, if any, will be taken — and they have 50 hostages to take reprisals on."

Robert Hohman of West Sacramento, the father of hostage Donald Hohman, 38, an Army medic, said:

"I heard the news briefings, but I really have no comment on

Back Page Col. 1

Furor Over TV Show on S.F. Gays

By Marshall Kilduff

Gay and straight political leaders included in a national television documentary on San Francisco gay politics, scheduled to be shown this weekend, charged yesterday that the show is biased and sensationalized.

The furor surrounds an hour-long news special titled "Gay Power — Gay Politics," which will be shown at 10 p.m. tomorrow on the CBS network, including KPIX (Channel 5) in San Francisco.

The program portrays gay voters as the pivotal factor in last year's mayoral race and as a community that appears to dictate how the city's decisions are made.

Both gay and straight leaders disputed the political analysis and contended the show exaggerates gay lifestyles and is unfairly edited to show city officials — most prominently Mayor Dianne Feinstein — as political opportunists.

Feinstein said she was refused an opportunity to see the show in advance, but read the script.

"Based on my reading, this

Back Page Col. 6

Index

Bridge 42
Business World 33
Chess 42
Comics 38
Deaths 43
Entertainment 64
People 40
TV-Radio 62
Weather 44

THE VOLCANO BLOWS UP

By Charles Petit
Science Correspondent

Vancouver, Wash.

Mount St. Helens burst into a frenzied eruption yesterday with a shattering blast that rocked thousands of square miles of the Pacific Northwest, killed at least seven persons, lofted a boiling, black cloud of ash 12 miles into the stratosphere, flooded nearby streams and washed out several bridges.

Scientists estimated last night that the volcano is now 1200 feet shorter than it was before the explosive eruption, which leveled almost every tree in an area spreading 15 miles north and west of the peak.

By late last night winds carried volcanic ash as far east as Great Falls, Mont., and the Weather Service expects it to cover the Great Plains and some Southern states during the next few days.

The awesome display, coming as the volcano 40 miles northeast of here seemed to have settled down after eight weeks of fitful activity, began with an earthquake and massive explosion from the mountain's summit and north flank at 8:32 a.m.

The quake, measuring 5.0 on the Richter Scale, was easily the most severe seismic disturbance since Mount St. Helens began erupting March 27, its first activity in 123 years.

The roar sent shock waves for hundreds of miles. "Our house was just shaking, and it sounded like artillery," said Jay Collins of Bellingham, Wash., 200 miles away.

There were no confirmed sightings of molten lava bubbling from the volcano — experts say volcanos such as Mount St. Helens seldom produce lava — but mudflows raced down the flanks of the 9000-plus-foot mountain and flooded the south fork of the nearby Toutle River, washing out several bridges on the Spirit Lake Highway.

In the late evening there was a continuous, dark gray stream of pyroclastics — a mixture of superheated gas, dust and volcanic ash — spurting from the top of the mountain.

The 1000-degree Fahrenheit mixture was flowing steadily from the top at speeds estimated up to 80 miles an hour, according to Carolyn Driedger, a Tacoma, Wash., geologist who works for the U.S. Geological Survey.

The crater at the summit grew to at least half a mile in diameter, and its rim dropped 1200 feet below Mount St. Helens' pre-eruption height of 9677 feet. The timberline is at 5000 feet.

There were reports that 2000 feet of the north side of the mountain, which took the

Back Page Col. 4

San Francisco Chronicle

The Largest Daily Circulation in Northern California

116th Year No. 106 ★★★★ MONDAY, MAY 19, 1980 777-1111  20 CENTS

7 Die in Eruption

Miami Riot Grows — Death Toll at 18

A cloud 12 miles high burst from Mount St. Helens and spread from Washington into Montana

Police Say 350 Arrested

Miami

Rioting blacks set hundreds of fires and looted stores and pawnshops for guns and other goods for a second straight night. Whites began to retaliate, and by late last night the death toll had reached at least 18.

The deaths included a 33-year-old black man who was gunned down by four white men and a 14-year-old black youth who was shot to death by a white man driving a blue pickup.

The number of injured is estimated at 350 persons, including five policemen and a National Guardsman wounded by gunfire.

City officials announced yesterday that public transportation had been suspended and that schools would not open today. An 8 p.m. to 6 a.m. curfew was imposed, and the sale of alcoholic beverages and gasoline was restricted.

Police said more than 350 people have been arrested — at least half of them for violating the curfew.

The riot has resulted in billions of dollars in property damage, primarily to the predominantly black Liberty City section of Miami.

(The Watts riot, in August 1965, left 34 people dead in the predominantly black section of Los Angeles, with property damage estimated at more than $40 million.)

The rioting in Miami began Saturday night after an all-white jury in Tampa acquitted four Dade County policemen in the beating death last December of Arthur McDuffie, a black insurance agent, in Miami. The trial was moved from Miami to Tampa because of the tense racial atmosphere in Miami.

In an attempt to try to halt the rioting, the Justice Department announced yesterday in Washington that it would examine the

Back Page Col. 1

Miami police brought a riot victim with a head wound to the emergency room of a hospital

Brezhnev and Giscard In Poland for Talks

Warsaw

Presidents Leonid I. Brezhnev of the Soviet Union and Valery Giscard d'Estaing of France arrived in Poland yesterday for a brief meeting — Brezhnev's first reported talk with a Western head of state since the Soviet intervention in Afghanistan.

Both leaders were greeted at the military section of Okecie Airport by Polish Communist Party chief Edward Gierek, who has met several times with Giscard d'Estaing and, according to the Polish news agency Interpress, issued the invitations for this conference.

The leaders planned an "informal meeting" today without the traditional diplomatic preparation, said a statement from the Elysee Palace in Paris. French sources here said the meeting probably would be brief, with little press access to the visitors.

The French statement said the meeting was called to correct a communications breakdown between East and West. France joined its Western allies in condemning the Soviet intervention in Afghanistan, although it argued that in the interests of detente the lines of communication must be kept open.

Even before it began, the

Page 10 Col. 1

Index

Bridge 27
Business World 29
Chess 27
Comics 34
Deaths 39
Entertainment 60
People 22
TV-Radio 58
Weather 39

Top of the News is on Page 20

Climber Tells How Mountain Blew Up on Him

Cougar, Wash.

Free-lance photographer Don Plumb said he was climbing "when the mountain blew up on me."

Escaping in oppressive heat, he said, he ran 12 miles down the side of Mount St. Helens yesterday and through the brush to the village of Cougar.

"I saw Goat Rock get blown up and the main crater fell in about 500 feet. It was hot. I'd say about 100 degrees or more. There were some people who died in cars not far from me.

"I think it was from gas. They were a little closer to it (the volcano) than I was, I guess. I could taste the gas but I kept moving and it never got too bad."

He was one of hundreds of eyewitnesses filled with a mixture of fear and awe when they saw the eruption and its aftermath.

The eruption sent what was described as walls of water and mud thundering down on the Toutle River.

"I could hear it crackling from my house," said Tom Huntington, who lives at the mountain's base. He said he drove to a vantage point overlooking the Toutle River and saw a sea of logs traveling at about 25 mph.

"It was wall-to-wall logs, millions of dollars worth of timber," he said.

An airline pilot flying near the volcano when it erupted described the awesome clouds that belched out of the volcano as "the biggest I've ever seen."

"It was a huge, grayish-black mushroom cloud," said Captain Joe

Back Page Col. 5

ELECTION EXTRA

REAGAN SWEEP

San Francisco Chronicle

The Largest Daily Circulation in Northern California

116th Year No. 251 ★★★★•• WEDNESDAY, NOV. 5, 1980 777-1111 20 CENTS

Huge Gains for the GOP

President-elect Ronald Reagan and his wife, Nancy, waved to the crowd at the Century Plaza Hotel in Los Angeles AP Wirephoto

Carter Gives Up Before Polls Close

ELECTORAL VOTES	
Needed to Win: 270	
Won or Leading	
Reagan	475
Carter	63
Anderson	0

Washington

Ronald Reagan won the White House from President Carter last night in a surprising landslide that changed the face of American government. Carter promised Reagan his "fullest support and cooperation" in the transition to Republican rule.

The Republican runaway that renounced the president cost Democrats dearly in Congress as well. The GOP gained at least six Senate seats in their bid to end a generation of Democratic control there. In the House, Democrats held onto their majority, but by a

Back Page Col. 4

CALIFORNIA

Alan Cranston

Cranston Trounces Gann

See Page 3

Anti-Smoking Initiative Defeated

See Page 6

CONGRESS

Republican Dan Quayle, who defeated Indiana Senator Birch Bayh, greeted the crowd in Indianapolis with his family

McGovern, Church, Bayh Lose

Demos Hold On To the House

See Page 1A

BAY AREA

District Elections Defeated

See Page 1D

Quentin Kopp led the field for the S.F. Board of Supervisors

Media's Projections Irk Voters

See Page 9

HEADLINE NEWS

Anti-U.S. Rally in Tehran

See Page 19

Soviet Link to Iran-Iraq War

See Page 22

State College Kidnap-Slaying

See Page 12

Index

Bridge 25
Business World 27
Chess 25
Comics 32
Deaths 42
Entertainment 59
Food 34
People 23
TV-Radio 58
Weather 43

Top of the News on Page 18

Ex-Beatle Shot in N.Y.

JOHN LENNON SLAIN

San Francisco Chronicle

The Largest Daily Circulation in Northern California

116th Year No. 280 ★★★★ TUESDAY, DEC. 9, 1980 777-1111 20 CENTS

REPORTER'S OWN STORY

'I Infiltrated the KKK'

(This is the first of a special series of reports by a newsman who infiltrated the Ku Klux Klan. It is published by special arrangement with the Nashville Tennessean.)

By Jerry Thompson

Copyright 1980 The Tennessean

The Ku Klux Klan today holds a strange, disturbing attraction for frustrated, fearful middle-income men and women — and a dangerous potential for violence and terror.

I know. For the last year I have been a Klansman. I have worn the white robe and hood. I have twice taken the oath pledging my life to the Klan. I have twice been "naturalized" into separate Klan empires. I have paid my Klan initiation fees and my Klan dues.

I have fired Klan crosses, collected contributions at Klan roadblocks, marched in Klan street demonstrations and helped disrupt order at a public meeting with shouts in a Klan chorus. I have attended KKK den meetings where men

AP Wirephoto

JERRY THOMPSON
Tennessean reporter

armed with pistols and automatic rifles mouthed their routine racist rhetoric: "The niggers and the Jews are ruining the country."

Clad in Klan garments, I have picketed the president of the United States, demonstrated against a television station showing a documentary about the KKK, and been jeered by black citizens. And I have concealed the pistol of an ungarbed fellow Klansman beneath my flowing robes when he thrust it at me as policemen approached.

Through it all I was acting out a role — working as an investigative reporter for The Tennessean: striving to discover just how dangerous the Klan is, endeavoring to penetrate the secrecy veil that has obscured much of the Klan's life since its founding in Pulaski, Tenn., more than a century ago.

I attended my last Klan function Saturday night — a meeting in Cullman, Ala., of a local den of Bill Wilkinson's Invisible Empire, Knights of

Page 4 Col 1

Police Hold Suspect

Gunman Blasts Lennon Outside His Apartment

New York

Former Beatle John Lennon was shot to death in front of his luxury apartment building in Manhattan last night by a deranged man who had apparently been stalking him for several days, police said.

A police spokesman said Lennon, 40, was shot shortly before 11 p.m. as he returned to his home in the Dakota, a cooperative building, from a late-night recording session.

Police sources close to the investigation said the gunman walked up to Lennon as he was leaving his limousine.

"Mr. Lennon?" the man said, pulling a gun from under his coat and firing.

Lennon staggered about five feet to a small guard's booth in the courtyard of the building.

"Do you know what you just did?" the doorman asked the man.

"I just shot John Lennon," the gunman responded, throwing down a pistol.

Chief of Detectives James Sullivan said a suspect in custody, was "apparently a wacko."

Sullivan announced about three hours after the shooting that Mark David Chapman, 25, of Hawaii, had been charged with murder in the case.

He said Chapman had arrived in the city about a week ago and had been seen at least three times near the Dakota in the past three days. Sullivan said Chapman had gotten Lennon's autograph when the singer left the building about 5 p.m. and then waited outside the Dakota until the Lennons returned.

Police were questioning the gunman, who sources said was "coherent," and were attempting to interview Lennon's wife, Yoko Ono, who was with him at the time of the shooting.

"Tell me it isn't true," Ono screamed in the police car on the way to the hospital, said a police officer. "Tell me he's all right."

Ono apparently was not hurt by the bullets that struck her husband as they entered the archway that led into the courtyard of the complex where they worked and lived.

Sullivan said the assailant fired five shots at Lennon with a .38-caliber pistol, hitting him several times. There were bullet holes in the structure and blood on the bricks of the building.

Immediately after Lennon was shot, hundreds of persons began to gather at West 72nd Street and Central Park West. A number of them were crying. By 1 a.m. the crowd had grown to 500.

Several police sources said the suspect had been seen in the vicinity of the Dakota for several days.

"This was no robbery," a police spokesman said, adding that Lennon was apparently shot by a "cuckoo."

A spokesman at Roosevelt Hos-

Back Page Col. 3

AP Wirephoto

JOHN LENNON
His wife was with him

New Harsh Soviet Words On Poland

By R. W. Apple Jr.

New York Times

Moscow

The Soviet Union asserted explicitly for the first time yesterday that independent trade unions in Poland are conducting a counter-revolutionary struggle against that country's Communist government.

Tass, the official news agency, said in a brief report from Warsaw that "counter-revolutionary groups, operating under the cover of branches of the 'Solidarity' union, have turned to open confrontation" with the Communist Party and the managements of factories and institutions.

The Tass story, which was broadcast by Moscow Radio and scheduled for prominent display in all the major Soviet newspapers, was by far the most ominous official comment from Moscow during the five months of the Polish crisis. Diplomats in Moscow were unanimous in declaring that it increased the possibility of armed Warsaw Pact intervention in Poland.

Last Friday, Poland's six allies in the pact expressed guarded

Back Page Col. 6

Tests Show Jeep Prone To Flip Over

By Michael Taylor and Rick Carroll

Copyright 1980 Chronicle Publishing Co.

The basic four-wheel-drive Jeep, whose roll bar system has been under fire in the courts for several years, is also more likely to flip over than any other passenger car on the roads today, two recents studies have concluded.

One of the tests, including a critical series of filmed rollover tests, has not been publicly released, but its results were made available to The Chronicle.

Both tests were underwritten by the Insurance Institute for Highway Safety, an independent organization supported by the insurance industry.

The first study, completed last February at the University of Michigan, examined accident records involving nine different off-road utility vehicles and found the Jeep CJ-5 and the early model of Ford Broncos to be inherently unsafe on the road. Manufacture of the Bronco model involved in the study was discontinued in 1978.

The tests found "there were indications that Jeeps and old Ford Broncos were the worst of the bunch . . . and that ultimately the Jeep CJ-5 was the worst in highway analysis. It didn't take much to roll one over," according to Brian O'Neill, the insurance institute's vice president for research.

After the first study — which was based on the accident reports of 12,000 utility vehicle crashes in nine states — the institute decided to see how Jeeps alone performed in real, on-the-road tests.

It hired Dynamic Sciences of Phoenix, a well-known vehicle and aircraft testing firm, to measure a Jeep's stability.

The results of the tests have not yet been made public, but O'Neill told The Chronicle last week that, after several months of testing in the Arizona desert where a Jeep CJ-5 was simply driven down a road and turned sharply, the

Back Page Col. 1

By John O'Hara

The usually busy Powell Street Station was deserted during the morning rush hour

Computer Breakdown

BART Foulup — Big Traffic Jams

By Carl Nolte

BART suffered one of the worst breakdowns in its troubled history yesterday when both of its main computers broke down at the start of the morning rush hour. Thousands of commuters were stranded.

The trouble was eventually traced to a 30-inch-long piece of computer hardware called a power supply unit. It failed at 6:27 a.m. and caused a series of electronic disasters inside BART's highly sophisticated computers, and a massive traffic jam on the freeways leading to San Francisco.

The failure shut down the transit system completely for an hour. BART started running again on manual control at 7:30, and service went back to normal at 2:30 p.m. — eight hours after the trouble started.

BART was able to operate normally at the evening rush hour.

In the morning, thousands of BART passengers decided to drive because of the shutdown, and traffic on the MacArthur Freeway backed up to the Mills College campus. The jam on the Bay Bridge did not subside until almost noon.

Bay Bridge toll captain John Sant said the tieup on the freeway was one of the worst in a long time. "We had more traffic than when the BART tube closed, or when AC Transit went on strike," he said.

"People had a little notice then, and they could plan ahead of time. But this morning people just had to make the best they could of it."

BART sent out an emergency call for help to AC Transit to help carry its passengers, but AC could scrape up only a dozen buses on short notice. "Our manpower was all committed already," AC's Mike Curry said. "We did the best we could, but we were jammed. It was standing room only.

"We just don't have the manpower and equipment necessary to meet that kind of crisis," he said. "It just can't be done."

AC, which carries about 22,500 passengers a day to San Francisco in the morning, compared to about

Back Page Col. 1

Index

Bridge	39
Business World	29
Chess	39
Comics	40
Deaths	41
Entertainment	60
People	36
TV-Radio	58
Weather	41

Assassination Try

REAGAN O.K. — BULLET IS REMOVED FROM LUNG

A Secret Service agent (foreground), a Washington policeman (center), and press secretary James Brady lay wounded as agents pinned suspect against wall

San Francisco Chronicle

The Largest Daily Circulation in Northern California

117th Year No. 63 ★★★★ TUESDAY, MAR. 31, 1981 777-1111 20 CENTS

Pawnshop Pistol Used

Reagan Aide Shot in Head — Suspect Arrested at Scene

A moment after the shootings, President Reagan was shoved into the back of his limousine by Secret Service agents

Two Others Are Wounded Outside Washington Hotel

Washington

A young gunman ambushed President Reagan at close range yesterday and fired six shots from a .22-caliber pistol — one of them piercing the president's lung inches from his heart. Doctors removed the bullet in a two-hour operation and said Reagan will recover.

The would-be assassin, identified by police as John Warnock Hinckley Jr., 25, of Evergreen, Colo., was tackled and pinned to the pavement, whisked away in a squad car and booked for attempted murder. There was no known motive for the shooting, and authorities said the suspect apparently acted alone.

The gun used in the assassination attempt was a "Saturday Night Special," FBI agent Roger Young said. Agents from the FBI and the Bureau of Alcohol, Tobacco and Firearms said Hinckley had bought two .22-caliber revolvers October 13 at a pawnshop in Dallas, and that one of the $47 guns was used to shoot Reagan yesterday.

The shots outside the Washington Hilton Hotel crackled through a dismal rainfall like balloons bursting at a child's birthday party. Presidential press secretary James Brady was gravely wounded in the head, and a Secret Service agent and a police officer were injured and in serious condition.

The stunning murder attempt occurred one mile from the White House at the sprawling hotel complex, where Reagan had just delivered a speech to a union convention.

Waving and smiling, Reagan emerged from the hotel by a public side door — as he usually leaves the hotel — and neared the bulletproof presidential limousine. A small crowd stood watching.

Then the gunfire crackled.

At the sixth shot, uniformed and plainclothes agents piled on a blond young man in a raincoat, pinning him against a stone wall.

The grin on Reagan's face turned to frozen horror as a Secret Service agent shoved him into the car.

Pandemonium erupted. Bystanders screamed. Guns were drawn in an instant. The suspect struggled fiercely under a mass of agents.

But the gunman had hit Reagan with one shot; another hit the door of the car. Brady, caught between Reagan and the gunman,

Back Page Col. 4

'Quiet, Friendly' Suspect Had Earlier Arrest for Weapons

Washington

John W. (Jack) Hinckley Jr., 25, the man accused of trying to assassinate President Reagan, was arrested last fall for trying to board an airliner with firearms in Nashville, Tenn., when President Carter was in town.

The husky, blond-haired Hinckley, described by acquaintances as quiet and friendly, has a history of psychiatric care.

A sketchy portrait of the suspect's background indicated that he had worked summers as a bartender, a salesman for a Hollywood portrait photographer and for a Dallas book publisher while sporadically attending Texas Tech University from 1974 to 1980.

NBC News reported that Hinckley once worked as a disc jockey at a country music station in Denver under the name John Warlek.

Much of the information came from a job application Hinckley filed last October 20 with the Denver Post, when he applied for "any writing, proofreading" job.

Hinckley, the son of "top-drawer" conservative Republicans who live in affluent Evergreen, Colo., was charged with attempting

Back Page Col. 1

John Hinckley Jr. left the courthouse after arraignment

Inside

Death Penalty Upheld. Page 8.

Academy Awards Delayed. Page 9.

Hijacked Jet Stormed. Page 11

Polish Strike Averted. Page 12.

Index

Bridge	21	Entertainment	41
Business World	51	People	19
Chess	21	TV-Radio	40
Comics	44	Weather	24
Deaths	24		

Top of the News is on Page 22

SHUTTLE'S TRIUMPH

117th Year No. 76 ★★★★ WEDNESDAY, APRIL 15, 1981 777-1111 20 CENTS

Columbia Glides In Perfectly

Throng Cheers Landing

By Paul Liberatore
Chronicle Correspondent

Edwards AFB

Lured into this forbidding desert by the rare chance to see history being made, a happy crowd that may be remembered here as the Woodstock of the space age got what it came for yesterday — a clear and spectacular view of the space shuttle Columbia coming back to earth.

Hundreds of thousands of people, who had arrived in vehicles of every description, filled a dusty square-mile inlet on the edge of Rogers Dry Lake, about three miles from the landing strip.

They overflowed the designated "public viewing area" with their recreational vehicles, trucks, cars, tents and campers by mid-morning and packed the roads cutting through the slow rising hills east of the Dryden Flight Research Center of the National Aeronautics and Space Administration.

Shortly after 10 a.m., as thousands of radios tuned to a special NASA channel resounded through the desolate desert with glowing reports on the progress of the historic flight, a pair of sonic booms cracked through the vast open spaces, announcing the imminent arrival of the Columbia.

A cheer went up, followed by an eerie silence as tens of thousands of faces turned upward toward the brilliant blue Mojave sky, searching for the first glimpse

Page 7 Col. 1

The Photo

San Francisco Chronicle photographer Peter Breinig was at Edwards Air Force Base to take the photograph at the top of the page of the space shuttle Columbia descending for a landing accompanied by a NASA T-38 chase plane.

AP Wirephoto

Astronauts John Young and wife Susy (left) and Bob Crippen and wife Virginia made brief remarks after landing

Dramatic End to U.S. Space Lull

America Back in the Race

By Charles Petit
Science Correspondent

Edwards AFB

When the 75-ton space shuttle Columbia, crackling from residual re-entry heat, rolled to a halt on Rogers Dry Lake yesterday it pushed America back into the manned space race — but perhaps not yet far out in front.

The Russians were in space first, have never slackened the pace of their manned orbit program, and have big plans for the future.

The shuttle's launch came, coincidentally, on the 20th anniversary of the first manned space flight by the late Yuri Gagarin on April 12, 1961. Americans were the first and so far only spacefarers to go to the moon, but the last previous U.S. manned flight included a symbolic rendezvous and handshake with cosmonauts aboard a Soviet Soyuz in July 1975.

And, as astronauts John Young and Robert Crippen tested the Columbia's wings for the first time, hurtling to a 215 mph wheeled landing here, they left behind in orbit two Russians, Vladimir V. Kovalenok and Viktor Savinykh, aboard the 42-ton, 76-foot-long Salyut 6 space station.

The Salyut has been in orbit since September 29, 1977. Kovalenok and Savinykh have been aboard since March 12 this year, the 32nd and 33rd Soviet cosmonauts to visit the station in 15 trips by the Soviet's reliable, use-once-and-throw-away Soyuz space vehicles.

And, perhaps symbolic of the Russians' current edge in experience, if not necessarily technology, the two cosmonauts would have had to look down about 45 miles from their orbit to see the Columbia dashing by at its height of 172 miles from the Earth's surface.

Where America now most certainly holds leadership is in its proven ability to fly a major payload into orbit and recover it intact — with enough cargo room to carry heavy equipment, multiple crews, lots of instruments, and even the ingredients to erect a full-scale permanent military space station.

Columbia is the prototype of other ships that will do these jobs, then fly back to land for more loads. In effect this country now has the potential to run a freight line to outer space and to keep space stations regularly supplied.

The shuttle schedule calls for placing 14 classified Defense Department satellites into space during the next five years. Some will be so big that only the hydrogen-fueled shuttle could lift them, while the Russians are still using rockets that sent their early

Back Page Col. 2

SHUTTLE INSIDE

- Bay Area reaction. Page 4.
- Tile inventor's story. Page 5.
- Launch pad damaged. Page 6.
- Next space crew. Page 6.
- The shuttle's future. Page 8.

A Tense Re-entry Blackout

By Charles Petit
Science Correspondent

Edwards AFB

The space shuttle Columbia plummeted through a blazing re-entry and skimmed to a perfect landing yesterday morning in a heart-stirring climax to the maiden test of NASA's gamble that reusable spaceships make better sense than throwaway rockets.

"What a way to come to California!" exclaimed astronaut Robert Crippen 120,000 feet over Big Sur.

The space-going freighter performed "right on the money," NASA mission control reported as the flight ended, more than two years later than the original date chosen in 1972 for the first flight of what is planned to be the mainstay of America's space program for the rest of the century.

The nose-down Columbia looked from the ground like a fat airborne shark diving eagerly toward Rogers Dry Lake and the 5.2-mile runway painted on its bleak surface. Two T-38 chase aircraft shadowed it like pilot fish.

For the first time in history a craft had lifted from Earth aboard a thundering rocket, orbited in the vacuum of space like a satellite, then descended into the planet's enveloping atmosphere under the

Back Page Col. 1

Index

Bridge	39
Business World	29
Chess	39
Comics	40
Deaths	41
Entertainment	60
Food	21
People	36
TV-Radio	58
Weather	41

Top of the News on Page 20

POPE SURVIVES

Surgery After Shooting at Vatican

Pope John Paul II slumped bleeding and seriously wounded as assistants came to his aid in his open car moments after the shooting in St. Peter's Square

UPI Telephoto

San Francisco Chronicle

The Largest Daily Circulation in Northern California

117th Year No. 101 ★★★★ THURSDAY, MAY 14, 1981 777-1111 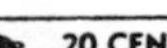 20 CENTS

Suspect Quickly Seized

'Mistake' Raid on Soviet Jet

Washington

In what appears to be an embarrassing mistake, U.S. Customs agents boarded a Soviet airliner Tuesday, seized some ordinary electronic equipment they believed to be related to defense, and created an international incident.

The Soviet government yesterday accused the agents of using brute force and filed an official protest, contending that "terror and banditism have been elevated in the United States to the status of official policy."

U.S. authorities defended the legality and conduct of the search and seizure, but were hard-pressed to explain the basis for the sudden

Back Page Col. 5

How Reagan's Son Uses Dad's Name

Washington

Michael Reagan, the president's son, has sent eight to 10 business solicitation letters to U.S. military bases in which he invokes the name of his father on behalf of a private military equipment supplier.

"I know that, with my father's leadership at the White House, this countries (sic) Armed Services are going to be rebuilt and strengthened," young Reagan wrote in identical letters mailed in late March. "We at Dana Ingalls Profile want to be involved in that process. . . . we look forward to becoming an approved supplier of machine parts and small assemblies."

Reagan, 35, signed the letters as the vice president of marketing and sales for the Burbank firm, which manufactures small machine-tool parts for aircraft and missiles.

In a telephone interview yesterday, young Reagan said he was

Back Page Col. 6

Turkish Terrorist, Murderer

By R.W. Apple Jr.
New York Times

Rome

The first reports said only that he spoke no Italian, that he was young and that he had dark hair.

But within a matter of minutes, a picture of the man accused of shooting Pope John Paul II in St. Peter's Square yesterday afternoon, began to emerge — a picture of a militant Turkish terrorist, already convicted of one murder, who escaped from a maximum-security prison in 1979 and then threatened in a letter to assassinate the pope.

The Turkish ambassador in Washington, Sukru Elekdag, said after the news of the shooting had flashed around the world, "The Turkish police have been under instruction to shoot him on sight."

Moments after he was wrestled to the ground by pilgrims who had been standing near him the alleged assailant told the Italian police that his name was Mehmet Ali Agca. He gave his age as 23 and said he was Turkish. He said also that he was a student at the University for Foreigners in Perugia in central Italy, but the records of the university showed no such registration.

A dark-haired young man, clean-shaven, with an angular face, Agca was wearing an open-neck white shirt under a lightweight jacket.

Sources said Agca was convicted in February 1979 of murdering Abdi Ipekci, the editor of the independent Turkish daily newspaper Milliyet. He was jailed. But in late November, he escaped from the military prison and had apparently been in hiding ever since.

When he fled from the prison, he left behind a letter, addressed to Milliyet, threatening the life of the

Back Page Col. 1

AP Wirephoto

Mehmet Ali Agca, the suspect, was led away by Italian police

Outpouring of Grief

Prayers in Bay Area

By Jerry Carroll

Millions of Californians paused in private or paid visits to cathedral, church and synagogue to pray for the recovery of Pope John Paul II after he was wounded yesterday by a would-be assassin.

"Restore him to health," the Rev. Howard Rasmussen, vicar general of the San Francisco Archdiocese, asked in a prayer of petition at a Mass for the fallen pontiff at St. Mary's Cathedral that drew Mayor Dianne Feinstein and other civic leaders

Hundreds of thousands of the state's 4.5 million Roman Catholics attended special noon Masses at the request of church leaders, and many more attended services after work. Clergy and congregations in other denominations offered up special prayers for the pope.

The outpouring of appeals for the pope's well-being began when the initial horror over the shooting in St. Peter's Square began to ebb. Amid the fervent prayers for the pope's recovery was threaded the Christian message of forgiveness.

"I think we should also pray for the person who did it," Rasmussen told the people who half filled the starkly modern cathedral. There were 41 priests, ministers and rabbis taking part in the Mass.

Speaking of Pope John Paul, Rasmussen said, "I suspect he would follow the example of his Lord and Master when He was on the

Page 4 Col. 1

Pope's Condition Is 'Guarded'

Rome

Pope John Paul II was shot and seriously wounded yesterday as he was standing in an open car moving slowly among more than 10,000 worshipers in St. Peter's Square.

The pontiff, who was struck by two bullets and wounded in the abdomen, arm and hand, underwent five hours and 25 minutes of surgery in which parts of his intestine were removed. A hospital bulletin at midnight said he was in "guarded" condition, but a surgeon expressed confidence that "the pontiff will recover soon."

Police arrested an armed Turkish citizen who was later identified as an escaped murderer who had previously threatened the pope's life in the name of Islam.

More about the attack on pope, Pages 2-7

The attack occurred as the pope, dressed in white, was shaking hands and lifting small children in his arms while being driven around the square. Suddenly, as he reached a point just outside the Vatican's bronze gate, there was a burst of gunfire.

One hand rising to his face and blood staining his garments, the pope faltered and fell into the arms of his Polish secretary, the Rev. Stanislaw Dziwisz, and his personal servant, Angelo Gugel, who were in the car with him.

The 60-year-old pope, the spiritual leader of nearly 600 million Roman Catholics around the world, was taken by ambulance to Gemelli Hospital, two miles

Back Page Col. 1

Index

Bridge	38
Business World	29
Chess	37
Comics	34
Deaths	39
Entertainment	58
People	36
Tales of the City	37
TV-Radio	56
Weather	39

Top of the News is on Page 18

THE ASSASSINATION OF SADAT

AP Wirephoto

EGYPTIAN PRESIDENT ANWAR SADAT
He smiled as the parade began

HOW HIS KILLERS MADE THE ATTACK

- Sadat reviews a military parade, marking the anniversary of the 1973 Arab war against Israel.
- At about 1 p.m., men in Egyptian uniforms, riding in a military vehicle in the parade, suddenly start firing automatic weapons and throwing grenades. They jump from the vehicle and charge the reviewing stand.
- Sadat and seven others are killed and 27 are wounded.
- Two assassins apparently are killed and four reportedly are captured. There is confusion about their exact number and identity
- Vice President Hosni Mubarak is favored to replace Sadat.

By John Boring

San Francisco Chronicle

The Largest Daily Circulation in Northern California

117th Year No. 226 ★★★★ WEDNESDAY, OCTOBER 7, 1981 777-1111 20 CENTS

Seven Others Die in Bloody Assault

Guards gathered at a building where Sadat was taken minutes after the attack; helicopter (left) later flew him to the hospital

Mystery Soldiers Seized as Slayers

By William E. Farrell
New York Times

Cairo

Anwar Sadat was shot and killed yesterday by a group of soldiers who hurled hand grenades and fired rifles at the Egyptian president as he watched a military parade commemorating the 1973 surprise attack against Israel.

The assassins' bullets ended the life of a humbly born, rural Egyptian who earned world renown for innovation and boldness in foreign affairs. It was a reputation that he gained when he stunned the West and angered the Arab world by going to the camp of the foe, Israel, to sue for peace.

As jet fighters roared overhead, the assassins sprayed the reviewing stand with bullets while thousands of horrified people — officials, diplomats, journalists and other guests — looked on.

The 62-year-old Sadat, shot in the chest and shoulder, was rushed to the Maadi military hospital in a coma, his uniform covered with blood. He died two hours later after undergoing surgery and open-heart massage, an official medical bulletin said.

The bulletin, signed by 11 doctors, said there were two wounds below Sadat's left nipple, a third in his neck and a fourth in his right arm. His left hip was also fractured.

"The president's death was ascribed to severe nervous shock, internal bleeding in the chest cavity and damage to the left lung," the report said.

As many as a dozen other spectators sitting

Back Page Col. 1

Inside

GOP Lieutenant Governor Mike Curb formally announces his candidacy for governor.

Page 14.

Wayne Gross hits a three-run homer to lead the Oakland A's past the Royals 4-0 in the opener of the American League West playoffs.

See Sports.

Houston catcher Alan Ashby's two-out, two-run homer in the ninth inning beats the Dodgers 3-1 in the National League West playoff.

See Sports.

Confusion On Motives In the Slaying

Washington

In the confusion swirling around the assassination of President Anwar Sadat of Egypt, little reliable information could be obtained about the killers.

Egyptian authorities were reported to have four uniformed men in custody last night, but the Egyptians revealed nothing about their prisoners.

"Islamic fundamentalists" was the characterization offered late yesterday afternoon by Secretary of State Alexander Haig to a group of senators.

A U.S. intelligence official went further and said at least one assassin had links to the Takfir

Back Page Col. 5

Witness' Report

The Attack Up Close

By David B. Ottaway
Washington Post

Cairo

It was toward the end of what had been a spectacular military parade, and nobody was paying much attention to the shiny, slow-moving Russian trucks pulling the new South Korean artillery pieces that were on display for the first time.

Instead, all eyes were turned toward the Mirage jets that swooped only feet above the reviewing stand, leaving behind trails of bright red, blue and white smoke as they climbed up and over to make a colorful loop in the blue sky before flying away.

Suddenly, one of the trucks came to an abrupt halt right in front of the reviewing stand where President Anwar Sadat and the entire Egyptian military and political hierarchy were seated.

I wondered whether there was another embarrassing breakdown in store in yesterday's parade, which marked Egypt's initial victory in 1973 over the Israelis along the Suez Canal. Already, one motorcycle had conked out just before passing the review stand, and the driver had had to push it along by hand.

We all thought it was just another parade special as a big bang went off, then another, and several soldiers leaped out of the back of the truck and started running toward the stands.

Then there was another huge bang and

Back Page Col. 5

More on Sadat — Pages 2-7 and 10-12

Index

Bridge	41	Entertainment	64
Business World	31	Food	23
Chess	41	People	[illegible]
Comics	45	TV-Radio	[illegible]
Deaths	46	Weather	[illegible]

Top of the News on Page 20

ARGENTINA SURRENDERS

San Francisco Chronicle

The Largest Daily Circulation in Northern California

118th Year No. 128 ★★★★ TUESDAY, JUNE 15, 1982 777-1111 25 CENTS

Guerrillas Dig In

Israeli Tanks Corner PLO In West Beirut

Beirut

Israeli tank columns completed their encirclement of Moslem west Beirut yesterday, trapping PLO leader Yasser Arafat and 7000 other guerrillas in the Lebanese capital. Arafat took refuge in a foreign embassy, Israel said.

At the same time, other Israeli armored units, greeted with rice and flowers by sympathetic Lebanese Christians, began driving still deeper into Lebanon in an apparent effort to push Syrian troops east into the Bekaa Valley, off the high ground northeast of the capital.

Officials of the Palestine Liberation Organization said yesterday that they would not give up without a fight, and that if the Israelis wanted them they were going to have to come in and get them.

George Habash, the leader of the Popular Front for the Liberation of Palestine, said in a statement that the guerrillas would turn west Beirut into a "a new Stalingrad" if the Israelis tried to enter the PLO camps and neighborhoods clustered near the airport.

The siege of the capital came as the Lebanese government of President Elias Sarkis announced the formation of a six-member national salvation board to deal with the political repercussions of the invasion. The board was formed by Sarkis and Prime Minister Chefik Wazzan to determine a response to Israel's conditions for withdrawal.

Those terms were delivered last night to Sarkis by Philip Habib, the special U.S. envoy. Habib arrived at the presidential palace in Baabda, five miles southeast of downtown Beirut, from Damascus, where he had flown earlier yesterday from Jerusalem. He would not make any statements to the press.

The conditions reportedly included the creation of a demilitarized zone stretching 25 miles north of the Israeli border, to prevent attacks by Palestinian guerrillas; and the withdrawal of Syria's 30,000-man peacekeeping force from Lebanon.

Lebanese government sources said the Israelis also wanted the board to order Lebanon's 25,000-man army into west Beirut to disarm the guerrillas and the various private Moslem militias.

In a report from Paris that quoted Palestinian sources, ABC

Back Page Col. 1

FBI Linked Donovan, Mob in '81

Washington

Incoming Reagan White House officials were informed by the FBI last year, on the first day of Secretary of Labor Raymond Donovan's Senate confirmation hearings, that Donovan had "close personal and business ties with known La Cosa Nostra figures."

The FBI report, dated Jan. 12, 1981, was hand-delivered that day to White House counsel Fred Fielding, who was then the Reagan transition team's conflict-of-interest counsel. According to informed sources, the report also stated that "this information was corroborated by independent interviews of confi-

Back Page Col. 4

A Blockade At the U.N. — 1600 Arrested

New York

Carrying daisies, holding hands and singing peace songs from the '60s, more than 1600 anti-nuclear demonstrators were arrested yesterday as they tried to erect a human blockade in front of the U.N. missions of five major nuclear powers.

The day-long protests resulted in the largest number of arrests for a political demonstration in New York history.

The participants, who came from 34 states and seven countries, had been schooled in passive resistance, taking courses of four hours or more. Police, according to Sergeant James Mullaly, had "specifically been told no force, no cuffs, no search and no taking anyone with children."

In front of the U.S. Mission across from the United Nations, where the greatest number of arrests was made, police officers in riot helmets put a hand on the shoulder of each demonstrator — none of whom was actually blocking an entrance — and asked if the

Back Page Col. 3

Britain Recaptures The Falkland Islands

UPI Telephoto

Prime Minister Thatcher left 10 Downing Street to announce the British victory to Commons

Thatcher Says War Is Over

London

Britain said the beleaguered Argentine forces on the Falkland Islands surrendered early today and returned the colony to British rule, 74 days after Argentina's dawn invasion started the bloody South Atlantic war.

"The Falkland Islands are once more under the government desired by their inhabitants. God save the Queen," said a message from British commander Major General Jeremy Moore to Prime Minister Margaret Thatcher. Moore said Major General Mario Menendez, the Argentine commander, "surrendered to me in East and West Falkland all Argentine forces in East and West Falkland, together with their impedimenta."

There was no immediate reaction from Argentina's military junta, which earlier said an unofficial cease-fire was in force on the South Atlantic islands Argentina seized more than two months ago.

Moore's message said "arrangements are in hand to assemble the men for return to Argentina to gather in their arms and equipment and to mark and make safe their munitions."

White flags flew over Stanley, the islands' capital, during the eerie hours of negotiation between the cease-fire, announced late yesterday, and the formal surrender.

Royal Marines and paratroopers, the Scot and Welsh guards and Nepalese Gurkhas were poised on the outskirts of the capital after overrunning Argentina's fragile "Galtieri line" of trenches, foxholes and machine-gun posts yesterday, routing the 7000-strong garrison.

Thatcher told cheering members of Parliament that surrender talks followed a cease-fire declared at noon (PDT) with sudden swiftness after a two-week siege of the capital.

Looking flushed and radiant, Britain's "Iron Lady" then joined a group of citizens triumphantly singing patriotic songs outside her No.

Back Page Col. 5

Holland Luxury Liners Make S.F. Home Port

By Scott Blakey

Holland America, one of a handful of the world's luxurious cruise lines, announced yesterday that it will base its West Coast operations in San Francisco at least through 1983 — a move that means a big financial boost for the port and the city.

The line's flagship, Rotterdam, sailed last night on the first cruise to Alaska from its new home port. It will serve passengers sailing Pacific waters through the rest of the 1982 cruise season, and in the fall of 1983 it will be joined by the Nieuw Amsterdam, the line's newest vessel, for cruises to Mexico, said Vincent Wasik, the company's president and chief executive officer.

"Holland American's decision could mean as much as $40 million a year in additional revenue for the city and add 25 to 30 more sailings from the port," said Eugene Gartland, president of the city's port commission.

Holland America's marketing director, Jon Firestone, said the line picked San Francisco because the city best reflected the image the 110-year-old firm is trying now to project — "upscale," he called it.

Holland America ships previously used New York or Fort Lauderdale for its American home ports and only called at San Francisco. The line's three ships other than the Rotterdam will continue to be based at those ports.

The announcement was made at an elegant luncheon, replete with international delicacies, an orchestra, flowers, open bar, swans and model ships sculpted from ice or butter, aboard the line's 25-year-old Rotterdam, docked at Pier 35.

It was greeted with enthusiasm by city and port officials who have for the past several years witnessed the loss of maritime trade to the Port of Oakland.

Leading the cheering section was Mayor Dianne Feinstein. After slipping away unnoticed from the official festivities for a 15-minute tour of the first-class and owner's

Back Page Col. 5

INDEX

Books 39
Bridge 21
Business World 51
Chess 20
Comics 44
Deaths 24
Entertainment 40
People 19
TV-Radio 38
Weather 18

Top of the News on Page 22

Soviet Leader Was 75

BREZHNEV DIES

San Francisco Chronicle

The Largest Daily Circulation in Northern California

118th Year No. 256 ★★★★• THURSDAY, NOVEMBER 11, 1982 777-1111 25 CENTS

Remembering Vietnam

UPI Telephoto

Fred Strother of Maine, a veteran who lost a leg in 1966 during the Vietnam War, paused beside the Vietnam Veterans Memorial in Washington yesterday — the first day the monument was open

By Richard Harwood and Haynes Johnson
Washington Post

Washington

From this day on, generations of Americans will come upon the black granite memorial to the veterans of Vietnam on the greensward of the Washington Mall and find there, first in the ranks of the dead, the names of Dale Buis and Chester Ovnard.

At dusk, on July 8, 1959, they sat down in a small mess hall 20 miles north of Saigon to watch a Jeanne Crain movie, "The Tattered Dress." Buis, an Army major from Imperial Beach, Calif., had been in that sliver of a country in Southeast Asia only two days on assignment as a military adviser. Ovnard, a master sergeant from Copperas Cove, Texas, had been around longer. That day he had mailed a letter to his wife telling of his experience there.

As the lights dimmed, peasant guerrillas

crept from the shadows to the mess hall windows. A few minutes later they opened fire. Buis and Ovnard were dead when they fell to the floor. They were the first American casualties of what was to become America's war in Vietnam.

The U.S. involvement in that distant place had begun nine years earlier with a decision by America's 33rd president, Harry S. Truman, to provide military assistance to the French.

Now, in the way of all wars, it enters a more permanent page of history with the consecration of a memorial this week in Washington so that those who fought and died will not be forgotten.

The memorial, set in the most peaceful of places in the graceful quiet park along the banks of the Potomac, stands surrounded by other symbols of the American past and present: the white shrine of the brooding Lincoln, the towering marble of the Washington Monument, the

Page 20 Col. 1

Sudden Illness

Struggle for Leadership Is Expected

Moscow

Communist Party chief Leonid Brezhnev, under whose iron rule the Soviet Union moved to crush dissidents in the Eastern bloc and achieved nuclear parity with the United States, died yesterday at the age of 75.

The official Tass news agency reported today that Brezhnev, whos death opens a competition for a successor, died a "sudden death" at 8:30 a.m. (9:30 a.m. PST) yesterday.

LEONID BREZHNEV
He ruled for 18 years

Brezhnev had led the Soviet Union for 18 years, taking over in October 1964, after Nikita Khrushchev was ousted. He had been rumored to be in ill health for years with heart troubles, a stroke and cancer.

No official announcement was made about who will assume Brezhnev's dual roles as general secretary of the Communist Party and the more ceremonial role of president.

Western experts believe the power vacuum will be filled in the short run by a collective leadership including longtime Brezhnev associate Konstantin Chernenko; former KGB chief Yuri Andropov; Defense Minister Dmitri Ustinov, and Foreign Minister Andrei Gromyko.

Also expected to play important roles are Premier Nikolai Tikhonov and Moscow Communist Party Chief Viktor Grishin.

But Chernenko and Andropov are considered the top contenders to replace Brezhnev as general secretary, the crucial post in the Soviet Union. Their ascendancy in the shadowy Kremlin hierarchy followed the death last January of chief Kremlin ideologist Mikhail Suslov.

The Tass statement said: "The Central Committee of the Communist Party of the Soviet Union, the presidium of the U.S.S.R. Supreme Soviet and the Council of Ministers of the U.S.S.R. hereby inform with deep sorrow the party and the entire Soviet people that Leonid I. Brezhnev, general secretary of the CPSU Central Committee and president of the Presidium of the U.S.S.R. Supreme Soviet, died a sudden death at 8:30 a.m. on Nov. 10, 1982.

"The name of Leonid Ilyich Brezhnev, a true continuer of Lenin's great cause and an ardent champion of peace and communism, will live forever in the hearts of the Soviet people and the entire progressive mankind."

In Washington, deputy press secretary Larry Speakes said today that the White House had been monitoring the official reports from Tass and Moscow television but did not have any immediate comment.

Brezhnev made his last public appearance on Sunday, standing with all his key associates atop the Lenin mausoleum during the military parade in Red Square which marked the 65th anniversary of the Soviet state. In an address to military leaders and the Soviet hierarchy, Brezhnev declared his desire for peace but warned any potential aggressors would receive "a crushing retaliatory strike."

He said the Soviet Union was

Back Page Col. 1

Cory Warns Of $3 Billion State Deficit

By Michael Harris

State Controller Ken Cory said yesterday that California faces a budget deficit of $2 billion to $3 billion in the next fiscal year, beginning July 1, unless there are new tax revenues and further sharp cuts in state spending.

The deficit would come on top of a still-unresolved deficit for the current fiscal year, in which Cory said tax returns have been coming in so far below estimate that the state may wind up as much as $1.2 billion in the red by June 30, the end of the fiscal year.

"If we don't solve the problem correctly, we can wind up with a New York situation," Cory said, referring to the federal bailout that

Back Page Col. 2

Demos, GOP Rush to Pass Funds for Jobs

Washington

A growing bipartisan consensus developed in Congress yesterday to pass during the post-election session a public works bill that would provide jobs for the unemployed.

There were indications that President Reagan may support a version of such a program if it is limited to repair of highways.

Responding to what they considered a mandate of last week's congressional elections, both Democrats and Republicans vied to claim authorship of jobs legislation, and began a bidding war to determine who could come up with a program that would put the most people to

Back Page Col. 5

Solidarity Strike Foiled

Polish Riot Cops Battle Thousands

Warsaw

Thousands of Poles shouting "Solidarity lives!" and "Down with the junta!" battled riot police in Warsaw, Wroclaw and Nowa Huta yesterday. But tough measures by the martial law regime apparently stymied nationwide work stoppages called by the union's underground leaders.

Workers staged sporadic minor protests and stoppages in about 20 towns and cities, and there were student protests in four cities, according to reports from Western correspondents, the official news agency PAP and government sources.

Polish television said police detained more than 300 people in Warsaw, more than 250 in Wroclaw and 94 in Nowa Huta and Krakow after street clashes. The broadcast also said police seized more than 60 people in Legnica, 40 in Poznan, 28 in Lodz and 16 in Dzierzoniow, near Walbrzych, but the broadcast gave no further details.

The rioting injured 17 police officers and sent 10 civilians to hospitals, the broadcast said.

"There was such a panic and fear that people worked," said a shipbuilder leaving the Lenin Shipyards in Gdansk, where Solidarity was formed during August 1980 strikes. "They were watched closely, but the work was not very efficient."

The official PAP news agency acknowledged sporadic attempts to slow down factories but said "honest, efficient work" prevailed.

"This positive balance of events allows us to hope ... that martial law can be lifted before the end of this year if political, economic and social conditions are still favorable," government spokesman Jerzy Urban told a news conference.

In Washington, President Reagan accused the Polish government of "declaring war on its own people." He added: "One can imprison protesters, club and disperse demonstrators with tear gas or water cannons, but the specter remains: never again will the self-appointed representatives of the workers be able to pretend that they represent anyone but themselves.

"Our hearts go out to the brave Polish people. By struggling for freedom and social justice against overwhelming odds, they fight for

Back Page Col. 3

INDEX

Books	69
Bridge	69
Business World	33
Chess	69
Comics	53
Deaths	54
Entertainment	70
People	50
TV-Radio	68
Weather	48
Top of the News On Page 24	

SENATOR HENRY JACKSON DIES/See Below

HOW RUSSIAN MISSILE SHOT DOWN AIRLINER

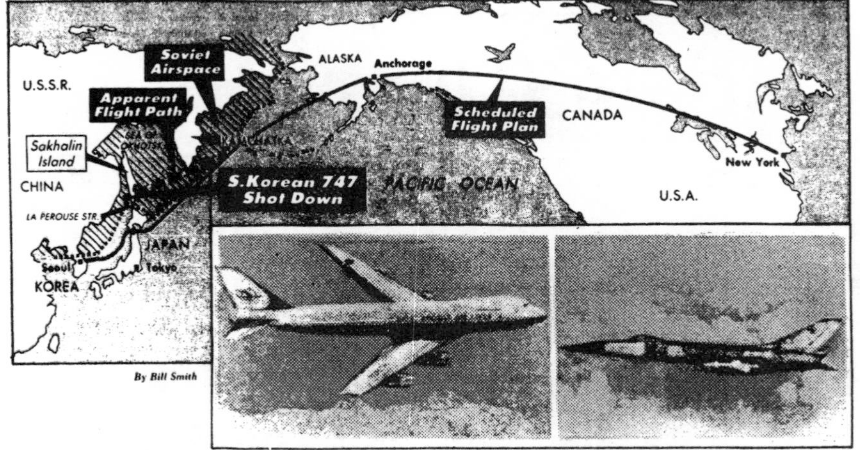

Pentagon officials said that the Korean Air Lines jumbo jet was shot down by a Soviet SU-15 fighter (right)

Wreckage Traces 'Seen'

Washington

A missile fired by a Soviet jet fighter downed a Korean Air Lines jet with 269 people aboard over the Soviet island of Sakhalin on Wednesday, American officials charged yesterday, asking Moscow to explain "this appalling act."

Early today, Soviet officials in Japan said Russian patrol boats found "traces of an airline crash" off Sakhalin.

The Boeing 747, whose passengers included Representative Larry McDonald, D-Ga., among an estimated 30 Americans, apparently plunged into the Sea of Japan, with no sign of any survivors.

Soviet officials, facing mounting international outrage, did not acknowledge downing the plane. A brief statement issued in Moscow by the official Tass news agency said only that Soviet fighter planes had tried to guide "an unidentified plane," which twice "violated the airspace of the U.S.S.R.," but that "the intruder plane did not react to the signals and warnings from the Soviet

Back Page Col. 1

San Francisco Chronicle

The Largest Daily Circulation in Northern California

119th Year No. 197 ★★★★★★• FRIDAY, SEPTEMBER 2, 1983 777-1111 25 CENTS

YITZHAK SHAMIR
Israeli foreign minister

Begin's Party Names Shamir New Leader

Tel Aviv

Foreign Minister Yitzhak Shamir, a former guerrilla leader and secret agent, won his party's approval early today to attempt to succeed outgoing Prime Minister Menachem Begin, Israel Radio reported.

Shamir was elected by a majority of his Herut Party's central committee.

Shamir, 68, defeated Deputy Premier David Levy by 437 to 302 votes in a secret ballot, election chairman Yohanan Vinitzky announced. Seven votes were void.

If he can form a coalition, Shamir is expected to continue Begin's tough nationalist policies, which the two men forged when they fought together in the underground for Israeli independence in the 1940s.

Begin, 70, did not leave his official residence in Jerusalem to attend the central committee meeting in a Tel Aviv theater, and he did not endorse either candidate, letting the Herut Party he created chose his successor.

"He feels a little weak. Not sick, but he's tired," said his old

Back Page Col. 5

Sen. Jackson Dies After Heart Attack

Everett, Wash.

Senator Henry (Scoop) Jackson, a Washington Democrat who had served in the Senate for 30 years, died last night after suffering a massive heart attack. He was 71.

The death of Jackson, known for his liberal views on social issues and hawkish stand on national defense, was confirmed by Willis Tucker, Snohomish County executive. A county law enforcement official said the senator was "dead on arrival" at Providence Hospital.

Mayor Bill Moore, a family friend, told radio station KIRO, "The senator is gone."

Moore said Jackson had been stricken by a heart attack at his home here at 7:47 p.m. He arrived at the hospital at 8:22.

Jackson's wife, Helen, arrived at the hospital at 9:04 p.m. along with one of their two children, hospital official Diane Kempf said.

Senate minority leader Robert Byrd, D-W.Va., said, "The nation has lost one of its best and wisest leaders. He was more than a colleague in the Senate."

Jackson, twice a candidate for the Democratic presidential nomination, was a staunch supporter of Israel and an advocate for Soviet Jews. He was his party's ranking member on the Senate Armed Services Committee and was third on the Senate seniority list.

In July, he cast his 11,000th roll call vote as a senator and drew an ovation from his colleagues for the milestone.

Jackson did not smoke, drank little and exercised religiously. The son of Norwegian immigrants, he

Back Page Col. 5

Pilots Aware of Route's Danger

INSIDE

■ Reagan demands a 'full explanation from the Soviet Union, Page 6.

■ Angry Bay Area Koreans are ignored at the Soviet Consulate in S.F., Page 6.

■ U.S. intelligence network detected Soviet fighter's movements, Page 6.

■ Family and friends of victims react with shock and anger, Page 7.

■ Right-wing leaders praise Rep. Larry McDonald, who died in the crash, Page 7.

■ A similar episode with a Korean jet occurred in 1978, Page 8.

■ Congressmen fear the incident may harm arms control talks, Page 9.

WARNING
Aircraft infringing upon Non Free Flying Territory may be fired on without warning. Consult NOTAMS and Flight Information Publications for the latest air information.

Navigational chart carries a warning for pilots flying near Soviet territory

Heavily Traveled Air Link

By Susan Sward

Commercial airline pilots who fly the route used by the Korean jet shot down over the Soviet Union consider it one of the most "navigationally sensitive" in the world because of its proximity to Soviet territory and airspace.

The route comes as close as 30 miles to Soviet airspace just east of the Kamchatka Peninsula and is 80 miles from the Soviet-held Kurile Islands, several pilots interviewed by The Chronicle said yesterday.

This is one of the most heavily traveled air routes in the world, linking North America and Europe with Asia.

On a typical day, an estimated 70 planes may fly west to Asia on the route, with the European carriers touching down in Anchorage for refueling and the North American carriers joining the flight path toward Asia at the end of the Aleutian Islands off Alaska.

Traditionally, pilots who fly the route say they assume the Russians are monitoring their planes' radio contact with air traffic control centers at Anchorage and Tokyo. For a stretch of about 1700 miles, the

Page 12 Col. 1

'Strategic' Area

Experts Ponder the Attack

By Drew Middleton
New York Times

New York

Soviet sensitivity over foreign radar penetration of defenses guarding La Perouse Strait south of Sakhalin Island may have been the motivation for the destruction of a South Korean airliner by a Soviet fighter.

In war, the strait would be the most direct route for the movement of the Pacific Fleet in the northwest Pacific, American officers said.

Over the last 27 months, U.S. and Japanese intelligence services have reported a steady expansion of Soviet military power on Sakhalin Island, the Siberian mainland, and on the island of Etorofu in the Kurile Islands chain.

Etorofu lies 10 miles northeast of Hokkaido, the northernmost Japanese island. The entire area, one officer said, is now of major importance to Soviet strategic planning.

A squadron of MiG-23s was on Etorofu about a month ago, according to intelligence sources.

American and NATO intelligence analysts rejected the idea that the shooting down of the Boeing airliner could have been the impulsive act of a Soviet pilot. They cited the rigid, centralized command system of all Soviet forces and argued that an attack on a civilian airliner, even when it was flying in Soviet military airspace, could not have been carried out without the approval of a higher headquarters.

They noted that the elapsed time between the first pickup of the airliner by Soviet radar and the attack was sufficient for an exchange of messages between the local commander and headquarters either in Vladivostok, headquarters of the Pacific fleet, or in Moscow.

Air Force sources were puzzled by the fact that the stricken airliner issued no mayday call signal after being hit. One interpretation is that the missile destroyed the cockpit and with it the communications system.

Reinforcement of the Soviet air force in the region has accompanied the expansion of the Pacific fleet's bases. Soviet military writings emphasize the importance of adequate fighter forces to cover the emergence of the fleet into the Pacific. The writers appear to be aware that American aircraft strewing mines in La Perouse Strait could impede or perhaps halt that operation. One Soviet army division has been located on Sakhalin Island. It is equipped with anti-aircraft missiles and guns.

There are four important naval bases in the region. The main fleet

Back Page Col. 4

Ex-Cop Named as Park 'Barrel Killer'

By Bill Workman

A former Millbrae policeman — already under investigation for three murders in San Mateo County — was named yesterday by San Francisco homicide inspectors as the killer of a man and two women whose nude bodies were found stuffed in oil drums in Golden Gate Park last May.

Police said three additional counts of murder will be filed next week against Anthony J. Sully, 39, of Burlingame, an electrical contractor now being held without bail in San Mateo county jail in the slaying of an Oakland escort service employee.

Sully is also a suspect in the

Page 4 Col. 1

INDEX

Books 69
Business World 35
Bridge 69
Chess 69
Comics 41
Deaths 48
Entertainment 70
People 44
Tales of the City 45
TV-Radio 68
Weather 49
Top of the News on Page 22

San Francisco Chronicle

The Largest Daily Circulation in Northern California

119th Year No. 241 ★★★★★★ MONDAY, OCTOBER 24, 1983 777-1111 25 CENTS

161 MARINES DEAD IN BEIRUT

A Marine whose leg was deeply torn in the explosion was carried off for emergency medical treatment

Suicide Attacks — 31 French Troops Also Die

Beirut

Suicide terrorists driving trucks loaded with TNT attacked the peacekeeping force in Lebanon yesterday and blew up U.S. Marine headquarters at Beirut airport, killing at least 161 Marines and injuring 75 others in the single largest loss of American military personnel since the Vietnam War.

Almost simultaneously, another bomb-laden truck slammed into a French paratroop barrack two miles away. At least 31 French paratroopers were killed, 12 were wounded and 53 were missing and believed to be buried in the rubble.

Pentagon officials said a Mercedes truck filled with 2000 pounds of TNT broke through a series of steel fences and sandbag barricades and detonated in the heart of the Marines' administrative headquarters shortly after dawn. The explosion collapsed all four floors of the building and turned it into a burning mound of broken cement pillars and cinderblocks.

Although a Marine sentry was able to fire five shots at the suicide driver and another Marine threw himself in front of the speeding, bomb-filled truck, neither was able to block its entry into the Marine headquarters, where it exploded in a fireball that left a crater 30 feet deep and 40 feet wide.

Gunnery Sergeant Herman Lange was one of the first Marines to reach the bombed headquarters.

"Bodies were lying around all over," he said. "Other people were trapped under the concrete. I could hear them screaming: 'Get us out. Don't leave us.' I just started digging, picking men out and taking them away on a jeep. It was total devastation."

Classified papers were blown all over the area, and Marines scrambled to pick them up. The pile of rubble was peppered with personal items — a can of deodorant, a jack of hearts from a deck of playing cards and a U.S. quarter, twisted out of shape by the blast.

In a haunting scene late last night, rescue workers using blow torches, pneumatic drills and

Back Page Col. 3

49ERS BEAT RAMS

The 49ers scored four touchdowns in the final quarter to defeat the Los Angeles Rams, 45-35, yesterday in Anaheim. The come-from-behind win moved San Francisco into sole possession of first place in its division.

Details in The Sporting Green

CBS Airs Tape Of De Lorean Drug Arrest

Los Angeles

An FBI videotape showing automaker John De Lorean examining contents of a suitcase purportedly containing cocaine was broadcast nationally last night by CBS News, which had won a court battle about the tape earlier in the day.

The tape is thought to be key evidence against De Lorean, who is facing a trial on drug trafficking charges. An attorney for De Lorean had warned that showing the tape would "unleash a circus unprecedented in court history."

The tape showed De Lorean on a couch in a hotel guest room, talking to a man across from him.

Another man, identified by CBS as an undercover agent, entered carrying a suitcase, which he placed on a coffee table and opened. "This is the other batch that's going out of here," the agent is heard to say, adding, "It'll generate about four and a half, not less than four and a half mil."

De Lorean responded "(unintelligible) . . . good as gold. Gold weighs more than this, for God's sake."

Then the suitcase was put out

Back Page Col. 1

Reagan Says U.S. Won't Back Off

Washington

President Reagan vowed yesterday to maintain a U.S. military presence in Lebanon in the wake of the suicide bombing attack that killed 161 Marines in Beirut, but his advisers discussed a plan to make the Marines less vulnerable by moving many of them to ships offshore.

The proposal to have the Marines live on U.S. warships when they are not on patrol at the Beirut airport emerged from a day of intense discussion by the president and his advisers about how to protect the Marines from further attacks and to head off congressional criticism.

Senator Dan Evans, R-Wash., said he was told by White House officials that this was one of two options under consideration. He said the other was expanding the territory occupied by the Marines to give them a more defensible perimeter.

Defense Secretary Caspar Weinberger said there was "circumstantial evidence" linking the bombing to a radical Moslem Shiite sect with ties to Iranian leader Ayatollah Ruhollah Khomeini. The organization, known as Hezballah, is also suspected of bombing the U.S. Embassy in Beirut last April 18, which killed 63 people, including 17 Americans.

"We intend to respond to this criminal act when the perpetrators are identified," White House

Page 2 Col. 1

Stunned, Grieving Survivors Search the Gruesome Rubble

By J. Michael Kennedy
Los Angeles Times

Beirut

Major Robert Jordan led the way through the rubble. His voice was mechanical and weary; he had heard the same questions many times yesterday morning.

The man in the truck, Jordan said, drove to the airport parking lot, whipped the vehicle around, crashing through fences and gates and gunfire with his deadly cargo. A Marine sergeant on guard duty tried to radio the target, command center of the Battalion Landing Team of the 24th Marine Amphibious Unit. But it was too late.

Jordan snapped his fingers. "It was that quick," he said.

As Jordan stood at the edge of the rubble, Marines using hacksaws, sledgehammers and their hands tried to uncover their buddies who might still be alive, the ones who had been sleeping in the upper floors of the four-story building. They listened for voices and then began digging. They stopped, listened, then went on.

The Marines who had been on the lower floors when the truck plowed into the building at 6:20 a.m. had died in their sleep. They died because someone in this brutal country thought that taking their lives was worth losing his own, that somehow killing Marines would help some political cause.

"I have not seen carnage like this since Vietnam," said Jordan, who had come into the Public Affairs Office earlier in the morning with his hands covered with the blood of a man he had helped pull from the wreckage.

On top of the building, or what was left of it, the Marines found one of their own and heaved away

Back Page Col. 3

INSIDE: Bombing of the Marines

The Marines have few military options, given the constraints of their role as a peacekeeping force. **Page 1A**

The building attacked by a suicide bomber is the hub of the Marines' activities and record-keeping. **Page 1A**

French soldiers cursed and wept over the attack on their base in Beirut, which left 31 dead. **Page 1B**

U.S. officials said evidence points to Iran as responsible for the attack. **Page 1B**

The text of President Reagan's statement on the attack on the Marines in Beirut. **Page 1B**

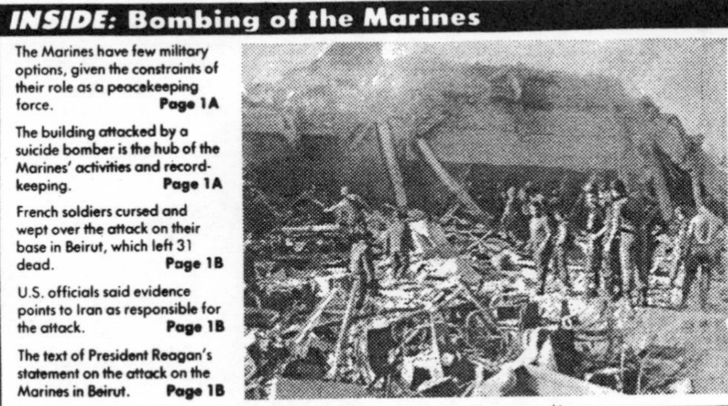

Congressmen reacted angrily to the attack and called on President Reagan to explain the U.S. presence in Lebanon. **Page 2**

A chronology of the events that led up to the attack on the Marines. **Page 2**

The attack came as Lebanese officials were preparing for new peace negotiations. **Page 2**

Marines to replace the victims of the bombing attack left Camp Lejeune, N.C. **Page 3**

Leaders of nations around the world denounced the massive bombings of the American and French troops. **Page 3**

INDEX

Books 41
Bridge 41
Business World 54
Chess 41
Comics 58
Deaths 22,23
Entertainment 42
People 16
TV-Radio 40
Weather 23
Top of the News on Page 20

Fierce Battles With Cubans

U.S. INVADES GRENADA

San Francisco Chronicle

The Largest Daily Circulation in Northern California

119th Year No. 243 ★★★★★★ WEDNESDAY, OCTOBER 26, 1983 777-1111 25 CENTS

Why the President Did It

Concern About Marxists

By Robert C. Toth
Los Angeles Times

Washington

The specter of another Iranian hostage crisis, more than calls for help from neighboring islands, precipitated the U.S. invasion of Grenada in association with six small Caribbean states, a key administration official said yesterday.

President Reagan referred to a "brutal group of leftist thugs" endangering the estimated 1000 American medical students and other U.S. citizens there. Secretary of State George Shultz spoke of the need of invading before Americans were "hurt or taken hostage."

But the roots of the invasion lie much deeper than the week-old series of events that led to what Shultz called "an atmosphere of violent uncertainty" on Grenada. And, despite its assurances yesterday, the Reagan administration may find it difficult to remove U.S. troops quickly and still keep its pledge to restore stable, democratic government to the island.

The administration had been openly hostile to Grenada's Marxist regime, warning that the small volcanic island — on which Cubans and Soviet technicans have worked for four years — could be used as an air and naval base to support Fidel Castro's foreign adventures and to threaten U.S. tanker routes through the Caribbean and the Panama Canal.

The administration thus had short-term as well as strategic reasons for sending Army Rangers and Marines to Grenada — after a final decision taken just one day earlier — when the radical new regime did not open the island's two airports for Americans and other foreigners to leave, officials said.

Having put troops ashore, the administration will come under immediate pressure to get them out as soon as possible, both to demonstrate the sincerity of its aims — "to restore order and democracy," Reagan said — and to avoid casualties from terrorist attacks by followers of the deposed radicals.

The 1900-man U.S. force will be withdrawn "as soon as order is restored to the island," a senior administration official told reporters at the White House, and Shultz indicated that the task of rebuilding a government that is responsive to the people of Grenada will be left primarily to the Organization of Eastern Caribbean States.

But the eastern Caribbean states have contributed only 300 men — many of them constables,

Back Page Col. 6

UPI Telephoto

President Reagan announced the invasion of Grenada alongside Dominica Prime Minister Mary Eugenia Charles as Secretary of State George Shultz, Defense Secretary Casper Weinbereger and White House press aide David Gergen listened in the wings

HIGHLIGHTS: The Invasion of Grenada

THE INVASION

Nearly 2000 U.S. Marines and Army Rangers and smaller forces from six Caribbean states invaded Grenada early yesterday morning. The bulk of the forces parachuted onto the island of 110,000 people. There was fighting with Cuban personnel, and 2 U.S. servicemen were reported dead. **Page 1.**

Students at St. George's Medical School first heard planes at 4:30 a.m. yesterday. **Page 3.**

Preparations for the invasion had secretly been under way for a week and possibly as long ago as two years. **Page 5.**

REAGAN'S REASONS

The president said the operation was intended to protect some 1000 Americans on the island and to thwart a bloody takeover of Grenada by Marxists. **Page 1.**

Reagan said he received "an urgent, formal request" from the Organization of Eastern Caribbean States to assist in restoring order and democracy on Grenada. **Page 1.**

Complete text of Reagan's statement. **Page 2.**

DECISION MAKING

President Reagan's crucial planning for the invasion took place Saturday at the Augusta National Golf Course. **Page 6.**

Reagan said the landing of U.S. troops in Grenada was consistent with international law, but critics disagreed. **Page 6.**

THE REACTION

Members of Congress debated whether Reagan should have committed the United States to another military conflict. **Page 2.**

British Prime Minister Margaret Thatcher said she personally warned President Reagan against invading Grenada. **Page 2.**

Latin American nations harshly criticized the United States, with not one supporting the Grenada action. **Page 4.**

The Soviet Union, which had some personnel captured on the island, demanded the immediate withdrawal of U.S. troops and called the invasion a "bandit-style armed intervention." **Page 4.**

A huge protest in Berkeley — called by some the biggest since anti-Vietnam War protests — assailed the invasion as a brazen power grab. **Page 4.**

U.S. Troops Suffer Casualties

Bridgetown, Barbados

Almost 2000 U.S. troops, joined by forces from six Caribbean nations, invaded Marxist-ruled Grenada yesterday, seizing the island's two airports and capturing Soviet and Cuban personnel in fierce battles that left two U.S. servicemen dead and 23 wounded.

Jamaican Prime Minister Edward Seaga, whose country contributed troops to the invasion force, said 12 Cubans and three civilians were killed in the fighting and a "vast quantity" of Soviet weapons was captured at an airport being built on Grenada with Cuban help.

The force of 1900 U.S. Marines and Army Rangers, backed by 11 U.S. ships, led the invasion, and was followed by 300 troops and policemen from the Caribbean nations. There were reports that two U.S. helicopters were shot down.

The Pentagon said at least two U.S. military men were killed and 23 wounded in the fighting. A terse statement said U.S. troops had encountered resistance, "but most objectives have been taken" during the first 12 hours after the predawn invasion.

Administration and congressional sources in Washington said three members of Grenada's 1200-man armed forces were killed, and 30 Soviet advisers and about 200 armed Cubans were captured.

One administration official, speaking on the condition that he not be named, said the Cubans would be taken to a Cuban ship in a Grenadian harbor, and that arrangements would be made for the Russians to leave.

Meanwhile, at an emergency meeting of the United Nations Security Council late last night, Grenadan deputy representative Ian Jacobs, at times close to tears, asked whether the time had come when size and power of one nation decided what government was chosen in another.

He called on the council to "condemn in the strongest manner this onslaught that is costing hundreds, maybe thousands of lives."

The Security Council meeting was called by Nicaragua, whose Deputy Foreign Minister, Victor Tinoco, dismissed the invasion as illegal and rejected Washington's justification for the landing.

"When is it legal for seven

Back Page Col. 1

INDEX

Books 55
Bridge 55
Business World 27
Chess 55
Comics 60
Deaths 39
Entertainment 56
Food 17
People 36
Tales of the City 38
TV-Radio 54
Weather 25
Top of the News on Page 16

Top Marine Calls Beirut Security 'Adequate'

Beirut

Marine Commandant Paul X. Kelley said yesterday he is "totally satisfied" with security procedures in effect before Sunday's terrorist bombing that has left at least 214 Marines and other U.S. servicemen dead.

Amid mounting complaints in the United States that the Marines were not prepared to deal with the kind of suicide bombing mission that flattened their Battalion Landing Team headquarters at Beirut International Airport, General Kelley, who arrived here yesterday, said he inspected the base twice before the blast.

"I think we had very adequate security measures," he said. "One has to realize if you have a determined individual who is willing to give up his life, chances are he's going to get through and do that."

Other peacekeeping force officers echoed Kelley's view.

One unidentified official, not an American, said: "Whoever is doing this job, they can choose when, where and how. We are just the targets. We can build bunkers and pile sandbags, but they will always choose when, where and how. You cannot defend yourself..."

Shortly before Kelley spoke, the Marine compound was on full alert after reports that three vehicles that might be carrying bombs had been spotted on an airport perimeter road near the base. Marines and reporters took to sandbag bunkers and foxholes as nervous Marines in full combat gear sealed off the base and searched suspi-

Back Page Col. 1

ASSASSINS KILL INDIRA GANDHI

India's Prime Minister Indira Gandhi

San Francisco Chronicle

The Largest Daily Circulation in Northern California

120th Year No. 248 ★★★★★★• WEDNESDAY, OCTOBER 31, 1984 777-1111 25 CENTS

Big 5th Day for Baby Fae

Baboon Heart Recipient 'Improving'

By Robert Bartlett

Baby Fae became the longest-surviving recipient of an animal heart yesterday, drinking from an infant bottle and napping in an oxygen tent on the fifth day after her operation at Loma Linda University Medical Center.

Physicians at the medical center were feeding the infant glucose and water from a bottle in preparation for formula-feeding later, said Brenda Pfeiffer, spokeswoman for the San Bernardino County institution.

Last night, Pfeiffer said Baby Fae, whose real name has not been made public at her parent's request, was "improving." Baby Fae's condition was listed as serious but stable.

At a news conference yesterday, a panel of three doctors said the 7-month-old healthy baboon's heart used in the transplant was about the size of a walnut. They said that Baby Fae, who weighed about five pounds when she was born three weeks prematurely, was the smallest human ever to receive a

Back Page Col. 1

AP Wirephoto

This is the first photo of Baby Fae, the longest-surviving recipient of an animal heart

Eight Wounds

India's Leader Is Shot by Her Security Guards

New Delhi

Prime Minister Indira Gandhi died today after being gunned down by a hail of bullets from members of her own security force.

Gandhi was shot at least eight times in an assassination outside her home. Sikh extremists claimed responsibility.

The 66-year-old prime minister was rushed to the All-India Institute of Medical Sciences, the country's most prestigious hospital, immediately after the attack. The United News of India quoted doctors as saying she died less than two hours later.

She reportedly was shot in the heart, abdomen and thigh.

An assistant cabinet secretary said by telephone that the cabinet was meeting today in emergency session.

An aide in the prime minister's office said that all armed forces have been put on a security alert and all military personnel on leave were ordered to report to duty.

In Washington, White House press aide Anson Franklin said President Reagan has been notified of Gandhi's death and "expressed deep personal sorrow."

There is currently no deputy prime minister in India, and there was no formal announcement of who was in charge of the government. Some sources said Home Minister P. V. Narasimha Rao might take over temporarily. A general election is expected to be held before the end of the year, but no dates have been announced.

Several hours after the shooting, which occurred at 9:20 a.m. in the morning, an unidentified caller told the Associated Press: "We have taken our revenge. Long live the Sikh religion."

Asked who he was and what organization he was from, the man said: "This is the action of the entire Sikh sect." Then the caller hung up.

Gandhi incurred the wrath of India's Sikh minority in June, when army troops besieged and then assaulted the Golden Temple, the Sikhs' holiest place of worship, in Amritsar.

The news agency said Gandhi was shot at by two members of her own security detail and that the two were killed on the spot by other security guards. Without elaborating, the agency also said an officer of the security police was injured and "overpowered."

The news agency said the at-

Page 11 Col. 5

Indira's Son A Possible Successor

New Delhi

One eventual possible successor to Indian Prime Minister Indira Gandhi is her son Rajiv, who has been his mother's closest aide. The death of a brother transformed Rajiv Gandhi from an airline pilot into his role as a political leader.

Rajiv, for 14 years a pilot for the domestic Indian Airlines, unexpectedly found himself in the political limelight when his politically popular younger brother, Sanjay, was killed in the crash of a stunt

Page 12, Col. 1

Yerba Buena Project Gets A Go-Ahead

By Reginald Smith

Yerba Buena Gardens, the $1 billion project that took nearly 20 years of controversy to put together, was unanimously approved last night by the San Francisco Redevelopment Agency.

The proposal, strongly backed by Mayor Dianne Feinstein, now goes before the Board of Supervisors for almost certain approval, and some construction is expected to begin early next year.

Considered the single biggest and most complex business transaction in the city's history, Yerba Bue-

Back Page Col. 4

Imprisoned Black Panther Wins Murder Case Hearing

By Jack Viets

A federal magistrate has reopened the murder case against Elmer (Geronimo) Pratt, the former Southern California Black Panther Party leader who was sent to prison for life more than 12 years ago.

Magistrate John R. Kronenberg of the U.S. District Court in Los Angeles ordered a hearing to review the validity of some of the key evidence that was used to convict Pratt for what became known as the "tennis court" murder in Santa Monica.

The hearing will determine whether some of the evidence was tainted by the FBI's Cointelpro program, the secret program of the late J. Edgar Hoover's secret program to neutralize radical groups like the Black Panthers during the turmoil and racial unrest of the late 1960s and early '70s.

"Pratt was set up," retired FBI Special Agent Wesley Swearingen told The Chronicle in an interview.

Seven current or former FBI agents have been ordered to testify at the hearing — six of them members of the Los Angeles FBI Black Extremist Squad 2, which had been ordered to disrupt the Black Panther Party in Southern California.

They include Special FBI Agent Richard E. Bloeser, the supervisor of Squad 2, Agent Richard W. Held, the Los Angeles Cointelpro coordinator, and former San Francisco Agent Raymond Byers, who gathered information on the Black Panther Party in the Bay Area from informants operating through the Oakland Police Department.

But the magistrate denied the request by Pratt's volunteer defense attorneys that Julio (Julius) Butler, a key prosecution witness against Pratt, be subpoenaed to testify. The date for the hearing has yet to be set.

Pratt stood trial in 1972 for the murder of a young schoolteacher, Carolyn Olsen, during a $30 robbery on a Santa Monica tennis court on the evening of Dec. 18, 1968.

The victim's husband, Kenneth, who was wounded in the attack, testified that the couple had

Page 4 Col. 1

Polish Divers Recover Body Of Slain Priest

Warsaw

Police frogmen found the body of the Rev. Jerzy Popieluszko in the icy waters of a reservoir yesterday, 11 days after three secret police officers kidnaped the pro-Solidarity priest, the official news media reported.

Polish authorities suggested that the kidnap-murder might be part of a broader conspiracy, and placed the Interior Ministry officers accused of the crime under special protection.

There were no reports of disturbances after the announcement on state-run television's evening newscast that the 37-year-old priest had been murdered and that his body had been recovered.

The government announced Friday that the three suspects — a captain and two lieutenants — had

Back Page Col. 5

GALLUP POLL

President's Lead Is Holding Steady

By George Gallup

Princeton, N.J.

In its next-to-the-last election survey, completed yesterday, the Gallup Poll found no statistical change in the standings of the two major-party tickets. The Reagan-Bush Republican ticket is the choice of 57 percent of registered voters. Forty percent favor the Mondale-Ferraro Democratic slate, and 3 percent are undecided.

In an October 15-17 survey the Reagan ticket received 58 percent of the vote and the Mon-

Back Page Col. 1

Prisons May Raise Research Puppies

Sacramento

The Deukmejian administration, searching for new ways to give prisoners productive work, has plans for inmates at a new Kern County prison to raise more than 2000 puppies a year for laboratory research.

Under state law and policies of Governor Deukmejian and the Legislature, California has embarked on a program to put to work as many inmates as possible, on grounds that jobs fight idleness and offer rehabilitation. Inmates now can cut their sentences in half by working.

The problem is that most kinds of productive work except making

Back Page Col. 3

INDEX

Books	53	Datebook	54
Bridge	53	[illegible]	35
Business	25	Food	17
Chess	53	People	18
Comics	34	Weather	64

Top of the News, Page 16

ELECTION SPECIAL

REAGAN LANDSLIDE

AP Wirephoto

President Reagan, accompanied by his wife, Nancy, gave the thumbs-up sign at a victory celebration in Beverly Hills

President Wins 49 States, 59% of Vote

GOP Keeps Senate; Demos Hold House

See Page 2

San Francisco Chronicle

The Largest Daily Circulation in Northern California

120th Year No. 254 ★★★★★★•• WEDNESDAY, NOVEMBER 7, 1984 777-1111 25 CENTS

ELECTION RESULTS

NATIONAL

Mondale Accepts Loss With Grace, Style

See Page 3

UPI Telephoto

Walter Mondale got a hug from his daughter Eleanor after he conceded the election

Inside Reagan's Big Victory See Page 8

KEY STATE PROPOSITIONS	YES	NO
36 Property Tax Initiative	☐	☒
37 State Lottery Proposal	☒	☐
38 English-Only Ballots	☒	☐
39 Reapportionment Initiative	☐	☒
40 Campaign Contribution Limits	☐	☒
41 Limits on Welfare Programs	☐	☒

BAY AREA

Marks Defeats Belli by Wide Margin See Page 4

Boxer, Burton, Dellums Win Re-Election See Page 5

Molinari Tops in S.F. Supervisors Race See Page 6

U.S. Concern Over 'MiG Shipment'

Washington

Administration officials said yesterday that a Soviet freighter that left a Black Sea port in September is being watched closely because of intelligence reports that the ship contains Soviet fighter planes that might be destined for Nicaragua.

It was not immediately clear, however, how reliable administration officials considered those intelligence reports or how seriously they were reacting to them.

Some officials, who would normally be attuned to any such information, said there was no unusual level of concern. Others, however, were uncharacteristically cryptic when asked about reports that the Soviet freighter might be carrying fighters to Nicaragua.

In Los Angeles, deputy White House press secretary Larry

Back Page Col. 3

Electoral College Victory Is the Biggest Since 1936

Mondale Wins D.C., Minnesota

By Larry Liebert
Political Correspondent

President Reagan won re-election yesterday with a landslide of breathtaking proportions.

With more than 95 percent of the popular vote counted, Reagan was trouncing Walter Mondale 59 percent to 41 percent. Even more important, Reagan captured 49 states in a virtual electoral shutout.

Reagan was the projected winner of 525 electoral votes, almost two times the 270 needed to win.

Mondale claimed only 13 electoral votes. He won the mostly black District of Columbia, with three electoral votes, and his home state of Minnesota, with 10.

It was a worse political disaster than Democrat George McGovern's defeat to Richard Nixon in 1972. McGovern won 17 electoral votes by capturing Massachusetts and the District of Columbia.

The only showing worse than Mondale's was Alf Landon's eight electoral votes against Franklin D. Roosevelt in 1936.

Reagan was the clear winner in his home state of California.

At 9:30 p.m., Reagan went before a screaming crowd of supporters at the same Beverly Hills hotel where he celebrated his election four years ago.

Reagan supporters waved American flags and chanted, "Four more years." The president, smiling broadly, responded, "I think that's just been arranged."

Claiming victory, he vowed, "America's best days lie ahead."

Repeating his favorite line of the campaign, he said, "You'll forgive me, I'm going to do it one more time — you ain't seen nothing yet."

"We want to make every family

Back Page Col. 1

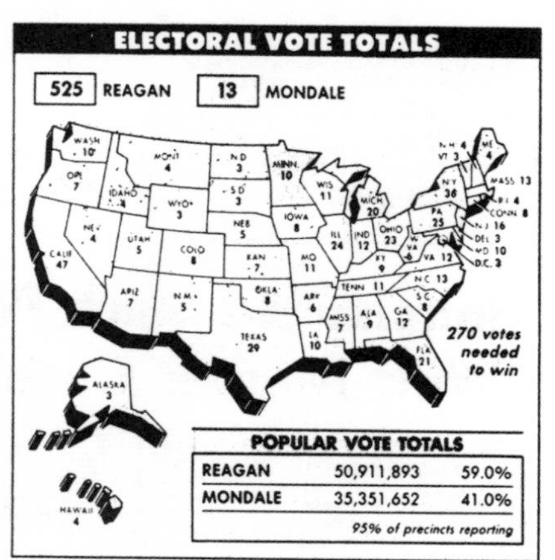

POPULAR VOTE TOTALS		
REAGAN	50,911,893	59.0%
MONDALE	35,351,652	41.0%

95% of precincts reporting

Californians Approve Lottery by Big Margin

By Steve Wiegand

California voters gave their blessing yesterday to creation of a state lottery, unswayed by warnings that it would lead to more crime and moral decay.

With 56 percent of the vote counted, Proposition 37 was winning by a substantial ratio of 58 percent to 42 percent and ahead in every county in the state.

The measure, which was supported by some educators and local government leaders and opposed by most top state elected officials and many law enforcement and religious groups, amends the state Constitution to call for the start of a government-run lottery by late March.

On a ballot that was unusually crowded with controversial propositions, voters rejected Proposition 36, the Howard Jarvis-sponsored measure that would provide tax refunds to some property owners, and Proposition 39, the initiative sponsored by Governor Deukmejian that would wrest reapportionment power away from the Legislature and give it to a panel of retired judges.

Voters also rejected Proposi-

Back Page Col. 4

INDEX

Books	67	Datebook	68
Bridge	67	Deaths	50
Business	31,79	Food	23
Chess	67	People	47
Comics	40	Weather	78

Top of the News, Page 22

66 Feared Dead in Reno Air Crash

— See Below

San Francisco Chronicle

The Largest Daily Circulation in Northern California

121st Year No. 4 ★★★★★★•• MONDAY, JANUARY 21, 1985 777-1111 25 CENTS

49ERS WIN IT

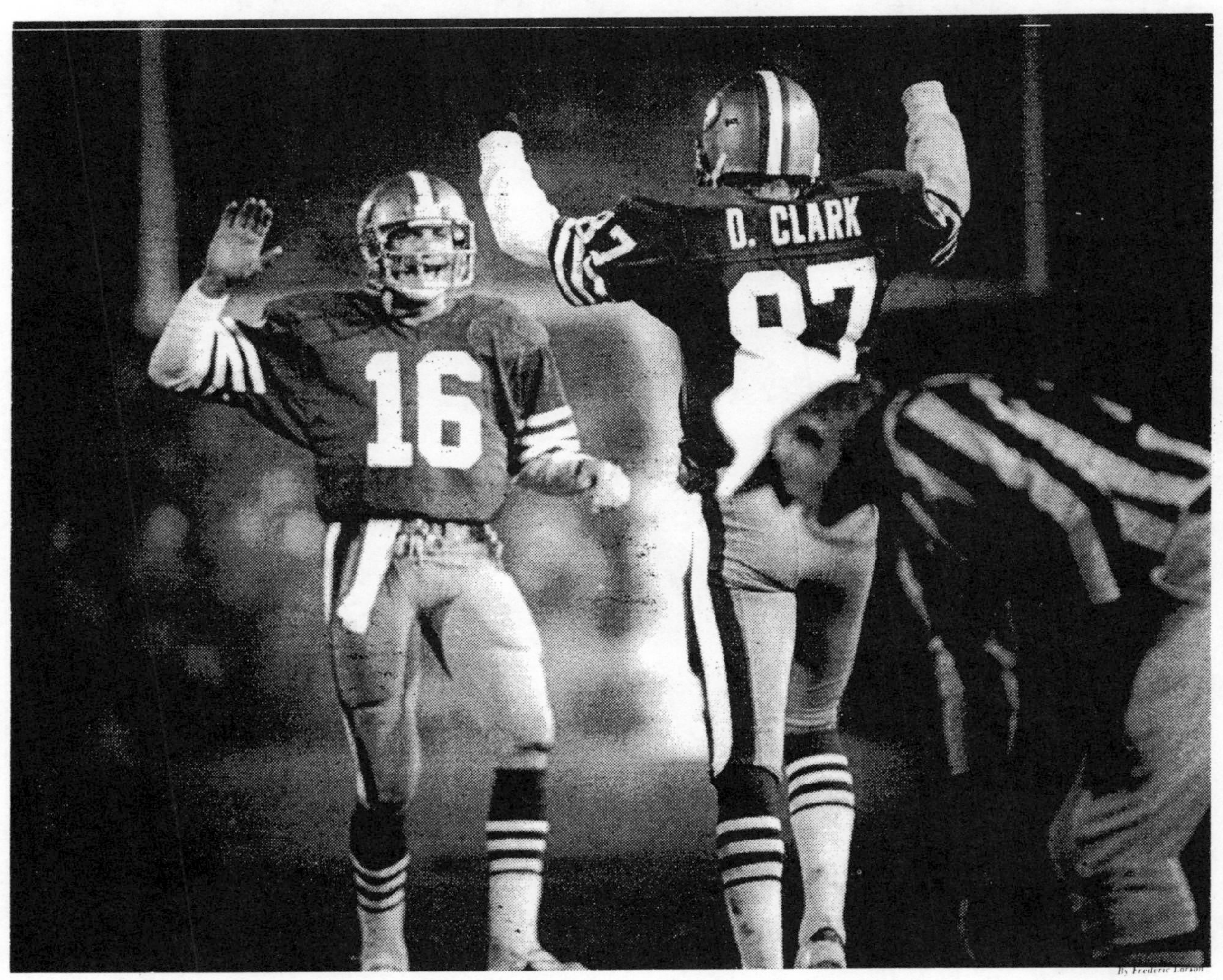

By Frederic Larson

A jubilant Joe Montana, the Super Bowl's most valuable player, saluted Dwight Clark yesterday after their 34-yard pass play on the 49ers' final possession of the game

Bay Area Celebrates — Victory Parade Today

By Larry Liebert

The San Francisco 49ers won the Super Bowl in a rout yesterday, and the triumph in their own back yard set off an exuberant celebration throughout the Bay Area.

Their 38-16 trouncing of the Miami Dolphins capped the winningest season in National Football League history, with 18 wins and only one loss

Minutes after the game at Stanford Stadium, the celebration shifted to San Francisco, where the streets were jammed into the morning hours with celebrants who honked their car horns, screamed themselves hoarse, broke a few windows, jumped on the hoods of automobiles, climbed onto buses, set off firecrackers and even lit bonfires in the streets.

By late last night, San Francisco police reported 184 arrests, most of them described as "happy

Back Page Col. 1

Charter Plane Plunges After Takeoff

Reno, Nev.

As many as 66 people died early today when a chartered plane with 68 passengers aboard crashed as it tried to land on a main thoroughfare outside Reno.

The plane slammed into a field south of downtown and burst into flame, a Federal Aviation Administration spokesman said.

A newsman on the scene con-

Back Page Col. 5

Reagan Sworn In — No Parade

Washington

Ronald Reagan took the oath of office for a second term as president yesterday but, because of the bitter cold, today's traditional outdoor inaugural events have been canceled.

Today's oath-taking ceremony and Reagan's speech, planned for in front of the Capitol, will be held indoors — and there will be no parade. Officials said it was the first inaugural parade to be canceled by weather since Andrew Jackson's second, in 1833.

The inaugural committee decided yesterday afternoon to recommend canceling the parade down Pennsylvania Avenue when it learned that the wind-chill factor would be 30 degrees below zero and could cause thousands of spectators to suffer frostbite or worse, said inaugural chairman Ron Walker.

He said participants in the parade, including hundreds of young people, would have had to begin lining up in pre-dawn cold at 4 a.m.

"I want to tell you, I want to

Back Page Col. 3

INDEX

Books	57	Chess	57	Deaths	43	Television	56
Bridge	57	Comics	22	Editorials	54	Weather	20
Business	67	Datebook	58	People	40	Top of News	14

SPECIAL REPORT ON SHUTTLE DISASTER/9 PAGES

San Francisco Chronicle

The Largest Daily Circulation in Northern California

122nd Year No. 11 ★★★★★★ WEDNESDAY, JANUARY 29, 1986 777-1111 25 CENTS

WHAT WENT WRONG

7 Killed In Shuttle Explosion

By Boyce Rensberger
Washington Post

Cape Canaveral

The space shuttle Challenger, carrying a crew that included schoolteacher Christa McAuliffe, exploded in a burst of flames 74 seconds after liftoff yesterday, killing all seven aboard and stunning a world made witness to the event by television.

The unexplained explosion occurred without warning as the flight seemed to be proceeding flawlessly at about 2900 feet per second, 10 miles above Earth and eight miles downrange from Cape Canaveral.

The spacecraft disintegrated into bits of debris that rained into the Atlantic Ocean. Those aboard, still strapped into their seats, had no means of escape.

It was the worst accident in the history of space exploration and the first time anyone has been killed during an American space flight.

The tragedy occurred 19 years and one day after U.S. astronauts Virgil (Gus) Grissom, Roger Chaffee

Back Page Col. 5

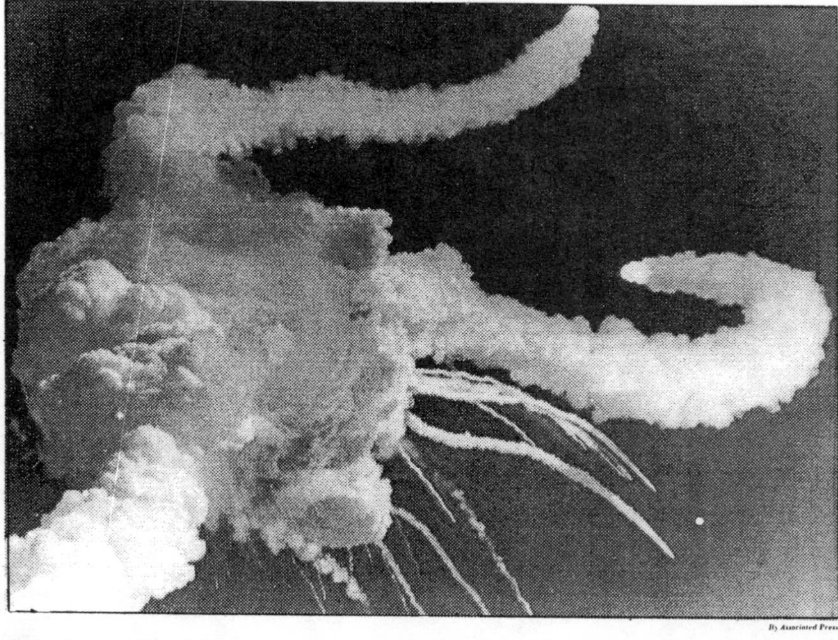

By Associated Press

Smoke plumes trailed the solid fuel rockets (upward, right) as they continued skyward after the liquid fuel tank and shuttle exploded

2 Areas on Fuel Tanks Suspected

By Thomas H. Maugh II
Los Angeles Times

Cape Canavaral

A little more than a minute after the space shuttle Challenger lifted off from pad 39B at the Kennedy Space Center yesterday morning a thin tongue of flame appeared between the left booster rocket and the shuttle's main fuel tank.

The flame was not seen by observers on the ground, but slow motion videotapes of the launch show it clearly.

Less than a second later, nearly 200,000 pounds of liquid hydrogen in the main fuel tank exploded in a massive fireball that enveloped the shuttle orbiter and sent both solid rocket boosters flying off in near opposite directions. The explosion destroyed the orbiter.

Although there is little doubt about what happened, exactly how it happened remained a major mystery. Yesterday, however, most of the speculation centered on two possibilities.

One is that a defect in the solid rocket booster caused exhaust

Back Page Col. 1

THE SHUTTLE CHALLENGER'S FATEFUL LIFTOFF

Orlando
Intended Route
CAPE CANAVERAL
Atlantic Ocean
FLORIDA
Lake Okeechobee
Fort Myers
Miami
Gulf of Mexico
50 MILES

8:39:12 TV tracking camera spots fireball near bottom of Challenger main fuel tank as the spaceship is 10.4 miles high and 8.0 miles from its Florida coast launching site. The shuttle is traveling at 1977 miles per hour.

8:39:13 Challenger explodes, spewing burning pieces like a fireworks display.

8:39:09 Last transmission from Challenger responding to command from Mission Control to increase throttle: "Challenger. Go at throttle up."

10.4 miles

8:38:52 Shuttle is traveling at 1539 miles per hour; altitude is 4.9 miles; distance from shore is 3.4 miles. Mission Control spokesman reports "Engines are throttling up. Three engines are at 104 percent."

8:38:07 Spacecraft begins its normal flight pattern that puts the shuttle on its back in a pre-planned maneuver.

8.0 miles

Launch pad 39 B

8:38:00 a.m. (PST) Challenger lifts off from launch pad, all systems appear normal.

Main fuel tank
Solid fuel boosters

Tracking equipment reports debris hit the water in an area approximately located at 28.64° North, 80.28° West; the water in the area is 75 to 150 feet deep.

KENNEDY SPACE CENTER

Chronicle graphic by Eric Jungerman and Chris Peterson

Serious Doubts Raised Over Future Space Flights

By David Perlman
Science Editor

The Challenger disaster yesterday forced a long delay in America's manned space program and fueled new controversy over its future.

This year was to have been one of the greatest and most adventurous for American space exploration since the space age began nearly 30 years ago, but now the adventure is on hold.

The speedup of the shuttle program's crowded schedule — strongly prodded by the White House — must await the results of NASA specialists who are probing the cause of the explosion that destroyed the Challenger and killed all seven aboard.

Another and even more ambitious effort, a program to put a huge space station in orbit by 1993, may be in far greater jeopardy, experts said.

Until yesterday, 15 space shuttle missions were scheduled for this year, including three to send dramatic scientific payloads into orbit and deep space. At least three secret military flights also were planned from the new shuttle spaceport at California's Vandenberg Air Force Base.

NASA's annual budget, running at nearly $8 billion, has more than $3.5 million earmarked for "space transportation" — the shuttle program with its high-technology development, expensive launches and corps of astronauts.

With the number of shuttles now reduced to three, the fleet has been grounded by President Reagan until the cause of the catastrophe has been pinpointed. That may take many months, experts say — and the answer may never be fully known.

Among the major space projects indefinitely delayed because they were due to be launched from shuttle orbiters this year are:

■ An unmanned probe called Galileo, which is to orbit the planet Jupiter and parachute instruments into its atmosphere.

■ The 10-ton Hubble Space Telescope, whose 94-inch mirror should enable astronomers to peer out to the very edges of the universe billions of light-years distant.

■ The European-built Ulysses space probe that will orbit the sun from pole to pole to measure solar particles and magnetic fields never before observed.

Postponing the Galileo mission, which was due to be launched in May, is a particular blow to scientists because the trajectory to Jupiter is only possible during a 20-day period in which the planet's orbit is in the right position to be reached from Earth.

It now appears the mission will

Page 3 Col. 1

President Postpones State of Union Talk

Washington

Saying "today is a day for mourning and remembering," President Reagan postponed the State of the Union address because of the space shuttle explosion.

In brief, nationally televised remarks from the Oval Office late yesterday afternoon, Reagan promised "to continue our quest in space."

"There will be more shuttle flights and more shuttle crews and, yes, more volunteers, more civilians, more teachers in space," he said. "This is truly a national loss. We mourn seven heroes. We mourn their loss as a nation together."

Concerned that schoolchildren across the nation had watched the explosion on television and had witnessed the death of Christa McAuliffe, the teacher from Concord, N.H., who was to have been the first ordinary citi-

Page 4 Col. 1

INSIDE

Actress Lilli Palmer Dies at 71

See Page 9

Books.......53
Bridge.......53
Business.......23
Caen.......31
Carroll.......49
Chess.......53
Classified.......36
Comics.......35
Crossword.......51
Datebook.......54
Dear Abby.......51
Deaths.......9, 36
Delaplane.......49
Dickey.......59
Editorials.......50
Food.......17
Hoppe.......51
Horoscope.......35
Letters.......50
Mellinkoff.......50
Movies
Bay Area.......56
S.F.......55
O'Flaherty.......53
People.......32
Personals.......10
Radio.......52
Rosenbaum.......60
Sports.......57
Stocks,
N.Y.......29
Amex.......30
TV.......52
Weather.......48
White.......24

Top of the News on Page 14

INSIDE THE ABANDONED PALACE/ SEE BELOW

San Francisco Chronicle

The Largest Daily Circulation in Northern California

122nd Year No. 35 ★★★★★★● WEDNESDAY, FEBRUARY 26, 1986 777-1111 25 CENTS

Celebrations in the Philippines

U.S. Flies Marcos to Guam

By Associated Press

A Filipino youth slashed an oil painting of Ferdinand Marcos with a stick as looters stormed Malacanang Palace

Inside the Marcos Palace

By Mark Fineman
Los Angeles Times

Manila

The Marcos family's once-private living chambers in the Malacanang presidential palace were testimony last night to the haste of a fleeing dictator.

The parquet floors of former President Ferdinand Marcos' quarters were strewn with private papers and decrees. Emptied drawers stood half-open.

The mirrored dressing room of former first lady Imelda Marcos was still filled with hundreds of her costly silk dresses and large wicker baskets overflowing with scented soaps from around the world. Dozens of quart- and gallon-size bottles of the most expensive French perfume scented the room more than two hours after their owner, with her husband and family, had fled a nation that no longer wanted them after two decades of rule.

The Marcoses fled so hastily that they abandoned scores of precious family mementos — from a six-foot oil painting of Marcos half nude in a Philippine jungle and photographs of the former president and first lady embracing to videotapes of Marcos family gatherings and a private visit between Mrs. Marcos and Nancy Reagan.

They also left behind a lavish, half-eaten meal on their silver service, a half-dozen wide-screen television sets, costly stereo units, a double freezer stuffed with imported,

Page 6 Col. 6

He's Due In Hawaii Today

Manila

Twenty years of dictatorship ended in an explosion of street celebrations today as Ferdinand Marcos surrendered the presidency of the Philippines and flew into exile aboard a U.S. Air Force plane.

Washington immediately recognized the new government of Corazon Aquino, and President Reagan guaranteed Marcos "his peace, his safety and his dignity" in the United States.

As crowds of jubilant Filipinos stormed his vacated presidential palace, Marcos flew from Clark Air Base in the Philippines to the American Pacific island of Guam. U.S. Defense Department officials said Marcos was to leave Guam this morning for Hickam Air Force Base in Honolulu.

His final destination was unclear last night, but Secretary of State George Shultz said Marcos could find "safe haven" in the United States.

In all, 55 people — family members and political supporters — went into exile with the man who dominated the Philippines for 20 years, Pentagon officials said.

Marcos was carried on a stretcher onto a U.S. Air Force C-9 medical evacuation plane with Red Cross markings, and he took off from Clark at 5:03 a.m. Wednesday local time (1:03 p.m. PST yesterday). His plane landed at 10:40 a.m. Wednesday Guam time (4:40 p.m. PST yesterday) at Andersen Air Force Base, where half a dozen anti-Marcos protesters demonstrated outside the sealed gates.

Marcos' wife, Imelda, and his former military chief of staff, General Fabian Ver, flew on the same plane with the former president. A second plane, a C-141 Starlifter, carried other members of the party on the 1500-mile flight to Guam, 3700 miles west-southwest of Hawaii.

A State Department spokesman said Marcos, 68, was exhausted and "physically frail," although he walked off the airplane in Guam without assistance. He had been treated by a doctor aboard the plane.

The State Department spokesman said he did not know details of Marcos' condition. However, U.S. officials have said that they believe that Marcos suffers from a series of afflictions, including a disease called lupus, in which healthy organs, including the kidneys, are sometimes attacked by the body's immune system.

Once in Guam, Marcos' party, in blue military cars with a police motorcycle escort, went to the Hilton Hotel in Agana, taking an isolated back road.

Marcos had been forced to surrender power in the face of wide-

Page 6, Col. 1

Marcos Family Finances
Page 7
U.S. Ready to Send Aid
Page 8
Exiles Can Go Home
S.F. Consul's Conversion
Page 9

The Phone Call That May Have Swayed Marcos

By Bernard Gwertsman
New York Times

Washington

It was about 3 a.m. Tuesday in Manila and President Ferdinand Marcos was telephoning to find out whether the message he had received from Washington calling for "a peaceful transition" to a new government actually meant he should quit.

Senator Paul Laxalt, who received the call in Washington — it was 2 p.m. Monday here — said later that Marcos was "a desperate man, clutching at straws," even though he would be formally sworn in for another term as president in a matter of hours.

He told the Nevada Republican, whom he seemed to trust as a Reagan confidant, that he did not want to resign, and he did not want to come to the United States where he might be harassed by congressional committees.

Marcos was scared, Laxalt said. He could not sleep. He feared the Malacanang Palace was about to be overrun by rebel troops. He said he had heard that U.S. Navy ships were offshore waiting to aid the rebels.

He asked Laxalt whether the

Page 6 Col. 1

Gorbachev Links Next Summit To Progress in Arms Control

Moscow

Addressing a landmark meeting of the Soviet Communist Party yesterday, Mikhail Gorbachev criticized President Reagan's recent response on arms reduction and said the timing of the next summit meeting could hinge on progress in arms control.

The Soviet leader's comments were included in a speech of 5½ hours on the state of the Soviet Union in the opening session of the 27th congress of the ruling party.

Addressing 5000 delegates and 152 foreign delegations, Gorbachev presented a sweeping view of the problems facing the nation, most of which he blamed on stagnation under the 18-year rule of Leonid Brezhnev, which ended in 1982. Gorbachev said the key to the future was a qualitatively new approach to Soviet economic development.

On Sunday, Reagan had responded in a letter to a proposal made January 15 by Gorbachev to eliminate nuclear arms by the year 2000 in a three-stage sequence. Reagan focused on the first of these stages, involving the elimination of medium-range nuclear missiles.

Gorbachev said that Reagan's proposal "seems to contain some reassuring opinions and theses," but that these "are swamped in various reservations, 'linkages' and 'conditions.'"

"To put it in a nutshell," Gorbachev said, "it is hard to detect in the letter we have just received any serious readiness of the United States administration to get down to solving the cardinal problems involved in eliminating the nuclear threat."

On the question of a summit

Back Page Col. 3

2 From Chronicle Win Top Photo Awards

San Francisco Chronicle photographers have won the first and third prizes in the nation's most prestigious news photo competition, a dual victory unprecedented in the 43-year history of the contest.

Photographer Steve Ringman was named the winner of the annual Newspaper Photographer of the Year award. It was the second time in three years that Ringman, 32, had won photojournalism's top honors — and the $1000 prize money that goes with it. He first won in 1983.

Chronicle photographer Eric Luse captured the third-place award, the first time any American newspaper has had two winners among the top three in the Photographer of the Year category.

The second-place award

Back Page Col. 1

ACT Quickly Replaces William Ball

By Steven Winn

American Conservatory Theatre founder William Ball was replaced yesterday by veteran ACT director Edward Hastings.

Hastings agreed to take charge of the company after the board of trustees swiftly ended Ball's 20-year reign in a dramatic six-hour meeting Monday night.

The abruptly called board meeting was attended also by a representative of the state attorney general's office, who said an inquiry into the theater's operation is continuing.

In a surprise announcement on Friday, Ball had said he intended to resign as general director at the end of the current season. Yesterday, the board quickly accepted Ball's resignation as both general director and president of the trustees and selected Hastings to take charge.

Hastings, former ACT executive director and a frequent guest stage director, accepted the newly created position of artistic director and declared his intention to plan

Back Page Col. 1

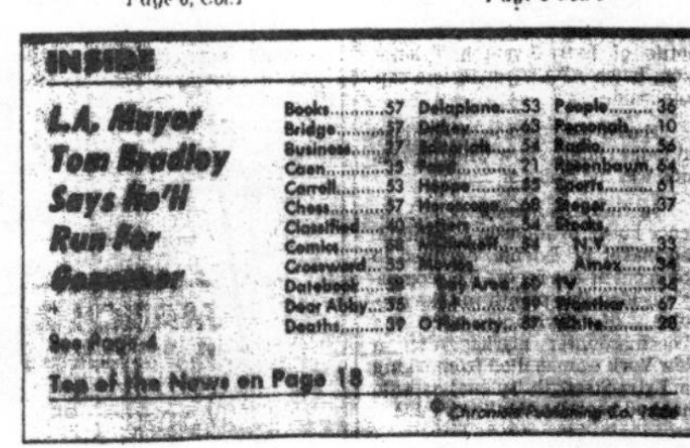

U.S. BOMBERS ATTACK 5 TARGETS IN LIBYA

San Francisco Chronicle

The Largest Daily Circulation in Northern California

122nd Year No. 76 ★★★★★★• TUESDAY, APRIL 15, 1986 777-1111 25 CENTS

Reagan Reply to Terrorism

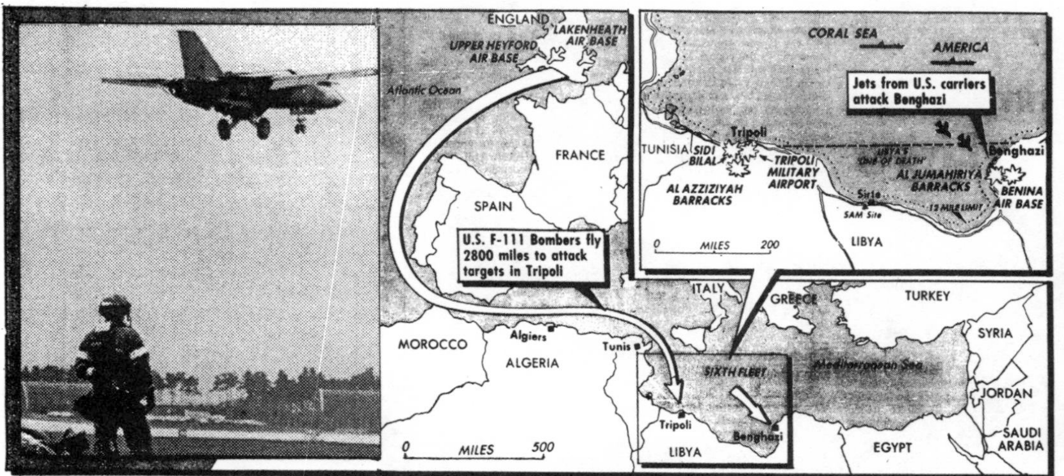

By Bruce Krefting

An F-111 fighter-bomber took off from the U.S. Air Base at Lakenheath, England, on its way around Europe to attack Libyan targets yesterday

One U.S. Plane Missing

Washington

U.S. planes attacked at least five targets in Libya yesterday in retaliation for the April 5 terrorist bombing in West Berlin in which an American serviceman was killed. President Reagan declared that "when our citizens are abused or attacked, anywhere in the world, ... we will respond, so long as I am in this Oval Office."

The bombers, flying from aircraft carriers in the Mediterranean and U.S. bases in Great Britain, set off fiery explosions in two cities and ignited what observers on the ground believed was a large fire at an oil storage facility outside Tripoli.

Defense Secretary Caspar Weinberger said one U.S. plane, an F-111 with a crew of two, "is not accounted for at this time."

He speculated that the plane could have had mechanical trouble during the long trip back to Britain. As of early this morning, the Pentagon said it still had no word on the missing plane. There were no confirmed American casualties.

"Today we have done what we had to do," Reagan said in an address to the nation last night. "If necessary, we will do it again."

Evidence of Libyan leader Moammar Khadafy's responsibility for the West Berlin incident, in which a Turkish woman also was killed and more than 200 people were injured, "is direct, it is precise, it is irrefutable," the president said.

"Despite our repeated warnings, Khadafy continued his reckless policy of intimidation, his relentless pursuit of terror," Reagan said. "He counted on America to be passive. He counted wrong."

Squadrons of F-111 fighter-bombers, flying from Air Force bases in Great Britain, hit targets described by White House spokesman Larry Speakes as the command and control centers and intelligence, communications, logistics and training facilities used by terrorists.

In addition, Navy F-14 interceptors, FA-18 fighter-bombers, A-6 attack bombers and planes equipped with electronic radar-jamming and surveillance gear were dispatched from two aircraft carriers that had taken up positions in the Mediterranean Sea just beyond Khadafy's "Line of Death" marking the boundary of the Gulf of Sidra.

The targets of the U.S. raid included Khadafy's suspected head-

Page 11A, Col. 1

Bombers Were Refused Passage

France Made U.S. Job Tougher

Washington

A complex nighttime military operation against Libya, involving at least five dozen aircraft and probably many more, was made more difficult by France's refusal to permit U.S. F-111 fighter-bombers based in the United Kingdom to fly over France, Defense Secretary Caspar Weinberger said last night.

Weinberger said U.S. planes had to fly about 2800 miles over water to reach their targets in western Libya, a round trip of at least 14 hours. Pentagon officials said the bombing plan called for each F-111 to be refueled in the air four times on the way to Libya and twice on the return trip, when the bombers could travel farther on less fuel because they had dropped their bombs.

The F-111Es from Royal Air Force Base Upper Heyford and the F-111Fs from RAF Lakenheath could have shortened their trips by 1200 nautical miles each way by flying over France, which, Weinberger said pointedly, would have presented "less risk to the pilots." A Pentagon official said two or three dozen tanker aircraft, mostly giant KC-10s, had to be put into the air to keep the F-111s fueled.

"Obviously, if we had permission to fly a direct route, we would have not subjected the pilots to such a long route," Weinberger said.

In addition to 18 F-111 fighter-bombers and dozens of tankers, at least some of which

Page 11A Col. 2

LIBYA INSIDE

How Decision Was Made	Page 11A
The Scene in Tripoli	Page 11B
The U.S. Evidence	Page 11B
Soviet Press Reaction	Page 11B
World Reaction	Page 12
What the Experts Say	Page 13
Shock in the Bay Area	Page 13
Reaction in Congress	Page 13
Khadafy-Reagan Feud	Page 14
Chronology of Problems	Page 14

Peninsula Ballpark Proposal Strikes Out

By Bill Workman and Reginald Smith

The San Mateo City Council has rejected Mayor Dianne Feinstein's proposal for a possible San Francisco Giants ballpark next to Bay Meadows, apparently killing hopes for a Peninsula stadium.

The council yesterday sent a letter to Feinstein, advising her that San Mateo has no room for a stadium at the Highway 101-92 interchange because of the added traffic, noise and congestion a ballpark would impose on nearby neighborhoods.

The council voted 5 to 0 on Saturday to end negotiations about a stadium after more than 150 of the track's neighbors and other San Mateo residents crowded into a special City Hall meeting.

"I really felt we should do everything we could to keep major league baseball in the Bay Area," said San Mateo Councilman Hugh Wayne. "But with the track and county fairgrounds already there, a 35,000-seat stadium would be a little more than our town could handle."

The meeting was held after Mayor Feinstein last week pushed for a quick decision on the Bay Meadows idea from San Mateo County officials. The officials had been holding private stadium talks with Feinstein and other San Francisco officials since February.

Feinstein said yesterday that she was disappointed by the San Mateo council's action. But, she said, the Bay Meadows site "was always a fallback position."

She said that she is "moving ahead full tilt" on possible downtown stadium sites in the South-of-

Back Page Col. 5

Gas Dealers Say Shortage Is Contrived

By Polly Ross Hughes

California service station dealers, angered by a sudden gasoline shortage in the state, accused major oil companies yesterday of conspiring to drive up prices by as much as five cents a gallon.

At least 50 percent of Bay Area service stations have already increased pump prices by one to two cents a gallon, said Jim Campbell, executive director of the California Service Station Association. He predicted that prices will continue rising next week as dealers pass on recent wholesale price boosts.

Gasoline dealers, middlemen and major oil companies agree that gasoline supplies have tightened on the West Coast in the past week, even though the world is awash in oil and prices of crude are plunging.

Major oil companies dismissed the collusion charge as "ridiculous." They blamed the shortage on a coincidental host of man-made and natural disasters — from earthquakes

Back Page Col. 5

Inside Nicaragua — Both War and Dissent

By Daniel Rosenheim
Chronicle Correspondent

Managua

Many people here simply call it "The Aggression."

Others say the United States is "removing the Soviet boot" from Central America.

Whatever their political persuasion, 2.2 million inhabitants of this embattled nation are deeply preoccupied with U.S. aid to the Nicaraguan rebels known as the Contras. Today, the eyes of Nicaragua are riveted on Washington, where the House of Representatives is supposed to resume debate on a proposal to provide $100 million in new funds for the Contras.

If, as many here predict, the aid is approved this week, it will undoubtedly intensify the bloody struggle between government troops and the rebels. That, in turn, will mean new hardship and deprivation for the people of this impoverished nation.

"We really can't solve our economic problems until the aggression against us is resolved," said William Huper, Nicaraguan minister of finance, who estimated that 35 percent of his government's total spending will be devoted to the military this year. "War is dislocating our entire economic, political and social life."

Nearly seven years after Sandinista guerrillas ousted dictator Anastasio Somoza, the Nicaraguan revolution is experiencing its darkest hour.

Although the Contras have fail-

Back Page Col. 1

INSIDE

A's Rally To Beat Minnesota, 7-6

Books 55 · Bridge 55 · Business 65 · Caen 17 · Carroll 51 · Chess 55 · Classified 38 · Comics 33 · Crossword 83 · Datebook 56 · Dear Abby 53 · Deaths 37
Delaplane 51 · Dickey 61 · Editorials 52 · Hoppe 53 · Horoscope 33 · Letters 52 · Manners 38 · Mellinkoff 52 · Movies, Bay Area 58 · S.F. 57 · O'Flaherty 55
People 20 · Personals 10 · Radio 54 · Rosenbaum 62 · Sports 59 · Steger 39 · Stocks, N.Y. 66 · Amex 67 · TV 54 · Weather 30 · White 26

SEE SPORTS
Top of the News on Page 16

Bay Area

A **Marin County** jury convicted Leslie Arthur Byrd of murder in the bathtub bondage slaying of a prostitute. Page 2.

The S.F. supervisors voted for a new study on building a downtown stadium. Page 2.

San Mateo sheriff's candidate Jim White talked of the 16-year-old shooting that has clouded his candidacy. Page 3.

Friends of Stephen Bingham formed to support the lawyer on trial for alleged complicity in a prison bloodbath. Page 4.

Environmentalists and fishermen said new state proposals to protect the bay could study its health to death. Page 5.

TOP OF THE NEWS

American President Cos., the Oakland-based container shipping firm, lost $10.1 million in the first quarter. Page 54.

State

Former California Supreme Court Justice Louis Burke died in a Mendocino hospital at the age of 81. Page 4.

Senator Alan Cranston's campaign takes off this week with a series of "statesmanlike" television commercials. Page 7.

Rep. Robert Badham said his opponent in the GOP primary may be a front for est founder Werner Erhard. Page 9.

Great Western Financial Corp. said its hostile takeover offer for Citadel Holding Corp. has been terminated. Page 54.

Nation

Michael Deaver, faced with criticism of his lobbying, urged an independent counsel to probe his work. Page 9.

A Senate committee gave the Navy permission to build 13 new battleship ports, including one at Treasure Island. Page 11.

President Reagan said the U.S. must be willing to defend its values "unflinchingly" in the face of terrorism. Page 17.

Personal computers are breaking new ground with landscape gardening. Page 18.

World

The worst nuclear accident that ever occurred was so hidden from the public that few people know about it. Page 12.

A Russian who mysteriously disappeared two months ago from his job at Radio Liberty surfaced in Moscow. Page 12.

A bomb went off at a park in Tokyo as radicals pledged to wreck celebrations in honor of Emperor Hirohito. Page 17.

Weather

Bay Area: Patchy coastal fog, otherwise mostly sunny and continued breezy Tuesday. Highs, 60s to mid-70s. Page 38.

Californians Feel Good, Poll Finds

See Below

San Francisco Chronicle

The Largest Daily Circulation in Northern California

122nd Year No. 88 ★★★★★★• TUESDAY, APRIL 29, 1986 777-1111 25 CENTS

Big Nuclear Accident At Reactor in Russia

Fallout As Far As Norway

Moscow

The Soviet Union announced yesterday that there has been an accident at a nuclear power plant in the Ukraine and that "aid is being given to those affected."

The severity of the accident, which spread discernible radioactive material over Scandinavia, was not immediately clear. But a terse statement by the news agency Tass suggested a major accident at Chernobyl nuclear plant in Pripyat, 60 miles north of Kiev.

The announcement, the Soviet Union's first official disclosure of a nuclear accident, came hours after Sweden, Finland, Norway and Denmark reported abnormally high radioactivity in their skies, and after Sweden demanded information.

The Soviet announcement said that one reactor was damaged and that a government commission had been set up to investigate, reinforcing indications that the accident was a serious one.

Residents of Kiev, contacted by telephone from Moscow, said early today that all bus service in the city had been stopped so that the vehicles could be used to evacuate those in the disaster area. "They're bringing them to Kiev, but we haven't seen anyone yet," a university student said. "We didn't see or hear any explosion."

Specialists in the United States said the accident probably posed no danger outside the Soviet Union. However, in the absence of detailed information, they said it will be difficult to determine the gravity of the accident, although they said environmental damage might be disastrous.

Charlie Porter, an Environmental Protection Agency radiation specialist in Montgomery, Ala., said radioactive material could drift over the North Pole to the U.S. West Coast in three to 14 days, depending on winds and the altitude of the debris. Without a radiation reading, he said, there was no way of know-

Back Page Col. 5

Experts Suspect A Meltdown

By Charles Petit
Science Correspondent

Most Soviet nuclear plants do not have the massive steel and concrete containment structures Western plants use to guard against radiation leaks, experts said yesterday.

The unprecedented admission by the Soviet government of an accident at one of the four reactors in Chernobyl led the American experts to theorize that some of the uranium-oxide fuel melted, releasing radioactive isotopes into the atmosphere in the type of accident that nuclear engineers fear the most.

The trickle of information from Soviet authorities left the experts with few hints of what happened or how many people might have been affected in the region north of the city of Kiev. But the experts said it seemed likely that cooling water, required to keep the reactor core below melting temperature, may have been lost.

All nuclear power plants work like boilers. Heat from the splitting of uranium atoms is carried off by water or other coolants to generate steam, which runs electric turbines. If the cooling water is

Back Page Col. 5

INSIDE NICARAGUA

By Steve Ringman

A Sandinista soldier hoisted a Russian-made AK-47 at the Totagalpa camp, six miles from the Honduran border

A Country Sacrifices To Keep On Fighting

By Daniel Rosenheim
Chronicle Correspondent

Totogalpa, Nicaragua

Francisco Serrano is a big admirer of things American.

When he is not in military uniform, the 18-year-old Nicaraguan favors running shoes, a

First of a series

loose-fitting shirt with the Playboy bunny insignia and a 10-speed Schwinn bike.

He even prefers to be called "Frank," rather than Francisco.

But Serrano's affection for the United States stops cold when it comes to America's support of the Nicaraguan rebels known as the Contras.

Serrano, who was wounded three times during his first 18 months in the Sandinista army, will carry Contra grenade fragments in his leg for the rest of his life.

"U.S. support for the Contras will not defeat our revolution," he says. "But it is creating many martyrs, killing many Nicaraguans, hurting our economy."

The brutal, 5-year-old struggle between the Sandinista government and Contra rebels is exacting a terrible toll on this nation — sapping an already enfeebled economy, forcing

Page 8 Col. 1

San Jose Superintendent Picked to Head S.F. Schools

By Diane Curtis

San Jose schools Superintendent Ramon Cortines was chosen last night to become the next schools chief for the San Francisco Unified School District.

During a four-hour closed-door meeting, the Board of Education voted 5 to 2 to offer Cortines the job he lost 11 years ago to Robert F. Alioto. Alioto was forced out last July by a bitterly divided board.

"I'm very pleased," Cortines, 53, said when reached at his San Francisco apartment. Asked if he thought he would take the job heading the 65,000-student San Francisco district, he replied, "Yes."

However, he said he has promised San Jose board members, who want him to complete the remaining three years on his contract, to meet with them before responding to any offer from San Francisco. "But I'm very pleased," he repeated.

San Jose Board President Joseph Wilson did not rule out legal action if Cortines decides to take the job. "It's a disappointing decision if that's the one he makes," Wilson said.

Calling Cortines "the best superintendent that we're aware of now," Wilson said last night in a telephone interview that the San Jose board's position was that Cor-

Page 6 Col. 4

Assembly OKs Bill Linking Grades, Sports

By Steve Wiegand
Chronicle Correspondent

Sacramento

The Assembly approved a bill yesterday requiring students to keep their grades at "C-level" if they want to play football, toot a tuba in the school band or participate in other extracurricular activities.

The measure, sent to the state Senate on a 54-to-13 vote, would require students in grades seven through 12 to maintain a 2.0 (or C) average on a 4.0 scale in order to take part in any school-sponsored extracurricular events. Students with learning disabilities would be exempt.

"We want to make sure that extracurricular activities do not overshadow academic perfor-

Back Page Col. 4

Whitworth Is Confronted by His Accuser in S.F. Spy Trial

By William Carlsen

In a dramatic courtroom confrontation yesterday, self-confessed master spy John Walker testified that Jerry Whitworth "had enough larceny in his heart that he would be interested in espionage."

It was the first face-to-face meeting of the two former Navy buddies since before their arrest last May on charges of selling Navy secrets to the Soviet Union.

Walker pleaded guilty to the charges last year and agreed to testify against his alleged partner Whitworth.

Whitworth, 46, stared intently

Back Page Col. 1

Public Thinks the Economy Is Great and Getting Better

By Mervin Field

CALIFORNIA POLL

For the third straight year, a majority of Californians indicate a very positive feeling about their economic well-being.

This year, as was the case in 1985 and 1984, majorities say they are both financially better off now than they were one year ago and expect to be even better off next year. In each year, no more than one in five adults reports being worse off economically than 12 months ago.

This buoyant public mood as it relates to the economy translates into a high proportion of the public (68 percent) saying now is a good time to buy major household items. Even larger majorities say this is a good time either to buy or sell a home.

The feeling that the state is in good economic times is close to being at its highest level since the poll

Back Page Col. 1

INSIDE

2nd Degree Murder Conviction In Bathtub Slaying

SEE PAGE 2

Books	43	Delaplane	39	People	18
Bridge	43	Dickey	49	Personals	10
Business	54	Editorials	40	Radio	42
Caen	23	Hoppe	41	Rosenbaum	50
Carroll	39	Horoscope	41	Sports	47
Chess	43	Letters	40	Steger	19
Classified	25	Mellinkoff	40	Stocks,	
Cohn	47	Movies,		N.Y.	62
Comics	64	Bay Area	46	Amex	51
Crossword	41	S.F.	45	TV	42
Datebook	44	Nachman	18	Weather	33
Dear Abby	41	O'Flaherty	43	White	49
Deaths	25				

THE VOYAGER DOES IT

BY ERIC LUSE/THE CHRONICLE

With the rising sun glinting from its wingtip, the Voyager touched down just after 8 a.m. yesterday at Edwards Air Force Base, where the historic round-the-world flight began nine days ago

San Francisco Chronicle

The Largest Daily Circulation in Northern California

122nd Year No. 293 ★★★★★★• WEDNESDAY, DECEMBER 24, 1986 777-1111 25 CENTS

Casey Memo Reportedly Linked Arms to Hostages

Washington

In a memorandum written at the beginning of the U.S. arms sales to Iran, CIA Director William Casey explicitly described the program as a trade of arms for hostages, according to a high-ranking official who has seen the document.

In addition, the government official asserted, the memo said that if the matter became public, President Reagan was prepared to portray the secret operation as a political opening to Tehran.

The document, written about a year ago, acknowledged that the arms sales conflicted with administration policy on terrorism, but described Reagan as determined to rescue the U.S. hostages in Lebanon, the official said.

The disclosure seems to contradict Reagan's assertions in the past two months that he approved the arms sales only as part of a diplomatic initiative aimed at making contact with "moderates" in Iran.

It could not be learned to whom the memorandum was addressed.

Senior officials at the White House and Justice Department said they had not seen the memo and one congressional official who has read many of Casey's other memos

Back Page Col. 5

North Was Once Hospitalized For Stress

Washington

Lieutenant Colonel Oliver North was hospitalized for 10 days in 1974 for emotional distress, but the White House was unaware of his medical history when it hired him in 1981 for the staff of the National Security Council, according to an authoritative Pentagon source.

Richard Allen, who was President Reagan's national security ad-

Back Page Col. 4

Pilots Set World Flight Record

BY ERIC LUSE/THE CHRONICLE

Pilots Jeana Yeager and Dick Rutan waved to the throngs gathered to welcome them at Edwards

Plane Lands Safely After Some Trouble

By Jack Viets
Chronicle Correspondent

Edwards Air Force Base

The pilots of the round-the-world Voyager made aviation history yesterday — and became instant American heroes.

Nine days, three minutes and 44 seconds after they took off to circle the globe nonstop without refueling, Dick Rutan and Jeana Yeager landed their long-wing experimental craft here shortly after 8 a.m. in front of a nationwide television audience.

Their return to earth was a scene reminiscent of astronauts bringing back a space shuttle. Tens of thousands of onlookers cheered, and the cameras of hundreds of TV stations and press photographers focused on the white craft.

But the graceful plane that Rutan, 48, and Yeager, 34, carefully brought down on the huge dry lake bed at Edwards in the Mojave Desert had little in common with the multibillion-dollar space shuttle that carried the banner of U.S. technological supremacy until the Challenger disaster early this year.

The Voyager is a tiny plane, with a cockpit roughly the size of a telephone booth, conceived on a paper napkin six years ago by its innovative designer, Burt Rutan, 43, the pilot's brother.

Built from lightweight composite materials, such as woven fiberglass honeycomb, graphite fibers and plenty of epoxy glue, the Voyager cost about $2 million, which was raised privately and took more than five years of work by a dedicated band of several hundred volunteers.

Although it was incapable of atmospheric re-entry like the near-

Page 5 Col. 1

Voyager's 2 Heroes Tell How They Feel

Edwards Air Force Base

Shrugging off accolades and saying he felt uncomfortable being called a hero, Voyager pilot Dick Rutan said yesterday the epic flight of the experimental aircraft taught him that man's achievements are limited only by his dreams.

"There were times I would have traded it all in. . . . I don't know that I would do it over again if I had the opportunity, but I'm glad I had the opportunity to do it once," the 48-year-old former fighter pilot told a press conference.

He said the most important thing he learned is that "no matter what age you are or what endeavor you're involved in, life is an opportunity and it's only limited by your imagination."

"What you want to do and what you can achieve are only limited by what you can dream about. . . . If you can conceive it, it's possible."

Rutan and co-pilot Jeana Yeager, who together dreamed of being the first pilots to fly around the world nonstop without refueling, spent six years making it a reality. Using a design of Rutan's brother Burt, they built a delicate plane with long spindly wings and a cockpit so cramped that one pilot had to lie on his back on the floor while the other occupied the only seat.

Fatigue etching deep lines in his craggy face, Rutan told reporters three hours after his historic landing that he had always had complete confidence in Yeager.

"She's a real sharp little pilot. When it was my turn to sleep, I had

Back Page Col. 1

2 Bay Hospitals End Free Rides For Drinkers

By Birney Jarvis

Two Bay Area hospitals have dropped out of the nationwide program that gives free cab rides to tipplers too drunk to drive during the Christmas and New Year holidays.

San Jose Hospital and Alta Bates Hospital in Berkeley will not participate in the CareCab campaign.

The free taxi rides will still be available in several Bay Area cities — including San Francisco, where Mayor Dianne Feinstein has strongly endorsed the program.

San Jose Hospital provided free rides for more than 1000 drinkers during the Christmas holiday and New Year's Eve in 1985 and during this year's Saint Patrick's Day, Memorial Day and Labor Day holidays.

The hospital said yesterday that the money that had been set aside for the program will be used during 1987 for public-service pro-

Back Page Col. 1

Reagan to Seek More Aid For Homeless in Lean Budget

Washington

Aid for the homeless and expanded trade assistance programs for U.S. workers laid off because of foreign competition will be among the few proposals for higher domestic spending in President Reagan's fiscal 1988 budget, James Miller, director of the Office of Management and Budget, said yesterday.

The White House will propose an increase in federal spending for the nation's homeless to more than $100 million from the current $70 million, reversing the administration's previous opposition to federally financed assistance.

The New York Times, quoting administration officials, reported that the budget also proposes changes in farm programs that are designed to save more than $16 billion over the next five years.

These officials said the proposals seeks to break the link between federal income-support payments and farmers' production, which gives farmers "incentives to overproduce," according to a report by the president's Council of Economic Advisers.

The officials also said the proposal would reduce payments to farmers by lowering the target

Back Page Col. 4

SEE PAGE 4

INSIDE

IRS Ready To Mail 1986 Tax Forms

See Page 6

Books.......32
Bridge.......11
Business.......41
Caen.......12
Carman.......32
Carroll.......25
Chess.......11
Classified.......14
Comics.......48
Crossword.......27
Datebook.......26
Dear Abby.......27
Deaths.......14
Delaplane.......25
Editorials.......26
Hoppe.......27
Horoscope.......48
Kahn.......9
Letters.......26
Manners.......10
Movies
Bay Area.......34
S.F.......31
Nevius.......35
People.......9
Radio.......33
Rosenbaum.......38
Sports.......35
Steger.......10
Stocks,
N.Y.......46
Amex.......45
TV.......33
Weather.......24

Top of the News on Back Page

SHIP SURVIVORS' DRAMATIC STORIES / SEE PAGE 9

San Francisco Chronicle

The Largest Daily Circulation in Northern California

123rd Year No. 105 ★★★★★★• TUESDAY, MAY 19, 1987 777-1111 25 CENTS

Frigate Knew Attack Was On — 'Ghastly Error' Left 28 Dead

Iraq Says It Was A Mistake

Chronicle Wire Services

Washington

Iraq apologized last night for its mistaken attack on the Navy frigate Stark, which killed 28 U.S. sailors and prompted a warning from President Reagan that any Iranian or Iraqi planes threatening U.S. vessels in the Persian Gulf will be shot down.

Iraqi President Saddam Hussein, formally apologizing for the "unintentional incident," and asked Reagan to extend his sorrow to the families of those killed and injured in the attack on Sunday.

Reagan ordered U.S. forces in the troubled gulf region on a higher state of alert and authorized them to fire at Iranian or Iraqi aircraft showing hostile intent.

The move was announced after a White House meeting where Reagan and a team of senior national security advisers discussed the first spillover of violence from the Iran-Iraq war to U.S. forces in the region.

In a written statement, White House spokesman Marlin Fitzwater said Iran and Iraq — the belligerents in a 6½-year-old war that has shaken Persian Gulf stability — had been notified of the "change in status" for U.S. ships in the area.

"Under this status," Fitzwater said, "aircraft of either country flying in a pattern which indicates hostile intent will be fired upon, unless they provide adequate notification of their intentions."

Pentagon spokesman Robert Sims said the change does not mean an enlarged U.S. force in the gulf, but "an increased readiness" to deal with the kind of threat that "proved to be a hostile one" in the case of the Stark.

A similar showing of apparent or even inadvertent hostility by Iraqi or Iranian warplanes "would not be tolerated," he said.

Despite the high death toll —

Back Page Col. 4

ATTACK ON THE FRIGATE STARK

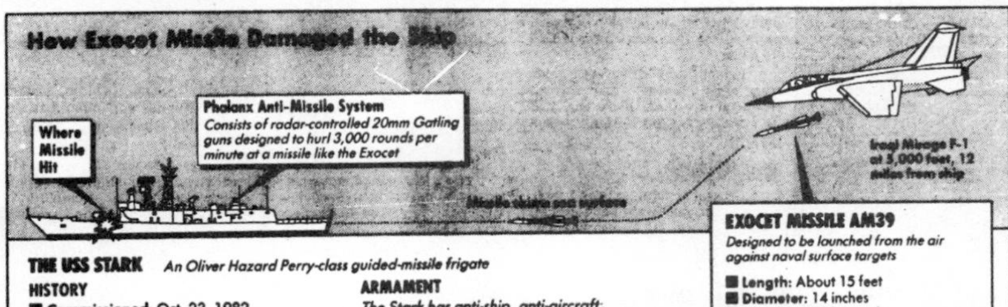

THE USS STARK *An Oliver Hazard Perry-class guided-missile frigate*

HISTORY

- **Commissioned:** Oct. 23, 1982
- **Builder:** Todd Shipyards Corp., Seattle
- **Base:** Mayport, Fla.

SPECIFICATIONS

- **Displacement:** 3,585 tons, fully loaded
- **Length:** 445 feet with a 45-foot beam
- **Maximum speed:** 29 knots
- **Crew:** About 200 officers and sailors
- **Cost:** $200.6 million

ARMAMENT

The Stark has anti-ship, anti-aircraft, anti-missile and anti-submarine capabilities

- Single-arm missile launcher firing Standard surface-to-air and Harpoon surface-to-surface missiles
- Two triple torpedo tubes
- One 76mm gun, 90 rounds per minute
- One 20mm Phalanx rapid-fire cannon

Sources: Jane's All the World's Aircraft, Weapons Systems and Fighting Ships, Reuters, Associated Press

EXOCET MISSILE AM39

Designed to be launched from the air against naval surface targets

- **Length:** About 15 feet
- **Diameter:** 14 inches
- **Weight:** 1,430 pounds
- **Warhead:** 363 pounds
- **Propulsion:** Two-stage solid rocket motor
- **Range:** 35-45 miles, depending on launch aircraft's height and speed
- **Flight speed:** About 500 mph
- **Guidance:** Radar homing system
- **Cost:** About $170,000

Highlights

THE TOLL

Sunday's attack on the frigate Stark by Iraqi jets killed 28 American sailors and injured at least 21.

THE SHIP

The Stark was being towed toward Bahrain yesterday. The ship is capable of steaming under its own power, the Navy said, but is being towed by the destroyer Conyngham.

THE REACTIONS

- **PRESIDENT REAGAN:** "We have protested this attack in the strongest terms and are investigating the circumstances of the incident. This tragic incident underscores the need to bring the Iran-Iraq war to the promptest possible end."
- **WHITE HOUSE STATEMENT:** "We expect an apology and compensation for the men who died in this tragic incident. We also seek compensation for the ship."
- **IRAQ REACTION:** President Saddam Hussein sent a letter to President Reagan expressing "deepest regret over the painful incident."
- **ALERT STATUS:** "The president has ordered a higher state of alert for U.S. vessels in the area" and Iran and Iraq were being officially notified of the change, White House spokesman Marlin Fitzwater said. "Under this status, aircraft of either country flying in a pattern which indicates hostile intent will be fired upon, unless they provide adequate notification of their intentions."
- **IRAN REACTION:** Prime Minister Hussein Musavi of Iran said Washington should avoid the "quicksands" of the Iran-Iraq war, and he threatened to cut off oil shipments through the gulf if the United States and Soviet Union continue to back Iraq, as Iran accuses them of doing.

BY ASSOCIATED PRESS

A tugboat pumped water onto the damaged area of the Stark

Puzzling Failure to Fire Back

Chronicle Wire Services

Washington

The U.S. frigate Stark issued two warnings to an attacking Iraqi warplane Sunday night, but despite more than a minute's alert, it failed to take other action against a Exocet missile, which killed at least 28 crew members and injured 21, Pentagon officials said yesterday.

The Iraqi Mirage F-1 fighter was tracked from its takeoff in Iraq by a U.S. Air Force Airborne Warning and Control System (AWACS) plane orbiting near the Persian Gulf and also was detected by the Stark's radar.

The frigate twice warned the fighter over an international radio frequency to veer away, but Pentagon officials said they are uncertain whether the Iraqi pilot heard the instructions.

At a distance of 12 miles and altitude of 5,000 feet, the Iraqi pilot launched an Exocet, which flew toward the ship at 500 miles per hour.

For reasons that Navy officials said yesterday are still unexplained, Commander Glenn R. Brindel, the Stark's skipper, failed to launch his long-range anti-aircraft missiles against the plane, to fire at the incoming missile with the frigate's anti-missile Phalanx Gatling guns or try to confuse the missile's homing radar by flinging up clouds of metal chaff.

Pentagon officials estimated that the Stark may have had one to two minutes between detection of the missile launch and impact but that the ship's officers apparently did not react.

Defense Secretary Caspar Weinberger described the attack on the Stark as a "ghastly error of some kind. . . . The ship's perfectly capable of defending itself."

About one-third of the crew was on watch under what the Navy calls "condition readiness three," which is a heightened alert used by U.S. warships on patrol in the gulf.

"It's his judgment. . . . It was the captain's call," said Air Force Lieutenant General Richard A. Burpee, director of operations for the Joint Chiefs of Staff. "We don't know what he was experiencing at that moment."

Officials said Brindel was "still pretty busy fighting fires," and "the last thing he needs is somebody from Washington to bother him while he's in an extremely tense situation."

Pentagon sources, meanwhile, told the Associated Press that the ship had been engaged in a sonar search for underwater mines at the time of the attack and thus was barely moving through the water. The sources, who asked not to be named, said it was not clear wheth-

Back Page Col. 5

Kidnaped Reno Models Safe — 2 Women Dead

By Dawn Garcia

South Lake Tahoe

A mysterious kidnaping ended late yesterday when police broke into a mobile home in South Lake Tahoe, rescued two young models and arrested their captor as he stood with the dead bodies of two other women.

FBI spokesman Mike McHale said a posse of law enforcement officers from eight agencies tracked

A posse tracked the suspect to a South Lake Tahoe mobile home

down Herbert James Coddington, 28, of South Lake Tahoe at the mobile home. Coddington, in custody at the El Dorado County sheriff's office in Lake Tahoe, was charged with violating federal kidnaping statutes and with homicide.

Alecia Thoma, 14, of Reno and Monica Berge, 12, of Sparks were found unharmed and were back with their families late last night, an FBI spokesman said.

FBI officials declined to say whether the two bodies found in the mobile home were Reno modeling school owner Maybelle (Mabs) Martin, 69, and her friend, Dottie Walsh, 67, also missing since Saturday.

The four were last seen leaving Reno on Saturday morning for a camera session at South Lake Tahoe. The camera session was arranged by a man claiming to be photographer Mark Clayton Bloomfield of Atlanta.

Investigators had circulated a composite drawing of the photographer through the Reno-Tahoe area. Reno Police said there were no ransom calls or messages.

Police had found Martin's

Back Page Col. 2

Singleton Goes To Richmond 'Permanently'

By Kathy Bodovitz

Paroled rapist Lawrence Singleton was moved yesterday to what state corrections officials called a "permanent" home in Richmond, although police there said they had been told that the arrangement is temporary.

Department of Corrections spokesman Robert Gore, refusing to specify where Singleton is staying, said he "has been placed permanently in Northern California."

Richmond police said they were notified about 10:30 a.m. that Singleton would be inside the city limits temporarily, for up to three days.

"There is no cause for public alarm," said Sergeant Ray Howard.

But reaction from Richmond leaders to Singleton's presence was quick, loud and negative.

"I am very disappointed, very displeased, about the decision that was made," Mayor George Living-

Back Page Col. 1

S.F. May Vote in Fall On Downtown Stadium

By J. H. Doyle

San Francisco Mayor Dianne Feinstein's dream of building a $70 million downtown baseball stadium is still alive.

On behalf of the mayor, Supervisor Jim Gonzalez asked the Board of Supervisors yesterday to reserve space on the November ballot for a proposition "authorizing the construction of a new baseball stadium using revenue bonds."

The ballot proposal, which calls for financing through a nonprofit corporation, must get a final go-ahead from Feinstein and the board. Under the proposal that may be put to voters, the Giants must agree to lease the ballpark for at least 25 years.

This is the fourth year in a row that Feinstein has introduced a bond measure to build a new stadium. Each year, financing has fallen through and the mayor has withdrawn the proposition before the November election.

"I haven't struck out yet," said Deputy Mayor Jim Lazarus, who cautioned that the city is still in a "preliminary" stance. "We're looking at a number of different financing options, including money from the private sector."

The mayor's office is studying the feasibility of building a stadium at Seventh and Townsend streets to replace the windblown and sparsely attended Candlestick Park. The stadium would cost "around $70 million" to build, Lazarus said.

Construction would be financ-

Back Page Col. 2

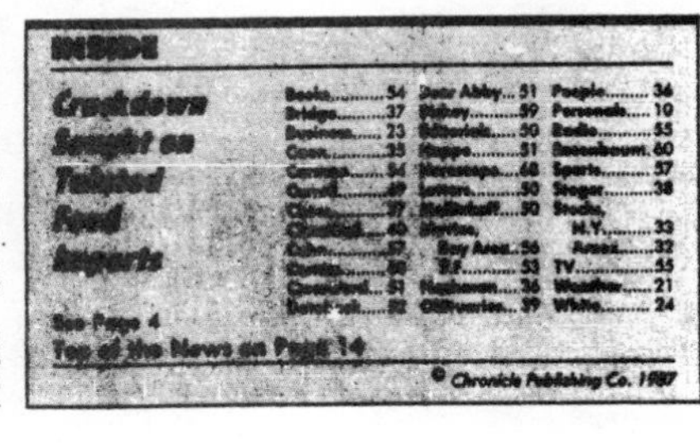
Books 54
Bridge 37
People 36
Radio 55
Sports 57
TV 55
White 24
Top of the News on Page 14

San Francisco Chronicle

The Largest Daily Circulation in Northern California

123rd Year No. 210 ★★★★★ FRIDAY, SEPTEMBER 18, 1987 415-777-1111 25 CENTS

Pope's Dramatic Day in S.F.

BY STEVE RINGMAN THE CHRONICLE

Pope John Paul II stood near the Golden Gate Bridge with (from left) Archbishop Pio Laghi, San Francisco Archbishop John Quinn, Cardinal Agostino Casaroli and Archbishop Eduardo Martinez

Hijack Suspect Seized by FBI in Mediterranean

New York Times

Washington

A Lebanese man was arrested in international waters in the Mediterranean Sea and flown to the United States to face charges of hijacking a Jordanian airliner in 1985, Attorney General Edwin Meese announced yesterday.

Meese said it was the first time a suspected terrorist had been arrested overseas by U.S. law enforcement officials.

The man, Fawaz Younis, 28, was arraigned yesterday under heavy security at U.S. District Court here. He was charged with hostage-taking, conspiracy and destruction of an aircraft. The plane had carried 70 people, including at least four Americans.

Justice Department officials, not wanting to compromise intelligence sources, declined to give details of Younis' arrest, but they emphasized that no other country had been involved and that the operation had been executed entirely by U.S. law enforcement and military officials.

They also insisted that the action was legal.

According to Justice Department officials, Younis "voluntarily" boarded a vessel manned by FBI

Back Page Col. 4

INSIDE

Bork Defends 'Conversions' On Issues

SEE PAGE A14

Biden Admits Law School Plagiarism

SEE PAGE A11

Judge Robert Bork

Arms Accord Near — Summit Likely in '87

New York Times

Washington

Major obstacles to a U.S.-Soviet treaty eliminating land-based medium- and short-range missiles were cleared away yesterday, and the two sides agreed tentatively to hold a summit meeting before the end of the year, senior Reagan administration officials said last night.

No firm date has been set for a visit to the United States by Soviet leader Mikhail Gorbachev, one official said, and several issues in the treaty have yet to be resolved, including details of verification procedures and a schedule for dismantling the missiles.

Intensive, all-day talks between Soviet Foreign Minister Eduard Shevardnadze and Secretary of State George Shultz overcame the

Back Page Col. 1

Pope Tells AIDS Sufferers They Have God's Love

By Carl Nolte

Pope John Paul II looked into the face of the AIDS epidemic in San Francisco yesterday and embraced its victims.

The first papal visit in the city's history came on a day of drama played out before disappointing crowds.

Only 50,000 people — a fraction of the numbers expected — lined Geary Boulevard to get a glimpse of the pontiff as he drove by in his bulletproof "popemobile," after a quick stop at the Golden Gate Bridge.

But Mission Dolores Basilica was packed to its ornate rafters when the pope arrived a little while later for a face-to-face meeting with a congregation that included 100 people with AIDS and AIDS-Related Complex.

He walked up slowly up the aisle, blessing, touching and reaching out to the congregation.

The pontiff held and kissed a 4-year-old child who contracted AIDS from a blood transfusion, and blessed and talked to many others who suffer from the fatal disease.

"God loves you all, without distinction, without limit . . ." he said. "He loves those of you who are sick, those who are suffering from AIDS and AIDS-Related Complex. . . . He loves all with an unconditional and everlasting love."

It was the third time in a week that the pope had spoken of AIDS. Earlier, he had said that homosexuals were "in the heart of the church" that people should have compassion for AIDS patients, and that the church welcomed homosexuals as long as they practiced chastity.

Yesterday, the pope laid his hands on David Glassberg, who went to the welcoming ceremony at the basilica with Tristano Palermino, his lover.

"I was going to tell the pope my lover and I had AIDS," Glassberg said later. "But his aura, his power when he touched us was so overwhelming I was speechless."

Two of the AIDS patients in the

Page A16 Col. 1

Only 50,000 Turn Out For Geary Motorcade

By Kevin Leary and Harre W. Demoro

Church officials said yesterday they are not concerned about the small crowds that greeted Pope John Paul II in San Francisco, because he "is not running for office."

The Rev. Miles O'Brien Riley, chief publicist for the Archdiocese of San Francisco, said it was "sad" that only about 50,000 people lined the route of the pope's motorcade on Geary Boulevard. Authorities were prepared for hundreds of thousands of spectators along the barricaded boulevard.

"I think we cried 'wolf' with all of these predictions of crowds and freaky people," Riley said. "I think we scared people off, but this isn't a popularity contest. The pope is not running for office."

The Rev. Ken Doyle, spokes-

Back Page Col. 1

Senate OKs Restraint on Star Wars Testing

Los Angeles Times

Washington

The Democratic-led Senate, ignoring the threat of a White House veto, voted yesterday to prohibit any tests of the Star Wars space defense system that would violate the traditional interpretation of the 1972 Anti-Ballistic Missile Treaty with the Soviet Union.

The Reagan administration had not formally proposed to conduct any such tests during the next two years, but Republicans had nevertheless mounted a four-month filibuster against congressional restraints on the Star Wars effort, known officially as the Strategic Defense Initiative.

The 58-to-38 vote along party lines was a setback for President Reagan's nuclear weapons strategy, occurring as Soviet Foreign Minister Eduard Shevardnadze ended a Washington visit to pin down details of a pending treaty to eliminate medium-range nuclear missiles.

The White House said the vote will "undermine our negotiating position" in Secretary of State George Shultz's talks with Shevardnadze, and it warned that Reagan would veto the $303 billion defense spending bill to which the prohibition is attached if the testing ban is approved by both houses.

The leading Democratic advo-

Back Page Col. 6

INSIDE

Exclusive Interview With Protester Brian Willson

See Page A4

Books.......E11 Bridge.......B5 Business.......C1 Caen.......B1 Carman.......E1 Chess.......B5 Classified.......B8 Cohn.......D1 Comics.......B2 Crossword...A35 Datebook.......E1 Dear Abby..A35

Dickey.......D3 Editorials.....A34 Hoppe.......A35 Horoscope.......B2 Letters.......A34 Mellinkoff...A34 Miss Manners B7 Movies, Bay Area....E10 S.F.......E11 Obituaries.....B7 People.......B3

Personals....A10 Radio.......E15 Restaurant..E14 Rubenstein..E18 Sports.......D1 Steger.......B5 Stocks, N.Y.......C7 Amex.......C6 TV.......E15 Weather....C26 White.......C2

Top of the News on Back Page

U.S. Ships Destroy Iran Outpost

Chronicle Wire Services

Washington

Four U.S. destroyers demolished an armed Iranian oil platform in the Persian Gulf yesterday in response to Iran's missile attack Friday against a U.S.-flagged Kuwaiti tanker, the Defense Department said.

A few hours later, Navy commandos boarded a similar Iranian rig nearby and destroyed radar and communications equipment, the Pentagon said.

The United States said there were no reports of casualties in the attacks. But Iran said some civilians aboard the first rig had been hurt, and it promised a "crushing blow" against the United States in revenge.

President Reagan described the actions as a "prudent yet restrained response" to Iranian attacks, and Defense Secretary Caspar Weinberger warned of "stronger countermeasures" if those attacks continued.

The Pentagon said the destroyers Kidd and Hoel and the smaller guided-missile destroyers Young and Leftwich fired 1,065 five-inch shells at their target, an inactive oil drilling rig called Rashadat, which stood on stilts near the gulf's main shipping lanes, 90 miles northeast of Qatar and 120 miles east of Bahrain.

Twenty minutes before the attack, the Navy radioed this warning to the 20 or 30 Iranians aboard the platform: "Rashadat, Rashadat, this is the U.S. Navy. We will commence firing on your position at 1400 hours (2 p.m.) You have 20 minutes to evacuate the platform."

Iranians were seen abandoning the rig on boats before the 85-minute attack began, the Navy said.

The Pentagon said that no fire was returned and that there were no Iranian casualties.

But Iran's official news agency said that "some of the civilian crew

Back Page Col. 1

San Francisco Chronicle

The Largest Daily Circulation in Northern California

123rd Year No. 237 ★★★★★★● TUESDAY, OCTOBER 20, 1987 415-777-1111 25 CENTS

THE MARKET'S BIG DROP

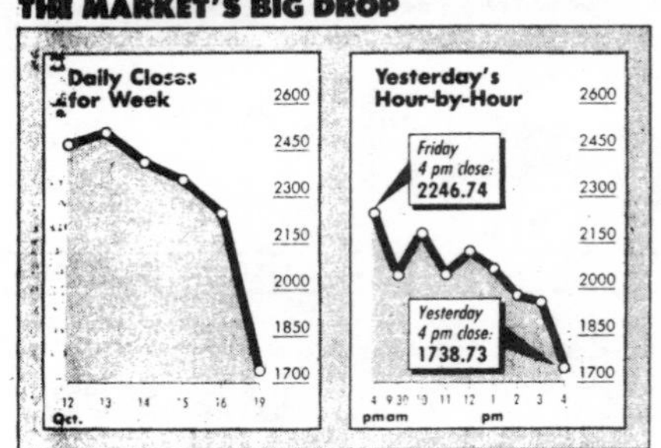

'A Financial Meltdown'

Dow Falls 508 — $500 Billion Loss

This Is Not Another 1929, Experts Say

By David Dietz

Wall Street's wicked drop yesterday parallels the infamous 1929 crash in some instances, but observers said the recent investment panic does not presage economic collapse.

At worst, local economists said, the record drop in the stock market in recent days may be signaling a mild economic decline early next year. A slump would raise unemployment and slow spending.

"The market is certainly signaling a lot of fundamental problems in the economy," said Joseph Wahed, chief economist at Wells Fargo Bank.

"We do have some imbalances, but not the type that will lead us into the severe and long-lasting depression that followed the '29 episode," Bank of America economist Daniel Van Dyke said.

In 1929, as in recent days, investors panicked, knocking $50 billion off the value of stocks in eight days — a phenomenal sum 58 years ago. The crash heralded the Great Depression, an apocalyptic period when banks and factories shut, unemployment lines bulged and real estate values plummeted.

Unlike today, however, the economy in the late

Back Page Col. 1

BY STEVE RINGMAN/THE CHRONICLE

William Farrell, a floor broker at the Pacific Stock Exchange, bowed his head as Dow continued its plunge

Reagan Says Don't Panic

By Vlae Kershner

Waves of panic selling sent the stock market to its worst crash of modern times yesterday, casting a cloud over the longest peacetime economic expansion since World War II.

The Dow Jones industrial average plummeted 508.33 points to 1,738.41, a 22.6 percent decline that was nearly double the worst of the October 1929 days that ushered in the Great Depression.

Tokyo's stock market plunged to its biggest one-day fall today, losing more than 14 percent of its value by late afternoon. The Hong Kong exchange suspended trading for the rest of the week after suffering heavy losses.

In Sydney, the Australian stock exchange lost a phenomenal 20 percent of its value in the first 45 minutes of trading before edging back up again slightly.

The total value of American stocks fell $503 billion yesterday, an average of $2,100 for every person in the United States. Some 604.4 million shares changed hands on the New York Stock Exchange, nearly double the record of 338.5 million set on Friday.

"There's absolute, outright financial panic," said San Francisco investment adviser John Osterweis. "People are willing to sell at any price just to get liquid, and I think it will feed on itself for a while."

The crash is expected to reverberate through the U.S. economy, which had been rising in tandem with stocks since 1982.

Investors nursing losses in stocks or people worried about a potential economic slump may put off planned purchases of cars, appliances or vacation homes, sending ripples through those industries. Companies that can't raise new capital because of the crash may scale back expansion plans. Those sorts of events could lead to higher unemployment and possibly a recession.

"The stock market always has been a leading indicator of the economy," said John Markese, vice president of the American Associa-

Page A4 Col. 4

MORE STOCKS NEWS

Tokyo Market Down Again Today

Hong Kong Exchange Closes D1

What It Means to You	A4	Takeover Targets Hit	D1
Why the Market Plunged	D1	The Dollar Bounces Back	D2
The Bond Market Recovers	D1	Reaction in Washington	D3
Option Traders' Nightmare	D1	Impact on Housing	D3
Logjam of Sell Orders	D1	Bankers Assess Damage	D4

Small-Time Investors in Shock

By Michael McCabe

The crowd of small-time investors stared up in disbelief at the big numbers racing across the ticker.

"I just never believed everyone would panic like this," Mark Childes, a mechanic for United Airlines, said quietly. "I kept waiting and waiting for the market to recover, but it just kept going down."

Childes, who joined the nervous crowd yesterday morning at Charles Schwab & Co. brokerage office in San Francisco's Financial District, finally sold his Allegis and Gillette stocks at 10:40 a.m.

"I lost about $3,000 — a big amount of money for me."

All day long, people like Childes marched into the brokerage office to check on the condition of their nest-eggs, as if the brokerage office were a hospital emergency room.

Not many looked like high-rollers. Some were elderly women carrying shopping bags and canes; some wore hard hats or work uniforms; some were in business suits or 49ers jackets.

Peering nervously at scraps of paper on which they had scrawled the names of their stocks, they watched as prices plummeted — and some lost what for them was a fortune.

Shortly after 10 a.m., the Dow Jones industrial average was down 183 points, an astounding

Page A4 Col. 1

Japan's Nakasone Picks His Successor

New York Times

Tokyo

Noboru Takeshita, a former finance minister and a master of political compromise, was virtually assured today of becoming Japan's next prime minister when the incumbent, Yasuhiro Nakasone, designated him to be his successor.

Takeshita's ascension came after an unusual turn of events in which Nakasone was given carte

Back Page Col. 5

6 Months in Jail for N.Y. Gunman Goetz

Chronicle Wire Services

New York

Subway gunman Bernhard Goetz was sentenced yesterday to six months in jail, ordered to see a psychiatrist and fined $5,000 by a judge who rejected a probation report recommending that he go free.

Goetz, whose shooting of four youths nearly three years ago touched off a nationwide debate over vigilantism, stood impassively as acting state Supreme Court Justice Stephen G. Crane sentenced him on the single count on which he was convicted — gun possession.

The crime carries a maximum penalty of seven years in prison, although most first-time offenders such as Goetz do not go to jail.

'A nonjail sentence for Mr. Goetz would invite others to violate the law'

Goetz, who was acquitted of more serious charges in the shootings, also was sentenced to five years of probation and 280 hours of community service at New York University Medical Center.

"A nonjail sentence for Mr. Goetz would invite others to violate the gun law," Crane said. "Whether you agree with the law or not, it is the law, and it was the law on Dec. 22, 1984, and it remains the law."

Goetz remains free on $50,000 bail pending appeal.

After the sentencing, Goetz's lawyer, Barry Slotnick, said: "I think Mr. Goetz has been victimized one more time, and unfortunately we have to go to another court and undo the wrong that's been done."

Mayor Edward Koch called the sentence "tough" but "correct."

William Kunstler, a lawyer for Darrell Cabey, one of the youths Goetz shot, said: "The judge brought some rationality into the proceedings. I hope people out in the streets will be deterred from doing what Goetz did."

Goetz, who had been seriously injured in a mugging four years earlier, claimed he gunned down the

Back Page Col. 3

INSIDE

Piniella Out, Billy Martin Back as Yankees' Manager

See Sports

Books	E4	[illegible]	E12	People	B3
Bridge	B5	[illegible]	C3	Personals	A10
Business	D1	Editorials	A16	Radio	E5
[illegible]	B1	[illegible]	A17	Rosenbaum	C4
[illegible]	E1	Horoscope	B2	Sports	C1
[illegible]	E12	Letters	A16	[illegible]	B5
[illegible]	B5	[illegible]	A16	Stocks,	
[illegible]	B6	Movies,		N.Y.	D12
[illegible]	B2	S.F.	E4	Amex	D13
[illegible]	A17	Bay Area	E3	TV	E5
[illegible]	E1	[illegible]	C1	Weather	D18
[illegible]	A17	Obituaries	B7		

Top of the News on Page A18

S.F.-Bound Jet Crashes

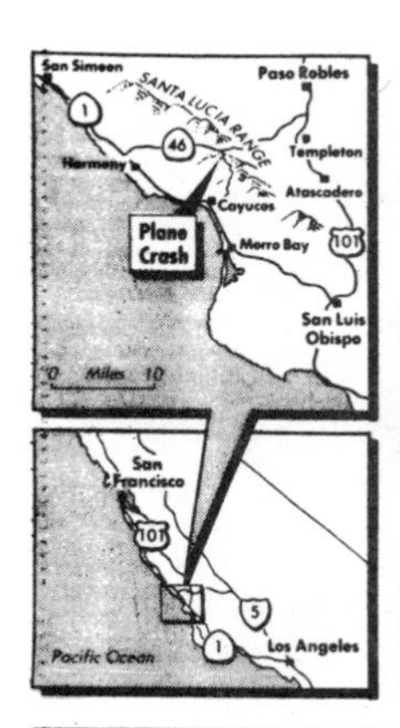

44 Die — PSA Crew Reported Gunshots

By Steve Massey and Ray Tessler

Paso Robles,
San Luis Obispo County

All 44 people on a San Francisco-bound Pacific Southwest Airlines jetliner were killed yesterday when the plane crashed after its crew reported gunfire on board, authorities said.

The crash of Flight 1771 from Los Angeles was preceded by reports of smoke in the cockpit and flames visible from the ground, and there were conflicting opinions about what might have caused the crash. Some experts said that the noise from certain types of engine failure might be mistaken for gunshots.

The flight, a regular 3:30 p.m. commuter run, was flying at 22,000 feet shortly before it plummeted into a hillside near Paso Robles at 4:14 p.m., according to the Federal Aviation Administration. The 83-seat plane was carrying 39 passengers and five crew members, according to PSA spokesman Mike Doering.

Among those killed were the president of Chevron U.S.A. Inc., James R. Sylla, 53, of San Rafael,

Page A8 Col. 1

The Pacific Southwest Airlines plane that crashed was similar to this BAe-146 four-engine jet

San Francisco Chronicle

The Largest Daily Circulation in Northern California

123rd Year No. 279 ★★★★★★• • TUESDAY, DECEMBER 8, 1987 415-777-1111 25 CENTS

'May God Help Us'

Gorbachev Arrives, Pushes For Long-Range Arms Pact

BY UNITED PRESS INTERNATIONAL

Secretary of State Shultz shook hands with Mikhail Gorbachev at Andrews Air Force Base in Maryland as Raisa Gorbachev looked on

2 Leaders To Sign INF Treaty Today

By Larry Liebert
Chronicle Washington Bureau Chief

Washington

Soviet leader Mikhail Gorbachev, arriving yesterday for three days of summit talks, promptly challenged President Reagan to offer new ideas to reduce strategic nuclear weapons.

"We have much to say to the American leaders, to the president of the United States," Gorbachev declared, minutes after his blue-and-white Ilyushin 62 Aeroflot jet set down at Andrews Air Force Base near here, "and we are hoping that we will hear some new words on their side."

In his brief remarks, Gorbachev emphasized that long-range strategic arms, which include intercontinental ballistic missiles and submarine- and bomber-launched warheads, pose the "pivotal questions" in U.S.-Soviet relations. The comments seemed intended to raise the ante for the summit meeting beyond the ban on short- and medium-range weapons that is set to be signed today.

On a chilly late afternoon, Gorbachev, in a dapper felt hat, and his wife Raisa, in a mid-length silver fox fur coat, stepped from their plane onto a red carpet for a ceremonial greeting from Secretary of State George Shultz.

"We are ready," Shultz said of the superpower talks that begin today at the White House.

"And now, we are ready too," the 56-year-old Soviet leader replied. He quietly added: "May God help us."

The American and Soviet flags flew at the airfield as Mrs. Gorbachev gave a kiss to a young girl and accepted a bouquet.

Two hours after the Gorbachevs' dramatic arrival, Reagan and

Back Page Col. 1

WASHINGTON SUMMIT

■ **TODAY** — President Reagan is to welcome Soviet leader Mikhail Gorbachev formally in ceremonies on the South Lawn of the White House. The two leaders will then meet privately before signing the treaty banning short- and medium-range nuclear weapons. After the treaty is signed, they will again meet privately.

■ **TONIGHT** — President and Mrs. Reagan host a state dinner for the Gorbachevs at the White House.

■ **LIVE TV COVERAGE** — Spokesmen for ABC, CBS, NBC and CNN said they will carry live, at 7 a.m. PST, Gorbachev's arrival and welcome at the White House. They also said they will broadcast live, beginning at 10:30 a.m. PST, the signing of the arms control treaty. NBC, ABC and CNN said they planned some coverage of the state dinner, beginning at 4 p.m. PST.

Complete Summit Coverage
PAGES A12, A13, A14 AND B4

Nancy, Raisa — A Little Chill At the Summit

Chronicle Wire Services

Washington

Raisa Gorbachev came to Washington yesterday in a white silver fox coat amid signs that she and Nancy Reagan are waging a cold war just as relations between their husbands were warming.

Nancy and Raisa will join their spouses at several official events during the summit, including two dinners and the witnessing of the signing of the treaty eliminating all medium- and short-range nuclear weapons.

But the two first ladies have only one private meeting scheduled — a coffee break and tour of the White House's private quarters —

Back Page Col. 4

Feinstein's Message for New Mayor

She Says S.F. Should End 2-Term Limit at City Hall

By Dave Farrell

Even as voters select her successor, Mayor Dianne Feinstein confessed she does not want to leave her City Hall command post.

"Two terms are not enough," Feinstein said in a quiet pre-election day interview. "It's just not enough time to do all the things the mayor of a major American city needs to do."

Although she has barely four weeks to go, the workaholic mayor said she plans to firm up details of a vast Mission Bay housing and office complex, offer to raise money for a downtown stadium and push ahead with studies to improve Fisherman's Wharf.

As for her own future, Feinstein said she will give speeches in China, work on a book about her political experiences and take a serious look at running for governor in 1990.

In the interview, the mayor said she was dissatisfied with the ci-

Page A4 Col. 3

S.F. Voters Choose Today Between Agnos, Molinari

By Jerry Roberts
Political Editor

Capping a multimillion dollar marathon campaign, San Francisco voters today will select a successor to Mayor Dianne Feinstein.

Polls will be open from 7 a.m. to 8 p.m.

With the National Weather Service forecasting a strong chance of rain, Registrar Jay Patterson said voter turnout will be between 40 and 45 percent, depending on the weather.

"That's pretty good for a runoff in December," Patterson said.

Assemblyman Art Agnos, who nearly won the mayor's office outright in a November 3 election, is considered the favorite to replace Feinstein. Elected by the Board of Supervisors as mayor after the 1978 assassination of George Moscone and elected by voters twice since then, Feinstein is prohibited by law

Back Page Col. 5

Supervisors Freeze Some S.F. Housing Demolitions

By Thomas G. Keane

The San Francisco Board of Supervisors slapped a temporary freeze on housing demolitions yesterday, stepping up the crusade to preserve the unique Victorian character of the city's neighborhoods.

The resolution, which passed by a 9-to-2 vote, could be followed next year by an even tougher one-year citywide moratorium on residential demolitions that is backed by several supervisors and Art Agnos, the heavy favorite in today's mayoral election.

The freeze suspends city permit applications submitted after August 27 for "demolitions or major alterations" of residential units. It expires February 2.

The measure grew out of mounting concern among residents that their elegant neighborhoods of stylish single-family homes are being torn down and replaced by ugly multi-unit buildings known derisively as "Richmond specials."

Although builders opposed any form of a freeze, yesterday's vote was considered something of a victory for them because a last-minute amendment proposed by Supervisor Bill Maher limited the measure to neighborhoods dominated by single-family homes and duplexes.

Supervisor Richard Hongisto, who authored the freeze and who has spearheaded the neighborhood groups' fight, wound up voting

Back Page Col. 5

INSIDE

McMahon Doubtful Starter Against The 49ers

SEE SPORTS

Books E4
Bridge B6
Business C1
Caen B1
Carman E1
Carroll E12
Chess B6
Classified C13
Cohn D1
Comics B2
Crossword A23
Datebook E1
Dear Abby A23
Delaplane E12
Dickey D3
Editorials A22
Horoscope B2
Letters A22
Mellinkoff A22
Movies,
S.F. E3
Bay Area E4
Nachman B3
Obituaries B7
People B3
Personals A10
Radio E5
Rosenbaum D4
Sports D1
Steger B4
Stocks,
N.Y. C10
Amex C12
TV E5
Theaters B2
Weather C16
[illegible] C2

Top of the News on Page A16

GIANTS, A's WIN—3 HOMERS FOR CANSECO/See Sports

San Francisco Chronicle

The Largest Daily Circulation in Northern California

124th Year No. 145 ★★★• MONDAY, JULY 4, 1988 415-777-1111 25 CENTS

U.S. Downs Iran Airliner — 290 Die in 'Mistake'

WHERE AND HOW IT HAPPENED

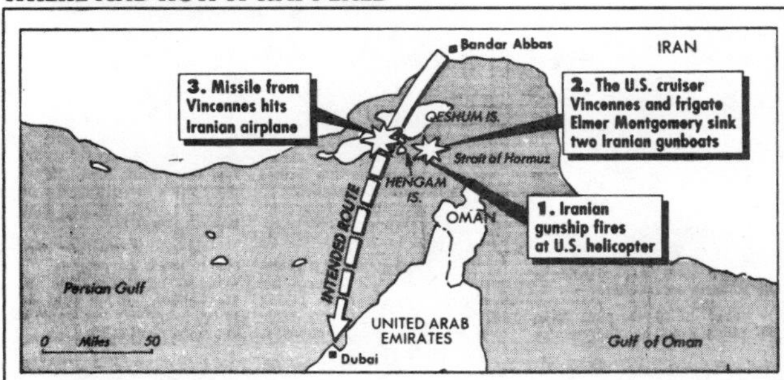

The following is the Pentagon chronology of events on the shooting down yesterday of an Iranian civilian jet by a Navy cruiser:

■ **Early morning, local time:** The Aegis-class cruiser Vincennes and the Navy frigate Elmer Montgomery are in the western curve of the Persian Gulf near the Strait of Hormuz. The Navy ships offer assistance to two merchant vessels; the offer is not accepted. Nearby are 13 to 15 small boats, believed to be Swedish-made Boghammar patrol boats owned by Iran. A short time later, the Vincennes dispatches a Navy helicopter to investigate further.

■ **10:10 a.m. (11:10 p.m. Saturday PDT):** The small Iranian boats fire guns at the Navy helicopter. The Vincennes returns to the scene.

■ **10:42 a.m. (11:42 p.m. Saturday PDT):** The Vincennes and the Montgomery fire their 5-inch guns at the Iranian boats.

■ **10:47 a.m. (11:47 p.m. Saturday PDT):** Radar on the Vincennes detects an aircraft over Iran heading out over the water. Admiral William Crowe, chairman of the Joint Chiefs of Staff, said the Vincennes had picked up "electronic indications" that led it to believe the aircraft was an American-built, swing-wing Iranian F-14 jet fighter. He declined to elaborate on that aspect of the incident, saying such information is classified.

■ **10:49 a.m. (11:49 p.m. Saturday PDT):** The Vincennes sends the first of seven warnings to the aircraft on military and civilian frequencies. The aircraft is heading directly for the Vincennes at about 500 mph.

■ **10:51 a.m. (11:51 p.m. Saturday PDT):** Getting no response from the craft, which is losing altitude and gaining speed, the Vincennes declares the aircraft hostile.

The U.S. cruiser Vincennes

■ **10:54 a.m. (11:54 p.m. Saturday PDT):** The Vincennes fires two Standard anti-aircraft missiles, at least one of which hit the aircraft while it was about six miles away.

Cruiser thought it was shooting at an F-14

An Airbus 300 was the type of plane shot down

Missile Attack Over Gulf

Cox News Service

Washington

A U.S. Navy cruiser, firing missiles at what it thought was an attacking Iranian warplane, shot down a commercial Iranian jet yesterday in the Persian Gulf, killing an estimated 290 people.

President Reagan called the incident "a terrible human tragedy" and said, "We deeply regret any loss of life."

Iran promised immediate retaliation for the incident and U.S. embassies around the world went on alert.

The Pentagon defended the ship's actions and said the commercial jet, an Air Iran A-320 Airbus, would not identify itself and acted in a "threatening manner" before the American warship reacted.

Admiral William Crowe, chairman of the Joint Chiefs of Staff, said the flight profile and "electronic emissions" from the commercial jetliner led the commander of the U.S. cruiser Vincennes to believe he was firing on an Iranian F-14 fighter.

There was no immediate explanation for the mistaken identity. The decision to fire was made seven minutes after the plane was spotted on radar and after it decreased altitude and headed toward the Vincennes, the Pentagon said. The plane failed to respond to seven radio warnings, officials said.

Reagan was at Camp David, Md., yesterday, where he was briefed on the developments. The president is expected to return to Washington about noon today as originally planned. He and Nancy Reagan are scheduled to hold a Fourth of July party this evening for the White House staff.

Although promising a full investigation of the incident, both the White House and the Pentagon yesterday pointed a finger of blame at Iran for the crash, the sixth worst aviation disaster in history and the deadliest recorded military downing of a civilian plane.

"I don't understand the responsibility of a country that, while it is attacking other ships and making a war zone out of a certain area of the

Back Page Col. 1

INSIDE

■ How an Advanced Warship Could Have Erred	PAGE A6
■ U.S. Policy on Iran Not Expected to Change	PAGE A6
■ Text of the U.S. Statement	PAGE A6
■ How Congress and Presidential Candidates Reacted	PAGE A6
■ Comparisons With Soviet Downing of Korean Airliner	PAGE A7
■ Relatives of Victims Furious at U.S.	PAGE A7
■ Other Incidents Involving Civilians	PAGE A7
■ Shock Among Bay Area Iranians	PAGE A7
■ Allies Say U.S. Has Right to Self Defense	PAGE A7
■ Chronology of U.S. involvement in the Gulf	PAGE A16
■ Will Rogers III, Commander of Vincennes, does not think of Iran as an enemy of U.S.	PAGE A16

Iran Calls U.S. 'Barbaric' — Hints at Retaliation

New York Times

Paris

Iran reacted to the U.S. downing of an Iranian jetliner yesterday by accusing the United States of barbarism and by hinting strongly that it will retaliate.

"The United States is responsible for the consequences of its barbaric massacre of innocent passengers," Foreign Minister Ali Akbar Velayati was quoted by IRNA, the official Iranian press agency, as saying.

Tehran Radio reported that there were 290 people aboard Flight 655, an Iran Air Airbus A-300 en route to Dubai from Bandar Abbas in Iran.

Those on board included 66 children and a crew of 16, the radio said, adding that Iranian rescuers had recovered 110 bodies. There appeared to be no survivors.

Iranian television showed helicopters shooting flares across the crash area and small motor boats moving in to pick up floating corpses.

A camera zeroed in on a rescue ship. On the ship's deck, a rescue worker held up the corpse of an infant and shook his fist.

"We will not leave the crimes of America unanswered," said a radio commentary monitored by Reuters in Cyprus.

"We will resist the plots of the Great Satan and avenge the blood of our martyrs from criminal mercenaries." Iran refers to the United States as the Great Satan. The radio did not say what the retaliation will be.

Tehran Radio said that today will be a day of mourning for the victims.

Before the airliner was shot down yesterday, the speaker of the Iranian Parliament, Hojatolislam Hashemi Rafsanjani, had stated that a priority of Iranian foreign policy will be to break the country's international isolation and to make new friends abroad, although not with the United States.

It was not known whether the downing of the airliner will alter

Back Page Col. 4

'65 Immigration Reform Opened Door for Asians

By Ramon G. McLeod
Chronicle Staff Writer

During 1964 hearings on the liberalization of U.S. immigration laws, Attorney General Robert Kennedy testified that Asian immigration would virtually disappear.

The landmark 1965 law has instead opened the door for more than 3 million legal Asian immigrants, including 250,000 last year.

The Bay Area alone drew 25,000 Asians as well as an additional 15,000 people from other areas of the globe in 1987, according to recently released Immigration and Naturalization Service statistics.

This influx made the Bay Area the third most popular destination for legal immigrants in the United States behind the New York and Los Angeles metropolitan areas.

The flood of immigrants also has led to a new proposal in Congress to limit the number of immigrants annually to 590,000, set aside 25 percent of immigrant visas for people with occupations or skills in short supply in this country and help new "seed" immigrants from Europe who could otherwise not enter the United States under family reunification preferences.

As Americans celebrate their

Page 5 Col. 1

Chronicle Fireworks Show Tonight

Sparkling lights and resounding explosions will fill the air beginning at 9:15 tonight when The Chronicle's annual fireworks display — one of the state's largest — gets under way at Crissy Field.

Weather experts said patchy fog is likely tonight, but they are not sure whether it will dim the pyrotechnic splendors planned along San Francisco Bay.

"There's a 50-50 chance it could be clear," said Steve Newman, The Chronicle's meteorologist. "We just

Back Page Col. 1

Fireworks Schedule
SEE PAGE D16

'L'Affaire Lia'— Melvin's View

By Bill Gordon
Chronicle Staff Writer

Melvin Belli lashed back at his estranged wife yesterday with charges that she spent more than $1 million of his money in six months on clothes, jewelry and other luxuries while cavorting with a boyfriend who threatened to kill him.

Belli dismissed as "ridiculous" charges that he beat and verbally abused his wife of 16 years, Lia Belli.

He vowed to file immediately for divorce. Last week, Mrs. Belli filed for a legal separation and obtained a court order barring him from the couple's Pacific Heights mansion.

"I want out," Belli said in an interview yesterday. "I should have gotten out when the people of San Francisco rejected her (in an unsuccessful 1984 state Senate bid)."

Mrs. Belli, 39, in seeking the legal separation, said she feared for the safety of the couple's 15-year-old daughter, Melia. She took the legal action two days after reporting to police that she narrowly escaped

Belli accuses wife of million-dollar spending spree with 'boyfriend'

from a man who entered the Belli mansion shortly before dawn and fired two shots at her.

Melvin Belli's remarks yesterday provided the lastest episode in a soap opera of cheating spouses, armed intruders and wild credit-card sprees.

"It's such a vile, venomous thing," he said about what he calls "l'affaire Lia."

Belli, 80, denounced the claims that he struck Mrs. Belli. "Violence is not in my nature," he said.

According to the internationally known lawyer, black eyes and bruises suffered by his wife in recent months were the result of her relationship with Alexander Montagu, an Australian-born Los Angeles resident who claims the title "viscount."

"She would come in after weekends with Montagu, bruised and beaten," said Belli. "He beat her on many occasions."

He said his relationship with his wife completely fell apart about two years ago.

Belli returned on Saturday

Back Page Col. 6

INSIDE

Brush Fires Rage Throughout The State
See Page A2

Books F5	Dear Abby A15	People B3
Bridge [illegible]	Dickey D3	Personals A8
Business C1	Editorials A14	[illegible] C3
[illegible] F1	Hoppe A15	Radio F6
[illegible]	Horoscope B2	[illegible]
[illegible]	Letters A14	Sports D1
Classified C4	Movies:	[illegible] B4
[illegible]	S.F. F3	[illegible] B3
[illegible]	Bay Area F4	TV F6
[illegible]	Obituaries B7	Theaters F2
[illegible]	Outdoors D1	Weather C8

Top of the News on Back Page